State Geological and Natural History Survey of Connecticut
Department of Environmental Protection

The Honorable John G. Rowland
Governor of Connecticut

Sidney J. Holbrook
Commissioner of the Department of Environmental Protection

Richard Hyde
Director, Natural Resources Center

Leslie J. Mehrhoff
Supervising Biologist,
State Geological and Natural History Survey

Allan N. Williams
Publisher, Technical Publications Program

Mary Crombie, Acorn Studio — *Cover Design*

Michael Oliver, Ph.D. — *Scientific Editor*

Julie Tamarkin — *Text Editor*

Additional copies may be purchased from:
DEP Maps and Publications Office
79 Elm Street
Hartford, Connecticut 06106
(203) 424-3555

ISBN 0-942081-06-4

Printed in Connecticut
United States of America

To my wife, Irene,

my parents, Lillian and Isadore,

and my children, Lara and Jennifer,

who have shared my interest in the

wonderful diversity of living things

and have provided patience

and encouragement

throughout this

project.

CONTENTS

CREDITS AND ACKNOWLEDGEMENTS

I wish to thank the many biologists, teachers, artists and students who have assisted in the preparation and review of this book over the past decade. I owe a special debt of gratitude to **Ralph Yulo** (Eastern Conn. State Univ.) and **Eileen Jokinen** (Univ. of Conn.) who extensively field-tested earlier drafts of this book with their students. I very much appreciate the careful reviews and thoughtful suggestions made by the following individuals: **Robert Bachand** (Norwalk Maritime Center), **Linda Bireley** (N.E. Utilities Environ. Lab.), **Diane Brousseau** (Fairfield Univ.), **Janine Caira** (Univ. of Conn.), **Donald Danila** (N.E. Utilities Environ. Lab.), **Paul Fell** (Conn. College), **Christine Gauthier** (N.E. Utilities Environ. Lab.), **Michael Klemens** (American Museum of Natural History), **Timothy Lynch** (R.I. Dept. Environ. Mgt.), **Joseph Pelczarski** (Mass. Office of Coastal Zone Mgt.), **Ron Rozsa** (Conn. Dept. Environ. Prot.), **Jack Schneider** (Norwalk Maritime Center), **David Simpson** (Conn. Dept. Environ. Prot.), **Richard Sisson** (R.I. Dept. Environ. Mgt.), **Maura Tyrrell** (Stonehill College), and **Joseph Vozarik** (N.E. Utilities Environ. Lab.) I am also very grateful to **Allan Williams** and **Hugo Thomas** (Conn. Dept. Environ. Prot.) for their support, assistance, and patience in publishing this book.

This book was funded in part by grants from the Oceanic Society, the Woman's Seamen's Friend Society of Connecticut, and Dwight D. Eisenhower Mathematics and Science Education Program through the Massachusetts Higher Education Coordinating Council, and the Long Island Sound License Plate Program.

In the credits that follow, figure numbers refer to the page within the chapter. For example, in the section for chapter 2, fig. 5F refers to figure F on page 2.05, fig.11G refers to figure G on page 2.11, fig. 0E refers to figure E on page 2.00, etc.

Chapter 2
Getting Started

TEXT: **Eileen Jokinen** is coauthor of these keys. **Jeffrey Pondick** wrote the portions of this chapter concerning the parasites and symbionts.

ILLUSTRATIONS: **Patricia May** drew all figures except as otherwise noted. **Lauren Churchill** drew figs. 1A, 1D, 2A, 3C (stalked jellyfish), 3G, 4C, 5F, 5K, 7H, 7I, 7J, 9D, 18C, 20B, 23B, 23J, 23L, 26D and 26E. **Carmela Venti** drew figs. 3C (anemone and hydroids), 7E, 7L (on rock), 9J, 9K, 11B, 11C, 11N, 13D, 13H, 13I, 13K, 13L, 15I, 15J, 15K, 15L, 15M, 15N, 17B, 17D, 17E, 17F, 17G, 17H, 17I, 17K, 17N, 17P, 25A and 27A. **Margaret Vose** drew most of the parasites and symbionts, figs. 18A, 18B, 19D, 19E, 19F, 19H, 19I, 20A, 20C, 20D, 21E, 21F, 21G, 21H and 21I. **Barbara Williams** drew figs. 9E and 23C. The illustrations were drawn from the following sources: **Abbott (1954)**: figs. 23E, 23F, 23G, 23H, 23K, 23M, 24B, 24C and 24E. **Barnes (1968)**: fig. 18B. **Daniels and Sawyer (1975)**: fig. 19E. **Gosner (1971)**: fig. 6C. **Gosner (1979)**: figs. 2B, 3D, 3E and 9O. **Miner (1950)**: fig. 27F. **Nichols and Cooke (1971)**: figs. 0E (snail) and 0F. **W. R. Taylor (1957)**: figs. 3G and 3I. From specimens or from illustrations on other pages: all figures not listed above.

Chapter 3
Sponges

TEXT: The key is adapted from **Hartman (1964)** and **Gosner (1971)**. Some descriptions are from **Hartman (1958)** and **Gosner (1979)**. The scientific names and classification system are according to **Gosner (1971)**.

ILLUSTRATIONS: **Patricia May** drew all figures except as otherwise noted. **Lauren Churchill** drew figs. 0C, 3A (microscleres), and 5D (spicules). **Carmela Venti** drew figs. 1D (on rock), 2A, 4A, 4C (flat form), 3C (sponge), 4A, 4C (flat) and 5C (sponge). Figures indicated with a prime mark (') were reproduced directly from their sources. All others were drawn by the above artists from the following sources: **Crowder (1931)**: fig. 2C'. **Gosner (1971)**: figs. 1J and 1K. **Hartman (1958)**: figs. 2D, 3B' (spicules), 4A' (spicules), 4B' (spicules), 5B' (spicules) and 5C' (spicules). **Hartman (1964)**: figs. 1I', 2B (encrusting form), 2E, 2F, 3A (spicules), 4B (sponge), and 5D (spicules). **Hyman (1940a)**: fig. 3B (sponge). **Meinkoth (1981):** fig. 0C. **Miner (1950)**: figs. 3A (sponge), 3C, 5A (sponge), and 5A (spicules). **Wells, Wells and Gray (1960)**: figs. 4C (on eelgrass) and 5D (sponge). From specimens or from illustrations on other pages: all figures not listed above.

Chapter 4
Cnidarians and Ctenophorans

TEXT: The keys are adpated from **Hand (1964)** and **Gosner (1971)** for the anemones, and from **Smith (1964)** and **Gosner (1971)** for the hydroids, jellyfishes, and ctenophores. Some descriptions of the hydroids are from **Fraser (1944)**, **Gosner (1979)**, **Miner (1950),** and **Nutting (1899)**. Anemone descriptions are based on **Gosner (1979)**, **Meinkoth (1981)**, and **Miner (1950)**. Ctenophore descriptions are from **Gosner (1979)**, **Mayer (1912)**, and **Miner (1950)**. The scientific names, common names, and classification system are according to **Cairns et al. (1991)**. Additional information regarding synonyms was provided in personal communications from **Steven Cairns** for scleractinians, **Dale Calder** for hydrozoans, **Daphne Fautin** for anthozoans, **Richard Harbison** for ctenophorans, and **Ron Larson** for scyphozoans.

ILLUSTRATIONS: **Patricia May** drew all figures except as otherwise noted. **Lauren Churchill** drew all figures on pages 4.02-4.03 and figs. 0A, 5H, 5I, 7E, 8A, 9D, 9E (polyp), 9F (polyp), 10B (*Hybocodon*), 11E, 11F, 11G, 13C, 13F, 14A (top view), 14B (in mud) 15F, 15G, 16A, 17C (comb rows), and 17D. **Carmela Venti** drew figs. 0B, 4A, 4D, 5F, 5G, 7A (40X), 7B (40X), 7C (40X), 7D (40X), 8B (40X), 9C (40X), 9E (40X), 9F (40X), 11I, 12B (closed), 12B (full extension), 13D (open), and 13E. Figures indicated with a prime mark (') were reproduced directly from their sources. All others were drawn by the above artists from the following sources: **Agassiz (1862)**: figs. 1C, 1F and 11I (actual size). **Fraser (1944)**: figs. 6C'(40X), 7A (40X), 7B (1/3 size), 7C (40X), 7D (40X), 8B (reproductive structure), 9E (40X), 9F (40X), 11C (40X), and 11H (actual size). **Gosner (1971)**: figs. 0B, 2A, 2B,2C, 3E, 3F, 3I, 3L, 5I (*Opercularella* polyp), and 8A. **Gosner (1979)**: figs. 16A (spicule), 17A, 17B, 17C (comb jelly), and 17D. **Hand**

(1964) after **Crowell (1946)**: fig.13F. **Hand (1964)** after **Hargitt (1914)**: figs. 14B' (whole anemone) and 15D. **Hickman (1967)**: fig. 17C (comb rows). **Hincks (1868)**: figs. 7A (40X), 7B (actual size), 7C (actual size), 7D (one third size), 8B (actual size), and 9E (actual size). **Hyman (1940b)**: figs. 9C (40X), 9F (actual size), and 11D' (actual size). **Larson (1976):** fig. 4A. **Meinkoth (1981)**: fig. 14B (in mud). **Miner (1950)**: figs. 3D, 3G, 3H, 3J, 3K, 5H (*Calycella* colony, *Cuspidella* polyp), 5I (colonies), 7E, 8B (40X), 9D, 9E (collar), 9F (collar), 10B (*Hybocodon*), 11C (actual size), 11E, 11F, 11G, 13C (oral view), 13F (closeup), 14A, 14B (closeup), 15C, 15E', 15F, 15G', and 16B (polyps). **Naumov (1960)**: fig. 10A (actual size). **Nutting (1899)**: figs. 6A' (40X), 9C (2X), 10A'(10X), 10B'(*Corymorpha*), 11D (40X), 11H (40X) and 11I (40X). **Sigerfoos (1899)**: figs. 6B (actual size) and 6B' (40X). **R. I. Smith (1964)**: figs. 5H (*Calycella* polyp), and 6C (actual size). **Smith and Carlton (1975)**: fig. 13D (open). **Stephenson (1928, 35)**: fig. 12B (full extension). **Verrill (1922)**: fig. 12B (normal extension). **Verrill and Smith (1873)**: fig. 1D. From specimens or from illustrations on other pages: all figures not listed above.

Chapter 5
Unsegmented Worms

TEXT: **Jeffrey S. Pondick** wrote the portions of this chapter concerning the parasitic worms. Life cycles and species descriptions for the cestodes and trematodes are based on **Schmidt (1970)**, **Cable (1977)**, **Cheng (1967)**, **Cheng (1973)**, **Meyer and Olsen (1980)**, **Noble and Noble (1982)**, **Pritchard and Kruse (1982)**, **Schell (1970)**, and **Schmidt and Roberts (1981)**. The key to the turbellarians is adapted from **Bush (1964)**, **Bush (1981)**, and **Gosner (1971)**. Additional information about the turbellarians is from **Hyman (1940b)** and **Miner (1950)**. The key to the nemertines is based on **R. I. Smith (1964)** and **Gosner (1971)**. Other sources of information about the nemertines include **Coe (1943)**, **Gosner (1979)**, **Miner (1950)**, and **Verrill (1892a)**. Scientific names and descriptions of the sipunculids are based on **Cutler (1977)**.

ILLUSTRATIONS: **Margaret Vose** drew most of the parasitic and symbiotic worms, including figs. 0A, 0B, 1D, 1J, 2A, 2B, 3C, 3D, 4A, 4B, 4C, 5D, 5E, 6A, 7J, 8A, and 9A. **Patricia May** drew figs. 1G, 1L, 1M, 6B, 7D, 7E, 7F, 7G, 7H, 7I, 8A (seal), and 8B. **Lauren Churchill** drew the peanut worms and many flatworms, figs. 1C, 1D, 1E, 1F, 1H, 1I, 1K, 6C, 9B, and 9C. **Carmela Venti** drew figs. 9G and 0H. The illustrations were drawn from the following sources: **Barnes (1968)**: fig. 8B. **Bush (1964)**: figs. 0A, 0B and 1E, 1F, 1G (eye pattern), 1H,1I, and 1K. **Cheng (1973)**: fig. 7J. **Coe (1943)**: fig. 6A. **Dawes (1946)**: fig. 3C (cercariae). **Gosner (1971)**: figs. 7H (head) and 7I (head). **Gosner (1979)**: figs. 7F (head) and 9C (tentacles). **Hyman (1939)**: fig. 1G (body shape). **Joyeux and Baer (1936)**: fig. 5D (segment). **Meglitsch (1967)**: fig. 5E (procercoid, coracidium, pleurocercoid). **Miner (1950)**: figs. 1C and 1D. **Nichols and Cooke (1971)**: figs. 4A (worm) and 5E (adult). **Noble and Noble (1982)**: fig. 3C (metacercaria, redia, sporocyst). **Schell (1970)**: fig. 2A (attachment organs). **Schmidt (1970)**: fig. 5D (head). **R. I. Smith (1964)**: figs. 6C, 7D (head), 9B. **Verrill (1892a)**: figs. 7D (worm), 7E (worm), 7F (worm), 7G, 7H (worm) and 7I (worm). **Verrill (1892b)**: fig. 1M. **Verrill and Smith (1873)**: figs. 1L, 4C, and 5E (scolexes). From specimens or from illustrations on other pages: all figures not listed above.

Chapter 6
Bryozoans and Entoprocts

TEXT: The keys, descriptions, scientific names, and classification system for the bryozoans and entoprocts are adapted from **Ryland and Hayward (1991), Rogick (1964a,b)**, and **Gosner (1971)**. Additional descriptive information is from **Rogick and Croasdale (1949)**, **Gosner (1979)**, and **Meinkoth (1981)**.

ILLUSTRATIONS: **Patricia May** drew all figures except as otherwise noted. **Lauren Churchill** drew figs. 1C, 1D, 1E, 1F, 1H, 2A 3D, 3F, 3H, 3J, 3K, 4A, 5A, 5C, 5G, 6C, 6D, 7F, 7H, 7G, 6A, and 6B. Figures indicated with a prime mark (') were reproduced directly from their sources. All others were drawn by the above artists from the following sources: **Gosner (1971)**: figs. 3H, 4A, 4F, 5H, and 7H. **Gosner (1979)**: figs. 2A (*L.verrucaria*), 3D, 3E, 3I, 4D, 4E, 5A (colony), and 7B. **Hyman (1951)**: fig. 7A (colony). **Miner (1950)**: fig. 1H. **Osburn (1912)**: figs. 4B and 5C (zooids). **Rogick and Croasdale (1949)**: figs. 0A' (10X,40X), 0B' (10X,40X), 1G' (actual size), 2A (*L. hispida*), 3C, 3F, 3J, 3K, 4C, 5A (zooids), 5B', 5I, 6C, 6D, 6E, 7A (zooid), 7F, and 7G. **Ryland and Hayward (1991)**: figs. 1C, 1D, 1E, 1F, 3G, 6A, and 6B. **Verrill and Smith (1873)**: fig. 1G' (10X). From specimens: figs. 0A (half size), 0B (half size), 5C (colony) and 5G.

Chapter 7
Mollusks

TEXT: The keys and the descriptions for the snails and bivalves are adapted from **Abbott (1954)**, **Gosner (1971)**, **Hunter and Brown (1964)**, **Jacobson and Emerson (1971)**, **Long Island Shell Club (1988)**, and **Morris (1975)**. The nudibranch and sacoglossan keys and descriptions are based on **Moore (1964)**, **Gosner (1971)**, and **Clark (1971)**. The scientific names, common names, and classification system are according to **Turgeon et al. (1988)**.

ILLUSTRATIONS: **Patricia May** drew all figures except as otherwise noted. **Barbara J. Williams** drew figs. 11C, 12A, 12B, 13N, and 13O. **Lauren Churchill** drew figs. 0B, 0D, 2B, 3E, 3F, 3G, 4D, 4E, 6A (teeth), 6F, 7B, 9G, 9I, 10A, 10D, 11E, 12C, 13G, 13I, 13J, 17D, 17G, 17H, 18C, 20B (*A. squamula*), 20D, 21F, 22C, and 23E. **Carmela Venti** drew figs. 0C, 5A, 5C, 5D, 17K, 21B, 21C, and 21D. Figures indicated with a prime mark (') were reproduced directly from their sources. All others were drawn by the above artists from the following sources: **Alder and Hancock (1845-55)**: figs. 11C, 12A, 12B, 13N, and 13O. **Arnold (1901)**: figs. 13E and 14B'. **Coe (1936)**: fig. 1B (stack). **Dall (1899)**, drawings by **A. E. Verrill** and **J. C. McConnell**: figs. 1E', 7A, 8A', 8B', 10F', and 21B (end view). **Galtsoff (1964)**: fig. 15D'(external views). **Gosner (1971)**: figs. 6A (teeth), 11F, and 12D (cerrata). **Gosner (1979)**: figs. 1D (side view), 6C (top whorl), 7D, 7F, 9I, 10D, 11A, 11B, 16A (inside and top views), 16B (inside and top views), 17G, 17H, 18A (inside view), 19E (outside view), 21A (top view), 22D (inner edge), 23C, and 23E. **Gould and Binney (1870)**, drawings by **E. S. Morse**: figs. 0C, 1A', 1D (underside), 4A (side view), 4B (side view), 9D, 10B', 10C', 14C', 16A'(side view), 16B'(side view), 17C', 17E', 17F, 18A' (outside view), 18A (juvenile), 18B' (side view), 19G', 19H', 19I', 20E', 22A' (outside view), 22B' (outside view), 23A', 23B' (outside view), and 23D. **Grimm (1975)**: fig. 7B. **Hunter and Brown (1964)**, drawings by **R. L. von Arx**: figs. 4B (bottom view), 10E', 18A (end view), 18B (end view), 21D (top view), and 4A (bottom view). **Jacobson and Emerson (1971)**, drawings by **A. D'Attilio**: figs. 1B' (underside), 1C (underside), 4C, 5A, 5C, 5D, 6A, 6B', 6D', 6E', 7C', 7E, 8C', 9E (juvenile), 9F',9G, 9H', 9J', 9K', 15D' (inside view), 17I, 17J, 17K, 19F, 20B (*A. simplex*), 20D, 21A (side view), 21B (side view), 21C, 21D (side view), 22A (inner edge), and 23B (inner edge). **Marcus (1958)**: fig. 13M. **Marcus (1972)**: fig. 11G. **Meinkoth (1981)**: fig. 7D. **Miner (1950)**: figs. 6F and 12C. **Moore (1964)**, drawings by **M. P. Morse** after **Alder and Hancock (1845-55)**: figs. 11E, 13D', 13E', 13G, 13H', 13I, 13J, 13K, and 13L'. **Morris (1975)**: figs. 20A, 20B (*A.squamula*), 20C, 21F, 22D (outside view), and 22E. **Verrill (1880-81)**: figs. 0A' and 0B. **Verrill and Smith (1873)**: figs. 6C'(shell), 19D'(outside view), and 22A'(siphon extended). **Weiss (1970)**: figs. 3E (operculum) and 3G (operculum). From specimens or from illustrations on other pages: all figures not listed above.

Chapter 8
Annelid Worms

TEXT: **Eileen Jokinen** is coauthor of the oligochaete section of this chapter and **Jeffrey S. Pondick** wrote the leech and lobster gill worm sections. The keys and descriptions for the polychaetes are based on **R. I. Smith (1964)**, **Pettibone (1963)**, **Gosner (1971)**, and **Miner (1950)**. The names of polychaete genera and the classification system are according to **Fauchald (1977)**. Information about the leeches is from **Sawyer, Lawler and Overstreet (1975)**. The oligochaete key and descriptions are adapted from **Cook and Brinkhurst (1973)**.

ILLUSTRATIONS: **Patricia May** drew all figures except as otherwise noted. **Lauren Churchill** drew figs. 4A (end view), 5C (side view), 5E (crown of tentacles), 6B (tail), 6C (tentacles), 7H, 7J, 8A, 11F, 14A, 15C, 16A, 16B, 17B, 17D, 17E, 19B, 19C (head), 19D, 19G (worm), 21G, 22A 22C, and 24A. **Margaret Vose** drew figs. 23A, 23B, 23C, and 23D. **Carmela Venti** drew figs. 3F (whole worm), 4B (tubes), and 20C. Figures indicated with a prime mark (') were reproduced directly from their sources. All others were drawn by the above artists from the following sources: **Arnold (1901)**: figs. 15A and 18A (worm). **Barnes (1968)**: figs. 0A, 5D (worm), 10B (tube), 13D (head), and 18A (head and proboscis). **Cook and Brinkhurst (1973)**: figs. 21H, 24A, 24B, 24C, 24D, 24E, and 24F. **Crane (1973)**: fig. 14A (heads). **Daniels and Sawyer (1975)**: fig. 23D. **Fauvel (1923)**: fig. 9E. **Gosner (1971)**: figs. 6D (tentacles), 7E (tentacles), 9A (scales and cirri), 10F, and 11G (papillae). **Gosner (1979)**: figs. 10B (worm), 10C, 14C, 14E, 16A (anterior end) 16B, 19B (papillae), 19C, and 22C. **Hartman (1944)**: figs. 5C (side and top view) and 15F. **Hartman (1945)**: figs. 12A and 22A' (tail). **Hartman (1957)**: fig. 20A' (top view). **Hartman (1966)**: fig. 20A (side view). **Light et al. (1954)** after **McIntosh (1879)**: figs. 6C, 9B' (worm), 11E' (worm), 17B, 19E' and 20C (worm). **Meinkoth (1981)**: fig. 4A (end view) **Miner (1950)**: figs. 5F' (crown of tentacles), 5G (worm), 6A, 6B, 6D (head), 7E (head), 7G, 8A (worm), 9B (head), 9D, 10E (tubes), 10F (head and tail), 11G (worm), 11H, 13G (body and tail), 16C' (whole worms), 17A, 19F, 19G (worm), and 22B. **Niemeyer and Martin (1967)**: fig. 13D (worm). **Nichols and Cooke (1971)**: fig. 23C. **Pettibone (1963)**: figs. 9A'(worm), 10A, 12C, 14B (head), 15B, 15D', 15E', 17D, 17E, 18A (parapodia), 19B (*Glycinde*), 19G (head), 20B', 20C (jaws), 21D, 21E' (head), 21E (parapodium), 21F' (head), and 21F (parapodium and setae). **R. I. Smith (1964)**: figs. 2A, 2B, 4A' (worm), 4A (tube), 4B' (worm), 5C (*S. borealis* and *S. spirillum*), 5E, 5F (collar and eyespots), 5G (collar and eyespots), 5H', 7H (gills), 7J, 8A (head), 8C, 8D, 11D, 12B', 13F, 13G (head), 14A' (parapodium), 14B' (parapodium), 14D' (parapodium), 15C, 16A (head), 16C (heads), 17C, 19B (*Goniada*), 22D, and 22E. **Ushakov (1955)**: fig. 21G. **Uzmann (1967)**: fig. 23A. **Verrill (1881)**: figs. 7F (worm) and 19D. **Verrill and Smith (1873)** with most drawings by **E. H. Emerton**: figs. 7H (worm), 7I, 8B, 14D' (worm), 16C' (worm), and 17B (heads). From specimens or from illustrations on other pages: all figures not listed above.

Chapter 9
Chelicerates

TEXT: The key to the pycnogonids is adapted from **McCloskey (1973)** with additional information about pycnogonid species from **Hedgpeth (1948)**. The spider keys and descriptions are based on **Kaston (1981)**. Spider descriptions are also derived from **Comstock (1940a)**, **Emerton (1902)**, and **Levi and Levi (1968)**. Information about terrestrial mites and ticks is from **Baker and Wharton (1952)**, **Anderson and Magnarelli (1980)**, **Baker et al. (1956)**, **Burgdorfer et al. (1982)**, and **Magnarelli et al. (1984)**. **Newell (1947)** is the source of information about water mites. The scientific names, common names and classification system are according to **McCloskey (1973)** for the pycnogonids, **Kaston (1981)** for the spiders, and **Anderson and Magnarelli (1980)** for the ticks.

ILLUSTRATIONS: **Margaret Vose** drew all figures except as otherwise noted. **Lauren Churchill** drew figs.2B, 3D, 3E, 5I (face), and 9A *(Ixodes)*. **Patricia May** drew figs. 1A (claws), 2A (side and dorsal), and 9B. **Carmela Venti** drew figs. 1A (ventral view) and 2A (dorsal view). Figure 1A (dorsal view) was reproduced directly from its source. All others were drawn by the above artists from the following sources: **Barnes (1968)**: figs. 1A (dorsal) and 9A *(Dermacentor)*. **Comstock (1940a)**: figs. 4C (face), 5G, 6C, 7E, 7I (face), and 7K (dorsal). **Crosby and Bishop (1925)**: fig. 7J (dorsal). **Emerton (1902)**: figs. 4C (dorsal views), 5D (dorsal), 5H (dorsal), 5I (dorsal), 5J (dorsal and underside), 7H (dorsal), 7I (dorsal), 8A and 8C. **Kaston (1981)**: figs. 5H (face), 6A, 6B, 6D (dorsal), 7F, 7G, 7K (face), and 8B. **Levi and Levi (1968)**: figs. 4A, 4B, 5D (face), 5E, 5F, 5I (face), 5J (face), 6D (face), 7H (face), 7J (face), and 9C. **McCloskey (1973)**: figs. 2A (oblique), 2B, 3D, 3E, 3F, 3G, and 3H. **Miner (1950)**: fig. 9B. **Snodgrass (1952)**: fig. 1A (ventral). **Wilson (1878)**: figs. 2A (side and dorsal), and 3C. From specimens or from illustrations on other pages: all figures not listed above.

Chapter 9
Insects

TEXT: **Don Bennett** and **Jane O'Donnell** are coauthors of the adult insect keys. **Eileen Jokinen** wrote the larval insect keys. The key to orders of adult insects is adapted from **Borror and DeLong (1971)** and **Jaques (1947)**. Information about many of the orders is from **Borror and White (1970)** and **Urquhart (1949)**. Keys and descriptions for the lepidopterans are based on **Ehrlich and Ehrlich (1961)**, **Holland (1968)**, and **Klots (1951)**; **Britton and Walden (1911)** for the orthopterans; **Britton et al. (1923)** and **Olmstead and Fell (1974)** for the homopterans and hemipterans; **Arnett (1968)**, **Dillon and Dillon (1961)**, and **Jaques (1951)** for the coleopterans; **Crampton et al. (1942)** for the dipterans; **Fairchild (1950)**, **Jamnback and Wall (1959)**, and **Pechuman (1972)** for the tabanids; **Headlee (1945)** and **Matheson (1945)** for the culicids; and **Viereck et al. (1916)** for the hymenopterans. The keys to larval insects are adapted from **Chu (1949)** and **A. Peterson (1939)**. Information about tabanid larvae is from **Freeman (1987)**, **Jamnback and Wall (1959)** and **Tesky (1969)**.

ILLUSTRATIONS: **Lauren Churchill** drew all of the figures from the following sources: **Arnett (1968)**: figs. 19C, 19D, 19E, 21E, 21F, and 21G. **Borror and DeLong (1971)**: figs. 14A, 14E and 28A. **Borror and White (1970)**: figs. 10A, 10D (grasshopper), 11G (head), 11H (head), 12A (head), 13C, 13D, 13E (side views), 13F, 15B, 16B, 18C (hopper and head, side view), 19B, 21C, 21H, 22A (head, antenna with arista), 22D (fly, antenna), 22E, 23F (fly, wing), 23H, 23I (fly), 23J (fly), 24A (faces), 25B, 25C, 25D, 25E, 25F, 25G, 26A, 26B, 27E, 27F, 27G, 27I, 27J (head), 28B (side view), 29C, 29D, 29E, 29F, 29G, 29H, 29I (wasp) and 29J. **Britton et al. (1923)**: figs. 17C (pointed shoulders), 17D, 17E (bug), 17G, 17H, and 18B. **Chu (1949)**: figs. 31E, 31F, 32A (carabids, heterocerids, coccinelids), 33D, and 34E. **Comstock (1940b)**: figs. 12A (butterfly, moth, scales, antenna), 15C (dorsal view), 17F (wing), 22A (antenna with style), 22C, 22D (foot), 23G (face), 23I (wing), 24A (wing), 25E, 26C, and 29I (galls). **Crampton et al. (1942)**: figs. 22B, 23F *(Tabanus)*, and 23G (foot). **DeLong (1926)**: fig. 18A (hopper). **Fairchild (1950)**: fig. 23F *(Chrysops)*. **Green (1968)**: fig. 14D. **Headlee (1945)**: figs. 24A (mosquitoes) and 33E. **Howard (1916)**: figs. 11H (wings extended, oblique view), 13E (dorsal view), 13G, 14C, 18D, 23G (fly), and 27J (fly). **Jaques (1947)**: figs. 10B, 11E (wings extended), 11F (wings extended), 11G (wings extended), 13B, 17E (tarsus), 17F (head), 18A (heads), and 18C (head, front view). **Jaques (1951)**: figs. 19A, 20A, 20B, and 21D *(Hippodamia)*. **McAlpine (1981)**: figs. 23I (antenna), 23J (antenna), 26D, and 27H. **Olmstead and Fell (1974)**: figs. 17C (rounded shoulders), 17F (bug), 21D *(Naemia)* and 28B (top view). **Pennak (1953)**: figs. 31H (side view), 32A (hydrophilids, chrysomelids), 32B, 33F, 33G, 33H, and 34B. **A. Peterson (1939)**: figs. 30B, 31C, 31G, 31H (underside), 31I, and 33C. **Urquhart (1949)**: figs. 15A, 15C (side view), and 16A. From specimens or from illustrations on other pages: all figures not listed above.

Chapter 10
Crustaceans

TEXT: **Jeffrey S. Pondick** wrote the keys and descriptions to the parasitic and commensal crustaceans. Information is from **Ho (1977)** and **Kabata (1979)** for the parasitic copepods and **Cressy (1978)** for the branchiurans. The keys and descriptions for the amphipods are adapted from **Bousfield (1973)** and **Kunkel (1918)**; **R. I. Smith (1964)**, **Kunkel (1918)**, **Menzies and Frankenberg (1966)**, and **Richardson (1905)** for the isopods; **Wigley (1964a)** for the mysids; **Wigley (1964b)** for the cumaceans; **Zullo (1964)** and **Zullo (1979)** for the barnacles; and **Williams (1984)** and **R. I. Smith (1964)** for the decapod crustaceans (shrimps, lobsters and crabs). **Gosner (1971)** was utilized in the preparation of many of the crustacean keys. The scientific names, common names, and classification system are according to **Bousfield (1973)** for the amphipods, **Manning (1974)** for the stomatopods, **Manning and Felder (1991)** for *Gilvossius*, **Zimmer (1980)** for the cumaceans, **Zullo (1979)** for the barnacles, **Williams et al. (1989)** for the decapods, and **Gosner (1971)** and **Bowman and Abele (1982)** for all other crustaceans. Additional information regarding synonyms was provided in personal communications from **E. L. Bousfield** for amphipods, **Brian Kensley** for isopods, and **Austin Williams** for decapods.

ILLUSTRATIONS: **Patricia May** drew all figures except as otherwise noted. **Lauren Churchill** drew figs. 1L (leg), 1M, 2A (fish with lice), 3H (shrimp), 3H (bopyrid), 4B (top view), 5C, 7E, 9F, 11D, 11I (telson), 12B, 13A, 13C (colony), 13D (scutum), 14B (telson tip), 14D, 14E, 14F, 14G, 15E, 18A (ventral view), 18B (*Axius* and *Gilvossius*), 19D, 22B, 23B (teeth), 23C (teeth), and 25C. **Carmela Venti** drew figs.1B, 2B, 4A, 4B,10A, 11G, 11I, 11J, 11K, 13D (cross sections), 15G, 15H, 17A (claw), 17B, 17C, 17D, and 17E. **Margaret Vose** drew the parasitic crustaceans, figs. 2A (*Brachiella*), 2A (*Lernaeenicus*), 2A (*Penella*), 2B (on snail shell), 2C, 3D, 3E, 3G and 3H (*Aega*). **Barbara J. Williams** drew figs. 13B (barnacle) and 13D (top view). Figures indicated with a prime mark (') were reproduced directly from the sources listed below. All others were drawn by the above artists from the following sources: **Barnes (1968)**: figs. 2A (fish with lice) and 3E (ventral view). **Bousfield (1973)**: figs. 7E, 8A, 9E (appendages), 9F, and 9G (appendages). **Calman (1912)**: figs. 1K and 14A (side views). **Crane (1973)**: fig. 18B. **Gosner (1971)**: figs. 10B (telson), 11H (telson), and 23B (ventral views). **Gosner (1979)**: figs. 2A, 3H, 11C, 11J, 18B, 19E (top view), 21D (shell), and 25C (maxilliped). **Ho (1977)**: fig. 2A (*Brachiella*). **Kabata (1979)**: figs. 2C and 3D. **Kunkel (1918)**: figs. 0D', 1E', 1F, 3G, 4B (side view), 5G'(side view), 5H', 5I', 6B', 6C', 7D, 7F, 7G, 7H, 7I, 8B, 9C, 9D, 9E' (amphipod), 9G (amphipod), 9H', 9I, 10A, 11C, 11F, 11G (isopod), 11H, 11I , 11K, 12A, 12B (side view), 12C', and 12D'. **Meinkoth (1981)**: fig.13C. **Menzies and Frankenberg (1966)**: fig. 10B' (top view). **Miner (1950)**: figs. 2A (*Penella*), 3E (dorsal view), and 3H (bopyrid). **Paulmier (1905)**: figs. 5G' (top view) and 19A' (out of shell). **Pilsbry (1916)**: figs. 0A, 13B (barnacle), 13C and 13D (top view). **Rathbun (1884)**: The exquisite illustrations in this source were drawn by **H. L. Emerton**: figs. 16A', 17B, 18A (dorsal view), 19A' (in shell), 21E, 21F, 22C, 22D, 23A', 23B (dorsal view), 24A, 24B (crab), and 24C (crab). **Richardson (1905)**: figs. 10B (side view) and 12B (dorsal view). **S. I. Smith (1882)**: fig. 17C. **R. I. Smith (1964)**: figs. 11D, 11E, 17D (leg), 17E (leg), 24B (teeth), and 24C (teeth). **Verrill and Smith (1873)**: figs. 1M, 15B (side view), 17A (shrimp), 17D (shrimp), and 17E (shrimp). **Watling (1979)**: figs. 14D, 14E, and 14G. **Wigley (1964a)**: figs. 1L (leg), 15A (top view), 15C, 15D, 15E, 15F, 15G, and 15H. **Wigley (1964b)**: figs. 14A (top view), 14B, 14C, 14D, 14E, 14F, and 14G. **Williams (1965)**: figs. 17A (claw), 17E (*P. pugio*), 17E' (*P. vulgaris*), 19B, 19C, 19E (side view), 21A, 21B, 21C, 21D (claw), 22A, 23C, 25A, 25B, 25C (shells and claw), 25D, 26A', 26B, 26C, and 26D. **Williams (1984)**: figs. 18B (*Axius* and *Gilvossius*), 19D, 22B, 23B (teeth), and 23C (teeth). **Zullo (1964)**: figs. 13A, 13B' (diagram), and 13D' (diagram). **Zullo (1979)**: fig. 13D. From specimens or from illustrations on other pages: all figures not listed above.

Chapter 11
Echinoderms and Hemichordates

TEXT: The keys and descriptions for the echinoderms are adapted from **Coe (1912)**, **Gosner (1971)** and **R. I. Smith (1964)**. The description of the acorn worm is based on **R. I. Smith (1964)**. The scientific names and classification systems are according to **Pawson (1977)** for the Holothuroidea, **Fell (1982)** for the Stelleroidea, **Serafy and Fell (1985)** for the Echinoidea, and **Gosner (1971)** for all others.

ILLUSTRATIONS: **Lauren Churchill** drew figs. 2A, 2B, 2C, 3D, 3E, 3F, 4A, 4B (spines), 4C, 4D, 5E (insets of disc and arms), 5G (disc inset), 6A, 6B, 7E (ossicles), 7F, and 7G. **Patricia May** drew figs. 1B, 1C, 3G, 3H, 3I, 5G (spines), 7C, 7D, and 7E. **Carmela Venti** drew figs. 1A (with spines), 4B, 5E, 5F, and 5G. **Margaret Vose** drew fig. 5A. Illustrations were drawn from the sources listed below. Figure 1A was reproduced directly from its source. **Coe (1912)**: figs. 1A (with spines), 1A (shell), 1B (shell), 1C (shell), 3G, 3H (aboral view), 4B, 5E, 5F, 5G, 7C, and 7E. **Crowder (1931)**: figs. 3I, 7D. **Gosner (1979)**: figs. 1B (hole pattern), 1C (hole pattern), 5E (arm segments), and 5G (disc). **Meinkoth (1981)**: figs. 2A, 2B, 2C, 3F and 4A. **Miner (1950)**: figs. 3E, 4C (disc), 4D (disc), 5E (disc), 6A and 7F. **Pawson (1977)**: figs. 6B, 7E (ossicle) and 7F (ossicles). **R. I. Smith (1964)**: figs. 4B (spines), 5E (spines), 5G (spines), and 7G. From specimens: figs. 1B (with spines), 1C (with spines), and 3H (oral view).

Chapter 12
Tunicates

TEXT: The keys and species descriptions are adapted from **Gosner (1971)** and **R. I. Smith (1964)**. **Richard Malatesta** provided information about *Botrylloides*, the Pacific colonial tunicate, and *Styela clava*, the Pacific rough sea squirt. The scientific names and classification system are according to **Gosner (1971)**.

ILLUSTRATIONS: **Lauren Churchill** drew figs. 0A, 0B, 0C, 1F, 1G, 1H, 1I, and 3C. **Margaret Vose** drew figs. 0D, 1E, 1F, 2A, 2B, and 3D. Illustrations were drawn from the following sources: **Barnes (1968)**: fig. 2B (zooids). **Gosner (1979)**: figs. 0B, 0D, 1I, 2A (spicule), and 3D. **Meinkoth (1981)**: figs. 0A and 1G. **R. I. Smith (1964)**: fig. 1F. From specimens: figures not listed above.

Chapter 13
Fishes

TEXT: The keys are adapted from **Bigelow and Schroeder (1953)**. Descriptions of fishes are based on **Bigelow and Schroeder (1953)**, **Leim and Scott (1966)**, **Scott and Scott (1988)**, and **Thomson, Weed, Taruski and Simanek (1978)**. The scientific names, common names, and classification system are according to **Robins et al. (1991)**.

ILLUSTRATIONS: Figures indicated with a prime mark (') were reproduced directly from their sources. **Lauren Churchill** drew figs. 06B (tail inset), 6C, 9B, 10A (faces), 11F, 12C, 12D, 13E (*A. brevirostrum*), 14A (gill), 15I, 18B, 24B, 27D (gill), and 27E (gill). All other illustrations were redrawn by **Patricia May** from the following sources: **Bigelow and Schroeder (1953)**. Many of these drawings are by **H. L. Todd** and were originally published in **Goode (1884)** and **Jordan and Evermann (1896-1900)**: figs. 1B, 4A, 4B, 5C, 5D, 5E, 5F, 5G, 6A', 6B, 6D, 6E, 7F', 7G', 7H', 7I', 8A', 8B', 8C', 8D', 8E', 8F', 8G', 9A', 9C', 9E', 10A', 10B', 10C', 11E', 11G', 11H', 12A', 12B', 13E', 13F', 13G', 13H', 13I', 13J', 14C', 14D', 15E', 15F', 15G', 15H', 15J', 15K', 15L', 16A', 17D', 17F', 18A', 18B', 18D', 19A', 19B', 19C', 19E', 19F', 20A', 20B', 21C', 21D', 21E', 21F', 21G', 21H', 21I', 22A', 22B', 22C', 23E', 23G', 23H', 23I', 24A', 25C', 25D', 25E', 25F', 25G', 25H', 25I', 25J', 26A', 26B', 26C', 26D', 26E', 27A', 27B', 27C', 27D', 27E', 28A', 28B', 28C', and 28D'. **Böhlke and Chaplin (1968)**: figs. 9B, 18B, and 24B. **Flescher (1980)**: figs. 6B (tail), 6C, 11F, 14A, 15I, 27D (gill arch), and 27E (gill arch). **Jordan and Evermann (1896-1900)**: figs. 11F', 13K', 16B, and 26F'. **Leim and Scott (1966)**: figs. 12D, 17E, and 18C'. **Scott and Scott (1988):** figs. 12C (ventral fin) and 12D (ventral fin). **C. L. Smith (1985)**: fig. 14B. **Thomson, Weed, Taruski and Simanek (1978)**: figs. 9D, 14A, 16C, 19C', 23D', and 23F. From specimens or from illustrations on other pages: all figures not listed above.

Chapter 14
Amphibians and Reptiles

TEXT: **Ellen Dawley** and **Michael Klemens** are coauthors of this chapter. Sources of information used in the preparation of this chapter include **Babbitt (1937)**, **Conant and Collins (1991)**, **Klemens (1993)**, **Lamson (1935)**, and **King (1979)**. Scientific names, common names, and classification system are according to **Collins (1990)**.

ILLUSTRATIONS: **Lauren Churchill** drew all snakes, all amphibians, and the turtle figs. 4B (bridge), 5C, 5D, and 5E. **Roy T. McDonald** drew all other turtles. The illustrations were drawn from the following sources: **Conant (1975)**: figs. 1A, 1B, 1C, 1D, 2A, 2B, 4B, 5C, 5D, 5E, 7E, 7G, 7H, and 7I. **Logier (1958)**: figs. 6A, 6B (actual size), 7F (underside), and 7I (underside). **Simon (1979)**: figs. 6C and 6D. **Zim and Smith (1953)**: figs. 6B (4X), and 7F (snake). From specimens or from illustrations on other pages: all figures not listed above.

Chapter 15
Birds

TEXT: **Margaret Rubega** is coauthor of the bird chapter. Bird descriptions are based on **Farrand (1983)**, **Farrand (1988)**, **R. T. Peterson (1980)**, and **Robbins, Bruun and Zim (1966)**. The scientific names, common names, and classification system are according to **American Ornithologists' Union (1983, 1989)**.

ILLUSTRATIONS: All illustrations were drawn by **Lauren Churchill** from the following sources: **Farrand (1983)**: figs. 5A, 5B, 6B, 7B, 9E, 13D, 13F, 13H,15D, 17F (hovering), 17G, 19G, 21H, 24A, 24B, 24D, 25B, 27C, 27I, 28B, and 29B. **Farrand (1988)**: figs. 6C, 23G, 23H, 24C, 25E, 28C, 29A, 32A (rock dove), 34A (perching), 34C, 35D, 35F, 35G, 35I, and 35K. **R. T. Peterson (1980)**: figs. 1F, 1I, 2C (foot), 3E (flying), 3F (foot), 3G (flying formation), 3I (taking off), 3J (taking off), 4A (adults), 4B, 6A, 7A, 7B (*P. grisegna*), 7C, 7D, 8A, 8B, 9C, 9D, 9F, 9G, 10A, 10B, 10C, 11A, 11B, 11C, 11D, 11E, 12A, 12B, 13C, 13E, 13G, 14A, 14B, 14C, 14D, 15A, 15B, 15C, 15D, 16A, 16B, 16C, 17D, 17E, 17F, 17G (head), 18A, 18B, 19C, 19D, 19E, 20A, 20B, 20D, 21E, 21F, 21G, 22A, 22B, 23C, 23D (adult), 23E, 23F, 25A, 25C, 25D, 26A, 26B, 27D, 27E, 27F, 27G, 27H, 28A, 28D, 28E, 28F, 29C, 29D, 29E, 29F, 30A, 30B, 31C, 31E, 31F, 31G, 32A (mourning dove), 33B, 33C, 33D, 33E (northern flicker), 33F, 34B, 34C, 35E, 35H, 35J, 36A, 36B, 36C, 36D, 36E, 36F, 37A, 37B, 37C, and 37D. **Robbins, Bruun and Zim (1966)**: figs. 1E, 4A (immature), 21C, 23D (immature), 31D, 33E (hairy woodpecker), and 34A (chasing crow). From specimens or from illustrations on other pages: all figures not listed above.

Chapter 16
Mammals

TEXT: The marine mammal key and descriptions are adapted from **Leatherwood, Caldwell and Winn (1976)**, **Katona, Rough and Richardson (1983)**, and **Goodwin (1935)**. Descriptions of terrestrial mammals are based on **Burt and Grossenheider (1964)**, **Godin (1977)**, **Goodwin (1935)**, **Hall and Kelson (1959)**, and **Wetzel (1979)**. Most scientific and common names are according to **Conn. D.E.P. Wildlife Bureau (1988)**. The classification system for terrestrial mammals is from **Godin (1977)**. The classification system in **Leatherwood, Caldwell and Winn (1976)** is used for marine mammals.

ILLUSTRATIONS: All illustrations were drawn by **Patricia May** except as otherwise noted. **Lauren Churchill** drew figs. 0A (heads), 0B, 1C, 1E (*Delphinus, Lagenorhynchus, Stenella*), 1F (*Delphinapterus*), 3F, 7F, and 7G. **Margaret Vose** drew the bats. Illustrations were redrawn from the following sources: **Burt and Grossenheider (1964)**: figs. 5F, 7G. **Goodwin (1935)**: figs. 1C, 1D, 1E (*Delphinus, Tursiops*), and 1F. **Hall and Kelson (1959)**: figs. 0A, 2D, 3E, 5C, 5D, 5E, 5G, 5H, 5J, 6A, and 6C. **Katona et al. (1983)**: figs. 0A (heads), 0B, and 1E (*Lagenorhynchus* and *Stenella*). **Keith (1969)**: fig. 4A. **Murie (1954)**: figs. 2A, 2B, 6B, 7D, 7E, and 7F. **Palmer (1957)**: fig. 4B. **R. L. Peterson (1966)**: figs. 2C and 5I.

INTRODUCTION
AND
KEYS

INTRODUCTION

HOW TO USE THIS BOOK

A key requires the user to make a series of decisions which, if made correctly, will lead to the identification of the organism. Usually each decision involves a choice between two alternatives, called a couplet. Occasionally there are three or more alternatives to choose from. Each decision must be made carefully because it will determine all of the decisions presented thereafter and can lead to an incorrect identification.

After each of the alternative choices in a couplet, you are told what to do next. You may be told to go to another couplet, indicated with the number symbol (#), or to another page.

The following is a sample key with four couplets:

Key to American Coins Dated after 1965

#1.Coin is copper-brown color .... **penny**
#1.Coin is silver color .... #2

#2.One side of coin displays an eagle .... #3
#2.Neither side of coin displays an eagle .... #4

#3.Coin is less than 2.5 cm (1") in diameter .... **quarter**
#3.Coin is greater than 2.5 cm (1") in diameter .... **half-dollar**

#4.The word "liberty" appears behind the head on one side of the coin .... **nickel**
#4.The word "liberty" appears in front of the head on one side of the coin .... **dime**

For practice, identify a nickel using this key. Start with couplet #1. You must decide if the coin is copper-brown or silver colored. Since it is silver, proceed to couplet #2. Your response to decision #2 should be that the coin does not display an eagle and therefore proceed to couplet #4. Your response to decision #4 should be that the coin has "liberty" behind the head and therefore you have identified the coin as a nickel. Note that if you had made an error in decision #2, you would have incorrectly concluded that the coin was a quarter in couplet #3. Now try "keying out" a different coin.

Use both the text and the drawings to make an identification. The illustrations are an important aid in using these keys. ALL technical terms mentioned in the keys are labeled in an accompanying illustration. References to figures are given throughout the keys, e.g., (Fig."X"). Always look at these figures whenever you need help in making a decision and to confirm your final identification. The page and figure number of the color photographs are indicated with reverse type, e.g., **17.05 A**. However, do not rely on the line drawings or the color photographs alone to make an identification. This can lead to serious errors because important diagnostic characteristics may not be immediately obvious in the pictures.

Start off your identification with the Getting Started Key, on page 2.00, unless you are absolutely sure which group key to begin with. Animals in different phyla often look very similar. For example, burrowing anemones and sea cucumbers look wormlike and some worms live in calcareous tubes and look snail-like. Sometimes you may not even be sure if you have a plant or an animal. For example, some bushy bryozoans are often mistaken for algae and some calacareous algae look like sessile animals. The Getting Started Key will help you find the correct chapter key and many chapters begin with an introductory key to guide you to the correct group key. Starting from the beginning can avoid time consuming errors in trying to make an identification using the wrong key.

The identification of a plant or animal is usually much easier when it is alive and undisturbed. Whenever possible for aquatic species, place the living organism in a dish of seawater and leave it alone for a few minutes. Once the organism relaxes, you may begin to observe tentacles, antennae, legs, and other important structures which had been contracted and withdrawn. Distinctive colors and patterns are also often much more obvious when the animal is alive.

PURPOSE OF THIS BOOK

"What's in a name? That which we call a rose by any other name would smell as sweet." [Shakespeare, Romeo and Juliet]

The marine environment is an exceptional educational resource which is readily available to enormous numbers of teachers and students at all levels, as well as to the general public. Furthermore, the harbors, bays, sounds, and estuaries of this region are an important subject of scientific investigation. However, many teachers feel inhibited from bringing a class to the shore because they do not know the names of the organisms their students will find there. Many scientists, such as ecologists and geologists, often need to identify the dominant biota on their study sites but are not taxonomic specialists.

The purpose of these keys is to enable these non-specialists to easily identify the common marine animals of this region. The keys have been written for anyone with a good high school or introductory college level background in biology. Junior and senior high school students should be able to use the keys with some guidance and assistance by their teacher. All technical terms used in the manual are defined in the text or explained through an appropriate illustration.

This book is intended to have a level of technical difficulty between that of the very rigorous and comprehensive keys, such as R. I. Smith (1964) or Gosner (1971), and the more popular field guides. The rigorous keys require a fairly high level of training to use and can be quite frustrating to the nonspecialist. The popular guides depend primarily on the illustrations for making identifications and often result in mistaken identifications from the use of nondiagnostic characteristics, such as color, which in fact may not truly distinguish between a number of the different species.

The keys in this book provide an instructional tool that can be used in invertebrate zoology, marine biology, and other courses to teach about the diversity in form and function that distinguishes one group of marine animals from another. The use of the keys also insures that attention is focused on the truly diagnostic characteristics. However, the illustrations are designed to be used interactively with the keys. All technical terms mentioned in the keys are labeled in an accompanying illustration.

This format is also well suited for use as a self-teaching guide by graduate students and other marine scientists who are new to this region and want to become familiar with these animals. By using this book first, nonspecialists will learn enough of the terminology necessary to proceed to the more comprehensive and technical manuals which will provide the positive identification needed for their scientific work.

The key format is very efficient for identification because it eliminates all but the essential information needed to discriminate between the different organisms. The lack of supplemental information about the life histories, biogeography, ecology, and physiology of the organisms is necessary to keep the book to a reasonable size useful for field work and classroom identification. However, this format might lead one to think that memorizing the names of the animals is a meaningful end in itself. Unless you are a taxonomic specialist, knowing the proper common or scientific name of an organism does not tell very much more about it than using a made-up name. However, once the correct name is known, more valuable information about the organism can be obtained from other references and from laboratory or field studies. These keys should enable the user to move quickly beyond the naming stage and into learning about the important processes and interrelationships that involve these animals.

It cannot be overemphasized that the unneccessary collecting and killing of marine animals should be strongly discouraged. The repeated scavenging of specimens by biology and oceanography classes can destroy the ecology of shoreline areas. In many states it is illegal to collect marine animals without a permit and without obeying strict rules.

A large number of students can share the specimens in a good classroom collection so there is usually no need for each student to have a personal set. Obtain and preserve only one or a few specimens of each species for a classroom collection and leave the other animals alive and undisturbed at your study sites. Rare or endangered species should never be taken, even if they are missing from the collection. Methods for collecting and preserving marine animals are described in Weiss and Dorsey (1979). This reference also contains many nondestructive activities which can be used to study marine animals after they have been identified with these keys.

In an ideal key the decisions should be based on those characteristics that establish the phylogenetic (evolutionary) relationships of the organisms. Broadly speaking, many of these keys do reflect this goal and, whenever possible, closely related species are found together. Even the best keys are only an approximation of the ideal because many phylogenetic relationships are still being studied by biologists. In the keys in this book the most obvious differences were often used in making up the choices even if these differences (such as color) are not the most important in terms of the evolutionary history of the group. For this reason these keys are called "artificial" and the decisions are by no means the only ones that could have been used to distinguish between the organisms. You might find it a worthwhile exercise to make up your own key to recent American coins and see how it differs from the one presented at the beginning of this chapter.

SCOPE OF THIS BOOK

These keys include only the most common animals occurring in the geographic region covered by this book. Less common species will be occasionally found that are not in this book and these species may be rather abundant in certain locales or at certain times of the year. To identify these species, refer to the more comprehensive identification manuals and technical literature listed at the end of this book (pages 18.01-18.05).

Groups that are primarily terrestrial, such as spiders, insects, birds, and mammals, are not covered as completely as animals that are strictly marine. Species that have a special relationship with the marine environment, such as gulls and waterfowl, are treated in greater detail than species that may be occasional visitors from upland sites, such as many perching birds. Frequently, however, these visitors may be quite abundant in coastal habitats.

Whenever possible, these keys can be used to make identifications to the species level. Identification of species in certain groups of organisms, such as amphipods, requires an examination of rather minute anatomical detail and a level of technical training that is beyond the scope of this book. In these cases, the keys may only go to the family or even class level.

The selection of animals included in this book is based on the animals reported to occur in Long Island Sound (Weiss et al., 1995), the Woods Hole region (R. I. Smith, 1964) and Boston Harbor. This book, however, is useful throughout southern New England, New York, and New Jersey (see Fig.A) wherever the environment is shallow (less than about 20 meters or 60' deep), estuarine (salinity of 15-30 o/oo), or semi-protected (restricted access to open ocean).

The Virginian marine biogeographical province extends from Cape Hatteras to Cape Cod. This province is predominantly inhabited by species that are adapted to temperate thermal regimes. The Boreal marine biogeographical region extends from Cape Cod north and contains predominantly cold water species. At Cape Cod, the confluence of the Labrador Current, flowing from the north, and the Gulf Stream, flowing from the south, does function somewhat as a thermal barrier to certain species. However, there are many other factors besides temperature that influence the distribution of marine animals such as geological substrate (sand, rock, mud, etc.), salinity, current speed, wave action, tidal amplitude, nutrient levels, and pollutants. All of these factors must be considered when considering the percentage of species shared in common by different locations within the region covered by this book. For example, Long Island, New York and the Cape Cod peninsula are part of a terminal moraine, the southernmost extent of the last glacial advance. The coast is predominantly rocky north of this moraine and sandy to its south. This transition has a considerable influence on the kinds of animals that colonize the intertidal zone.

Taking all of these factors into consideration, this book is most accurate in places such as Long Island Sound, Narragansett Bay, Buzzards Bay, Great South Bay, the Peconic Bays, the lower Hudson River estuary, Barnegat Bay, Plymouth Bay, and Boston Harbor and most protected harbors and estuaries between Cape Ann, Massachusetts and Cape May, New Jersey. It is much less accurate and should be used with care in open ocean or exposed marine environments such as Block Island Sound, Rhode Island Sound, Massachusetts Bay, Cape Cod Bay, Nantucket Sound, and the New York Bight. For example, the book does not include many of the sharks or whales that are found nearby in open waters but rarely stray into shallow, estuarine waters.

CLASSIFICATION SYSTEM AND NOMENCLATURE

The standard classification system developed by Linnaeus in the eighteenth century organizes living organisms into groups and subgroups as follows:

Kingdom
Phylum
Class
Order
Family
Genus
Species

According to standard practice, the genus and species names are indicated in italics.

Systematists, biologists who study the evolutionary relationships of particular groups of animals, determine how they should be classified based on these relationships. Since this is an ongoing and active field of scientific inquiry, the classification of certain animals may be revised from time to time as our knowledge about these animals improves. For example, animals that were once thought to be the same species may turn out to belong to several different species. The changes in names and classification of animals can be a source of frustration to nontaxonomists who have become used to a particular name. Many species included in this book have been known by different names in the past. Wherever it appears that this may cause some confusion, the previous names are indicated in parenthesis after the currently accepted name. For example, the genus name for the bay scallop has changed several times in recent years but the species name has remained the same. This is indicated in the following manner: *Argopecten irradians (=Aequipecten i. = Pecten i.).*

Although the revision of scientific names may cause some confusion, the variations in common names are much worse. People within a few miles of each other may have many different common names for the same species. For example, in New England, bergall, cunner, and choggy all refer to the same fish, *Tautogolabrus adspersus*. Furthermore, many of the less obvious marine animals do not have any common names. Therefore, most marine animals should be identified by their scientific name to avoid misunderstandings. The American Fisheries Society, the American Ornithologists' Union, and other organizations are attempting to standardize the common names for some groups of animals. Whenever possible, the common names used in this book are based on these standardized names.

The sources of information used for the scientific names, common names, and classification system in each chapter of this book are cited in the Credits and Acknowledgements section.

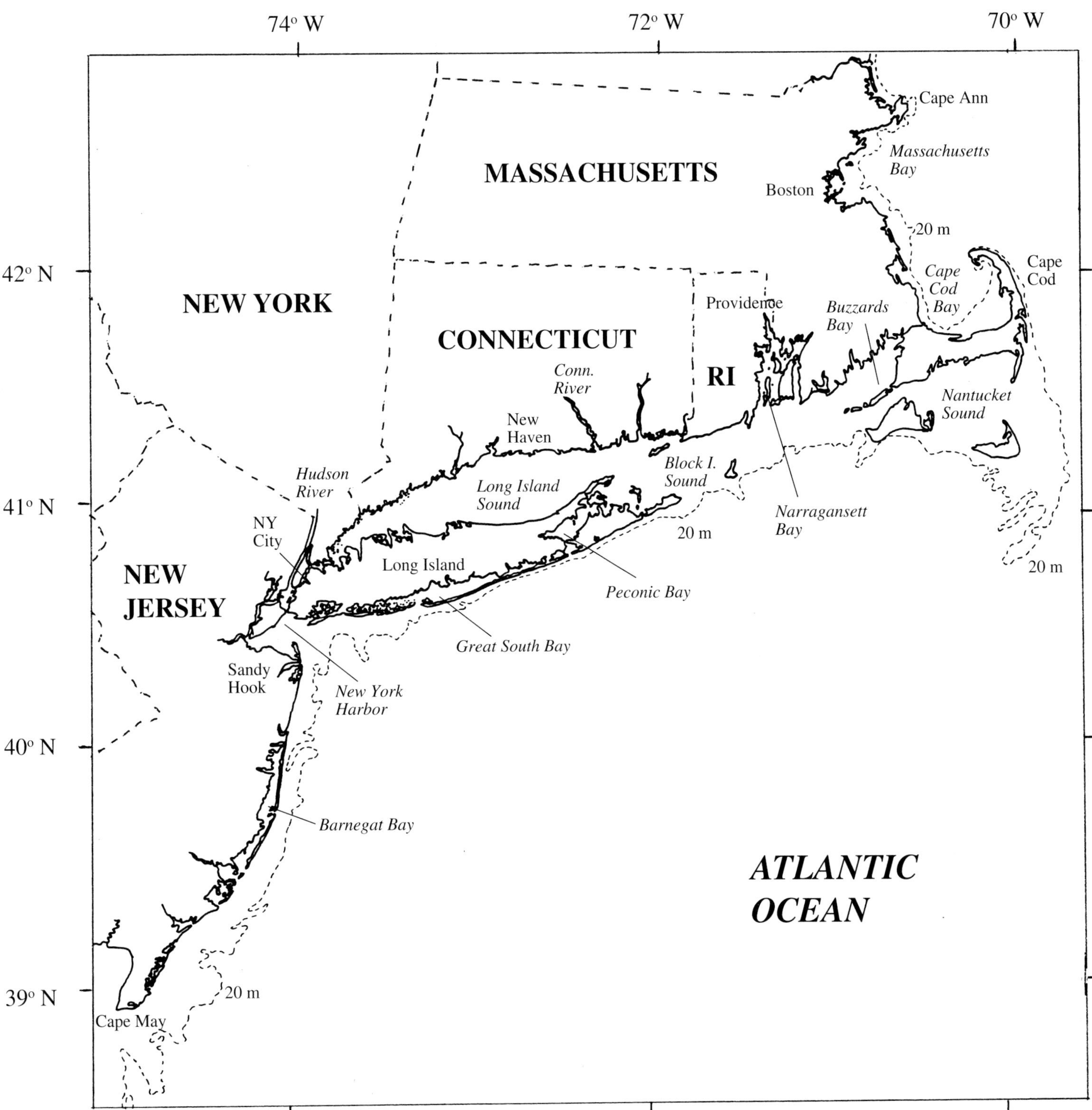

Fig.A. This book can be used in the region shown above wherever the waters are shallow (less than about 20 meters or 60' deep), estuarine (15 - 30 o/oo salinity), or semi-protected (restricted access to open ocean). The 20 meter depth contour is indicated with a dotted line.

GETTING STARTED KEY[1]

(Refer to page 1.01 if you do not know how to use an identification key)

#1.Microscopic size plants and animals, less than 2 mm (1/16") long .... #2

#1.Individuals or colonies of plants and animals larger than 2 mm (1/16") .... **macrofauna and macroflora**, #3

#2.Animals that live inside the body cavity, shell or tissue of another animal .... **parasites and other symbionts**, page 2.18

#2.Free-living, not found living inside another animal. Refer to identification books for **plankton** (organisms in water) and **meiofauna** (organisms in sediments)

#3.Animals that can move about by swimming (Fig.A), floating (Fig.B), walking (Fig.C), flying (Fig.D), crawling (snails, starfish, sea urchins, etc. See Fig.E), burrowing (worms, clams, and any animal buried in mud or sand. See Fig.F). Animals with fins (Fig.A), legs (Fig.C), wings (Fig.D), tube feet (Fig.E), a muscular foot (Figs.E,F) or other structures used in locomotion .... **motile animals**, page 2.12

#3.All plants and sessile animals (animals that attach firmly to one spot on rocks, pilings, seaweeds, eelgrass, shells, etc.) and parasites (animals that live inside other animals) and any nonmoving objects (e.g. egg cases, sand tubes, holes) made by animals. (If in doubt, try this choice) .... **plants, sessile animals, and nonmoving objects**, page 2.01

[1]The identification of a plant or animal is usually much easier when it is alive and undisturbed. Whenever possible, place the living organism in a dish of seawater and leave it alone for a few minutes. Once the organism relaxes, you may begin to observe tentacles, antennae, legs and other important structures which had been contracted and withdrawn. Distinctive colors and patterns are often lost when an organism is dead.

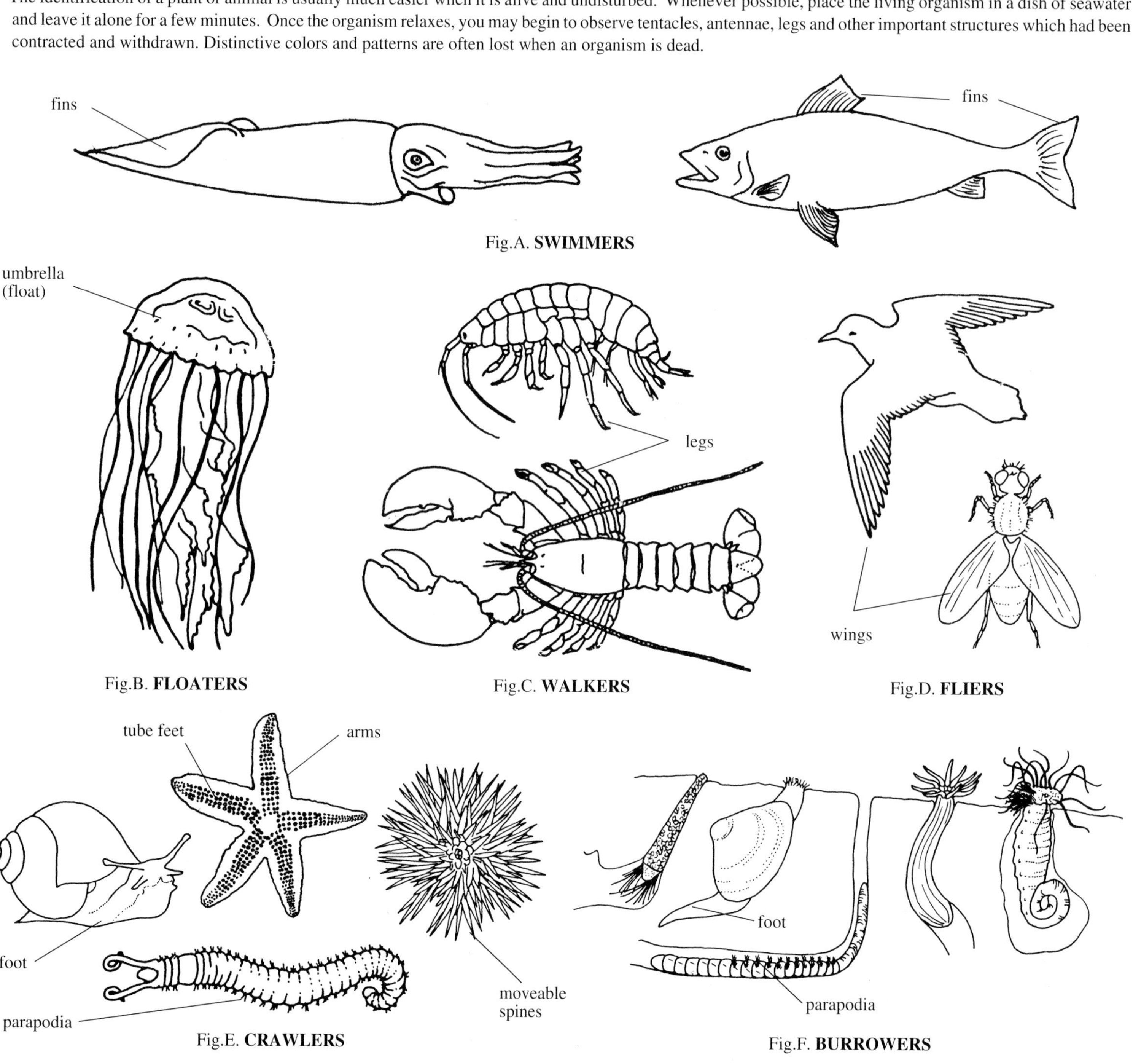

Fig.A. **SWIMMERS**

Fig.B. **FLOATERS**

Fig.C. **WALKERS**

Fig.D. **FLIERS**

Fig.E. **CRAWLERS**

Fig.F. **BURROWERS**

PLANTS AND SESSILE ANIMALS

(Getting started key begins on page 2.00)

#1.Looks typically plantlike (page 2.02, Figs. A-I); seaweeds, grasses, bushes, flowers, lichens, plantlike animals; may be leafy, stringy, bladelike, bushy, branched, or ropelike .... **plants and plantlike animals**, page 2.02
#1.Does not look plantlike (Figs.A-D, this page) .... #2

#2.Forms a thin layer or coating (less than 3 mm (1/8") thick) on the surface of rocks, seaweeds, shells, eelgrass, pilings, etc. and assumes the shape of whatever it is growing on (Fig.A); may be hard or soft (rubbery, leathery, gelatinous, spongy, fuzzy) .... **thin encrusting organisms**, page 2.06
#2.Has a distinct shape and thickness of its own (Figs.B-D) .... #3

#3.Tubes, cones, or other objects of sand, mud, shell fragments, mucus, piles of coiled mud (Fig.B) .... **tubes and castings**, page 2.25
#3.Not a tube and not a pile of mud .... #4

#4.With hard shells (barnacles, limpets, coral, oysters, mussels, etc.) (Fig.C) .... page 2.10
#4.Without hard shells (Fig.D), soft, leathery or parchmentlike[1] to the touch; also irregularly shaped lumpy objects .... #5

#5.Animals that live inside the body cavity, shell, or tissue of another animal .... **parasites and other symbionts**, page 2.18
#5.Not found living inside another animal .... page 2.08

[1]Parchment is a paperlike material that is a bit stiffer and thicker than the pages of this book.

Fig.A. **THIN-LAYERED ENCRUSTING ORGANISMS**

Fig.B. **TUBES, CASTINGS, AND EGG CASES MADE OF MUD, SAND, OR SHELL-LIKE MATERIAL**

Fig.C. **HARD SESSILE ORGANISMS**

Fig.D. **SOFT SESSILE ORGANISMS**

PLANTS AND PLANTLIKE ANIMALS

(Getting started key begins on page 2.00)

#1.All plants with leaves (usually green) and true roots (Fig.A); includes all plants above the high tide level; also includes subtidal grasses (e.g. eelgrass) and intertidal saltmarsh plants .... **vascular plants**[1]
#1.Without leaves or true roots (Figs.B-I); always found in the intertidal zone or below .... **algae and plantlike animals**, #2

#2.Very flat and thin in most parts; may be bladelike, sheetlike, leafy, or membranous (Fig.B) .... **flat algae**[2]
#2.Not flat and thin (Figs.C-I); may be somewhat round or irregular in cross section; may be thick and fingerlike or thin and threadlike .... #3

#3.Not branched (Figs.C,D) .... #4
#3.Branched (Figs.E-I); branches may be thick and fingerlike or thin and threadlike; branch pattern may be bushy, clustered, stolonate, twiglike or featherlike..#6

#4.With a flowerlike cluster of tentacles[3] at the end of a stemlike stalk (Fig. C) .... #5
#4.No tentacles (Fig.D) .... **unbranched algae**[2]

#5.Column ("stalk") is narrow and long; at least 4 times as long as wide (Fig.C) .... **hydroids**, page 4.04
#5.Column is wide; less than 3 times as long as wide (Fig.C) .... **anemones**, page 4.12
#5.Column is narrow and short; with 8 arms each ending in a cluster of tentacles (Fig.C) .... **stalked jellyfishes**, page 4.00

#6.With thick, spongy and porous branches (Figs.E,F) usually greater than 2 mm (1/16") in diameter; may or may not have microscopic spicules[4]. .... #7
#6.With thin, threadlike, twiglike, featherlike or filamentous branches (Figs.G-I) usually less than 2 mm (1/16") in diameter; no microscopic spicules .... #8

#7.Color dark green; branches very limp when out of water; no microscopic spicules[4] (Fig.E) .... ***Codium fragile*, an alga**[2]
#7.Color variable, rarely dark green; branches may be firm when out of water; microscopic spicules always present (Fig.F) .... **sponges**, page 3.00

#8.A colony made up of numerous zooids[5] (cup shaped, tubular, boxlike or funnel shaped structures which can be seen at the branch tips or along the branches when examined under a microscope or magnifying lens at 20X); most zooids have tentacles[6] but the tentacles are often withdrawn or contracted and may not be easily observed (see page 2.04, Figs.A-N) .... **branching plantlike animals**, page 2.04
#8.No zooids or tentacles can be seen when branches are examined at 20X magnification[6] (Fig.I); cells have chromatophores (organelles containing green, red or brown pigments) which can be seen at 100X or higher magnifications; some species, such as *Corallina* (Fig.G), are heavily calcified (shell-like) .... **algae**[2]

[1]Refer to a guide to the identification of seashore vascular plants such as Army Corps of Engineers (1977), Duncan and Duncan (1987), Moul (1973), Petry (1968), or Silberhorn (1982).
[2]Refer to an algae identification guide such as Hylander (1928), Taylor (1957), or Taylor and Villalard (1979).
[3]See footnote 1 on page 2.00.
[4]Spicules are microscopic skeletal structures. See page 3.00 for directions on preparing spicules for microscopic examination.
[5]In this key, "zooids" are defined as the individual members of a colony of animals and refer to both the polyps of a hydroid and the zooecia of a bryozoan.
[6]The colonies of some bushy bryozoans and hydroids (Fig.H) are often mistaken for algae. Some calcareous algae (Fig.G), especially when bleached white by the sun, look like sessile branched animals. For easiest identification, place a fresh, living specimen in seawater and leave undisturbed for at least 5 minutes. Examine carefully under a dissecting microscope at 20X and look for zooids (see page 2.04, Figs.A-N) and the movement of tentacles, avicularia, and other structures shown on pages 2.04-2.05.

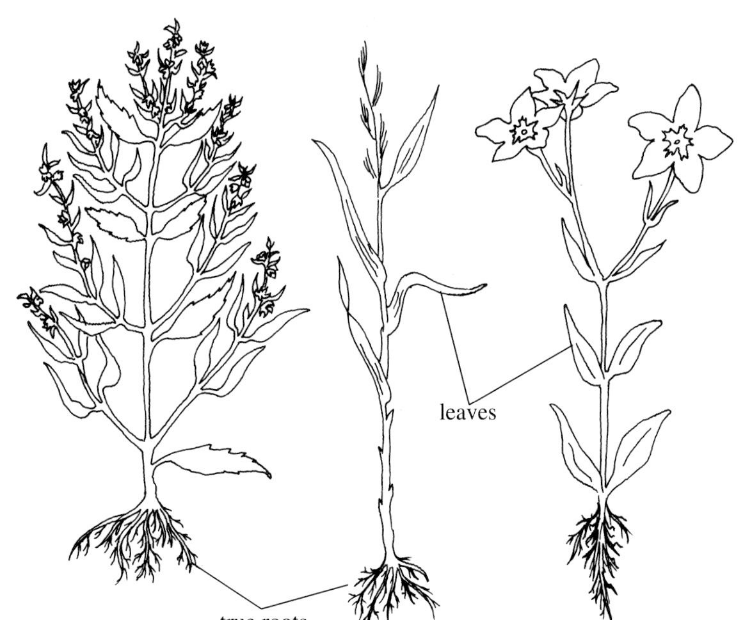

Fig.A. **VASCULAR PLANTS**

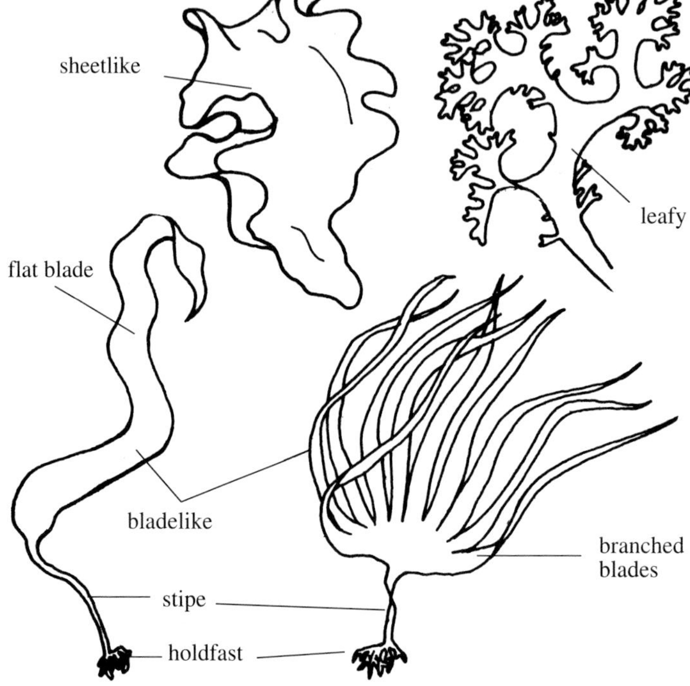

Fig.B. **FLAT ALGAE**

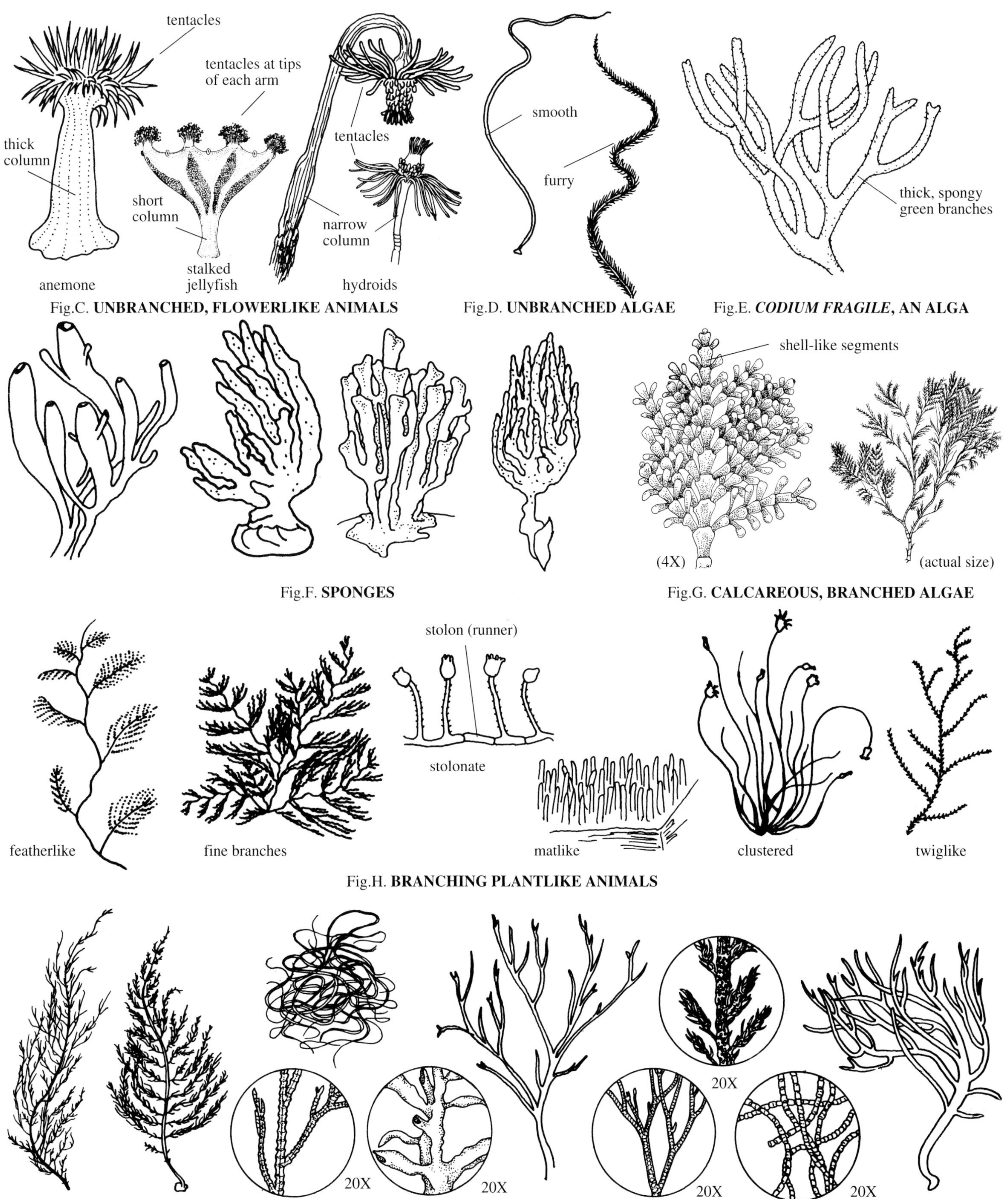

Fig.C. **UNBRANCHED, FLOWERLIKE ANIMALS**

Fig.D. **UNBRANCHED ALGAE**

Fig.E. ***CODIUM FRAGILE*, AN ALGA**

Fig.F. **SPONGES**

Fig.G. **CALCAREOUS, BRANCHED ALGAE**

Fig.H. **BRANCHING PLANTLIKE ANIMALS**

Fig.I. **FILAMENTOUS, BRANCHED ALGAE**

BRANCHING PLANTLIKE ANIMALS[1]

(Getting started key begins on page 2.00)

#1.Colony has a bushy, featherlike or twiglike branching pattern (see Fig.H on page 2.03) with a main stem dividing into branches which further subdivides into smaller branches (Figs A-D) .... #2

#1.With a stolonate, clustered or matlike branching pattern (see Fig.H on page 2.03); stolonate type branching has a threadlike runner or rootlike network (stolon) which connects individual upright zooids[2] or branches (Figs.E-K); matlike (Figs.L,M) and clustered (Fig.N) types of branching have a number of unbranched stems arising from a common base .... #5

#2.Main stems made out of zooids[2] (tubular or boxlike "cells", Fig.A); may have beaklike structures (avicularia) on some of the branches (avicularia are often difficult to find) .... **bushy bryozoans**, page 6.00

#2.Zooids are attached to stems or branches (Figs.B-D); main stems are not constructed from zooids .... #3

#3.Zooids do not have a stem or stalk; zooids are somewhat tubular or cylindrical in shape (Fig.B) .... **some hydroids**, page 4.07

#3.Zooids have a long or short, narrow stem or stalk; zooids are somewhat goblet, vase or funnel shaped (Figs.C,D) .... #4

#4.Zooids are paired opposite each other on branches or spiral around branches; zooid stems very short or absent (Fig.C) .... **some bryozoans**, page 6.06

#4.Zooids are arranged alternately or irregularly on branches; the stem or stalk of each zooid usually is long (Figs.D,N) .... **some hydroids**, page 4.08

#5.Zooids do not have any stem or stalk; zooids are somewhat tubular or cylindrical in shape (Fig.E) .... **some bryozoans**, page 6.06

#5.Zooids have a narrow stem or stalk; zooids are somewhat goblet or flower shaped (Figs.F-N) .... #6

#6.Erect or upright portion of colony is branched (Figs.G,N) .... **some hydroids**, page 4.04

#6.Erect or upright portion of colony is not branched (Figs.H-N) .... #7

#7.With tentacles scattered all over head of zooid (Fig.H) or with two circles of tentacles at top of zooid (Fig.N) .... **some hydroids**, page 4.10

#7.With one circle of tentacles at top of zooid (Figs.I-M) .... #8

#7.With no tentacles (Fig.F); with two siphons (short tubular openings) .... **creeping stolonate tunicate**, page 12.01

#8.Colony forms a dense, fuzzy mat usually found growing on living snail shells or snail shells occupied by hermit crabs (Fig.L); the base mat is crustlike or rootlike and has tiny spines .... **some hydroids**, page 4.06

#8.Not usually found on living snail shells or snail shells occupied by hermit crabs .... #9

#9.Zooids arise from a rubbery or gelatinous base mat (Fig.M) that may be spiny or may have rounded puckered openings .... **rubbery bryozoans**, page 6.05

#9.Zooids arise from a threadlike runner (stolon) (Figs.I-K) .... #10

#10.Tentacles can be withdrawn into a goblet shaped, protective collar (Fig.I) .... **some hydroids**, page 4.08

#10.Tentacles cannot be withdrawn into a protective collar; when disturbed, tentacles curl up rather than contract (Fig.J) .... **entoprocts**, page 6.07

#10.Tentacles can be withdrawn into a spoon shaped or club shaped collar (Fig.K); stalk may be snakelike with spiral lines .... **some bryozoans**, page 6.06

[1]The branched animals shown here are often mistaken for algae. Some calcareous algae look like sessile branched animals. Refer to couplet #8 and footnote 6 on page 2.02 to distinguish between these plants and animals.

[2]In this key, "zooids" are defined as the individual members of a colony of animals and refer to both the polyps of a hydroid and the zooecia of a bryozoan.

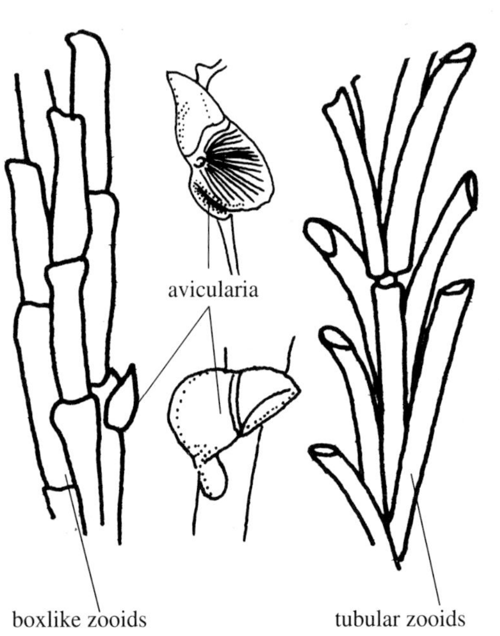

Fig.A. **BUSHY BRYOZOANS (20X)**

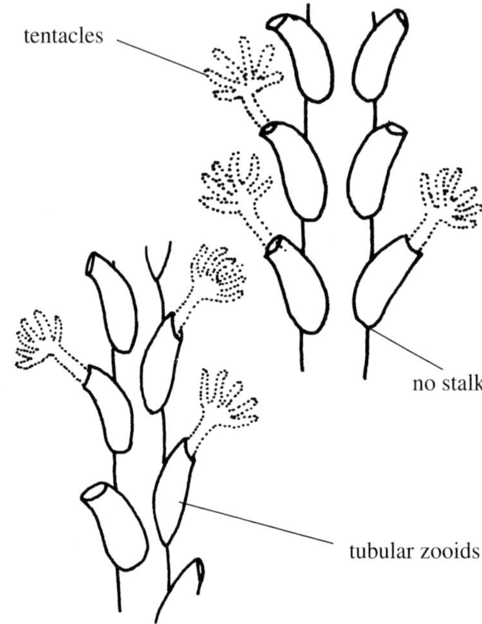

Fig.B. **BRANCHING HYDROIDS WITH STALKLESS ZOOIDS (20X)**

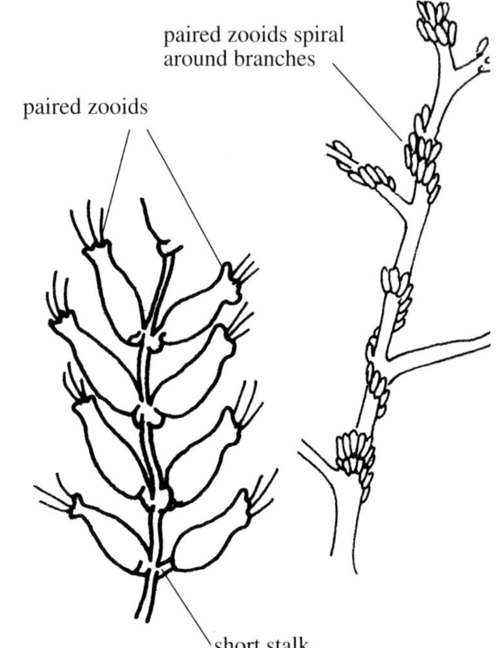

Fig.C. **BRANCHING BRYOZOANS (20X)**

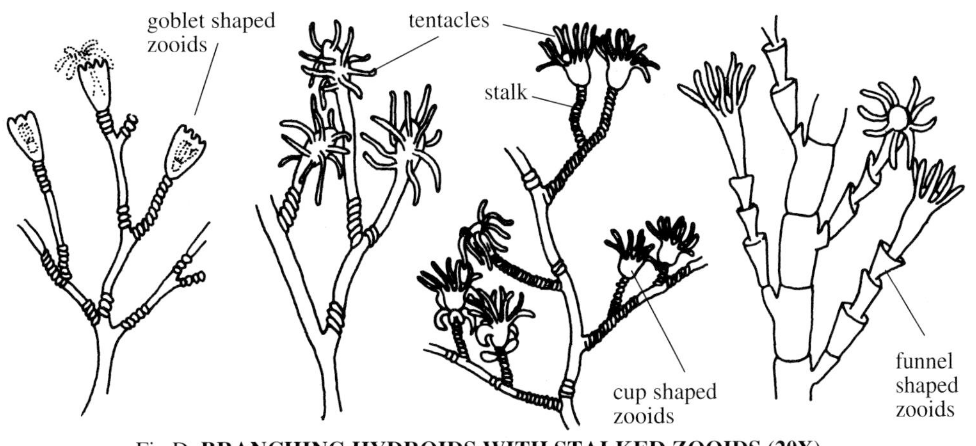

Fig.D. **BRANCHING HYDROIDS WITH STALKED ZOOIDS (20X)**

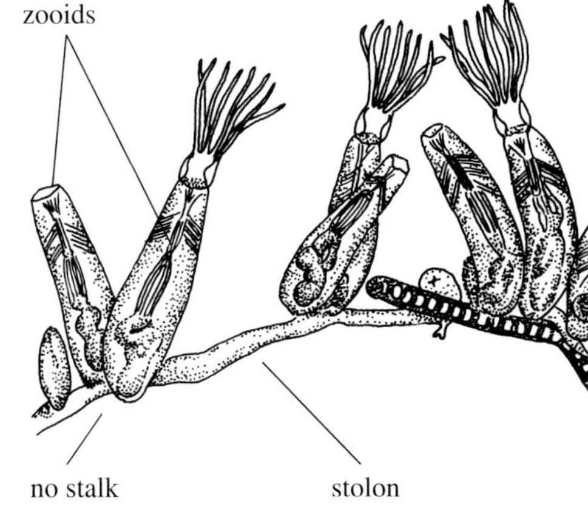

Fig.E. **STOLONATE BRYOZOAN (20X)**

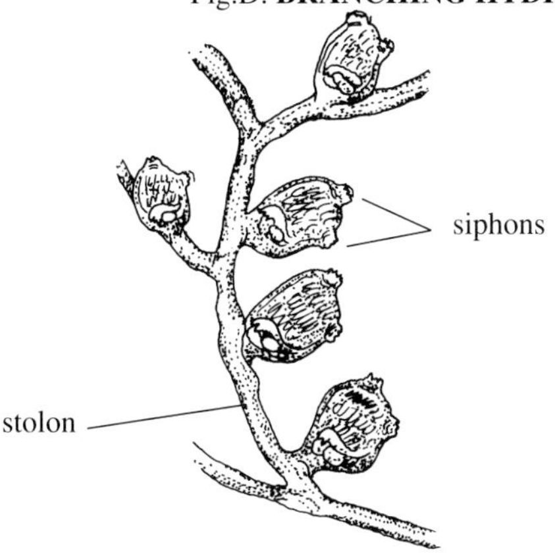

Fig.F. **STOLONATE TUNICATE (4X)**

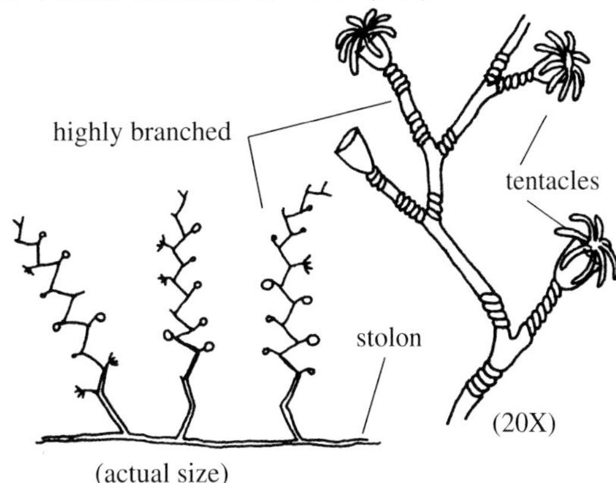

Fig.G. **STOLONATE, BRANCHED HYDROIDS**

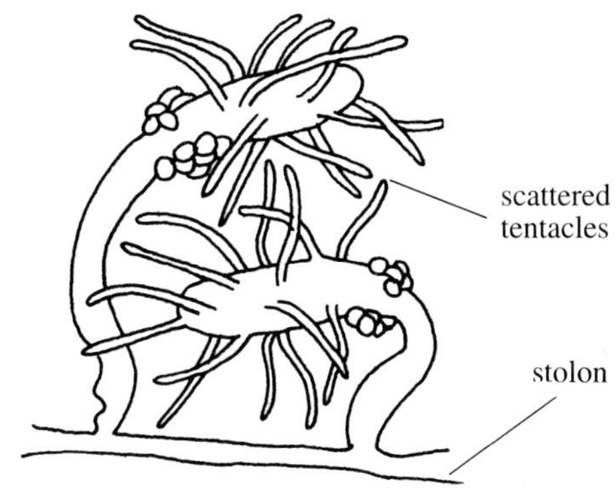

Fig.H. **STOLONATE, UNBRANCHED HYDROID (20X)**

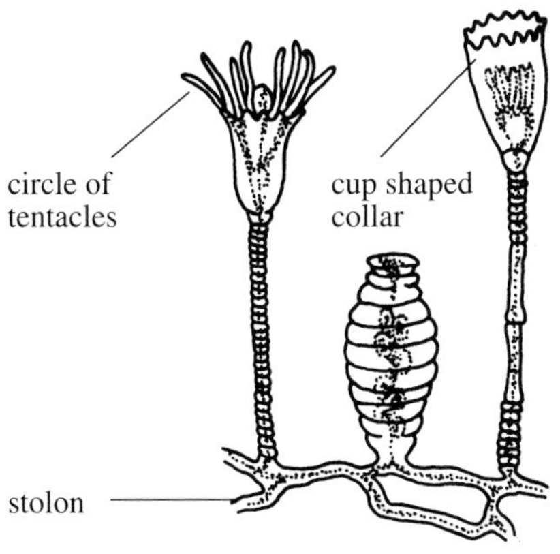

Fig.I. **STOLONATE, UNBRANCHED HYDROID (20X)**

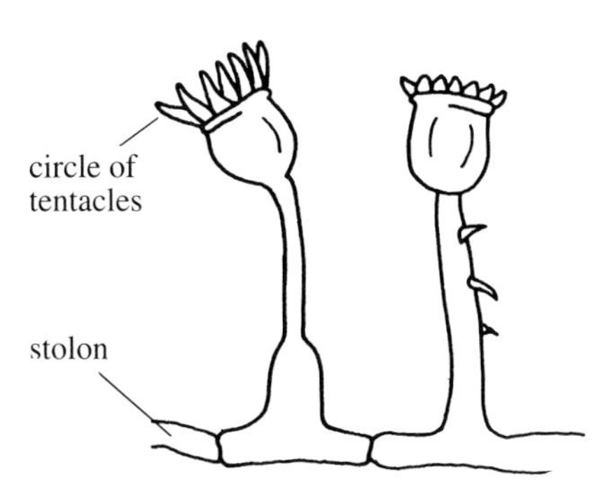

Fig.J. **STOLONATE ENTOPROCTS (20X)**

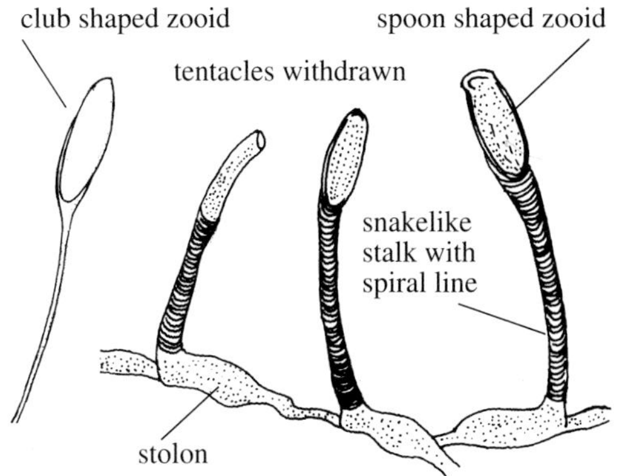

Fig.K. **STOLONATE BRYOZOANS (20X)**

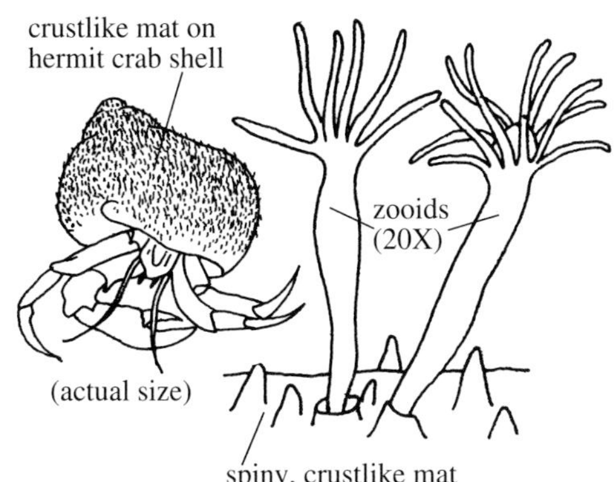

Fig.L. **MATLIKE HYDROIDS**

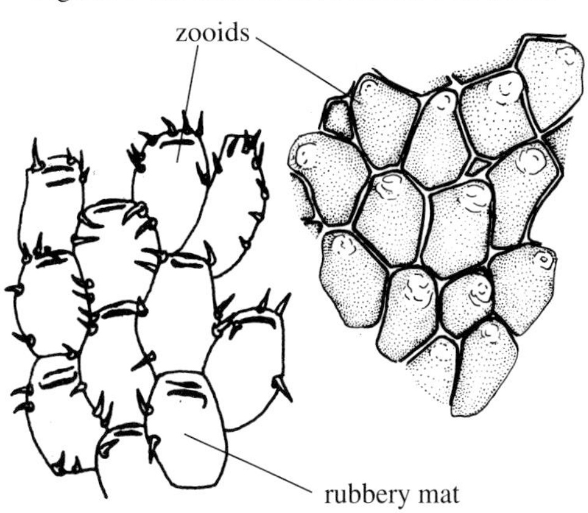

Fig.M. **RUBBERY BRYOZOANS (20X)**

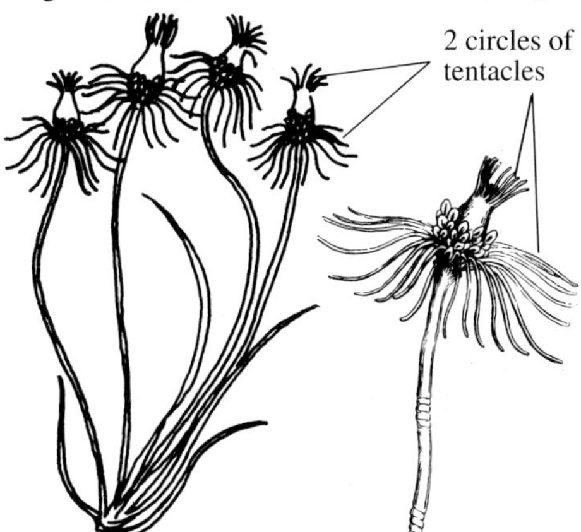

Fig.N. **CLUSTERED HYDROIDS**

THIN ENCRUSTING ORGANISMS

Hard or soft animals and plants growing as a thin layer or coating over a substrate

(Getting started key begins on page 2.00)

#1.Very thin film, crust, stain or enamel-like coating on rocks, shells, seaweeds and other substrates (Fig.A); too thin to be easily scraped off with a knife (less than 1 mm (1/32") thick), often appears to be painted onto the substrate; may be red, black, green purple, white or other colors .... **encrusting algae**[2]
#1.Organism usually thicker than 1 mm (1/32"); usually can be scraped off substrate (Figs.B-L) .... #2

#2.Made of shelly (calcareous) material; often white but may be orange, brown or other colors (Figs.B-F) .... #3
#2.Soft, leathery, slimy, furry, spongy, rubbery, or gelatinous; not calcareous (Figs.G-L) .... #7

#3.Roughly circular in outline (Figs.B,C); appears to have radiating lines or holes .... #4
#3.Usually irregular or tubular or lacelike (Figs.D-F) .... #5

#4.Lines in shelly material radiate from center of disc (Fig.B); entire disc may be larger than 3 mm (1/8") in diameter .... **barnacle basal plate**, page 10.13
#4.Pores (holes) in shelly material radiate from center of disc (Fig.C); entire disc is less than 3 mm (1/8") in diameter .... **disc shaped bryozoans**, page 6.02

#5.Delicately lacelike or moderately porous (Fig.D) .... **lacy encrusting bryozoans**, page 6.02
#5.Without numerous pores; may be tubelike or platelike .... #6

#6.Twisted or coiled calcareous (shell-like) tubes (Fig.E) attached to rocks, algae, eelgrass, etc .... page 2.25
#6.Thin, oval, white shells (Fig.F) which attach firmly to hard objects such as rocks, bottles, etc.; often attaches to the inside of large snail shells and the underside of horseshoe crab shells; with a shelf on underside that can be seen when shell is pried off .... ***Crepidula plana*, eastern white slippersnail**, page 7.01

#7.Fuzzy, furry, hairlike or threadlike in texture (this can be best determined when it is submerged in seawater and examined at 10X magnification) .... #8
#7.Rubbery, spongy, gelatinous or leathery in texture .... #9

#8.Forms a dense fuzzy mat usually found on hermit crab or living snail shells (Fig.G); when submerged in sea water and undisturbed, tentacle bearing polyps may be seen (at 20X magnification) arising from the base mat; the base mat is crustlike or rootlike and has tiny spines (examine the spines at 20X magnification with the colony out of the water and the polyps contracted) .... **hydroids**, page 4.06
#8.Not usually found on living snail shells or snail shells occupied by hermit crabs; rootlike network, if present, without spines .. **branching animals**, page 2.04

#9.Individual zooids can be distinguished when colony is examined at 20X magnification (Figs.H-J); no spicules[1]; each zooid usually has at least one pore or opening; some zooids may have tentacles (Fig.J); some zooids may be arranged in star shaped clusters (Fig.H) or wavy lines (Fig.I); surface texture is usually rubbery or gelatinous .... #10
#9.Individual zooids cannot be distinguished when colony is examined at 20X magnification (Figs.K,L); with spicules[1] which may be needle or star shaped; surface may have numerous pores and/or wartlike bumps; surface texture may be soft and spongy, leathery or rubbery but not usually gelatinous .... #12
#9.Individual zooids cannot be distinguished when colony is examined at 20X; no spicules[1]; smooth slimy film with tiny pores .... **slime sponge,** page 3.00

#10.Zoolds arranged in numerous star shaped (radiating) structures (this pattern is much more obvious on living animals than preserved specimens) (Fig.H) .... **colonial tunicates**, page 12.02
#10.Zooids are not arranged in star shaped clusters (Figs.I,J) .... #11

#11.Colony usually bright orange, but may be yellow, white or red; no tentacle bearing structures ever emerge from the openings; zooids may be arranged in wavy, twisted lines (Fig.I); colony is never spiny .... **colonial tunicates**, page 12.02
#11.Not usually bright orange; tentacle bearing zooids may be seen (at 20X magnification) emerging from the openings when the undisturbed living colony is submerged in sea water; a rubbery or gelatinous layer composed of numerous tiny (up to 3 mm (1/8") high) conical projections having puckered openings and sometimes bristling with small spines (Fig.J) .... **rubbery bryozoans**, page 6.05

#12.Tough white crust; has tiny star shaped spherical spicules with numerous points (Fig.K); rubbery or leathery in texture, without any tubules or projections . ... ***Didemnum candidum*, colonial tunicate**, page 12.02
#12.Color variable, never pure white; spicules have 3 or fewer rays; usually spongy and porous in texture; may or may not have chimneylike tubules, fingerlike projections or wartlike bumps (Fig.L) .... **sponges**, page 3.00

[1]Spicules are microscopic skeletal structures rarely over 700 µm long. See page 3.00 for directions on preparation of spicules for microscopic examination.
[2]Refer to an identification guide to the algae. See footnote 2 on page 2.02.

Fig.A. **VERY THIN FILMS, CRUSTS, STAINS**

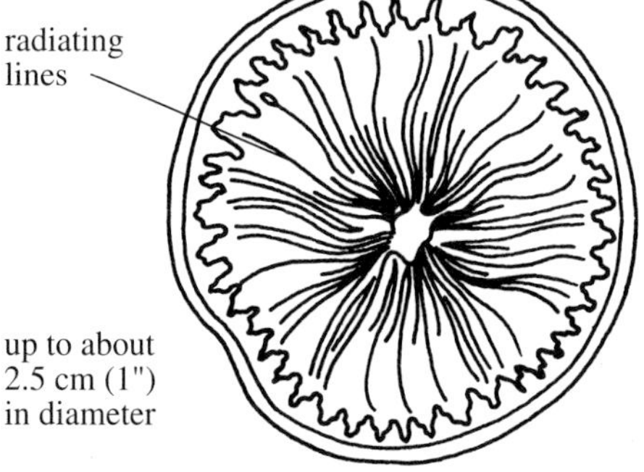

radiating lines

up to about 2.5 cm (1") in diameter

Fig.B. **BARNACLE BASAL PLATE**

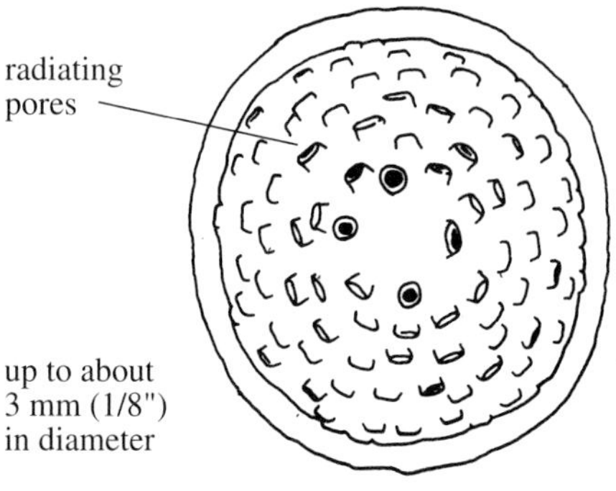

radiating pores

up to about 3 mm (1/8") in diameter

Fig.C. **DISC SHAPED BRYOZOANS**

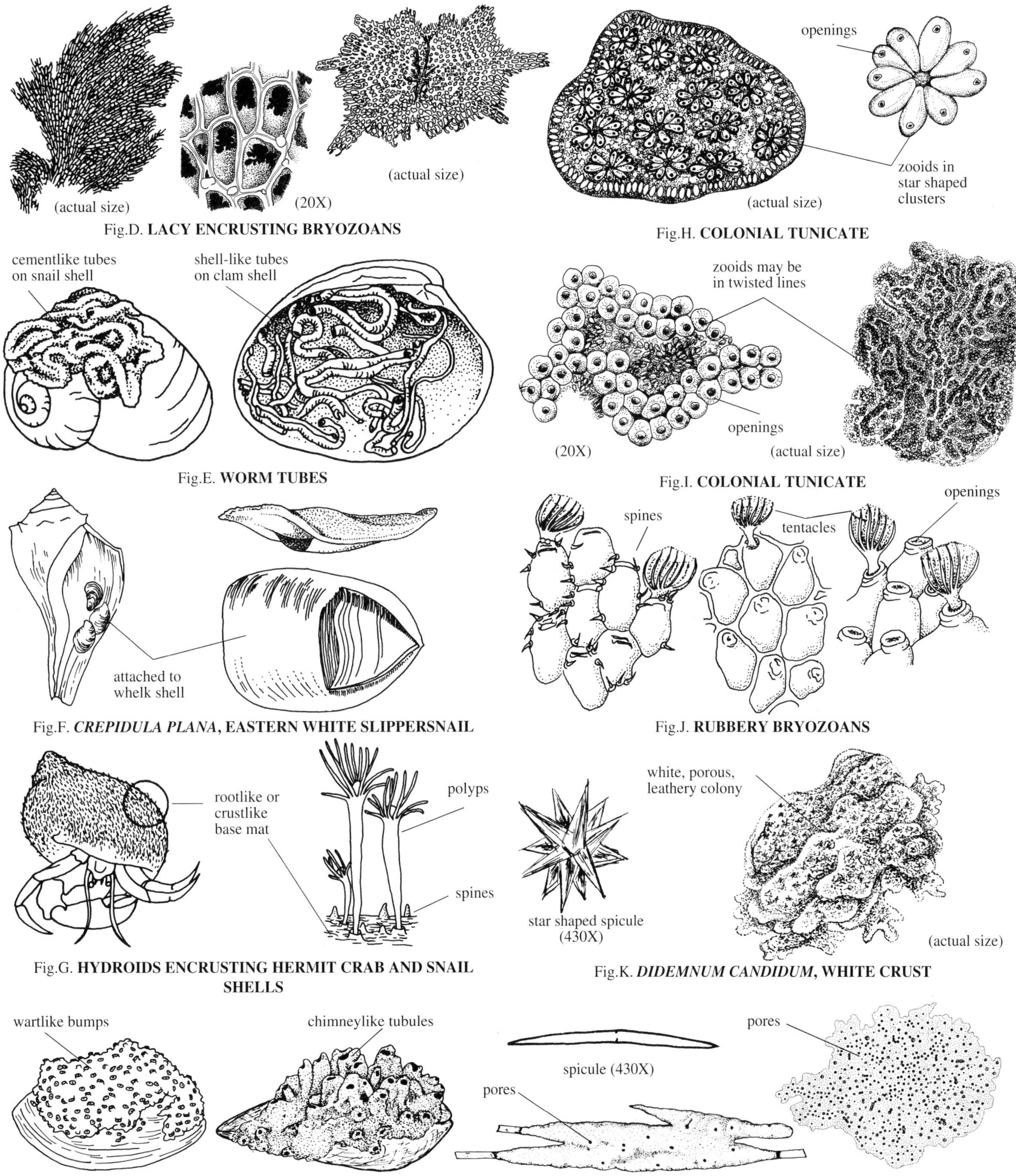

Fig.D. **LACY ENCRUSTING BRYOZOANS**

Fig.H. **COLONIAL TUNICATE**

Fig.E. **WORM TUBES**

Fig.I. **COLONIAL TUNICATE**

Fig.F. ***CREPIDULA PLANA*, EASTERN WHITE SLIPPERSNAIL**

Fig.J. **RUBBERY BRYOZOANS**

Fig.G. **HYDROIDS ENCRUSTING HERMIT CRAB AND SNAIL SHELLS**

Fig.K. ***DIDEMNUM CANDIDUM*, WHITE CRUST**

Fig.L. **SPONGES**

NONMOTILE[1] ANIMALS AND EGG CASES - WITHOUT SHELLS

(Getting started key begins on page 2.00)

#1.Numerous rubbery or gelatinous spheres (Fig.A) stuck together to form a round, or ribbonlike or irregularly shaped mass; may be attached to rocks, seaweeds, eelgrass, etc. or may be unattached .... **egg masses**, page 2.22
#1.Not made up of numerous rubbery or gelatinous spheres .... #2

#2.Less than 8 mm (5/16") in height, width and length .... #3
#2.More than 8 mm (5/16") in height, width, or length .... #5

#3.Gelatinous (jellylike), semitransparent; may be ribbonlike, coiled, threadlike, doughnut shaped or dropletlike (Fig.B); often found in rows or clusters on eelgrass, algae, hydroids, etc.; no openings; sometimes with one or more spherical eggs visible inside at 20X magnification .... **snail eggs**, page 2.22
#3.Leathery, rubbery, spongy or parchmentlike[2]; may have one or more openings (which may be closed or plugged) .... #4

#4.Wine glass, vase or goblet shaped (Fig.C); stands erect on a stalk or stem; with a single opening (which may be closed) at top; no tentacles or bristles around opening; often in rows or clusters on rocks, shells and other hard substrates; parchmentlike[2] covering .... **snail eggs**, page 2.22
#4.Not wine glass shaped (Figs.I-R) .... #7

#5.Gelatinous (jellylike), semitransparent; may be a large clump of clear, cigar shaped lobes, about 5 cm (2") long, with tiny spherical eggs or embryos visible inside (Fig.D) or may be greenish, pear shaped, and loosely attached to mud by a threadlike stalk with total length about 2.5 cm (1") (Fig.E) .... **eggs**, page 2.22
#5.Not gelatinous; not shaped as described above (Figs.F-R) .... #6

#6.Parchmentlike[2] or vinyl plasticlike; may be a light colored string of discs (Fig.F) about 20 cm (8") long, or a dark colored rectangular pouch about 10 cm (4") long with hornlike projections (Fig.G) or a light colored "popcorn ball" shaped mass of hollow spheres (Fig.H) about 10 cm (4") in diameter; not firmly attached to a substrate but may be entangled in seaweed .... **egg cases**, page 2.22
#6.Leathery, rubbery or spongy; not shaped as described above (Figs.I-R) .... #7

#7.Buried or burrowed in sand, mud or other bottom sediments .... **motile animals**, page 2.12
#7.Firmly attached[1] to rocks, shells, seaweed, pilings, eelgrass or other substrates .... #8

#8.With one or more circles of tentacles at the end of a cylindrical or stemlike column (Figs.I,J); tentacles may contract or withdraw when disturbed .... #9
#8.Without obvious tentacles (Figs.K-R) .... #10

#9.Stem or stalk is slender, more than 4 times as long as wide (Fig.I); stem may or may not be branched .... **hydroids**, page 4.04
#9.Column ("body") is thick, less than 3 times as long as wide (Fig.J) and is not branched .... **anemones (open)**, page 4.12
#9.Stem or stalk is short; with 8 arms each ending in a cluster of tentacles .... **stalked jellyfishes**, page 4.00

#10.Globular, vase shaped or a rounded conical mound shape (Figs.K-M) with one or two openings at top (openings may be closed) .... #11
#10.May be flat and thin or sluglike (Fig.R) or lumpy (Figs.O-Q) or with upright projections (Fig.N); with no openings or with numerous pores .... #13

#11.A rounded conical mound with a single opening at the top (Fig.K) .... **anemones (closed)**, page 4.12
#11.Globular, club shaped or vase shaped (Figs.L,M) .... #12

#12.With two openings (Fig.L); each opening is at the end of a short tube (siphon) (openings may be closed and siphons contracted when animal is disturbed); may be yellowish with coiled orange intestines visible inside or may be rough, bumpy and brownish; without spicules[3]. .... **sea squirts**, page 12.00
#12.With one opening surrounded by a fringe of bristles or hairs (Fig.M); white, soft and flexible; with calcareous spicules having 3-4 radiating rays .... **vase sponge**, page 3.00

#13.With erect projections (Fig.N) which may be fingerlike, chimneylike or pillarlike and may be branched or unbranched; with spicules[3]. .... #14
#13.Without erect projections; may or may not have spicules .... #15

#14.With zooids (polyps) having featherlike tentacles (polyps withdraw when disturbed); spicules[3] are calcareous, tooth shaped, spiny .... **soft coral**, page 4.16
#14.No zooids (polyps); spicules[3] are usually siliceous with 1 or 2 rays but may be calcareous with 3 or 4 rays .... **sponges**, page 3.00

#15.Thick, massive and lumpy (Figs.O-Q); may be smooth or covered with wartlike bumps; usually yellowish or brownish .... #16
#15.Thin, not lumpy .... #18

#16.Hollow (Fig.O); up to 10 cm (4") in diameter; no spicules .... **sea potato, algae**[4]
#16.Solid; may be firm or spongy; may or may not have spicules; may grow larger than 10 cm (4") in diameter .... #17

#17.With spicules[3]; may have wartlike bumps (Fig.P) or may be smooth and liverlike; no tentacle bearing zooids emerge from openings .... **sponges**, page 3.00
#17.No spicules; surface covered with puckered openings (Fig.Q); tentacle bearing zooids may emerge when undisturbed .... **rubbery bryozoans**, page 6.05

#18.Sluglike, somewhat oval in outline (Fig.R); moves very slowly and may seem to be immobile unless observed carefully; often responds to touch by moving or contracting .... **wormlike, motile animals**, page 2.16
#18.Irregular in outline; firmly attached to substrate and does not move .... **encrusting organisms**, page 2.06

[1]Some very slow moving animals may appear to be nonmotile (nonmoving, firmly attached to substrate). If the animal does not key out on this page then try page 2.16 which includes all wormlike and sluglike animals which creep on the substrate (rocks, seaweeds, pilings, etc.) or burrow into the bottom (mud, sand, etc.).
[2]Parchment is a paperlike material that is a bit stiffer and thicker than the pages of this book.
[3]Spicules are microscopic skeletal structures. See page 3.00 for instructions on how to prepare spicules for microscopic examination.
[4]Refer to an identification guide to the algae. See footnote 2 on page 2.02.

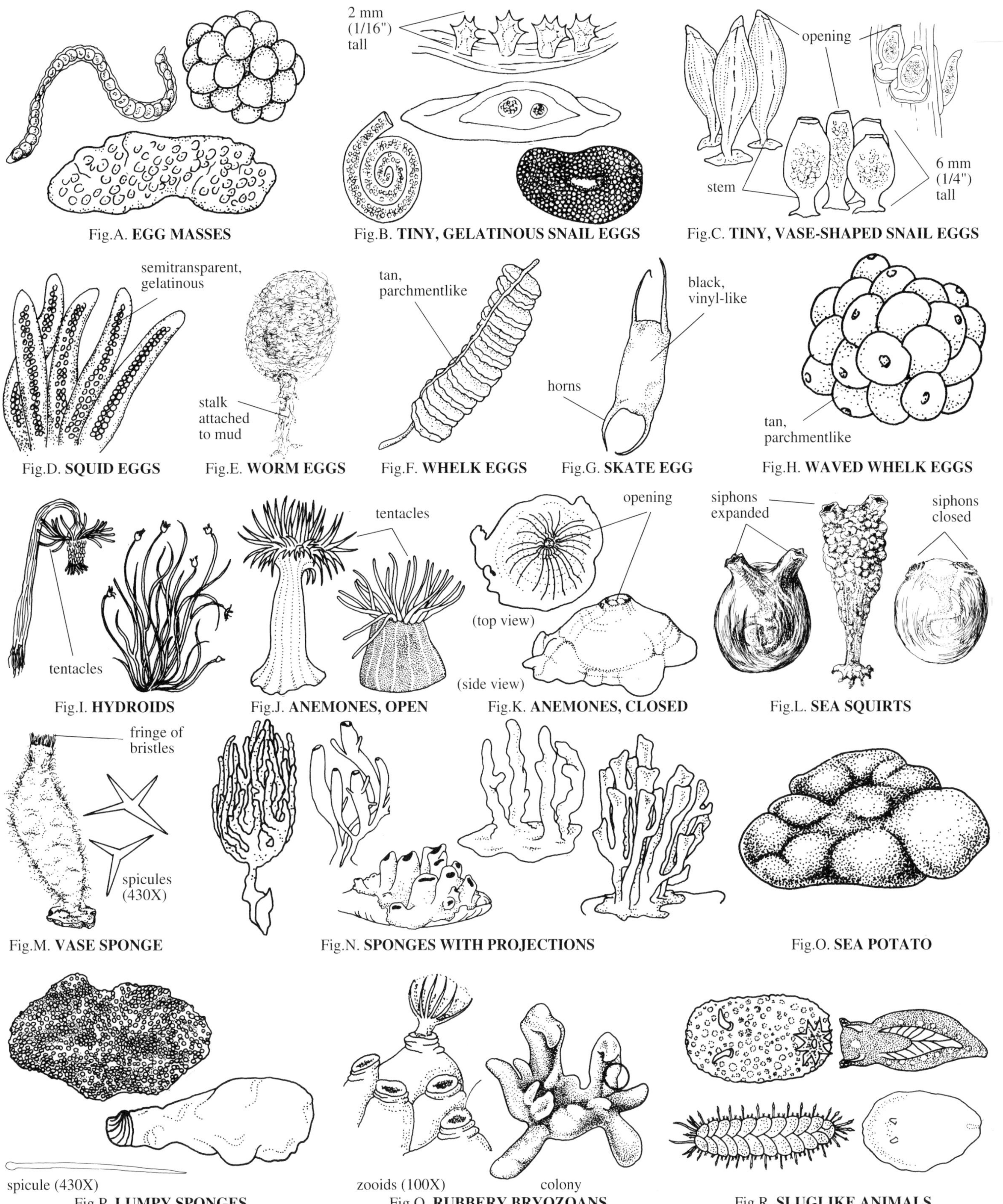

Fig.A. **EGG MASSES**

Fig.B. **TINY, GELATINOUS SNAIL EGGS**

Fig.C. **TINY, VASE-SHAPED SNAIL EGGS**

Fig.D. **SQUID EGGS**

Fig.E. **WORM EGGS**

Fig.F. **WHELK EGGS**

Fig.G. **SKATE EGG**

Fig.H. **WAVED WHELK EGGS**

Fig.I. **HYDROIDS**

Fig.J. **ANEMONES, OPEN**

Fig.K. **ANEMONES, CLOSED**

Fig.L. **SEA SQUIRTS**

Fig.M. **VASE SPONGE**

Fig.N. **SPONGES WITH PROJECTIONS**

Fig.O. **SEA POTATO**

Fig.P. **LUMPY SPONGES**

Fig.Q. **RUBBERY BRYOZOANS**

Fig.R. **SLUGLIKE ANIMALS**

LEGLESS ANIMALS - WITH SHELLS

Legless, shell covered animals that are attached firmly to the substrate (rocks, algae, pilings, etc.) or creep very slowly on the substrate or burrow into the substrate (mud, sand, etc.)

(Getting started key begins on page 2.00)

#1.Branched and jointed (Fig.A); erect fan shaped or bushlike tufts; usually white and calcareous (shell-like) .... **branched calcareous organisms**, page 2.02
#1.Not branched (Figs.B-O) .... #2

#2.With numerous long spines[1] attached to a somewhat spherical shell (Fig.B) or tiny fuzzlike spines attached to a flat disc shaped shell (Fig.C) .... **sea urchins and sand dollars**, page 11.01
#2.Without numerous long or short spines (Figs.D-O) .... #3

#3.Shell is a single piece (Figs.D-I); shell is not made up of more than one plate or valve; shell may or may not have a "shelf" (Fig.H) on underside .... #4
#3.Shell is made up of two or more plates or valves (Figs.J-O) which can be separated if pried apart with a sharp knife; the lines separating the different plates or valves can be seen if examined carefully .... #11

#4.Shell is coiled, snail-like (Figs.D,E) .... #5
#4.Shell is not coiled (Figs.F-J) .... #6

#5.Shell is firmly cemented to eelgrass, algae or other substrates and cannot move around; when alive and undisturbed a crown of featherlike tentacles (Fig.D) may extend from opening of shell; shell is tiny, never larger than 2 mm (1/16") in diameter; shell is white .... ***Spirorbis* spp., coiled worms**, page 8.04
#5.Animal grips substrate by means of a muscular, fleshy foot (Fig.E) and can move about by means of a slow creeping motion; when animal is alive and undisturbed, a single pair of tentacles, a proboscis and a muscular foot may extend from the opening of the shell; shell may be larger than 2 mm (1/16") in diameter; shell may or may not be white .... **snails**, page 7.02

#6.With numerous circular, cuplike depressions in a lumpy stony mass; each depression contains a tentacle bearing polyp which can be observed when the animal is alive and undisturbed (Fig.F) .... **coral**, page 4.16
#6.Without cuplike depressions; without tentacle bearing polyps (Figs.G-J) .... #7

#7.Shell is tubular (Fig.G); may be twisted or straight .... **worm tubes**, page 2.25
#7.Shell is not tubular (Figs. H-J); may be flat, conical, hat shaped, clamshell shaped, etc .... #8

#8.With a shelflike structure (Fig.H) on underside[2] of shell .... **slippersnails**, page 7.01
#8.Without a shelflike structure on underside of shell (Figs.I,J) .... #9

#9.Shell is squat and conical, shaped somewhat like a Chinese cap, with the point (apex) near the center (Fig.I); usually with tortoise shell coloring, greenish white with brown lines and patches .... **limpets**, page 7.01
#9.Not shaped or colored as above .... #10

#10.Thin crust, firmly attached to rocks or other substrates .... **thin, encrusting organisms**, page 2.06
#10.Not a thin crust (Fig.J) .... **bivalves**[3], page 7.14

#11.Shell consists of two parts ("valves") joined together by a hinge (Fig.J); one of the valves may be cemented to the substrate or anchored by threads or a very short stalk; the two valves may or may not be the same size and shape .... **bivalves**[3], page 7.14
#11.Shell consists of more than 2 plates (Figs.K-O) .... #12

#12.Shell consists of 8 or more overlapping plates (Figs.K,L) arranged in one or two rows along the back of an oval or worm shaped body; without any openings on top; animal may curl up like a pill bug when pried off the substrate .... #13
#12.Plates are not arranged in rows along the back (Figs.M-O); with an opening at the top (which may be closed); with 6 pairs of feathery appendages (cirri) which extend through the opening and rhythmically sweep through the water pulling food inside the shell (cirri are only extended when the living animal is submerged in seawater and is undisturbed) .... #14

#13.With 8 overlapping plates in a single row (Fig.K); margin of body ("girdle") is fleshy, not covered by the shell .... **chitons**, page 7.00
#13.With 12 or more pairs of plates (scales) arranged in two rows (Fig.L); with tiny bristles (setae) and threadlike extensions (cirri) around margins .... **scale worms**, page 8.09

#14.Squat, conical shell (Fig.M) or an elongate, tubular shell[4] (Fig.N) consisting of 6 side plates; with a central opening on top which, when alive, is covered by a beaklike trap door that consists of four tiny plates; shell is attached directly to substrate; no fleshy stalk .... **acorn barnacles**, page 10.13
#14.With a beaklike shell at the end of a soft bodied fleshy stalk (Fig.O); shell consists of 5 white plates .... **gooseneck barnacles**, page 10.13

[1]The spherical shell of a sea urchin or the disclike shell of a sand dollar is often found without any spines. The spines usually detach from the shell when the animal dies. See page 11.01 for illustrations of sea urchin and sand dollar shells with and without the spines.
[2]The shelf on the underside of a living slippersnail is covered over by tissue and cannot be seen unless the tissue is removed.
[3]When a bivalve dies, the two shells often come apart. If you find a single uncoiled shell that does not have a shelf like the slippersnails (Fig.H) or is not hat shaped and tortoise shell colored like the limpet (Fig.I) then you probably have a single valve from a bivalve. Refer to the key on page 7.14.
[4]Acorn barnacles are usually squat and conical. When growing in crowded conditions, however, they may become quite tall and tubular (Fig.N).

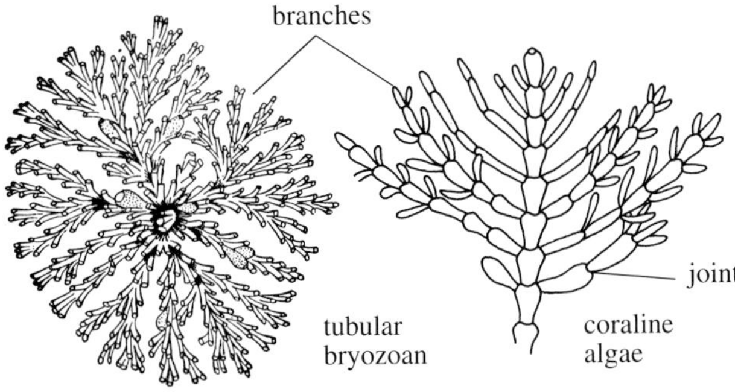

branches
joints
tubular
bryozoan
coraline
algae

Fig.A. **BRANCHED, CALCAREOUS ORGANISMS**

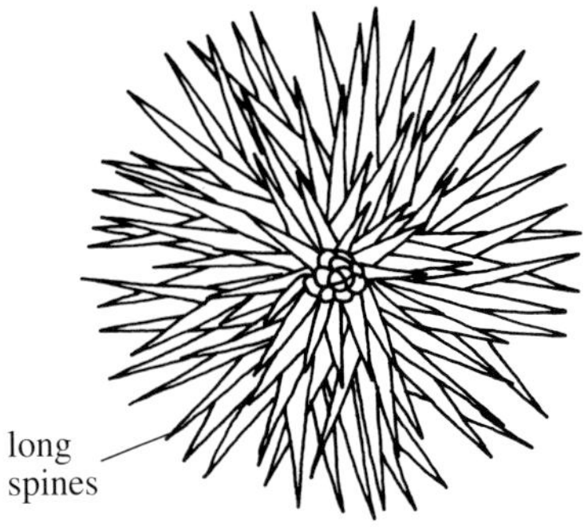

long
spines

Fig.B. **SEA URCHIN**

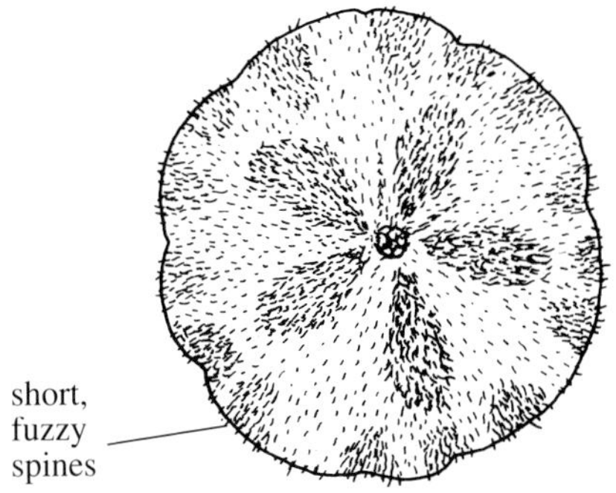

short,
fuzzy
spines

Fig.C. **SAND DOLLAR**

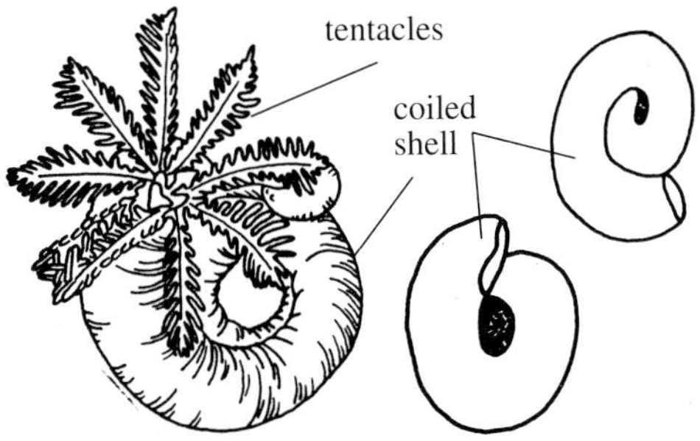

tentacles
coiled
shell

Fig.D. ***SPIRORBIS* SPP., COILED WORMS**

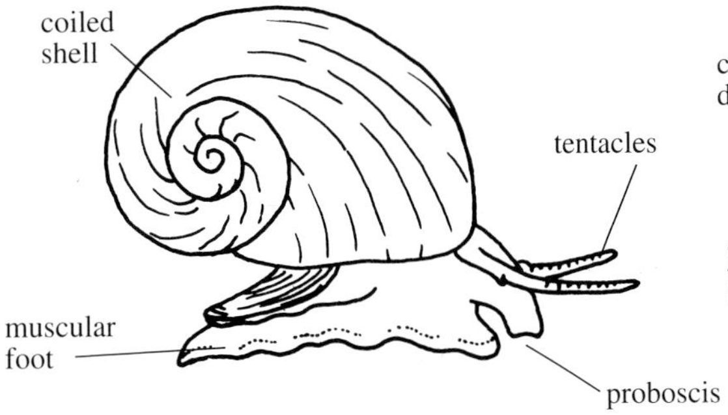

coiled
shell
tentacles
muscular
foot
proboscis

Fig.E. **SNAIL, SIDE VIEW**

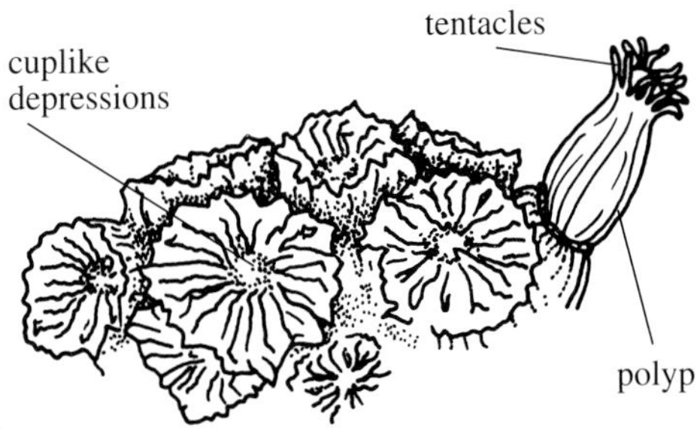

tentacles
cuplike
depressions
polyp

Fig.F. **CORAL**

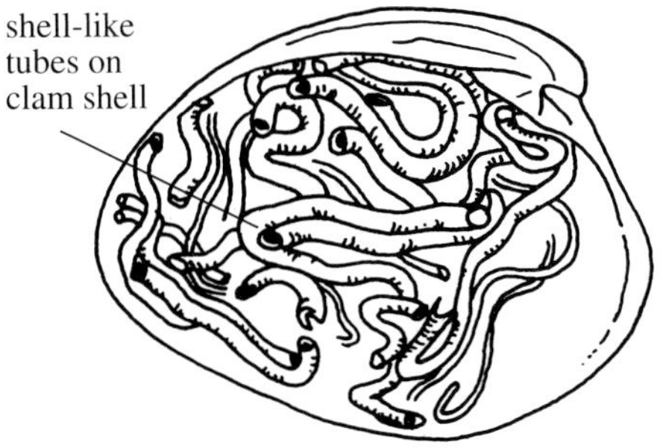

shell-like
tubes on
clam shell

Fig.G. **WORM TUBES**

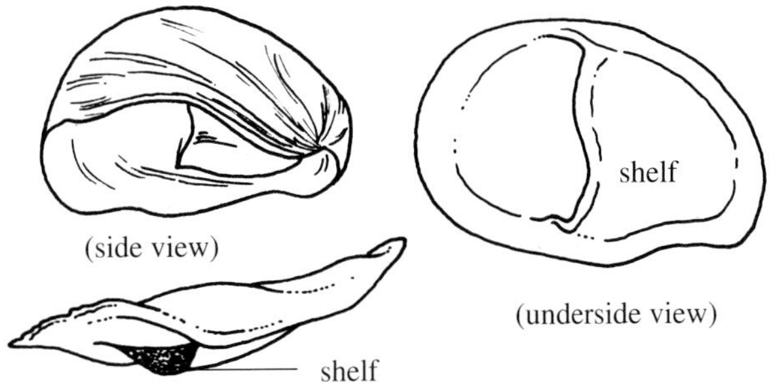

(side view)
shelf
(underside view)
shelf

Fig.H. **SLIPPERSNAILS**

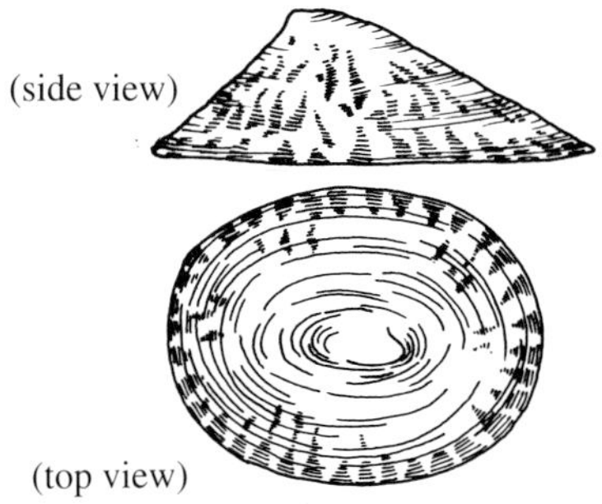

(side view)
(top view)

Fig.I. **LIMPET**

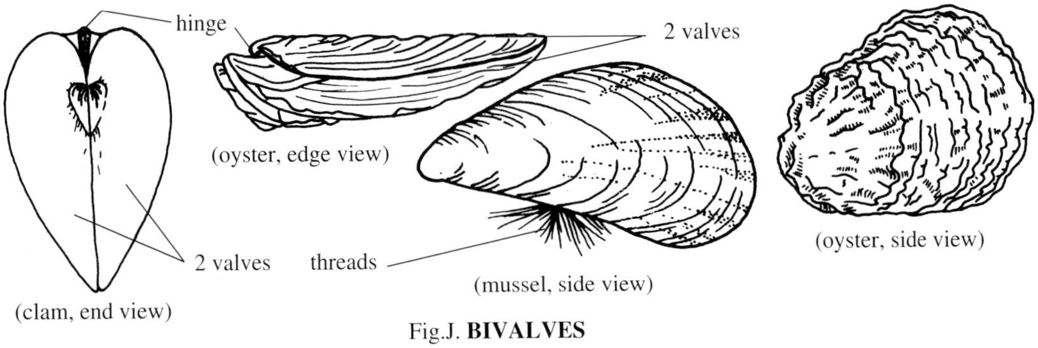

hinge
2 valves
(oyster, edge view)
2 valves
threads
(clam, end view)
(mussel, side view)
(oyster, side view)

Fig.J. **BIVALVES**

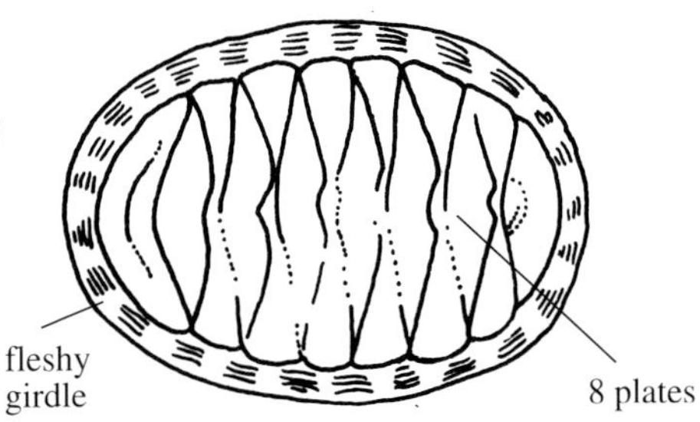

fleshy
girdle
8 plates

Fig.K. **CHITON**

setae (bristles)
scales
cirri (filaments)

Fig.L. **SCALE WORM**

cirri
extended
beak
(closed, top view)

Fig.M. **ACORN BARNACLES, NORMAL FORM**

side
plates

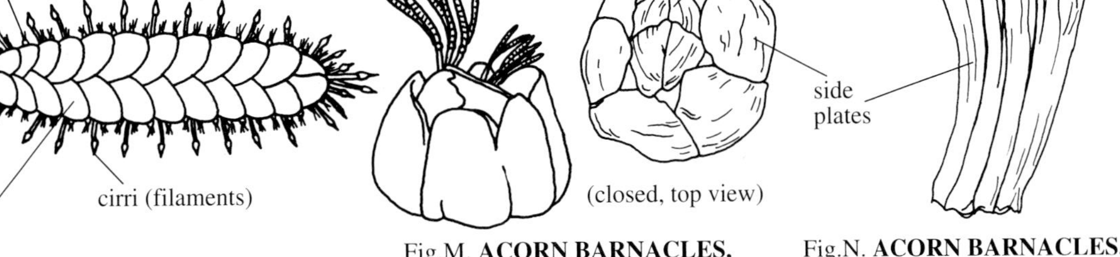

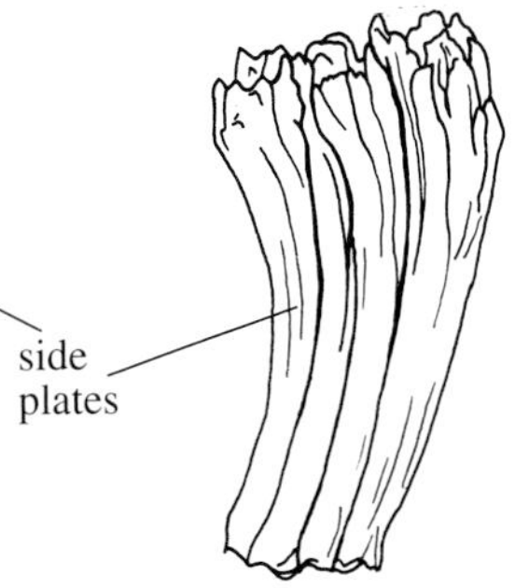

Fig.N. **ACORN BARNACLES, CROWDED FORM**

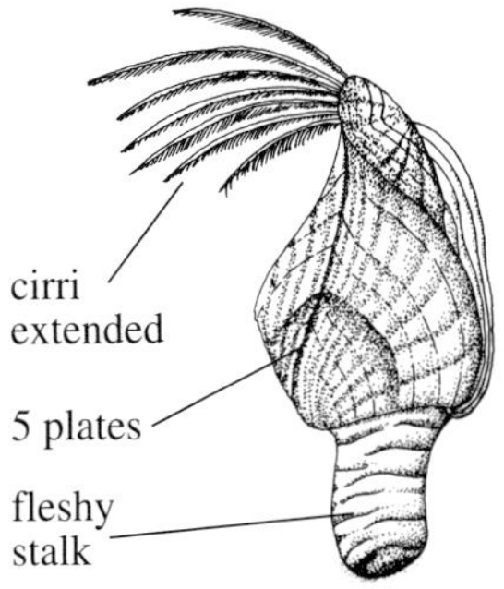

cirri
extended
5 plates
fleshy
stalk

Fig.O. **GOOSE NECK BARNACLE**

MOTILE ANIMALS

Animals which can move about by swimming, walking, crawling, burrowing, flying, etc.

(Getting started key begins on page 2.00)

#1.With legs .... page 2.14
#1.Without legs (Figs.A-M); may have other structures used for locomotion such as fins, tentacles, flippers, a muscular foot, radiating arms, tube feet or movable spines .... #2

#2.With arms or tentacles (Figs.A,B,F,J,K) .... #3
#2.Without any arms or tentacles .... #5

#3.Arms (usually five[1]) radiate out from a central body (Figs.A,B) which may be somewhat flattened or disclike; most species have short spines on arms and body giving skin a rough texture .... **sea stars (starfishes) and brittlestars**, #4
#3.Body is umbrella shaped (Fig.F), wormlike (Fig.H), saclike (Fig.J), or tubular (Fig.K); surface of body and tentacles is smooth, not spiny .... #7

#4.Arms are relatively wide and fleshy (Fig.A); arms merge together at the central disc; with a groove on the underside of each arm; groove contains rows of tube feet .... **sea stars (starfishes)**, page 11.02
#4.Arms are thin (Fig.B) and are spaced apart where they emerge from the central disc; no grooves on the underside of the arms .... **brittlestars**, page 11.04

#5.With numerous long spines[2] attached to a somewhat spherical shell (Fig.C) or tiny fuzzlike spines attached to a flat, disc shaped shell (Fig.D) .... **sea urchins and sand dollars**, page 11.01
#5.Without numerous spines (Figs.E-M) .... #6

#6.Enclosed in one or more shells (Fig.E); with a muscular foot used to creep or burrow very slowly on or into the substrate; snail-like, clamlike, limpetlike animals .... **mollusks**, page 2.10
#6.Soft bodied; body not enclosed in a shell or hard case (Figs.F-M) .... #7

#7.With a jellylike or gas filled float (Figs.F,G) which may be shaped like an umbrella, balloon or bag; body is transparent or semitransparent; floats or swims with a pulsating motion .... **jellyfishes and comb jellies**, #8
#7.Without a jellylike or gas filled float (Figs.H-M) .... #9

#8.With four or more tentacles (Fig.F) or with 2 unbranched tentacles; no comblike plates; float is shaped like an umbrella or is a gas filled sac; float may be pink, red, milky white, blue or transparent and colorless .... **jellyfishes[3]**, page 4.00
#8.With only one pair of branched tentacles or no tentacles; with 8 rows of comblike plates (Fig.G) that are made up of tiny cilia (short "hairs") which create water currents by rapidly vibrating; body is globular, saclike or lobed; usually transparent and colorless .... **comb jellies**, page 4.17

#9.Wormlike (Fig.H), sluglike (Fig.I), snakelike, or saclike (Fig.J) animals adapted for crawling, creeping, or burrowing; no fins or flippers .... page 2.16
#9.With fins or flippers (Figs.K-M); free swimming animals .... #10

#10.With 8 arms and 2 tentacles surrounding the mouth (Fig.K) .... **squid**, page 7.00
#10.No arms or tentacles surrounding the mouth (Figs.L,M) .... #11

#11.With gills (Fig.L) used for underwater respiration .... **fishes**, page 13.00
#11.With nostrils or a blowhole (Fig.M) used for breathing air .... **marine mammals: seals, porpoises, dolphins and whales**, page 16.00

[1]Seastars and brittlestars in this region usually have five arms but are occasionally found with more or less than five. Normally, all of the arms are the same length but a new arm that is regenerating (replacing one that has broken off) may be smaller than the others.

[2]Often the spherical shell of a sea urchin or the disclike shell of a sand dollar is found without any spines. The spines usually detach from the shell when the animal dies. See page 11.01 for illustrations of sea urchin and sand dollar shells with and without the spines.

[3]**WARNING:** The tentacles of some jellyfishes can inflict a painful sting. Handle jellyfishes with care, even when they are washed up on shore and appear to be dead.

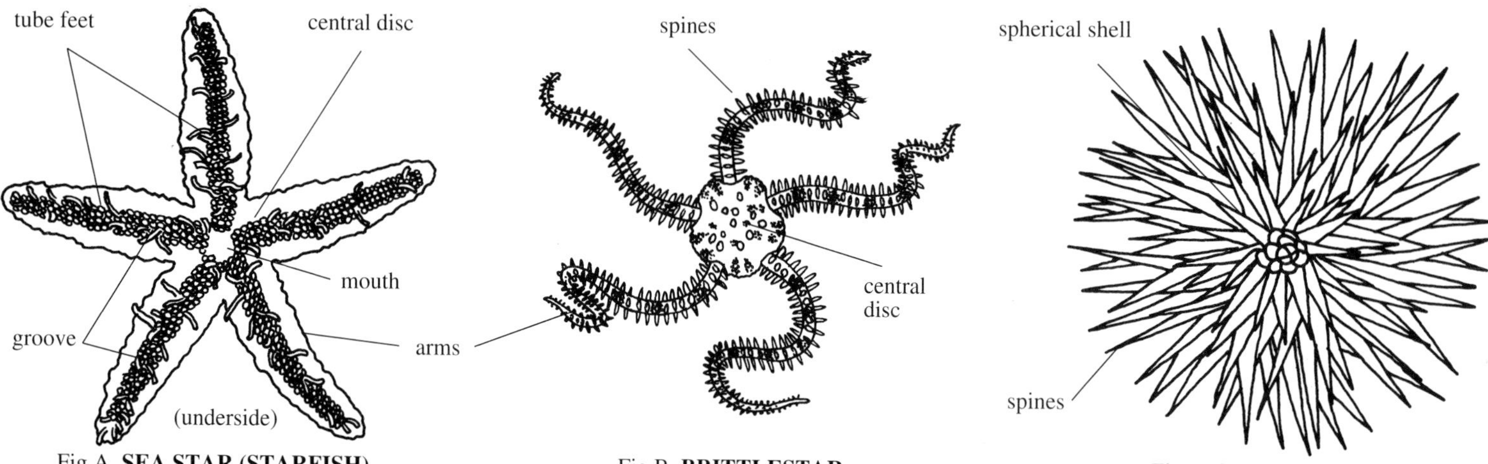

Fig.A. **SEA STAR (STARFISH)** Fig.B. **BRITTLESTAR** Fig.C. **SEA URCHIN**

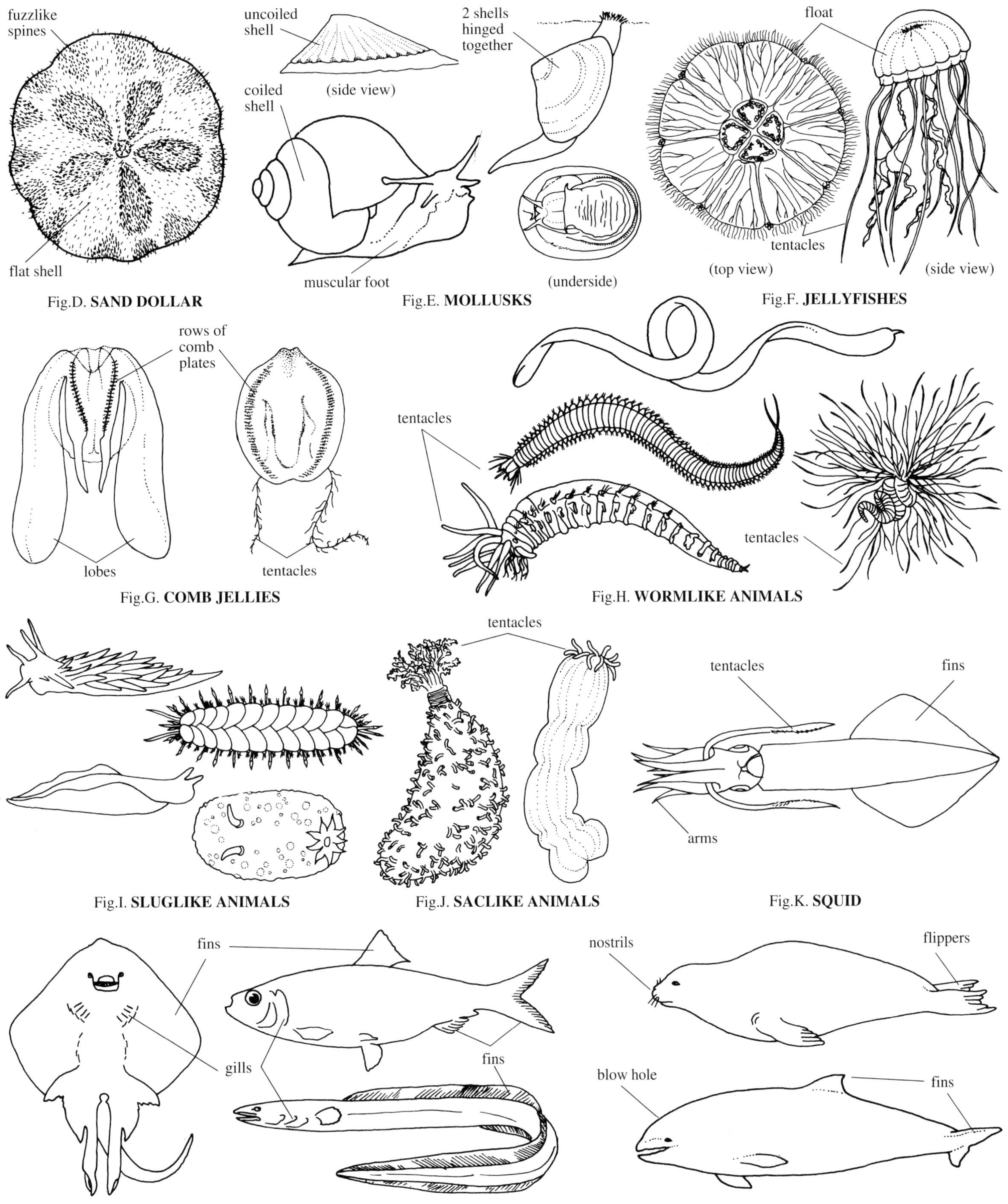

Fig.D. **SAND DOLLAR**

Fig.E. **MOLLUSKS**

Fig.F. **JELLYFISHES**

Fig.G. **COMB JELLIES**

Fig.H. **WORMLIKE ANIMALS**

Fig.I. **SLUGLIKE ANIMALS**

Fig.J. **SACLIKE ANIMALS**

Fig.K. **SQUID**

Fig.L. **FISHES**

Fig.M. **MARINE MAMMALS**

ANIMALS WITH LEGS

(Getting started key begins on page 2.00)

#1.With wings (Figs.A,B) .... #2
#1.No wings (Figs.C-N) .... #3

#2.With one pair of legs and wings (Fig.A); with feathers .... **birds**, page 15.00
#2.With one pair of wings; with hairy body and membranous wings; no feathers; mouselike body and face .... **bats**, page 16.03
#2.With three pairs of legs and one or two pairs of wings (Fig.B); no feathers .... **winged insects**, page 9.10

#3.With two pairs of legs (Figs.C-E) .... #4
#3.With three or more pairs of legs (Figs.F-N) .... #6

#4.With fur, hair (Fig.C) .... **terrestrial mammals**, page 16.02
#4.Without fur or hair (Figs.D,E) .... #5

#5.Body covered by a bony or leathery shell (Fig.D) .... **turtles**, page 14.02
#5.Without a bony shell (Fig.E) .... **amphibians (frogs, toads, salamanders)**, page 14.01

#6.Legs (Fig.F) are fleshy, stubby, unjointed and may be paddle shaped, bumplike or leafy; body is wormlike, caterpillarlike or maggotlike; usually more than 8 pairs of legs but may have fewer .... **wormlike animals**, page 2.16
#6.Legs are jointed, usually slender; with 3 to 8 pairs of legs; body not wormlike (Figs.G-N) .... **arthropods**, #7

#7.Lives in a snail shell (Fig.G); with two pairs of walking legs and one pair of claws .... **hermit crabs**, page 10.19
#7.Does not live in a snail shell; with 3 or more pairs of legs (Figs.H-N) .... #8

#8.With three pairs of legs[1] (Fig.H); with one pair of antennae .... **wingless insects**, page 9.14
#8.With four or more pairs of legs (Figs.I-N) including appendages with large claws; with no antennae or two pairs of antennae .... #9

#9.Body covered by a hard, horseshoe shaped shell (Fig.I); with a long, sharply pointed tail spike (telson) .... **horseshoe crab**, page 9.01
#9.Body not horseshoe shaped and tail not a sharp spike (Figs.J-N) .... #10

#10.With five or more pairs of legs[3] (Figs.J,K) including appendages with large claws; with two pairs of antennae[2]; primarily aquatic animals which usually live underwater or in moist habitats below the high tide level .... **some crustaceans (lobsters, crabs, shrimps, amphipods, isopods, etc.)**, page 10.00
#10.With four pairs of legs including appendages with large claws; may or may not have two pairs of antennae; may live on land or live in water .... #11

#11.With swimmerets (somewhat feathery appendages, see Fig.J) under the abdomen ("tail"); with two pairs of antennae[2] .... **some crustaceans**, page 10.00
#11.No swimmerets under abdomen; no true antennae but with fanglike, needlelike or clawlike head appendages (chelicerae) (Figs.L-N) .... **chelicerates**, #12

#12.Animal is divided into two distinct regions (Fig.L), a cephalothorax ("head and body") and an abdomen ("tail") with a narrow stalk or pedicel ("waist") in between (Fig. L); with a pair of fanglike head appendages (chelicerae) and eight simple eyes; strictly terrestrial animals which always live above the water level .... **spiders**, page 9.04
#12.Body not divided into two distinct regions (Figs.M,N); body may be oval or globular or reduced to a skeletonlike base for the legs; body may consist of a single segment or may be divided into more than two segments; may be found on land or in the water .... #13

#13.Legs are at least twice as long as body (Fig.M); legs are divided into 8 segments and, in most species, end with a claw; head has a proboscis ("snout") and/or a pair of chelifores ("claws") and/or one pair of palpi ("antennae"); strictly aquatic, only live below the high tide level .... **pycnogonids**, page 9.02
#13.Legs are less than twice as long as body (Fig.N); legs have five joints; head appendages are needlelike for piercing and sucking, and are attached to a projecting gnathosoma ("snout"); most species are found in the intertidal zone or above but several species live submerged in water .... **mites and ticks**, page 9.09

[1]When counting legs, include the appendages bearing large claws as well as the walking legs.
[2]Insects have one pair of true antennae. Crustaceans have two pairs. (Some crabs are able to withdraw their antennae into grooves along the front margin of the shell, making the antennae difficult to observe). The pycnogonids (sea spiders) and arachnids (spiders, mites and ticks) do not have true antennae but do have head appendages that may look similar to antennae. If in doubt, rely on the head count, body segmentation and other characteristics given in the keys.
[3]All male pycnogonids and some females have ovigers, leglike appendages under their body used for carrying eggs (see Fig.M). Do not include the ovigers in the leg count. Refer to the first half of couplet #13 for a description of the pycnogonids.

wings
1 pair of legs

Fig.A. **BIRDS**

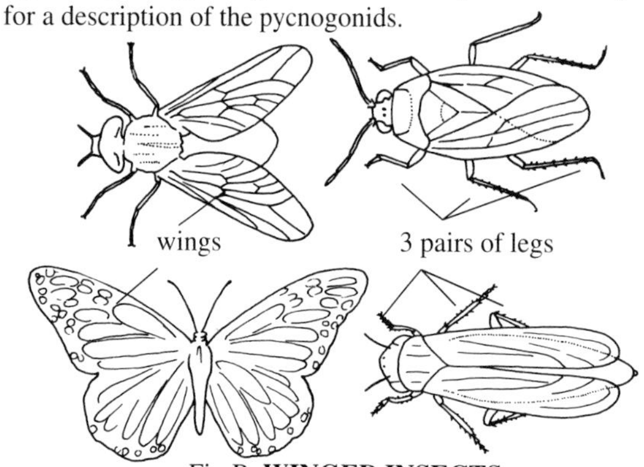

wings
3 pairs of legs

Fig.B. **WINGED INSECTS**

fur
2 pairs of legs

Fig.C. **MAMMALS**

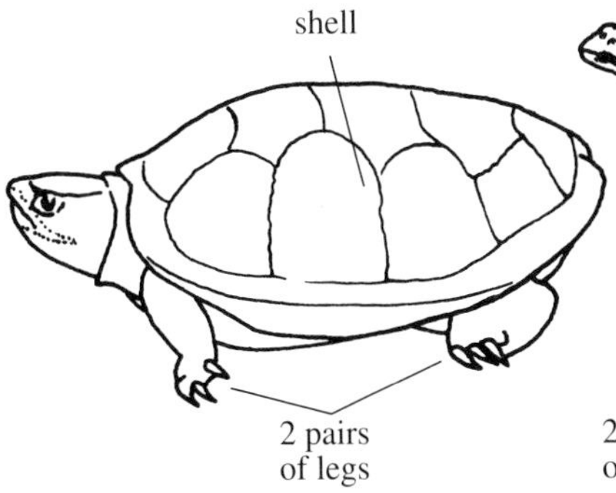

shell

2 pairs of legs

Fig.D. **TURTLE**

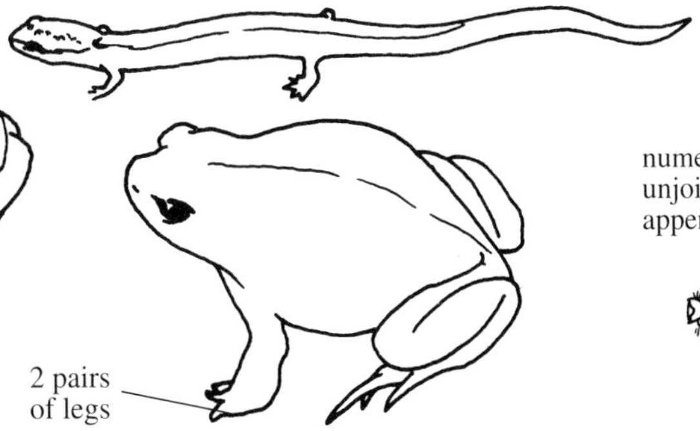

2 pairs of legs

Fig.E. **AMPHIBIANS**

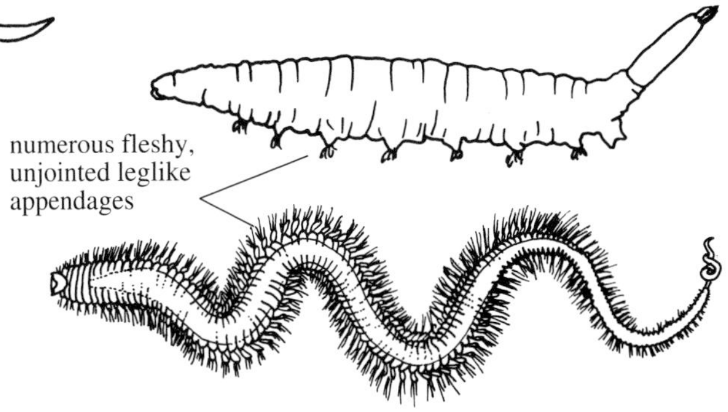

numerous fleshy, unjointed leglike appendages

Fig.F. **WORMLIKE ANIMALS**

in snail shell

Fig.G. **HERMIT CRABS**

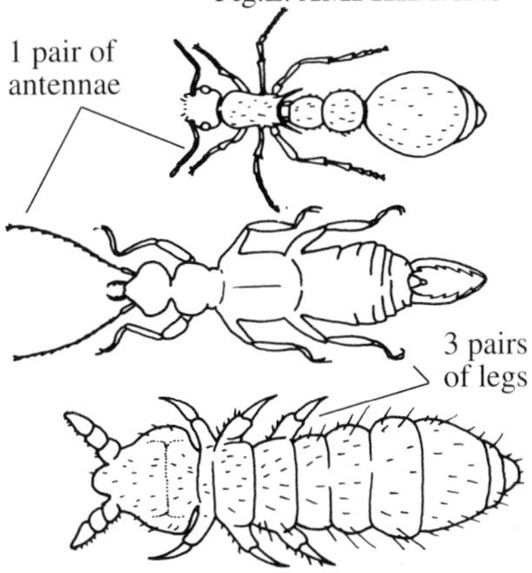

1 pair of antennae

3 pairs of legs

Fig.H. **WINGLESS INSECTS**

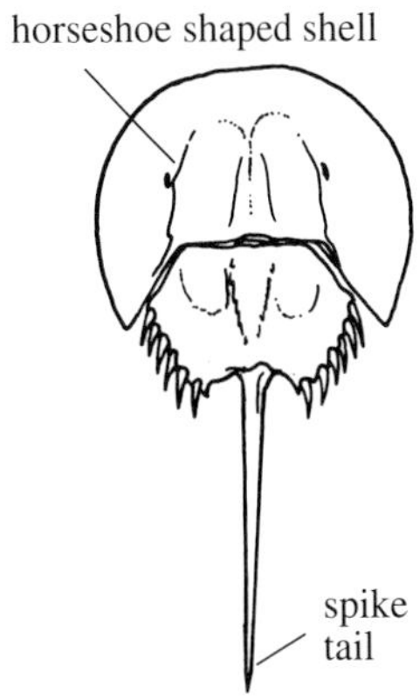

horseshoe shaped shell

spike tail

Fig.I. **HORSESHOE CRAB**

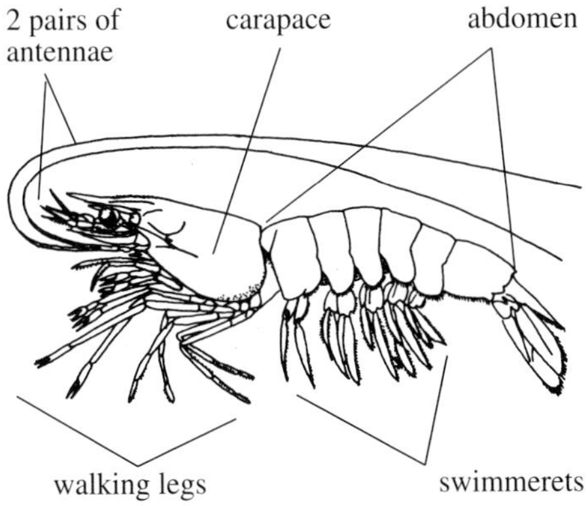

2 pairs of antennae

carapace

abdomen

walking legs

swimmerets

Fig.J. **CRUSTACEAN APPENDAGES**

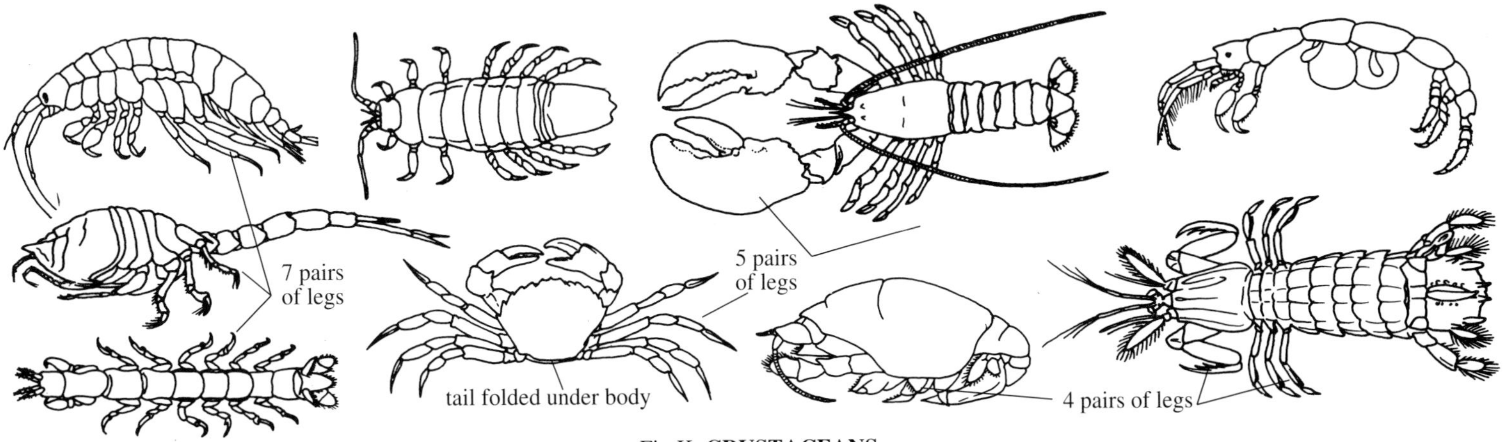

7 pairs of legs

tail folded under body

5 pairs of legs

4 pairs of legs

Fig.K. **CRUSTACEANS**

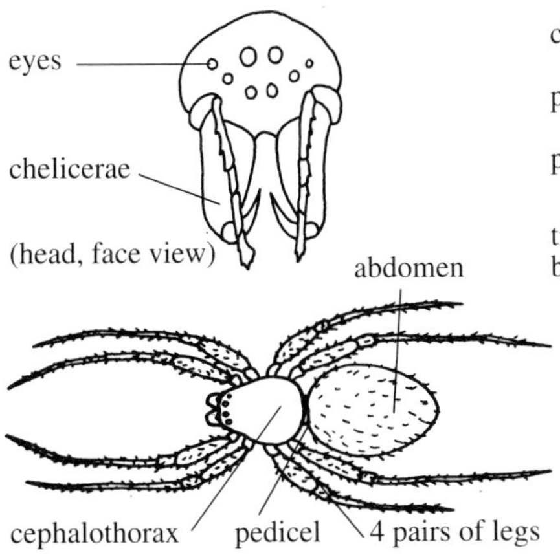

eyes

chelicerae

(head, face view)

abdomen

cephalothorax

pedicel

4 pairs of legs

Fig.L. **SPIDERS**

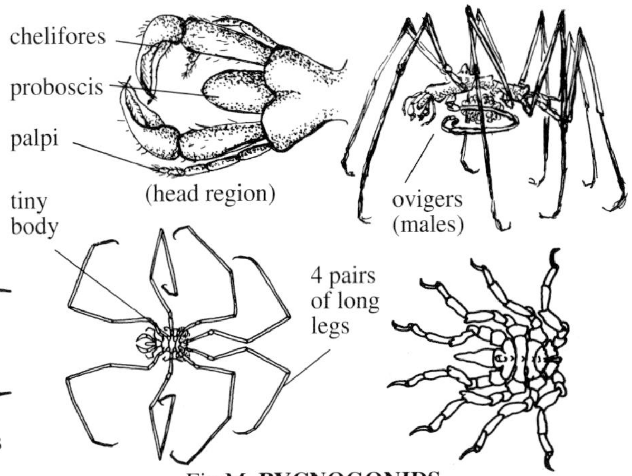

chelifores

proboscis

palpi

(head region)

ovigers (males)

tiny body

4 pairs of long legs

Fig.M. **PYCNOGONIDS**

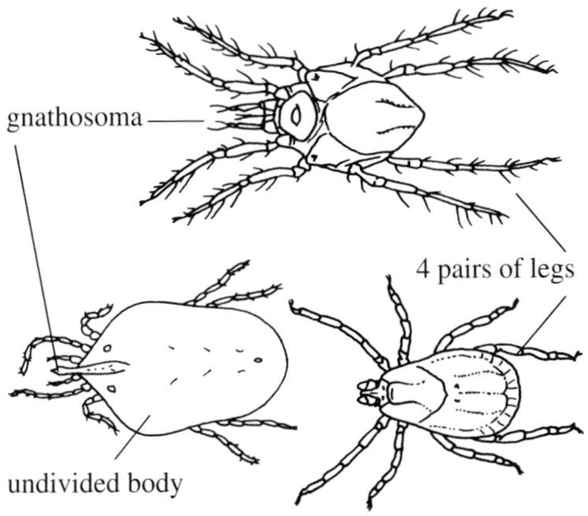

gnathosoma

4 pairs of legs

undivided body

Fig.N. **MITES AND TICKS**

WORMLIKE, SLUGLIKE, AND SNAKELIKE ANIMALS[1]

Soft-bodied, motile animals, without legs

(Getting started key begins on page 2.00)

#1. With a sucker disk or an attachment organ (see Figs.A-I, page 2.20) at one or both ends; attaches to another animal .... **parasites and symbionts**, page 2.20
#1. Without a sucker disk or an attachment organ; does not live attached to another animal .... #2

#2. Body region with obvious appendages or projections (Figs.A-C) along the back (dorsal surface) or sides, such as fleshy paddlelike or leglike lobes (parapodia or prolegs), threads, tube feet, featherlike gills, clublike or fingerlike structures on back (cerata), sides folded up onto back, etc. .... #3
#2. Body region without obvious appendages or projections (Figs.D-P) giving the body a smooth, naked, featureless appearance. (The head region, however, may or may not have obvious tentacles, gills, or other appendages) .... #5

#3. Body not segmented (Figs.A,B); sluglike or saclike animals .... #4
#3. Body composed of numerous segments with fleshy paddlelike or leglike lobes (parapodia or prolegs), threadlike filaments or hairs extending from many of the segments; wormlike or maggotlike animals (Figs.C,F) .... #6

#4. Saclike animals (Fig.A) with tube feet[2] on body and a crown of branched tentacles[2] surrounding mouth; lies on the bottom or buries in the bottom sediments with only the crown of tentacles visible; when disturbed the animal often becomes ball shaped[1] .... **sea cucumbers**, page 11.06
#4. Sluglike animals (Fig.B) with a flattened muscular foot and at least one pair of tentacles on head; with cerata (fingerlike, clublike, or leafy projections) on back or with sides folded up onto back; glides along on rocks, seaweeds or hydroids .... **nudibranchs**, page 7.11

#5. With tiny bristles (setae) extending from the sides of the body (Figs.D-F); body with true segmentation[3] (Use 10X magnification to look for bristles) .... #6
#5. Body without any tiny bristles (setae) extending from the sides (Figs.G-P); body not segmented .... #8

#6. With more than 14 body segments (Figs.C,D) .... **annelid worms**, page 8.00
#6. With 14 or fewer body segments (Figs. E,F) .... #7

#7. Back (dorsal surface) covered with overlapping plates or scales (Fig.E) .... **scale worms**, page 8.09
#7. No plates or scales on back (Fig.F); may look somewhat caterpillarlike or maggotlike; may have a breathing tube or gills on the posterior (rear end); may have stubby bumplike prolegs .... **insect larvae and pupae**, page 9.30

#8. All or part of body distinctly flattened (Figs.G-I) .... #9
#8. Body not particularly flat; may be cylindrical, threadlike or saclike (Figs. J-P) .... #11

#9. Back (dorsal surface) is covered with tiny cone shaped or rounded bumps (Fig.G); with a circle of gills[2] near one end and a pair of tentacles[2] near the other .... **dorid nudibranchs**, page 7.11
#9. Body is smooth (Figs.H-I); without a circle of gills near posterior end .... #10

#10. Never grows longer[1] than 38 mm (1.5") and rarely longer than 25 mm (1"); with a single opening ("mouth") which is located on underside near middle or front of body; no anus; no pointed projection (cirrus) at posterior end; no grooves along sides of head; no long proboscis; with at least two tiny eyespots at front end or along margins; looks like a freshwater planarian; often found gliding smoothly along on rocks and other objects .... **flatworms** (Fig.H), page 5.00
#10. Often grows longer than 25 mm (1") and some species may grow over 1 m (3') long[1]; with a mouth and an anus; some species have a pointed projection (cirrus) at posterior end and others do not; some species have a groove along the sides of the head and others do not; with a long, threadlike, eversible proboscis[2] ("tongue") which can be thrust out to impale prey; some species have eyespots and others do not; often found buried in the sand or mud or under rocks .... **nemerteans (ribbon or proboscis worms)** (Fig.I), page 5.06

#11. With a pair of nostrils, a pair of well developed eyes and a large hinged jaw (Fig.J); skin is scaly; with an internal bony skeleton .... **snakes**, page 14.06
#11. No nostrils; no internal skeleton; no well developed eyes but may have simple eyespots (Figs.K-P) .... #12

#12. Worm is divided into three regions (Fig.K): a slender whitish proboscis, a short orange collar and a large, brownish trunk .... **acorn worms**, page 11.07
#12. Not divided into three distinct regions as described above (Figs.L-P) .... #13

#13. With no tentacles[2] (Figs.L,M); 1 or no tail cirrus (pointed projection); very slender and threadlike, usually less than 3 mm (1/8") wide .... #14
#13. With 2 tentacles[2]; 2 tail cirri (pointed projections); very slender and threadlike .... ***Polygordius* spp., archiannelid worms,** page 8.11
#13. With more than 2 tentacles[2] (Figs.N-P); no tail cirrus; thick bodied, more than 3 mm (1/8") wide .... #15

#14. No eyespots or grooves on head; very smooth and sharply pointed at both ends (Fig.L); whitish or transparent; many species move by coiling in loops and figure eights .... **nematodes (roundworms)**, page 5.08
#14. With eyespots on head and/or a groove along sides of head (Fig.M); may be whitish or may have tinges of brighter colors .... **nemerteans**[1], page 5.06

#15. Composed of an introvert[2] and a trunk region (Fig.N) which may be separated by a necklike constriction when the introvert is fully extended; the introvert can be withdrawn inside the trunk and is slightly more slender and pointed than the trunk; the mouth is surrounded by a ring of tiny, fingerlike, unbranched tentacles[2]; skin is silky, smooth and not transparent .... **peanut worms**, page 5.09
#15. Not divided into an introvert and trunk (Figs.O,P); skin may be transparent or opaque, smooth or bumpy; tentacles[2] may be branched or unbranched .... #16

#16. With branched, featherlike tentacles[2] (Fig.O); with microscopic anchor and plate shaped deposits embedded in the skin (use 25X magnification to see these deposits); skin often feels sticky and is very thin, almost transparent, so that insides are visible .... **burrowing sea cucumbers**, page 11.06
#16. Tentacles are not branched (Fig.P); with no microscopic anchor or plate shaped deposits in skin; most species have an opaque skin with longitudinal grooves or bumpy ridges, but a few species have a smooth and transparent skin .... **burrowing anemones**, page 4.14

[1]Handle these animals with great care. They may break into pieces if they are disturbed. Whenever possible, examine them while they are alive and relaxed. They can quickly change their shape by elongating or contracting. They are especially difficult to identify if they are preserved, contracted or missing parts. If the head or tail end is missing then appendages such as the proboscis or cirrus will also be missing.

[2]This structure is usually withdrawn and cannot be seen unless the animal is alive, active, and completely undisturbed. See footnote #1 on page 2.00.

[3]Examine the sides of the animal carefully at 10X or 20X magnification to determine if there are tiny bristles (setae) extending from the body. Most truly segmented worms have these bristles. Unsegmented worms do not have any bristles but may have creases, wrinkles and folds which look superficially like true segments.

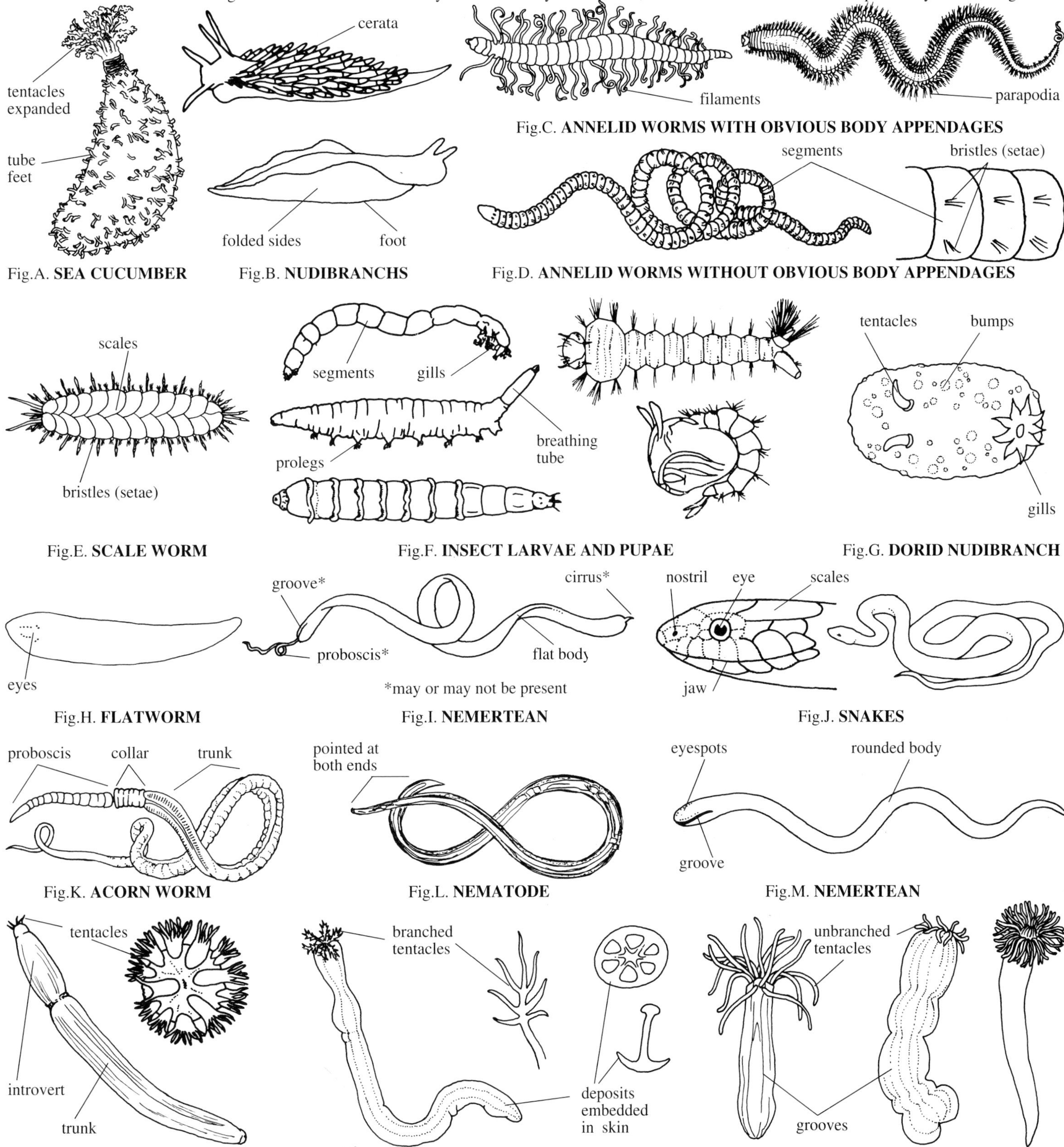

Fig.A. **SEA CUCUMBER**

Fig.B. **NUDIBRANCHS**

Fig.C. **ANNELID WORMS WITH OBVIOUS BODY APPENDAGES**

Fig.D. **ANNELID WORMS WITHOUT OBVIOUS BODY APPENDAGES**

Fig.E. **SCALE WORM**

Fig.F. **INSECT LARVAE AND PUPAE**

Fig.G. **DORID NUDIBRANCH**

Fig.H. **FLATWORM**

Fig.I. **NEMERTEAN**

Fig.J. **SNAKES**

Fig.K. **ACORN WORM**

Fig.L. **NEMATODE**

Fig.M. **NEMERTEAN**

Fig.N. **PEANUT WORM**

Fig.O. **BURROWING SEA CUCUMBER**

Fig.P. **BURROWING ANEMONES**

PARASITES AND OTHER SYMBIONTS[1]

Animals found living on or in another animal

(Getting started key begins on page 2.00)

#1.Found within a cyst (a sac or capsule, usually oval in shape, that forms in the host animal's tissue surrounding the larval stage of a parasite) (Figs.A,B) .... #2
#1.Not encysted (Figs.C-J) .... #3

#2.Cysts are tiny black dots visible in the skin of fish (Fig.A) .... **metacercarial stage of *Cryptocotyle lingua*, a digenetic trematode worm**, page 5.03
#2.Cysts[2] found within the muscles (Fig.B), organs and internal tissues of vertebrates and invertebrates .... #3

#3.With jointed legs (Fig.C,D) .... **parasitic arthropods**, #4
#3.No legs or may have fleshy, unjointed leglike appendages (Figs.E-J) .... #5

#4.Found attached to mammals, including humans; with 4 pairs of legs; without antennae; unsegmented body (Fig.C) .... **ticks**, page 9.09
#4.Found attached to fish, crabs, shrimp, jellyfish and other aquatic animals; with more than 4 pairs of legs and/or with antennae and/or with a segmented body (Fig.D) .... **parasitic crustaceans**, page 10.02

#5.A cluster of cocoons (Fig.E) along the back edge of a crab shell .... **cocoons of the parasitic leech, *Myzobdella lugubris***, page 8.23
#5.Not a cluster of cocoons on a crab shell .... #6

#6.With one or more attachment organs (hooks, suckers, claspers, spiny proboscis, adhesive disc, anchors, etc.) (Fig.F) .... page 2.20
#6.Without any attachment organs (Figs.G-J) .... #7

#7.A pink wormlike animal living inside the comb jelly, *Mnemiopsis leidyi* (Fig.G) .... **parasitic anemone, *Edwardsia leidyi***, page 4.15
#7.Not found inside a comb jelly .... #8

#8.Body usually tapering to a point at each end (Fig.H); elongate, round in cross section; body may be extended or folded back on itself within a cyst; found in the digestive tract and internal organs of vertebrates and invertebrates .... **roundworms (nematodes)**, page 5.08
#8.Not tapered to a point at both ends (Figs.I,J) .... #9

#9.Tiny worms, less than 1 mm (1/32") long; usually oval or cylindrical in shape (Fig.I) and round in cross section; found inside the tissues of molluscs (snails, clamlike animals, etc.) and rarely annelids (segmented worms) .... **sporocyst and redial larval stages of flukes, digenetic trematode worms**, page 5.02
#9.Longer than 1 mm (1/32"); found crawling on or in the shell of molluscs and crustaceans (e.g., crabs, lobsters); may or may not be somewhat flattened in cross section (Fig.J) .... **free living worms**, page 2.16

[1]Parasitism, mutualism, and commensalism are different types of animal associations included under the general term symbiosis, which means "living together". If neither partner benefits at the other's expense, the association is called commensalism. If both partners benefit, the association is called mutualism. When one partner (the parasite) benefits at the expense of the other (the host), the association is called parasitism. It is often very difficult to determine which type of symbiotic relationship is actually involved when two animals are found living together. For example, the harm being done to the host by a parasitic relationship may not be obvious without careful study. Therefore, this key includes all three types of symbionts. Refer to a textbook such as Schmidt and Roberts (1981), Cheng (1973), or Noble and Noble (1982) for more background on the biology of parasitism.

The identification of many symbiotic species is not possible without considerable expertise and the use of special techniques which are beyond the scope of this book. Many parasites are so highly modified that they bear little or no resemblance to other members of their group. Thus, the keys that follow provide representative examples of species for each phylum but are not intended for identification at the species level. An expert should be consulted if more precision is required. The specimen must be brought to the expert in good condition if it is to be of any value. If possible, keep the animal alive in seawater and have it identified within a day. Preservatives such as alcohol or formalin usually render the specimen unidentifiable. For proper fixation methods, refer to a parasitology manual such as Pritchard and Kruse (1982), Meyer and Olsen (1980), or Cable (1977).

[2]Open the cyst and examine the animal living inside. It may be possible to identify the animal using these keys. If not, an expert should be consulted. Larger cysts can be teased apart with a needle. Small cysts can sometimes be popped open by applying pressure with a cover slip on a microscope slide.

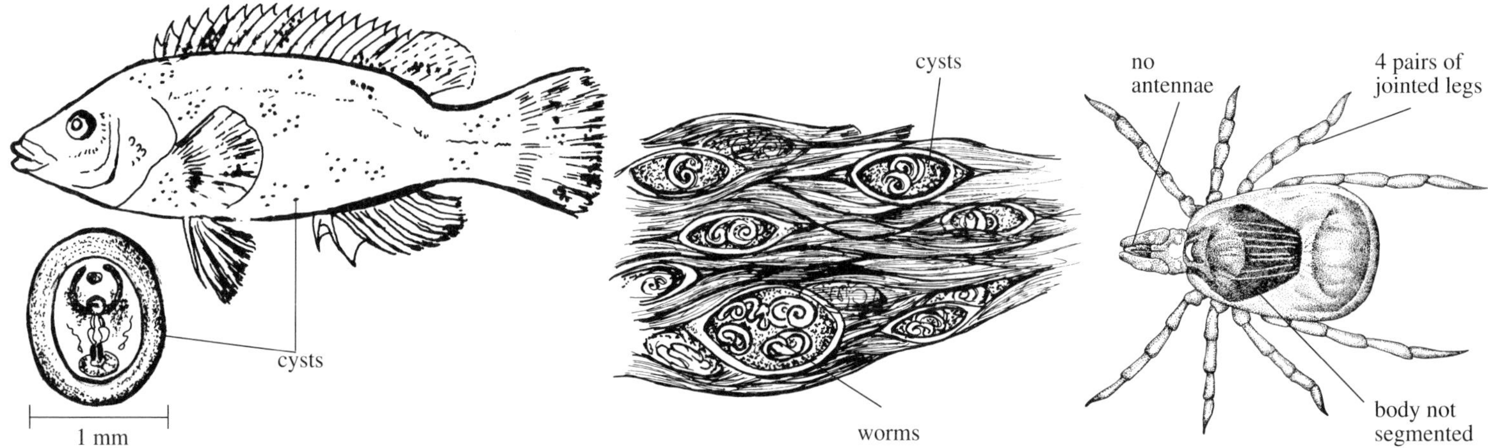

Fig.A. **METACERCARIA CYSTS OF TREMATODE WORM**

Fig.B. **CYSTS IN MUSCLE TISSUE, HIGHLY MAGNIFIED**

Fig.C. **TICK**

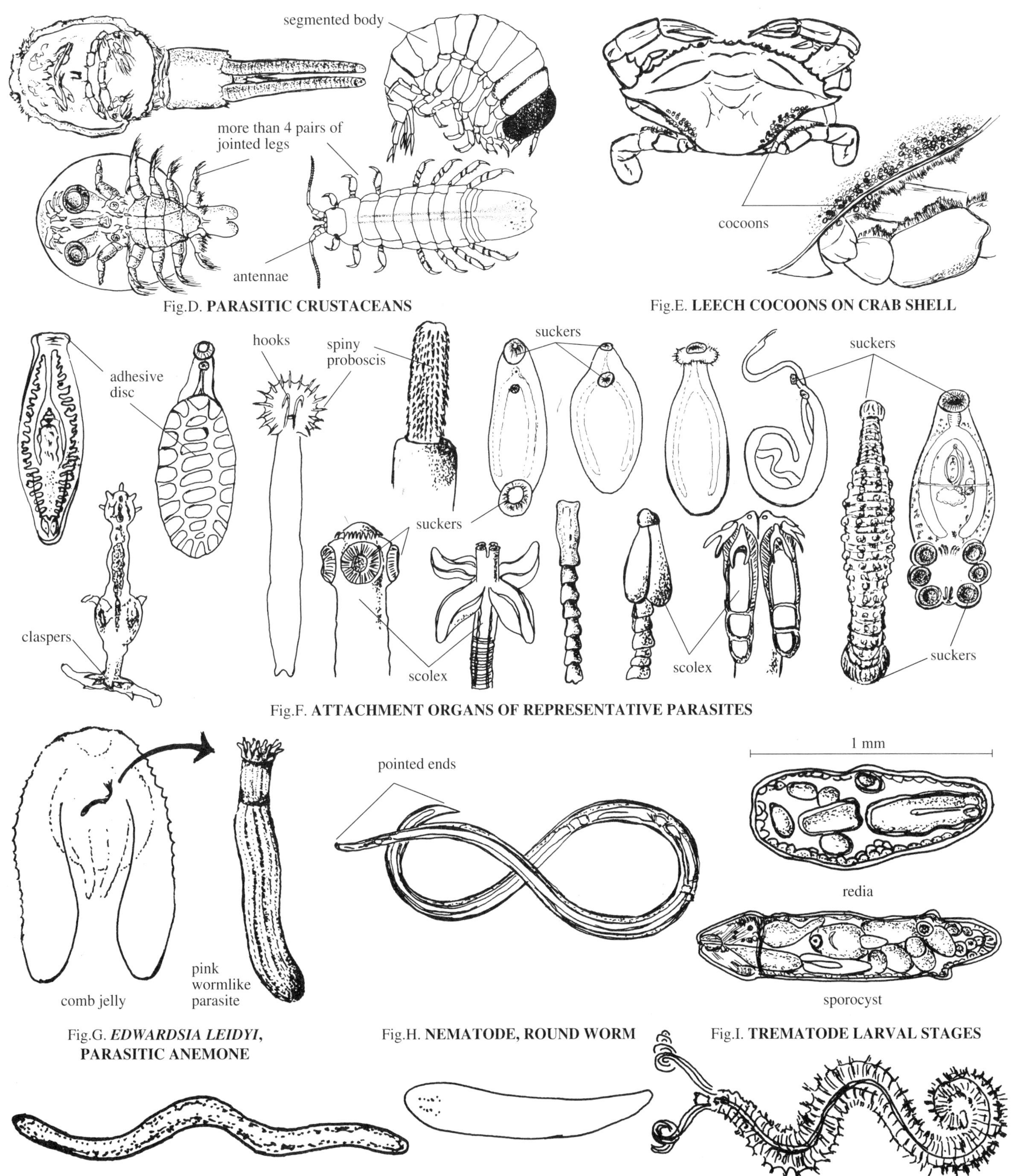

Fig.D. **PARASITIC CRUSTACEANS**

Fig.E. **LEECH COCOONS ON CRAB SHELL**

Fig.F. **ATTACHMENT ORGANS OF REPRESENTATIVE PARASITES**

Fig.G. ***EDWARDSIA LEIDYI*, PARASITIC ANEMONE**

Fig.H. **NEMATODE, ROUND WORM**

Fig.I. **TREMATODE LARVAL STAGES**

Fig.J. **FREE LIVING WORMS**

PARASITES AND OTHER SYMBIONTS WITH ATTACHMENT ORGANS

(Key to parasites and other symbionts begins on page 2.18)

#1. With a sucker (Fig.A) at each end of a heavy walled, segmented, wormlike body; sucker at tail end is somewhat disc shaped and sucker at head end usually surrounds the mouth; found attached to the external surface of fish, crabs, and other invertebrate and vertebrate hosts .... **leeches**, page 8.23

#1. Not as above (Figs.B-I) .... #2

#2. Head end attached to or buried into the gills, fins or body of fish; with a wormlike body extending outside of the fish (Fig.B); often with a pair of egg sacs at the external end .... **parasitic copepods**, page 10.02

#2. Completely contained within the intestinal tract or gill chamber of the host .... #3

#3. With a retractile proboscis armed with hooks or spines (Fig.C) (Note: the proboscis may be withdrawn into body and may not be obvious); adults found in the intestinal tract of vertebrates; larval stages found in the internal organs and body cavities of crustaceans and sometimes vertebrates .... **thorny-headed or spiny-headed worms, acanthocephalans**, page 5.09

#3. Without a spiny retractile proboscis (Figs.D-I) .... #4

#4. With claspers and posterior limbs (Fig.D) used for attaching and walking on the gills and egg masses of lobsters; very tiny, about 1 mm (1/32") in length .... ***Histriobdella homari*, lobster gill worms**, page 8.23

#4. Without claspers and posterior limbs (Figs.E-I); not usually found on lobster gills or egg masses .... #5

#5. Body divided into many segments (proglottids) (Fig.E); worm may be very long, sometimes exceeding 1 m (3'); with a scolex (Fig.F) attachment organ; usually found in the intestinal tract of fishes, birds and mammals .... **tapeworms, cestodes**, page 5.04

#5. Body not segmented (Figs.G-I) (Note: some worms have wrinkled skin which may look like segments); rarely exceeding 5 cm (2") in length .... #6

#6. With a scolex type attachment organ similar to one of those shown in Fig.F .... **larval and unsegmented adult tapeworms, cestodes**, page 5.04

#6. Attachment organ is not similar to those shown in Fig.F (Figs.G-I) .... #7

#7. With one or more more suckers (Fig.G); one sucker usually located at anterior (head) end; one or more suckers usually located ventrally (underside) and/or at posterior end; may or may not have hooks at posterior end .... **monogene and trematode worms**, page 5.02

#7. With a single adhesive disc (Figs.H,I) at the posterior end; no hooks .... #8

#8. Found on the book gills of horseshoe crabs; mouth and proboscis (Fig.H) located in middle of body; intestines with 3 main branches and numerous side branches .... **horseshoe crab flatworms (turbellarians)**, page 5.00

#8. Found in the mantle cavity of clams, mussels and other bivalves; with a retractile proboscis (Fig.I) that extends from the anterior end; intestines not branched .... ***Malacobdella grossa*, nemertean worm**, page 5.07

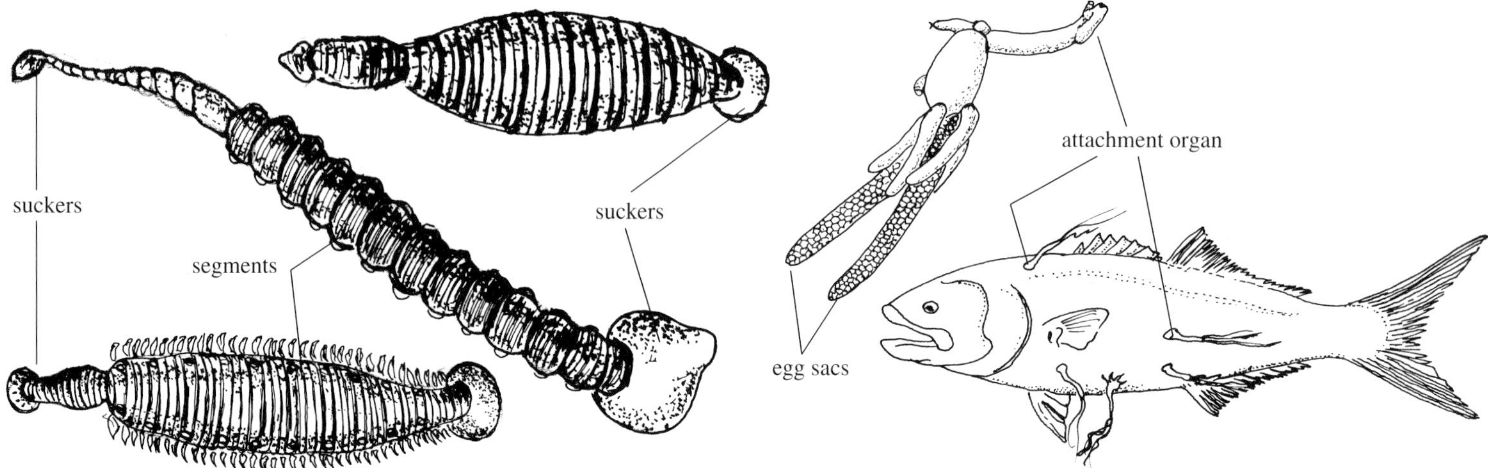

Fig.A. **LEECHES**

Fig.B. **PARASITIC COPEPODS**

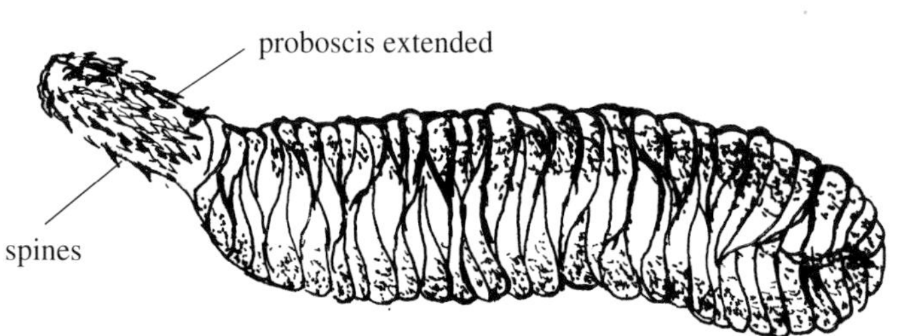

Fig.C. **THORNY OR SPINY-HEADED WORMS**

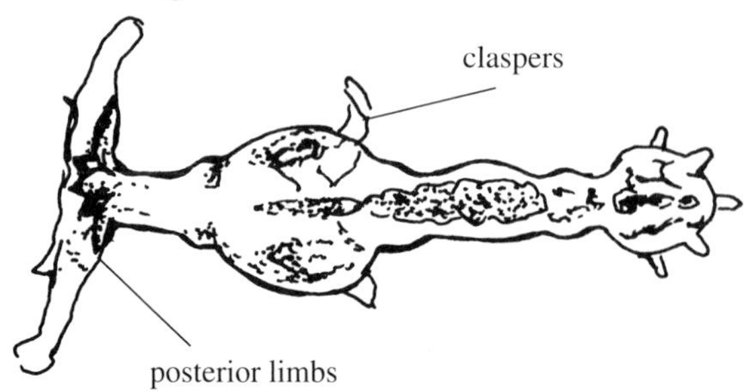

Fig.D. ***HISTRIOBDELLA HOMARI*, LOBSTER GILL WORM**

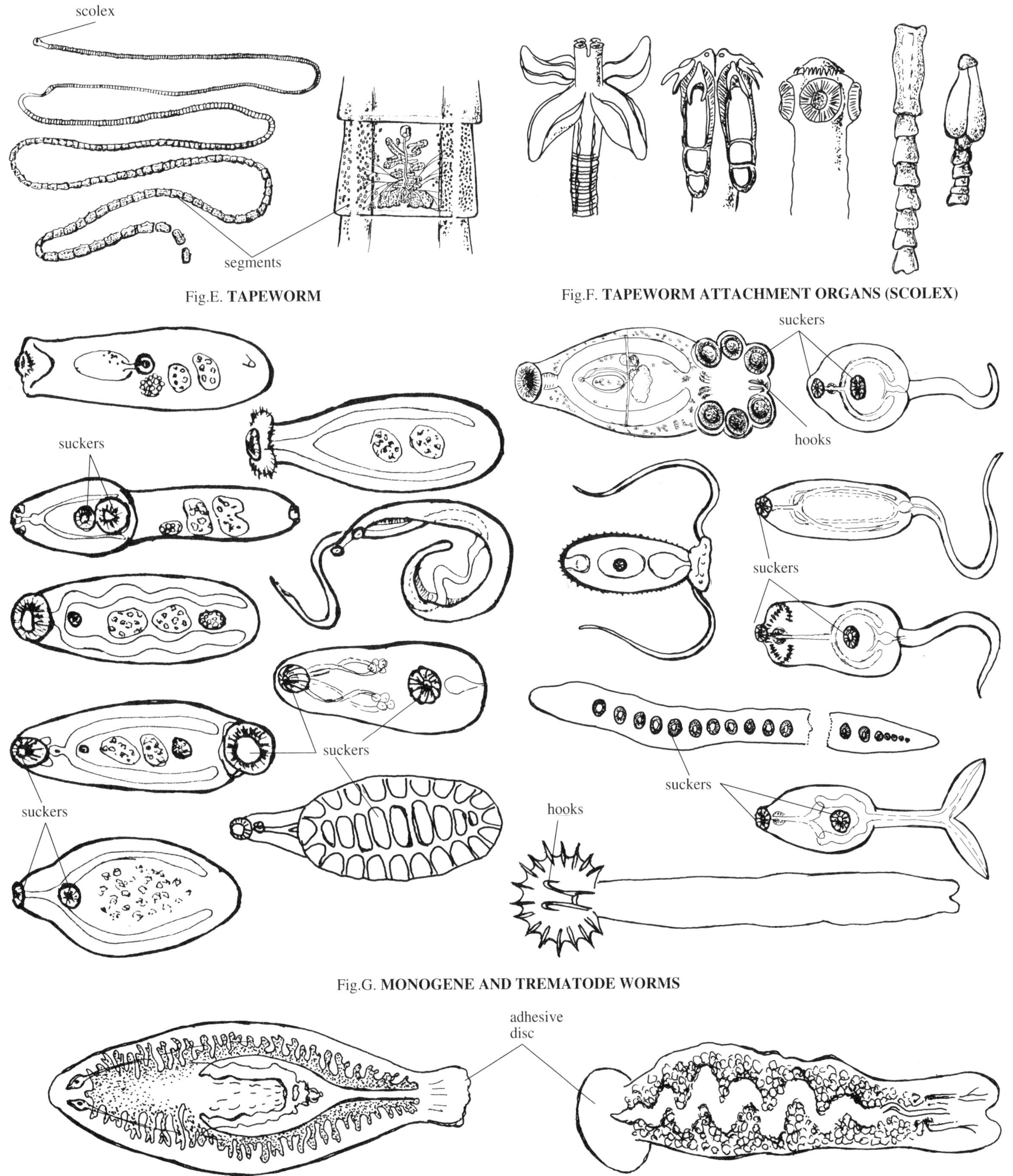

Fig.E. **TAPEWORM**

Fig.F. **TAPEWORM ATTACHMENT ORGANS (SCOLEX)**

Fig.G. **MONOGENE AND TREMATODE WORMS**

Fig.H. ***BDELLOURA CANDIDA*, HORSESHOE CRAB FLATWORM**

Fig.I. ***MALACOBDELLA GROSSA*, NEMERTEAN WORM**

EGGS AND EGG CASES[1]

(Getting started key begins on page 2.00)

#1.More than 12 mm (1/2") in height, width OR length (Figs.A-K) .... #2
#1.Less than 12 mm (1/2") in height, width AND length (Figs.J-N) .... #11

#2.Collar shaped (Fig.A); made out of sand and mucus; when dry, becomes very brittle and crumbles easily; often over 7.5 cm (3") in diameter with a hole that is usually over 2.5 cm (1") in diameter; eggs are embedded in underside of collar .... **egg cases of moonsnails**, page 7.04
#2.Not collar shaped (Figs.B-K); not made out of sand and mucus .... #3

#3.Gelatinous (jellylike or Jellolike); semitransparent, may be colorless, whitish or greenish; may be composed of cigar or pear shaped lobes (Figs.B,C) or may be stringlike or ribbonlike (Fig.J) .... #4
#3.Leathery, rubbery, spongy, or parchmentlike[2] (Figs.D-I); not transparent; not composed of cigar or pear shaped lobes .... #6

#4.Stringlike or ribbonlike (Fig.J); less than 6 mm (1/4") in width .... **egg masses of various species of sea slugs or nudibranchs**, page 7.11
#4.Composed of one or more cigar, torpedo or pear shaped lobes (Figs.B,C); lobes are more than 6 mm (1/4") in width .... #5

#5.Cigar or torpedo shaped lobes (Fig.B); many lobes are usually stuck together to form clumps or masses that often exceed 30 cm (1') in diameter; individual lobes are colorless and are about 10 cm (4") in length; numerous tiny spherical eggs or embryos can be seen embedded in each lobe when examined under 10X magnification .... **egg cases of *Loligo pealeii*, longfin squid**, page 7.00
#5.Pear shaped lobes (Fig.C); individual lobes are loosely attached to muddy or sandy bottoms by a threadlike stalk; often somewhat greenish; usually less than 5 cm (2") in length .... **egg cases of polychaete worms such as *Lumbrineris*,** page 8.21, ***Leitoscoloplos*,** page 8.19, ***Arenicola*,** page 8.19

#6.A rectangular pouch (Fig.D) with hornlike tendrils at each corner; pouch is leathery or parchmentlike[2], usually black, and exceeds 7.5 cm (3") in length; a single well developed skate develops inside the egg case and hatches out through a slitlike opening along one edge of the pouch between the tendrils; development takes place while the egg case is entangled in seaweed on the ocean bottom; after hatching, these egg cases are found washed up on shore and are called "mermaid's purses" .... **egg case of *Raja*, skates**, page 13.06
#6.Not a black rectangular pouch .... #7

#7.A row of disclike or irregularly shaped objects joined together on a stringlike attachment (Figs.E-G) .... #8
#7.A ball or irregular clump of somewhat spherical eggs (Figs.H,I) .... #10

#8.String of somewhat triangular or irregularly shaped egg masses (Fig.E); string may reach over 12 mm (1/2") in length and egg masses are about 3 mm (1/8") long .... **egg mass of *Epitonium*, wentletrap snails**, page 7.06
#8.String of disc shaped, parchmentlike[2] capsules (Figs.F,G); string may reach over 15 cm (6") in length and capsules are about 2.5 cm (1") in diameter; numerous tiny whelks (snails) develop inside each capsule and hatch out through a tiny pore located at the edge of the capsule on the side opposite the stringlike attachment; if the pore is plugged then the egg yolk and developing whelks can usually be found inside when the capsule is torn open; the whelks develop and hatch while the egg case is submerged on the ocean bottom but the egg cases are often found washed up on shore, especially after hatching .... **whelk egg case**, #9

#9.Discs are blunt, double edged, like a coin (Fig.F) .... **egg case of *Busycon carica*, knobbed whelk**, page 7.10
#9.Discs are sharp, single edged (Fig.G) .... **egg case of *Busycotypus canaliculatus* (=*Busycon canaliculatum*) , channeled whelk**, page 7.10

#10.Parchmentlike[2], somewhat flattened eggs, in a spherical clump resembling a "popcorn ball" (Fig.H) that may be 7.5 cm (3") or more in diameter; occasionally found dried and washed ashore with holes in many of the egg capsules .... **egg case of *Buccinum undatum*, waved whelk**, page 7.09
#10.Rubbery and membranous; eggs are nearly perfect spheres (Fig.I); eggs are usually found attached to seaweeds and under rocks offshore .... **fish eggs, such as *Hemitripterus americanus*, the sea raven**, page 13.21

#11.Gelatinous (jellylike or Jellolike); lies flat, not upright; may be stringlike, ribbonlike, platelike or irregularly shaped (Figs.J-M); transparent, usually colorless or a milky white .... #12
#11.Parchmentlike[2], rubbery, leathery or fuzzy; upright and erect; may be vaselike or chimneylike (Figs.N); may or may not be transparent; often found in rows or clusters on rocks, seaweeds, eelgrass, shells, etc .... page 2.24

#12.Long ribbonlike or stringlike strand of even diameter (Fig.J); often deposited on seaweeds and hydroids .... **egg masses of various species of nudibranchs (sea slugs)**, page 7.11
#12.Coiled, doughnut or irregularly shaped (Figs. K-M) .... #13

#13.Coiled gelatinous string (Fig.K); attached to seaweed or eelgrass; coil is approximately 3 mm (1/8") in diameter .... **egg mass of the snail *Bittium alternatum*, alternate bittium**, page 7.06
#13.Doughnut or irregularly shaped (Figs.L,M) .... #14

#14.Doughnut shaped (Fig.L); about 8 mm (5/16") in diameter .... **eggs of the snail *Lacuna vincta*, northern lacuna**, page 7.05
#14.Irregularly shaped (Fig.M); deposited on seaweeds near the low tide level .... **egg mass of *Littorina obtusata*, yellow periwinkle**, page 7.05

[1]This key does not include eggs or egg cases which are normally attached to the parent or are planktonic. Only the most obvious and common eggs are included in this key. Some soft bodied sessile (attached) animals such as sea squirts, anemones and sponges might be confused with egg cases. Refer to page 2.08 if you are not sure you have an egg case.

[2]Parchment is a paperlike material that is a bit stiffer and thicker than the pages of this book.

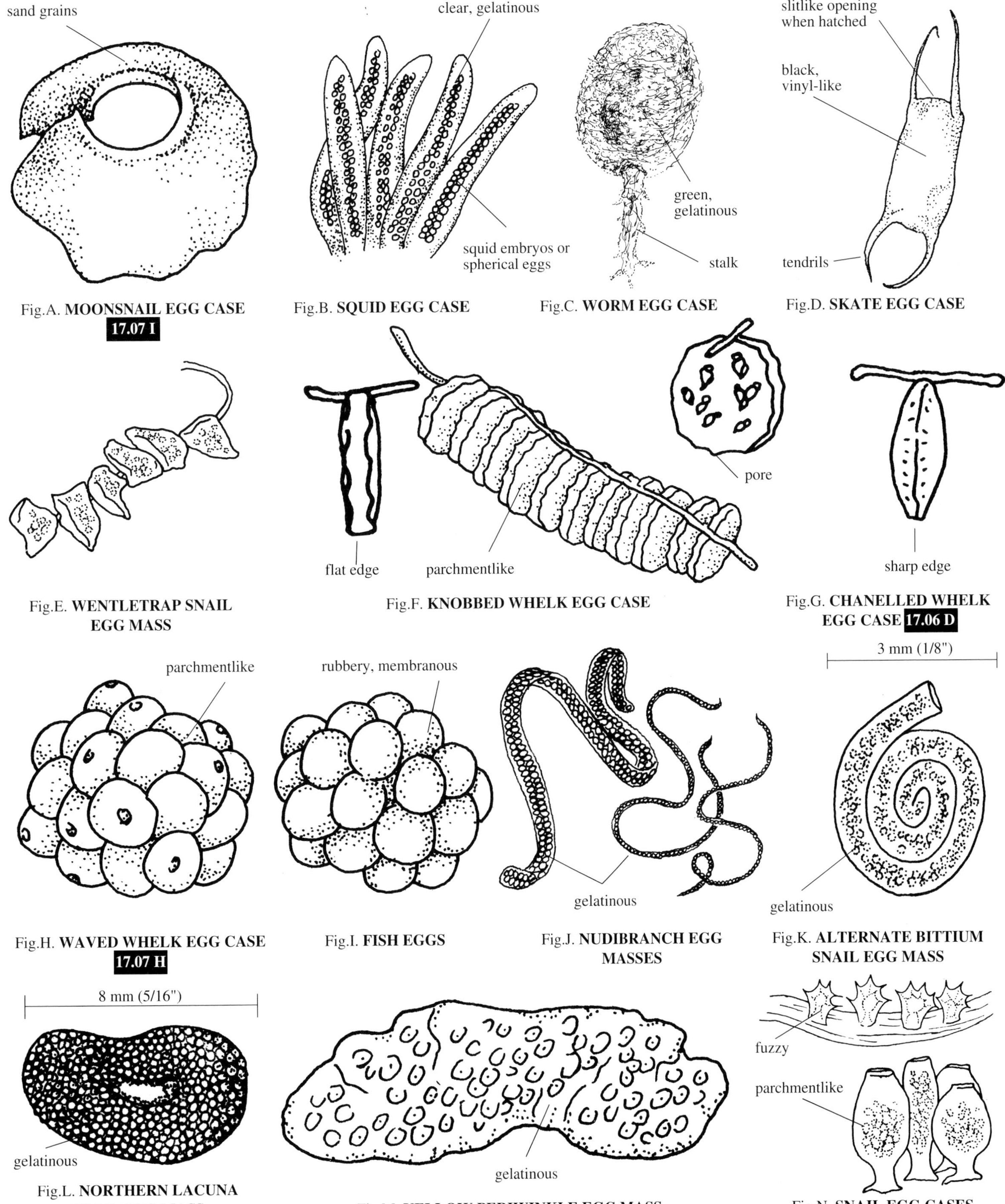

Fig.A. **MOONSNAIL EGG CASE** **17.07 I**

Fig.B. **SQUID EGG CASE**

Fig.C. **WORM EGG CASE**

Fig.D. **SKATE EGG CASE**

Fig.E. **WENTLETRAP SNAIL EGG MASS**

Fig.F. **KNOBBED WHELK EGG CASE**

Fig.G. **CHANELLED WHELK EGG CASE** **17.06 D**

Fig.H. **WAVED WHELK EGG CASE** **17.07 H**

Fig.I. **FISH EGGS**

Fig.J. **NUDIBRANCH EGG MASSES**

Fig.K. **ALTERNATE BITTIUM SNAIL EGG MASS**

Fig.L. **NORTHERN LACUNA SNAIL EGG MASS**

Fig.M. **YELLOW PERIWINKLE EGG MASS**

Fig.N. **SNAIL EGG CASES**

EGGS AND EGG CASES (CONTINUED)

(Key to eggs and egg cases begins on page 2.22)

#1.Stalked, somewhat wineglass shaped (Figs.A-C); attached end narrower than free end; often found on hard substrates (shells, rocks, pilings, etc.); parchmentlike, not transparent .... #2
#1.Attached end the same width or wider than free end (Figs.D,E); often found in rows on eelgrass and seaweed; transparent or whitish .... #4

#2.Opening is off to one side, not centered at top (Fig.A) (opening is plugged until snails hatch) .... **egg case of *Eupleura caudata*, thick-lip drill**, page 7.08
#2.Opening (may be plugged) is centered at top (Figs.B,C) .... #3

#3.Somewhat pointed at top (Fig.B); up to 8 mm (5/16") long .... **egg case of *Nucella lapillus (=Thais lapillus)* , Atlantic dogwinkle**, page 7.09
#3.Rounded or blunt at top (Fig.C); up to 6 mm (1/4") long .... **egg case of *Urosalpinx cinerea*, Atlantic oyster drill**, page 7.08

#4.With short spines (Fig.D) .... **egg case of *Ilyanassa obsoleta (=Nassarius obsoletus)* , eastern mud snail**, page 7.09
#4.Without spines (Fig.E) .... **egg case of *Nassarius vibex*, bruised nassa (snail)**, page 7.09

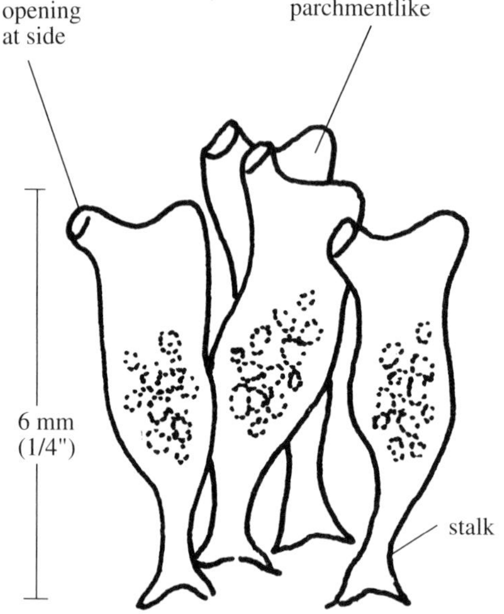

Fig.A. **THICK-LIP DRILL EGG CASES**

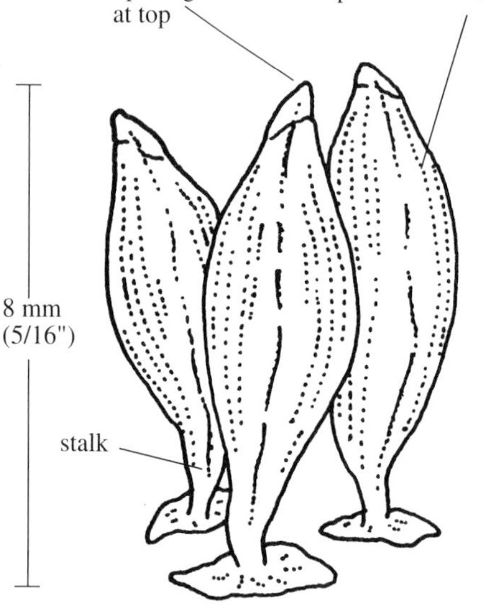

Fig.B. **ATLANTIC DOGWINKLE EGG CASES**

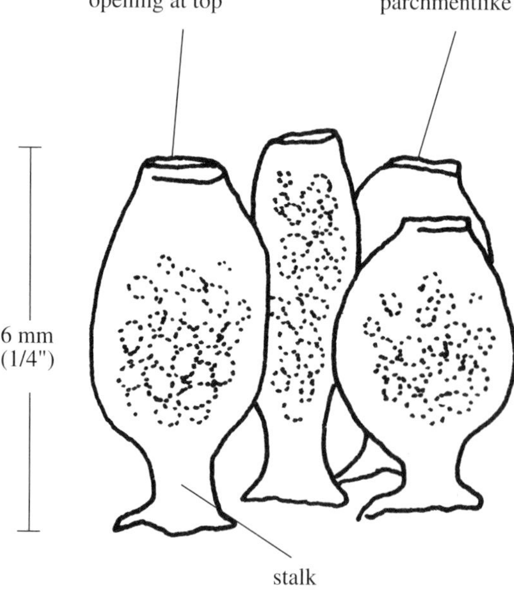

Fig.C. **ATLANTIC OYSTER DRILL EGG CASES** **17.06 E**

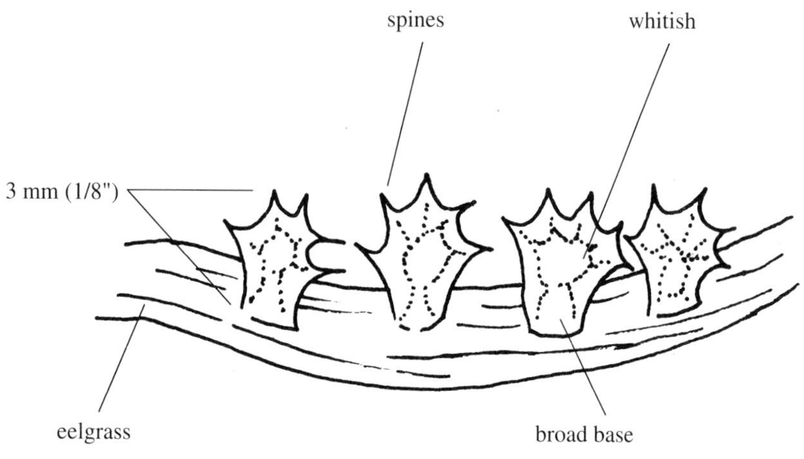

Fig.D. **EASTERN MUDSNAIL EGG CASES**

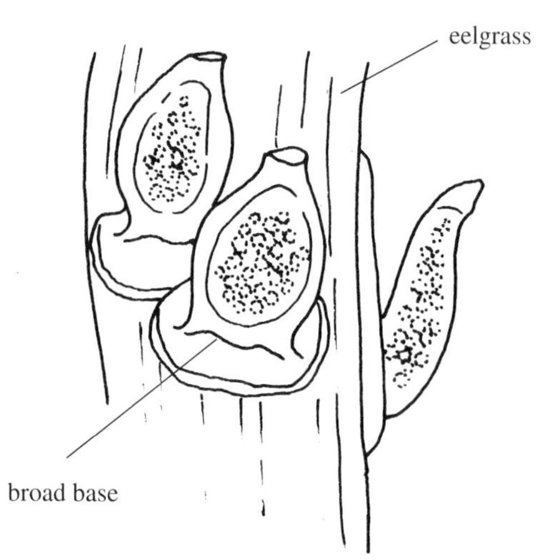

Fig.E. **BRUISED NASSA (SNAIL) EGG CASES**

TUBES AND CASTINGS

(Getting started key begins on page 2.00)

#1.Flexible, bends easily without breaking; parchmentlike[1], leatherlike or membranous (page 2.26, Figs.A-E) .... page 2.26
#1.Hard or brittle, will not bend; will break or crumble if bent or squeezed .... #2

#2.Hard and thick walled; (Fig.A) made out of a concretelike material consisting of a mixture of fine sand and cement; tubes are bent, coiled and twisted, usually with a number of tubes cemented together; tubes may form holes in a reeflike structure up to 30 cm (12") across or in a smaller lumplike mass attached to shells and rocks .... **tube of *Sabellaria vulgaris*, cement-tube worm**, page 8.04
#2.Not made out of a concretelike material; not thick walled .... #3

#3.Made out of sand or mud (page 2.27, Figs.A-F), sometimes consisting of a single layer of sand or mud cemented together .... page 2.27
#3.Calcareous, made out of shell-like material (this page, Figs. B-D) .... #4

#4.Erect and upright (Fig.B) attached at one end only; sides of tube made out of 6 plates; opening of tube, when animal is alive, has a beaklike "trapdoor" made out of 4 plates; tubes usually packed closely together .... **barnacles, crowded form**, page 10.13
#4.Most or all of the tube lies flat (Figs.C-D) and is attached directly to the substrate (rock, shell, seaweed, eelgrass, etc.); one end of the tube may or may not be erect; sides of tube are one continuous piece, not 6 separate plates; tube is coiled or twisted .... #5

#5.Twisted (Fig.C) and often over 2.5 cm (1") in length; common on shells, rocks and other hard objects; firmly attached for all or most of length; may occur singly or in a tangled mass .... **tube of *Hydroides dianthus*, carnation worm**, page 8.05
#5.Tightly coiled and tiny (Figs.D); coils are nearly flat or slightly raised; coil diameter less than 3 mm (1/8") across and tube diameter less than 1 mm (1/32"); often found in large numbers on eelgrass, seaweeds, rocks, etc .... **tube of *Spirorbis*, coiled worm**, #6

#6.Coiled clockwise (Fig.D) .... **tube of *Spirorbis borealis*, clockwise coiled worm**, page 8.05
#6.Coiled counterclockwise (Fig.D) .... **tube of *Spirorbis spirillum*, counterclockwise coiled worm**, page 8.05

[1]Parchment is a paperlike material that is a bit thicker and stiffer than the pages of this book.

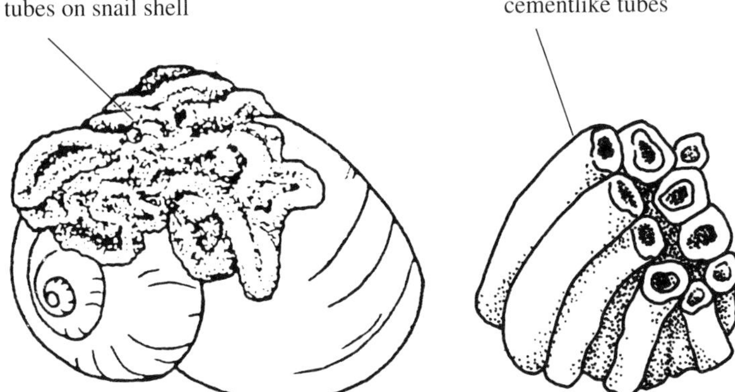

Fig.A. ***SABELLARIA VULGARIS*, CEMENT-TUBE WORM TUBES**

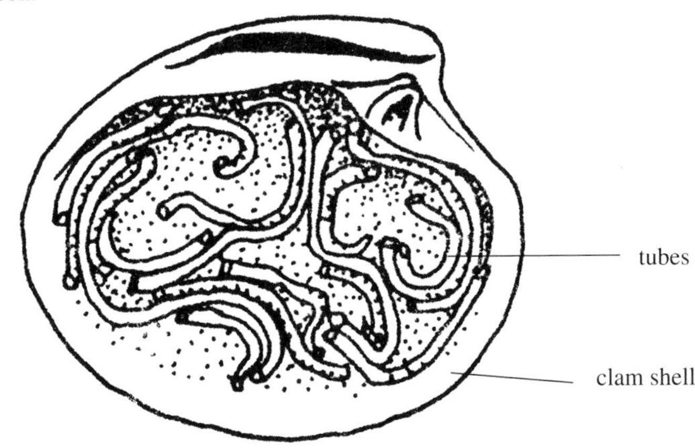

Fig.C. ***HYDROIDES DIANTHUS*, CARNATION WORM TUBES** **17.08 D**

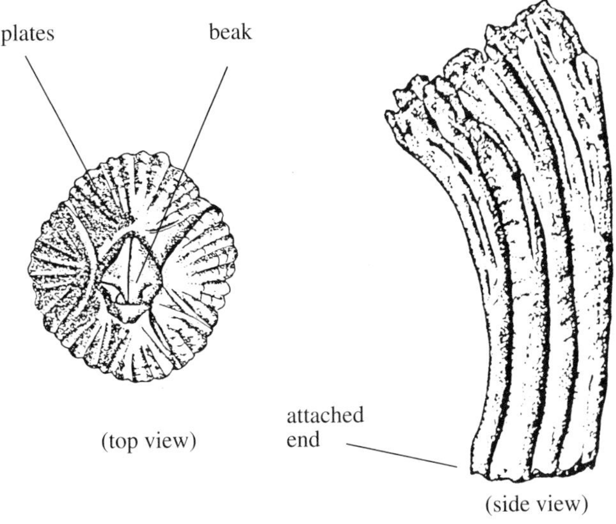

Fig.B. **BARNACLES, CROWDED FORM**

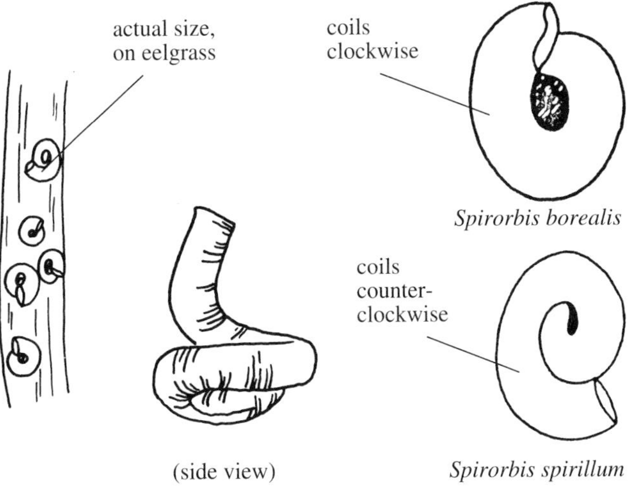

Fig.D. ***SPIRORBIS*, COILED WORM TUBES**  and 

FLEXIBLE TUBES AND CASTINGS

(Key to tubes and castings begins on page 2.25)

#1.Collar shaped (page 2.27, Fig.A); made out of sand and mucus .... **moonsnail egg case**, page 7.04
#1.Not collar shaped .... #2

#2.Coils of solid mud, often forming mounds (page 2.27, Fig.B) .... page 2.27
#2.Hollow tubes (Figs.A-E, this page). .... #3

#3.With pieces of shell, seaweed, eelgrass, pebbles and other debris (Fig.A) attached to a flexible but tough, skinlike tube; tube often extends 5-8 cm (2"-3") above the bottom, like a chimney .... **tube of *Diopatra cuprea*, junk worm**, page 8.13
#3.Smooth tube; without debris attached (Figs.B-E) but may have some sand grains embedded in tube wall .... #4

#4.Transparent, whitish tube with bamboolike rings (Fig.B); found in mudflats and among roots of eelgrass .... **tube of *Spiochaetopterus oculatus*, glassy tube worm**, page 8.10
#4.Tube is not transparent and does not have bamboolike rings (Figs.C-E) .... #5

#5.U-shaped tube (Fig.C) with tapered ends that extend up to 2.5 cm (1") above the bottom; tube is parchmentlike[1]. .... **tube of *Chaetopterus variopedatus*, parchment worm**, page 8.10
#5.Not U-shaped; ends not tapered; membranous, skinlike tubes made out of mucus coated with mud (Figs.D,E) .... #6

#6.Tubes attached to hard objects such as shells, pilings, rocks; may occur as individual tubes or may be colonial; may grow together forming an extensive mat overgrowing the substrate; tubes may be erect and chimneylike or may lie flat against the substrate ....
tubes[2] of polychaete worms such as featherduster worms, *Potamilla* and *Sabella*, page 8.05, terebellid worms, page 8.06, and fringed worms, page 8.08; OR **amphipods** such as *Corophium insidiosum*, page 10.05 and *Jassa marmorata*, page 10.07; OR **anemones** such as *Fagesia lineata*, page 4.13.
#6.Tubes buried in mud or sand or attached to soft objects such as seaweeds and hydroids .... #7

#7.Tubes buried in mud or sand ....
tubes[2] of polychaete worms belonging to the families Terebellidae, page 8.06, Ampharetidae, page 8.06, Spionidae, page 8.11, Lumbrineridae, page 8.21 and Maldanidae, page 8.22; OR **amphipods** belonging to the families Corophiidae and Ischyroceridae, page 10.05; OR **burrowing anemones,** page 4.14.
#7.Tubes attached to algae, branches of hydroids, sponges and other soft objects ....
tubes[2] of amphipods belonging to the families Corophiidae, page 10.05, Ampithoidae, page 10.09 and others; OR **polychaete worms**, such as *Autolytus cornutus*, page 8.16.

[1]Parchment is a paperlike material that is a bit thicker and stiffer than the pages of this book.
[2]These tubes and castings cannot be easily distinguished without first identifying the animal inside.

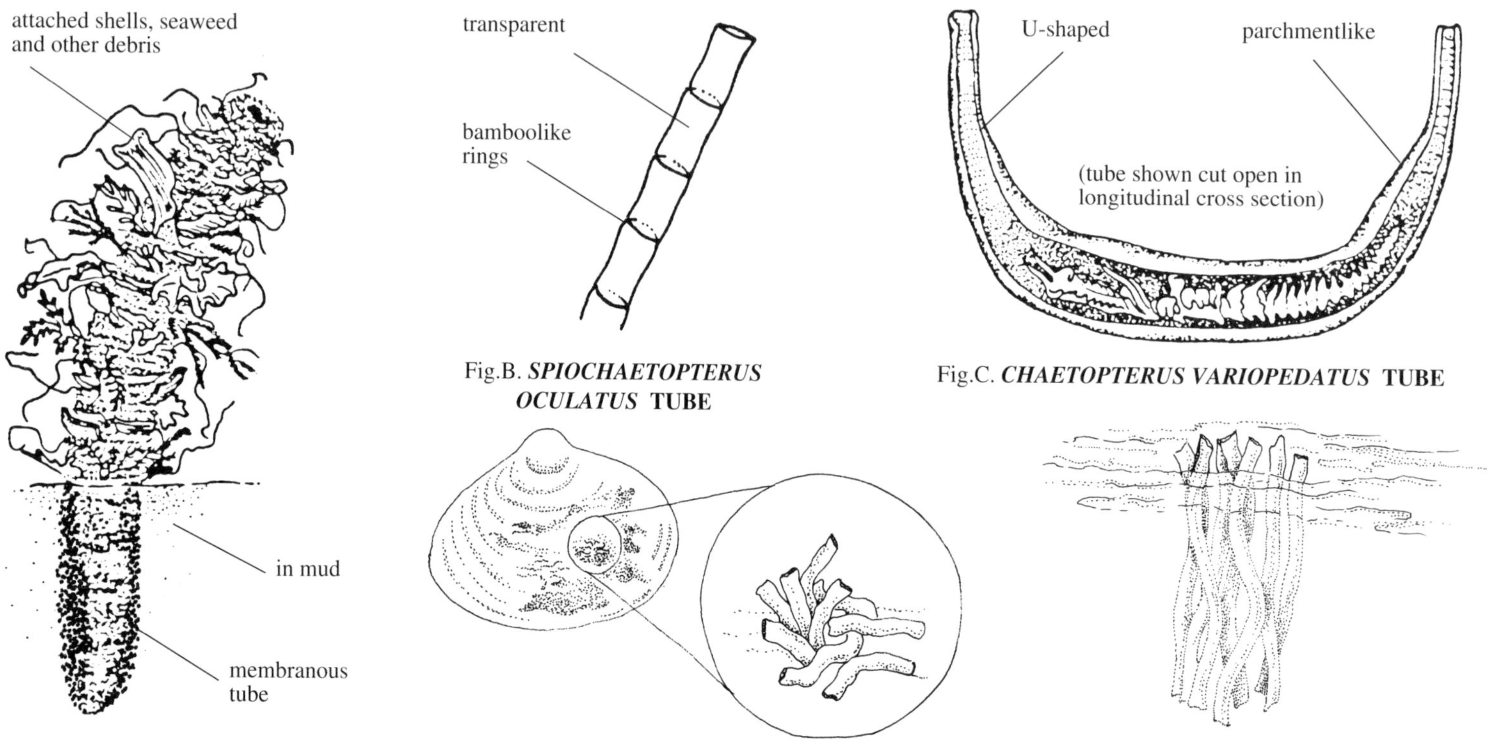

Fig.A. ***DIOPATRA CUPREA* TUBE**

Fig.B. ***SPIOCHAETOPTERUS OCULATUS* TUBE**

Fig.C. ***CHAETOPTERUS VARIOPEDATUS* TUBE**

Fig.D. **FLEXIBLE TUBES ON SHELL**

Fig.E. **FLEXIBLE TUBES BURIED IN MUD**

SAND OR MUD TUBES AND CASTINGS

(Key to tubes and castings begins on page 2.25)

#1.Collar shaped (Fig.A); made out of sand and mucus; often over 7.5 cm (3") in diameter with a hole that is usually over 2.5 cm (1") in diameter .... **moonsnail egg cases**, page 7.04

#1.Not collar shaped (Figs. B-F); hole is usually less than 2.5 cm (1") in diameter .... #2

#2.Coils of solid mud, often forming mounds (Fig.B) ....
castings or deposits of polychaete worms[1], such as *Arenicola,* lug worms, page 8.19; OR **unsegmented worms**, such as *Saccoglossus kowalewskii,* the acorn worm, page 11.07. These burrowing animals eat sand and mud, digest the organic matter and expel the undigested sediment in a ropelike or stringlike casting held together by mucus. The castings are ejected at intervals with a rapid squirt from the hole in the center of the pile.

#2.Hollow inside, not solid; may be coiled, twisted or straight (Figs.C-F) .... #3

#3.Egg shaped or spherical (Fig.C); with a single opening .... **cocoon of long-legged fly pupae and larvae**, pages 9.31, 9.34

#3.Cylindrical or cone shaped (Figs.D-F) .... #4

#4.Cone shaped (Fig.D) .... **tube of *Pectinaria gouldii*, cone worm**, page 8.04

#4.Cylindrical (Figs.E-F) .... #5

#5.Rough tube made out of coarse sand grains or pebbles (Fig.E) cemented together by hardened mucus ....
tubes[1] **of polychaete worms** such as *Pista cristata*, the pom-pom worm, page 8.07 or *Clymenella torquata,* the bamboo worm, page 8.22; OR **tubes of the burrowing anemones**, *Ceriantheopsis americana* and *Cerianthus borealis,* page 4.14.

#5.Smooth tube made out of fine sand grains (Fig.F); end of tube sometimes extends 6 mm (1/4") or more above the bottom, like a chimney ....
tubes[1] **of polychaete worms**, such as *Clymenella torquata*, the bamboo worm, page 8.22 or *Spio setosa*, a spionid worm, page 8.11; OR **tubes of amphipods,** such as *Leptocheirus pinguis,* in the amphipod family Aoridae, page 10.07.

[1]These tubes and castings cannot be easily distinguished without first identifying the animal inside.

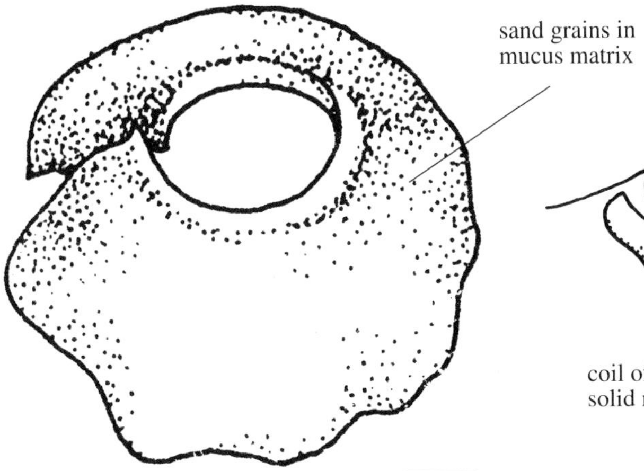

sand grains in mucus matrix

Fig.A. **MOONSNAIL EGG CASE** **17.07 I**

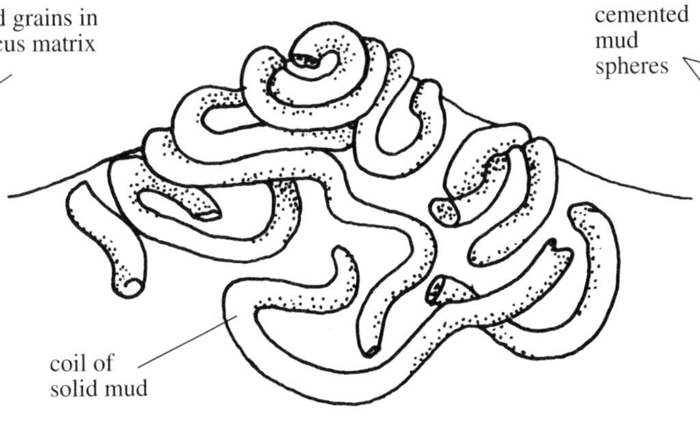

coil of solid mud

Fig.B. **WORM CASTINGS** **17.09 A**

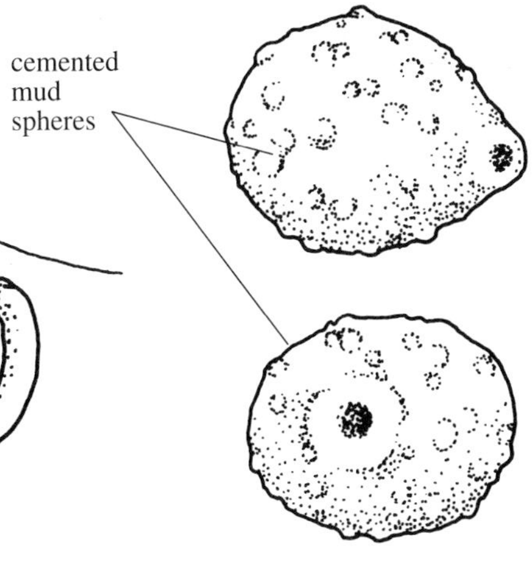

cemented mud spheres

Fig.C. **LONG-LEGGED FLY COCOON**

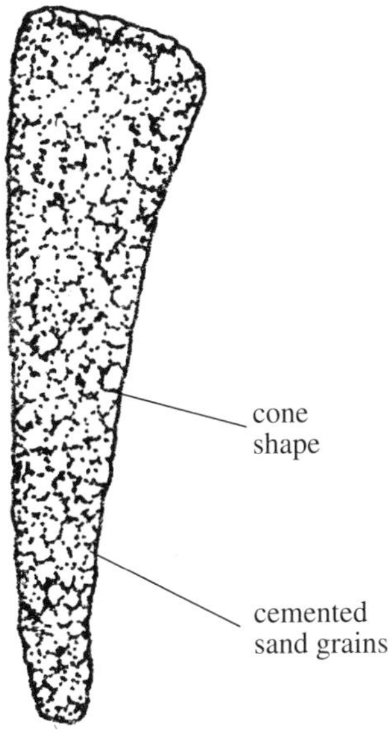

cone shape

cemented sand grains

Fig.D. ***PECTINARIA GOULDII* TUBES** **17.08 B**

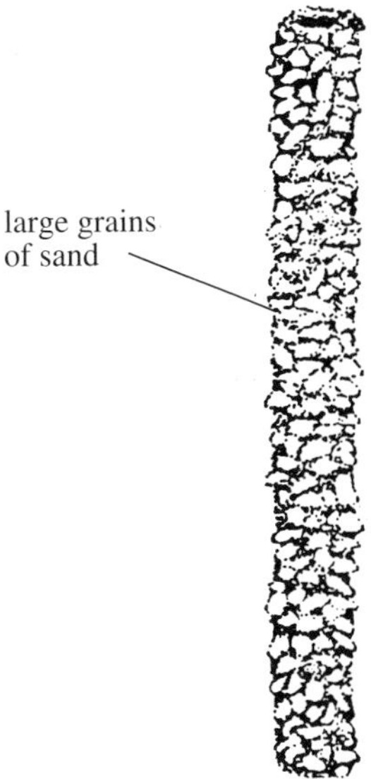

large grains of sand

small grains of sand

Fig.E. **COARSE SAND TUBES** **17.09 G**

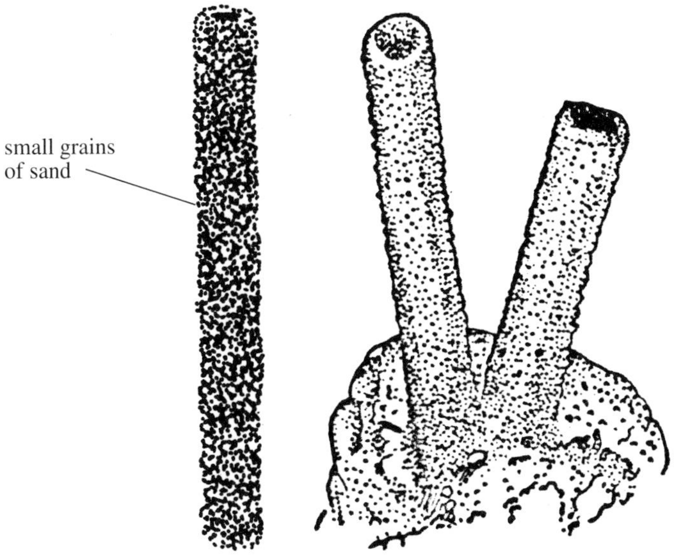

Fig.F. **FINE SAND TUBES**

SPONGES: PHYLUM PORIFERA

Sponges are animals that form encrusting or plantlike colonies attached to rocks, shells, seaweed, pilings, and other objects. They have a porous structure consisting of a system of canals, cavities, and openings to the outside. Seawater is pumped through this system by flagella, microscopic filaments. The sponge body is supported by a skeletal framework composed of spicules[1], tiny needlelike structures made up of either carbonate or silicate.

(Use the key on page 2.01 to determine if you have a sponge.)

#1.Sponges without any raised projections, tubes or branches; sponge surface may have wartlike bumps (Fig.A) or pores (Figs.C,D) or may be smooth and shiny (Fig.B); sponges may be thick and massive (Figs.A,B) or thin and encrusting (Fig.C,D) .... #2

#1.Sponges with branches, tubes or other raised projections; projections may be bushy or fingerlike (Fig.E), chimneylike (Fig.F), slender (Fig.G), vaselike (Fig.H), or tubular (Fig.I) .... #4

#2.With numerous wartlike bumps on surface (Fig.A); bright yellow; may be thick, lumpy and massive or may be thin and encrusting; these sponges bore holes in shells and may completely overgrow and dissolve away the shells .... ***Cliona* spp., boring sponges**, page 3.02

#2.Without wartlike bumps (Figs.B-D); surface may be smooth and shiny (Fig.B) or may have numerous pores (Fig.C,D); may or may not be yellow .... #3

#3.Thick and lumpy (Fig.B), often more than 2.5 cm (1") thick; without any obvious pores; rubbery and firm in texture, with smooth, shiny surface; yellowish; often attaches to shells .... ***Suberites ficus,* fig sponge**, page 3.05

#3.Thin and encrusting (Fig.C,D), less than 2.5 cm (1") thick; with pores; soft, fuzzy or slimy in texture; may or may not be yellowish .... #7

#4.With broad handlike or bushlike branches (Fig.E) often growing over 8 cm (3") tall; sponges usually stand erect, upright; branches may arise from a single narrow stalk near the base .... page 3.03

#4.Without broad fingerlike or bushlike branches; projections with various other shapes (Figs. F-I); projections less than 8 cm (3") long .... #5

#5.Whitish; individual projections are vaselike (Fig.H) or branched and tubular (Fig.I); tiny sponges, individual projections are less than 6 mm (1/4") thick or 25 mm (1") tall; spicules[1] are calcareous and some spicules have 3 or 4 radiating rays (Fig.J) .... **calcareous sponges**, #6

#5.Not white, may be pale yellow or other colors; projections may be chimneylike (Fig.F) or slender (Fig.G); spicules[1] are siliceous and have only 1 or 2 rays (Fig.K) .... **siliceous sponges**, #7

#6.Vase or urn shape; with fringe of "hairs" around opening .... ***Scypha ciliata,* tufted vase sponge** (Fig.H)

#6.Branching, cylindrical tubes arising from network of tubes at base .... ***Leucosolenia botryoides,* organ pipe sponge** (Fig.I)

#7.Most spicules[1] are pointed at both ends (Fig.K); sponge not red in color .... page 3.04

#7.Most spicules[1] are rounded or knobbed at one or both ends (Fig.K); sponge may or may not be red in color .... page 3.05

#7.Without any spicules; smooth, slimy film with tiny pores; tan or light brown; occurs north of Cape Cod .... ***Halisarca* spp., slime sponge** (Fig.C)

[1]The shape, form, and color of many sponge species are highly variable and often cannot be used for making identifications. The positive identification of a sponge usually requires an examination of its microscopic skeletal structures called spicules.

A temporary slide mount of sponge spicules can be prepared by placing a tiny piece (2 mm x 2 mm) of the sponge on a microscope slide and adding a few drops of bleach such as Chlorox. Gently squeeze the sponge several times with a probe so that the bleach is absorbed. After the soft tissue has completely dissolved, place a coverslip on the slide and examine the spicules with a compound microscope at low power (100X) and high dry power (430X). Be sure to base your identification on intact spicules only, not on any broken spicule fragments. Test the spicules with 10% acetic acid (or vinegar) to determine if they are calcareous (made out of calcium carbonate) or siliceous (glassy). Acetic acid will dissolve calcareous spicules but not siliceous spicules.

The length of a spicule can be easily estimated by comparing it to the diameter of the microscope's field of view (Fig.L). Measure the diameter of the field of view by looking at a metric ruler through the microscope. Divide the diameter length by the number of times the spicule will fit end to end across the field of view. For example, at 100X (10X eye piece, 10X objective) the diameter of the microscope's field of view might be 1500 μm and at 430X (10X eye piece, 43X objective) the diameter might be 340 μm. At high power, a spicule which can fit 3 times across the field of view would be about 113 μm long (340/3 = 113). A μm (micrometer) = 0.001 mm = 10^{-6} m. This unit is also sometimes called a micron and given the symbol μ.

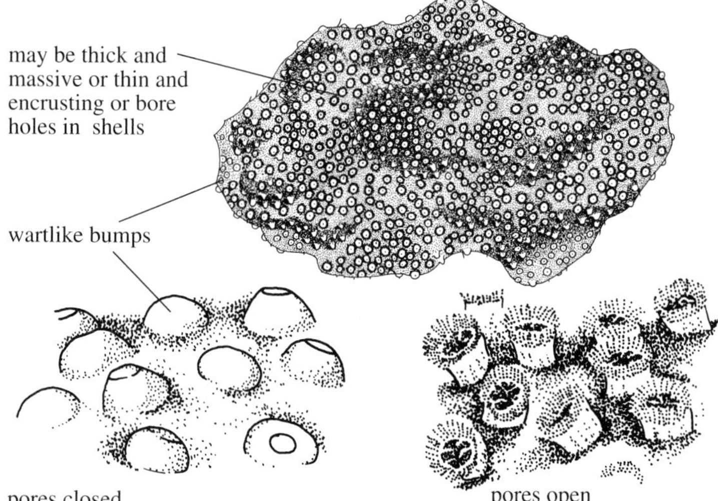

Fig.A. ***CLIONA* SPP., BORING SPONGES**

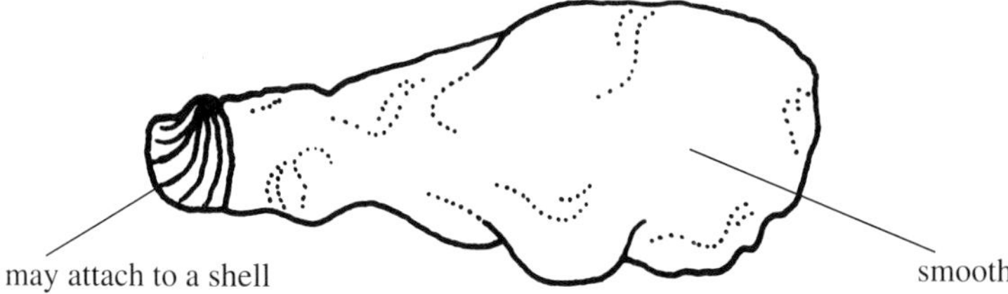

Fig.B. ***SUBERITES FICUS,* FIG SPONGE**

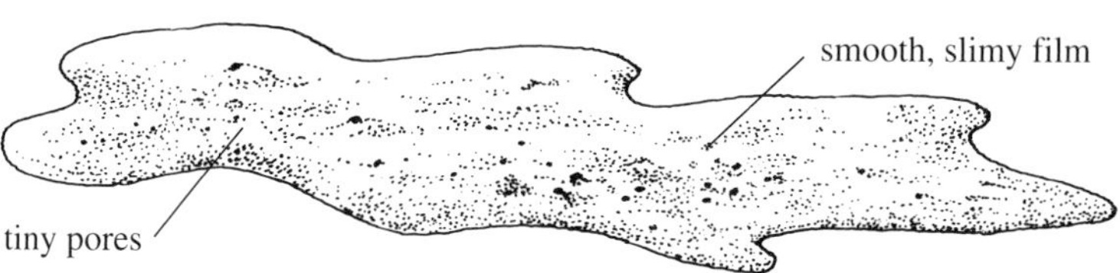

Fig.C. ***HALISARCA* SPP., SLIME SPONGE:** Tan or light brown; about 10 cm (4") long, 3 mm (1/8") thick; attaches to underside of rocks, shells and algae holdfasts in shallow water; occurs from Cape Cod north.

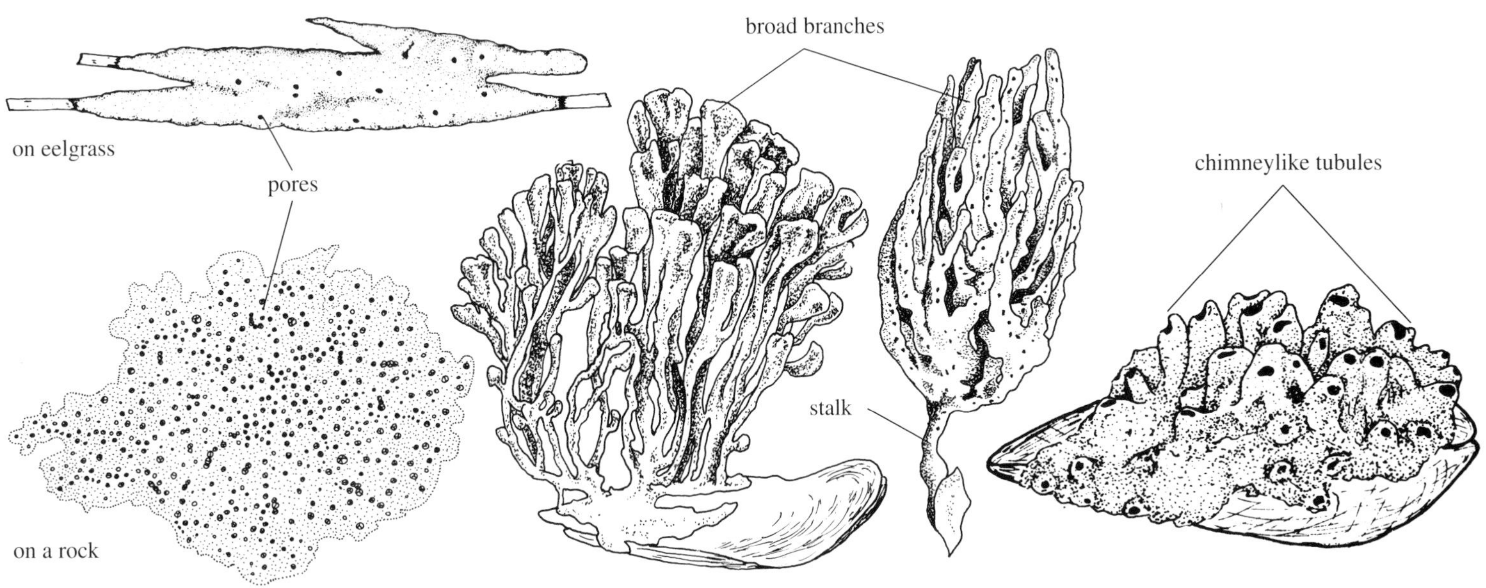

Fig.D. **THIN AND ENCRUSTING SPONGES**

Fig.E. **SPONGES WITH BROAD BUSHLIKE OR FINGERLIKE BRANCHES**

Fig. F. **ENCRUSTING SPONGE WITH RAISED CHIMNEYLIKE TUBULES**

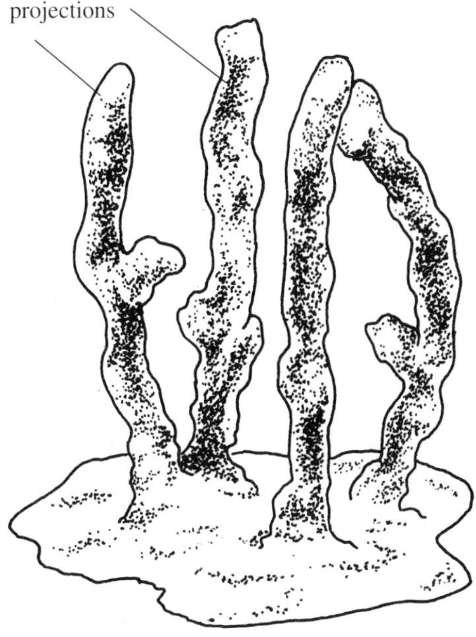

Fig.G. **ENCRUSTING SPONGE WITH SLENDER PROJECTIONS**

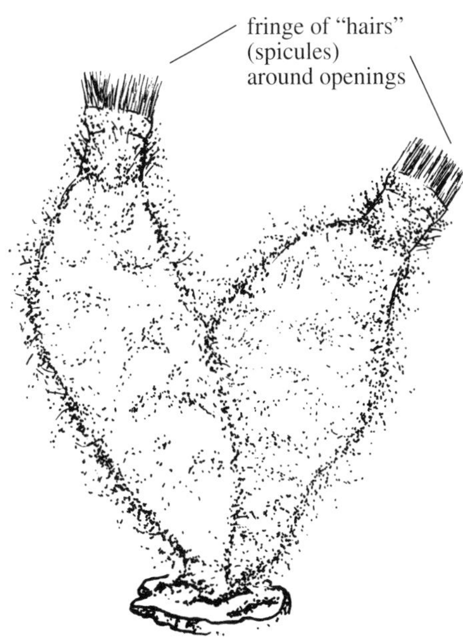

Fig.H. ***SCYPHA CILIATA*, TUFTED VASE SPONGE:** Cream white; fuzzy; up to 2.5 cm (1") tall and 6 mm (1/4") in diameter; grows in small clusters on eelgrass, seaweeds, shells and rocks.

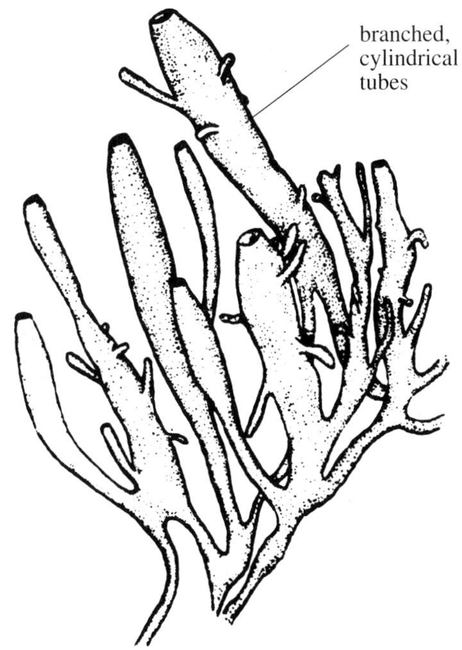

Fig.I. ***LEUCOSOLENIA BOTRYOIDES*, ORGAN PIPE SPONGE:** White; each tube up to 13 mm (1/2") tall and 1.5 mm (1/16") in diameter; lives in intertidal zone on rockweeds and rocks.

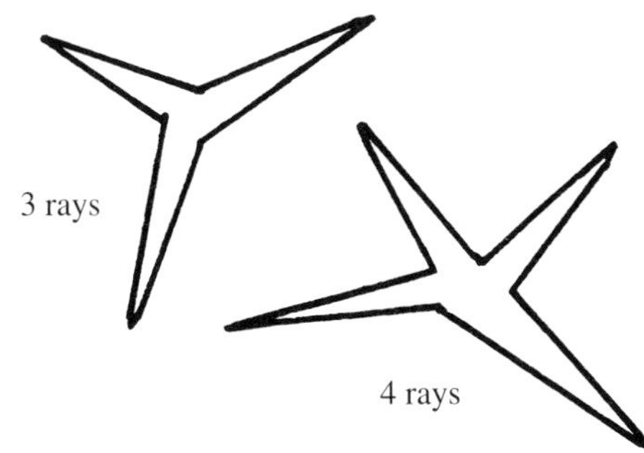

Fig.J. **CALCAREOUS SPICULES**

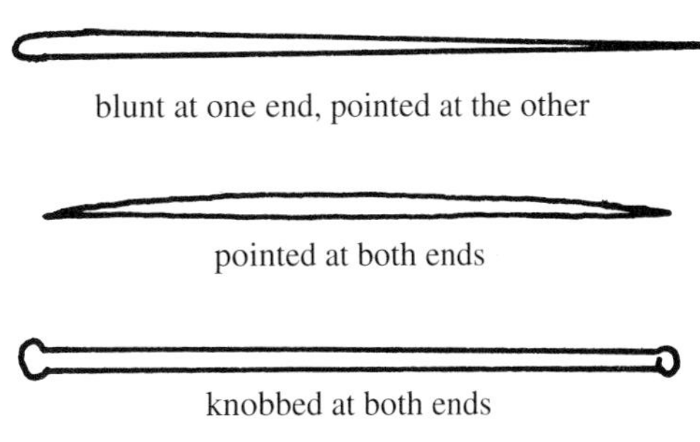

Fig.K. **SILICIOUS SPICULES**

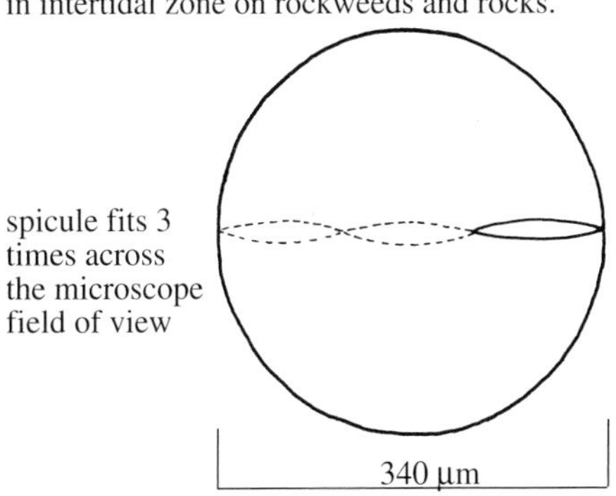

Fig.L. **MEASURING A SPICULE**

BORING OR SULFUR SPONGES: PHYLUM PORIFERA, GENUS *CLIONA*

Yellowish sponges which are thick and massive and/or have wartlike bumps on their surface. May bore into or attach to shells.

(Sponge key begins on page 3.00)

#1.Thick, massive, lumpy form (Fig.A) .... ***Cliona celata*, boring sponge**[1]
#1.Thin, encrusting form (Fig.B) which bores holes in shells (Fig.C) .... #2

#2.Diameter of holes bored into shells (Fig.C) may be larger than 2 mm (about 1/16"); all spicules[4] are Type I only, knobbed at one end, pointed at the other (Fig.D); may grow into massive form (Fig.A) .... ***Cliona celata*, boring sponge**[1]
#2.Diameter of holes bored into shells is smaller than 1.6 mm (1/16"); some spicules are Type III, twisted and spiny (Fig.F); does not grow into massive form, remains in boring (Fig.C) or encrusting form (Fig.B) .... #3

#3.Some spicules are Type II, pointed at both ends (Fig.E); these spicules may be smooth or spiny .... ***Cliona vastifica* or *Cliona truitti*, boring sponge**[2]
#3.No spicules are Type II .... ***Cliona lobata*, boring sponge**[3]

[1]***CLIONA CELATA*, BORING OR SULFUR SPONGE**: Bright sulfur yellow; the most common boring sponge in southern New England, usually found below the low tide level growing on boulders and on the bottom. Colonies begin by penetrating into mollusc shells, riddling the shells with many tunnels and holes (Fig.C). As the sponge gets larger, it may cover over the entire surface of the shell (Fig.B). It may then grow into a massive irregular shape (Fig.A), sometimes over 30 cm (12") in diameter, which completely dissolves the mollusc shell. Spicules are Type I only (Fig.D). **17.01 D** **17.01 G**

[2]***CLIONA VASTIFICA*, BORING SPONGE**: Light or pale yellow; found on oyster and other mollusc shells. Colonies begin as described above for *Cliona celata* but do not grow into the massive form. Spicules are Type I, II and III (Figs.D-F). ***CLIONA TRUITTI*** is nearly identical to *Cliona vastifica* and may not be a distinct species. *Cliona truitti* tends to occur in waters of low salinity.

[3]***CLIONA LOBATA*, BORING SPONGE**: Light or pale yellow; found on oyster and other mollusc shells. Colonies begin as described for *Cliona celata* but do not grow into the massive form. Spicules are Type I and III only (Figs.D,F).

[4]See footnote on page 3.00 for information on examining and measuring spicules.

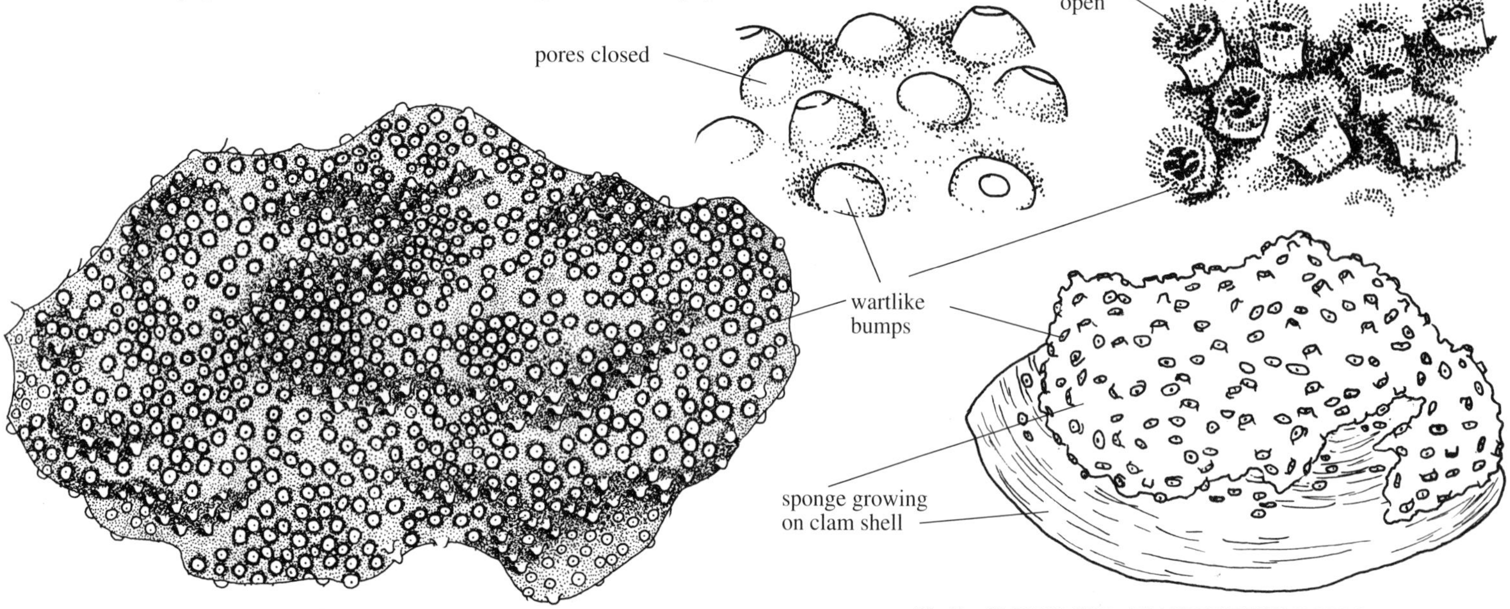

Fig.A. ***CLIONA CELATA*, MASSIVE FORM** **17.01 D** **17.01 G**

Fig.B. ***CLIONA* SPP., ENCRUSTING FORM**

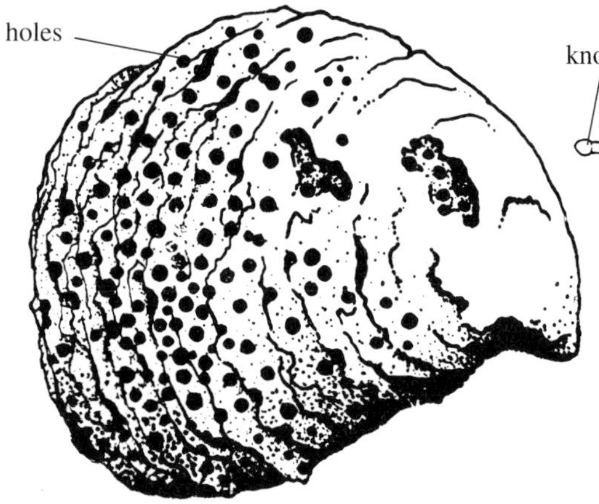

Fig.C. ***CLIONA* SPP., HOLES BORED IN SHELL**

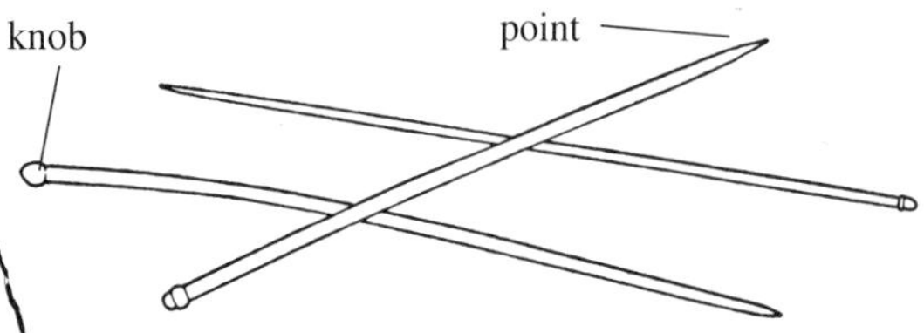

Fig.D. **TYPE I SPICULES**

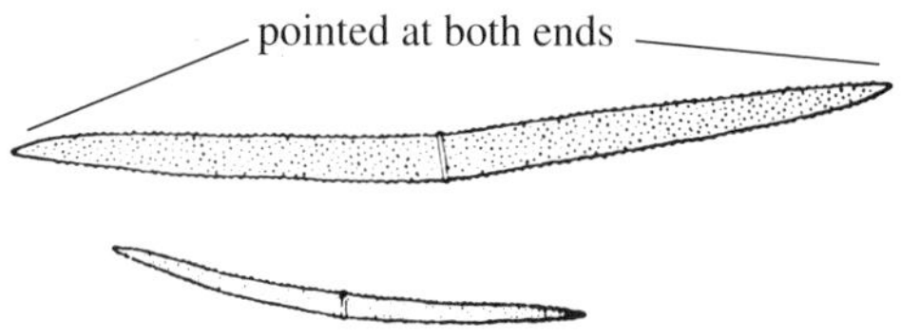

Fig.E. **TYPE II SPICULES**

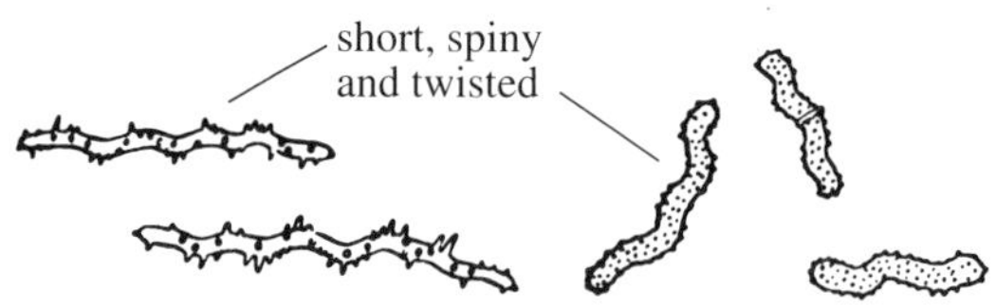

Fig.F. **TYPE III SPICULES**

ERECT SPONGES WITH BROAD FINGERLIKE OR BUSHLIKE BRANCHES: PHYLUM PORIFERA

(Sponge key begins on page 3.00)

#1.Bright red to orange brown; pores are small and inconspicuous; branch tips may be flattened, giving sponge a fanlike or bushlike appearance; branches may be interconnected; spicules[1] have a spiny or smooth knob at one end and are pointed at the other end .... ***Microciona prolifera,* red beard sponge** (Fig.B)

#1.Not bright red or orange brown; pores are usually large and conspicuous; branches are broad and fingerlike (Figs.A, C), giving the sponge a handlike appearance; spicules do not have a knob at either end .... #2

#2.With full size spicules <u>and</u> with microscleres (tiny spicules[1], about 25 µm long) which are C-shaped with pointed anchorlike tips (Fig.A) ..***Isodictya* spp.**, #3

#2.With no C-shaped microscleres; with full size (longer than 50 µm) spicules only .... #4

#3.Most spicules[1] are blunt at one end and are pointed at the other .... ***Isodictya deichmannae*** (Fig.A)

#3.Most spicules are pointed at both ends .... ***Isodictya palmata*** (Fig.A)

#4.Spicules[1] are blunt at one end and are pointed at the other .... ***Hymeniacidon heliophila*** (not shown)[2]

#4.Spicules are pointed at both ends (Figs. C,D) .... #5

#5.Many spicules are longer than 200 µm .... ***Halichondria* spp., bread-crumb sponges** (page 3.04, Fig.A)

#5.Most spicules are shorter than 150 µm .... ***Haliclona oculata,* deadman's fingers sponge** (Fig.C)

[1]See footnote on page 3.00 for instructions on examining and measuring spicules. Use highest power (oil immersion) lens to examine microscleres.

[2]*Hymeniacidon heliophila:* Orange or olive; colony up to about 10 cm (4") wide; may be branching, encrusting or lobular; surface with cone shaped projections.

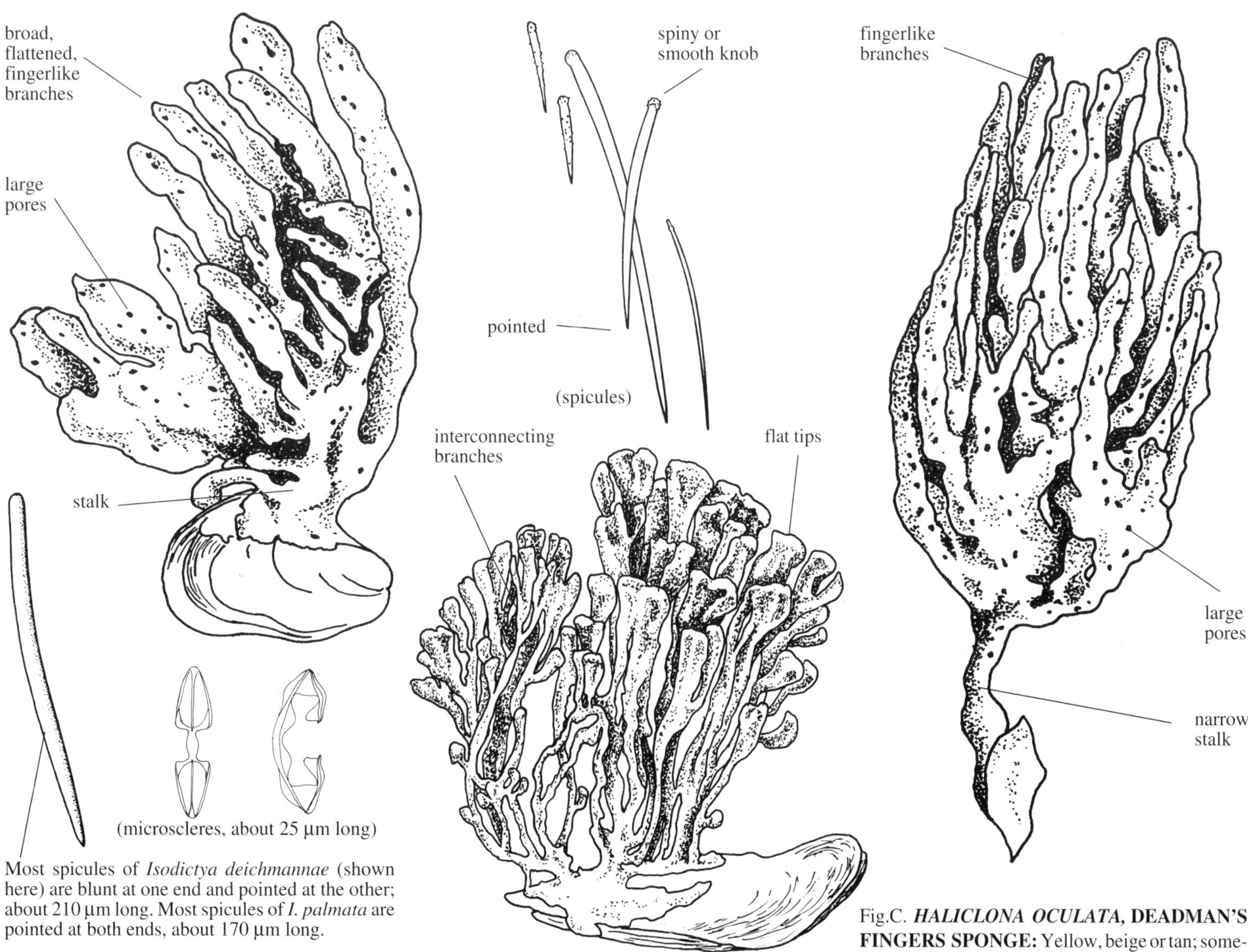

Most spicules of *Isodictya deichmannae* (shown here) are blunt at one end and pointed at the other; about 210 µm long. Most spicules of *I. palmata* are pointed at both ends, about 170 µm long.

Fig.A. ***ISODICTYA* SPP.:** Yellow, beige or reddish; may reach 30 cm (12") in height; upright form with broad fingerlike branches. Examine spicules to identify the species.

Fig.B. ***MICROCIONA PROLIFERA,* RED BEARD SPONGE:** See page 3.05 for description.
17.01 C **17.01 E**

Fig.C. ***HALICLONA OCULATA,* DEADMAN'S FINGERS SPONGE:** Yellow, beige or tan; sometimes tinged with violet; average length is 15 cm (6") but may grow to 45 cm (18"); very common offshore, often washes up on shore after storms. See page 3.04 for other species of *Haliclona.*

SPONGES WITH SPICULES[1] WHICH ARE POINTED AT BOTH ENDS
PHYLUM PORIFERA

(Sponge key begins on page 3.00)

#1. Many spicules[1] are longer than 200 µm .... ***Halichondria* spp., bread-crumb sponge** (Fig.A)
#1. Most spicules are shorter than 150 µm .... ***Haliclona* spp.**, #2

#2. With raised tubules (Fig.B) .... ***Haliclona* spp.** (Fig.B)
#2. Without raised tubules (Fig.C) .... ***Haliclona canaliculata*** (Fig.C)

[1]See footnote on page 3.00 for information on examining and measuring spicules.

spicules pointed at both ends
slender projections
thin encrusting form
many spicules longer than 200 µm

Fig.A. ***HALICHONDRIA* SPP., BREAD-CRUMB SPONGES:** ***Halichondria bowerbanki*** is very common from Cape Cod south. Its colors and forms are extremely variable. It may be brown, yellow, beige, olive green or bronze. Young colonies form thin encrustations. Older colonies may have thin branches or fingerlike projections and may reach 8 cm (3") in height and 15 cm (6") in width. ***Halichondria panicea*** is common north of Cape Cod. It forms thin yellowish or greenish crusts with low volcano shaped tubules each ending in a large pore, similar to Fig.B below. Both species attach to rocks, algae and pilings. They live in tidepools, in the intertidal zone and in deeper water. Refer to W. D. Hartman (1964) to distinguish between these species. **17.01 B** **17.01 F**

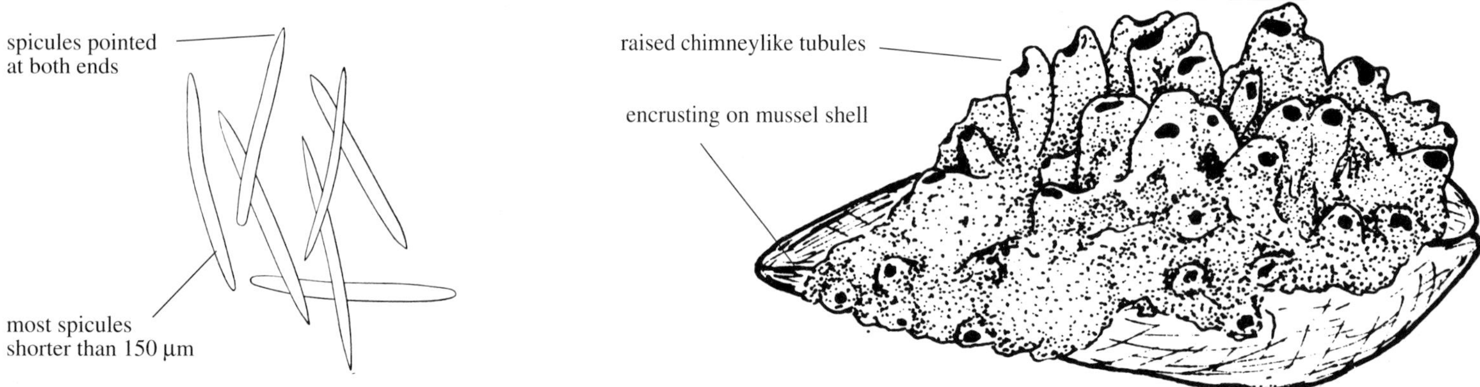

Fig.B. ***HALICLONA* SPP.:** ***Haliclona loosanoffi*** is usually dark tan, beige, or gold; grows up to 3 cm (1") thick and 15 cm (6") across; common from Cape Cod south; forms mats on rocks, shells and algae in the lower intertidal zone and offshore; produces gemmules, reproductive structures which can survive during the winter and germinate in the spring (Fell, 1974). Gemmules look like white cushionlike specks and are particularly conspicuous on eelgrass and algae during the late summer and early fall after the parent sponge has degenerated. ***Haliclona permollis*** is pink, lavender, or purple; occurs north and south of Cape Cod. **17.01 A**

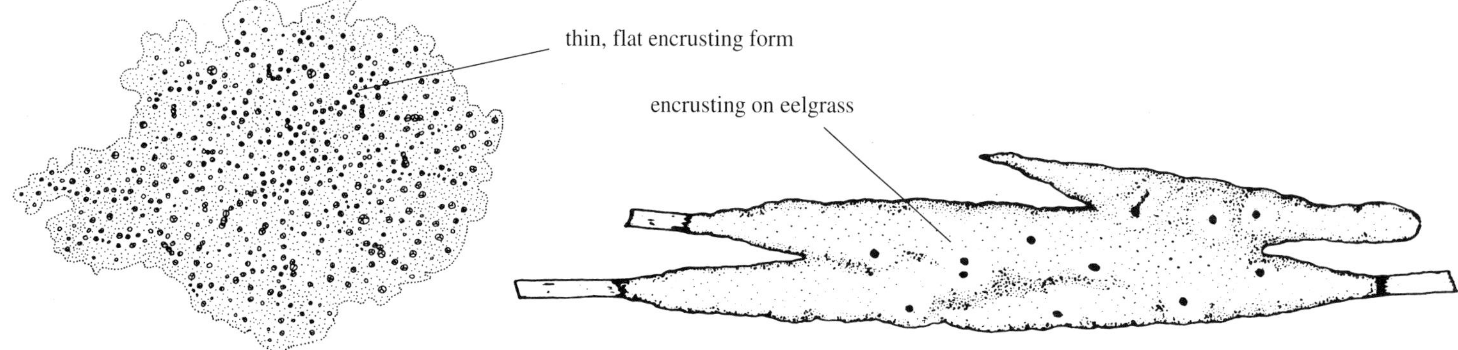

Fig.C. ***HALICLONA CANALICULATA:*** May be beige, tan, brown or gold; grows up to 8 mm (1/3") thick and 10 cm (4") across; spicules are pointed at both ends and are generally shorter than 150 µm; forms thin crusts on rocks, shells, algal holdfasts, and eelgrass.

SPONGES WITH SPICULES[1] WHICH ARE ROUNDED OR KNOBBED AT ONE OR BOTH ENDS PHYLUM PORIFERA

(Sponge key begins on page 3.00)

#1.Many spicules are longer[1] than 700 µm .... ***Polymastia robusta*** (Fig.A)
#1.Spicules are shorter than 500 µm (Figs.B-D) .... #2

#2.Bright red to orange-brown; spicules have a spiny or smooth knob at one end and are pointed at the other ... ***Microciona prolifera*, red beard sponge** (Fig.B)
#2.Yellow, olive, tan, brown or greenish; without spiny knobs on spicules, spicules may have smooth knobs or may be blunt at one or both ends and may be pointed at one end .... #3

#3.Some spicules have knobs at both ends, others are pointed at one end and blunt at the other .... ***Lissodendoryx isodictyalis*** (Fig.C)
#3.Spicules have a knob at one end only, other end is pointed .... #4

#4.With microscleres (tiny spicules[1], about 25 µm long, which may be C-shaped, S-shaped, hook-shaped or rod-shaped) .... #5
#4.No microscleres .... ***Prosuberites epiphytum*** (not shown)[2]

#5.Microscleres are rod-shaped with a knob or swelling in the middle (Fig.D) .... ***Suberites ficus*, fig sponge** (Fig.D)
#5.Microscleres are C-shaped, S-shaped and hook-shaped, some with an anchor-shaped swelling at one end .... ***Mycale fibrexilis*** (not shown)[3]

[1]See footnote on page 3.00 for instructions on examining and measuring spicules. Use highest power (oil immersion) lens to examine microscleres.
[2]*Prosuberites epiphytum* is orange-brown or olive-brown; forms a thin encrustation on rocks, algae and shells, including live snails; occurs from Cape Cod south.
[3]*Mycale fibrexilis* is yellow, brown, or gray; usually forms thin crusts but may become massive; common on pilings; occurs from Cape Cod south.

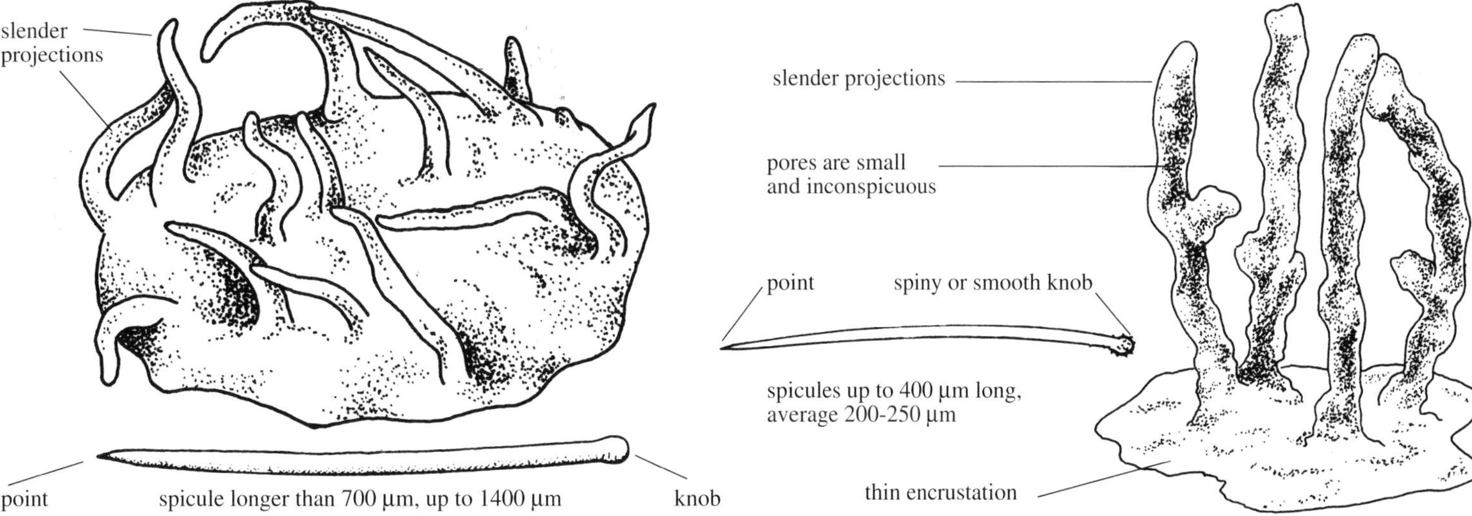

Fig.A. ***POLYMASTIA ROBUSTA:*** Red, yellow-orange, salmon color; forms thin encrustation with numerous slender projections; colony may reach 5 cm (2") across; found on rocks.

Fig.B. ***MICROCIONA PROLIFERA*, RED BEARD SPONGE:** Tomato red, burnt orange, orange brown; thin encrustation when young, develops vertical fingerlike projections and bushlike colonies with interwoven branches when old (page 3.03 Fig.B); may reach over 20 cm (8") in height; very common; found on shells, rocks, pilings in intertidal zone and offshore. **17.01 C** **17.01 E**

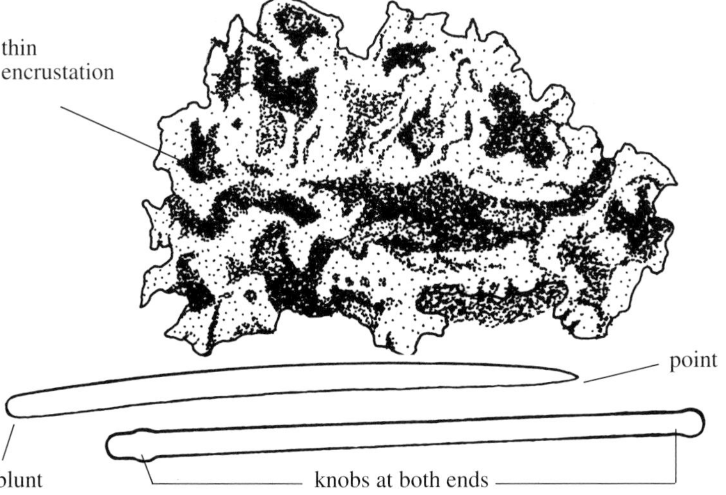

Fig.C. ***LISSODENDORYX ISODICTYALIS (=carolinensis):*** Olive, yellow, tan, or gray-brown; usually forms a thin encrustation up to 8 cm (3") long; found on dock pilings and rocks near low tide mark.

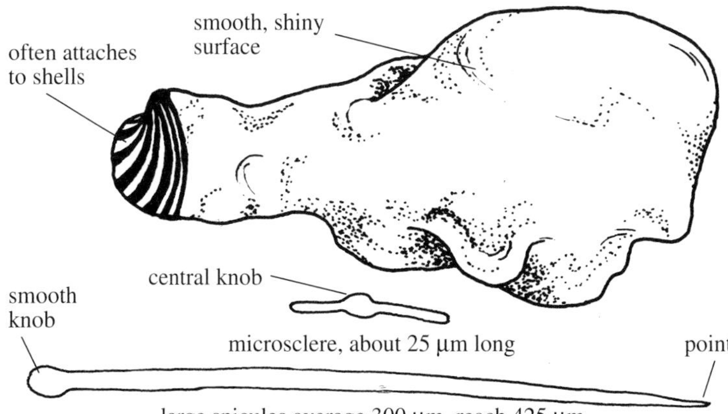

Fig.D. ***SUBERITES FICUS*, FIG SPONGE:** Yellowish; up to 35 cm (14") long, over 3 cm (1") thick; rubbery and firm in texture; surface is smooth and shiny without obvious pores; often attaches to shells.

STALKED JELLYFISHES
PHYLUM CNIDARIA, CLASS SCYPHOZOA, ORDER STAUROMEDUSAE

Jellyfishes that attach to rocks, seaweeds, and other solid objects with a narrow stalk. They have 8 arms, each with a cluster of clublike tentacles.

(Use key on page 2.02 to determine if you have a stalked jellyfish)

#1.With a bean shaped marginal anchor (adhesive disc) in notches between arms; arms are short; 100-120 tentacles per arm .... ***Haliclystus auricula*** (Fig.A)
#1.With a trumpet shaped marginal anchor in notches between arms; arms are long; 15-30 tentacles per arm .... ***Haliclystus salpinx*** (Fig.A)
#1.With no marginal anchors .... **other stalked jellyfishes** (Fig.A)

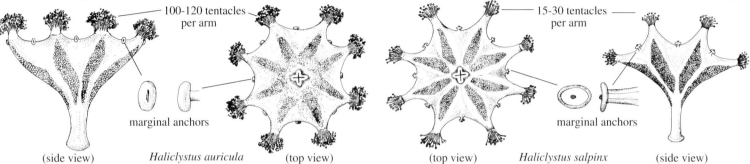

100-120 tentacles per arm
15-30 tentacles per arm
marginal anchors
marginal anchors
(side view) *Haliclystus auricula* (top view)
(top view) *Haliclystus salpinx* (side view)

Fig.A. ***HALICLYSTUS* SPP. AND ALLIES, STALKED JELLYFISHES:** Color variable; most species are under 3 cm (1 1/4") long; attach to seaweed, eelgrass, rocks and other solid objects; may be found in tide pools and offshore; not common south of Cape Cod. Refer to Larson (1976) to identify species.

JELLYFISHES
PHYLUM CNIDARIA, CLASSES SCYPHOZOA, HYDROZOA, AND CUBOZOA

Free swimming or floating animals with a gelatinous body that is usually umbrella or bell shaped. The typical jellyfishes are in the class Scyphozoa. The sea wasp, *Tamoya haplonema*, is in the class Cubozoa. The Portuguese man-of-war, *Physalia physalis*, is a siphonophore (class Hydrozoa, order Siphonophora). Siphonophores are a colony of polypoid and medusoid individuals. Hydromedusae are also in the class Hydrozoa. Some hydromedusae are medusoid (jellyfishlike) only. Others have a life cycle that includes a medusoid and a hydroid (polyp) stage (see Fig.F on page 4.05). The tentacles of all jellyfishes in the phylum Cnidaria have stinging cells, but the sting of most species cannot be felt by humans. Comb jellies (page 4.17) do not have stinging cells and are in a separate phylum, the Ctenophora.

(Use key on page 2.12 to determine if you have a jellyfish)

#1.With a balloonlike float, filled with air; usually pointed at both ends and may have a flattened sail-like ridge on top; bright blue or purple tinged with pink .... ***Physalia physalis*, Portuguese man-of-war**[1] (Fig.C)
#1.Float is umbrella shaped, radially symmetrical (like the spokes of a wheel) .... #2

#2.Umbrella opening is partially closed over by a shelflike membrane, the velum (Fig.B); usually transparent and colorless .... **hydromedusae**, page 4.02
#2.Umbrella opening does not have a velum[2]; usually has a distinct color (Figs.D-F) .... **class Scyphozoa, jellyfishes,** #3

#3.Umbrella is shallow, saucer shaped, with 4 horseshoe shaped gonads (Fig.D); marginal tentacles are very short and numerous; pale pink, orange or milky white color .... ***Aurelia aurita*, moon jelly** (Fig.D)
#3.Umbrella is deep or thick (Figs.E,F); with more than 8 long tentacles; common .... #4
#3.Umbrella is deep or thick; no tentacles or 8 long tentacles; Gulf Stream species which rarely stray into coastal waters ..... **other jellyfishes** (see Larson, 1976)

#4.Bell shaped umbrella with 32-48 clefts (indentations) around the edge; 24-40 tentacles attached to the clefts at the umbrella edge; often found in estuaries where the salinity is low; milky white color with tiny white dots or may be pinkish with radiating reddish bars .... ***Chrysaora quinquecirrha*, sea nettle**[1] (Fig.E)
#4.Thick, lens shaped umbrella with 8 major lobes and 32 smaller lobes; stripes of red, orange-brown or purple radiate from the center to the margin of each lobe; long reddish brown to yellowish tentacles are attached to the underside of the umbrella in 8 clusters .... ***Cyanea capillata*, lion's mane jellyfish**[1] (Fig.F)

[1]**HANDLE WITH CARE**. Tentacles can give painful sting even when jellyfish is found washed up on shore.
[2]*Aurelia aurita* (Fig.D) has a velumlike structure but is easily distinguished from the hydromedusae by its larger size, color, and 4 horseshoe shaped gonads.

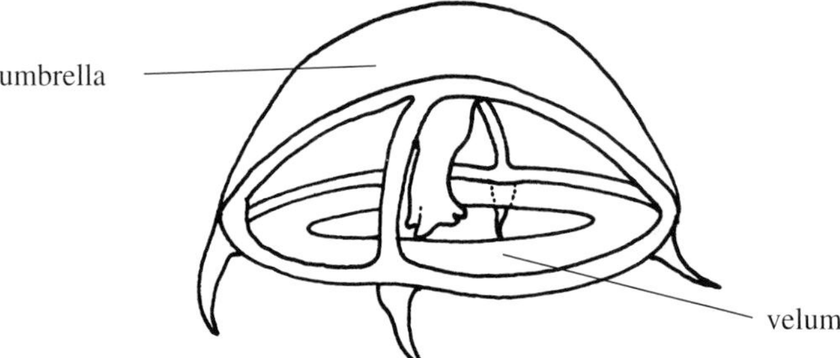

Fig.B. **HYDROMEDUSAE:** Most species are transparent, colorless, and are less than 2.5 cm (1") in diameter. Larger hydromedusae are identified on page 4.02. Refer to a plankton key to identify the smaller species. Many hydrozoans have life cycles that include a medusoid and a hydroid stage (see Fig.F on page 4.05).

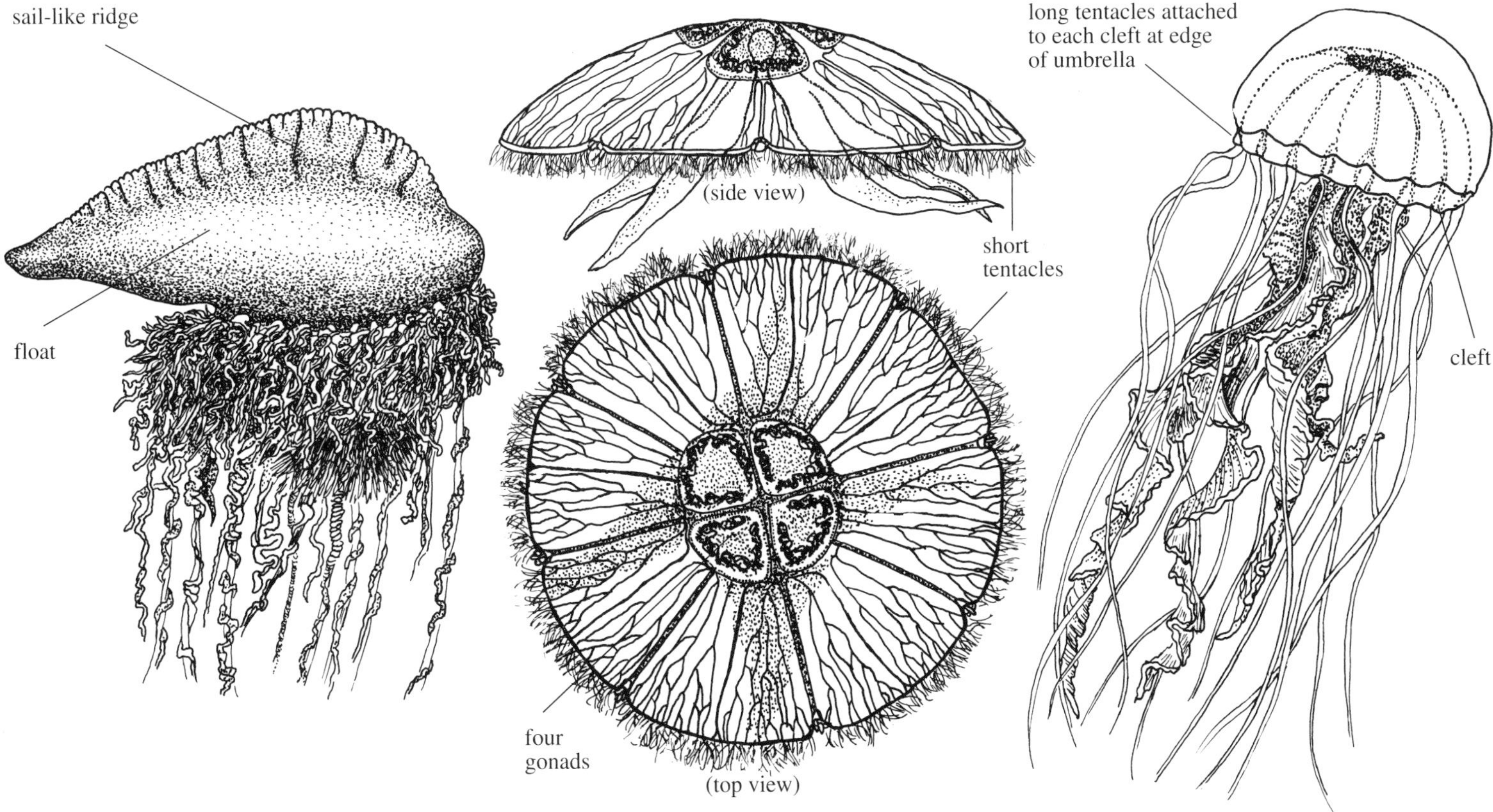

Fig.C. ***PHYSALIA PHYSALIS*, PORTUGUESE MAN-OF-WAR[1]:** Bright blue or purple tinged with pink; float grows over 30 cm (1') long and tentacles may be 12-15 m (40-50') long; a Gulf Stream species which rarely drifts into estuarine waters. (class Hydrozoa, order Siphonophora)

Fig.D. ***AURELIA AURITA*, MOON JELLY:** Pale pink, orange or milky white; up to 25 cm (10") in diameter; very common in this region during late spring. (class Scyphozoa, order Semaeostomeae) **17.02 B** **17.02 C**

Fig.E. ***CHRYSAORA QUINQUECIRRHA*, SEA NETTLE[1]:** Milky white with fine white pimples on umbrella; up to about 10 cm (4") in diameter; very common in estuaries and brackish waters. In saltier water, may be pinkish with 16 reddish radiating bars; up to 19 cm (7 1/2") in diameter; occurs in bays and open water, not common. (class Scyphozoa, order Semaeostomeae) **17.02 A** **17.02 F**

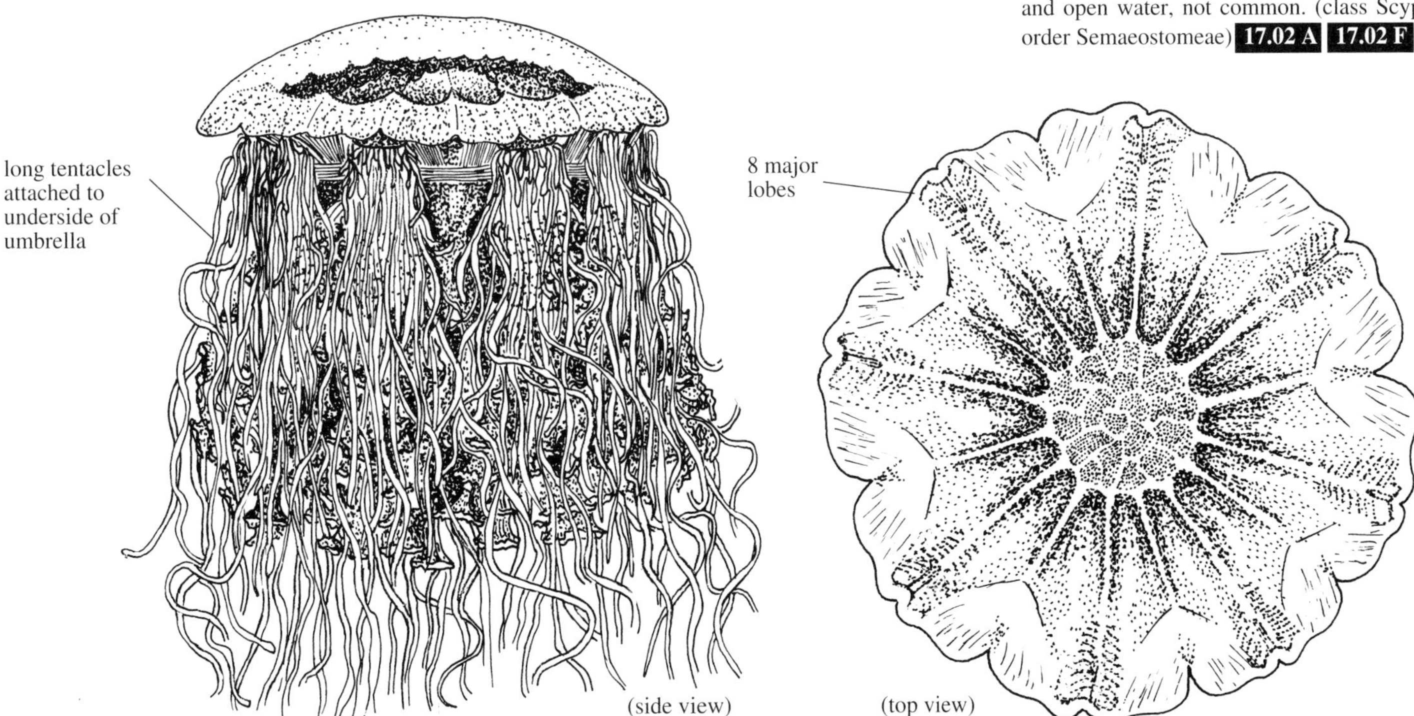

Fig.F. ***CYANEA CAPILLATA*, LION'S MANE JELLYFISH[1]:** Stripes of red, orange-brown, or purple radiate from center of the umbrella, tentacles are reddish brown to yellowish; up to about 30 cm (12") in diameter in this region but may reach over 2.5 m (8') in northern waters; very common throughout this region during summer and early fall. (class Scyphozoa, order Semaeostomeae) **17.02 D** **17.02 E**

JELLYFISHES (CONTINUED)
PHYLUM CNIDARIA, CLASSES HYDROZOA AND CUBOZOA

(Jellyfish key begins on page 4.00)

#1.Less than 2.5 cm (1") in diameter and length .... **small hydromeduse**[2]
#1.At least 2.5 cm (1") in diameter or length .... #2

#2.With 2 tentacles .... ***Stomotoca pterophylla*** (Fig.A)
#2.With 4 tentacles .... #3
#2.With 10-40 tentacles .... #5
#2.With more than 40 tentacles .... #6

#3.Tentacles have an enlarged paddle shaped section at their base, where they attach to the umbrella .... ***Tamoya haplonema*, sea wasp**[1] (Fig.B)
#3.Tentacles are not enlarged at their base; with a long manubrium (stomach) extending below mouth of umbrella .... #4

#4.With 1-3 centripetal canals (short, dead end canals attached to the ring canal. see Fig.C) between the 4 radial canals .... ***Liriope tetraphylla*** (Fig.C)
#4.With no centripetal canals; 4 radial canals only .... ***Eutima mira*** (Fig.D)

#5.With a long manubrium (stomach) with 4 frilly lips at the mouth; umbrella is round at the top; umbrella is clear, transparent .... ***Tima formosa*** (Fig.E)
#5.With a long frilly 4-lobed stomach; with 30-50 clefts (indentations) around the edge of the umbrella; umbrella is milky white with white dots .... page 4.00
#5.Manubrium is short; umbrella has a pointed projection on top .... ***Catablema vesicarium*, constricted jellyfish** (Fig.F)

#6.With 4 horseshoe shaped gonads at the center of the umbrella .... ***Aurelia aurita*, moon jelly**, page 4.01
#6.Without 4 horseshoe shaped gonads .... #7

#7.With 4 radial canals .... #8
#7.With 8 radial canals .... ***Aglantha digitalis*, pink helmet** (Fig.G)
#7.With 12-16 radial canals (in 4 clusters) .... ***Halopsis ocellata*** [3] (not shown)
#7.With more than 20 radial canals .... #10

#8.Tentacles are long and have a sharp bend near outer end; no eyespots on circular canal .... ***Gonionemus vertens*, clinging jellyfish** (Fig.H)
#8.Tentacles are long and are coiled at outer end; with eyespots on circular canal .... ***Laodicea undulata*** (Fig.I)
#8.Tentacles are short; with eyespots on circular canal .... #9

#9.Umbrella is about 6 times wider than high; mouth opening has slitlike extensions down the radial canals . ***Staurophora mertensi*, whitecross jellyfish** (Fig.J)
#9.Umbrella is about 2 times wider than high; mouth opening does not extend down the radial canals .... ***Tiaropsis multicirrata*** (Fig.K)

#10.With rows of tiny bumps on underside of umbrella between the radial canals .... ***Rhacostoma atlanticum*** (Fig.L)
#10.Without tiny bumps on underside of umbrella between the radial canals .... ***Aequorea* spp.**[2] (Fig.L)

[1]**HANDLE WITH CARE**. Tentacles can give a painful sting even when jellyfish is found washed up on shore.
[2]Many different species of small hydromedusae are common in the plankton. They are difficult to identify. Use Gosner (1971) or a plankton guide.
[3]*Halopsis ocellata:* up to 7 cm (2 3/4") in diameter; occurs north of Cape Cod during the summer and fall; uncommon. (class Hydrozoa, order Leptomedusae)

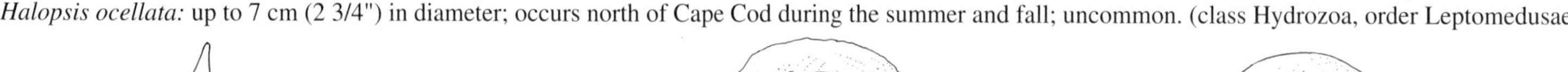

Fig.A. ***STOMOTOCA PTEROPHYLLA:*** Transparent; up to 3 cm (1/1/4") wide; occurs in spring and summer. (class Hydrozoa, order Anthomedusae)

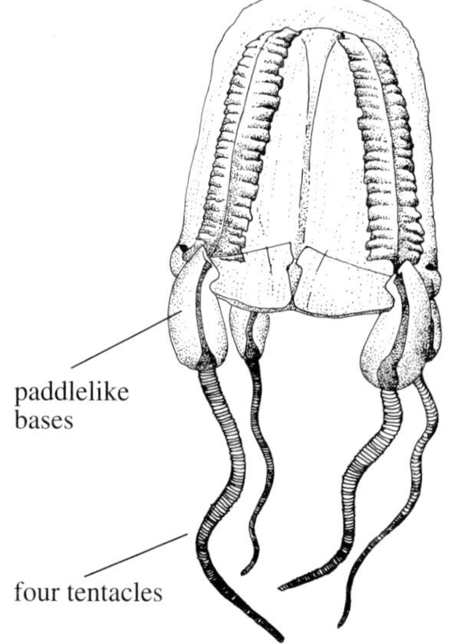

Fig.B. ***TAMOYA HAPLONEMA*, SEA WASP**[1]**:** Umbrella transparent, tentacles and organs yellowish; up to 9 cm (3 1/2") wide; rarely strays as far north as Connecticut in summer. (class Cubozoa)

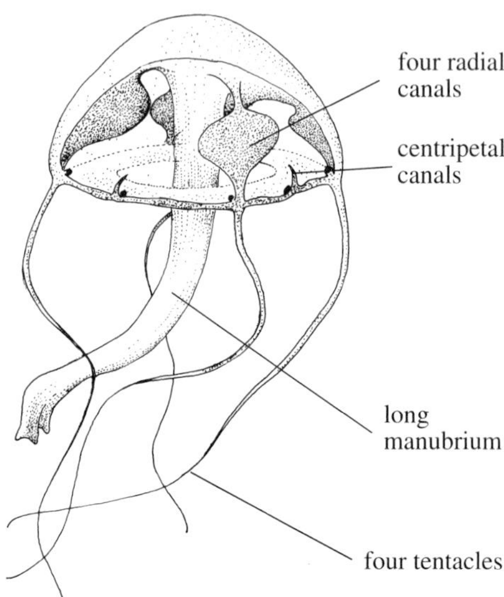

Fig.C. ***LIRIOPE TETRAPHYLLA:*** Umbrella transparent, gonads on radial canals greenish; up to 3 cm (1 1/4") wide; occurs south of Cape Cod in fall. (class Hydrozoa, order Trachymedusae)

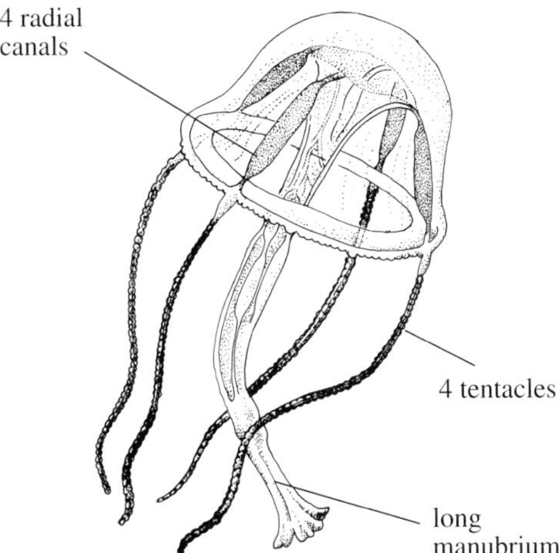

Fig.D. ***EUTIMA MIRA:*** Light blue tinged with green; up to 3 cm (1 1/4") wide; strays north as far as Cape Cod in summer. (class Hydrozoa, order Leptomedusae)

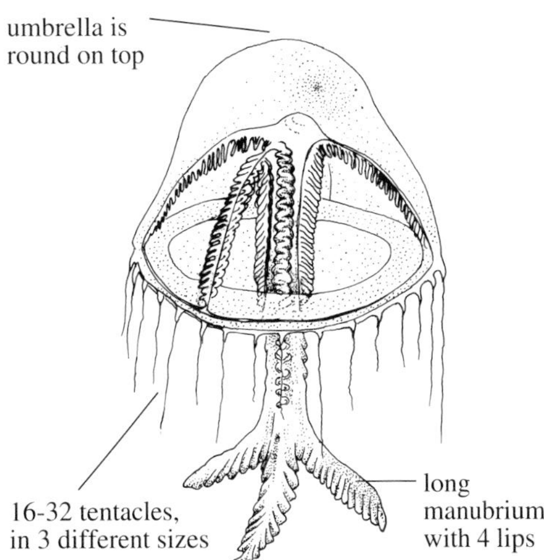

Fig.E. ***TIMA FORMOSA:*** Umbrella transparent, organs cream or pink; up to 10 cm (4") in diameter; south of Cape Cod in spring-summer, north in fall-winter. (class Hydrozoa, order Leptomedusae)

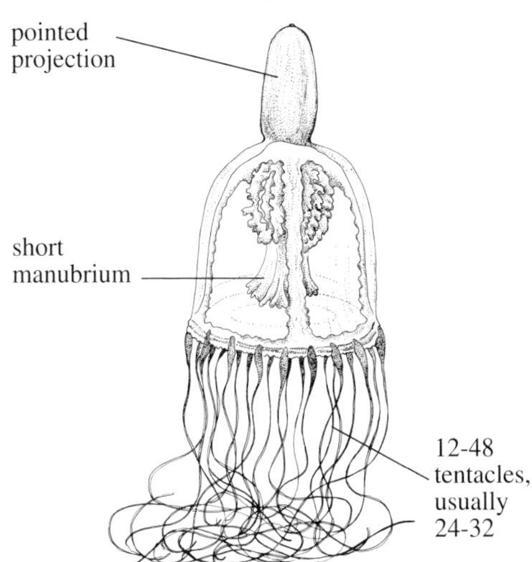

Fig.F. ***CATABLEMA VESICARIUM,* CONSTRICTED JELLYFISH:** Umbrella transparent, manubrium and tentacle bases brown; up to 2.5 cm (1") wide; south to Cape Cod in summer. (class Hydrozoa, order Anthomedusae)

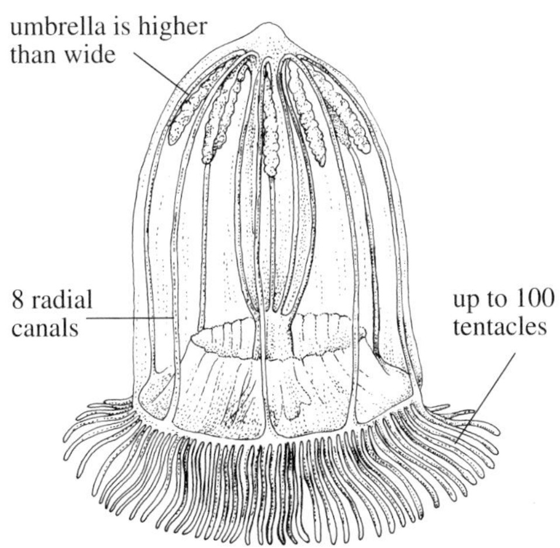

Fig.G. ***AGLANTHA DIGITALIS,* PINK HELMET:** Umbrella transparent, stomach and tentacles pink; up to 3 cm (1 1/4") tall; occurs year-round north of Cape Cod, in winter and spring to the south. (class Hydrozoa, order Trachymedusae)

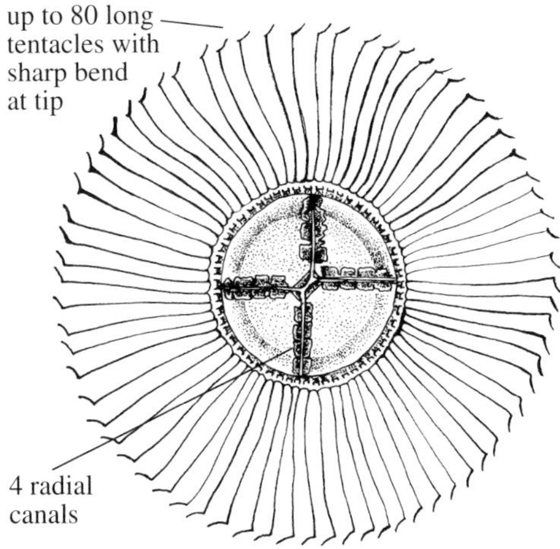

Fig.H. ***GONIONEMUS VERTENS,* CLINGING JELLYFISH:** Transparent umbrella, brown manubrium, green pigment spot at base of each tentacle; diameter of umbrella to 2 cm (3/4"). (class Hydrozoa, order Limnomedusae)

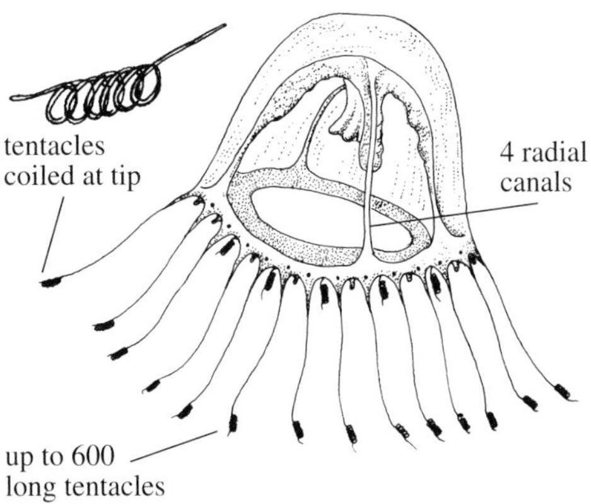

Fig.I. ***LAODICEA UNDULATA:*** Transparent umbrella; up to 4 cm (1 1/2") wide; occurs in summer and fall as far north as Boston harbor. (class Hydrozoa, order Leptomedusae)

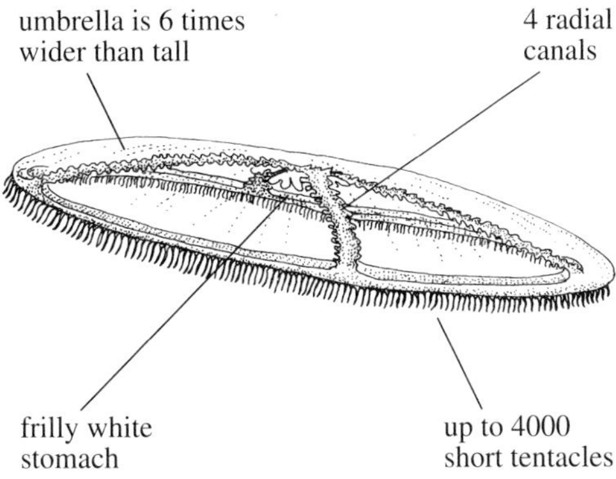

Fig.J. ***STAUROPHORA MERTENSI,* WHITE-CROSS JELLYFISH:** Umbrella transparent with bluish tinge, whitish cross shaped stomach; up to 23 cm (9") wide; usually occurs north of Cape Cod in spring and summer, rare to the south. (class Hydrozoa, order Leptomedusae)

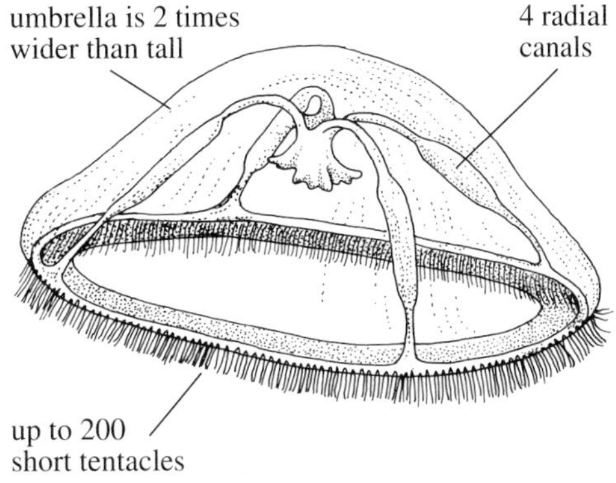

Fig.K. ***TIAROPSIS MULTICIRRATA :*** Umbrella transparent, stomach and bases of tentacles are yellowish, 8 black eyespots along margin; 3 cm (1 1/4") diameter; usually occurs north of Cape Cod in spring, rare to the south. (class Hydrozoa, order Leptomedusae)

Rhacostoma has rows of tiny bumps on underside between radial canals. *Aequorea* does not.

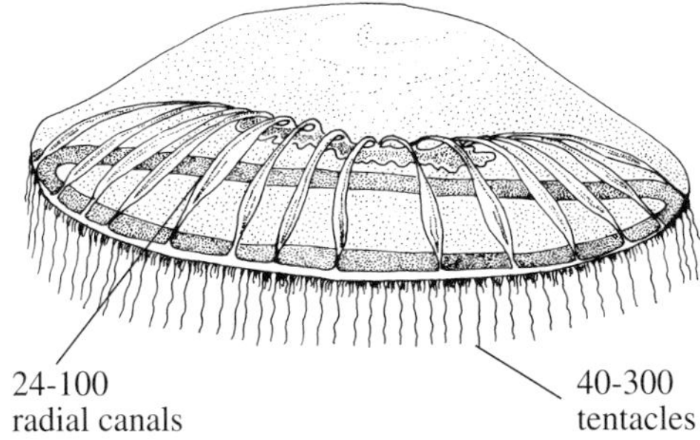

Fig.L. ***AEQUOREA* SPP.[2]:** Up to 18 cm (7") in diameter. ***RHACOSTOMA ATLANTICUM:*** Pinkish; up to 11 cm (4 1/2") in diameter south of Cape Cod and up to 30 cm (12") to the north. Both genera are usually oceanic, but stray nearshore in summer and fall. (class Hydrozoa, order Leptomedusae)

HYDROIDS: PHYLUM CNIDARIA, CLASS HYDROZOA[1]

Hydrozoans occur in either a hydroid form (somewhat similar to a sea anemone) or a hydromedusoid form (somewhat like a jellyfish) or have a life cycle that includes alternating generations of each stage (Fig.F). Only the hydroid stage of each species is included in this key. Hydroids usually occur in plantlike colonies attached to rocks, seaweed, eelgrass, shells, pilings, and other objects. Hydroid colonies are visible without a microscope and look like a crustlike mat (Fig.A), a fuzzy growth (Fig.B), a threadlike network (Fig.C), or a flowerlike cluster (Fig.D). A hydroid individual consists of a stem and a flowerlike polyp (Fig.E) which usually can only be seen under magnification[2]. Some polyps have tentacles used for feeding while other polyps have a reproductive function and produce the hydromedusa stage. Hydromedusae are found in the plankton (see page 4.02) and most species are microscopic in size.

(Use the key on page 2.04 to determine if you have a hydroid)

#1.Colonies arise from a crustlike or rootlike mat; usually found on living snail shells or snail shells occupied by hermit crabs (Fig.A), but also may be found on rocks, pilings and other objects .... page 4.06

#1.Colonies have a somewhat plantlike, threadlike or bushy appearance (Figs. B-I); not usually found on living snail or hermit crab shells .... #2

#2.Feeding polyps[2] (tentacle bearing individuals) can withdraw all or part way into a hydrotheca (collar) shaped like a cup, tube or funnel (Figs.F-I) .... #3

#2.Feeding polyps do not have a hydrotheca (collar) into which the tentacles can be withdrawn (Fig.E) .... page 4.10

#3.With a cone shaped operculum (lid) which closes over the hydrotheca opening when the tentacles are withdrawn (Figs.H,I) .... page 4.05

#3.No operculum (Figs. F,G) .... #4

#4.Hydrotheca (collar) is shaped like a goblet, wine glass or funnel, with a narrow stem (Fig.F) .... page 4.08

#4.Hydrotheca (collar) is somewhat tubular or cylindrical; the base of the collar is attached directly to the main branch (Fig.G) .... page 4.07

[1]**WARNING: Only the more common hydroid species are included in these keys.** Refer to Gosner (1971) for positive identification.

[2]The polyps of most hydroids are microscopic in size and should be examined under a dissecting microscope or hand lens at least at 10X magnification. Hydroids should be identified while they are still alive. Place the hydroid colony in seawater and leave it undisturbed for a few minutes until the polyps are fully extended.

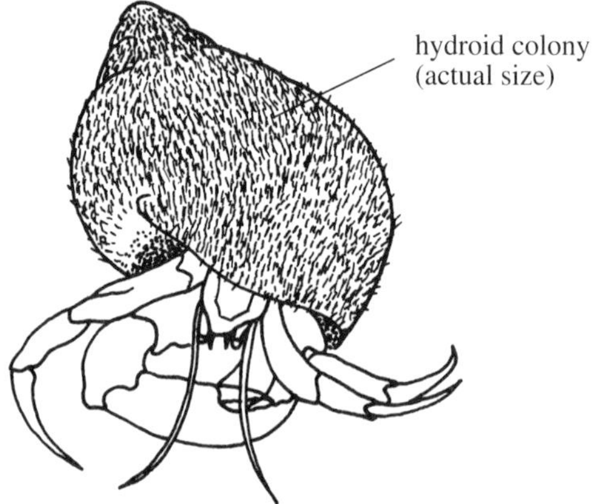

Fig.A. **CRUSTLIKE HYDROID COLONY**

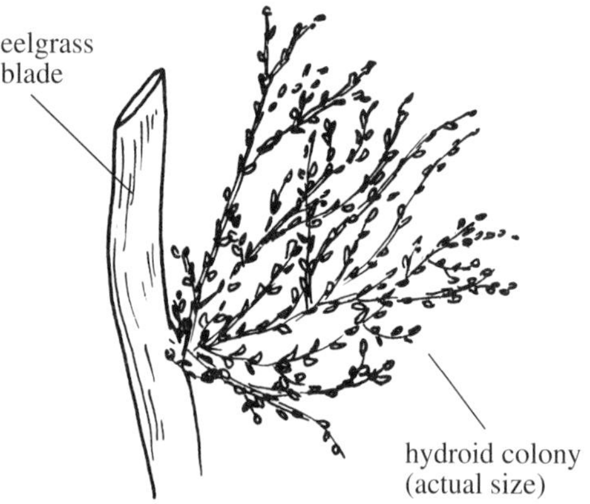

Fig.B. **BUSHY HYDROID COLONY**

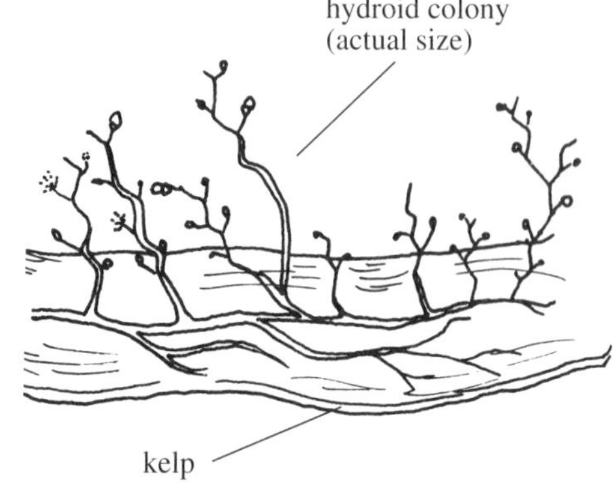

Fig.C. **THREADLIKE HYDROID COLONY**

Fig.D. **FLOWERLIKE HYDROID COLONY**

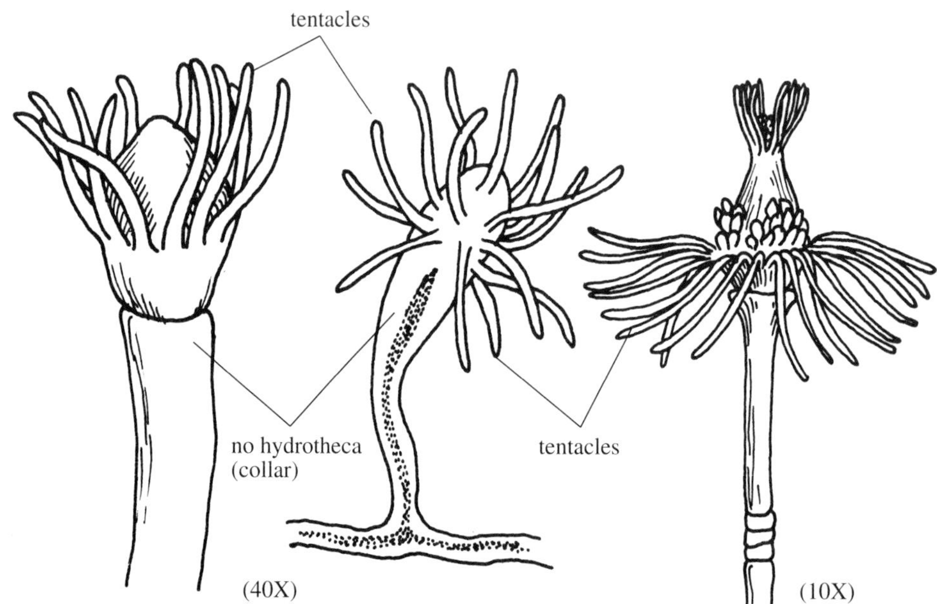

Fig.E. **HYDROID POLYPS WITHOUT A HYDROTHECA (COLLAR)**

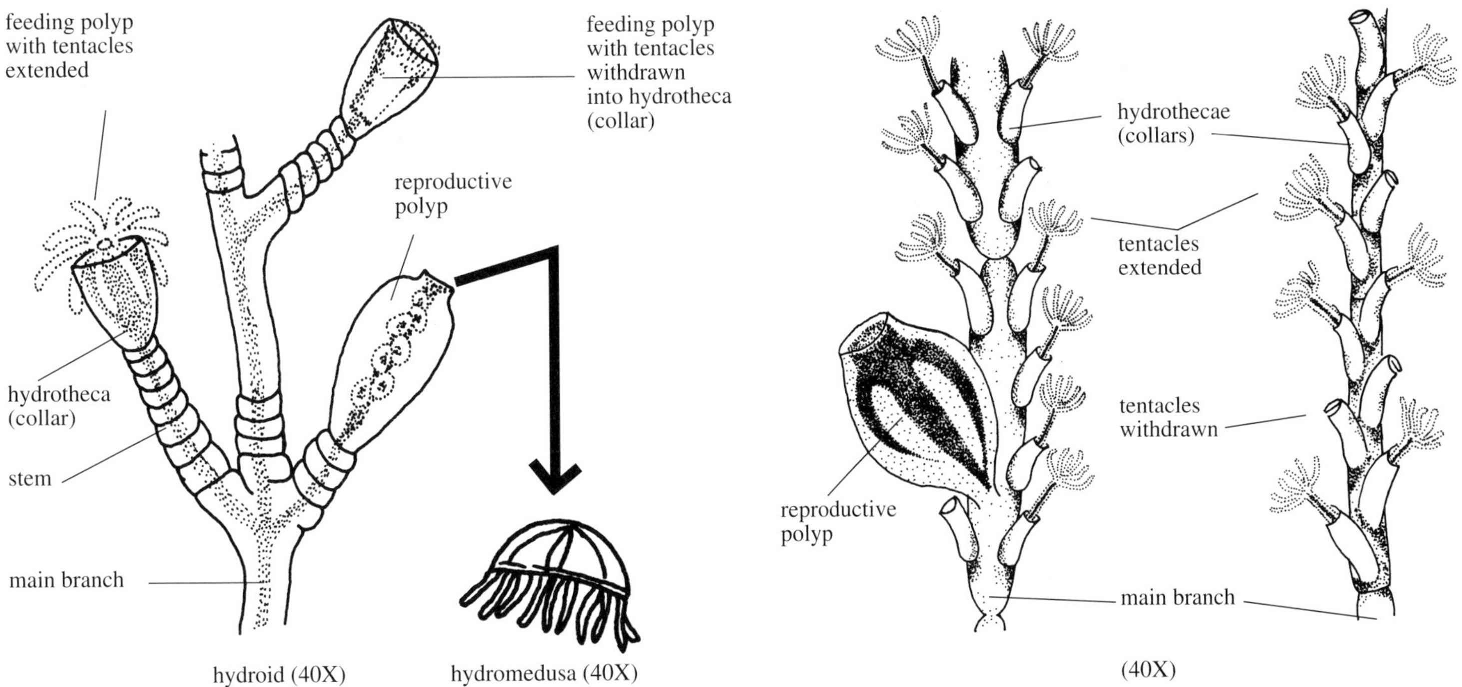

Fig.F. **HYDROID WITH GOBLET SHAPED HYDROTHECAE**

Fig.G. **HYDROIDS WITH TUBELIKE HYDROTHECAE**

HYDROIDS WITH OPERCULUM (LID)

#1.Polyps are attached to branches by a narrow stem (base of polyp is narrower than the polyp head); stem may be long or short .... #2
#1.Polyps are attached directly to branches, without a narrow stem (base of polyp is about the same width as the polyp head) .... ***Cuspidella* spp.**[1] (Fig.H)

#2.Segments of operculum are hinged at the base, creating a hinge line around the polyp .... #3
#2.Without a hinge line at base of operculum segments .... ***Opercularella* spp.**[1] (Fig.I)

#3.Polyps are connected by a creeping stolon (rootlike runner) which lies flat against the surface to which it is attached; stolon is not highly branched and polyps are solitary; with 8 or 9 opercular segments; colony is minute and inconspicuous .... ***Calycella syringa*, creeping bell hydroid** (Fig.H)
#3.Polyps are attached to erect, upstanding stalks; stalks may be highly branched in some species; most species have 10 or more operculum segments; the colonies of some species reach 5 cm (2") long .... ***Lovenella* spp.**[1] (Fig.I)

[1]Refer to Gosner (1971) or other identification guides to identify the species.

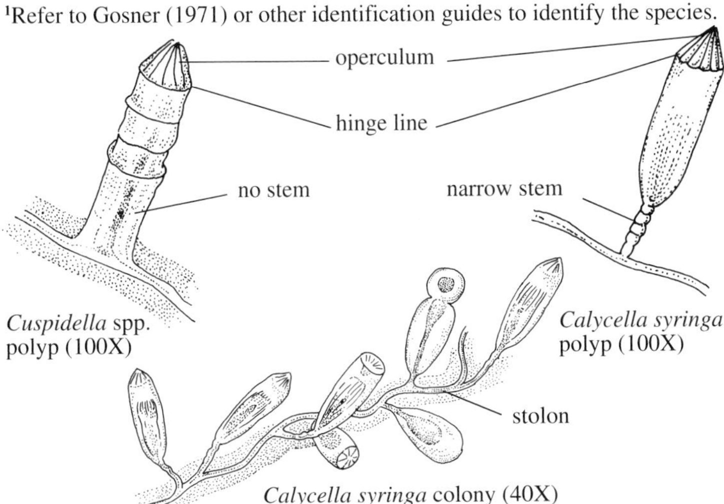

Fig.H. ***CALYCELLA SYRINGA*, CREEPING BELL HYDROID and *CUSPIDELLA* SPP.**[1]**:** These species are fairly common but are often overlooked because their polyps are tiny, less than 1 mm (1/32") tall. They attach to the surface of algae, bryozoans, and other hydroids with a creeping stolon (rootlike runner). Use the key above to distinguish between these species.

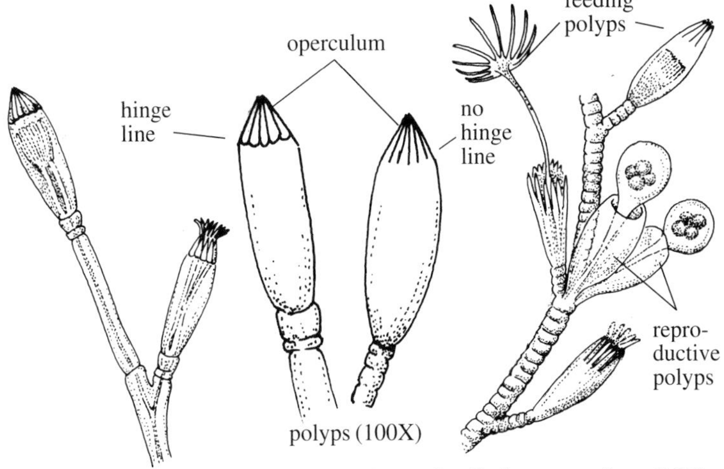

Fig.I. ***OPERCULARELLA* SPP.**[1] **and *LOVENELLA* SPP.**[1]**:** *Opercularella lacerata* has a highly branched colony; up to 25 mm (1") long. *Lovenella grandis* colonies have unbranched rigid stems growing from a common stolon (runner); up to 5 cm (2") long. These species have erect, upright colonies. Other species are much smaller and may have branched, unbranched or stolonate colonies.

HYDROIDS ARISING FROM A CRUSTLIKE OR ROOTLIKE MAT
PHYLUM CNIDARIA, CLASS HYDROZOA, FAMILY HYDRACTINIIDAE
Colonies often grow on snail or hermit crab shells

(Hydroid key begins on page 4.04)

#1.Spines[1] on base mat are rough and jagged; colony includes many different kinds of polyps[2]. .... ***Hydractinia echinata,*** **roughspined snailfur** (Fig.A)
#1.Spines on base mat (Figs.B,C) are smooth; colony includes only a few different kinds of polyps .... #2

#2.Base mat is rootlike (Fig.B); usually found on living snail shells .... ***Stylactaria*** **spp.**, #3
#2.Base mat is crustlike (Fig.C); usually found on snail shells occupied by hermit crabs .... ***Podocoryna carnea,*** **smoothspined snailfur** (Fig.C)

#3.About 20 tentacles in a single circle .... ***Stylactaria hooperi*** (Fig.B)
#3.About 12-16 tentacles divided into 2 circles .... ***Stylactaria arge*** (Fig.B)

[1]Examine the spines and the base mat with the snail shell out of the water so that the polyps contract and do not hide the spines. Use a dissecting microscope or hand lens with at least 10X magnification.
[2]Refer to footnote 2 on page 4.04.

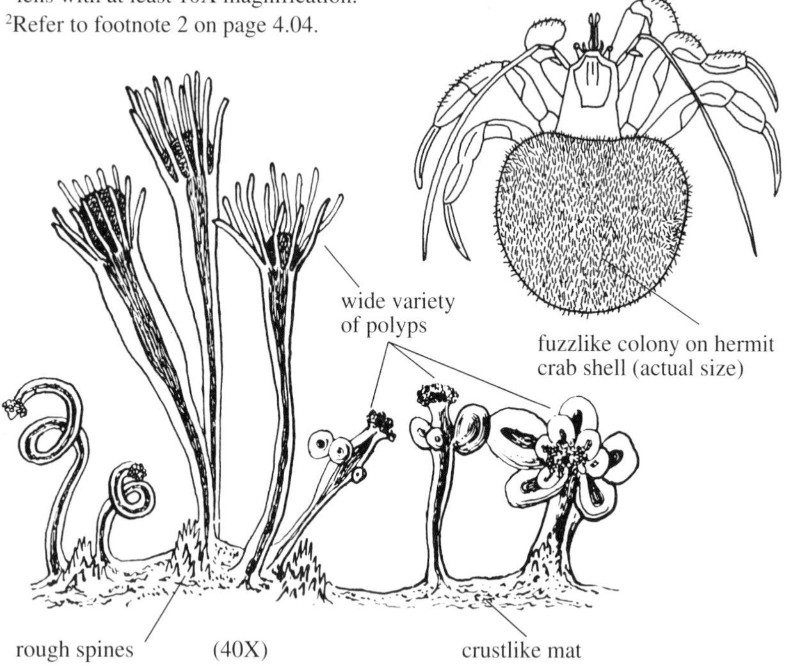

Fig.A. ***HYDRACTINIA ECHINATA,*** **ROUGHPINED SNAILFUR:** Overall color of colony may be brown, pink, beige, orange, or white; feeding polyps up to 5 mm (3/16") tall; one of the most common hydroids; usually found on shells occupied by hermit crabs but also common on rocks, pilings, etc.

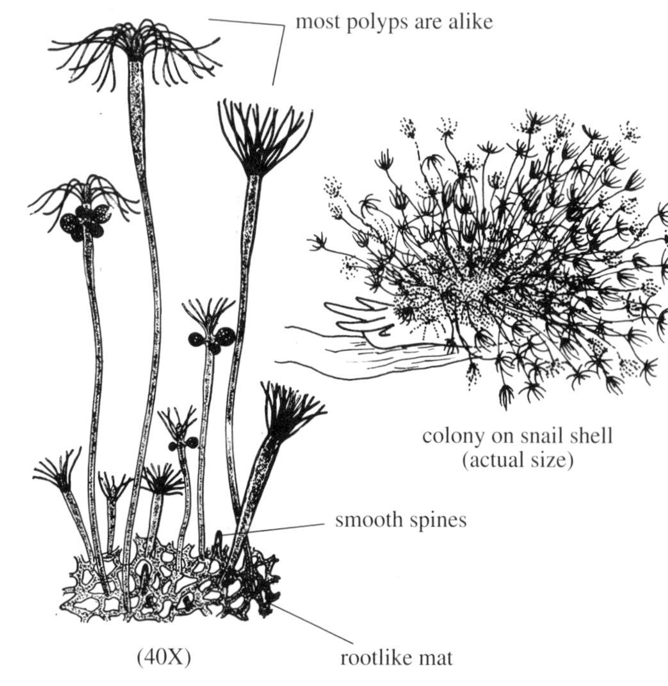

Fig.B. ***STYLACTARIA (=Stylactis)*** **SPP.:** *Stylactaria hooperi* is pinkish white; polyps up to 5 cm (2") tall; usually found on living snails; has 20 tentacles in a single circle. *Stylactaria arge* is similar except has 12-16 tentacles divided into 2 circles.

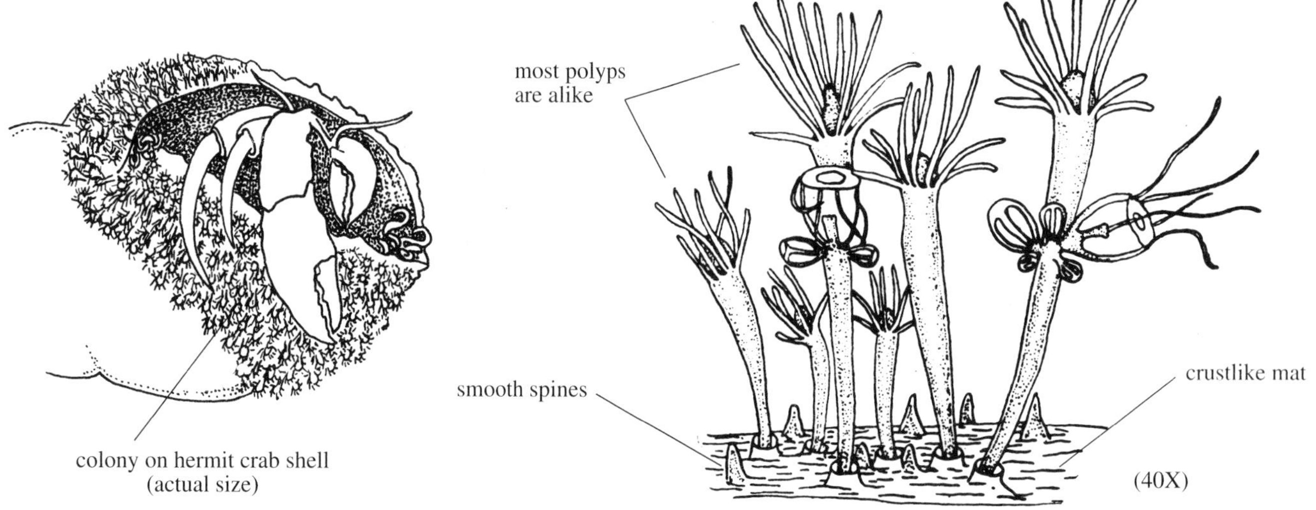

Fig.C. ***PODOCORYNA CARNEA,*** **SMOOTHSPINED SNAILFUR:** Overall color of colony is white or pink; polyps up to 5 mm (3/16") tall; usually found on snail shells occupied by hermit crabs. **17.02 H**

HYDROIDS WITH TUBE SHAPED HYDROTHECAE[1] (COLLARS)
PHYLUM CNIDARIA, CLASS HYDROZOA

(Hydroid key begins on page 4.04)

#1.With nematophores (tiny spoutlike structures) between hydrothecae (collars); hydrothecae are very short, cup shaped .... **family Halopterididae**[2] (Fig.E)
#1.Without nematophores; hydrothecae are longer than wide, cylinder shaped (Figs. A-D) .... **family Sertulariidae,** #2

#2.Hydrothecae are all attached in a row to one side of the branches, but may bend alternately from side to side ..***Hydrallmania falcata,*** **sickle hydroid** (Fig.A)
#2.Hydrothecae (collars) are attached to both sides of the branches (Figs.B-D) .... #3

#3.Hydrothecae are paired and are directly opposite each other on either side of the branches .... ***Dynamena pumila*** **and allied species**[2] (Fig.B)
#3.Hydrothecae alternate from side to side of the branches (Figs.C,D) .... #4

#4.Only one hydrotheca per section of branch .... ***Sertularella*** **spp.**[2] (Fig.C)
#4.More than one hydrotheca per section of branch .... ***Sertularia cupressina*** **and allied species**[2] (Fig.D)

[1]Follow the instructions in footnote 2 on page 4.04 for the microscopic examination of hydroids. Refer to Figs.F and G on page 4.05 for terms used in hydroid key.
[2]The identification of these hydroids to the species level is beyond the scope of this book, requiring specialized knowledge and detailed microscopic examination of reproductive and other structures. Use Gosner (1971) or other identification books to determine the species.

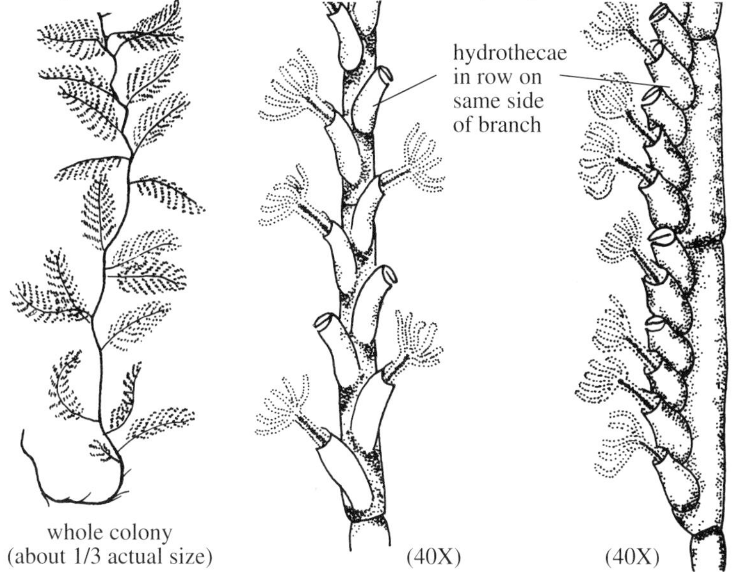

Fig.A. ***HYDRALLMANIA FALCATA,*** **SICKLE HYDROID:** Fernlike colony, may reach 30 cm (12") in length.

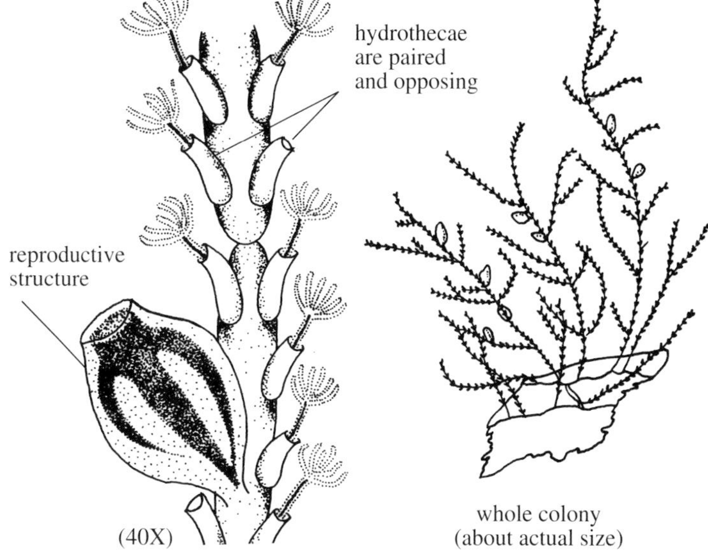

Fig.B. ***DYNAMENA PUMILA*** **AND ALLIED SPECIES**[2]**:** *Dynamena pumila (=Sertularia p.),* sea oak, shown here, is dark brown; up to 5 cm (2") tall; colonies grow in stiff, upright tufts; common on seaweed and shells.

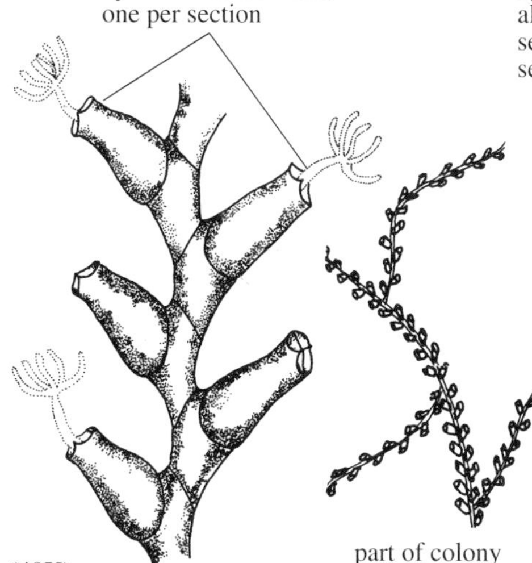

Fig.C. ***SERTULARELLA*** **SPP**[2]**.:** Colonies reach 15 cm (6") in length; often attaches to seaweeds.

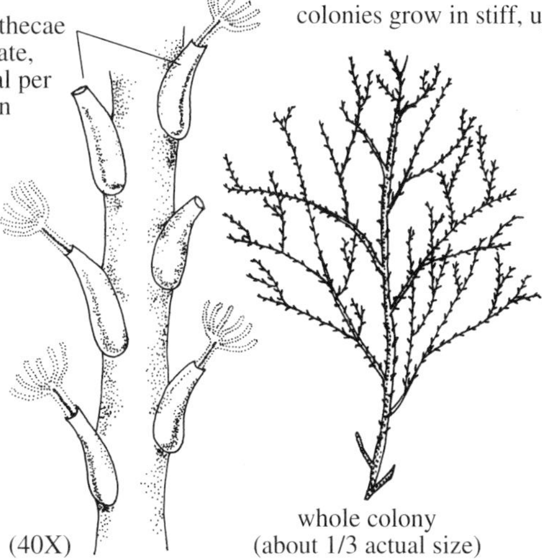

Fig.D. ***SERTULARIA CUPRESSINA*** **AND ALLIED SPECIES**[2]**:** *Sertularia cupressina (=Thuiaria argentea),* whiteweed hydroid, has bushy colonies with silvery branches; up to 30 cm (12") long; common on seaweed, rocks and pilings.

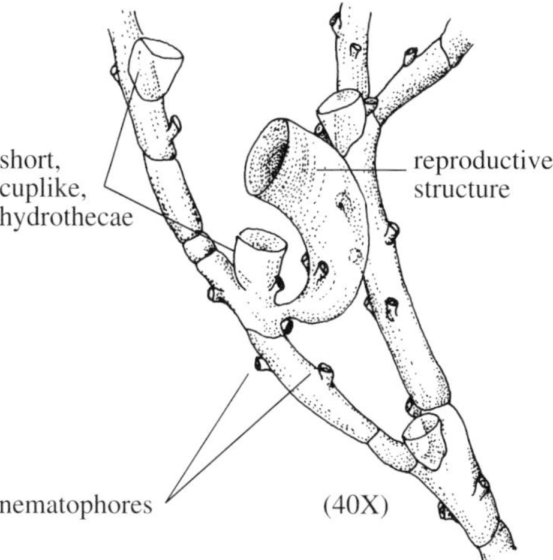

Fig.E. **FAMILY HALOPTERIDIDAE**[2]**:** One common species, *Schizotricha tenella*, has a white, delicate, feathery colony; up to about 7.5 cm (3") long; found on pilings, seaweeds in shallow waters.

HYDROIDS WITH GOBLET SHAPED OR FUNNEL SHAPED HYDROTHECAE (COLLARS)
PHYLUM CNIDARIA, CLASS HYDROZOA

Tentacles can be completely or partially withdrawn into hydrothecae[1]

(Hydroid key begins on page 4.04)

#1.Hydrothecae[1] (collars) are funnel or cylinder shaped; tentacles can only be partially withdrawn into hydrothecae; reproductive polyps are in rows on upper side of branches and have a pair of polyps with tentacles on top .... ***Halecium* spp.** (Fig.B)
#1.Hydrothecae are cuplike; tentacles can be withdrawn completely into hydrothecae (Figs.C-F) .... **family Campanulariidae[2]**, #2

#2.Rim of hydrotheca (cuplike collar) is smooth (Fig.E) .... #3
#2.Rim of hydrotheca is toothed (Figs.C,D,F) .... #4

#3.Reproductive structures have a narrow-necked opening and broad shoulders (Fig.A, #1); reproductive structures release medusae (tiny "jellyfish") with 12-16 tentacles; colony is often zigzagged with an extensive threadlike runner system; often found on kelp .... ***Obelia* spp.[2]** (Fig.E)
#3.Reproductive structures are shaped like Fig.A, #2-#4; medusae are very tiny and are not released from reproductive structure .... ***Campanularia* spp.[2]** (Fig.F)

#4.Colony is irregularly branched or unbranched; reproductive structures are ringed like a Japanese lantern; medusae (tiny "jellyfish") are released from the reproductive structure and have 4-8 tentacles .... ***Clytia* spp.[2]** (Fig.C)
#4.Colony is highly branched; reproductive structures are not ringed (Fig.A,D); medusoids are reduced and remain within or attached to reproductive structure (Fig.D) .... ***Gonothyraea loveni*** (Fig.D), ***Campanularia* spp. and allied species[2]** (Fig.F)

[1]Follow the instructions in footnote 2 on page 4.04 for the microscopic examination of hydroids. Refer to Fig.F on page 4.05 for terms used in hydroid key.
[2]**WARNING**: The identification of the genera or species in the family Campanulariidae is beyond the scope of this book, requiring specialized knowledge of their sexual stages and detailed microscopic examination of reproductive and other structures. Several species in each of these genera occur in this region (see Weiss et al., 1995). If a positive identification to genus or species is necessary, refer to Gosner (1971) or other identification sources.

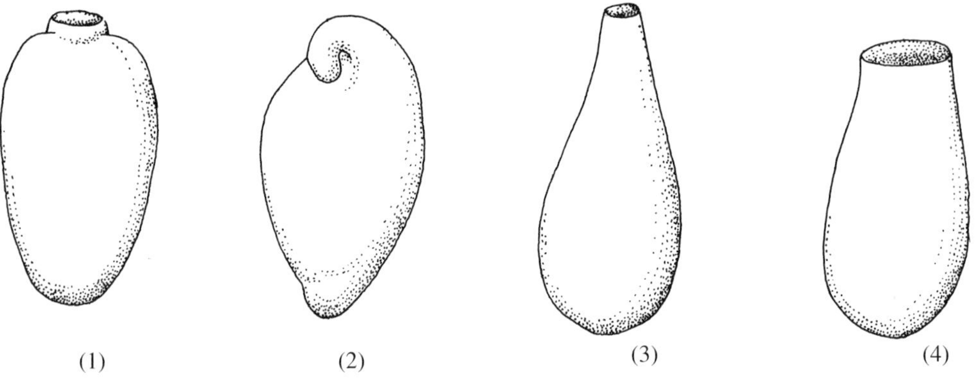

Fig.A. **REPRODUCTIVE STRUCTURES (100X)**

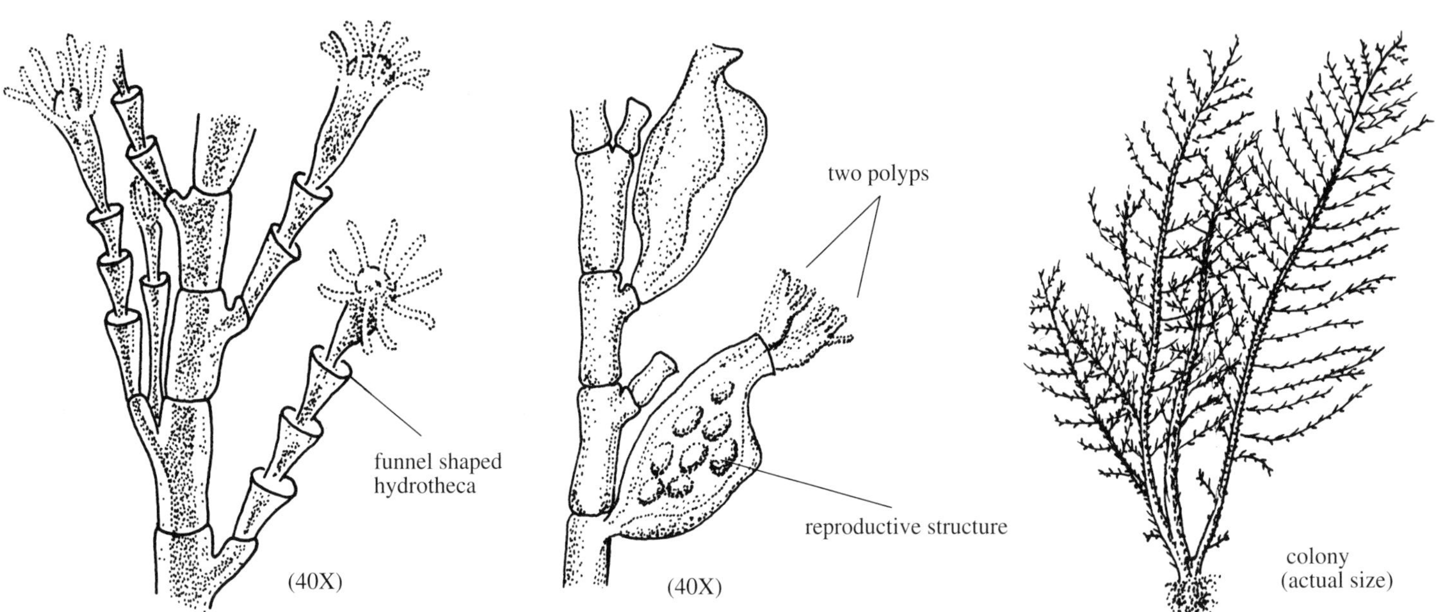

Fig.B. ***HALECIUM* SPP.:** A bushy or fanlike colony, highly branched; up to 25 cm (10") long; found on rocks, shells and other hard objects in shallow water.

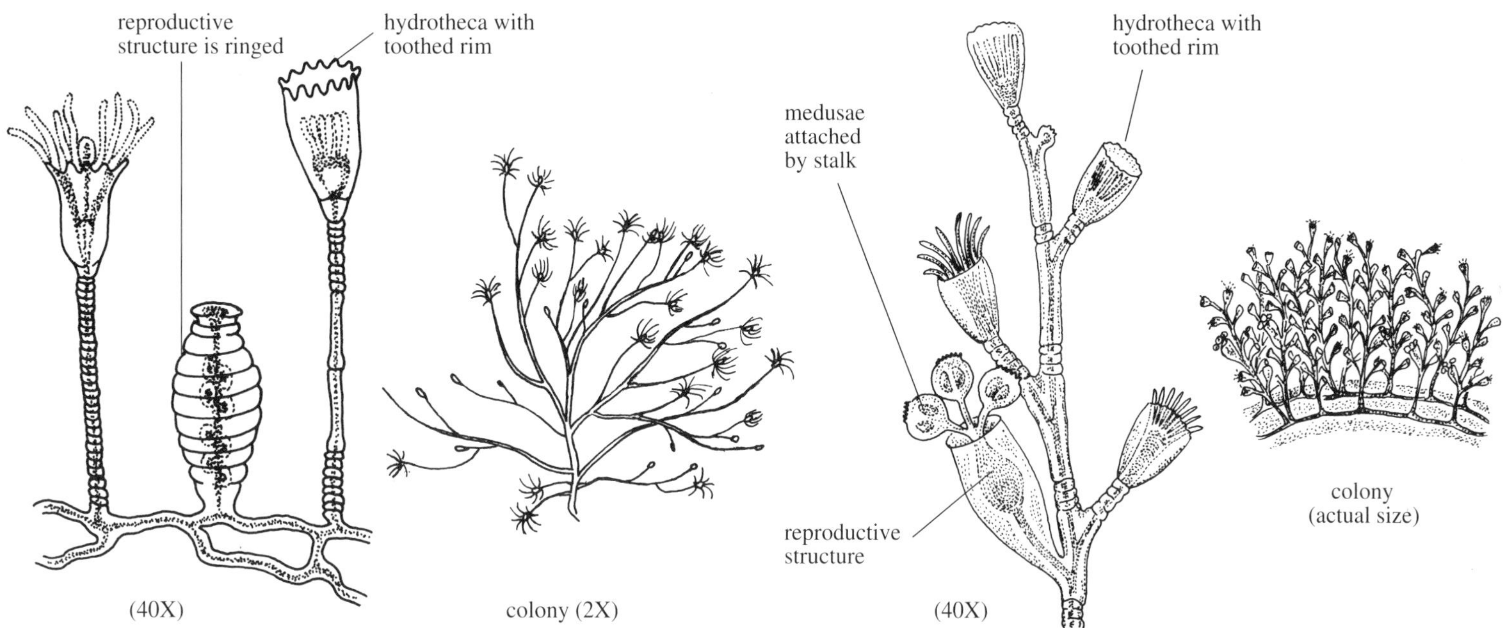

Fig.C. ***CLYTIA* SPP.**[2]**:** White; colony up to 2.5 cm (1") in height; found on rocks, seaweeds, pilings.

Fig.D. ***GONOTHYRAEA LOVENI***[2]***:*** Colonies are about 2.5 cm (1") tall; the medusae remain attached by a stalk to the reproductive structure.

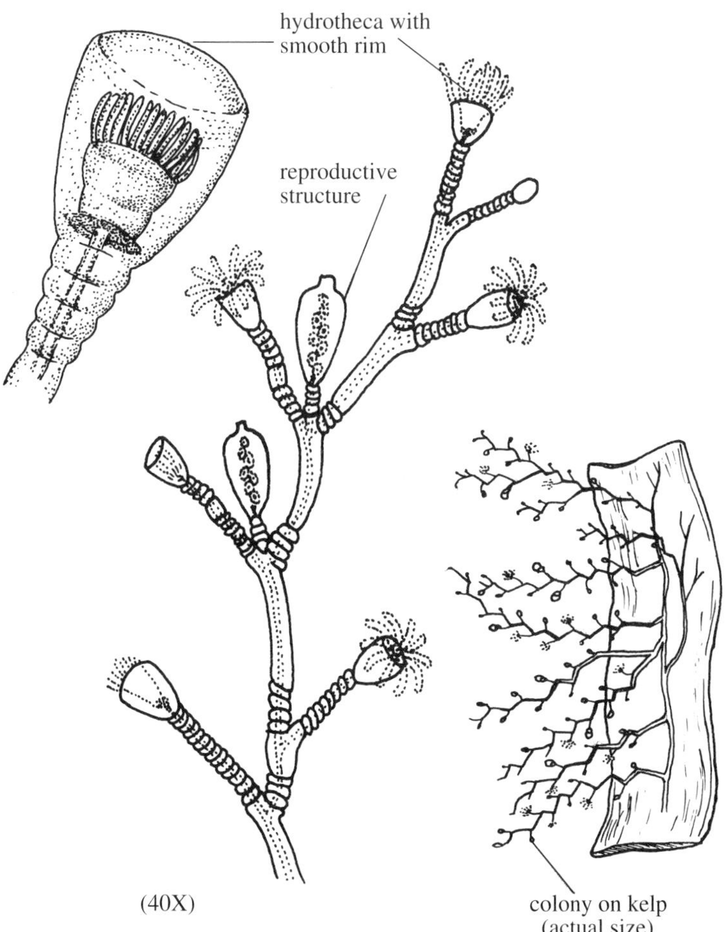

Fig.E. ***OBELIA* SPP.**[2]**:** *Obelia geniculata,* the knotted thread hydroid, (shown here) is one of the most common hydroids in this region. It is white or beige; zigzagged colony reaches a height of 2.5 cm (1"); grows from an extensive threadlike runner system often found on kelp, *Laminaria*, and on pilings, rocks and other seaweeds. Other *Obelia* species are also common. **17.03 A**

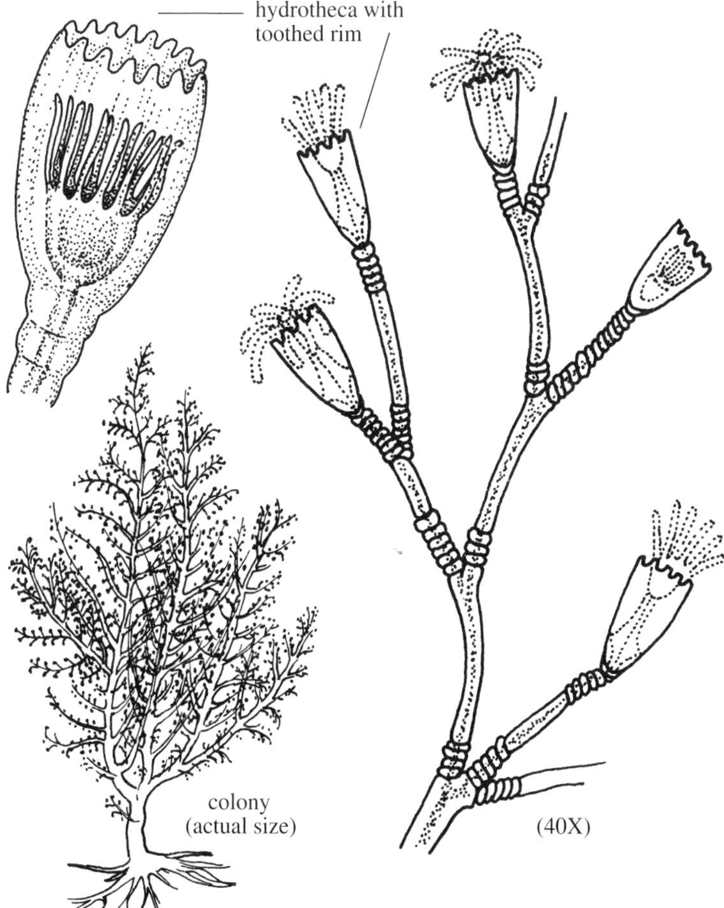

Fig.F. ***CAMPANULARIA* SPP.**[2] **AND ALLIED SPECIES**[2]**:** Colonies may reach 25 cm (10") in height; attach to pilings, seaweeds, eelgrass. The species shown here is highly branched and has hydrothecae with toothed rims. Other species may have smooth rimmed hydrothecae and/or may have zigzagged or unbranched colonies. None of these species release medusae. **17.03 B**

HYDROIDS WITHOUT HYDROTHECAE[1] (COLLARS)
PHYLUM CNIDARIA, CLASS HYDROZOA

(Hydroid key begins on page 4.04)

#1.Tentacles are arranged in one or two crownlike circles around the head of the polyp (Figs.A-D) ... #2
#1.Tentacles are scattered all over the head of the polyp (Figs.E-I) ... #8

#2.Two circles of tentacles on polyp (Figs.A,B), one circle near base of polyp head and other near tip; polyp large and showy ... #3
#2.One circle of tentacles on polyp (Figs.C,D) ... #7

#3.Polyps are solitary, occurring separately, not colonial ... #5
#3.Colonial hydroids, forming masses of tangled stems ending in bright red or pink flowerlike polyps (Fig.A) ... ***Tubularia (=Ectopleura)* spp.**, #4

#4.Pink color; stems are highly branched; with rings around stem ... ***Tubularia larynx*** (Fig.A)
#4.Rose color; stems have few or no branches; without rings around stem ... ***Tubularia crocea*** (Fig.A)
#4.Scarlet color; stems are not branched; with rings around stem ... ***Tubularia indivisa*** (Fig.A)

#5.Stalk is wider at base than at neck; base is somewhat bottle or club shaped ending in a rootlike holdfast (Fig.B) ... #6
#5.Stalk is slender along its entire length ... ***Tubularia* spp. and allied species** (Fig.A)

#6.With rings around the base of the head of the polyp; lives in tidepools and intertidal zone; up to 5 cm (2") long ... ***Hybocodon prolifer*** (Fig.B)
#6.Without rings around the base of the head of the polyp; lives offshore in subtidal waters; up to 10 cm (4") long ... ***Corymorpha pendula*** (Fig.B)

#7.Cone shaped structure (hypostome) in center of tentacles; 10-12 tentacles on polyp ... ***Bougainvillia* spp.**[2] (Fig.C)
#7.Trumpet or funnel shaped structure (hypostome) in center of tentacles; 20-32 tentacles on polyp ... ***Eudendrium* spp.**[2] (Fig.D)

#8.Some or all of the tentacles have knobs at the tips (Figs.E-G) ... #9
#8.Tips of tentacles are all pointed; none of the tentacles have knobs at the tips (Figs.H-I) ... #11

#9.Tentacles at the base of the polyp are pointed, other tentacles have knobs at the tips ... ***Halocordyle disticha*** (Fig.E)
#9.All of the tentacles have knobs at the tips (Figs.F,G) ... #10

#10.Polyp body is longer than polyp stem; with more than 30 tentacles ... ***Zanclea costata*** (Fig.F)
#10.Polyp body is shorter than polyp stem; with about 16 tentacles ... ***Sarsia tubulosa*** (Fig.G)

#11.Colony highly branched; color is brownish; reproductive buds not clustered; found in fresh or brackish water ... ***Cordylophora caspia (=lacustris)*** (Fig.H)
#11.Polyps arise from an unbranched, vinelike network; reproductive buds in berrylike clusters; found in seawater ... ***Clava multicornis (=leptostyla)*** (Fig.I)
#11.Solitary, unbranched stalks; stalks are wider at base than at neck; base is somewhat club or bottle shaped; saltwater species ... ***Corymorpha pendula*** (Fig.B)

[1]Follow the instructions in footnote 2 on page 4.04 for the microscopic examination of hydroids. Refer to Fig.F on page 4.05 for terms used in hydroid key.
[2]Refer to Gosner (1971) for a positive identification to species. Also, note warning in footnote 1 on page 4.04.

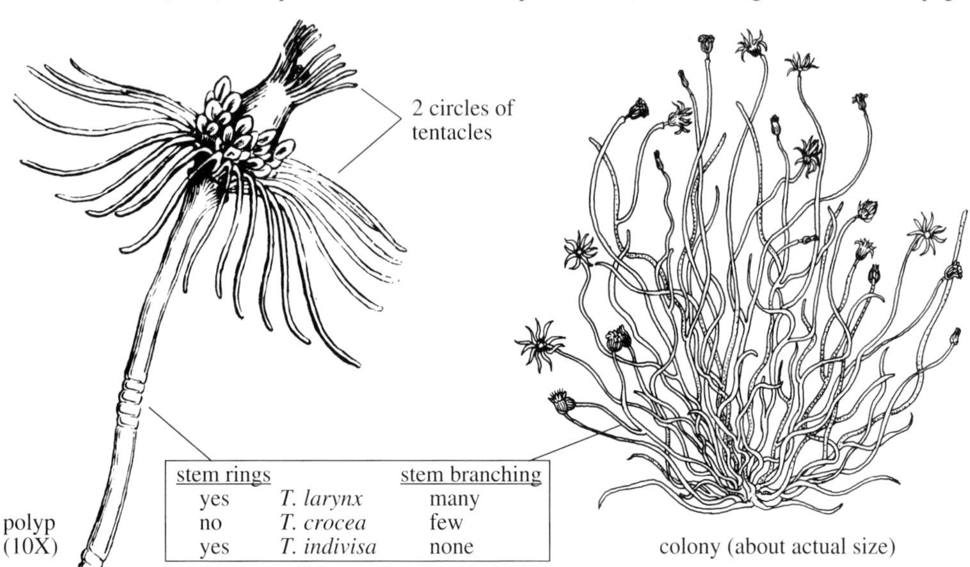

Fig.A. ***TUBULARIA (=ECTOPLEURA)* SPP.:** Very common during the spring, uncommon at other times. *Tubularia crocea* has rose colored polyps; up to 13 cm (5") tall; found on pilings, lobster pots, rocks, etc. *Tubularia larynx* has bright pink polyps; up to 5 cm (2") tall; found on rocks, pilings, algae, etc. *Tubularia indivisa (=couthouyi)* has scarlet red polyps; up to 15 cm (6") tall; occurs on sandy or stony bottoms. Other species of *Tubularia* may also occur in this area. *Ectopleura dumortierii*, a brackish water species which has a maximum length of 12 mm (1/2"), closely resembles *Tubularia*. **WARNING:** For a positive identification of any of these species, refer to Gosner (1971) or other identification sources.

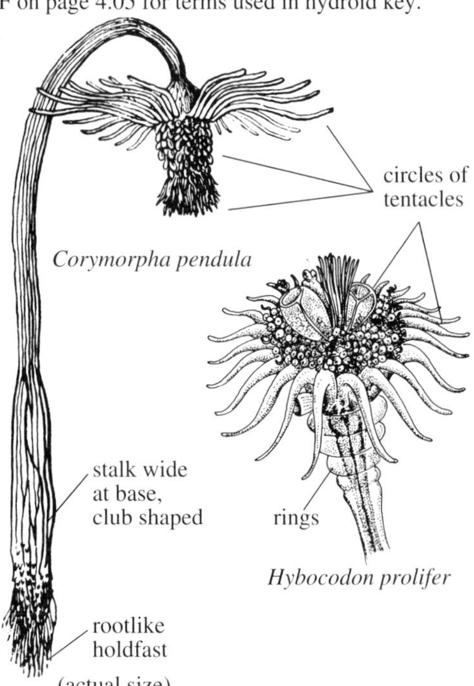

Fig.B. ***CORYMORPHA PENDULA:*** Up to 10 cm (4") tall; lives offshore on sand or mud bottoms. ***HYBOCODON PROLIFER:*** Up to 5 cm (2") tall; lives in tidepools; common north of Cape Cod.

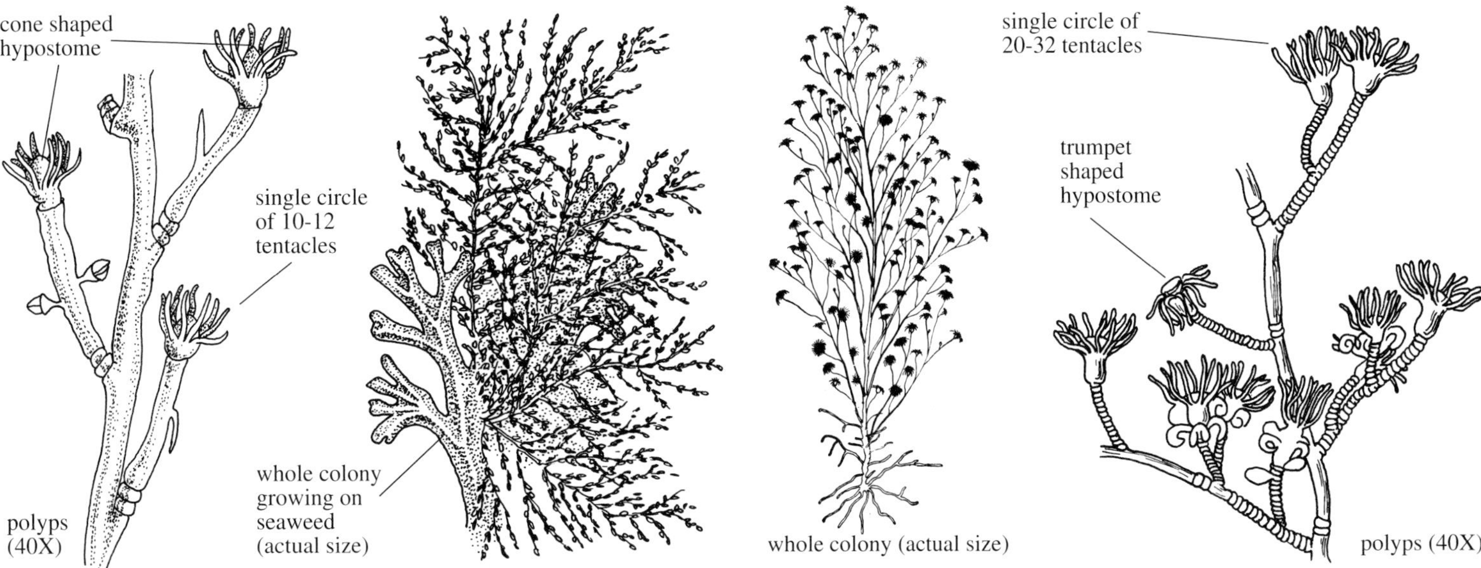

Fig.C. ***BOUGAINVILLIA* SPP.[2] :** The most common species, *Bougainvillia carolinensis*, has green branches with red polyps; the colony grows up to 30 cm (12") long; attaches to seaweeds, rocks, and pilings.

Fig.D. ***EUDENDRIUM* SPP.[2] :** Colonies are less than 1 cm (3/8") to over 30 cm (12") long.

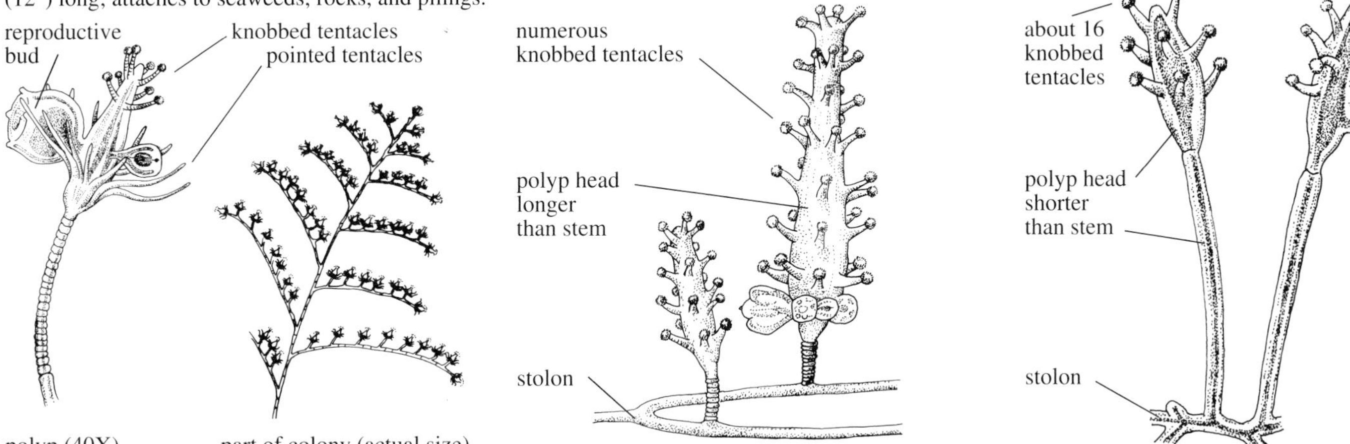

Fig.E. ***HALOCORDYLE DISTICHA (=Pennaria tiarella),* FEATHER HYDROID:** Pink or white polyps; up to 15 cm (6") long; occurs in shallow water on eelgrass, rocks.

Fig.F. ***ZANCLEA COSTATA:*** Pink; up to about 1 cm (3/8") tall; often found attached to encrusting bryozoans on subtidal rocks.

Fig.G. ***SARSIA TUBULOSA,* CLAPPER HYDROID:** Rose red internally; up to 2 cm (3/4") tall; occurs in winter and early spring.

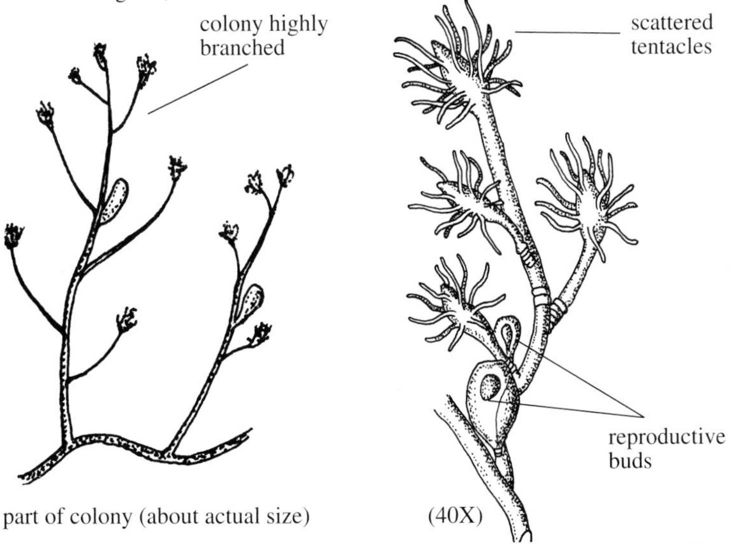

Fig.H. ***CORDYLOPHORA CASPIA (=C. lacustris),* FRESHWATER HYDROID:** Brownish; up to 6 cm (2 1/2") tall; found in fresh or brackish water.

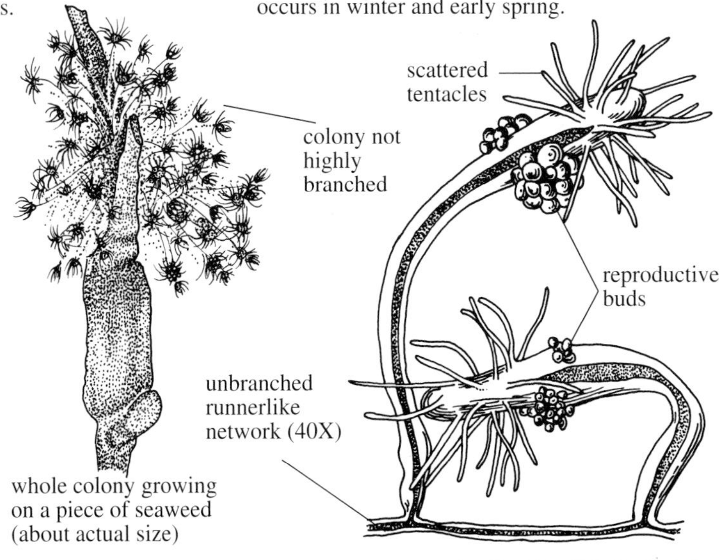

Fig.I. ***CLAVA MULTICORNIS (=C. leptostyla),* CLUB HYDROID:** Reddish pink; polyps up to 1 cm (3/8") long; grows in patches on rockweed near low tide level, also in tide pools and on rocks.

ATTACHED ANEMONES
PHYLUM CNIDARIA, CLASS ANTHOZOA, ORDER ACTINIARIA
Anemones that attach to rocks and other solid objects

(Use the key on page 2.08 to determine if you have an anemone)

#1. More than 100 tentacles (Figs.B,C); body often grows larger than 2.5 cm (1") in diameter; with a strong oral sphincter muscle[1] .... #2
#1. Fewer than 65 tentacles (Figs.D,E,F); body rarely grows larger than 2 cm (3/4") in diameter; oral sphincter muscle is weak or absent .... #3

#2. Tentacles are slender and pointed, too numerous to count (about 1000); tentacles are arranged in wavy or frilled lobes; color may be brown, orange or white; acontia[1] are present .... ***Metridium senile*, clonal plumose anemone** (Fig.B)
#2. Tentacles are thick and may be blunt at the tips; tentacles number about 160 and are arranged in 5 concentric circles; color usually red; no acontia .... ***Urticina felina*, northern red anemone** (Fig.C)

#3. Green or gray-black body, may have orange or white vertical lines; body is usually wider than tall .... ***Diadumene lineata* (=*Haliplanella luciae*), orangestriped green anemone** (Fig.D)
#3. Orange, pink or white body; body is usually 2 or 3 times taller than wide (Figs.E,F) .... #4

#4. Base is enclosed in a mucus or parchmentlike tube (Fig.F) sometimes encrusted with sand grains; with 40 or fewer tentacles; acontia are absent[1] .... #5
#4. Base of anemone is not enclosed in a tube; has 40-60 tentacles; acontia are present .... ***Diadumene leucolena*, white anemone** (Fig.E)

#5. With about 40 tentacles arranged in three concentric rings, with the innermost tentacles longer than the others; base is enclosed in a thin mucus tube; column is smooth; pedal (attachment) end is flat or rounded; attaches to rocks, sometimes in large matlike colonies .... ***Fagesia lineata*, lined anemone** (Fig.F)
#5. With 16-20 tentacles in a single ring; forms parchmentlike tube often encrusted with sand grains; middle of column with wartlike bumps and 8 longitudinal grooves; pedal end is rounded and inflatable, used for digging; usually found burrowed into sandy mud underneath rocks .... ***Edwardsia elegans*, tube building anemone** (page 4.14, Fig.B)

[1]Refer to Fig. A for terms used in anemone key.

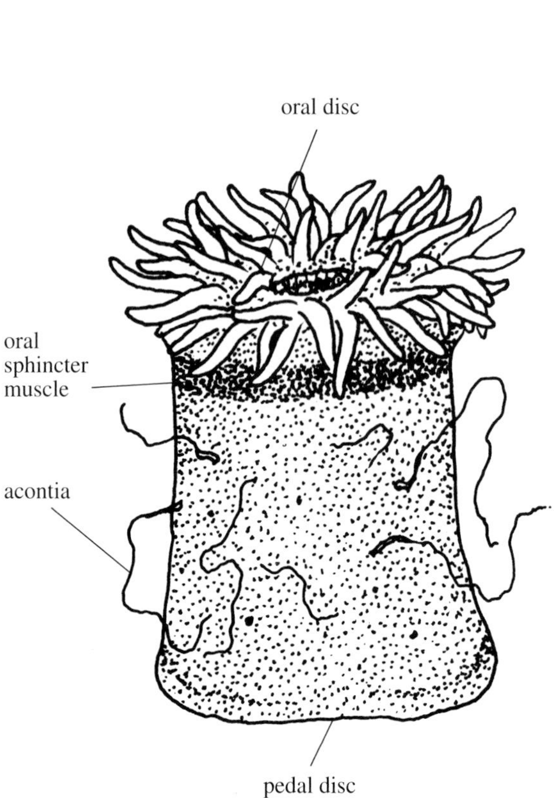

Fig.A. **TYPICAL ANEMONE:** Acontia are threadlike filaments which normally remain inside the anemone but may stick out if it is handled roughly. Some anemone species have a strong oral sphincter muscle and are able to close up completely (see Fig.B). The oral sphincter muscle is weak in other species and the tentacles may protrude when the anemone is closed (see Fig.D).

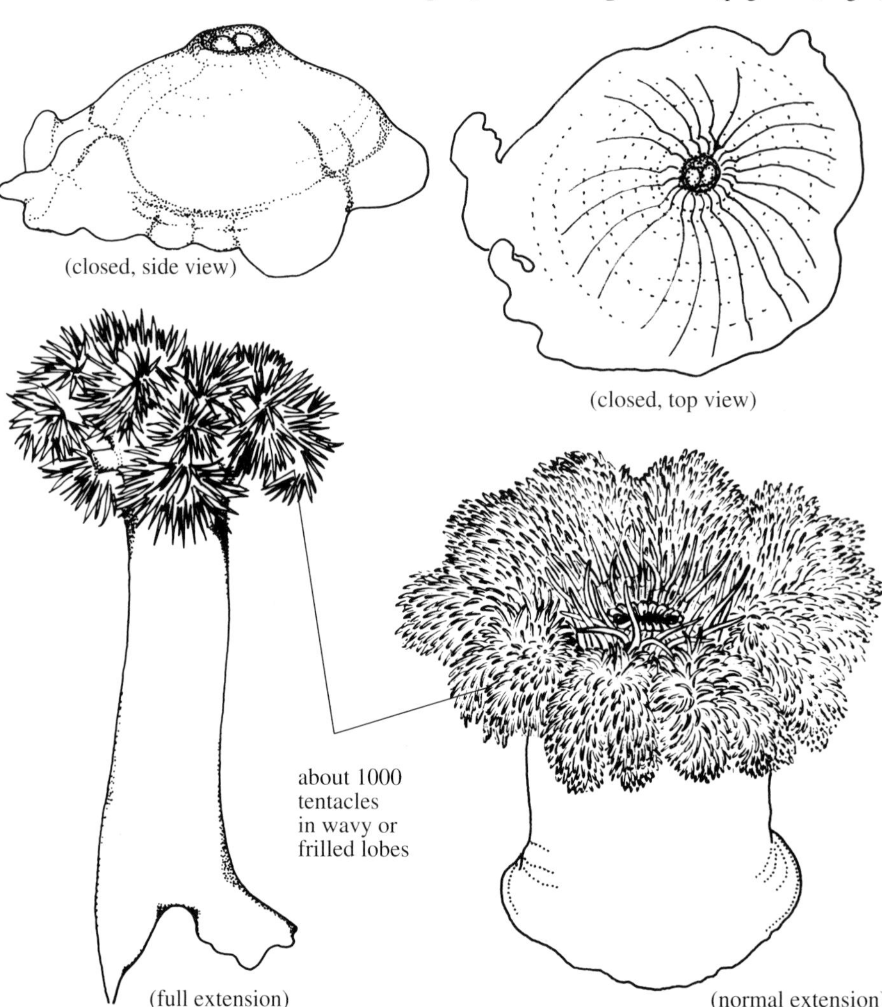

Fig.B. ***METRIDIUM SENILE*, CLONAL PLUMOSE ANEMONE:** May be dark brown, orange or white; up to 10 cm (4") tall and 7.5 cm (3") in diameter; extremely common throughout this region, found at low tide level and offshore attached to rocks, dock pilings and other solid objects.

17.03 E **17.03 F**

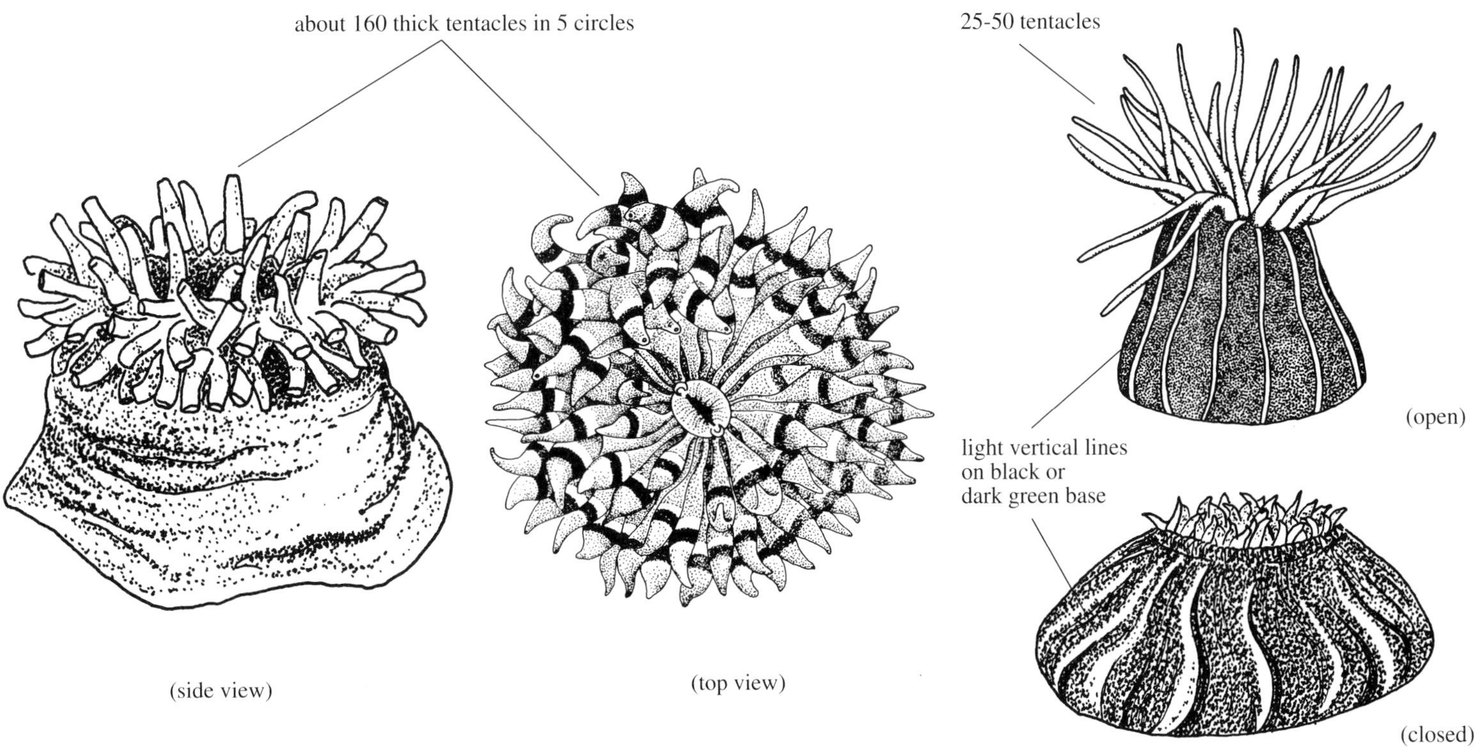

Fig.C. ***URTICINA FELINA (=Tealia felina),*** **NORTHERN RED ANEMONE:** Red, may be streaked or banded with green; tentacles may have one or two dark rings; up to 5 cm (2") tall and 12 cm (5") wide; not common south of Cape Cod.

Fig.D. ***DIADUMENE LINEATA (=Haliplanella luciae),*** **ORANGESTRIPED GREEN ANEMONE:** Green to blackish body with orange, yellow, red or white vertical lines; up to 2 cm (3/4") tall, 5 mm (1/4") wide; very common in tidal marshes and on seaweeds and rocks, especially in tide pools and rock crevices in intertidal zone. **17.03 C**

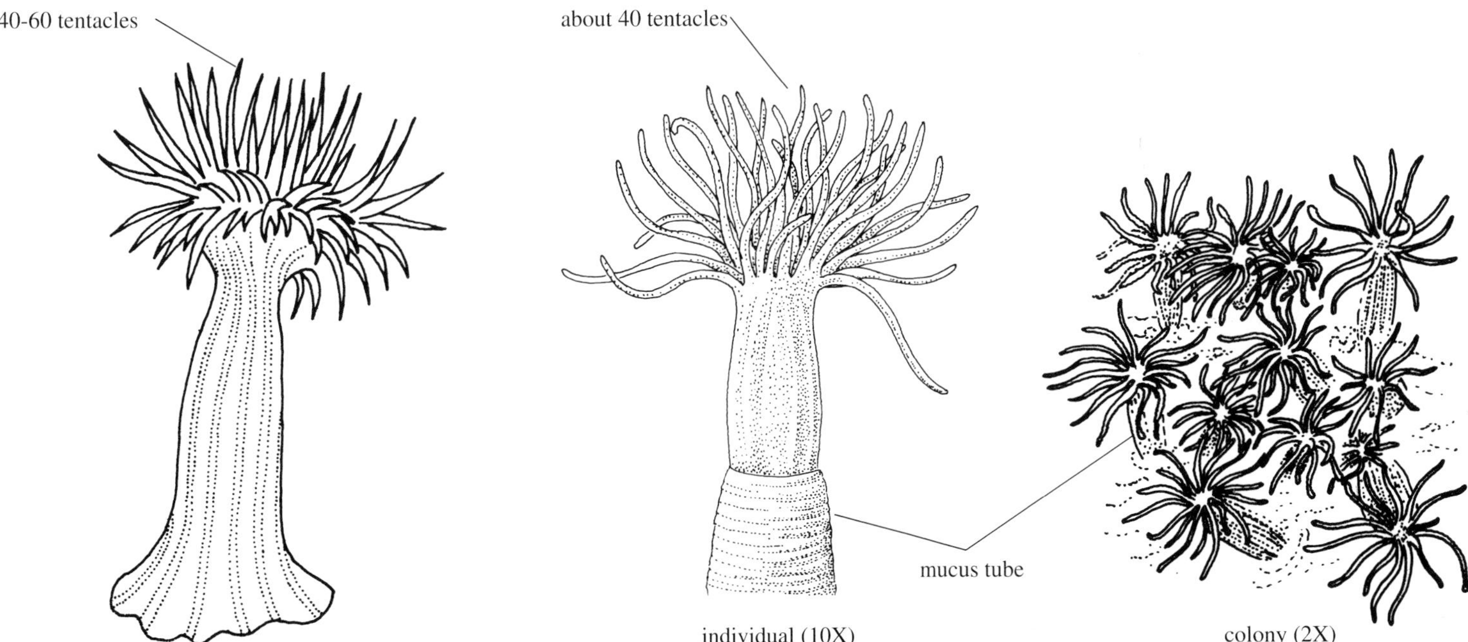

Fig.E. ***DIADUMENE LEUCOLENA,*** **WHITE ANEMONE:** Translucent orange, pink or white; membranes inside can sometimes be seen through body wall and look like light vertical stripes; up to 4 cm (1.5") tall; common on rocks, shells and seaweeds. **17.03 G**

Fig.F. ***FAGESIA LINEATA (=Edwardsia l.),*** **LINED ANEMONE:** Tentacles and oral end are whitish or tan; basal end enclosed in a brownish mucus tube; attaches to rocks, especially on the underside, sometimes forming large matlike colonies; occurs below the low tide level and in deeper water. **17.03 D**

BURROWING ANEMONES
PHYLUM CNIDARIA, CLASS ANTHOZOA, ORDERS CERIANTHARIA AND ACTINIARIA

Anemones that live buried in mud or sand, usually with only the tentacles exposed; body often elongate or wormlike.

(Use the key on page 2.16 to determine if you have a burrowing anemone)

#1.Two concentric circles of tentacles (Fig.A); body is smooth, no longitudinal grooves or ridges; no attachment disc .... **order Ceriantharia,** #2
#1.Single circle of tentacles (Figs.B-F); body may or may not have longitudinal grooves or ridges; may or may not have attachment disc ... **order Actiniaria,** #3

#2.Marginal tentacles all the same length; up to 20 cm (8") long; occurs Cape Cod and south .... ***Ceriantheopsis americana*** (Fig.A)
#2.Marginal tentacles different lengths; up to 45 cm (18") long; occurs Cape Cod and north .... ***Cerianthus borealis*** (Fig.A)

#3.With 20 or fewer tentacles; no attachment disc but may have an inflatable digging "foot" (Figs.B-D) .... #4
#3.More than 50 tentacles; with an attachment disc (Figs.E,F) .... #6

#4.Body has 20 longitudinal rows of tiny bumps; with 20 blunt tentacles which may have knobs at their tips .... ***Haloclava producta*** (Fig.C)
#4.Body has 8 longitudinal grooves (Figs.B,D), no bumps; with 12-16 slender, pointed tentacles .... #5

#5.Body is divided into three sections (Fig.B), top section forms a smooth, whitish or clear collar, middle section has a rough brown covering which often has sand grains stuck to it, bottom section forms a somewhat pointed inflatable digging "foot" .... ***Edwardsia elegans*** (Fig.B)
#5.Body is not divided into three sections; entire body is smooth and transparent .... ***Nematostella vectensis*** (Fig.D)

#6.With 140 or more tentacles; fine longitudinal grooves on body; no acontia[1] .... ***Paranthus rapiformis*** (Fig.E)
#6.With fewer than 100 tentacles (Fig.F); body is smooth but sand grains may be stuck to sides; with acontia .... ***Actinothoe*** **spp.,** #7

#7.With about 64 tentacles .... ***Actinothoe modesta*** (Fig.F)
#7.With about 48 tentacles .... ***Actinothoe gracillima*** (Fig.F)

[1]Refer to Fig. A on page 4.12 for terms used in anemone key.

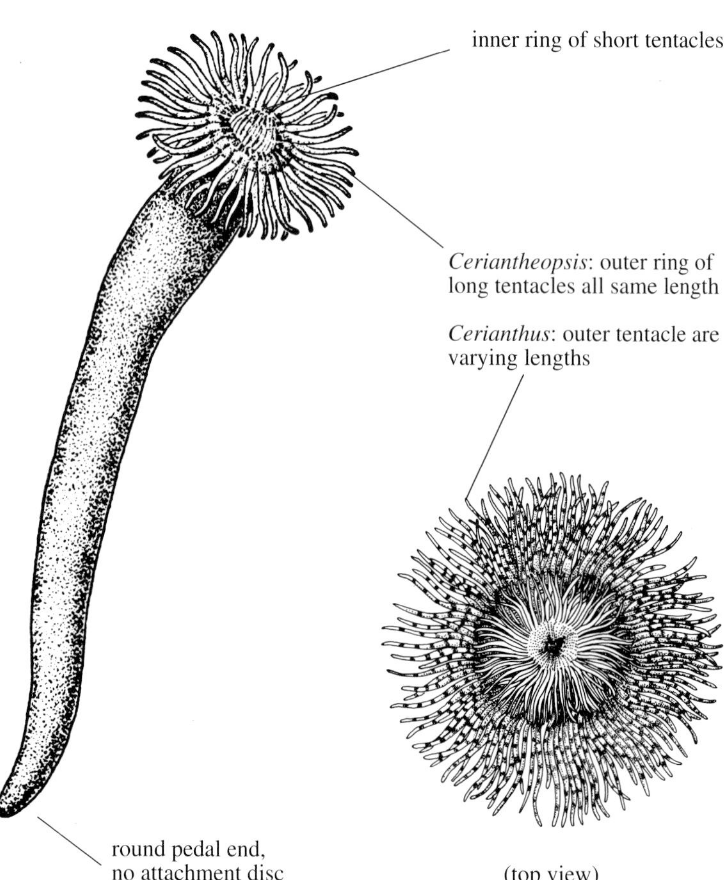

Fig.A. ***CERIANTHEOPSIS AMERICANA:*** Brown; up to 20 cm (8") long; common south of Cape Cod in depths under 30 m (100'). ***CERIANTHUS BOREALIS:*** Brown; up to 45 cm (18") long; common north of Cape Cod in depths over 12 m (40'). Both species burrow into bottom sediments and build thick tubes made of sand, mud and mucus. (class Anthozoa, order Ceriantharia)

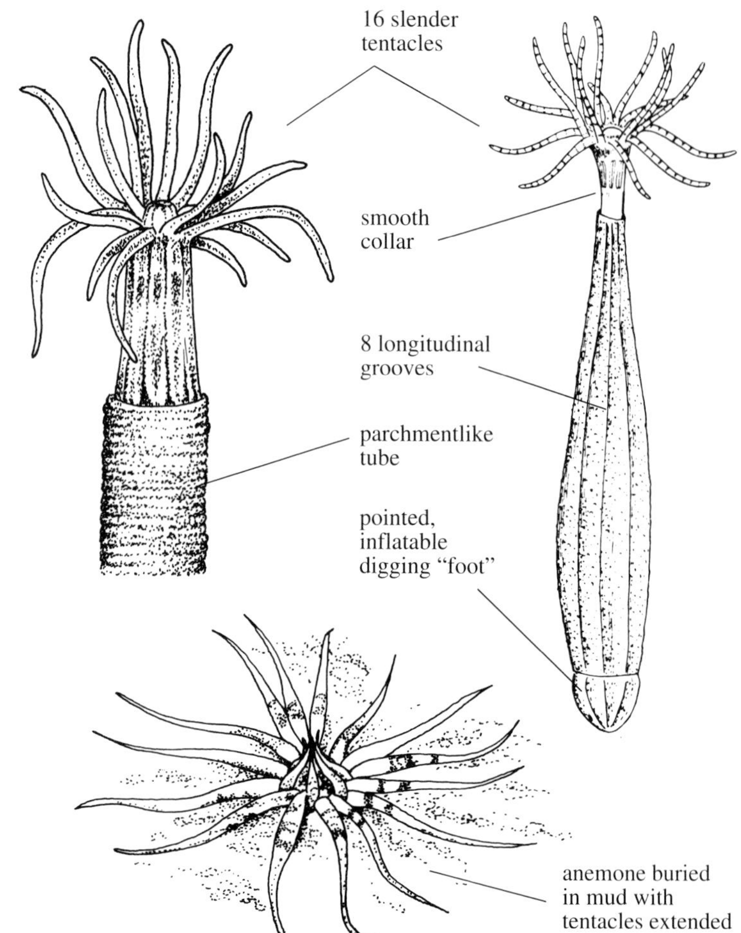

Fig.B. ***EDWARDSIA ELEGANS:*** Collar and tentacles are white or pale pink, body enclosed in a brown parchmentlike tube encrusted with sand; up to 15 cm (6") in length and 2.5 cm (1") in diameter; found buried in sandy mud under stones from low tide level and into deeper water. (class Anthozoa, order Actiniaria)

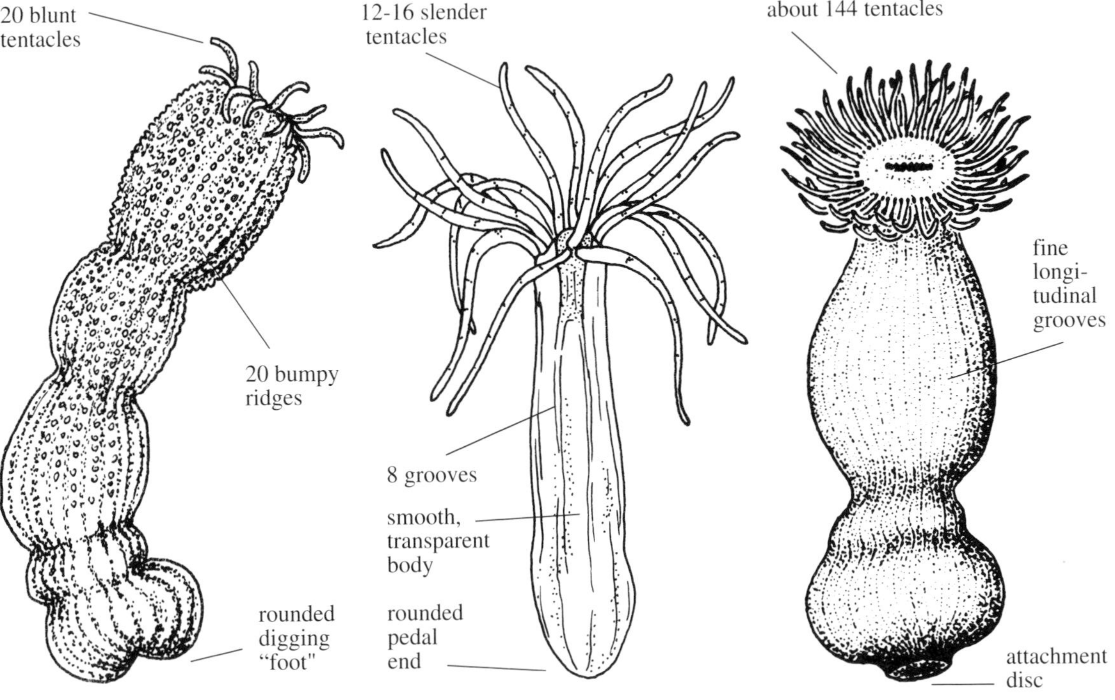

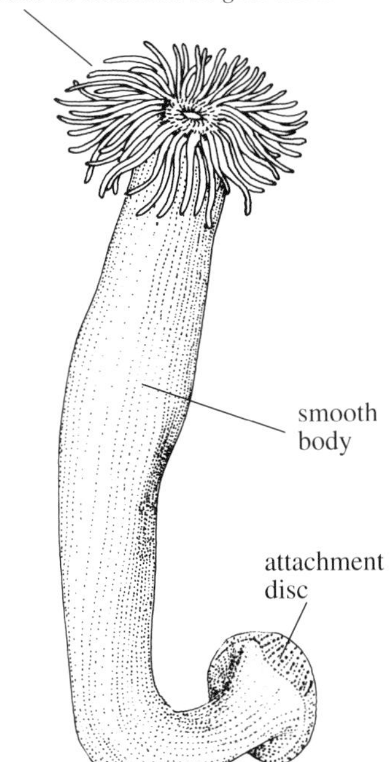

Fig.C. ***HALOCLAVA PRODUCTA:*** Whitish or salmon color; up to 10 cm (4") long, 2 cm (3/4") in diameter; commonly found buried in intertidal sand and mud flats. (class Anthozoa, order Actiniaria)

Fig.D. ***NEMATOSTELLA VECTENSIS:*** Transparent; up to 2 cm (3/4") long and 3 mm (1/8") in diameter; lives buried in soft mud where salinity is less than 20 o/oo. (class Anthozoa, order Actiniaria)

Fig.E. ***PARANTHUS RAPIFORMIS:*** Pale yellow or pink; up to 7.5 cm (3") long; 2.5 cm (1") in diameter; found buried in sand near low tide level. (class Anthozoa, order Actiniaria)

Fig.F. ***ACTINOTHOE MODESTA:*** Body is pale white or pink, tentacles are gray-green; up to 6.5 cm (2.5") long. ***ACTINOTHOE GRACILLIMA:*** up to 25 mm (1") long. Both species bury in sand or pebbles at or below low tide level, from Cape Cod south (class Anthozoa, order Actiniaria)

COMB JELLY PARASITE ANEMONE
CLASS ANTHOZOA, ORDER ACTINIARIA

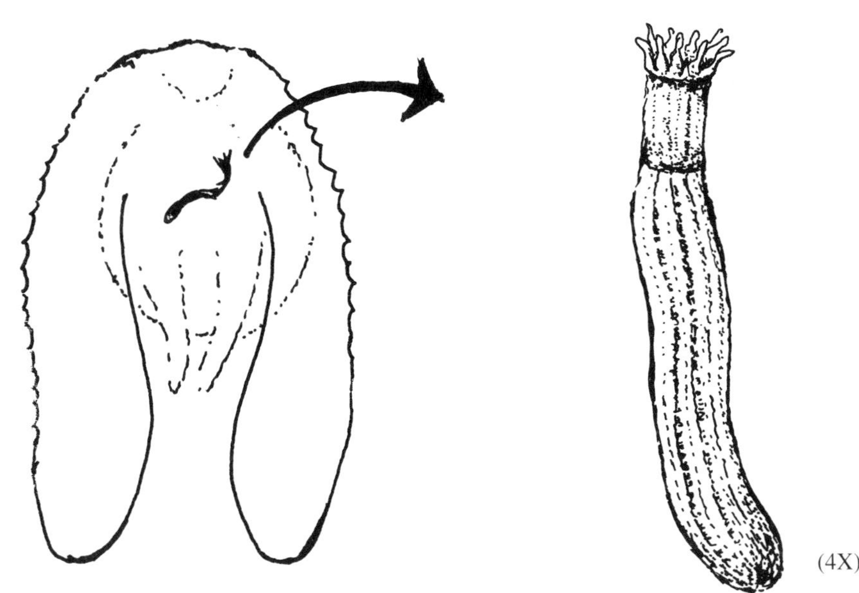

Fig.G. ***EDWARDSIA LEIDYI,*** **COMB JELLY PARASITE ANEMONE:** Pink; up to about 2.5 cm (1") long; the larval stage of this anemone is a common parasite of the ctenophore *Mnemiopsis leidyi,* the sea walnut or common southern comb jelly (see page 4.17). It looks like a thin pink worm or thread within the clear comb jelly. Little is known about the life cycle or the adult stage of this anemone.

SOFT CORALS
PHYLUM CNIDARIA, CLASS ANTHOZOA, ORDER ALCYONACEA

Colonial cnidarians with a skeleton of calcareous spicules and polyps with 8 featherlike branching tentacles

(Use key on page 2.08 to determine if you have a soft coral)

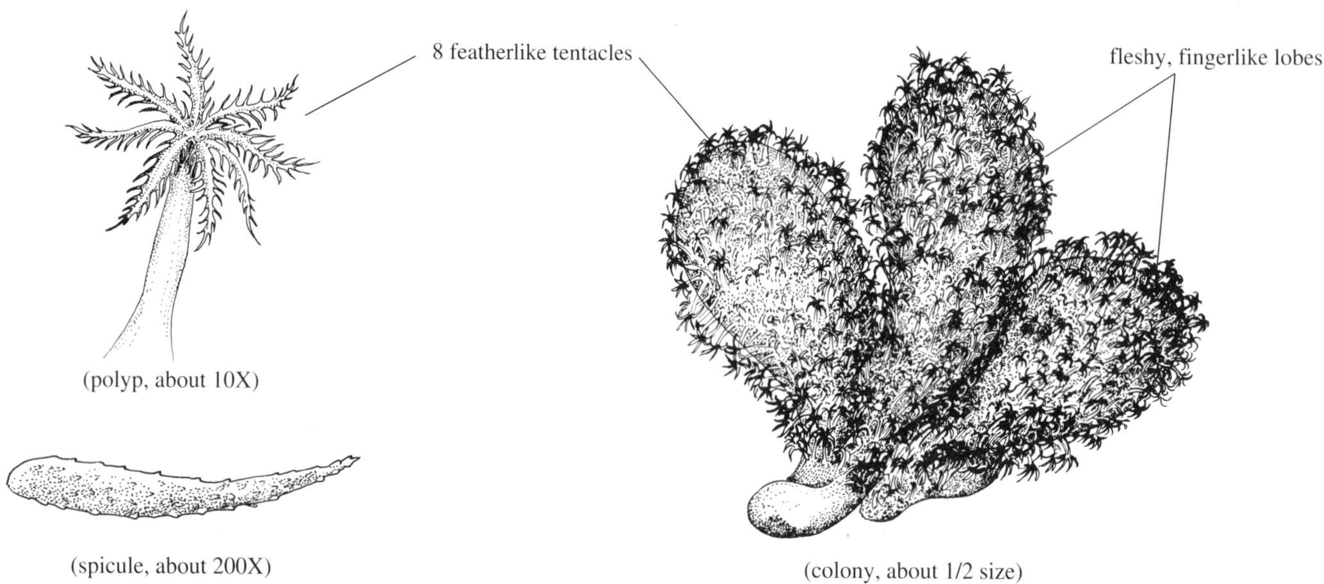

Fig.A. ***ALCYONIUM DIGITATUM*****, DEAD MAN'S FINGERS:** White, pink, pale orange or yellowish; polyps are translucent white; forms lobed colonies up to 20 cm (8") long; attaches to rocks, shells and other solid objects in depths greater than 15 m (50'). This is the only species of soft coral that occurs in southern New England at depths under 30 m (100'). Refer to Gosner (1971) to identify deep water species.

STONY CORALS
PHYLYM CNIDARIA, CLASS ANTHOZOA, ORDER SCLERACTINIA

Colonial cnidarians that build a calcareous formation with cuplike depressions.

(Use key on page 2.10 to determine if you have a stony coral)

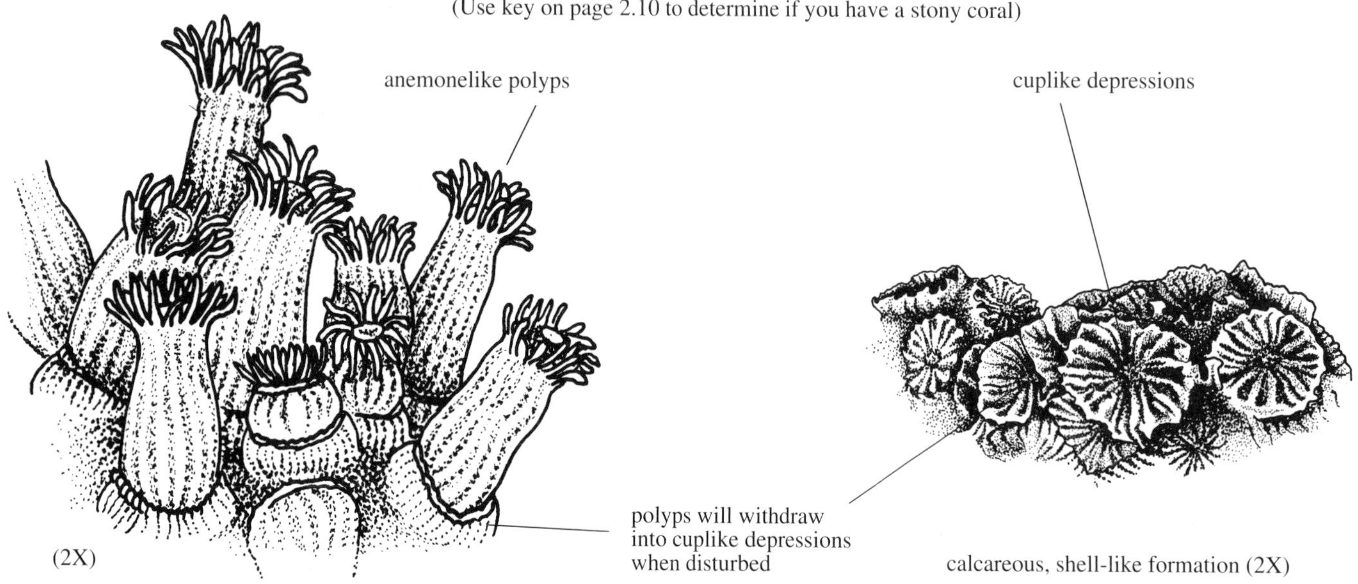

Fig. B. ***ASTRANGIA POCULATA (=A. danae)*****, NORTHERN STAR CORAL:** Whitish, shell-like skeleton; transparent white polyps; cuplike depressions in skeleton are about 6 mm (1/4") in diameter; entire colony may reach up to 10 cm (4") across; common on rocks and other hard objects below the low tide level to about 35 m (120'). Other species of stony coral occur only in much deeper water off our coast. Refer to Cairns (1981) to identify these other species. **17.02 G**

COMB JELLIES
PHYLUM CTENOPHORA

Free swimming or floating animals with a clear gelatinous body that has 8 rows of comblike plates. The comb plates are made up of tiny cilia (short "hairs") that create water currents by making a waving motion. Comb jellies have biradial symmetry (body has 2 lobes or 2 tentacles or a flattened saclike shape). Unlike the true jellyfishes, the comb jellies do not have stinging cells.

(Use the key on page 2.12 to determine if you have a comb jelly)

#1.Spherical or egg shaped; with a pair of obvious tentacles, each with small side branches .... ***Pleurobrachia pileus*, sea gooseberry** (Fig.A)
#1.With a lobed or flattened saclike body; without obvious tentacles .... #2

#2.Flattened saclike body without any lobes; with a wide mouth .... ***Beroe* spp., Beroe's comb jellies** (Fig.B)
#2.Body with 2 large lobes .... #3

#3.Occurs from Cape Cod south; lobes are attached to body only near the top of the body, not on the sides; lobes longer than body; auricles (4 fingerlike structures around mouth) arise from deep grooves .... ***Mnemiopsis leidyi*, sea walnut or common southern comb jelly** (Fig.C)
#3.Occurs from Cape Cod north; lobes are attached to body on the sides and top of the body; lobes shorter than body; auricles arise from side of body .... ***Bolinopsis infundibulum*, common northern comb jelly** (Fig.D)

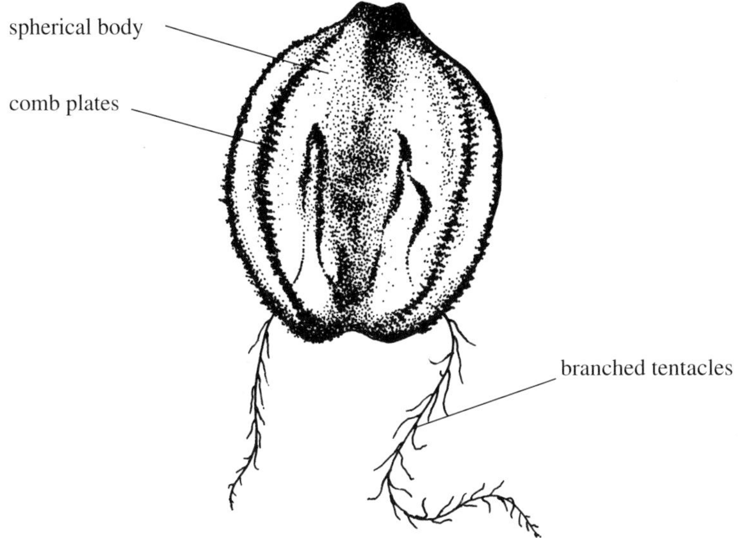

Fig.A. ***PLEUROBRACHIA PILEUS*, SEA GOOSEBERRY:** Clear; up to 2 cm (3/4") in diameter; occurs in winter and spring, not common in coastal waters in summer. (class Tentaculata, order Cydippida)

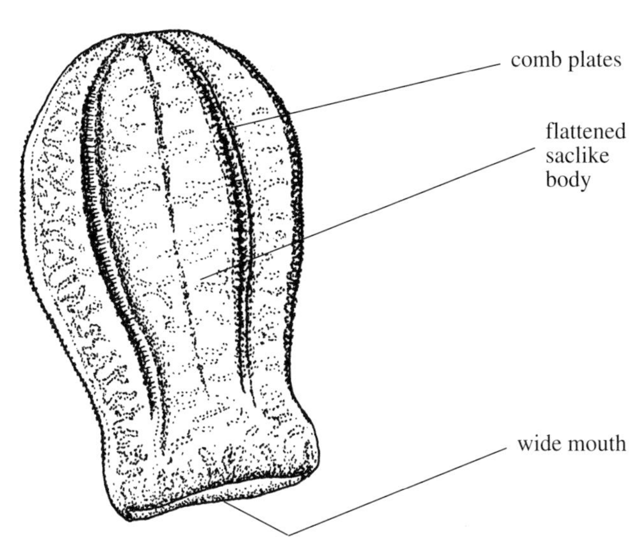

Fig.B. ***BEROE* SPP., BEROE'S COMB JELLIES**: Pinkish or reddish brown; up to 10 cm (4") in length; not common. *Beroe ovata* occurs from Cape Cod south. *Beroe cucumis* occurs from Cape Cod north. Refer to Gosner (1971) to distinguish these very similar species. (class Nuda, order Beroida)

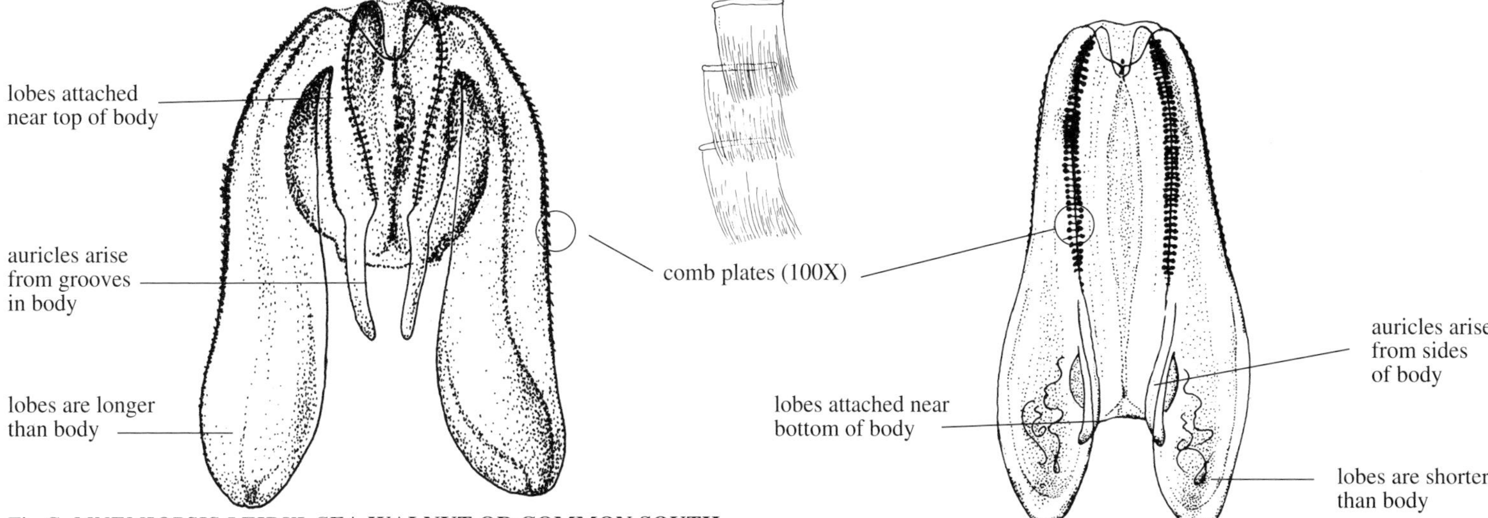

Fig.C. ***MNEMIOPSIS LEIDYI*, SEA WALNUT OR COMMON SOUTHERN COMB JELLY:** Clear, colorless; up to 10 cm (4") long; when disturbed, produces a blue-green bioluminescent glow visible in dark; often has a pink wormlike anemone inside body (see page 4.15); occurs from Cape Cod south; very abundant from August through early fall. (class Tentaculata, order Lobata)

Fig.D. ***BOLINOPSIS INFUNDIBULUM*, COMMON NORTHERN COMB JELLY:** Transparent, iridescent; up to 15 cm (6") long; the most common comb jelly north of Cape Cod; occurs in Massachusetts Bay and north. (class Tentaculata, order Lobata)

FLATWORMS: PHYLUM PLATYHELMINTHES, CLASS TURBELLARIA

Free living or symbiotic; flattened, unsegmented worms without appendages; digestive system present, without an anus, with a mouth located ventrally usually near middle or anterior end; with a ciliated epithelium

(Use key on page 2.16 to determine if you have a flatworm)

#1.Found on book gills and around leg bases of the horseshoe crab, *Limulus polyphemus* (Figs.A,B) .... #2
#1.Free living or associated with animals other than horseshoe crabs (Figs.C-M) .... #3

#2.With a distinct adhesive disc (sucker) at rear end; posterior branches of intestines[2] are separate; up to 16 mm (5/8") long; a horseshoe crab will often have many of these worms on its gills and leg bases .... ***Bdelloura*** **spp., horseshoe crab flatworm** (Fig.A)
#2.No adhesive disc; branches of intestines are joined together at posterior ends; up to 3 mm (1/8") long; not as common as *Bdelloura* .... ***Syncoelidium pellucidum*****, horseshoe crab flatworm** (Fig.B)

#3.Tiny worms, under 5 mm (3/16") long .... #4
#3.Larger worms, 5 mm (3/16") or longer, up to about 38 mm (1 1/2") long .... #8

#4.Without a clearly defined gut[2] (intestines); no eyes[2]; no tentacles[2] (Figs.C-F)) .... **order Acoela,** #5
#4.Gut has a clearly defined outer wall; gut has 3 main branches and many smaller branches (see Fig.A); with more than 2 eyes, eyes are often in rows or clusters; tentacles may or may not be present (Figs.G-M) .... **order Polycladida**, #8
#4.Gut has a clearly defined outer wall; with 1 pair of eyes or no eyes; no tentacles .... **other orders[1]**

#5.With 1-5 tail-like appendages at rear of worm .... ***Polychoerus caudatus*** (Fig.C)
#5.No tail-like appendages (Figs.D-F) .... #6

#6.With hairs or spines on surface of body; yellowish body .... ***Childia groenlandica*** (Fig.D)
#6.No hairs or spines on body (Figs.E-F) .... #7

#7.Yellow at front end, dark reddish-purple to black pigment scattered in middle of body; somewhat pointed at both ends ..... ***Aphanostoma diversicolor*** (Fig.E)
#7.Orange or reddish brown .... ***Anaperus gardineri*** (Fig.F)
#7.Pale tan, transparent or other colors .... **other species in the order Acoela[1]**

#8.No tentacles[2] (Figs.G,H) .... #9
#8.With tentacles (tentacles may arise from front edge or on top of head[2]) (Figs.I-M) .... #10

#9.With two rows of 4-5 eyespots[2] and a pair of eyespots behind each row, occurs north and south of Cape Cod ..... ***Euplana gracilis*****, slender flatworm** (Fig.G)
#9.Eyespots in 4 clusters; occurs north of Cape Cod only .... ***Notoplana atomata*****, speckled flatworm** (Fig.H)

#10.Tentacles arise from front margin of head .... ***Prosthecereaus maculosus*****, horned flatworm** (Fig.I)
#10.Tentacles arise from top of head, above brain (Figs.J-M) .... #11

#11.No marginal eyes (Figs.J,K) .... #12
#11.With marginal eyes (tiny eyespots around body edge, Figs. L,M) .... #13

#12.Body oval; no eyes on tentacles; lives in the mantle cavity of the whelk, *Busycotypus*, and other snails .... ***Hoploplana inquilina*****, whelk flatworm** (Fig.J)
#12.Body elongate; with eyes scattered on tentacles; lives on eelgrass and sand; occurs south of Cape Cod only .... ***Gnesioceros floridana*** (Fig.K)

#13.Marginal eyes on front half of body only; not banded .... ***Stylochus ellipticus*****, tide pool flatworm** (Fig.L)
#13.Marginal eyes go all around body; with a distinct pattern of white or yellowish and brown cross bands .... ***Stylochus zebra*****, striped flatworm** (Fig.M)

[1]This key does not include the rarer species of flatworms, particularly those which are less than 5 mm (3/16") long and are unlikely to be noticed. The identification of flatworms to species often requires specialized techniques, including serial sectioning. Refer to Bush (1981) to make a positive identification of worms in the orders Acoela and Nemertodermatida. Refer to Gosner (1971) for worms in the orders Tricladida and Polycladida. The other orders have undergone major revisions in recent years but Bush (1964) can be used to identify some of the more common local species.

[2]The eyes, tentacles and internal organs can be best observed while the animal is alive. Use a dissecting microscope at 10-30X and adjust the substage and incident lighting to various angles until you find the best view. Dorsal tentacles can be difficult to see when examined directly from above. Try oblique views.

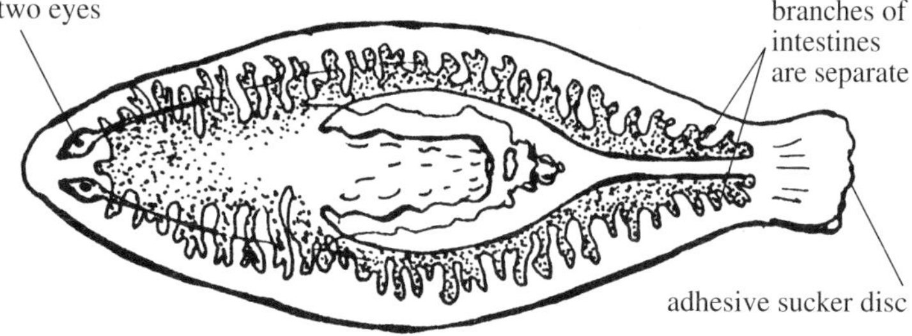

Fig.A. ***BDELLOURA*** **SPP., HORSESHOE CRAB FLATWORMS:** Grayish white to yellow, with brown intestines; symbiotic, found on book gills and leg bases of the horseshoe crab. *B. candida,* the most common species, grows to 16 mm (5/8") long; *B. propinqua* to 8 mm (5/16"). (order Tricladida)

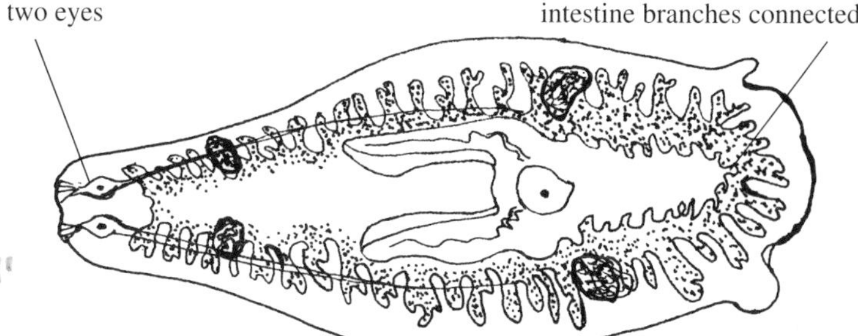

Fig.B. ***SYNCOELIDIUM PELLUCIDUM*****, HORSESHOE CRAB FLATWORM:** Up to 3 mm (1/8") long; symbiotic, found on horseshoe crabs; not as common as *Bdelloura*. (order Tricladida)

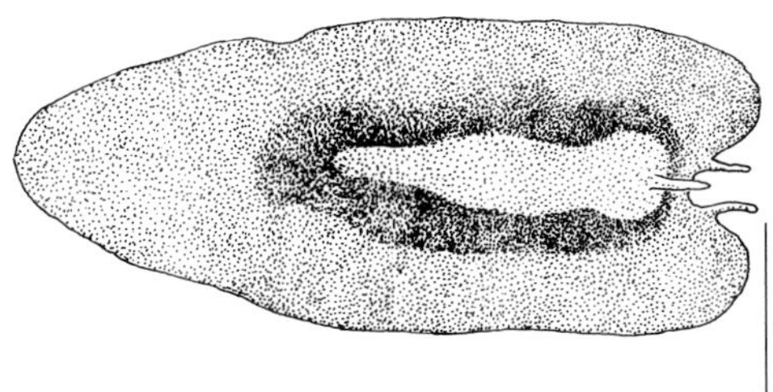

Fig.C. ***POLYCHOERUS CAUDATUS:*** Orange or red; up to 5 mm (3/16") long; occurs on sea lettuce, eelgrass, pilings and rocks. (order Acoela)

Fig.D. ***CHILDIA GROENLANDICA (=C. spinosa):*** Light yellow; about 1 mm (1/32") long; occurs on sea lettuce. (order Acoela)

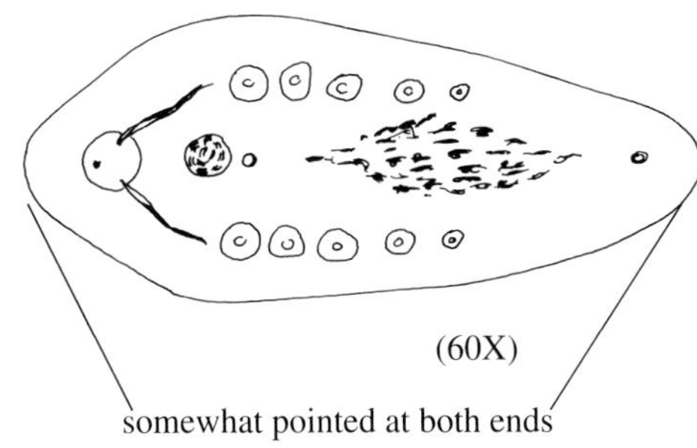

Fig.E. ***APHANOSTOMA DIVERSICOLOR:*** Yellow at front, reddish purple to black in middle; 2 mm (1/16") long; occurs on algae. (order Acoela)

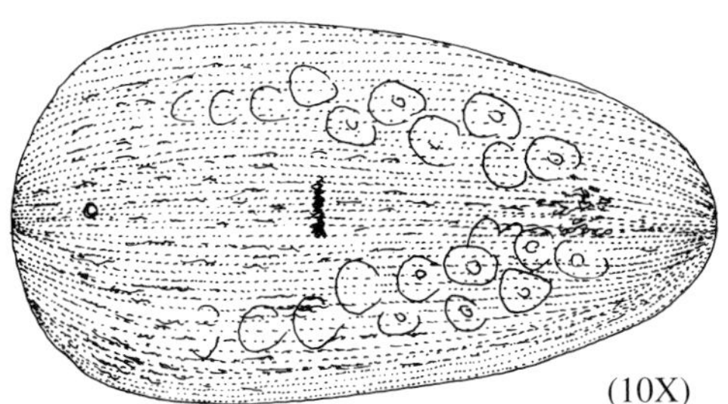

Fig.F. ***ANAPERUS GARDINERI:*** Orange or reddish brown; up to 5 mm (3/16") long; creeps on surface of subtidal mud. (order Acoela)

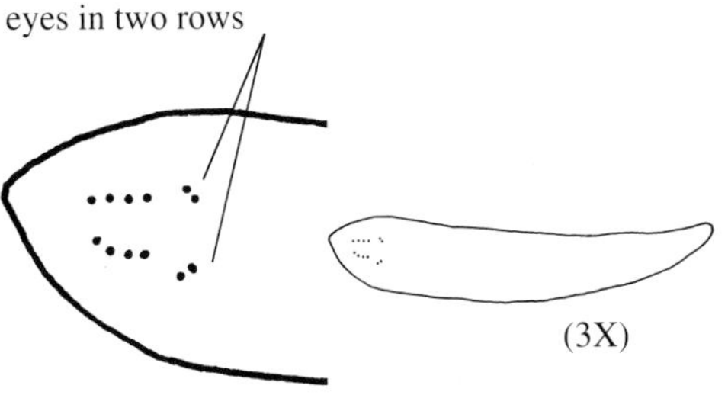

Fig.G. ***EUPLANA GRACILIS*, SLENDER FLATWORM:** Body yellowish to gray-brown; up to 13 mm (1/2") long; lives on pilings, eelgrass, sponges and hydroids; one of the most common flatworms throughout this region. (order Polycladida)

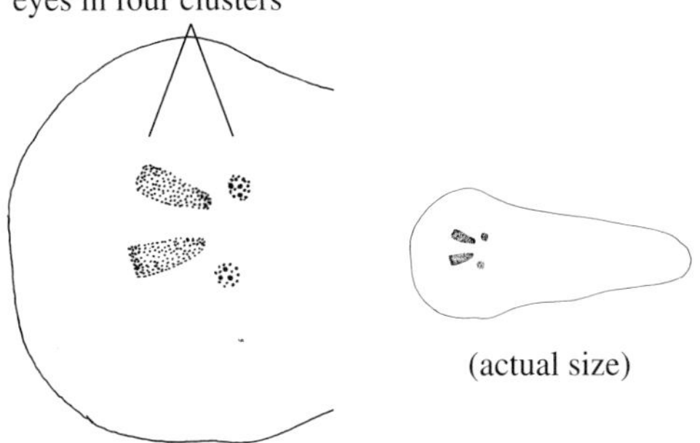

Fig.H. ***NOTOPLANA ATOMATA*, SPECKLED FLATWORM:** Light brown with orange speckles; up to 25 mm (1") long; lives under rocks from lower intertidal zone to deep water; the most common flatworm north of Cape Cod. (order Polycladida)

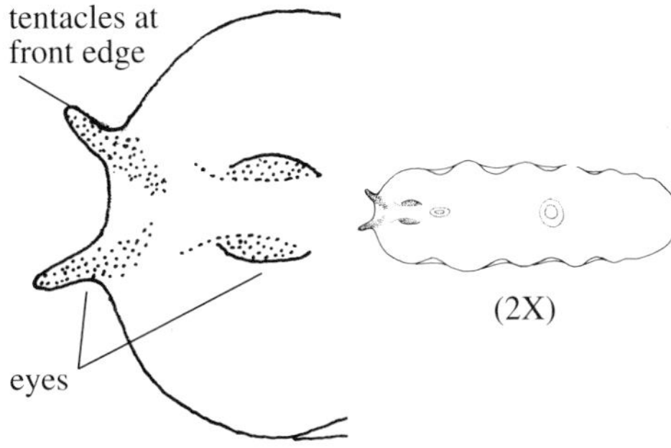

Fig.I. ***PROSTHECEREAUS MACULOSUS*, HORNED FLATWORM:** Tan or pink with brown tentacles; up to 12 mm (1/2") long; on seaweed and pilings near low tide level. (order Polycladida)

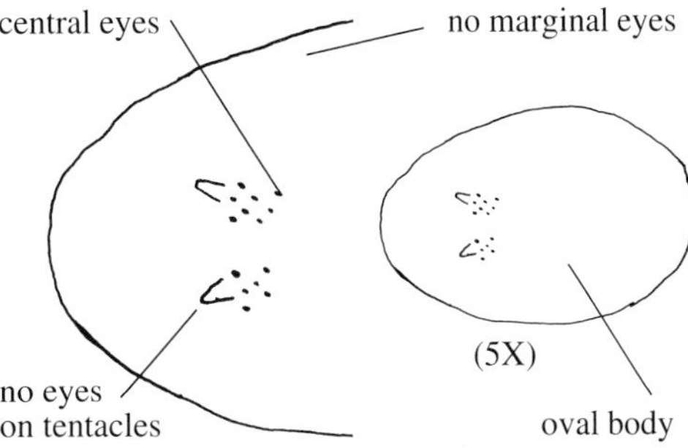

Fig.J. ***HOPLOPLANA INQUILINA*, WHELK FLATWORM:** White; up to 6 mm (1/4") long; symbiotic, lives in the mantle cavity of the whelk, *Busycotypus*, and other snails. (order Polycladida)

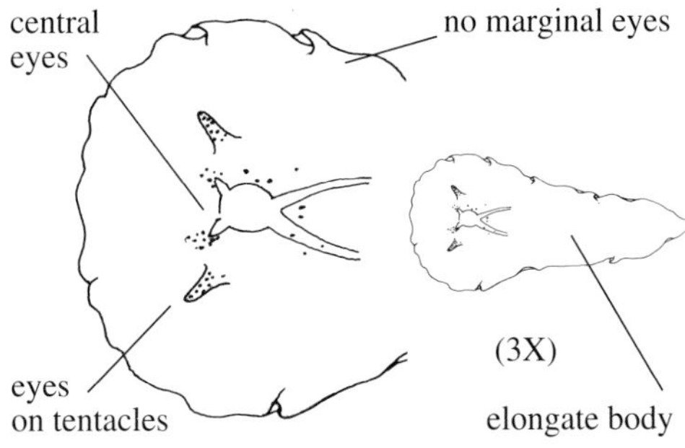

Fig.K. ***GNESIOCEROS FLORIDANA*, SOUTHERN FLATWORM:** Yellowish with brownish spots; up to 8 mm (5/16") long; occurs on eelgrass and sandy bottoms. (order Polycladida)

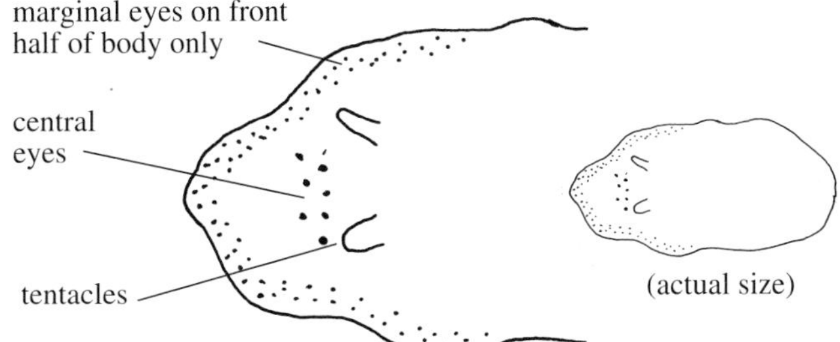

Fig.L. ***STYLOCHUS ELLIPTICUS*, TIDE POOL FLATWORM:** Beige, yellow, gray or brown; up to 2.5 cm (1") long; lives under stones in shallow water and tide pools; feeds on barnacles, oysters and other bivalves; one of the most frequently observed flatworms throughout this region. (order Polycladida)

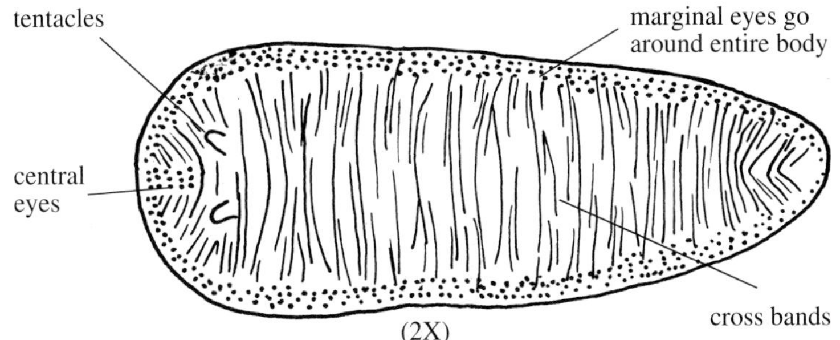

Fig.M. ***STYLOCHUS ZEBRA*, STRIPED FLATWORM:** Distinct pattern of white or yellowish and brown cross bars; up to 38 mm (1 1/2") long; found free living on rocks and pilings, also found in hermit crab shells. (order Polycladida)

TREMATODE AND MONOGENETIC WORMS (FLUKES)
PHYLUM PLATYHELMINTHES, CLASSES TREMATODA AND MONOGENEA

Unsegmented, parasitic flatworms

(Use the key on page 2.18 to determine if you have a trematode or monogenetic worm)

#1.With a relatively large posterior attachment organ (opisthohaptor) with anchors, hooks or suckers (Fig.A) .. **class Monogenea[1], monogenetic worms** (Fig.A)
#1.Without large posterior attachment organ; usually with one or more suckers, but suckers may be lacking (Figs.B-D) .... **class Trematoda**, #2

#2.With a large ventral (located on underside) attachment organ resembling a waffle iron, or a longitudinal row of suckers (Fig.B) .... **subclass Aspidogastrea[1], aspidogastrid trematodes** (Fig.B)
#2.Lacking a large ventral attachment organ as described above (Figs.C,D) .... **subclass Digenea[1], digenetic trematodes**, #3

#3.No attachment organ; tiny worms, less than 1 mm (1/32") long; found in the tissues of snails, bivalves and rarely polychaete worms .... **sporocyst and redia larval stages of digenetic trematodes** (Figs.C,D)
#3.With an oral sucker and usually an additional ventrally located sucker (Fig.C) .... #4

#4.Tail usually present (Fig.C); found within and emerging from sporocysts and redia (Fig.C) in snails, bivalves and rarely polychaete worms; mature forms are active swimmers or crawlers .... **cercaria larval stage of digenetic trematodes** (Fig.C,D)
#4.Tail absent (Fig.C) .... #5

#5.Tiny worms less than 1 mm (1/32") long; usually found in cysts (Figs.C,D) which are very frequently observed as black dots embedded in the skin of fish; may occur in or on vertebrates, invertebrates and occasionally on any available solid object .... **metacercaria[2] larval stage of digenetic trematodes** (Figs.C,D)
#5.Usually larger than 1 mm (1/32"); not encysted; found in the digestive tract of birds, fish and other vertebrates .... **adult digenetic trematodes** (Figs.C,D)

[1]The classification scheme used here divides the class Trematoda into only two subclasses, the Aspidogastrea and the Digenea, with the Monogenea placed in a separate class. Some biologists divide the class Trematoda into three subclasses: Monogenea, Aspidogastrea, and Digenea. Still others treat these subclasses as orders. The Aspidogastrea are called Aspidobothrea in some texts. The identification of monogenetic and trematode worms to the species level is beyond the scope of this book. Refer to Schell (1970) for a more detailed guide to the identification of these parasites.
[2]Some metacercaria do not form cysts and are very difficult to distinguish from cercaria that lack tails.
[3]Cilia are very short hairlike structures. Ciliated forms move with a gliding motion while nonciliated forms move with a creeping or swimming motion.

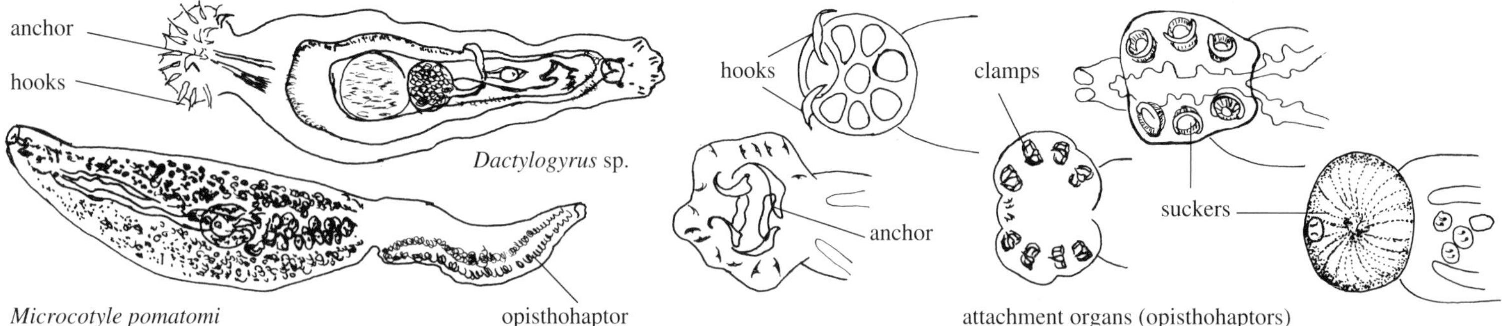

Fig.A. **CLASS[1] MONOGENEA, MONOGENETIC WORMS:** Adults are small, 0.03-20 mm long; lack cilia[3]; with a large posterior attachment organ, the opisthohaptor (shown above) that is muscular and usually bears hooks, anchors, clamps, or suckers; life cycle direct with one host; a ciliated[3] larva (oncomiracidium) is the infective stage; primarily parasites of the skin and gills of fishes. One common species, *Dactylogyrus* sp. (shown above), is a small parasite with large anchors on the opisthohaptor which attaches to the gills of a variety of fishes. Heavy infections of this parasite can cause loss of blood followed by secondary infections by bacteria and fungi which can kill host. Massive fish die offs can occur from outbreaks of this parasite in crowded situations such as in fish culture ponds or aquaria. *Microcotyle pomatomi* (shown above), another monogenetic trematode, is a common gill parasite of bluefish. It is approximately 1 cm (3/8") in length with numerous clamps but no anchors on the opisthohaptor.

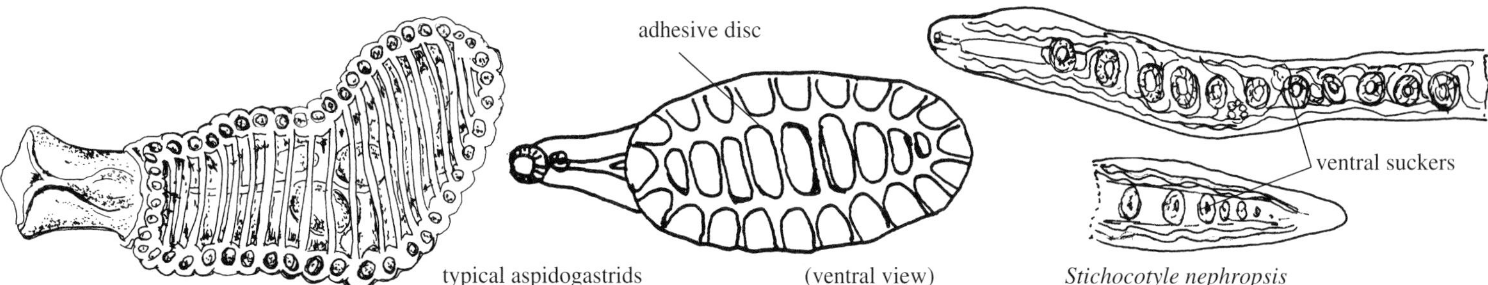

Fig.B. **SUBCLASS[1] ASPIDOGASTREA, ASPIDOGASTRID TREMATODES:** Parasites of mollusks, turtles, and fish; direct development; most species with a single host but species parasitic in vertebrates require an intermediate host. Many aspidogastrid trematodes have a characteristic ventral sucker with longitudinal and transverse muscle ridges. Some species, such as *Stichocotyle nephropsis* (shown above), have a longitudinal row of 24-30 suckers along the ventral surface. This species reaches 11.5 cm (4 1/2") in length and is a parasite in the bile duct of skates and rays with lobsters and other crustaceans serving as intermediate hosts.

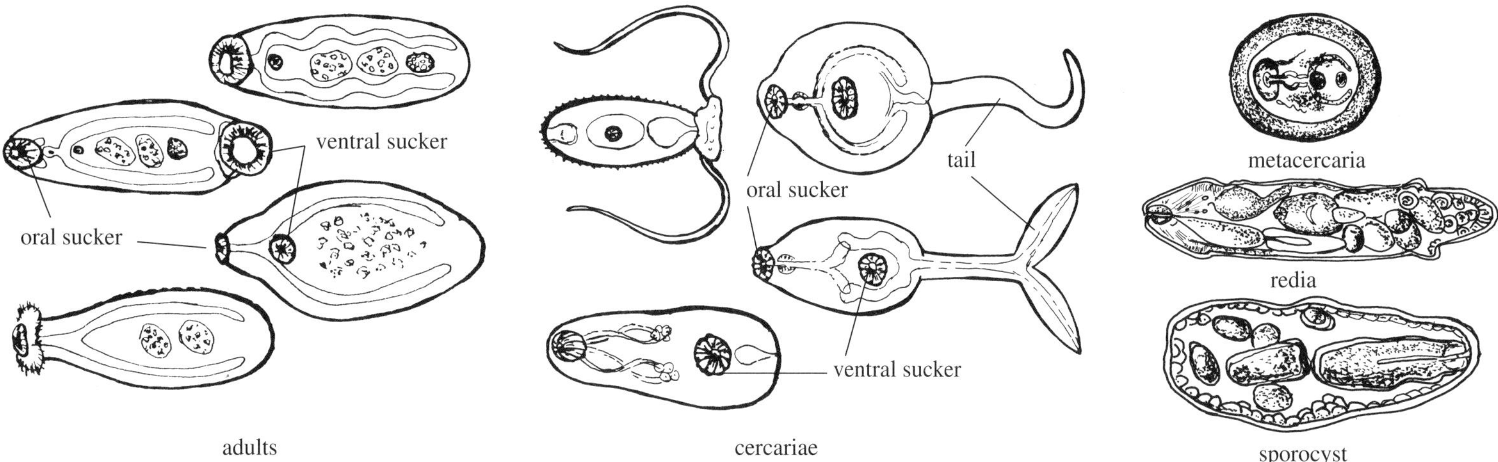

Fig.C. **SUBCLASS[1] DIGENEA, DIGENETIC TREMATODES (FLUKES):** Adults are 2 mm (1/16") to 6 cm (2 1/2") in length; with an oral sucker and a ventral sucker usually present; life cycle indirect and complex with at least two intermediate hosts and a number of larval stages. The life cycles of three common species are described in Fig.D.

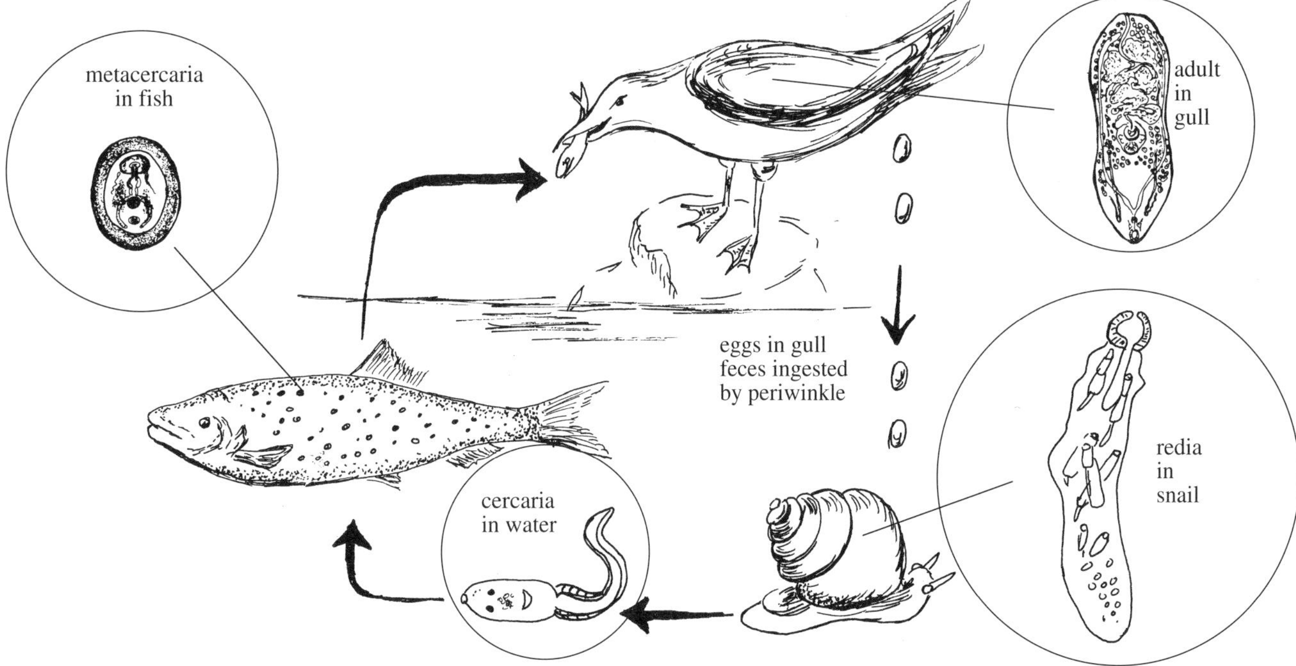

Fig.D. **DIGENETIC TREMATODE LIFE CYCLES:** *Cryptocotyle lingua* is a very common species in southern New England and its life cycle is diagramed above. Adults are intestinal parasites of birds such as gulls. The adults produce eggs which are deposited on rocks and in the water with the bird droppings. The common shore periwinkles, *Littorina* spp., become infected when they ingest these eggs. The first larval stage, called miracidia, hatch from the eggs and metamorphose into rediae which are found in the digestive gland of the snails. Rediae produce cercaria which leave the snails and penetrate the skin of fishes forming cysts, the metacercaria stage. Fish respond to this invasion by depositing a pigment around the metacercaria cysts causing them to appear black. This condition, called "black spot", can often be observed in a variety fish species. When an infected fish is eaten by a bird the metacercariae excyst ("hatch") and mature into adults, completing the life cycle. If humans eat the skin of raw or improperly cooked fish, they can become infected.

Austrobilharzia variglandis is another digenetic trematode that is quite common around mudflats. The adult trematode parasitizes the mesenteric veins of birds, commonly gulls. The adults produce eggs that are passed out into the water with the feces of the birds and hatch into free swimming miracidium larvae. These larvae penetrate the eastern mudsnail, *Ilyanassa obsoleta*, and metamorphose into sporocysts, which are found in the haemocoel of the snails' digestive gland. Sporocysts produce cercariae which leave the snail and actively swim around in search of their normal final host, a gull or other bird. Infection is accomplished by burrowing through the host's skin. Occasionally, the free swimming cercariae will accidently encounter a human who is wading or swimming in the water. The cercariae can penetrate the person's skin and cause an intense itching and a rash known as "swimmer's itch" or "clam digger's itch." Fortunately, the human body has defense mechanisms which prevent the cercaria from maturing into the parasitic adult stage.

Proctoeces maculatus is a digenetic trematode that, in temperate waters, can complete its entire life cycle in one host, the blue mussel, *Mytilus edulis.* In the summer and fall, the most prevalent stages include sporocysts, which are very active, cercariae, and unencysted metacercariae. Adults appear in greater numbers in the winter. This parasite is very common and causes the condition known as "orange disease" due to the coloration of mussel tissue infected with sporocysts, which are usually bright orange. However, it is also possible to find uninfected mussels with bright orange tissue. In subtropical waters, the life cycle of this species usually involves more than one host with the adult an intestinal parasite of labrid fishes (wrasses) and various mussels serving as intermediate hosts.

TAPEWORMS: PHYLUM PLATYHELMINTHES, CLASS CESTOIDEA (CESTODA)

Parasitic worms with three body regions (Fig.A): a scolex (attachment organ), a neck and a strobila (series of body segments); adults are long, attaining lengths of 12 m (40') in some species; digestive system absent; development can be indirect (with larval stages) or direct (without larval stages); life cycles can be indirect (with intermediate hosts) or direct (without intermediate hosts)

(Use the key on page 2.18 to determine if you have a tapeworm)

The identification of a tapeworm to species is beyond the scope of this book. Refer to Schmidt (1970) for a more detailed guide to the identification of tapeworms. A parasitologist should be consulted if it is necessary to make a positive identification of a tapeworm species. The species described here are encountered in marine hosts and are representative of the major tapeworm orders. Fortunately, in southern New England, tapeworms rarely occur in humans as the result of eating seafood. A few cases have been reported, however, and thorough cooking of fish is a recommended precaution.

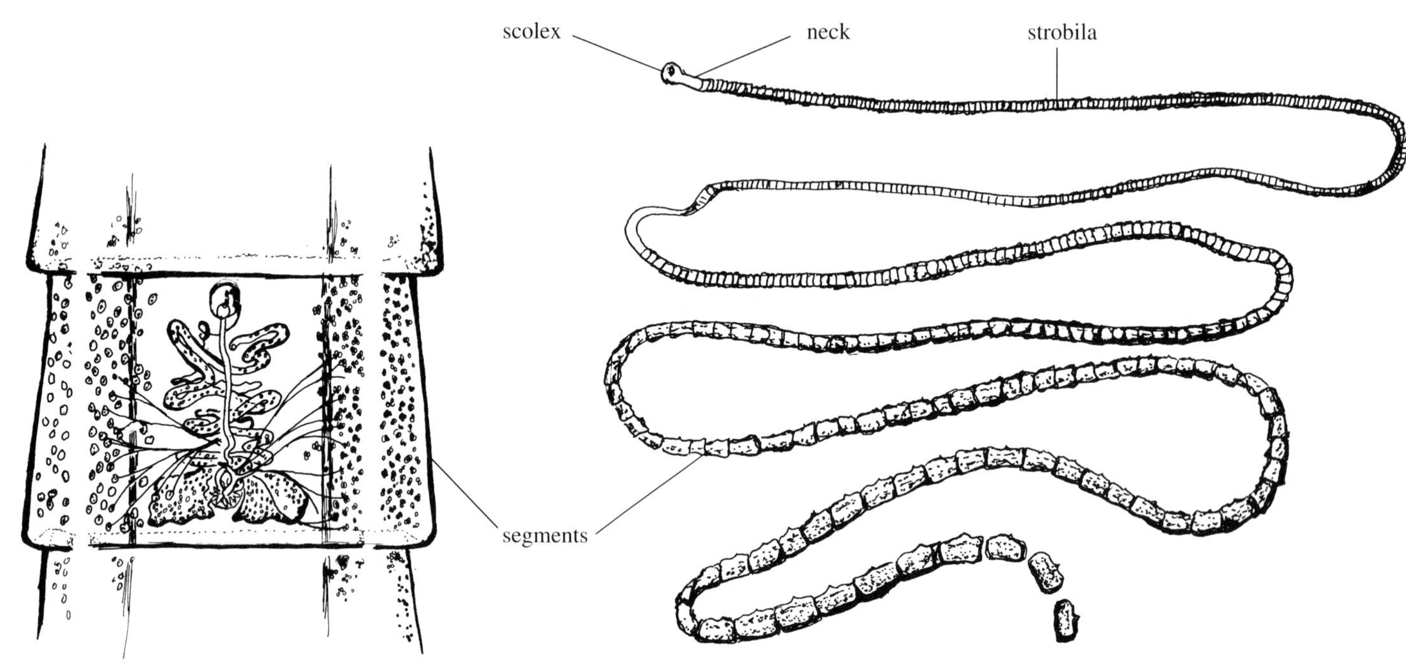

Fig.A. **TYPICAL ADULT TAPEWORM**

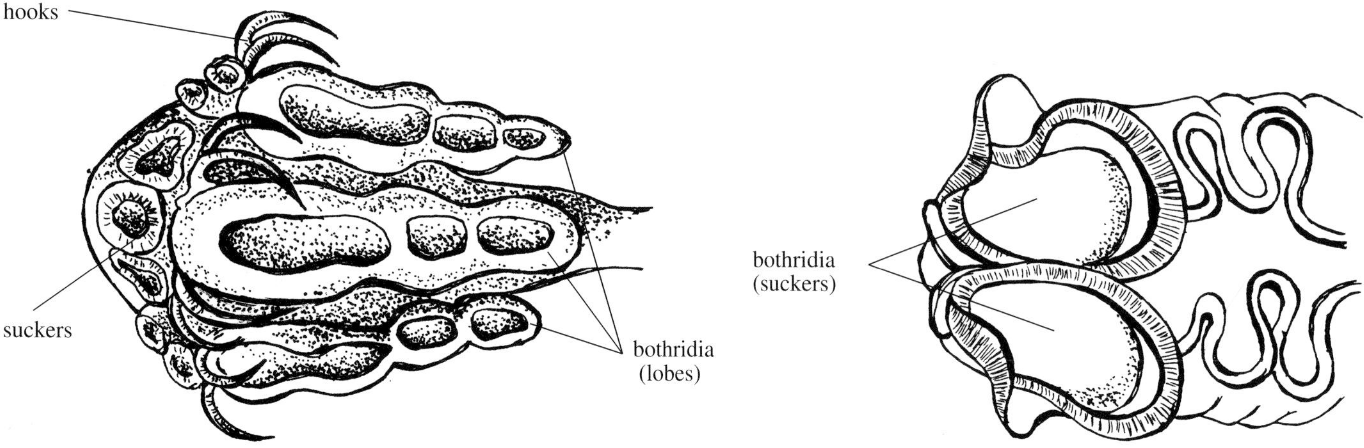

Fig.B. **SCOLEX OF *CALLIOBOTHRIUM VERTICILLUM*, TETRAPHYLLIDEAN TAPEWORM:** Adults are spiral valve parasites of sharks and are common in the smooth dogfish, *Mustelus canis*. Their life cycle is similar to *Bothriocephalus* (Fig.E) except that the pleurocercoid stage occurs in a hermit crab, *Pagurus pollicaris*, rather than a fish. The scolex of a tetraphyllidean tapeworm has four lobes known as bothridia and usually has hooks.

Fig.C. **SCOLEX OF *TETRABOTHRIUS CYLINDRACEUS*, TETRAPHYLLIDEAN TAPEWORM:** Adults are intestinal parasites of birds and mammals. They are found in the herring gull, *Larus argentatus*. Their life cycle is unknown but is thought to involve copepods. The scolex of this tapeworm has four sucker shaped muscular bothridia with an anterior flap.

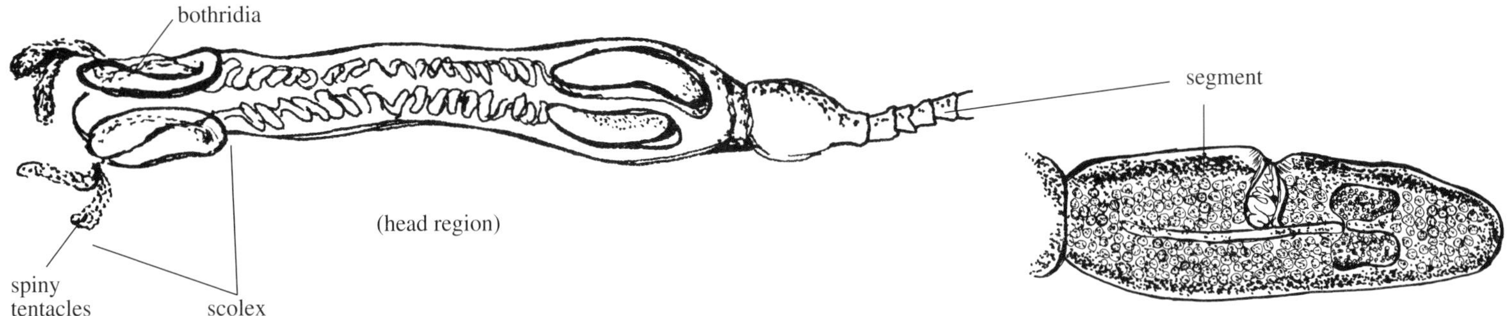

Fig.D. ***LACISTORHYNCHUS TENUIS*, TRYPANORHYNCHAN TAPEWORM:** Adults are parasites in the spiral valves of sharks, skates, and rays. They are common in the smooth dogfish, *Mustelus canis*. Their life cycle is similar to *Bothriocephalus* (Fig.E). Pleurocercoids of this species have been reported from squids. The scolex of a tapeworm in the order Trypanorhyncha has two or four lobes known as bothridia and spiny tentacles that can be retracted into sheaths.

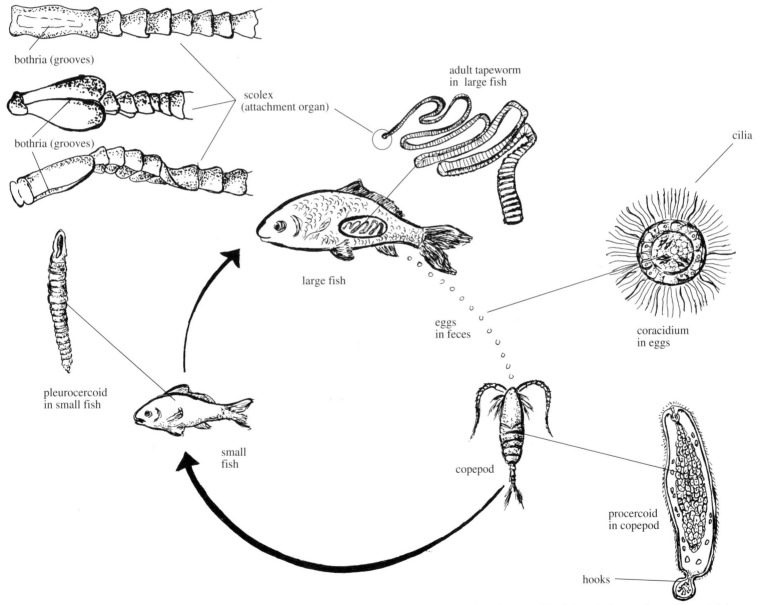

bothria (grooves)

scolex
(attachment organ)

adult tapeworm
in large fish

bothria (grooves)

cilia

large fish

eggs
in feces

coracidium
in eggs

pleurocercoid
in small fish

small
fish

copepod

procercoid
in copepod

hooks

Fig. E. ***BOTHRIOCEPHALUS* SP., PSEUDOPHYLLIDEAN TAPEWORM:** The life cycle and larval stages of *Bothriocephalus* are shown above. Adults are intestinal parasites of fishes. The adult worms reach up to 9 m (30') in length and produce eggs that pass into the water along with the fishes' feces. In the water, a larval stage, a coracidium, develops inside the eggs and hatches out. If a coracidium is eaten by a copepod it develops into a procercoid stage. If the copepod is eaten by a small fish, the procercoid migrates into the muscle of the fish and develops into a pleurocercoid. Larger fish are infected and become the final hosts when they eat the smaller fish. Tapeworms in the order Pseudophyllidea have a scolex (attachment organ) with one or two bothria, elongate groove shaped structures.

RIBBON OR PROBOSCIS WORMS: PHYLUM NEMERTINEA (RHYNCHOCOELA, NEMERTEA)

Unsegmented worms; no appendages; with retractile proboscis; with mouth at anterior end on ventral side; with anus at posterior end.

(Use key on page 2.16 to determine if you have a ribbon or proboscis worm)

#1.With 2 eyespots on head[1] (Figs. A,B)........#2
#1.With 4 or more eyespots on head (Figs.C-F) ....#3
#1.Without any eyespots on head (Figs.G-J) ....#6

#2.Found on the gills and egg masses of crabs, such as the green crab, blue crab and lady crab .... ***Carcinonemertes carcinophila*** (Fig.A)
#2.Free living worms; found offshore .... ***Amphiporus bioculatus*** (Fig.B)

#3.With a groove (cephalic groove) running lengthwise along both sides of the head; no cirrus[1] (pointed tail-like projection) .... ***Lineus* spp.** (Fig.D)
#3.With a groove (cephalic groove) running lengthwise along both sides of the head; with a cirrus[1] (pointed tail-like projection) .... ***Micrura affinis*** (Fig.I)
#3.Without a longitudinal groove on sides of head (Figs.C,E,F); grooves may be absent or may run across head or at an angle behind rear corner of head ....#4

#4.With more than 12 eyespots on each side of head (older worms have up to 40); eyespots extend behind brain region .... ***Zygonemertes virescens*** (Fig.C)
#4.With 6-12 eyespots on each side of head; eyespots do not extend behind brain; eyespots may be in rows or scattered on head .... ***Amphiporus* spp.** (Fig.E)
#4.With four eyespots set in a square pattern on head (Fig.F); often colorful worms ....#5

#5.Body is slender and cylindrical; head not demarcated from body by any transverse grooves .... ***Oerstedia dorsalis***[2]
#5.Body is short and flattened; head is demarcated from body by inconspicuous transverse grooves .... ***Tetrastemma* spp.** (Fig.F)

#6.With a groove (cephalic groove) along the sides of the head (Figs.H,I); worm may be longer than 15 cm (6") and wider than 6 mm (1/4"); with a pointed projection (cirrus) at posterior end[1]........#7
#6.Without a groove along the sides of the head; worm is never longer than 15 cm (6") or wider than 6 mm (1/4"); with or without a pointed projection (cirrus) at posterior end ....#9

#7.Mouth is large, slotlike (Fig.H); body may be flattened, ribbonlike with thin edges, or may be thick ....#8
#7.Mouth is small, round (Fig.I); body is slender, may be flattened in intestinal region but edges are not thin and ribbonlike .... ***Micrura* spp.** (Fig.I)

#8.Front end narrow and thick, posterior broad and flat; brown, olive, purple or red; up to 25 cm (10") long, 1.2 cm (1/2") wide .... ***Cerebratulus luridus*** (Fig.G)
#8.Ribbonlike, with thin edges; beige or cream, tinged with pink or yellow; up to 1 m (3') long, 2.5 cm (1") wide ... ***Cerebratulus lacteus*, ribbon worm** (Fig.H)

#9.With a posterior sucker disc; found in the mantle cavity of clams, mussels and other bivalves .... ***Malacobdella grossa*** (Fig.J)
#9.Without a posterior sucking disc; not usually found inside bivalves ....#10

#10.Body is flattened, at least in posterior region; may be up to 5 mm (3/16") in width ....#11
#10.Body is threadlike, rounded in cross section; not more than 1 mm (1/32") thick ....#12

#11.Tail with long cirrus[1] (pointed projection); head tapers to point .... ***Zygeupolia rubens***[3]
#11.Tail without any cirrus; head is rounded at tip .... ***Carinoma tremaphoros***[4]

#12.Body coils into a tight spiral; grows up to 10 cm (4") long; head is long and pointed; does not live in tubes .... ***Procephalothrix spiralis***[5]
#12.Body does not usually coil into a spiral; up to 2.5 cm (1") long; head is broad; found in thin, delicate tubes .... ***Tubulanus pellucidus***[6]

[1]These worms break up into pieces very easily when they are handled, making it difficult to obtain the entire worm. Be sure to examine the worm carefully to determine whether or not the anterior and/or posterior end of the worm is present. The anterior end of the worm is essential for conclusive identification. Often the posterior end and/or the cirrus breaks off and is missing.
[2]*Oerstedia dorsalis* is variable in color and pattern; 2 cm (3/4") long by 2 mm (1/16") wide; occurs on rocks and pilings among other fouling organisms.
[3]*Zygeupolia rubens* is white or rose; up to 8 cm (3") long by 5 mm (3/16") wide; abundant in sand in shallow waters.
[4]*Carinoma tremaphoros* has a whitish head region, the posterior region is yellowish, reddish or beige; up to 15 cm (6") long and 5 mm (3/16") wide; found in shallow, protected water in silty clay.
[5]*Procephalothrix spiralis* is white, tinged with red, yellow or green; up to 10 cm (4") long and 0.8 mm (1/32") wide; lives under stones and in sand in intertidal zone.
[6]*Tubulanus pellucidus* is whitish, sometimes with a pale yellow or orange line; grows up to 2.5 cm (1") long and 0.8 mm (1/32") wide; found in delicate, thin walled tubes among bryozoans and colonial tunicates.

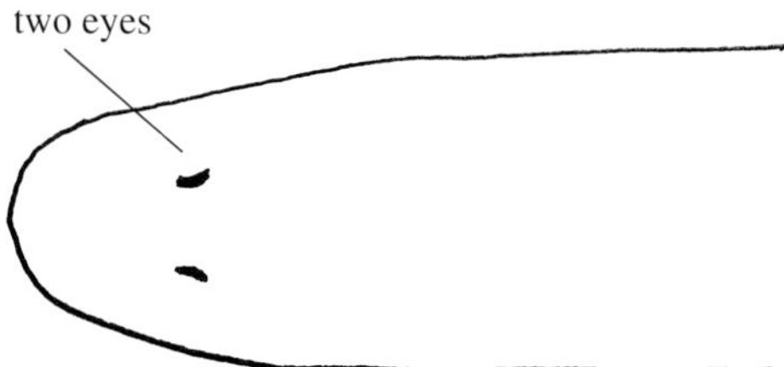

Fig.A. ***CARCINONEMERTES CARCINOPHILA:*** Yellowish, rosy or brick red; up to 4 cm (1 1/2") long; found on gills and eggs of crabs.

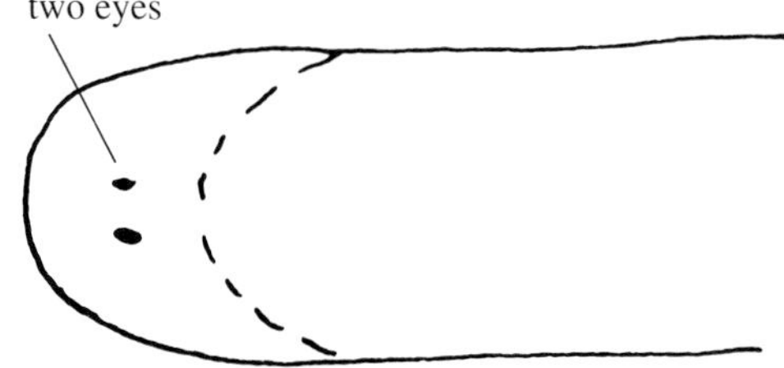

Fig.B. ***AMPHIPORUS BIOCULATUS:*** Orange, yellow, red or pinkish; up to 4 cm (1 1/2") long by 3 mm (1/8") wide; found offshore.

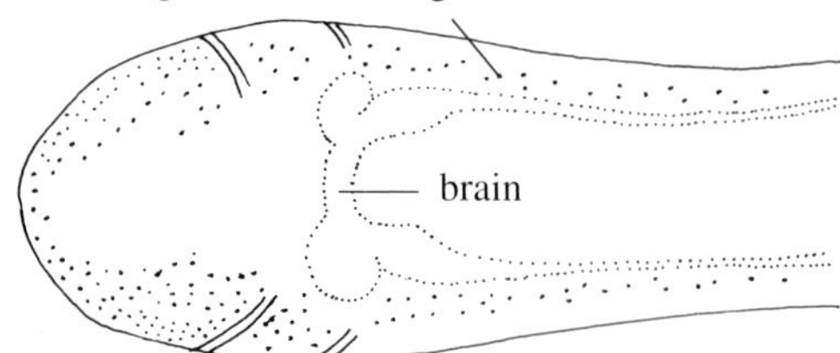

Fig.C. ***ZYGONEMERTES VIRESCENS:*** Color variable; up to 4 cm (1 1/2") long by 2 mm (1/16") wide; common in intertidal zone or shallow water.

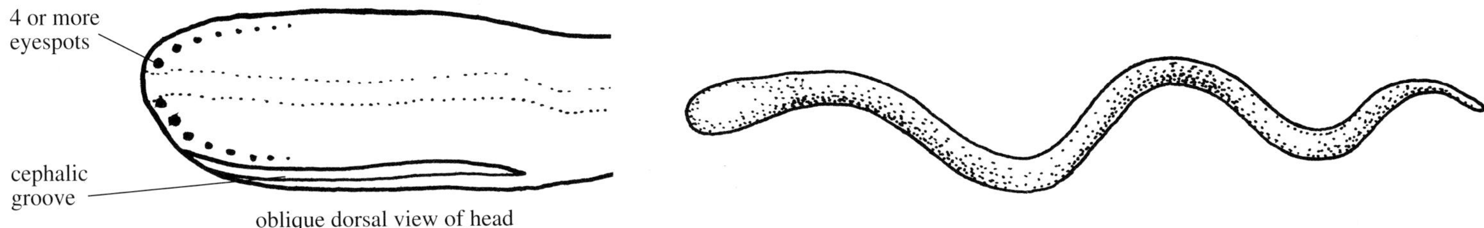

Fig.D. ***LINEUS* SPP.:** *Lineus bicolor* is green with a white or yellow midstripe; grows up to 5 cm (2") long and 1.5 mm (1/16") wide; found offshore. *Lineus arenicola* is pale red; grows up to 10 cm (4") long and 2 mm (1/16") wide; found in intertidal zone in sand and among rocks. This species has 4 eyespots whereas some of the others have up to 16. *Lineus socialis* is brown tinged with green or red; grows up to 15 cm (6") long and 3 mm (1/8") wide; found in intertidal zone in sand and among pebbles. This species contracts in coils and is sometimes found with many worms tangled together in a mass. The other species do not coil. They contract by getting thicker and shorter. *Lineus ruber* is variable in color, ranging from dark red to green to brownish green; 15 cm (6") long and 4 mm (3/16") wide; found in intertidal zone in sand and among pebbles.

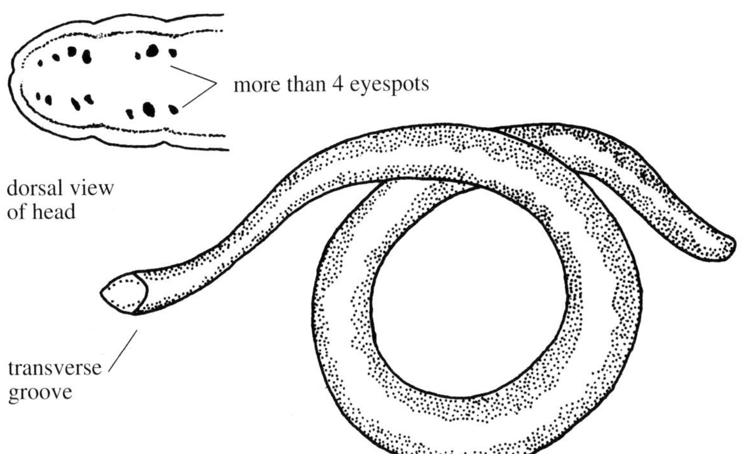

Fig.E. ***AMPHIPORUS* SPP.:** The most common local species grow up to 4 cm (1 1/2") long and 3 mm (1/8") wide; found in intertidal zone in tide pools, among seaweed, hydroids and on pilings. Numerous species occur in this region. Refer to Gosner (1971) to identify.

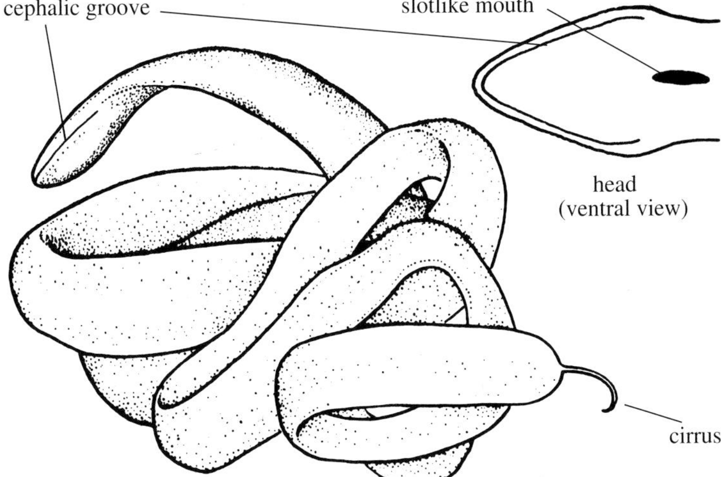

Fig.H. ***CEREBRATULUS LACTEUS,* RIBBON WORM:** Red, pink, beige, or milky white; often grows over 1 m (3') long and 1.2 cm (1/2") wide; found in intertidal zone under rocks and in mud. **17.04 A** **17.04 B**

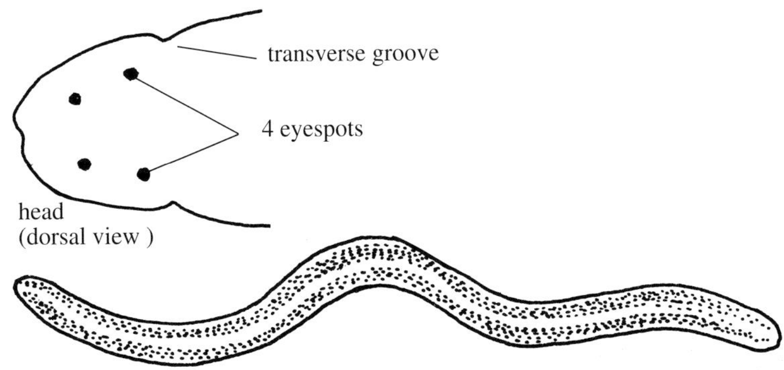

Fig.F. ***TETRASTEMMA* SPP.:** Occur on rocks, pilings, and eelgrass beds. Two species are striped and are up to 3 cm (1 1/4") long. *T. vittatum* is usually green with 2 yellow stripes on body and 6 green stripes on head. *T. elegans* is yellowish with brown stripes. The other species are unstriped and are usually under 2 cm (3/4") long. *T. candidum* is pale green or yellowish with a white head. *T. vermiculus* is yellowish to red, often with brown flecks, and dark bands connecting eyespots. *T. wilsoni* is white or translucent with white flecks.

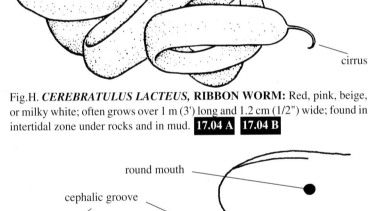

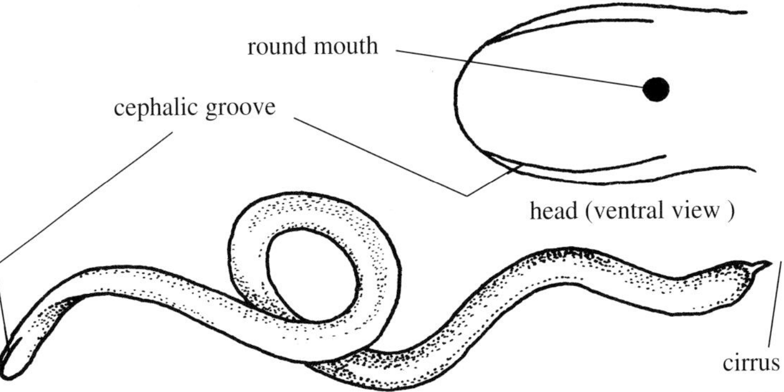

Fig.I. ***MICRURA* SPP.:** Two species occur under stones and in sand in intertidal zone. *Micrura leidyi* is deep red or purple red, paler on underside and edges of the head; up to 30 cm (12") long and 6 mm (1/4") wide. *Micrura caeca* is pale red, yellowish red or brownish red; up to 12 cm (5") long and 3 mm (1/8") wide. *Micrura affinis* occurs in water over 10 m (30') deep north of Cape Cod. It is red or brown; up to 15 cm (6") long; has 4-6 eyes on each side of head.

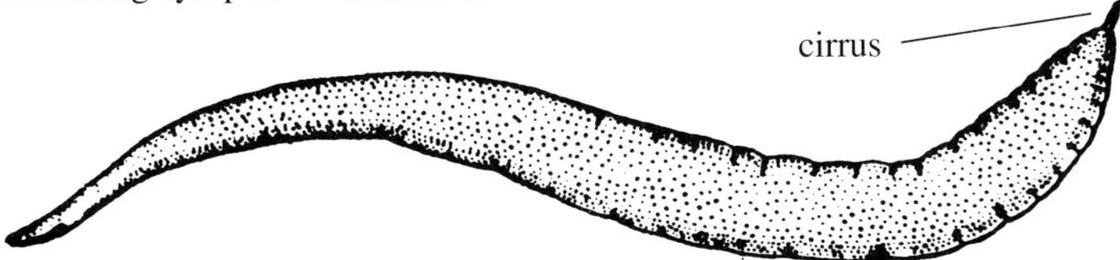

Fig.G. ***CEREBRATULUS LURIDUS:*** Chocolate brown, olive or purplish brown; up to 30 cm (12") long; found in sandy mud offshore.

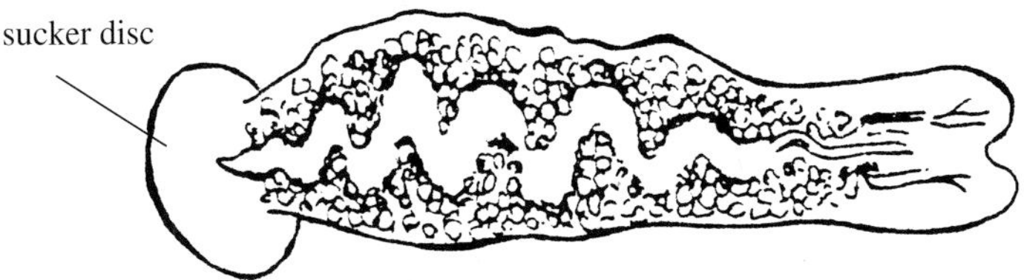

Fig.J. ***MALACOBDELLA GROSSA:*** Yellowish white; up to 39 mm (1 1/2") long; symbiont in the mantle cavity of clams, mussels and other bivalves.

ROUNDWORMS: PHYLUM NEMATODA

Unsegmented worms which taper at both ends and lack appendages; body cavity filled with fluid; digestive system is complete with a mouth and an anus; body wall has longitudinal muscles only, which accounts for characteristic whiplike motion; sexes are separate; life cycles range from free living to parasitic with all intermediate possibilities occurring.

(Use the key on page 2.16 to determine if you have a free living nematode worm. Use the key on page 2.18 if it is a parasite)

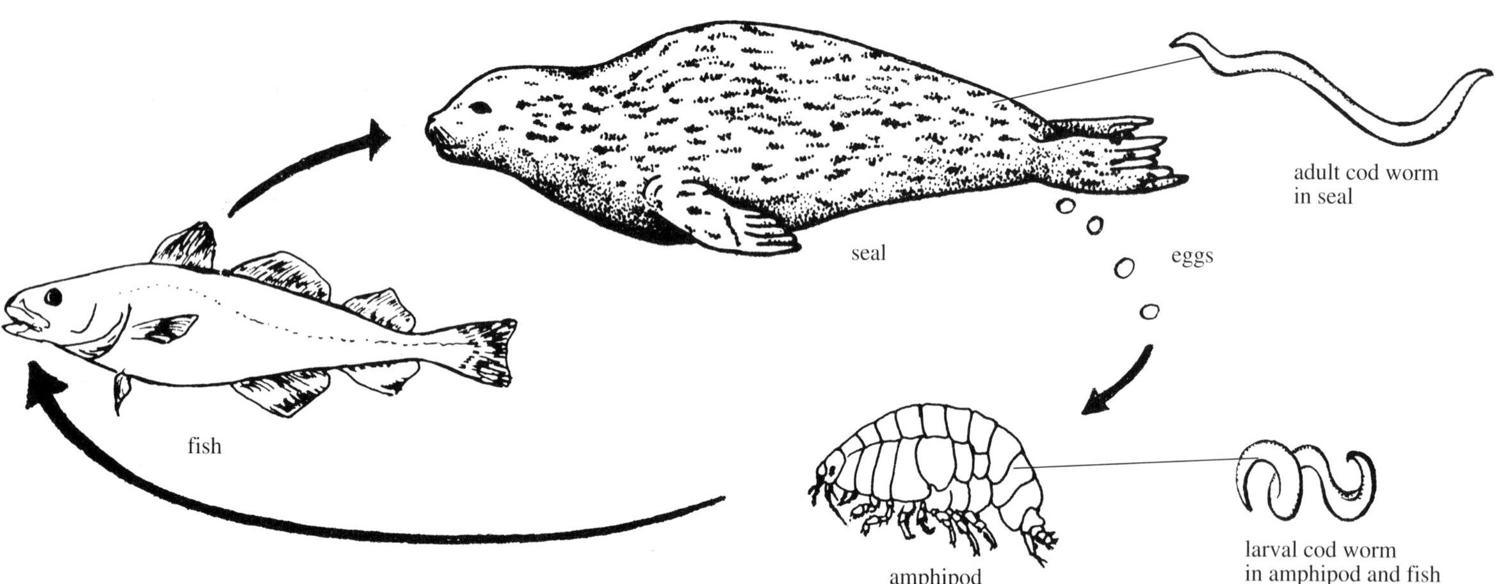

Fig.A. **PARASITIC AND SYMBIOTIC NEMATODES:** Life cycles of parasitic nematodes can be direct, involving just one host, or indirect with a number of intermediate hosts. Consult a parasitologist to identify parasitic and symbiotic nematodes. The cod worm, *Phocanema decipiens*, is an example of a common parasitic nematode found in marine fishes and its life cycle is diagramed above. Larval cod worms are beige to brown; about 4 cm (1 1/2") long; loosely coiled in the musculature of a fish host. These worms live as adults in the stomachs of seals where they deposit up to 400,000 eggs per female. Eggs pass out in the feces of the seal and the larval stages molt, hatch, and infect invertebrates, mostly tiny crustaceans such as amphipods. If eaten by a small fish, the larvae burrow through the fish's stomach wall and enter the body muscles. If this fish is eaten by a larger fish, such as a codfish, the process of migration to the musculature is repeated. Larvae remain in the fish and do not develop until eaten by a seal. In the seal's stomach the larvae molt and mature into adults. This species is quite common and, if looked for carefully, can be found in fish purchased at fish markets. Cod worms have been reported to occur in humans but these infections have not led to serious illness and were eliminated naturally. A closely related genus, *Anisakis,* is infective to humans and can be fatal. Most cases have been reported from Japan and Europe where raw fish is eaten. **LARVAE OF THESE WORMS ARE KILLED WHEN FISH IS PROPERLY COOKED!**

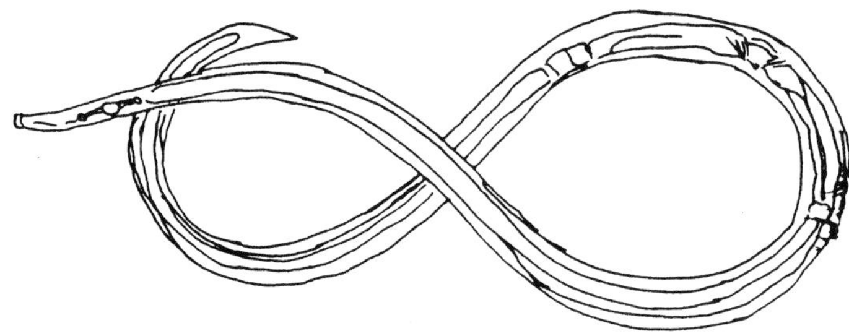

Fig.B. **FREE LIVING NEMATODES:** Usually tiny, microscopic in size, less than 1 mm (1/32") in length; often white or colorless and transparent. Free living nematodes are extremely abundant, with a great many different species occuring in enormous numbers at all depths in the water and in bottom sediments. Over 200 species representing 25 families of nematodes have been reported (Tietjen, 1977) in the bottom sediments of this region. Refer to Keppner and Tarjan (1989) for a key to the genera of free living marine nematodes of the order Enoplida and for a list of references useful for the identification of other marine nematodes.

SPINY-HEADED WORMS: PHYLUM ACANTHOCEPHALA

Unsegmented worms lacking appendages; with a neck, a trunk, and a proboscis armed with recurved spines used to attach to the intestinal wall of the host; body cavity filled with fluid; digestive system absent; sexes are separate; all known species are parasitic; life cycle involves at least two hosts and often employs paratenic hosts (temporary hosts used for transport only).

(Use key on page 2.18 to determine if you have a spiny-headed worm)

The identification of a spiny-headed worm to species is beyond the scope of this book and a parasitologist should be consulted. The following is an example of a a spiny-headed worm that has marine hosts.

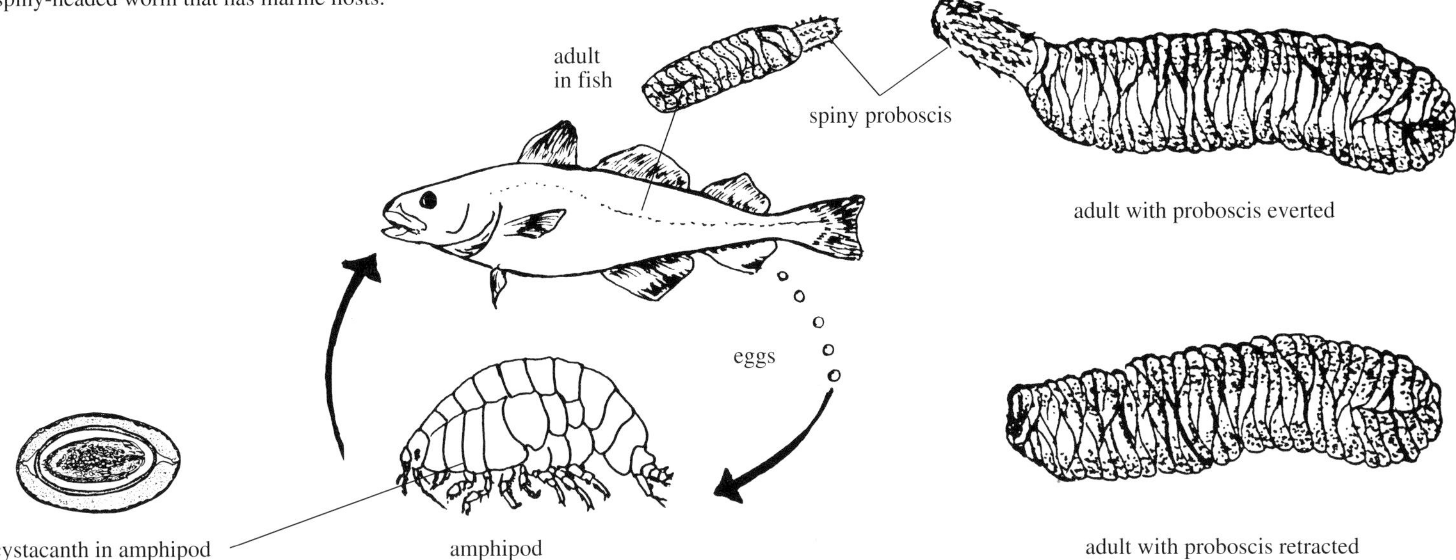

Fig.A. ***ECHINORHYNCHUS GADI:*** Adults are intestinal parasites of cod, flounder and many other fish species. Males grow up to 2 cm (3/4") long, females up to 8 cm (3 1/4") long. Eggs of this parasite are voided with the feces of the fish. If an egg is eaten by an amphipod (first intermediate host), several larval stages develop. The worm then forms a cystacanth, a juvenile stage which is enclosed within a cyst and has a retracted proboscis. If an infected amphipod is eaten by an appropriate fish, the cystacanth develops into an adult. If the amphipod is eaten by an inappropriate fish (a paratenic host), the proboscis of the cystacanth everts and penetrates the intestinal wall. The cystacanth remains dormant until this temporary host is eaten by an appropriate host fish.

PEANUT WORMS: PHYLUM SIPUNCULOIDEA

Unsegmented worms with a two part body consisting of a retractible introvert and a thicker trunk; without appendages.

(Use the key on page 2.16 to determine if you have a peanut worm)

#1.Lives in empty snail shells and worm tubes; usually under 12 mm (1/2") long .... ***Phascolion strombi*** (Fig.B)
#1.Lives in sand or mud in intertidal zone or shallow water; often up to 15 cm (6") long .... ***Phascolopsis gouldii*, peanut worm**[1] (Fig.C)

[1]Several other species occur on the outer continental shelf and slope of this region. Refer to Cutler (1977) to identify sipunculids collected in deep water.

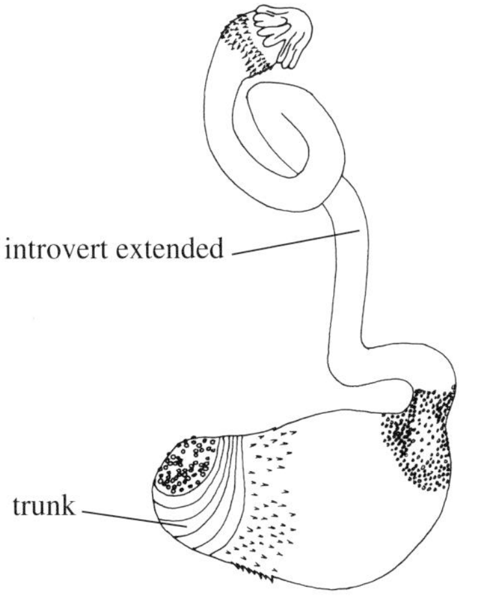

Fig.B. ***PHASCOLION STROMBI:*** Whitish or brownish; usually less than 12 mm (1/2") long; lives in empty snail shells and worm tubes.

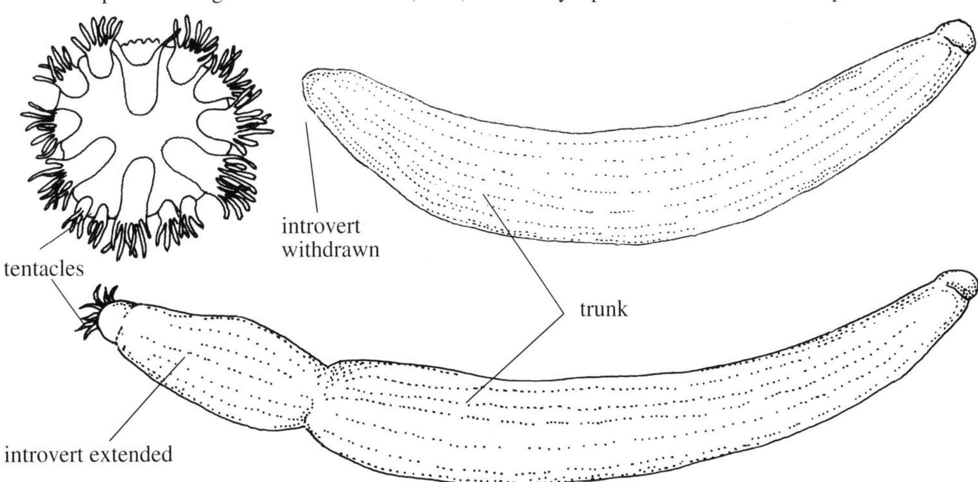

Fig.C. ***PHASCOLOPSIS GOULDII (=Golfingia g. =Phascolosoma g.),* PEANUT WORM:** Gray, green, tan, pink, or whitish; trunk may reach 30 cm (12") long but rarely over 15 cm (6"); introvert is about 1/3 trunk length when extended; found in sand or mud at low tide level and offshore in shallow water.

BUSHY AND ERECT BRYOZOANS: PHYLUM BRYOZOA (ECTOPROCTA)[1]

Bryozoans that are highly branched and grow in erect tufts.

(Use key on page 2.04 to determine if you have a bushy bryozoan)

#1. Individual zooids (cells) are very lightly calcified (not shell-like); colonies are soft and bushy, very similar to branching seaweeds; occasionally with beaklike structures (avicularia) on some portions of the colony (Figs.A-F) .... #2
#1. Individual zooids (cells) highly calcified (shell-like), with numerous pores; colonies are stiff, twiglike or encrusting (Figs.G,H) .... #7

#2. With no spines or very short spines; spines, if present, are shorter than zooid (Figs. A-D) .... #3
#2. With long spines extending from each zooid (Figs.E,F), spines are as long as the zoids (Note: spines can be easily broken by careless treatment) .... #6

#3. Zooids are paired back to back with oval openings facing opposite directions; colonies are tree shaped; no avicularia .... ***Eucratea loricata*** (Fig.C)
#3. Zooids are joined side by side with openings facing in same direction; colonies are bushy; with beaklike avicularia (Figs.A,B,D) .... #4

#4. With 4-7 spines on the sides and top edges of each opening; with 4-12 rows of zooids on each branch .... ***Dendrobeania murrayana*** (Fig.D)
#4. Spines, if any, only at the corners of the top edges of openings, none on sides; with 2-6 rows of zooids on each branch, usually 2-3 rows ..... ***Bugula* spp.**, #5

#5. Branches of colony are spiraled or whorled; 2 rows of zooids per branch; 1-3 spines at top edge of opening; very common .... ***Bugula turrita*, spiral-tufted bushy bryozoan** (Fig.A)
#5. Branches of colony are somewhat flattened and fanlike; 3-6 rows of zooids per branch; 1-3 spines at top edge of opening; less common .... ***Bugula simplex*, fan-tufted bushy bryozoan** (Fig.B)
#5. Branches of colony are fanlike or cup shaped; 2 rows of zooids per branch; 4-7 spines at top edge of opening; rare .... **other *Bugula* spp.**[1] (not shown)

#6. Zooids are trumpet shaped with openings nearly at the outer end; with 4-8 long spines per zooid; with beaklike avicularia .... ***Bicellariella ciliata*** (Fig.E)
#6. Zooids are cylindrical with oval openings on the sides; with 1-2 long spines per zooid; with shieldlike plate in front of opening .... ***Tricellaria gracilis*** (Fig.F)

#7. With narrow flexible joints (nodes) between tubular zooids; colonies are erect, twiglike .... ***Crisia* spp.**[1]**, jointed-tube bryozoans** (Fig.G)
#7. Without flexible joints (nodes) between tubular zooids; colonies are encrusting or fanlike with individual zooids projecting above surface .... **family Tubuliporidae, panpipe bryozoans**[1] (Fig.H)

[1] **WARNING:** This key includes all of the common bushy or erect bryozoans that occur in southern New England, but rarer species have been omitted. Refer to Ryland and Hayward (1991) for a positive identification, especially for species collected in deep waters or in the northern end of this region.

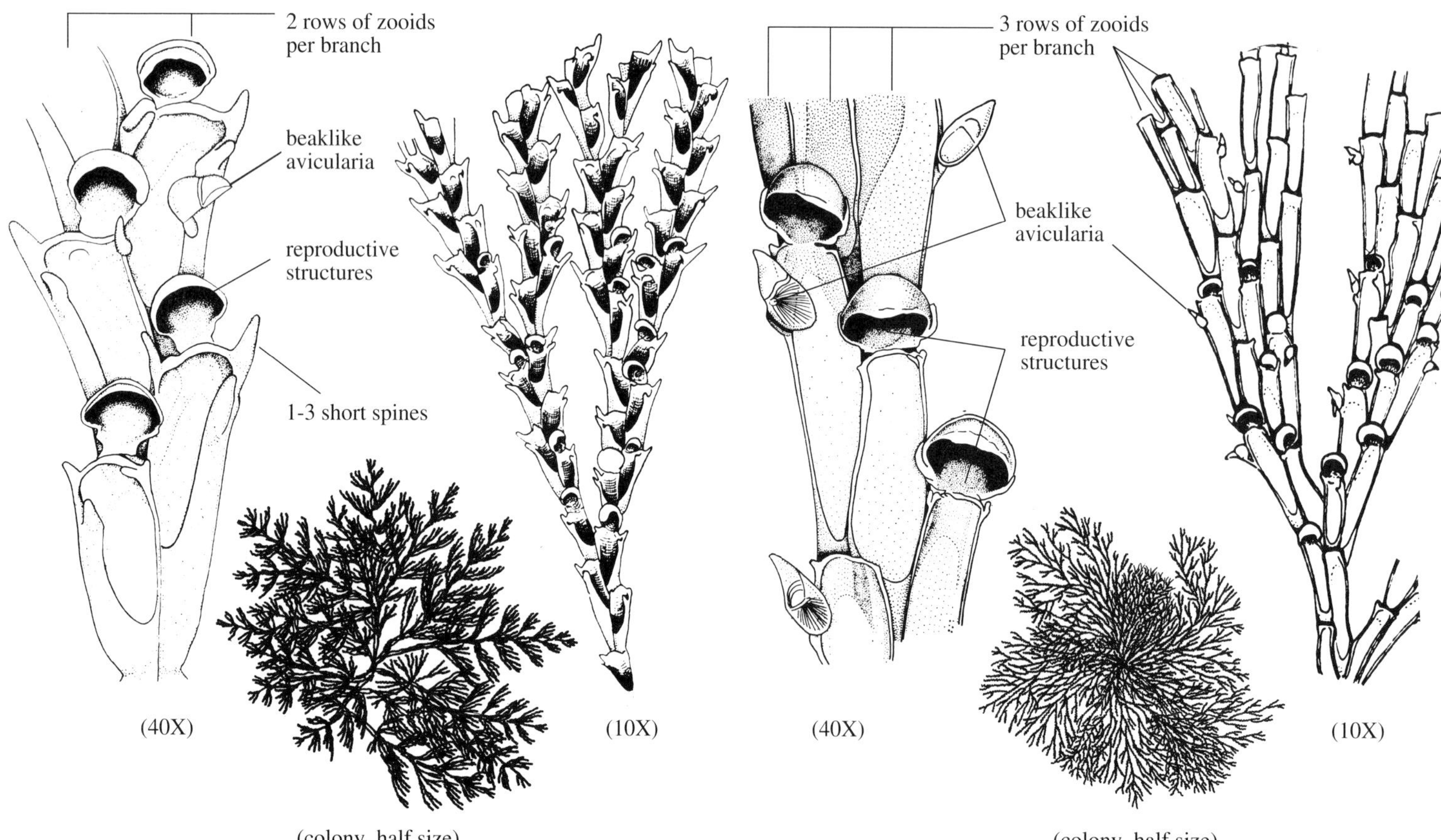

Fig.A. ***BUGULA TURRITA*, SPIRAL-TUFTED BUSHY BRYOZOAN:** Yellow to orange-brown; colonies up to 30 cm (12") long; common on pilings, rocks, and other hard objects. **17.10 H**

Fig.B. ***BUGULA SIMPLEX*, FAN-TUFTED BUSHY BRYOZOAN:** Tan or beige; colonies up to 2.5 cm (1") long; common fouling organism attached to lobster pots, boat hulls, mooring lines, pilings, and other substrates.

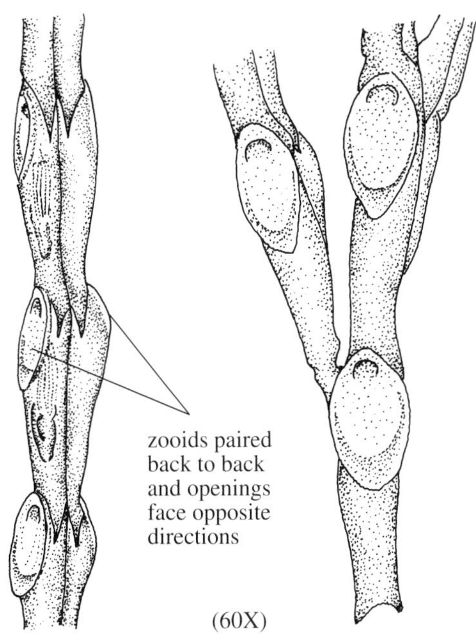

Fig.C. ***EUCRATEA LORICATA:*** Buff or light brown; colony forms tall, dense clump, with treelike branching, usually up to 10 cm (4") long but may reach 25 cm (10"); lower intertidal and offshore; Cape Cod and north.

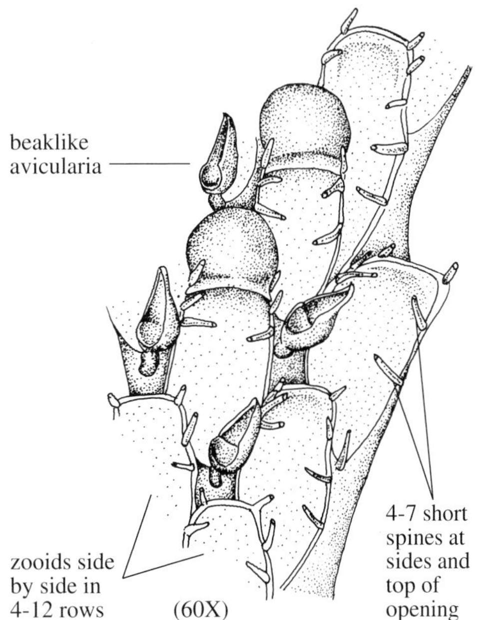

Fig.D. ***DENDROBEANIA MURRAYANA:*** Colony forms a dense, bushy tuft with broad, flat, square ended branches, up to 3 cm (1 1/4") tall; lives on stones, shells, and other bryozoans in shallow waters and offshore.

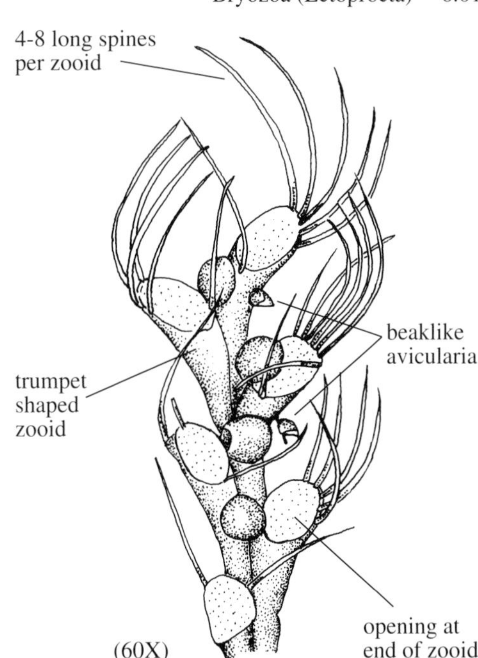

Fig.E. ***BICELLARIELLA CILIATA:*** White; colony forms a feathery tuft, up to 3 cm (1 1/4") tall; occurs from lower intertidal zone into deep waters.

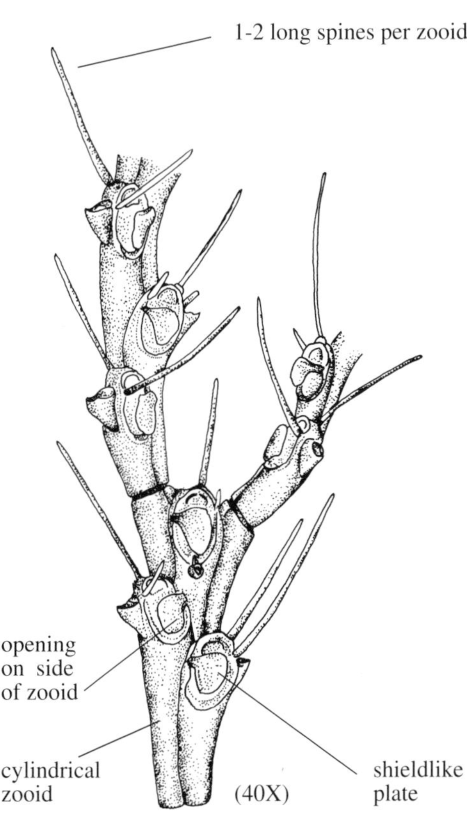

Fig.F. ***TRICELLARIA GRACILIS:*** White; colony forms delicate tuft, up to 3 cm (1 1/4") tall; occurs in shallow waters attached to algae, rocks, and other hard substrates; Cape Cod and north.

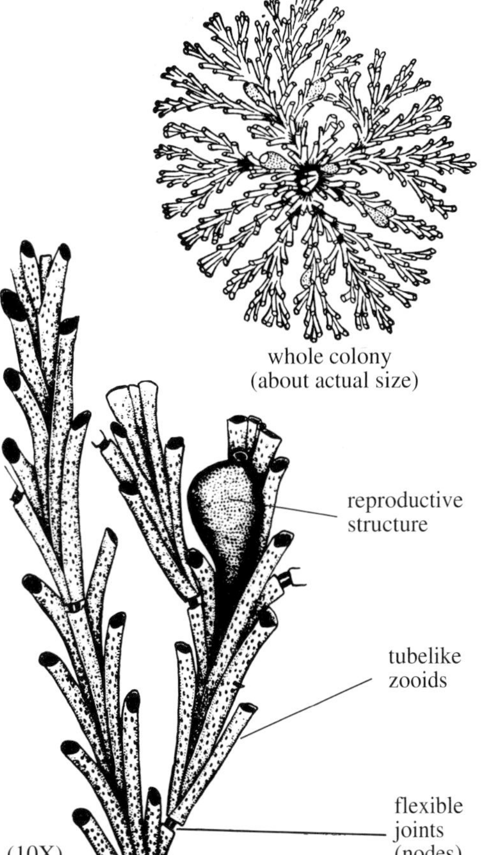

Fig.G. ***CRISIA* SPP[1]., JOINTED-TUBE BRYOZOANS:** White with yellow or brown nodes; colonies up to 4 cm (1 1/2") high; attaches to rocks, algae, pilings, and other firm substrates; common.

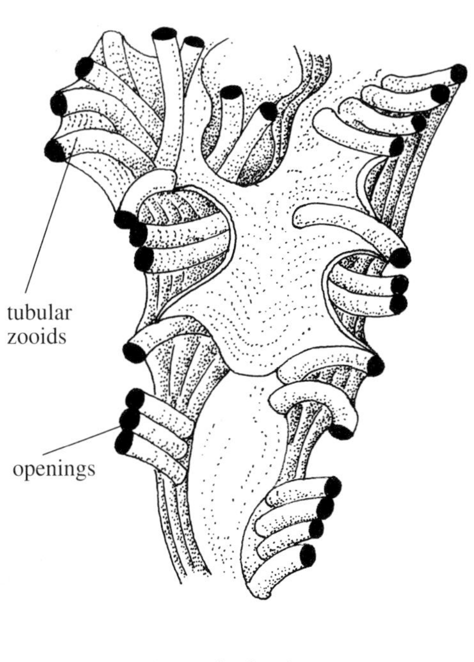

Fig.H. **FAMILY TUBULIPORIDAE[1], PANPIPE BRYOZOANS:** White or purple; colonies of some species are erect and branching, antlerlike, reaching about 25 mm (1") in height; not common.

ENCRUSTING BRYOZOANS: PHYLUM BRYOZOA (ECTOPROCTA)[1]

Bryozoans that form a calcareous (shell-like) crust.

(Use key on page 2.06 to determine if you have an encrusting bryozoan)

#1. Tiny white, disclike or wartlike colonies (Fig.A); less than 3 mm (1/8") in diameter; openings radiate from center like the spokes of a wheel; individual zooids (cells) are tubular with rounded openings .... ***Lichenopora* spp.**, #2

#1. Colonies may grow much larger than 3 mm (1/8") in diameter; shape of colony may be irregular; openings do not radiate from the center of the colony; openings may or may not be round (Figs.B-K) .... #3

#2. With pores, tubes and bumps at center of colony; colony has layered appearance .... ***Lichenopora hispida*** (Fig.A)

#2. Without pores, tubes or bumps at center of colony; colony does not have layered appearance .... ***Lichenopora verrucaria*** (Fig.A)

#3. The opening of each zooid (cell) is very large with shelly material forming a thin rim or wall around the opening (Fig.B); at least half of the opening is uncovered or covered only with a membrane[2]; some species have spines that point into or surround the openings, other species do not have spines; the large openings and thin white calcareous walls give the colony a lacelike appearance .... **lacy bryozoans**, page 6.04

#3. The opening to each zooid (cell) is small with more than half of the top of each zooid covered with a calcareous (shell-like) lid (Figs.C-K); colonies may be red, white, orange or brown .... #4

#4. Calcareous lid of each zooid is solid except for the opening (ovicells have pores); no avicularia (tiny beak shaped structures) .... ***Hippothoa hyalina*** (Fig.C)

#4. Calcareous lid with numerous pores on borders and/or in center of each zooid (Figs.D-K); many species have avicularia (tiny beak shaped structures) .... #5

#5. Opening is keyhole shaped, with a distinct notch at bottom (Figs.D-F) .... #6

#5. Opening has a distinct tooth projecting into opening from bottom; tooth may be pointed or flat (G-I) .... #8

#5. Opening is round, semicircular or bell shaped; without a notch or tooth at bottom (Figs.J,K) .... #10

#6. Avicularia (beak shaped structures) on midline directly beneath notch in openings .... ***Schizomavella auriculata*** (Fig.D)

#6. Avicularia, if present, not on midline beneath openings .... #7

#7. Avicularia sharply pointed (avicularia may be lacking on large parts of the colony) .... ***Schizoporella unicornis*** (Fig.E)

#7. Avicularia oval, usually located on one or both sides of openings .... ***Stephanosella* spp.** (Fig.F)

#8. Avicularia located directly beneath opening and mounted on a raised bump .... ***Rhamphostomella* spp.** (Fig.G)

#8. Avicularia located to the sides of the openings .... #9

#9. With spines attached to the outer edge of some or most of the openings; calcareous lid with 2 rows of flattened ribs .... ***Cribrilina punctata*** (Fig.H)

#9. No spines above openings; pores in calcareous lid are along the border of each zooid (cell), not in center .... ***Parasmittina nitida*** (Fig.I)

#10. Opening is somewhat bell shaped; no avicularia or ovicells; without spines bordering the openings .... ***Cryptosula pallasiana*** (Fig.J)

#10. Opening is round or semicircular; with avicularia (beak shaped or oval structures); with tiny spines above some openings .... ***Microporella ciliata*** (Fig.K)

[1]**WARNING:** This key includes the most common species of bryozoans reported to occur in southern New England, but many less common species have been omitted (see Weiss et al., 1995 or Rogick, 1964b). Numerous taxonomic revisions have made the identification of bryozoans especially confusing and difficult. For a positive identification, refer to Gosner (1971) or the most up-to-date sources available.

[2]Place a drop of bleach (such as Chlorox) on the colony to determine if the zooids are covered with membranous or calcareous lids. If the lids are membranous they will dissolve away in the bleach, leaving a large uncovered opening. Calcareous lids will not dissolve.

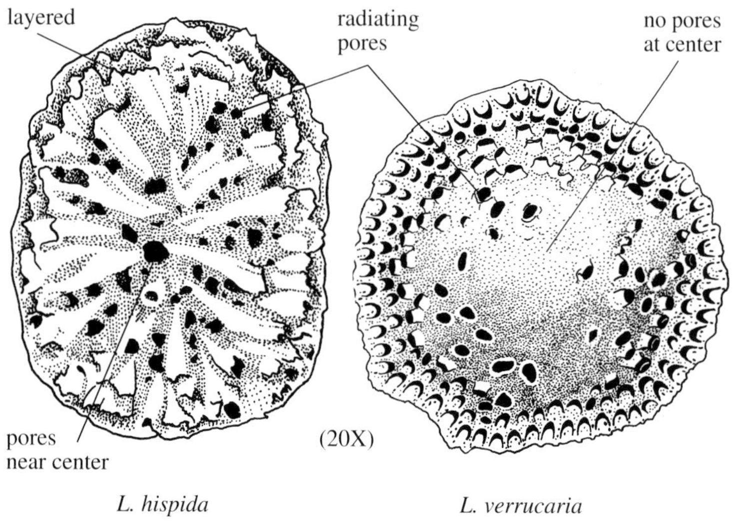

Fig.A. ***LICHENOPORA* SPP.:** White; colony about 3 mm (1/8") in diameter; found on algae, hydroids, bryozoa and stones. Use above key to identify species.

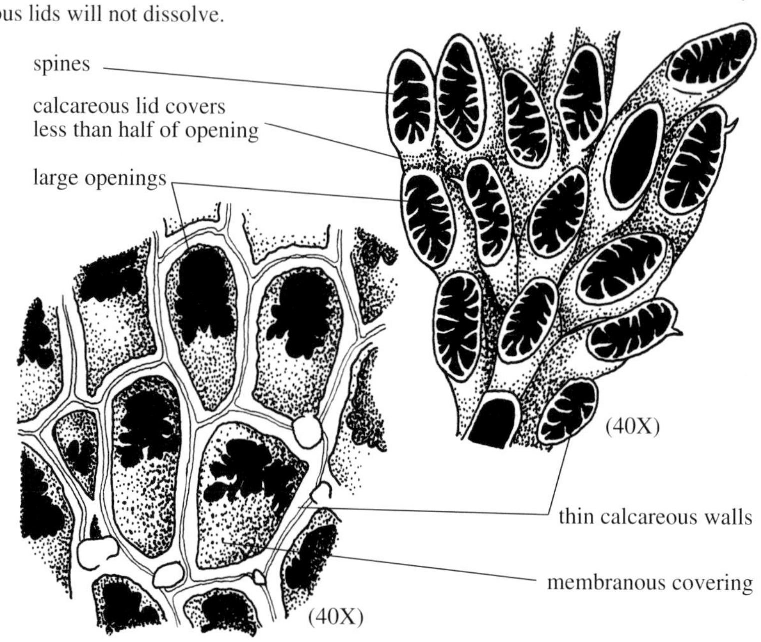

Fig.B. **LACY BRYOZOANS:** White colonies. Use key on page 6.04.

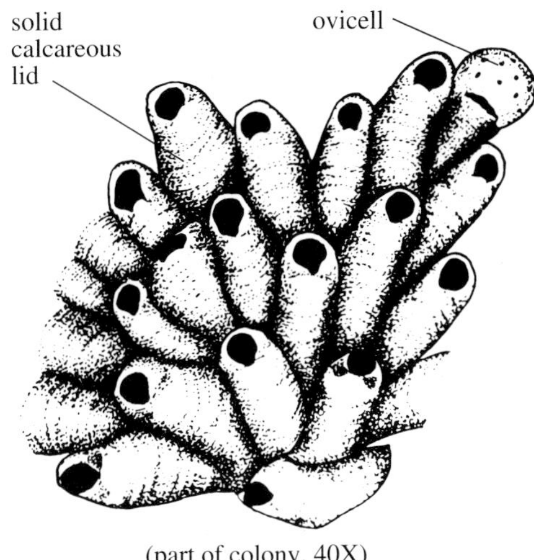

(part of colony, 40X)

Fig.C. ***HIPPOTHOA HYALINA:*** Colonies are shiny, glassy white, or iridescent; up to 2.5 cm (1") in diameter, but usually much smaller, found on algal stems and holdfasts in shallow water.

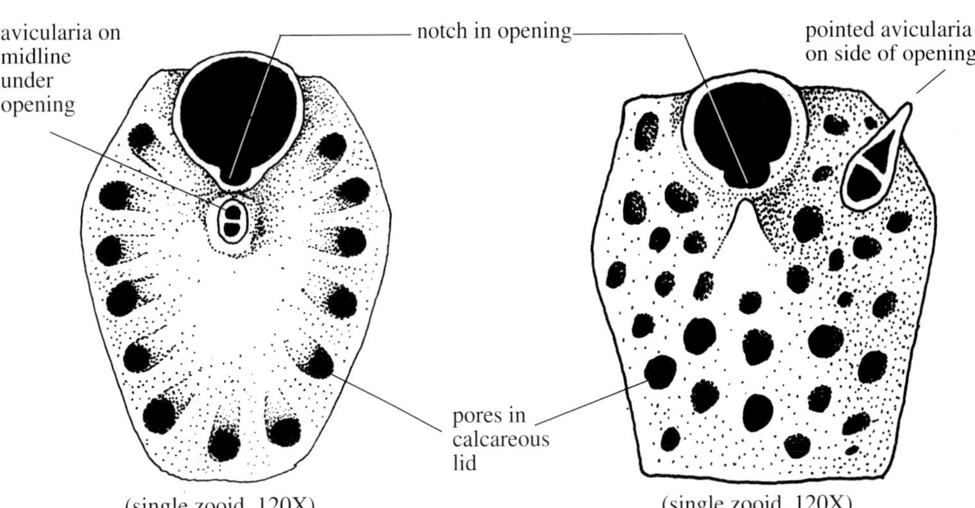

(single zooid, 120X)

Fig.D. ***SCHIZOMAVELLA AURICULATA:*** Red, yellow, or white; encrusts stones and shells; occurs in deeper water in southern New England.

(single zooid, 120X)

Fig.E. ***SCHIZOPORELLA UNICORNIS:*** Pale orange to brick red; found on shells, stones, pilings, and seaweeds; very common. **17.10 B D E**

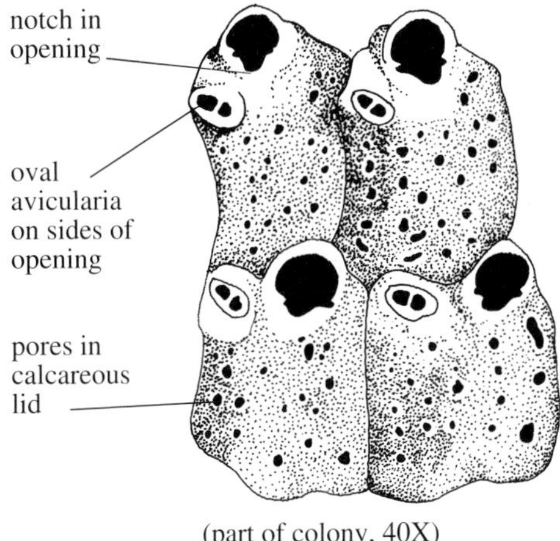

(part of colony, 40X)

Fig.F. ***STEPHANOSELLA* SPP.:** Colonies are layered and ruffled; red, orange, or white; attach to algae, shells, rocks and many other substrates.

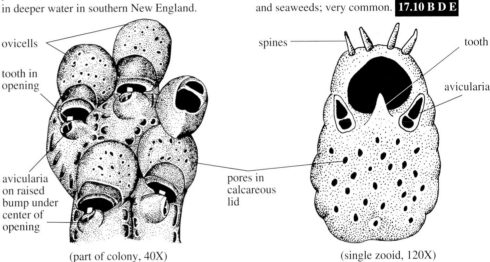

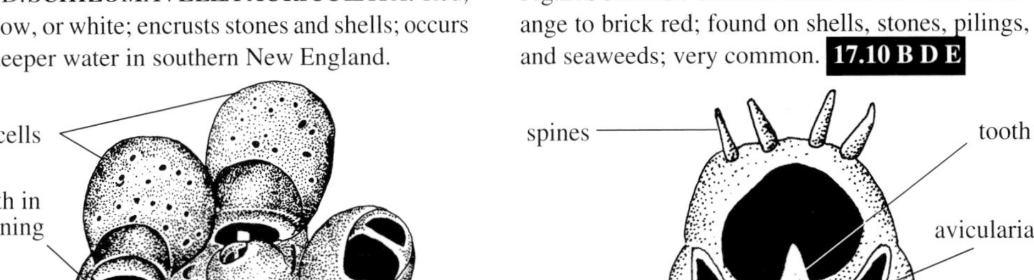
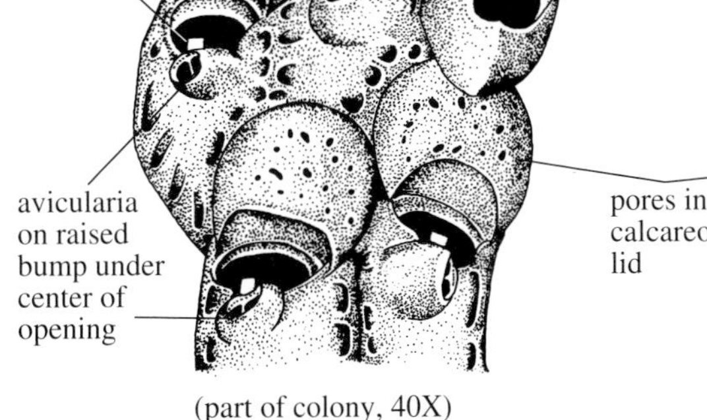

(part of colony, 40X)

Fig.G. ***RHAMPHOSTOMELLA* SPP.:** White, gray, or pink; colony is mostly flat but may have erect folds; encrusts hydroids and other substrates.

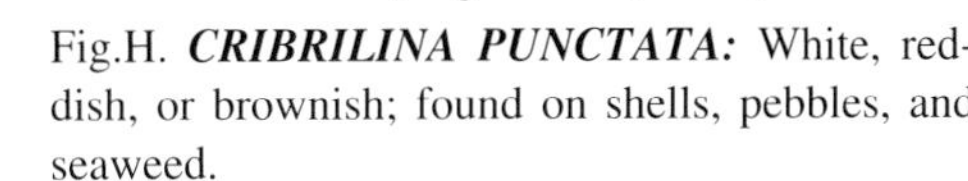

(single zooid, 120X)

Fig.H. ***CRIBRILINA PUNCTATA:*** White, reddish, or brownish; found on shells, pebbles, and seaweed.

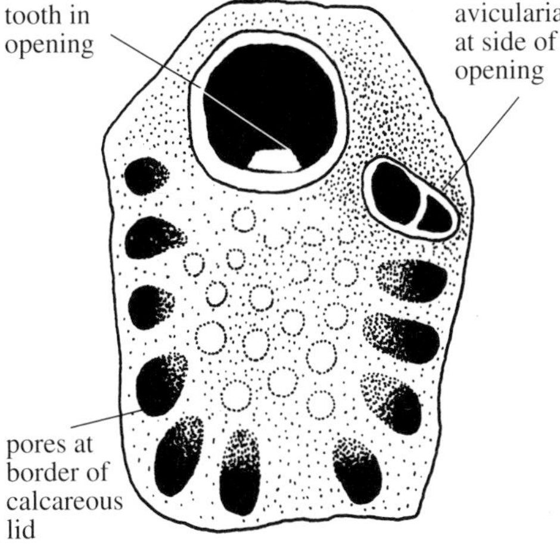

(single zooid, 120X)

Fig.I. ***PARASMITTINA NITIDA:*** White, gray, or yellow; colonies grow up to about 5 cm (2") in diameter; found on rocks offshore.

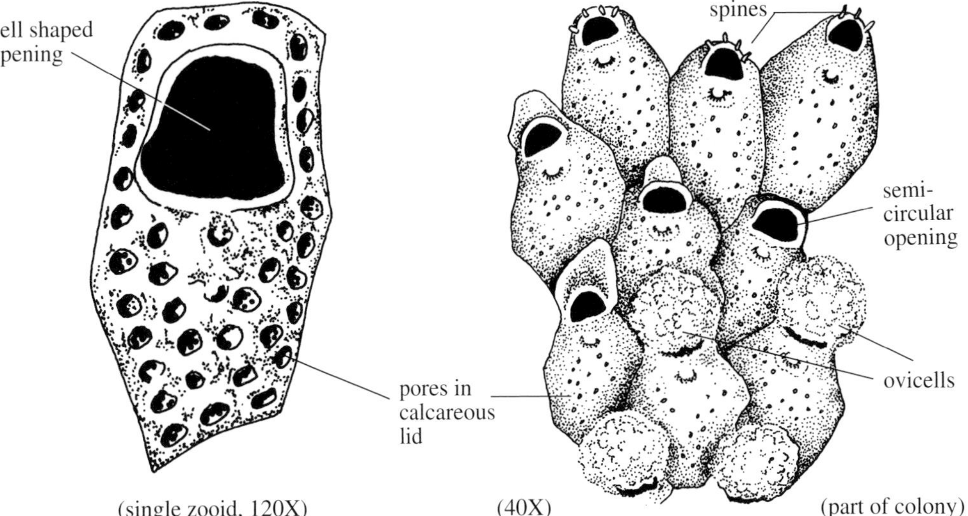

(single zooid, 120X)

Fig.J. ***CRYPTOSULA PALLASIANA:*** Orange; colonies up to about 2 cm (3/4") in diameter; found on rocks, shells, and seaweeds; very common.

(40X) (part of colony)

Fig.K. ***MICROPORELLA CILIATA:*** Silvery or frosty colored; colonies grow up to about 2.4 cm (1"); found on rocks, shells, and seaweeds.

LACY BRYOZOANS: PHYLUM BRYOZOA (ECTOPROCTA)

Encrusting bryozoans with large openings and thin calcareous walls that form a lacy crust.

(The key to the encrusting bryozoans begins on page 6.02)

#1. Without any spines surrounding the openings (Figs.A,B) .... #2
#1. With 2 or more pointed spines or rounded knobs which point into or surround the opening of each zooid (cell); (the spines or knobs often stand erect) .... #3

#2. With small triangular enclosures with erect chitinous tubes at two of the corners of each zooid (cell) .... ***Conopeum truitti*** (Fig.A)
#2. Without any triangular enclosures at the corners of the zooids .... ***Membranipora tenuis*** (Fig.B)

#3. With ovicells (reproductive structures) and avicularia (beaklike structures), (Figs.C-E) .... #4
#3. Without ovicells or avicularia (Figs.F-I) .... #6

#4. Ovicells are triangular; usually with 2-4 tiny spines surrounding the opening .... ***Callopora aurita*** (Fig.C)
#4. Ovicells are round (Figs.D,E) .... #5

#5. With 2-4 spines .... ***Tegella unicornis*** (Fig.D)
#5. With 12-14 spines .... ***Callopora craticula*** (Fig.E)

#6. Zooids partially covered with a calcareous (shell-like) lid (Figs.H,I) .... #7
#6. Zooids without a calcareous lid; with small delicate pointed spines surrounding oval opening .... ***Electra crustulenta*** (Fig.F)
#6. Zooids without a calcareous lid; with a knob at each corner of rectangular zooids .... ***Membranipora membranacea*** (Fig.G)

#7. Calcareous lid has many tiny pores; spine at bottom of opening may be much longer than the spines at the sides .... ***Electra pilosa*** (Fig.H)
#7. Calcareous lid not porous; all spines are about the same size .... ***Electra monostachys*** (Fig.I)

[1]**WARNING:** See footnote 1 on page 6.02. The classification of the lacy bryozoans is particularly unstable and subject to change.

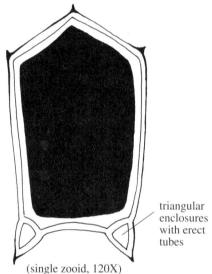

Fig.A. ***CONOPEUM TRUITTI:*** White; found on rocks and shells and sometimes algae.

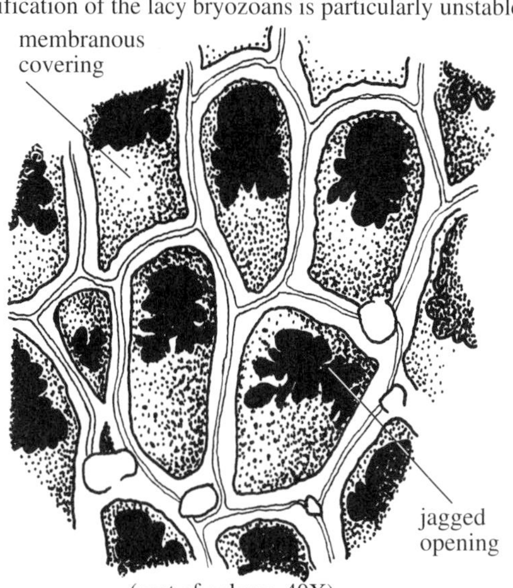

Fig.B. ***MEMBRANIPORA TENUIS:*** White; found in shallow water and estuaries with lower salinity.

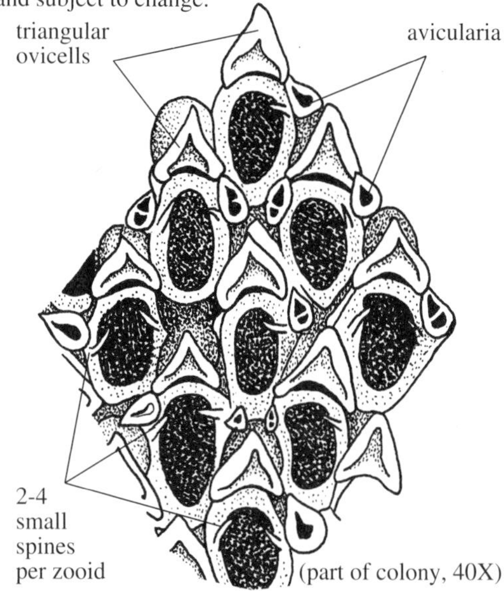

Fig.C. ***CALLOPORA AURITA:*** White; forms small colonies on rocks, shells, and seaweed.

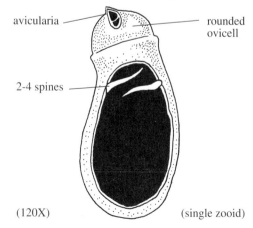

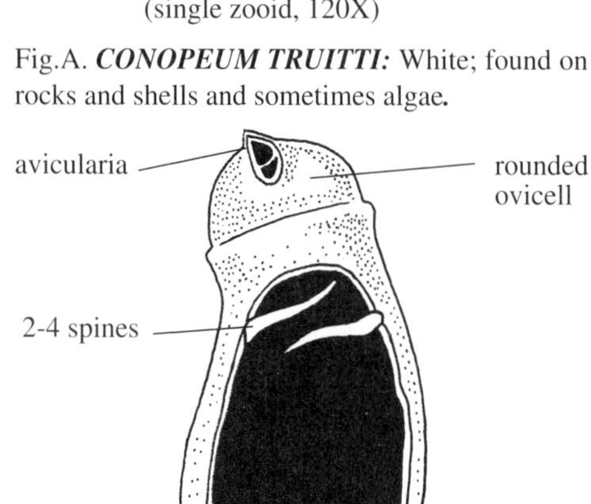

Fig.D. ***TEGELLA UNICORNIS:*** White; found on shells offshore.

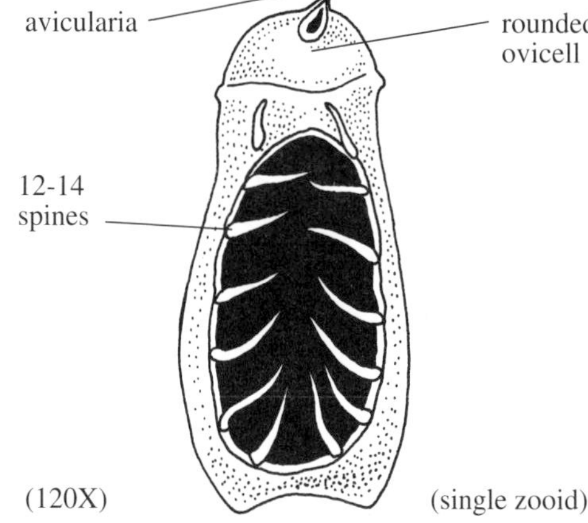

Fig.E. ***CALLOPORA CRATICULA:*** White; found on shells and stones in shallow and deep water.

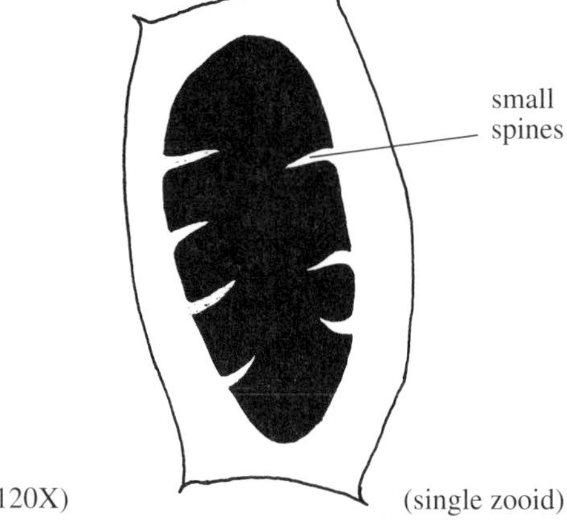

Fig.F. ***ELECTRA CRUSTULENTA:*** White; may be found in estuaries with low salinity.

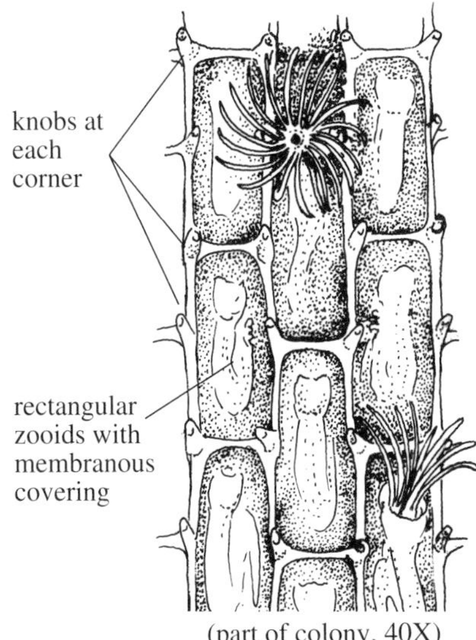

Fig.G. ***MEMBRANIPORA MEMBRANACEA:*** White; colonies expand somewhat fanlike and can cover large portions of kelp *(Laminaria)* blades; introduced from Pacific, now very common.
17.10 A **17.10 C**

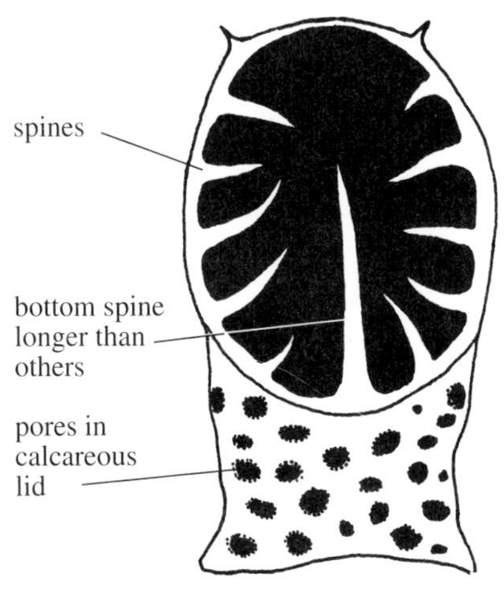

Fig.H. ***ELECTRA PILOSA:*** White; irregularly shaped colonies to 30 cm (12") long; very common on kelp (*Laminaria*), other seaweeds, shells, rocks, etc.; also found in estuaries with reduced salinity.
17.10 F **17.10 G**

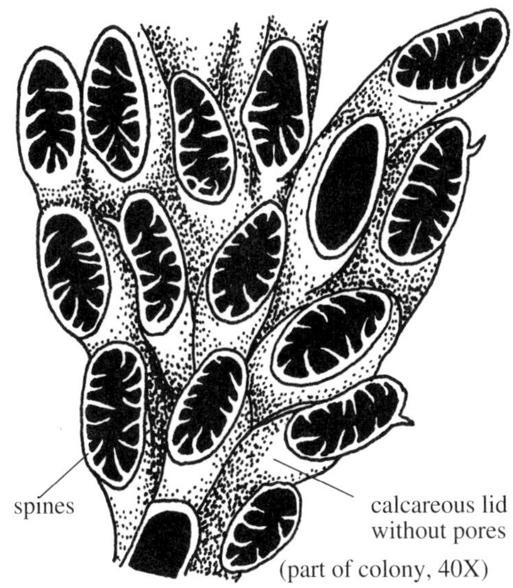

Fig.I. ***ELECTRA MONOSTACHYS:*** White; found on shells and rocks, occasionally on seaweed.

RUBBERY AND BRISTLY BRYOZOANS: PHYLUM BRYOZOA (ECTOPROCTA)

Bryozoans that form a gelatinous, leathery, or rubbery colony that is usually encrusting but may be erect with round lobes.

(Use key on page 2.06 to determine if you have a rubbery bryozoan)

#1.Colony is bristly, with short spines; individual zooids ("cells") are spiny; openings are slitlike when closed.. ***Flustrellidra hispida*, bristly bryozoan** (Fig.A)
#1.Colony is smooth, rubbery and glossy; zooids ("cells") do not have spines; openings are rounded and puckered when closed ....***Alcyonidium* spp.**, #2

#2.Forms a crustlike colony; not erect, not branched ....***Alcyonidium polyoum*, rubbery bryozoan** (Fig.B)
#2.Forms an erect, highly branched, shrublike or antlerlike colony; branches may be cylindrical or flattish ......***Alcyonidium verrilli*, rubbery bryozoan** (Fig.C)

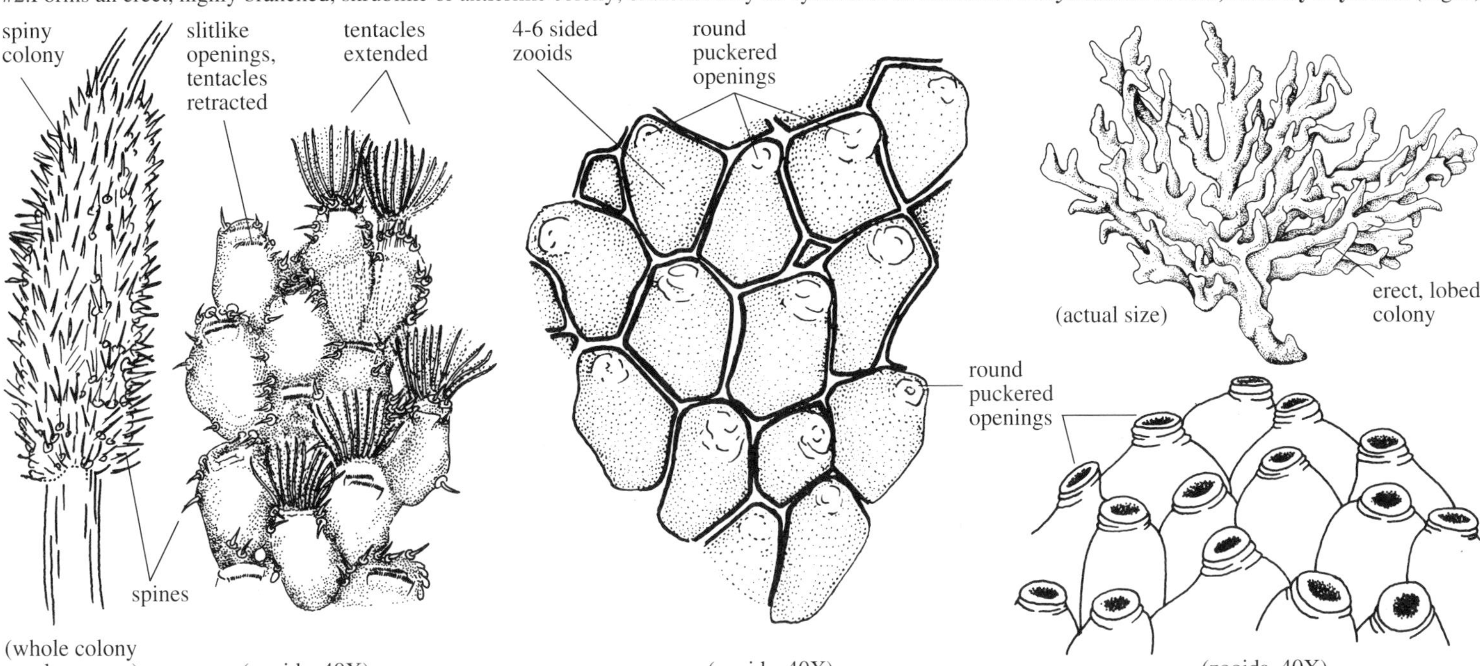

Fig.A. ***FLUSTRELLIDRA HISPIDA*, BRISTLY BRYOZOAN :** Brown or reddish brown; colonies may be 2 mm (1/16") or more in thickness, 5 cm (2") or more in length; forms a bristly, encrusting colony on rockweeds and other seaweeds.

Fig.B. ***ALCYONIDIUM POLYOUM,* RUBBERY BRYOZOAN:** Color variable, may be gray, yellow, red, or brown; colonies up to 38 cm (15") in diameter; encrusts on pilings, stones, algae, shells, and other objects.

Fig.C. ***ALCYONIDIUM VERRILLI*, RUBBERY BRYOZOAN:** Gray, brown, or reddish; colony reaches up to 30 cm (12") in height; found in lower intertidal zone and in shallow water, occurs in estuaries in brackish water.

STOLONATE BRYOZOANS: PHYLUM BRYOZOA (ECTOPROCTA)

Zoids have a circlet of tentacles that encloses the mouth but not the anus of their U-shaped digestive tract.
Zooids are connected by a stolon (rootlike network).

(Use the key on page 2.04 to determine if you have a stolonate bryozoan)

#1.Zooids (individuals) are horn shaped and connected in a chain .... ***Scruparia* spp.**[1] (Fig.A)
#1.Zooids are not horn shaped; zooids are not connected in a chain .... #2

#2.Zooids are tubular or cylindrical, without a stalk .... #3
#2.Zooids connected to stolon (rootlike network) by a stalk (narrow stemlike base) .... #6

#3.Colony with treelike branching; groups of zooids spiral around the stolon in double rows; zooids stiff .... ***Amathia vidovici*** (Fig.B)
#3.Colony is not highly branched; zooids occur singly or in clumps along stolon .... #4

#4.Stolon may have an expanded section with spiny projections beneath each zooid; zooids often have more than 10 tentacles; stolon is not segmented except where zooids are attached .... ***Nolella* spp.**[1] (Fig.C)
#4.Stolon is not expanded beneath zooids; zooids have 8-10 tentacles; stolon is divided into one or more segments between zooids .... ***Bowerbankia* spp.**, #5

#5.With a circlet of 8 tentacles .... ***Bowerbankia gracilis*** (Fig.D)
#5.With a circlet of 10 tentacles .... ***Bowerbankia imbricata*** (Fig.E)

#6.Stalk is snakelike and encircled by a fine spiral thread; with a spoon shaped zooid at end of stalk .... ***Aetea* spp.**[1] (Fig.F)
#6.Stalk is threadlike; with a vase shaped or club shaped zooid at end of stalk .... #7

#7.Stalk is very short; zooids are paired and are vase shaped; colony is erect and branching .... ***Aeverrillia* spp.**[1] (Fig.G)
#7.Stalk is long; zooids are club shaped and arise singly or in pairs from stolon; often found attached to legs, shells or gills of crabs .... ***Triticella* spp.**[1] (Fig.H)

[1] Refer to Gosner (1971) or Ryland and Hayward (1991) to determine species.

horn shaped zooids
zooids form a chain
stolon

Fig.A. ***SCRUPARIA* SPP.**[1]**:** Colony is white; attaches to stones, shells, algae, hydroids, bryozoans, and crabs in shallow and deep water.

branching stolon
zooids spiral around stolon in double rows

Fig.B. ***AMATHIA VIDOVICI:*** Colony is colorless to light brown; 2-3 cm (1") tall; common on rocks, shells, algae, and pilings in shallow waters.

8-22 tentacles
stolon unsegmented
stolon expanded under some zooids

Fig.C. ***NOLELLA* SPP.**[1]**:** Opaque gray brown; zooids up to 4 mm (3/16") tall; occurs on shells, stones, hydroids, and bryozoans in shallow water.

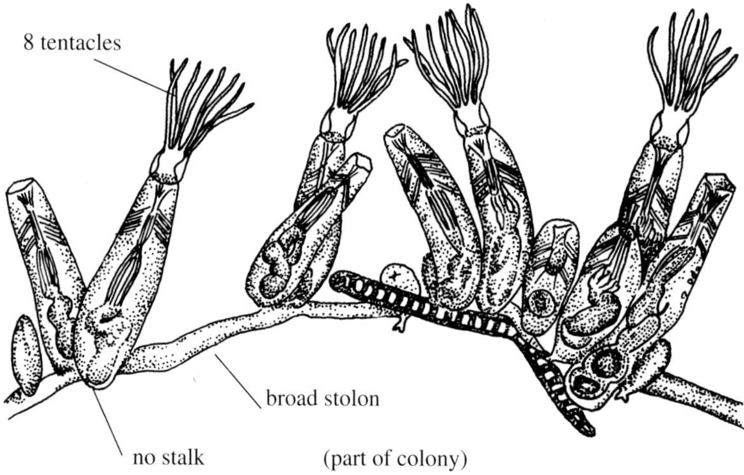

Fig.D. ***BOWERBANKIA GRACILIS:*** Transparent, gray; individuals up to 1 mm (1/32") long; found on stones, pilings, seaweeds.

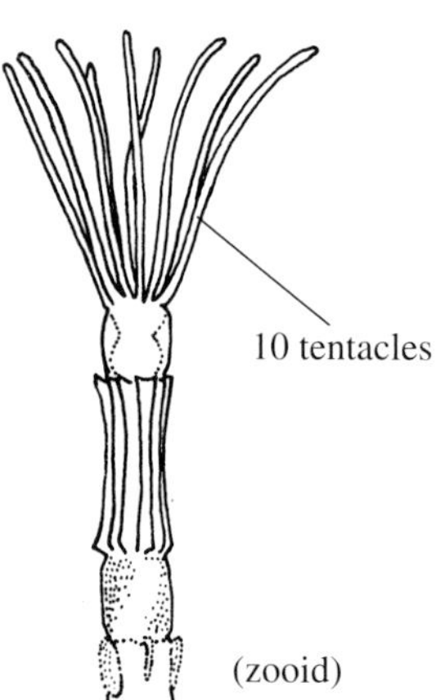

Fig.E. ***BOWERBANKIA IMBRICATA:*** Transparent, may be pinkish during breeding season because of reddish larvae; individuals up to 1 mm (1/32") long; found on stones, pilings, seaweeds; not as common as *Bowerbankia gracilis*.

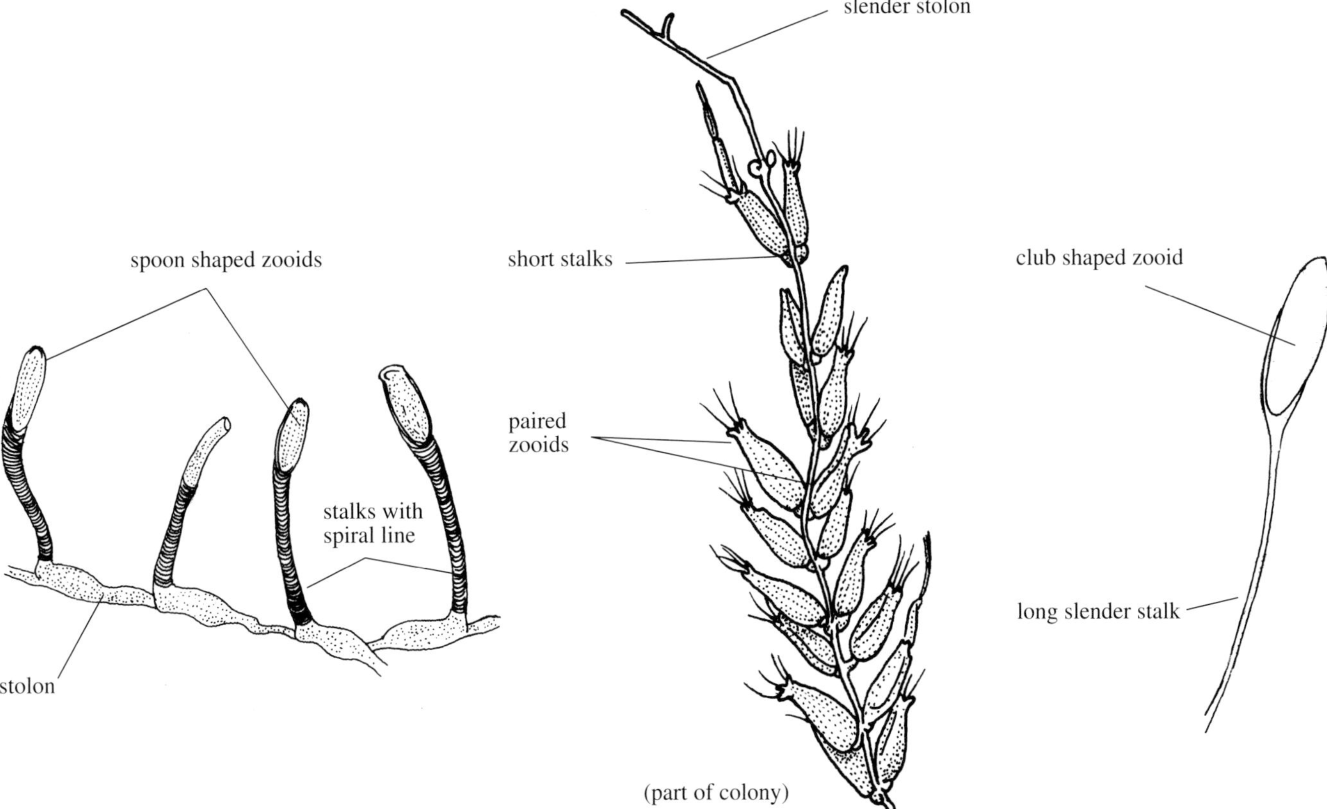

Fig.F. ***AETEA* SPP.[1]:** Colony is white, sometimes pinkish; zooids are glassy, up to 0.6 mm (1/64") tall; common on stems of bushy bryozoans, hydroids, algae as well as stones and shells.

Fig.G. ***AEVERRILLIA* SPP.[1]:** Zooids yellowish; colonies up to 15 cm (6") long; found on pilings and seaweed.

Fig.H. ***TRITICELLA* SPP.[1]:** Zooids up to 2 mm (1/8") tall; sometimes lives attached to the legs, shells, or gill chambers of crabs.

ENTOPROCTS: PHYLUM ENTOPROCTA

The cuplike upper portion of these tiny colonial animals has a circle of tentacles that encloses both the mouth and anal opening of its U-shaped digestive tract. The upper portion is mounted on a stalk that is connected to other individuals by a stolon (rootlike network).

(Use the key on page 2.04 to determine if you have an entoproct)

#1. With spines on stalk; base of stalk not swollen .... ***Pedicellina cernua*** (Fig.A)
#1. Without spines on stalk; base of stalk is swollen .... ***Barentsia* spp.** (Fig.B)

Fig.A. ***PEDICELLINA CERNUA:*** Whitish; individuals up to 6 mm (1/4") long; found on pilings, rocks, and other objects

Fig.B. ***BARENTSIA* SPP.:** Whitish; up to 1 cm (3/8") long; found on pilings, rocks, shells, and leg bases of spider crabs and horseshoe crabs.

SQUID: PHYLUM MOLLUSCA, CLASS CEPHALOPODA

Mollusks having no external shell; with fins, 8 arms, 2 tentacles, well developed eyes, and a torpedo shaped body

#1.Fins are long, more than half of the mantle length; eyelids are transparent; common south of Cape Cod .... ***Loligo pealeii,* longfin squid**[1] (Fig.A)
#1.Fins are short, about 1/3 of the mantle length; eyelids with notch in front; common north of Cape Cod .. ***Illex illecebrosus,* northern shortfin squid**[1] (Fig.B)

[1]Squid are often caught in bottom trawl nets offshore and schools of squid are also frequently seen nearshore. They swim backwards (with the tentacles trailing behind) by jet propulsion, squirting water out of the mantle through a tube near the base of the head. They produce a cloud of black ink when disturbed. Females lay gelatinous, cigar shaped egg cases in large communal clusters (see Fig.B, page 2.23). During breeding, the suckers on the fourth arm on the left side of the male become swollen papillae (pimplelike projections) which are used to transfer sperm capsules to the female.

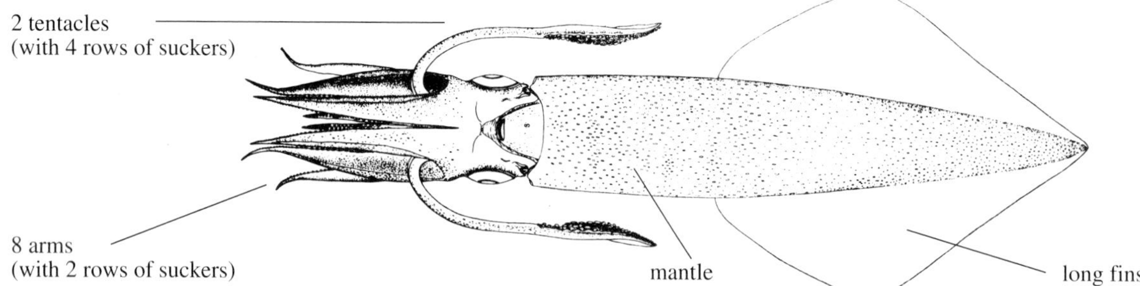

Fig.A. ***LOLIGO PEALEII,* LONGFIN SQUID:** White or translucent gray with tiny red or purple spots which expand and contract, making squid appear to "blush"; may grow up to 60 cm (2') long, but rarely exceeds 30 cm (1'); common south of Cape Cod. (family Loliginidae) **17.04 C**

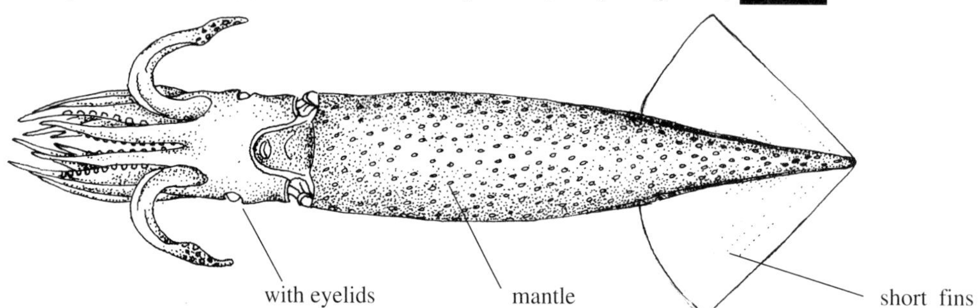

Fig.B. ***ILLEX ILLECEBROSUS,* NORTHERN SHORTFIN SQUID:** White with red, brown or gold speckles; overall color ranges from blue to red; up to about 45 cm (18") long; feed voraciously on schools of small fish; common north of Cape Cod. (family Ommastrephidae)

CHITONS: PHYLUM MOLLUSCA, CLASS POLYPLACOPHORA

Mollusks with 8 overlapping valves (plates)

(Use the key on page 2.10 to determine if you have a chiton)

#1.Valves (plates) have a triangular central region stippled with rows of tiny beads; girdle (fleshy portion of body surrounding the valves) has sparsely scattered short transparent hairs; overall color usually whitish, tan, brown or gray .... ***Chaetopleura apiculata,* eastern beaded chiton** (Fig.C)
#1.Valves are uniformly smooth except for growth rings and a central ridge; no hairs on girdle; overall color usually mottled red or reddish-brown .... #2

#2.Girdle is granular, with a texture like sandpaper; girdle covered with tiny scales (visible with 20X lens) .... ***Tonicella marmorea,* mottled red chiton** (Fig.D)
#2.Girdle is smooth, leathery, without scales .... ***Tonicella rubra,* northern red chiton** (Fig.D)

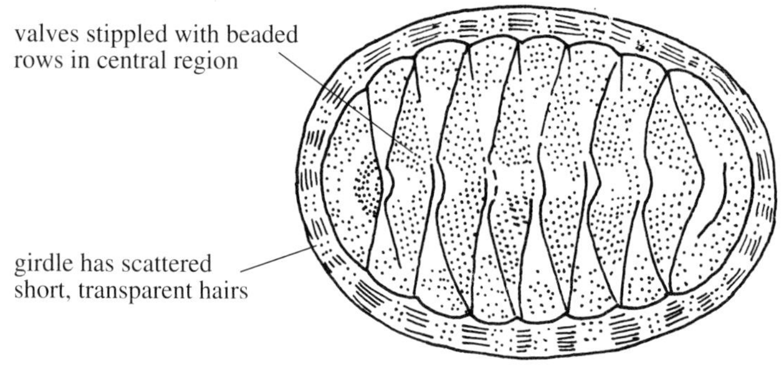

Fig.C. ***CHAETOPLEURA APICULATA,* EASTERN BEADED CHITON:** Tan, brown or gray; up to 19 mm (3/4") long; found in shallow water on stones or shells; curls up when removed.

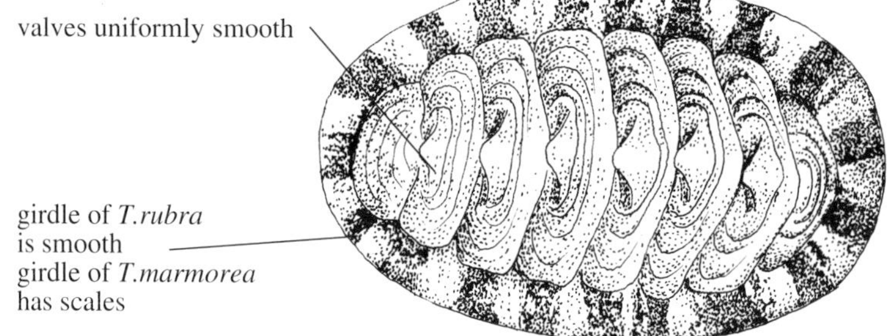

Fig.D. ***TONICELLA* SPP.:** Usually mottled with red or brown but sometimes with blue or green; common north of Cape Cod. *Tonicella rubra (=Ischnochiton rubra),* northern red chiton, occurs in the rocky intertidal zone and is up to 19 mm (3/4") long. *T. marmorea,* mottled red chiton, occurs on subtidal rocks and is up to 3.8 cm (1 1/2") long. Use key to identify the species. **17.04 D**

LIMPETS AND SLIPPERSNAILS
PHYLUM MOLLUSCA, CLASS GASTROPODA, FAMILIES ACMAEIDAE AND CALYPTRAEIDAE

Limpets and slippersnails are gastropods, like snails, with a single shell. Unlike snails, however, their shell is not coiled.

(Refer to the key on page 2.10 to determine if you have a slippersnail or limpet)

#1.With a shelflike structure on underside of shell (Fig.E); apex (point) of shell is near edge (Figs.B-D) .... **family Calyptraeidae, slippersnails**, #2
#1.Without a shelflike structure on underside of shell; apex is near center of shell .... ***Notoacmea testudinalis,* plant limpet** (Fig.A)

#2.Shell is arched, cup shaped (Figs.B,C) .... #3
#2.Shell is very flat and thin (Fig.D) .... #4

#3.Shelf is about 1/2 the shell length; edge of the shelf is wavy; grows up to 5 cm (2") long; apex usually does not overhang the edge of the shell; sometimes attach on top of each other forming long stacks .... ***Crepidula fornicata*, common Atlantic slippersnail**[1] (Fig.B)
#3.Shelf is about 1/3 the shell length; edge of shelf is a smooth curve, not wavy; apex often overhangs beyond edge of shell; may attach to one another, but does not form long stacks; does not grow longer than 1.3 cm (1/2") .... ***Crepidula convexa*, convex slippersnail** (Fig.C)

#4.Shell is pearly white; shelf is less than 1/2 shell length; apex points straight back .... ***Crepidula plana*, eastern white slippersnail** (Fig.D)
#4.Shell is whitish with reddish brown markings; shelf is about 1/2 shell length; apex turns to one side..***Crepidula fornicata*, common Atlantic slippersnail**[1] (Fig.B)

[1]Shell may be very flat or deeply arched, depending on the shape of the object it is attached to.

apex near center

(side view) (top view)

Fig.A. ***NOTOACMEA TESTUDINALIS (=Acmaea testudinalis),* PLANT LIMPET:** Greenish white with brown lines and patches, tortoise shell coloring; up to 1.5 cm (5/8") long; attaches to rocks at low tide mark. (family Acmaeidae: limpets) **17.12 G**

stack of slipper shells

shelf is half shell length, edge is wavy

apex curves, at shell edge

(side view) (underside)

Fig.B.***CREPIDULA FORNICATA*, COMMON ATLANTIC SLIPPER-SNAIL**[1]**:** Beige or whitish with reddish brown spots, blotches and wavy markings; largest slippersnail; up to 5 cm (2") long; very common, attaches to rocks, shells, and other hard objects; forms stacks; changes sex, with females at the bottom of the stack, males at top, and hermaphrodites in between. **17.06 B**

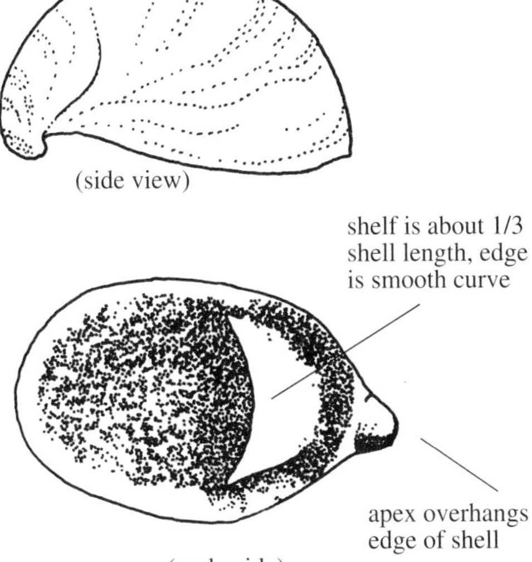

Fig.C. ***CREPIDULA CONVEXA*, CONVEX SLIPPERSNAIL:** Brown with stripes or dots of reddish brown; tiny, up to 1.3 cm (1/2") long; less common than other slippersnails; attaches to shells, rocks and other hard objects.

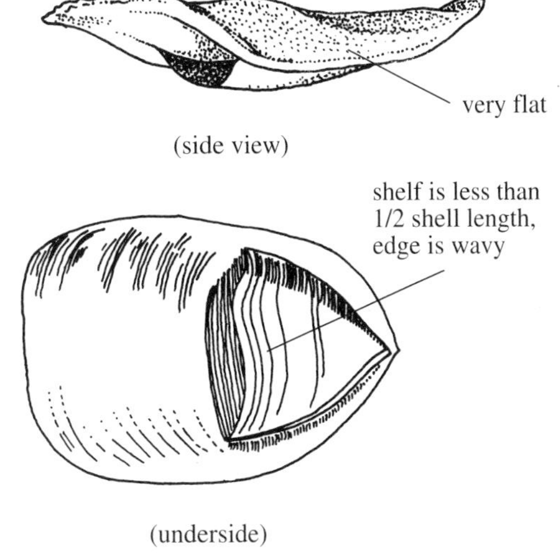

Fig.D. ***CREPIDULA PLANA*, EASTERN WHITE SLIPPERSNAIL:** Pearly white; up to 3.3 cm (1 1/4") long; often found attached to the underside of horseshoe crab shells and inside large snail shells occupied by hermit crabs. **17.06 C**

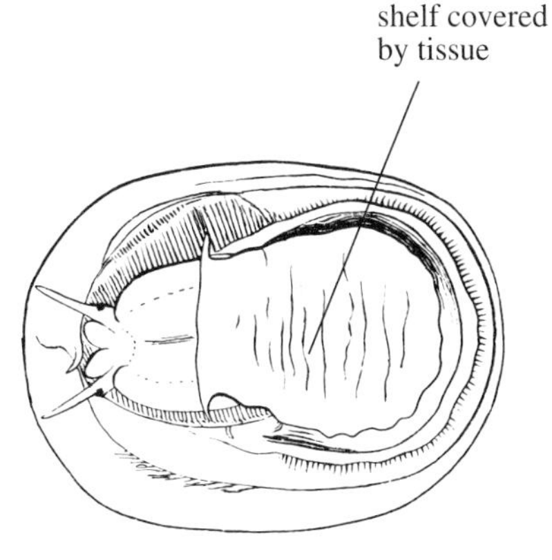

Fig.E. **UNDERSIDE OF LIVE SLIPPER-SNAIL:** The shelf is covered over by tissue and cannot be seen when the animal is alive. Remove the tissue to examine the shelf underneath.

SNAILS: PHYLUM MOLLUSCA, CLASS GASTROPODA

Mollusks with coiled shells

(Use the key on page 2.10 to determine if you have a snail)

#1.Bottom of shell has a siphonal canal[1] or siphonal notch (Figs.B-D) .... #2
#1.Bottom of shell is round (Figs.E-H), without a siphonal canal or notch .... #5

#2.Siphonal canal is long (nearly 1/4 total shell length), forming an obvious extension to lower lip of opening (Fig.B) .... #3
#2.Siphonal canal is short or absent (Fig.C,D) .... #4

#3.Shell is mostly smooth, without vertical ribs or spiral grooves, except grooves between whorls; large, often over 5 cm (2") long (Fig.B) .. **whelks,** page 7.10
#3.Shell is heavily sculptured with vertical ribs and/or spiral ridges (Figs.C,D); never grows more than 3.5 cm (1 1/2") long .... #4

#4.Opening is tiny, less than 1/4 total shell length; cone shaped shell is extremely pointed, narrow and elongate (Fig.C) .... **ceriths**, bottom of page 7.10
#4.Opening is longer than 1/4 total shell length; shell is egg or spindle shaped (Fig.D) .... **drills, dog whelks, mudsnails, and dovesnails**, page 7.08

#5.Round shells with circular or D-shaped openings (Figs.E,G) .... #6
#5.Cone shaped, egg shaped or cylindrical shells (Fig.F,H); opening may be round or elongate .... #7

#6.With an umbilicus (small hole) and/or a callus (Fig.E) near inner lip; with a D-shaped opening and operculum plate; often grow larger than 3 cm (1 1/4") in diameter .... **moonsnails**, page 7.04
#6.Without an umbilicus or callus; with a circular or teardrop shaped opening and operculum plate (Fig.G); inner lip of opening somewhat broad or thickened; never grow longer than 3 cm (1 1/4") .... **periwinkles**, page 7.05

#7.Opening is round or oval and is about 1/3 or less than the length of the shell (Fig.F) .... **bittium, rice and similar snails**, page 7.06
#7.Opening is elongate and is at least 1/2 the length of the shell (Fig.H) .... **marsh and bubble snails**, page 7.07

[1]Refer to Fig. A for terms used in snail key.

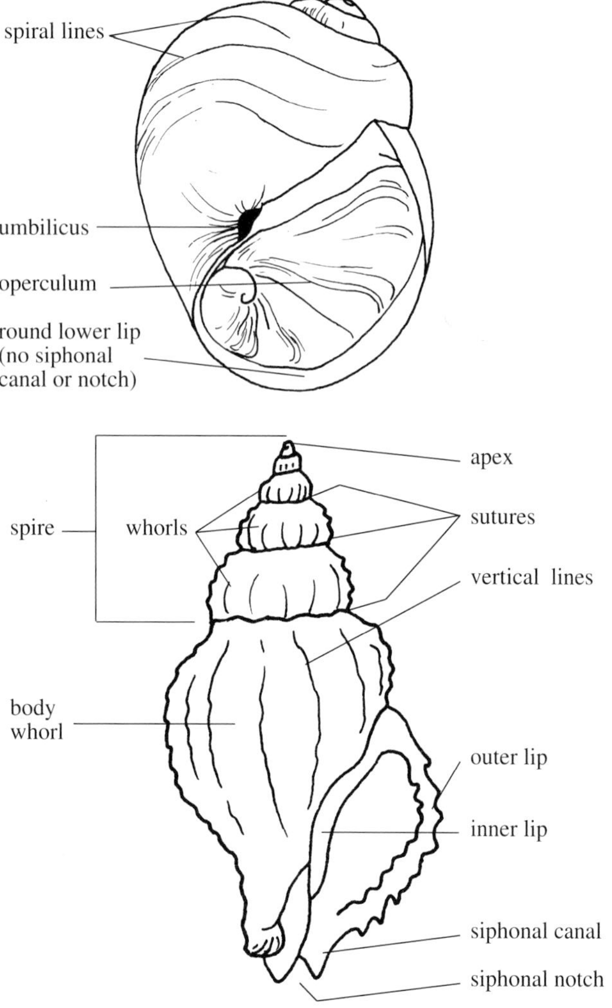

Fig.A. **TERMS USED IN SNAIL KEY**

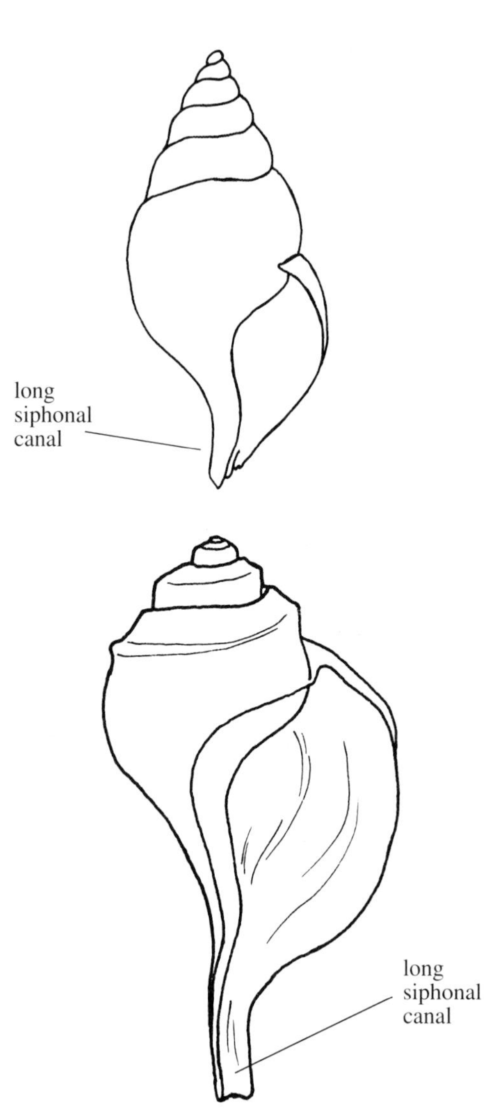

Fig.B. **WHELKS**

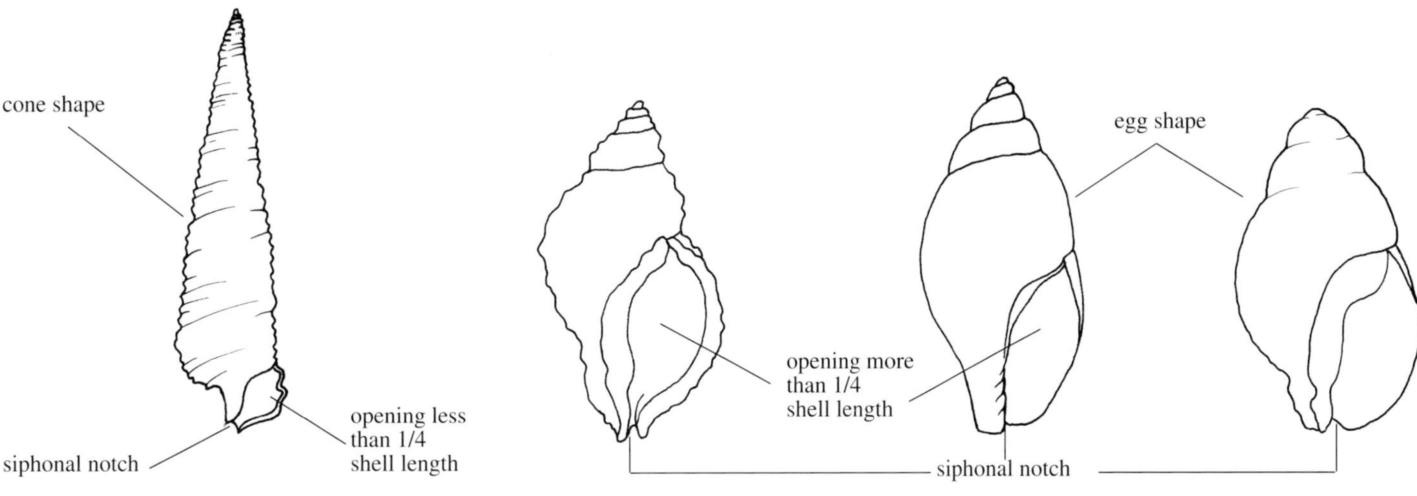

Fig.C. **CERITHS**

Fig.D. **DRILLS, DOG WHELKS, MUDSNAILS, AND DOVESNAILS**

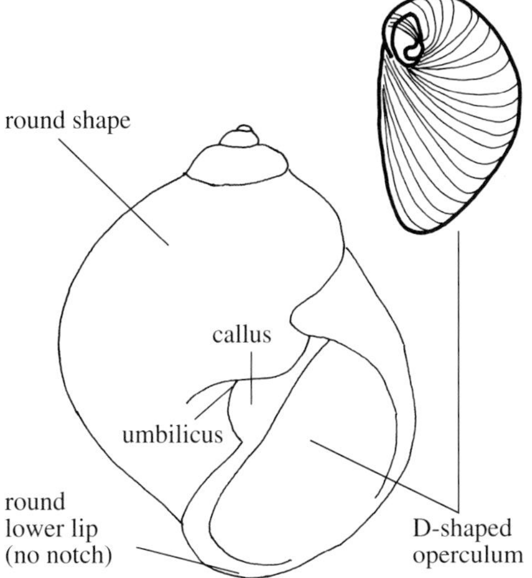

Fig.E. **MOONSNAILS**

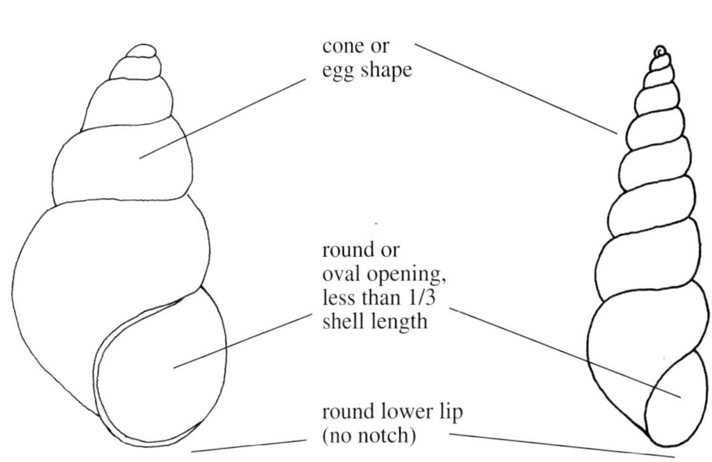

Fig.F. **BITTIUM, RICE, AND SIMILAR SNAILS**

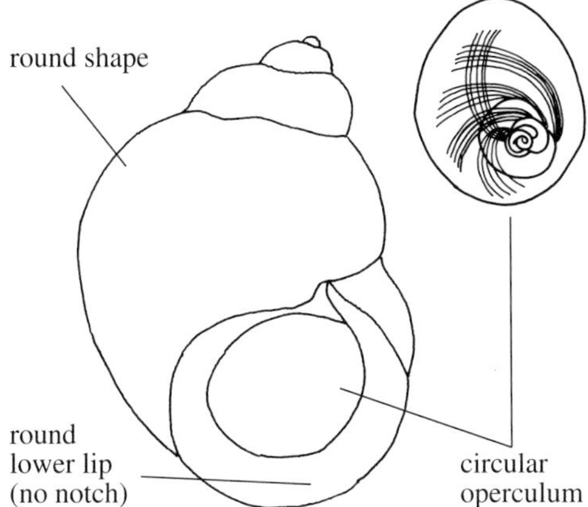

Fig.G. **PERIWINKLES**

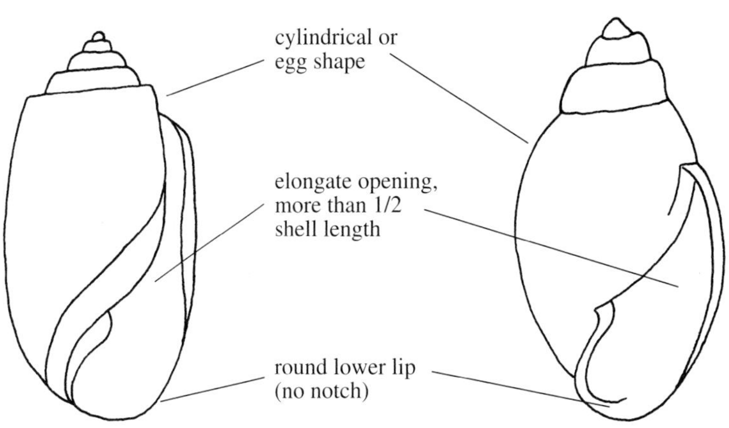

Fig.H. **MARSH AND BUBBLE SNAILS**

MOONSNAILS: PHYLUM MOLLUSCA, CLASS GASTROPODA, FAMILY NATICIDAE

Round snails without a siphonal notch[1]; with a D-shaped opening and operculum; with an umbilicus and/or a callus

(Snail key begins on page 7.02)

#1.Callus is large and obvious (Figs.A,E); umbilicus is almost completely covered over by the callus .... #2
#1.Callus is small or absent; umbilicus is not covered over by the callus (Figs.B-D) .... #4

#2.Callus is purple or brown; shell is wider than high with low flat spire[1]; up to 7.5 cm (3") in diameter .... ***Neverita duplicata*, shark eye** (Fig.A)
#2.Callus is white; shell is slightly higher than wide; up to 3.8 cm (1 1/2") high .... #3

#3.Grows up to 6 mm (1/4") high; operculum is calcareous (shell-like); umbilicus is usually visible; uncommon north of Cape Cod .... ***Tectonatica pusilla*, miniature moonsnail** (Fig.E)
#3.Grows up to 38 mm (1 1/2") high; operculum is horny and thin; umbilicus is completely obscured by callus; uncommon south of Cape Cod .... ***Natica clausa*, Arctic moonsnail** (not shown)

#4.No callus; grows up to 10 cm (4") high; shell is grayish with beige periostracum (outer coating); no spots .... ***Euspira heros*, northern moonsnail** (Fig.B)
#4.With small white callus; less than 2.5 cm (1") high; with dark brown spots or bands .... ***Euspira triseriata*, spotted moonsnail** (Fig.C)
#4.With small white callus; less than 1 cm (1/2") high; shiny white with greenish periostracum, no spots . ***Euspira immaculata*, immaculate moonsnail** (Fig.D)

[1]Refer to Fig.A on page 7.02 for explanation of terms used in snail key.

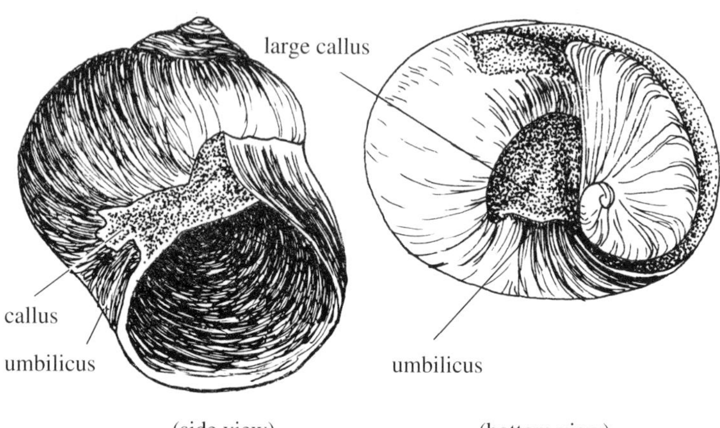

Fig.A. ***NEVERITA DUPLICATA (=Polinices d.)*, SHARK EYE (=lobed moonsnail):** Brown or beige with purple or brown callus; up to 7.5 cm (3") in diameter; occurs in shallow water and the intertidal zone on sandy bottom; produces distinctive collar shaped egg case (see page 2.23, Fig.A); common from Cape Cod south.

umbilicus umbilicus

(bottom view) (side view)

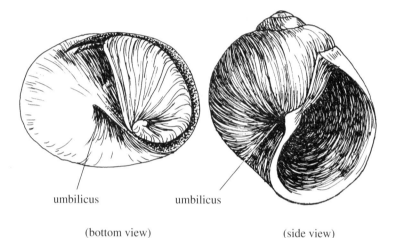

Fig.B. ***EUSPIRA HEROS (=Lunatia h., =Polinices h.)*, NORTHERN MOONSNAIL:** Brown, beige, or gray; up to 10 cm (4") in diameter; common in shallow water on sandy bottom; produces distinctive collar shaped egg case (see page 2.23, Fig.A); common from Long Island, N.Y. north.
17.07 I **17.12 F** **17.12 G**

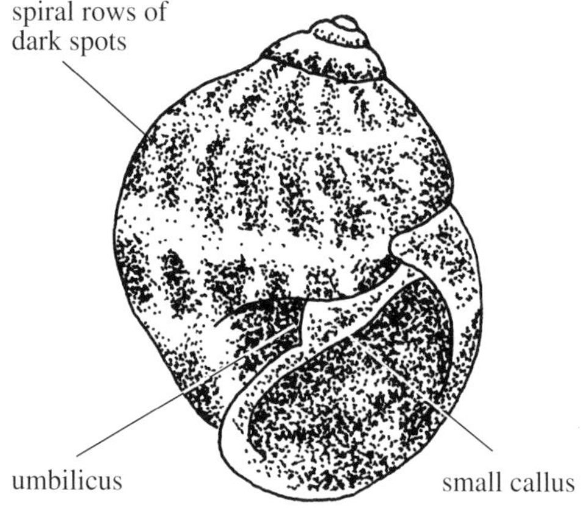

Fig.C. ***EUSPIRA TRISERIATA (=Lunatia t., =Polinices t.)*, SPOTTED MOONSNAIL:** Yellowish-white with spiral bands of squarish dark brown or purplish spots; up to 2.5 cm (1") long; found in shallow water on sandy bottom.

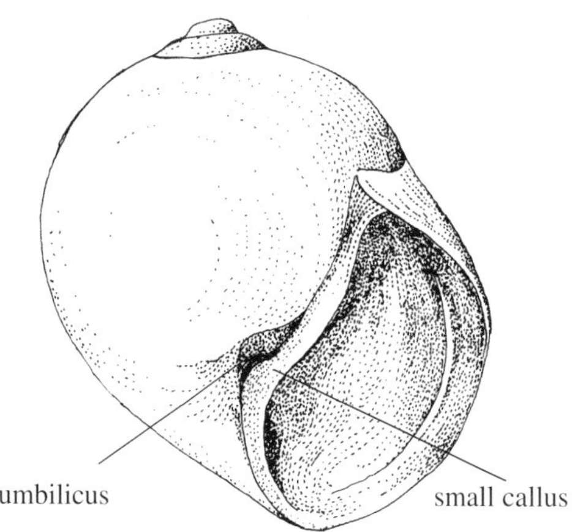

Fig.D. ***EUSPIRA IMMACULATA (=Polinices i.)*, IMMACULATE MOONSNAIL:** Shiny white with greenish periostracum; up to 9 mm (3/8") high; subtidal.

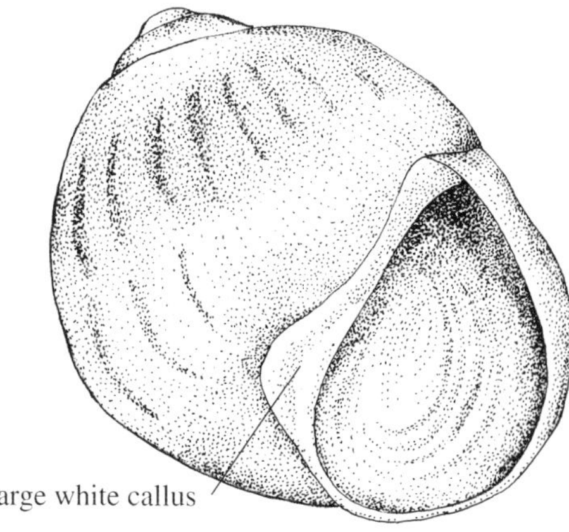

Fig.E. ***TECTONATICA PUSILLA (=Natica p.)*, MINIATURE MOONSNAIL:** With faint light brown bands or spots; up to 6 mm (1/4") high; occurs from Cape Cod south in subtidal waters.

PERIWINKLES: PHYLUM MOLLUSCA, CLASS GASTROPODA

Round snails without a siphonal notch[1]; with a circular opening and operculum plate; no callus or umbilicus

(Snail key begins on page 7.02)

#1.Spire (Fig.A) very flat and low; top of shell is round .... *Littorina obtusata*, **yellow periwinkle** (Fig.A)
#1.Raised spire; top of shell comes to sharp or rounded point (Figs.B-D) .... #2

#2.Sutures (Figs.C,D) are deep and distinct; shell has a terraced appearance; never grows larger than 1.6 cm (5/8") long .... #3
#2.Sutures are very shallow so there is little or no indentation between whorls; grows up to 3 cm (1 1/4") long; the most common periwinkle on the rocky shore .... *Littorina littorea*, **common periwinkle** (Fig.B)

#3.Thick outer lip (Fig.C); no groove on inner lip; grows up to 1.6 cm (5/8") long; found in intertidal zone .... *Littorina saxatilis*, **rough periwinkle** (Fig.C)
#3.Thin, sharp outer lip; crescent shaped groove in inner lip (Fig.D); rarely found larger than 6 mm (1/4") long; found on eelgrass and seaweed below low tide level, usually with distinct white and brown spiral bands but may be all brown .... *Lacuna vincta*, **northern lacuna** (Fig.D)

[1]Refer to Fig.A on page 7.02 for explanation of terms used in snail key.

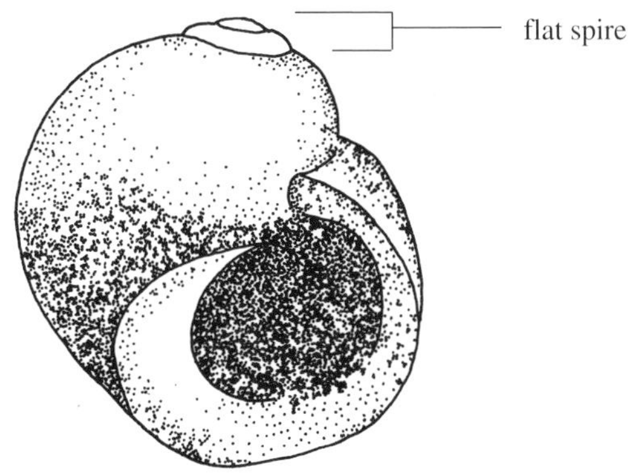

pointed spire
shallow sutures
rounded spire
spiral ridges
(young snail)
(older snail)

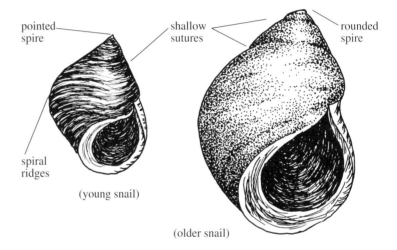

Fig.A. ***LITTORINA OBTUSATA*, YELLOW PERIWINKLE:** Usually green or yellow but also may be orange, brown, or black; less than 1.2 cm (1/2") long; found on rockweed in rocky intertidal zone; eggs shown on page 2.23. (family Littorinidae) **17.07 A**

Fig.B. ***LITTORINA LITTOREA*, COMMON PERIWINKLE:** Usually brown, black or gray; sometimes with whitish spiral lines; up to 3 cm (1 1/4") long; the most common periwinkle in the rocky intertidal zone, also found in saltmarshes; when young, shell has fine spiral ridges and a sharp point at top; when older, it is smooth with top rounded and worn away. (family Littorinidae) **17.07 B** **17.07 C**

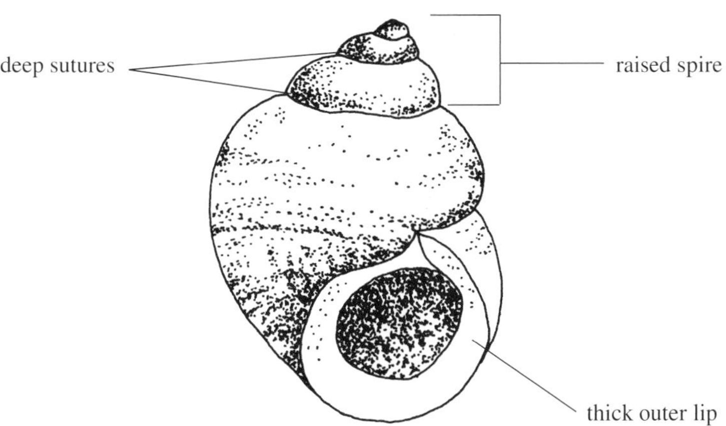

Fig.C. ***LITTORINA SAXATILIS*, ROUGH PERIWINKLE:** Yellow, green, or brown, sometimes with white or colored bands; less than 1.3 cm (1/2") long; found in mid to upper tide level in rocky intertidal zone and tidal marshes. (family Littorinidae) **17.07 D**

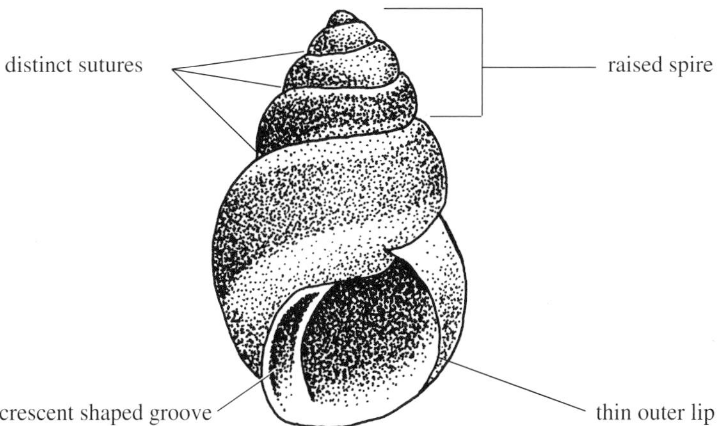

Fig.D. ***LACUNA VINCTA*, NORTHERN LACUNA (=chink shell, =lesser periwinkle):** Usually light brown with four dark brown spiral bands, but may be all brown; may grow up to 10 mm (3/8") high but usually under 6 mm (1/4"); often found in large numbers on eelgrass and algae in shallow water; eggs shown on page 2.23. (family Lacunidae) **17.07 E**

BITTIUM, RICE AND SIMILAR SNAILS: PHYLUM MOLLUSCA, CLASS GASTROPODA

Cone shaped and egg shaped snails without an obvious siphonal notch[1]; opening is round or oval, less than 1/2 the length of the shell.

(Snail key begins on page 7.02)

#1.With one or more folds ("teeth") on columella (inner lip of opening) .... **family Pyramidellidae[2] (in part)** (Fig.A)
#1.Without any folds on columella .... #2

#2.With bladelike vertical ribs; up to 2.5 cm (1") long .... ***Epitonium* spp.[2], wentletraps** (Fig.B)
#2.Without bladelike vertical ribs; tiny snails, less than 6 mm (1/4") long .... #3

#3.Top whorl[1] stands on edge (top whorl sometimes breaks off or wears down); some species have more than 8 whorls .... ***Turbonilla* spp.[2], turbonilles** (Fig.C)
#3.Top whorl does not stand on edge; all species have 8 or fewer whorls .... #4

#4.Shell is smooth, shiny and translucent; without sculptured or etched lines .... ***Hydrobia totteni*, minute hydrobia** (Fig.D)
#4.Shell is sculptured or etched with vertical and/or spiral lines; shell is not shiny or translucent .... #5

#5.Shell is distinctly sculptured with a crisscrossing network of fine lines and grooves giving shell surface a "waffle" texture; dull gray or brownish color; with 6 to 8 whorls; lip of opening has a barely perceptible siphonal notch; very common .... ***Bittium alternatum*, alternate bittium** (Fig.E)
#5.Shell is lightly etched with vertical and/or spiral lines; with 6 or fewer whorls; lip of opening has no siphonal notch; usually white or light yellow; not common .... **family Rissoidae[2]** (Fig.F)

[1]Refer to Fig.A on page 7.02 for explanation of terms used in snail key.
[2]Refer to a good shell book to identify the species. This group includes a number of very similar species which occur in this region (see Weiss et al., 1995).

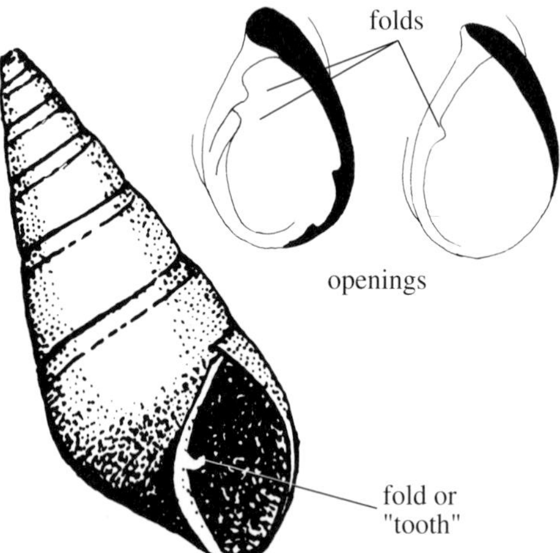

Fig.A. **FAMILY PYRAMIDELLIDAE[2]:** Usually white; tiny, up to 6 mm (1/4") long; occur in intertidal zone and in shallow water; some species are parasitic on slippersnails and other mollusks.

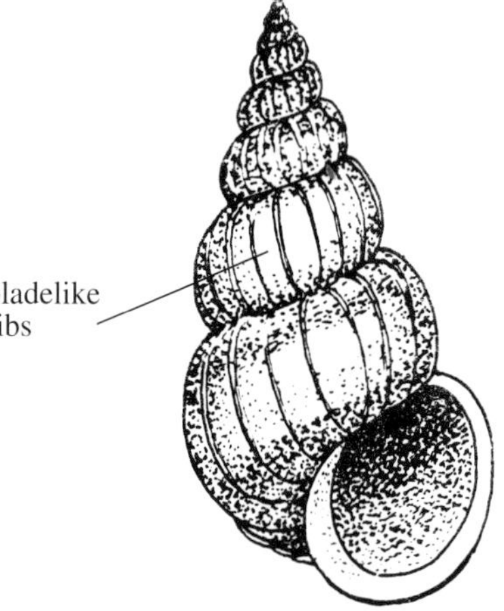

Fig.B. ***EPITONIUM* SPP.[2], WENTLETRAPS:** White or gray, with brown bands on some species; up to 2 cm (3/4") long; not common. (family Epitoniidae: wentletraps)

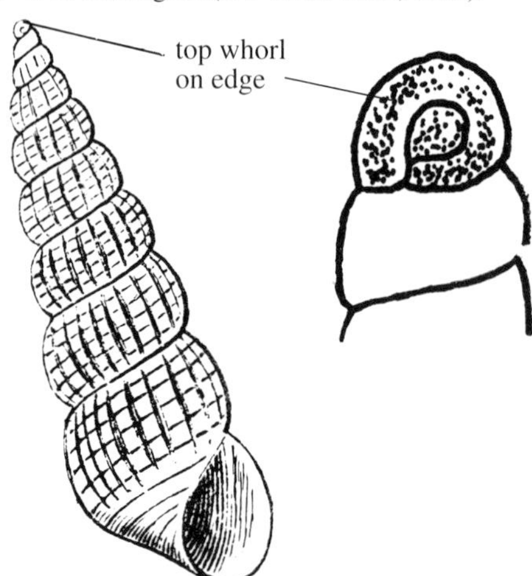

Fig.C. ***TURBONILLA* SPP.[2], TURBONILLES:** Often shiny, yellowish white; tiny, up to about 6 mm (1/4") long; live in deeper water, not common. (family Pyramidellidae: odostomes, turbonilles)

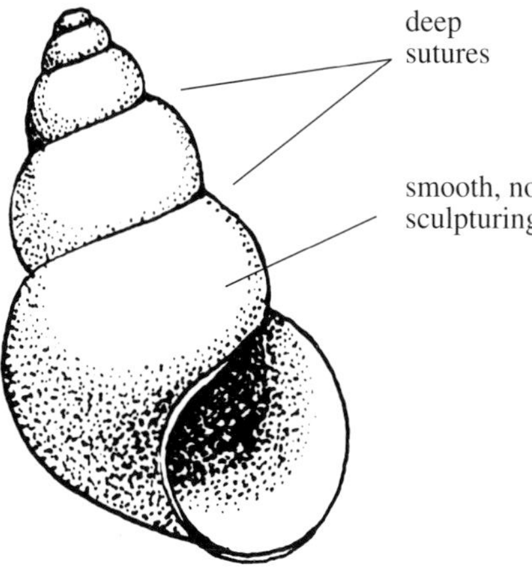

Fig.D. ***HYDROBIA TOTTENI*, MINUTE HYDROBIA:** Shiny, translucent, yellowish brown; tiny, up to 3 mm (1/8") long; found in saltmarsh pools and on seaweeds. (family Hydrobiidae)

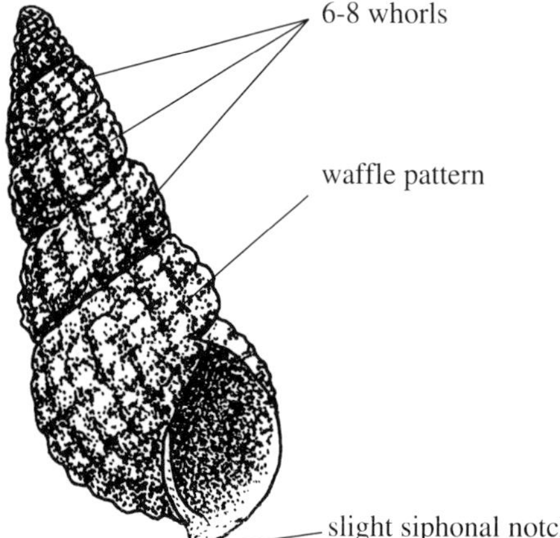

Fig.E. ***BITTIUM ALTERNATUM*, ALTERNATE BITTIUM:** Gray, brown or dull brick color; up to 6 mm (1/4") long; common in shallow water on eelgrass, also in intertidal zone; see eggs on page 2.23. (family Cerithiidae: ceriths)

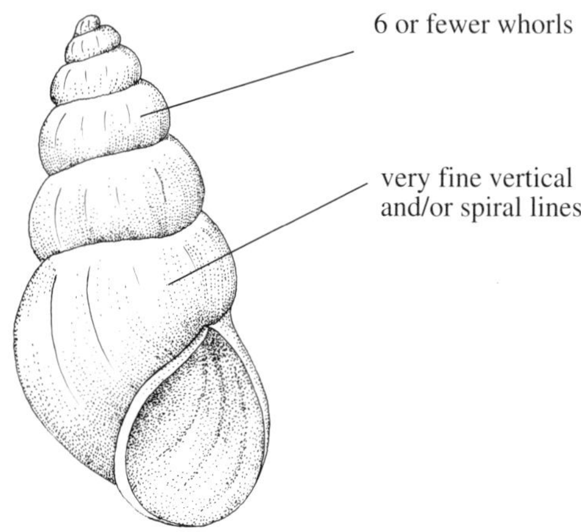

Fig.F. **FAMILY RISSOIDAE[2]:** The most common species is *Onoba aculeus (=Cingula a.)*, the pointed cingula. It is light yellow or brown; tiny, up to 3 mm (1/8") long; occurs in shallow water .

MARSH AND BUBBLE SNAILS: PHYLUM MOLLUSCA, CLASS GASTROPODA

Cylindrical or egg shaped snails without a siphonal notch[1]; opening is elongate, at least 1/2 the length of the shell

(Snail key begins on page 7.02)

#1.Opening is about 2/3 or less of the length of the shell (Figs.A-D) .... #2
#1.Opening is about 3/4 or more of the length of the shell (Figs.E,F) .... #4

#2.With two small teeth or folds on inner lip of opening (Figs.C,D); usually found in saltmarshes; brown color .... #3
#2.Without small teeth on inner lip; not found on saltmarshes; shiny white with spiral dotted lines .... ***Rictaxis punctostriatus*, pitted baby-bubble** (Fig.A)
#2.Without small teeth on inner lip; found at upland border of saltmarshes and on brackish water marshes .... ***Succinea wilsoni*, golden ambersnail[2]** (Fig.B)

#3.Egg shaped, with short spire; 5-6 whorls; up to 15 mm (5/8") long; with shallow sutures; very common on saltmarshes .... ***Melampus bidentatus*, eastern melampus[2]** (Fig.C)
#3.Top shaped, with elongate spire; 7-8 whorls; up to 8 mm (3/8") long, with deep sutures; not common .... ***Ovatella myosotis*, mouse ear marsh snail[2]** (Fig.D)

#4.With small but distinct spire; opening does not extend to the top of the shell .... ***Acteocina canaliculata*, channeled barrel-bubble** (Fig.E)
#4.No obvious spire; opening extends to the top of the shell .... **order Cephalaspidea, bubble snails[3]** (Fig.F)

[1]Refer to Fig.A on page 7.02 for explanation of terms used in snail key.
[2]This is a pulmonate (air breathing) snail belonging to the subclass Pulmonata.
[3]Over 8 different species of bubble snails are found in this region (see Weiss et al., 1995). They are all very similar to Fig.F. Refer to a shell book such as Morris (1975) for specific identification. When extended, their body almost completely encloses the shell and sometimes cannot be fully retracted into the shell. *Haminoea solitaria*, the solitary glassy-bubble, is the largest and most common bubble snail. It is whitish; up to 12 mm (1/2") long; and occurs on intertidal mudflats.

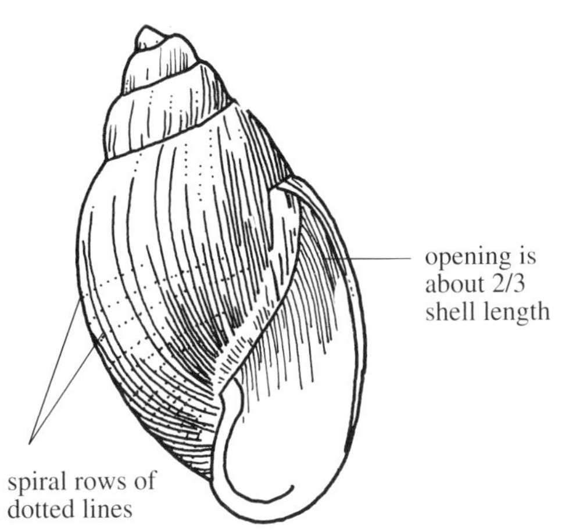

Fig.A. ***RICTAXIS PUNCTOSTRIATUS (=Acteon p.),* PITTED BABY-BUBBLE:** Shiny white; up to 6 mm (1/4") long; not common. (family Acteonidae: baby-bubbles)

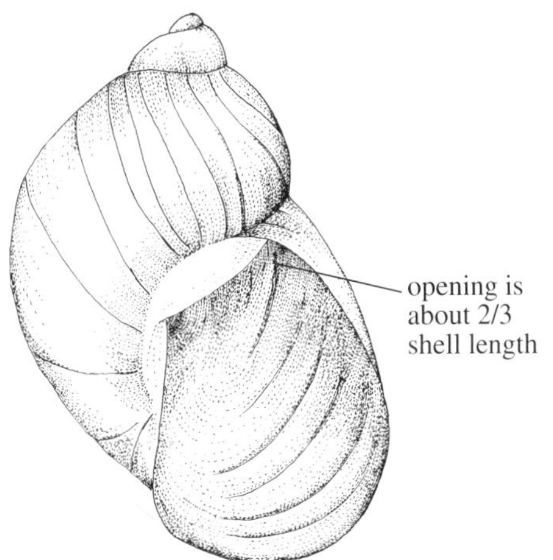

Fig.B. ***SUCCINEA WILSONI,* GOLDEN AMBERSNAIL:** Up to 12 mm (1/2") long; occurs at the upland border of saltmarshes and on brackish water marshes[2]. (family Succineidae: ambersnails)

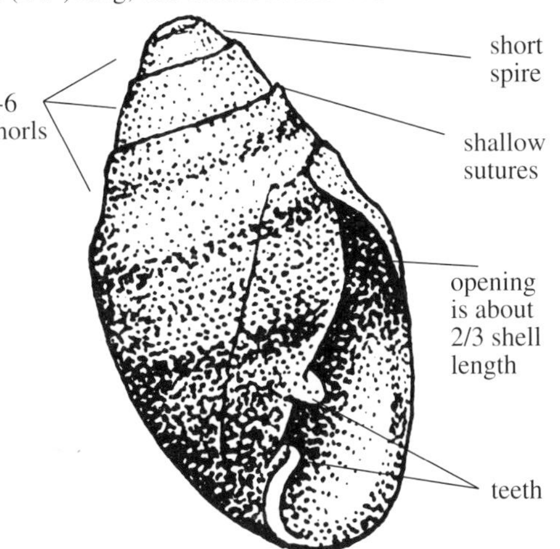

Fig.C. ***MELAMPUS BIDENTATUS,* EASTERN MELAMPUS:** Smooth and shiny; brown to olive green, sometimes with brown spiral bands; up to 12 mm (1/2") long; very common on tidal marshes near high tide level[2]; climbs up on marsh grasses to stay above water level as tide rises; found at base of grasses and under vegetation when tide is out. (family Melampodidae: marsh snails)

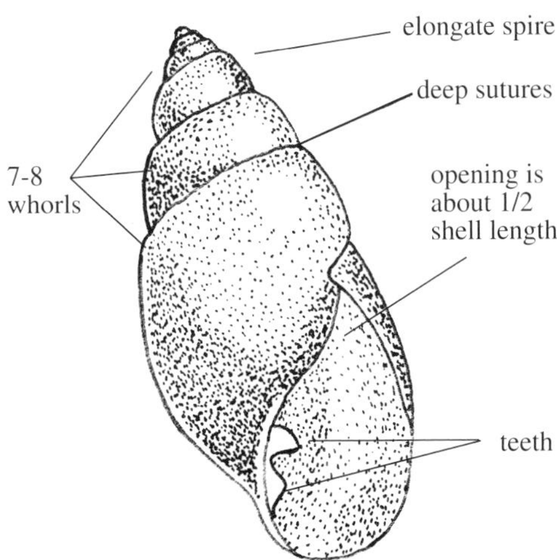

Fig.D. ***OVATELLA MYOSOTIS,* MOUSE EAR MARSH SNAIL:** Translucent brownish; up to 6 mm (1/4") long; lives near high tide level on marshes, pilings, rocks[2]. (family Melampodidae: marsh snails)

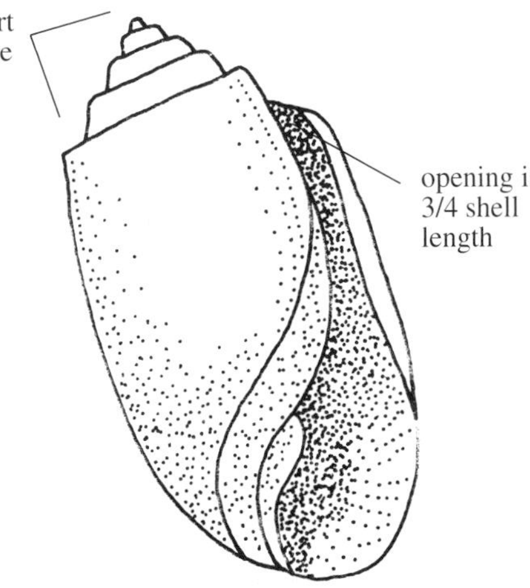

Fig.E. ***ACTEOCINA CANALICULATA (=Retusa c.),* CHANNELED BARREL-BUBBLE:** Shiny white; up to 4 mm (3/16") long; found on sand and mudflats. (family Scaphandridae)

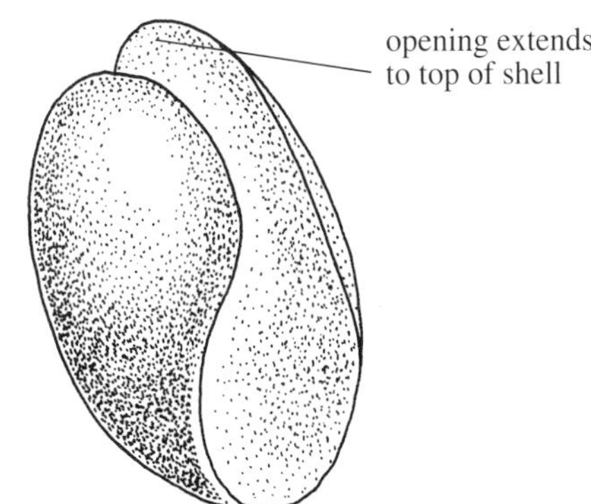

Fig.F. **ORDER CEPHALASPIDEA, BUBBLE SNAILS:** Often whitish; up to 12 mm (1/2") long. A number of species occur in this region[3].

DRILLS, WHELKS, MUDSNAILS, AND DOVESNAILS: PHYLUM MOLLUSCA, CLASS GASTROPODA

Egg or spindle shaped snails with a siphonal canal[1] or notch

(Snail key begins on page 7.02)

#1.With a distinct siphonal canal (Figs. A,B), forming a pointed extension to lower lip of opening (if in doubt, make this choice) .... #2
#1.With a siphonal notch but no siphonal canal, lower lip of opening is somewhat blunt (Figs. C-K) .... #4

#2.With sharp, angular spiral ridges and transverse ribs giving shell a jagged appearance; siphonal canal is nearly 1/4 the total shell length and is extremely narrow; bottom end of shell is sharply pointed .... ***Eupleura caudata*, thick-lip drill** (Fig.A)
#2.Edges of whorls are rounded (Figs.B,D); siphonal canal is about 1/8 the total shell length and is not very narrow; bottom of shell is moderately pointed .... #3

#3.With deep distinct ribs running lengthwise from the top to the bottom of the shell; ribs are crisscrossed by fine spiral ridges giving the shell a knobby texture; lips of opening rather thin and sharp .... ***Urosalpinx cinerea*, Atlantic oyster drill** (Fig.B)
#3.Without distinct ribs running length of shell .... #4

#4.Shell is stout and thick walled; inner lip is somewhat flattened and often looks polished (Figs. C-G) .... #5
#4.Shell is slender and thin walled; inner lip is rounded (Figs.H-K) .... #9

#5.Large snail, up to 10 cm (4") shell length; body flesh is white with black spots and blotches; shell has distinct longitudinal rounded ribs crisscrossed by finer spiral ridges, creating a wavy appearance; very rare south of Cape Cod except offshore in deep waters; common subtidal snail north of Cape Cod, rarely occurring in intertidal zone .... ***Buccinum undatum*, waved whelk** (Fig.G)
#5.Under 35 mm (1 1/2") long; body not white with black spots; shell does not have distinct longitudinal ribs; common in intertidal zone on rocks and mud .. #6

#6.With spiral ridges, giving shell a corrugated texture; outer lip of opening rather thick; siphonal canal is variable in length and bottom end of shell may appear more or less pointed; very common on rocks in intertidal zone .... ***Nucella lapillus*, Atlantic dogwinkle** (Fig.D)
#6.Without spiral ridges; outer lip of opening thin walled; usually found on sandflats and mudflats .... #7

#7.Inner lip is dark; extremely common on intertidal mudflats; grooves in shell usually worn and indistinct so shell looks smooth or "dirty"; apex ("point") often worn and rounded; no groove between siphonal canal and body whorl .... ***Ilyanassa obsoleta*, eastern mudsnail** (Fig.E)
#7.Inner lip is light; not common on intertidal mudflats, usually found offshore on sandflats; distinct, "clean," pattern of grooves in shell; apex usually pointed; may have groove between siphonal canal and body whorl .... #8

#8.Upper and outer lips are thin; shell has distinct waffle pattern created by sharp spiral and vertical grooves; 6 or more whorls[1] .... ***Ilyanassa trivittata*, threeline mudsnail** (Fig.C)
#8.Upper and outer lips are thick; inner lip is very broad and flattened; 5 or fewer whorls .... ***Nassarius vibex*, bruised nassa** (Fig.F)

#9.With a notch at the top of the outer lip; each whorl sharply rounded .... ***Kurtziella cerina*, waxed-colored mangelia** (Fig.H)
#9.No notch at top of outer lip; whorls are only slightly rounded (Figs.I-K) .... #10

#10.With 2-3 rows of glassy beads on each whorl .... ***Cerithiopsis greeni*, Green's miniature cerith** (Fig.I)
#10.Without beads (Figs.J-K) .... #11

#11.Smooth and glossy; crescent shaped markings; smaller than 6 mm (1/4") in length .... ***Mitrella lunata*, lunar dovesnail** (Fig.J)
#11.With low, rounded ribs on each whorl; blotched markings; grows up to 18 mm (3/4") long .... ***Anachis* spp., dovesnails** (Fig.K)

[1]Refer to Fig. A on page 7.02 for explanation of terms used in snail key.

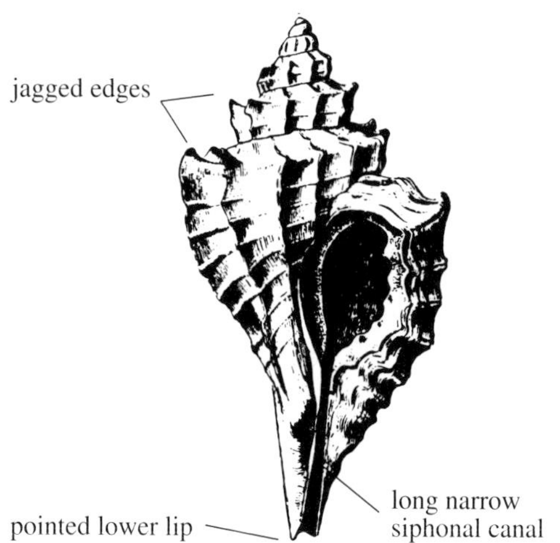

Fig.A. ***EUPLEURA CAUDATA*, THICK-LIP DRILL:** Grayish or reddish brown; up to 25 mm (1") long; found on rocky shores but not as common as other drills; egg case shown on page 2.24. (family Muricidae: drills)

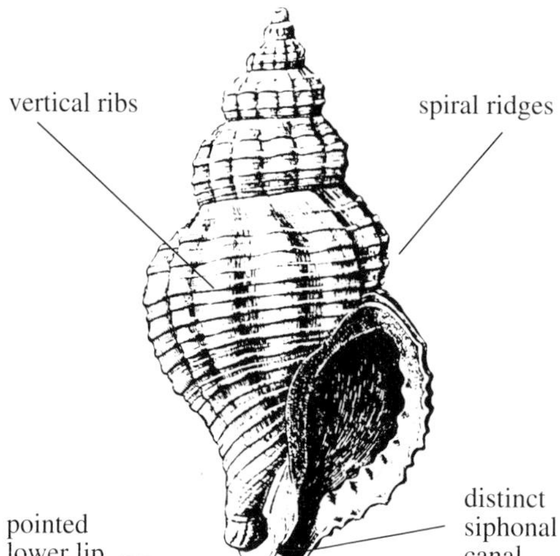

Fig.B. ***UROSALPINX CINEREA*, ATLANTIC OYSTER DRILL:** Gray; up to 3 cm (1 1/4") long; the most common of the drills; found on rocks and shellfish beds; egg case shown on page 2.24. (family Muricidae: drills) **17.06 E**

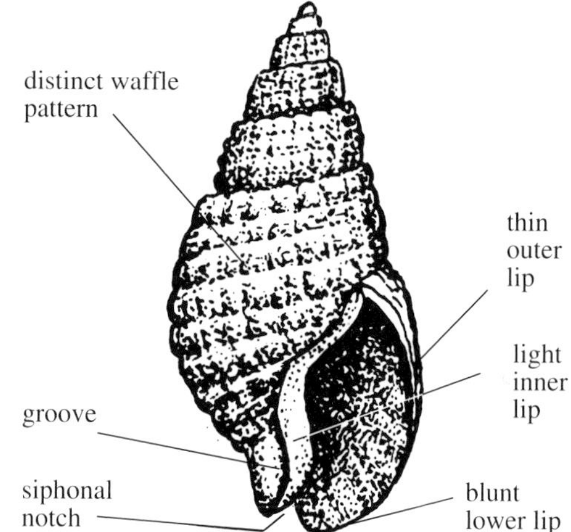

Fig.C. ***ILYANASSA TRIVITTATA* (=*Nassarius t.*), THREELINE MUDSNAIL (=New England dog whelk):** White or beige; up to 2 cm (3/4") long; common offshore on sandy bottom, not usually on mudflats. (family Nassariidae) **17.07 F**

spiral ridges
thick, flattened inner lip
pointed form with longer siphonal canal
thick outer lip
blunter form with shorter siphonal canal

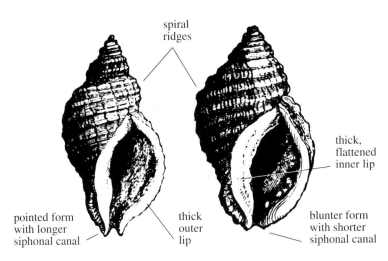

Fig.D. ***NUCELLA LAPILLUS (=Thais l.),*** **ATLANTIC DOGWINKLE:** Color variable including white, gray, purple, brown, and yellow; up to 3.5 cm (1 1/2") long; the most common drill on some rocky shores; egg case shown on page 2.24. (family Muricidae: drills)

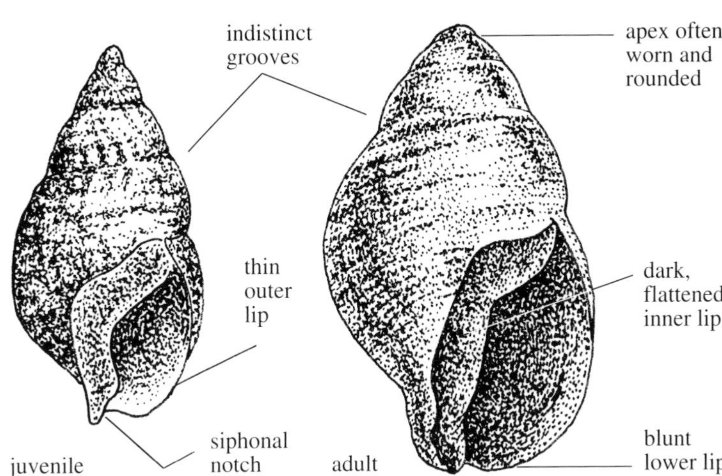

Fig.E. ***ILYANASSA OBSOLETA (=Nassa o., =Nassarius o.),*** **EASTERN MUDSNAIL**: Gray-black or dark brown; often covered with a fuzzy, moldlike, or enamel-like growth that may be greenish, whitish, or pinkish (growth may be a hydroid colony, see page 4.06); up to 2.5 cm (1") long; very common on mudflats; egg case shown on page 2.24. (family Nassariidae) **17.07 G**

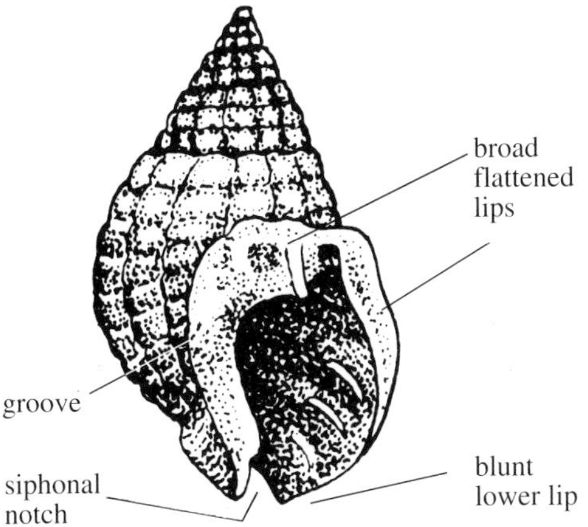

Fig.F. ***NASSARIUS VIBEX,*** **BRUISED NASSA**: Gray or brown; up to 13 mm (1/2") long; found in shallow water on mud-sand bottoms; much less common than the two species of *Ilyanassa*; egg case shown on page 2.24. (family Nassariidae)

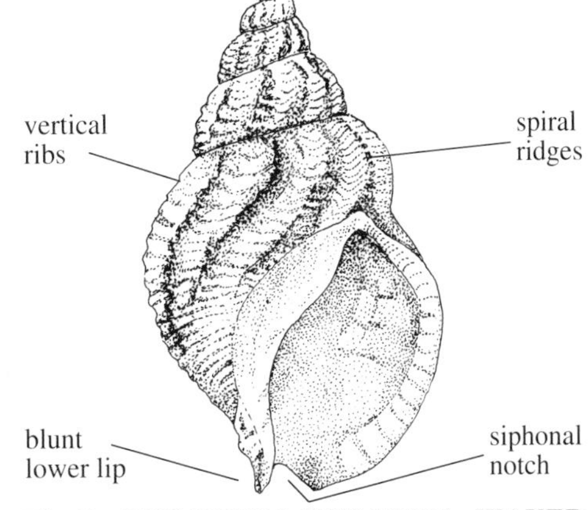

Fig.G. ***BUCCINUM UNDATUM,*** **WAVED WHELK:** Dull white or tan with yellowish outer layer, body white with black spots; up to 10 cm (4") long; common in shallow water north of Cape Cod; egg case on p. 2.23. (family Buccinidae) **17.07 H**

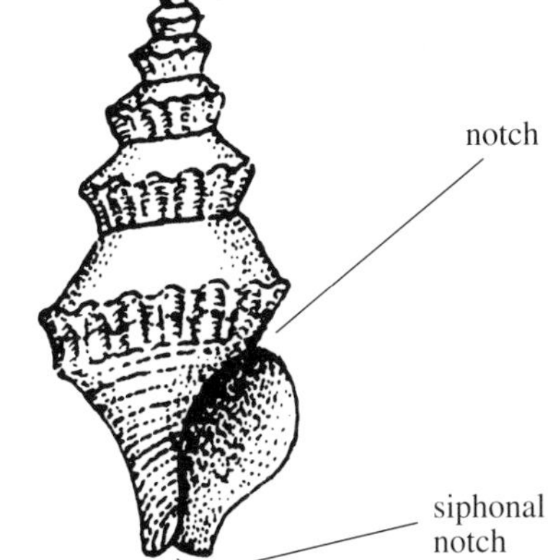

Fig.H. ***KURTZIELLA CERINA (=Mangelia c.),*** **WAX-COLORED MANGELIA:** White; up to 13 mm (1/2") long; not common. (family Turridae: turret shells)

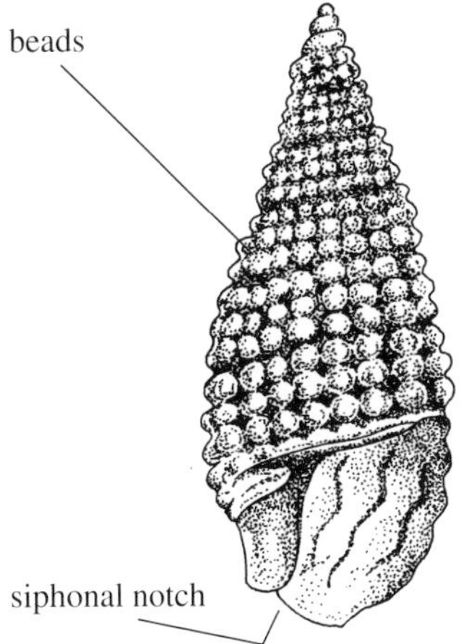

Fig.I. ***CERITHIOPSIS GREENI,*** **GREEN'S MINIATURE CERITH:** Brown; length up to 3 mm (1/8") long; not common. (family Cerithiopsidae: miniature ceriths)

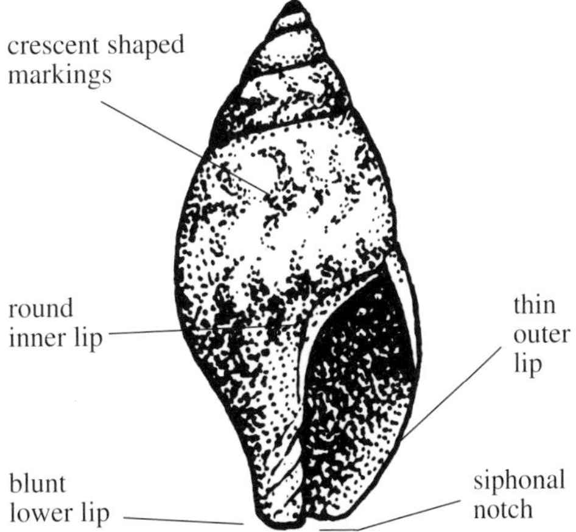

Fig.J. ***MITRELLA LUNATA,*** **LUNAR DOVESNAIL:** Beige with brown crescent shaped markings; tiny, less than 5 mm (1/4") long; common on eelgrass and seaweed in shallow waters. (family Columbellidae: dovesnails)

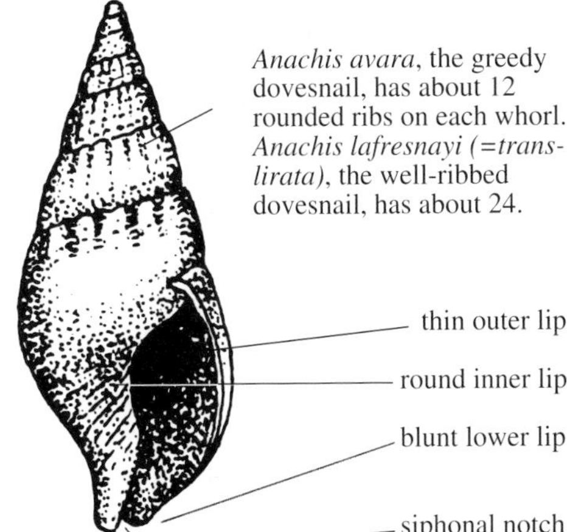

Fig.K. ***ANACHIS*** **SPP., DOVESNAILS:** Light brown with darker reddish-brown blotches; up to 18 mm (3/4") long; common on seaweeds near low tide level. See above to distinguish the two local species. (family Columbellidae: dovesnails) **17.06 F**

WHELKS: PHYLUM MOLLUSCA, CLASS GASTROPODA

Large snails with a long siphonal canal[1]

(Snail key begins on page 7.02)

#1.Opening (including siphonal canal) is about 1/2 the shell length .... ***Colus* spp., whelks** (Fig.A)
#1.Opening (including siphonal canal) is about 3/4 the shell length (Figs.B,C) .... #2

#2.A deep groove or "channel" (Fig.B) spirals around top of shell; outer edge ("shoulder") of body whorl is broad and flat, without knobs .... ***Busycotypus canaliculatus*, channeled whelk** (Fig.B)
#2.No groove around top of shell; outer edge ("shoulder") of body whorl has a row of knobs or bumps .... ***Busycon carica*, knobbed whelk** (Fig.C)

[1]Refer to Fig. A on page 7.02 for terms used in snail key.

opening about 1/2 shell length

Fig.A. ***COLUS* SPP.:** Occurs near shore north of Cape Cod but only offshore and in deep water to the south. *Colus stimpsoni*, Stimpsons whelk, the largest and most common species, has a white shell with a thin brown outer shell covering; grows up to 13 cm (5") long. The other two local *Colus* species are under 62 mm (2 1/2") long. (family Buccinidae)

groove or "channel"

opening about 3/4 shell length

Fig.B. ***BUSYCOTYPUS CANALICULATUS (=Busycon c.)*, CHANNELED WHELK:** Beige or yellowish gray; often covered with a hairy outer shell layer; up to 20 cm (8") long; very common in shallow water on sand; has distinctive egg case (see Fig.G on page 2.23). (family Melongenidae)
17.06 C **17.06 D**

knobs

opening about 3/4 shell length

Fig.C. ***BUSYCON CARICA*, KNOBBED WHELK:** Gray, sometimes with purplish streaks; largest snail in this region, up to 23 cm (9") long; lives in shallow water on sand, not as common as channeled whelk; produces distinctive egg case (see Fig.F on page 2.23). (family Melongenidae)

CERITHS AND TRIPHORAS: PHYLUM MOLLUSCA, CLASS GASTROPODA

Cone shaped snails with a siphonal notch[1] and small opening

(Snail key begins on page 7.02)

#1.Shell has a left handed coil; opening is to your left side when facing the shell .... ***Triphora nigrocincta*, black-line triphora** (Fig.D)
#1.Shell has a right handed coil; opening is to your right side when facing the shell (Figs.E,F) .... #2

#2.With a sharp ridge spiraling around the shell so it looks like a tiny wood screw .... ***Seila adamsi*, Adams' miniature cerith** (Fig.E)
#2.Rows of tiny, raised beads spiral around shell .... ***Cerithiopsis emersonii*, awl miniature cerith** (Fig.F)

[1]Refer to Fig.A on page 7.02 for terms used in snail key.

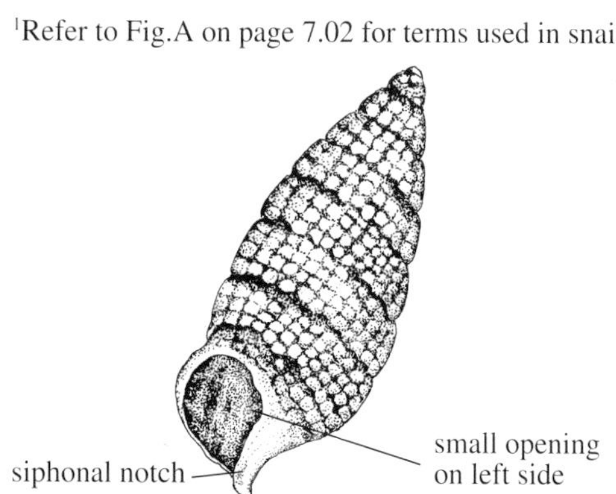

Fig.D. ***TRIPHORA NIGROCINCTA*, BLACK-LINE TRIPHORA:** Blackish-brown with glassy, grayish beads; up to 6 mm (1/4") long; lives on algae and under rocks. (family Triphoridae)

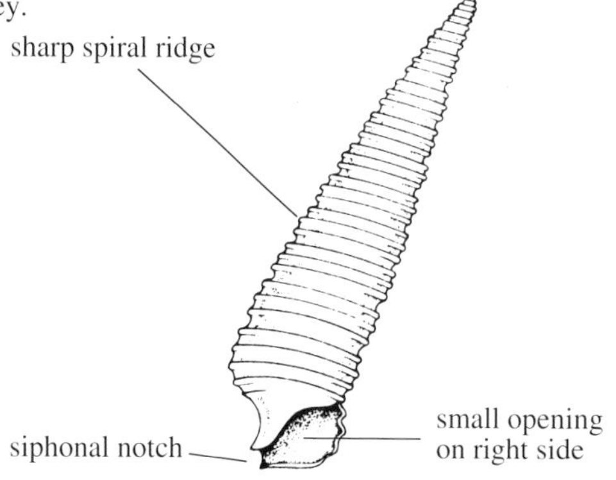

Fig.E. ***SEILA ADAMSI*, ADAMS' MINIATURE CERITH:** Chocolate brown or yellowish; up to 1.3 cm (1/2") long; not common. (family Cerithiopsidae)

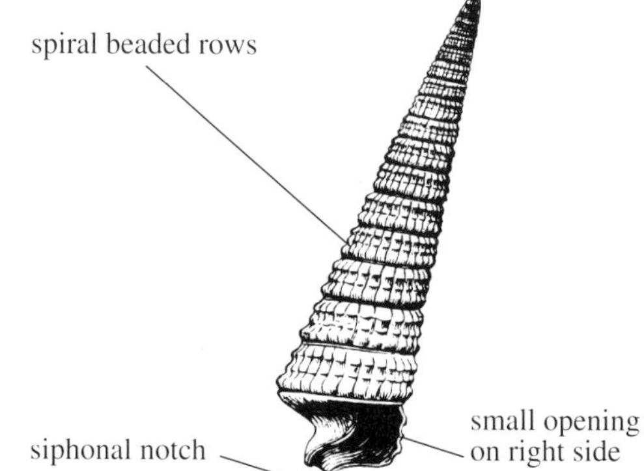

Fig.F. ***CERITHIOPSIS EMERSONII*, AWL MINIATURE CERITH:** Chocolate brown with lighter colored, shiny beads; up to 1.5 cm (5/8") long; not common. (family Cerithiopsidae)

SEA SLUGS (NUDIBRANCHS AND SACOGLOSSANS)
PHYLUM MOLLUSCA, CLASS GASTROPODA, ORDERS SACOGLOSSA AND NUDIBRANCHIA

Gastropods without shells

(Use the key on page 2.16 to determine if you have a sea slug)

#1.With a circle of gills[1] near middle or posterior end (Figs.A-C) ... #2
#1.Without a circle of gills (Figs.D-G) ... #6

#2.Circle of gills near posterior end; broad, oval, flattened body (Fig.A) ... **family Onchidorididae, dorid nudibranchs,** #3
#2.Circle of gills near middle of back; slender, elongate body (Figs.B,C) ... #5

#3.Surface with cone shaped bumps, all about the same size; gills are featherlike with numerous branchlets ... ***Acanthodoris pilosa*, hairy spiny doris** (Fig.A)
#3.Surface with rounded bumps, varying in size; gills are featherlike without secondary branchlets ... #4

#4.With dark brown and whitish markings ... ***Onchidoris bilamellata*, barnacle-eating onchidoris** (Fig.A)
#4.Yellow or white body ... ***Onchidoris muricata*, fuzzy onchidoris** (Fig.A)

#5.With a low bumpy rim or ridge along each side of body ... **family Polyceridae** (Fig.B)
#5.Without any rim along sides of body ... ***Ancula gibbosa*, Atlantic ancula** (Fig.C)

#6.With cerata[1] (leafy, clublike or fingerlike projections on the back) (Fig. D) ... **eolid and other nudibranchs,** page 7.12
#6.Without cerata (Figs.F,G) ... #7

#7.With a mantle which covers the head and foot; with a pair of gills on the underside near the rear end between the foot and the mantle; sides of body do not fold upward; with a pair of tentacles[1] on the upper surface near the front of the mantle ... ***Doridella obscura*, obscure corambe** (Fig.E)
#7.No mantle; no gills on underside; sides of body fold upward (Figs. F,G); with a pair of short tentacles at tip of head ... ***Elysia* spp., sacoglossans,** #8

#8.Sides of body fold up along entire length of body; folds may overlap at top ... ***Elysia chlorotica*, emerald elysia** (Fig.F)
#8.Sides of body fold up in front 2/3 of body; fold does not extend to posterior tip of foot; folds do not meet at top ... ***Elysia catulus*** (Fig.G)

[1]Nudibranchs should be examined and identified while they are alive and relaxed. Their physical features are greatly distorted when preserved. Some nudibranchs can withdraw their gills and tentacles when disturbed.

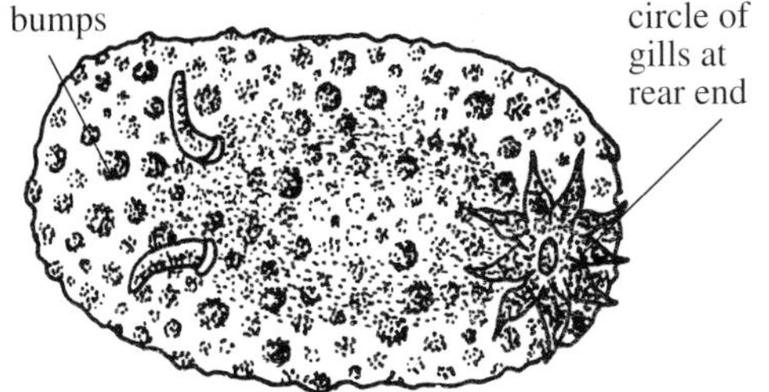

Fig.A. **FAMILY ONCHIDORIDIDAE:** *Acanthodoris pilosa*, hairy spiny doris, may be white, yellow, purple, brown, or black; up to 3 cm (1 1/4") long; found under rocks in lower intertidal zone and offshore. *Onchidoris bilamellata (=fusca)*, barnacle-eating onchidoris, has white and dark brown markings; up to 2.5 cm (1") long; midtide level to offshore; found on barnacle covered rocks. *Onchidoris muricata (=aspera)*, fuzzy onchidoris, is white or yellow; up to 1.2 cm (1/2") long; found under rocks in lower intertidal zone and offshore.

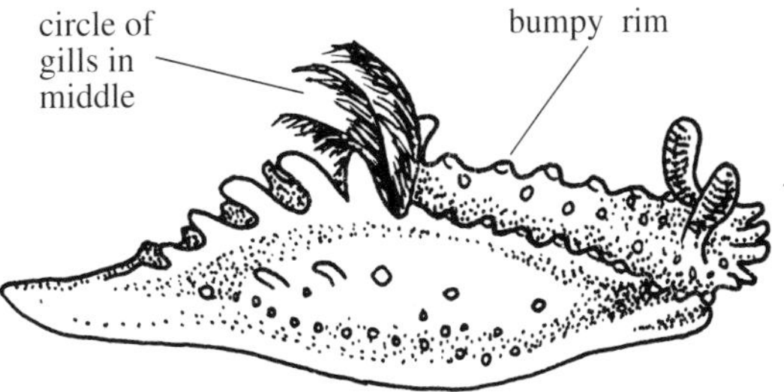

Fig.B. **FAMILY POLYCERIDAE:** A common species, *Polycera dubia*, is yellowish green with bright yellow bumps; up to 2 cm (3/4") long; lives under rocks in lower intertidal zone and below.

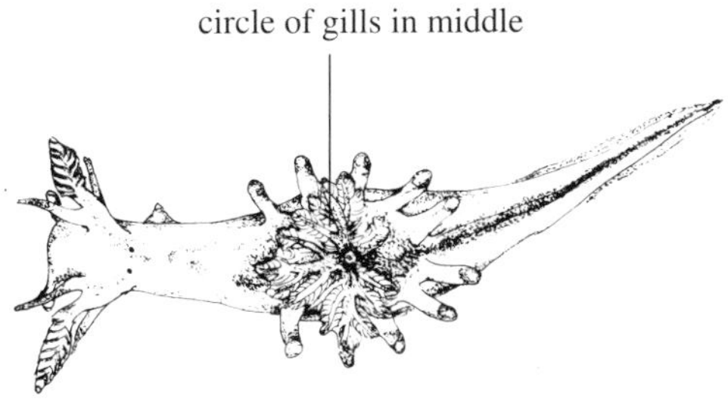

Fig.C. ***ANCULA GIBBOSA*, ATLANTIC ANCULA:** Whitish; up to 1.2 cm (1/2") long; found in lower intertidal zone and offshore. (family Goniodorididae)

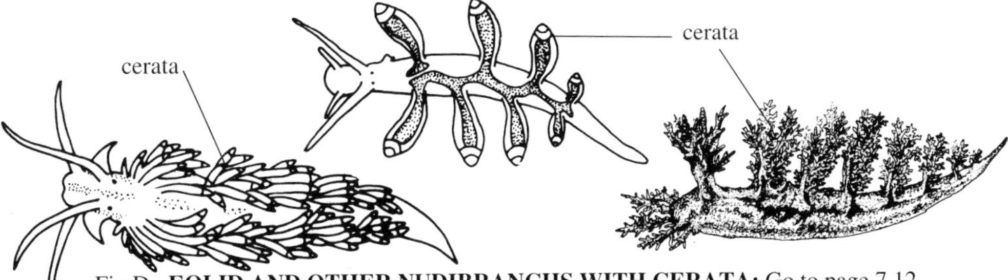

Fig.D. **EOLID AND OTHER NUDIBRANCHS WITH CERATA:** Go to page 7.12

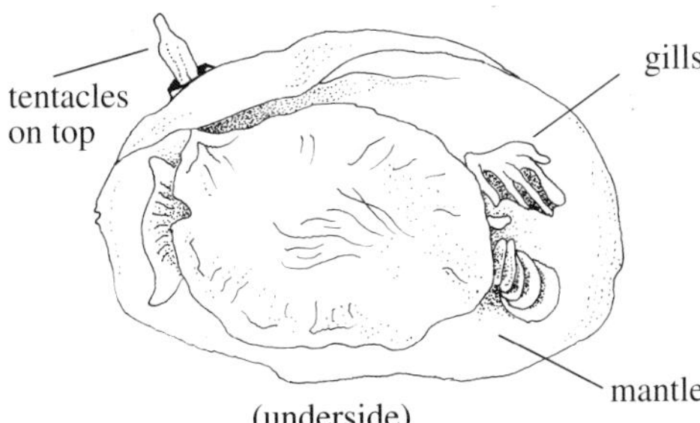

Fig.E.***DORIDELLA OBSCURA* (=*Corambe o.*):** Up to 8 mm (5/16") long; common on encrusting bryozoans. (family Corambidae)

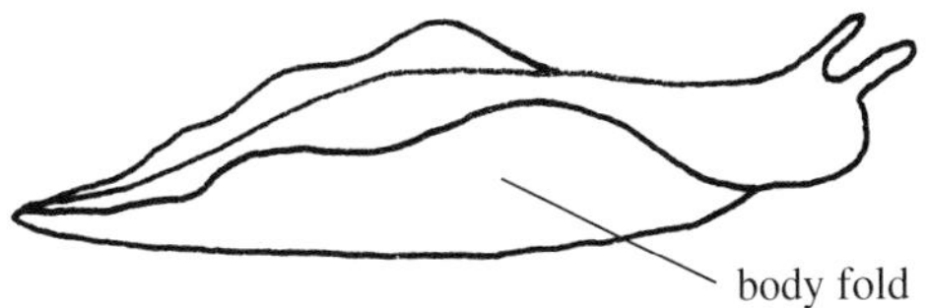

Fig.F. ***ELYSIA CHLOROTICA*, EMERALD ELYSIA:** Green; up to 3 cm (1 1/4") long found in saltmarshes. (family Elysiidae)

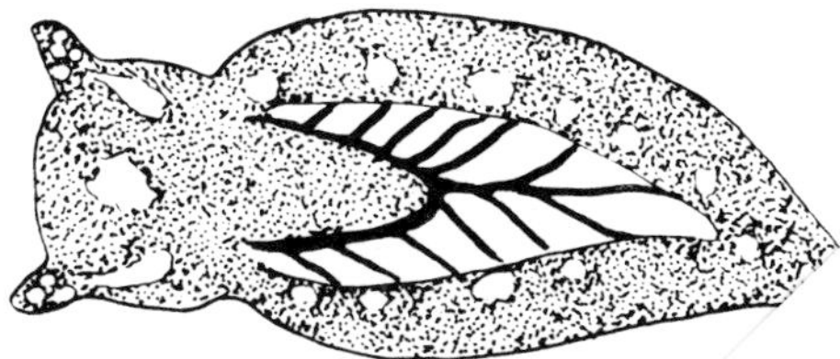

Fig.G. ***ELYSIA CATULUS*:** Green; u
(3/8") long; found on eelgrass. (fam

SEA SLUGS (NUDIBRANCHS) WITH CERATA PHYLUM MOLLUSCA, CLASS GASTROPODA, ORDER NUDIBRANCHIA, SUBORDERS EOLIDACEA AND DENDRONOTACEA

(Sea slug key begins on page 7.11)

#1.Cerata[1] are branched and bushy .... ***Dendronotus frondosus*, frond-aeolis** (Fig.A)
#1.Cerata are not branched (Figs.B-O) .... #2

#2.Front of head is flattened to form a velum .... ***Tenellia fuscata*** (Fig.B)
#2.No velum (Figs.C-O) .... #3

#3.With two pairs of tentacles (Figs.C-L) .... #4
#3.With one pair of tentacles (Figs.M-O) .... #13

#4.With club shaped cerata; fewer than 15 cerata on each side (Figs.C-E) .... #5
#4.With slender cerata; more than 20 cerata on each side (Figs.F-L) .... #7

#5.Tentacles extend from a trumpetlike sheath at the base; cerata are club shaped and are ringed with tubercles .... ***Doto coronata*, crown doto** (Fig.C)
#5.Tentacles do not have basal sheaths; cerata are not ringed with tubercles (Figs.D,E) .... #6

#6.With 4-5 cerata per side; transparent white body .... ***Tergipes tergipes*** (Fig.D)
#6.With 5-10 cerata per side; green or brown spotted body .... ***Eubranchus exiguus*, dwarf balloon aeolis** (Fig.E)

#7.Broad, oval, flattened body with up to 400 cerata on each side .... ***Aeolidia papillosa*, shag-rug aeolis** (Fig.F)
#7.Slender, elongate body; with fewer than 100 cerata on each side (Figs.G-L) .... #8

#8.Front edge of foot extends out at sides forming sharply angled winglike or tentaclelike projections (Fig.G-I) .... #9
#8.Front edge of foot is rounded or bluntly angled and does not extend much beyond sides (Fig.J-L) .... #11

#9.Dorsal (second or rear) pair of tentacles are ringed with sharp ridges (like the threads on a screw) .... ***Facelina bostoniensis*, Boston facelina** (Fig.G)
#9.Dorsal tentacles are smooth or only slightly wrinkled .... #10

#10.Body gray with white edges and a row of brown spots on midline; central core of cerata is gray .... ***Cratena pilata*** (Fig.H)
#10.Body is transparent white; central core of cerata is bright red .... ***Coryphella* spp.** (Fig.I)

#11.Dorsal (second or rear) pair of tentacles are almost twice as long as the first (front) pair .... ***Eubranchus pallidus*** (Fig.J)
#11.Both pairs of tentacles are about the same length (Figs.K,L) .... #12

#12.Front edge of foot is rounded .... ***Cuthona aurantia*, orange-tip cuthona** (Fig.K)
#12.Front edge of foot is bluntly angled .... ***Cuthona concinna*** (Fig.L)

#13.Cerata are short and stubby .... ***Ercolania fuscata*, dusky stiliger** (Fig.M)
#13.Cerata are elongate (Figs.N,O) .... #14

#14.Two rows of cerata on each side .... ***Alderia modesta*, modest alderia** (Fig.N)
#14.One row of about 20 cerata per side .... ***Placida dendritica*** (Fig.O)

[1]Nudibranchs should be examined and identified while they are alive and relaxed. Their physical features are greatly distorted when preserved. Some nudibranchs can withdraw their gills and tentacles when disturbed.

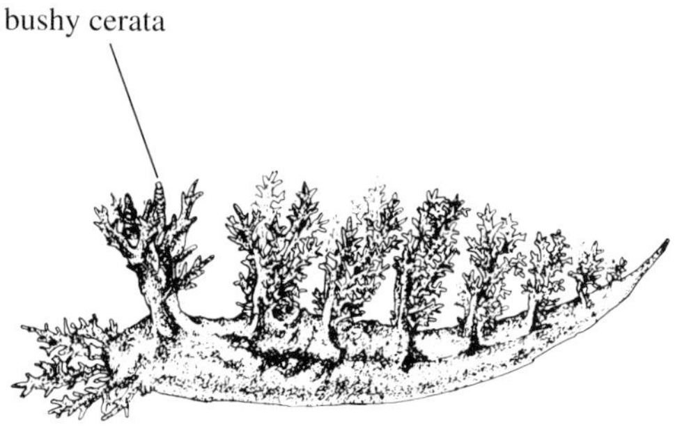

Fig.A. ***DENDRONOTUS FRONDOSUS*, FROND-AEOLIS**: Brown to reddish with white spots; up to 5 cm (2") long; found in lower intertidal zone and offshore among fine seaweeds and hydroids, such as *Tubularia*. (family Dendronotidae)

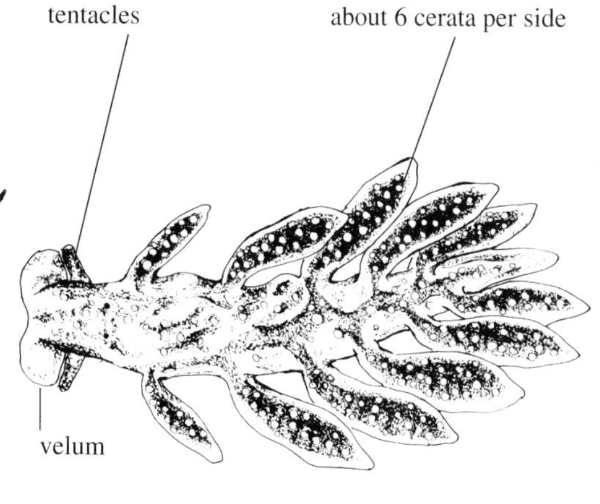

Fig.B. ***TENELLIA FUSCATA (=Embletonia f.)*:** Up to 6 mm (1/4") long; found on hydroids and filamentous green algae. (family Tergipedidae)

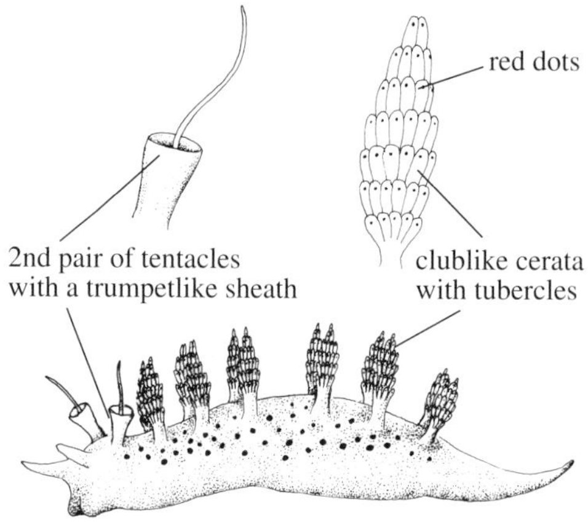

Fig.C. ***DOTO CORONATA (=Idulia c.)*, CROWN DOTO:** Pale rose or yellow with many brown dots; each tubercle on cerata has a red core and is tipped with a red dot; up to 12 mm (1/2") long; lives on hydroids and bryozoans. (family Dotoidae)

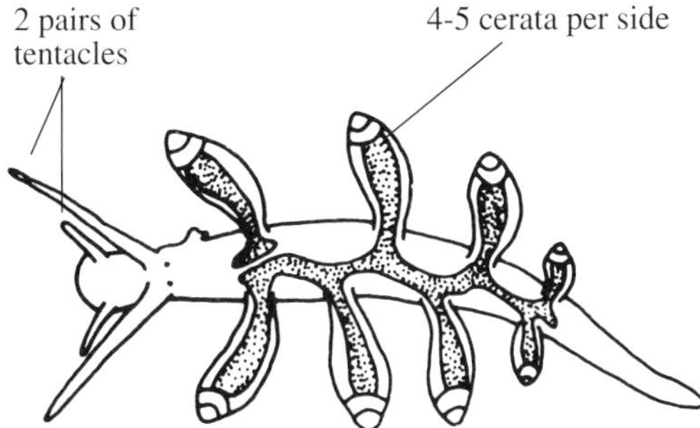

Fig.D. ***TERGIPES TERGIPES (=T. despectus):*** Transparent, milky body; cerata have an orange ring near tip and dark core; up to 8 mm (5/16") long; found on hydroids growing on kelp or eelgrass. (family Tergipedidae)

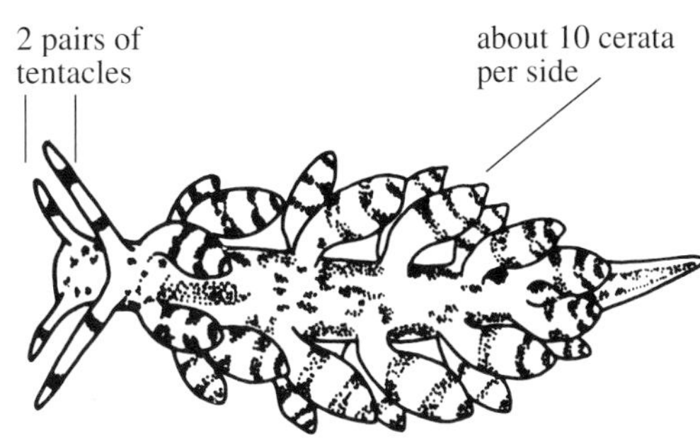

Fig.E. ***EUBRANCHUS EXIGUUS,*** **DWARF BALLOON AEOLIS:** Green or brown spots; up to 8 mm (5/16") long; found on hydroids growing on eelgrass. (family Eubranchidae)

Fig.F. ***AEOLIDIA PAPILLOSA (=Aeolis p.):*** Orange or gray; up to 10 cm (4") long; found in lower intertidal zone and offshore. (family Aeolidiidae)

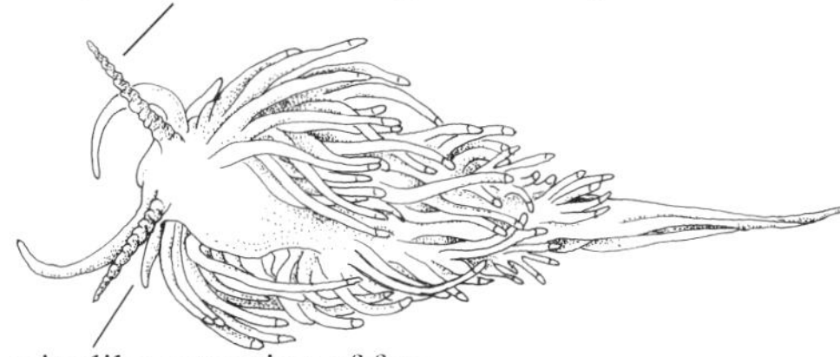

Fig.G. ***FACELINA BOSTONIENSIS,*** **BOSTON FACELINA:** Grows to 25 mm (1") long; lives on hydroids, such as *Tubularia.* (family Facelinidae)

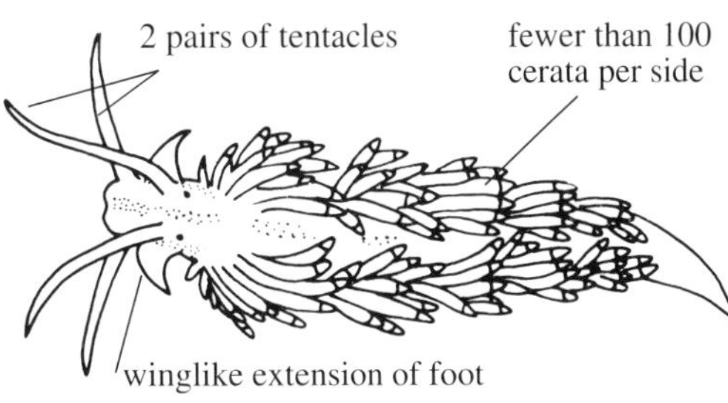

Fig.H. ***CRATENA PILATA:*** Gray body with white edges and a stripe or row of brown spots on midline; central core of cerata are gray; up to 3 cm (1 1/4") long; found on hydroids and red seaweeds in shallow water. (family Facelinidae)

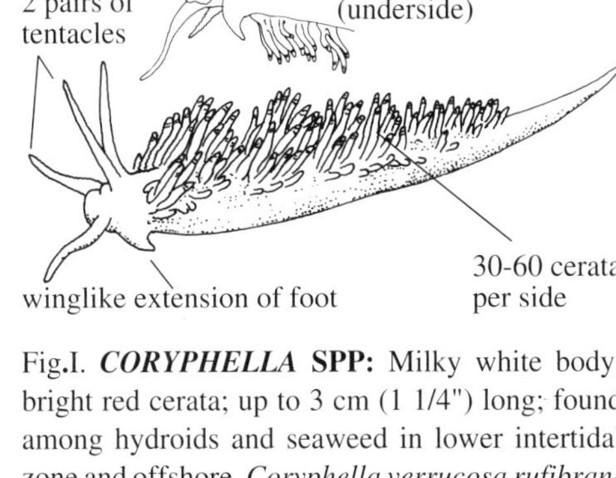

Fig.I. ***CORYPHELLA*** **SPP:** Milky white body, bright red cerata; up to 3 cm (1 1/4") long; found among hydroids and seaweed in lower intertidal zone and offshore. *Coryphella verrucosa rufibranchialis*, the red-finger aeolis, is the most common species. (family Coryphellidae) **17.06 A**

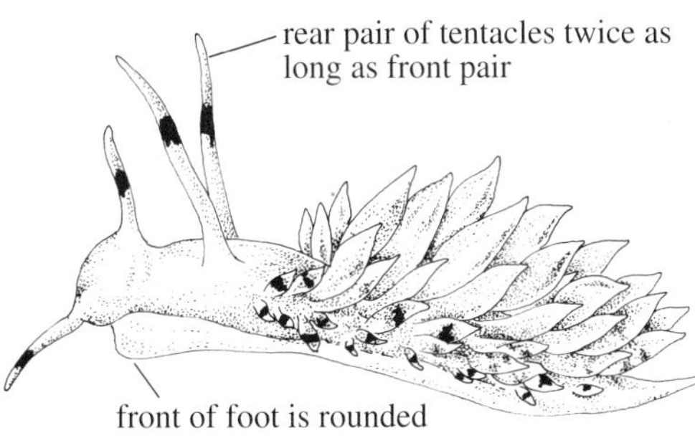

Fig.J. ***EUBRANCHUS PALLIDUS:*** With gold and red blotches on cerata and back; up to 12 mm (1/2") long; lives among hydroids; occurs in winter and spring. (family Eubranchidae)

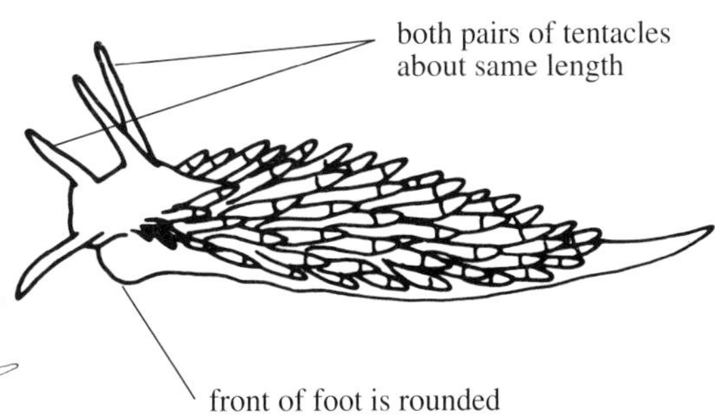

Fig.K. ***CUTHONA AURANTIA (=Cratena a., =Catriona a.),*** **ORANGE-TIP CUTHONA:** Cerata may be orange tipped; up to 16 mm (5/8") long; found on *Tubularia* and other hydroids. (family Tergipedidae)

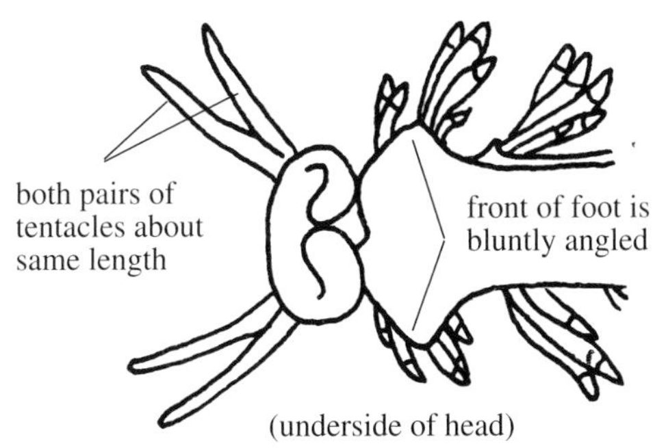

Fig.L. ***CUTHONA CONCINNA:*** Grows up to 12 mm (1/2") long. (family Tergipedidae)

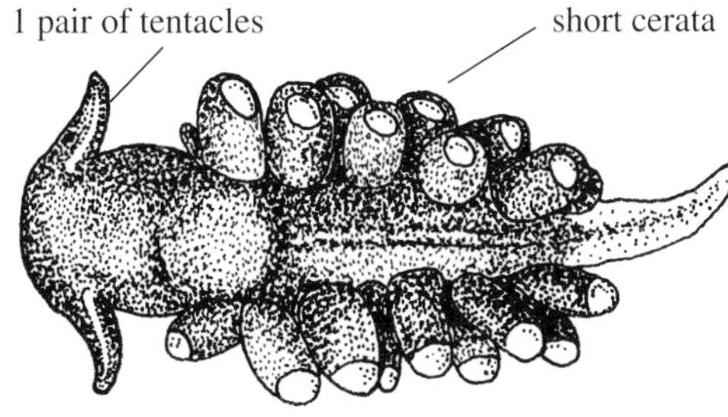

Fig.M. ***ERCOLANIA FUSCATA (=Stiliger f.),*** **DUSKY STILIGER:** Up to 6 mm (1/4") long; lives on filamentous green algae. (family Stiligeridae)

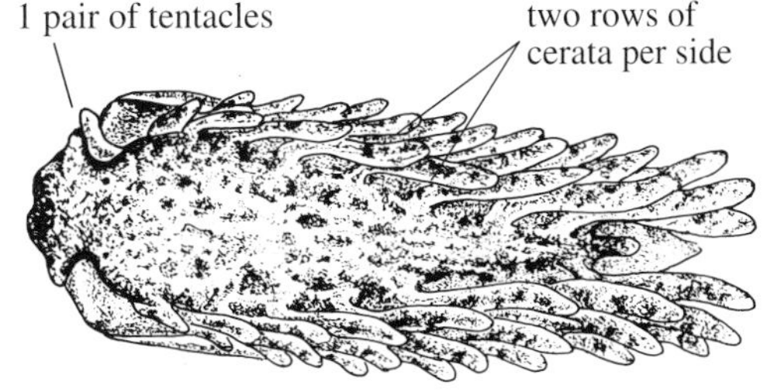

Fig.N. ***ALDERIA MODESTA (=A. harvardiensis),*** **MODEST ALDERIA:** Up to 15 mm (5/8") long; found in marshes and estuaries north of Cape Cod. (family Stiligeridae)

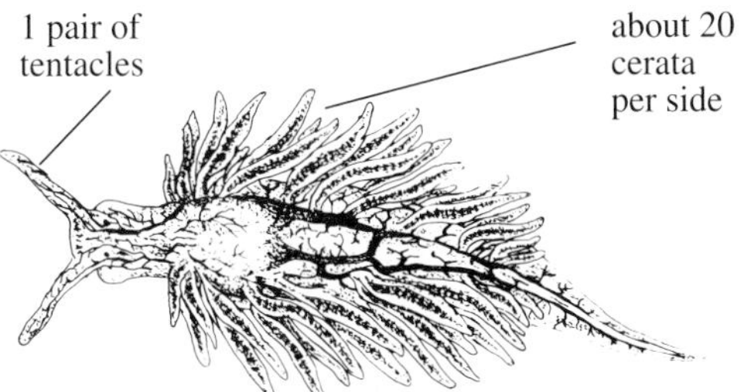

Fig.O. ***PLACIDA DENDRITICA (=Hermaea d.):*** Up to 1 cm (3/8") long; found on the seaweed *Codium.* (family Hermaeidae)

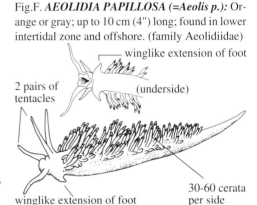

BIVALVES: PHYLUM MOLLUSCA, CLASS BIVALVIA (PELECYPODA)

Mollusks with two shells (valves) joined by a hinge

(Use the key on page 2.10 to determine if you have a bivalve)

#1.Found in tubes bored into water soaked wood, such as submerged pilings, boat hulls, driftwood, etc. (Figs.B,C) .... **wood borers**[1], #2
#1.Not found bored into wood .... #3

#2.Long wormlike body; tiny shell about 6 mm (1/4") in diameter at one end of body .... ***Teredo navalis*, naval shipworm** (Fig.B)
#2.Typical bivalve type shell, up to 5 cm (2") long; shell gapes widely at both ends; large siphons[2]. .... ***Zirfaea crispata*, great piddock** (Fig.C)

#3.Shell surface is very flaky, jagged and layered (Fig.D); shell is flattened and somewhat elongate; attaches to submerged objects such as pilings, rocks and other shells .... ***Crassostrea virginica*, eastern oyster** (Fig.D)
#3.Not as above .... #4

#4.Wedge shaped shell (Fig.E); most species are dark colored (blue, brown), but one tiny species is white; often attaches by threads (byssal fibers) to the bottom, rocks, shells, dock pilings, and other objects .... **mussels**, bottom of page 7.19
#4.Not as above .... #5

#5.Distinct grooves or ribs radiate out (like a fan) from the umbo[2] to the edges of the shell (Fig.F) .... page 7.16
#5.No radiating lines on shell; shell may have no lines at all or may have lines that form concentric[2] rings .... #6

#6.Elongate shells, at least twice as long as wide (Fig.G) .... page 7.23
#6.Shell length is less than twice its width (Figs.H-L) .... #7

#7.Umbones recurve or point back at a distinct angle (Fig.H); shells are somewhat triangular in shape .... page 7.18
#7.Umbones point up, away from opposite edge of shell (Fig.I); shells may be triangular, oval, or circular .... #8

#8.Shell has a prominent spoon shaped structure (chondrophore) (Fig.K) on the inside of one or both of the shells beneath the umbo; shell may grow larger than 5 cm (2") .... page 7.22
#8.Without a chondrophore; shell is never longer than 5 cm (2") .... #9

#9.Shell is symmetrical (Fig.J) (both ends have about the same shape and umbo is about equal distance from either end of shell); shell width and length are about equal, shell is circular or triangular in shape .... page 7.20
#9.Shell is asymmetrical (Fig.L) (one end is more rounded, pointed, or flattened than the other and umbo may be closer to one end of the shell than the other); shell is distinctly longer than wide; may be oval or rectangular in shape .... page 7.21

[1]Other bivalves that may bore into wood are described on page 7.16-7.17. In this region they are usually found in mud, clay, and peat, not wood.
[2]Refer to Fig.A for explanation of terms used in bivalve key. Bivalve siphons are shown on page 7.22, Fig.A and page 7.23, Fig.E.

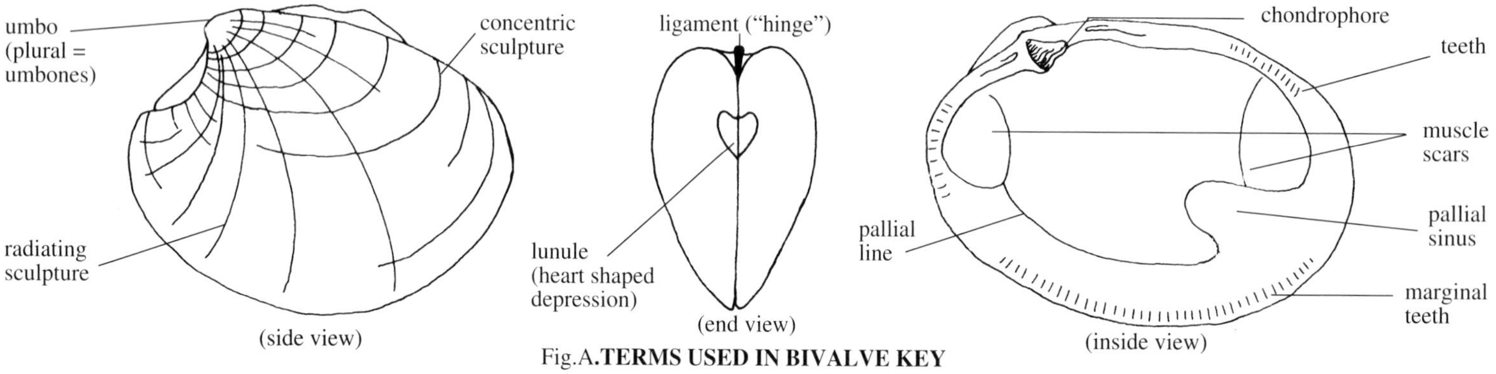

Fig.A.**TERMS USED IN BIVALVE KEY**

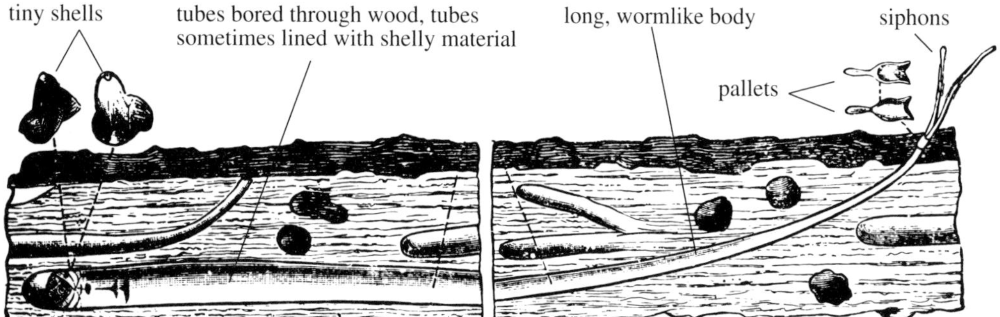

Fig.B. ***TEREDO NAVALIS,* NAVAL SHIPWORM:** Whitish shells; shells and tubes about 6 mm (1/4") in diameter; driftwood, old pilings and docks, and other waterlogged wood often found honeycombed with shipworm tubes. (family Teredinidae: shipworms)

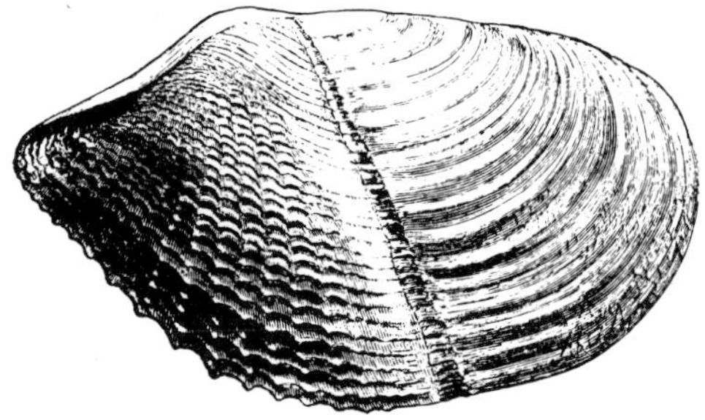

Fig.C. ***ZIRFAEA CRISPATA,* GREAT PIDDOCK:** Whitish; up to 5 cm (2") long; found in burrows in waterlogged driftwood and in peat, clay, and shale. (family Pholadidae: piddocks)

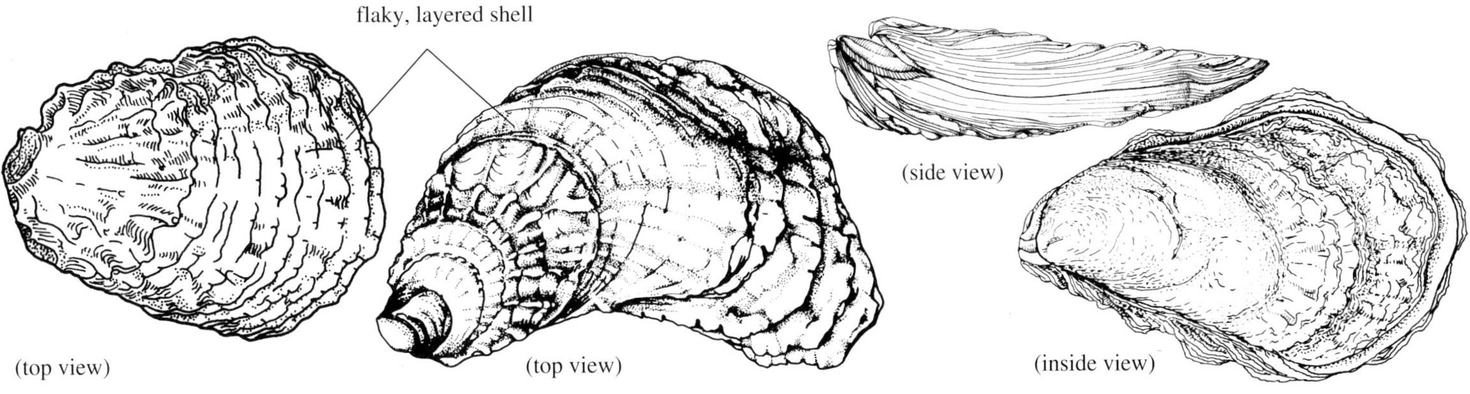

Fig.D. ***CRASSOSTREA VIRGINICA*, EASTERN OYSTER:** Grayish white; up to about 15 cm (6") long; found at or below low tide level attached to rocks, pilings, other shells, etc.; shape is variable (see above); very common; supports a large commercial fishery. (family Ostreidae: oysters) **17.04 E**

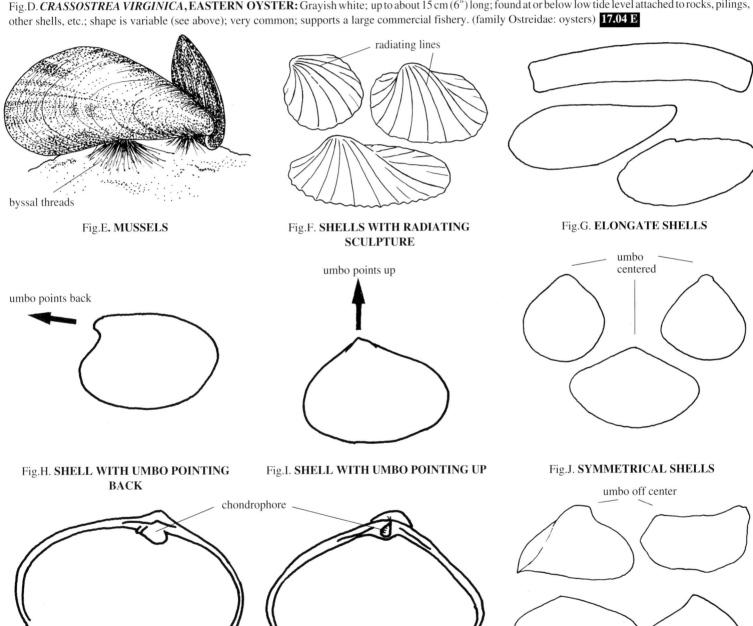

byssal threads

Fig.E. **MUSSELS**

radiating lines

Fig.F. **SHELLS WITH RADIATING SCULPTURE**

Fig.G. **ELONGATE SHELLS**

umbo points back

Fig.H. **SHELL WITH UMBO POINTING BACK**

umbo points up

Fig.I. **SHELL WITH UMBO POINTING UP**

umbo centered

Fig.J. **SYMMETRICAL SHELLS**

chondrophore

Fig.K. **SHELLS WITH CHONDROPHORE**

umbo off center

Fig.L. **ASYMMETRICAL SHELLS**

BIVALVES WITH RADIATING SCULPTURE
PHYLUM MOLLUSCA, CLASS BIVALVIA (PELECYPODA)

(Bivalve key begins on page 7.14)

#1.With winglike extensions (Figs.C,D) on either side of umbo[1] .... **scallops**, #2
#1.Without winglike extensions on either side of umbo .... #3

#2.With deep, rounded, radiating ribs and grooves; up to 7.5 cm (3") in diameter; common in bays in eelgrass beds ..***Argopecten irradians*, bay scallop** (Fig.C)
#2.With fine radiating lines; up to 20 cm (8") in diameter; common in deep water offshore on sandy bottoms .....***Placopecten magellanicus*, sea scallop** (Fig.D)

#3.With a row of filelike teeth on inside edge (hinge) of shell to either side of umbo (Figs.A,B); with broad, squared off "shoulders"; shell has a somewhat quadrangular shape .... **arks**, #10
#3.Without a row of filelike teeth on hinge; shell is oval, triangular, or circular (Figs.E-K) .... #4

#4.Round, triangular, or teardrop shaped shell (Figs.E-G); less than twice as long as wide; umbo about equal distance from either end of shell .... #5
#4.Elongate shell, about twice as long as wide (Figs.H-K); umbo closer to one end of shell than the other .... #6

#5.Dark brown outer covering; 20 or fewer distinct rounded ribs and deep grooves; shell is thick, sturdy ....***Cyclocardia borealis*, northern cyclocardia** (Fig.E)
#5.Beige or white; 22-28 weak, scaly (bumpy) ribs; shell is thin and fragile ....***Cerastoderma pinnulatum*, northern dwarf-cockle** (Fig.F)
#5.Light brown or yellowish; more than 30 very fine radiating lines ....***Crenella* spp., crenellas** (Fig.G)

#6.With a shiny brown outer shell covering that often extends beyond the shell; yellowish radiating lines or slits in the shell covering give a fringed appearance to edge; umbo is very low and indistinct ....***Solemya velum*, Atlantic awningclam** (Fig.K)
#6.White shell, without brown covering; umbo is raised and distinct (Figs.H-J) .... #7

#7.Both ends of shell are rounded (Figs.H,I) .... #8
#7.Longer end of shell is blunt and flattened (Figs.H,J) .... #9

#8.With a winglike plate extending above umbones; ribs are distinct and scaly (bumpy or spiny) over entire shell; up to 18 cm (7") long; valves (shells) gape (do not touch each other at the ends when the valves are closed); siphons are thick and fused ....***Cyrtopleura costata*, angelwing** (Fig.H)
#8.No winglike plate above umbones; ribs more distinct and scaly at short end than long end; up to 5 cm (2") long; valves do not gape; siphons are separate and extensible ....***Petricola pholadiformis*, false angelwing** (Fig.I)
#8.With a winglike plate above umbones; shell divided in half by radial groove; radial ribs on one half of shell only; up to 7.5 cm (3") long; valves gape; siphons are thick and fused ....***Zirfaea crispata*, great piddock** (page 7.14, Fig.C)

#9.With very fine radiating lines and wrinkles; glassy, semitranslucent, pearly white ....***Lyonsia hyalina*, glassy lyonsia** (Fig.J)
#9.With deep scaly (bumpy) radiating ribs; chalky white ....***Barnea truncata*, Atlantic mud-piddock** (Fig.H)

#10.Ligament is broad (Fig.A); with a space between the umbones of the shells; with a gray-brown outer shell layer that is usually partially worn off; with 30-50 ribs; bottom edge of shell is rather straight; grows up to 3.8 cm (1 1/2") long ....***Anadara transversa*, transverse ark** (Fig.A)
#10.Ligament is narrow (Fig.B); umbones are in close contact; with a hairy black-brown outer shell layer that does not usually wear off; with 26-35 ribs; bottom edge of shell is curved; grows up to 6 cm (2 1/4") long ....***Anadara ovalis*, blood ark** (Fig.B)

[1]Refer to Fig.A on page 7.14 for explanation of terms used in bivalve key.

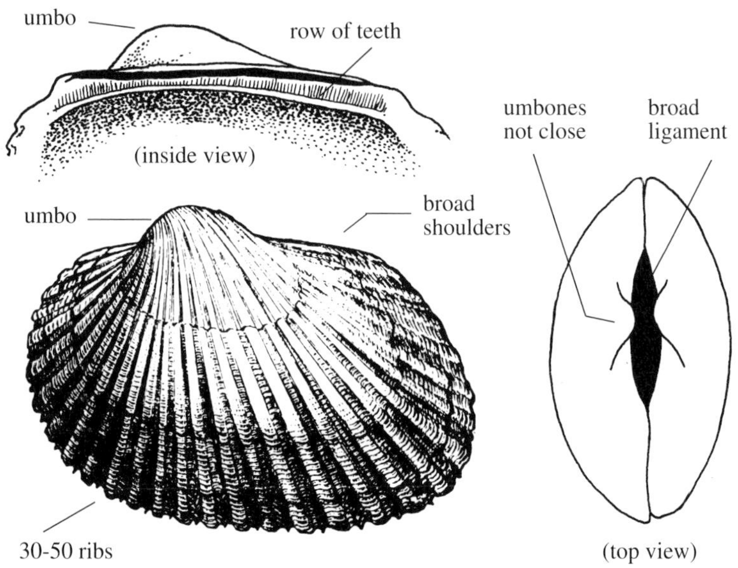

umbo
row of teeth
(inside view)
umbo
broad shoulders
30-50 ribs
umbones not close
broad ligament
(top view)
umbones almost touch
narrow ligament
(top view)
umbo
row of teeth
(inside view)
umbo
broad shoulders
26-35 ribs
hairs

Fig.A. ***ANADARA TRANSVERSA*, TRANSVERSE ARK:** Whitish shell with gray-brown outer covering which is usually all or partially worn off; up to 3.8 cm (1 1/2") long; quite common in mud. (family Arcidae: arks)

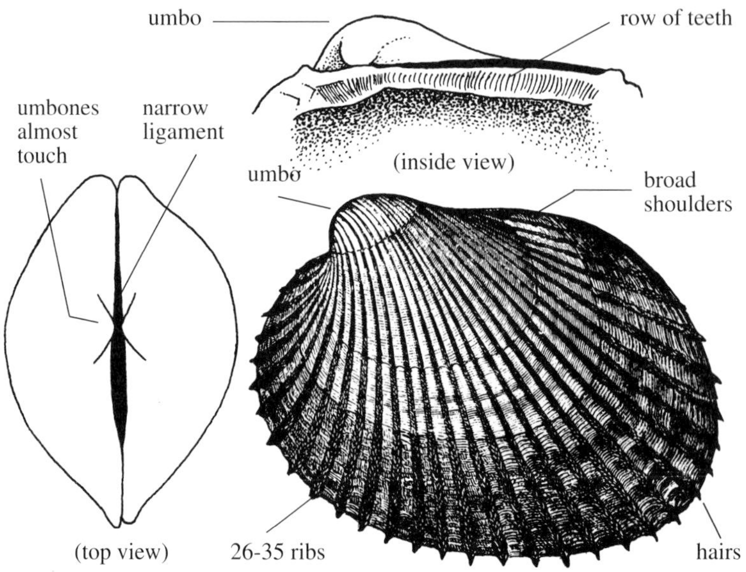

Fig.B. ***ANADARA OVALIS*, BLOOD ARK:** Whitish shell with hairy dark brown outer covering; soft tissue is red because, unlike most bivalves, blood contains hemoglobin; up to 6 cm (2 1/2") long; rare. (family Arcidae: arks)

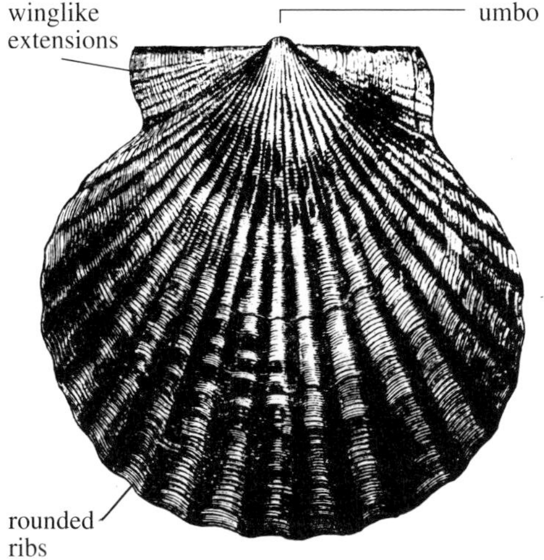

Fig.C. ***ARGOPECTEN IRRADIANS (=Pecten i., =Aequipecten i.),*** **BAY SCALLOP:** Color variable, usually tan or beige, but may be gray, brown, orange, green, or reddish; up to 7.5 cm (3") long; common in shallow bays and estuaries; lives in eelgrass beds. (family Pectinidae: scallops) **17.05 F**

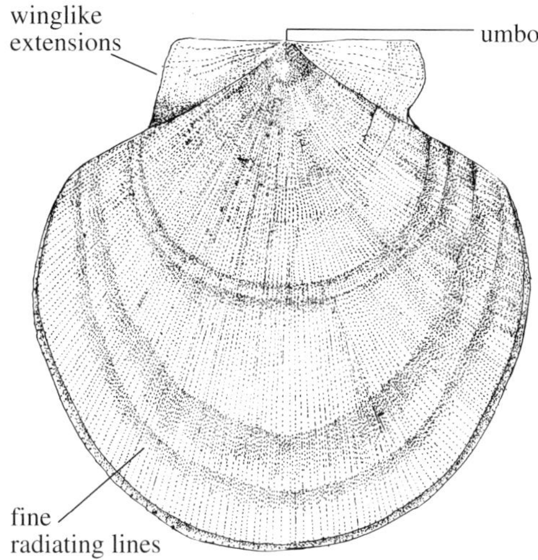

Fig.D. ***PLACOPECTEN MAGELLANICUS,*** **SEA SCALLOP:** Upper valve (shell) is reddish or purplish brown, lower valve pinkish white to white; up to 20 cm (8") in diameter; rare in nearshore waters but common and commercially very important offshore. (family Pectinidae: scallops)

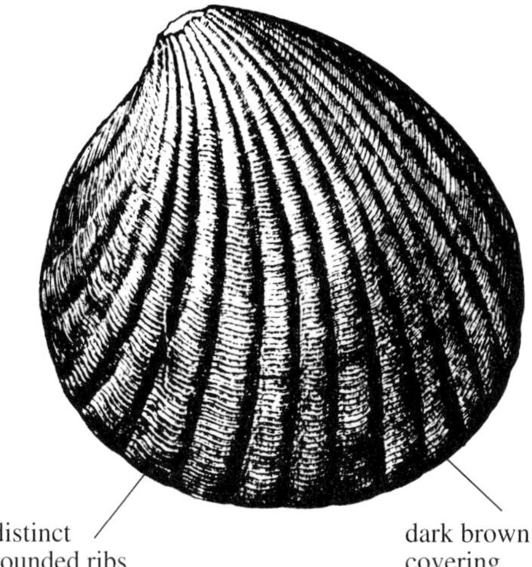

Fig.E. ***CYCLOCARDIA BOREALIS (=Venericardia b.),*** **NORTHERN CYCLOCARDIA:** Dark brown outer covering; up to 3.8 cm (1 1/2") long; common offshore in bottom mud. (family Carditidae: carditas)

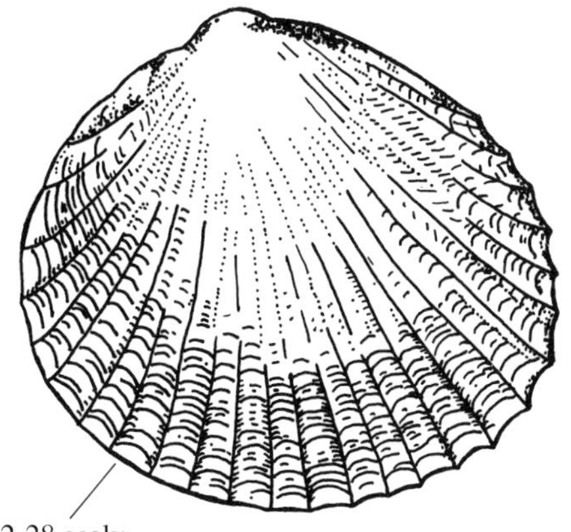

Fig.F. ***CERASTODERMA PINNULATUM,*** **NORTHERN DWARF-COCKLE:** Beige or creamy white with irregular brown markings; up to 1.3 cm (1/2") long; not common; found offshore. (family Cardiidae: cockles)

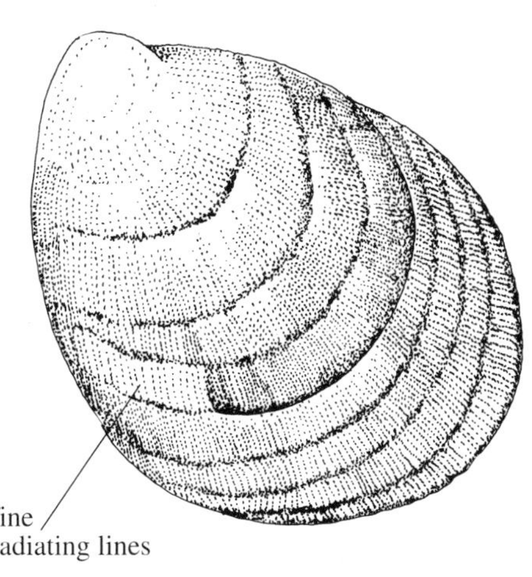

Fig.G. ***CRENELLA*** **SPP., CRENELLAS:** *Crenella glandula*, glandular crenella, is olive brown; up to 13 mm (1/2") long; subtidal in mud. A less common species, *C. decussata,* is yellowish gray; up to 3 mm (1/8") long. (family Mytilidae: mussels)

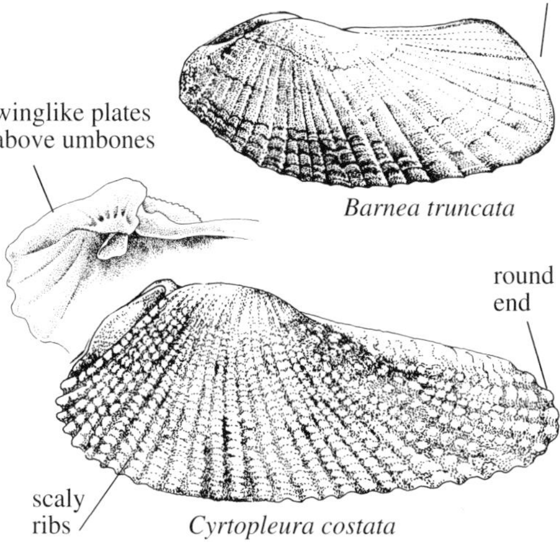

Fig.H. ***CYRTOPLEURA COSTATA (=Barnea c.),*** **ANGELWING:** White; up to 18 cm (7") long; uncommon. ***Barnea truncata,*** **Atlantic mud-piddock:** white or gray; up to 5 cm (2") long; bores into clay, peat or wood. (family Pholadidae)

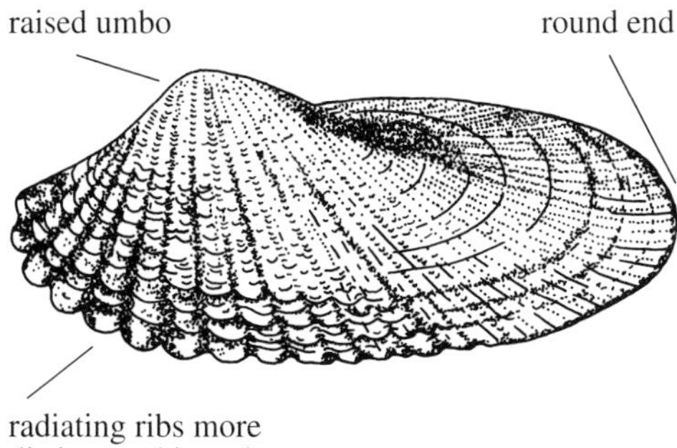

Fig.I. ***PETRICOLA PHOLADIFORMIS,*** **FALSE ANGELWING:** White; up to 5 cm (2") long; shells often wash up on shore; bores into peat, clay and occasionally wood. (family Petricolidae)

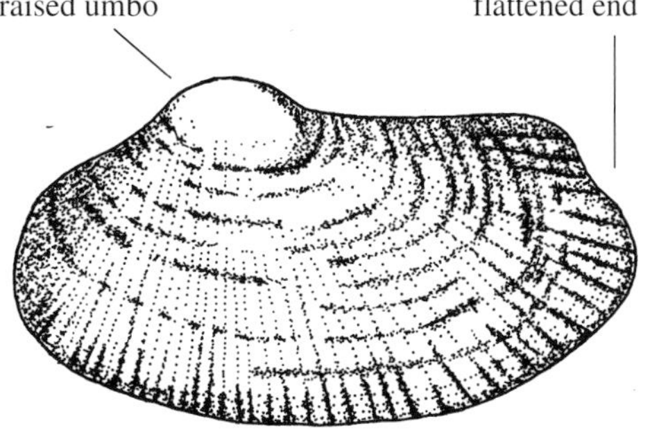

Fig.J. ***LYONSIA HYALINA,*** **GLASSY LYONSIA:** Glassy or pearly white; up to 2 cm (3/4") long; found in bottom clay in shallow water. (family Lyonsiidae)

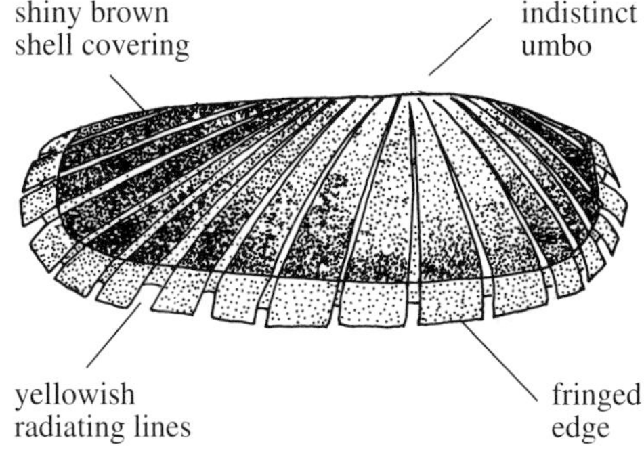

Fig.K. ***SOLEMYA VELUM,*** **ATLANTIC AWNINGCLAM:** Shiny brown with yellowish radiating lines; up to 2.5 cm (1") long; common in mudflats. (family Solemyidae: awningclams)

BIVALVES WITH RECURVING UMBO
PHYLUM MOLLUSCA, CLASS BIVALVIA (PELECYPODA)

Bivalves that are circular or triangular and do not have radiating sculpture

(Bivalve key begins on page 7.14)

#1.Periostracum (outer shell layer or coating) is yellowish white; with a low ridge extending from umbo[1] to bottom of shell, making one end of shell somewhat flattened; shell is rather thin and delicate .... ***Mulinia lateralis*, dwarf surfclam** (Fig.F)

#1.Periostracum is black, gray, or brown; without a ridge extending from umbo (Figs.A-E); shell is thick and sturdy .... #2

#2.With a lunule[2] (Figs. A,B); periostracum is usually light or dark gray but may be black; shell is distinctly longer than wide, oval shaped .... #3

#2.No lunule (Figs.C-E); periostracum is usually light or dark brown but may be black; shell is nearly as wide as long; circular or triangular shaped .... #4

#3.Bottom inner edge of shell has marginal teeth (Fig.A); lunule[2] is deeply cut and distinctly heart shaped (Fig.A); inside of shell has purple area; gray periostracum on umbones not usually worn through; grows up to 13 cm (5") long .... ***Mercenaria mercenaria*, northern quahog** (Fig.A)

#3.No marginal teeth on bottom inner edge of shell; lunule is shallow and is not distinctly heart shaped (Fig.B); no purple areas on inside of shell; gray periostracum on umbones usually worn through exposing chalky white shell beneath; grows up to 5 cm (2") long .... ***Pitar morrhuanus*, false quahog** (Fig.B)

#4.No marginal teeth on bottom inner edge of shell (Fig.C) .... #5

#4.With marginal teeth on bottom inner edge of shell (Figs. D,E) .... #6

#5.Maximum diameter is 4.5 cm (1 3/4"), rarely over 2.5 cm (1"); shell is more triangular than circular .... ***Astarte* spp.**[3]

#5.Maximum diameter is 13 cm (5"), frequently over 2.5 cm (1"); shell is more circular than triangular .... ***Arctica islandica*, ocean quahog** (Fig.C)

#6.With 10-20 distinct, rounded concentric grooves and ridges; shell is wider than long, umbones moderately pointed ...... ***Astarte undata*, wavy astarte** (Fig.D)

#6.Concentric lines are very shallow, only weakly etched into surface of shell; shell is about as long as it is wide; umbones very pointed; foot is bright red .... ***Astarte castanea*, smooth astarte** (Fig.E)

[1]Refer to Fig.A on page 7.14 for explanation of terms in bivalve key.
[2]The lunule is a depression in the shell beneath the umbones, see Figs. A and B.
[3]Refer to Gosner (1971) or a good shell book to identify the species.

sharp concentric ridges
(young clam)
deep heart shaped lunule
(end view)
marginal teeth
purple area

Fig.A. ***MERCENARIA MERCENARIA*, NORTHERN QUAHOG (=hardshell clam, =cherrystone clam** when small): Periostracum (outer covering of shell) is light or dark gray or nearly black, inside of shell is white with large purple area; up to 13 cm (5") long; very common in shallow water and offshore; shell may have sharp bladelike concentric ridges when young but is smooth with irregular growth lines when older. (family Veneridae: hardshell clams) **17.05 A**

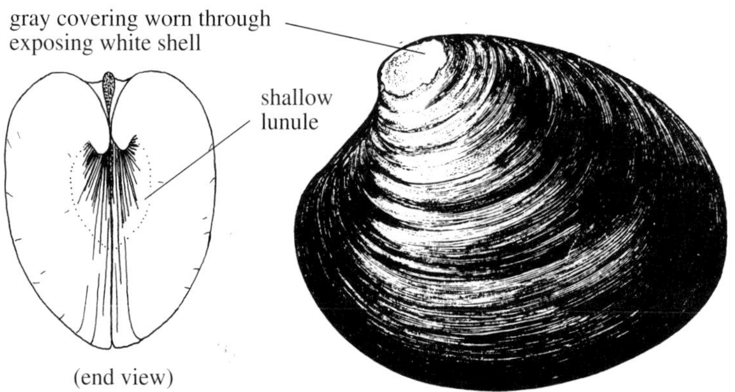

Fig.B. ***PITAR MORRHUANUS*, FALSE QUAHOG:** Gray outer shell covering which is often worn through on umbones exposing chalky white shell beneath; up to 5 cm (2") long; common in bottom mud. (family Veneridae)

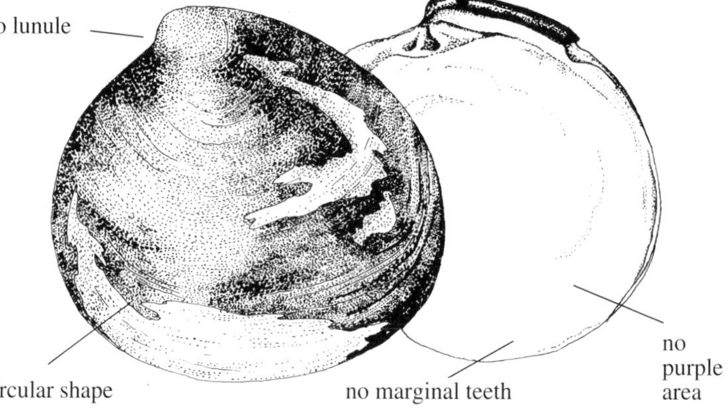

Fig.C. ***ARCTICA ISLANDICA*, OCEAN QUAHOG:** Dark brown or black thick periostracum (outer coating) covering white shell; up to 13 cm (5") in diameter; common in deeper waters offshore in muddy sand. (family Arcticidae)

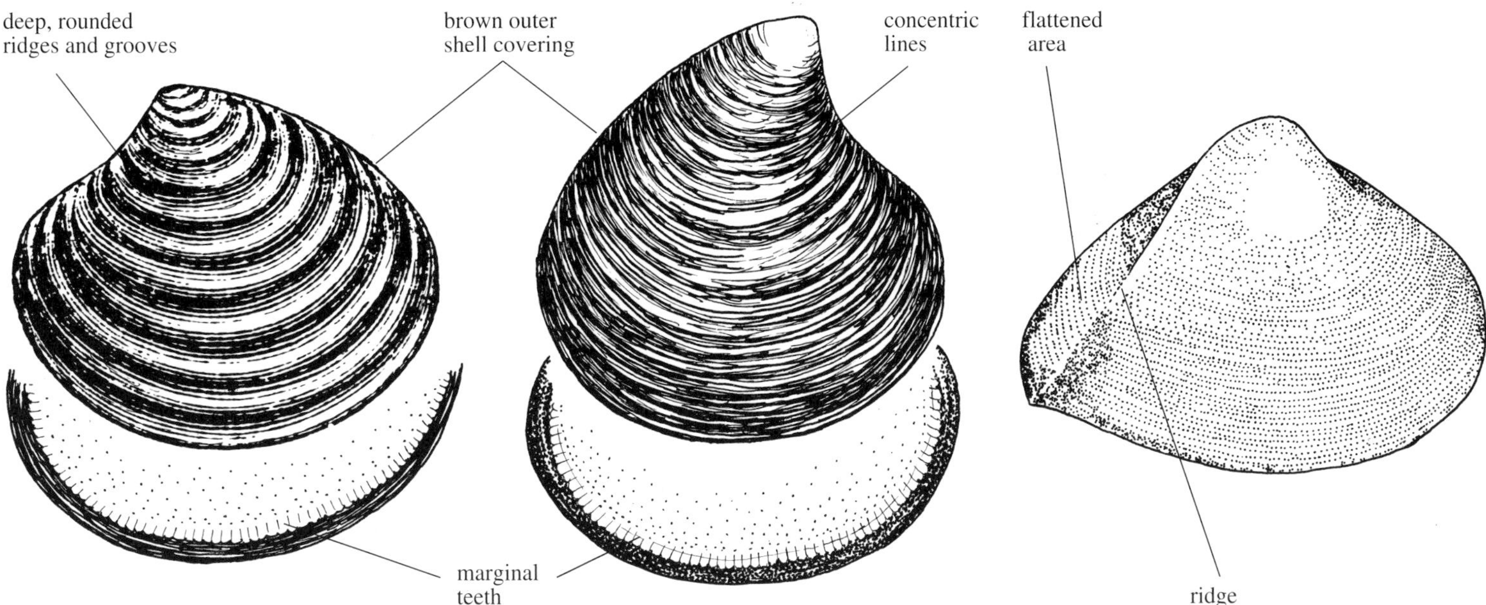

Fig.D. ***ASTARTE UNDATA*, WAVY ASTARTE:** Reddish brown or dark brown covering, often glossy; up to 3 cm (1 1/4") long; common in bottom muds; has 10-20 ridges. *Astarte crenata (=subaequilatera)*, crenulate astarte, is similar but has 25-40 ridges; less common. (family Astartidae) **17.05 E**

Fig.E. ***ASTARTE CASTANEA*, SMOOTH ASTARTE:** Chestnut or reddish brown outer shell layer, inside of shell is shiny white; foot and soft tissue are bright red; up to 2.5 cm (1") long; burrows in subtidal sand and mud; not common. (family Astartidae: astartes)

Fig.F. ***MULINIA LATERALIS*, DWARF SURFCLAM:** Thin yellowish white outer shell layer with shiny white shell beneath; flattened end is sometimes a bit darker and rougher than the rest of the shell; up to 1.8 cm (3/4") long; very common in bottom mud. (family Mactridae: surfclams)

MUSSELS: PHYLUM MOLLUSCA, CLASS BIVALVIA (PELECYPODA), FAMILY MYTILIDAE

Bivalves with wedge shaped shells; most species are dark colored (blue, brown) but one is white; shell is often attached by byssal threads (see Fig. E on page 7.15) to the substrate or to other shells.

(Bivalve key begins on page 7.14)

#1. Umbo ("beak") is at extreme end of shell (Fig.G); shell surface is shiny and smooth, sometimes with very fine concentric lines; blue-black outer shell color; forms large intertidal and subtidal mussel beds .... ***Mytilus edulis*, blue mussel** (Fig.G)

#1. Umbo is near but not at very end of shell (Figs.H,I); shell surface may have radiating ribs or "hairy" outer covering; brown or yellow-brown outer shell color .... #2

#2. With radiating ribs; common in tidal marshes, partially embedded in peat; dark shell; up to 10 cm (4") long .... ***Geukensia demissa*, ribbed mussel** (Fig.H)

#2. Without radiating ribs; may have rough "hairy" looking dark outer shell covering; lives in deeper water .. ***Modiolus modiolus*, northern horsemussel** (Fig.I)

#2. Without radiating ribs; shiny white shell; tiny, up to 3 mm (1/8") long (shaped like Fig.I) .... ***Dacrydium vitreum*, glassy mussel** (not shown)

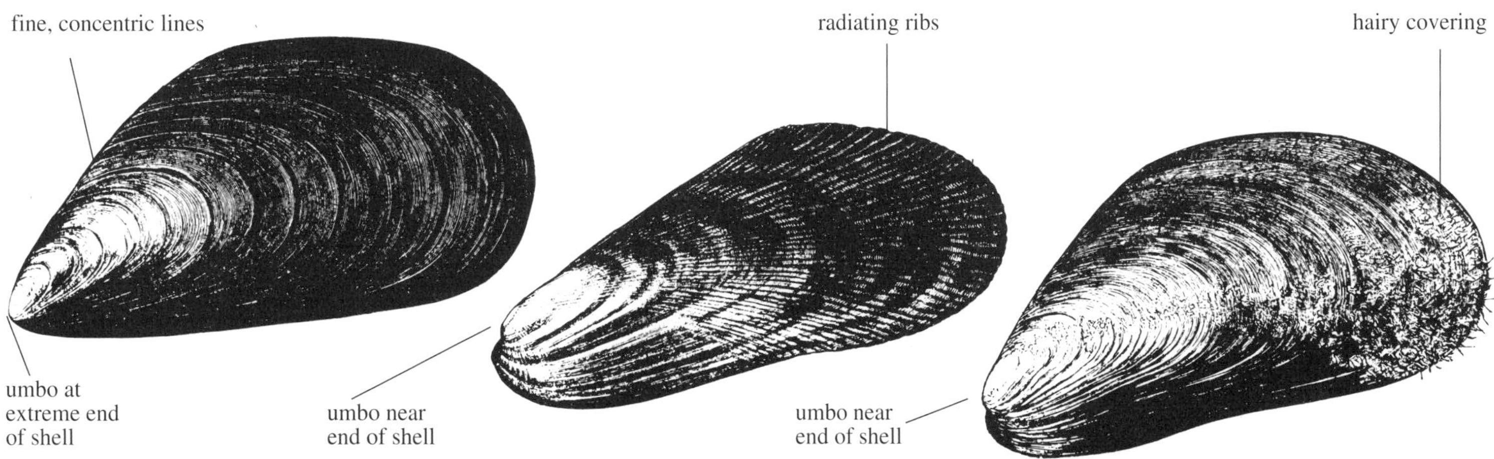

Fig.G. ***MYTILUS EDULIS*, BLUE MUSSEL:** Blue or blue-black; up to 7.5 cm (3") long; common in beds near low tide level and offshore; attaches to rocks and shells with byssal fibers. **17.05 D**

Fig.H. ***GEUKENSIA DEMISSA (=Modiolus d.)*, RIBBED MUSSEL:** Yellow-brown outer covering; up to 10 cm (4") long; very common in tidal marshes partially embedded in the peat. **17.05 G**

Fig.I. ***MODIOLUS MODIOLUS*, NORTHERN HORSEMUSSEL:** Dark brown outer covering; up to 15 cm (6") long; less common than *Mytilus* or *Geukensia*; lives in deeper water.

CIRCULAR OR TRIANGULAR BIVALVES
PHYLUM MOLLUSCA, CLASS BIVALVIA (PELECYPODA)

Symmetrical bivalves that do not have radiating sculpture or a chondrophore[1]

(Bivalve key begins on page 7.14)

#1. With an angular ridge from the umbo to the margin (see Figs.B and C on page 7.21) giving one end of shell a somewhat flattened appearance .... page 7.21
#1. Without an angular ridge .... #2

#2. Grows larger than 1 cm (3/8") long; circular shaped shells (Figs.A-C) .... #3
#2. Tiny bivalves[2], less than 1 cm (3/8") long; triangular shaped shells (Figs.D,E) .... #6

#3. Upper shell is translucent, thin and deeply arched (Fig.B); may be yellow, gold, beige, brown, silvery gray or black; lower shell is flat, dull white and has a hole near the umbo; attaches to submerged objects .... ***Anomia* spp.**, #4
#3. Both shells are about the same shape and color (Figs.A,C); lives in bottom mud and sand .... #5

#4. Upper shell is smooth, glossy or pearly; common south of Cape Cod .... ***Anomia simplex*, common jingle** (Fig.B)
#4. Upper shell is rough, covered with prickly scales arranged in radiating rows; common north of Cape Cod .... ***Anomia squamula*, prickly jingle** (Fig.B)

#5. Dull white shell with grayish or yellowish outer covering that is usually worn away at umbones; shells are longer than wide and rather flat .... ***Macoma balthica*, Baltic macoma** (Fig.A)
#5. Yellowish white shell sometimes with zigzagged brown or orange markings; shells are wider than long and are deeply arched .... ***Laevicardium mortoni*, Morton eggcockle** (Fig.C)

#6. With a row of teeth on inside edge of shell to either side of umbo (Fig.D) .... ***Nucula* spp., nutclams**, #7
#6. Without a row of teeth on inside edge of shell to either side of umbo .... ***Gemma gemma*, amethyst gemclam** (Fig.E)

#7. With very fine, tiny teeth along inside ventral edge (bottom edge, opposite umbo) of shell .... ***Nucula proxima*, Atlantic nutclam** (Fig.D)
#7. With no teeth along inside ventral edge of shell, edge is smooth .... ***Nucula delphinodonta*, dolphintooth nutclam** (Fig.D)

[1]Refer to Fig A. on page 7.14 for explanation of terms used in the bivalve key.
[2]If you have a tiny bivalve that doesn't key out here, it may be a juvenile of a larger species. Go to couplet #3.

Fig.A. ***MACOMA BALTHICA*, BALTIC MACOMA:** Dull white shell with grayish or yellowish outer covering that is usually worn away at umbo; up to 2.5 cm (1") long; not common, found in black bottom muds offshore in bays. (family Tellinidae: tellins and macomas)

hole
upper shell is arched, fragile, translucent. It is smooth and pearly in *A. simplex*
(10X)
upper shell of *A. squamula* has radiating rows of prickly scales
flat, white bottom shell
(side view)

Fig.B. ***ANOMIA* SPP., JINGLES:** The upper shell of *Anomia simplex*, the common jingle, is translucent, pearly, and may be yellow, gold, beige, brownish, silvery gray or black; up to 5 cm (2") long; common south of Cape Cod. The upper shell of *Anomia squamula (=A. aculeata)*, the prickly jingle, is rough and yellowish or brownish; up to 2 cm (3/4") long; common north of Cape Cod. The upper shell of both species often washes up on beaches; the white lower shell attaches to rocks, shells and other submerged objects and is rarely found. A short bundle of fine attachment threads passes through the hole in the bottom shell. (family Anomiidae)

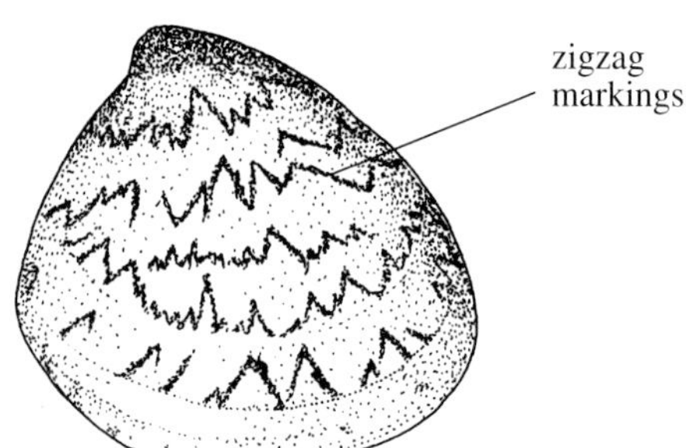

Fig.C. ***LAEVICARDIUM MORTONI*, MORTON EGGCOCKLE:** Beige or whitish shell with brownish or orange markings, sometimes in a zigzagged pattern; inside of shell usually has a blotch of purple; up to 2.5 cm (1") long; not common, found in muddy sand in sheltered shallow waters such as eelgrass beds. (family Cardiidae: cockles)

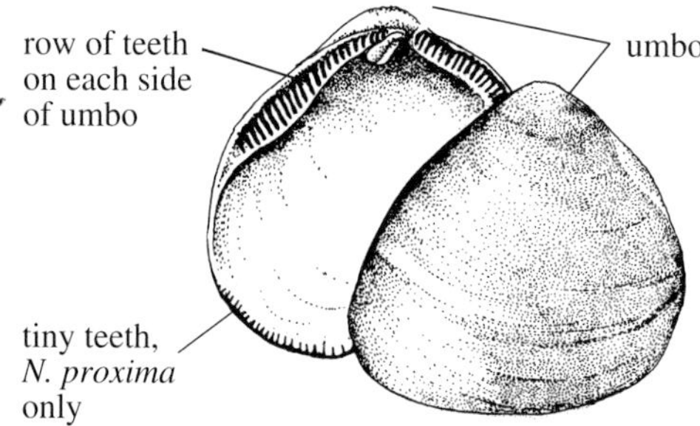

Fig.D. ***NUCULA* SPP., NUTCLAMS:** Olive green or grayish, shiny; tiny, up to 6 mm (1/4") long; very common in bottom muds. The most common species, *Nucula proxima*, the Atlantic nutclam, has tiny teeth on ventral inside edge of shell. *N. delphinodonta*, the dolphintooth nutclam, does not. (family Nuculidae) **17.05 B**

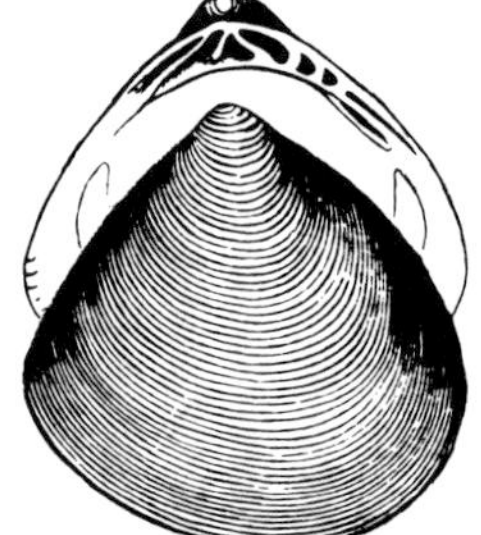

Fig.E. ***GEMMA GEMMA*, AMETHYST GEMCLAM:** Whitish or beige, often with blue or purplish areas; tiny, up to 3 mm (1/8") long; very common in sand and silty sand, especially in bays and estuaries; found in intertidal zone and offshore in shallow water. (family Veneridae: hardshell clams)

ASYMMETRICAL BIVALVES WITHOUT RADIATING SCULPTURE
PHYLUM MOLLUSCA, CLASS BIVALVIA (PELECYPODA)

Bivalves with one end more pointed or flattened than the other; umbo[1] may be closer to one end than the other.

(Bivalve key begins on page 7.14)

#1.Extremely flat, thinner than a coin; top of shell is saddle shaped and one end has a spoutlike projection .... ***Pandora gouldiana*, Gould pandora** (Fig.A)
#1.Not extemely flat; top of shell not saddle shaped (Figs.B-F) .... #2

#2.With an angular ridge that runs from umbo to margin of shell (Figs.B,C) giving one end of shell a somewhat flattened appearance .... #3
#2.Without an angular ridge (Figs.D-F) .... #4

#3.One shell fits into the other and shells do not meet edge to edge when closed; shell has concentric ridges...... ***Corbula contracta*, contracted corbula** (Fig.B)
#3.Shells meet edge to edge; shell is smooth, shiny .... ***Mulinia lateralis*, dwarf surfclam** (Fig.C)

#4.With a slight but obvious twist to shell .... ***Macoma tenta*, elongate macoma** (Fig.D)
#4.Without a twist (Figs.E,F) .... #5

#5.White, yellowish or pink; pallial[1] line with sinus .... ***Tellina agilis*, northern dwarf-tellin[2]** (Fig.E)
#5.Shell is covered with brownish periostracum (thin outer shell layer); pallial[1] line with no sinus .... ***Mysella planulata*, plate mysella** (Fig.F)

[1]Refer to Fig.A on page 7.14 for explanation of terms used in bivalve key.
[2]*Donax variabilis,* the variable coquina, is a southern species that occasionally can be found as far north as the New York City area. It occurs in large numbers in the surf zone of sandy ocean beaches. It is similar to *Tellina agilis*. *Donax* has tiny, fine teeth along the bottom inside edges of the shells. *Tellina* does not.

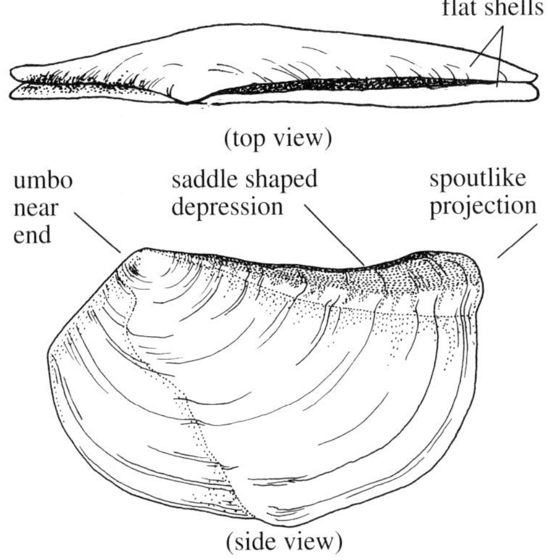

Fig.A. ***PANDORA GOULDIANA*, GOULD PANDORA:** White; up to 2.5 cm (1") long, extremely thin; common. (family Pandoridae)

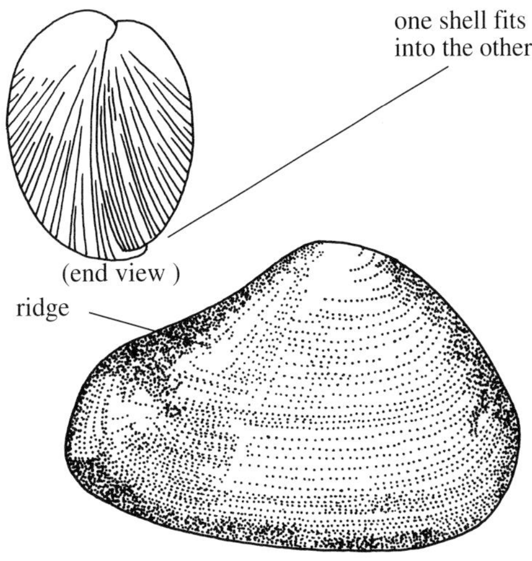

Fig.B. ***CORBULA CONTRACTA*, CONTRACTED CORBULA:** White shell; up to 1.3 cm (1/2") long; not common. (family Corbulidae)

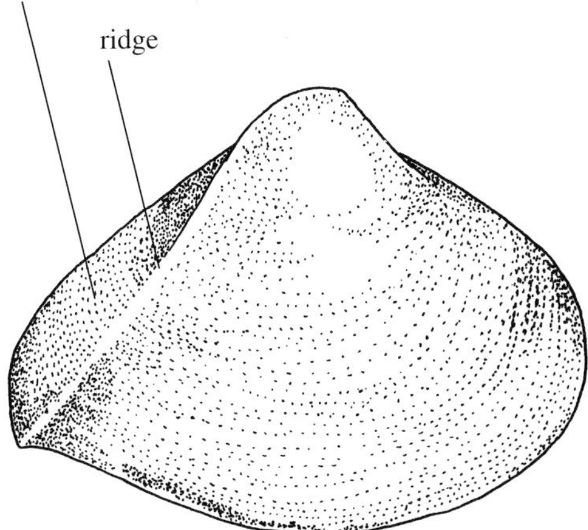

Fig.C. ***MULINIA LATERALIS*, DWARF SURFCLAM:** Thin yellowish-white outer shell layer on shiny white shell; up to 1.8 cm (3/4") long; very common in bottom mud. (family Mactridae)

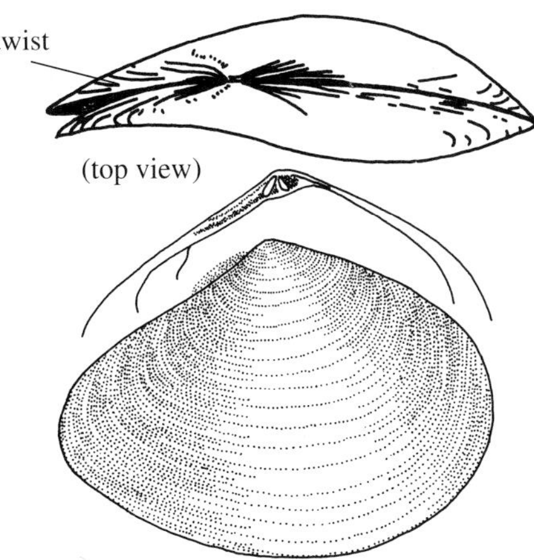

Fig.D. ***MACOMA TENTA*, ELONGATE MACOMA:** Pinkish white, iridescent shell; up to 1.8 cm (3/4") long; not common, found in offshore bottom muds. (family Tellinidae)

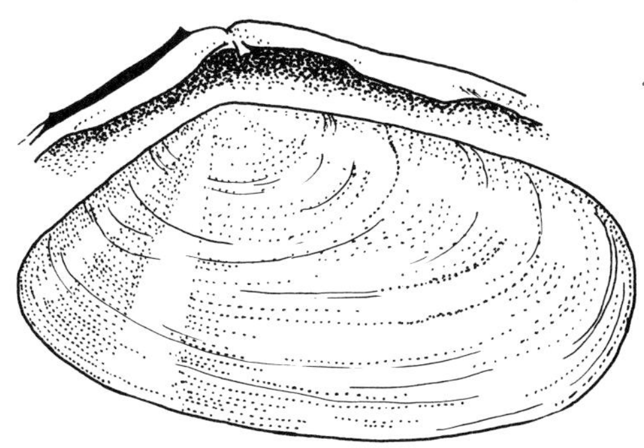

Fig.E. ***TELLINA AGILIS*, NORTHERN DWARF-TELLIN[2]:** White, yellowish or pink; sometimes with pink blotches; up to 1.3 cm (1/2") long; common in fine sand and mud; found in the intertidal zone and offshore. (family Tellinidae)

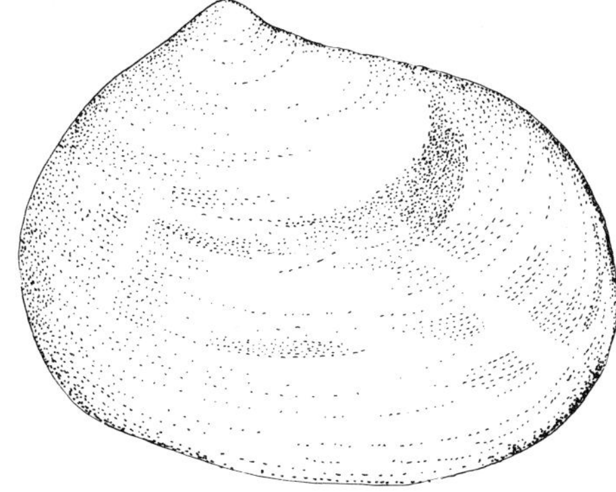

Fig.F. ***MYSELLA PLANULATA*, PLATE MYSELLA:** White shell is covered by thin yellowish-brown periostracum; up to 5 mm (1/4") long; attaches to submerged objects; also commensal with worms and crustaceans. (family Montacutidae)

BIVALVES WITH A CHONDROPHORE
PHYLUM MOLLUSCA, CLASS BIVALVIA (PELECYPODA)

Bivalves with a spoon shaped structure, the chondrophore, on the inner edge of the shell beneath the umbo[1].

(Bivalve key begins on page 7.14)

#1.Shell is nearly symmetrical (both ends of shell have about the same shape, the umbo is near center) (Figs.A,B); may grow longer than 40 mm (1 1/2") ...... #2
#1.Shell is asymmetrical (one end of shell is flatter or more pointed than the other and/or umbo is closer to one end) (Figs.C-E); less than 40 mm (1 1/2 ") .... #3

#2.Shell is somewhat oval shaped; chondrophore (projecting tooth) is only found in one shell, with a heart shaped pit in the other; siphon of living clam, when extended, is very long and cannot be completely retracted into shell. As a result, the shells do not touch at the ends when the clam closes up; grows up to 10 cm (4") long .... ***Mya arenaria*, softshell** (Fig.A)
#2.Shell is somewhat triangular shaped; chondrophore is the same in both shells; siphon is not unusually long and shells do touch when clam closes up; grows up to 20 cm (8") long .... ***Spisula solidissima*, Atlantic surfclam** (Fig.B)

#3.Shell is sturdy, thick walled; both ends of shell are rounded but umbo is much closer to one end than the other; periostracum (thin outer shell covering) is pale brown .... ***Mesodesma arctatum*, Arctic wedgeclam** (Fig.C)
#3.Shell is fragile, thin walled; one end of shell is flatter or more pointed than the other (Figs.D,E); shell is glossy white or periostracum is yellowish .... #4

#4.One end is round, the other somewhat pointed; shell has concentric ridges; dull white on outside .... ***Cumingia tellinoides*, Tellin semele** (Fig.D)
#4.One end is round, the other somewhat flattened; shell is smooth; white with yellowish periostracum .... ***Periploma papyratium*, paper spoonclam** (Fig.E)

[1]Refer to Fig.A on page 7.14 for explanation of terms used in bivalve key.

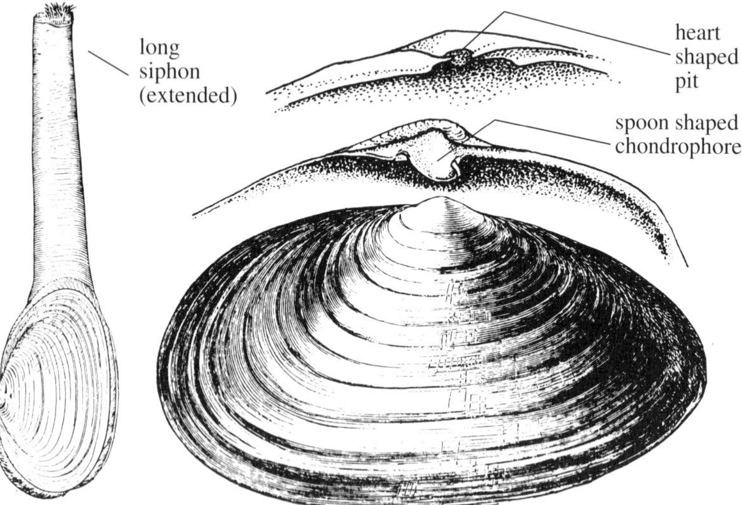

Fig.A. ***MYA ARENARIA*, SOFTSHELL (=steamer, =long-neck):** Chalky white shell, sometimes with grayish outer covering; up to 10 cm (4") long; very common in the intertidal zone and in shallow water; lives in a deep burrow and shoots up a spurt of water when disturbed. (family Myidae) **17.13 E**

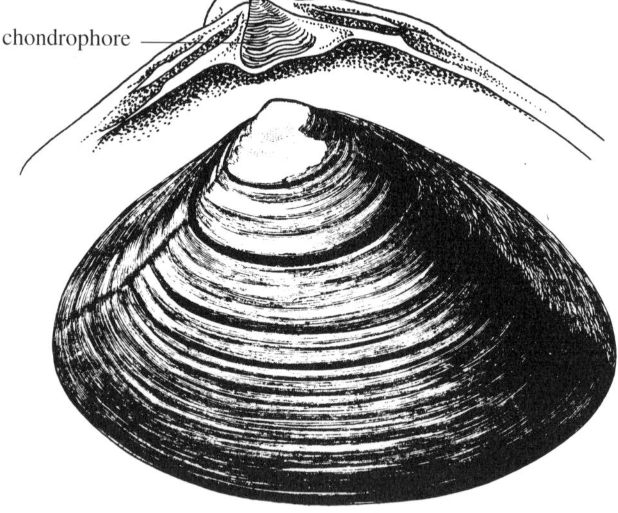

Fig.B. ***SPISULA SOLIDISSIMA*, ATLANTIC SURFCLAM:** Dull white shell, often with beige or yellow outer covering; up to 20 cm (8") long; common offshore in sand; a large commercial fishery harvests these clams for chowder and other food products. (family Mactridae: surfclams)

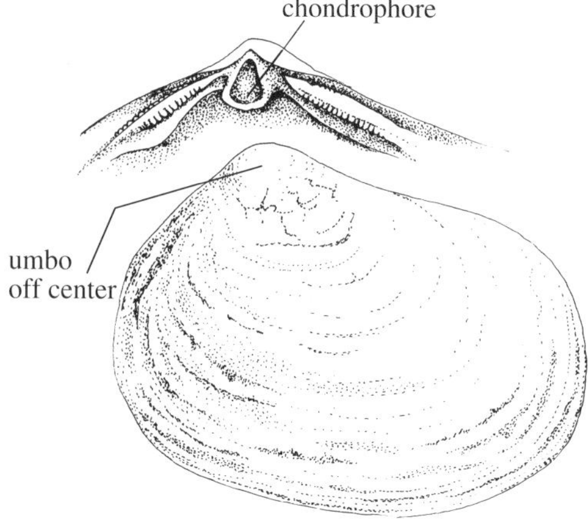

Fig.C. ***MESODESMA ARCTATUM*, ARCTIC WEDGECLAM:** White shell with a pale brown thin covering; up to 40 mm (1 1/2") long; common north of Cape Cod. (family Mesodesmatidae)

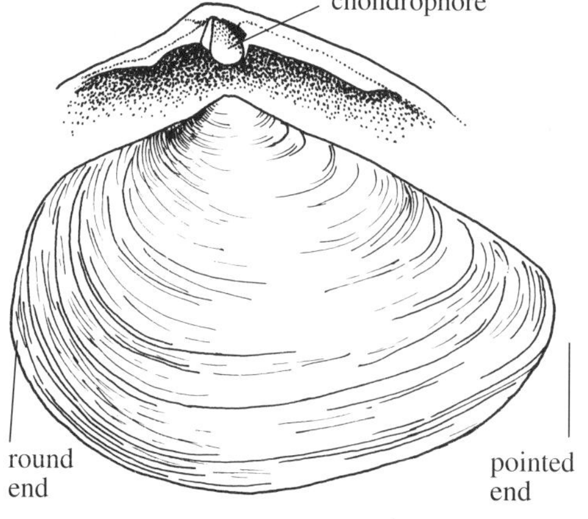

Fig.D. ***CUMINGIA TELLINOIDES*, TELLIN SEMELE:** Chalky white; up to 2 cm (3/4") long; occurs in mud and eelgrass beds; not common. (family Semelidae: semeles and abras)

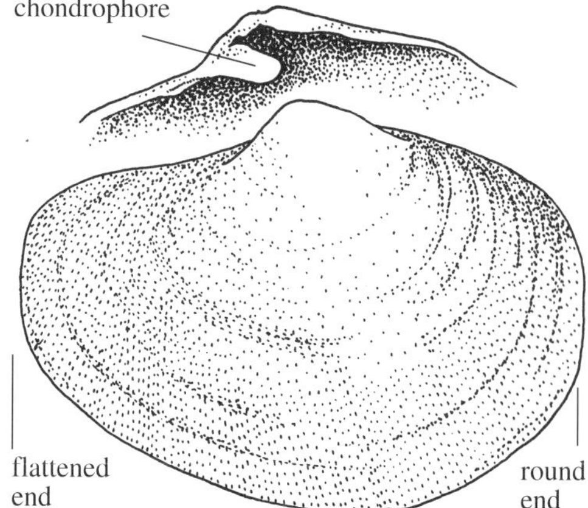

Fig.E. ***PERIPLOMA PAPYRATIUM*, PAPER SPOONCLAM:** White and pearly, with yellowish periostracum; up to 2.5 cm (1") long. (family Periplomatidae: spoonclams)

ELONGATE BIVALVES WITHOUT RADIATING SCULPTURE
PHYLUM MOLLUSCA, CLASS BIVALVIA (PELECYPODA)

Bivalves with shells that are at least twice as long as wide

(Bivalve key begins on page 7.14)

#1.Shell is over 5 times as long as wide .... ***Ensis directus*, Atlantic jackknife** (Fig.A)
#1.Shell is about twice as long as wide (Figs.B-E) .... #2

#2.One end of shell is pointed, the other end is rounded; with a row of teeth inside of shell on each side of umbo (Fig.B) .... ***Yoldia* spp., yoldias,** #3
#2.Neither end of shell is pointed; without a row of teeth on inside edge (Figs.C-E) .... #4

#3.With about 20 teeth on each side of the umbo; up to 62 mm (2 1/2") long; very common .... ***Yoldia limatula*, file yoldia** (Fig.B)
#3.With about 50 very fine teeth on each side of the umbo; up to 25 mm (1") long; less common .... ***Yoldia sapotilla*, short yoldia** (Fig.B)
#3.With 12-14 teeth on each side of umbo; up to about 50 mm (2") long; uncommon .... ***Yoldia* spp., other yoldias**[2]

#4.Umbo is closer to one end of the shell than the other (Figs.C,D) .... #5
#4.Umbo is nearly central (Fig.E) .... #7

#5.Both ends of shell are rounded (Fig.C); surface of shell is smooth .... #6
#5.One end of shell is flattened, other end is rounded; shell is rough, dull and irregular; siphons are bright red .... ***Hiatella* spp., hiatellas**[2] (Fig.D)

#6.With a distinct rib on inside of shell .... ***Siliqua costata,* Atlantic razor** (Fig.C)
#6.With a spoon shaped structure (chondrophore) on the inside of one shell beneath the umbo (see Figs.A-E on page 7.22) .... page 7.22

#7.Ligament (flexible "hinge" near umbo) is external; no chondrophore[1]; siphons are separate .... ***Tagelus* spp., tageluses**[2] (Fig.E)
#7.Ligament is internal; with a chondrophore[1] (see Figs.A-E on page 7.22); siphons may be fused or separate .... page 7.22

[1]Refer to Fig.A on page 7.14 for explanation of terms used in bivalve key.
[2]Refer to Gosner (1971) or a good shell book to distinguish between these species.

Fig.A. ***ENSIS DIRECTUS*, ATLANTIC JACKKNIFE (=common razor clam):** Shiny, yellow-green outer shell covering; up to 25 cm (10") long; common in sand and mud near low tide level; rapidly digs a deep burrow which has a keyhole shaped opening; very good to eat and often harvested by clam diggers. (family Solenidae: razors and jackknives) **17.04 F**

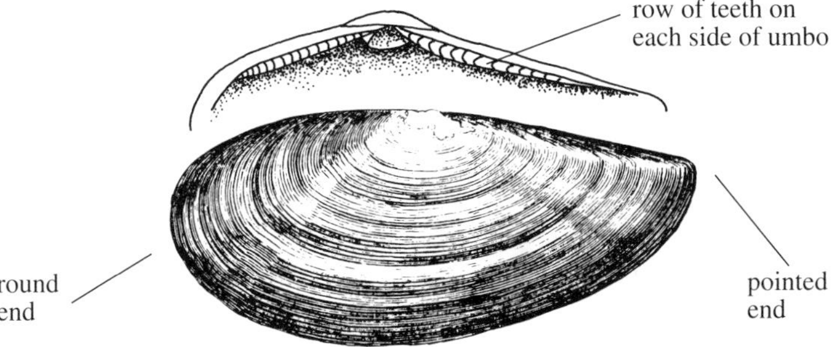

Fig.B. ***YOLDIA LIMATULA*, FILE YOLDIA:** Shiny, smooth, olive green outer covering; up to 62 mm (2 1/2") long; very common in bottom mud and often eaten by flounder. ***Yoldia sapotilla*, short yoldia**, is similar in color to *Yoldia limatula*; up to 25 mm (1") long; less common. Use key to distinguish these and other yoldias. (family Nuculanidae: nutclams and yoldias) **17.05 C**

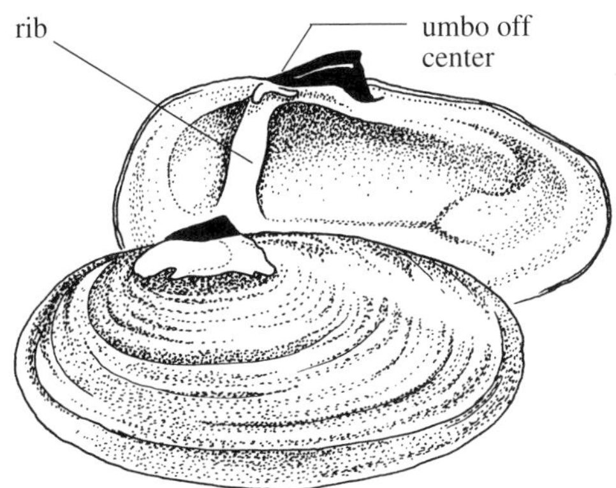

Fig.C. ***SILIQUA COSTATA*, ATLANTIC RAZOR (=ribbed pod)**: Pinkish white with thin yellowish-green outer shell covering; up to 5 cm (2") long; not common. (family Solenidae: razors and jackknives)

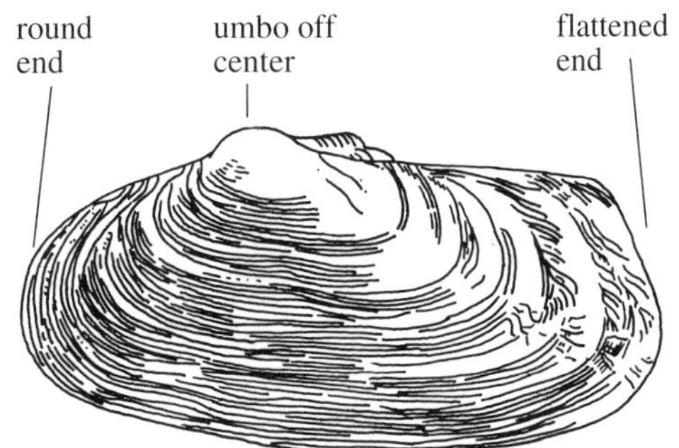

Fig.D. ***HIATELLA* SPP., HIATELLAS:** Chalky white shell with grayish outer covering; siphons are bright red; up to 3.8 cm (1 1/2") long; found in crevices in rocks and among seaweed holdfasts. The two local species, *Hiatella arctica*, Arctic hiatella, and *Hiatella striata*, striate hiatella, are very difficult to distinguish[2]. (family Hiatellidae)

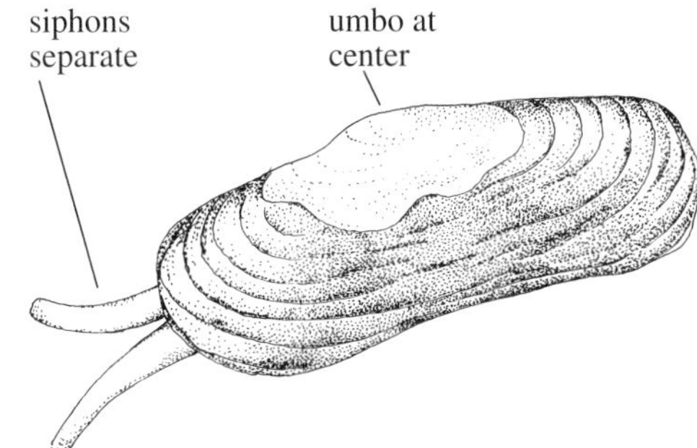

Fig.E. ***TAGELUS* SPP.:** *Tagelus plebeius*, stout tagelus, has a yellowish-brown or greenish periostracum (outer shell covering); up to 10 cm (4") long. *Tagelus divisus*, the purplish tagelus, is often pale purple; up to 3.8 cm (1 1/2") long. Both species burrow into muddy sand in shallow water and intertidal mudflats. (family Solecurtidae)

ANNELID (SEGMENTED) WORMS: PHYLUM ANNELIDA[1]

Worms that are segmented (divided into numerous ringlike sections) and have setae (bristles) on each of the segments[2].

(Use the key on page 2.16 to determine if you have an annelid worm)

#1.Dorsal (upper) surface with overlapping scales or plates (Fig.B) .... **scale worms**, page 8.09
#1.Dorsal surface without scales .... #2

#2.Head[3] region with one or more obvious tentacles, long bristles, lobes, antennae or filaments (this page, Figs.A-I and page 8.02, Figs.A-E) .... #3
#2.Head region with no obvious tentacles, bristles, antennae, or filaments (see page 8.03, Figs.A-F) (several pairs of microscopic antennae may be present which are much smaller than the head segment) .... page 8.03

#3.With long stiff bristles pointing forward from head (Fig.C) .... **broom worms**, bottom of page 8.11
#3.Head without long stiff bristles .... #4

#4.With tentacles usually too numerous to count; head segment (prostomium) may be overgrown and hidden by tentacles (Figs.D-I) .... #5
#4.No more than about 12 tentacles, antennae, palps etc.; head segment not hidden by tentacles (Fig.A) .... page 8.02

#5.Tentacles are arranged in a fanlike (Fig.D) or crownlike (Fig.E), or padlike (Fig.F) pattern; worms live in tubes (Fig.G) made of cemented sand grains, or parchmentlike or shell-like material .... page 8.04
#5.Tentacles are stringy or spaghettilike (Fig.H,I); tentacles are often blood red color; worms may or may not live in tubes .... #6

#6.Stringy tentacles or gill filaments occur on the head segment only, not on any of the body segments (Fig.H) .... page 8.06
#6.Stringy tentacles or gill filaments occur on one or more body segments (Fig.I) .... **family Cirratulidae**, page 8.08

[1]**WARNING: The identification of many annelid worms to the species level is beyond the scope of this book, requiring microscopic examination of the parapodia and setae.** For a positive identification of polychaete worms, use Fauchald (1977) to determine the family and genus. Use Pettibone (1963), Gosner (1971), or R. I. Smith (1964) to determine the species in many families. Other references useful for leeches and oligochaetes are provided on the appropriate pages.

[2]See Fig.A for terms used in annelid worm key.

[3]The identification of most segmented worms requires a careful examination of the head region with a hand lens or dissecting microscope. Unfortunately, finding the head of a worm is not always easy. If you are not sure which end is the head, check both ends carefully on the topside (dorsal) and the underside (ventral). Identification may not be possible if a worm has been broken during collection and no head is present. Therefore, be as gentle as possible when collecting and handling worms to prevent breakage. Some worms have a proboscis, a tonguelike extension, which they can stick out or withdraw into their mouth (for example, see Fig.A). The proboscis often remains in the extended position when the worm is dead, especially if it has been preserved. Check very carefully to be sure that you are examining the head of the worm and not the end of the extended proboscis. Some worms have jaws or teeth at the end of the proboscis but these may be covered over if the proboscis is withdrawn or only partially extended. Whenever possible examine the worm while it is alive to avoid confusing the proboscis with the head segment or the head with the tail.

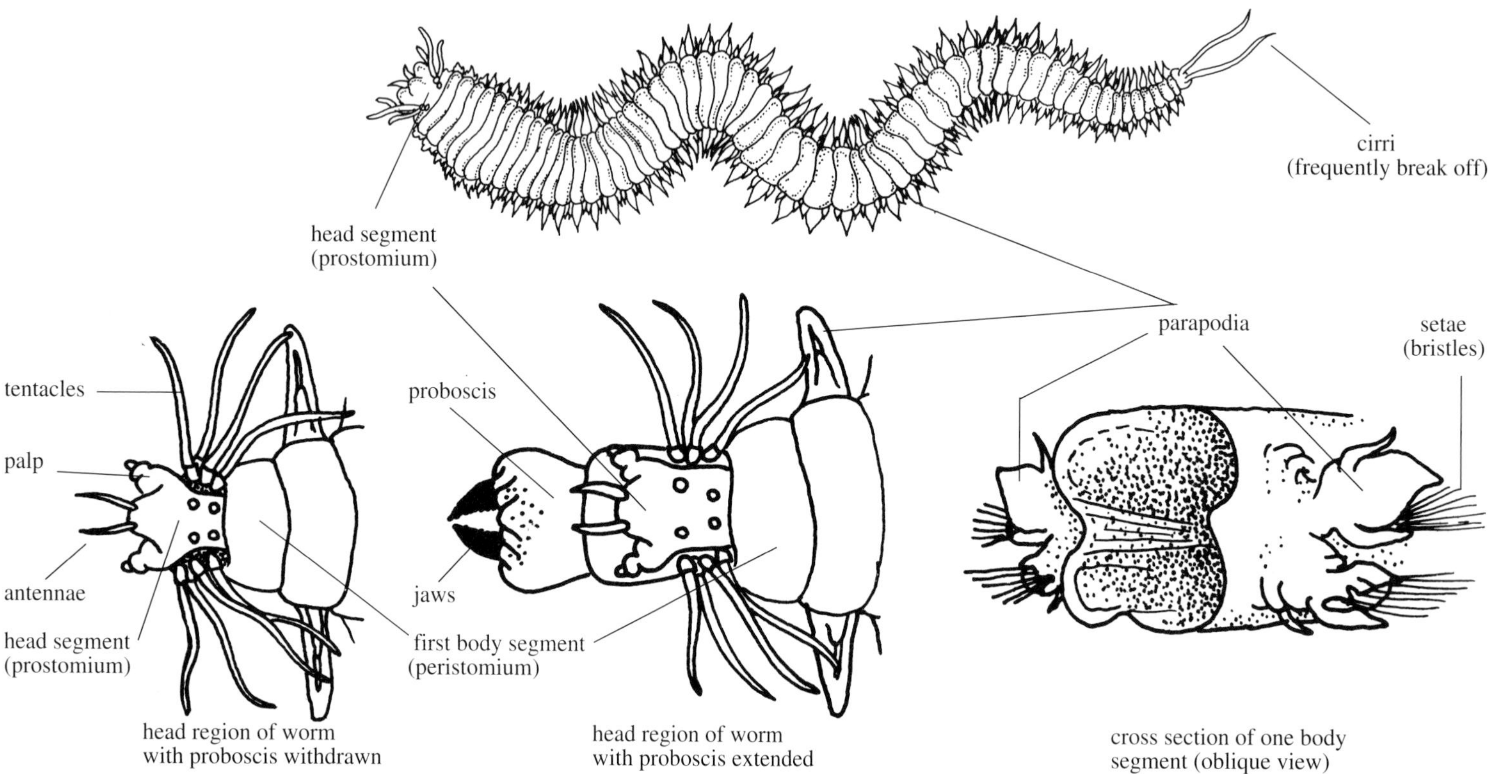

Fig.A. **TERMS USED IN ANNELID WORM KEY**

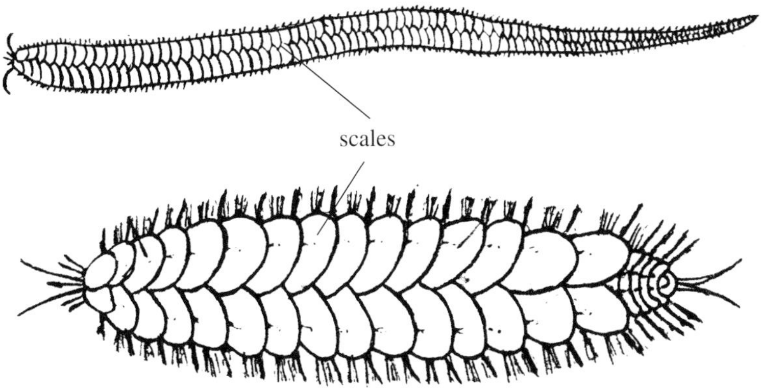

Fig.B. **SCALE WORMS**

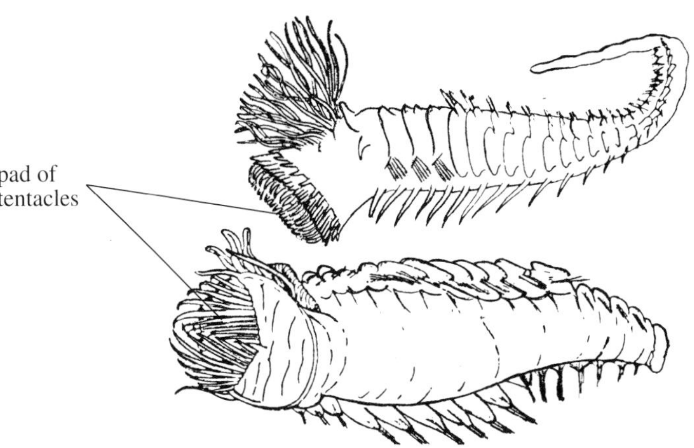

Fig.F. **WORMS WITH A PAD OF SHORT, GOLDEN TENTACLES**

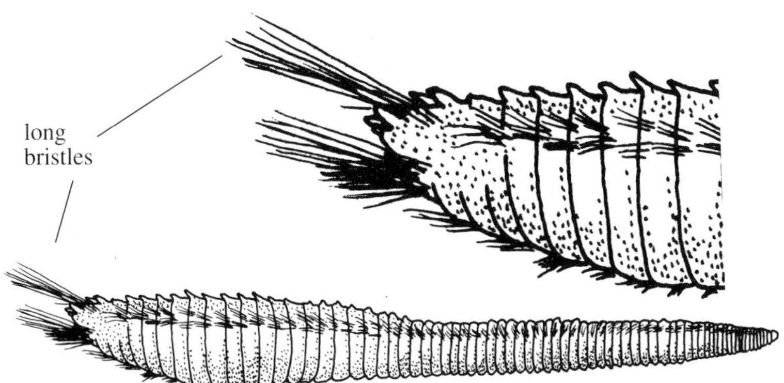

Fig.C. **BROOM WORMS**

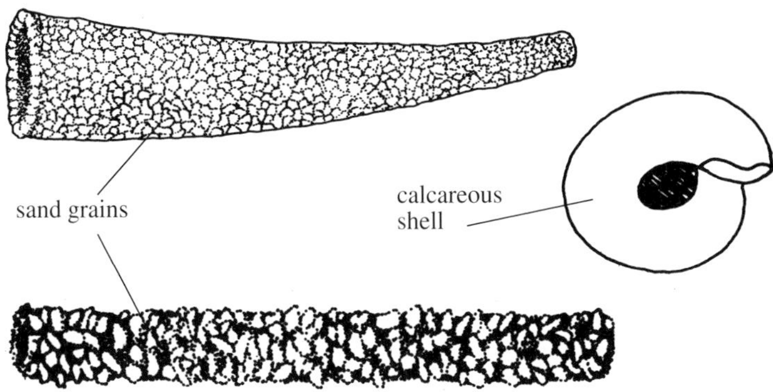

Fig.G. **WORM TUBES**

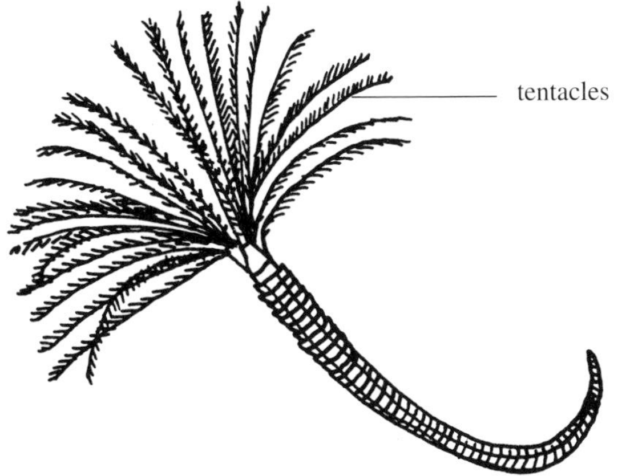

Fig.D. **WORMS WITH FANLIKE TENTACLES**

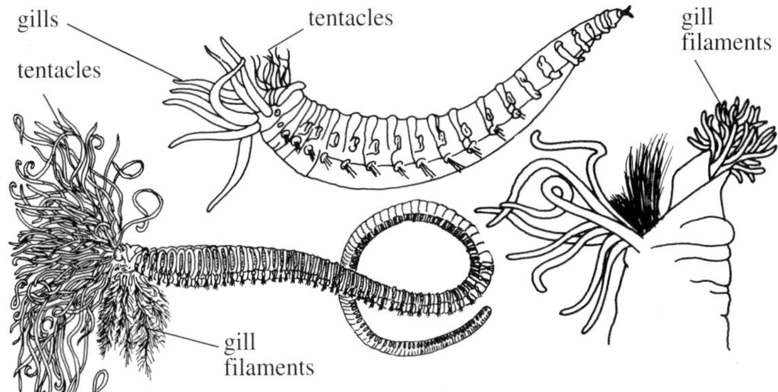

Fig.H. **WORMS WITH STRINGY GILL FILAMENTS AND TENTACLES ON HEAD SEGMENT ONLY**

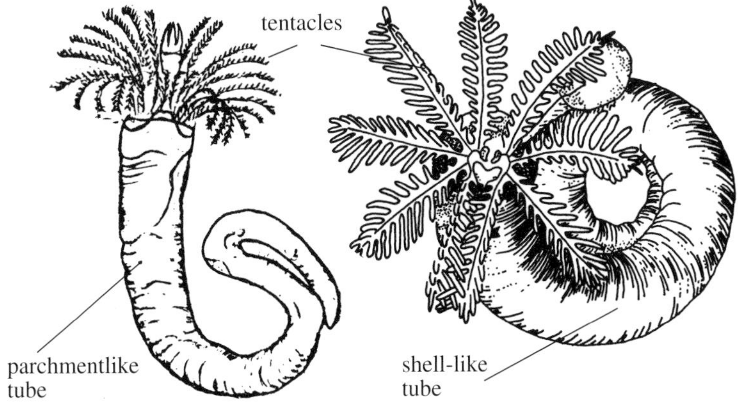

Fig.E. **WORMS WITH CROWNLIKE CIRCLE OF TENTACLES**

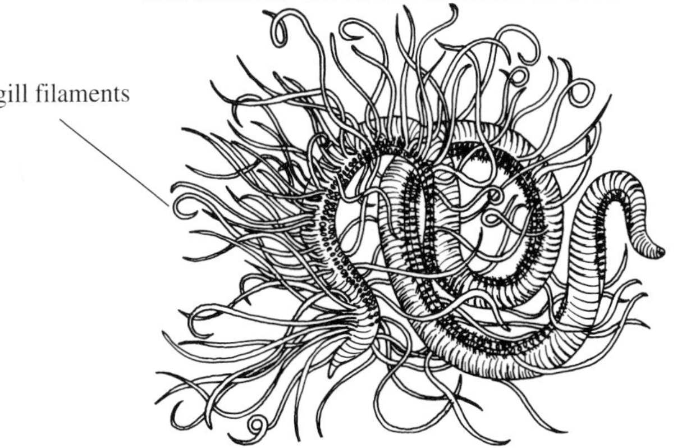

Fig.I. **WORMS WITH STRINGY GILL FILAMENTS ON BODY SEGMENTS**

ANNELID (SEGMENTED) WORMS WITH HEAD APPENDAGES[1]: PHYLUM ANNELIDA

(Annelid worm key begins on page 8.00)

#1.Head region[2] with 1 or 2 tentacles (one pair) or tentaclelike appendages (Fig.A) .... page 8.10
#1.Head region with more than 2 tentacles or tentaclelike appendages (Figs.B-E) .... #2

#2.Head region with 3 to 5 tentacles or tentaclelike appendages (Fig.B) .... page 8.12
#2.Head region with more than 5 tentacles or tentaclelike appendages (Figs.C-E) .... #3

#3.Head region with a pair of fleshy lobes (palps), 4 pairs of tentacles and 1 pair of tiny antennae (Fig.C); with an extensible proboscis having dark, sharply pointed jaws at the tip .... **family Nereidae, clam worms**, page 8.14
#3.Head region not as described above (Figs.D,E) .... #4

#4.Head region with 2-4 pairs of tentacles and 4-5 antennae (Fig.D); parapodia ("legs") are leaflike and overlapping; usually with 2 eyes .... **family Phyllodocidae, paddle worms**, page 8.15
#4.Head region with 2-3 antennae, 2 oral palps, and 1-8 pairs of peristomial cirri (Fig.E); parapodia ("legs") have long thread or rodlike extensions (parapodial cirri); usually with 4 eyes .... **families Syllidae, Pilargiidae, and Hesionidae** page 8.16

[1]See Fig.A on page 8.00 for terms used in annelid worm key.
[2]See footnote 3 on page 8.00 for important instructions concerning the examination of the head and the proboscis.

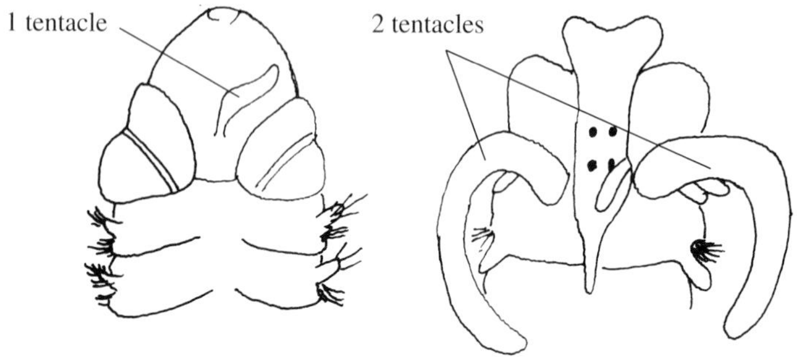

Fig.A. **WORMS WITH 1-2 TENTACLES ON HEAD**

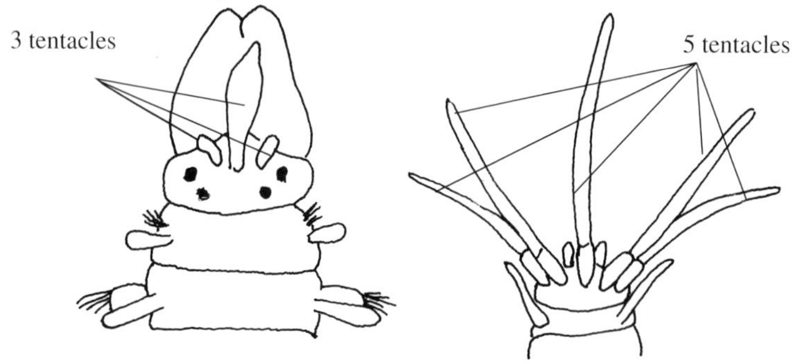

Fig.B. **WORMS WITH 3-5 TENTACLES ON HEAD**

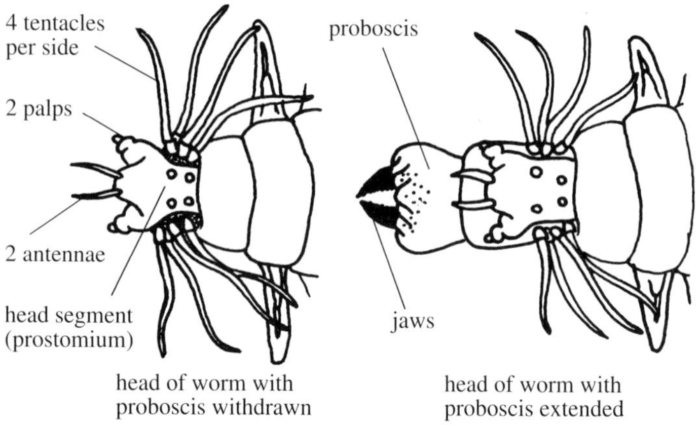

Fig.C. **CLAM WORMS, FAMILY NEREIDAE**

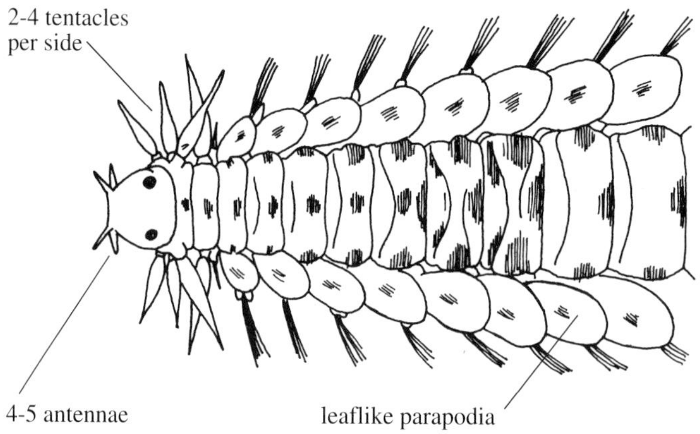

Fig.D. **PADDLE WORMS, FAMILY PHYLLODOCIDAE**

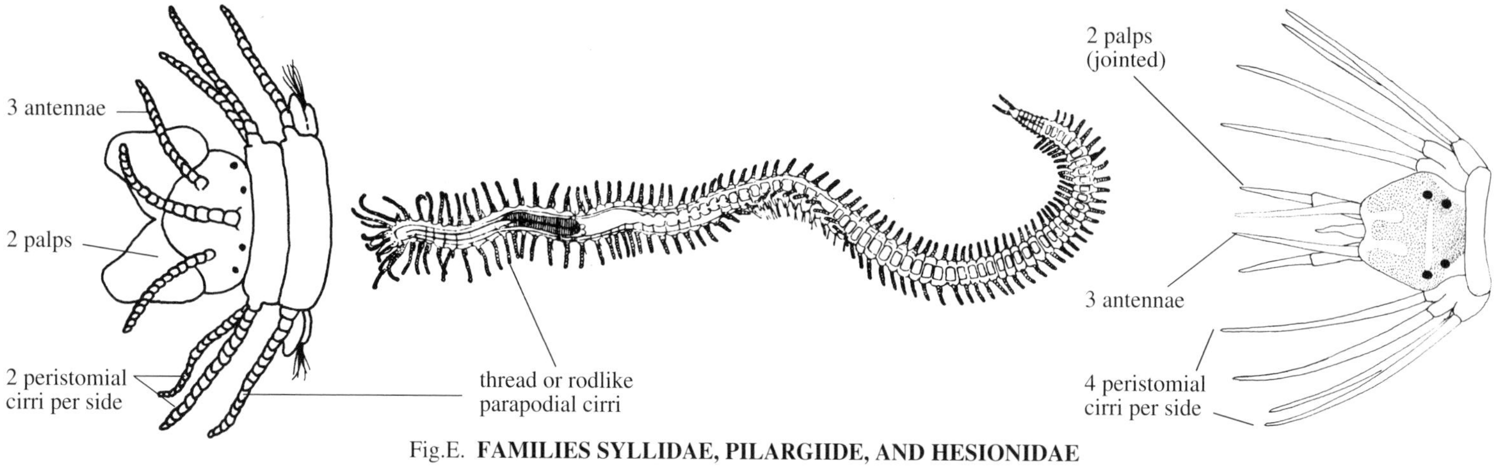

Fig.E. **FAMILIES SYLLIDAE, PILARGIIDE, AND HESIONIDAE**

ANNELID (SEGMENTED) WORMS WITH NO HEAD APPENDAGES[1]: PHYLUM ANNELIDA

(Annelid worm key begins on page 8.00)

#1.Body segments are usually longer than wide, bamboolike; head segment[2] is hoodlike or rounded; tail segment is funnel or spoon shaped (Fig.A) .... **bamboo worms**, page 8.22

#1.Body segments are generally wider than long; head segment is not hoodlike; tail segment is not funnel or spoon shaped (Figs.B-F) .... #2

#2.Head segment[2] is somewhat flattened in front with pointed front corners .... **painted worms** (Fig.B) **and T-headed worms** (Fig.C), page 8.17

#2.Head segment is pointed (Fig.D) or rounded (Figs.E,F) .... #3

#3.Thick bodied worms that are thicker at their midsection (Figs.D,E) and narrower at their head and tail ends; tip of head may be rather sharply pointed (Fig.D) or blunt (Fig.E) .... page 8.18

#3.Thin, threadlike worms, width never exceeding 6 mm (1/4"), body of worm is nearly the same thickness over its entire length (Fig.F); tip of head is usually somewhat rounded or conical .... page 8.20

[1]See Fig.A on page 8.00 for terms used in annelid worm key.

[2]See footnote 3 on page 8.00 for important instructions concerning the examination of the head and the proboscis.

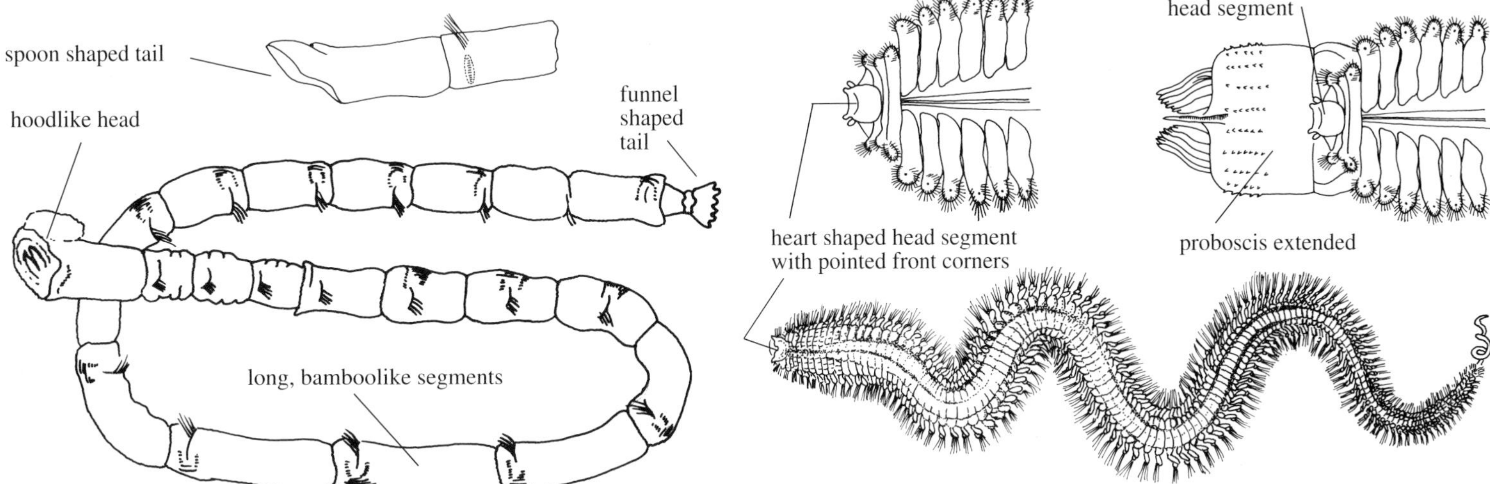

Fig.A. **BAMBOO WORMS, FAMILY MALDANIDAE**

Fig.B. **PAINTED WORMS, FAMILY NEPHTYIDAE**

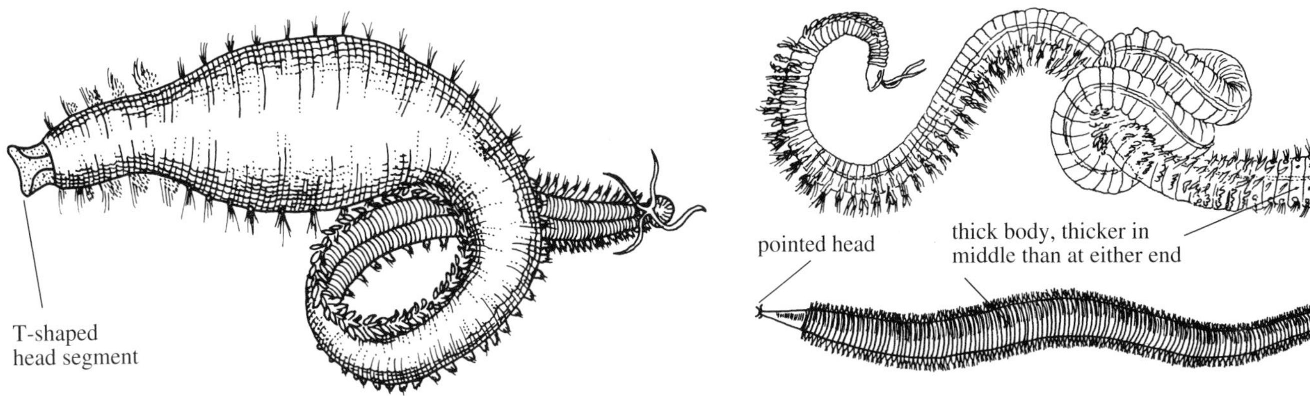

Fig.C. **T-HEADED WORM, FAMILY SCALIBREGMIDAE**

Fig.D. **THICK BODIED WORMS WITH POINTED HEAD AND NO OBVIOUS TENTACLES**

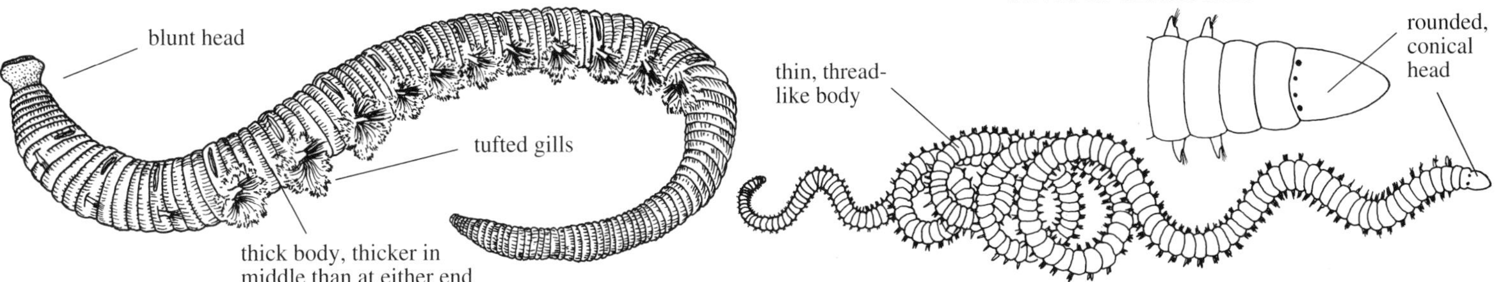

Fig.E. **LUGWORM, FAMILY ARENICOLIDAE**

Fig.F. **THIN, THREADLIKE WORMS WITH ROUNDED HEAD AND NO TENTACLES**

CONE WORMS, COILED WORMS, FAN WORMS AND RELATED SPECIES
PHYLUM ANNELIDA, CLASS POLYCHAETA

Segmented worms with fanlike, crownlike, or padlike tentacles; build tubes made of cemented sand grains, parchmentlike or shell-like material.

(Annelid worm key begins on page 8.00)

#1.Head end is flattened (Figs.A,B) .... #2
#1.With featherlike tentacles (Figs.C-H) arranged like a fan or in a circular crown .... #3

#2.Lives in a delicate cone shaped tube made out of sand grains; head has two comblike rows of golden bristles .... ***Pectinaria gouldii*, cone worm** (Fig.A)
#2.Lives in hard, twisted tubes made of sand grains cemented to shells and to other worm tubes; head has a pad of tentacles arranged in two concentric semicircles .... ***Sabellaria vulgaris*, cement-tube worm** (Fig.B)

#3.Tubes (Figs.C,D) are calcareous (made out of a white, shell-like material); worm has an operculum ("trap door") that plugs up the opening of the tube when the worm is withdrawn .... **family Serpulidae**[1], #4
#3.Tubes are flexible, leathery, parchmentlike or sandy; worm does not have an operculum (Figs.E-H) .... **family Sabellidae, fan worms**[1], #6
#3.Tubes are coated with overlapping flattened sand grains and shell bits, like shingles; worm segments are long, bamboolike ...... ***Owenia fusiformis*,** page 8.22

#4.Tiny, flat, coiled, snail-like tubes (Fig.C) on stones, algae, eelgrass, etc .... ***Spirorbis* spp., coiled worms,** #5
#4.Irregular, twisted tubes (Fig.D) often over 2.5 cm (1") long .... ***Hydroides dianthus*, carnation worm** (Fig.D)

#5.Tubes coil counterclockwise .... ***Spirorbis spirillum*, counterclockwise coiled worm** (Fig.C)
#5.Tubes coil clockwise .... ***Spirorbis borealis*, clockwise coiled worm** (Fig.C)

#6.Tiny, less than 5 mm (1/4") long; with 10-12 body segments bearing setae (bristles); with a pair of eye spots on first and last body segments .... ***Fabricia sabella*, little fan worm** (Fig.E)
#6.With more than 12 body segments bearing setae; often longer than 5 mm (1/4"); no eye spots on body (Figs.F-H) .... #7

#7.Without eye spots on tentacles; collar lobed; tube leathery, covered with sand or mud .... ***Potamilla neglecta*, eyeless fan worm** (Fig.F)
#7.With eye spots on tentacles (Figs.F-H) .... #8

#8.With eyes in a single row on each tentacle; tube leathery and sand covered .... ***Potamilla reniformis*, fan worm** (Fig.F)
#8.With eyes in two rows on each tentacle (Figs.G,H) .... #9

#9.Eye spots are not paired, arranged in two irregular rows; collar is divided into 2 lobes .... ***Sabella microphthalma*, fan worm** (Fig.G)
#9.Eye spots are in pairs on each tentacle; collar is divided into 4 lobes .... ***Sabella crassicornis*, fan worm** (Fig.H)

[1]**WARNING:** This key does not include some of the rarer species in this family. Refer to Gosner (1971) for a positive identification, especially for species found in deeper water or in the northern portion of this region.

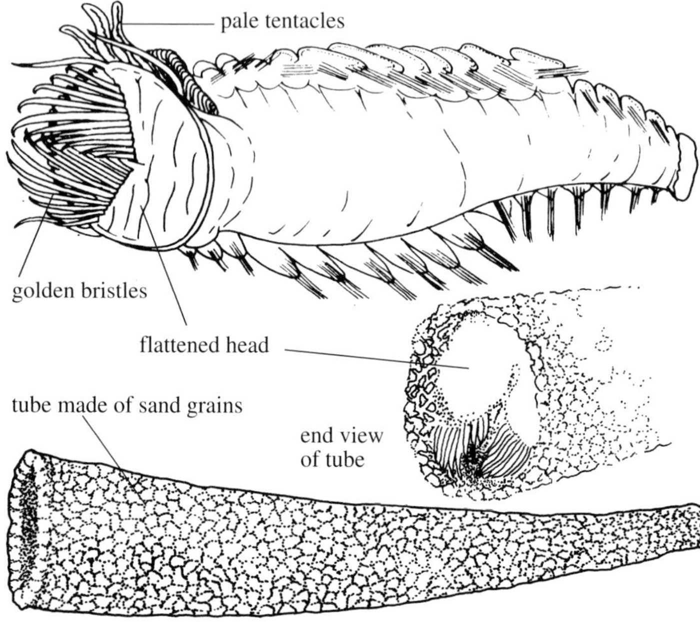

Fig.A. ***PECTINARIA GOULDII*, CONE WORM:** Pink or beige body mottled with red and blue; two comblike rows of golden bristles on head, red gills on sides of head; pale pinkish tentacles; up to 5 cm (2") long; constructs distinctive cone shaped tubes made out of a single layer of sand grains; lives vertically, with head down and pointed end of tube facing up; very common in intertidal zone and offshore in bottom mud. (family Pectinariidae) **17.08 A** **17.08 B**

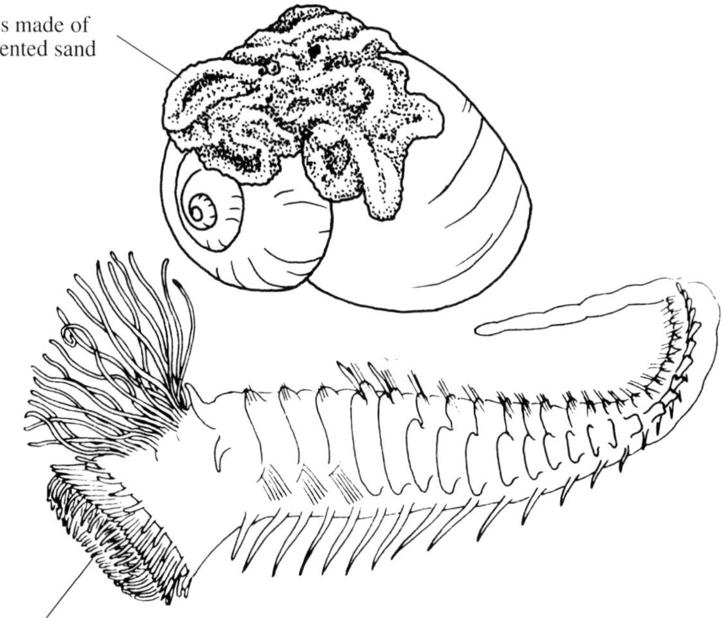

Fig.B. ***SABELLARIA VULGARIS*, CEMENT-TUBE WORM:** Pink or beige colored body with tinge of yellow; golden tentacles are arranged in a pad of concentric semicircles; up to 2.5 cm (1") long; builds well cemented sand tubes which form reeflike structures up to 30 cm (12") across; often colonial with several tubes cemented together; common on shells and rocks in southern New England. (family Sabellariidae)

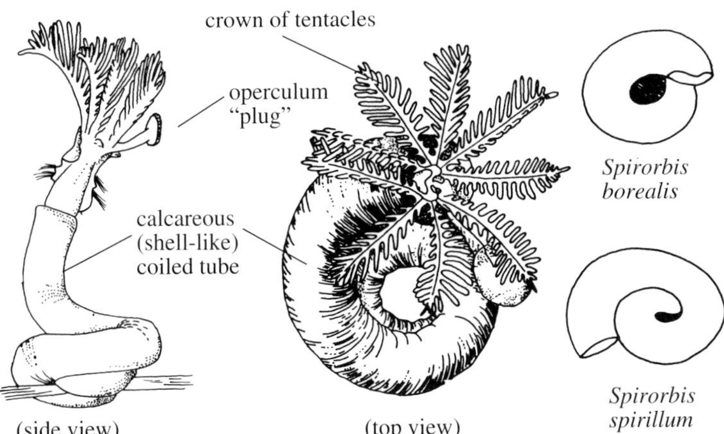

Fig.C. ***SPIRORBIS* SPP., COILED WORMS:** Build tiny white calcareous (shell-like) coiled tubes, up to 2 mm (1/16") in diameter. *Spirorbis borealis* has a dull chalky tube coiling clockwise; very common near shore on eelgrass, seaweeds, etc. *Spirorbis spirillum* has a smooth, shiny tube coiling counter-clockwise; found offshore. (family Serpulidae[1]) **17.08 C** **17.09 E**

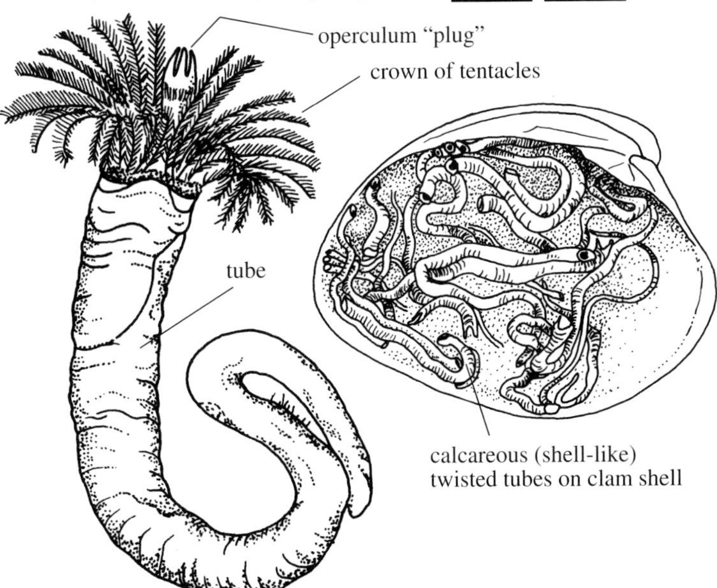

Fig.D. ***HYDROIDES DIANTHUS*, CARNATION WORM:** Crown of tentacles may be brown or purple banded with white; green or yellow translucent collar; branching veins often appear green due to green colored blood; up to 7.5 cm (3") long; twisted, snaky, white tubes are very common on shells, stones and other hard objects. (family Serpulidae) **17.08 D**

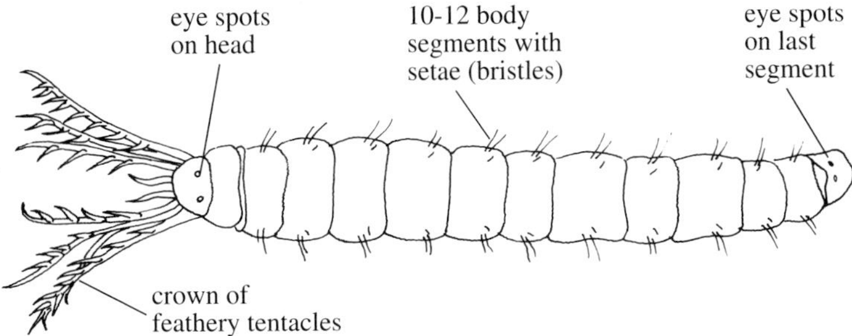

Fig.E. ***FABRICIA SABELLA*, LITTLE FAN WORM:** Yellowish body; tiny, up to about 3 mm (1/8") long; lives in soft parchmentlike tubes near low tide level, embedded in mud or entwined within the branches of coralline algae growing on rocks; can leave tube and freely move about. (family Sabellidae[1])

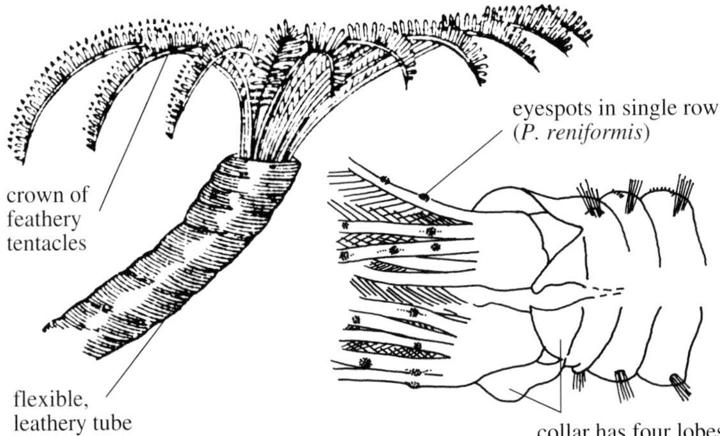

Fig.F. ***POTAMILLA* SPP., FAN OR FEATHER-DUSTER WORMS:** Live in leathery tubes attached to shells and covered with sand or mud. *Potamilla neglecta*, eyeless fan worm, is reddish or brown; up to 6 cm (2 1/2") long; found offshore. *Potamilla reniformis* has red eye spots, tentacles are reddish brown tinged with white and tipped with yellowish gray, body is yellowish green; up to 10 cm (4") long. (family Sabellidae[1])

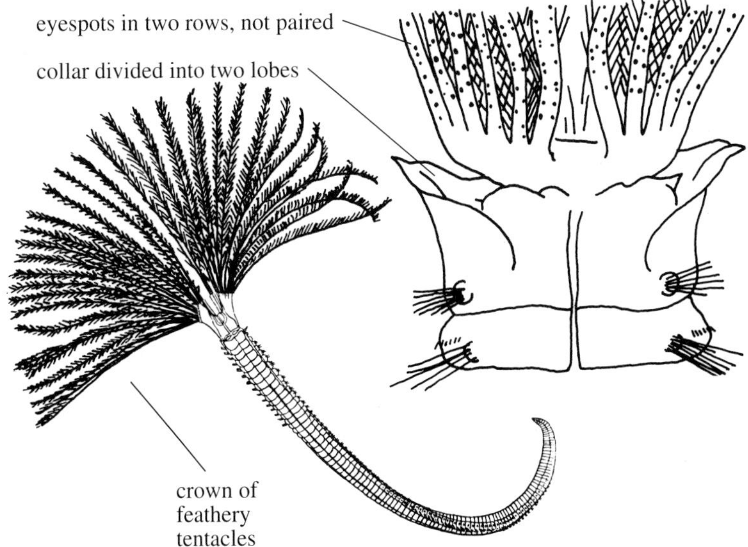

Fig.G. ***SABELLA MICROPHTHALMA*, FAN OR FEATHER-DUSTER WORM:** Reddish brown eye spots, whitish body; up to 3 cm (1 1/4") long; found in intertidal zone and in shallow water on shells. (family Sabellidae[1])

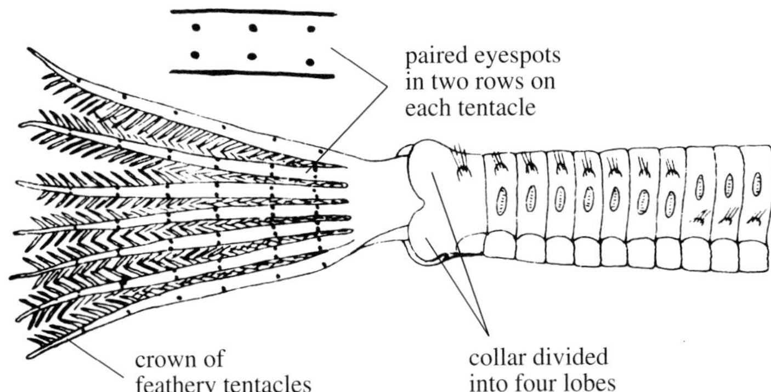

Fig.H. ***SABELLA CRASSICORNIS*, FAN OR FEATHER-DUSTER WORM:** Up to 5 cm (2") long; tube is transparent and flexible on top, rigid below; found offshore. (family Sabellidae[1])

PHYLUM ANNELIDA, CLASS POLYCHAETA, FAMILIES TEREBELLIDAE AND AMPHARETIDAE

Segmented worms with numerous stringy tentacles and gill filaments on head segment only

(Annelid worm key begins on page 8.00)

#1.Some of the threadlike or branched tentacles can be withdrawn[1] into the mouth leaving the thicker, pointed, unbranched tentaclelike gills extended (Figs.A-E) .... **family Ampharetidae**[2], #2

#1.None of the tentacles can be withdrawn into the mouth; gills may or may not be branched (Figs.F-J) .... **family Terebellidae**[2], #6

#2.With 40 or more posterior (rear) segments that do not have setae (bristles); about 18 of the anterior (front) segments have setae .... ***Melinna cristata*** (Fig.A)

#2.With 12 or fewer posterior segments that do not have setae (bristles); about 14 of the anterior segments have golden yellow setae (Figs.B-E) .... #3

#3.With 10-14 cirri (short projections) at the tail end (Fig.B) .... ***Ampharete acutifrons*** (Fig.B)

#3.With 2 cirri at the tail end (Fig.C) .... #4

#3.With no cirri at the tail end .... ***Hobsonia florida (=Hypaniola grayi)*** (Fig.C)

#4.Tentacles that can be withdrawn into mouth are not branched; tentacles are threadlike .... ***Amage auricula*** (Fig.C)

#4.Tentacles that can be withdrawn into mouth have short, featherlike branches (Figs.D,E) .... #5

#5.Without a bundle of long golden setae (bristles) in front of gills .... ***Asabellides oculata*** (Fig.D)

#5.With a bundle of long golden setae (bristles) in front of gills .... ***Ampharete arctica*** (Fig.E)

#6.With branched gills on head segment in addition to threadlike tentacles (Figs.F-H) .... #7

#6.With only threadlike tentacles on head segment; no branched gills on head segment; body is blood red color (Figs.I,J) .... #9

#7.Gills are spirally branched; when contracted the gills look like red pompoms on a stalk .... ***Pista cristata*, pom-pom worm** (Fig.F)

#7.Gills are bushy or treelike, not spirally branched (Figs.G,H) .... #8

#8.With 2 pairs of branching gills; setae (bristles) on 17 of the anterior (front) segments; grows up to 7 cm (2 3/4") long .... ***Pista palmata*** (Fig.G)

#8.With 3 pairs of branching gills; setae on 40-50 of the anterior segments; grows up to 38 cm (15") long .... ***Amphitrite ornata*, ornate worm** (Fig.H)

#8.With 1 pair of branching gills; setae on 16 of the anterior segments; grows up to 15 cm (6") long; with numerous eyespots .... ***Pista maculata*** (not shown)

#9.Parapodia are simple, not branched; small, bright red worm with long tentacles wrapped around body; worm looks like a drop of blood in the mud; grows up to 2.5 cm (1") long .... ***Polycirrus eximius*, blood droplet worm** (Fig.I)

#9.Midbody with branching red fleshy appendages (parapodia) that look like gills but have setae (tiny bristles); very long, threadlike, fragile, blood red worm which grows up to 35 cm (14") long .... ***Enoplobranchus sanguineus*, bloody thread worm** (Fig.J)

[1]Leave the living worm undisturbed in a dish of seawater for about half an hour. The tentacles will begin to extend and can be examined with a hand lens or dissecting microscope. Touch the tentacles with a probe to determine if they can be withdrawn into the mouth or not.

[2]**WARNING:** This key does not include some of the rarer species in these families. Refer to Gosner (1971) for a positive identification.

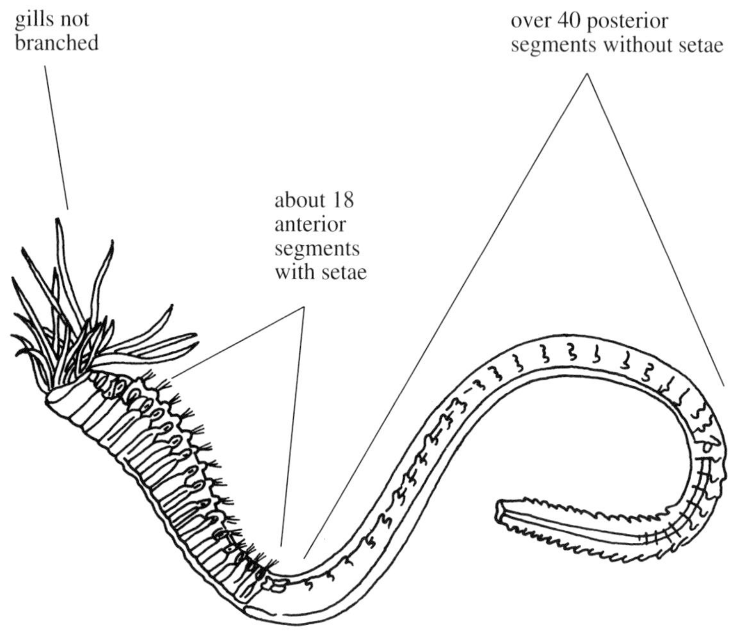

Fig.A. ***MELINNA CRISTATA:*** Up to 5 cm (2") long; builds cylindrical membranous tube with a thick black cover of fine silt; common offshore in bays and sounds, also found in estuaries and eelgrass beds.

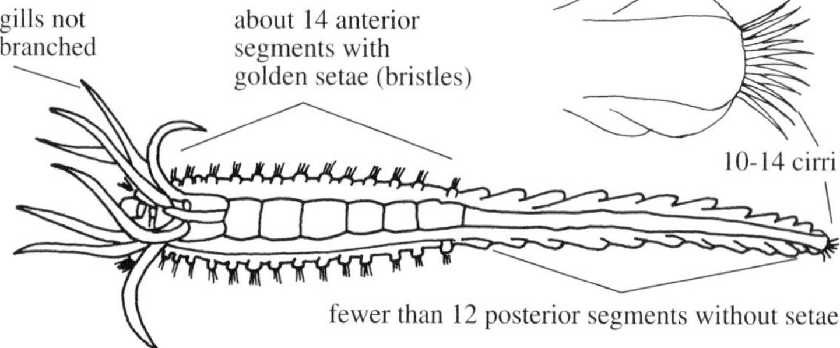

Fig.B. ***AMPHARETE ACUTIFRONS:*** Translucent yellow-green body, red near head, with golden yellow setae; up to 2.5 cm (1") long; builds membranous tube covered with sand and mud; found near low tide level and offshore.

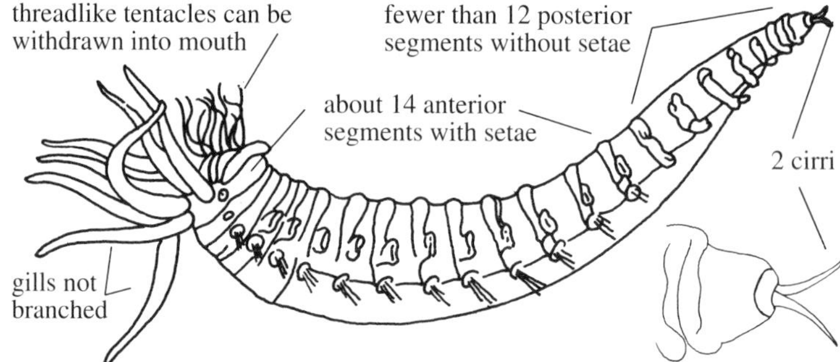

Fig.C. ***AMAGE AURICULA:*** Up to 2 cm (3/4") long; builds membranous tube covered with soft mud. ***Hobsonia florida (=Hypaniola grayi)*** lacks anal cirri; has about 20 segments with setae; occurs in shallow waters of low salinity.

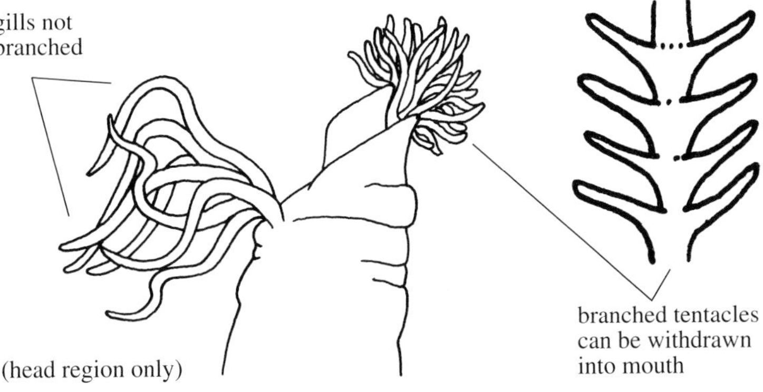

Fig.D. ***ASABELLIDES OCULATA:*** Up to 1 cm (3/8") long; found offshore on sandy silt and in brackish water.

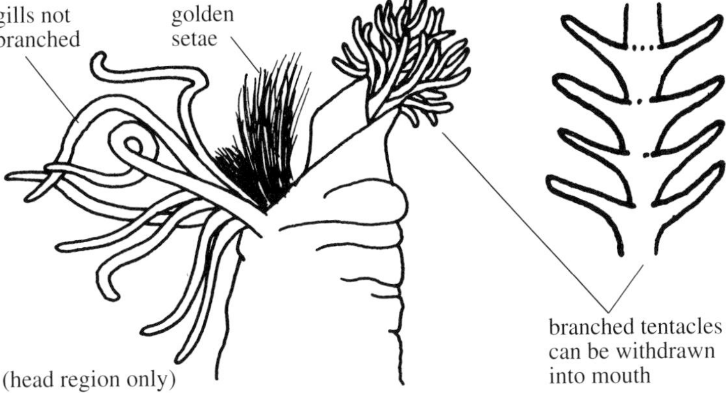

Fig.E. ***AMPHARETE ARCTICA:*** Up to 2.5 cm (1") long; with bundle of golden setae (bristles) on either side of head.

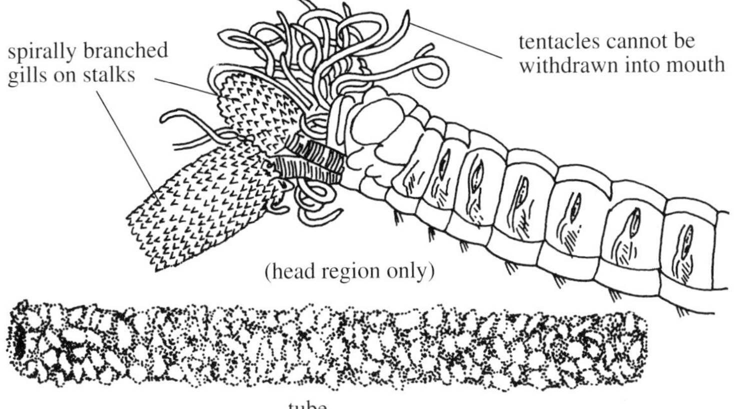

Fig.F. ***PISTA CRISTATA*, POM-POM WORM:** Body and gills are red; up to 9 cm (3 1/2") long; burrows into mud, builds tube which is rough and encrusted with coarse pebbles.

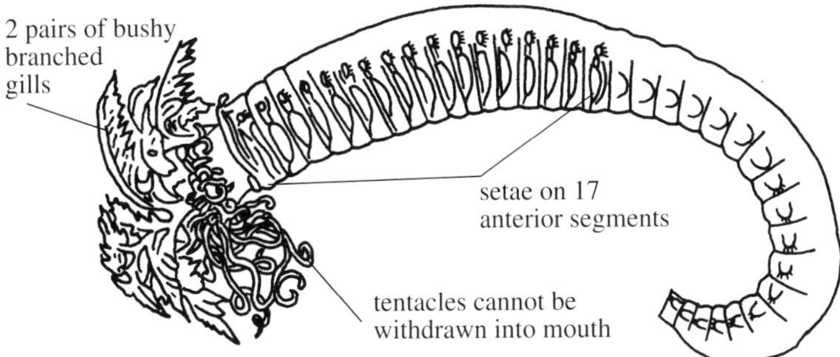

Fig.G. ***PISTA PALMATA:*** Light red to dark reddish brown, body has white spots and a row of rectangular red spots, gills are green; up to 7 cm (2 3/4") long; found in mud near low tide level and offshore[2].

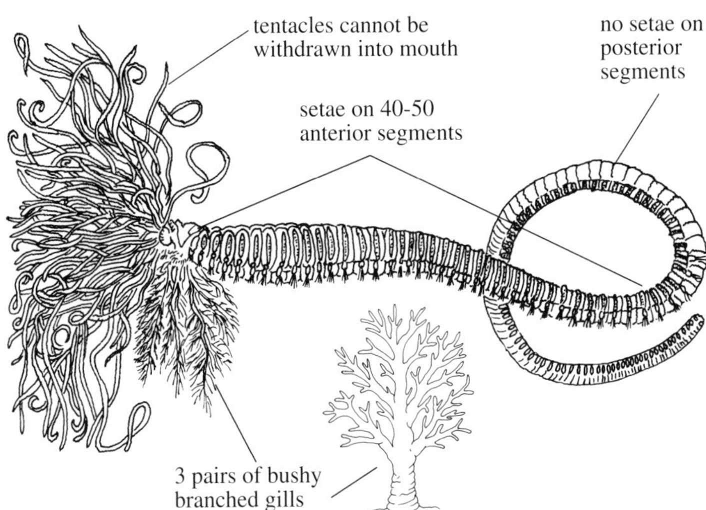

Fig.H. ***AMPHITRITE ORNATA*, ORNATE WORM:** Body is orange-red, tentacles are pale and translucent, gills are bright red; up to 38 cm (15") long; builds tube of black mud or sand near low water level and offshore. Other species with 3 pairs of branched gills occur in this region[2] but are much less common, smaller, and usually have setae on fewer than 40 segments.

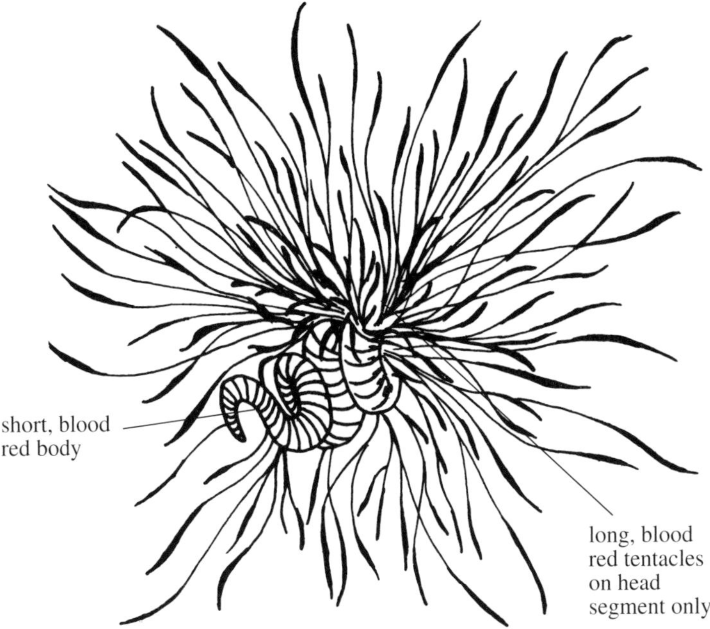

Fig.I. ***POLYCIRRUS EXIMIUS*, BLOOD DROPLET WORM:** Bright red; up to 2.5 cm (1") long; common in mud and sand near low water level and offshore, also found under rocks. Other species of *Polycirrus* occur in this region, but are much less common. *P. medusa* is also red but has setae on 11-13 segments whereas *P. eximius* has setae on 18-25 segments. *P. phosphoreus* is yellow and has setae on 14-32 segments. **17.08 E** **17.09 C**

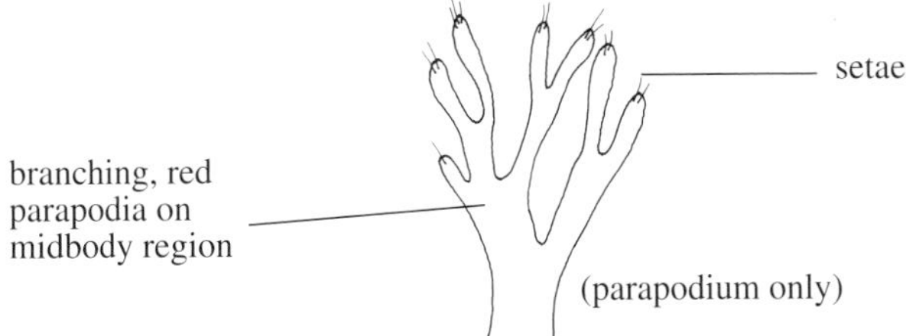

Fig.J. ***ENOPLOBRANCHUS SANGUINEUS*, BLOODY THREAD WORM:** Blood red; up to 35 cm (14") long; found in mud and sand near low water level and offshore.

FRINGED AND CORAL WORMS
PHYLUM ANNELIDA, CLASS POLYCHAETA, FAMILY CIRRATULIDAE

Segmented worms with numerous stringy tentacles and gill filaments on body segments

(Annelid worm key begins on page 8.00)

#1.The first appendage-bearing segment has a cluster of numerous (more than 2) stringy red gill filaments (Figs. A,B); most of the following segments have one or more pairs of long gill filaments which often wrap around the body forming a tangled mass; large worms, up to 15 cm (6") long .... #2

#1.The first appendage-bearing segment has 1 or 2 tentacles; with gill filaments on all or some of the remaining segments; small, up to 16 mm (5/8") long .... #3

#2.With 2-9 eyes on each side of head segment; head segment is somewhat blunt; gill filaments begin on first bristle-bearing body segment; occurs from Cape Cod north .... ***Cirratulus cirratus*, eyed fringed worm** (Fig.A)

#2.No eyes; head segment pointed; no gill filaments on the first 7 segments; common from Cape Cod south .. ***Cirriformia grandis*, large fringed worm** (Fig.B)

#3.With a single tentacle on the first appendage-bearing segment .... ***Cossura longocirrata*** (not shown)

#3.With 2 grooved tentacles (Figs.C,D) on first appendage-bearing segment .... #4

#4.With short threadlike gill filaments on first 4-6 segments only; found in shells or on coral .... ***Dodecaceria corallii*, coral worm** (Fig.C)

#4.Threadlike gill filaments occur over nearly the entire body; found in bottom muds .... ***Tharyx* spp. and related species[1]** (Fig.D)

[1]The identification of these worms to the species level is beyond the scope of this book, requiring microscopic examination of the parapodia and setae. Refer to Pettibone (1963), Gosner (1971), or R. I. Smith (1964) to determine the species

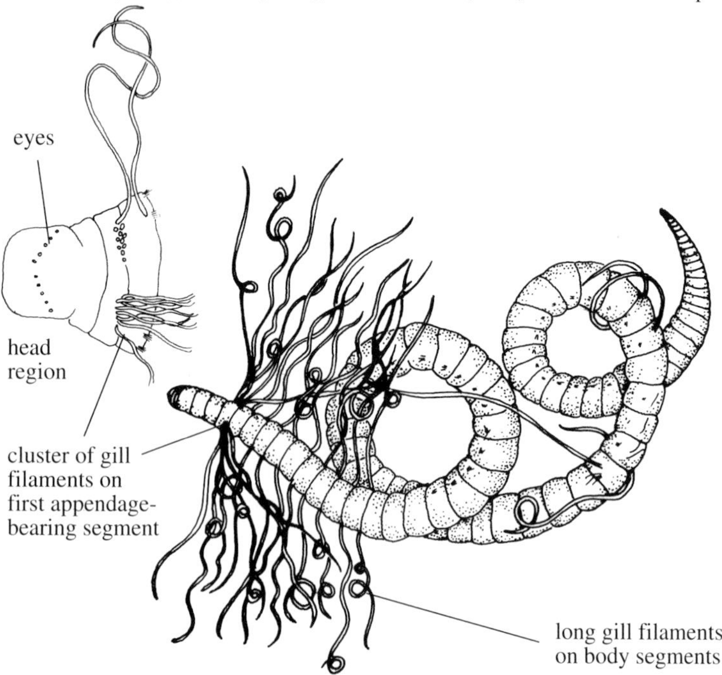

Fig.A. ***CIRRATULUS CIRRATUS*, EYED FRINGED WORM:** Orange to yellowish with red gill filaments; up to 12 cm (5") long; lives in burrows in mud or under rocks, sponges and mussels in lower intertidal zone and shallow waters; filaments extend out and sweep over surface of mud to collect particles of food; occurs from Cape Cod north.

Fig.B. ***CIRRIFORMIA GRANDIS (=Cirratulus g.)*, LARGE FRINGED WORM:** Orange-red, orange-brown or yellowish body; tentacles are yellow or orange with a central bright red blood vessel; up to 15 cm (6") long; lives near low tide mark and offshore burrowed into mud and gravel beneath stones; common from Cape Cod south but can be found throughout New England.

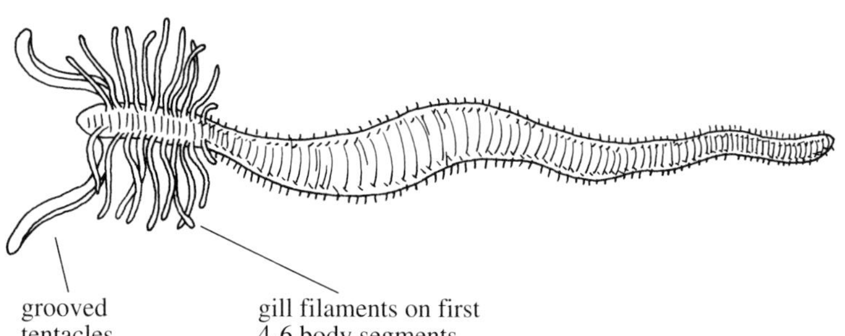

Fig.C. ***DODECACERIA CORALLII*, CORAL WORM:** Dark green to black; up to 12 mm (1/2") long; burrows into dead shells, *Astrangia poculata*, northern star coral (page 4.16), or coralline algae.

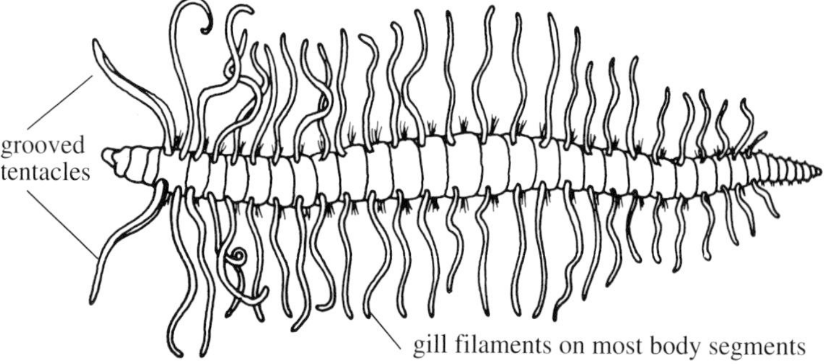

Fig.D. ***THARYX* SPP. AND RELATED SPECIES[1]:** The most common species, *Tharyx acutus*, is pale colored; grows up to 16 mm (5/8") long; occurs on dredge spoil dump sites and other impacted or polluted areas.

SCALE WORMS: PHYLUM ANNELIDA, CLASS POLYCHAETA, FAMILIES POLYNOIDAE AND SIGALIONIDAE[1]

Segmented worms with overlapping scales or plates[2] on dorsal surface.

(Annelid worm key begins on page 8.00)

#1.With 12-15 pairs of scales (Figs.A,B); with threadlike cirri (cirri may be withdrawn if worm is disturbed or not alive) .... **family Polynoidae[1] (in part), #2**
#1.With 16 or more pairs of scales (Figs.C-E); with or without threadlike cirri .... #5

#2.With 12 or 13 pairs of scales (Fig.A) .... ***Lepidonotus* spp., #3**
#2.With 15 pairs of scales (Fig.B) .... ***Harmothoe* spp., #4**

#3.Found free-living, under rocks, in tide pools, etc.; bumps on scales are close together .... ***Lepidonotus squamatus*, twelve-scaled worm** (Fig.A)
#3.Usually found in hermit crab shells; bumps on scales are widely spaced .... ***Lepidonotus sublevis*, hermit crab scale worm** (Fig.A)

#4.Two pairs of eyes on top (dorsal surface) of head[2]. .... ***Harmothoe extenuata*, fifteen-scaled worm** (Fig.B)
#4.One pair of eyes on top (dorsal surface) of head and one pair on bottom (ventral surface) of head .... ***Harmothoe imbricata*, fifteen-scaled worm** (Fig.B)

#5.Lives in tubes with other worms; with threadlike cirri .... ***Lepidametria commensalis*, tube dwelling scale worm** (Fig.C)
#5.Does not live in tubes with other worms; without threadlike cirri .... **family Sigalionidae[1], #6**

#6.With 16-60 pairs of scales; lives under stones, on seaweed, etc.; up to 2.5 cm (1") long .... ***Pholoe minuta*, slender many-scaled worm** (Fig.D)
#6.With 100 or more pairs of scales; burrows in bottom mud; up to 20 cm (8") long .... ***Sthenelais boa*, burrowing scale worm** (Fig.E)

[1]**WARNING:** This key does not include some of the rarer species in these families. Refer to Gosner (1971) for a positive identification, especially for species found in deeper water or in the northern portion of this region.

[2]Scales often fall off if worm is handled roughly or is not alive. Remove scales to examine eyes.

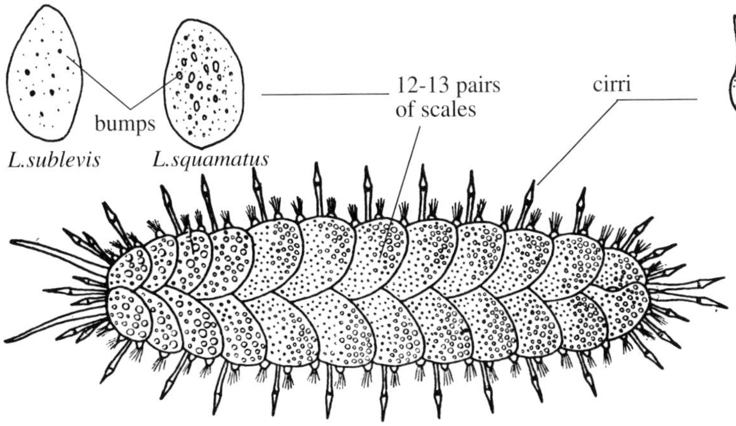

Fig.A. ***LEPIDONOTUS* SPP., TWELVE-SCALED WORMS:** *Lepidonotus squamatus*, the twelve-scaled worm, is variable in color, may be brown or tan and mottled with yellow, red, or green; up to 5 cm (2") long and 1.6 cm (5/8") wide; very common, found on rocks, shells, pilings, seaweeds, etc. in intertidal zone and offshore. *Lepidonotus sublevis*, the hermit crab scale worm, is up to 3.5 cm (1 3/8") long and 1 cm (3/8") wide; lives in hermit crab shells. **17.09 D**

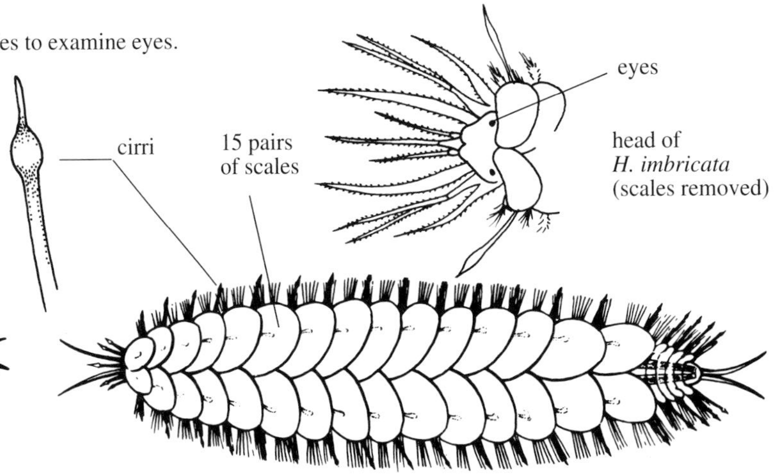

Fig.B. ***HARMOTHOE* SPP., FIFTEEN-SCALED WORMS:** *Harmothoe extenuata* is brown, black, green, or gray, sometimes mottled or banded; up to 7.5 cm (3") long and 2 cm (3/4") wide; found in intertidal zone and offshore on rocks, shells, pilings, etc. *Harmothoe imbricata* is brown, dark green, black, or gray, sometimes mottled or banded; up to 6.5 cm (2 1/2") long and 2 cm (3/4") wide; very common, found clinging to rocks, shells, pilings, seaweed, etc. in intertidal zone, in tide pools and on the bottom in deeper water.

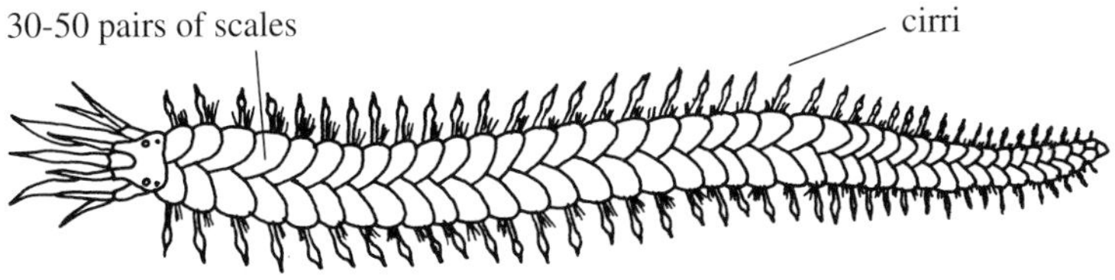

Fig.C. ***LEPIDAMETRIA COMMENSALIS*, TUBE DWELLING SCALE WORM**: Dark colored; up to 10 cm (4") long and 1 cm (3/8") wide; lives in the tube of the ornate worm, *Amphitrite ornata* (see page 8.07), and other tube worms. (family Polynoidae)

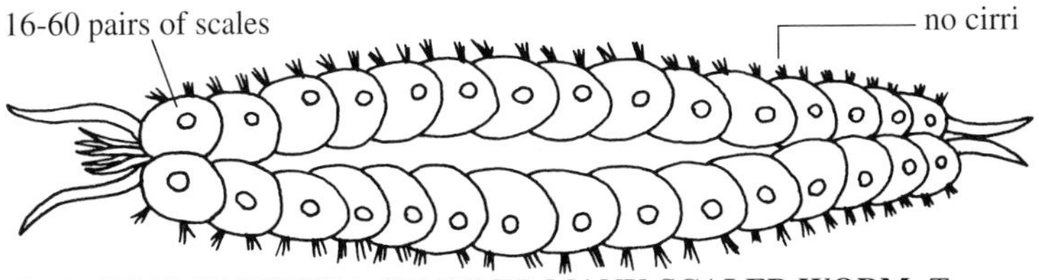

Fig.D. ***PHOLOE MINUTA*, SLENDER MANY-SCALED WORM:** Translucent, yellowish brown to pale pink, mottled with brown; up to 2.5 cm (1") long and 5 mm (3/16") wide; found offshore under stones, on seaweeds, etc.

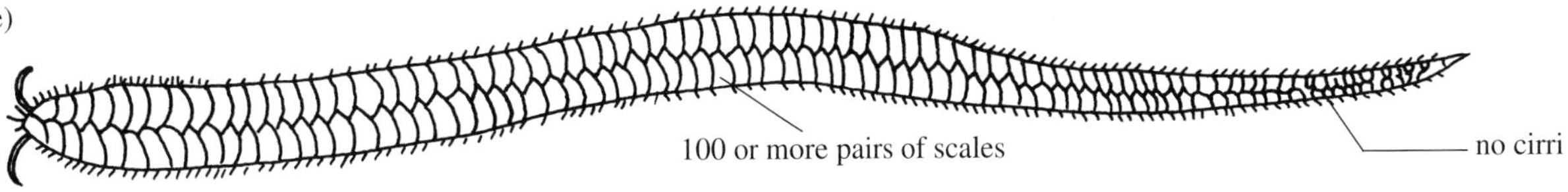

Fig.E. ***STHENELAIS BOA*, BURROWING SCALE WORM:** Mottled gray, sometimes with a stripe down the back; up to 20 cm (8") long and 5 mm (3/16") wide; often found among eelgrass roots, burrows in mud, from lower intertidal zone to offshore.

SEGMENTED WORMS WITH ONE OR TWO TENTACLES OR HEAD APPENDAGES[1]
PHYLUM ANNELIDA, CLASS POLYCHAETA

(Annelid worm key begins on page 8.00)

#1.With a single antenna[1], arising from center of head .... ***Aricidea catherinae*** (Fig.A)
#1.With a pair of tentacles, antennae or other head appendages[1] (Figs.B-F) .... #2

#2.Head appendages (tentacles, antennae, etc.) are extremely tiny, much shorter than head segment, barely visible without magnification .... page 8.03
#2.Head appendages are as long or longer than head segment .... #3

#3.Body of worm divided into 3 distinct regions, with segments in each region highly specialized for different functions (Fig.C) ...... **family Chaetopteridae**, #4
#3.Body segments similar in size, shape and function; not divided into distinct regions; with two long, coiling tentacles (Figs.D,E) .... **family Spionidae**, #5
#3.Body segmentation indistinct; no parapodia; with a pair of anal cirri (tail appendages) .... ***Polygordius* spp.** (Fig.F)

#4.Lives in a vertical tube which is long, transparent and ringed like bamboo; only the top of the tube opens to surface of sediment; worm is very thin, grows up to 6 cm (2 1/2") long and 1 mm (1/32") wide; long tentacles .... ***Spiochaetopterus oculatus*, glassy tube worm** (Fig.B)
#4.Lives in a U-shaped tube made out of parchmentlike material; both ends of the tube open to surface of sediment; grows up to 25 cm (10") long and 2.5 cm (1") wide; head appendages (palps) moderate length .... ***Chaetopterus variopedatus*, parchment worm** (Fig.C)

#5.Fifth body segment is unlike other body segments; fifth segment has long setae (bristles) on top .... ***Polydora* spp., mud or blister worms**[2] (Fig.D)
#5.Fifth body segment is the same as the other body segments; setae are on sides, not top .... **other Spionidae**[2] (Fig.E)

[1]Tentacles often break off if worm is roughly handled.
[2]The identification of these worms to the species level is beyond the scope of this book, requiring microscopic examination of the parapodia and setae. Refer to Pettibone (1963), Gosner (1971), or R. I. Smith (1964) to determine the species.

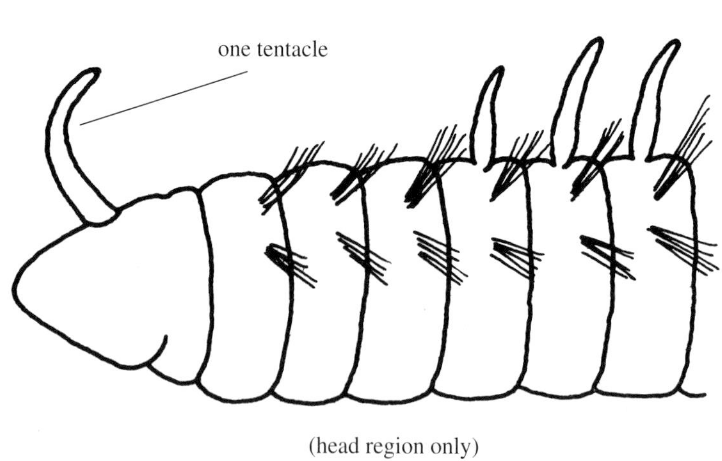

Fig.A. ***ARICIDEA CATHERINAE:*** Darkly pigmented; up to about 2 cm (3/4") long; burrows in mud near low tide level. (family Paraonidae)

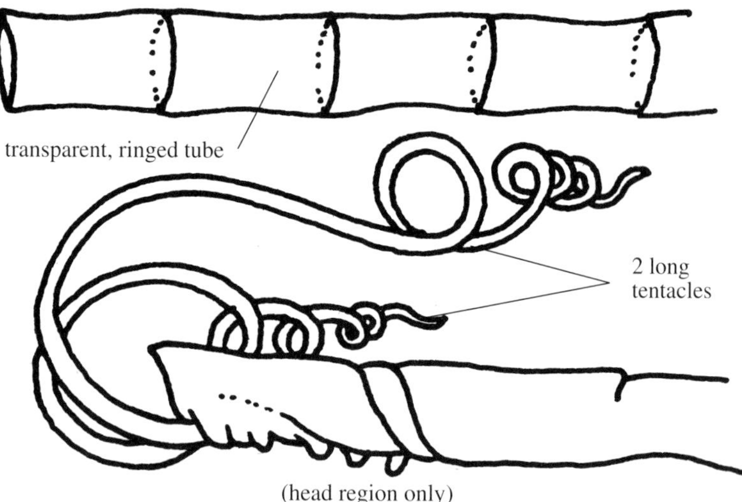

Fig.B. ***SPIOCHAETOPTERUS OCULATUS*, GLASSY TUBE WORM:** White, yellowish, light brown; up to 6 cm (2 1/2") long and 1 mm (1/32") wide; lives in a transparent, whitish tube ringed like bamboo; found in mudflats and in shallow water. (family Chaetopteridae)

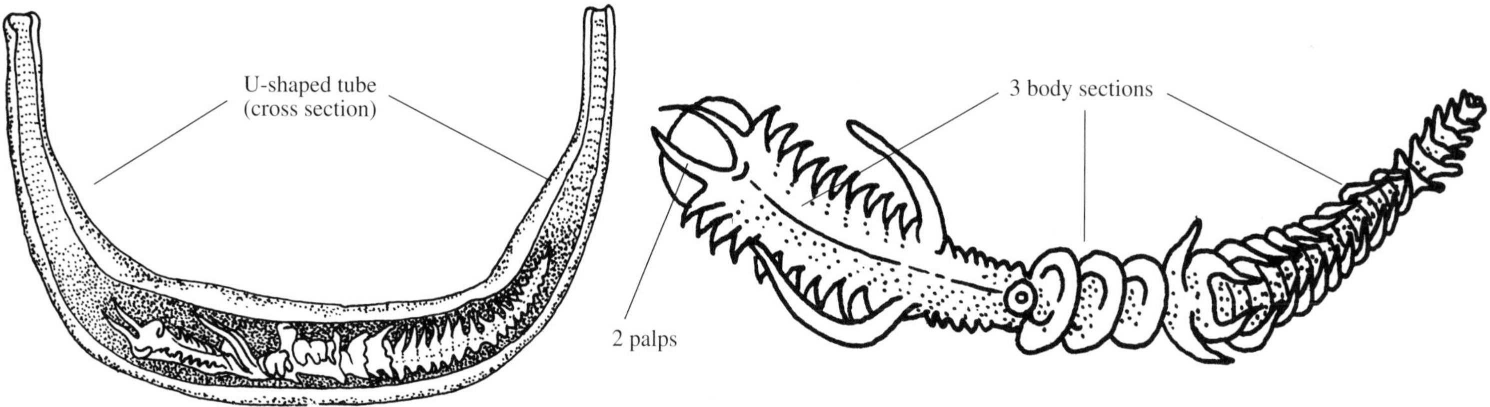

Fig.C. ***CHAETOPTERUS VARIOPEDATUS*, PARCHMENT WORM:** Yellow, brightly luminescent in dark; up to 25 cm (10") long; lives in U-shaped parchmentlike tube; found offshore in muddy bottoms. (family Chaetopteridae) **17.09 B**

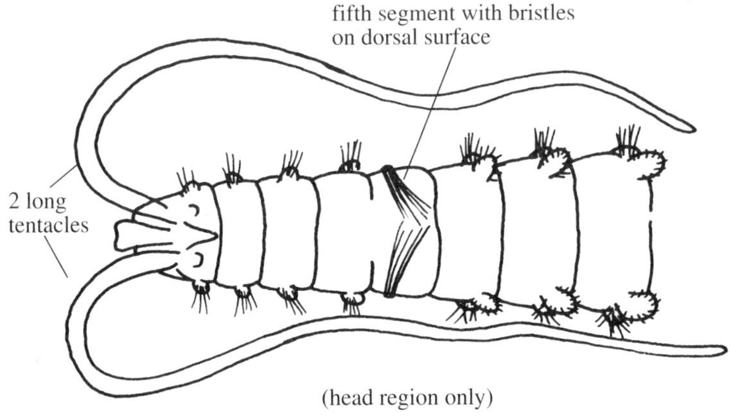

Fig.D. ***POLYDORA* SPP., MUD OR BLISTER WORMS[2]:** The most common free-living species of *Polydora* in this region, *Polydora ligni*, grows up to 2.5 cm (1") long and builds soft mud covered vertical tubes (see Fig.E) attached to shells, bottom mud and hard objects in shallow water and near the low tide level. Large colonies of mud worms occur on offshore mudflats and oyster beds, completely covering the surface of the bottom in a layer of mud tubes. Several other *Polydora* species are commensals, dwelling within the shells of other living animals. *Polydora websteri* lives in oyster shells. The oysters react to the worm by producing a blister within the shell. *Polydora commensalis*, a bright red worm, lives inside snail shells occupied by hermit crabs. (family Spionidae)

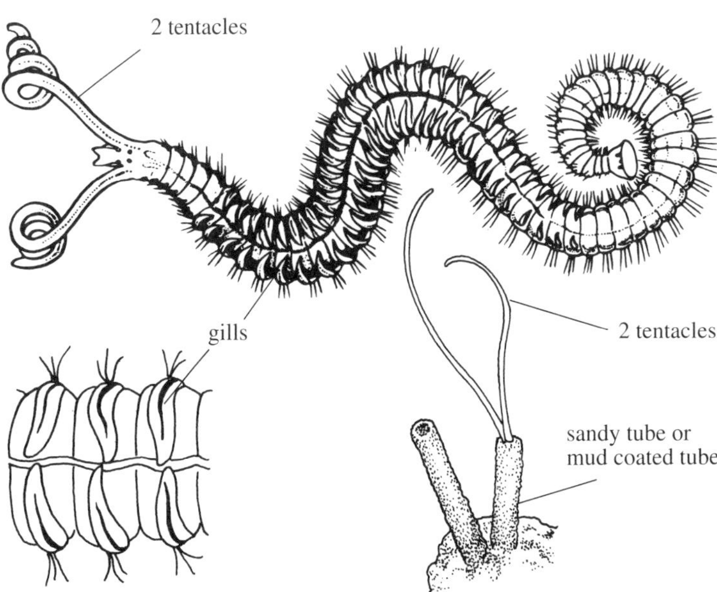

Fig.E. **FAMILY SPIONIDAE[2]:** A number of species of worms in this family, in addition to *Polydora* (Fig.D), occur in this region. *Spio setosa*, one of the most common, grows up to 7.5 cm (3") long and builds distinctive, sandy, chimneylike tubes on protected beaches and sand flats. Another common species, *Scolecolepides viridis*, grows up to 10 cm (4") long and 3 mm (1/8") wide and can be found in mud in brackish water.

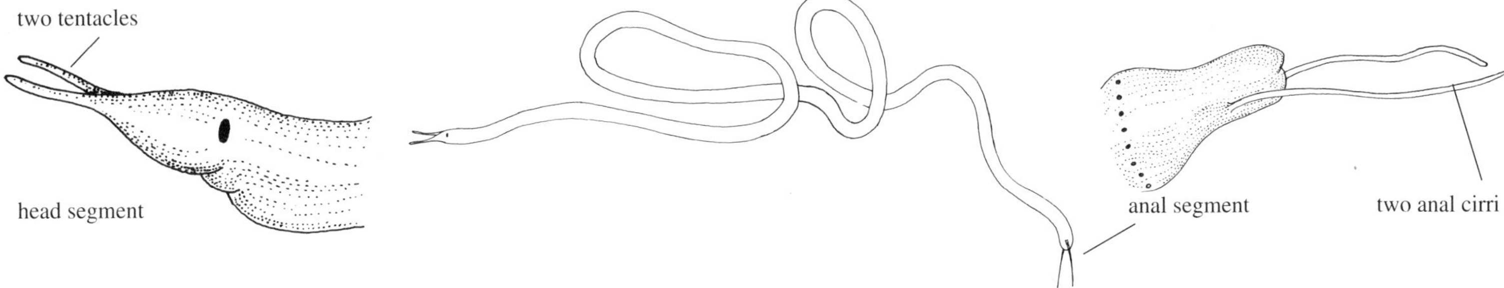

Fig. F. ***POLYGORDIUS* SPP.:** The most common species in southern New England, *Polygordius appendiculatus*, is salmon red; up to 2 cm (3/4") long. These worms are classified in the order Archiannelida because they have relatively simple characteristics that many biologists consider similar to the primitive ancestral worms from which other polychaetes may have evolved. (family Polygordiidae)

BROOM WORMS: PHYLUM ANNELIDA, CLASS POLYCHAETA, FAMILY FLABELLIGERIDAE

Segmented worms with long bristles pointing forward from head.

(Annelid worm key begins on page 8.00)

#1.Body enclosed in thick mucus mantle; papillae ("pimplelike" bumps) on body are on stalks .... ***Flabelligera affinis*, mantled broom worm** (Fig.G)
#1.Body not enclosed in thick mucus mantle; papillae on body are not stalked .... ***Pherusa* spp., common broom worm** (Fig.H)

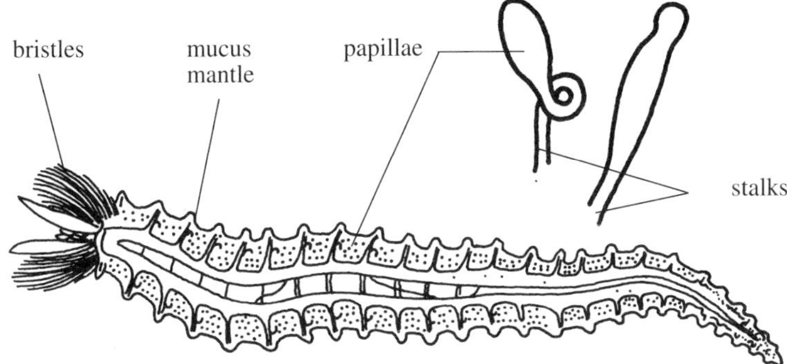

Fig.G. ***FLABELLIGERA AFFINIS*, MANTLED BROOM WORM:** Up to 6 cm (2 1/2") long and 1 cm (3/8") wide; found offshore in bottom mud.

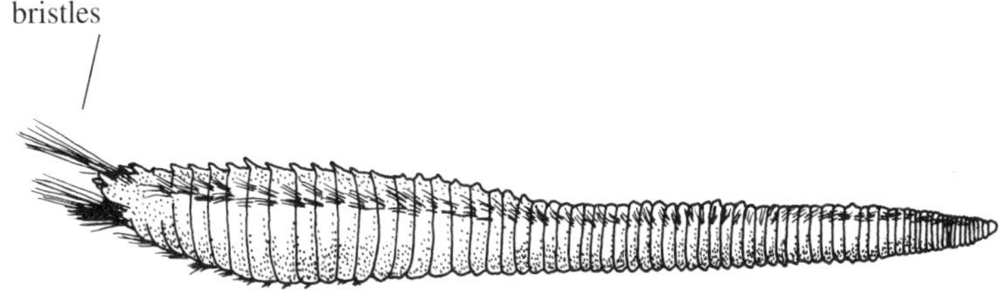

Fig.H. ***PHERUSA* SPP., COMMON BROOM WORM:** Brownish or greenish; up to 6 cm (2 1/2") long and 1 cm (3/8") wide; very common in mud offshore; *Pherusa affinis* is the most common species. Refer to Gosner (1971) or R. I. Smith (1964) to determine the species. **17.08 F**

SEGMENTED WORMS WITH THREE TO FIVE TENTACLES OR HEAD APPENDAGES[1] PHYLUM ANNELIDA, CLASS POLYCHAETA

(Annelid worm key begins on page 8.00)

#1.With four tentacles or tentaclelike head appendages (Figs.A,B) .... #2
#1.With 3 or 5 tentacles or tentaclelike head appendages (Figs. C-G) .... #4

#2.Head appendages are extremely tiny, much shorter than head segment, barely visible without magnification .... page 8.03
#2.Head appendages are as long as or longer than head segment .... #3

#3.With setae (bristles) on first two segments; tentaclelike gills are often distinctively banded .... ***Streblospio benedicti*** (Fig.A)
#3.No setae (bristles) on first two segments; with a pair of segmented antennae and a thicker pair of palps .... ***Schistomeringos* spp.**[2] (Fig.B)

#4.With 5 tentacles or antennae; with conspicuous featherlike or frilled gills (Figs.C,D) .... #5
#4.With 3 antennae and 1-2 fleshy lobes (palps) projecting in front of head; no conspicuous gills (Figs.E-G) .... #6

#5.Antennae are short; lives in mucus lined tunnels but no permanent tubes, gills have 2-8 filaments at tips .... ***Marphysa* spp.**[2] (Fig.C)
#5.Antennae are long; lives in a distinctive parchmentlike tube which has bits of shells, seaweed, eelgrass, and other "junk" attached to it; with long, featherlike, spiraled gills on anterior (front) end of body .... ***Diopatra cuprea*, plumed worm or junk worm** (Fig.D)

#6.Parapodia (leglike appendages) have long rodlike or threadlike extensions (parapodial cirri, Fig.E); palps separated, not fused; body not threadlike, usually wider than 0.5 mm (1/32") .... **families Syllidae (in part) and Hesionidae,** page 8.16
#6.Parapodia without long extensions (Figs.F,G); palps fused for at least 1/3 of length; threadlike, less than 0.5 mm (1/32") wide...**family Syllidae**[2] **(in part)**, #7

#7.With 2 pairs of short tentaclelike processes (cirri) on segment just behind head; with 2 or 3 pairs of eyes .... ***Brania* spp.**[2] (Fig.F)
#7.With 1 or no pairs of short tentaclelike processes (cirri) on segment just behind head; with 2 pairs of eyes .... ***Exogone* spp.**[2] (Fig.G)

[1]Tentacles often break off if worm is handled roughly. See footnote 3 on page 8.00.
[2]The identification of these worms to the species level is beyond the scope of this book, requiring microscopic examination of the parapodia and setae. Refer to Pettibone (1963), Gosner (1971), or R. I. Smith (1964) to determine species.

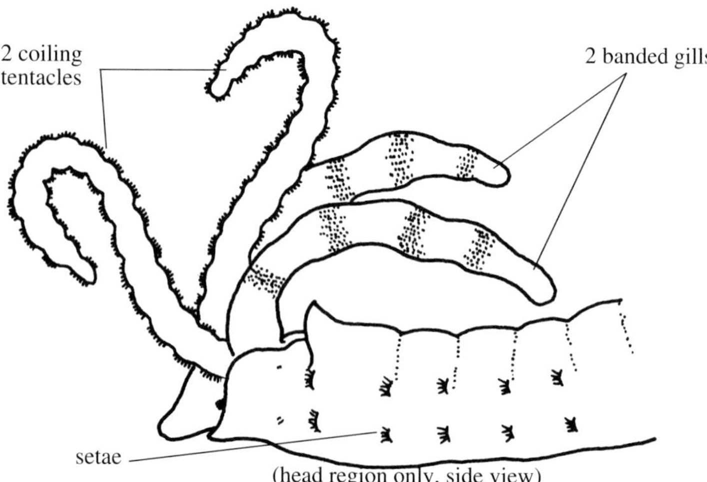

Fig.A. ***STREBLOSPIO BENEDICTI:*** Translucent reddish-brown body, gills with wide bands of dark green; up to 6 mm (1/4") long; found in sandy mud, inhabits soft gray mucoid tubes which lie flat on surface or are slightly buried in mud. (family Spionidae)

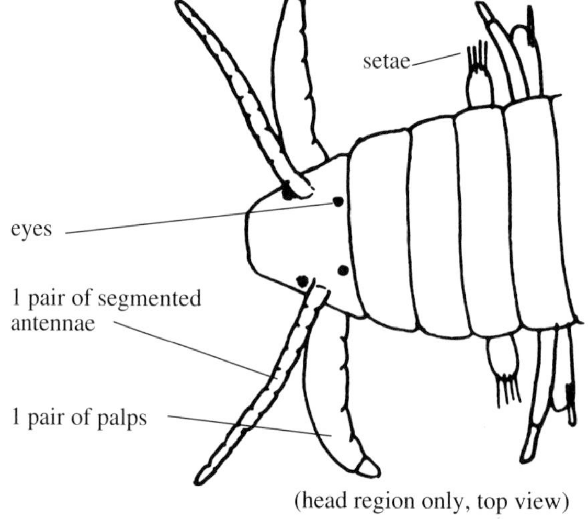

Fig.B. ***SCHISTOMERINGOS (=Stauronereis)* SPP.**[2]**:** Red, purple, pale pink, yellowish, or white; up to 5 cm (2") long; burrows into mud or under rocks. *Schistomeringos rudolphi* has 4 reddish eyes. *Schistomeringos caecus* does not have any eyes. (family Dorvilleidae)

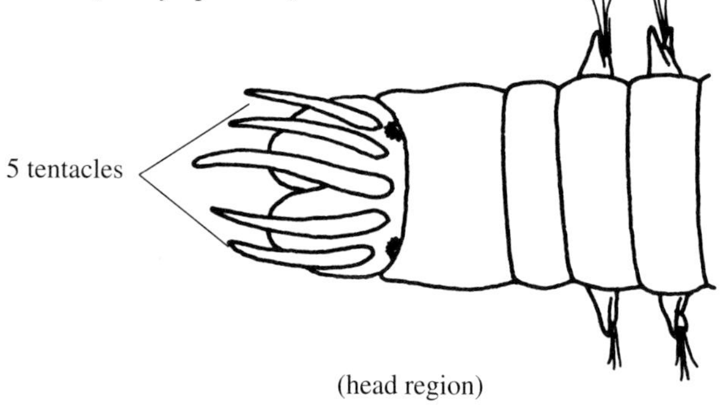

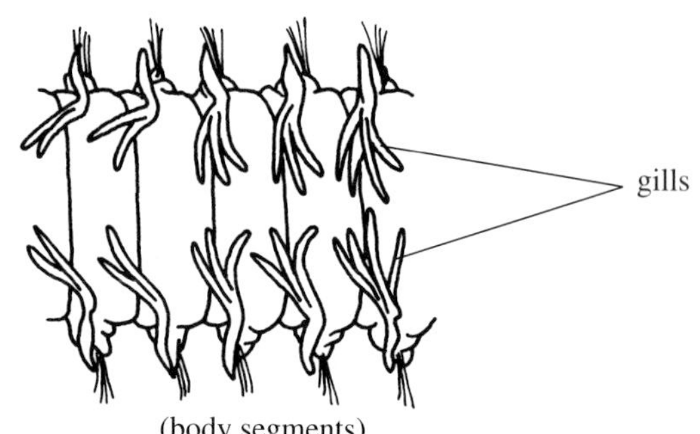

Fig.C. ***MARPHYSA* SPP.**[2]**:** Yellowish to brownish red body; iridescent, bright red gills; up to 15 cm (6") long; found in clay and muddy banks that are exposed at low tide, lives in well defined burrows. (family Eunicidae)

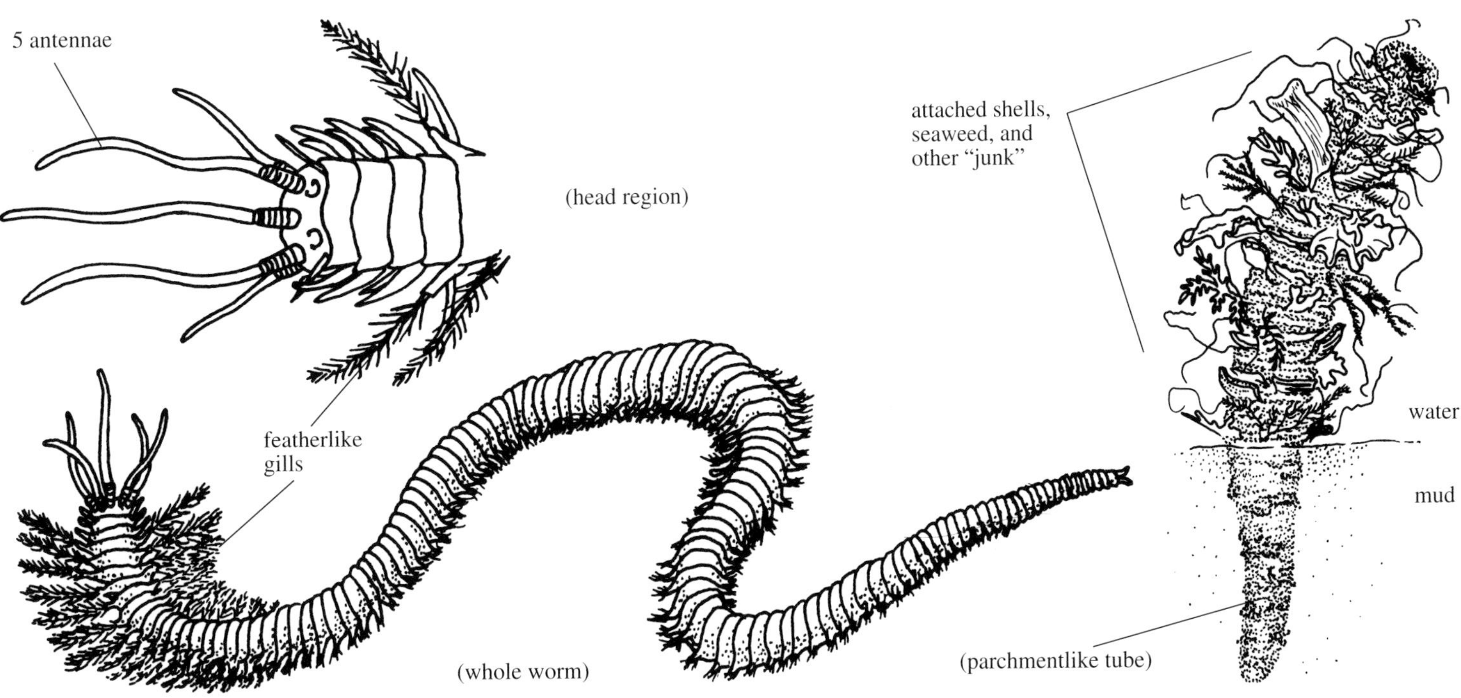

Fig.D. ***DIOPATRA CUPREA*, PLUMED WORM OR JUNK WORM:** Bright red, iridescent; up to 30 cm (12") long; builds distinctive parchmentlike tubes that have bits of shells, pebbles, seaweed, eelgrass, and other "junk" attached; tubes extend 5-8 cm (2-3") above the surface of the sand or muddy bottom; very common. (family Onuphidae)

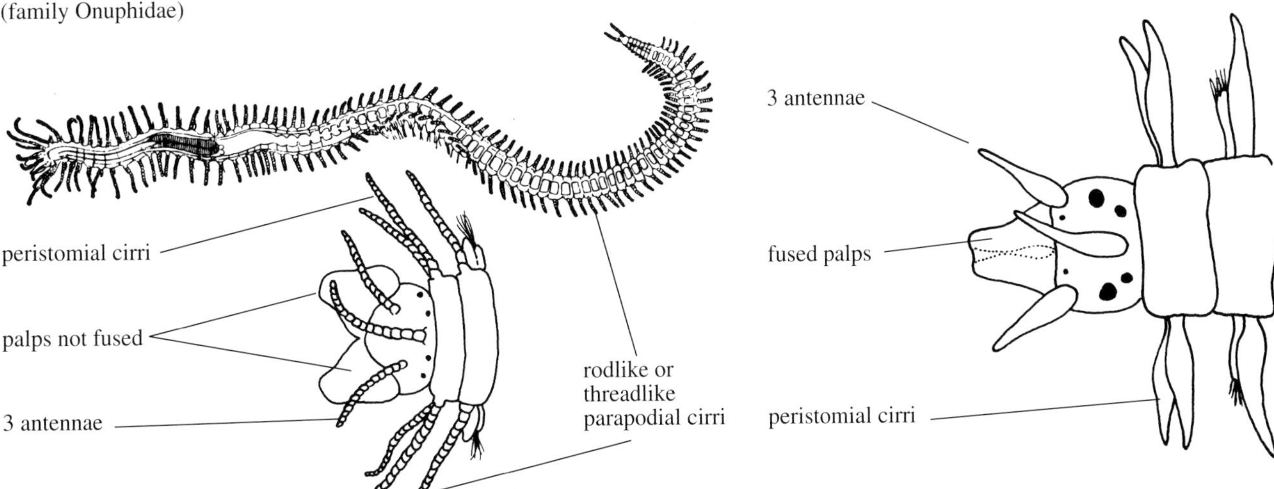

Fig.E. **FAMILIES SYLLIDAE (in part) AND HESIONIDAE:** Worms with rodlike or threadlike parapodial cirri, palps not fused.

Fig.F. ***BRANIA* SPP.[2]:** Up to 7 mm (1/4") long and 0.4 mm (1/64") wide; found in mud and mussel beds. (family Syllidae)

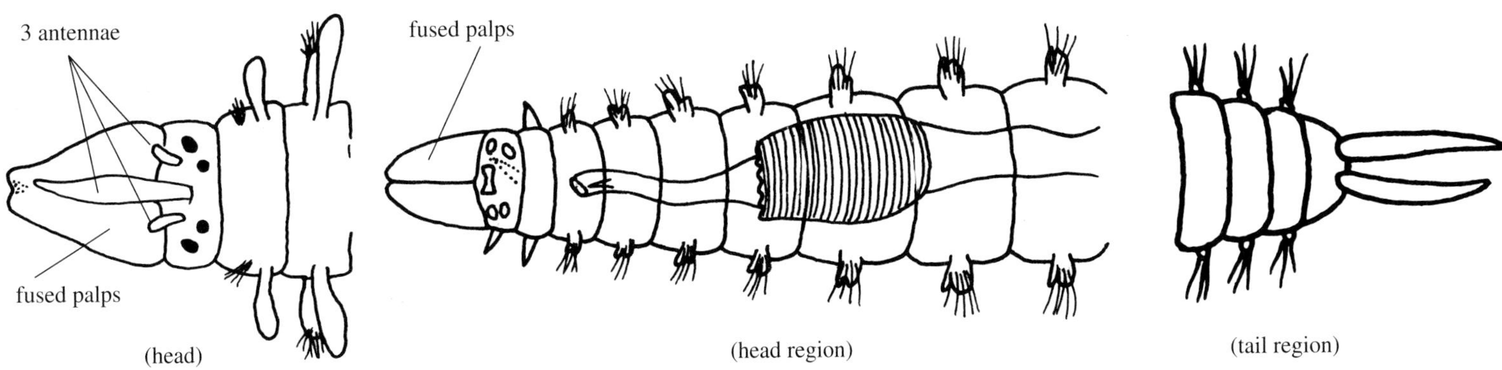

Fig.G. ***EXOGONE* SPP. AND SIMILAR SPECIES[2]:** A common species, *Exogone dispar*, is white or colorless, tinged with red and marked with a white line between segments; up to 8 mm (5/16") long; found offshore on shells and stones and in mussel beds. (family Syllidae)

CLAM WORMS: PHYLUM ANNELIDA, CLASS POLYCHAETA, FAMILY NEREIDAE

Segmented worms with 4 pairs of tentacles, one pair of antennae, and one pair of fleshy lobes (palps) on head region[1]

(Annelid worm key begins on page 8.00)

#1. Upper lobes of all parapodia[1] (fleshy leglike appendages) are broad and leaflike (Fig.A); jaws are dark brown or black (can only be seen when proboscis is extended); often grows over 20 cm (8") long .... ***Nereis virens*, common clam worm** (Fig.A)

#1. Upper lobes of parapodia are not broad and leaflike (Figs.B-E); jaws may or may not be dark brown or black; rarely over 15 cm (6") long .... #2

#2. Upper lobes of parapodia near posterior end of worm are long and straplike, with cirrus (projection) near tip (Fig.B); anterior parapodia are much smaller; jaws are yellowish (can only be seen when proboscis is extended); common in saltmarshes and estuaries .... ***Nereis succinea*, yellow-jawed clam worm** (Fig.B)

#2. Upper and lower lobes of all parapodia are about the same size (Figs.C-E) .... **other Nereidae[2]**, #3

#3. Found in mud, usually living in tubes of bamboo worms .... ***Nereis grayi*, tube-dwelling clam worm** (Fig.C)

#3. Found on pilings, buoys, rocks, seaweed, etc .... #4

#4. Iridescent greenish brown or reddish brown .... ***Nereis pelagica*, fouling clam worm** (Fig.D)

#4. Transparent or whitish color .... ***Nereis acuminata (=arenaceodonta)*, white clam worm** (Fig.E)

[1]Refer to Fig. A on page 8.00 for terms used in annelid worm key. Examine sides of parapodia to observe shape and structure.

[2]**WARNING:** This key does not include some of the rarer species in this family. The identification of these worms to the species level is beyond the scope of this book, requiring microscopic examination of the parapodia and setae. Refer to Pettibone (1963), Gosner (1971), or R. I. Smith (1964) to determine species.

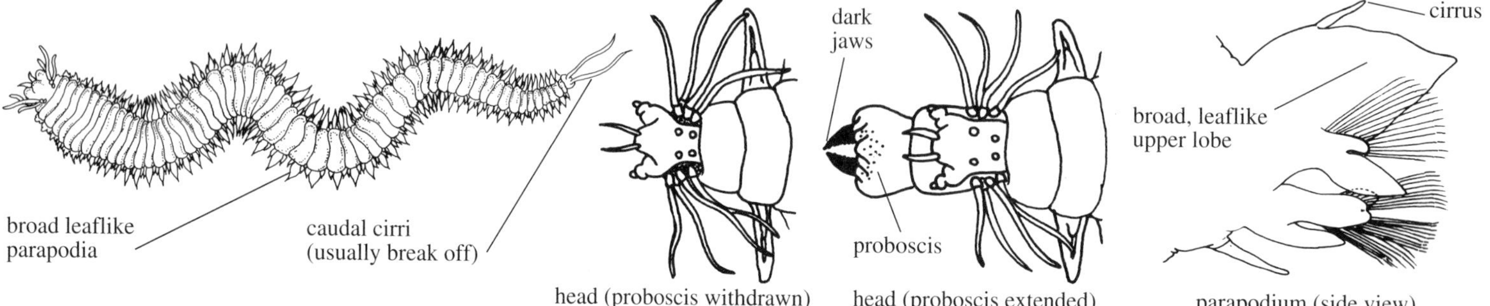

Figs.A. ***NEREIS VIRENS*, COMMON CLAM WORM:** Males are steel blue with green parapodia, females are dull green tinged with orange and red, jaws are dark brown or black; reportedly up to 90 cm (3') long but rarely over 25 cm (10") long in local waters; common in mudflats and sandflats in the intertidal zone, also found under rocks; prefers higher salinity waters. **17.08 G**

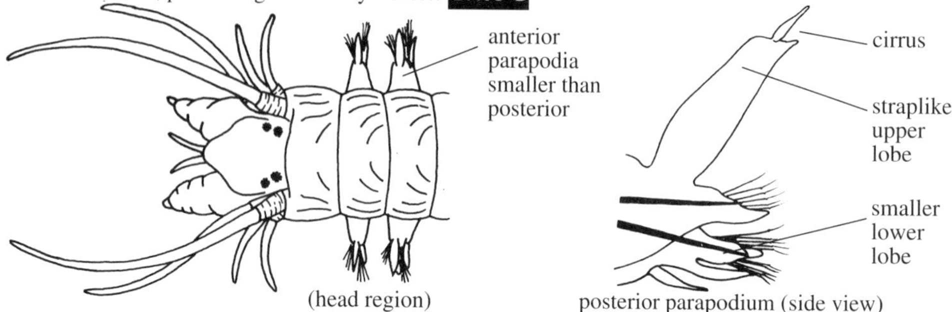

Fig.B. ***NEREIS SUCCINEA*, YELLOW-JAWED CLAM WORM:** Brownish in front with darker colored head segment; greenish, greenish-yellow or pale red toward rear; distinct red blood vessel on midline; jaws are yellowish; up to 20 cm (8") long but rarely over 15 cm (6"); found in marshes and estuaries in salinities as low as 9 parts per thousand.

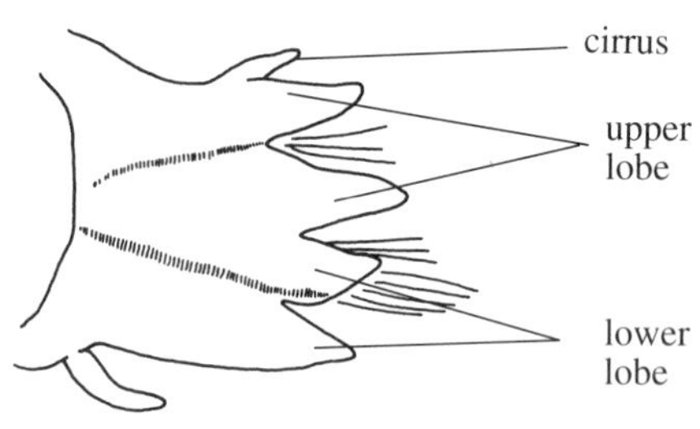

Fig.C. ***NEREIS GRAYI*, TUBE-DWELLING CLAM WORM:** Up to 6 cm (2 1/2") long; found in mud, usually living in bamboo worm tubes (see page 8.22 for bamboo worms).

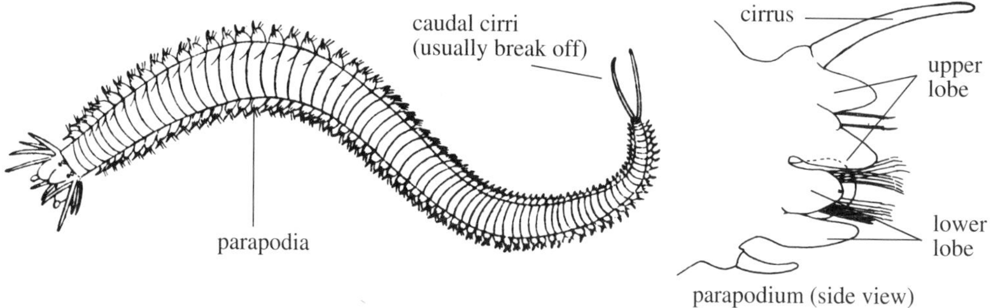

Fig.D. ***NEREIS PELAGICA*, FOULING CLAM WORM**: Iridescent greenish brown or reddish brown body, black jaws; up to 16 cm (6 1/2") long; found near low tide level and offshore on algae, pilings, bouys, rocks, etc. among other fouling organisms.

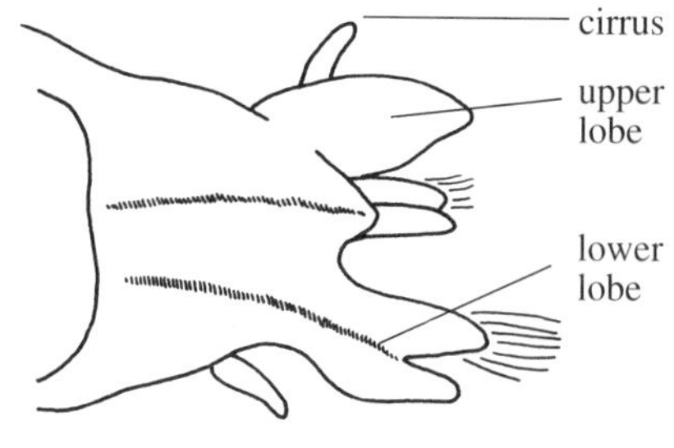

Fig.E. ***NEREIS ACUMINATA*, WHITE CLAM WORM:** Transparent or whitish; grows up to 7 cm (2 3/4") long; lives on pilings and algae.

PADDLE WORMS: PHYLUM ANNELIDA, CLASS POLYCHAETA, FAMILY PHYLLODOCIDAE

Segmented worms with 2-4 tentacles, 4-5 antennae, and with overlapping leaflike parapodia (fleshy leglike appendages)[1].

(Annelid worm key begins on page 8.00)

#1.Two tentacles on each side of head; 4 antennae at tip of head; head segment is triangular .... ***Eteone*** **spp.**[2] (Fig.B)
#1.Four tentacles on each side of head; 4-5 antennae at tip of head; head segment may be oval, triangular or heart shaped (Figs.C-F) .... #2

#2.Five antennae at tip of head (Figs. C,D) .... #3
#2.Four antennae at tip of head (Figs.E,F) .... #4

#3.With 3 tentacle-bearing segments distinctly visible dorsally (when viewed from above) .... ***Eulalia*** **spp.**[2] (Fig.C)
#3.With 2 tentacle-bearing segments distinctly visible dorsally .... ***Eumida sanguinea*** (Fig.D)

#4.Head segment (prostomium) is heart shaped; worm grows longer than 2 cm (3/4") .... ***Phyllodoce*** **spp.**[2] (Fig.E)
#4.Head segment (prostomium) is oval or triangular, not heart shaped; worm does not grow longer than 2 cm (3/4") .... ***Paranaitis speciosa*** (Fig.F)

[1]Refer to Fig. A on page 8.00 for terms used in annelid worm key.
[2]Refer to Pettibone (1963), Gosner (1971), or R. I. Smith (1964) to determine species.

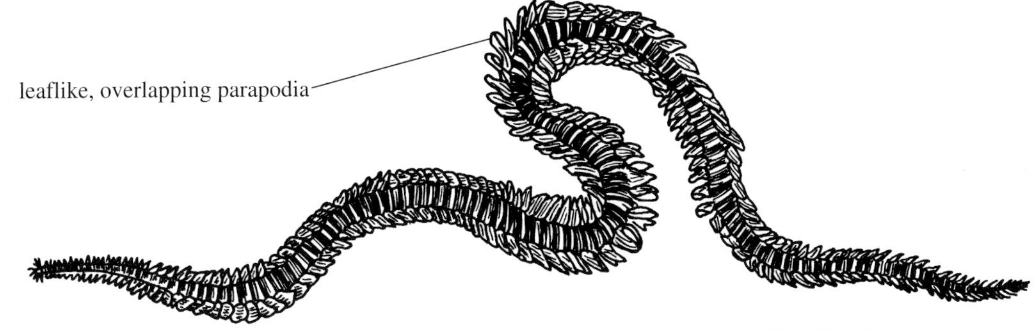

Fig.A. **TYPICAL PADDLE WORM, FAMILY PHYLLODOCIDAE**

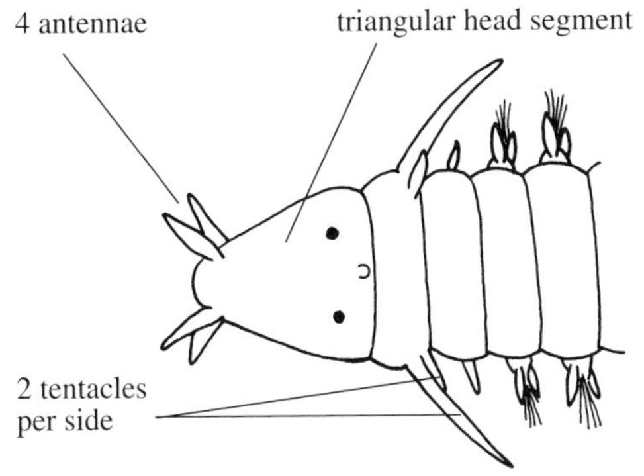

Fig.B. ***ETEONE*** **SPP.**[2]**:** One common species, *Eteone lactea,* is milky white or pale yellow; up to 23 cm (9") long and 3 mm (1/8") wide; occurs offshore and in the intertidal zone in mud and sand.

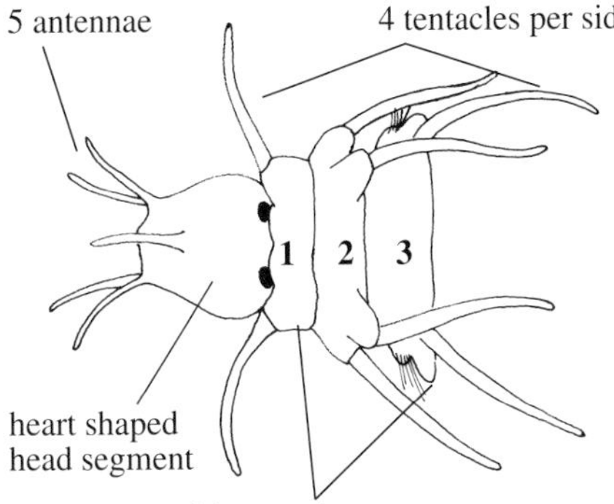

Fig.C. ***EULALIA*** **SPP.**[2]**:** Green, brown, or tan sometimes spotted with darker brown or green; up to 15 cm (6") long; found on shells, rocks, pilings in intertidal zone and offshore.

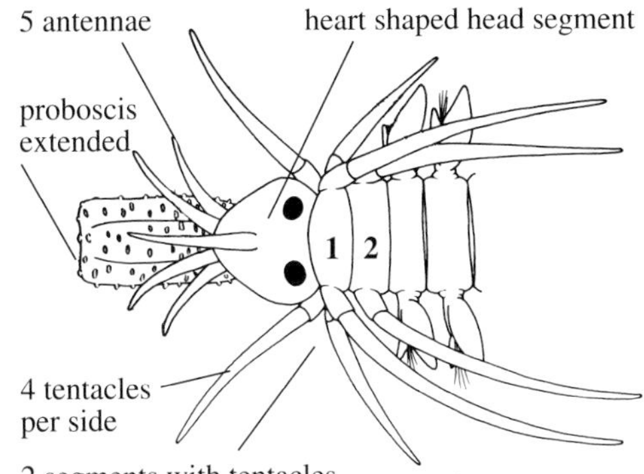

Fig.D. ***EUMIDA SANGUINEA:*** Green or yellow body with brown or gray bands; up to 6 cm (2 1/2") long; common on pilings

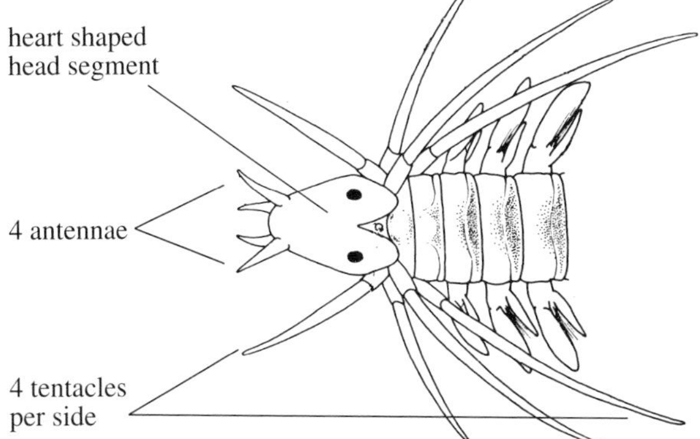

Fig.E. ***PHYLLODOCE*** **SPP.**[2]**:** Yellow, green, or white, and may have brown spots or stripes; rarely over 15 cm (6") long or 3 mm (1/8") wide; found near low tide level and offshore.

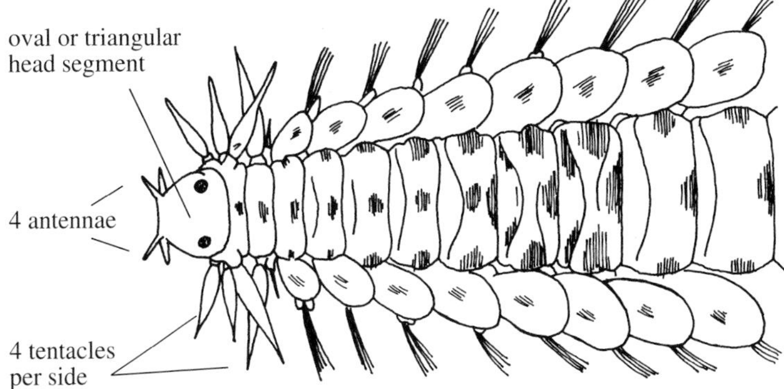

Fig.F. ***PARANAITIS SPECIOSA:*** Iridescent, greenish-yellow, with reddish spots; up to 1.8 cm (3/4") long and 3 mm (1/8") wide; found in mussel beds and in shallow water on sand, clay, mud, and shells.

FAMILIES SYLLIDAE, HESIONIDAE, AND PILARGIIDAE
PHYLUM ANNELIDA, CLASS POLYCHAETA

Segmented worms with 3 antennae, 2-4 cirri and 2 palps in head region and with long threadlike extensions (cirri) on the parapodia ("legs")[1].

(Annelid worm key begins on page 8.00)

#1.Palps are slender and jointed (Fig.A); with 2-8 pairs of peristomial cirri (long appendages attached to segment just behind head)...**family Hesionidae**[2] (Fig.A)
#1.Palps consist of 1 or 2 fleshy lobes which are not jointed (Figs.B-C); with 1-2 pairs of peristomial cirri .... #2

#2.Two palps are distinct and separate for most of their length; palps form two fleshy lobes projecting from head segment ..... **family Syllidae**[2] **(in part)** (Fig.C)
#2.Palps are fused to the head segment and/or are fused to each other for at least 2/3 of their length .... #3

#3.Palps are fused to head segment (prostomium) and to each other and are difficult to distinguish from the head segment; palps are separated near the front with a pointed tip at the end of each palp; head of worm appears to be notched; usually with long tentaclelike peristomial cirri .... **family Pilargiidae**[2] (Fig.B)
#3.Palps are fused to each other but can be distinguished from the head segment (page 8.13, Figs.F,G); peristomial cirri are not long and tentaclelike .... **family Syllidae**[2] **(in part)** page 8.12
#3.Palps form a narrow rim at front edge of prostomium; with long tentaclelike peristomial cirri .... ***Autolytus* spp.**[2] (Fig.C)

[1]Refer to Fig. A on page 8.00 for terms used in annelid worm key. The peristomium is the first body segment just behind the head segment (prostomium).
[2]The identification of these worms to the genus or species level is beyond the scope of this book, requiring microscopic examination of the parapodia and setae. Refer to Fauchald (1977) to determine genus. Use Pettibone (1963), Gosner (1971), or R. I. Smith (1964) to determine species.

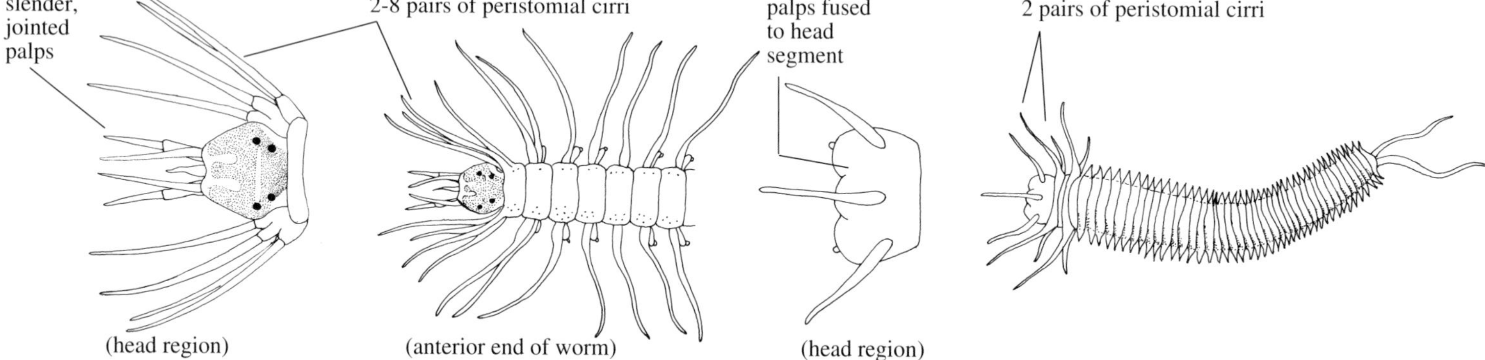

Fig.A. **FAMILY HESIONIDAE**[2]**:** The species shown here, *Podarke obscura*, is dark brown to black with yellow cross bands; up to 4 cm (1 1/2") long; common among eelgrass and bottom debris from intertidal zone to deep water; swarms to surface on summer nights.

Fig.B. **FAMILY PILARGIIDAE**[2]**:** The species shown here, *Sigambra tentaculata*, grows up to 16 mm (5/8") long; burrows in sand or mud from intertidal zone into deep water

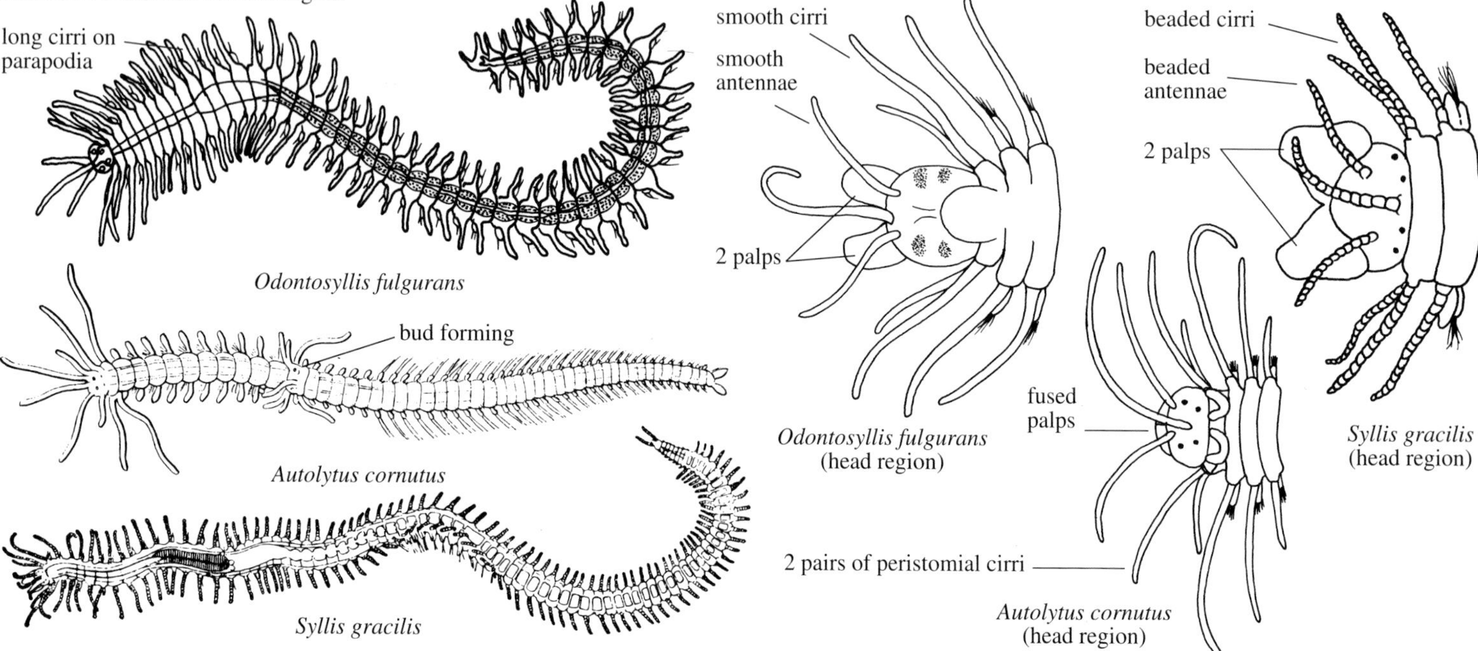

Fig.C. **FAMILY SYLLIDAE**[2]**:** Nearly two dozen species occur in this region. Some species grow up to 5 cm (2") long but most are much smaller; they are often found creeping under stones, shells, seaweeds, and among other benthic organisms from the lower intertidal zone into deep waters. *Syllis* spp. have beaded or segmented antennae and cirri. Other genera such as *Odontosyllis*, *Streptosyllis,* and *Syllides* have smooth antennae and cirri. *Autolytus cornutus* has fused and indistinct palps; is pink or beige with brown eyes; grows up to 2 cm (3/4") long; found on algae and hydroids; constructs cylindrical tubes; can reproduce by budding.

PAINTED WORMS AND T-HEADED WORMS
PHYLUM ANNELIDA, CLASS POLYCHAETA, FAMILIES NEPHTYIDAE[1] AND SCALIBREGMIDAE

Segmented worms with head segment[2] that is flattened in front with pointed corners; no obvious tentacles or other head appendages[3].

(Annelid worm key begins on page 8.00)

#1.Head segment (prostomium) is T-shaped; anterior portion of body appears swollen; body is cylindrical .... ***Scalibregma inflatum*, T-headed worm** (Fig.A)
#1.Head segment[2] (prostomium) is squarish (Figs.B-E), with two tiny, pointed antennae at front corners; body is not inflated at front end; body is flattened; bristles (setae) appear to be in two distinct rows when worm is viewed from side, particularly near front end .... ***Nephtys* spp.[1]**, #2

#2.Tiny projections (cirri) on both upper and lower lobes of parapodia on first body segment (Fig.C) .... #3
#2.Cirri only on lower lobes of parapodia on first body segment (Figs.D,E) .... #4

#3.Setae (bristles) are dark bronze or black; very common .... ***Nephtys incisa*, common painted worm** (Fig.C)
#3.Setae are light, yellow color; less common .... ***Nephtys caeca,* yellow-bristled painted worm** (Fig.C)

#4.Cirri on first body segment are forward of the widest part of the segment; cross bands are crescent shaped; common .... ***Nephtys picta*** (Fig.D)
#4.Cirri on first body segment are at the tips of the widest part of the segment; cross bands are V-shaped; less common .... ***Nephtys bucera*** (Fig.E)

[1]**WARNING:** The identification of these worms to the species level is beyond the scope of this book, requiring microscopic examination of the parapodia. Furthermore, this key includes only the most common species and at least 5 other species also occur in this region. Refer to Pettibone (1963), Gosner (1971), or R. I. Smith (1964) for a positive identification.

[2]The head segment of *Nephtys* is difficult to locate, especially if the proboscis is extended (see Fig.B). Examine the anterior (front) of the worm on its dorsal (upper) surface very carefully with a hand lens or dissecting microscope. Adjusting the angle of the microscope light often helps. Look at both ends and turn the worm over if you are not sure which end and/or surface you are looking at.

[3]Refer to Fig. A on page 8.00 for terms used in annelid worm key.

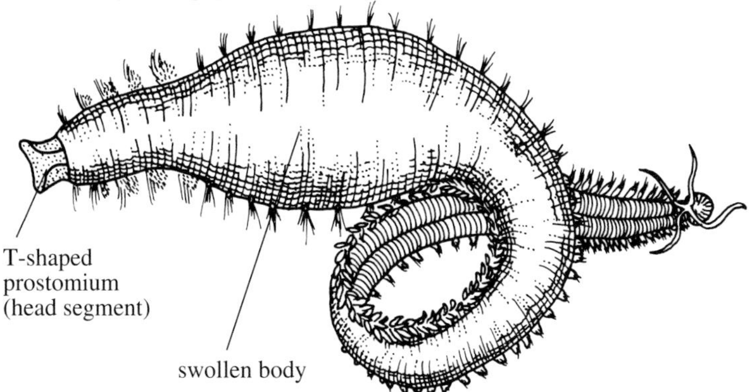

Fig.A. ***SCALIBREGMA INFLATUM*, T-HEADED WORM:** Brick red; up to 7.5 cm (3") long; found in muddy sand in intertidal zone and offshore. (family Scalibregmidae)

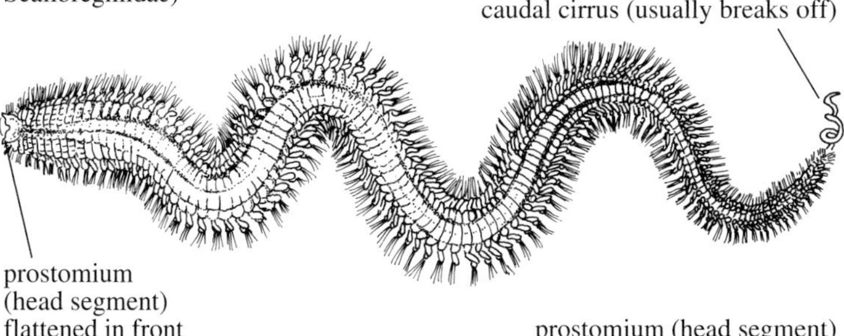

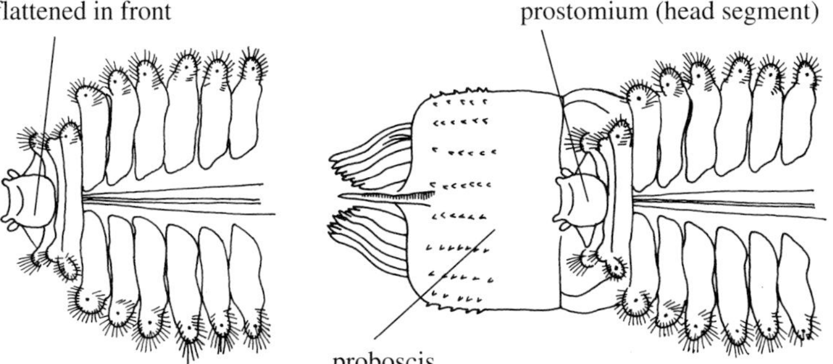

Fig.B. ***NEPHTYS* SPP., PAINTED WORMS, TYPICAL FORM**

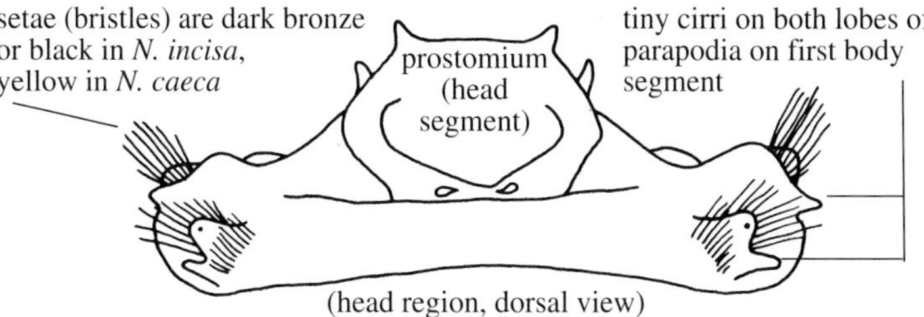

Fig.C. ***NEPHTYS INCISA*, COMMON PAINTED WORM[1]:** White or brownish, with a red blood vessel running down midline of the back and underside, with dark bronze or black setae (bristles); up to 15 cm (6") long; very common offshore in mud, occasionally near low tide level. ***Nephtys caeca*:** white, greenish, or dark body; yellow setae; up to 25 cm (10") long; occurs in mud or sand, usually offshore. A number of other very similar but less common species also occur in this region[1]. **17.09 F**

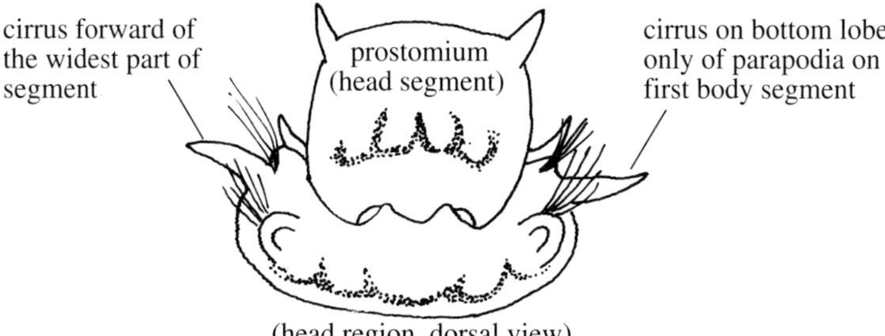

Fig.D. ***NEPHTYS PICTA*, PAINTED WORM:** With brown crescent shaped crossbands near the head; up to 30 cm (1') long; common in sand and mud.

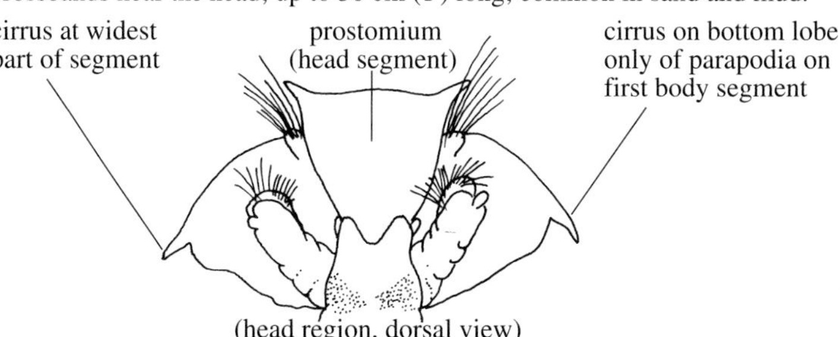

Fig.E. ***NEPHTYS BUCERA*, PAINTED WORM:** With brown V-shaped crossbands near the head; up to 30 cm (1') long; occurs in sand.

THICK BODIED WORMS WITH NO HEAD APPENDAGES
PHYLUM ANNELIDA, CLASS POLYCHAETA

Segmented worms that are much thicker in the midsection than at either end, usually with a pointed or blunt head segment[1].

(Annelid worm key begins on page 8.00)

#1.No gills on dorsal surface ("back"); gills absent or gills on the sides only (Figs.A-E) .... #2
#1.With gills on the dorsal surface of the midbody of the worm; gills are in 2 rows of tufts (Fig.F) or cover the back like a furry coat (Fig.G) .... #8

#2.With small but well developed parapodia (fleshy leglike appendages) (Fig.A); with 4 tiny antennae at tip of head segment (antennae are usually not visible without the aid of a microscope or hand lens); with a long extensible proboscis (proboscis is usually withdrawn into mouth) (Figs.A,B) .... #3
#2.Without any obvious parapodia (Figs.C-E); gills and setae (bristles) may or may not be present; without any antennae; without a long proboscis .... #6

#3.Proboscis has four black jaws at the end (jaws can only be seen when proboscis is fully extended); all parapodia very similar (Fig.A)...**family Glyceridae**, #4
#3.Proboscis with a bushy patch along one edge, or a ring of papillae (tiny bumps) at the tip, or rows of tiny black V's near base; parapodia near head of worm have one lobe, others have two lobes ,........ **family Goniadidae** (Fig.B)

#4.Without any gills[3] above or below the parapodia; not as common as other blood worms; up to 15 cm (6") long .... ***Glycera capitata*, blood worm** (Fig.A)
#4.With gills[3] above parapodia (Fig.A), but gills may be withdrawn into body; common blood worms, up to 37 cm (15") long .... #5

#5.Gills are branched, can be withdrawn into body .... ***Glycera americana*, blood worm** (Fig.A)
#5.Gills are not branched, cannot be withdrawn into body .... ***Glycera dibranchiata*, blood worm** (Fig.A)

#6.With a long, slender earthwormlike body (Fig.C); the first 5-11 segments behind the head are somewhat swollen and also bear slender, pointed setae (bristles); no obvious setae (bristles) on midbody segments; without a groove on ventral (underside) surface .... **capitellid threadworms**, page 8.20, couplet #7
#6.With a short, stubby body; with gills and/or obvious setae and/or a groove on ventral surface (Figs.D,E) .... #7

#7.No ventral groove .... ***Travisia carnea*** (Fig.D)
#7.With a ventral groove .... ***Ophelia* spp.[2]** (Fig.E)

#8.With 11-13 pairs of tufted gills on back (Fig.F); head segment is rounded .... **family Arenicolidae, lug worms**, #9
#8.Dorsal surface of midbody segments is covered with furry gills (Fig.G); head segment is pointed .... **family Orbiniidae[2]** (Fig.G)

#9.With 12-13 pairs of gills on back; occurs north of Cape Cod .... ***Arenicola marina,* lug worm** (Fig.F)
#9.With 11 pairs of gills on back; occurs south of Cape Cod .... #10

#10.Firm, stout; dark black-green; often 15-30 cm (6"-12") long; long, narrow gelatinous egg mass; castings formless....... ***Arenicola cristata,* lug worm** (Fig.F)
#10.Soft, limp; pale pink-tan; up to 15 cm (6") long; egg shaped, gelatinous egg mass; castings cylindrical, coiled ...... ***Arenicola brasiliensis,* lug worm** (Fig.F)

[1]Refer to Fig. A on page 8.00 for terms used in annelid worm key.
[2]The identification of these worms to the species level is beyond the scope of this book, requiring microscopic examination of the parapodia and setae. Refer to Pettibone (1963), Gosner (1971), or R. I. Smith (1964) to determine species.
[3]The gills are most easily located and examined when the worm is alive. Use a dissecting microscope (20X) to observe blood moving though the gills and to determine whether or not the gills can be withdrawn.

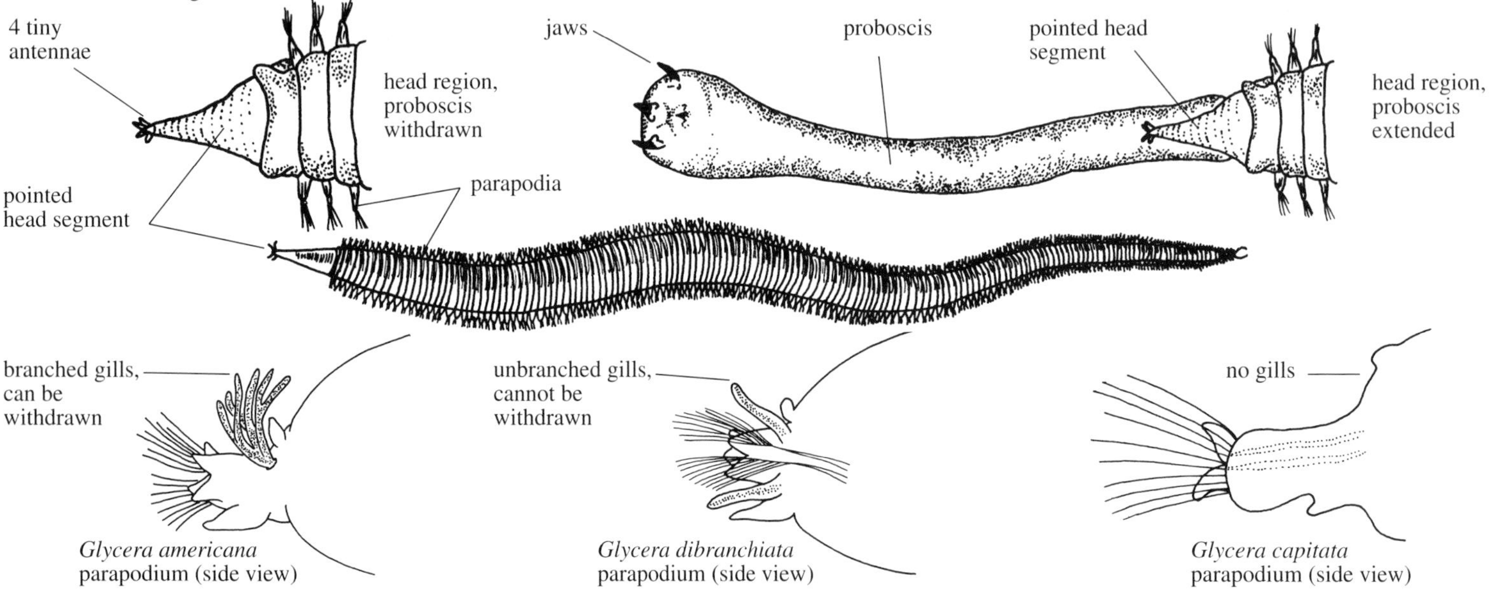

Fig.A. ***GLYCERA* SPP., BLOOD WORMS OR BEAK THROWERS:** Pink or beige in color; patches of red blood can be seen pulsating along the length of the body; with black jaws at the end of a long proboscis which shoots out of the mouth when the worm is disturbed or is feeding. The two most common species, *Glycera americana* and *Glycera dibranchiata*, grow up to 37 cm (15") long and 1 cm (3/8") thick, and occur near the low tide level in sand or mud, also found offshore. A less common species, *Glycera capitata,* grows up to 15 cm (6") long and is found offshore. Use key to distinguish these species. (family Glyceridae) **17.08 H**

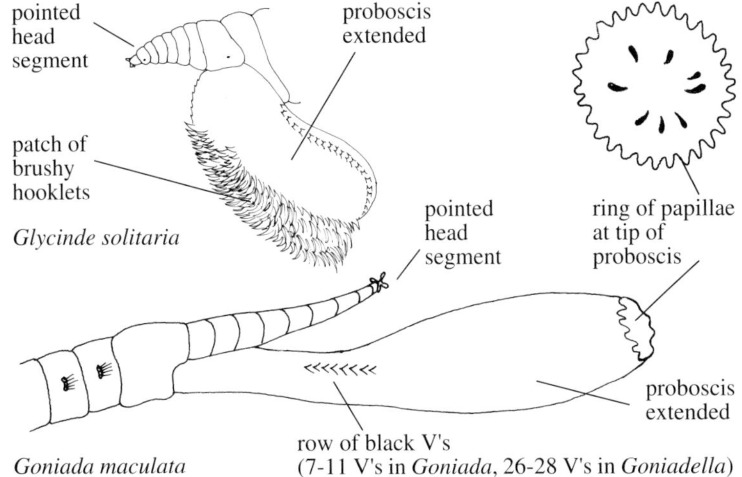

Fig.B. **FAMILY GONIADIDAE[2]:** *Glycinde solitaria* is pale yellow or greenish gray; up to 34 mm (1 1/4") long; occurs in the southern part of this region. *Goniada maculata* is pale green at head end and yellow or orange at tail end; up to 10 cm (4") long; occurs from R.I. north. *Goniadella gracilis* is iridescent pink or yellow; up to 5 cm (2") long; occurs south of Cape Cod. Other less common species[2] also occur in this region.

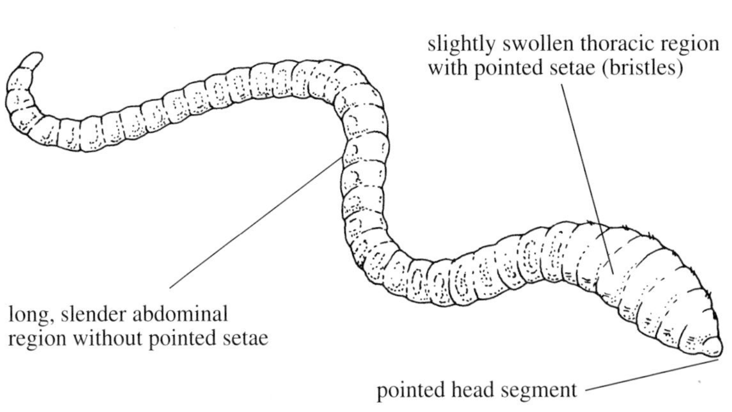

Fig.C. **FAMILY CAPITELLIDAE, CAPITELLID THREADWORMS:** Refer to page 8.20 couplet #7.

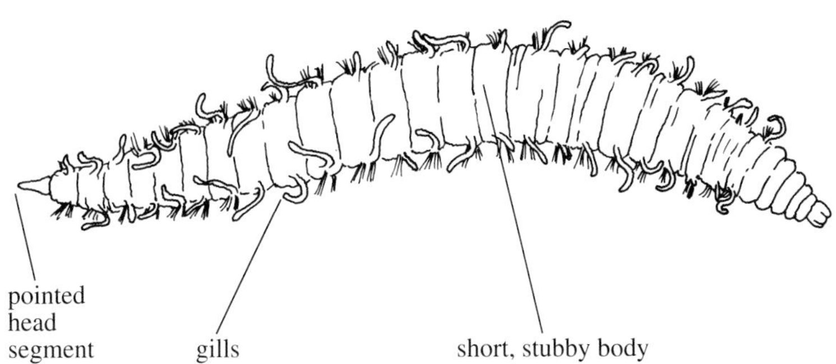

Fig.D. ***TRAVISIA CARNEA:*** Red or pinkish; up to 7.5 cm (3") long; found on sandflats and mudflats in estuarine waters; occurs from Cape Cod south. (family Opheliidae)

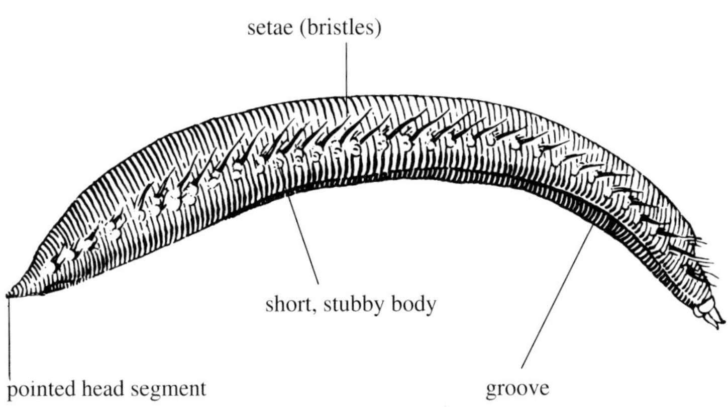

Fig.E. ***OPHELIA* SPP[2].:** Red with bluish iridescence; up to 7.5 cm (3") long; burrows head first into clean sand in intertidal zone and in shallow water. (family Opheliidae)

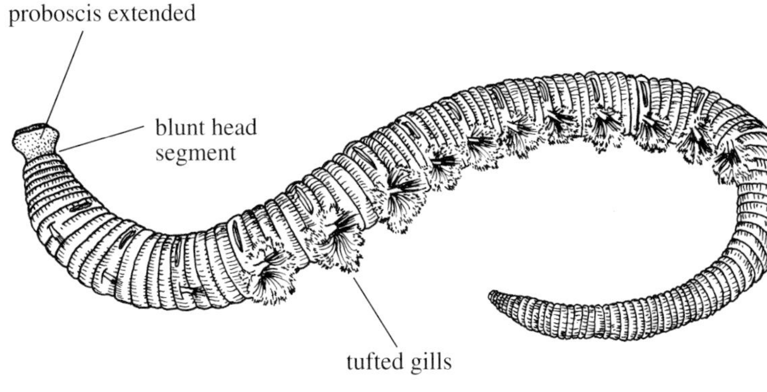

Fig.F. **FAMILY ARENICOLIDAE, LUG WORMS:** ***Arenicola marina*** is green with reddish-brown gills; up to 20 cm (8") long; occurs north of Cape Cod. ***Arenicola brasiliensis*** is pale pinkish-tan; up to 15 cm (6") long; occurs from Cape Cod south in sand and muddy sand; forms cylindrical, coiled piles of castings (see page 2.27) **17.09 A**; produces an egg shaped gelatinous egg mass (see page 2.22). ***Arenicola cristata*** is greenish black; up to 15 cm (6") long; occurs from Cape Cod south; produces a ribbon shaped gelatinous egg mass; castings are formless. Refer to the key to distinguish between these species.

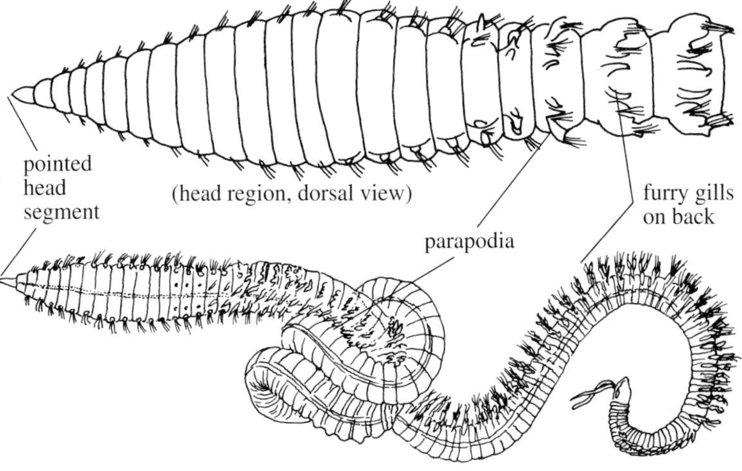

Fig.G. **FAMILY ORBINIIDAE[2]:** Orange, yellow, red, or brown; very common in mud and sand near the low tide level; also found offshore. The most common species, *Leitoscoloplos fragilis (=Haploscoloplos f., =Scoloplos f.)* grows up to 15 cm (6") long. *Haploscoloplos robustus (=Scoloplos r.)* is the largest species, reaching 37 cm (15") in length.

THREADWORMS AND OPAL WORMS
PHYLUM ANNELIDA, CLASS POLYCHAETA

Thin, threadlike, segmented worms with conical head having no tentacles or other appendages[1]; head is usually somewhat rounded at tip.

(Annelid worm key begins on page 8.00)

#1.With small but obvious parapodia[1] (fleshy leglike or paddlelike tabs, Figs.A-F) or tentaclelike gills (Figs.A) on many segments .... #2
#1.Without any obvious parapodia or gills (Figs.G,H) .... #7

#2.With small tentaclelike gills on the back of many body segments (Fig.A); without black jaws on proboscis[2].......... **family Paraonidae, threadworms**, #3
#2.No tentaclelike gills on the back of any body segments (Fig.C); with black jaws on proboscis[2]. .. **families Lumbrineridae and Arabellidae, opal worms**, #4

#3.Gills begin on the 6th or 7th body segment; with a total of 9-14 pairs of gills .... ***Paraonis gracilis*, threadworm** (Fig.A)
#3.Gills begin on the 4th body segment; with a total of 16-25 pairs of gills .... ***Paraonis fulgens*, threadworm** (Fig.A)

#4.With four eyes on head segment.......... ***Arabella iricolor*, opal worm** (Fig.B)
#4.No eyes on head segment (Figs.D-F) (Note: eyes may be hidden under a fold of the first body segment. Push fold back and examine head carefully) .... #5

#5.Head is flattened from top to bottom; all setae (bristles) on lower lobe of parapodia ("legs") are pointed, none hooked or hooded .... ***Drilonereis* spp.[3], opal worms** (Fig.D)
#5.Head is conical or rounded, not flattened; some setae (bristles) on lower lobe of parapodia ("legs") are hooked and hooded (tip enclosed in a droplet of clear material) (See Fig.F) .... #6

#6.With branched gills on some parapodia ("legs") .... ***Ninoe nigripes*, opal worm** (Fig.E)
#6.Without any gills on parapodia .... ***Lumbrineris* spp.[3], opal worms** (Fig.F)

#7.Some segments have swollen, raised areas called tori (Fig.G) which are vestigal parapodia; with a row of short hooklike setae (bristles) embedded in the tori; with slender pointed capillary setae on first 5-11 segments .... **family Capitellidae[3], capitellid threadworms** (Fig.G)
#7.Without tori (Fig.H); most segments usually have two bundles of setae projecting from each side, one bundle near the back (dorsolateral setae) and another bundle near the belly (ventrolateral setae) .... **class Oligochaeta, oligochaetes, aquatic earthworms**, page 8.24

[1]Refer to Fig. A on page 8.00 for terms used in annelid worm key.
[2]Jaw parts and proboscis can only be seen when proboscis is extended from mouth. Usually, proboscis is withdrawn inside of mouth. (See Fig.A on page 8.00)
[3]The identification of these worms to the species level is beyond the scope of this book, requiring microscopic examination of the parapodia and setae. Refer to Pettibone (1963), Gosner (1971), or R. I. Smith (1964) to determine species.

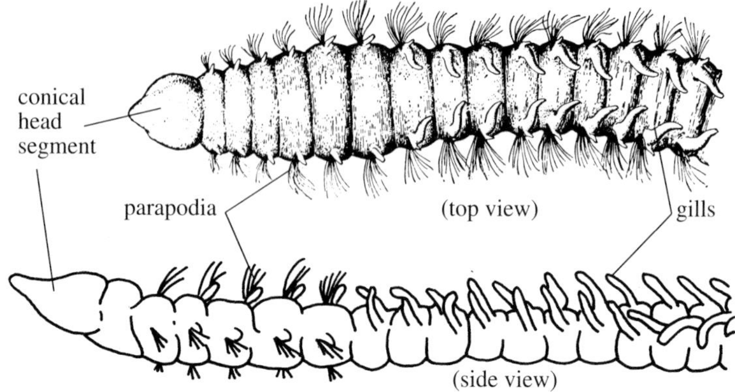

Fig.A. ***PARAONIS* SPP., THREADWORMS:** *Paraonis gracilis* (shown here) and *Paraonis fulgens* occur in this region. They both grow up to 2.5 cm (1") long and 0.5 mm (1/64") wide; found offshore in mud. Use the key above to distinguish between these two species. (family Paraonidae)

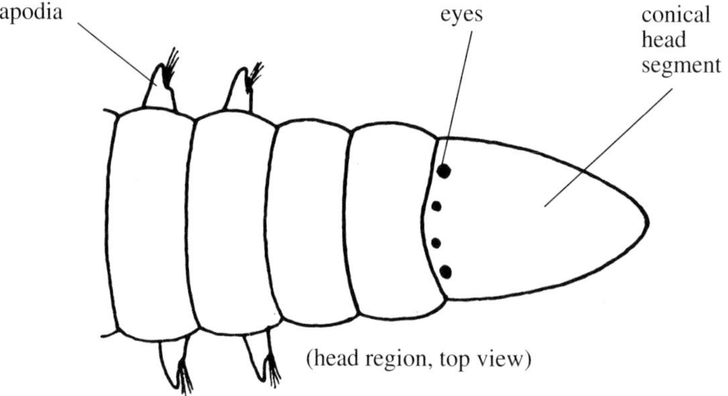

Fig.B. ***ARABELLA IRICOLOR*, OPAL WORM:** Reddish, brownish, or greenish, often with a brilliant iridescence; grows up to 60 cm (24") long and 5 mm (3/16") wide; very common near low tide level and offshore burrowing in sand, muddy sand, and under rocks. (family Arabellidae)

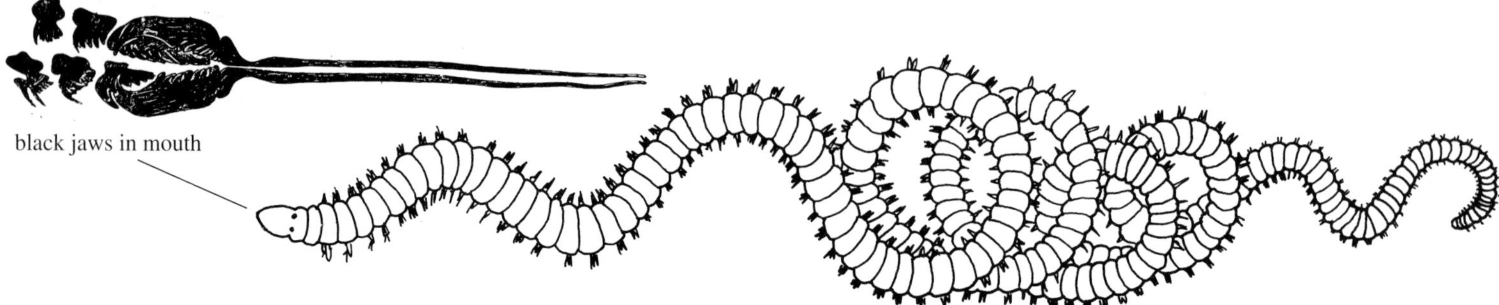

Fig.C. **TYPICAL OPAL WORM**

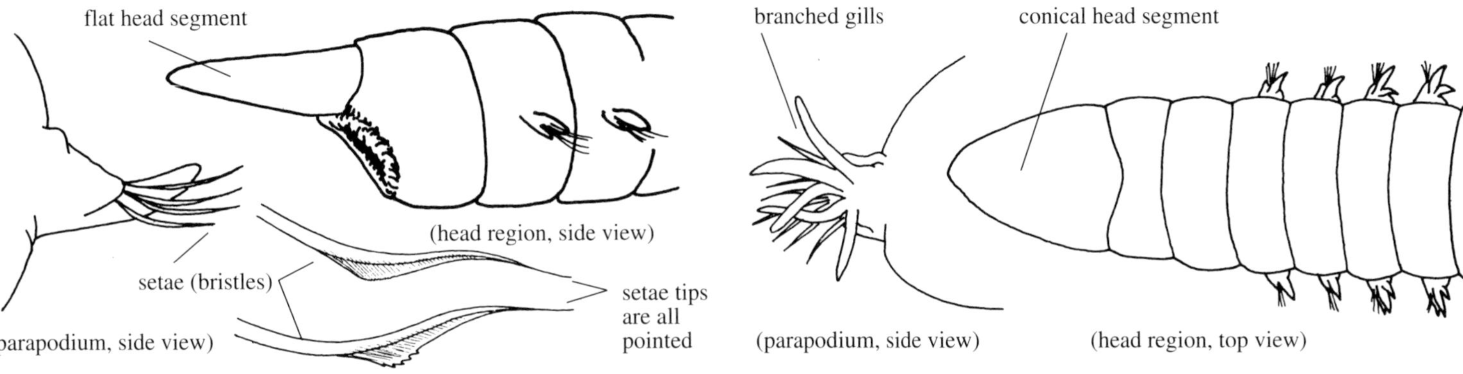

Fig.D. ***DRILONEREIS* SPP.**[3]**, OPAL WORMS:** Red; up to 60 cm (24") long and 3 mm (1/8") wide; found in fine sand and sandy mud in intertidal zone and offshore. (family Arabellidae)

Fig.E. ***NINOE NIGRIPES*, OPAL WORM:** Iridescent tan, sometimes with white dots; up to 10 cm (4") long; found at low tide level and offshore in mud; forms tubes of mucus mixed with sand and mud. (family Lumbrineridae)

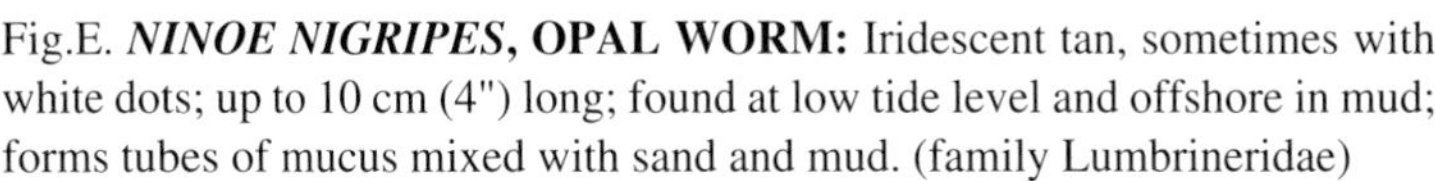

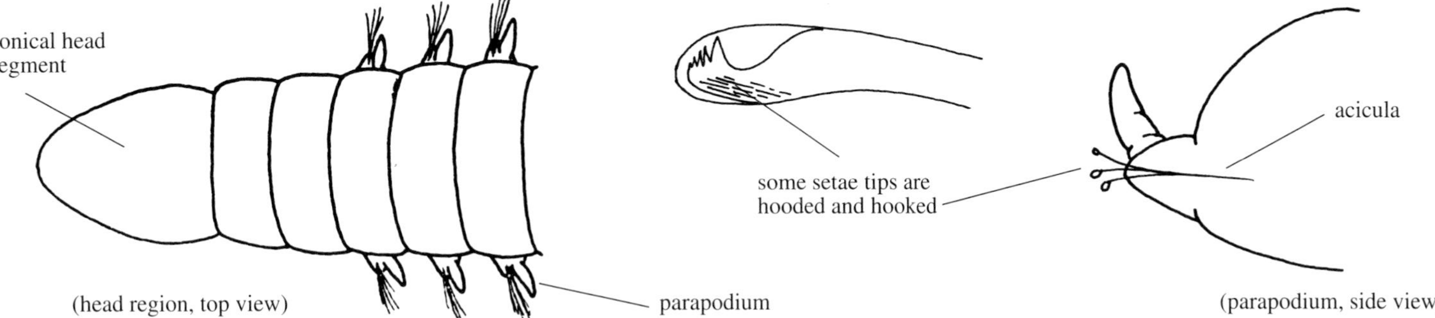

Fig.F. ***LUMBRINERIS* SPP.**[3]**, OPAL WORMS:** One common species is *Lumbrineris tenuis* which has a short conical head segment, yellow setae (bristles on parapodia) and yellow acicula (bristles inside parapodia). This species is reddish, orange, or brown; up to 15 cm (6") long; found at low tide level and offshore in mud and sand beneath stones. Other species have a very long head segment or black setae and acicula and may reach 38 cm (15") in length. (family Lumbrineridae)

17.08 I

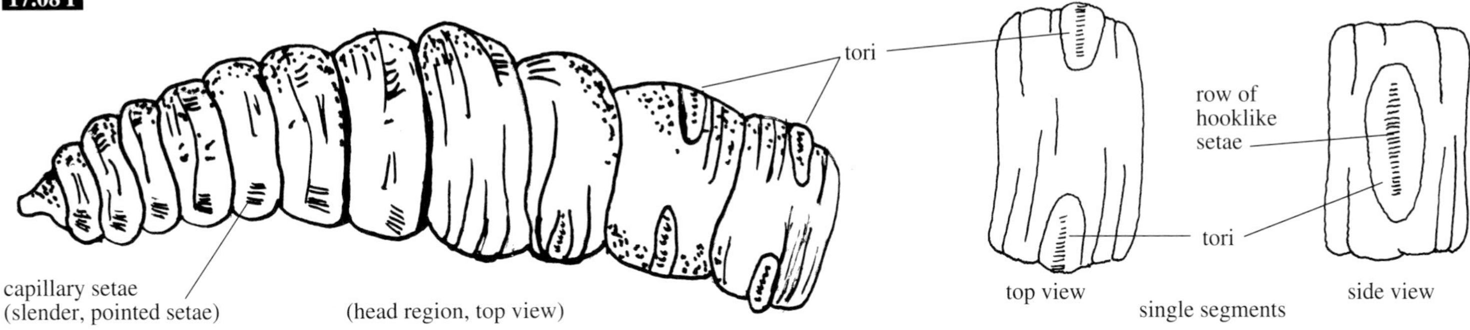

Fig.G. **FAMILY CAPITELLIDAE, CAPITELLID THREAD WORMS:** Several genera occur in this region, eating their way through sandy mud like an earthworm. They are particularly tolerant of polluted or stressed conditions in harbors and bays, often being one of the first animals to recolonize an area after it has been impacted by the dumping of dredge spoils or by an oil spill. See Fig. C on page 8.19 for the overall shape of a typical capitellid worm. *Mediomastus ambiseta* is one of the most frequently reported capitellid species in this region. It has capillary setae (slender, pointed bristles) only on the first 4 segments behind the head segment and has 11 thoracic segments. *Capitella capitata* is a blood red worm with golden-yellow capillary setae in 4 rows on the first 7 segments behind the head segment; up to 100 mm (4") long and 2 mm (1/16") wide; *Notomastus* spp. have capillary setae on 11 segments and are somewhat larger than the other capitellids, reaching 30 cm (12") in length. *Heteromastus filiformis* has capillary setae on 5 segments; with a dark red thorax and yellow or greenish-red abdomen. The taxonomy of this family is undergoing extensive revisions and identification to the species level is very problematic at this time. Refer to Fauchald (1977) for a key to genera.

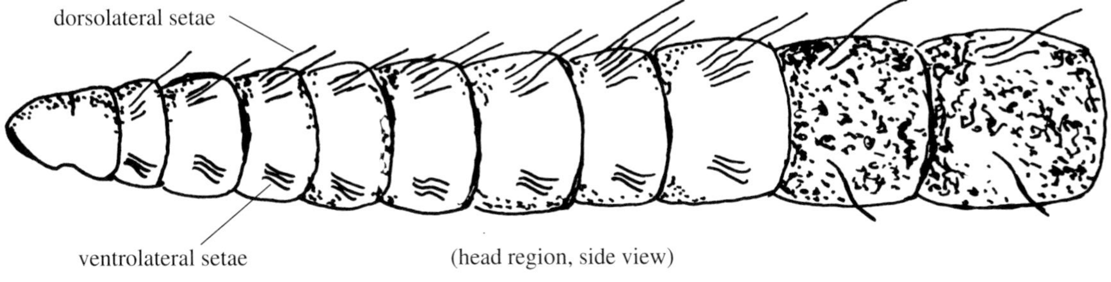

Fig.H. **OLIGOCHAETE, AQUATIC EARTHWORM**: Refer to page 8.24.

BAMBOO WORMS
PHYLUM ANNELIDA, CLASS POLYCHAETA, FAMILY MALDANIDAE[1] AND OWENIIDAE[1]

Segmented worms with long bamboolike segments; head without tentacles.

(Annelid worm key begins on page 8.00)

#1.With a funnel shaped tail (Figs.A,B) .... #2
#1.Tail is spoonlike or flat (Figs.D,E) .... #4
#1.Tail is round; head has a frilly membrane .... ***Owenia fusiformis*** (Fig.C)

#2.Head is hoodlike and flattened, with distinct rim (Fig.A) .... ***Clymenella* spp., #3**
#2.Head is rounded, not flattened, without a hood .... ***Nicomache lumbricalis*, round-headed bamboo worm** (Fig.B)

#3.Fourth body segment has a collar; 18 body segments have setae (bristles); up to 16 cm (6 1/2") long.... ***Clymenella torquata*, common bamboo worm** (Fig.A)
#3.Fourth body segment without a collar; 19-42 body segments have setae; less than 2 cm (3/4") long .... ***Clymenella zonalis*, little bamboo worm** (Fig.A)

#4.Tail segment longer than wide, forming spoonlike tail .... ***Asychis elongata*, spoon-tailed bamboo worm** (Fig.D)
#4.Tail segment about as long as wide, forming a flat, oval plate .... ***Maldane sarsi*, oval-tailed bamboo worm** (Fig.E)

[1]**WARNING:** This key does not include some of the rarer species in this family. Refer to Gosner (1971) for a positive identification, especially for species found in deeper water or in the northern portion of this region.

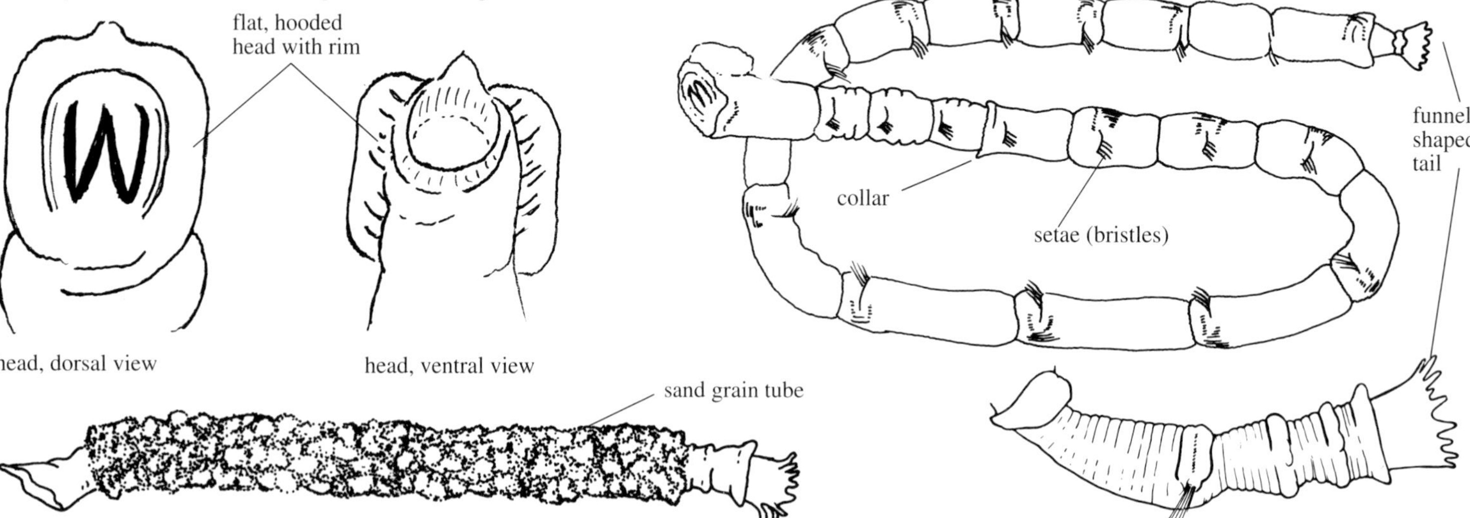

Fig.A. ***CLYMENELLA* SPP., BAMBOO WORMS**: *Clymenella torquata*, the common bamboo worm, is bright red or green; up to 16 cm (6 1/2") long; lives in tubes constructed out of sand grains cemented together. Very common in intertidal zone and offshore. *Clymenella zonalis*, the little bamboo worm, has dark red bands near head; up to 2 cm (3/4") long; found offshore. (family Maldanidae) **17.09 G**

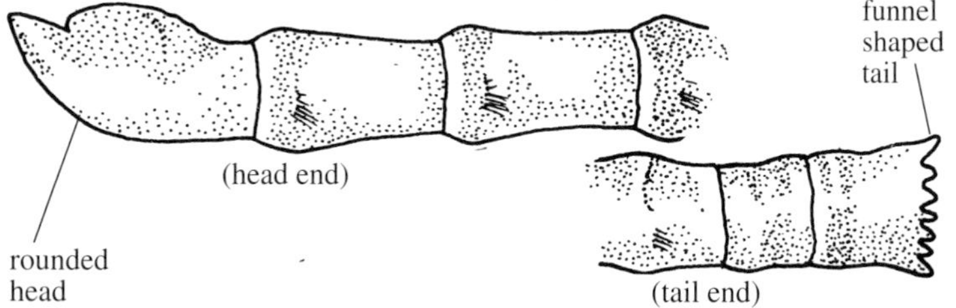

Fig.B. ***NICOMACHE LUMBRICALIS*, ROUND-HEADED BAMBOO WORM**: Pale yellow near tail and bright red near head; up to 16 cm (6 1/2") long; found in rock crevices and mud tubes. (family Maldanidae)

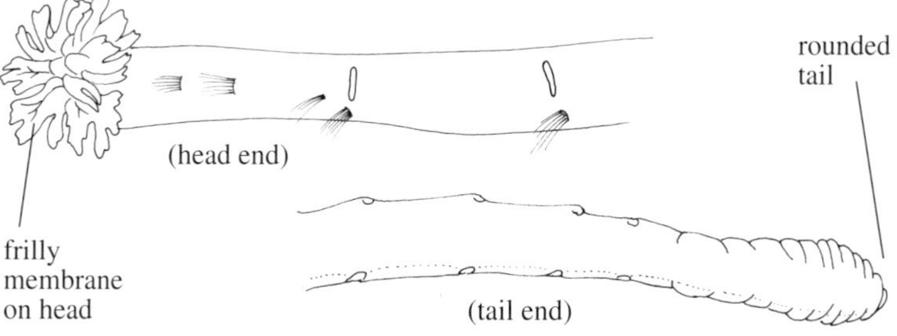

Fig.C. ***OWENIA FUSIFORMIS:*** Frilly membrane is translucent with greenish blue, yellow, and red tints; up to 10 cm (4") long; builds tube made of closely set shell fragments cemented together by a mucous secretion. (family Oweniidae)

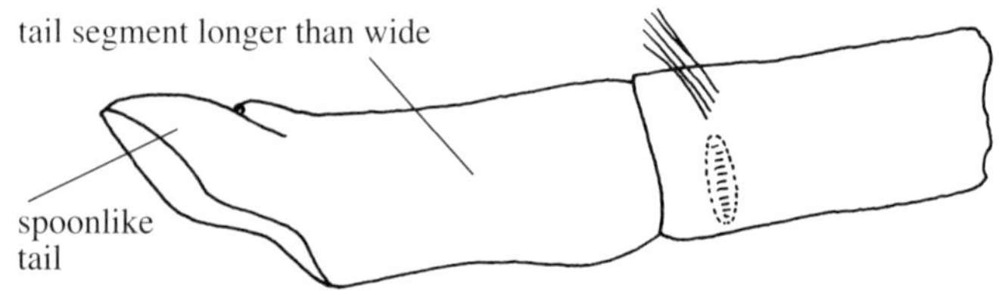

Fig.D. ***ASYCHIS ELONGATA (=Maldanopsis e.)*, SPOON-TAILED BAMBOO WORM**: Dark to reddish brown, often iridescent, anterior end speckled with black or dark purple; up to 30 cm (12") long; forms tubes of fine mud on sandy-muddy bottoms near low tide level. (family Maldanidae)

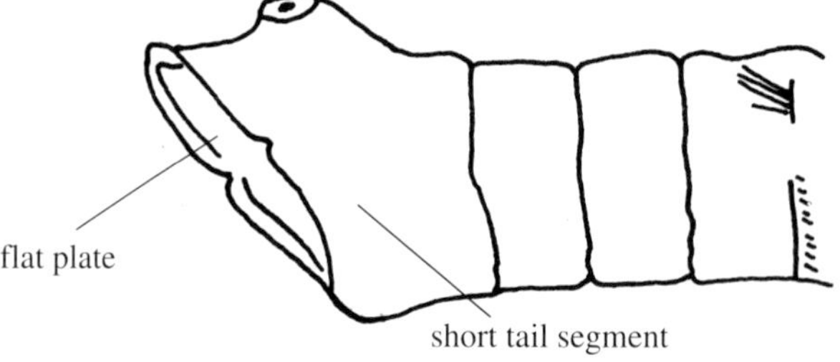

Fig.E. ***MALDANE SARSI*, OVAL-TAILED BAMBOO WORM**: Up to 10 cm (4") long; found in muddy sand. (family Maldanidae)

LOBSTER GILL WORMS
PHYLUM ANNELIDA, CLASS POLYCHAETA, FAMILY HISTRIOBDELLIDAE

Tiny parasitic worms living in the gill chamber and on the gills of the American lobster

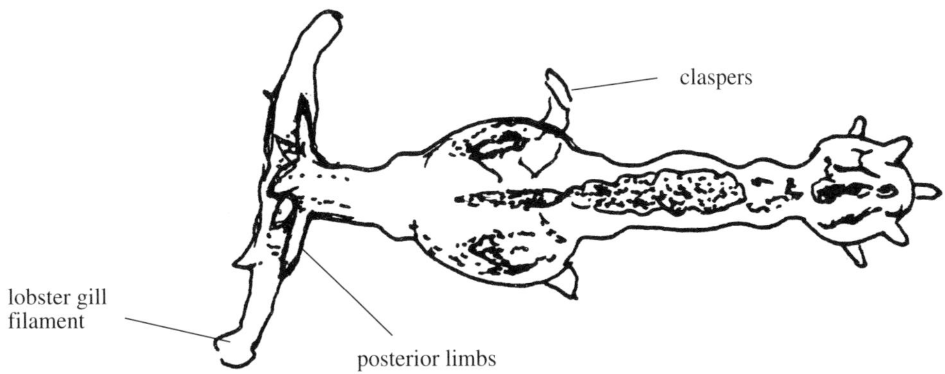

Fig.A. ***HISTRIOBDELLA HOMARI*, LOBSTER GILL WORM**: Colorless; about 1 mm (1/32") in length; lives in the gill chamber and on the gills of the American lobster. They are very difficult to detect because of their small size and lack of color. Isolate the worms by placing lobster gills in 50% seawater and refrigerating overnight. Discard the gills and carefully examine the bottom of the bowl with a dissecting microscope. The worms are not active and are easily missed.

LEECHES: PHYLUM ANNELIDA, CLASS HIRUDINEA

Segmented worms with a sucker at the anterior and posterior ends; lacking setae (bristles) or parapodia (fleshy leglike appendages)

(Use the key on page 2.20 to determine if you have a leech)

The marine leeches are not as common or as well studied as the fresh water leeches. Refer to Sawyer, Lawler and Overstreet (1975) for a key to the marine leech species of the eastern United States and to Gosner (1971) for a key to genera. All marine species belong to the family Piscicolidae. There is very little information available on the species of leeches to be found in southern New England. The following are presented only as examples of species that might be encountered.

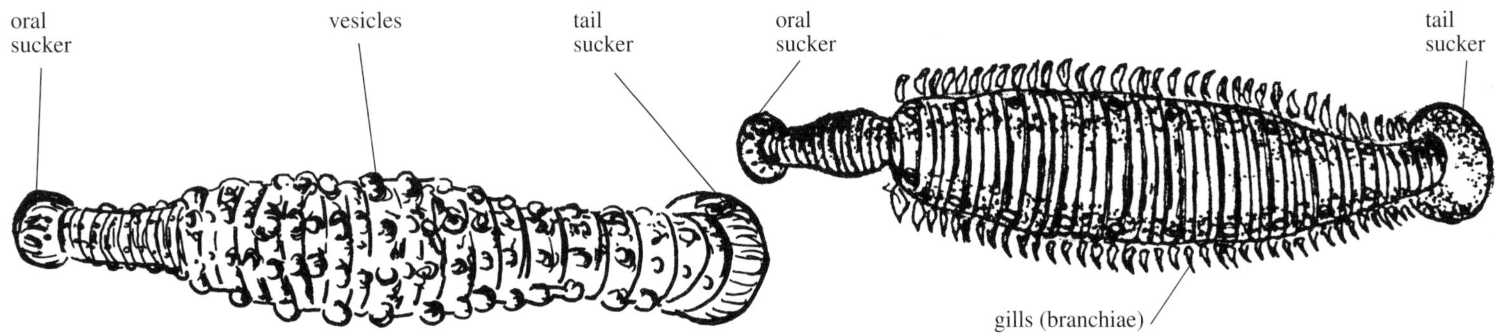

Fig.B. ***PISCICOLA* SPP., FISH LEECHES**: Elongate body; with eyes and vesicles (wartlike bumps) along the sides; found on a variety of fishes.

Fig.C. ***BRANCHELLION* SPP., SKATE LEECHES**: Elongate, flattened body; without eyes; with 33 pairs of leaflike gills (branchiae); found on skates.

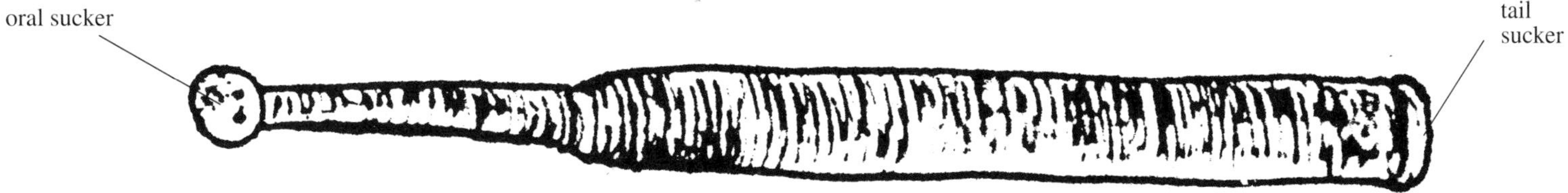

Fig.D. ***MYZOBDELLA LUGUBRIS*, CRAB LEECH**: Elongate, smooth body; without tubercles or vesicles (wartlike bumps); found in brackish water on crustaceans such as the blue crab, *Callinectes sapidus* and fish; deposits cocoons along the back edge of crab shells and legs (see Fig.E on page 2.19).

AQUATIC EARTHWORMS (OLIGOCHAETES): PHYLUM ANNELIDA, CLASS OLIGOCHAETA[1]

Segmented worms with no parapodia[2]; head segment without any antennae or other appendages; each body segment usually bears two dorsolateral and two ventrolateral bundles of setae with two or more setae in each bundle.

(Use the key on page 8.20 to determine if you have an oligochaete worm)

#1.Some standard size setae[2] (bristles, Fig.A) with bifid tips (two-pronged tips, Fig.B); hair setae (very long bristles, Fig.B) may or may not be present; body wall generally thin, worm appears to be very fragile .... #2

#1.All setae with simple pointed or rounded tips (Fig.B); no hair setae; body wall generally thick .... #3

#2.Dorsolateral setae (Fig.C) absent on first 4 or 5 segments or may be absent on all segments; eyes may or may not be present .... **family Naididae[1]** (Fig.C)

#2.Dorsolateral setae present on all but the first segment; eyes never present .... **family Tubificidae[1]** (Fig.D)

#3.Worms relatively large, body may be greater than 1.5 to 2.0 mm (1/16") in diameter; setae two per bundle (Fig.E) on all segments; clitellum (Fig.E) begins on thirteenth segment .... **family Megascolecidae[1], *Pontodrilus* spp.** (Fig.E)

#3.Worms usually less than 1.0 mm (1/32") in diameter; setae rarely two per bundle on every segment and may be totally absent on some parts of the body; clitellum begins on eleventh segment .... **family Enchytraeidae[1]** (Fig.F)

[1]Refer to Cook and Brinkhurst (1973) to determine species. Species identification requires special techniques and expertise which are beyond the scope of this book.
[2]Refer to Fig. A on page 8.00 for terms used in annelid worm key.

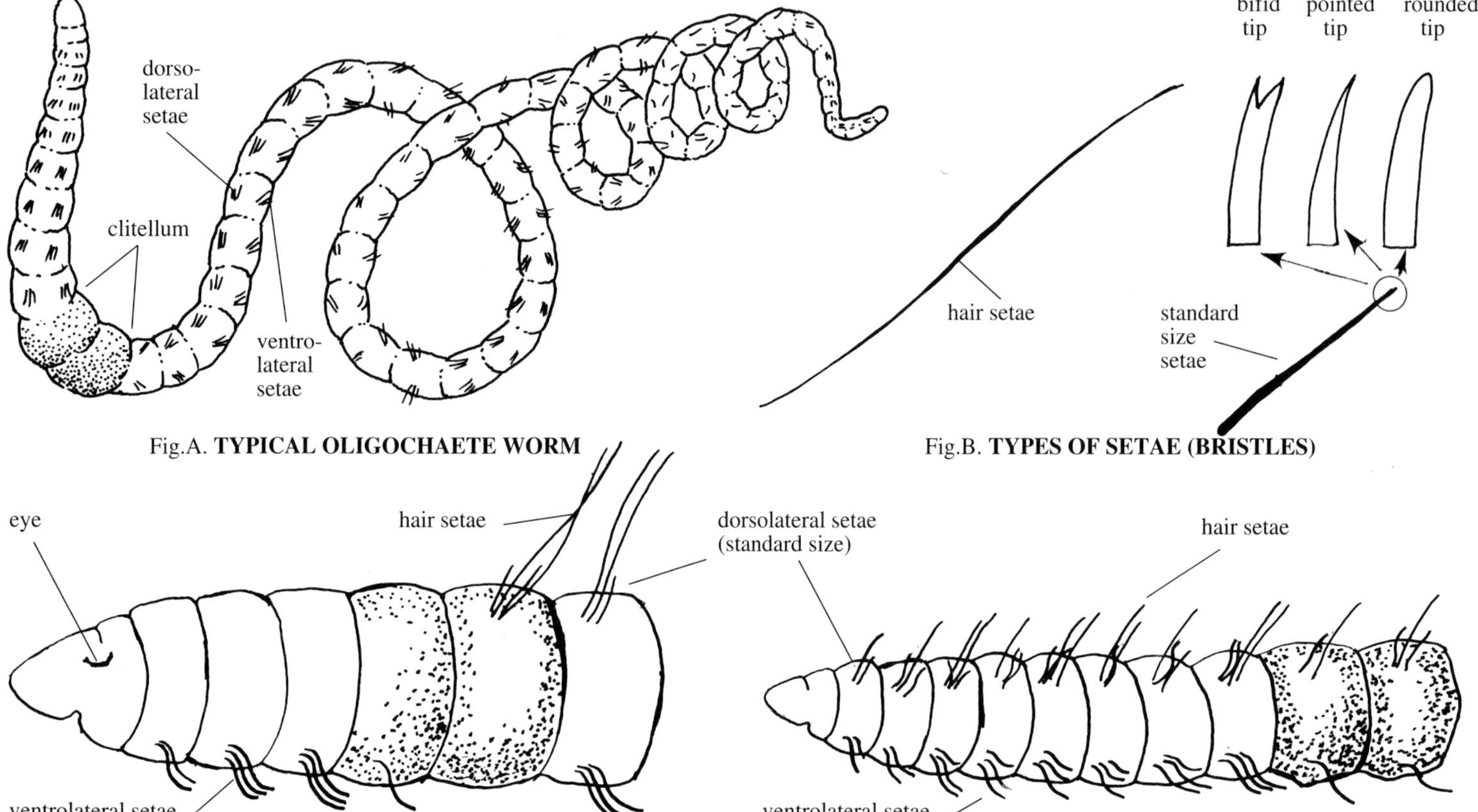

Fig.A. **TYPICAL OLIGOCHAETE WORM**

Fig.B. **TYPES OF SETAE (BRISTLES)**

Fig.C. **TYPICAL NAIDID OLIGOCHAETE WORM**

Fig.D. **TYPICAL TUBIFICID OLIGOCHAETE WORM**

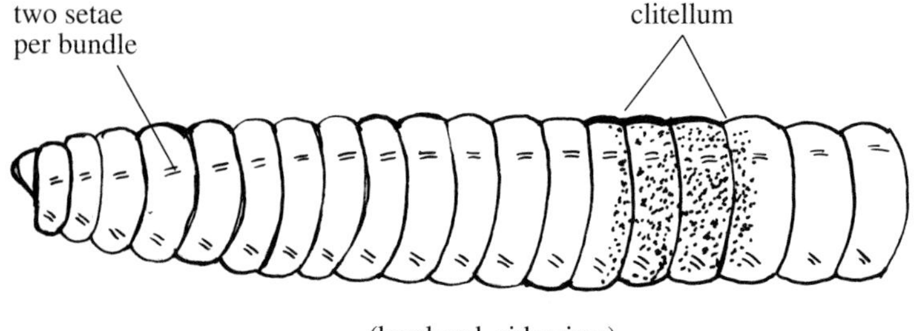

Fig.E. **TYPICAL MEGASCOLECID OLIGOCHAETE WORM**

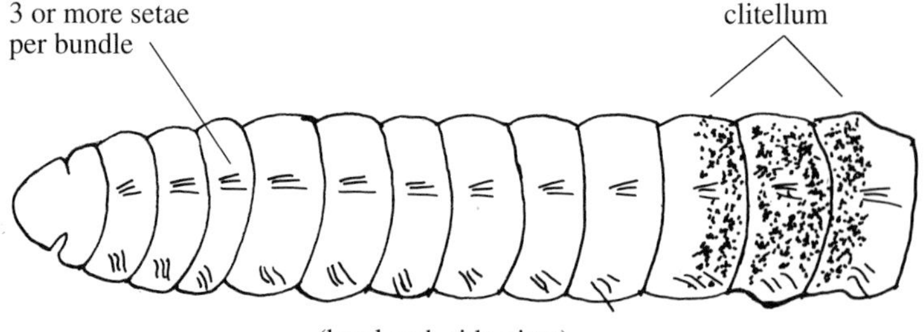

Fig.F. **TYPICAL ENCHYTRAEID OLIGOCHAETE WORM**

HORSESHOE CRABS: PHYLUM ARTHROPODA, SUBPHYLUM CHELICERATA, CLASS MEROSTOMATA (XIPHOSURA)

Aquatic arthropods with a large carapace, long pointed tail, chelicerae (clawlike first preoral appendages), and no antennae.

(Use the key on page 2.14 to determine if you have a horseshoe crab)

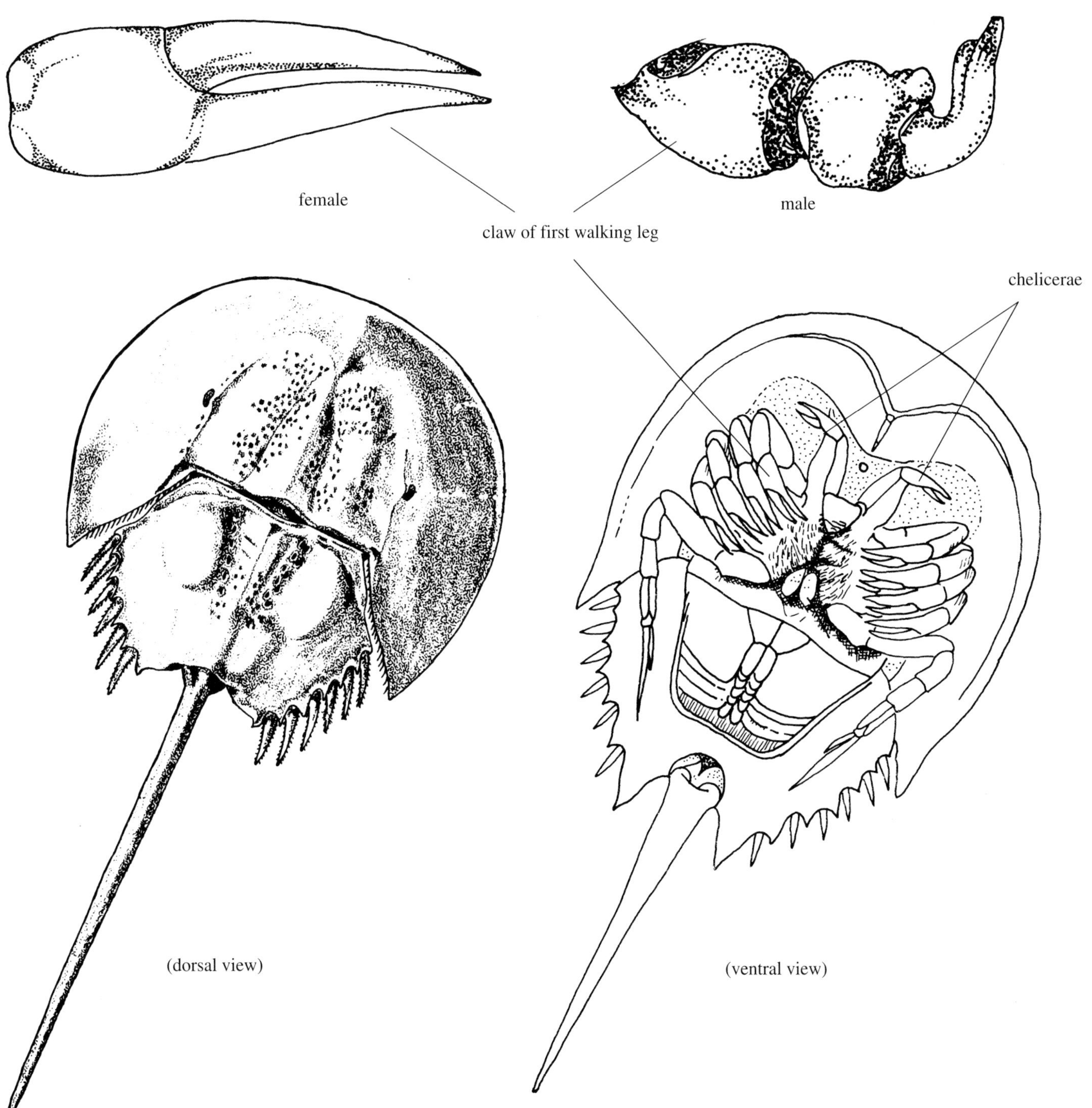

***LIMULUS POLYPHEMUS*, HORSESHOE CRAB:** Olive green or brownish color; up to 60 cm (24") long, males are usually somewhat smaller than mature females; very common in southern New England; males have hooklike first walking legs used to grasp a female, linking the pair together as as they crawl onto the beach where they mate and deposit their eggs; first walking legs of females are similar to the other walking legs, with pincerlike claws; horseshoe crabs grow by molting and their shed, empty shells are frequently found along the shore. Their long spikelike tail is used for turning right side up when the crab has been turned over. It is harmless to man. This is the only species of horseshoe crab found along our coast. **17.11 D**

PYCNOGONIDS OR SEA SPIDERS: PHYLUM ARTHROPODA, SUBPHYLUM CHELICERATA, CLASS PYCNOGONIDA

Spiderlike arthropods with 4 pairs of long legs; slender body that may appear to be no more than the base of each leg; legs are divided into 8 segments plus, in most species, a claw; strictly aquatic, never found above the high tide level; may be found on hydroids and anemones.

(Use the key on page 2.14 to determine if you have a pycnogonid)

#1.Head with only a conical proboscis[1] ("nose"); without chelifores (claw-bearing head appendages) or palpi ("antennae") .... ***Pycnogonum littorale*** (Fig.C)
#1.Head with chelifores[1] or palpi or both .... #2

#2.Chelifores are well developed with obvious claws (Figs.B,D-F) .... #3
#2.No claws on head appendages; chelifores are absent or stublike, much shorter than the palpi ("antennae"), and do not have claws (Figs.G,H) .... #7

#3.With palpi ("antennae") (Fig.B) .... #4
#3.Without palpi (Figs.D,E) .... #5

#4.Fingers on claws of chelifores are thick, shorter than the palm .... ***Nymphon grossipes*** (Fig.B)
#4.Fingers on claws of chelifores are slender, as long or longer than the palm .... ***Nymphon stromi*** (Fig.B)

#5.With a long thin neck; chelifores are about the same length as the neck .... ***Callipallene brevirostris*** (Fig.F)
#5.Neck is short or absent; chelifores are about twice as long as the neck (Figs.D,E) .... #6

#6.With a short but obvious neck which overhangs the basal end of the proboscis .... ***Anoplodactylus lentus*** (Fig.D)
#6.Without a neck .... ***Phoxichilidium femoratum*** (Fig.E)

#7.Chelifores are tiny, inconspicuous stubs .... ***Tanystylum orbiculare*** (Fig.G)
#7.Chelifores are about half the length of the palpi ("antennae") .... ***Achelia spinosa*** (Fig.H)

[1]Refer to Fig. B for the terms used in this key.
[2]This key only includes species that are common in waters under 30 m (100') deep. Refer to McCloskey (1973) to identify pycnogonids collected in deeper water or which drift into nearshore waters on floating *Sargassum*.

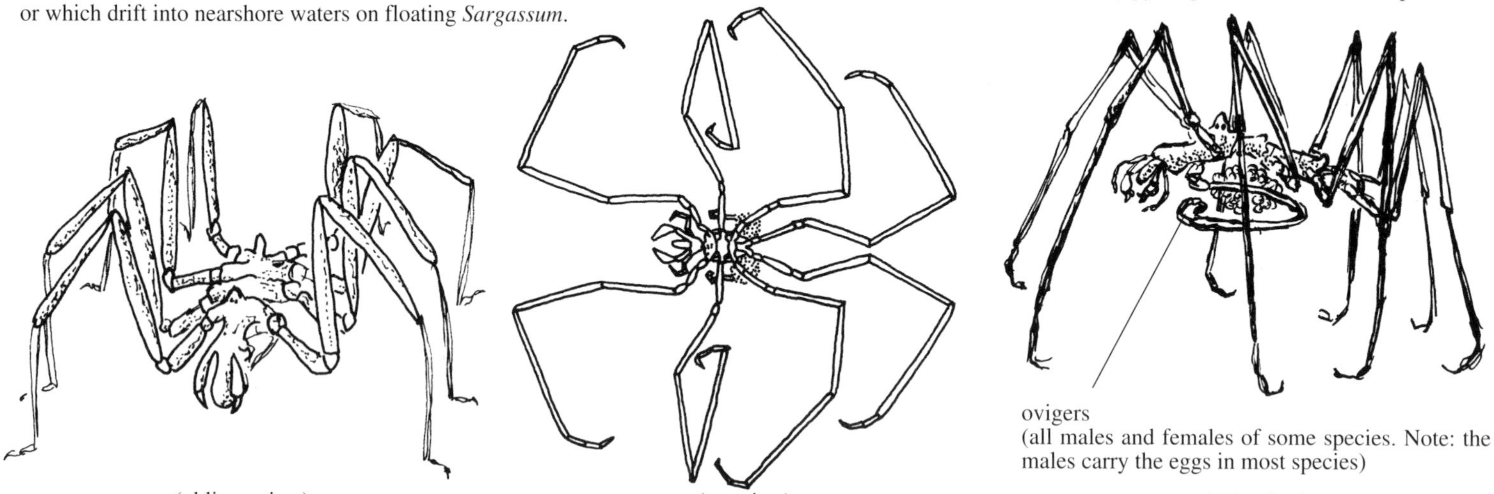

(oblique view)

(top view)

ovigers
(all males and females of some species. Note: the males carry the eggs in most species)

(side view)

Fig.A. **TYPICAL SEA SPIDERS**

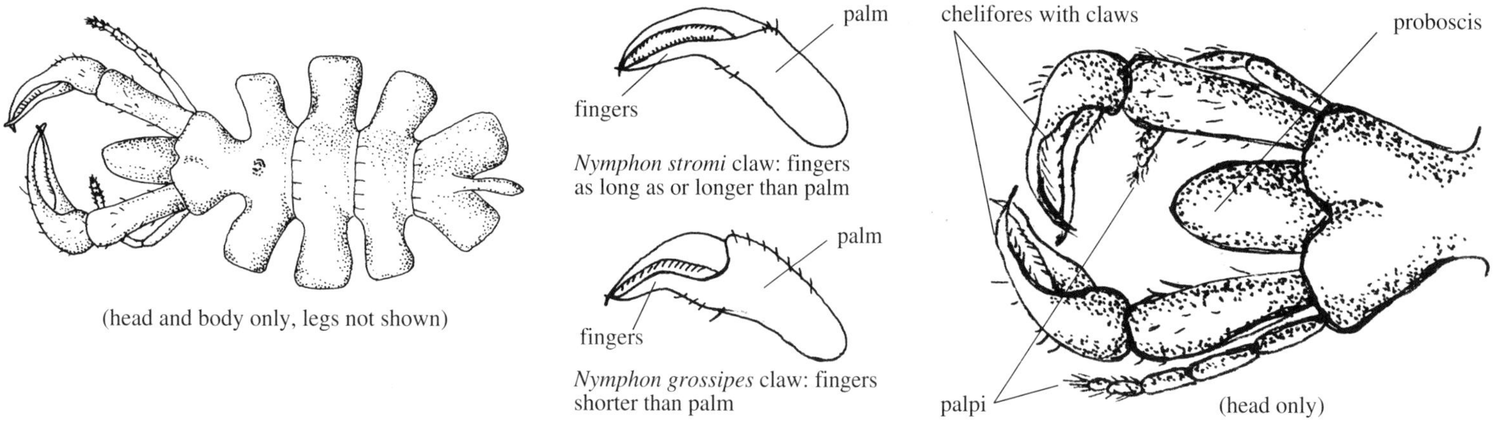

(head and body only, legs not shown)

palm

fingers

Nymphon stromi claw: fingers as long as or longer than palm

palm

fingers

Nymphon grossipes claw: fingers shorter than palm

chelifores with claws

proboscis

palpi

(head only)

Fig.B. ***NYMPHON* SPP.:** *Nymphon grossipes* is light pink-yellow, legs often banded with reddish to light purple; body up to 12 mm (1/2") long; occurs in water over 20 m (60') deep on rocky or muddy bottoms. *Nymphon stromi* is very similar but is less common; occurs in water over 12 m (40') deep.

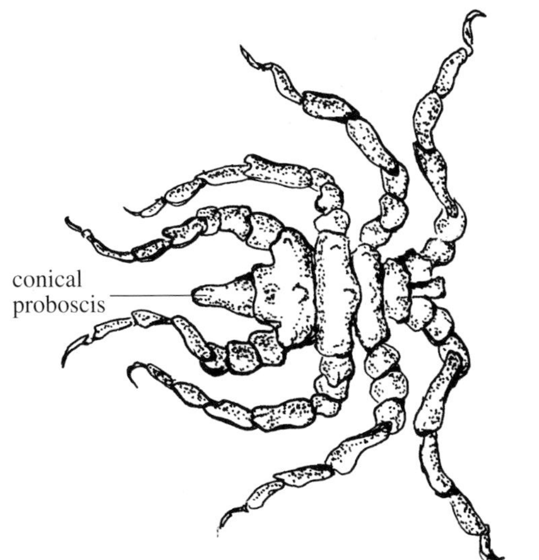

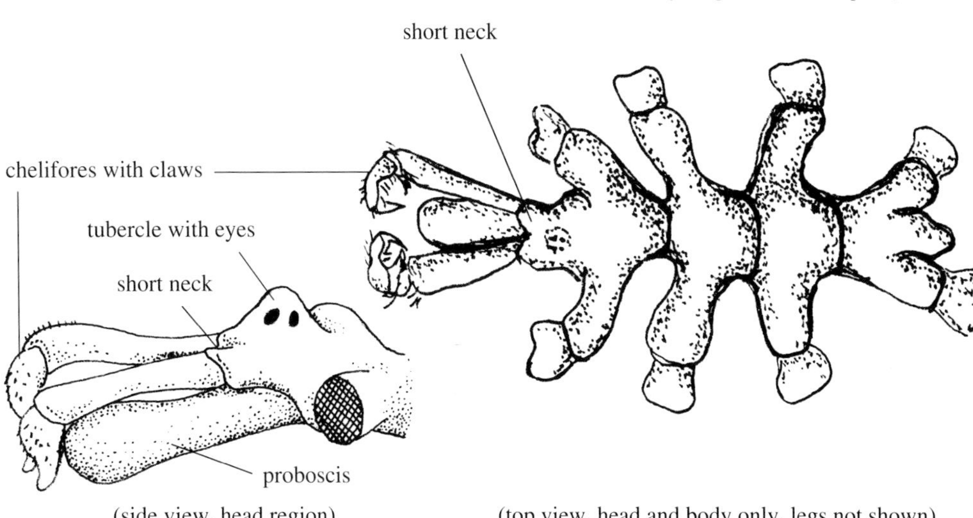

Fig.C. ***PYCNOGONUM LITTORALE:*** Body is yellowish brown to dark brown, legs are blackish toward tips; body length up to 5 mm (3/16"); found under stones and clinging to anemones below the low tide level.

Fig.D. ***ANOPLODACTYLUS LENTUS:*** Purple with brown or black eyes; body up to about 6 mm (1/4") long; found in the intertidal zone and offshore on hydroids, sea squirts, and seaweeds; occurs from Cape Cod south. 17.11 C

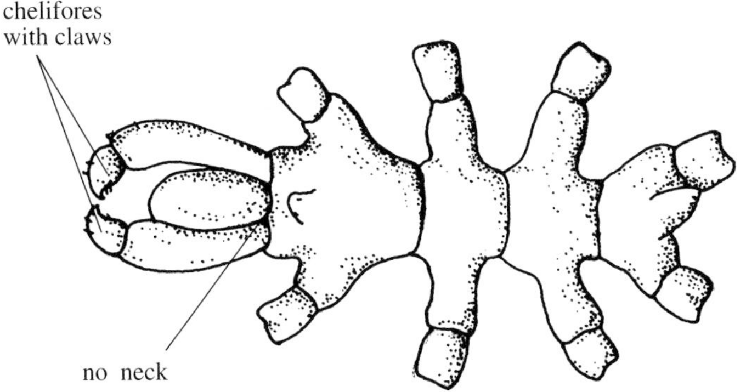

Fig.E. ***PHOXICHILIDIUM FEMORATUM:*** Body up to about 3 mm (1/8") long; occurs from Long Island Sound north in the intertidal zone and deep water; common on the hydroid *Tubularia*.

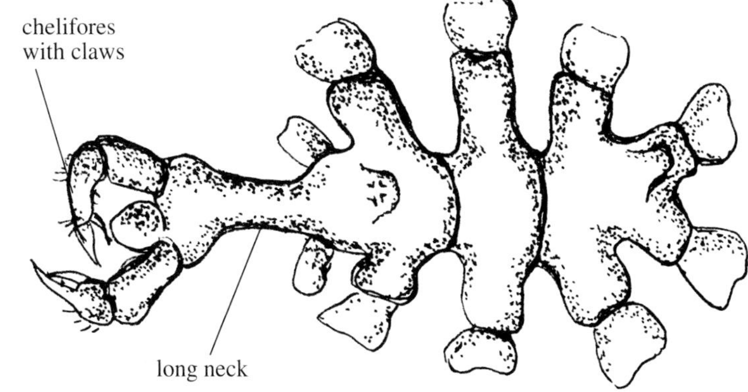

Fig.F. ***CALLIPALLENE BREVIROSTRIS****:* Eyes are bright red; body length to 1.6 mm (1/16"); common on pilings among fouling organisms, especially hydroids such as *Tubularia*.

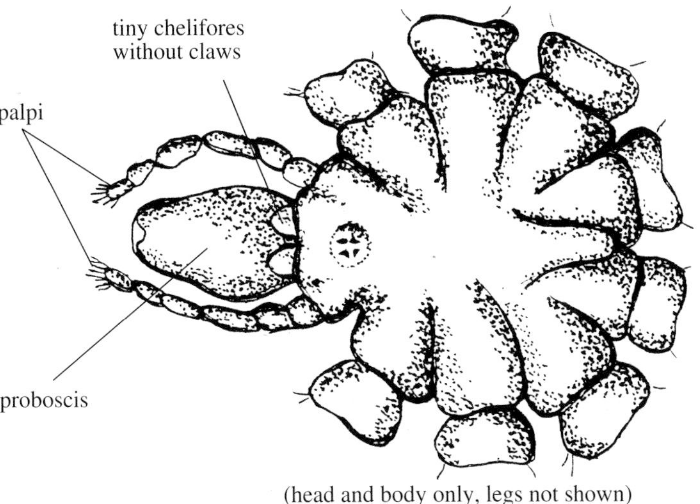

Fig.G. ***TANYSTYLUM ORBICULARE:*** Body length to 1 mm (1/32"); found among hydroids and sea squirts.

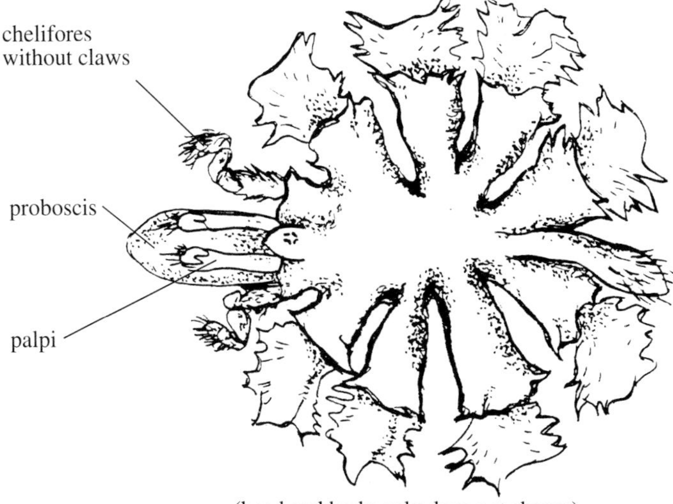

Fig.H. ***ACHELIA SPINOSA****:* Body length to 1 mm (1/32"); found beneath stones near low tide level and on hydroids and other fouling organisms.

SPIDERS: PHYLUM ARTHROPODA, SUBPHYLUM CHELICERATA, CLASS ARACHNIDA, ORDER ARANEAE

Arachnids having two distinct body regions (cephalothorax and abdomen) with a narrow stalk (pedicel) in between; with four pairs of walking legs; with a pair of fanglike head appendages (chelicerae) and eight simple eyes.

(Use the key on page 2.14 to determine if you have a spider)

#1.Eyes arranged in three rows (Fig.A) with a 4-2-2 pattern (lowest, frontmost row has four eyes; the next two rows each have two eyes and are higher up and further back) .... #2

#1.Eyes in two rows (Fig.B), rows may be straight or may be curved with eyes in a somewhat oval pattern or may be in two concentric U-shaped rows .... #3

#2.The four eyes in the first row are smaller than the eyes in the second or third rows .... **family Lycosidae, wolf spiders**[1] (Fig.C)

#2.The four eyes in the first row are larger than the eyes in the second or third rows .... **family Salticidae, jumping spiders**[1] (Fig.D)

#3.With two claws (Fig.E) at tip of walking legs; may or may not have a claw tuft (If leg tip has claw tuft, make this choice. If not, count the claws) .... #4

#3.With 3 claws (Fig.F) at tip of walking legs; without claw tuft .... #5

#4.First two pairs of legs are longer and stouter than rear two pairs of legs; legs are held out to the sides, crablike; sidemost eyes are often raised up on knobs or bumps (tubercles); with a knoblike projection (colulus) between the front two spinnerets (Fig.G) .... **family Thomisidae, crab spiders**[1] (Fig.H)

#4.Legs are all about the same size; legs do not extend sideways; eyes are not on raised tubercles; no colulus .... **family Clubionidae, sac spiders**[1] (Fig.I)

#5.Spinnerets in a single transverse row .... **family Hahniidae**[1] (Fig.J)

#5.Spinnerets in a cluster (Fig.G); not arranged in a single transverse row .... page 9.06

[1]The identification of spiders to the species level requires specialized knowledge and is beyond the scope of this book. Use Kaston (1981) to determine species. Refer to Weiss et al. (1995) for a list of the species in this family reported to occur along the coast.

1st row: 4 eyes
2nd row: 2 eyes
3rd row: 2 eyes
(cephalothorax, top view)
3rd row: 2 eyes
2nd row: 2 eyes
1st row: 4 eyes
(head, face view)

Fig.A. **SPIDERS WITH EYES IN THREE ROWS**

cephalo-thorax, top view
cephalo-thorax, top view
eyes in straight rows
eyes in oval pattern
eyes in U-shaped rows
head, face view
head, face view

Fig.B. **SPIDERS WITH EYES IN TWO ROWS**

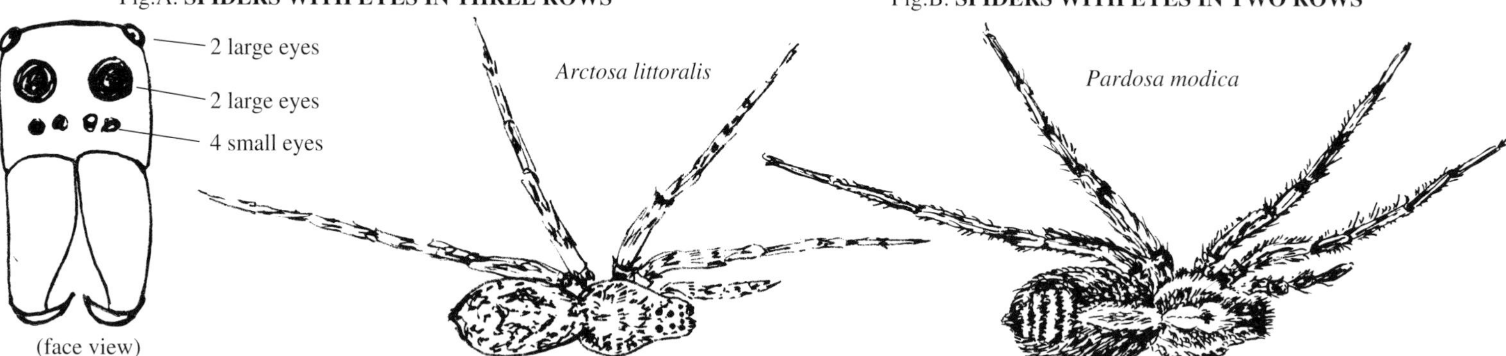

Fig.C. **FAMILY LYCOSIDAE, WOLF SPIDERS**[1]: A very common seashore family of spiders with a number of species occurring on tidal marshes, sandy beaches, and rocky shore areas; some species dig deep burrows; a few species are up to 21 mm (7/8") long but most are less than 12 mm (1/2") long; the color of these rather hairy spiders ranges from gray and black to yellowish and brownish. *Arctosa littoralis*, is commonly found on sandy beaches under driftwood and in tunnels 15-25 cm (6"-10") deep located near the top of sand dunes. This spider, which reaches 15 mm (5/8") in length, is colored like the sand on which it lives and is difficult to see when it is not moving. Several species of wolf spiders in the genus *Pardosa*, including *P. distincta*, *P. modica*, and *P. longispinata*, are common on saltmarshes. *P. distincta* reaches 7 mm (1/4") in length and has a distinctive pattern of light brown markings on a yellow background. *P. modica* is mostly dark brown with gray markings but has a pair of very distinct yellow stripes near each side of the carapace and a less distinct mid-stripe. This species grows up to 9 mm (3/8") in length. *P. longispinata*, which reaches 7 mm (1/4") in length, is yellow to yellow green with gray markings. The legs are yellow in the female and darker in the male. There is a Y-shaped black mark on the underside of the cephalothorax between the legs and a single black stripe on the underside of the abdomen.

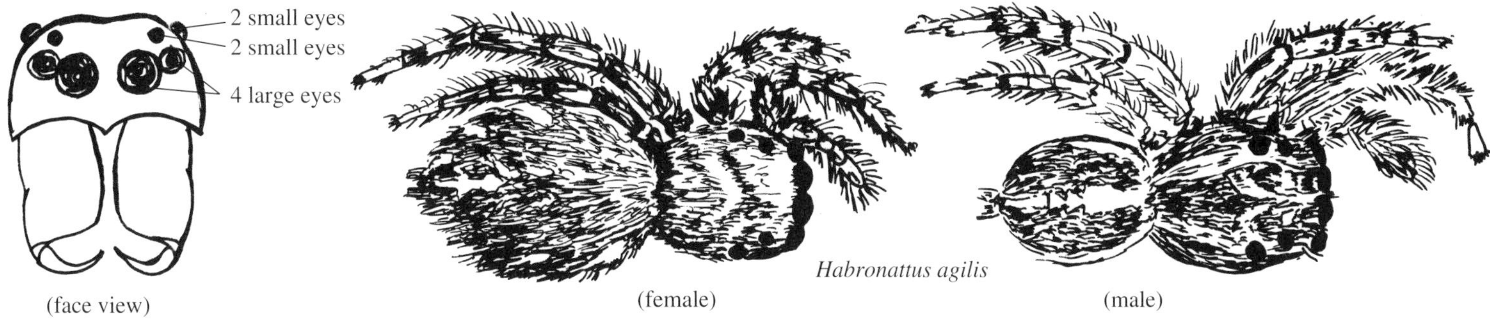

Fig.D. **FAMILY SALTICIDAE, JUMPING SPIDERS**[1]**:** Common on beaches and saltmarshes; most shore species are less than 7 mm (1/4") long and are brown, black or gray with white or yellow markings. Several species, including *Habronattus agilis*, are found in marsh grass, under driftwood and stones along the shore. *Habronattus agilis* males are brightly marked with black and white stripes and females are gray with indistinct white spots; they are up to 6 mm (1/4") long.

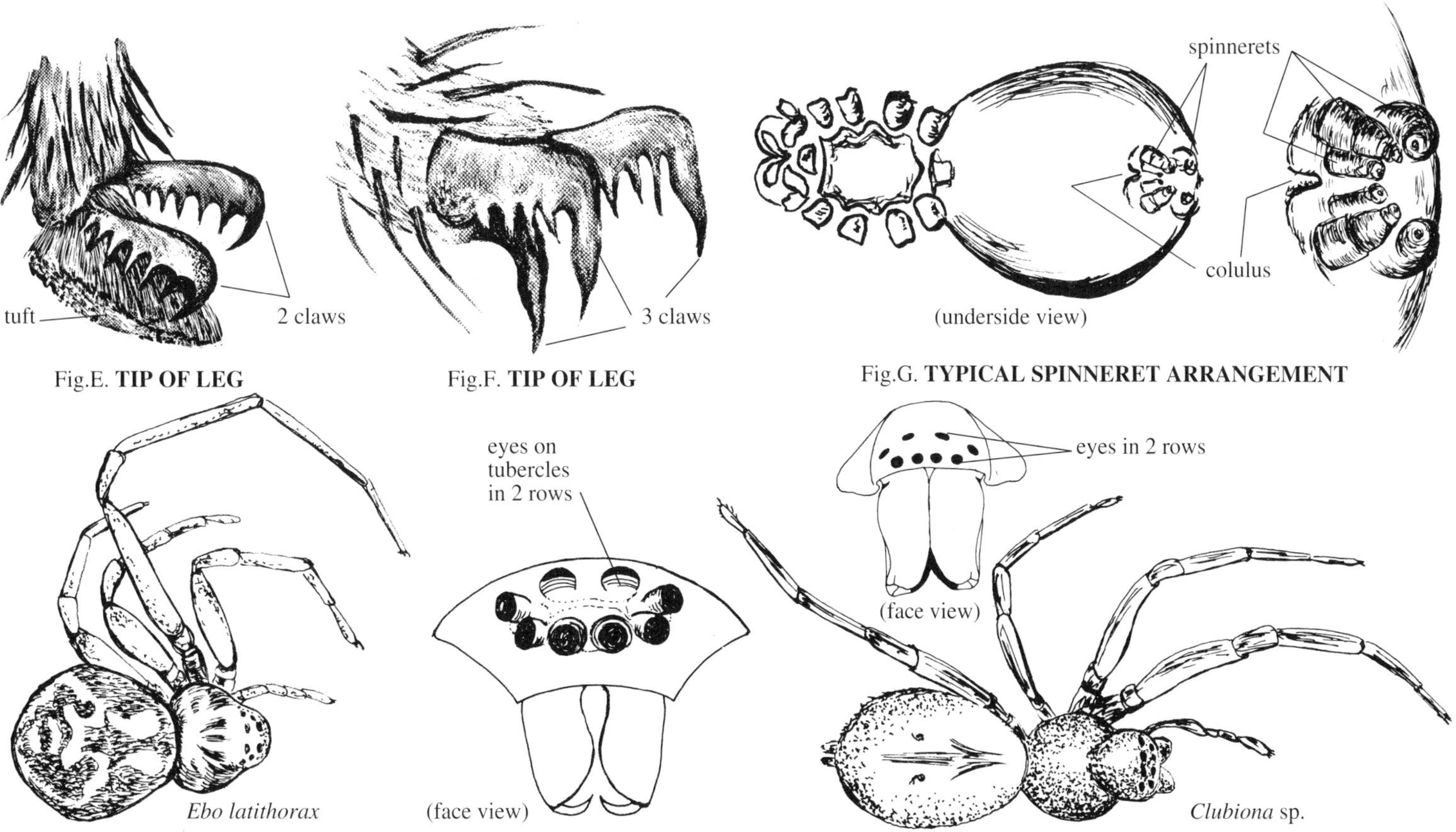

Fig.E. **TIP OF LEG**

Fig.F. **TIP OF LEG**

Fig.G. **TYPICAL SPINNERET ARRANGEMENT**

Fig.H. **FAMILY THOMISIDAE, CRAB SPIDERS**[1]**:** Yellowish brown; up to 3 mm (1/8") long; found under leaves near the shore.

Fig.I. **FAMILY CLUBIONIDAE, SAC SPIDERS**[1]**:** Common on marshes and beaches; length up to about 9 mm (3/8"); greenish yellow color.

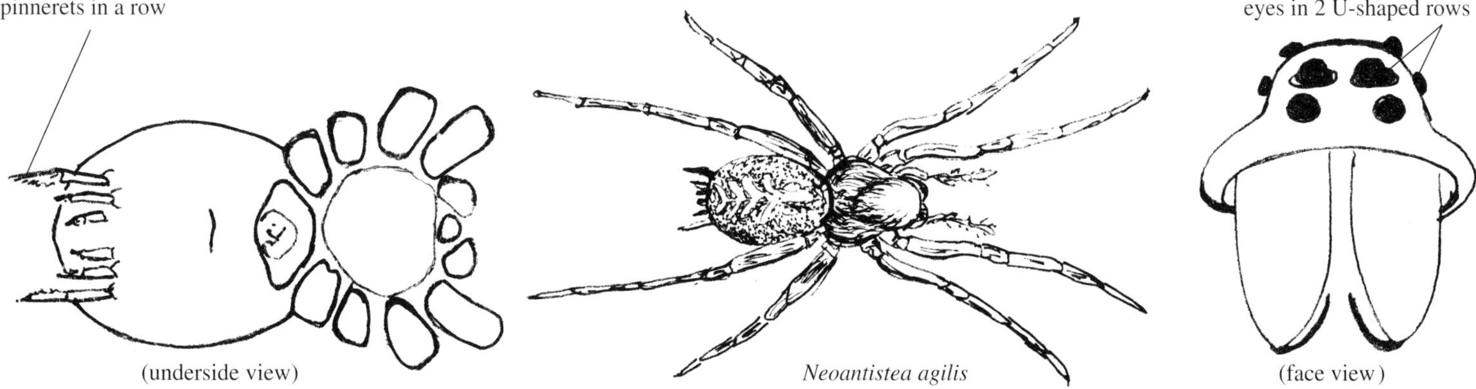

Fig.J. **FAMILY HAHNIIDAE**[1]**:** *Neoantistea agilis*, the most common species in this family, has a reddish or orange-brown cephalothorax and yellowish legs ringed with gray. The abdomen is gray with a pattern of yellow spots. These spiders reach 3 mm (1/8") in length and occur in saltmarshes.

SPIDERS (CONTINUED): PHYLUM ARTHROPODA, SUBPHYLUM CHELICERATA, CLASS ARACHNIDA, ORDER ARANEAE

(Spider key begins on page 9.04)

#1.Eyes are all about the same color; with a short clypeus (Fig.A) (the region in front of the first eyes and the front edge of the head), clypeus is shorter than the mid-eye region .... #2

#1.Some eyes are dark and others are light in color; with a long clypeus (Fig.B), clypeus is as long or longer than the mid-eye region sometimes giving forehead a bulging appearance .... #3

#2.Chelicerae (jaws) have a boss (a smooth, raised protuberance, "bump", at the base near the outer edge of the chelicerae, see Fig.A); chelicerae are not especially large .... **family Araneidae (=Epeiridae), orb-weaving spiders[1]** (Fig.C)

#2.Chelicerae are very large and powerful; chelicerae do not have a boss .... **family Tetragnathidae, thick-jawed spiders** (Fig.D)

#3.With a cribellum (a transverse plate in front of the spinnerets, see Fig.E) and calamistrum (one or two rows of curved spines on the dorsal surface of the metatarsus of the fourth walking legs, see Fig.F) .... **family Dictynidae, cribellate spiders[1]** (Fig.H)

#3.Without a cribellum or calamistrum .... #4

#4.With a comblike row of 6 to 10 curved, serrated (toothed) bristles (Fig.G) on the underside (ventral surface) of the tarsus (last segment before the claw) of the fourth walking legs .... **family Theridiidae, comb-footed spiders[1]** (Fig.I)

#4.Without a comb row of serrated bristles on the tarsus of the fourth walking legs .... #5

#5.Lives on or near the ground, usually under debris such as dead leaves and grass; up to 3 mm (1/8") long ...... **family Micryphantidae, dwarf spiders[1]** (Fig.J)

#5.Often found hanging beneath one side of a flat sheetlike web (see page 9.08, Fig.C) attached to shrubs and grasses; may grow up to 5 mm (1/4") in length .... **family Linyphiidae, sheet-web weavers[1]** (Fig.K)

[1]See footnote on page 9.04

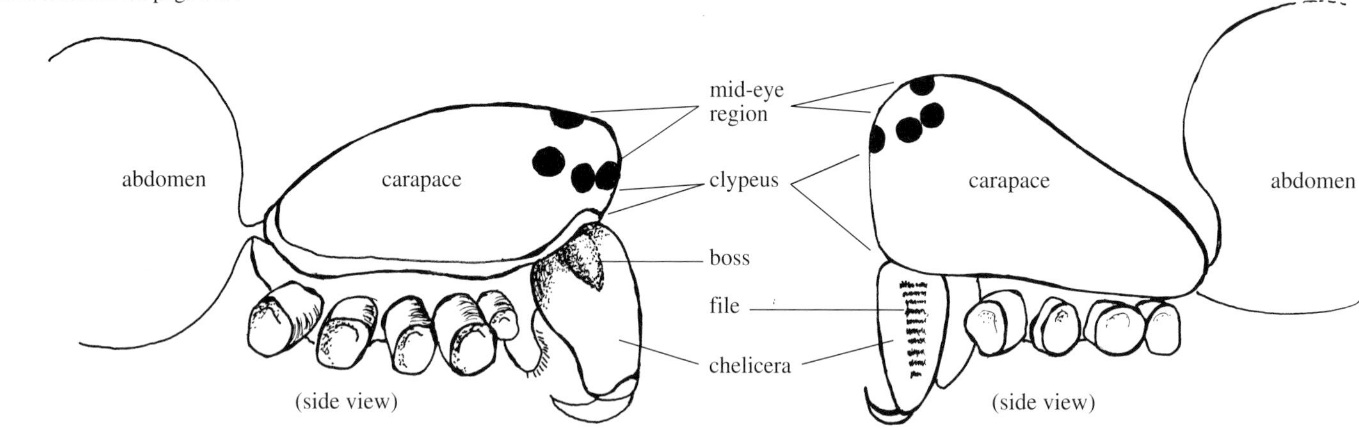

Fig.A. **SPIDER WITH A SHORT CLYPEUS AND A BOSS ON THE CHELICERAE**

Fig.B. **SPIDER WITH A LONG CLYPEUS AND A FILE ON THE CHELICERAE**

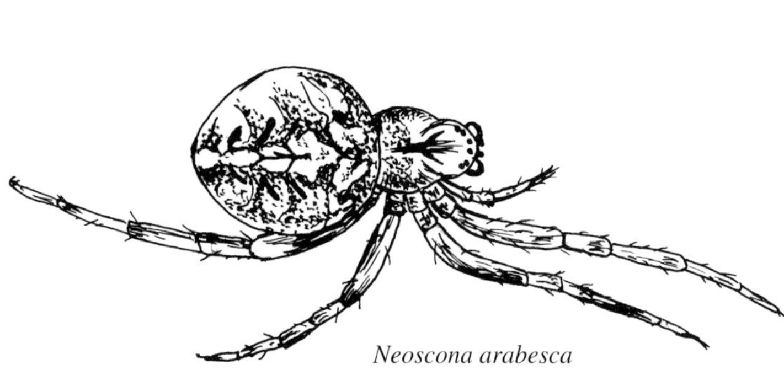

Fig.C. **FAMILY ARANEIDAE (=EPEIRIDAE), ORB-WEAVING SPIDERS[1]**: A number of species in this family are common in mid-Atlantic coastal regions on marsh grasses and on upper border shrubs, such as bayberry. *Eustala anastera* occurs throughout southern New England and is likely to occur along the shore. This species is gray, often with a scalloped triangle on the back of the abdomen. It grows up to 8 mm (5/16") long and builds a characteristic web (see page 9.08, Fig.B) among shrubs and bushes, often overhanging water.

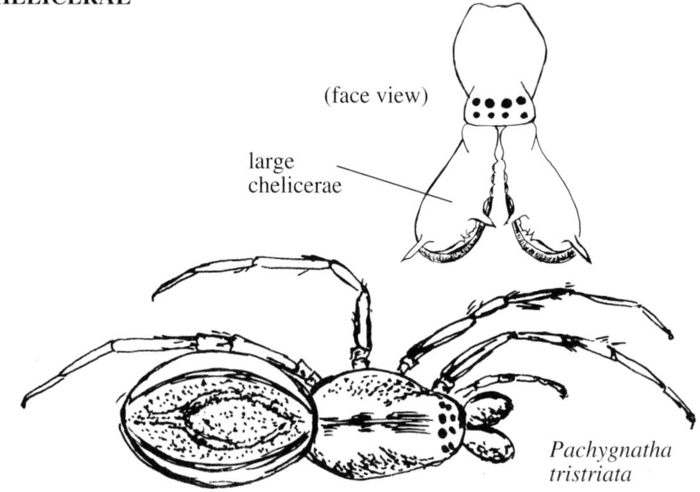

Fig.D. **FAMILY TETRAGNATHIDAE, THICK-JAWED SPIDERS[1]**: Several species in this family may occur along the shore. *Pachygnatha tristriata*, which has been found in saltmarshes, is yellowish brown with gray markings on the carapace. Its abdomen is silver and gray bordered with black. Maximum length of this species is 6.5 mm (1/4").

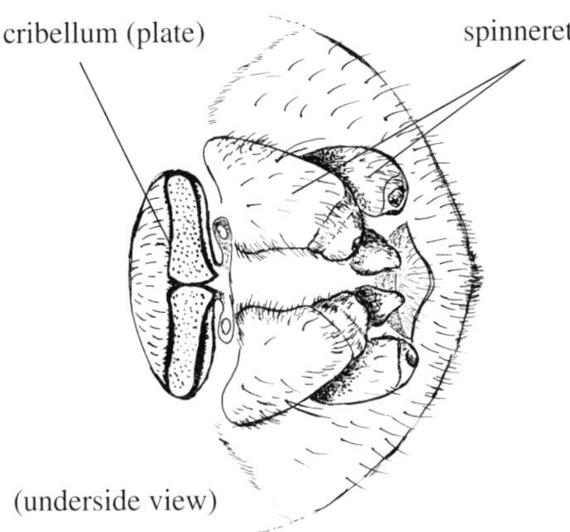

Fig.E. **ABDOMEN WITH CRIBELLUM**

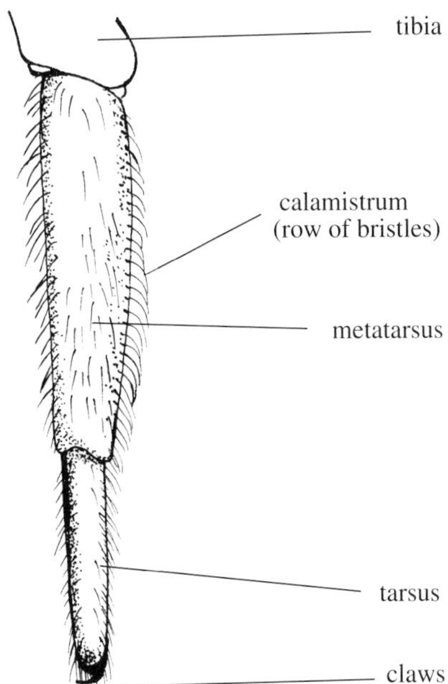

Fig.F. **FOURTH WALKING LEG WITH CALAMISTRUM**

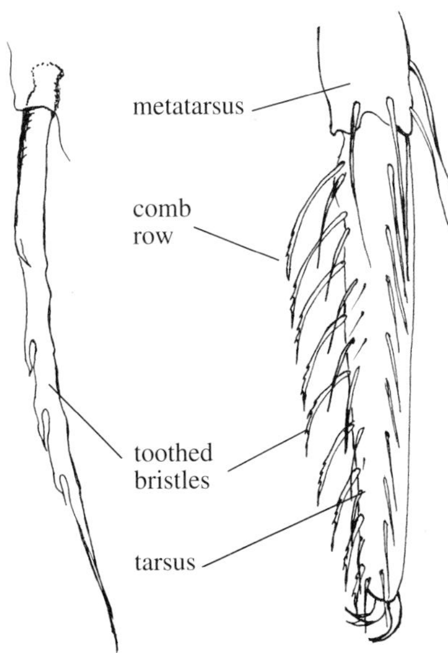

Fig.G. **FOURTH WALKING LEG WITH COMB ROW**

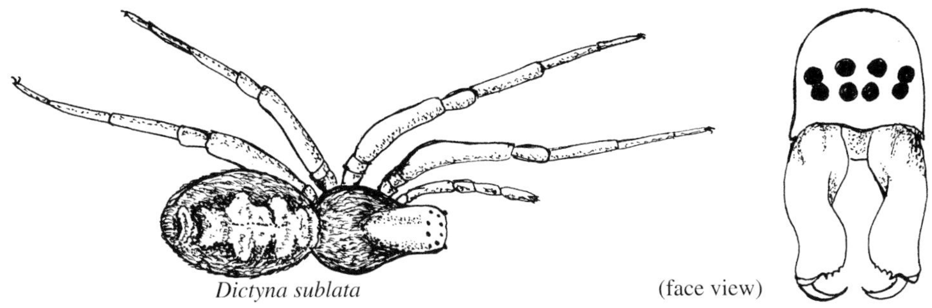

Fig.H. **FAMILY DICTYNIDAE, CRIBELLATE SPIDERS**[1]: *Dictyna sublata* and several other species in this family are extremely common throughout southern New England and are reported to occur in mid-Atlantic marine environments. *D. sublata* reaches a length of 3.7 mm (3/16"). Its cephalothorax (head-body region) is yellow in front and brown in back. Its abdomen (tail region) is brown with a broad yellow band running down the middle. It builds webs on the upper surface of large leaves in shrubs and vines.

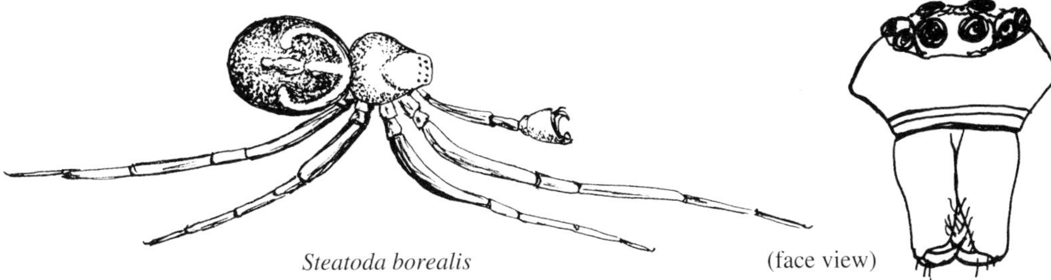

Fig.I. **FAMILY THERIDIIDAE, COMB-FOOTED SPIDERS**[1]: A number of species in this family occur throughout this region and are common in the shrubs along the upper border of marshes and the back dunes of the mid-Atlantic region. Most are less than 7 mm (1/4") in length. Web is shown on page 9.08, Fig.A.

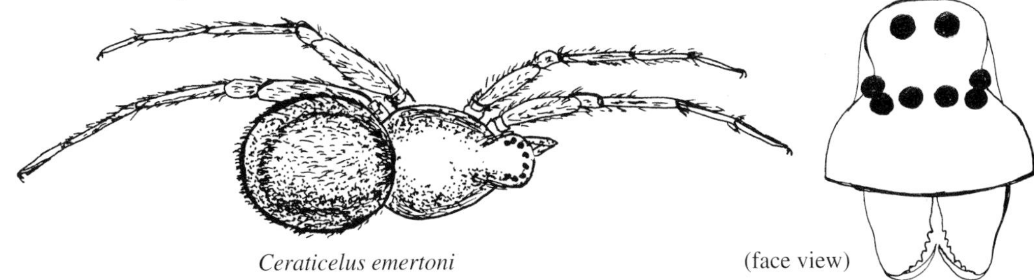

Fig.J. **FAMILY MICRYPHANTIDAE, DWARF SPIDERS**[1]: Perhaps the most common seashore spider family, a number of dwarf spider species live on tidal marshes, sandy beaches and other shoreline habitats and are often found under grass, litter, or stones; they are small spiders, generally under 3 mm (1/8") in length; the color of these spiders ranges from yellow-orange to reddish-brown. *Grammonota trivittata* is a dwarf spider that is found almost exclusively on saltmarshes, preferring the wetter regions, and is often collected under the moist grasses stranded at the high tide line. This species reaches 3 mm (1/8") in length, has a brown carapace, yellow legs, and a gray abdomen with two lighter broad longitudinal stripes. Another species, *Ceraticelus emertoni*, is common on saltmarshes as well as inland. This species reaches 1.5 mm (1/16") in length and is orange yellow with black around the eyes. Some species in this family have rows of parallel grooves, called a "file" (Fig.B), on the chelicerae. The file is rubbed with another part of the body to make a sound.

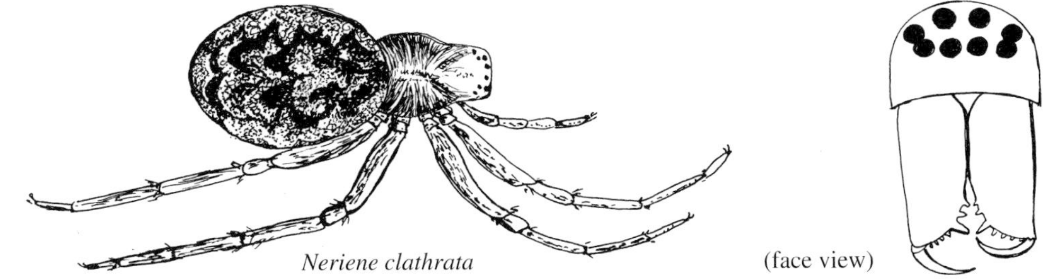

Fig.K. **FAMILY LINYPHIIDAE, SHEET-WEB WEAVERS**[1]: One species in this family, *Neriene clathrata*, occurs on saltmarshes. This species has a brown body with black markings and yellow to orange legs. It reaches 5.2 mm (3/16") in length. Other species are common in mid-Atlantic regions on upper marsh border and maritime upland shrubs, such as bayberry. Characteristic web is shown on page 9.08, Fig.C.

SPIDER WEBS: PHYLUM ARTHROPODA, SUBPHYLUM CHELICERATA, CLASS ARACHNIDA, ORDER ARANEAE

(Spider key begins on page 9.04)

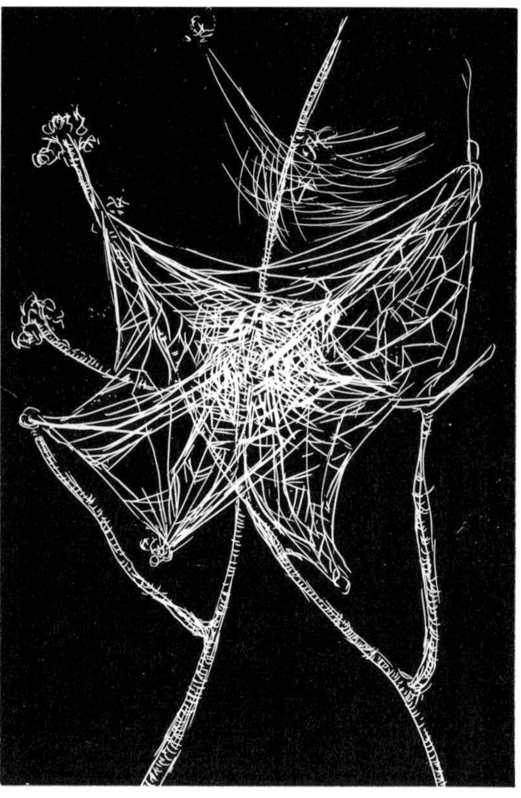

Fig.A. **FAMILY THERIDIIDAE, COMB-FOOTED SPIDER WEB:** This spider family is described on page 9.07.

Fig.B. **FAMILY ARANEIDAE (=EPEIRIDAE), ORB-WEAVING SPIDER WEB:** This spider family is described on page 9.06.

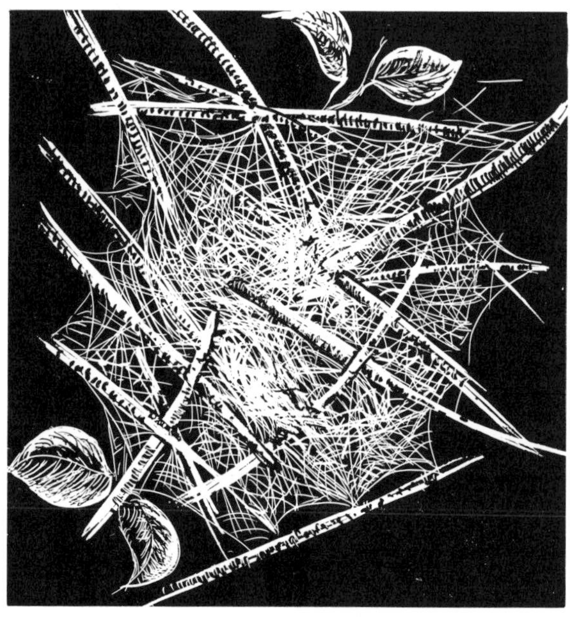

Fig.C. **FAMILY LINYPHIIDAE, SHEET-WEB WEAVERS WEB:** This spider family is described on page 9.07.

MITES AND TICKS: PHYLUM ARTHROPODA, SUBPHYLUM CHELICERATA, CLASS ARACHNIDA, ORDER ACARINA

Tiny arachnids with little or no distinction between body regions which are fused to form a single round or oval unit; adults have four pairs of legs but larvae may have only three pairs; mouth parts (chelicerae) are often needlelike for piercing and sucking and are attached to a projecting "snout" (gnathosoma)

(Use the key on page 2.14 to determine if you have a mite or tick)

#1. Usually found attached to mammals, including humans, who have been walking through grassy areas of marshes or dunes; external parasites that attach by embedding their mouth parts into the skin of the host .... **suborder Ixodides, ticks**[1] (Fig.A)

#1. Usually found free living; may be swimming in water or crawling on rocks, the surface of a marsh, or on grasses and seaweeds .... #2

#2. Primarily aquatic; usually found in water either free swimming or crawling on submerged vegetation and rocks .... **suborder Trombidiformes, family Halacaridae, marine water mites**[2] (Fig.B)

#2. Primarily terrestrial; usually found crawling on the surface of marshes, beaches or other shoreline areas and on seashore plants .... **suborder Trombidiformes, various families, trombidiid mites**[3] (Fig.C)

[1]Refer to Anderson and Magnarelli (1980) for a list of technical references used to determine the species of ticks. Refer to Baker et al. (1956) for detailed information on ticks and other parasitic mites.

[2]Refer to Newell (1947) for the identification, systematics, and ecology of the Halacaridae.

[3]Refer to Baker and Wharton (1952) for a review of mite and tick taxonomy, including keys to families.

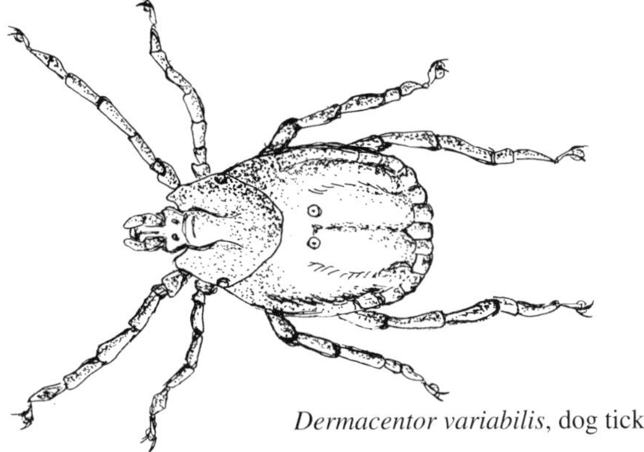

Dermacentor variabilis, dog tick

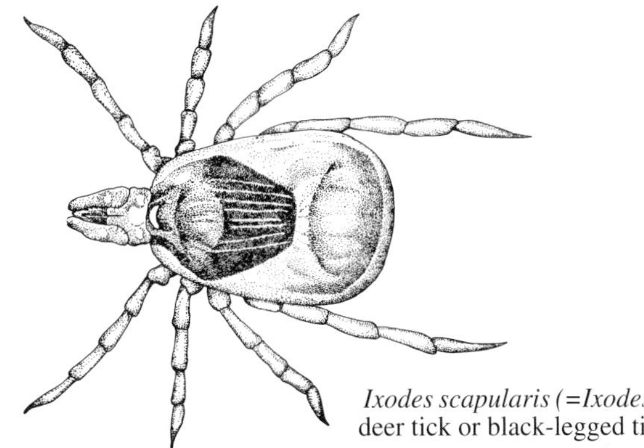

Ixodes scapularis (=Ixodes dammini), deer tick or black-legged tick

Fig.A. **SUBORDER IXODIDES, TICKS**[1]: Usually brown or black; average length about 4 mm (3/16"); quite common in shore areas with dense vegetation such as marshes, dunes, uplands. Give yourself a thorough examination, "tick check," after walking in these areas. Over fifteen species of ticks occur in this region but only the two species described below are encountered frequently on humans (Anderson and Magnarelli, 1980). The American dog tick, *Dermacentor variabilis*, is a serious pest and frequently parasitizes wild and domestic mammals of all sizes including humans. This tick is a vector of Rocky Mountain spotted fever. *Ixodes scapularis (=Ixodes dammini)*, the deer tick or black-legged tick, infests many different wild and domestic mammals including white-tailed deer and humans. This tick transmits a spirochaete causing Lyme disease (Burgdorfer et al.,1982; Magnarelli et al.,1984). Lyme disease, which occurs throughout the northeast, derives its name from Lyme, Connecticut where the disease was first recognized. After the tick bites, a circular lesion may develop followed by arthritic, nervous, and heart disorders. Most tick bites, including bites from the ticks described above, do not result in any illness and should not be cause for undue alarm. However, a physician should be consulted immediately if a tick bite produces any unusual symptoms.

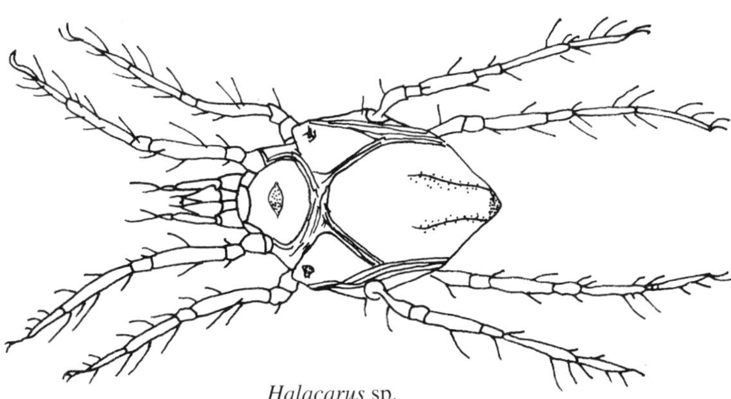

Halacarus sp.

Fig.B. **SUBORDER TROMBIDIFORMES**[2]**, FAMILY HALACARIDAE, MARINE WATER MITES:** Usually dark in color; generally less than 2 mm (1/16") in length; numerous species occur from the intertidal zone to offshore, often found crawling on seaweeds, rocks, hydroids, and eelgrass; several species are symbiotic, associated with mussels, chitons, and nemertean worms.

Fig.C. **SUBORDER TROMBIDIFORMES**[3]**, VARIOUS FAMILIES, TROMBIDIID MITES:** Most species are very tiny, less than 3 mm (1/8") in length and some are microscopic; many species are bright red; frequently found crawling on the surface of saltmarshes and on marsh grasses.

ADULT INSECTS
PHYLUM ARTHROPODA, CLASS INSECTA

Air breathing, primarily terrestrial arthropods usually with 1 pair of antennae and 3 pairs of legs. Wings often present but may be absent.

(Use the key on page 2.14 to determine if you have an insect)

#1.With well developed wings (wings may be folded tightly against body such as in bugs and beetles) .... #2

#1.Wings absent, or small and inconspicuous .... **wingless insects**, page 9.14

#2.With one pair of wings (Fig.C) .... **order Diptera, true flies**, page 9.22

#2.With two pairs of wings (Figs.E-H on this page and Figs. A-G on pages 9.12-9.13); hind pair often often folded underneath front pair .... #3

#3.Front (outer) wings thicker than hind wings (Figs.E-H, this page); front wings are leathery, hard, or parchmentlike at least near the base; front wings may serve as "wing covers" (elytra) and may be folded over the thin, membranous hind wings .... #4

#3.Front and hind wings are alike in texture (pages 9.12-9.13, Figs.A-G); both pairs of wings are usually thin, transparent, and membranous but may be thicker, covered with hairs or scales .... page 9.12

#4.Front (outer) wings are stiff and relatively hard (chitinous or hornlike) and meet in a straight line down the back (Fig.E); front wings without veins but may have parallel grooves .... **order Coleoptera, beetles**, page 9.19

#4.Front wings are leathery and/or membranous, not hard; wings at rest overlap or are held tentlike or rooflike over body (Figs.F-H); all or part of front wings with veins .... #5

#5.Rear legs usually very large and powerful (Fig.F), often used for hopping; mouthparts used for chewing (with sideways moving mandibles, "jaws", see Fig.D); entire front wings are leathery with veins .... **order Orthoptera, grasshoppers, crickets, and mantids**, page 9.15

#5.Rear legs not particularly powerful (Figs.G,H); mouthparts used for sucking (with an elongate segmented beak forming a sucking tube, see Figs.G,H) ...... #6

#6.Front (outer) wings are leathery at their base and are thinner, membranous, and overlapping at their tips (Fig.G); beak (sucking tube) arises from front of head and extends backward under head (Fig.G) .... **order Hemiptera, true bugs**, page 9.16

#6.Front wings are same texture over entire length; wings at rest do not usually overlap and are often held tentlike or rooflike over body (Fig.H); beak arises from rear of underside of head, often appearing to arise between base of front legs (Fig.H) .... **order Homoptera (in part), hoppers and aphids**, page 9.18

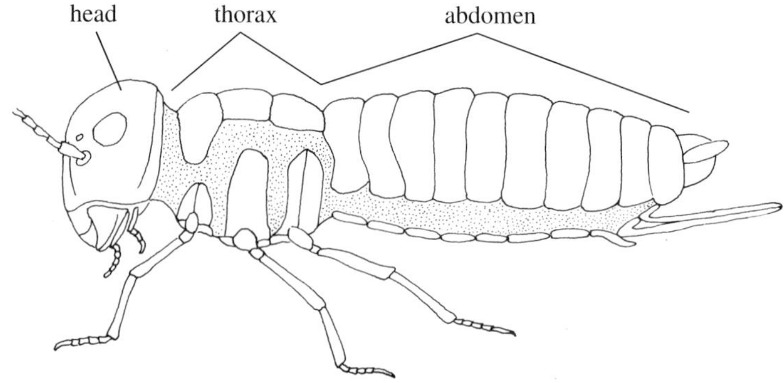

Fig.A. **TYPICAL INSECT BODY REGIONS**

tibia

tarsus

femur

tarsal claw

trochanter

coxa

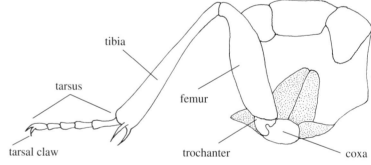

Fig.B. **TYPICAL INSECT LEG REGIONS**

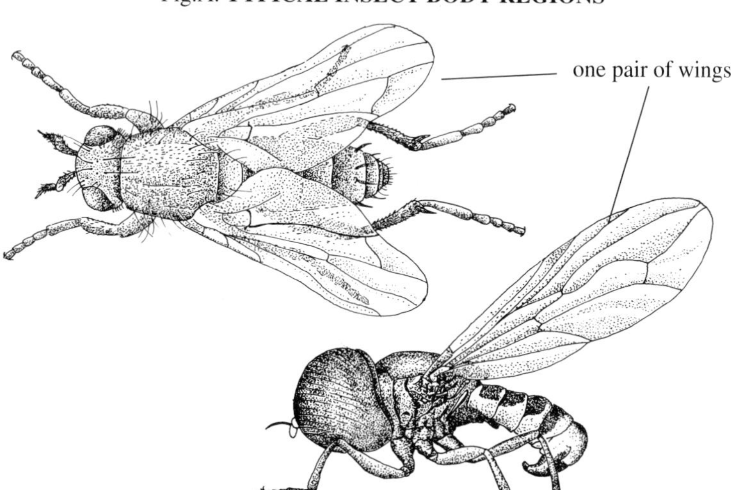

Fig.C. **ORDER DIPTERA, TRUE FLIES:** Go to page 9.22.

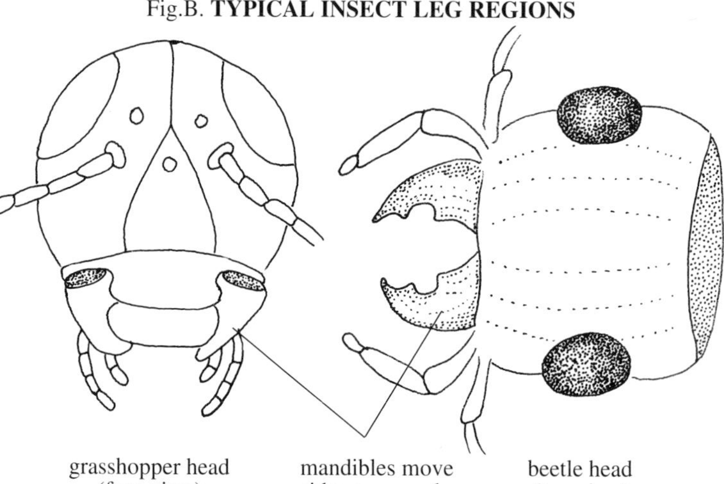

Fig.D. **INSECTS WITH MANDIBLES**

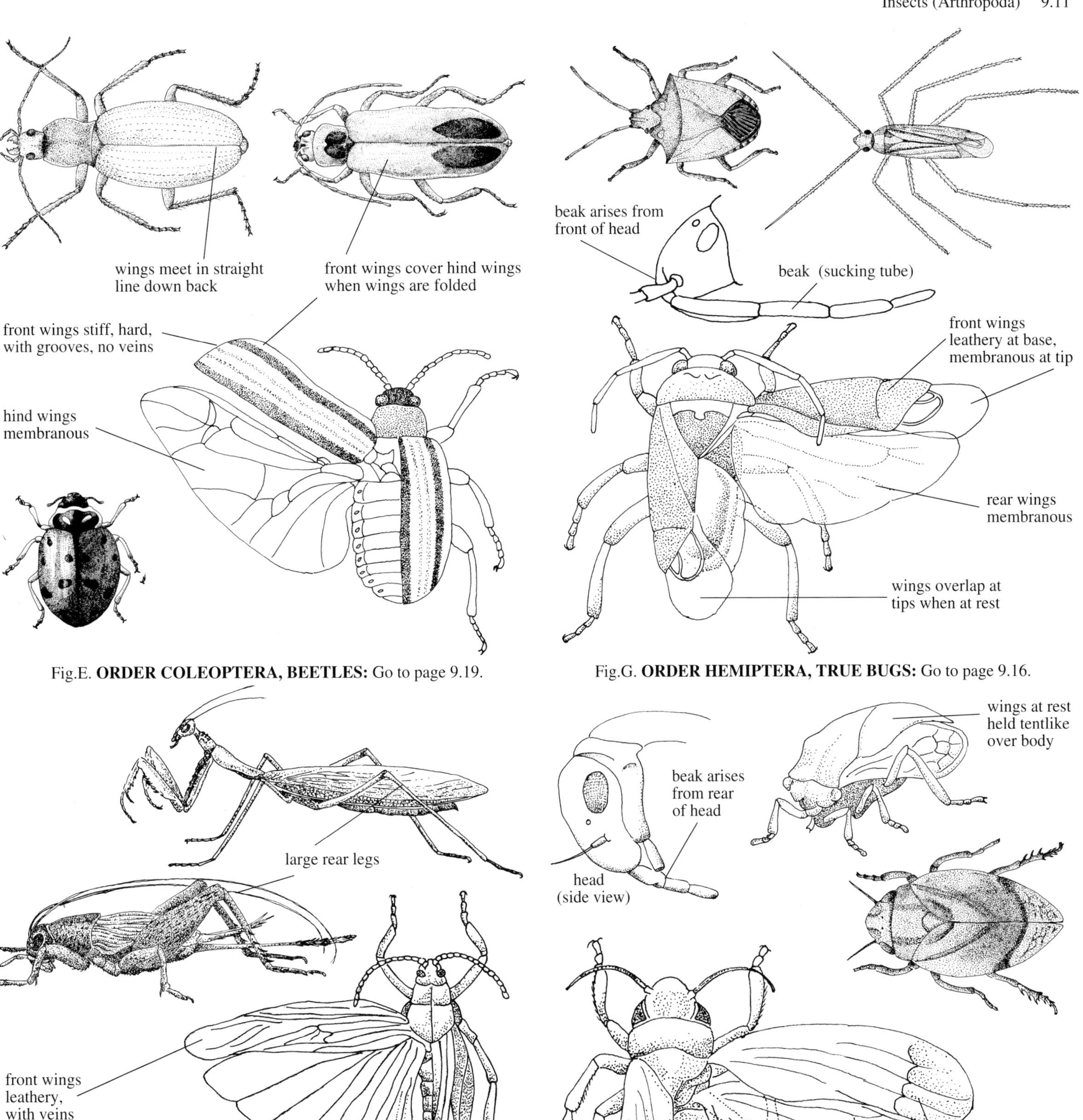

Fig.E. **ORDER COLEOPTERA, BEETLES:** Go to page 9.19.

Fig.G. **ORDER HEMIPTERA, TRUE BUGS:** Go to page 9.16.

Fig.F. **ORDER ORTHOPTERA, GRASSHOPPERS, CRICKETS AND MANTIDS:** Go to page 9.15.

Fig.H. **ORDER HOMOPTERA, HOPPERS AND APHIDS:** page 9.18

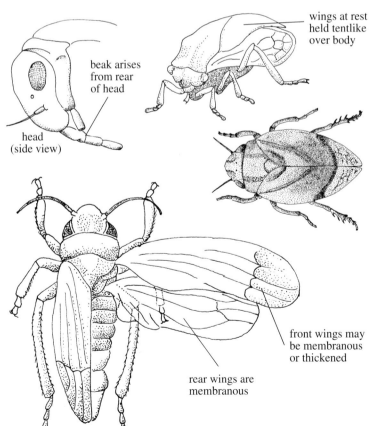

ADULT INSECTS WITH TWO PAIRS OF SIMILAR WINGS PHYLUM ARTHROPODA, CLASS INSECTA

Insects with two pairs of wings; both the front and rear pairs of wings are alike in texture, usually thin and membranous but may be covered with hairs or scales

(Insect key begins on page 9.10)

#1. Wings covered with scales; mouthparts form a coiled sucking tube (Fig.A) .... **order Lepidoptera, butterflies, moths, and skippers** (Fig.A)
#1. Wings not covered with scales, mouthparts not coiled (Figs.B-G) .... #2

#2. Wings narrow, with few veins, and with a fringe of long hairs around the edges (Fig.B); very small and slender insects, less than 1 cm (3/8") long, most species under 2 mm (1/8") long .... **order Thysanoptera, thrips** (Fig.B)
#2. Wings without a fringe of long hairs (Figs.C-G) .... #3

#3. Wings completely covered by dense hairs (Fig.C); wings often held rooflike over body; antennae very long and threadlike, sometimes longer than body; slender, elongate, mothlike insects .... **order Trichoptera, caddisflies** (Fig.C)
#3. Wings not covered with dense hairs; wings usually membranous (Figs.D-G) .... #4

#4. Mouthparts form an elongate, segmented beak (Fig.D) used as a sucking tube; beak (sucking tube) arises from rear of underside of head, often appearing to arise between base of front legs; wings, when at rest, are usually held tentlike or rooflike over body, sloping down and outward from center (Fig.D) .... **order Homoptera (in part), hoppers and aphids**, page 9.18
#4. Mouthparts used for chewing, with mandibles ("jaws"); wings may or may not be held rooflike over body (Figs.E-G) .... #5

#5. Front wings longer and larger than rear wings (Fig.E) (hind and front wings may be hooked together and may look like one wing); wings with relatively few cross veins; body length rarely over 3.5 cm (1 1/2"); with obvious antennae (Fig.E) .... **order Hymenoptera, bees, wasps, ants, and related insects**, page 9.28
#5. Front and rear wings nearly the same length and area (Figs.F,G); wings with numerous cross veins; with long, slender bodies, often over 3.5 cm (1 1/2") in length, and with long wings; may or may not have obvious antennae .... #6

#6. Antennae short and inconspicuous (Fig.F); wings at rest held out to sides or held together above body... **order Odonata, dragonflies and damselflies** (Fig.F)
#6. Antennae long and segmented (Fig.G); wings at rest usually folded rooflike over body .... **order Neuroptera, lacewings, fishflies and others** (Fig.G)

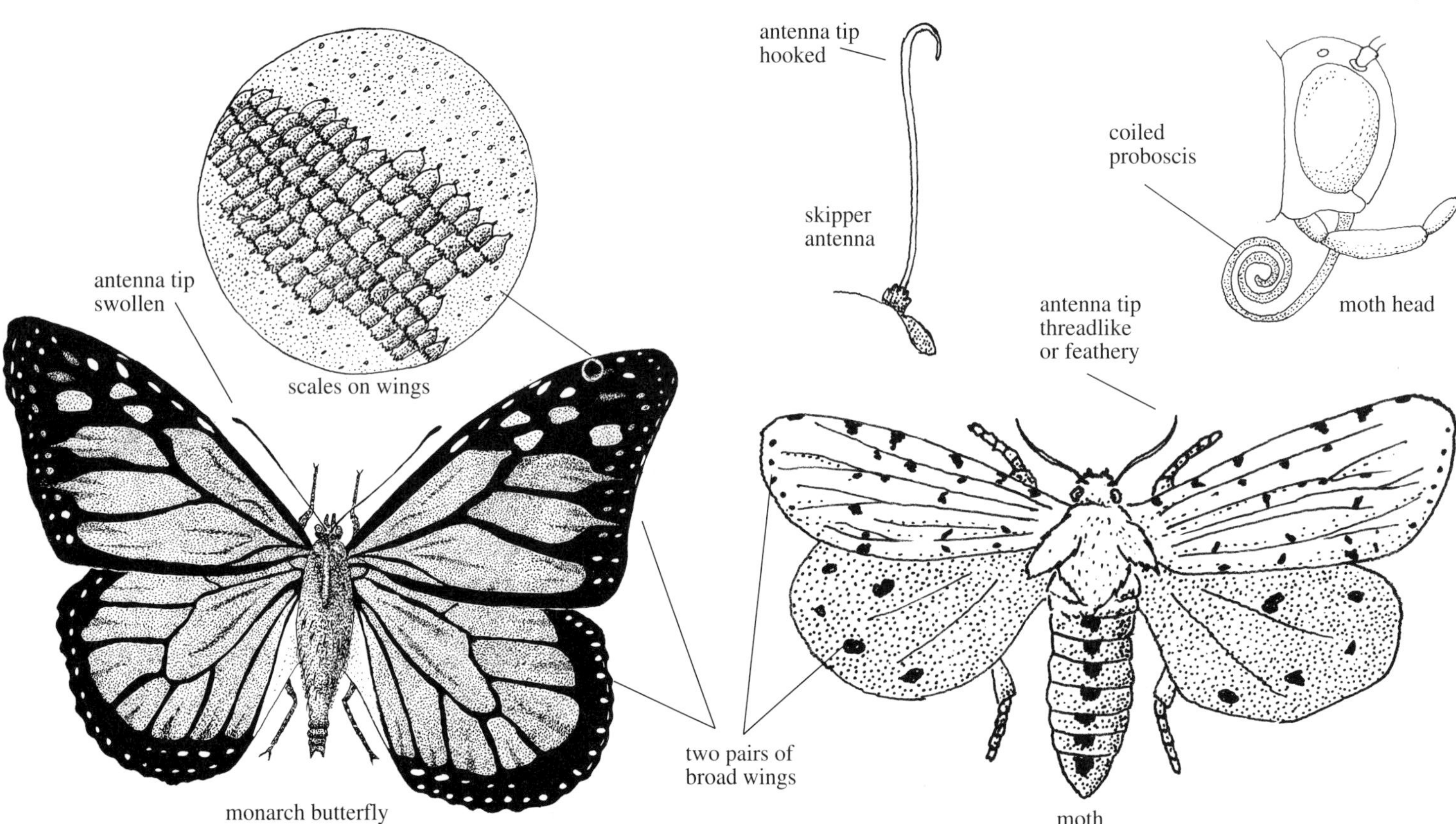

Fig.A. **ORDER LEPIDOPTERA, BUTTERFLIES, MOTHS, AND SKIPPERS:** Many species are very colorful with distinctive markings on wings; large insects, reaching over 4 cm (1.5") in length; a number of species can be found on tidal marshes, beaches, and other seashore environments. For example, the monarch butterfly, *Danaus plexippus*, shown here, is often observed along shore and over open water during its migration south in the fall. The antennae of butterflies are clubbed or swollen at their tip but are not hooked. Moths have feathery or threadlike antennae that are not swollen at the tip. The antennae of skippers are swollen and hooked at the tip. Most lepidopterans can be easily identified to species by comparing their wing patterns with illustrations in books such as Covell (1984), Ehrlich and Ehrlich (1961), Holland (1968), or Klots (1951). Caterpillars, the larvae of lepidopterans, are also common on saltmarshes (see page 9.30). **17.11 A**

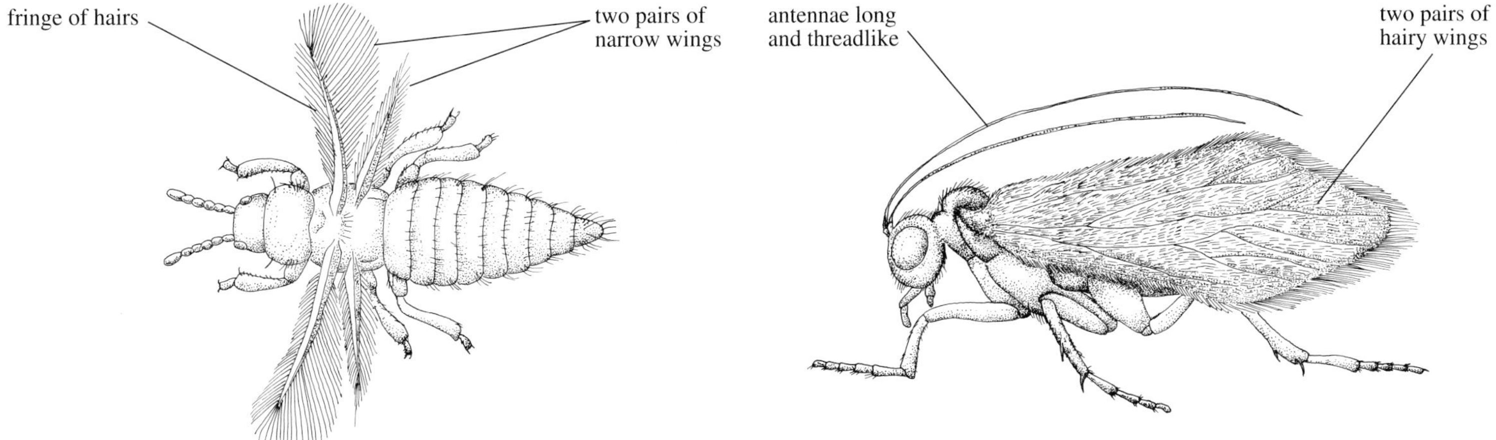

Fig.B. **ORDER THYSANOPTERA, THRIPS:** Often black but may be lighter color; most species tiny, under 2 mm (1/8") long; *Anaphothrips* sp. and *Thysanoptera* sp. occur on saltmarshes.

Fig.C. **ORDER TRICHOPTERA, CADDISFLIES:** Usually dull colored; up to 25 mm (1") long; common around freshwater environments but may occur in brackish waters; pupae (page 9.31) and larvae (page 9.32) are aquatic.

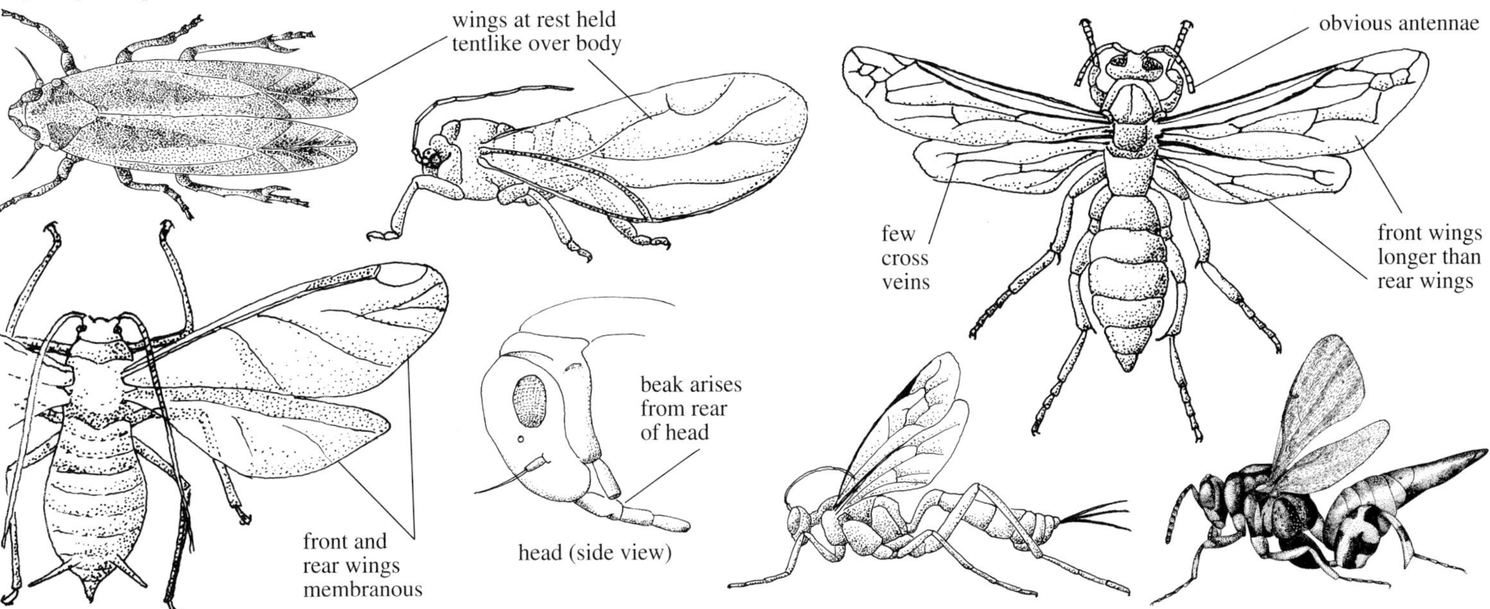

Fig.D. **ORDER HOMOPTERA, HOPPERS AND APHIDS**

Fig.E. **ORDER HYMENOPTERA, BEES, WASPS, ANTS, ETC.**

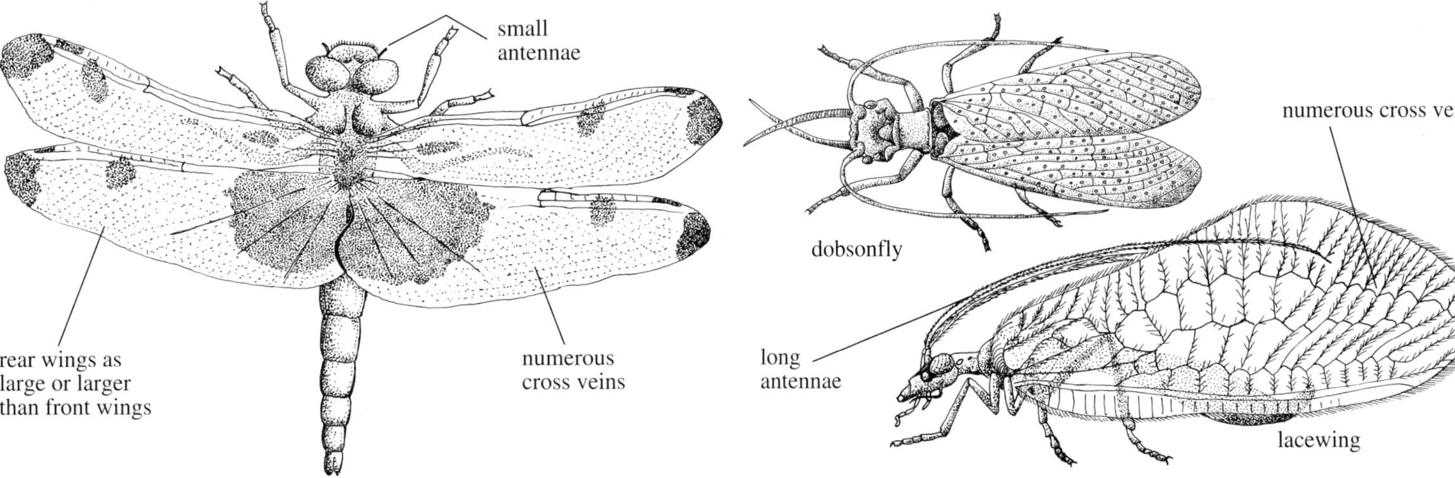

Fig.F. **ORDER ODONATA, DRAGONFLIES AND DAMSELFLIES:** Body may be black, gray, blue, green, and often metallic or colorful with spots or bands on silvery wings; many species reach over 6 cm in length (2.5"); common skimmers (shown here), dragonflies in the family Libellulidae, occasionally occur on tidal marshes.

Fig.G. **ORDER NEUROPTERA, LACEWINGS, FISHFLIES, AND RELATED INSECTS:** May be black or gray, sometimes greenish or brownish; some species reach over 2.5 cm (1") long; dobsonflies, shown here, are aquatic with larvae living under stones in streams; lacewings, also shown here, are found in grassy areas.

WINGLESS INSECTS
PHYLUM ARTHROPODA, CLASS INSECTA
Seashore arthropods with 1 pair of antennae and 3 pairs of legs

(Use the key on page 2.14 to determine if you have a wingless insect)

#1. With a pair of large pincers (Fig.A) at rear end of abdomen .... ***Anisolabis maritima*, seaside earwig** (Fig.A)
#1. Without pincers at tail end (Figs.B-E) .... #2

#2. With a slender "waist," a stalklike constriction between thorax and abdomen (Fig.B); antennae with an elbowlike bend (Fig.B) .... **order Hymenoptera, family Formicidae, ants**, page 9.28
#2. Without a narrow waist; antennae usually not elbowed (C-E) .... #3

#3. Tiny, soft bodied insects, less than 6 mm (1/4") in length .... #4
#3. Longer than 6 mm (1/4"), usually hard bodied insects .... #6

#4. With a pair of short tubes (cornicles) extending from abdomen (Fig.C); tiny, plump, somewhat pear shaped insects; mouthparts form a segmented beak (see Fig.D on page 9.13) .... **order Homoptera, family Aphididae, aphids**, page 9.18
#4. Without a pair of tubes extending from abdomen; mouthparts not distinctly segmented .... #5

#5. Abdomen with six segments (Fig.D); mouthparts indistinct; often found in large numbers under rocks in the intertidal zone and floating on surface of water in tidepools; light blue or blue-black color .... ***Anurida maritima*, seashore springtail** (Fig.D)
#5. Abdomen with more than 6 segments .... **other insect orders**[1]

#6. With 2 or 3 long, jointed threadlike tails (Fig.E) and long antennae with many segments .... ***Machilis maritima*, seashore bristletail** (Fig.E)
#6. Without long tails .... #7

#7. Mouthparts form a segmented beak used as a sucking tube (see Fig.G on page 9.11) .... **order Hemiptera, true bugs**, page 9.16
#7. Mouthparts used for chewing, with mandibles ("jaws") (see Fig.D on page 9.10) .... **order Coleoptera, beetles**, page 9.19

[1]Refer to an insect identification guide such as Arnett (1985), Borror and White (1970), or Jaques (1947).

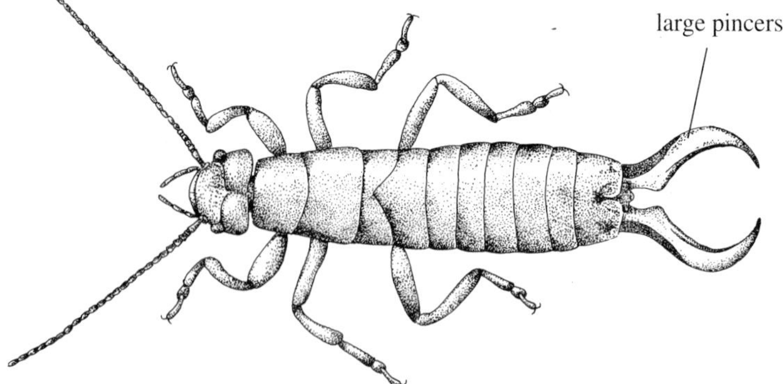

Fig.A. ***ANISOLABIS MARITIMA*, SEASIDE EARWIG:** Brownish black; up to 20 mm (3/4") long; common along shore. This species can be distinguished from other earwigs (insects in the order Dermaptera) by its larger size, lack of wings, and antennae having 24 segments.

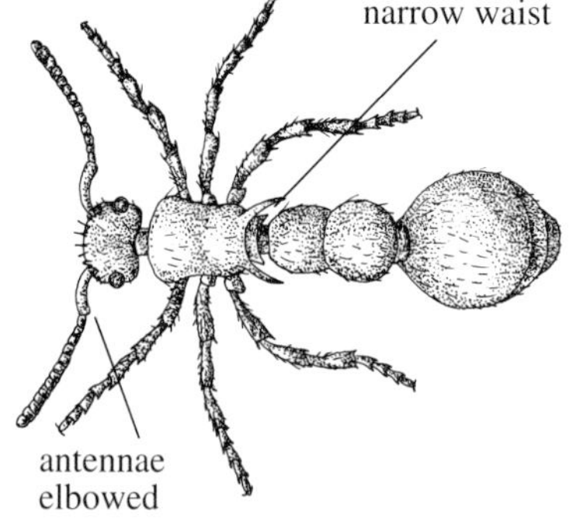

Fig.B. **ANT, ORDER HYMENOPTERA, FAMILY FORMICIDAE:** Go to page 9.28.

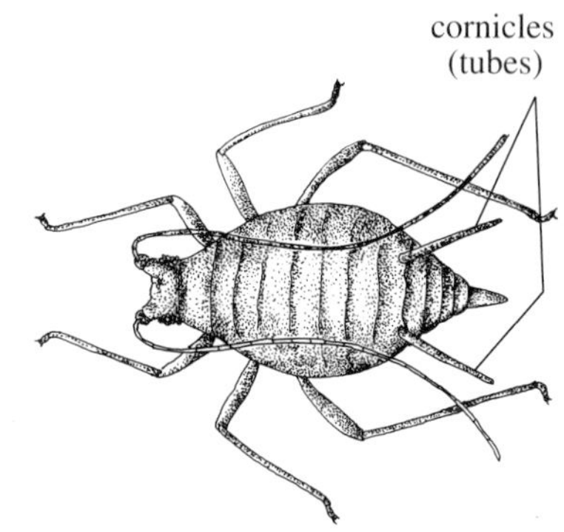

Fig.C. **APHID, ORDER HOMOPTERA, FAMILY APHIDIDAE:** Go to page 9.18.

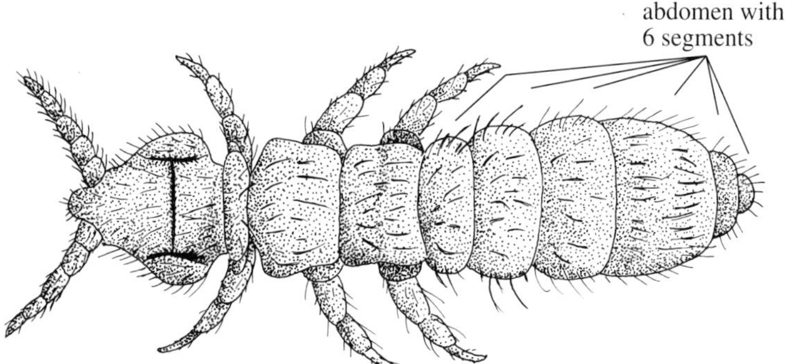

Fig.D. ***ANURIDA MARITIMA*, SEASHORE SPRINGTAIL:** Light blue or blue-black; small, up to about 3 mm (1/8") long; very common in tidepools and under rocks in the intertidal zone; often found in large numbers floating or walking on the surface of the water. This is the only species of springtail (insects in the order Collembola) common in the marine environment. **17.11 B**

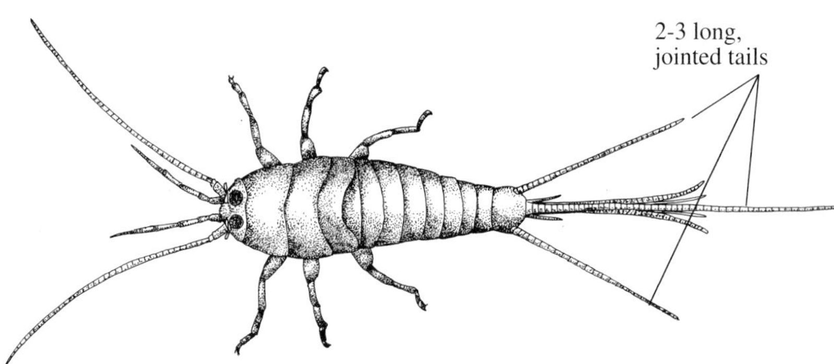

Fig.E. ***MACHILIS MARITIMA*, SEASHORE BRISTLETAIL:** Up to about 12 mm (1/2") in length; occurs around intertidal rocks; belongs to the insect order Thysanura.

GRASSHOPPERS, CRICKETS, AND MANTIDS
CLASS INSECTA, ORDER ORTHOPTERA

Insects with two pairs of wings (or wingless); the front (outer) wings are leathery with veins; mouthparts used for chewing (with mandibles that move sideways); rear legs are large

(Use the key on page 9.10 to determine if you have an orthopteran)

#1. Front legs large and powerful, armed with spines; front legs often folded in "praying" position, forming claws used for catching insects; middle and rear legs slender, used for walking; prothorax (Fig.A) very long; tarsi[1] with 5 segments .... **family Mantidae, mantids** (Fig.A)

#1. Front legs slender, without claws (Figs. B-C); rear legs enlarged, used for jumping; tarsi[1] with 4 or fewer segments .... #2

#2. Antennae long, usually as long as body or longer; females with elongate ovipositor[2] (Figs.B,C) .... #3

#2. Antennae short, less than half the body length; females with short ovipositor .... **other grasshoppers and crickets**[3]

#3. Tarsi[1] of middle legs, and usually all legs, with 4 segments; ocelli (simple eyes) as well as compound eyes usually present; females with sword shaped ovipositor[2] (Fig.B) .... **family Tettigoniidae, long-horned grasshoppers** (Fig.B)

#3. Tarsi[1] of all legs with 3 segments; ocelli may be present or absent; females with cylindrical or needle shaped ovipositor[2] (Fig.C); body somewhat flattened, wider than deep .... **family Gryllidae, crickets** (Fig.C)

[1]Refer to Fig.B on page 9.10 for the names of the regions of an insect leg. The tarsus (tarsi = plural) is the outermost region.

[2]Both males and females have a pair of cerci, appendages at the end of the abdomen (see Figs.B,C). The cerci of the grasshoppers are short. Cricket cerci are long and feelerlike. Ovipositors, which are used for laying eggs, occur only on the females.

[3]Refer to an insect identification guide such as Arnett (1985), Borror and White (1970), or Jaques (1947).

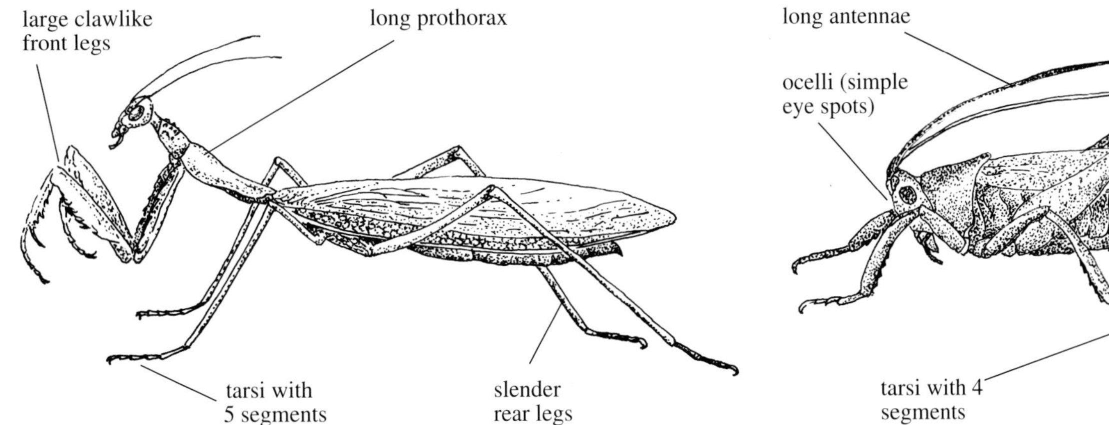

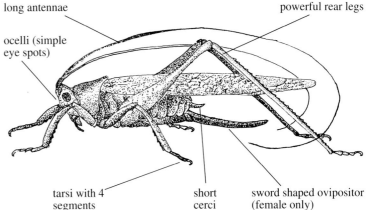

Fig.A. **FAMILY MANTIDAE, MANTIDS:** Pale green or brown; large insects; occasionally found on marsh grasses. The two common praying mantis species in southern New England, *Mantis religiosa* and *Tenodera aridifolia sinensis* are not native to this region. The former, introduced from Europe, reaches about 5 cm (2") long, and the latter, from China, grows up to 10 cm (4") in length.

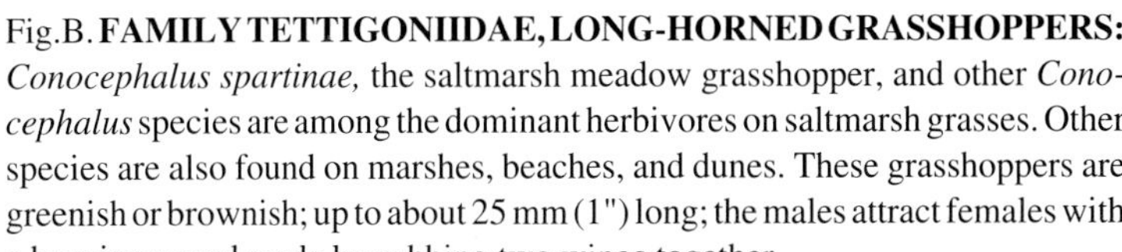

Fig.B. **FAMILY TETTIGONIIDAE, LONG-HORNED GRASSHOPPERS:** *Conocephalus spartinae,* the saltmarsh meadow grasshopper, and other *Conocephalus* species are among the dominant herbivores on saltmarsh grasses. Other species are also found on marshes, beaches, and dunes. These grasshoppers are greenish or brownish; up to about 25 mm (1") long; the males attract females with a buzzing sound made by rubbing two wings together.

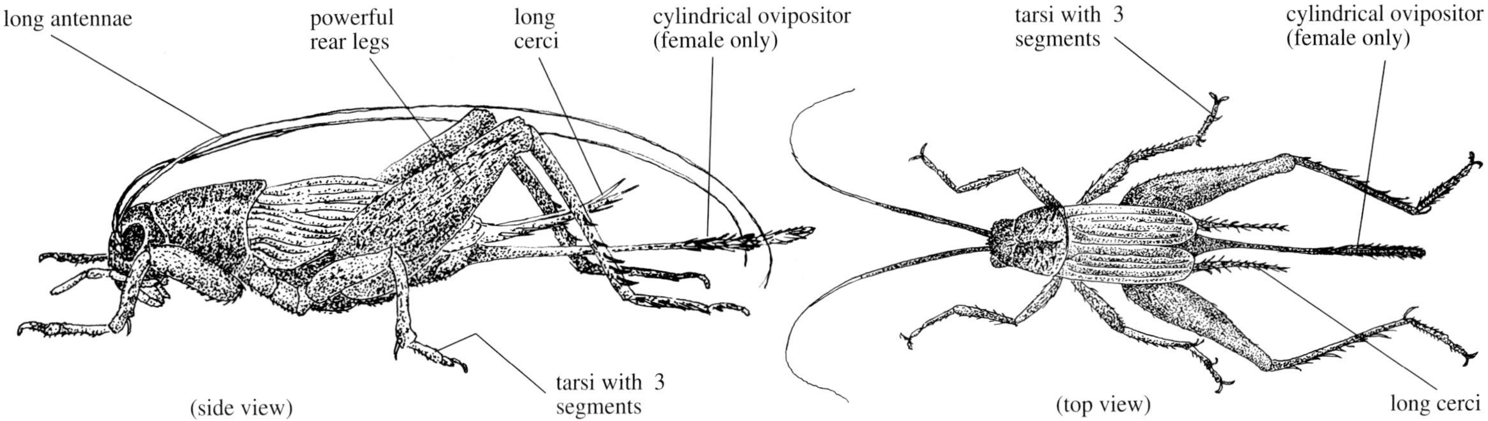

Fig.C. **FAMILY GRYLLIDAE, CRICKETS:** *Nemobius* sp., the ground cricket (shown here) is brown or black; up to 12 mm (1/2") in length; often found under the ground cover near the base of saltmarsh plants on which it grazes.

TRUE BUGS: CLASS INSECTA, ORDER HEMIPTERA

Insects with two pairs of wings (or wingless) with front (outer) wings that are leathery at their base and thinner, membranous, and overlapping at their tips; mouthparts form an elongate segmented beak or sucking tube that arises from front of head and extends backward under head

(Use the key on page 9.10 to determine if you have a true bug)

#1.Antennae are very short and are hidden in grooves on underside of head; rear legs may be elongate and flattened, used as oars for swimming (Fig.A) ....#2
#1.Antennae are longer than head and are visible from above (Figs.B-H); rear legs usually not flattened ....#3

#2.Back is crossed by many dark lines; front tarsi[1] short, composed of one scoop shaped segment ....**family Corixidae, water boatmen** (Fig.A)
#2.Back is not crossed by numerous dark lines; front tarsi not as described above ....**other bug families**[2]

#3.Antennae with 5 segments; overall shape of body is usually shieldlike or oval with rather broad shoulders (Figs.B,C) ....#4
#3.Antennae with 4 or fewer segments (Figs.D-H); body may or may not be shieldlike or oval shaped ....#7

#4.Scutellum (Fig.B), a large oval plate, extends to rear end of abdomen, covering most of wings ....**family Scutelleridae, shield-backed bugs** (Fig.B)
#4.Scutellum (Figs.C-H) does not extend to rear of abdomen, leaves most of wings exposed ....#5

#5.Scutellum (Fig.C) is large and triangular, nearly half the length of the abdomen ....#6
#5.Scutellum (Figs.D-H) is small, much less than half the length of the abdomen ....#7

#6.Tibiae[1] with weak or no spines, may have hairs; shoulders may be rounded or pointed ....**family Pentatomidae, stink bugs** (Fig.C)
#6.Tibiae[1] with one or more rows of stout spines; shoulders are rounded ....**other bug families**[2]

#7.Bugs which walk on surface film of water or on plants in the water; often wingless or with small wings, but may have full sized wings; body and legs are long and slender (Figs.D,E) ....#8
#7.Bugs which do not walk on water surface or on plants in the water; with wings; body and legs not especially long or slender (Figs.F-H) ....#10

#8.Head longer than thorax; usually creep or walk slowly on water surface ....**family Hydrometridae, water measurers** (Fig.D)
#8.Head shorter than thorax (Fig.E); may run, skate or walk across surface of water ....#9

#9.Base of middle legs closer to rear legs than to front legs; front claws (Fig.E) are attached to sides of last tarsal segment instead of the tip ....**family Gerridae, water striders** (Fig.E)
#9.Base of middle legs about equally spaced between front and rear legs; front claws may be attached to tip of leg or to sides ....**other bug families**[2]

#10.With a cuneus (a distinctly separate and somewhat triangular shaped section at the outer end of the thickened portion of the front wing, see Fig. F)........#11
#10.Without a cuneus (Fig.H) ....#12

#11.Without ocelli (simple eyespots), only compound eyes are present; beak with 4 segments ....**family Miridae, plant bugs** (Fig.F)
#11.With ocelli (simple eye spots, see Figs. G-H) and compound eyes; beak with 3 segments ....**other bug families**[2]

#12.Beak with 3 segments (Fig.G) ....#13
#12.Beak with 4 segments ....**other bug families**[2]

#13.Head is longer than wide, often pointed in front and with a distinct neck; beak usually curves under body, fitting into a distinct groove on underside of first thoracic segment (prosternum) ....**family Reduviidae, assassin bugs** (Fig.G)
#13.Head is wider than long and is not usually pointed; without a neck; no groove on prosternum; membranous portion of front wings with 4-5 long, closed cells ....**family Saldidae, shore bugs** (Fig.H)

[1]Refer to Fig.B on page 9.10 for the names of the regions of an insect leg. The tarsus (tarsi = plural) is the outermost region and the tibia (tibiae = plural) is next.
[2]Refer to an insect identification guide such as Arnett (1985), Slater and Baranowski (1978), Borror and White (1970), or Jaques (1947).

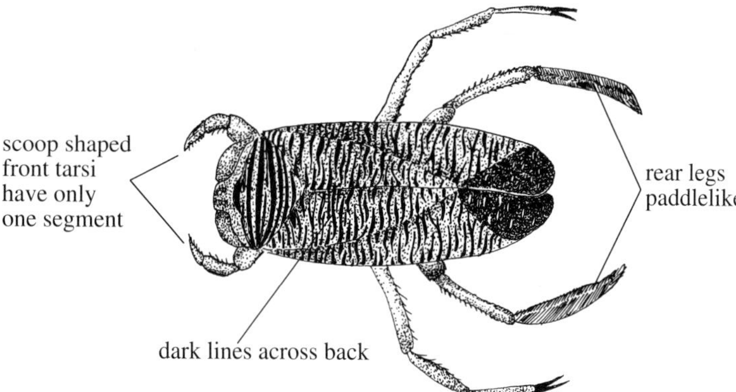

Fig.A. **FAMILY CORIXIDAE, WATER BOATMEN:** Usually gray or black with narrow, dark lines across back; up to about 12 mm (1/2") long; occasionally found in saltmarshes and in brackish water pools above the high tide level; swim with a quick darting motion using rear legs as paddles; often cling to submerged plants and other objects; when underwater, they respire using the oxygen in a coating of air which envelops their body.

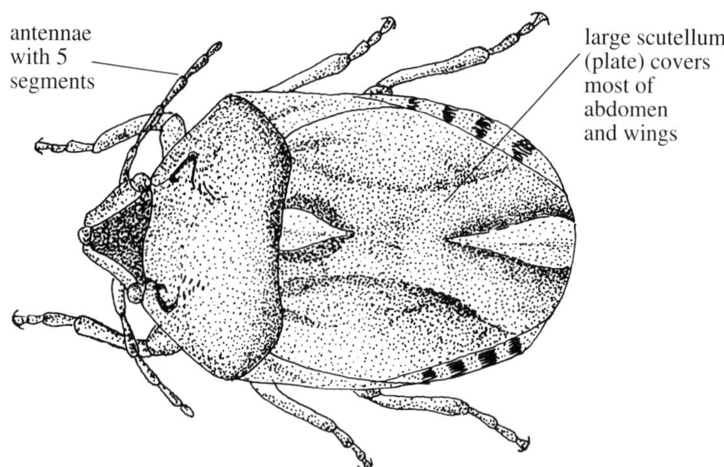

Fig.B. **FAMILY SCUTELLERIDAE, SHIELD-BACKED BUGS:** Usually brownish; up to about 10 mm (3/8") long; occurs in saltmarshes.

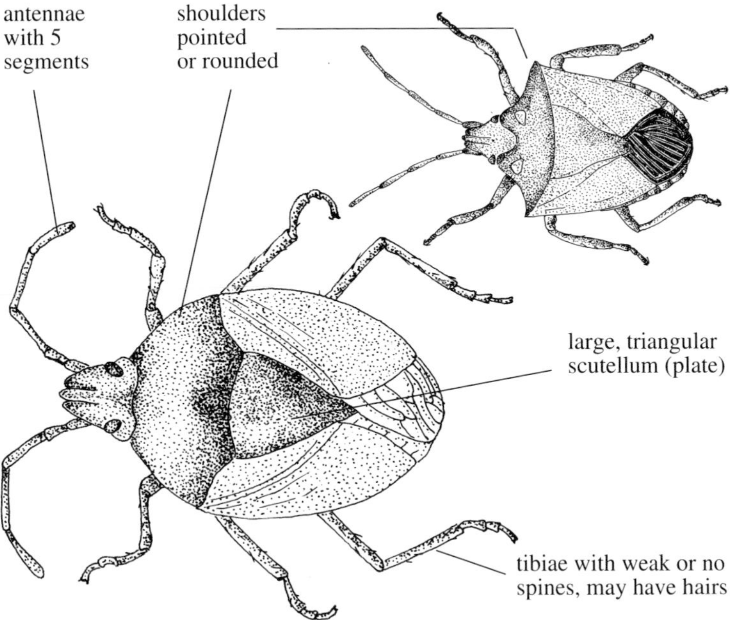

Fig.C. **FAMILY PENTATOMIDAE, STINK BUGS:** *Rhytidolomia saucia* is dark olive-green; about 10 mm (3/8") long; and occurs on saltmarsh grasses and upland border shrubs. Other stink bug species are brightly colored or plain; often over 7 mm (1/4") long; some species produce an unpleasant odor.

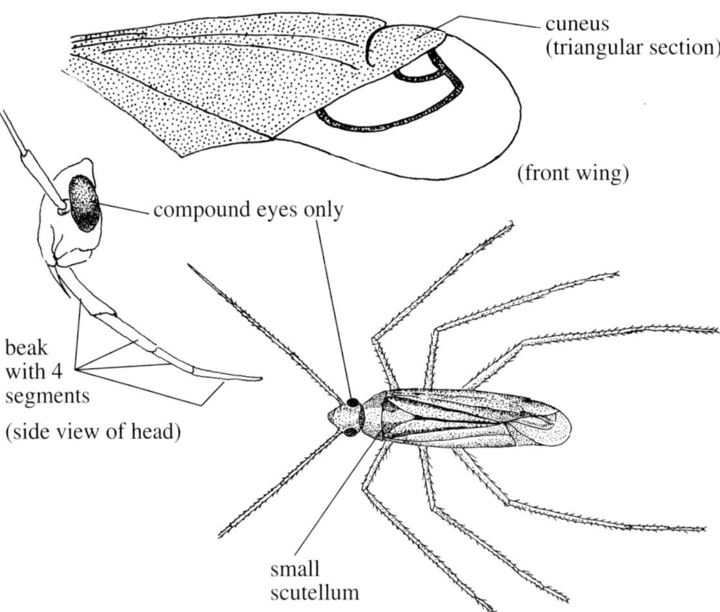

Fig.F. **FAMILY MIRIDAE, PLANT BUGS:** *Trigonotylus* sp., shown here, is bright green; about 5 mm (1/4") long; very common herbivore found on saltmarsh grasses.

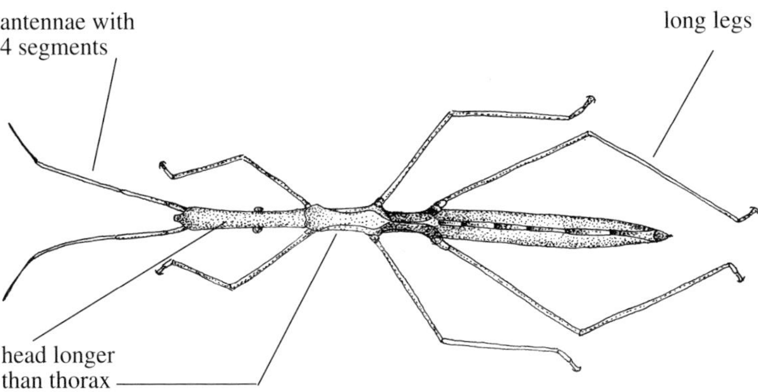

Fig.D. **FAMILY HYDROMETRIDAE, WATER MEASURERS:** Gray; about 8 mm (5/16") long; occasionally found in saltmarshes on aquatic plants or walking slowly on surface of water.

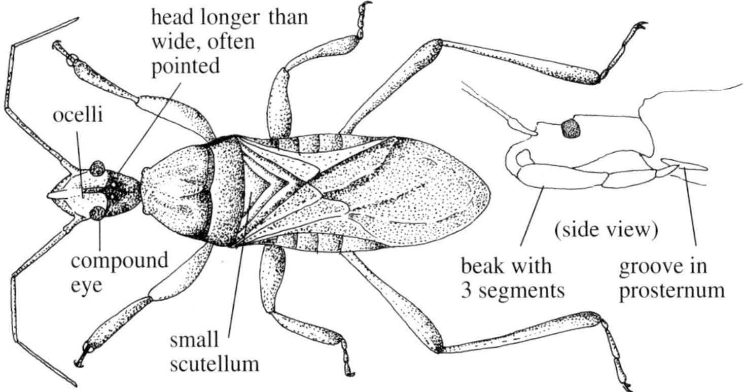

Fig.G. **FAMILY REDUVIIDAE, ASSASSIN BUGS:** Usually black or brown; up to 25 mm (1") long; occasionally found on saltmarshes; most species feed on other insects but some will bite people and should be handled carefully.

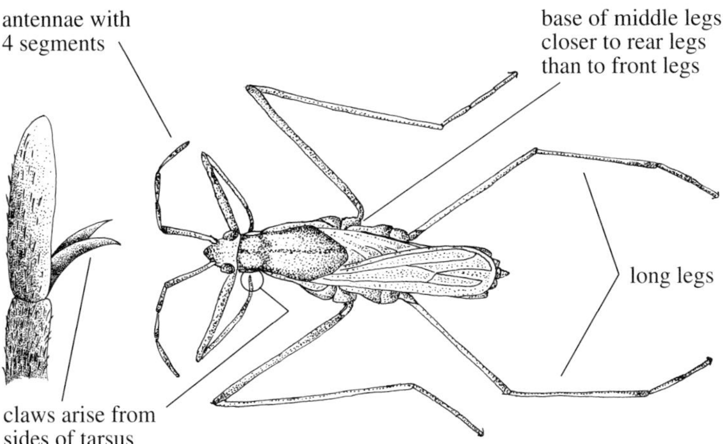

Fig.E. **FAMILY GERRIDAE, WATER STRIDERS:** Black; usually over 5 mm (1/4") long; will run or skate across surface of water; found occasionally on saltmarshes. Oceanic water striders, which are common among the plants floating in the Sargasso Sea, rarely drift near shore.

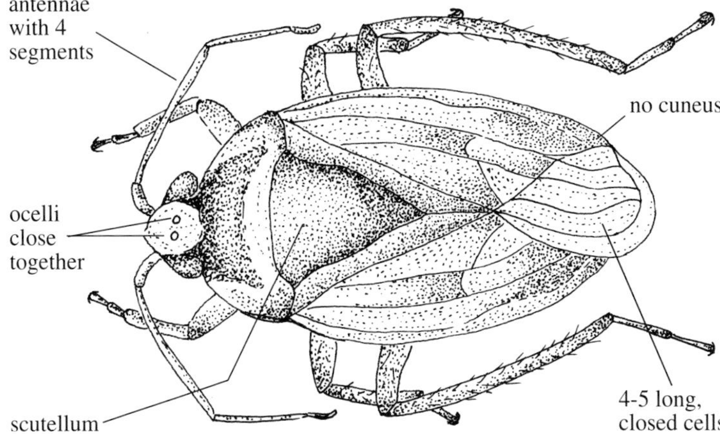

Fig.H. **FAMILY SALDIDAE, SHORE BUGS:** Usually black or brown with whitish markings; about 8 mm (5/16") long; common on saltmarshes and also found on beaches and mudflats; when disturbed, will fly a short distance and hide within grass or under other cover.

HOPPERS, APHIDS: CLASS INSECTA, ORDER HOMOPTERA

Insects with two pairs of wings (or wingless) with front (outer) wings either membranous or thickened; wings at rest usually held tentlike or rooflike over body; mouthparts form a beak or sucking tube which often appears to arise between the bases of the front legs

(Use the key on page 9.10 to determine if you have a homopteran)

#1.Tarsi[1] with three segments; antennae are short and bristlelike; wings usually present (Figs.A-C) .... #2
#1.Tarsi[1] with one or two segments; antennae usually long and threadlike; wings may or may not be present (Fig.D) .... #5

#2.Antennae are attached to front of head between eyes or in front of eyes (Figs.A,B) .... #3
#2.Antennae are attached to sides of head, beneath eyes (Fig.C) .... #4

#3.Tibiae[1] of rear legs with one or more rows of small spines .... **family Cicadellidae, leafhoppers** (Fig.A)
#3.Tibiae[1] of rear legs with one or two stout spines and usually a circle of spines at the tip .... **family Cercopidae, froghoppers or spittlebugs** (Fig.B)

#4.Tibiae[1] of rear legs with a broad, moveable spur at tip .... **family Delphacidae, planthoppers** (Fig.C)
#4.Tibiae[1] of rear legs without a broad spur at tip .... **other homopteran families[2]**

#5.With a pair of cornicles (tubes) extending near posterior end of abdomen (Fig.D); with pear shaped body .... **family Aphididae, aphids** (Fig.D)
#5.Without cornicles .... **other homopteran families[2]**

[1]Refer to Fig.B on page 9.10 for the names of the regions of an insect leg. The tarsus (tarsi = plural) is the outermost region and the tibia (tibiae = plural) is next.
[2]Refer to an insect identification guide such as Arnett (1985), Borror and White (1970), or Jaques (1947).

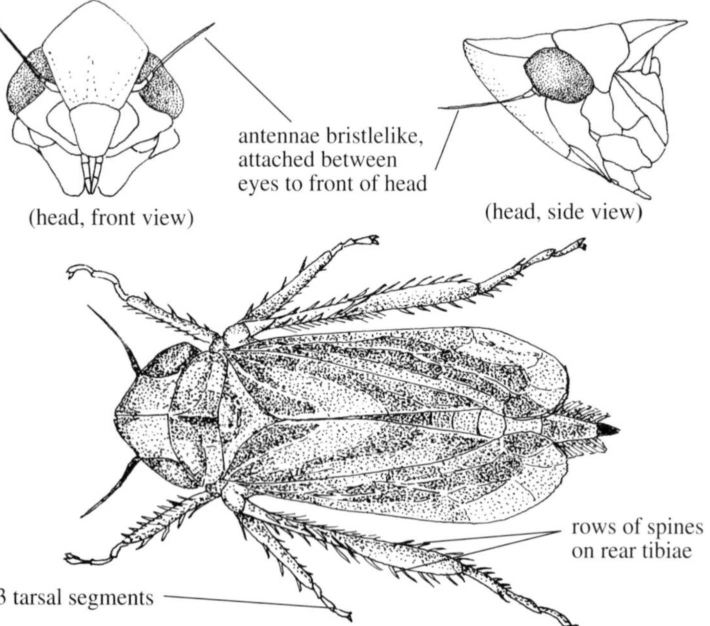

Fig.A. **FAMILY CICADELLIDAE, LEAFHOPPERS:** Various colors; up to 1 cm (3/8") long; a number of species, including several species of *Deltocephalus* (shown here), *Amplicephalus simplex,* and *Graminella nigrifrons* are very common on saltmarsh plants and beach grasses.

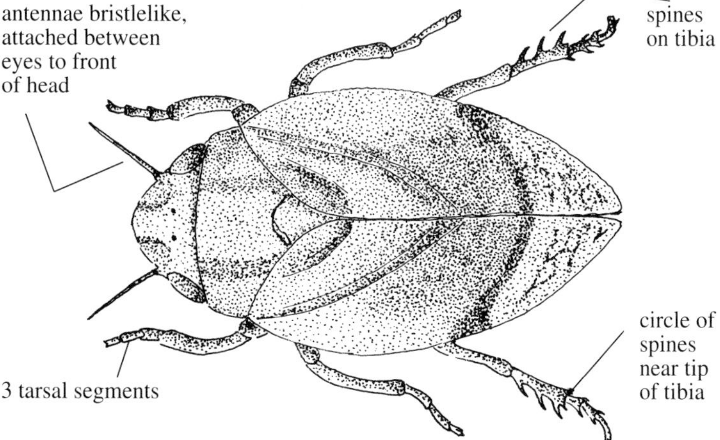

Fig.B. **FAMILY CERCOPIDAE, FROGHOPPERS OR SPITTLEBUGS:** Up to 12 mm (1/2") long; nymphs deposit a spittlelike mass on grass.

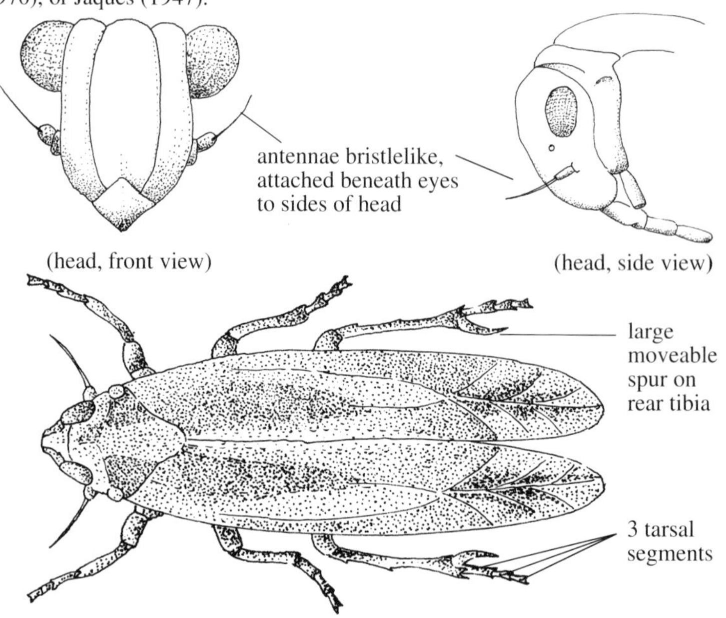

Fig.C. **FAMILY DELPHACIDAE, PLANTHOPPERS:** Up to about 5 mm (1/4") long; several species are very common on saltmarsh plants. *Prokelisia marginata* is the dominant herbivore on some saltmarshes with nymphs occurring throughout the year and winged adults in the warmer months.

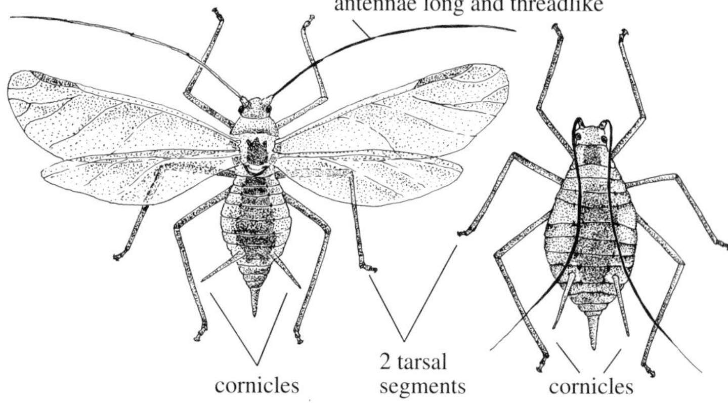

Fig.D. **FAMILY APHIDIDAE, APHIDS:** Green; tiny, under 8 mm (5/16") long; complex life cycle with winged and wingless forms; very common on the leaves of marsh elder and other plants at the upland border of saltmarshes.

BEETLES[1]: CLASS INSECTA, ORDER COLEOPTERA

Insects with two pairs of wings; the front (outer) pair of wings are hard (chitinous); wings meet in a straight line down back and do not have veins.

(Use the key on page 9.10 to determine if you have a beetle)

#1.The coxae (base segments, see Fig.A) of the rear legs completely divide the first abdominal segment. (Thus, the rear margin of the first abdominal segment is not continuous across the entire abdomen because it is interrupted by the coxal cavities[2] of the rear legs.); rear coxae are immovably fused to the metasternum (rear plate on underside of thorax, see Fig.A) .... **suborder Adephaga**, #2

#1.The coxae (base segments, see Fig.A) of the rear legs do NOT completely divide the first abdominal segment. (Thus, the sides of the first abdominal segment are only partially separated by the coxal cavities[2] of the rear legs and the rear margin of this segment extends across the entire abdomen.); rear coxae are not fused to metasternum .... **suborder Polyphaga**, page 9.20

#2.Rear coxae (base of hind legs) form large plates (Fig.B) covering 3 or more abdominal segments .... **family Haliplidae, crawling water beetles** (Fig.B)

#2.Rear coxae do not cover 3 abdominal segments (Fig.A) .... #3

#3.Rear legs flattened and with fringes of long hairs, modified for swimming .... **family Dytiscidae, predaceous diving beetles** (Fig.E)

#3.Rear legs not flattened and without fringes of long hairs .... #4

#4.Head, including eyes, usually wider than the thorax (Fig.C); the bases of the antennae (Fig.C) are located on the front of the head, above and closer together than the bases of the mandibles .... **family Cicindelidae, tiger beetles** (Fig.C)

#4.Head, including eyes, usually narrower than the thorax (Fig.D); the bases of the antennae (Fig.D) are located on the sides of the head, between eyes and bases of the mandibles .... **family Carabidae, ground beetles** (Fig.D)

[1]Refer to White (1983), Arnett, Downie and Jaques (1980), or Arnett (1968) to identify the most common species of beetles.

[2]Coxal cavities are the openings in the underside of the beetle where the legs are attached (see Fig.A).

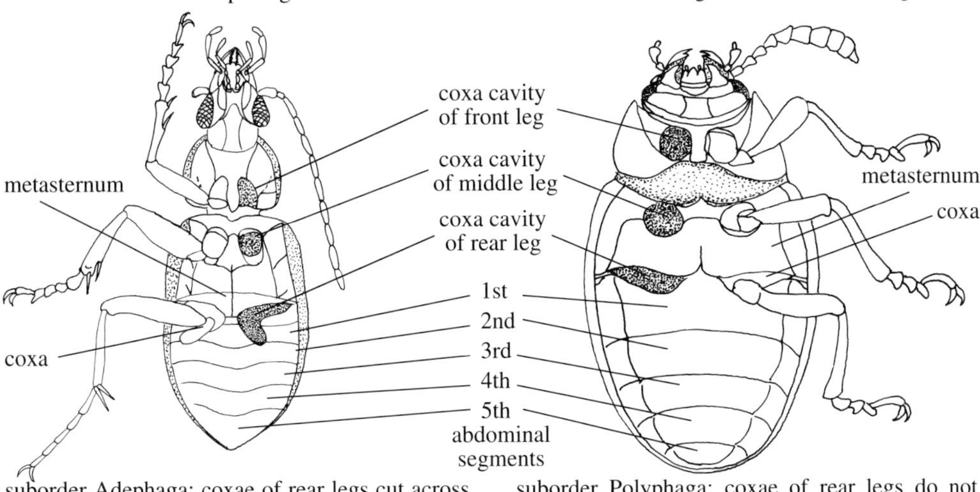

suborder Adephaga: coxae of rear legs cut across entire width of 1st abdominal segment.

suborder Polyphaga: coxae of rear legs do not completely divide 1st abdominal segment.

Fig.A. **VENTRAL (UNDERSIDE) VIEW OF TYPICAL BEETLES**

very large coxae

abdomen

(ventral view)

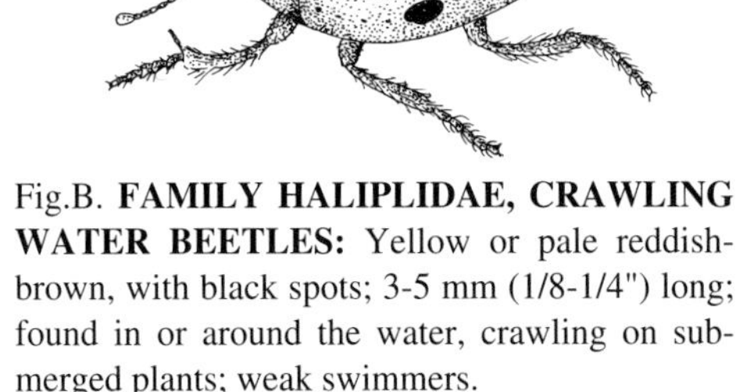

Fig.B. **FAMILY HALIPLIDAE, CRAWLING WATER BEETLES:** Yellow or pale reddish-brown, with black spots; 3-5 mm (1/8-1/4") long; found in or around the water, crawling on submerged plants; weak swimmers.

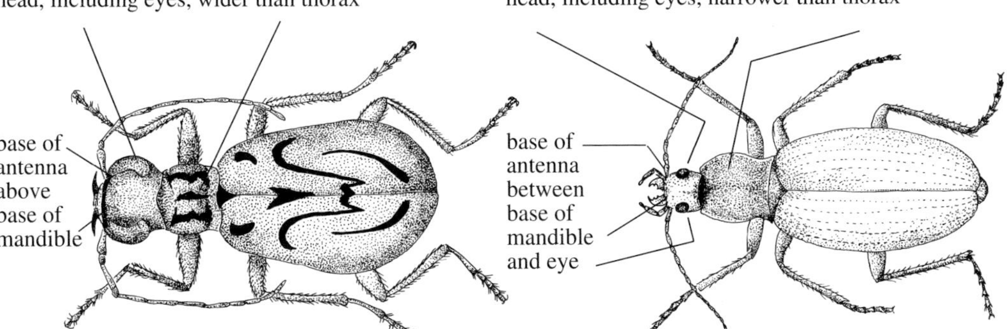

Fig.C. **FAMILY CICINDELIDAE, TIGER BEETLES:** Brightly colored, may be brown, bronze, black or green, often with distinctive markings; usually 10-20 mm (3/8-3/4") long but may be 6-40 mm (1/4-1 1/2"); found on sandy beaches; swift runners and fliers; some species bite; larvae dig deep vertical tunnels.

Fig.D. **FAMILY CARABIDAE, GROUND BEETLES:** *Bembidion* sp. is common on saltmarshes especially in piles of drifted eelgrass; it is shiny, dark brown with lines etched into outer wings; about 5 mm (1/4") long. Other species are usually black and shiny, sometimes brightly colored; 2-35 mm (1/16-1 3/8").

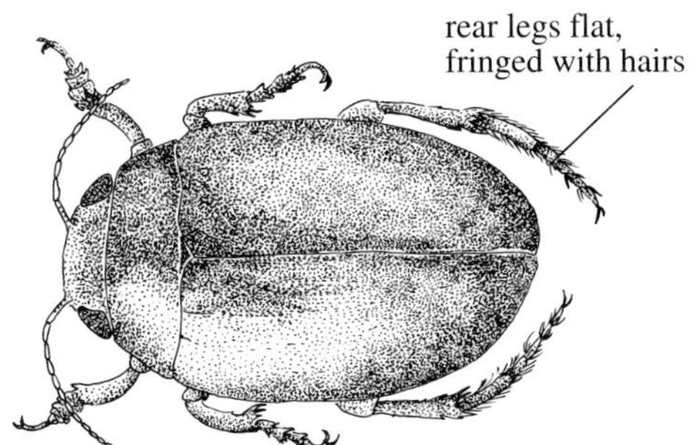

Fig.E. **FAMILY DYTISCIDAE, PREDACEOUS DIVING BEETLES:** Black, brown, or yellow, often with light markings; 1-35 mm (1/32-1 3/8") long; strong swimmers, both hind legs kick at same time; strong fliers, attracted to lights at night.

BEETLES (CONTINUED)
CLASS INSECTA, ORDER COLEOPTERA, SUBORDER POLYPHAGA

Beetles in which the rear margin of the first abdominal segment extends completely across abdomen, without the rear coxae separating the sides of the segment.

(Beetle key begins on page 9.19)

#1.Front wings (elytra) are short (Fig.A) and rear wings are folded under them, exposing at least three abdominal ("tail") segments beyond wings .... **family Staphylinidae, rove beetles** (Fig.A)
#1.Front wings (elytra) and/or rear wings cover all or most of the abdominal segments (Figs.B-H) .... #2

#2.Front of head elongated into a downward curving snout or beak (Fig.B); antennae elbowed (bent) .... **family Curculionidae, snout beetles** (Fig.B)
#2.Head without beak or snout (Figs.C-H); antennae not usually elbowed (bent) .... #3

#3.Rear legs usually flattened and with fringes of long hairs, modified for swimming; maxillary palps (Fig.C) long, usually longer than antennae; antennae are short, with 7-10 segments .... **family Hydrophilidae, water scavenger beetles**[2] (Fig.C)
#3.Rear legs not flattened and without fringes of long hairs (Figs.D-H); maxillary palps shorter than antennae .... #4

#4.The tarsi (see Fig.D) of all legs divided into 3 obvious[1] segments; small, oval, convex beetles which are often brightly colored (ie. yellow, red, or orange with black markings, or black with yellow or red markings) .... **family Coccinellidae, ladybird beetles** (Fig.D)
#4.All tarsi[1] with more than 3 segments (Figs E-H) .... #5

#5.Tarsi[1] of rear legs with 4 segments and tarsi of front legs with 5 segments; eyes usually notched .... **family Tenebrionidae, darkling beetles** (Fig.E)
#5.Tarsi[1] of rear legs with same number of segments as tarsi of front legs; eyes not usually notched .... #6

#6.Tarsi of all legs with 5 obvious[1] segments (Fig.F) .... #7
#6.Tarsi of all legs with 4 obvious[1] segments (Figs.G-H) .... #8

#7.Abdomen ("tail") with 7 or 8 segments visible from the underside; soft-bodied with leathery front wings (elytra); head is not concealed by thorax when viewed from above; antennae with 11 segments and are often serrate (with sawlike teeth along edges) .... **family Cantharidae, soldier beetles** (Fig.F)
#7.Abdomen with 5 or 6 segments visible ventrally (from the underside); body may or may not be soft; head may or may not be concealed by thorax when viewed dorsally (from above); antennae may or may not have 11 segments or be serrate .... **various beetle families**[3]

#8.Tibiae[1] of front and middle legs are flattened and spiny, adapted for digging; usually found burrowed in mud or sand .... **family Heteroceridae, variegated mud-loving beetles** (Fig.G)
#8.Tibiae[1] are not flattened or spiny; usually found living on plants .... **family Chrysomelidae, leaf beetles** (Fig.H)

[1]See Fig.B on page 9.10 for the names of the regions of an insect leg. The tarsus (tarsi = plural) is the outermost region and the tibia is next. The tarsus is subdivided into 3-5 obvious segments and ends in a pair of claws. In addition, some beetles, such as the ladybird beetles and the leaf beetles, have a tiny tarsal segment that is difficult to see and may be fused to one of the other segments. When using this key, only count the apparent, obvious segments.
[2]A similar family, the Limnebiidae, minute moss beetles, may occur in marshes. The Hydrophilidae have 5 abdominal segments. The Limnebiidae have 6-7.
[3]Refer to White (1983), Arnett, Downie and Jaques (1980), Arnett (1968), or Dillon and Dillon (1961) to identify these beetles.

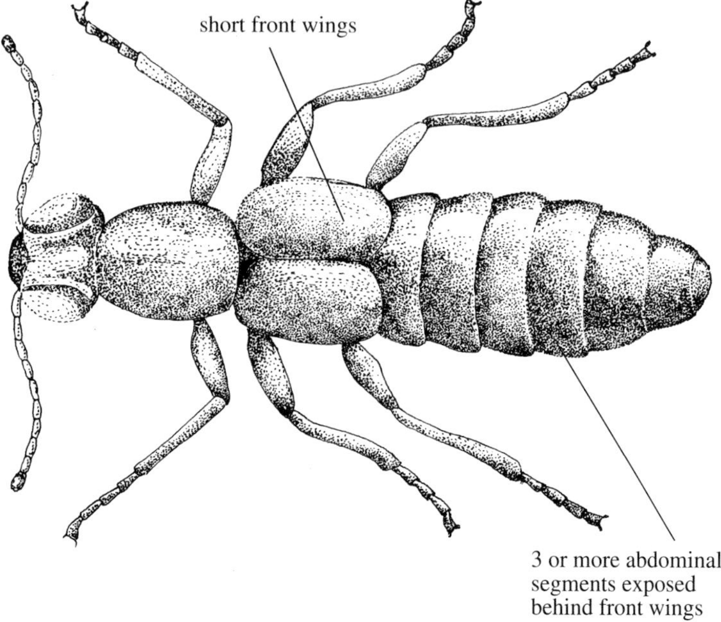

Fig.A. **FAMILY STAPHYLINIDAE, ROVE BEETLES:** Abdomen often bent upward, appearing to be poised to sting (but they won't); swift fliers and runners; 1-20 mm (1/32-3/4") long.

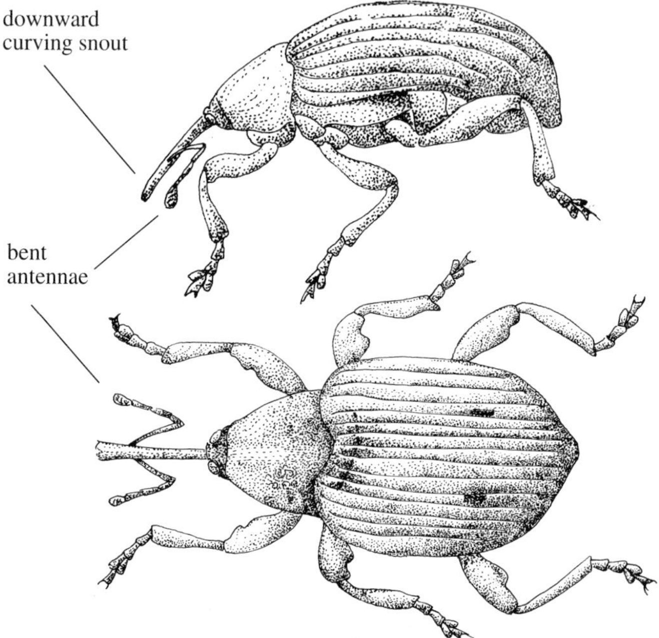

Fig.B. **FAMILY CURCULIONIDAE, SNOUT BEETLES:** Found on salt-marshes feeding on plants; 1-35 mm (1/32-1 3/8") long.

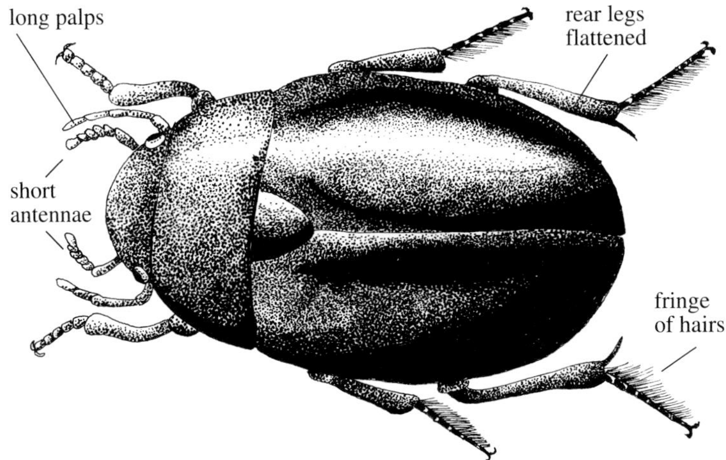

Fig.C. **FAMILY HYDROPHILIDAE, WATER SCAVENGER BEETLES:** *Enochrus hamiltoni* occurs in saltmarshes, especially very wet areas (pannes); it is dull brown, with rows of dots etched into front wings (elytra); about 5 mm (1/4") long. Other species, ranging up to 40 mm (1 1/2") in length, also live along the shore and some are good swimmers, kicking rear legs alternately.

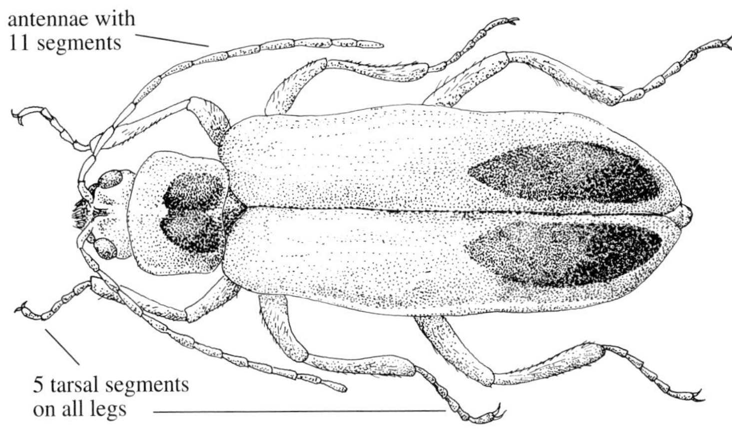

Fig.F. **FAMILY CANTHARIDAE, SOLDIER BEETLES:** Species in at least two genera of soldier beetles, *Cantharis* and *Silis*, are found at the upland edge of saltmarshes. The front wings (elytra) of these species are black and their pronotum (body segment behind head) is orange with a central brown area; they reach about 9 mm (3/8") in length.

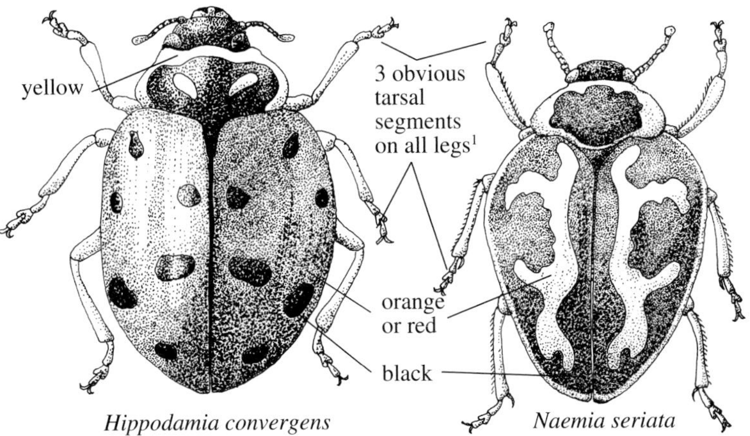

Fig.D. **FAMILY COCCINELLIDAE, LADYBIRD BEETLES:** Brightly colored with distinctive species specific pattern of spots and markings; often yellow, orange or red with black markings or black with yellow or red markings; about 6 mm (1/4") long. The species shown here are common in saltmarshes. In midsummer they are abundant on marsh elder where they feed on aphids. Later in the summer they are found on marsh grasses where they feed on pollen.

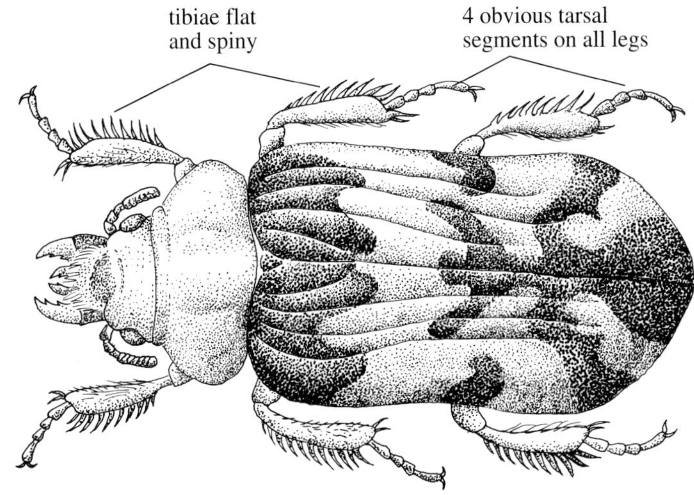

Fig.G. **FAMILY HETEROCERIDAE, VARIEGATED MUD-LOVING BEETLES:** *Heterocerus* sp. is found in the upper portions of saltmarshes and burrows in mud or sand; it is brown with wavy yellowish markings on front wings (elytra); about 6 mm (1/4") long.

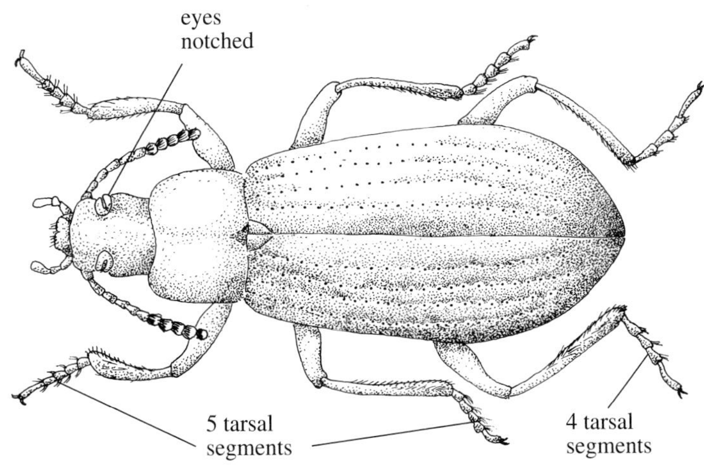

Fig.E. **FAMILY TENEBRIONIDAE, DARKLING BEETLES:** Usually black or brown; 2-35 mm (1/16-1 1/2") long.

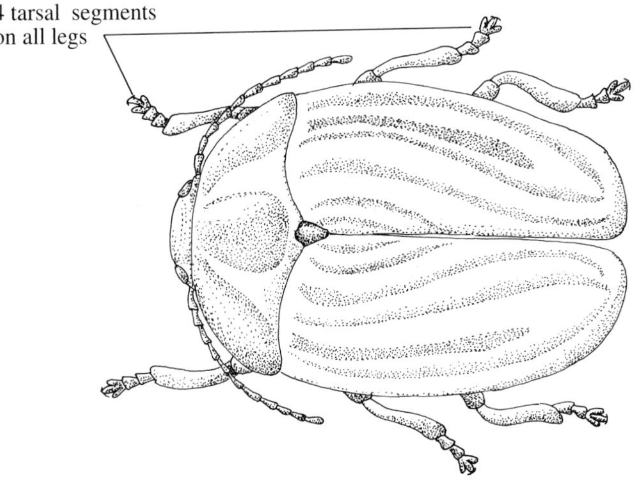

Fig.H. **FAMILY CHRYSOMELIDAE, LEAF BEETLES:** Color and shape widely variable; 1-20 mm (1/32"-3/4"); several species occur on saltmarshes.

TRUE FLIES: CLASS INSECTA, ORDER DIPTERA

Insects with a single pair of wings.

(Use key on page 9.10 to determine if you have a true fly)

#1. Antennae composed of 5 or fewer segments, usually 3 (Fig.A); antennae often with a long bristle (arista) or slender projection (style); third segment of antennae not subdivided into rings ... #3

#1. Antennae composed of 6 or more distinct segments or less distinct rings (Figs.B,F) ... #2

#2. Antennae composed of 3 segments with the third segment subdivided into rings (Fig.F) or subsegments (these rings are not as distinct as the 3 main segments but may give the appearance of being additional segments); relatively stout bodied, medium to large flies that often bite; wings with two large lobes (calypters, see Fig.F) near base on posterior side and with wing tips enclosed by a forked vein ... **family Tabanidae, horse, deer, and greenhead flies** (Fig.F)

#2. Antennae composed of 6 or more distinct segments (Fig.B); antennae may be long or feathery; mostly slender, soft-bodied, midgelike or mosquitolike flies with relatively long legs ... page 9.24

#3. With a frontal suture (an upside down U- or V-shaped line or groove on the face, see Fig.C) ... **muscoid flies,** page 9.26

#3. Without a frontal suture ... #4

#4. Feet with three pads (Fig.D) ... **family Rhagionidae, snipe flies** (Fig.D)

#4. Feet with two pads (Fig.G) ... #5

#5. Top of head between eyes is sunken or hollowed out, strongly concave as viewed from front (Fig.G); with three tiny simple eyes (ocelli) as well as two large compound eyes; face may be hairy, bearded; abdomen (tail) often rather long and sometimes pointed ... **family Asilidae, robber flies** (Fig.G)

#5. Top of head is not sunken between eyes ... #6

#6. Head very large and hemispherical, consisting almost entirely of eyes (Fig.E); face very narrow ... **family Pipunculidae, big-headed flies** (Fig.E)

#6. Head not unusually large; face not especially narrow ... #7

#7. Wings with strong, thick anterior veins, remainder of veins are weaker and slant obliquely toward rear wing margin (Fig.H); antennae with very small basal segments and ending in a long arista (bristle); hind legs long, with larger segments (femora) flattened from side to side; small or minute flies with humpbacked appearance ... **family Phoridae, humpbacked flies** (Fig.H)

#7. Wings with normal venation; antennae not as described above ... #8

#8. Body usually a metallic green or coppery color; cross vein (r-m) between radius (r) vein and media (m) vein (Fig.I) located in basal 1/4 of wing; male genitalia (Fig.I) often folded forward under abdomen; antennae usually with long bristle (arista) ... **family Dolichopodidae, long-legged flies** (Fig.I)

#8. Body not a metallic color; r-m cross vein (Fig.J) located beyond basal 1/4 of wing; male genitalia (Fig.J) not folded forward under abdomen; third antennal segment usually rounded with a long terminal projection (style) ... **family Empididae, dance flies** (Fig.J)

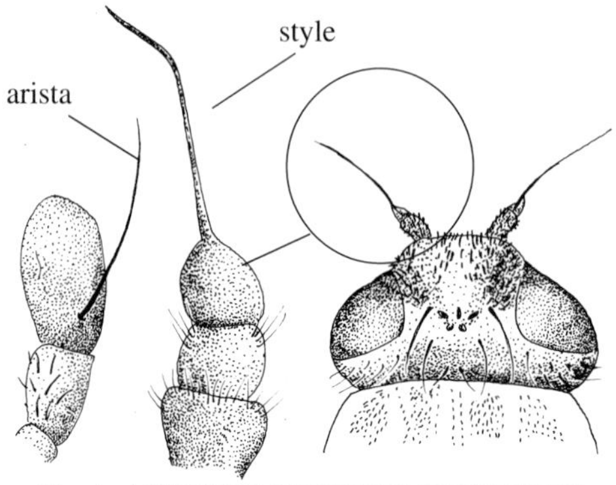

Fig.A. **ANTENNAE WITH 3 SEGMENTS**

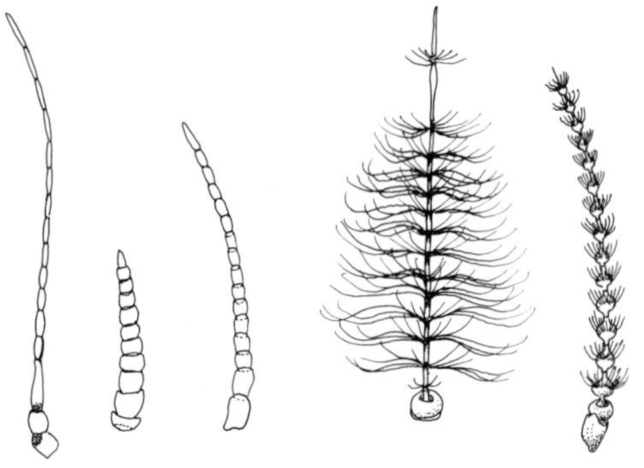

Fig.B. **ANTENNAE WITH 6 OR MORE SEGMENTS**

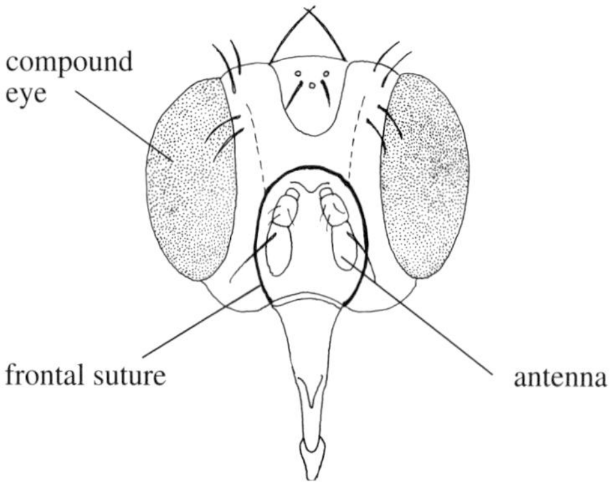

Fig.C. **FACE OF MUSCOID FLIES**

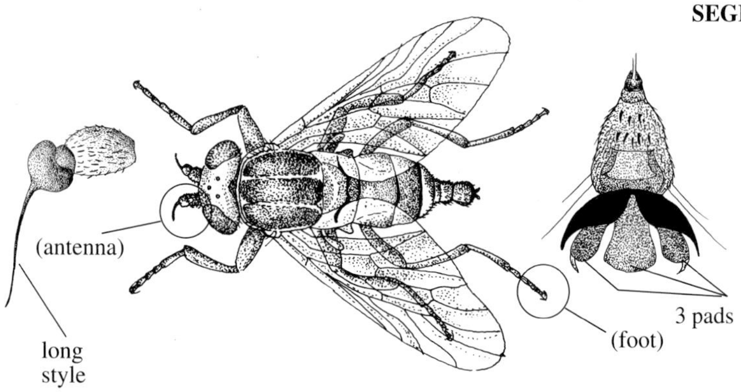

Fig.D. **FAMILY RHAGIONIDAE, SNIPE FLIES:** Most species are black or gray; 8-15 mm (3/8 - 5/8") long.

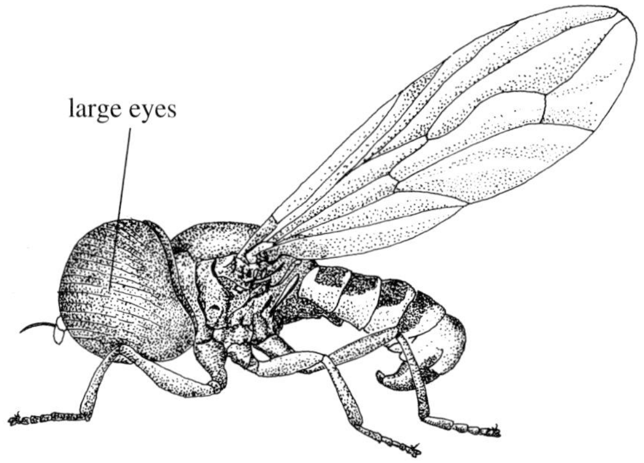

Fig.E. **FAMILY PIPUNCULIDAE, BIG-HEADED FLIES:** Small, up to about 5 mm (1/4" long); occur on saltmarshes.

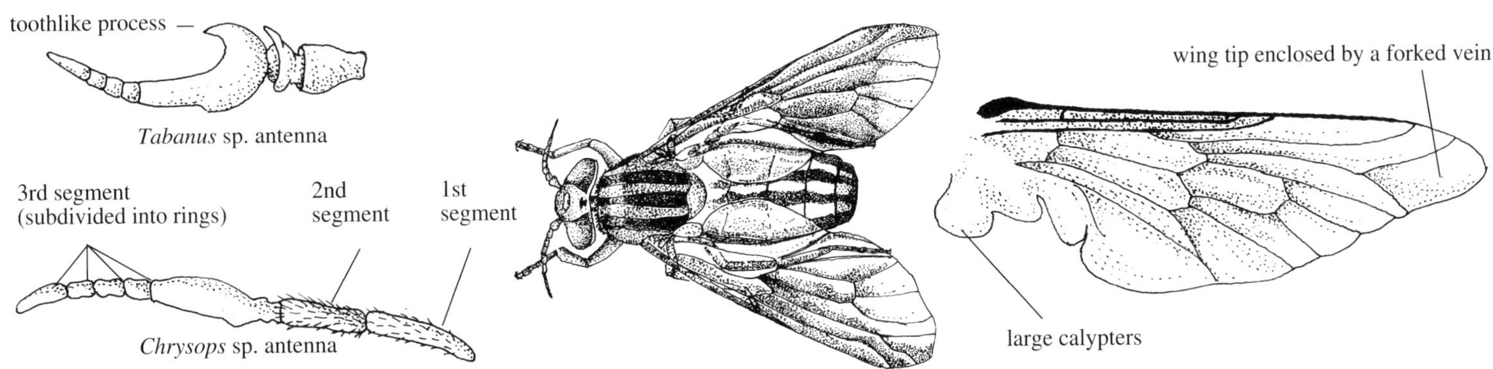

Fig.F. **FAMILY TABANIDAE, DEER, HORSE, AND GREENHEAD FLIES:** Several species of deer and horse flies are common along the coast, especially in saltmarshes and sand dunes, where they can be extremely annoying to people. (See Jamnback and Wall, 1959; Pechuman, 1972; or Fairchild, 1950). Females are blood seeking and can inflict a painful bite. Males do not bite, feeding on flowers such as beach pea and swamp rose. The eyes of males meet dorsally (at the top of the head) but are separated in females. They breed in saltmarshes where their larvae (see pages 9.30 - 9.34) can often be found during the summer months. One of the most abundant coastal species, the greenhead fly, *Tabanus nigrovittatus*, averages over 1 cm (1/2") in length and has bright green eyes. The antennae of *Tabanus* has a toothlike process near the base of the third segment (see above). The two most common coastal deer fly species, *Chrysops atlanticus* and *Chrysops fuliginosus*, are about the size of a house fly, up to about 8 mm (3/8") in length. Their antennae do not have a toothlike process near the base of the third segment.

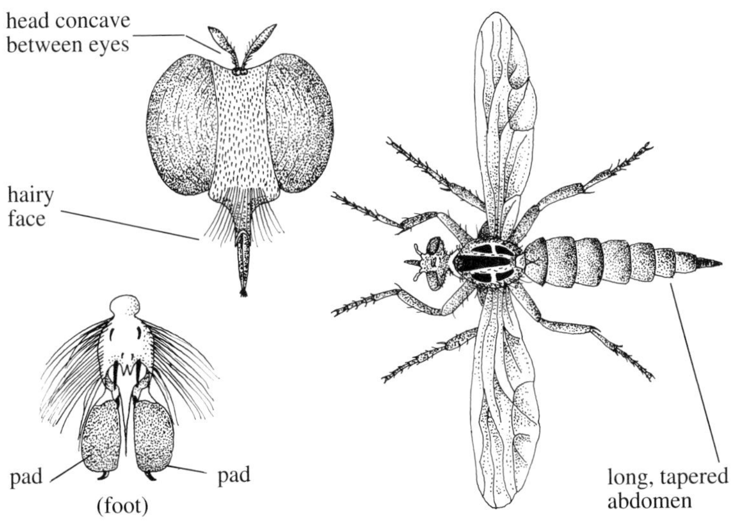

Fig.G. **FAMILY ASILIDAE, ROBBER FLIES:** Light grayish brown, abdomen may be partially whitish or silvery; up to about 2 cm (3/4") long; several species occur on open sandy beaches.

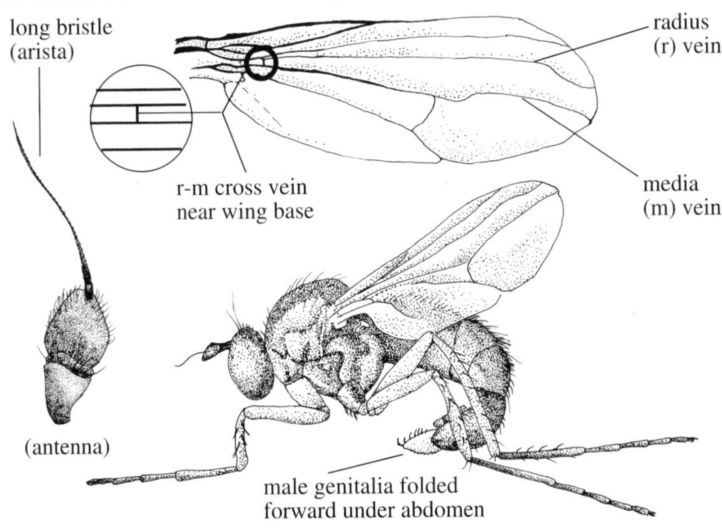

Fig.I. **FAMILY DOLICHOPODIDAE, LONG-LEGGED FLIES:** Often a metallic green or copper color; up to about 6 mm (1/4") long; adults and larvae (see pages 9.30-9.34) of several species occur in saltmarshes and mudflats.

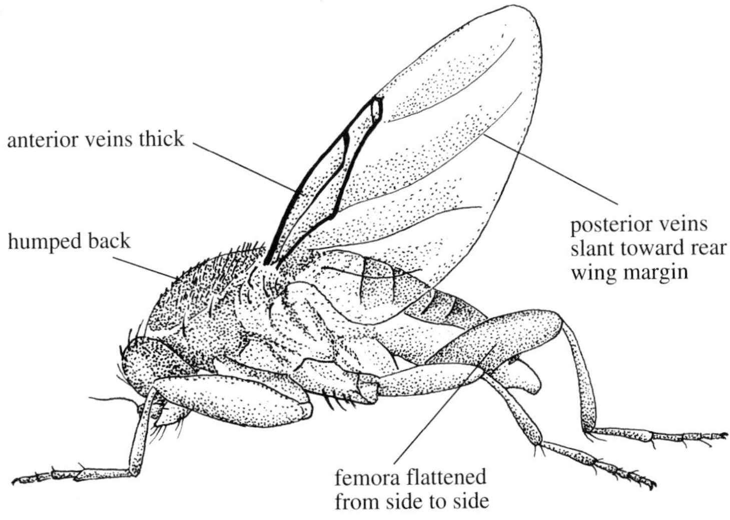

Fig.H. **FAMILY PHORIDAE, HUMPBACKED FLIES:** Usually black, brown or yellowish; small or minute, length usually less than 4 mm (3/16") long.

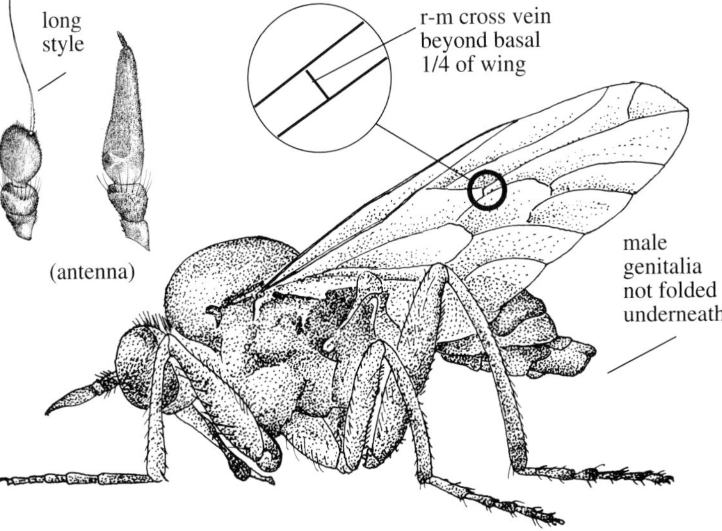

Fig.J. **FAMILY EMPIDIDAE, DANCE FLIES:** Up to about 6 mm (1/4") long; occur in saltmarshes.

MOSQUITOES, MIDGES, GNATS AND RELATED FLY FAMILIES
CLASS INSECTA, ORDER DIPTERA, SUBORDER NEMATOCERA

Flies having antennae with 6 or more segments; often with long legs and long antennae.

(Fly key begins on page 9.22)

#1. Wings are relatively long and narrow (Figs. A-C); legs are relatively long; mosquitolike insects (if in doubt, make this choice) .... #2
#1. Wings are relatively short and broad (Figs.D-G); legs are not particularly long .... #5

#2. With scales (Fig.A) on edges and veins of wings, body and legs; proboscis long, extending far beyond head .... **family Culicidae, mosquitoes** (Fig.A)
#2. Without scales on wings, body or legs; proboscis short, barely extending beyond head (Fig.B-G) .... #3

#3. With a distinct V-shaped line or groove (Fig.B) across the back of the midsection of the thorax ("body") .... **family Tipulidae, crane flies** (Fig.B)
#3. Without a V-shaped line across the back of the thorax (Figs.C-G) .... #4

#4. Antennae long and, in males, usually feathery (Fig.C); legs are long, particularly front legs; total length of fly may reach over 12 mm (1/2"); wings may be folded rooflike over the body in the resting position; do not bite .... **family Chironomidae, midges** (Fig.C)
#4. Antennae and legs not long or feathery (Figs.E-G); tiny flies, usually less than 4 mm (3/16") in length; wings lie flat over back when at rest; some species are vicious biters; often have a somewhat humpbacked appearance .... #6

#5. Wings, body and antennae are very hairy (Fig.D); wings are pointed at the tip and are often folded rooflike or together over the body in the resting position .... **family Psychodidae, moth or sand flies** (Fig.D)
#5. Wings and body not densely hairy (Figs.E-G); wings not pointed at the tip; wings usually held flat over body when at rest; many species have a somewhat humpbacked appearance .... #6

#6. With ocelli (simple eyespots) as well as compound eyes (Fig.E); do not bite humans; some species form galls on plants .... **superfamily Mycetophiloidea, fungus and gall gnats** (Fig.E)
#6. Without ocelli (simple eyespots), with compound eyes only; vicious biters and pests of humans; tiny flies, less than 4 mm (3/16") long .... #7

#7. Anterior wing veins thicker and stronger than posterior veins; wings are very broad .... **family Simuliidae, black flies** (Fig.F)
#7. Posterior wing veins thicker and stronger than anterior veins; wings are not particularly broad .... **family Ceratopogonidae, punkies** (Fig.G)

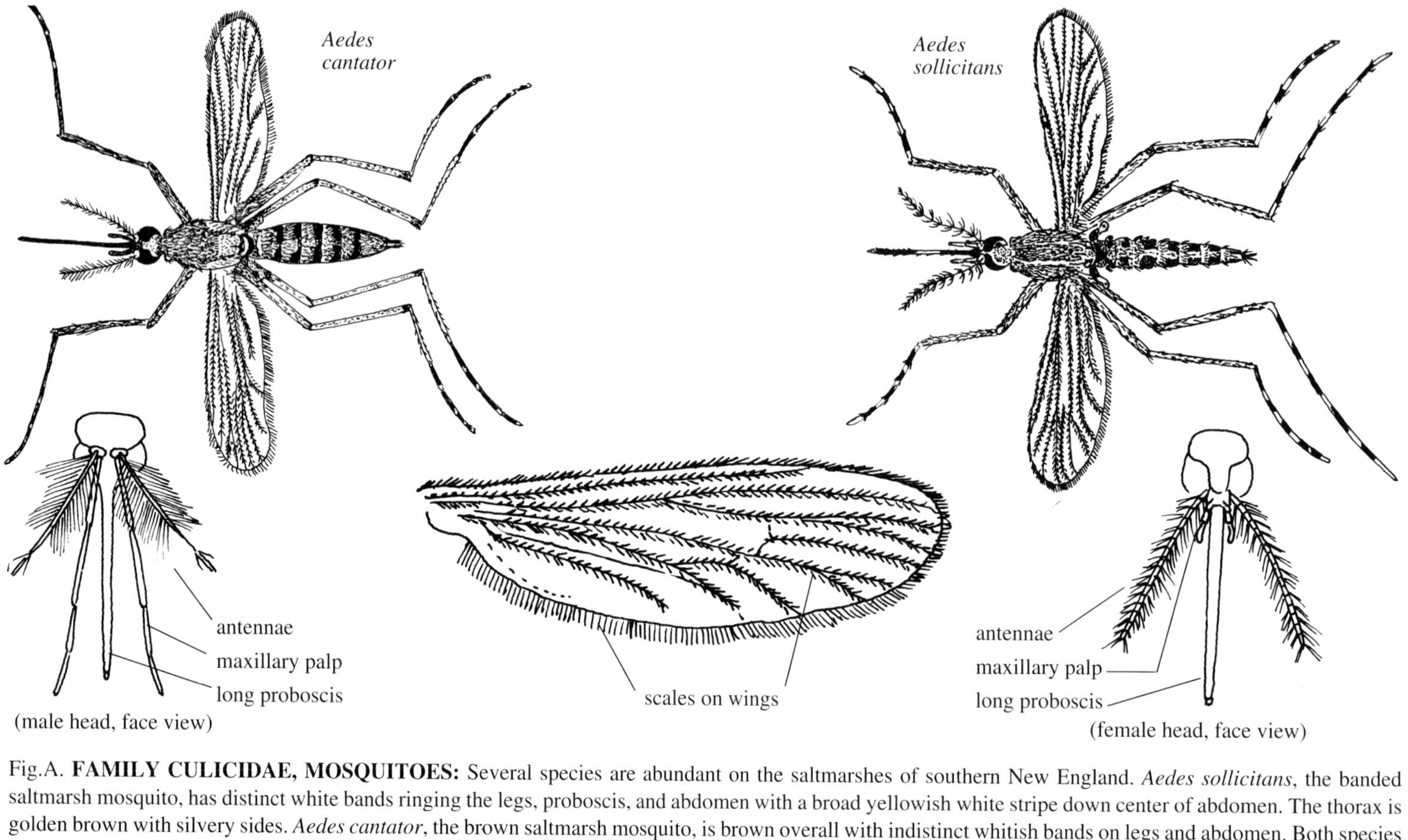

Aedes cantator

Aedes sollicitans

antennae
maxillary palp
long proboscis
(male head, face view)

scales on wings

antennae
maxillary palp
long proboscis
(female head, face view)

Fig.A. **FAMILY CULICIDAE, MOSQUITOES:** Several species are abundant on the saltmarshes of southern New England. *Aedes sollicitans*, the banded saltmarsh mosquito, has distinct white bands ringing the legs, proboscis, and abdomen with a broad yellowish white stripe down center of abdomen. The thorax is golden brown with silvery sides. *Aedes cantator*, the brown saltmarsh mosquito, is brown overall with indistinct whitish bands on legs and abdomen. Both species are about 6-7 mm (1/4") long, excluding proboscis, which is about 3 mm (1/8") long. Refer to Matheson (1945) or Headlee (1945) to identify adult mosquitoes to species. Female mosquitoes, which bite and are blood sucking, are annoying pests and can transmit diseases, such as equine encephalitis, to livestock and people. Males, which do not bite, have much more feathery antennae and, in most species, longer maxillary palps than females. Mosquito larvae (page 9.33) and pupae (page 9.31) are aquatic and occur in standing water on saltmarshes. Many saltmarshes have been diked, ditched, and drained to reduce mosquito breeding habitats.

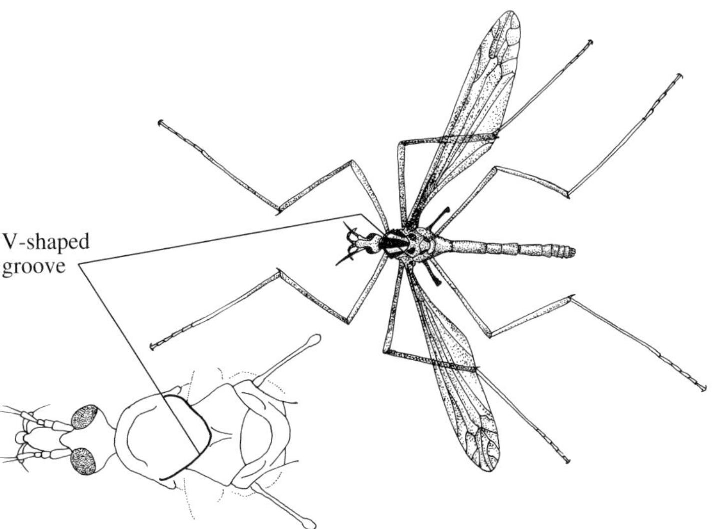

Fig.B. **FAMILY TIPULIDAE, CRANE FLIES:** Brownish or gray; up to 2.5 cm (1") long; crane flies do not bite people.

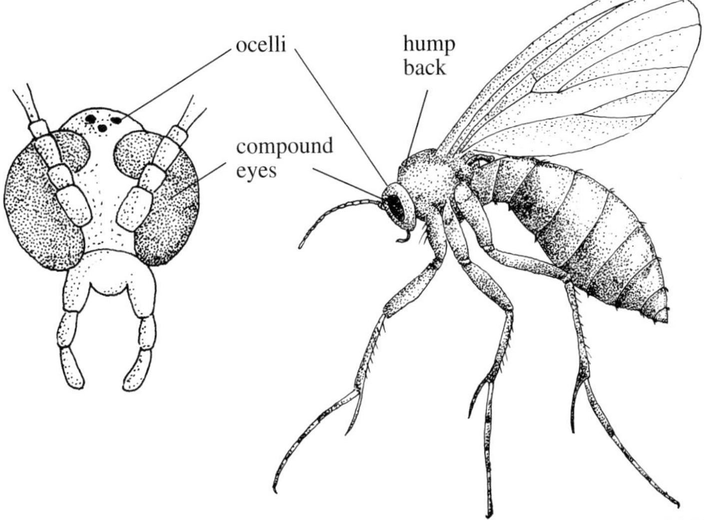

Fig.E. **SUPERFAMILY MYCETOPHILOIDEA, FUNGUS AND GALL GNATS:** Gall gnats, family Cecidomyiidae, are rarely over 3 mm (1/8") long and the larvae of most species form galls. Fungus gnats, family Mycetophilidae, may reach over 5 mm (1/4") long. Both families occur in saltmarshes.

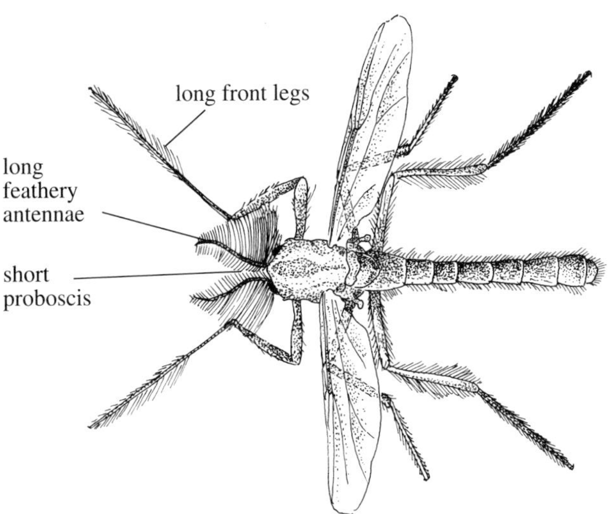

Fig.C. **FAMILY CHIRONOMIDAE, MIDGES:** Up to 12 mm (1/2") long; larvae (see page 9.33) are found in mudflats in the lower salinity portions of estuaries; midges do not bite people.

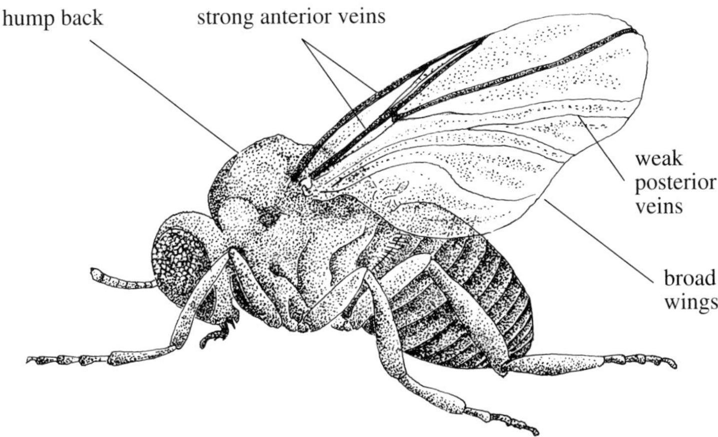

Fig.F. **FAMILY SIMULIIDAE, BLACK FLIES:** Usually gray or black; up to 4 mm (3/16") long; vicious biters; found on beaches and marshes.

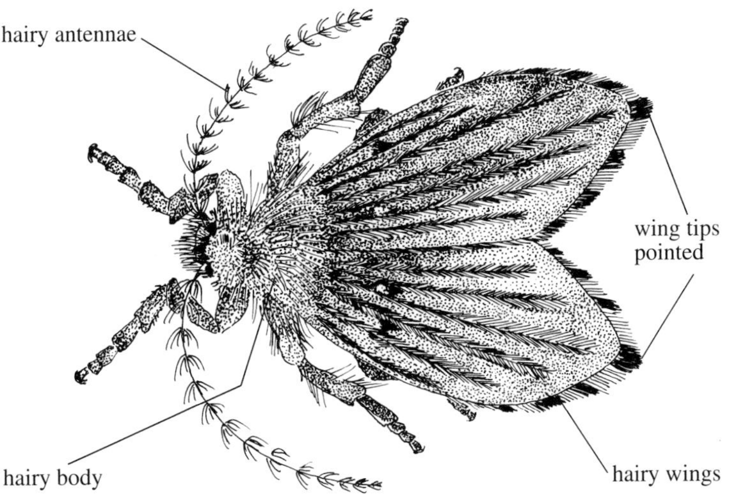

Fig.D. **FAMILY PSYCHODIDAE, MOTH OR SAND FLIES:** Very hairy overall; up to 5 mm (1/4") long; see pages 9.30-9.33 for larvae.

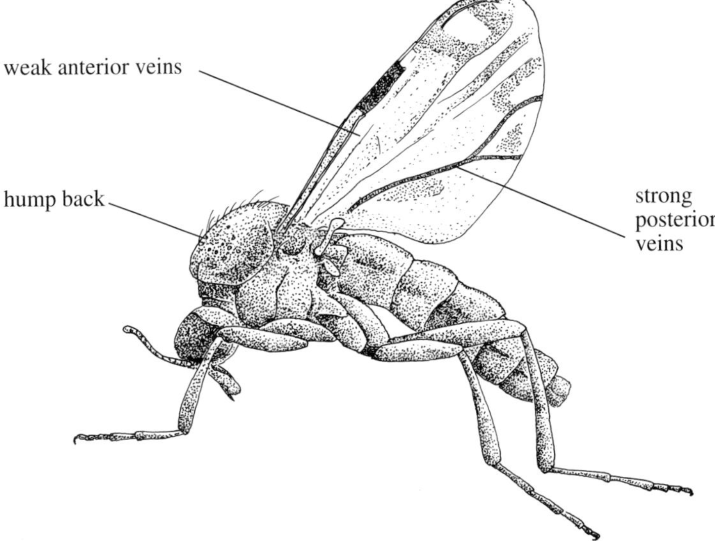

Fig.G. **FAMILY CERATOPOGONIDAE, PUNKIES:** Usually less than 3 mm (1/8") long; many species bite humans; see pages 9.30-9.33 for larvae.

MUSCOID FLIES
CLASS INSECTA, ORDER DIPTERA, SUBORDER CYCLORRHAPHA, DIVISION SCHIZOPHORA
Flies with a frontal suture

(Fly key begins on page 9.22)

#1.Second antennal segment (Fig.B) with a longitudinal suture (line or groove running lengthwise) on outer side; wings with two large lobes (calypters) near base on posterior side (Fig.A); thorax (body) usually with a suture (line or groove) going completely across the back near middle of thorax .... **superfamily Muscoidea[1], houseflies and related fly families** (Fig. E)

#1.Second antennal segment without a longitudinal suture (line or groove) on outer side; calypters (lobes near base of wings) are small or absent; thorax (body) usually without a complete suture (line or groove) going across the back near middle of thorax .... #2

#2.Subcosta vein in wing is complete, ending in costa vein (see Fig.A for diagram of wing veins) .... #3

#2.Subcosta vein is incomplete, not reaching the costa vein, sometimes dead-ending or fusing with the radius vein at the tip (see Fig.A) .... #5

#3.Back of body (dorsal surface of thorax) is flattened AND legs and abdomen very bristly; wings without bands, spots, or patterns .... **family Coelopidae, seaweed flies** (Fig.D)

#3.Dorsal surface of thorax is convex (rounded) or, if somewhat flattened, then legs are not bristly; wings are often banded, spotted or patterned .... #4

#4.Body usually yellowish or brownish; tibia (Fig.C) of leg with one or more bristles which extend from the tip (preapical bristles); femur leg segment (Fig.C) with bristles; anal cell (Fig.A) of wing usually rounded at outer end .... **superfamily Sciomyzoidea[1], marsh flies and related fly families** (Fig.F)

#4.Body usually blackish and shiny; without any preapical bristles on tibia (Fig.C); anal cell (Fig.A) of wing usually with a sharp projection at outer end .... **family Otitidae, picture-winged flies** (Fig.G)

#5.Anal cell (Fig.A) of wing is present .... **superfamily Milichioidea[1], beach flies, small dung flies, milichiid flies and related families** (Fig.H)

#5.Anal cell (Fig.A) of wing is absent .... #6

#6.Costa vein (Fig.A) of wing is broken twice, near end of radius vein AND near humeral cross vein; body usually blackish color; face bulges somewhat forward of eyes; .... **family Ephydridae, shore flies** (Fig.I)

#6.Costa vein (Fig.A) is broken only once, near end of radius vein; body may be black, gray or brightly colored with yellow; usually with a large and shiny triangular area on top of head which extends nearly to the bases of the antennae .... **family Chloropidae, frit flies** (Fig.J)

[1]Refer to an insect identification guide such as Arnett (1985) or Borror and White (1970) to distinguish between the fly families in this superfamily.

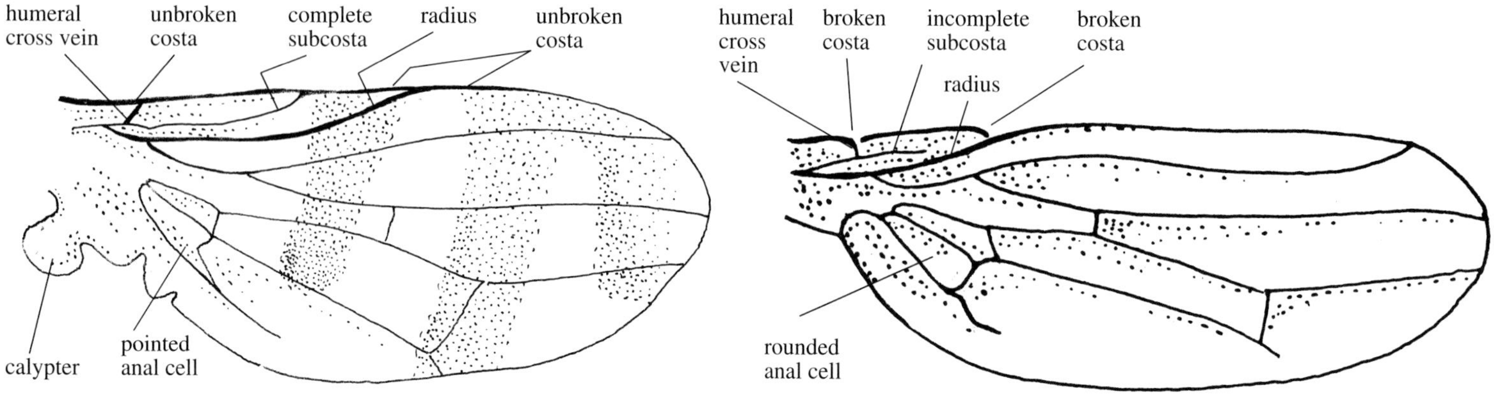

Fig.A. **WINGS OF MUSCOID FLIES**

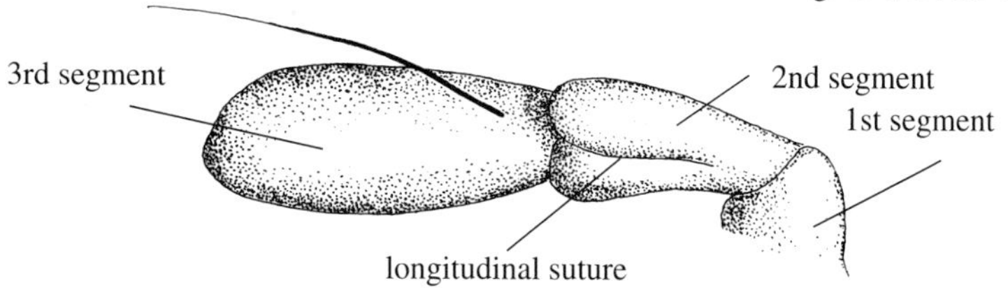

Fig.B. **ANTENNA OF MUSCOID FLIES**

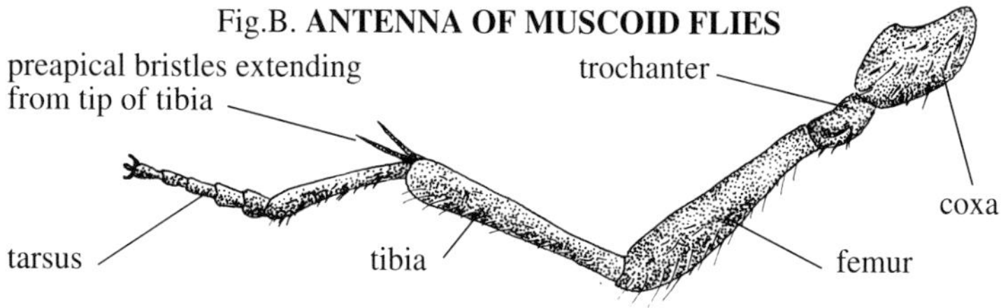

Fig.C. **LEG OF MUSCOID FLIES**

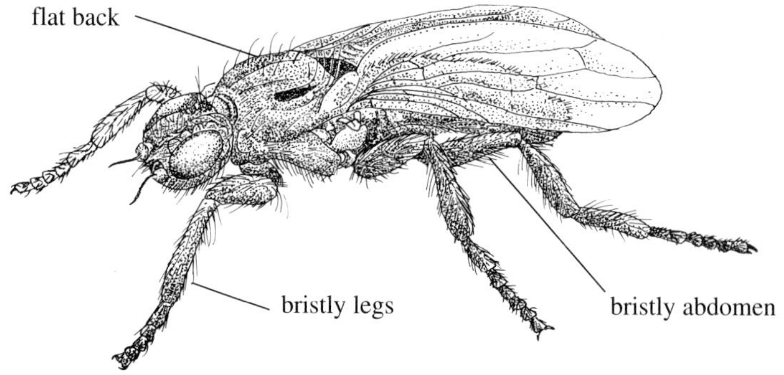

Fig.D. **FAMILY COELOPIDAE, SEAWEED FLIES:** Black or brown; up to about 5 mm (1/4") long; may be found in large numbers along the seashore, with larvae living in stranded algae.

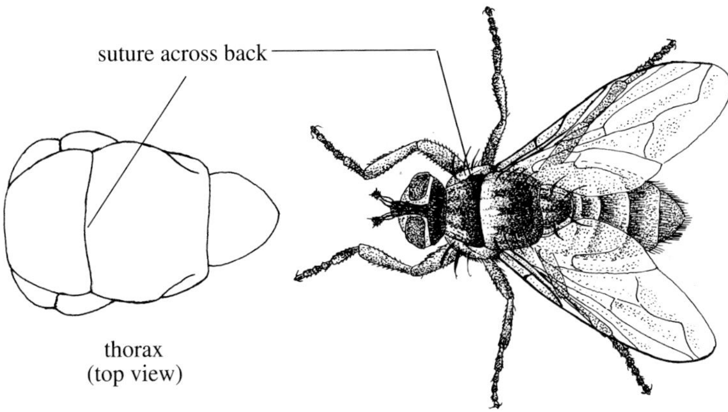

Fig.E. **SUPERFAMILY MUSCOIDEA, HOUSE FLIES AND RELATED FAMILIES[1]:** Many of these species resemble the house fly, somewhat hairy, black in color; about 5 mm (1/4") in length; breeding in decaying plant and animal matter. Other species may be much larger or smaller and vary widely in appearance and habits. This group contains a number of fly families which are very common and abundant along the shore and inland.

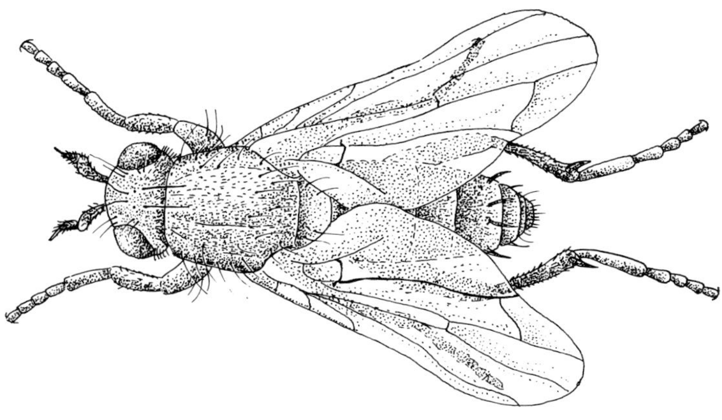

Fig.F. **SUPERFAMILY SCIOMYZOIDEA, MARSH FLIES AND RELATED FAMILIES[1]:** Yellowish or brownish flies, often with spots or patterns on wings; small to medium size, up to about 5 mm (1/4") long. Marsh flies occur in saltmarshes and dryomyzid flies occasionally are found along the shore. The larvae (see page 9.34) of some species feed on snails.

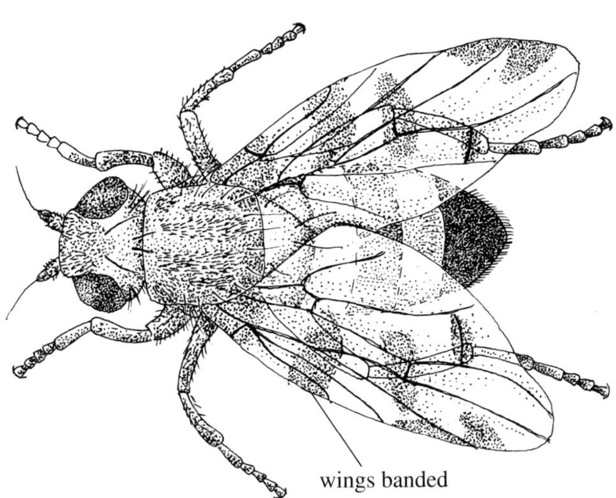

Fig.G. **FAMILY OTITIDAE, PICTURE-WINGED FLIES:** Body usually black and shiny, wings often banded or patterned; small to medium size, up to about 8 mm (3/8") long; often found in saltmarshes.

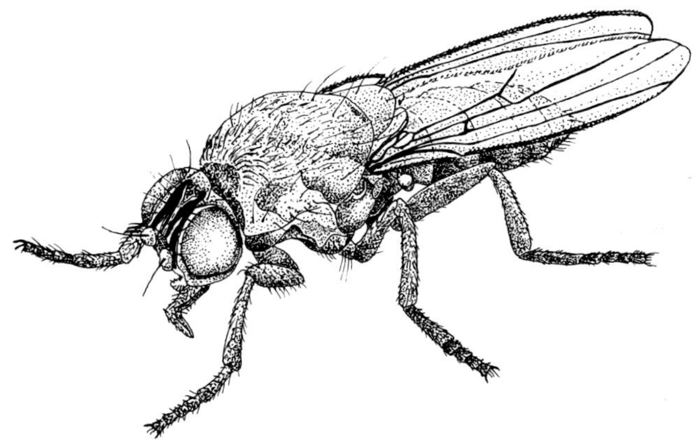

Fig.H. **SUPERFAMILY MILICHIOIDEA, BEACH FLIES AND RELATED FAMILIES[1]:** Most of these flies are black or brown; very small usually under 3 mm (1/8") long; found on saltmarshes, beaches and other intertidal environments. The larvae of some species feed on algae. The families Milichiidae (milichiids), Canaceidae (beach flies), Tethinidae (tethinids), and Sphaeroceridae (small dung flies) may occur along the shore.

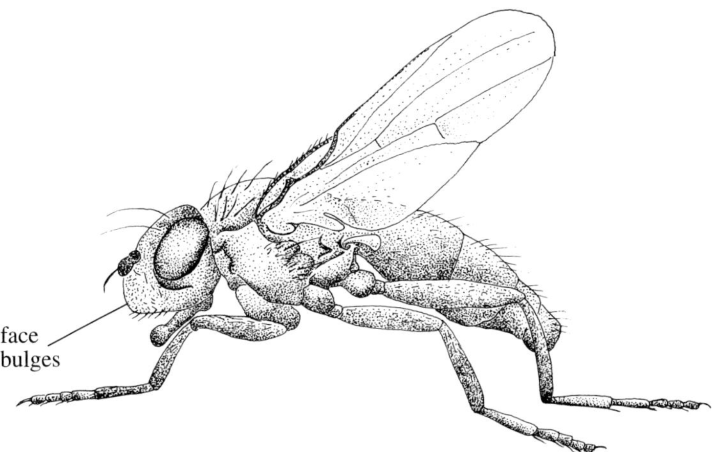

Fig.I. **FAMILY EPHYDRIDAE, SHORE FLIES:** Most species are black; usually small, under 3 mm (1/8") long; adults may occur in large numbers on tide pools above the high tide line; larvae (see page 9.34) occur in brackish water.

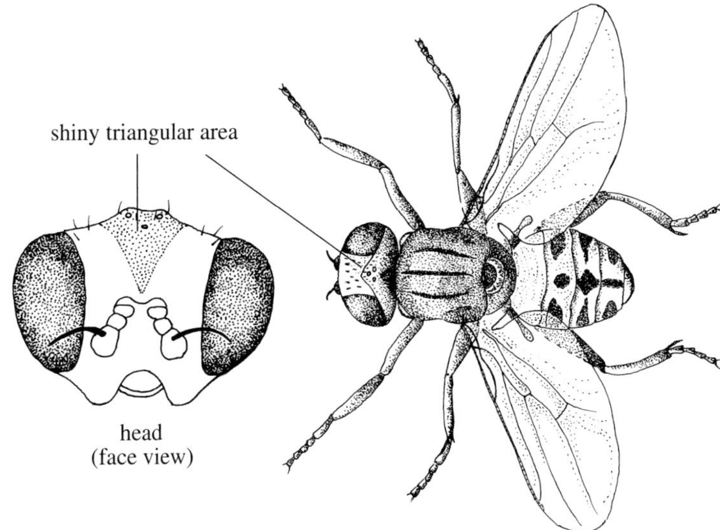

Fig.J. **FAMILY CHLOROPIDAE, FRIT FLIES:** Most species are small, under 3 mm (1/8") long and are variable in color, including black, gray and yellow; very common in saltmarsh grasses.

ANTS, WASPS, BEES AND RELATED INSECTS
CLASS INSECTA, ORDER HYMENOPTERA

Insects with two pairs of membranous wings (or wingless) that have relatively few veins; front wings larger than rear wings.

(Use the key on page 9.10 to determine if you have a hymenopteran)

#1.Wide "waist" (where abdomen joins thorax, see Fig.A); veins in hind wings form at least 3 closed[2] basal cells .... **suborder Symphyta, sawflies and related families** (Fig.A)

#1.Slender "waist," sometimes forming a petiole, a narrow stalk or stem (Figs.B-I); hind wings with 2 or fewer closed[2] basal cells .... **suborder Apocrita**, #2

#2.Petiole (stalklike "waist") with 1 or 2 humps or nodes (Fig.B); antennae distinctly elbowed (sharply bent) at least in females; often wingless .... **family Formicidae, ants** (Fig.B)

#2.First abdominal segments are not humped and nodelike; antennae may or may not be elbowed (Figs.C-I) .... #3

#3.Veins in front wing form at least 6 closed cells[2] (Figs.C-E); rear wings with at least 1 closed cell .... #4

#3.Veins in front wing form 5 or fewer closed cells[2] (Figs. F-I); rear wings may have no closed cells .... #7

#4.Pronotum (first dorsal plate of thorax, just behind head, see Fig.C) is somewhat triangular in shape when viewed from the side and extends nearly to the tegula (small scalelike structure overlying base of front wings, see Fig.C) .... #5

#4.Pronotum does not get close to the tegula; pronotum is short and collarlike with rounded lobes (see Fig.E) or is somewhat squarish (see Fig.F). .... #6

#5.With long threadlike antennae containing 16 or more segments; long ovipositor (female only) arises just forward of the tip of the tail (see Fig.J) and cannot be withdrawn into abdomen; usually does not sting .... **superfamily Ichneumonoidea, ichneumons, braconids and related families** (Fig.C)

#5.Antennae contain 12-13 segments; short ovipositor (see Fig.J) arises from tip of tail and functions as a sting .... **superfamily Vespoidea, yellowjackets, hornets and other vespoid wasps** (Fig.D)

#6.Body usually hairy; body hairs are branched or featherlike; first segment of tarsus on rear legs enlarged and flattened ..... **superfamily Apoidea, bees** (Fig.E)

#6.Body not hairy or, if hairy, body hairs are simple unbranched bristles; first segment of rear tarsi are slender .... **other hymenopterans[1]**

#7.Pronotum (first dorsal plate of the thorax just behind head, see Fig.F) is somewhat squarish and does not quite reach tegula (small scalelike structure overlying base of front wings, see Fig.F); antennae elbowed (bent sharply) with 5-13 segments .... **superfamily Chalcidoidea, chalcids** (Fig.F)

#7.Pronotum is somewhat triangular in shape when viewed from the side and extends nearly to the tegula (see Figs.G-I); antennae may or may not be elbowed and has 7-16 segments .... #8

#8.Antennae arise from a lip that protrudes from the front of the face .... **family Diapriidae, diapriids** (Fig.G)

#8.Antennae do not arise from a lip on the front of the face (Figs.H,I) .... #9

#9.Antennae arise low on face; antennae with 12 or fewer segments .... **superfamily Proctotrupoidea (in part), platygasterids and related families** (Fig.H)

#9.Antennae arise from middle or top of face (Fig.I); antennae with 13 or more segments .... #10

#10.Ovipositor (females only) arises just forward of the tip of the tail (Fig.J) and is permanently extended; thorax rather rough; abdomen oval and shiny; often produces galls on the leaves of various plants, including oak trees .... **family Cynipidae, gall wasps** (Fig.I)

#10.Ovipositor (Fig.J) arises from tip of tail and can be withdrawn into abdomen .... **other hymenopterans[1]**

[1]Refer to an insect identification guide such as Arnett (1985), Borror and White (1970), or Jaques (1947).

[2]Closed cells are areas of wing completely enclosed by veins. See Fig.A.

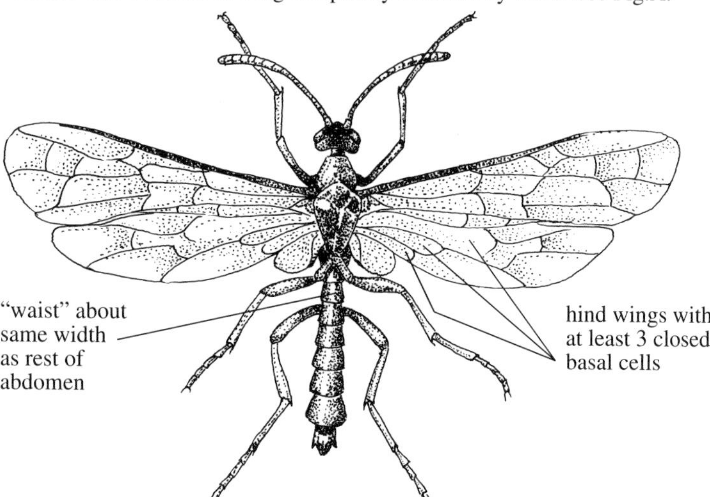

Fig.A. **SUBORDER SYMPHYTA, SAWFLIES AND RELATED FAMILIES:** Stem sawflies, family Cephidae, shown here, occur on saltmarshes. They are usually black, up to 13 mm (1/2") long; their larvae bore holes in the stems of grasses and shrubs. Other families in this suborder may be black, brown or brightly colored; usually under 20 mm (3/4") long.

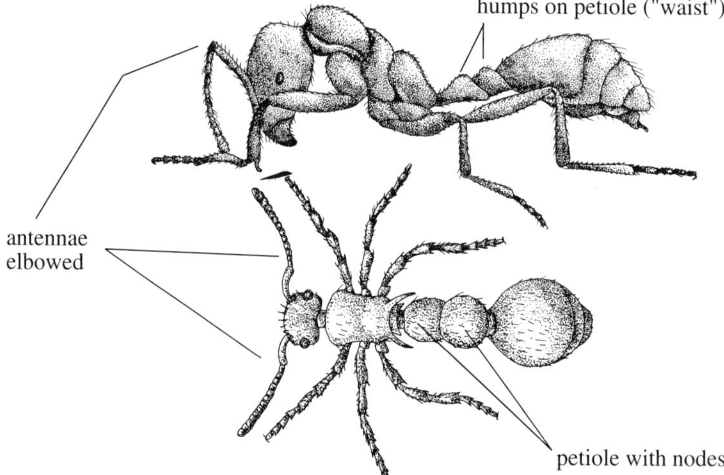

Fig.B. **FAMILY FORMICIDAE, ANTS:** Small ants in the subfamily Myrmicinae are common on saltmarshes, living at the base of grasses and among upper border shrubs. Other ants are common on sandy beaches and dunes. Myrmicine ants, shown here, are usually under 6 mm (1/4") long; dark in color; with an abdominal stalk made up of two segments. The other major subfamily of ants, the Formicinae, have an abdominal stalk with only one segment.

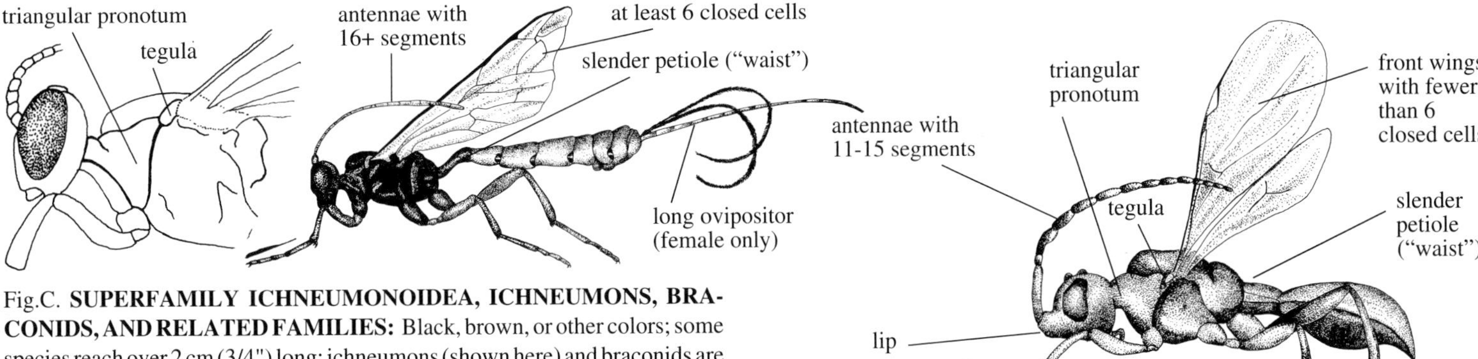

Fig.C. **SUPERFAMILY ICHNEUMONOIDEA, ICHNEUMONS, BRACONIDS, AND RELATED FAMILIES:** Black, brown, or other colors; some species reach over 2 cm (3/4") long; ichneumons (shown here) and braconids are found on saltmarshes. Their larvae parasitize other insects and help control harmful insect populations. Although these wasplike insects look formidible, especially the females with their long ovipositor, most species do not sting.

Fig.G. **FAMILY DIAPRIIDAE, DIAPRIIDS:** Shiny black; length under 7 mm (1/4"); occurs on saltmarshes.

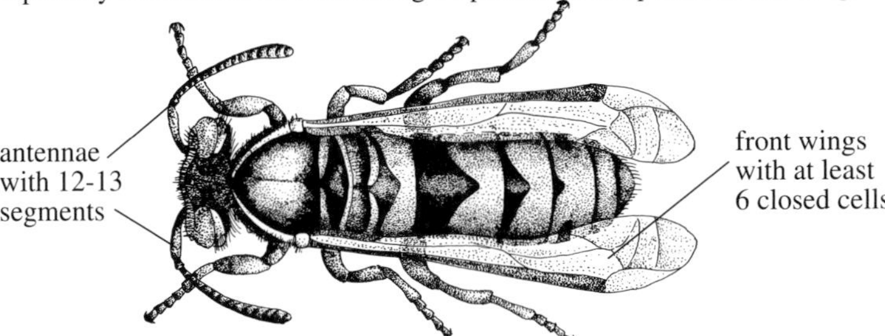

Fig.D. **SUPERFAMILY VESPOIDEA, YELLOWJACKETS, HORNETS, AND OTHER VESPOID WASPS**: Yellowjackets, shown here, have yellow and black bands across the abdomen; reach up to about 20 mm (3/4") in length; are common on beaches and other seashore environments; sometimes found off-shore where they will fly along behind a moving boat, apparently resting in the slipstream; females inflict a painful sting.

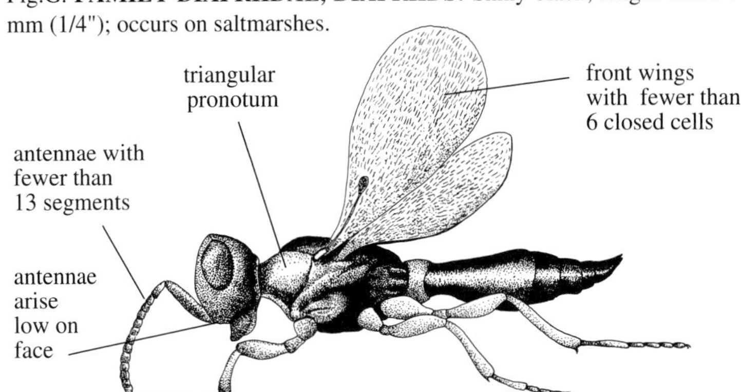

Fig.H. **SUPERFAMILY PROCTOTRUPOIDEA, PLATYGASTERIDS AND RELATED FAMILIES**: Shiny black; usually under 10 mm (3/8") long and many species are tiny, under 4 mm (3/16") long; occur on saltmarshes.

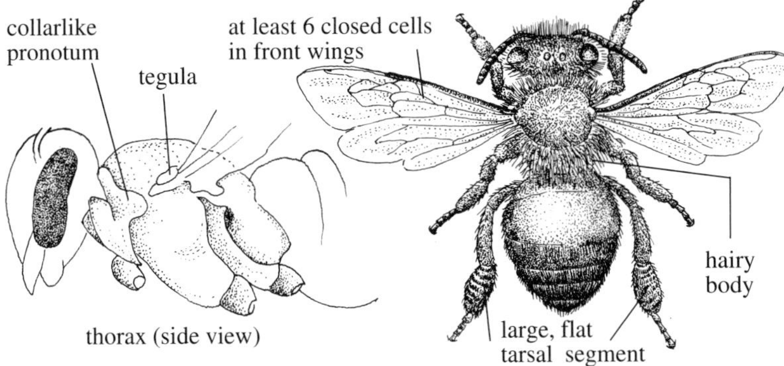

Fig.E. **SUPERFAMILY APOIDEA, BEES:** Many bees are solid black or have yellow or white markings; some species are up to 25 mm (1") long; may be found among flowers on marsh and dune plants; can inflict a painful sting.

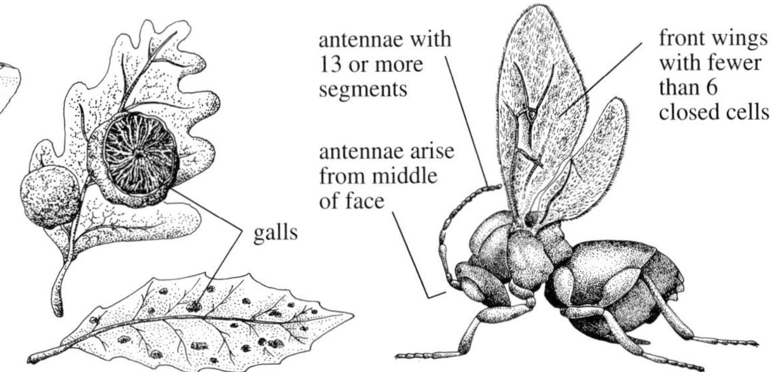

Fig.I. **FAMILY CYNIPIDAE, GALL WASPS:** Black with shiny abdomen; usually under 10 mm (3/8") long; forms galls which may be found on the leaves of shrubs and trees in the back dunes and along the upper border of saltmarshes.

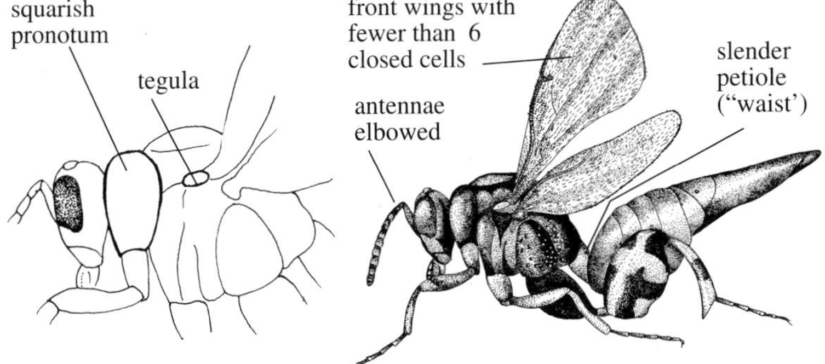

Fig.F. **SUPERFAMILY CHALCIDOIDEA, CHALCIDS:** Usually black, blue-black or green, sometimes metallic; small, usually under 7 mm (1/4") long; occur on saltmarshes.

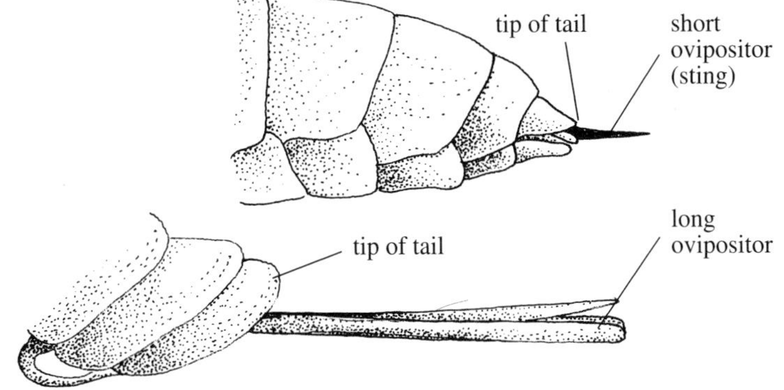

Fig.J. **OVIPOSITOR TYPES:** Short ovipositor (sting) can be withdrawn into abdomen when not in use. Long ovipositor cannot be withdrawn.

INSECT LARVAE AND PUPAE[1]

(Use the key on page 2.16 to determine if you have an insect larva or pupa)

#1.No wing buds or compound eyes; body usually wormlike, maggotlike or caterpillarlike (Fig.A); usually active, moving and feeding .... **larvae**, page 9.32
#1.With wing buds (Figs.B-I); resembles a mummy; with legs, antennae, wing buds and other structures often encased in a membrane and/or held tightly against the body; usually with compound eyes; usually an inactive resting stage but a few pupae, such as mosquito "wrigglers" (Fig.C) are active .... **pupae**, #2

#2.Appendages (legs, wings, mouthparts, etc.) are fused with each other and to the body to form a continuous covering (Figs.B,C) .... #3
#2.Appendages are free and not fused together, even though they are held in a fixed position (Figs.D-I) .... #4

#3.No breathing tubes or respiratory organs; with two pairs of wing buds but inner pair may be folded and hidden beneath outer .... **lepidopteran pupae** (Fig.B)
#3.With breathing tubes (Fig.C), gill filaments, or other respiratory organs located dorsally near head region; one pair of wing buds .... **dipteran pupae**, #5

#4.With one pair of wing buds (Figs.D-F) .... **pupae of true flies, order Diptera,** #5
#4.With no wing buds or with two pairs (You may need to lift up the outer pair to find the inner pair which are often hidden underneath) (Figs.G-I) .... #8

#5.Thorax ("body" region) considerably wider than abdomen ("tail" region); with trumpetlike breathing tubes on back of thorax; sometimes occurs in standing water areas on tidal marshes; found near water surface and may be quite active .... **pupae of mosquitoes ("wrigglers"), family Culicidae** (Fig.C)
#5.Thorax about the same width or only slightly wider than abdomen (Figs.D-F); pupae usually somewhat cylindrical; thorax may or may not have raised respiratory organs on back .... #6

#6.Dwells in a hollow egg shaped mud cocoon; with a pair of long hornlike respiratory organs that protrude outside through an opening in the cocoon; cocoons occasionally found in large numbers on mudflats .... **pupae of long-legged flies, family Dolichopodidae** (Fig.D)
#6.Without long hornlike respiratory organs (Figs. E-F); not found in a mud cocoon .... #7

#7.Prothorax (anterior segment of body region, just behind head) with a long slitlike opening connected to the spiracle (porelike opening to respiratory system).. .... **pupae of horse and deer flies, family Tabanidae** (Fig.E)
#7.Without a long, slitlike opening on prothorax .... **pupae of other true flies, order Diptera**[1] (Fig.F)

#8.With a distinct constriction ("waist") between the abdomen and thorax; mouthparts with a tonguelike extension used for lapping; with a pair of ovipositors (egg laying tubes or valves) at tail end .... **pupae of ants, bees, wasps, and related insects, order Hymenoptera** (Fig.I)
#8.Without a constriction between the abdomen and thorax (Figs. G,H); no distinct tongue; no paired ovipositors .... #9

#9.Antennae with 11 or fewer segments and usually shorter than body but may be much longer with numerous stout segments; wings buds are tough and hard or leathery, like the outer wing covers of adult beetles; wing buds wrap around to the underside of the body and pass between the rear two pairs of legs .... **pupae of beetles, order Coleoptera** (Fig.G)
#9.Antennae are long, with 12 or more segments; wing buds are not tough and leathery .... **pupae of caddisflies, order Trichoptera** (Fig.H)

[1]This key includes only the larvae and pupae most likely to be found in marine environments and excludes many others that you may occasionally encounter. Refer to Chu (1949) for the identification of immature insects to the family level. To go beyond the family level, use the references listed at the end of Chu (1949). Refer to Tesky (1969) and Jamnback and Wall (1959) to determine the species of tabanid (horse and deer fly) larvae. The groups of insects included in this key pass through immature stages in their development that are very different in appearance from their adult form. This type of development is called complete or complex metamorphosis and includes the egg, larva, pupa and adult stages. The development of other insect groups involves gradual or simple metamorphosis or no metamorphosis. The immature stages of these insects appear to be identical or very similar to the adult form, except for the lack of wings or the presence of wing buds. These immature insects will key out to the proper order with the wingless insects on page 9.14.

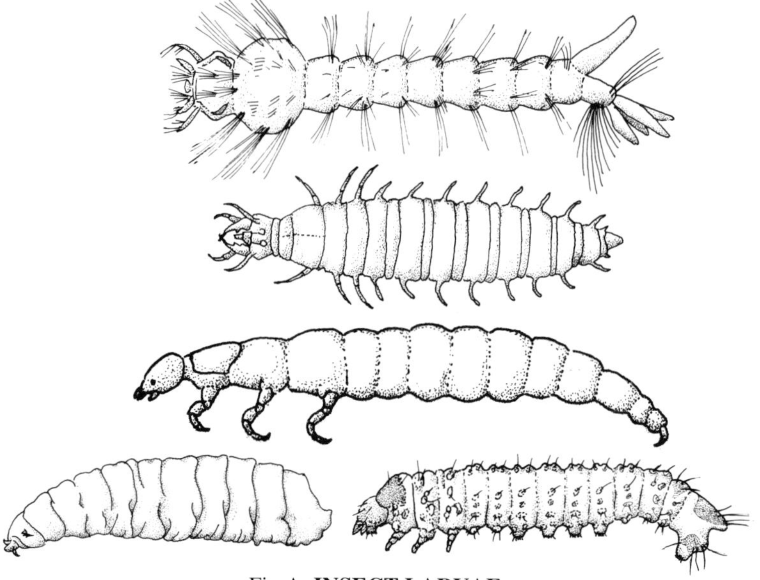

Fig.A. **INSECT LARVAE**

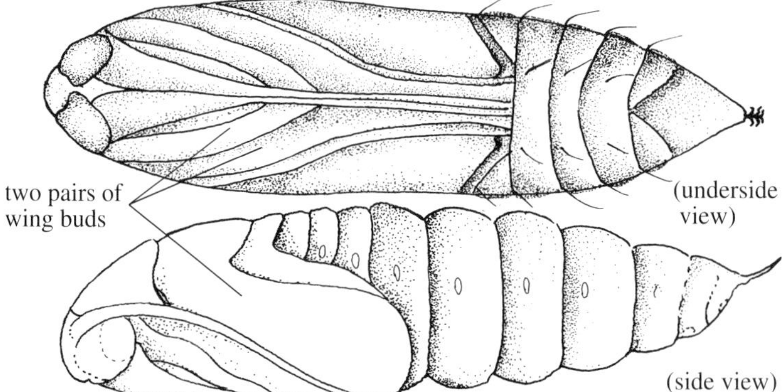

Fig.B. **MOTH AND BUTTERFLY PUPAE, ORDER LEPIDOPTERA:** Moth pupae are usually brown and smooth. Some butterfly pupae are encased in white cocoons made out of silk threads spun by the caterpillars' silk glands. Many butterfly pupae, called chrysalids, are not in cocoons and may be brightly colored. Most lepidopteran pupae are less than 2.5 cm (1") long. They are often attached to plants growing on sand dunes and upper tidal marshes.

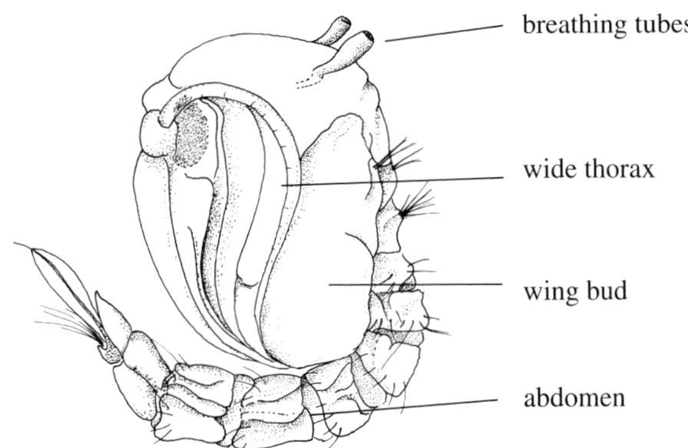

Fig.C. **MOSQUITO PUPAE, FAMILY CULICIDAE:** Usually beige; 6-9 mm (1/4-3/8") long; occurs in pools of standing water in tidal marshes; active, especially when disturbed. Sometimes called "wrigglers."

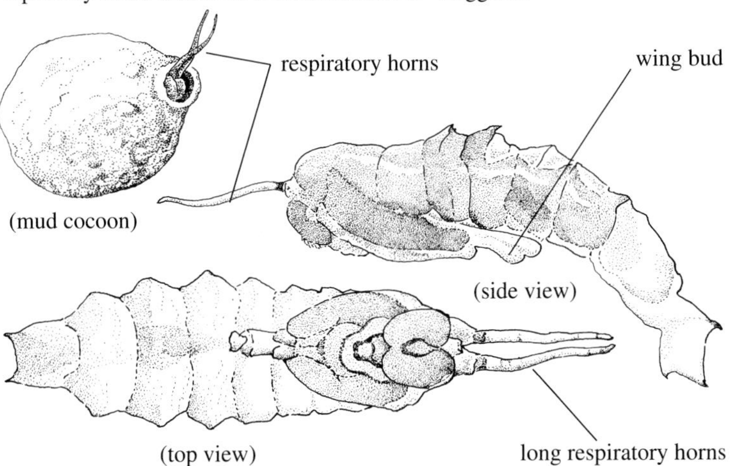

Fig.D. **LONG-LEGGED FLY PUPAE, FAMILY DOLICHOPODIDAE:** Yellow-white; up to about 1 cm (3/8") long; lives in spherical mud cocoons lying on surface of mudflats, among algae and in shallow water.

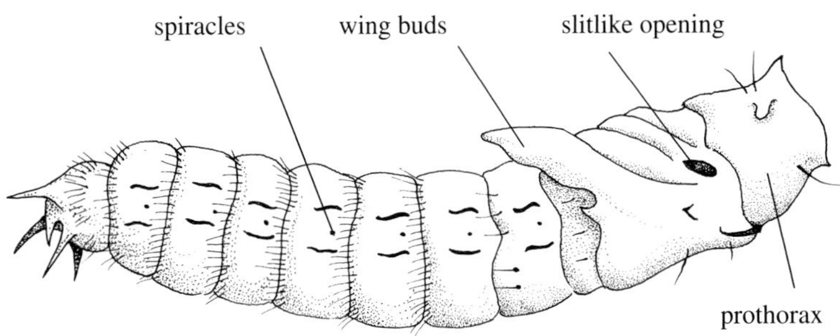

Fig.E. **HORSE AND DEER FLY PUPAE, FAMILY TABANIDAE:** Light tan to dark brown; up to about 2 cm (3/4") long; occurs among saltmarsh grasses.

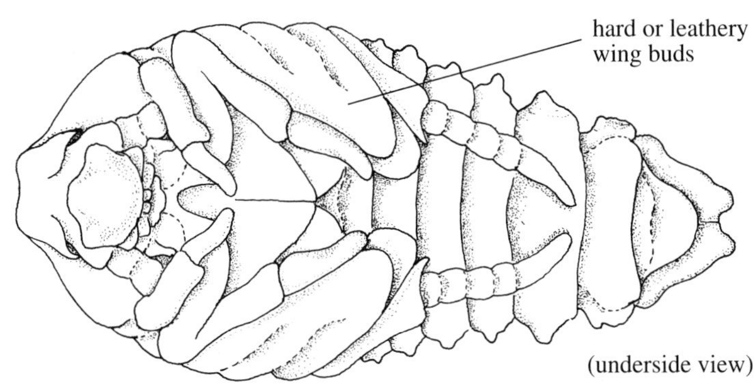

Fig.G. **BEETLE PUPAE, ORDER COLEOPTERA:** Beige, yellow-brown, black or various other colors; up to about 5 cm (2") long; found in saltmarshes and other aquatic habitats.

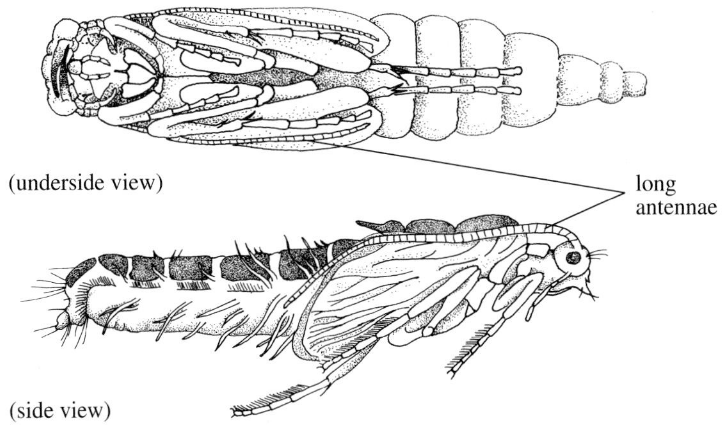

Fig.H. **CADDISFLY PUPAE, ORDER TRICHOPTERA:** Up to 2 cm (3/4") long; occurs in a case made up of sand grains, pebbles, or bits of plant material (see Fig.B on page 9.32); usually found submerged in fresh or brackish water.

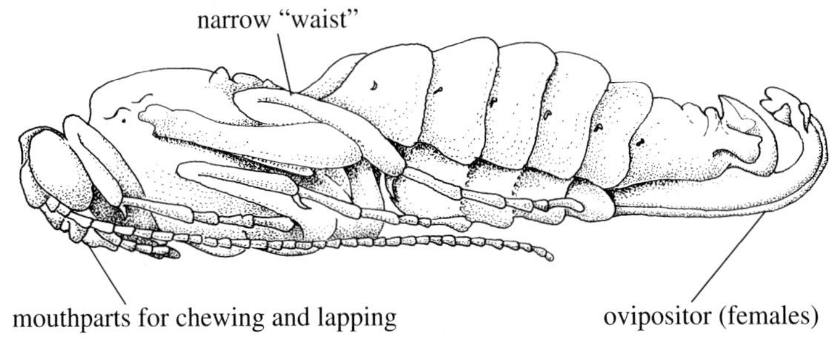

Fig.I. **HYMENOPTERAN PUPAE, ORDER HYMENOPTERA:** May reach over 4 cm (1 1/2 ") long but usually smaller. Sometimes enclosed in a cocoon or in the cells of a nest. Pupae of parasitic species may occur within the host.

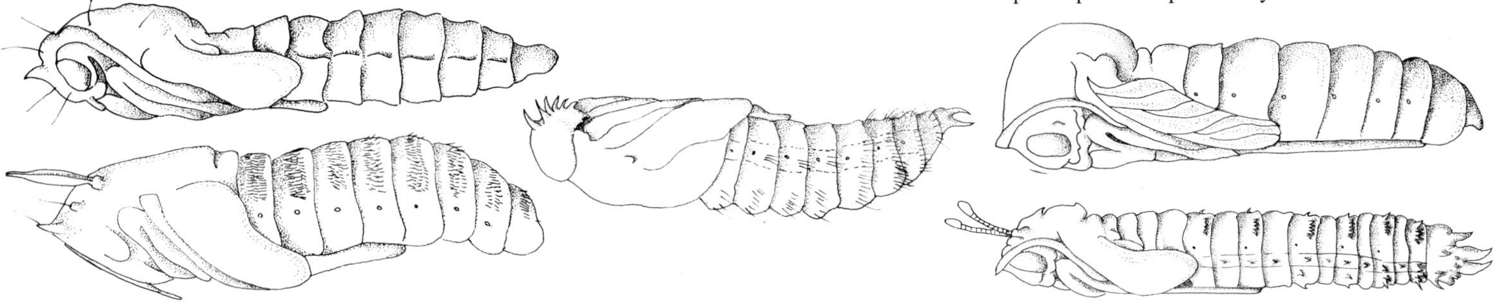

Fig.F. **FLY PUPAE, ORDER DIPTERA:** Often beige, yellowish, or brown but may be other colors; most species are under 20 mm (3/4") long; found in tidal marshes, on beaches among stranded algae, and other coastal habitats.

INSECT LARVAE[1]

(Insect larvae key begins on page 9.30)

#1.With three pairs of true legs (legs that are jointed and segmented) (Figs.A-C) on the thorax (midbody region just behind the head); abdomen (posterior region) may or may not have prolegs (fleshy bumplike legs that are not jointed or segmented) (Fig.C) .... #2
#1.Without any true legs (Figs.D-I); prolegs may or may not be present on abdomen or thorax .... #4

#2.With prolegs (fleshy, bumplike legs) (Fig.C) on 4-5 mid-abdominal (posterior region) segments and on last segment; prolegs with crochets (tiny hooks) often arranged in a circular or oval pattern .... **order Lepidoptera, moth and butterfly larvae, caterpillars** (Fig.C)
#2.Without any mid-abdominal prolegs or, if prolegs are present, they do not have crochets (Figs.A,B) .... #3

#3.End of abdomen ("tail") with a pair of hooked claws; larvae often build cases .... **order Trichoptera, caddisfly larvae** (Fig.B)
#3.End of abdomen without hooked claws; larvae do not live in a case .... **probably[1] order Coleoptera, beetle larvae** (Fig.A)

#4.With a complete, distinct head segment (Figs.D-H); head is about the same width as rest of body and is usually rounded or blunt but may be pointed .... #5
#4.Without any head segment or with a partial, tiny peglike or pointlike head segment that is much narrower than the rest of the body (Fig.I) .... page 9.34

#5.Without a breathing tube or other complex structures at posterior end (Fig.D) .... **probably[1] order Coleoptera, beetle larvae** (Fig.D)
#5.With a breathing tube, fingerlike projections or other complex structures at the posterior end (Figs.E-H) .... **order Diptera, true fly larvae**, #6

#6.Thorax (body region behind head) wider than abdomen ("tail" region) .... **family Culicidae, mosquito larvae** (Fig.E)
#6.Thorax same width as abdomen (Figs.F-H) .... #7

#7.With a breathing tube on tail end; with transverse plates or bands on the back of some or all segments .... **family Psychodidae, sand fly larvae** (Fig.F)
#7.Tail end with various structures but without an obvious breathing tube (Figs.G-H); without transverse plates or bands on the back of any segments .... #8

#8.With one or two prolegs (fleshy, bumplike legs) on prothorax (first segment behind head) .... **family Chironomidae, midge larvae** (Fig.G)
#8.With no prolegs on prothorax .... **family Ceratopogonidae, larvae of biting midges, punkies, no-see-ums** (Fig.H)

[1]See footnote on page 9.30.

mudloving beetle larva, family Heteroceridae

jointed legs

ground beetle larva, family Carabidae

jointed legs

ladybird beetle larva, family Coccinellidae

leaf beetle larva, family Chrysomelidae

water scavenger beetle larva, family Hydrophilidae

Fig.A. **BEETLE LARVAE, ORDER COLEOPTERA:** The larvae of ground beetles, family Carabidae, may be yellow, brownish or nearly black; length may be 10-45 mm (3/8-1 3/4"); occurs in tidal marshes. Mudloving beetle larvae, family Heteroceridae, are up to 1 cm (3/8") long and are found in muddy shores. The larvae of water scavenger beetles, family Hydrophilidae, are usually dark gray or yellow-brown; 3-60 mm (1/8-2 1/2") long; live in stagnant pools, lakes, streams, and brackish water. The larvae of ladybird beetles, family Coccinellidae, may be brightly colored with orange and black markings; found on saltmarsh plants where they feed on aphids, scale mites and other harmful insects. The larvae of leaf beetles, family Chrysomelidae, feed on the leaves and roots of saltmarsh plants.

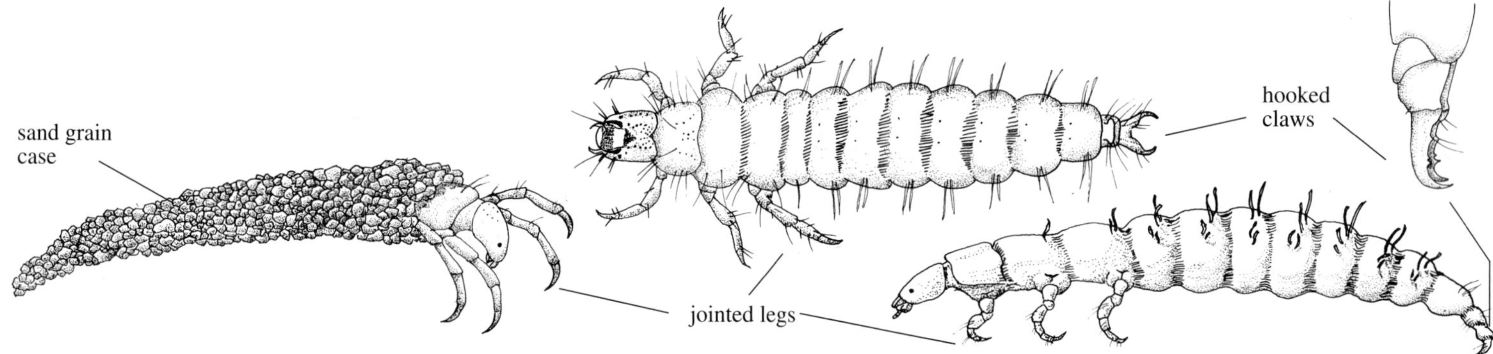

Fig.B. **CADDISFLY LARVAE, ORDER TRICHOPTERA:** Head and thorax may be darkly pigmented, abdomen may be whitish, green, tan, or gray; up to about 20 mm (3/4") long; occur in streams and other aquatic habitats under stones, gravel, and debris; build cases out of sand, pebbles, and plant matter.

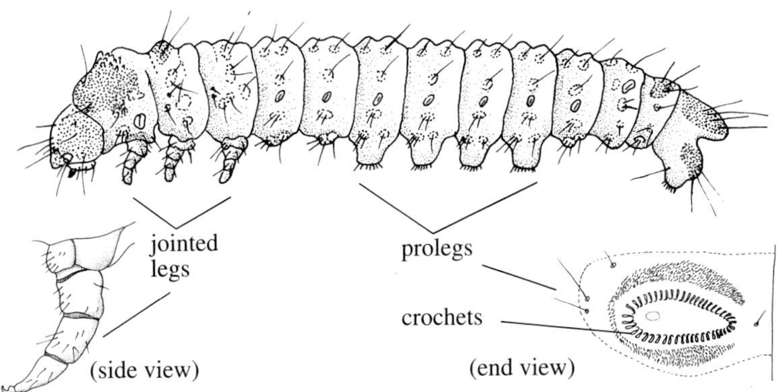

Fig.C. **MOTH AND BUTTERFLY LARVAE (CATERPILLARS), ORDER LEPIDOPTERA:** Many species very colorful including green, yellow, brown and other hues; usually about 25-50 mm (1-2") long; often found crawling and feeding on the foliage of marsh and dune plants.

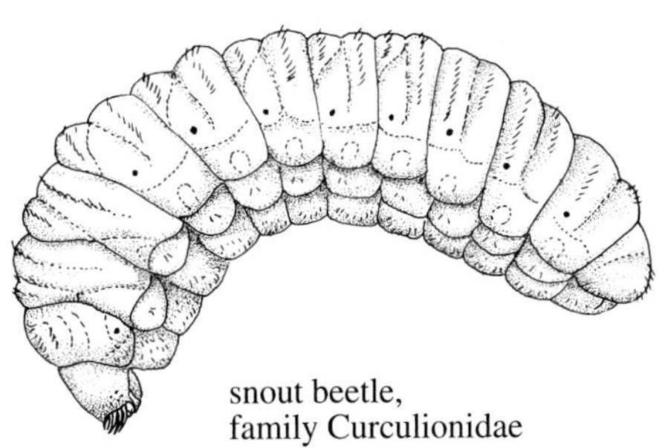

Fig.D. **BEETLE LARVAE, ORDER COLEOPTERA:** Beetle larvae live in the roots, fruits, and other parts of marsh and dune plants. The species shown here lives in wild rose hips.

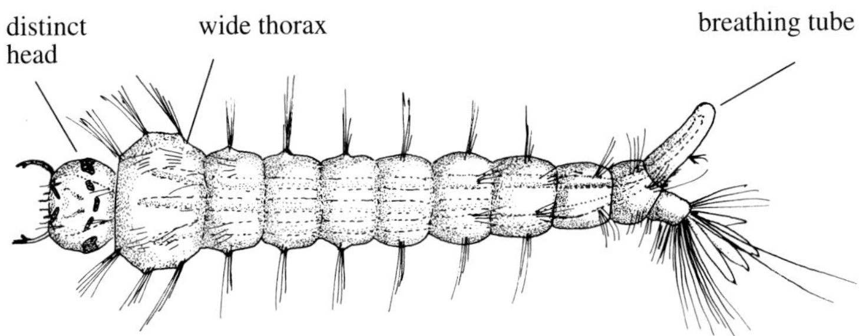

Fig.E. **MOSQUITO LARVAE ("WRIGGLERS"), ORDER DIPTERA, FAMILY CULICIDAE:** Usually yellowish-gray, whitish, or brown; 6-9 mm (1/4-3/8") long; found in pools of standing water in tidal wetlands; swim with wriggling motion when disturbed. Some states dig ditches and apply pesticides in saltmarshes to kill mosquito larvae and to eliminate their breeding habitat.

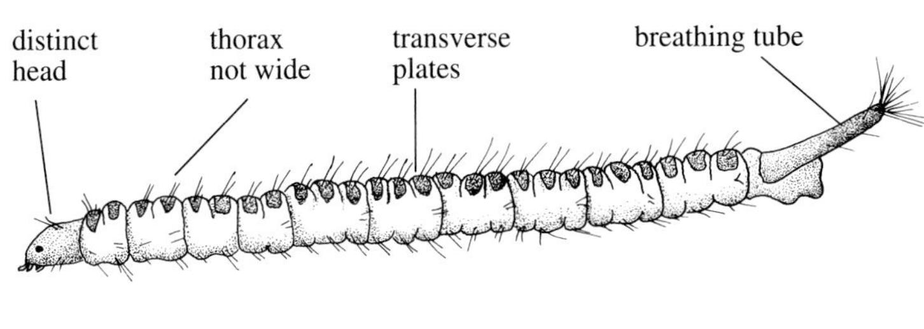

Fig.F. **SAND FLY LARVAE, ORDER DIPTERA, FAMILY PSYCHODIDAE:** Yellow, gray or nearly white; less than 6 mm (1/4") long; aquatic larvae, usually in fresh water, sometimes near sewer drains.

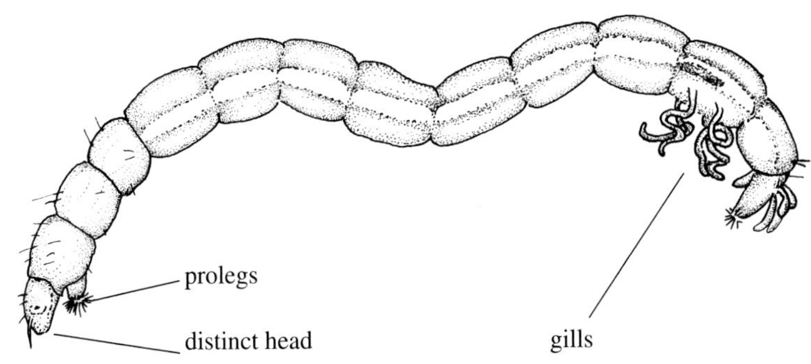

Fig.G. **MIDGE LARVAE, ORDER DIPTERA, FAMILY CHIRONOMIDAE:** Most species are red, some are other colors; up to 25 mm (1") long; live in bottom muds of rivers and estuaries; some species build cases.

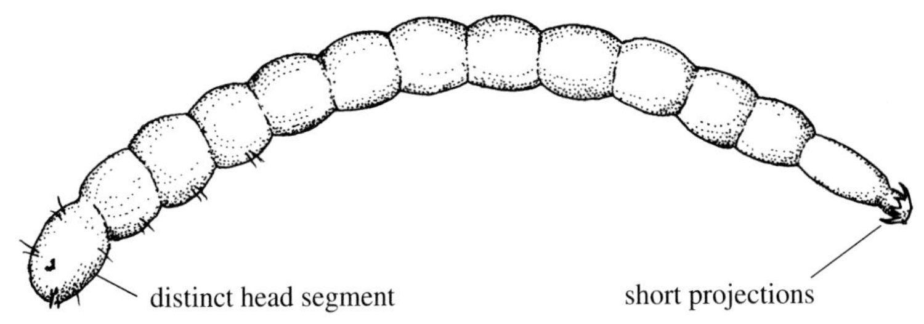

Fig.H. **BITING MIDGE ("NO-SEE-UM" OR "PUNKIE") LARVAE, ORDER DIPTERA, FAMILY CERATOPOGONIDAE:** Usually under 5 mm (1/4") long but may reach 15 mm (5/8"); live among algae and in mud bottoms, primarily in fresh water .

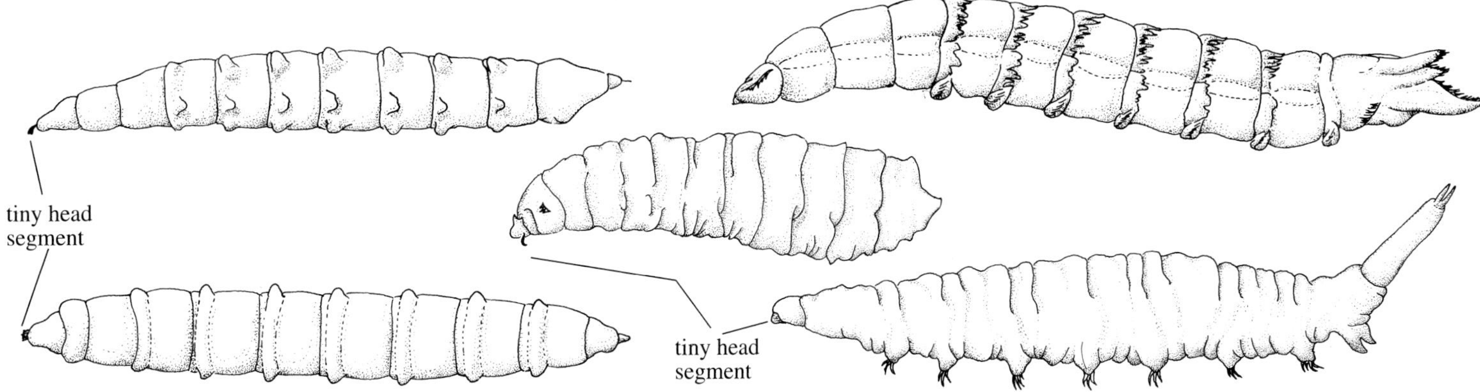

Fig.I. **INSECT LARVAE WITHOUT A DISTINCT HEAD SEGMENT, HEAD SEGMENT MAY BE ABSENT OR TINY AND POINTED**

INSECT LARVAE WITHOUT A DISTINCT HEAD SEGMENT[1]

(Insect larvae key begins on page 9.30)

#1.Tail end without a breathing tube or any projections (Figs.A,B); tail end may taper to a point or may be blunt .... #2
#1.Tail end with a breathing tube or with fingerlike or blunt projections (Fig.C-E) .... #3

#2.Body wedge shaped (Fig.A) with tail end wide and flat; generally found living in strand lines of seaweed, eelgrass, and other debris washed up onto shore .... **family Muscidae, stable and house fly larvae** (Fig.A)
#2.Body spindle shaped with both ends tapering to a point (Fig. B) .... **family Tabanidae[1], greenhead, horse, and deer fly larvae** (Fig.B)

#3.With an elongate breathing tube at tail end .... **family Ephydridae, shorefly larvae** (Fig.C)
#3.Tail end with blunt, tapering or fingerlike projections (Figs.D,E), without a breathing tube .... #4

#4.Tail end with thin pointed projections which fan out from body .... **family Sciomyzidae, marsh fly larvae** (Fig.D)
#4.Tail end with short blunt projections .... **family Dolichopodidae, long-legged fly larvae** (Fig.E)

[1]See footnote on page 9.30.

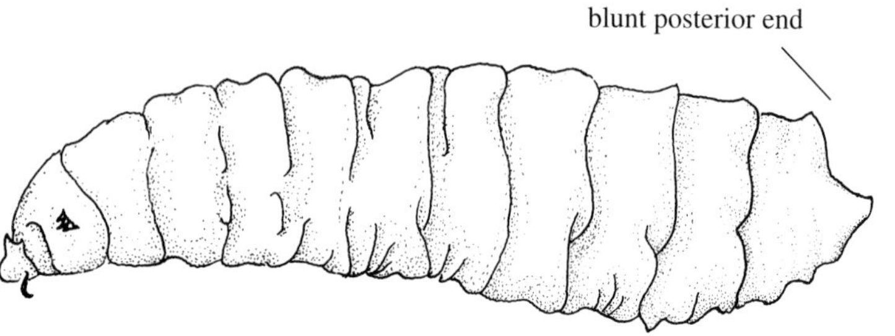

Fig.A. **STABLE AND HOUSE FLY LARVAE ("MAGGOTS"), ORDER DIPTERA, FAMILY MUSCIDAE:** Nearly white to cream colored; 5-12 mm (1/4-1/2") long; found on shore in decaying plants and animals.

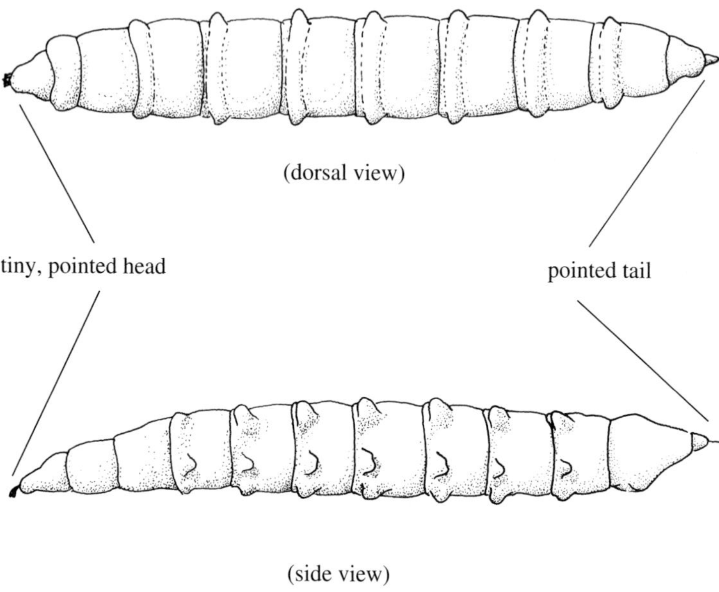

Fig.B. **GREENHEAD, HORSE, AND DEER FLY LARVAE, ORDER DIPTERA, FAMILY TABANIDAE:** Creamy white or amber color; the larvae of deer flies, *Chrysops* spp., are 14-16 mm (5/8") long; the larvae of green-head flies, *Tabanus* spp., are 18-50 mm (3/4-2") long; several species are common among saltmarsh grasses and some are aquatic.

tiny, pointed head

long breathing tube

prolegs

Fig.C. **SHORE FLY LARVAE, ORDER DIPTERA, FAMILY EPHYDRIDAE:** Color varies from dirty white to muddy green or brown; 5-16 mm (1/4-5/8") long; found in brackish water, stagnant pools, and in wet mud.

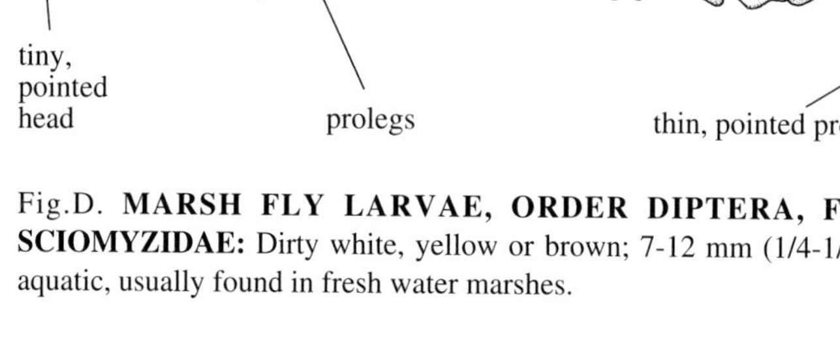

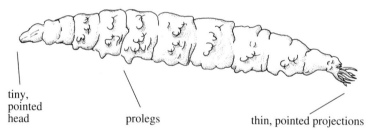

Fig.D. **MARSH FLY LARVAE, ORDER DIPTERA, FAMILY SCIOMYZIDAE:** Dirty white, yellow or brown; 7-12 mm (1/4-1/2") long; aquatic, usually found in fresh water marshes.

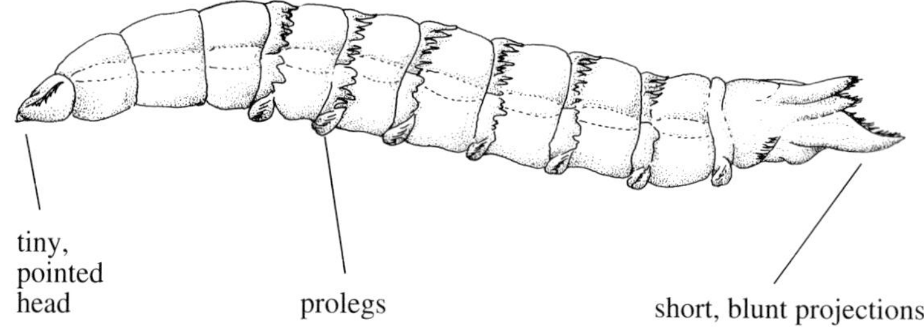

Fig. E. **LONG-LEGGED FLY LARVAE, ORDER DIPTERA, FAMILY DOLICHOPODIDAE:** White or yellow; 5-10 mm (1/4-3/8") long; found on mudflats at edge of pools, among algae, and in shallow water; builds spherical mud cocoons in which pupation takes place (see Fig.D on page 9.31).

CRUSTACEANS: PHYLUM ARTHROPODA, CLASS CRUSTACEA

Gill breathing, primarily aquatic arthropods usually with 2 pairs of antennae and 4 or more pairs of legs and/or claws.

(Use the key on page 2.00 to determine if you have a crustacean)

#1.Firmly cemented to rocks and other objects (Fig.A) .... **barnacles**, page 10.13
#1.Not cemented to rocks or other objects (Figs.B-O) .... #2

#2.Attaches to or lives inside another animal .... **parasitic crustaceans**, page 10.02
#2.Free living, not attached to or living inside another animal .... #3

#3.Carapace[1] is very small or lacking; segments of head, thorax ("body") and abdomen ("tail") are all about the same size; usually with 7 pairs of legs (including claws) but may have fewer (Figs.B-F) .... **amphipods, isopods, and tanaids**, page 10.04
#3.Carapace is obvious (Figs.G-O), covering the head and all or most of the thorax ("body"); the abdomen ("tail") is not covered by the carapace and its segments are much smaller than the carapace; the abdomen may extend out behind the body (Figs.J-O) or fold tightly underneath the body (Figs.G,I); usually with 5 pairs of legs (including claws) but may have 3 or more pairs .... **shrimps, mysids, crabs, and lobsters**, #4

#4.Lives in an empty snail shell; abdomen ("tail") is soft and has no shell; with 2 pairs of walking legs and 1 pair of claws (Fig.H) ..... **hermit crabs**, page 10.19
#4.Does not usually live in an empty snail shell; abdomen ("tail") has a shell and is not especially soft (Figs.G,I-O) .... #5

#5.Abdomen ("tail") is normally kept folded tightly underneath the body at an acute angle (Figs.G,I) .... **crabs**, #6
#5.Abdomen ("tail") is usually extended back behind the body (Figs.J-O) or is only slightly bent .... **shrimps, mysids, and lobsters**, #7

#6.Body is egg shaped; with 4 pairs of wide, flat, hairy legs none of which have claws; with a long, triangular, shieldlike plate (telson) at end of abdomen ("tail") which is tucked under body; burrows into wave swept sandy beaches (Fig.G) .... **sand (mole) crabs**, bottom of page 10.19
#6.Body is typically crablike, somewhat flattened and wider than deep, not egg shaped; with 5 pairs of legs, the first pair with large claws; abdomen is reduced in size, usually broadly rounded or triangular in females and narrow in males (Fig.I) .... **true crabs**, page 10.20

#7.Carapace does not cover all thoracic ("body") segments (rear 3 pairs of walking legs are attached to segments not covered by the carapace) (Figs.J,K) ...... #8
#7.Carapace covers all of the thoracic ("body") segments (all of the walking legs are attached to segments covered by the carapace) (Figs.L-O) .... #9

#8.Abdomen ("tail") is wider than carapace; eyes are large and are on stalks; large animals, reaching up to 25 cm (10") long; second pair of legs have large, powerful, spiny claws similar to the claws of a praying mantis (Fig.J) .... **mantis shrimp**, page 10.16
#8.Abdomen ("tail") is much narrower than carapace; eyes are very tiny or lacking, eyes are not on stalks; small animals, less than 15 mm (5/8") long; none of the legs have claws (Fig.K) .... **cumaceans**, page 10.14

#9.With 8 pairs of feathery legs; each leg is composed of two branches; none of the legs have claws (Fig.L) .... **mysids**, page 10.15
#9.With fewer than 8 pairs of legs; one or more pairs of legs end in small or large claws (Figs.M-O) .... #10

#10.Legs and claws are slender and delicate; body and tail are narrow; most species less than 7.5 cm (3") long (Fig.M) .... **true shrimps**, middle of page 10.16
#10.With a pair of large, powerful claws; legs are stout, primarily used for walking; body and tail are broad (Figs.N,O) .. **lobsters and mud shrimp**, page 10.18

[1]All crustacean bodies are divided into 3 sections, the head, thorax ("body"), and abdomen ("tail"). The head and thorax of some crustaceans are covered by a single shell called the carapace (Figs.G-O). The legs and claws are always attached to the thorax. The appendages attached to the underside of the abdomen are called pleopods or swimmerets. The appendages attached to the posterior end of the abdomen are called uropods.

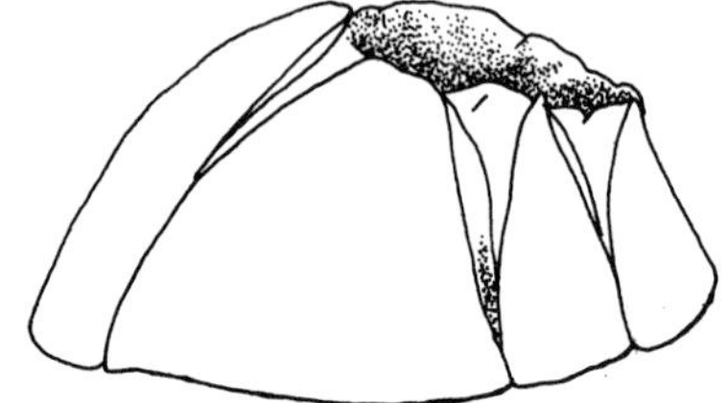

Fig.A. **BARNACLE**

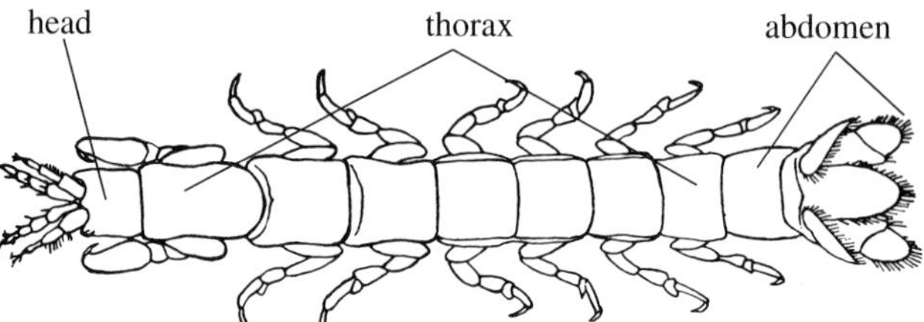

Fig.C. **ANTHURID ISOPOD**

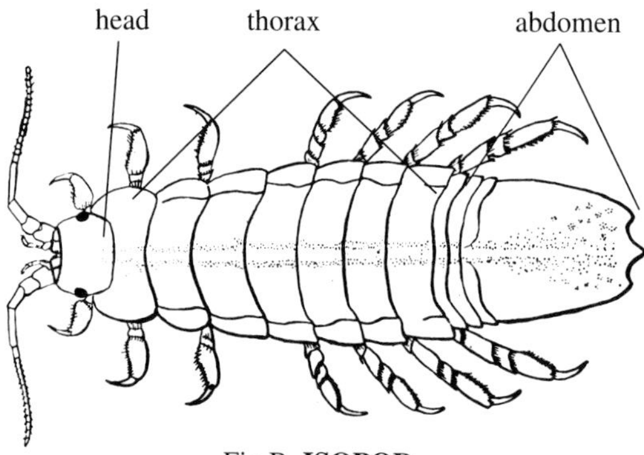

Fig.B. **ISOPOD**

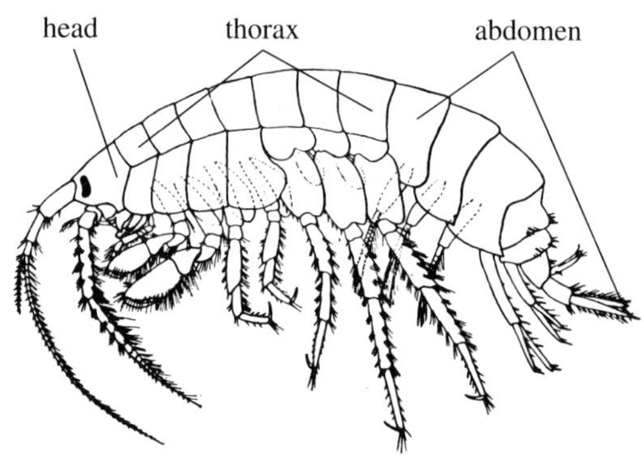

Fig.D. **GAMMARID AMPHIPOD**

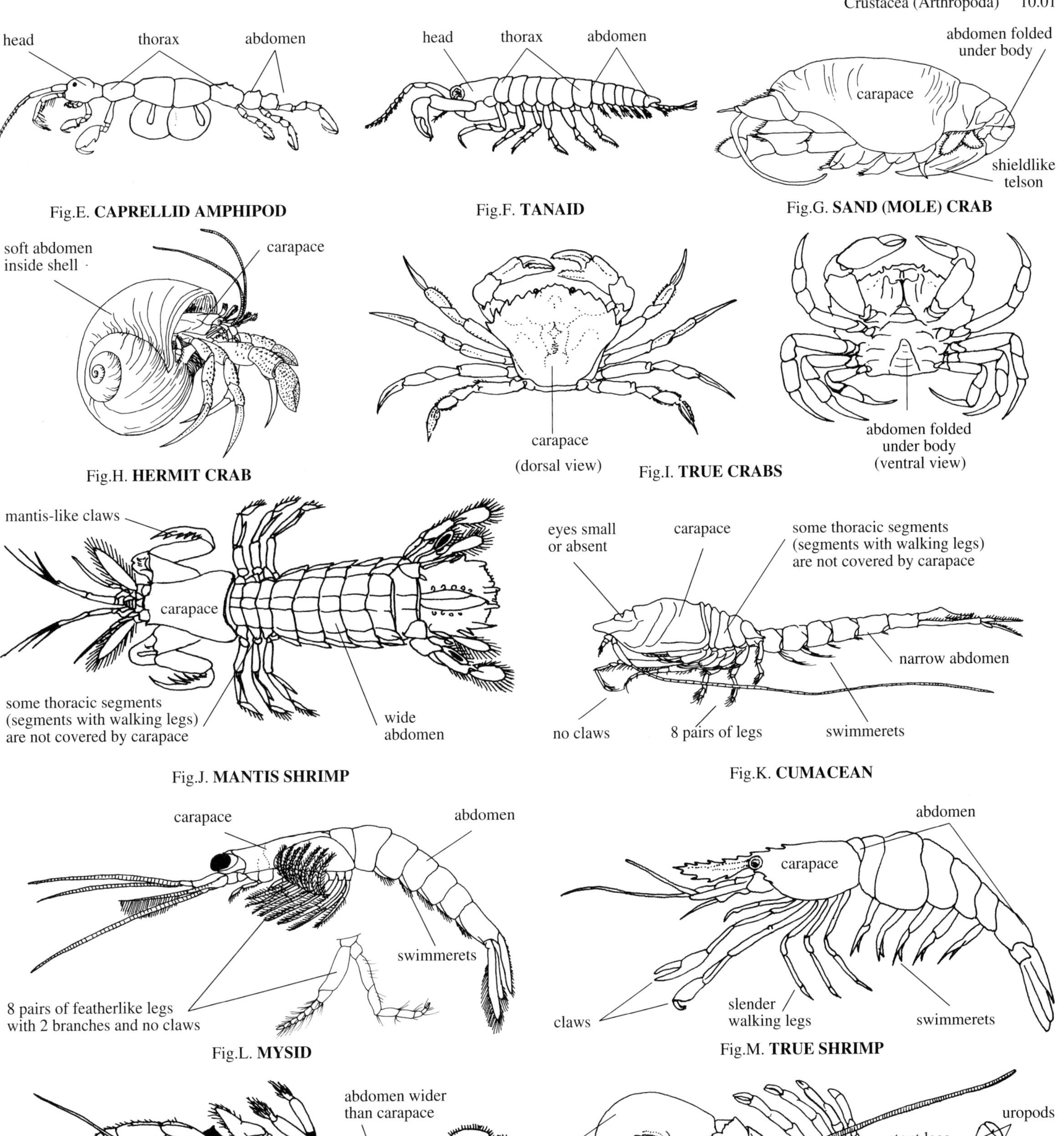

Fig.E. **CAPRELLID AMPHIPOD**

Fig.F. **TANAID**

Fig.G. **SAND (MOLE) CRAB**

Fig.H. **HERMIT CRAB**

Fig.I. **TRUE CRABS**

Fig.J. **MANTIS SHRIMP**

Fig.K. **CUMACEAN**

Fig.L. **MYSID**

Fig.M. **TRUE SHRIMP**

Fig.N. **MUD SHRIMP AND ALLIES**

Fig.O. **LOBSTER**

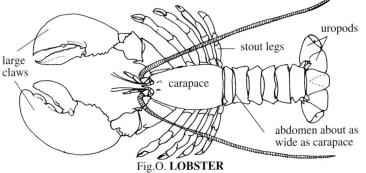

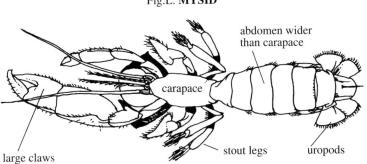

PARASITIC AND COMMENSAL CRUSTACEANS
PHYLUM ARTHROPODA, CLASS CRUSTACEA

Crustaceans living inside or attached to the outside of another animal

(Use the key on page 2.18 to determine if you have a parasitic crustacean)

#1.With a squat, conical shell (Fig.B) consisting of side plates and an opening at top which is covered by a beaklike trap door .... **acorn barnacles**, page 10.13
#1.Not with a conical shell as described above .... #2

#2.Head end attached to or buried into the gills, fins or body of fish; with a slender, wormlike body extending externally from the fish; often with a pair of egg sacs at the external end .... **subclass Copepopda, order Siphonostomatoida (in part), ribbon fish lice or gill maggots**[1] (Fig. A)
#2.Not as described above (Figs.C-H) .... #3

#3.Head and body (thorax) regions are covered by a single shell (carapace) (Figs.C-F) .... #4
#3.Segments of head and body regions are distinct and are not covered by a single shell (carapace) (Figs.G-H) .... #7

#4.With a shieldlike carapace (Figs.D,E); body somewhat flattened; common on fish gills and skin .... #5
#4.Carapace not shieldlike (Figs.C,F) .... #6

#5.Eyes are tiny and simple, not compound; without sucking discs .... **subclass Copepoda, order Siphonostomatoida (in part), caligiform fish lice**[1] (Fig.D)
#5.Eyes are compound (made up of many facets, like an insect); with 2 sucking discs on the underside .... **subclass Branchiura, arguloid fish lice** (Fig.E)

#6.With hooklike antennae used to attach to host; common fish gill parasites .... **subclass Copepoda, order Poecilostomatoida, fish lice**[1] (Fig.C)
#6.Without hooklike antennae; crablike or shrimplike animals (Fig.F) .... page 10.00, couplet #3

#7.Body is distinctly flattened from side to side (laterally) .... **order Amphipoda** (Fig. G)
#7.Body is distinctly flattened from top to bottom (dorsoventrally) .... **order Isopoda** (Fig.H)

[1]There are numerous species of free living copepods and they are very common in the plankton (refer to a plankton identification book). Some parasitic copepods closely resemble free living forms (Fig.C) and others are highly modified for parasitism (Figs. A,D). The classification system used here for parasitic copepods is from Kabata (1979). Refer to Ho (1977), Ho (1978) and Dudley and Illg (1991) to identify many of the species of copepods which are associated with fishes and ascidians in the northeastern United States. WARNING: Some of these references use a different classification system than Kabata (1979).

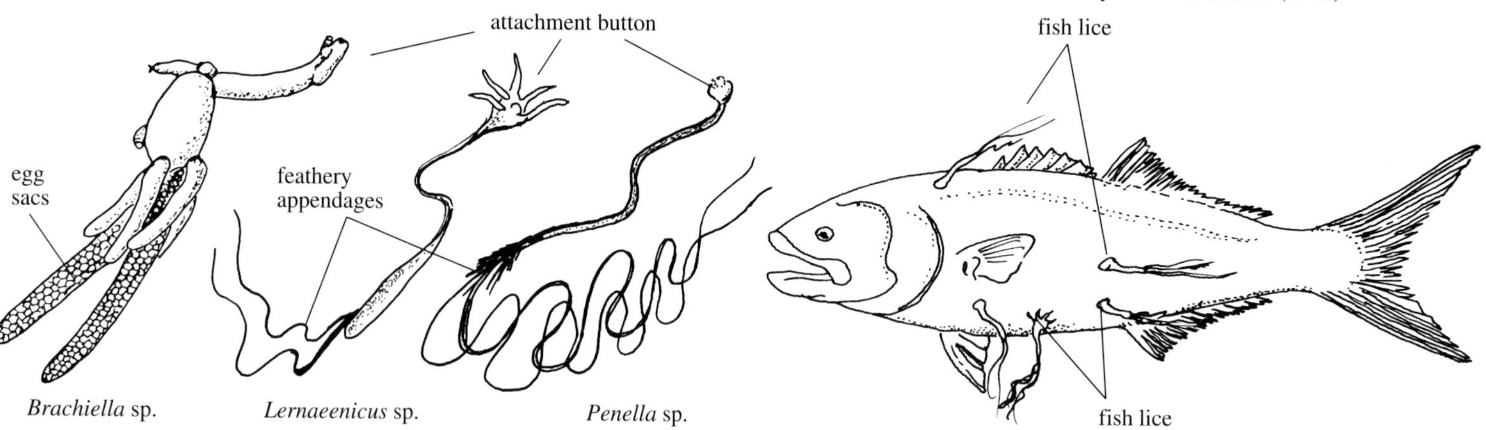

Fig.A. **COPEPOD ORDER SIPHONOSTOMATOIDA (in part), RIBBON FISH LICE OR GILL MAGGOTS:** Head embeds into the tissue of the host fish and feeds on the fish's blood by means of a special attachment button and thread; body extends externally from fish and is long and wormlike, often ending with a pair of stringlike egg sacs. *Lernaeenicus* sp. is up to 5 cm (2") long and parasitizes bluefish (*Pomatomus saltatrix*), Atlantic menhaden (*Brevoortia tyrannus*), and other common fishes. *Penella* sp. parasitizes swordfish (*Xiphias gladius*) and ocean sunfish (*Mola mola*) and may reach 20-25 cm (8-10") in length.

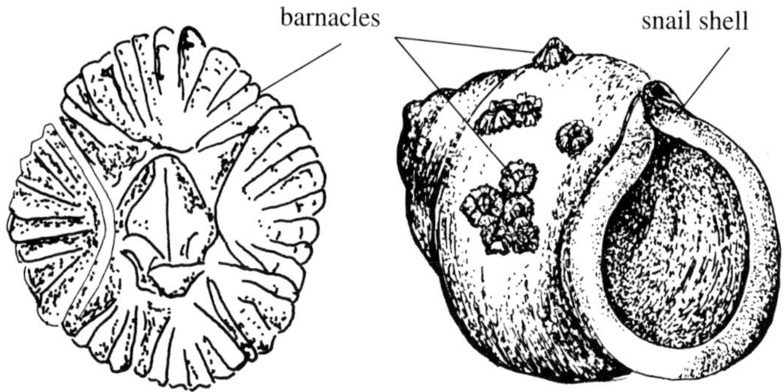

Fig.B. **SUBCLASS CIRRIPEDIA, ACORN BARNACLES:** Attach to many animals, such as mollusks, but are probably commensal without causing harm.

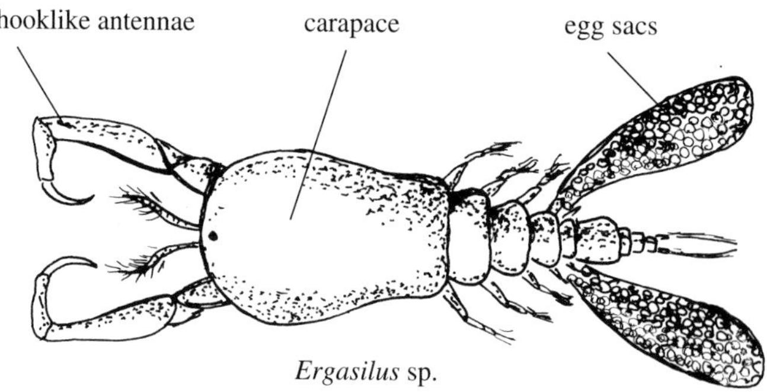

Fig.C. **COPEPOD ORDER POECILOSTOMATOIDA, FISH LICE:** Generally tiny and attach to the gills of fish using their hooklike antennae.

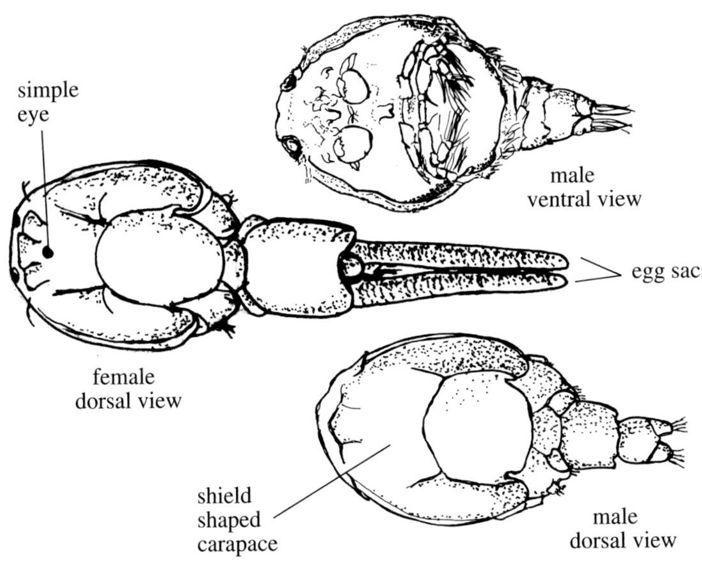

Fig.D. **COPEPOD ORDER SIPHONOSTOMATOIDA (in part), CALIGIFORM FISH LICE:** May exceed 5 mm (1/4") in length and some species may reach 5 cm (2"); commonly found crawling about on the skin of fish and occasionally found swimming free in the plankton.

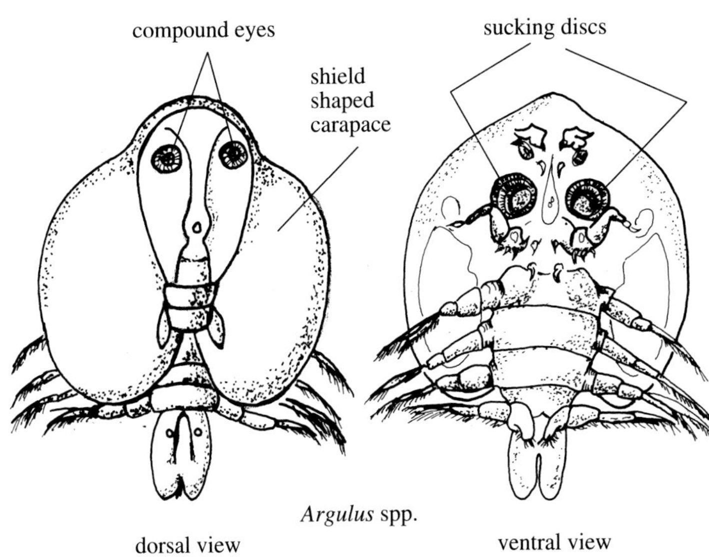

Fig.E. **SUBCLASS BRANCHIURA, ARGULOID FISH LICE:** Up to 1.2 cm (1/2") in length; common ectoparasites on the skin and in the gill cavity of fish; also found free swimming in the plankton. Refer to Cressy (1978) for the identification of the branchiurans of the northeastern United States.

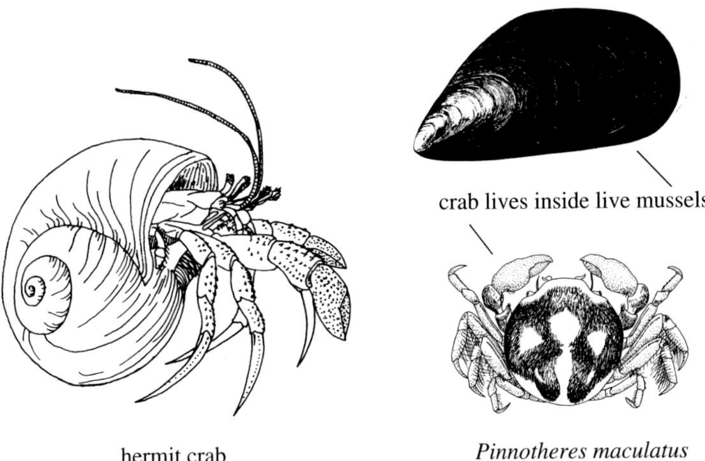

Fig.F. **CRABS:** Hermit crabs occupy snail shells after snails have died (see page 10.19). Several species of small crabs, such as pea crabs, *Pinnotheres* spp. live inside living mussels, oysters, and other bivalves as well as worm tubes (see page 10.26).

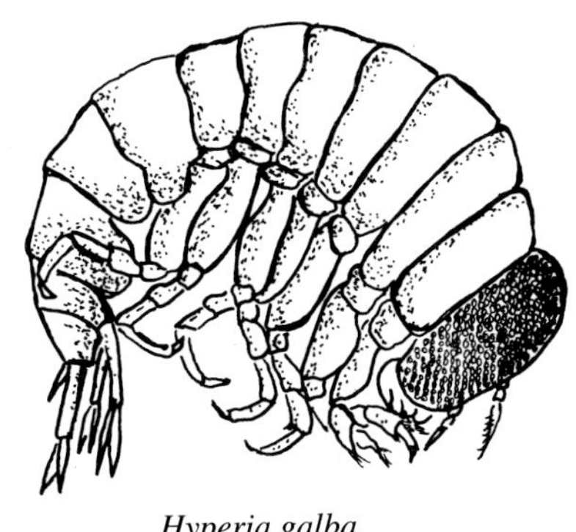

Fig.G. **ORDER AMPHIPODA, AMPHIPODS:** Most amphipods are free living (see pages 10.04-10.09) and only a few are completely parasitic. *Hyperia galba* parasitizes the lion's mane jellyfish, *Cyanea capillata* and moon jelly, *Aurelia aurita*. Other amphipods, included with the free living forms, are commensal with sponges, ascidians, polychaete worms, and sipunculids.

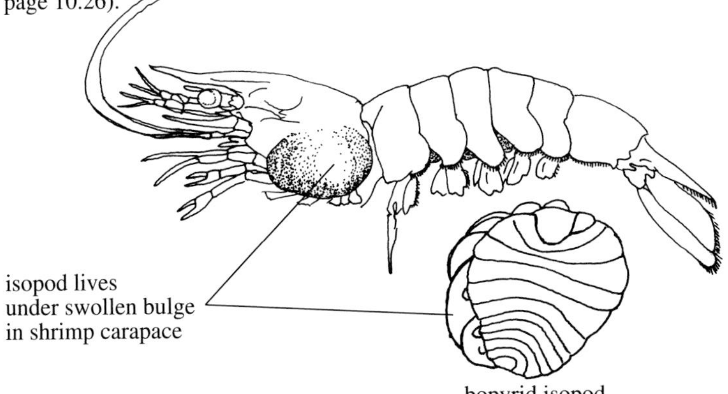

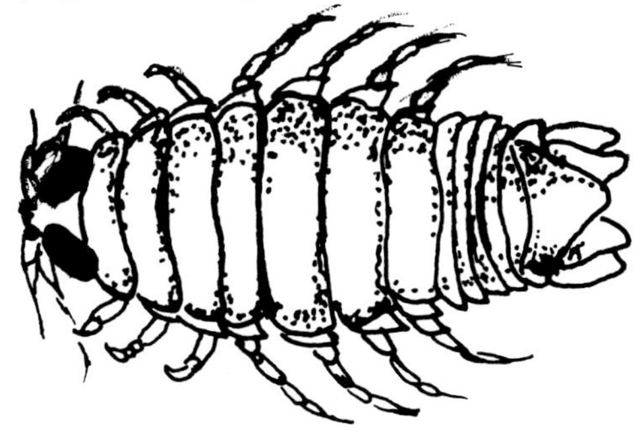

Fig.H. **ORDER ISOPODA, ISOPODS:** Most isopod species are free living (see pages 10.10-10.12). Isopods in the families Aegidae and Cymothoidae are ectoparasites on the skin and gills of Atlantic menhaden (*Brevoortia tyrannus*), bluefish (*Pomatomus saltatrix*), dogfishes (*Squalus*), skates (*Raja*), Atlantic cod (*Gadus morhua*) and many other fishes. *Aega psora,* shown above, reaches 5 cm (2") in length. Isopods in the family Bopyridae permanently attach to crabs and shrimp, sometimes forming a bump under the shell of the host. Adult female bopyrid isopods are often asymmetrical with one side of the body larger than the other.

AMPHIPODS, ISOPODS, AND TANAIDS
PHYLUM ARTHROPODA, CLASS CRUSTACEA, ORDERS AMPHIPODA, ISOPODA AND TANAIDACEA

Free moving crustaceans without an obvious carapace[1]

(Crustacean key begins on page 10.00)

#1.Body is distinctly flattened from top to bottom, much wider than deep (Fig.A); legs are all about the same size and shape .... **isopods**, page 10.10

#1.Body not distinctly flattened from top to bottom, not wider than deep (Figs.B-I); legs may all be similar or may vary in size and shape .... #2

#2.Body distinctly flattened from side to side (Fig.B) so that the animal often lies on its side; body is sturdy, narrower than deep, usually with an arched, banana shaped back; legs vary in size and shape, often with subchelate (trigger) type claws (Fig.C) on the first several pairs of legs; coxae (side plates) are medium or large and they overlap .... **typical gammarid amphipods**, #3

#2.Body is very slender, somewhat cylindrical or tubular in shape, not particularly flattened from top to bottom or from side to side; coxae (side plates) are lacking (Figs.E,F) or occur only on several segments (Fig.G) or are short and do not overlap (Figs.H,I); legs may all be similar or may vary in size and shape .... #4

#3.With an extra tip (accessory flagellum) on first antennae[2] (Fig.D) .... page 10.06

#3.Without an extra tip on first antennae .... page 10.08

#4.Legs are all about the same size and shape, except for the first pair which may have chelate (pincer) or subchelate (trigger) type claws (Fig.C); with 6 pairs of walking legs (legs without claws) that are not much longer than the body width; midsection of body has legs (Figs.E,F) .... **anthurid isopods and tanaids**, page 10.12

#4.Legs vary in length and shape, the first two pairs of legs usually have subchelate (trigger) type claws (Fig.C); legs are much longer than body width; midsection of body may or may not have any legs (Figs.G-I) .... #5

#5.Abdominal ("tail") segments are reduced to a short stub (Fig.G); with 3 pairs of hooklike legs at posterior end of body; midbody segments often do not have any legs but may have paddlelike gills and, in females, brood plates .... **caprellid amphipods**, #6

#5.With a well developed abdomen ("tail"); posterior appendages are not hooklike; midbody segments with legs (Figs.H,I); usually lives in soft, flexible tubes in bottom mud .... **slender gammarid amphipods**, #7

#6.No legs on midbody segments (segments having paddlelike gills); with a hornlike extension at front of top of head; body smooth, not spiny .... ***Caprella penantis (=C. geometrica)*** (Fig.G)

#6.With legs on midbody segments OR without a hornlike extension on head OR body is spiny .... **other caprellid amphipods**[3] (Fig.G)

#7.First antennae longer than second antennae[4] (Fig.H); first antennae with an extra tip[2] (Fig.D); may have bright red spots and blotches...***Unciola* spp.**[3] (Fig.H)

#7.Second antennae longer than first antennae[4] (Fig.I); no extra tip on first antennae; without bright red spots .... **amphipod families Corophiidae and Ischyroceridae (in part)**[3] (Fig.I)

[1]Refer to footnote on page 10.00 for a description of the three different sections of a crustacean and the appendages attached to each section.

[2]Examine the antennae very carefully with a dissecting microscope or hand lens since the extra tip is often very small and difficult to see. The structure of the antennae can be best observed when the amphipod is submerged in liquid so that the different parts of the antennae float apart and do not stick to each other.

[3]Use Gosner (1971) to identify the species of caprellid amphipods and Bousfield (1973) to identify gammarid amphipods. Refer to Weiss et al. (1995) for a check list of the species reported to occur in this region.

[4]The second antennae and the first or second claws of males are often much broader and more powerful than of females. Females are shown in Figs.H and I.

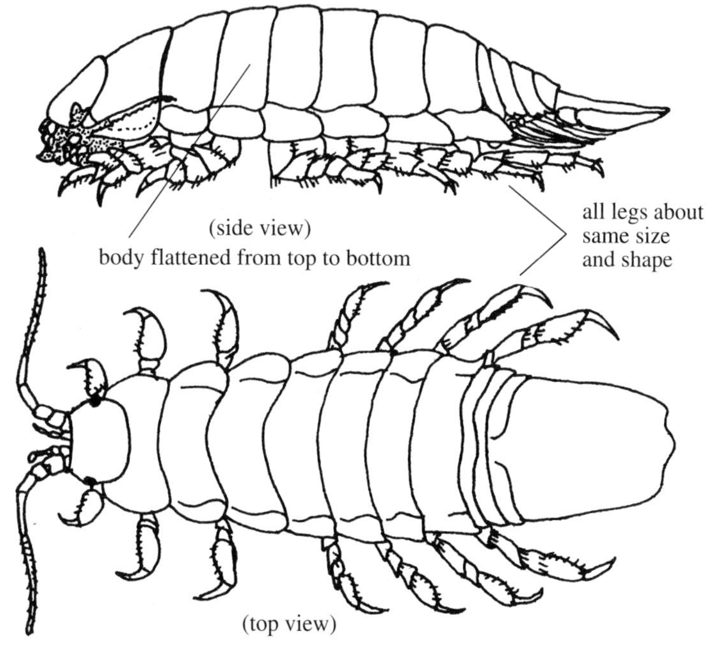

Fig.A. **TYPICAL ISOPOD**

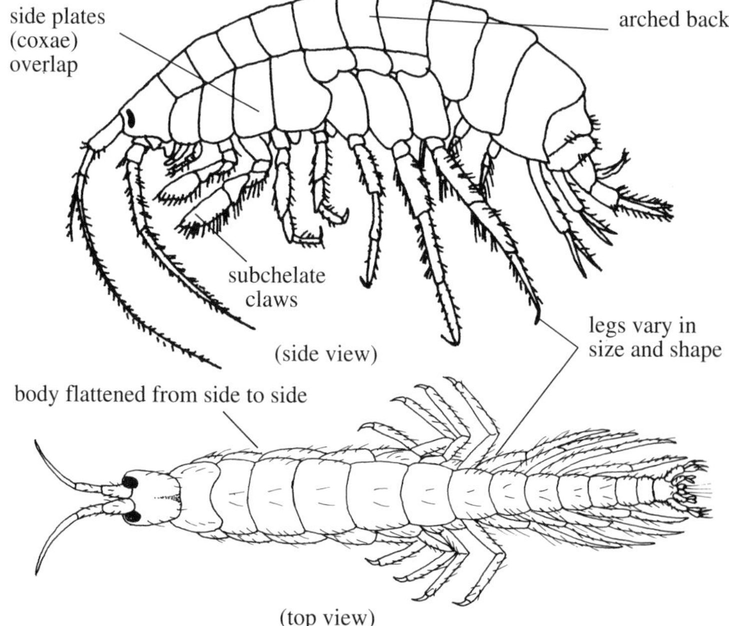

Fig.B. **TYPICAL GAMMARID AMPHIPOD**

subchelate "trigger" type claw
moveable spine
moveable finger
chelate, "pincer" type claw

Fig.C. **CRUSTACEAN CLAW TYPES**

first antenna
extra tip[2] (accessory flagellum)
second antenna

Fig.D. **GAMMARID AMPHIPOD HEAD**

subchelate claws
slender body
6 pairs of short walking legs on thorax

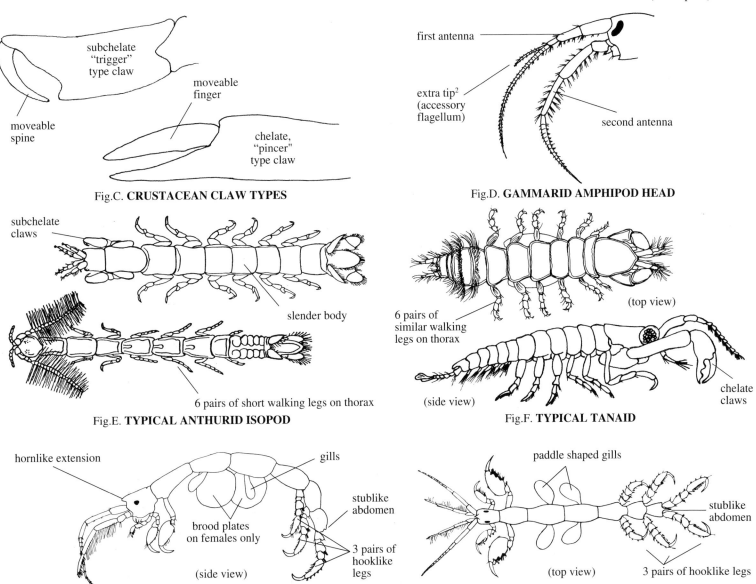

Fig.E. **TYPICAL ANTHURID ISOPOD**

6 pairs of similar walking legs on thorax
(top view)
(side view)
chelate claws

Fig.F. **TYPICAL TANAID**

hornlike extension
gills
brood plates on females only
stublike abdomen
3 pairs of hooklike legs
(side view)
paddle shaped gills
stublike abdomen
(top view)
3 pairs of hooklike legs

Fig.G. **FAMILY CAPRELLIDAE, CAPRELLID AMPHIPODS OR SKELETON SHRIMP:** *Caprella penantis (=C. geometrica)*, shown here, is one of the most common caprellid amphipods found in this region but other species also frequently occur[3]. They are usually colorless and transparent but may be reddish or mottled; up to about 1.5 cm (5/8") long; common on hydroids, eelgrass, sponges, seaweeds, and among other attached organisms on pilings and rocks.

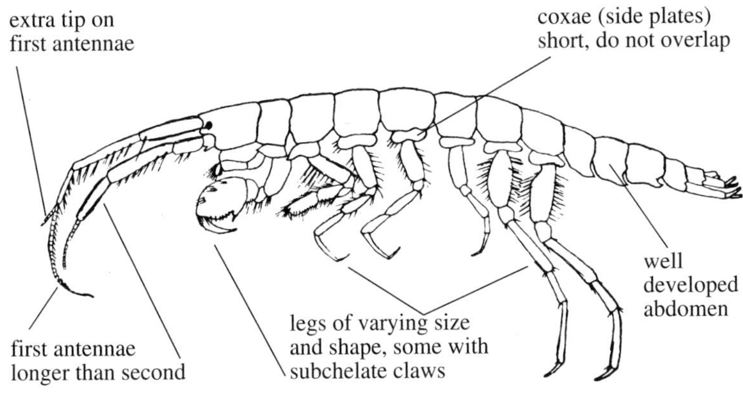

Fig.H. ***UNCIOLA* SPP., TUBE DWELLING AMPHIPODS[3]:** Grow up to 1.6 cm (5/8") long; found from the lower intertidal zone to offshore. *Unciola irrorata*, a very abundant species, has bright red spots and blotches on the body, claws, and antennae. It lives in the tubes of other amphipods and worms in sandy or muddy bottoms. (family Aoridae) 17.11 E

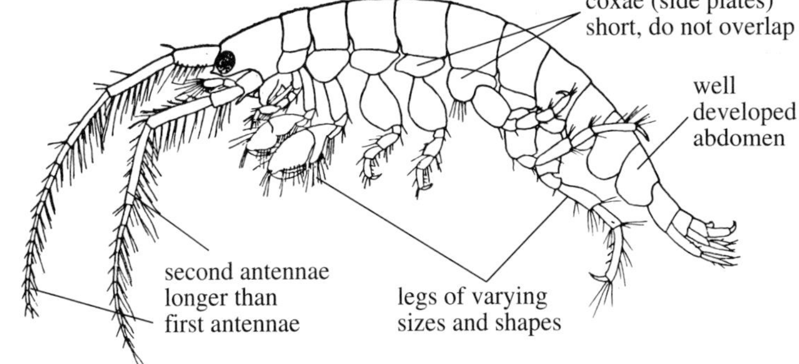

Fig.I. **AMPHIPOD FAMILIES COROPHIIDAE AND ISCHYROCERIDAE (in part), TUBE DWELLING AMPHIPODS[3]:** Most species in these families build soft, flexible tubes of mud and sand sometimes attached to hydroids, sponges, or rocks. They occur from the intertidal zone into deeper water. They are less than 6 mm (1/4") long. *Corophium insidiosum* is very common on sandy mudflats and its tubes are often found among eelgrass roots. It is purplish brown with a dark crossband at the rear edge of each segment.

GAMMARID AMPHIPODS WITH AN EXTRA TIP ON FIRST ANTENNAE[2]
PHYLUM ARTHROPODA, CLASS CRUSTACEA, ORDER AMPHIPODA

Crustaceans that are flattened from side to side, do not have a carapace, and have an extra tip on the first antennae

(Amphipod key begins on page 10.04)

#1.With a large hoodlike rostrum ("beak") overhanging the entire base of first antennae .... **family Phoxocephalidae, hood-headed amphipods**[1] (Fig.B)
#1.Rostrum ("beak") is small or lacking; rostrum, if present, does not cover more than half of the base segment of the first antennae (Figs.C-I) .... #2

#2.Legs are broad and very hairy (with long bristles), specialized for digging in sand (Fig.C); eyes may or may not be absent, tiny, or unpigmented; usually lives in clean sand in sand bars, wave exposed beaches, or subtidal sand flats .... #3
#2.Legs are not especially broad or hairy; eyes are obvious and have pigment (black or some other color) (Figs.D-I); not usually found in clean sand .... #4

#3.Body broad; eyes absent, tiny or unpigmented; no claws on last four pairs of walking legs .... **family Haustoriidae, digging amphipods**[1] (Fig.C)
#3.Body slender; eyes obvious and pigmented; with claws on last four pairs of walking legs .... **family Pontoporeiidae, digging amphipods**[1] (not shown)

#4.Rear edge of fourth coxal (side) plate (Fig.A) is concave (Figs.D-G) .... #5
#4.Rear edge of fourth coxal (side) plate (Fig.A) is straight (Figs.H-I) .... #8

#5.No large claws on legs; base of first antennae very stout; coxal plates long, covering all but the tips of the legs .... **family Lysianassidae**[1] (Fig.D)
#5.With large claws on one or both of the first two pairs of legs; base of first antennae not especially stout; coxal plates much shorter than legs (Figs.E-G) .... #6

#6.Rear legs (seventh pair) much longer than sixth; antennae are short, about same length or shorter than legs with large claws .... ***Listriella* spp.** (Fig.E)
#6.Sixth pair of legs are about as long or longer than rear legs; antennae are long and thin, much longer than legs with large claws (Figs.F,G) .... #7

#7.Eyes are large and kidney bean shaped; the claws on the first pair of legs are nearly as large or larger than the claws on the second pair of legs; first antennae usually same length or shorter than second antennae .... **family Gammaridae, scuds or sideswimmers**[1] (Fig.F)
#7.Eyes are nearly round; the claws on the first pair of legs are distinctly smaller and weaker than the claws on the second pair (especially in males); first antennae always longer than second antennae .... **family Melitidae**[1] (Fig.G)

#8.First antennae longer than second; claws are larger on the first pair of legs than the second pair, especially in males .... **family Aoridae**[1] (Fig.H)
#8.First antennae shorter than second; claws are larger on the second pair of legs than the first, especially in males .... **family Ischyroceridae**[1] (Fig.I)

[1]The identification of amphipods to the species level is beyond the scope of this book, requiring specialized knowledge and microscopic examination of appendages. Use Bousfield (1973) to determine species.
[2]See Fig.D on page 10.05 and footnote 2 on page 10.04.

rear edge of fourth coxal plate is straight

rear edge of fourth coxal plate is concave

Fig.A. **REAR EDGE OF FOURTH COXAL PLATE:** The rear edge of the fourth coxal plate of some amphipods (left) is straight and is concave (curves inward) in other species (right). Be sure to count all of the coxal plates starting from the head end. The first coxal plate is sometimes smaller than the others or points forward (left) but should be included in the count. If the fifth coxal plate overlaps the fourth then it must be lifted away to see the rear edge of the fourth.

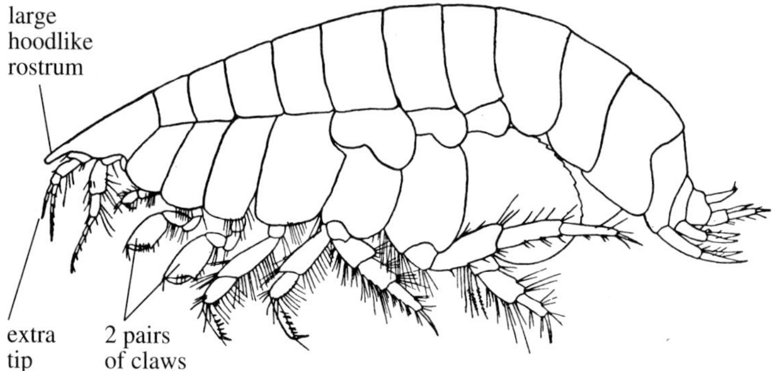

Fig.B. **FAMILY PHOXOCEPHALIDAE, HOOD-HEADED AMPHIPODS**[1]**:** Up to 8 mm (3/8") long; burrows in fine sand or sandy mud bottoms but does not construct tubes; found in the lower intertidal zone in protected bays and estuaries. *Phoxocephalus holbolli*, a common species, is beige or orange and has tiny, inconspicuous and unpigmented eyes. The other species in this family have either very conspicuous, pigmented eyes or no eyes at all.

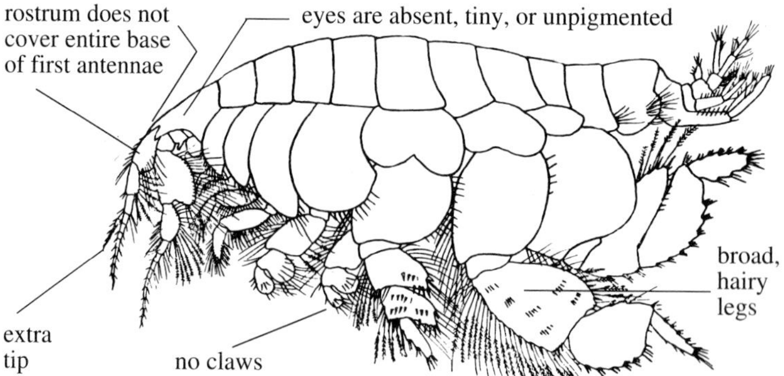

Fig.C. **FAMILY HAUSTORIIDAE, DIGGING AMPHIPODS**[1]**:** Most species burrow in clean sand on wave exposed beaches, sand bars, subtidal sand flats, or along the banks of tidal creeks. *Haustorius canadensis* is the largest species, growing up to 18 mm (3/4") long, but most are less than 8 mm (3/8") long. *H. canadensis* has a prominent rostrum ("beak"), is sandy colored, and is often found on fine sandy beaches digging rapidly in the swash zone.

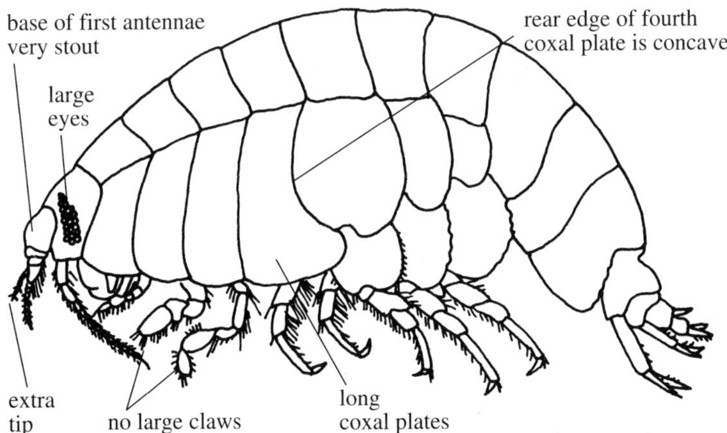

Fig.D. **FAMILY LYSIANASSIDAE[1]:** Up to 2.5 cm (1") long. One species, *Orchomenella pinguis*, is whitish; up to 7 mm (1/4") long; often found offshore in large numbers scavenging the bait from lobsters pots. Other species are common in protected bays in mud or in coarse, shelly sand among eelgrass roots.

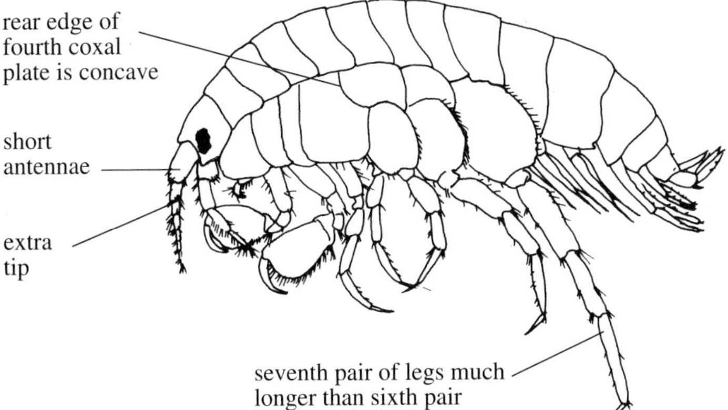

Fig.E. ***LISTRIELLA* SPP.[1]:** Up to 6 mm (1/4") long; lives in the tubes of *Clymenella*, *Amphitrite,* and other polychaete worms. (family Liljeborgiidae)

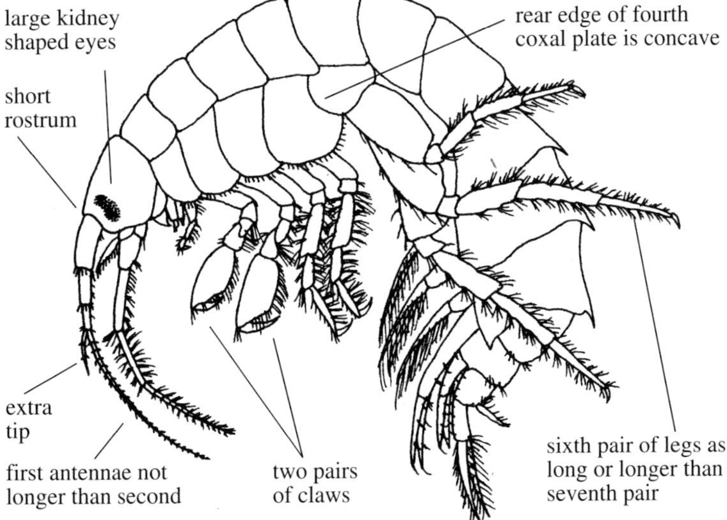

Fig.F. **FAMILY GAMMARIDAE, SCUDS OR SIDESWIMMERS[1]:** This family is probably the most common group of amphipods found in the rocky intertidal zone, under rockweed, stones and in tide pools. They are also found on beaches and tidal marshes under stranded seaweeds, grasses, driftwood, etc. Some species are common in deep water offshore. Most species are olive green or brown and some have red spots or brown bands. Some species reach 22 mm (7/8") in length but most are about 13 mm (1/2") long. Most of the species in this family are in the genus *Gammarus*.

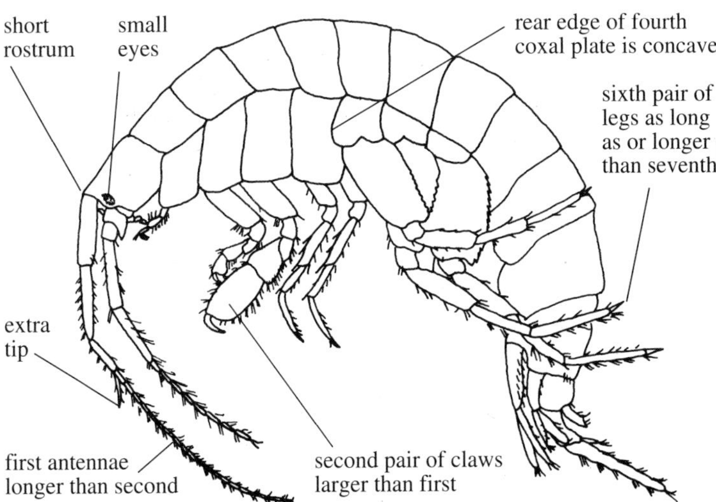

Fig.G. **FAMILY MELITIDAE[1]:** Green, yellow, or brown; up to 25 mm (1") long; found from the low tide level out into deeper water.

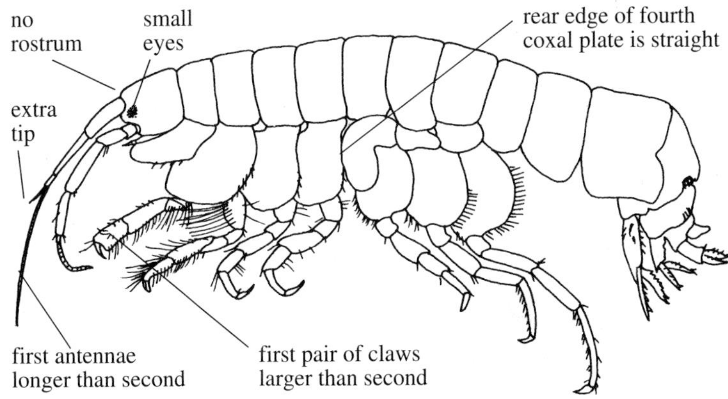

Fig.H. **FAMILY AORIDAE[1]**: *Leptocheirus pinguis*, in this family, is one of the most abundant amphipods in muddy and sandy bottoms in the lower intertidal zone and offshore. It grows up to 17 mm (5/8") long and has dark brown pigment granules forming distinctive broad transverse bands across the body segments. **17.11 F** Most other Aeoridae species are less than 10 mm (3/8") long and live among seaweeds, eelgrass, shellfish beds, and around docks and pilings.

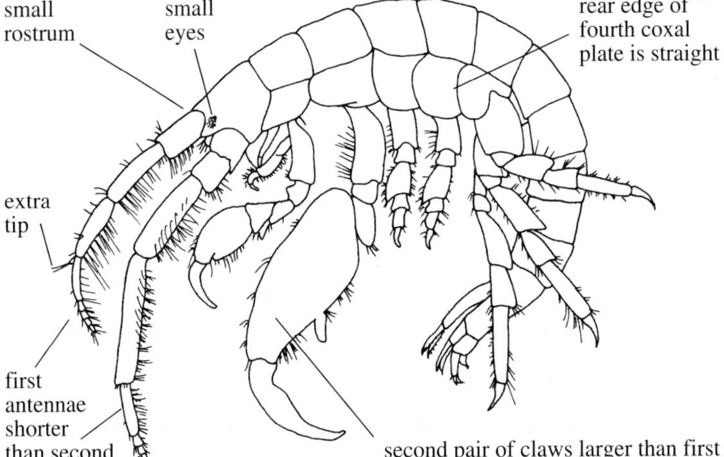

Fig.I. **FAMILY ISCHYROCERIDAE (in part), FOULING AMPHIPODS[1]:** Up to 12 mm (1/2") long; builds open ended mud tubes on pilings, wharves, bouys, and the bottom of boats; also common on eelgrass and soft sediments in channels. One of the most common species, *Jassa marmorata (=J. falcata)*, is conspicuously colored, with light spots on reddish background. Males have unusually large claws on their second pair of legs.

GAMMARID AMPHIPODS WITH NO EXTRA TIP ON FIRST ANTENNAE[1]
PHYLUM ARTHROPODA, CLASS CRUSTACEA, ORDER AMPHIPODA

Crustaceans that are flattened from side to side, do not have a carapace, and do not have an extra tip on the first antennae

(Amphipod key begins on page 10.04)

#1.With two or three tiny eyes on each side of the head .... **family Ampeliscidae, four-eyed amphipods**[2] (Fig.A)
#1.With one medium to large eye on each side of head (Figs.B-I) .... #2

#2.One or more of the coxal (side) plates are very large, covering over most of the legs .... **family Stenothoidae, seed-shrimp amphipods**[2] (Fig.B)
#2.None of the coxal plates are especially large; the coxal plates do not cover over most of the legs (Figs.C-I) .... #3

#3.Eyes touch each other or are fused together on top of head or rostrum ("beak"); eyes are large .... **family Oedicerotidae**[1] (not shown)
#3.Eyes are separated on each side of the head; eyes may be small or large but they do not touch .... #4

#4.First antennae are noticeably shorter than second antennae (Figs.C,D) .... #5
#4.First antennae about as long or longer than second antennae (Figs.E-I) .... #6

#5.Second antennae are at least three times as long as first (Fig.C); first coxal (side) plate is smaller and shorter than plates 2-4; usually found at or above the high tide level on tidal marshes or sand beaches .... **family Talitridae, beach hoppers or sand fleas**[2] (Fig.C)
#5.Second antennae are less than twice as long as the first; first coxal plate is about the same size as plates 2-4; usually found below the high tide level on rocky or stony shores .... **family Hyalidae**[2] (Fig.D)

#6.Telson (tip of tail) is split by a deep cleavage (Fig.F) .... #7
#6.Telson is not split by a deep cleavage .... #9

#7.The pointed tips of the rear 3 pairs of legs point to the rear .... ***Dexamine thea*** [3] (not shown)
#7.The pointed tips of the rear 3 pairs of legs point forward .... #8

#8.With claws on the first two pairs of legs; with 7 coxal (side) plates on each side (see Fig.A on page 10.06) .... ***Pontogeneia inermis*** [3] (not shown)
#8.With claws on only one pair of front legs; with 6 coxal plates on each side .... ***Batea catharinensis*** [3] (not shown)

#9.Rear edge of fourth coxal (side) plate is concave (see Fig.A on page 10.06); eyes are large, diameter of eyes at least half the head width (Figs.E,G) .... #10
#9.Rear edge of fourth coxal plate is not concave (see Fig.A on page 10.06); medium size eyes, eye diameter is less than half the head width (Figs.H,I) .... #11

#10.Branches of tail appendages (3rd uropods, see Fig.F) are about the same length and have featherlike bristles (setae); the third segment of the first antennae is pointed on its bottom edge .... ***Calliopius laeviusculus*** (Fig.E)
#10.Branches of tail appendages (3rd uropods, see Fig.F) are not the same length and have simple, pointed bristles (setae); the third segment of the first antennae is not pointed on the bottom .... **family Pleustidae**[2] (Fig.G)

#11.First and second antennae are about the same length; head bulges out to a point in front of eyes .... **family Photidae**[2] (Fig.H)
#11.First antennae longer than second antennae; head is round in front of eyes .... **family Ampithoidae, nest-building amphipods**[2] (Fig.I)

[1]See Fig.D on page 10.05 and footnote 2 on page 10.04.
[2]Use Bousfield (1973) to determine species.
[3]*Dexamine thea* (family Dexaminidae): up to 4 mm (3/16") long; nests among subtidal plants and stones. *Batea catharinensis* (family Bateidae): up to 8 mm (5/16") long; lives on subtidal stones and gravel. *Pontogeneia inermis* (family Pontogeneiidae): up to 11 mm (7/16") long; attaches to submerged plants in colder months.

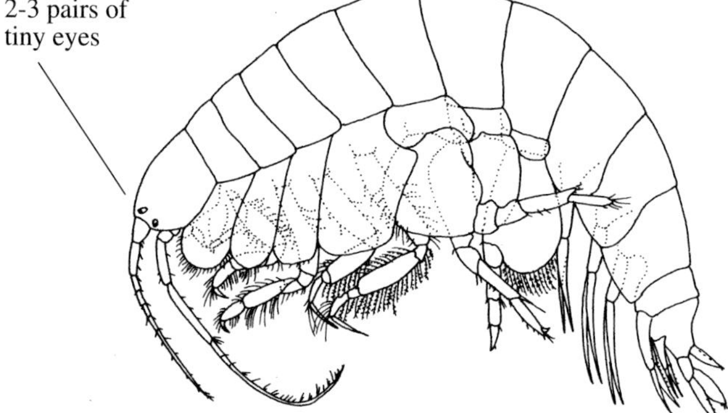

Fig.A. **FAMILY AMPELISCIDAE, FOUR-EYED AMPHIPODS**[2]**:** Up to 20 mm (3/4") long; color whitish, sometimes with red or purple spots and pink eyes; very abundant offshore and in the lower intertidal zone on muddy and sandy bottoms, especially in eelgrass beds; many species build parchmentlike tubes. Several species in the genus *Ampelisca* are very common. Their telson is deeply split (see Fig.F) and is at least two times longer than wide. Another common species is *Byblis serrata*. Its telson is about as long as it is wide and is split for only about half its length.

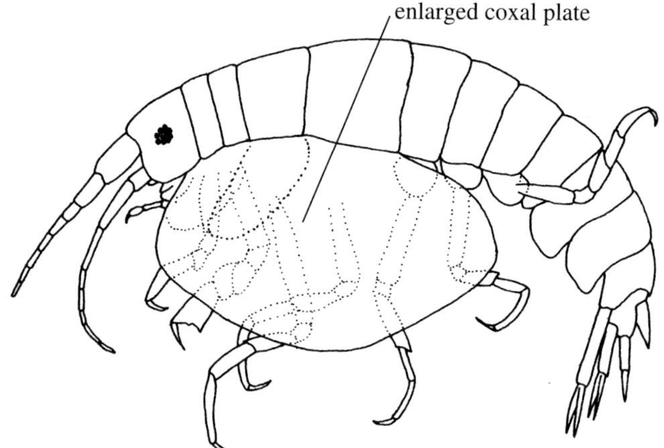

Fig.B. **FAMILY STENOTHOIDAE, SEED-SHRIMP AMPHIPODS**[2]**:** Translucent, sometimes with a row of red or brown marks along the back and red eyes; tiny, up to 4 mm (3/16") long; found on hydroids and sponges from the low tide level into deeper water. *Parametopella cypris*, a common species, has only one enlarged coxal plate; all other species have 2 or 3.

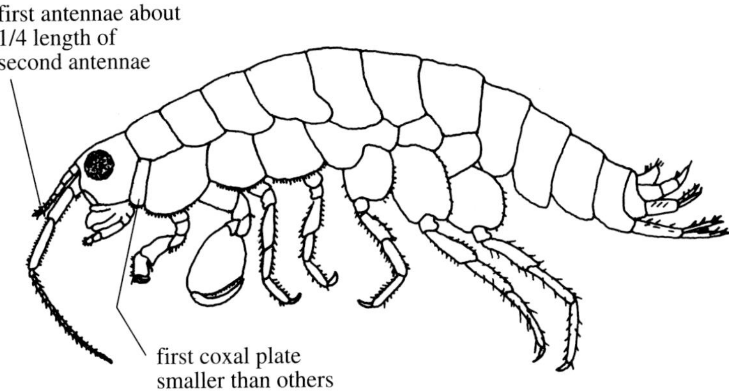

Fig.C. **FAMILY TALITRIDAE, BEACH HOPPERS OR SAND FLEAS:** These amphipods are semiterrestrial, often found well inland from the high tide level. Two species are the dominant amphipods on tidal marshes and are usually green or brown. *Orchestia grillus*, the American marsh hopper, is the larger species, growing up to 18 mm (3/4") long, and is found higher up on the marsh in drier places among the grasses. *Uhlorchestia spartinophila (=Orchestia uhleri)*, the banded marsh hopper, is under 10 mm (3/8") long. It remains near the high tide level in moist places among the grass roots and under dead seaweeds and other stranded debris. Two species of *Americorchestia* are the dominant amphipods on sandy beaches near or above the high tide level. They are whitish or sand colored and dig burrows into the sand that have circular openings. *A. megalophthalma (=Talorchestia m.)*, the big-eyed sandhopper, grows up to 24 mm (1") long and usually remains at or just below the mean high water level. *A. longicornis (=Talorchestia l.)*, the long-horned sandhopper, grows up to 27 mm (1 1/8") long and is often found well above the high tide level, sometimes more than 100 m (330') inland and in sand dunes.

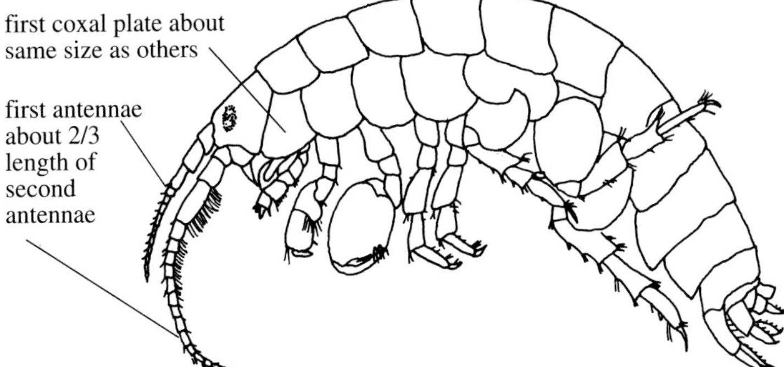

Fig.D. **FAMILY HYALIDAE[2]:** Up to 12 mm (1/2") long; some species are green to olive brown with reddish brown antennae; found in intertidal zone under stones, rockweed and marsh grass.

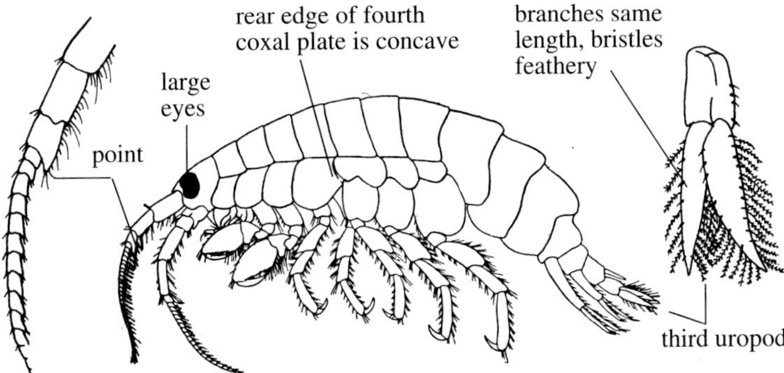

Fig.E. ***CALLIOPIUS LAEVIUSCULUS:*** Whitish body, mottled and banded with red, brown, or orange spots; up to 14 mm (5/8") long; swims in tide pools and often caught in plankton net tows offshore in water up to 20 m (65') in depth. (family Calliopiidae)

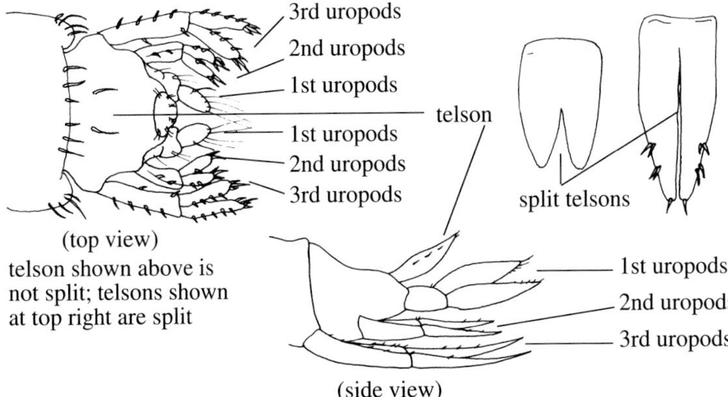

Fig.F. **AMPHIPOD TAIL APPENDAGES**

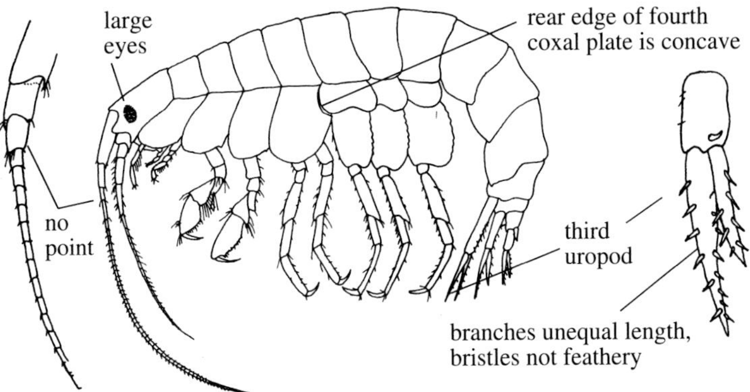

Fig.G. **FAMILY PLEUSTIDAE[2]:** Up to 6 mm (1/4") long; found on the bottom from the low tide level offshore into deeper water.

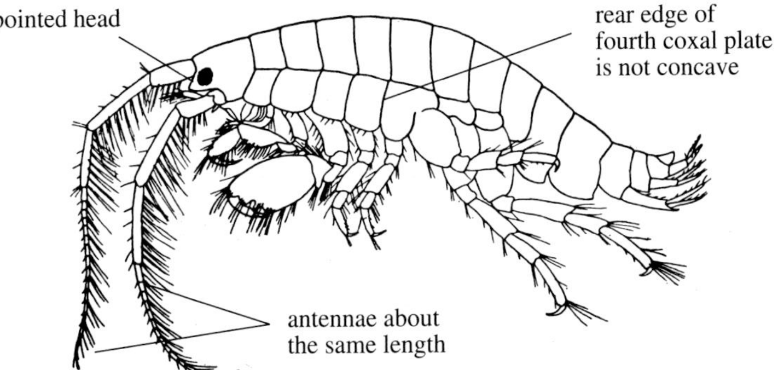

Fig.H. **FAMILY PHOTIDAE[2]:** Up to 8 mm (5/16") long; lives offshore on rocky or muddy bottoms.

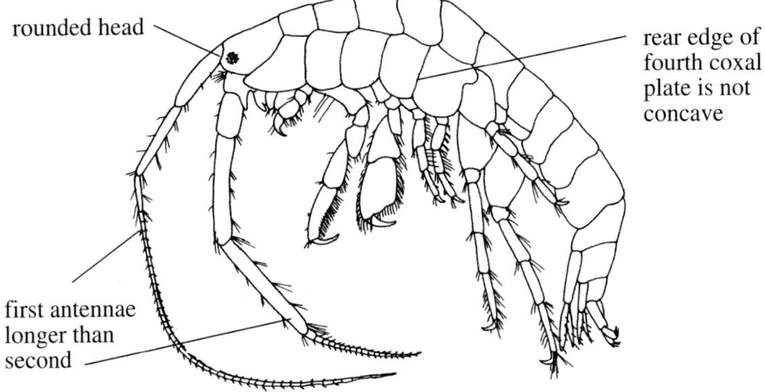

Fig.I. **FAMILY AMPITHOIDAE, NEST BUILDING AMPHIPODS[2]:** Up to 20 mm (3/4") long; builds nests and tubes among eelgrass and seaweeds in the intertidal zone and in shallow water; nests are constructed from bits of seaweed cemented on algae and eelgrass with a gluelike secretion.

ISOPODS: PHYLUM ARTHROPODA, CLASS CRUSTACEA, ORDER ISOPODA

Crustaceans flattened from top to bottom; legs on thorax[1] are all very similar; 5 pairs of pleopods on abdomen; no carapace

(Use key on page 10.00 to determine if you have an isopod)

#1.Without a large telson (tail plate); tail is divided into 6 segments with several small appendages (uropods) at end of tail .... ***Philoscia vittata*** (Fig.A)
#1.With a large telson (Figs.B-K) .... #2

#2.Uropods (tail appendages) are on the sides of the telson (tail plate) and are relatively large, forming a fanlike tail (Fig.B,D) .... #3
#2.Without a tail fan; uropods are either very small (Figs.E,F) or are underneath the telson (Figs. G-K, also see Fig.C) .... #5

#3.With 6 abdominal segments (posterior segments without walking legs) including the telson (Fig.B) .... ***Politolana* spp.,** #4
#3.With 2 abdominal segments including the telson .... **family Sphaeromatidae[2]** (Fig.D)

#4.Telson is rounded .... ***Politolana polita*** (Fig.B)
#4.Telson is notched .... ***Politolana concharum*** (Fig.B)

#5.With tiny uropods (tail appendages) on sides of telson (tail plate) (Fig.E) or at end of telson (Fig.F) .... #6
#5.Without any uropods at end or sides of the telson (Figs.G-K). The uropods fold underneath the telson to form a chamber (Fig.C) which encloses the pleopods (swimmerets); the uropods cannot be seen when viewing the animal from the dorsal (top) side .... **order Valvifera, valviferan isopods**, #7

#6.With tiny uropods (tail appendages) on sides of telson; telson (tail plate) is not notched; animals burrow in wood .... ***Limnoria lignorum*, gribble** (Fig.E)
#6.With tiny uropods set in notches in the telson; not found burrowed in wood .... ***Jaera marina*** (Fig.F)

#7.Sides of head have a deep notch or groove (Fig.G); eyes are on top of head; first 3 pairs of walking legs are clawlike but last 4 pairs are not; with 4 abdominal (tail) segments in front of telson .... ***Chiridotea* spp.,** #8
#7.Sides of head are not notched (Figs.H-K); eyes are on sides of head; all walking legs are the same, either with or without claws; with 0-3 abdominal segments in front of telson .... #9

#8.Found in marine environments; one pair of antennae much longer than the other pair .... ***Chiridotea tuftsi*** (Fig.G)
#8.Found in marine environments; both pairs of antennae are about the same length .... ***Chiridotea caeca*** (Fig.G)
#8.Found in brackish water environments (where water has low salinity) .... **other *Chiridotea* spp.[2]** (Fig.G)

#9.With 3 abdominal (tail) segments in front of telson; the second antennae (lower, longer pair) have a multisegmented tip (Fig.H) .... ***Idotea* spp.,** #10
#9.Without any abdominal segments in front of telson; the second antennae are not multisegmented (Figs.I-K) .... #11

#10.End of telson has 3 points .... ***Idotea balthica*** (Fig.H)
#10.End of telson has single point .... ***Idotea phosphorea*** (Fig.H)
#10.End of telson is almost straight across, no obvious points .... ***Idotea metallica*** (Fig.H)

#11.Second antennae only about 2 times as long as first antennae (Fig.I) .... ***Edotea* spp.,** #12
#11.Second antennae more than 3 times as long as first antennae (Figs.J,K) .... ***Erichsonella* spp.,** #13

#12.Side edges at tip of telson shaped with a compound curve (S-shaped curve) leading to the point at the end .... ***Edotea triloba*** (Fig.I)
#12.Side edges at tip of telson shaped with a simple curve (convex) leading to the point at the end .... ***Edotea montosa*** (Fig.I)

#13.Telson without distinct tubercles .... ***Erichsonella attenuata*** (Fig.J)
#13.With distinct tubercle (bump) on either side of telson .... ***Erichsonella filiformis*** (Fig.K)

[1]Refer to footnote on page 10.00 for a description of the three different sections of a crustacean and the appendages attached to each section.
[2]Refer to R. I. Smith (1964) or Schultz (1969) to identify these species.

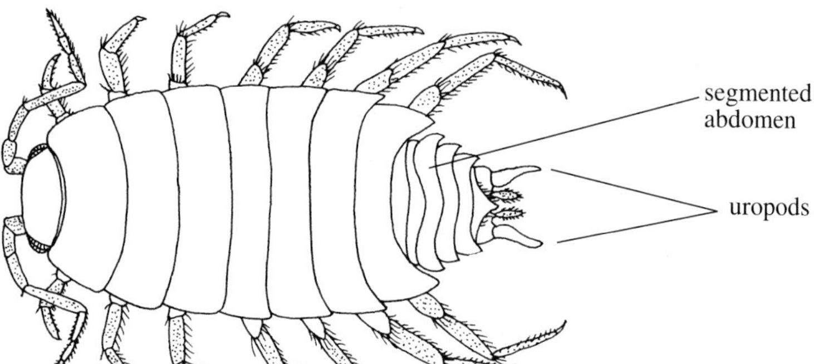

Fig.A. ***PHILOSCIA VITTATA:*** Mottled brown with yellowish sides; up to 8 mm (5/16") long; very common in saltmarshes among the grasses of the high marsh; usually hidden under debris. (family Oniscidae)

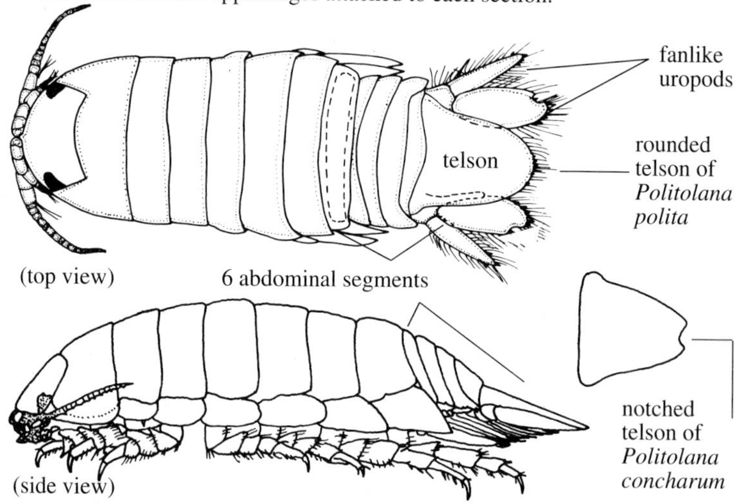

Fig.B. ***POLITOLANA* SPP. (=*Cirolana* spp.):** Scavengers of dead fish, crabs, etc.; found around fishing docks, lobster pots. *Politolana polita* is up to 16 mm (5/8") long; *P. concharum* is up to 25 mm (1") long. (family Cirolanidae)

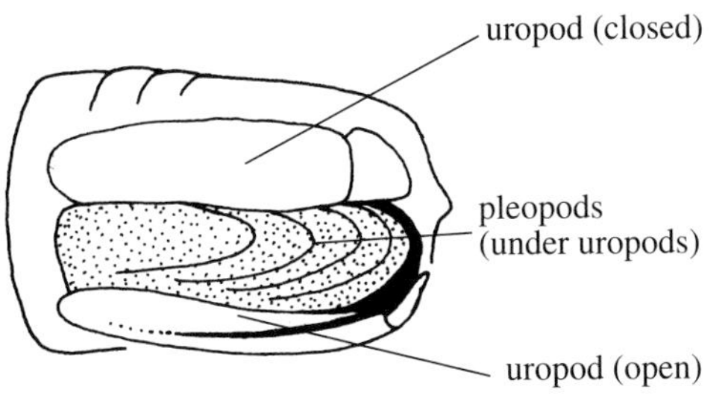

Fig.C. **TYPICAL VALVIFERAN ISOPOD TELSON (UNDERSIDE VIEW)**

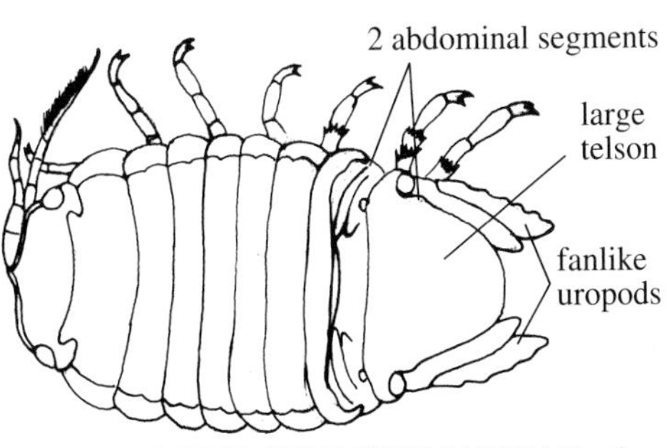

Fig.D. **FAMILY SPHAEROMATIDAE:** One species, *Sphaeroma quadridentata*, is mottled with white; up to 9 mm (3/8") long; occurs in the intertidal zone among seaweed and under stones; rolls up into a ball when disturbed.

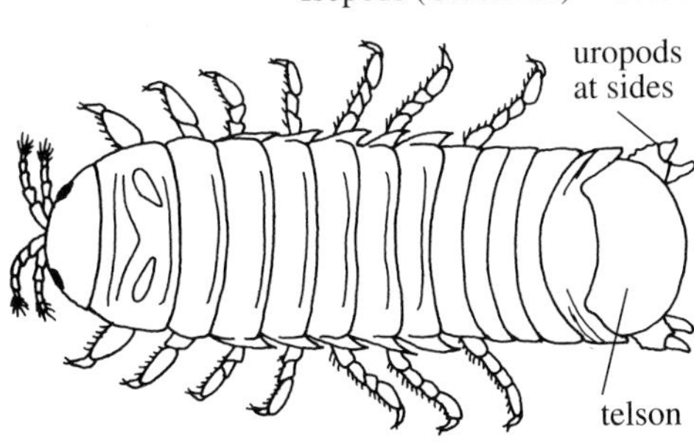

Fig.E. ***LIMNORIA LIGNORUM*, GRIBBLE:** Gray; up to 5 mm (3/16") long; a wood boring isopod, found in pilings and driftwood. (family Limnoriidae)

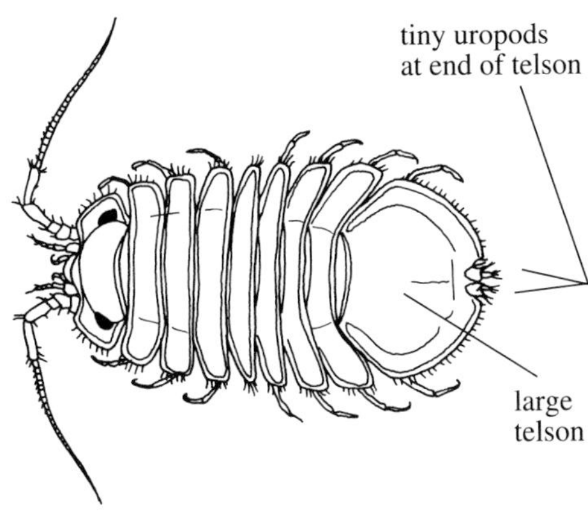

Fig.F. ***JAERA MARINA:*** Usually marbled gray; up to 5 mm (3/16") long; common in intertidal zone among seaweed, mussels and under stones. (family Janiridae)

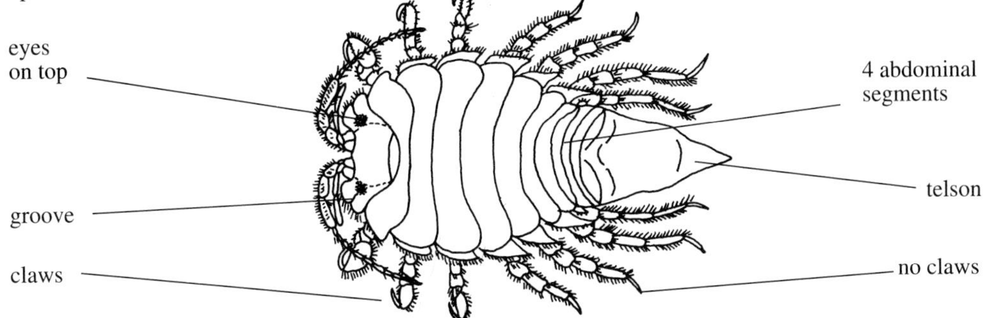

Fig.G. ***CHIRIDOTEA* SPP.:** *Chiridotea tuftsi*, shown here, is reddish brown; up to 6 mm (1/4") long; lives offshore in sand and mud. *Chiridotea caeca* is similar (see key); usually dark gray; up to 13 mm (1/2") long; burrows in intertidal sand flats. Use R. I. Smith (1964) or Schultz (1969) to identify brackish water species. (family Idoteidae)

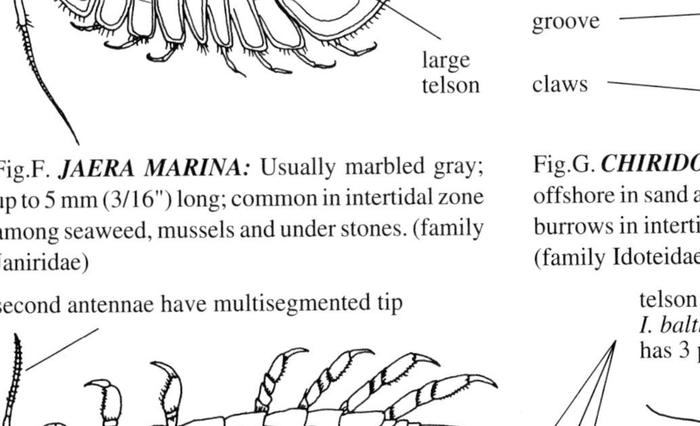

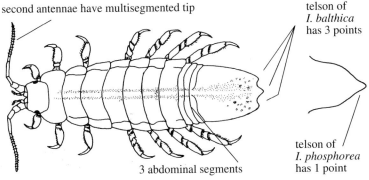

Fig.H. ***IDOTEA* SPP.:** Often green or brown, but color and pattern varies greatly; may have stripes, bands, or blotches of red, yellow, white, or black; up to 38 mm (1 1/2") long; clings to eelgrass, seaweed, and rocks. *Idotea balthica* and *Idotea phosphorea* occur in tidepools, the lower intertidal zone and shallow water. *Idotea metallica* often swims offshore. (family Idoteidae) **17.11 G**

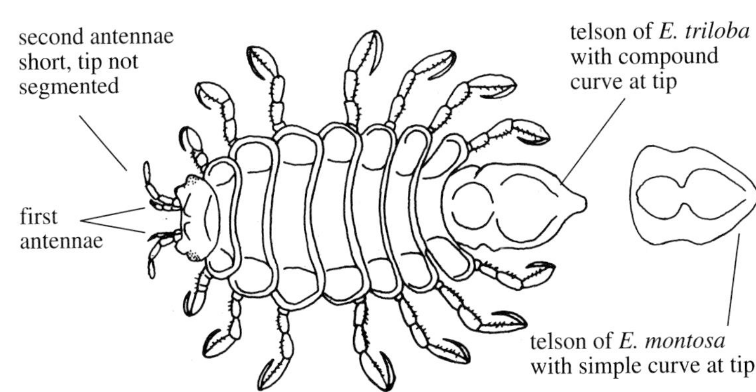

Fig.I. ***EDOTEA* SPP.:** *Edotea triloba* is muddy gray-black color; up to about 6 mm (1/4") long; found on muddy shores, pilings, and among decaying eelgrass and seaweeds. *Edotea montosa* is up to 9 mm (3/8") long; found offshore in mud and fine sand. (family Idoteidae)

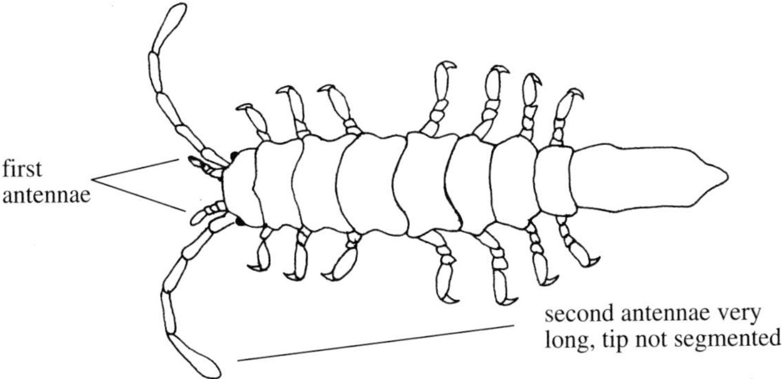

Fig.J. ***ERICHSONELLA ATTENUATA:*** Up to 15 mm (5/8") long; found on eelgrass and algae. (family Idoteidae)

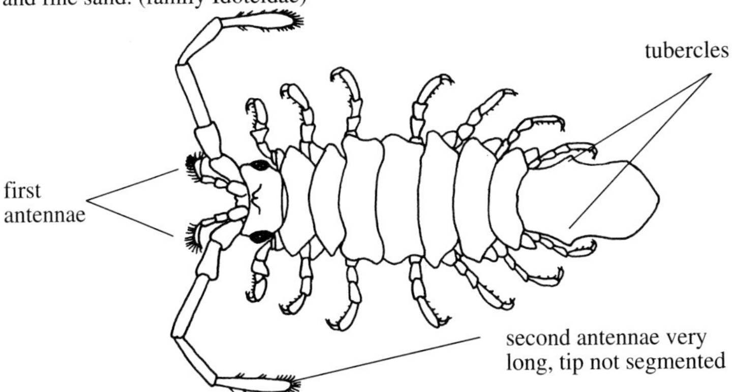

Fig.K. ***ERICHSONELLA FILIFORMIS:*** Up to 15 mm (5/8") long; common on eelgrass and algae. (family Idoteidae) **17.11 H**

ANTHURID ISOPODS AND TANAIDS
PHYLUM ARTHROPODA, CLASS CRUSTACEA, ORDERS ISOPODA AND TANAIDACEA

Crustaceans with a slender, tubular body; with six pairs of walking legs, all similar in size and shape; without an obvious carapace[1]

(Crustacean key begins on page 10.00)

#1.With large chelate[2] (pincer type) claws on first pair of legs; uropods (tail appendages) are not fanlike (Figs.A,B) .... **order Tanaidacea, tanaids**, #2
#1.First pair of legs have subchelate (trigger type) claws or no claws at all; uropods are fanlike (Figs.C,D)... **order Isopoda, family Anthuridae, anthurids**, #4

#2.No eyes .... ***Leptognathia caeca*, blind tanaid** [3]
#2.With a pair of eyes (Figs.A,B) .... #3

#3.With 3 pairs of pleopods (swimmerets), the featherlike appendages under the abdominal (tail) segments; uropods (2 pairs of appendages pointing back from posterior end) have only one branch; with rows of setae ("bristles") on abdomen .... ***Tanais cavolini*, tanaid** (Fig.A)
#3.With 5 pairs of pleopods; uropods have two branches; without rows of setae on abdomen .... ***Leptochelia savignyi*, tanaid** (Fig.B)

#4.The first five segments of the abdomen ("tail") are fused on top but are separated along the sides; second antennae of males are long and have many hairs .... ***Ptilanthura tenuis*, anthurid isopod** (Fig.C)
#4.The first six segments of the abdomen are fused completely together and cannot be distinguished on the top or sides; both pairs of antennae are short .... ***Cyathura polita*, anthurid isopod** (Fig.D)

[1]Refer to footnote on page 10.00 for a description of the three different sections of a crustacean and the appendages attached to each section.
[2]Refer to Fig.C on page 10.05 showing the difference between chelate and subchelate type claws.
[3]*Leptognathia caeca*, the blind tanaid (not shown), reaches up to 2.5 mm (1/8") in length.

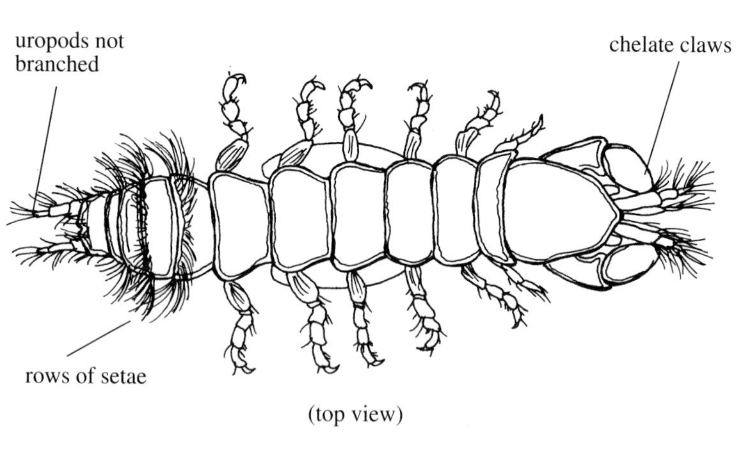

Fig.A. ***TANAIS CAVOLINI*, TANAID:** Brown with white underside; up to 5 mm (1/4") long; found on pilings, algae, eelgrass, shells, and sponges.

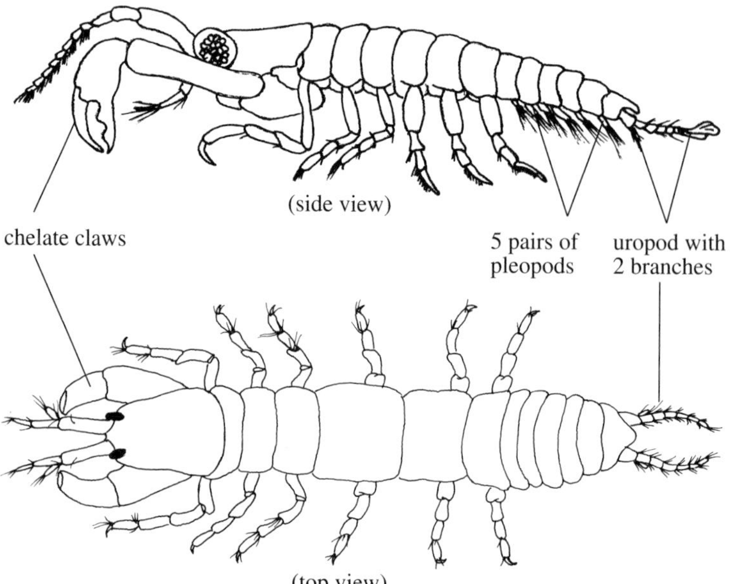

Fig.B. ***LEPTOCHELIA SAVIGNYI*, TANAID:** Up to 2 mm (1/16") long; lives on eelgrass and algae.

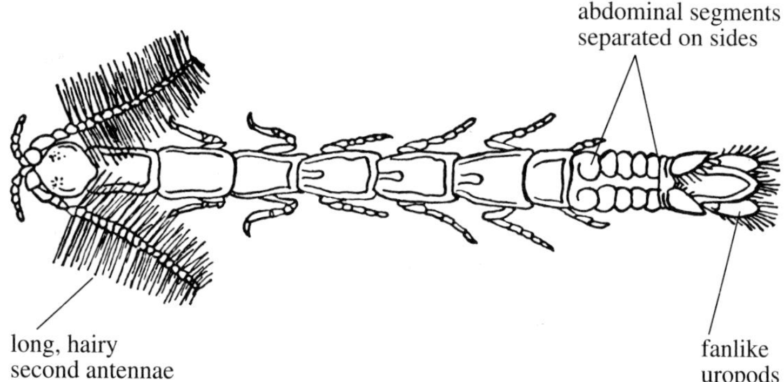

Fig.C. ***PTILANTHURA TENUIS*, ANTHURID ISOPOD:** Mottled brown; up to 1 cm (3/8") long; found in muddy and sandy bottoms offshore and at low tide level.

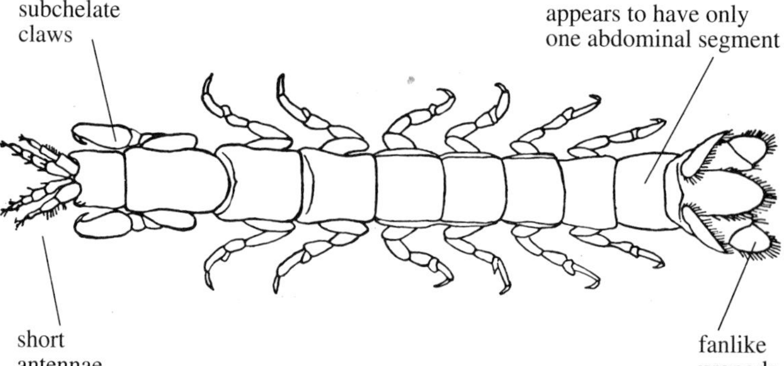

Fig.D. ***CYATHURA POLITA*, ANTHURID ISOPOD:** Up to 2.5 cm (1") long; common on shelly and muddy bottoms in the intertidal zone and offshore, also found in areas of low salinity on eelgrass and algae.

BARNACLES
PHYLUM ARTHROPODA, CLASS CRUSTACEA, SUBCLASS CIRRIPEDIA

Crustaceans cemented to substrate and enclosed by calcareous shell

(Use key on page 2.10 to determine if you have a barnacle)

#1.Shell attached by fleshy stalk to substrate (rock, piling, etc.) .... ***Lepas* spp., gooseneck barnacle** (Fig.A)
#1.Shell attached directly to substrate (Figs.B-D) .... #2

#2.Base[1] of barnacle is membranous (made out of soft tissue) .... #3
#2.With calcareous (shell-like) base plate .... #4

#3.Both end plates of shell[2] are about the same size and are overlapped by the plates to either side (Fig.B) ..... ***Chthamalus fragilis*, little gray barnacle** (Fig.B)
#3.One end plate is usually larger than the other and it overlaps the plates to either side (Fig.D) ...... ***Semibalanus balanoides*, northern rock barnacle** (Fig. C)

#4.Scuta (larger, triangular beak plates) with distinct lines running lengthwise and crosswise AND shell walls are smooth, without ribs .... ***Balanus eburneus*, ivory acorn barnacle** (FigD)
#4.Scuta with crosswise lines only, no distinct lengthwise lines AND/OR shell walls have distinct ribs .... **other *Balanus* spp., acorn barnacles** (Fig.D)

[1]Scrape the barnacle off the substrate (i.e. rock, piling) with a fingernail or knife. Examine the substrate and the underside of the barnacle and look for the remains of a calcareous (shelly) base plate (Fig.D). If none, then the barnacle had a membranous base (Fig.C). If a calcareous base is present, it may be solid or porous.
[2]Use the orientation of the beaks to determine which are the end plates and which are the side plates, as shown in Figs.B and D.

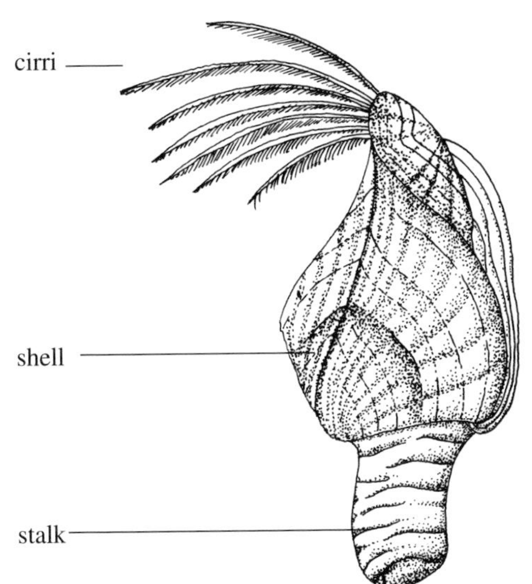

Fig.A. ***LEPAS* SPP., GOOSENECK BARNACLES[1]:** White shells sometimes edged with orange; up to 7.5 cm (3") tall, including stalk; very rarely found in estuarine waters, occasionally drifts into bays and sounds on floating weeds or wood. Refer to Zullo (1979) to determine species.

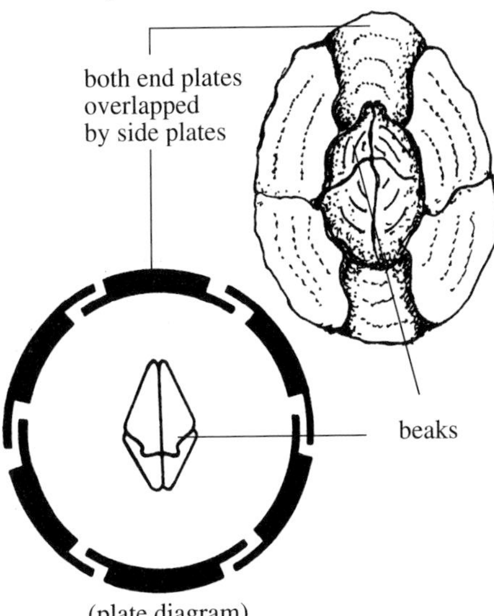

Fig.B. ***CHTHAMALUS FRAGILIS*, LITTLE GRAY BARNACLE:** Gray, beige, or brown; up to 1 cm (3/8") in diameter; common south of Cape Cod on rocks and other solid objects near the high tide level.

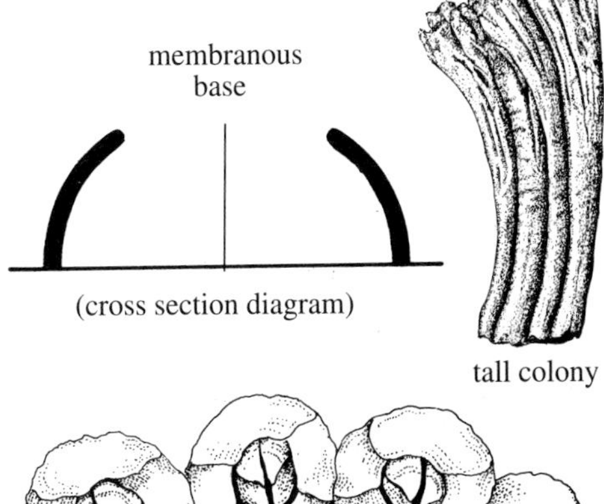

Fig.C. ***SEMIBALANUS BALANOIDES* (=*Balanus b.*) NORTHERN ROCK BARNACLE:** White; may reach 2.5 cm (1") in diameter but usually less than 1.3 cm (1/2"); under crowded conditions may grow taller than wide but usually not; the most common intertidal barnacle.

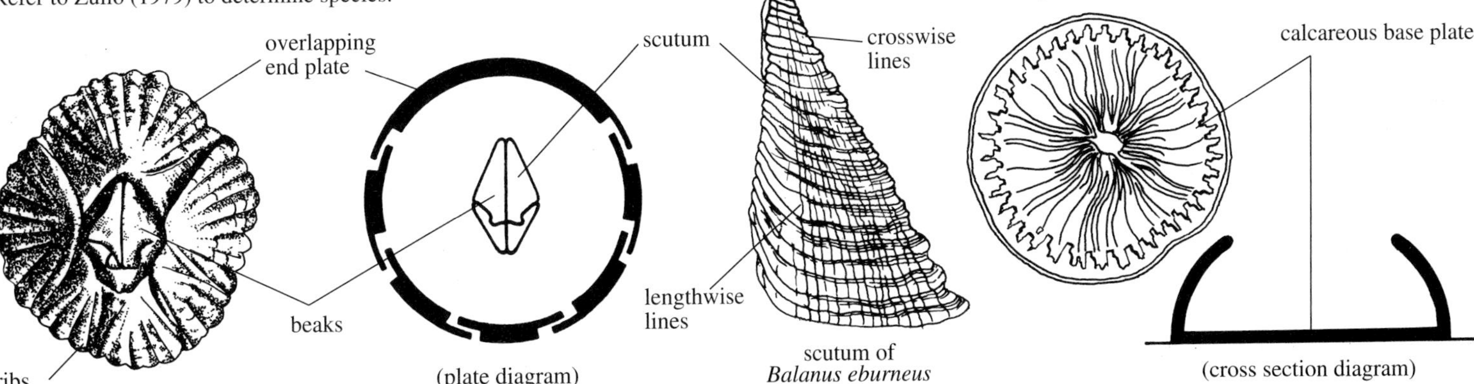

Fig.D. ***BALANUS* SPP., ACORN BARNACLES:** These species are less common along the open coast than *Semibalanus balanoides* (Fig.C) but may be dominant where the salinity is lower or beneath the intertidal zone. *Balanus eburneus*, the ivory barnacle, predominates in the intertidal zone and shallow waters of some estuaries. It is ivory white; up to 2.5 cm (1") high and wide; its base is porous, full of hollow tubes. Use the above key to identify this species. Six other *Balanus* species occur in southern New England. Refer to Zullo (1979) to identify these species. (Note: Both *Balanus* and *Semibalanus* have one overlapping end plate.)

CUMACEANS
PHYLUM ARTHROPODA, CLASS CRUSTACEA, ORDER CUMACEA

Tiny crustaceans with a short carapace that does not cover all of the thoracic ("body") segments[1]; thorax is much wider than abdomen ("tail"); eyes are tiny or lacking and are not on stalks; usually found burrowed in bottom sediments but may also occur in the plankton

(Use the key on page 10.00 to determine if you have a cumacean)

#1.Telson ("tail plate," see Fig.A) is long and somewhat pointed at the end (Figs.A-C); with spines on edges of telson .... #2
#1.Telson is short but obvious (Fig.D) and is rounded, not divided or pointed; without spines on edges of telson .... ***Petalosarsia declivis*** (Fig.D)
#1.Telson is absent (Figs.F,G) or is very small, divided, and without spines (Fig.E) .... #3

#2.With 5 spines at the tip of the telson; males have no pleopods (see Fig.A to determine sex and locate the pleopods) ...... ***Lamprops quadriplicata*** (not shown)
#2.With 2 spines at the tip of the telson; males have 2 pairs of pleopods; the tip of the telson is flat, straight .... ***Diastylis* spp.**[2] (Fig.B)
#2.No spines at the tip of the telson; males have 2 pairs of pleopods; the tip of the telson curves upward .... ***Oxyurostylis smithi*** (Fig.C)

#3.Inner branches of uropods (tail appendages, see Fig.A) have 2 segments .... #4
#3.Inner branches of uropods have 1 segment .... **other cumacean species**[2]

#4.Front of head comes to a beaklike point (pseudorostrum) which extends in the forward direction .... ***Leucon americanus*** (Fig.E)
#4.Front of head is rounded, blunt or squared off (some species may have a point on top of the head which extends upward, not forward) .... #5

#5.Outer branch of uropods (tail appendages, see Fig.A) are as long or longer than inner branch .... #6
#5.Outer branch of uropods are shorter than inner branch .... ***Eudorella* spp.**[2] (Fig.F)

#6.Males with 3 pairs of pleopods (see Fig.A to determine sex and locate the pleopods) .... ***Pseudoleptocuma minor*** (Fig.G)
#6.Males with 2 pairs of pleopods .... **other cumacean species**[2]

[1]Refer to footnote on page 10.00 for a description of the three different sections of a crustacean and the appendages attached to each section.
[2]Refer to Watling (1979) or Zimmer (1980) to identify the species.

Fig.A. **TYPICAL CUMACEANS:** Male cumaceans have long antennae and have 1-5 pairs of pleopods (abdominal appendages) in most species. Female cumaceans have very small antennae and do not have any pleopods. Cumaceans usually burrow in mud or sand. They sometimes swim in the water column at night.

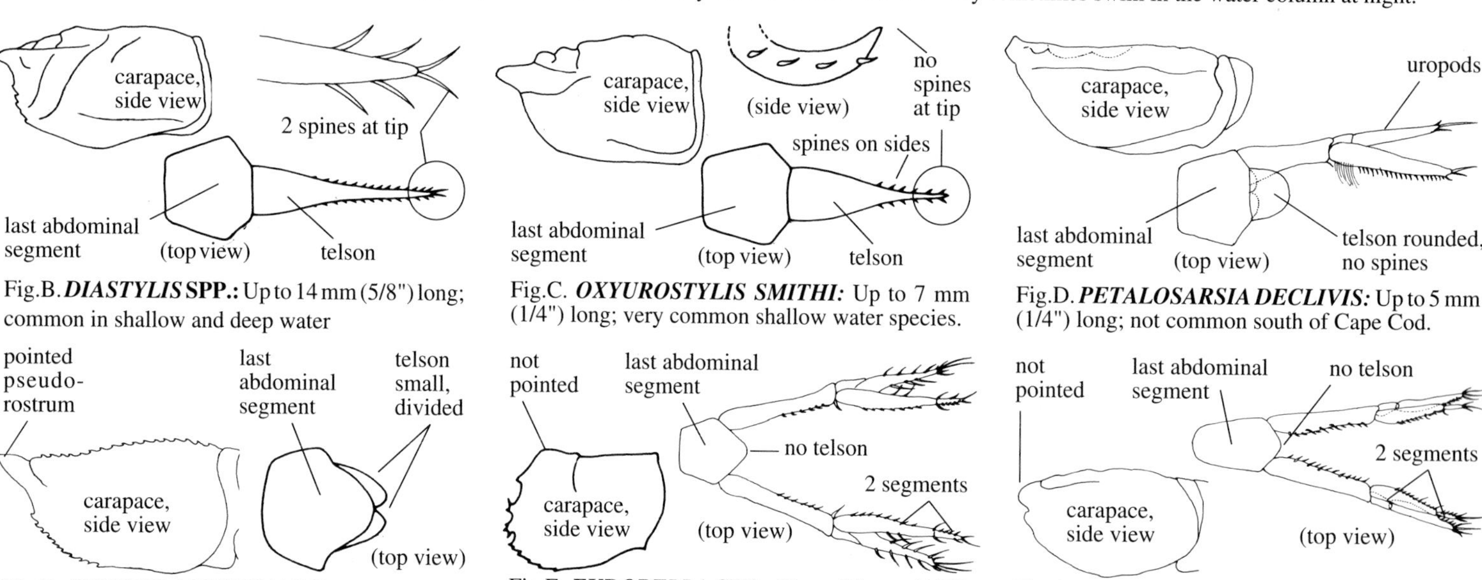

Fig.B. ***DIASTYLIS* SPP.:** Up to 14 mm (5/8") long; common in shallow and deep water

Fig.C. ***OXYUROSTYLIS SMITHI:*** Up to 7 mm (1/4") long; very common shallow water species.

Fig.D. ***PETALOSARSIA DECLIVIS:*** Up to 5 mm (1/4") long; not common south of Cape Cod.

Fig.E. ***LEUCON AMERICANUS:*** Up to 5 mm (1/4") long; in brackish water south of Cape Cod.

Fig.F. ***EUDORELLA* SPP.:** Up to 12 mm (1/2") long; more common north of Cape Cod.

Fig.G. ***PSEUDOLEPTOCUMA MINOR* (=*Leptocuma m.*):** Up to 7 mm (1/4") long.

MYSIDS (OPOSSUM SHRIMP)
PHYLUM ARTHROPODA, CLASS CRUSTACEA, ORDER MYSIDACEA

Free swimming shrimplike crustaceans with 8 pairs of feathery, two-branched legs.

(Use the key on page 10.00 to determine if you have a mysid)

#1.Telson ("tail plate," see Figs.A,B) has V-shaped notch at the tip (Figs. D-F) .... #2
#1.Telson is rounded or pointed at the tip, without a notch (Figs.G,H) .... #5

#2.Antennal scales (see Figs.A-C) are long and narrow (Figs.E,F); most of the telson has spines along its outside edges .... #3
#2.Antennal scales are broad and rounded; only the rear half of the telson has spines along its outside edges .... ***Heteromysis formosa*** (Fig.D)

#3.Tips of antennal scales are blunt .... ***Praunus flexuosus*** (Fig.E)
#3.Tips of antennal scales are sharply pointed (Fig.F) .... ***Mysis* spp., #4**

#4.With 25 spines on sides of telson; spines end where notch begins .... ***Mysis stenolepis*** (Fig.F)
#4.With more than 30 spines on sides of telson; spines continue to tip of telson .... ***Mysis mixta*** (Fig.F)

#5.Antennal scales (see Figs.A-C) are about 10 times as long as wide; tip of telson is somewhat pointed .... ***Neomysis americana*** (Fig.G)
#5.Antennal scales are about 5 times as long as wide; tip of telson is rounded .... ***Mysidopsis bigelowi*** (Fig.H)

Fig.A. **TYPICAL MYSID, TOP VIEW**

Fig.B. **TYPICAL MYSID, SIDE VIEW**

Fig.C. **TYPICAL MYSID HEAD**

Fig.D. ***HETEROMYSIS FORMOSA:*** Males are translucent, females partially rose colored; up to 9 mm (3/8") long; sometimes found in small swarms inside dead clam shells; occurs in intertidal zone and offshore.

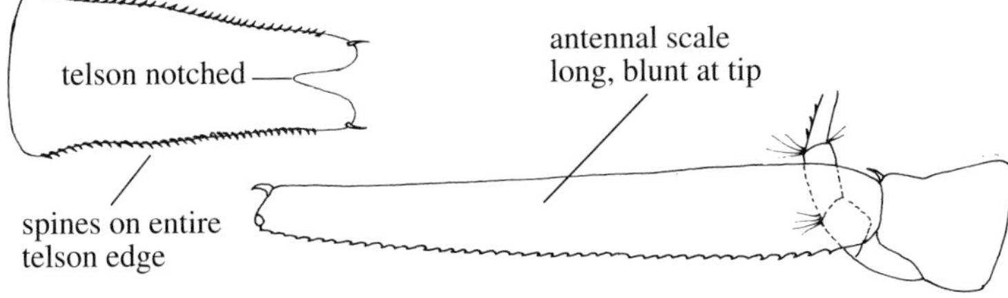

Fig.E. ***PRAUNUS FLEXUOSUS:*** Body is translucent greenish or yellowish with darker streaks and a pink tail; up to 25 mm (1") long; first observed on the American coast in 1960 on the north shore of Cape Cod, this European species has spread northward and now occurs throughout the Gulf of Maine.

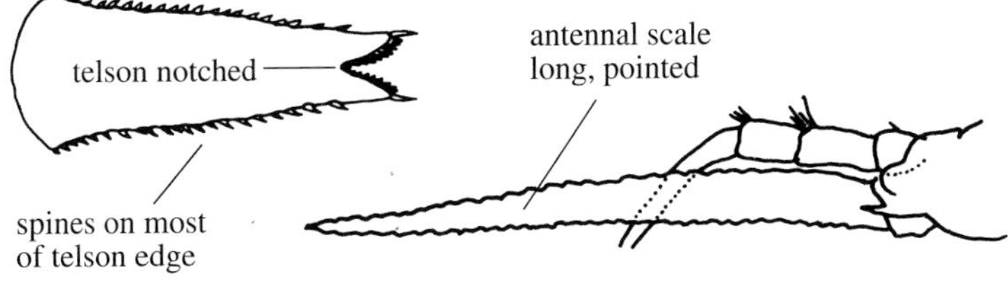

Fig.F. ***MYSIS* SPP.:** *Mysis stenolepis* has a translucent body with black star shaped spots; up to 30 mm (1 1/4") long; common among eelgrass and weeds in shallow water. *Mysis mixta* is up to 25 mm (1") long; common north of Cape Cod in areas without eelgrass or weeds; occurs in intertidal zone and offshore.

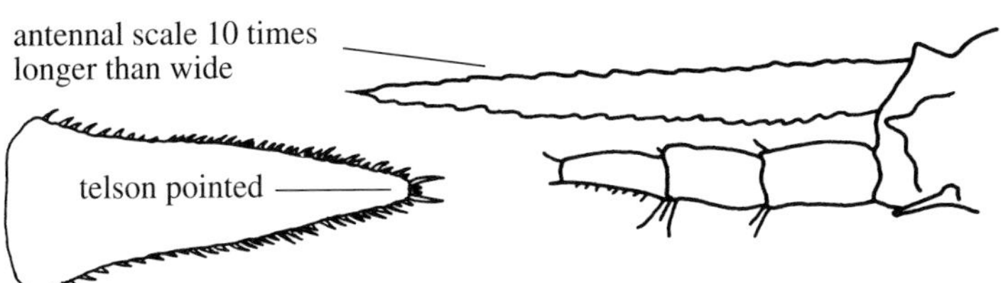

Fig.G. ***NEOMYSIS AMERICANA:*** Up to 12 mm (1/2") long; very common in shallow and estuarine waters.

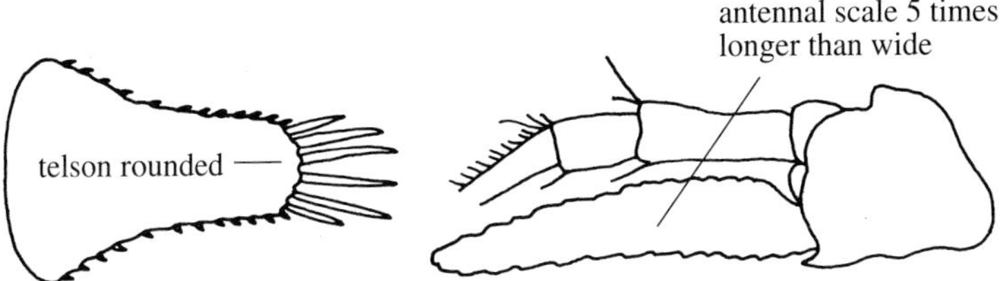

Fig.H. ***MYSIDOPSIS BIGELOWI:*** Up to 8 mm (5/16") long; usually found in deeper water.

MANTIS SHRIMPS
PHYLUM ARTHROPODA, CLASS CRUSTACEA, ORDER STOMATOPODA

Crustaceans with a short carapace that does not cover all of the thoracic segments (segments with legs); with powerful, spiny claws

(Use the key on page 10.00 to determine if you have a mantis shrimp)

#1.Large, grows up to about 19 cm (7 1/2") long; with a ridge on midline of carapace (ridge has tiny V at front end) ....***Squilla empusa,* mantis shrimp** (Fig.A)
#1.Small, grows up to about 4 cm (1 1/2") long; no ridge on midline of carapace; not common ....***Nannosquilla grayi*** (not shown)

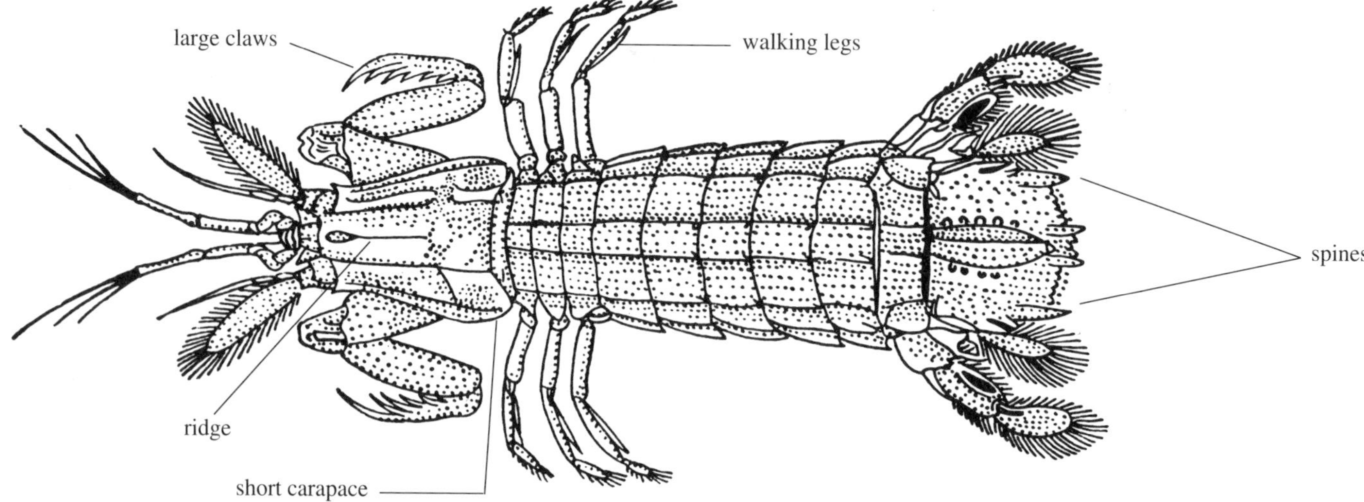

Fig.A. ***SQUILLA EMPUSA,* MANTIS SHRIMP**: Gray or green tinged with yellow and red; up to about 19 cm (7 1/2") long. Quite common in some parts of this region, such as western Long Island Sound. Not common in some other locations. WARNING: Mantis shrimp can stab you with the spines at the end of their tail by quickly flipping their tail forward under their body. Use Manning (1974) to identify stomatopods collected in waters over 30 m (100') deep. **17.12 A**

TRUE SHRIMPS
PHYLUM ARTHROPODA, CLASS CRUSTACEA, ORDER DECAPODA (in part)

Crustaceans with a carapace, extended abdomen ("tail") and with 5 pairs of slender, delicate legs and claws.

(Use the key on page 10.00 to determine if you have a true shrimp)

#1.Rostrum ("beak" or "nose") is very short, does not extend beyond eyes; claws on first pair of legs[1] are subchelate[2] ("trigger" type claws) .... ***Crangon septemspinosa,* sevenspine bay shrimp** (Fig.A)
#1.Rostrum is long and extends well in front of eyes (Figs.B-E); first pair of legs either with chelate ("pincer" type) claws or no claws at all ....#2

#2.The sides of the first abdominal ("tail") segment[3] overlap the second abdominal segment; the first three pairs of legs have small, nearly equal sized claws; grows up to 21 cm (8 1/2") in length ....***Penaeus aztecus,* brown shrimp** (Fig.B)
#2.The sides of the second abdominal segment have rounded lobes that overlap both the first and third segments (Figs.C-E); no claws on third pair[1] of legs; less than 10 cm (4") and rarely over 5 cm (2") long ....**caridean shrimp**, #3

#3.No obvious claws on first pair of legs; second pair of legs with tiny claws; carpus ("wrist" segment, leg segment above claw) of second pair of legs is divided into a large number of tiny segments; grows up to 10 cm (4") long .... **family Pandalidae, pandalid shrimp** (Fig.C)
#3.With small but obvious claws on both first and second pairs of legs; the carpus ("wrist" segment) of the second pair of legs is not divided into more than 3 segments (Figs. D,E); does not grow more than 5 cm (2") long ....#4

#4.Carpus ("wrist" segment) of second pair of legs divided into 3 short sections; abdomen ("tail") is sharply bent and is humped; claws on first pair of legs stronger but shorter than claws on second pair; often bright green but may be reddish brown; up to 1.9 cm (3/4") long ....***Hippolyte* spp., zostera shrimp** (Fig.D)
#4.Carpus of second pair of legs has one section and is not subdivided (Fig.E); abdomen is not sharply bent (Fig.E); claws on second pair of legs stronger and longer than on first; color never bright green; up to 5 cm (2") long ....***Palaemonetes* spp., grass shrimp**, #5

#5.With 2-3 teeth on underside of rostrum ("nose" or "beak"); teeth on top of rostrum do not go all the way to the tip; with only one rostral tooth behind eye socket; with no teeth on moveable finger of claws on second[1] legs; with yellowish eyestalks ....***Palaemonetes pugio*, daggerblade grass shrimp** (Figs.E)
#5.With 4-5 teeth on underside of rostrum; teeth on top of rostrum go all the way to the tip; with two rostral teeth behind eye socket; with two teeth on moveable finger of claws on second[1] legs; with reddish eyestalks ....***Palaemonetes vulgaris*, marsh grass shrimp** (Fig. E)
#5.With 4-5 teeth on underside of rostrum; teeth on top of rostrum go all the way to the tip; with one rostral tooth behind eye socket; with one tooth on moveable finger of claws on second[1] legs ....***Palaemonetes intermedius*, brackish grass shrimp** (Fig. E)

[1]Count shrimp legs backward, from rear to front (i.e. 5-4-3-2-1), to avoid confusion with mouth parts and other appendages that may look leglike. All shrimps have 5 pairs of walking legs.
[2]See Fig. C on page 10.05 for a comparison of the chelate and subchelate claw types.
[3]Refer to footnote on page 10.00 for a description of the three different sections of a crustacean and the appendages attached to each section.

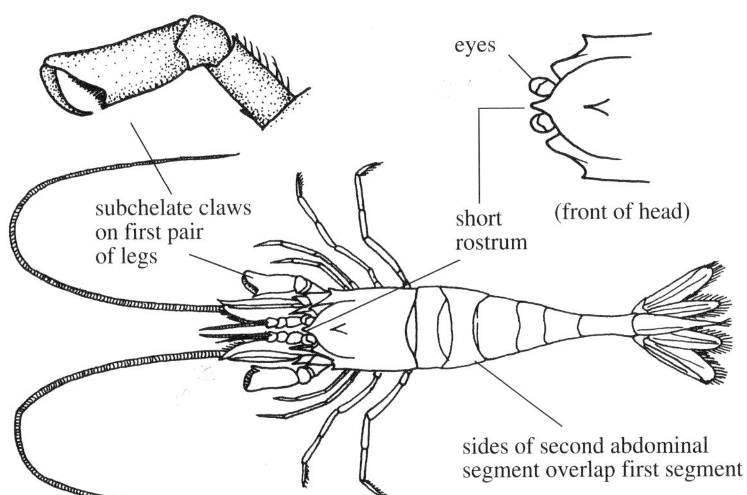

Fig.A. ***CRANGON SEPTEMSPINOSA*, SEVENSPINE BAY SHRIMP (=sand shrimp):** Light or dark brown or beige, often with speckles; color and pattern can vary to match the mud or sand it is on; up to 6 cm (2 1/2") long; the most common shrimp in this region. (family Crangonidae) **17.12 B**

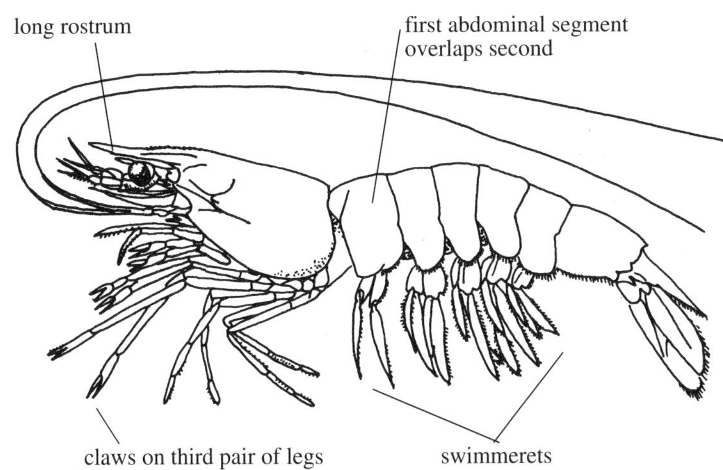

Fig.B. ***PENAEUS AZTECUS*, BROWN SHRIMP:** Brown; up to 21 cm (8.5") long; rarely found in southern New England; these shrimps are edible and are of commercial importance further south. (family Penaeidae)

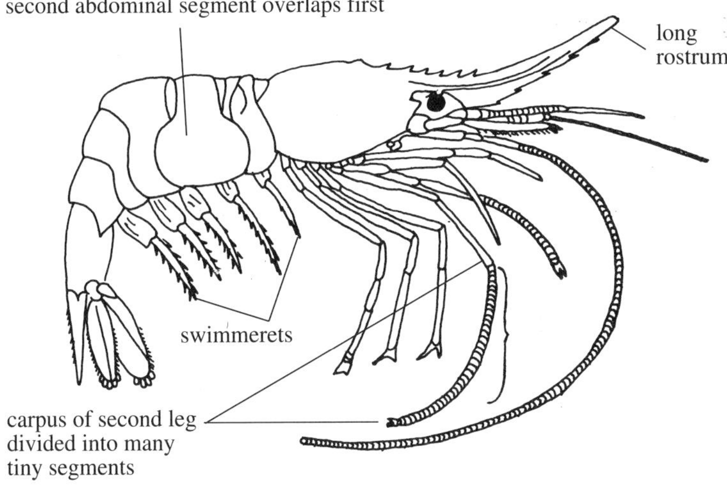

Fig.C. **FAMILY PANDALIDAE, PANDALID SHRIMP:** Up to 10 cm (4") long; rare in southern New England. One species, *Pandalus montagui*, Aesop shrimp, is pink or red or transparent with red spots and stripes; edible and commercially important further north.

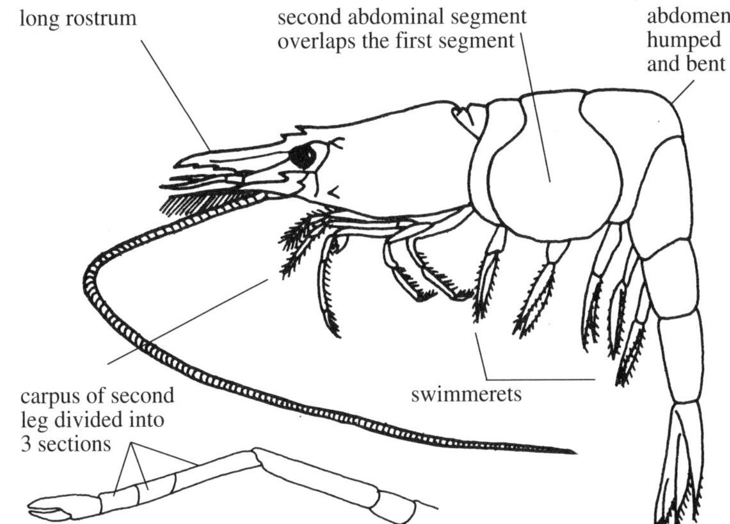

Fig.D. ***HIPPOLYTE* SPP., ZOSTERA SHRIMP:** Often bright green, sometimes dark or reddish brown; up to 1.9 cm (3/4") long; common in submerged beds of eelgrass (*Zostera*) and algae in shallow estuaries. (family Hippolytidae)

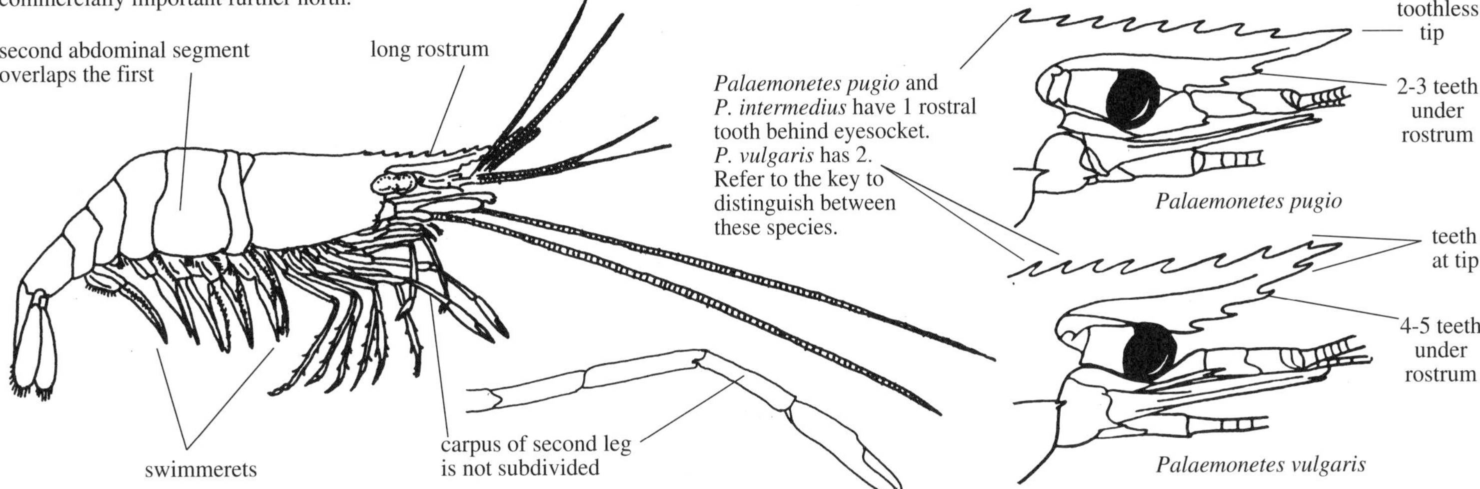

Fig.E. ***PALAEMONETES* SPP., GRASS SHRIMP:** Translucent with brownish or reddish spots and streaks; up to 5 cm (2") long; found in bays and estuarine habitats, especially eelgrass beds. *P. vulgaris*, the marsh grass shrimp, has reddish eyestalks. It is the most common species and prefers more saline waters. *P. pugio*, the daggerblade grass shrimp, which has yellowish eyestalks and *P.intermedius*, the brackish grass shrimp prefer brackish water. (family Palaemonidae)

LOBSTERS AND MUD SHRIMPS
PHYLUM ARTHROPODA, CLASS CRUSTACEA, ORDER DECAPODA (in part)

Crustaceans with a carapace covering the entire thorax[1]; with 5 pairs of legs including 4 pairs of stout walking legs and one pair of powerful claws; body and tail are broad

(Use the key on page 10.00 to determine if you have a lobster or mud shrimp)

#1. Abdomen ("tail") is about the same width as the carapace ("body") and is slightly longer; shell is hard and strong except just after molting; total length often exceeds 10 cm (4") .... ***Homarus americanus*, American lobster** (Fig.A)

#1. Abdomen is wider and nearly twice as long as the carapace (Fig.B); shell is weak and flexible; total length is less than 10 cm (4") .... **superfamily Thalassinoidea, mud shrimps and allies,** #2

#2. Rostrum ("nose" or "beak") is small, rounded and does not extend over eyes; large claws on first pair of legs are not the same size; with a much smaller pair of claws on second pair of legs (first pair of "walking" legs) .... ***Gilvossius setimanus*, ghost shrimp** (Fig.B)

#2. Rostrum is large, flat on top, covered with tufts of short bristles, and extends over the eyes; large claws on first pair of legs are the same size; no claws on the second pair of legs (first pair of "walking" legs) .... ***Upogebia affinis*, coastal mud shrimp** (Fig.B)

#2. Rostrum is long and pointed; large claws on first pair of legs are not the same size; with small claws on second pair of legs (first pair of "walking" legs) .... ***Axius serratus*, lobster shrimp** (Fig.B)

[1]Refer to footnote on page 10.00 for a description of the three different sections of a crustacean and the appendages attached to each section.

carapace length

(top, dorsal view)

hard, stiff
male
soft, featherlike
female
swimmerets (pleopods)
first swimmerets

(underside, ventral view)

Figs.A. ***HOMARUS AMERICANUS*, AMERICAN LOBSTER:** Greenish-brown with blue patches near joints of appendages; lobsters have been reported in excess of 80 cm (32") total length but most lobsters in the estuarine waters of southern New England do not grow much larger than the legal minimum catch size (8.26 cm (3 1/4") carapace length in 1994). (Carapace length is measured from the back of the eye sockets, as shown above). The lobster fishery in southern New England is a multimillion dollar industry. The first pair of swimmerets of the female lobster are soft and featherlike, similar to the other swimmerets but with only one branch. The first pair of swimmerets of the male lobster are hard and stiff. During the day, lobsters dwell in burrows under rocks and in the mud. They forage for food at night, actively preying on crabs, worms, bivalves, and other animals. Female lobsters carry large egg masses, containing up to 30,000 eggs, attached to the swimmerets under their tail. It is illegal to possess a lobster when in this "berried" condition. (family Nephropidae: clawed lobsters) **17.12 C**

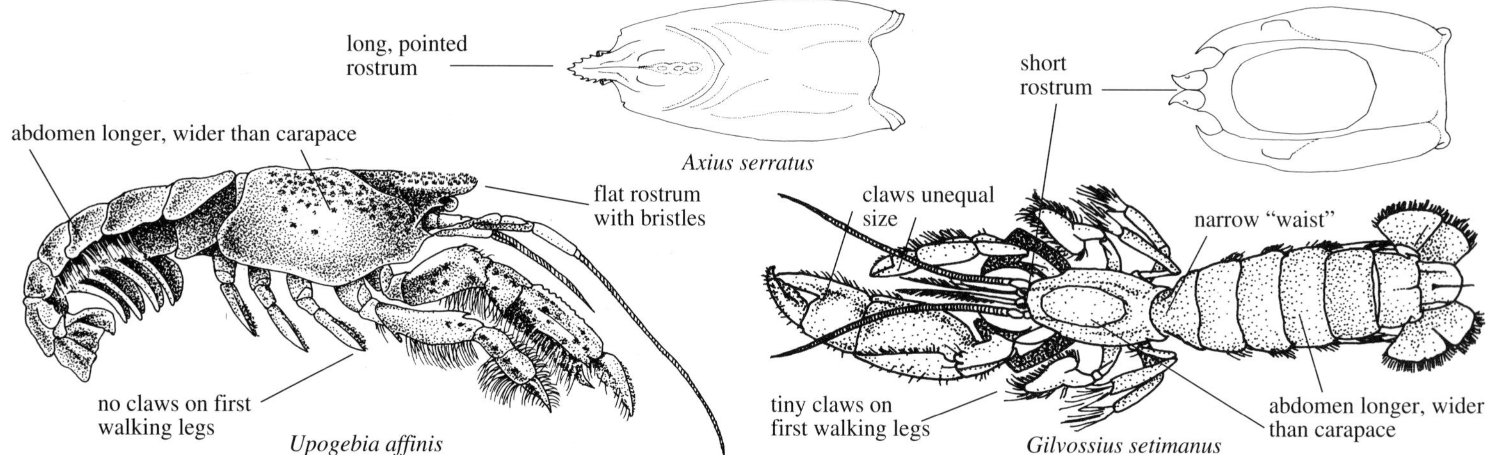

Fig.B. **SUPERFAMILY THALASSINOIDEA, MUD SHRIMPS AND ALLIES:** Up to 10 cm (4") long; burrow into mud or sand in the intertidal zone and in shallow water; not common. Refer to the above key to distinguish between the three most common species which occur in southern New England: *Gilvossius setimanus (=Callianassa atlantica)*, a ghost shrimp; *Upogebia affinis*, the coastal mud shrimp; and *Axius serratus*, a lobster shrimp.

HERMIT CRABS
PHYLUM ARTHROPODA, CLASS CRUSTACEA, ORDER DECAPODA, FAMILY PAGURIDAE

Crabs which live in empty snail shells (Fig.A); with soft, shell-less abdomen[1] ("tail").

(Use key on page 10.00 to determine if you have a hermit crab)

#1.Largest claw is slender (width less than 1/2 length), almost cylindrical, without saw-teeth on outer edge of claw; carapace[1] length up to 12 mm (1/2") .... #2
#1.Largest claw is broad (width more than 1/2 length), flat or oval in cross section, with saw-teeth on outer edge; carapace length may exceed 12 mm (1/2")..#3

#2.Large claws are nearly hairless and without purple bands (but may have a darkish longitudinal stripe); length of eyestalks are less than 3.5 times the greatest width; prefers shells of mudsnails (*Ilyanassa*), periwinkles (*Littorina*) and other small snails; very common ...***Pagurus longicarpus*, longwrist hermit crab** (Fig.B)
#2.Large claws are hairy and may have 4 or 5 distinct purplish bands; length of eyestalks are more than 3.5 times the greatest width; prefers shells of the greedy dovesnail (*Anachis avara*) or the bruised nassa (*Nassarius vibex*); tiny, up to 6 mm (1/4") carapace length; not common ....***Pagurus annulipes*** (not shown)

#3.Moveable finger of major claw with a projecting angle on outer edge; claws are bumpy, without many long spines or an orange stripe; very common; prefers shells of moonsnails (*Euspira*), whelks (*Busycon, Busycotypus*) and other large snails ....***Pagurus pollicaris*, flatclaw hermit crab** (Fig.C)
#3.Moveable finger of major claw is curved, not angled, on outer edge; claws have a broad longitudinal red-orange stripe; claws have many small bumps and spines; prefers shells of the waved whelk (*Buccinum undatum*) ....***Pagurus acadianus*, Acadian hermit crab** (Fig.D)
#3.Moveable finger of major claw is curved on outer edge; claws with many long spines, hairs and bumpy ridges ....***Pagurus arcuatus*** (not shown)

[1]See Fig.A showing the different regions of a crab. The carapace covers the head and thorax ("body") of the crab, but does not cover the abdomen ("tail").

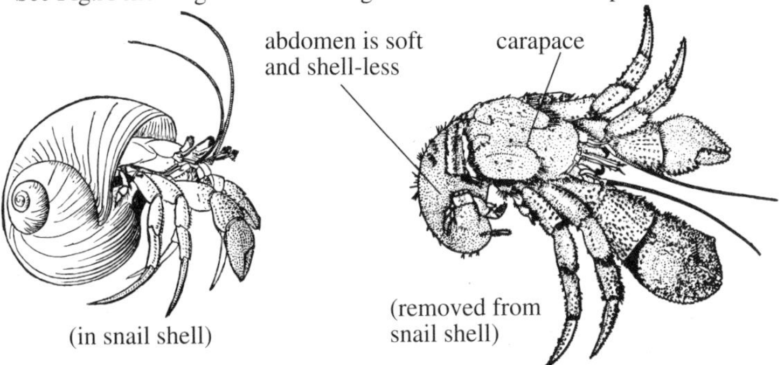

Fig.A. ***PAGURUS* SPP., HERMIT CRABS**

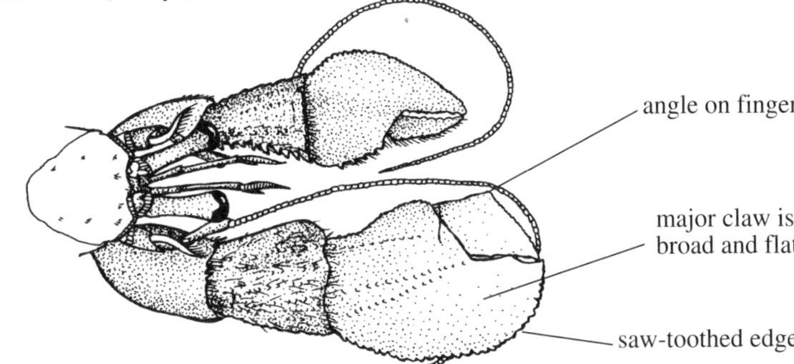

Fig.C. ***PAGURUS POLLICARIS*, FLATCLAW HERMIT CRAB:** Reddish brown, up to 3 cm (1 1/4") carapace length; very common. **17.12 F**

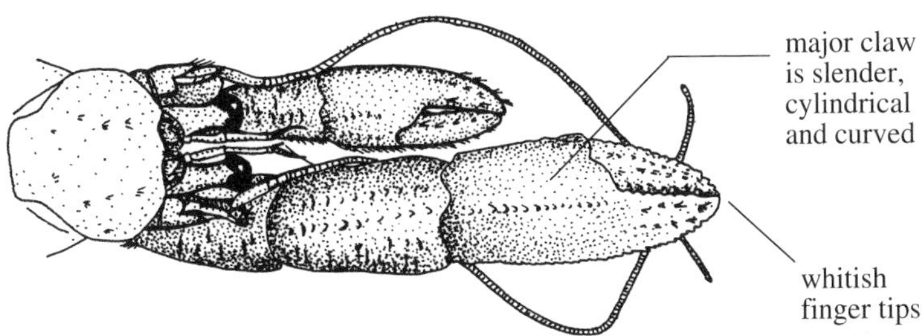

Fig.B. ***PAGURUS LONGICARPUS*, LONGWRIST HERMIT CRAB:** Body is gray or tan, large claw is whitish; up to 11 mm (1/2") carapace length; very common. **17.12 E**

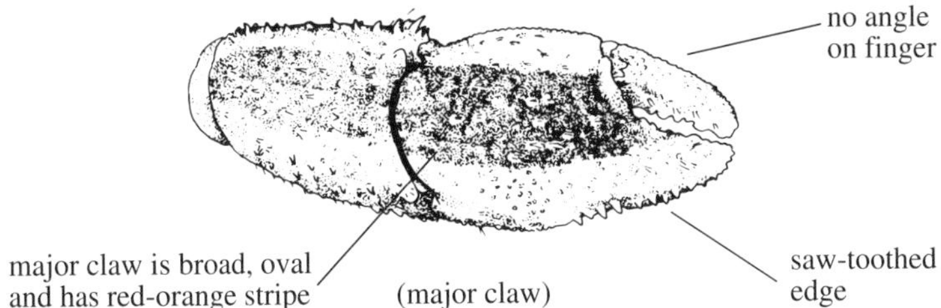

Fig.D. ***PAGURUS ACADIANUS*, ACADIAN HERMIT CRAB:** Body brown, legs orange or reddish-brown with white bases, claws with longitudinal red-orange stripe and whitish edges; up to 3 cm (1 1/4") carapace length. **17.12 G**

SAND CRAB
PHYLUM ARTHROPODA, CLASS CRUSTACEA, ORDER DECAPODA, FAMILY HIPPIDAE

Crustaceans with an egg shaped body, 3 pairs of legs, and with a triangular shieldlike plate (telson) at the end of the abdomen ("tail") which is usually tucked under the body.

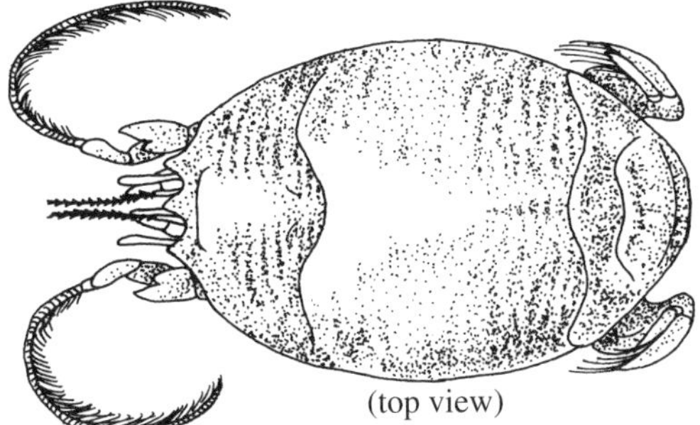

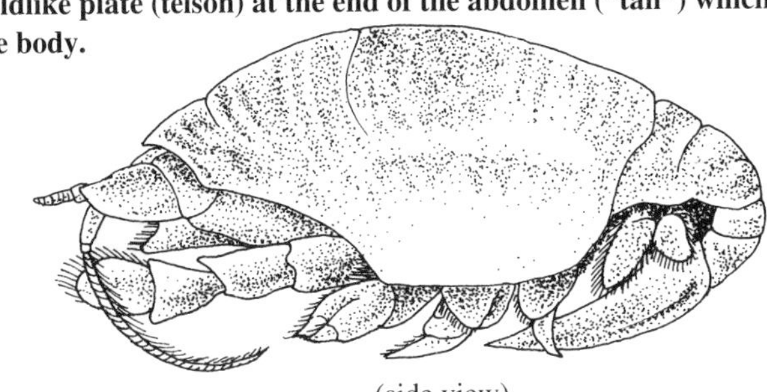

Fig.E. ***EMERITA TALPOIDA*, ATLANTIC SAND CRAB (=mole crab):** Pale yellowish brown; up to 2.5 cm (1") long; burrows into wave swept sandy beaches; not common in estuarine waters.

TRUE CRABS

PHYLUM ARTHROPODA, CLASS CRUSTACEA, ORDER DECAPODA, INFRAORDER BRACHYURA

Crustaceans with abdomen ("tail") that is folded tightly under body (Fig.A); with five pairs of legs including four pairs of walking legs and one pair with large claws.

(Use the key on page 10.00 to determine if you have a true crab)

#1.With a long, pointed rostrum ("nose" or "beak"); carapace ("body") somewhat triangular or bulbous in shape (Fig.B) .... **spider crabs**, page 10.22

#1.Front of shell is rounded or straight, not long and pointed; carapace ("body") is oval, round, or squarish, not triangular or bulbous (Figs.C-F) .... #2

#2.Last pair of legs are flattened and paddlelike with rounded tips for swimming (Fig.C), remaining legs are pointed .... **swimming crabs**, page 10.23

#2.All of the walking legs, including the last pair, are pointed .... #3

#3.With 3 small pointed or rounded teeth between eyes on front edge of shell (Fig.D); carapace width may exceed 4 cm (1 1/2") .... **cancer and green crabs**, page 10.24

#3.No teeth between the eyes on front edge of shell; may or may not have a single central notch or groove between the eyes (Figs.E,F); carapace width never greater than 4 cm (1 1/2") .... #4

#4.Semiterrestrial crabs which are active and move about on shore above the water level and dig burrows on marshes and mudflats; carapace outline is squarish with a straight and toothless front margin (see Figs.A-F on facing page, page 10.21); males may or may not have one claw which is much larger than the other .... **fiddler and marsh crabs**, page 10.21

#4.Crabs which are primarily aquatic, living below the low tide level or hiding beneath rocks and other wet places in the intertidal zone; do not actively move about on the shore above the water level; front margin of carapace is often curved and may have teeth (Figs.E-F); both claws of males are the same size .... #5

#5.With 3-5 distinct teeth to either side of eyes on front edge of shell (Fig.E); with a central notch or groove along midline of shell; eyes are well developed; some species have dark markings on the fingers of the claws; free living crabs, often found burrowed into mud; carapace width may be greater than 16 mm (5/8") .... **mud crabs**, page 10.25

#5.With no teeth to either side of eyes on front edge of shell (Fig. F); eyes are very small; without dark markings on fingers of claws; usually live inside oysters, mussels and other bivalves or in worm tubes; carapace width less than 16 mm (5/8") .... **pea crabs**, page 10.26

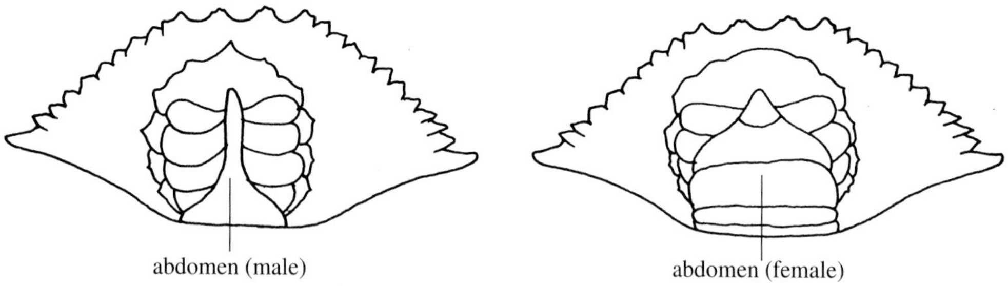

abdomen (male)

abdomen (female)

Fig.A. **UNDERSIDE OF TYPICAL CRABS:** Females usually have a broad abdomen ("tail" or "apron"); males have a narrow abdomen. Females carry eggs ("sponge") attached between the abdomen and the body. **17.13 D**

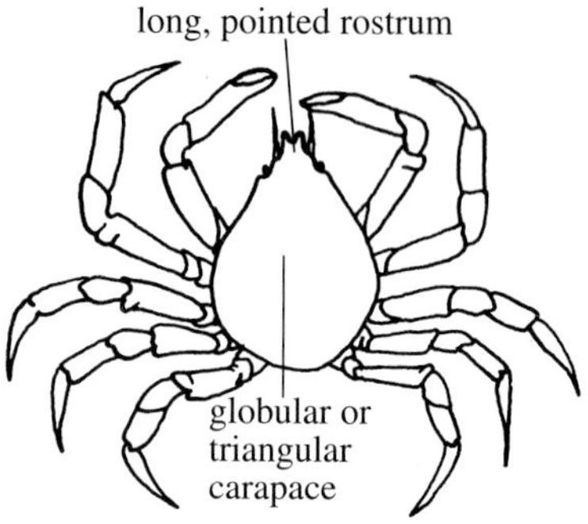

long, pointed rostrum

globular or triangular carapace

Fig.B. **SPIDER CRABS**

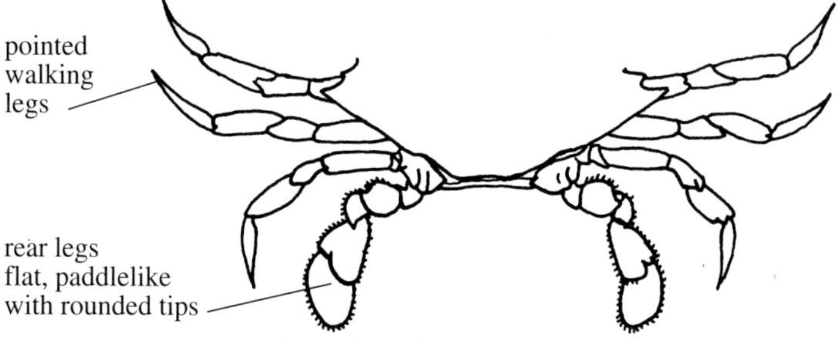

pointed walking legs

rear legs flat, paddlelike with rounded tips

Fig.C. **SWIMMING CRABS**

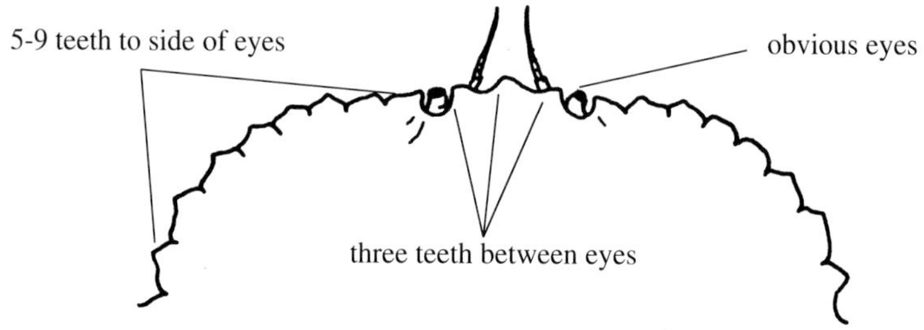

5-9 teeth to side of eyes

obvious eyes

three teeth between eyes

Fig.D. **CANCER OR GREEN CRABS**

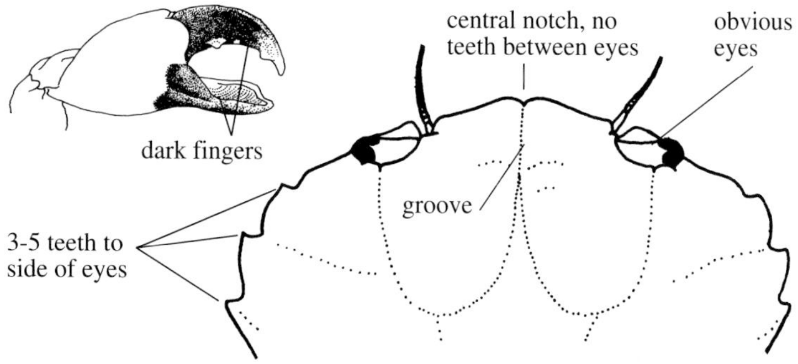

dark fingers

central notch, no teeth between eyes

obvious eyes

groove

3-5 teeth to side of eyes

Fig.E. **MUD CRABS**

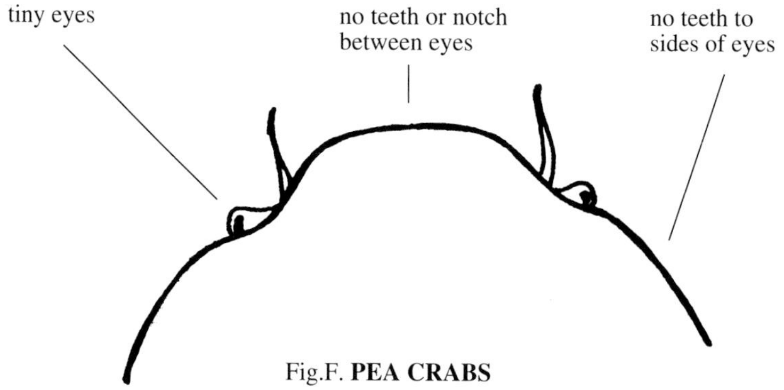

tiny eyes

no teeth or notch between eyes

no teeth to sides of eyes

Fig.F. **PEA CRABS**

FIDDLER AND MARSH CRABS
CLASS CRUSTACEA, ORDER DECAPODA, FAMILIES OCYPODIDAE AND GRAPSIDAE

Semiterrestrial crabs that actively move about and dig burrows on the shore above the low tide level; carapace ("shell") outline is squarish with a straight and toothless front margin.

(Use the key on page 10.20 to determine if you have a fiddler or marsh crab)

#1.Space between eyes is wide; eyestalks are shorter than space between eyes; front edge of shell has a small notch between eyes; both claws are about the same size in males and females .... ***Sesarma reticulatum*, heavy marsh crab** (Fig.A)

#1.Space between eyes is narrow; eyestalks are longer than space between eyes (Figs.D-F); shell is not notched between eyes; males (Fig.F) have one claw much larger than the other; both claws are the same size in females (Fig.E) .... **family Ocypodidae, fiddler crabs**, #2

#2.Inner palm of large claw of male[1] with a smooth ridge .... ***Uca pugilator*, Atlantic sand fiddler crab** (Fig.B)

#2.Inner palm of large claw of male[1] with a bumpy ridge (Figs.C,D) .... #3

#3.Shell does not have a groove behind each eye; joints of claws do not have red spots; shell width never exceeds 2.2 cm (7/8"); entire shell is very dark, almost black .... ***Uca pugnax*, Atlantic marsh fiddler crab** (Fig.C)

#3.Shell has a curved groove behind each eye (Fig.D); with reddish spots at joints of claws, especially in males; shell is often wider than 2.2 cm (7/8"); shell is usually grayish with brown mark in center .... ***Uca minax*, redjointed fiddler crab** (Fig.D)

[1]Refer to Williams (1984) to identify a female or capture and identify a male in the same colony and assume that the female is the same species. Males have one large claw and one small claw (Fig.F) and females have two small claws (Fig.E).

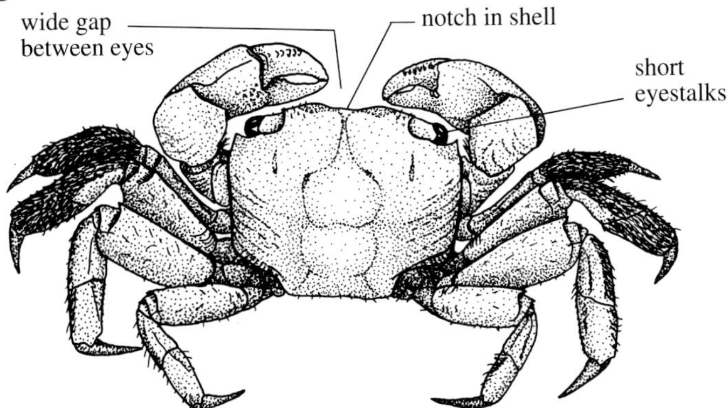

Fig.A. ***SESARMA RETICULATUM*, HEAVY MARSH CRAB:** Dark olive, purple, or nearly black; carapace width up to 2.8 cm (1 1/8"); digs burrows near edge of saltmarshes in or near cordgrass. A similar crab, *Planes minutus*, gulfweed crab, occasionally drifts into coastal waters from offshore on floating *Sargassum* seaweed and other flotsam. (family Grapsidae: shore and marsh crabs)

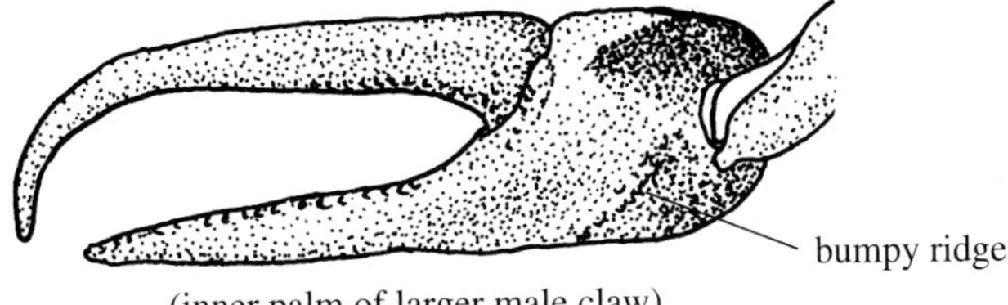

(inner palm of larger male claw)

Fig.C. ***UCA PUGNAX*, ATLANTIC MARSH FIDDLER CRAB:** Shell is uniformly dark gray, almost black; shell width up to 2.2 cm (7/8"); usually digs burrows in mud at edges of lower tidal marsh and along mosquito drainage ditches; very common. (family Ocypodidae: fiddler crabs) **17.12 D**

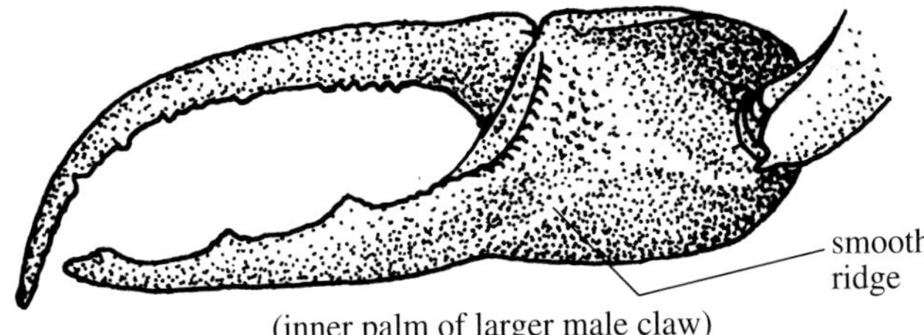

(inner palm of larger male claw)

Fig.B. ***UCA PUGILATOR*, ATLANTIC SAND FIDDLER CRAB:** Shell is mottled in grayish-blue and purple, front half of shell may have a large patch of deep purplish blue; shell width up to 2.6 cm (1"); burrows into sand and sandy mud at edges of saltmarshes and tidal creeks. (family Ocypodidae: fiddler crabs)

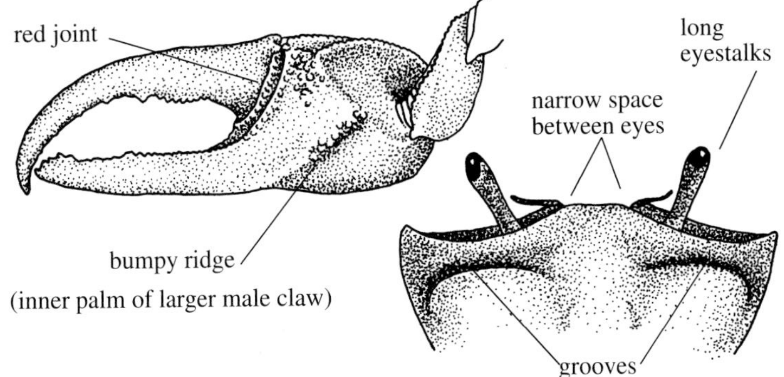

(inner palm of larger male claw)

Figs.D. ***UCA MINAX*, REDJOINTED FIDDLER CRAB:** Shell is grayish, lighter in front, with central brown mark; with reddish spots at joints of claws, especially the larger claw of males, shell width may grow up to 3.6 cm (1 1/2"); found in burrows along the ditches in the upper sections of tidal marshes where the salinity is low. (family Ocypodidae: fiddler crabs)

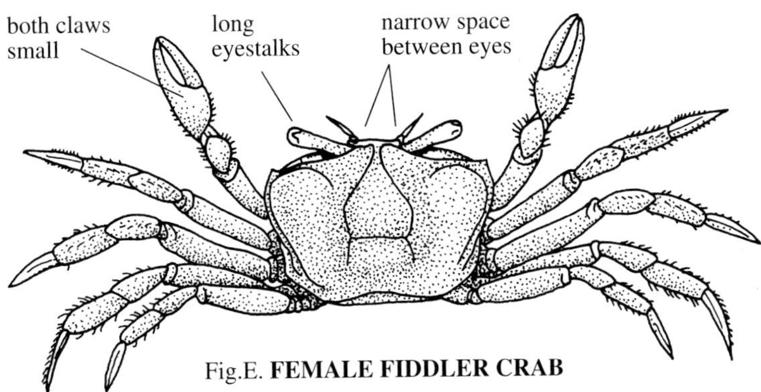

Fig.E. **FEMALE FIDDLER CRAB**

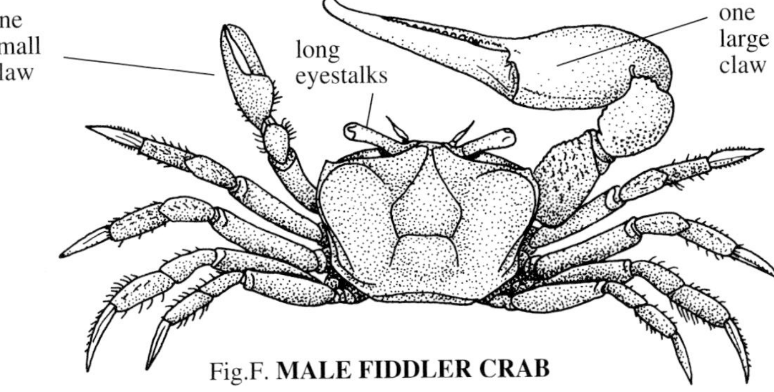

Fig.F. **MALE FIDDLER CRAB**

SPIDER CRABS
PHYLUM ARTHROPODA, CLASS CRUSTACEA, ORDER DECAPODA, FAMILY MAJIDAE

Crabs with long legs, a triangular, globular, or bulbous carapace, and a long, pointed rostrum

(Use the key on page 10.20 to determine if you have a spider crab)

#1.Carapace ("shell") is smooth, without any spines or bumps on back (but does have fuzzlike hairs); rostrum ("beak") has two pointed tips separated by a large, deep V-shaped notch; tiny crabs with a carapace length up to 1.3 cm (1/2") .... ***Pelia mutica*, cryptic teardrop crab** (Fig.A)

#1.Carapace with spines or sharp bumps[1] (Figs.B-D); rostrum has a tiny V-shaped notch or narrow slit at tip; carapace length often exceeds 1.3 cm (1/2") ..... #2

#2.With a wide triangular tooth at the rear of each eyesocket which projects beyond the curve of the shell; rostrum is divided into two tips separated by a very narrow slit; without a row of spines or bumps along the midline of the back of the shell; shell is reddish-brown .... ***Hyas* spp., lyre crabs** (Fig.B)

#2.Without a wide triangular tooth at the rear of each eyesocket (Figs.C,D); rostrum is divided into two tips separated by a tiny V-shaped notch; with a row of about 6-9 spines[1] or bumps along the entire midline of the back of the shell; shell is dirty grayish or brownish .... ***Libinia* spp., spider crabs**, #3

#3.With about 9 spines[1] or sharp bumps on midline of back of shell .... ***Libinia emarginata*, portly spider crab** (Fig.C)

#3.With about 6 spines[1] or sharp bumps on midline of back of shell .... ***Libinia dubia*, longnose spider crab** (Fig.D)

[1]The spines are often difficult to see because of the fuzzlike growth on the shell. Scrape your fingernail along the midline to feel the spines for an accurate count.

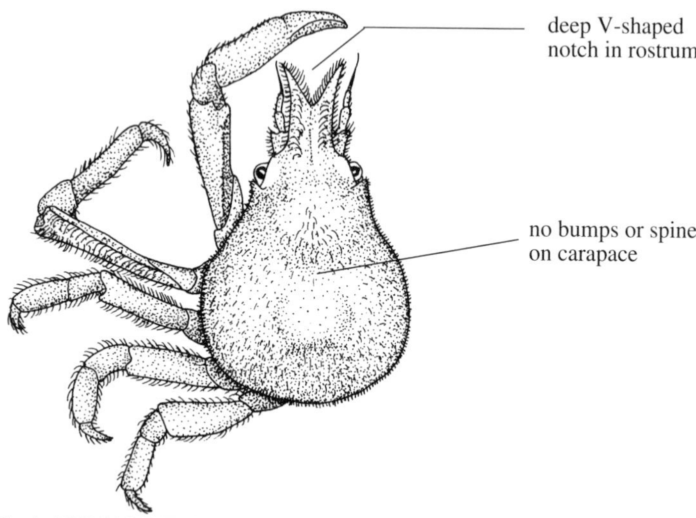

Fig.A. ***PELIA MUTICA*, CRYPTIC TEARDROP CRAB:** Bright red patches on carapace and legs; often covered with sponge; carapace up to 1.3 cm (1/2") long; found on gravelly or shelly bottoms and among fouling organisms on dock pilings; not common.

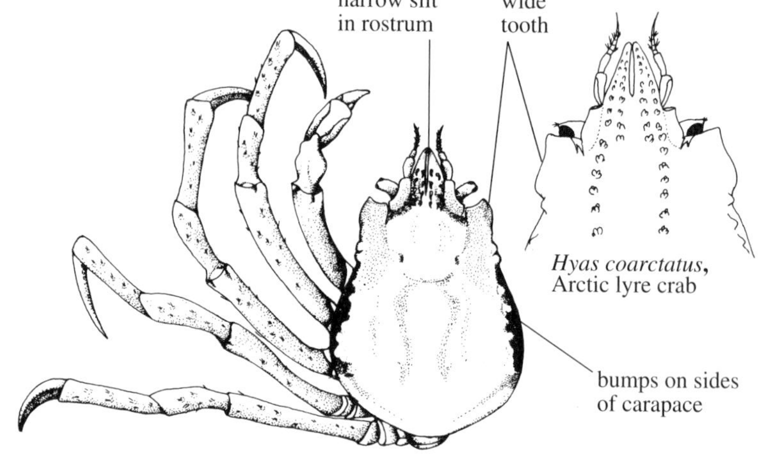

Fig.B. ***HYAS* SPP., LYRE CRABS (=toad crabs):** Reddish brown on upper side. The maximum carapace length is 3 cm (1 1/4") for *Hyas coarctatus* and 9.5 cm (3 3/4") for *Hyas araneus*. *H. araneus* is common north of Cape Cod.

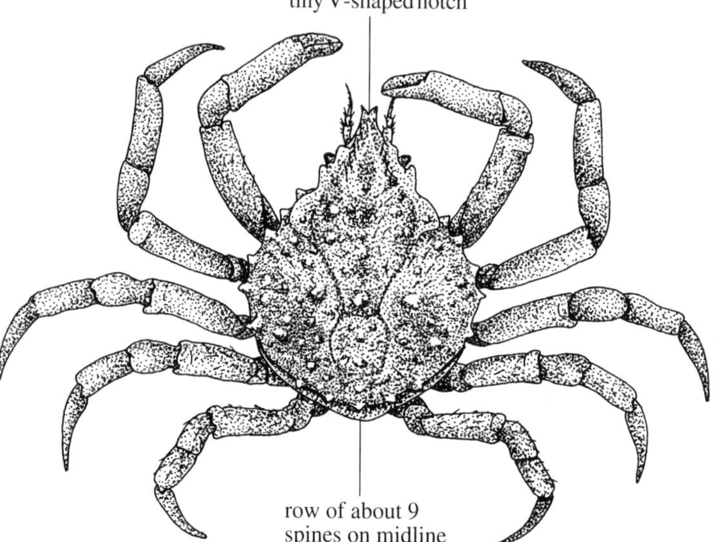

Fig.C. ***LIBINIA EMARGINATA*, PORTLY SPIDER CRAB:** Dirty, grayish brownish color; covered with small hairs; up to 10 cm (4") carapace length; claws and first legs of mature males are much larger than those of females; the most common spider crab in much of this region. **17.13 A**

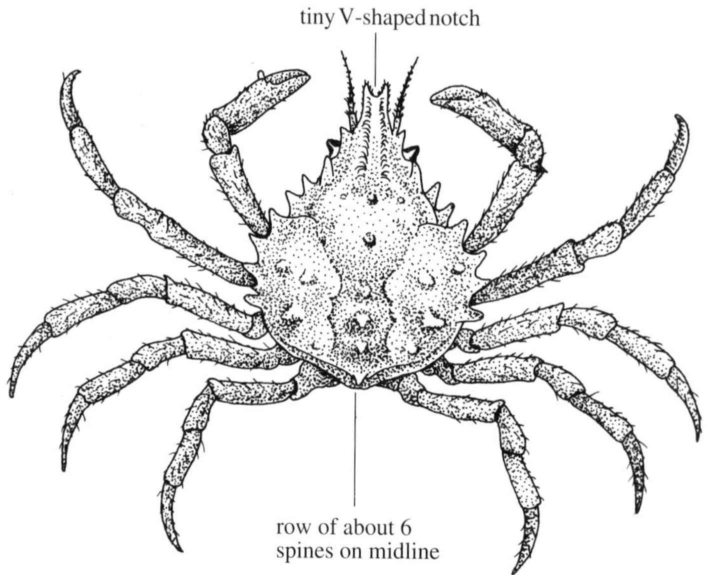

Fig.D. ***LIBINIA DUBIA*, LONGNOSE SPIDER CRAB:** Dirty, grayish brownish color; up to 10 cm (4") carapace length; not as common in our region as *L. emarginata,* the portly spider crab, but is more common further south.

SWIMMING CRABS[1]

PHYLUM ARTHROPODA, CLASS CRUSTACEA, ORDER DECAPODA, FAMILY PORTUNIDAE[2]

Crabs with rear legs which are flat and paddlelike, with rounded tips, and are adapted for swimming.

(Use the key on page 10.20 to determine if you have a swimming crab)

#1.Carapace ("shell") is only slightly wider than long; with 3-5 teeth on edge of shell to either side of eyes; with small rounded spots of reddish purple .... ***Ovalipes ocellatus*, lady crab**[1] (Fig.A)

#1.Carapace ("shell") is more than twice as wide as long (Figs.B,C); with 9 teeth on edge of shell to either side of eyes; the ninth (outermost) tooth is longer than the others and forms a strong, sharp spine; not speckled with red spots .... #2

#2.With 4 teeth on edge of shell between eyes (including the teeth at the inner corner of each eye socket); with 3 spines on front edge of claw "arms" (merus); often very common .... ***Callinectes sapidus*, blue crab**[1] (Fig.B)

#2.With more than 4 teeth on edge of shell between eyes; may or may not have more than 3 spines on front edge of claw "arms" (merus); rare .... **other swimming crabs**[1] (Fig.C)

[1]WARNING: These crabs are very quick, strong and aggressive. Their claws are sharp and can inflict a painful cutting bite.

[2]*Carcinus maenas*, the green crab, is also in this family. Its rear legs are somewhat flattened with pointed tips. See page 10.24.

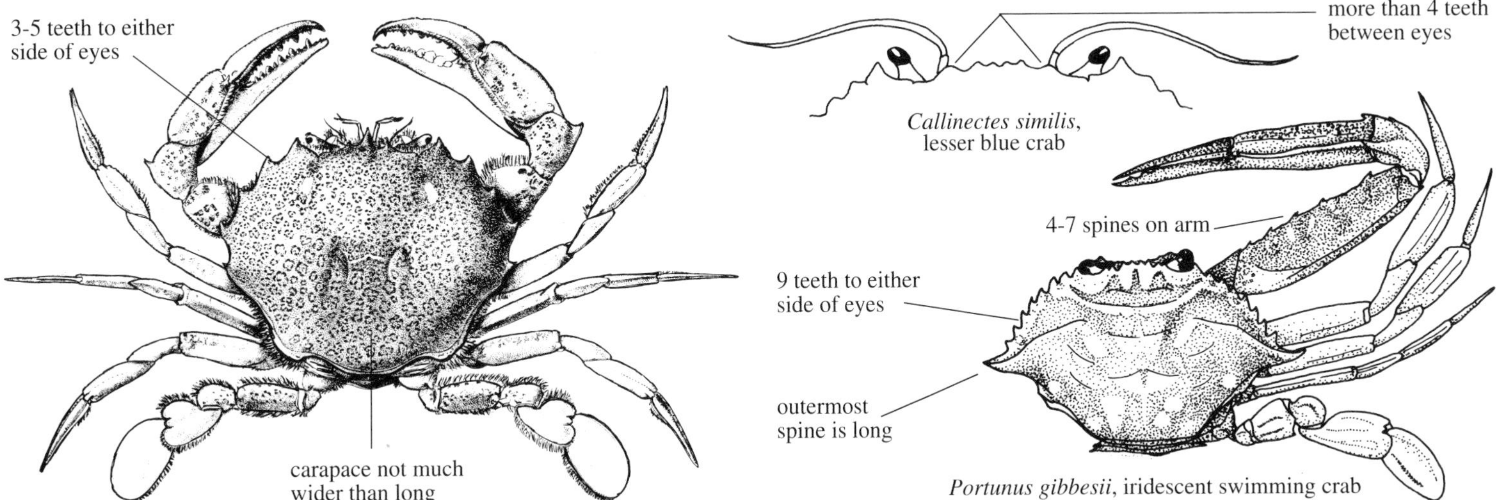

Fig.A. ***OVALIPES OCELLATUS*, LADY CRAB:** Small rounded spots of reddish purple on gray or beige background; up to 8 cm (3 1/4") carapace width; common on sandy bottoms in shallow water.

Fig.C. **OTHER SWIMMING CRABS:** Occasionally other swimming crabs such as *Portunus gibbesii* or *Callinectes similis* are found in southern New England. Refer to Williams (1984) to identify these crabs.

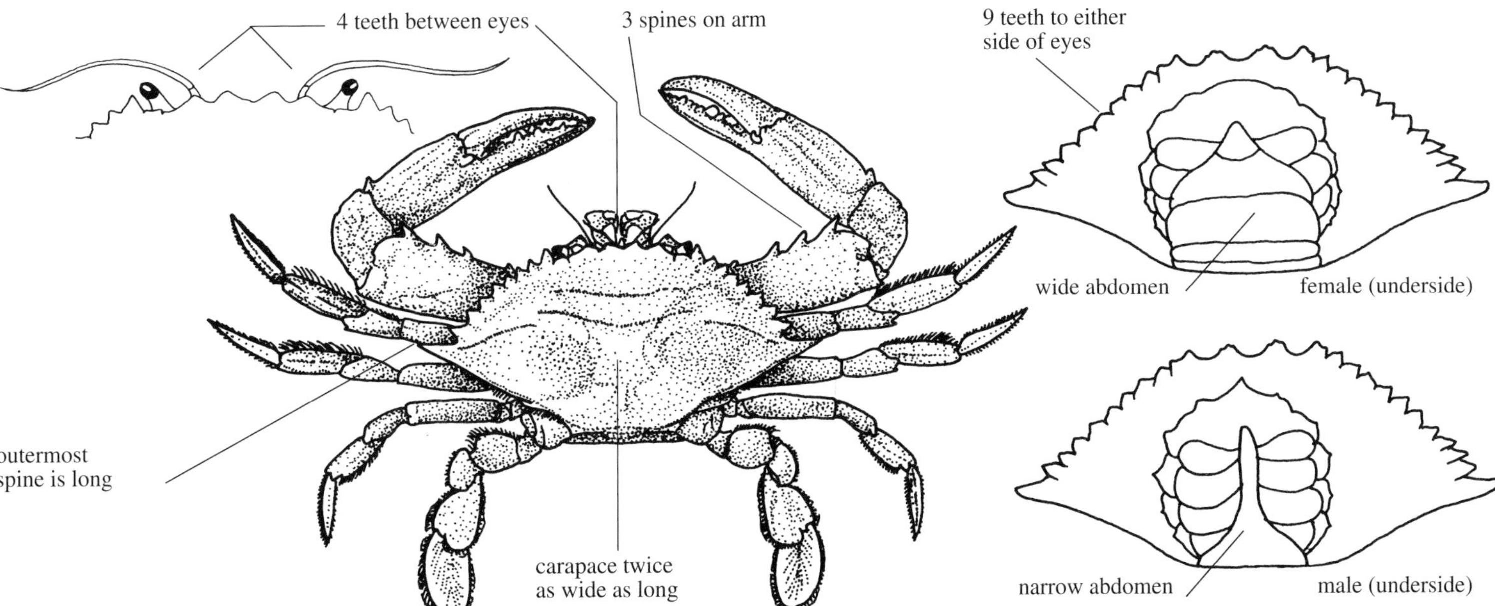

Fig.B. ***CALLINECTES SAPIDUS*, BLUE CRAB:** Grayish or bluish green carapace; fingers of claws are bright blue in males, red in females; may grow up to 23 cm (9") carapace width (from spine tip to spine tip); they mate in upper estuarine areas; females migrate to deeper water to spawn; some years they are very common, other years quite rare. **17.13 B**

CANCER AND GREEN CRABS
CLASS CRUSTACEA, ORDER DECAPODA, FAMILIES CANCRIDAE AND PORTUNIDAE

Crabs with pointed rear legs and with three pointed teeth between eyes on front edge of shell.

(Use the key on page 10.20 to determine if you have a cancer crab or green crab)

#1.With 5 teeth to the side of each eye on front edge of shell .... ***Carcinus maenas*, green crab** (Fig.A)
#1.With 9 teeth to the side of each eye on front edge of shell .... **family Cancridae, rock crabs,** #2

#2.Teeth on front edge of shell are smooth edged .... ***Cancer irroratus*, Atlantic rock crab** (Fig.B)
#2.Teeth on front edge of shell are rough, bumpy, jagged .... ***Cancer borealis*, Jonah crab** (Fig.C)

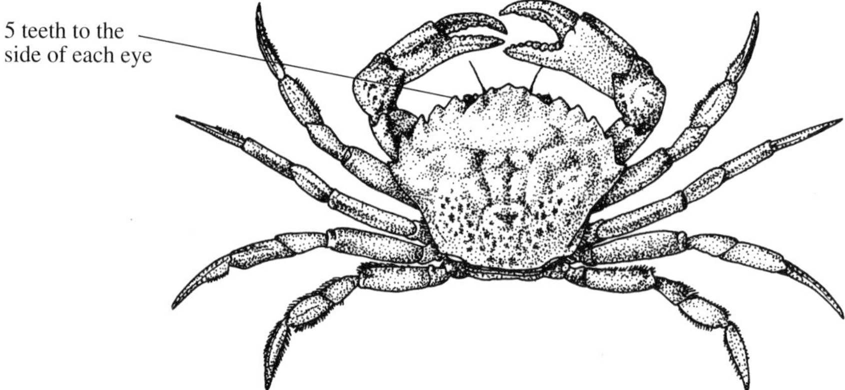

Fig.A. ***CARCINUS MAENAS*, GREEN CRAB:** Usually dark green, almost black, with yellow or brown blotches, sometimes with a brown hourglass shaped mark on shell; mature females are red-orange on underside, males and immature crabs are yellow or green underneath; shell width up to 8 cm (3 1/4"); very common throughout southern New England in intertidal zone and offshore; often found under rocks and along the banks of tidal creeks. This crab is in the family Portunidae, the swimming crabs (see page 10.23). The last segment of the rear walking legs is somewhat flattened, although the tips are pointed. **17.13 C, D, E**

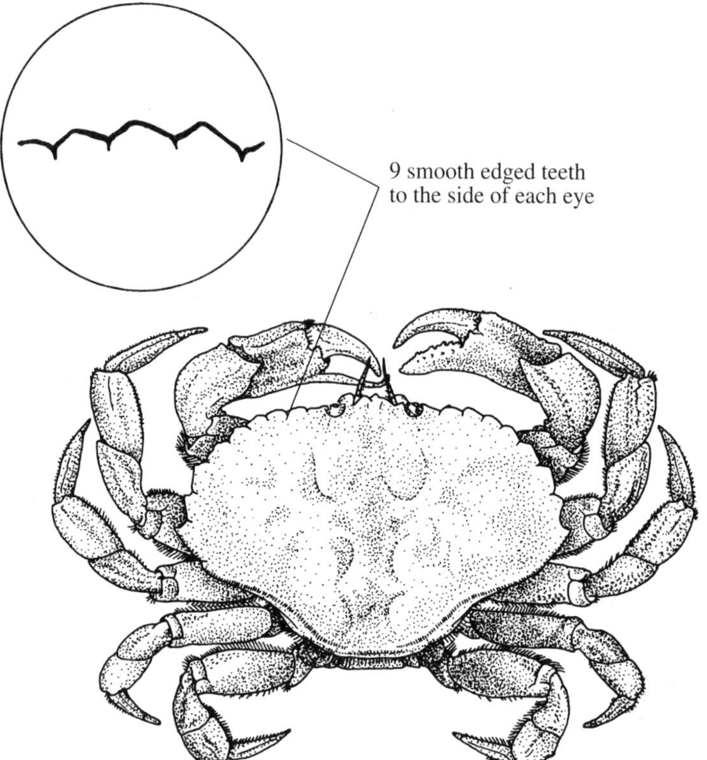

Fig.B. ***CANCER IRRORATUS*, ATLANTIC ROCK CRAB:** Beige or yellow with numerous closely spaced tiny dots of purple-brown giving crab an overall appearance of reddish-brown; shell width up to 13 cm (5 1/4"); very common, often found on subtidal sand flats and around rocks; usually quite aggressive when disturbed, assuming a wide legged stance with raised claws open and ready to pinch. (family Cancridae: rock crabs) **17.13 F**

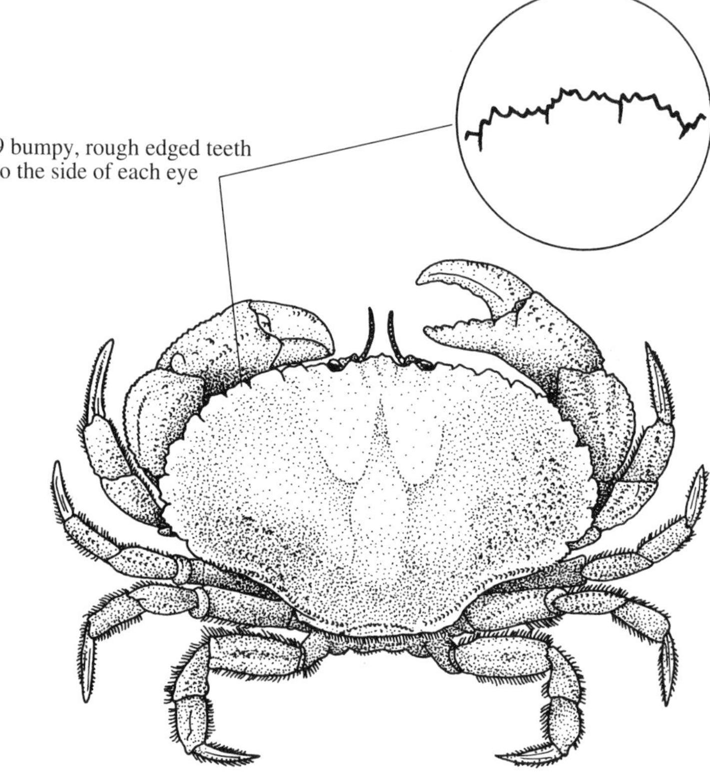

Fig.C. ***CANCER BOREALIS*, JONAH CRAB:** Red or purple overall on top, yellow or beige underneath, legs with purple blotches; shell width up to 16 cm (6 1/4"); very common throughout southern New England; often digs shallow burrows under large subtidal rocks; tends to tuck claws and legs under body and remain motionless when disturbed whereas *Cancer irroratus* (Fig.B) is usually more aggressive. (family Cancridae: rock crabs)

MUD CRABS
CLASS CRUSTACEA, ORDER DECAPODA, FAMILY XANTHIDAE

Crabs with pointed rear legs; with no teeth between eyes and with 4-5 teeth to either side of eyes on front edge of shell; with a single central notch or groove along midline of shell.

(Use the key on page 10.20 to determine if you have a mud crab)

#1.Fingers of claws are light colored, not black or brown; front of crab ("face") beneath eyes and above mouth is flattened, slightly concave, forming a broad groove that extends beyond the eyes and appears double edged when viewed from front .... ***Rithropanopeus harrisii*, Harris mud crab** (Fig.A)

#1.Fingers of claws are black or dark brown (Figs.B-D); front of shell has a single edge; face is not flattened or concave .... #2

#2.Moveable finger of larger claw with a large, molarlike tooth; dark marking on fixed finger does not extend up very far onto palm of claw .... ***Panopeus herbstii*, Atlantic mud crab** (Fig.B)

#2.No large tooth on moveable finger of larger claw (Figs. C,D); dark marking on fixed finger extends broadly up onto palm of claw .... #3

#3.With a dark red spot on the inner (concealed) surface of the third maxillipeds (outermost appendages covering mouth, Fig.C); finger tips of smaller claw with a hollowed out, spoon shaped depression; carapace somewhat flattened and oval; not common .... ***Eurypanopeus depressus*, flatback mud crab** (Fig.C)

#3.Without a red spot on maxillipeds; finger tips not hollowed out; carapace somewhat angular; very common .... ***Dyspanopeus sayi*, Say mud crab** (Fig.D)

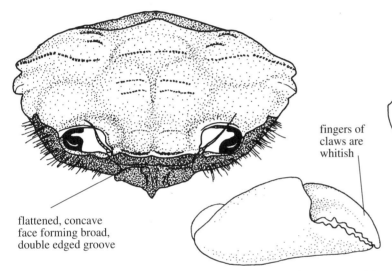

fingers of claws are whitish

flattened, concave face forming broad, double edged groove

Fig.A. ***RITHROPANOPEUS HARRISII*, HARRIS MUD CRAB:** Brownish above, paler below; shell width up to 2 cm (3/4"); not common; found in brackish waters of estuaries.

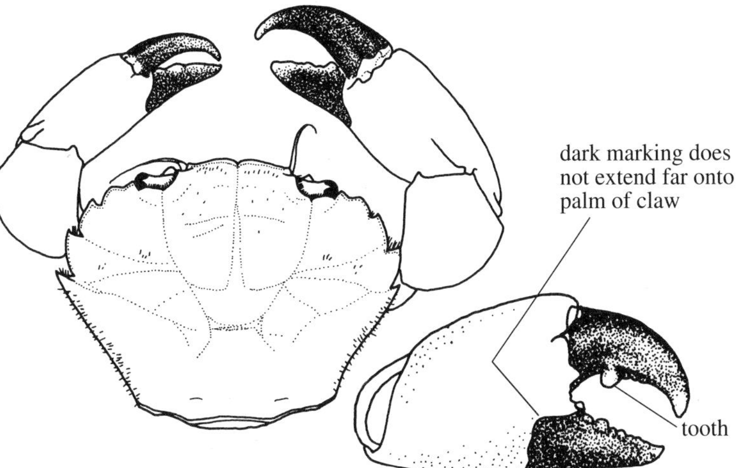

Fig.B. ***PANOPEUS HERBSTII*, ATLANTIC MUD CRAB:** Shell is usually muddy tan colored; shell width up to 3.8 cm (1 1/2"); found on muddy bottoms. Third maxilliped may have a red spot on inner surface like *Eurypanopeus depressus* (see Fig.C) but spot is much smaller and more circular.

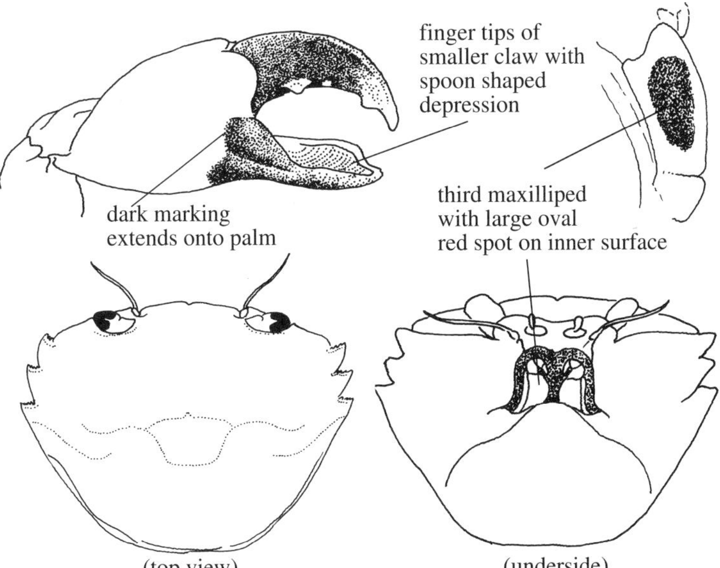

Fig.C. ***EURYPANOPEUS DEPRESSUS*, FLATBACK MUD CRAB:** Mottled grayish olive or dark olive brown; shell width up to 2.5 cm (1"); occurs on oyster beds, not common.

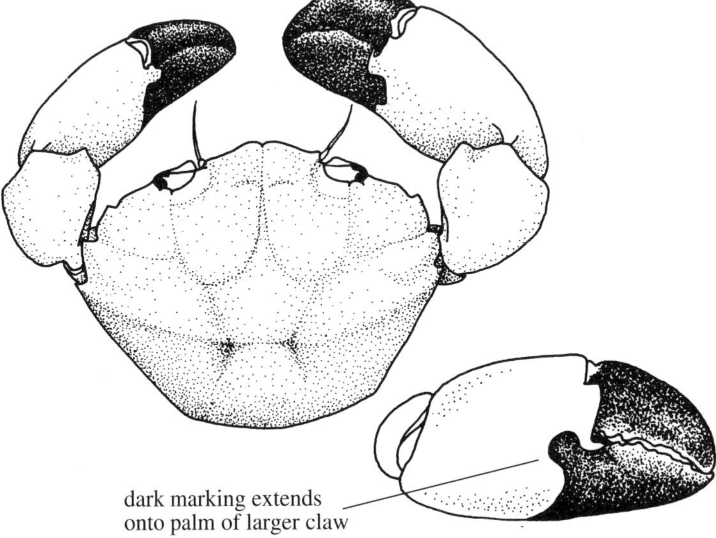

Fig.D. ***DYSPANOPEUS SAYI* (=*Neopanope s.*), SAY MUD CRAB:** Shell dark brown; shell width up to 3 cm (1 1/4"); very common in mud, under rocks, in sponge colonies, and among fouling organisms on pilings.

PEA CRABS
CLASS CRUSTACEA, ORDER DECAPODA, FAMILY PINNOTHERIDAE

Tiny crabs; front outline of shell is rounded and edge of shell is toothless; eyes are very small; lives inside bivalves or worm tubes or on sea urchins.

(Use key on page 10.20 to determine if you have a pea crab)

#1.With a double pointed tip at the end of the first three walking legs; shell has a somewhat rectangular outline; usually found clinging to sea urchins and sand dollars .... ***Dissodactylus mellitae*, sand-dollar pea crab** (Fig.A)

#1.With a single pointed tip at the end of each walking leg; shell has a round or oval outline (Figs.B-D) .... #2

#2.Third pair of walking legs are much longer and broader than the others; shell is oval, about twice as wide as long; some species live in worm tubes[1] but others may be free living .... ***Pinnixa* spp., pea crabs** (Fig.B)

#2.Walking legs are all about the same size; shell is roundish; lives in bivalves and parchment worm tubes[1]. .... ***Pinnotheres* spp., pea crabs, #3**

#3.Shell surface is covered with short, dense, dull brown hairs (females) or with a thick dark fuzz or fur (males) that may wear off in places leaving lighter colored bald spots (Fig.C); front edge of shell with small "eye sockets" so that tiny eyes can be seen from top of shell; usually found in mussels but may be found in other bivalves .... ***Pinnotheres maculatus*, squatter pea crab** (Fig.C)

#3.Shell surface is smooth and nearly hairless but edges of shell and legs may have hairs; front edge of shell overhangs and hides the eyes (females) or has deep "eye sockets" exposing large eyes (males); occurs in bivalves, especially oysters, or worm tubes .... ***Pinnotheres ostreum*, oyster pea crab** (Fig.D)

[1]The eastern tube crab, *Polyonx gibbesi*, also lives in the tubes of the parchment worm, *Chaetopterus variopedatus.* This crab, which is in the family Porcellanidae (porcelain crabs) has long antennae and only 3 pairs of walking legs. The pea crabs have short antennae and 4 pairs of legs.

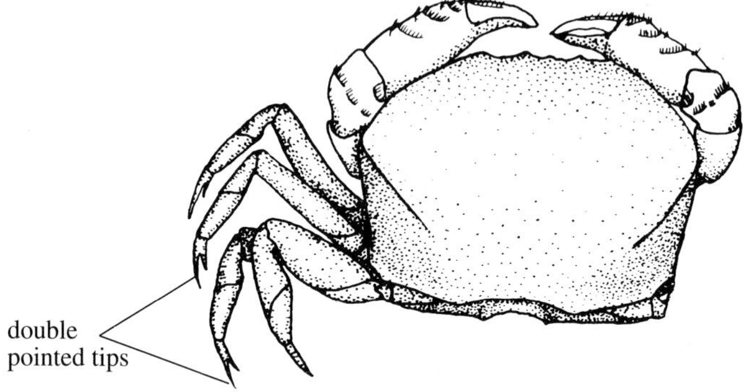

Fig.A. ***DISSODACTYLUS MELLITAE*, SAND-DOLLAR PEA CRAB:** Light color with darker blotches; very tiny, shell width up to 5 mm (3/16"); clings to sand dollars and sea urchins; rare.

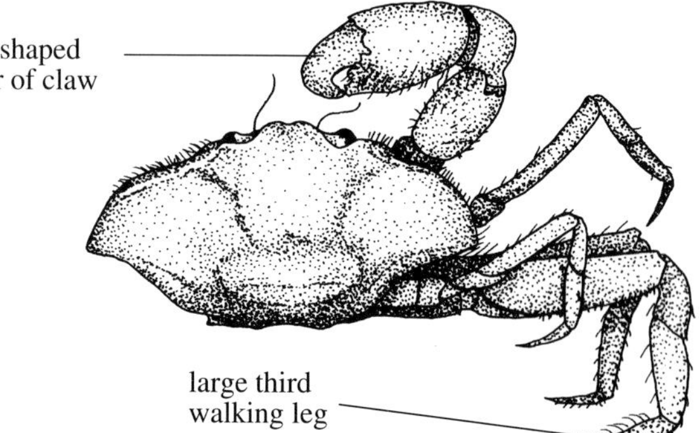

Fig.B. ***PINNIXA* SPP., PEA CRABS:** One species, *Pinnixa sayana*, shown here, is whitish with light brown stains; up to 1 cm (3/8") shell width; found free living in bottom muds; claw has a hook shaped finger. Other species live in the tubes of worms such as lugworms (*Arenicola*) and parchment tube worms[1]. Refer to Williams (1984) to identify these crabs.

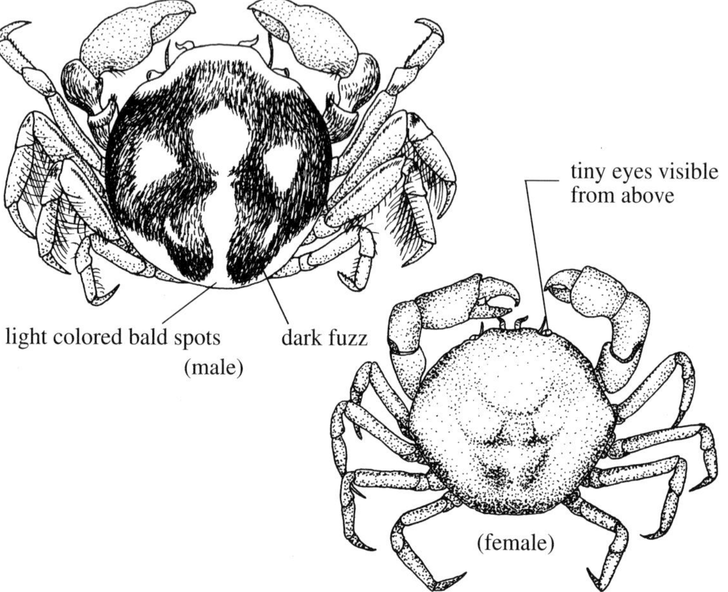

Fig.C. ***PINNOTHERES MACULATUS*, SQUATTER PEA CRAB:** Mature females are dull brown, mature males have distinctive light colored bald spots on a dark fuzzy background; females grow to 16 mm (5/8") carapace length, males to 9 mm (3/8"); commonly found in mussels but also occur in scallops, clams, oysters, and parchment worm tubes[1]; these crabs damage the gills of their bivalve hosts and are therefore considered to be parasitic.

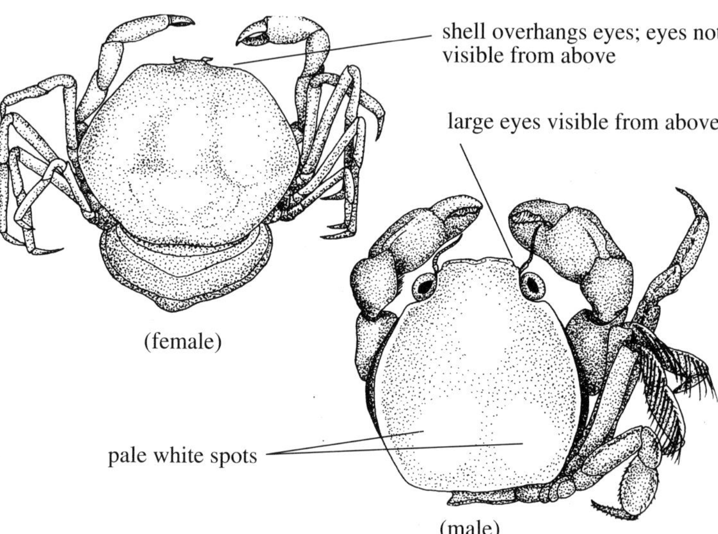

Fig.D. ***PINNOTHERES OSTREUM*, OYSTER PEA CRAB:** Mature females are shiny, whitish or salmon pink; mature males and immature females are dark or medium-dark brown with two large, almost circular, white spots on top and underside of shell; shell width of females reaches 16 mm (5/8") and grows to 5 mm (3/16") in males; parasitic primarily on the oyster but also reported to occur in scallops, mussels, and parchment worm[1] tubes.

SEA URCHINS AND SAND DOLLARS: PHYLUM ECHINODERMATA, CLASS ECHINOIDEA[1]

Echinoderms with numerous spines attached to a hard, spherical or disc shaped shell.

(Use the key on page 2.00 to determine if you have a sea urchin or sand dollar)

#1.Flat, disc shaped animal (Fig.A); spines are tiny, fuzzlike; with a flowerlike pattern of 5 petal shaped markings radiating from center of disc .... #2

#1.Somewhat spherical animal (Figs.B,C), shaped like a pincushion; with distinct and obvious spines .... **sea urchins**, #3

#2.Without holes penetrating through the entire width of the shell; common in this region .... ***Echinarachnius parma*, sand dollar** (Fig.A)

#2.With 5 long slitlike holes penetrating through the shell; very rare in this region .... ***Mellita quinquiesperforata*, keyhole urchin** (not shown)

#3.Spines are long and stout, about as long as shell radius; spines are not spaced closely together; color is purple or brown .... ***Arbacia punctulata*, purple sea urchin** (Fig.B)

#3.Spines are short and slender, shorter than shell radius; spines are spaced very closely together; color is green or yellow .... ***Strongylocentrotus droebachiensis*, green sea urchin** (Fig.C)

[1]Refer to Serafy and Fell (1985) to identify species found in waters deeper than 30 m (100').

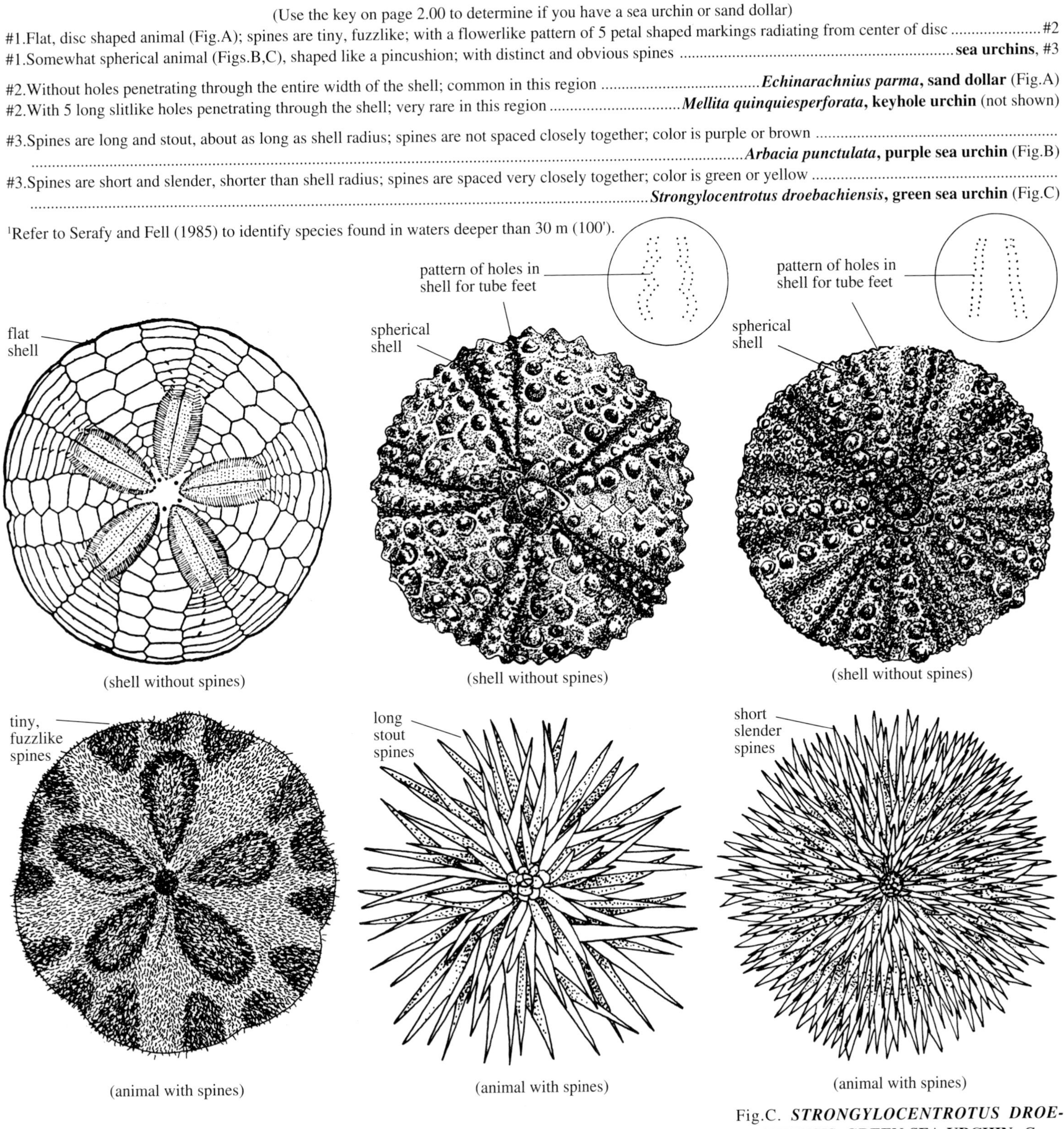

Fig.A. ***ECHINARACHNIUS PARMA*, SAND DOLLAR:** Purplish brown or reddish brown when alive, may turn green or brown when preserved, shell bleaches white; up to 7.5 cm (3") in diameter; found offshore on sandy bottoms. **17.14 F**

Fig.B. ***ARBACIA PUNCTULATA*, PURPLE SEA URCHIN:** Purple, brown, or black; diameter of shell (not including spines) up to about 5 cm (2"); found near rocks and on shelly bottom; occurs as far north as the south side of Cape Cod. **17.14 C**

Fig.C. ***STRONGYLOCENTROTUS DROEBACHIENSIS*, GREEN SEA URCHIN:** Green or yellow; diameter of shell (not including spines) up to about 7.5 cm (3"); occurs in subtidal rocky bottom areas, often on kelp beds; also lives in intertidal zone north of Cape Cod. **17.14 D**

SEA STARS (STARFISHES)[1]
PHYLUM ECHINDODERMATA, CLASS STELLEROIDEA, SUBCLASS ASTEROIDEA

Star shaped echinoderms, usually with 5 or more radiating arms; arms are wide, merge at the central disc, and have a groove on the underside.

(Use the key on page 2.12 to determine if you have a sea star)

#1.With 7 or more arms, usually 9-12 (Fig..A) .... **sunstars, #2**
#1.With 6 or fewer arms, usually 5 (Figs.B-I) .... #3

#2.With long, coarse, bristly spines arranged in brushlike bundles .... ***Crossaster papposus*, spiny sunstar** (Fig.A)
#2.With short, fine, prickly spines .... ***Solaster endeca*, purple sunstar** (Fig.A)

#3.Pentagon shaped (see Figs. B-D: arms are short, arm length is about the same as the arm width at the base; central disc is large, diameter of central disc is about the same as arm length) .... #4
#3.Star shaped (see Figs. E-I: arm length is greater than arm width at the base; diameter of central disc is less than arm length) .... #6

#4.With marginal plates forming a distinct border around the edges of the sea star (Figs. C,D); without a membrane covering upper surface .... #5
#4.Without marginal plates; with a membrane forming a tentlike covering over upper surface and enclosing a large space; this membrane has a large hole in center; with a winglike membrane connecting arms; membranes supported by spines .... ***Pteraster militaris*, winged sea star** (Fig.B)

#5.Yellow brown; marginal plates each have a single flattened spine. .... ***Ctenodiscus crispatus*, mud star** (Fig.C)
#5.Red with yellow border; marginal plates each have 1-3 beadlike spines and granular edges .... ***Hippasteria phrygiana*, horse star** (Fig.D)

#6.With a row of plates and spines forming a distinct margin around the edges of the starfish .... ***Pontaster tenuispinus*** (Fig.E)
#6.Without a distinct border of spines and plates .... #7

#7.Surface of arms relatively smooth, spines are tiny; upper side is usually bright red; 2 rows of tube feet in a narrow groove on the underside of each arm .... ***Henricia sanguinolenta*, blood star** (Fig.I)
#7.Spines on arms are obvious (Figs.F-H), surface very rough and bumpy; 4 rows of tube feet in a wide groove on the underside of each arm (Figs.G,H). ...... #8

#8.Madreporite[2] ("eye" spot) usually whitish; arms are firm, slender and tubular; arm radius is about 6-7 times as long as the radius of the central disc; arm radius may reach up to 4 cm (1.5"); spines on arms in no obvious pattern; color usually light red, pink, lavender or purple; not as common as the following 2 species .... ***Leptasterias tenera*, slender sea star** (Fig.F)
#8.Madreporite[2] ("eye" spot) usually light yellow; arms are somewhat soft, flabby and flattened; arm radius is about 5 times as long as the radius of the central disc; arm radius may reach up to 20 cm (8"); some spines may be arranged in a line running down the center of each arm; color usually light, such as pink, red, orange, tan, blue, lavender; not common in shallow water south of Cape Cod but becomes more common to the north ... ***Asterias vulgaris*, northern sea star** (Fig.G)
#8.Madreporite[2] ("eye" spot) usually bright orange-red; arms are firm, cylindrical or slightly flattened; arm radius is about 5 times as long as the radius of the central disc; arm radius may reach up to 13 cm (5"); spines on arms in no obvious pattern; overall color is brown or greenish black with tones of orange, red or pink; this is the most common shallow water sea star in this region, especially south of Cape Cod .... ***Asterias forbesi*, common sea star** (Fig.H)

[1]This key only includes species that occur in water under 30 m (100') deep in southern New England. Refer to Gosner (1971) to identify deeper water species.
[2]The madreporite is a sieve plate covering the opening to the series of tubes making up the sea star's water vascular system. It is *not* an eye.

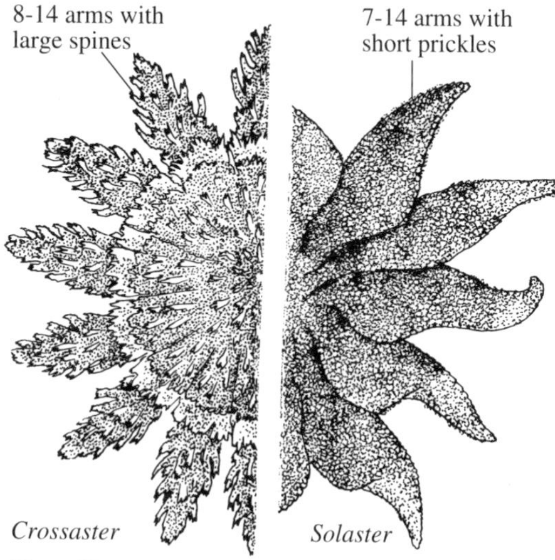

8-14 arms with large spines
7-14 arms with short prickles
Crossaster *Solaster*

Fig.A. **SUNSTARS:** *Crossaster papposus*, the spiny sunstar, is bright scarlet with concentric bands of pink, white, and red; up to 18 cm (7") radius. *Solaster endeca*, the purple sunstar, is purple, red, pink, or orange; up to 20 cm (8") radius. Both species only occur north of Cape Cod and rarely in water under 30 m (100') deep in southern New England.

tentlike and winglike membranes
hole on top
pentagonal shape

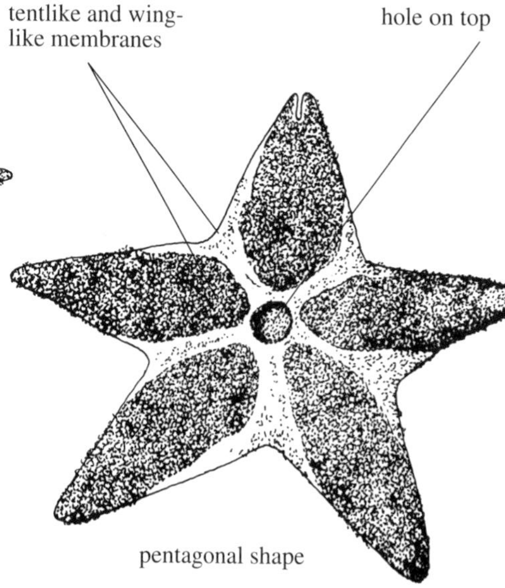

Fig.B. ***PTERASTER MILITARIS*, WINGED SEA STAR:** Yellow, orange, or red on upper surface, white or tan underneath; up to 7 cm (3") radius; occurs north of Cape Cod on rocky subtidal bottoms.

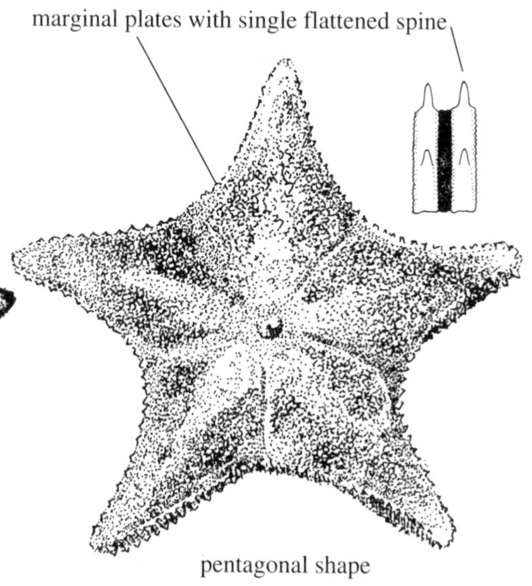

marginal plates with single flattened spine
pentagonal shape

Fig.C. ***CTENODISCUS CRISPATUS*, MUD STAR:** Pale yellow or tan; up to 5 cm (2") radius; occurs on muddy bottoms in water over 6 m (20') deep; not common in shallow water south of Cape Cod, but more common to the north.

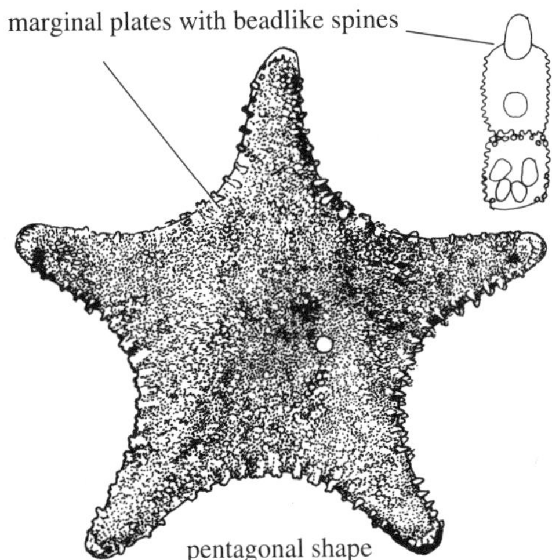

Fig.D. ***HIPPASTERIA PHRYGIANA*, HORSE STAR:** Upperside is red with yellow border, underside is beige; up to 20 cm (8") radius; occurs north of Cape Cod in water over 20 m (66') deep.

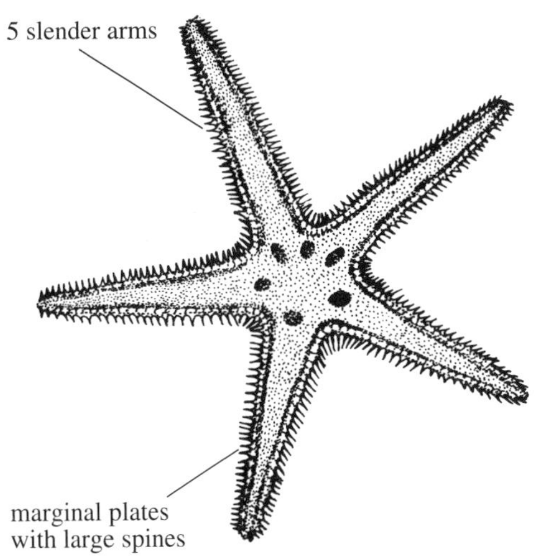

Fig.E. ***PONTASTER TENUISPINUS:*** Upperside is pink, orange, or red; underside is whitish; up to 13 cm (5") radius; occurs in water over 18 m (60') deep; not common.

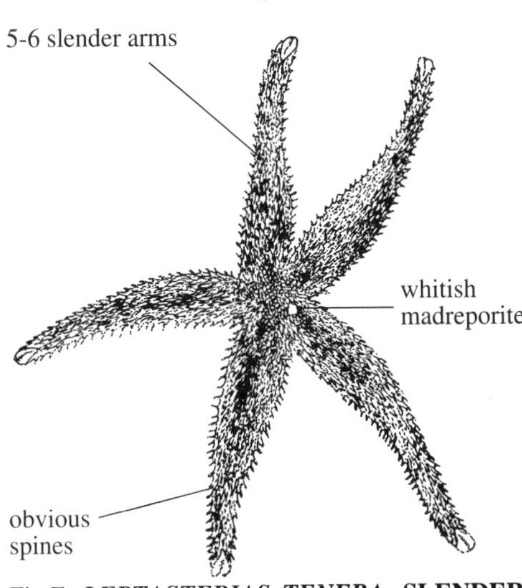

Fig.F. ***LEPTASTERIAS TENERA*, SLENDER SEA STAR:** Upperside is light red, pink, lavender, or purple; up to 4 cm (1 1/2") radius; rare in shallow water south of Cape Cod; other *Leptasterias* species also occur north of Cape Cod.

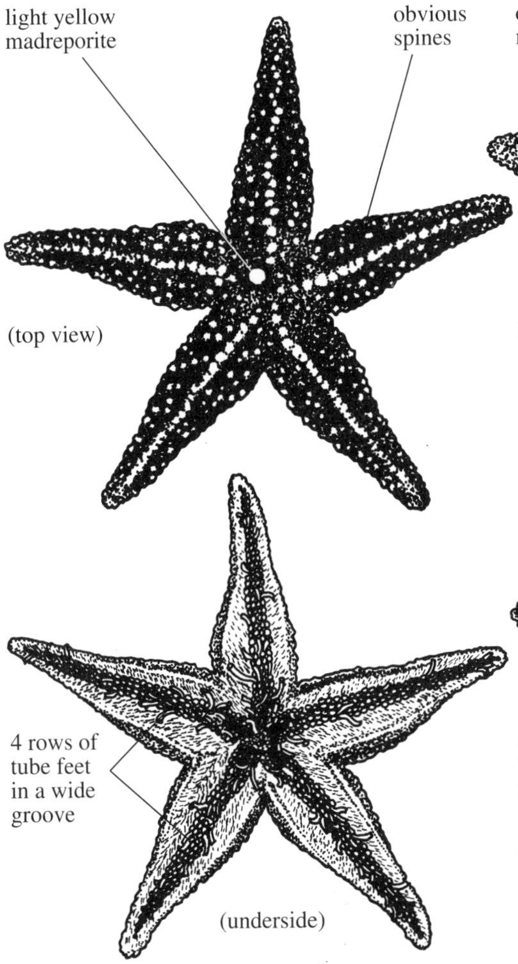

Fig.G. ***ASTERIAS VULGARIS*, NORTHERN SEA STAR:** Upperside light purple, yellow, pink, or red; madreporite pale yellow; up to 20 cm (8") radius; common north of Cape Cod; becomes more common than *A. forbesi* north of Boston; rare south of Cape Cod except in deeper water. **17.14 A**

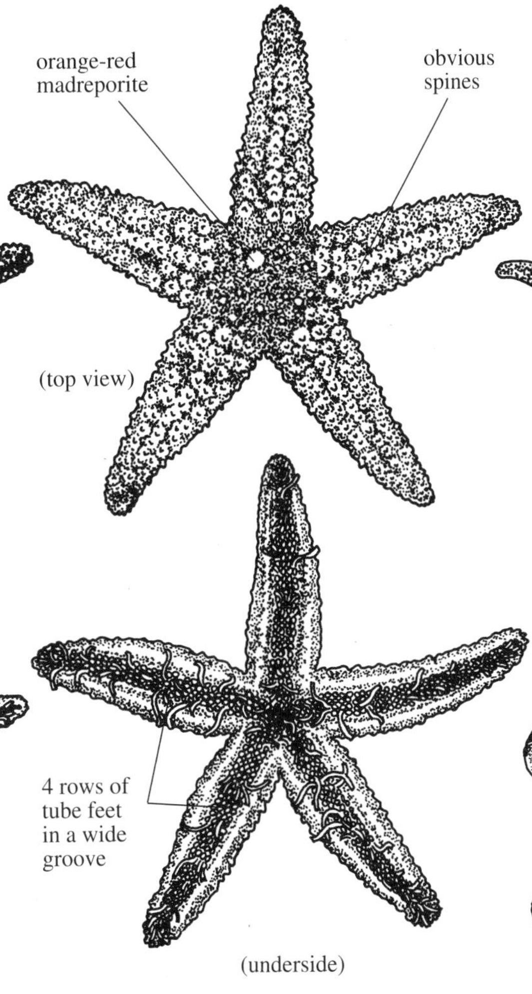

Fig.H. ***ASTERIAS FORBESI*, COMMON SEA STAR:** Upperside is dark brown or greenish black with tones of orange or red; spines are white; madreporite orange-red; underside is lighter, yellow or beige; up to 13 cm (5") radius; the most common sea star throughout this region. **17.14 B**

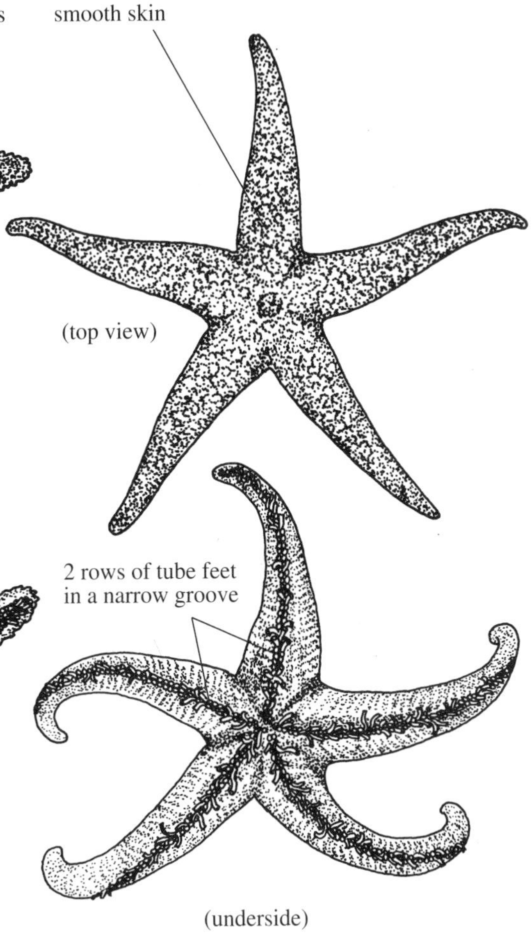

Fig.I. ***HENRICIA SANGUINOLENTA*, BLOOD STAR:** Color on upperside is usually red but may be orange, purple, or beige; underside is usually yellow or beige; up to 5 cm (2") radius; very common on rocky bottoms throughout this region from the low tide level into deeper water. **17.14 E**

BRITTLE STARS[1] AND BASKET STARS
PHYLUM ECHINODERMATA, CLASS STELLEROIDEA, SUBCLASS OPHIUROIDEA

Echinoderms with 5 wormlike radiating arms that are thin, separated at the central disc and without a groove on the underside.

(Use the key on page 2.12 to determine if you have a brittle star)

#1.Arms are branched, often entwining themselves and forming a tangled, coiling mass .... ***Gorgonocephalus arcticus*, northern basket star** (Fig.A)
#1.Arms are not branched .... #2

#2.With 7-8 tiny spines on each side of each arm joint; spines lie flat against arm so arms look smooth, not spiny; upper surface of central disc covered with fine granules .... ***Ophioderma brevispinum*, short-spined brittle star** (Fig.B)
#2.With 5-6 long spines on each side of each arm joint; spines project outward from arm so arms look spiny; each upper arm plate is surrounded by a ring of tiny scales; upperside of disc covered with large oval plates and fine, blunt spines .... ***Ophiopholis aculeata*, daisy brittle star** (Fig.E)
#2.With 3-4 short but obvious spines projecting outward on each side of each arm joint; upperside of disc covered with tiny scales visible with hand lens ...... #3

#3.Length of arms more than 10 times the diameter of the central disc .... ***Amphioplus abditus*, burrowing brittle star** (Fig.F)
#3.Length of arms less 3-5 times the diameter of the central disc .... #4

#4.Red color; disc diameter up to 35 mm (1 1/2") .... ***Ophiura sarsi*** (Fig.C)
#4.Gray or brown color, sometimes with lighter spots; disc diameter up to 9 mm (3/8") .... #5

#5.Small radial shields (pair of scales on upperside of disc at base of each arm), not much larger than other disc scales .... ***Ophiura robusta*** (Fig.D)
#5.Large radial shields much larger than other disc scales .... ***Axiognathus squamatus*, little brittle star** (Fig.G)

[1]This key only includes species which occur in water under 30 m (100') deep in southern New England. Refer to Gosner (1971) to identify deeper water species.

Fig. A. ***GORGONOCEPHALUS ARCTICUS*, NORTHERN BASKET STAR:** Upperside of disc yellowish-brown to brown; arms yellowish tan, white at tips; disc diameter up to 10 cm (4"), arm length up to 36 cm (14"); occurs from Cape Cod north.

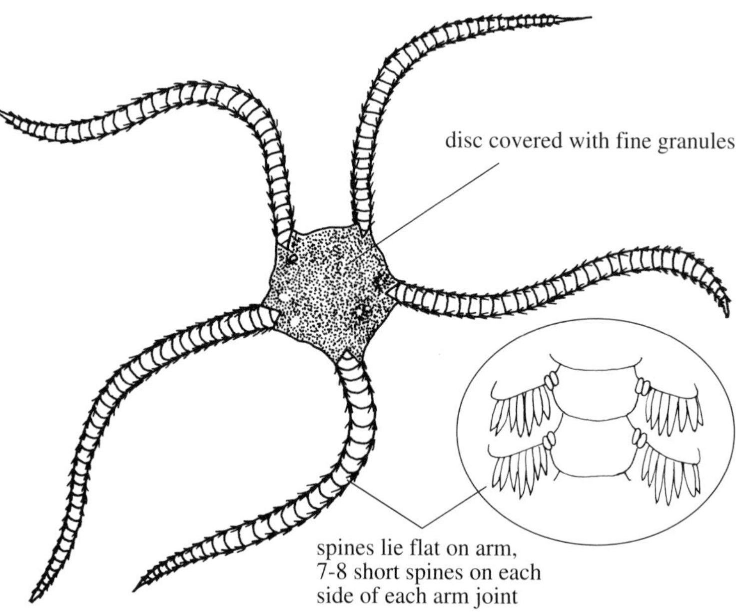

Fig.B. ***OPHIODERMA BREVISPINUM*, SHORT-SPINED BRITTLE STAR:** Usually dark green or brown but sometimes nearly black; central disc diameter up to 15 mm (5/8"); found in tide pools and among the roots of eelgrass in protected areas; occurs from Cape Cod south.

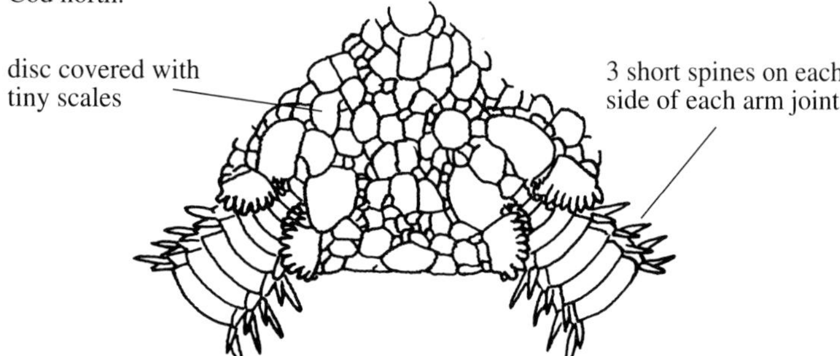

part of upperside of disc and base of two arms

Fig.C. ***OPHIURA SARSI:*** Red; central disc up to 35 mm (1 1/2") in diameter; arms about 15 cm (6") long; occurs in the Gulf of Maine in 10 m (30') or deeper water.

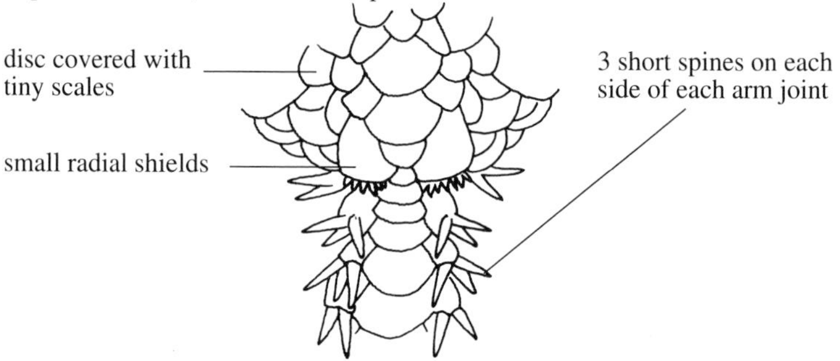

part of upperside of disc and base of one arm

Fig.D. ***OPHIURA ROBUSTA:*** Gray to brown, sometimes with lighter spots; central disc up to 9 mm (3/8") in diameter, arm length up to about 3 cm (1 1/4"); occurs from Cape Cod north and is subtidal in this region.

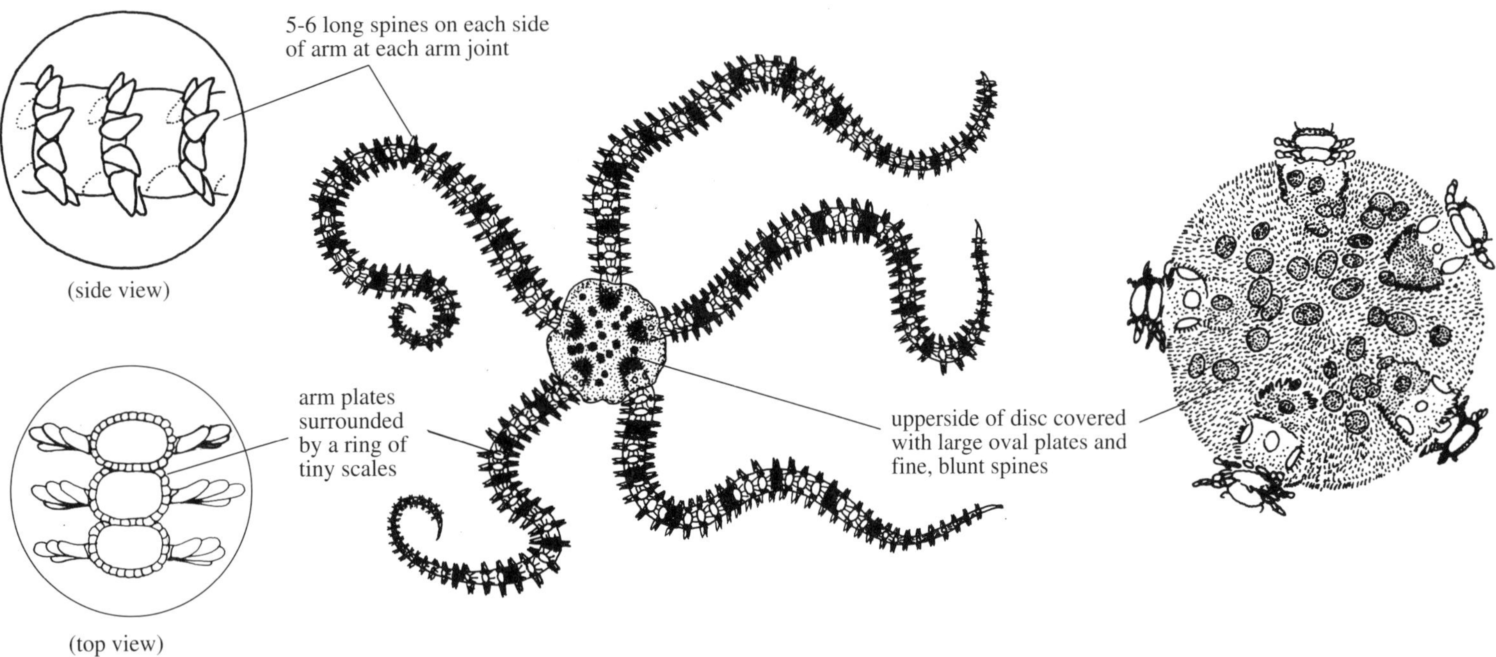

Fig.E. ***OPHIOPHOLIS ACULEATA*, DAISY BRITTLE STAR:** Color extremely variable, may be red, purple, brown, yellow, or green; the central disc may be spotted or blotched; the arms are usually banded or striped; central disc diameter up to 2 cm (3/4"); lives under rocks from low tide level to very deep water; not common south of Cape Cod.

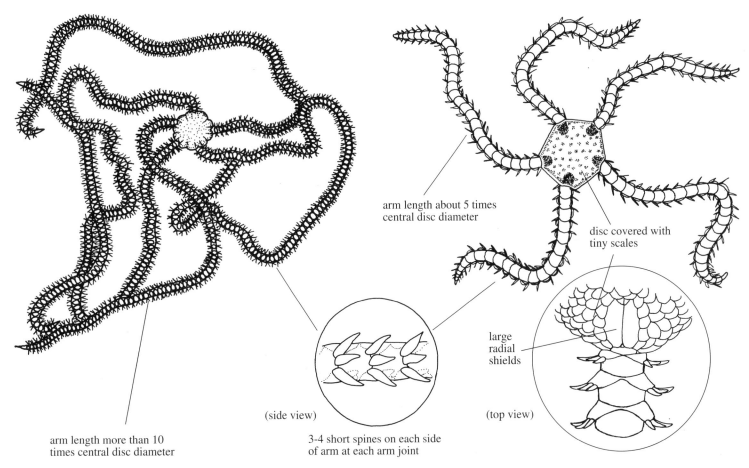

arm length about 5 times
central disc diameter

disc covered with
tiny scales

large
radial
shields

(side view)

(top view)

arm length more than 10
times central disc diameter

3-4 short spines on each side
of arm at each arm joint

Fig.F. ***AMPHIOPLUS ABDITUS*, BURROWING BRITTLE STAR:** Color variable, usually contrasting dark (black-reddish brown) and light (gray-tan); central disc diameter up to 12 mm (1/2"); burrows in soft mud.

Fig.G. ***AXIOGNATHUS SQUAMATUS*, LITTLE BRITTLE STAR:** Gray or pale brown, often with numerous white spots; central disc diameter up to 5 mm (1/4"); found in dead mollusk shells, under stones, in eelgrass beds.

SEA CUCUMBERS[1]
PHYLUM ECHINODERMATA, CLASS HOLOTHUROIDEA

Echinoderms with a soft wormlike or saclike body; circle of tentacles[2] surrounds mouth.

(Use the key on page 2.16 to determine if you have a sea cucumber)

#1.Body is opaque, thick; 10, 15 or 20 tentacles[2] surround mouth; with or without tube feet[2] (Figs.A-D) .... #2
#1.Body is thin, wormlike, transparent or translucent; 12 tentacles[2] surround mouth; no tube feet (Figs.E-F) .... #8

#2.Body ends in a long narrow tail region which is about 1/3 the total length; 15 tentacles, each tentacle has 4 short branches at the tip; without tube feet .... ***Caudina arenata*, rat-tailed sea cucumber** (Fig.A)
#2.With no tail or with only a short stubby tail (Figs.B-D); 10 or 20 highly branched tentacles; with tube feet .... #3

#3.Underside is flat, footlike; upperside is covered with scales; may have a short pointed tail .... ***Psolus* spp.** (Fig.B)
#3.Body is cylindrical or round, underside is not flattened(when alive and in water); without scales on upper side; no tail (Figs.C,D) .... #4

#4.Tube feet are scattered all over body, not in rows (Fig.C) .... #5
#4.All or some tube feet are in distinct rows or bands (Fig.D) .... #6

#5.Dark color (dark brown, green or nearly black) .... ***Sclerodactyla briareus*, hairy sea cucumber** (Fig.C)
#5.Light color (whitish, pale brown) .... **other sea cucumbers[3]**

#6.With 20 tentacles; tube feet are in 8 broad bands .... ***Duasmodactyla commune*** (not shown)
#6.With 10 tentacles; tube feet are scattered all over upper surface and are in a double row on underside .... ***Stereoderma unisemita*** (not shown)
#6.With 10 tentacles; tube feet arranged in 5 rows .... #7

#7.Occurs north of Nantucket; up to 50 cm (20") long; body usually brownish, tube feet orange ..... ***Cucumaria frondosa*, orange-footed sea cucumber** (Fig.D)
#7.Occurs south of Cape Cod; up to 5 cm (2") long; color usually white or dirty brown .... ***Pentamera pulcherrima*** (Fig.D)

#8.Color whitish; branches of tentacles in 4-6 pairs plus one on end; with anchor and oval shaped ossicles[2]. .... ***Leptosynapta tenuis*, white synapta** (Fig.E)
#8.Color pinkish; branches of tentacles in 2-4 pairs plus one on end; with anchor and oval shaped ossicles[2]. .... ***Epitomapta roseola*, pink synapta** (Fig.E)
#8.Color pinkish or whitish; each tentacle ends in a tuft of about 10 short, fingerlike branches radiating around the tip of each tentacle like the fronds on a palm tree; with wheel shaped ossicles[2]. .... ***Chiridota laevis*, silky sea cucumber** (Fig.F)

[1]This key only includes species which occur in water under 30 m (100') deep in southern New England. Refer to Pawson (1977) to identify deeper water species.
[2]Tentacles and tube feet of sea cucumbers may be withdrawn when the animal is disturbed or preserved. To observe these structures, a living sea cucumber should be placed in a dish of seawater and left undisturbed for at least half an hour. Ossicles are microscopic calcareous structures embedded in the skin. Place a tiny piece of skin on a microscope slide and add a drop of bleach (such as Chlorox) to dissolve away the soft tissue, leaving the ossicles. Examine under 100X magnification.
[3]Refer to Pawson (1977) or Gosner (1971) to identify these species.

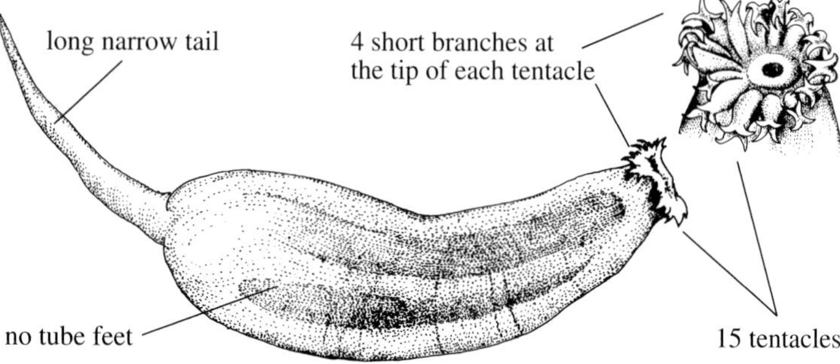

Fig.A. ***CAUDINA ARENATA*, RAT-TAILED SEA CUCUMBER:** Pinkish, red, or purple; up to 25 cm (10") long; buries in mud or sand in subtidal waters; occurs in Rhode Island and north.

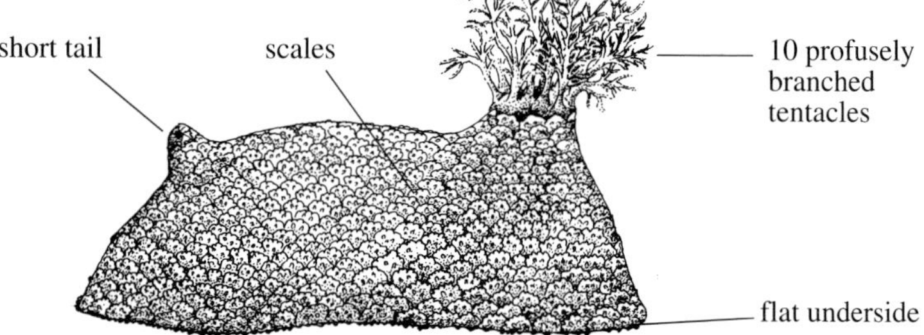

Fig.B. ***PSOLUS* SPP.:** *P. fabricii* is bright red; up to 19 cm (8") long; and has a short tail-like projection. *P. phantapus* is yellowish brown or black; up to 15 cm (6") long; and has a longer tail-like projection. Both species attach to rocks and other hard bottoms. They occur in subtidal waters from Cape Cod north.

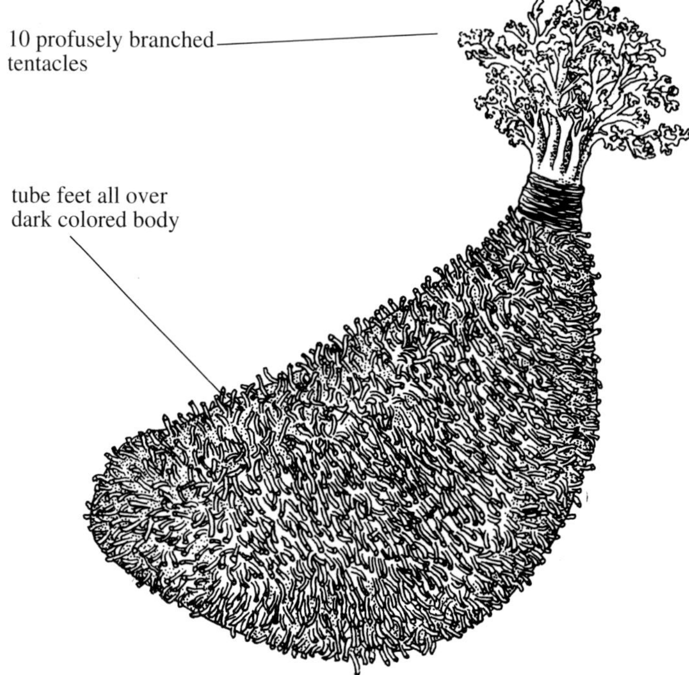

Fig.C. ***SCLERODACTYLA BRIAREUS* (=*Thyone b.*), HAIRY SEA CUCUMBER:** Black, brown, or purple; may reach 22 cm (8 1/2") long but usually up to 10 cm (4"); commonly found buried in soft mud in shallow water, often in eelgrass beds, with tentacles extended over surface of mud.

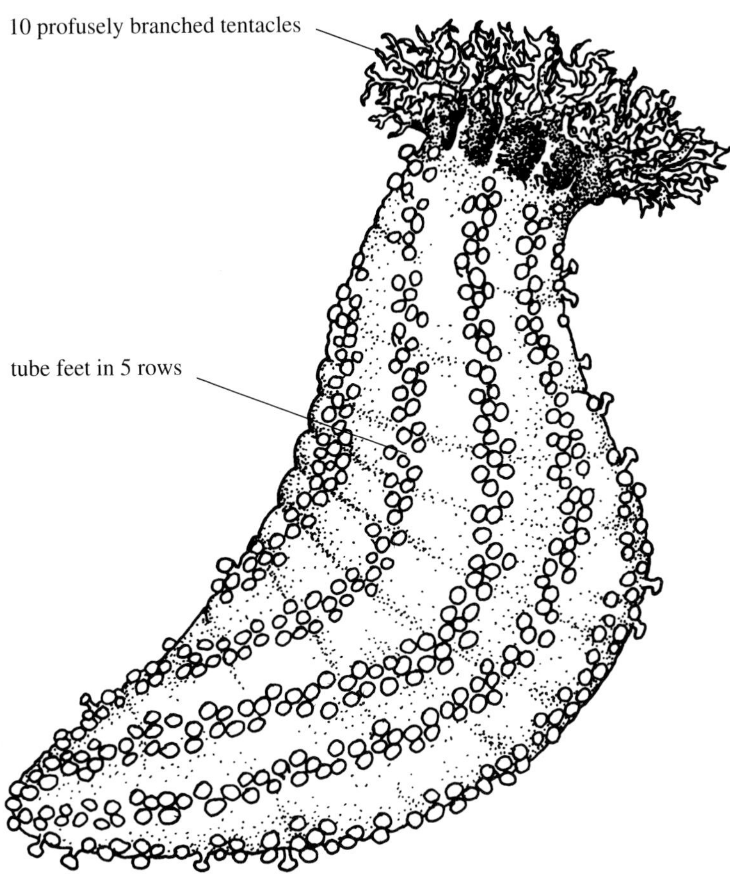

Fig.D. ***CUCUMARIA FRONDOSA,*** **ORANGE-FOOTED SEA CUCUMBER:** Adults are dark reddish brown or purple, often with orange tube feet; young are lighter brown and translucent; up to 50 cm (20") long, but usually under 25 cm (10") in nearshore waters; occurs from Nantucket north; very common on rocks below low water. ***PENTAMERA PULCHERRIMA:*** White or pale yellow; up to 5 cm (2") long; occurs from Cape Cod south; not common but may be found cast up on shore among seaweed after severe storms.

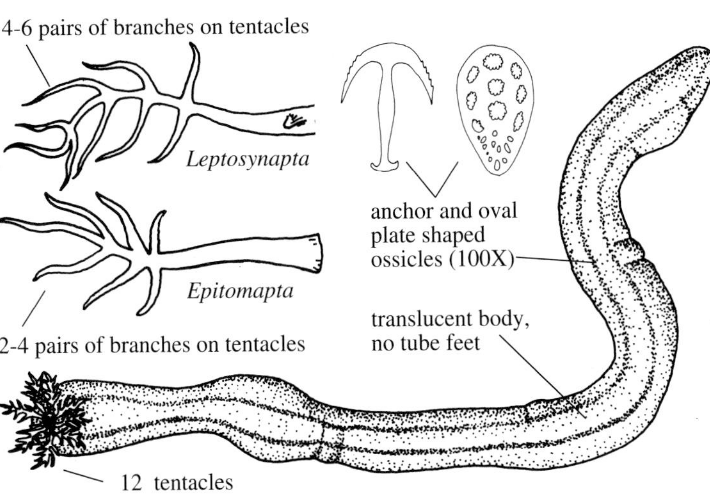

Fig.E. ***LEPTOSYNAPTA TENUIS (=L. inhaerens),*** **WHITE SYNAPTA:** Translucent white; up to 15 cm (6") long; very common. **17.14 G**
EPITOMAPTA ROSEOLA (=Leptosynapta r.), **PINK SYNAPTA**: Rose-pink color; up to 10 cm (4") long. Both species burrow into mudflats, sandflats, and gravel in intertidal zone and in deep water. Their skin feels sticky because the pointed ossicles cling to your hand.

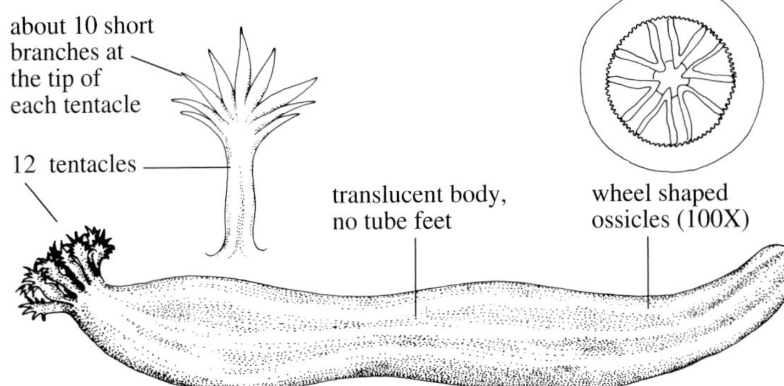

Fig.F. ***CHIRIDOTA LAEVIS,*** **SILKY SEA CUCUMBER:** Translucent pinkish or whitish; up to 15 cm (6") long; burrows in sand, mud and under rocks from the low tide level into deeper water; occurs from Cape Cod north.

ACORN WORM
PHYLUM HEMICHORDATA

Unsegmented worm with a three part body consisting of a proboscis, collar and trunk; without appendages. Larval stage of some species is similar to larval stages of the echinoderms. Because of the larval stage, hemichordates are considered to be closely related to the echinoderms and chordates.

(Use the key on page 2.16 to determine if you have an acorn worm)

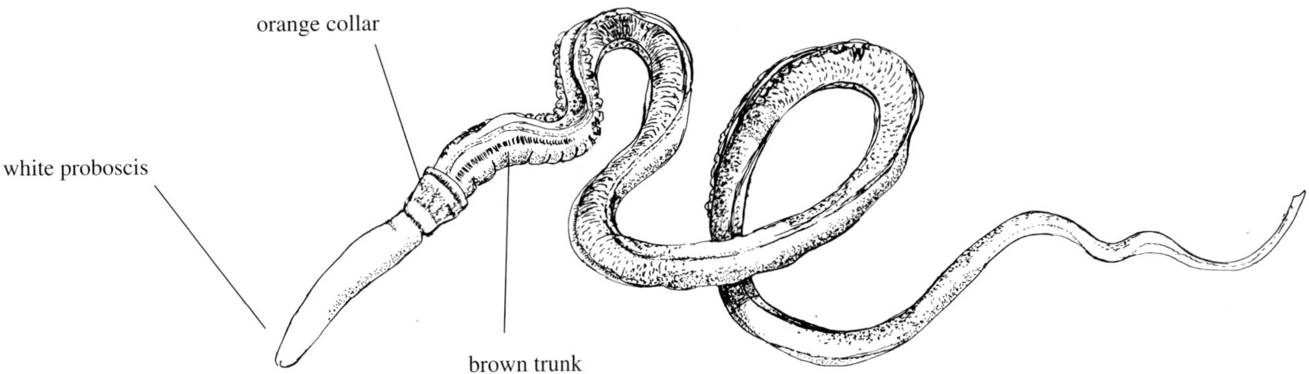

Fig.G. ***SACCOGLOSSUS KOWALEWSKII (=S. kowalevskyi),*** **KOWALEWSKY'S ACORN WORM:** Whitish proboscis, orange collar, brownish trunk; to 15 cm (6") long; lives in mud and sand in intertidal zone and in shallow water; produces small piles of stringlike mud castings (see page 2.27, Fig.B). **17.09 A**

SEA SQUIRTS[1]
PHYLUM CHORDATA, SUBPHYLUM UROCHORDATA, CLASS ASCIDIACEA

Globular or somewhat cylindrical animals with an opening at the end of two short siphons[2] (tubes)

(Use the key on page 2.08 to determine if you have a sea squirt)

#1.Individuals are connected by a stolon (creeping vinelike network); individuals are tiny, up to 3 mm (1/8") tall .. ***Perophora viridis*, creeping tunicate** (Fig.G)
#1.Individuals are separate, not connected by a stolon; individuals grow larger than 3 mm (1/8") .... #2

#2.With a stalk (Figs.H,I) .... #3
#2.Without a stalk (Figs.A-F) .... #4

#3.Vase or club shaped with tapering stalk; brown; body very rough, bumpy, wrinkled; siphons[2] on top .... ***Styela clava*, Pacific rough sea squirt** (Fig.H)
#3.Oval body on long ropelike stalk; smooth body is orange, red or yellow; siphons[2] on side .... ***Boltenia ovifera*, stalked sea squirt** (Fig.I)

#4.Surface is spiny, cactuslike (spines are somewhat flexible, with 4-8 branches at tip); siphons[2] are bright red ...... ***Boltenia echinata*, cactus sea squirt** (Fig.A)
#4.Surface is not spiny .... #5

#5.Pink to bright red body; dome shape, lower than high; resembles drop of blood .... ***Dendrodoa carnea*, blood drop sea squirt** (Fig.B)
#5.Brown, green or yellow; vase or spherical shape .... #6

#6.Outer covering (test or "skin") is very rough, bumpy, wrinkled and gristly; both siphons[2] have four lobes and the openings are somewhat square .... ***Styela partita*, Atlantic rough sea squirt** (Fig.C)
#6.Outer covering is smooth and semitransparent but may be encrusted with sand, mud or debris which can be scraped off; outer covering, when clean, is usually yellow or orange and darker internal organs can sometimes be seen inside; one siphon has 6 lobes and the other siphon has 4 or 8 lobes (Figs. D-F) .... #7

#7.Tall, slender, vaselike; one siphon has 8 lobes and the other siphon has 6 lobes .... ***Ciona intestinalis*, sea vase** (Fig.D)
#7.Globular, grapelike; one siphon has 4 lobes and the other siphon has 6 lobes .... #8

#8.Attaches to eelgrass, pilings, boats, floats, shells, seaweeds and many other solid substrates. .... ***Molgula* spp., sea grape** (Fig.E)
#8.Lives on or in sand and mud, unattached to solid objects .... #9

#9.Bases of siphons are close together; siphons are rather long .... ***Bostrichobranchus pilularis*** (Fig.F)
#9.Bases of siphons are separated by at least 1/5 of the body circumference; siphons are short .... ***Molgula arenata*** (not shown)

[1]**WARNING:** This key does not include many of the less common sea squirts, particularly species that occur from Cape Cod north. The identification of these species often requires dissection and examination of internal organs and is beyond the scope of this book. Refer to Gosner (1971) to make a positive identification.
[2]Siphons contract and close up tightly when the sea squirt is disturbed. To examine the siphons, place the animal in sea water and allow time for it to relax.

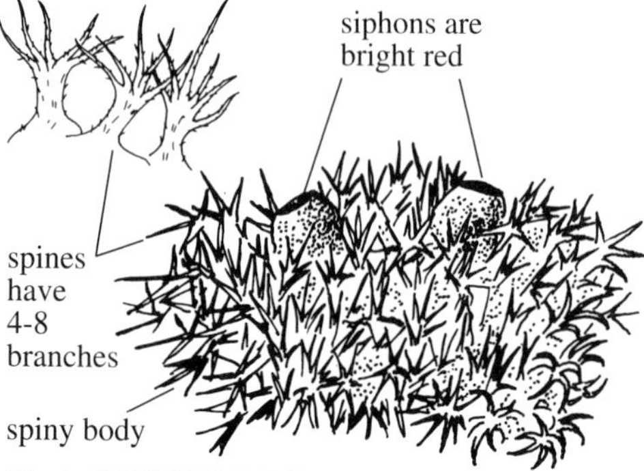

Fig.A. ***BOLTENIA ECHINATA*, CACTUS SEA SQUIRT:** Body pink or reddish, siphons bright red; up to 25 mm (1") tall; rare south of Cape Cod.

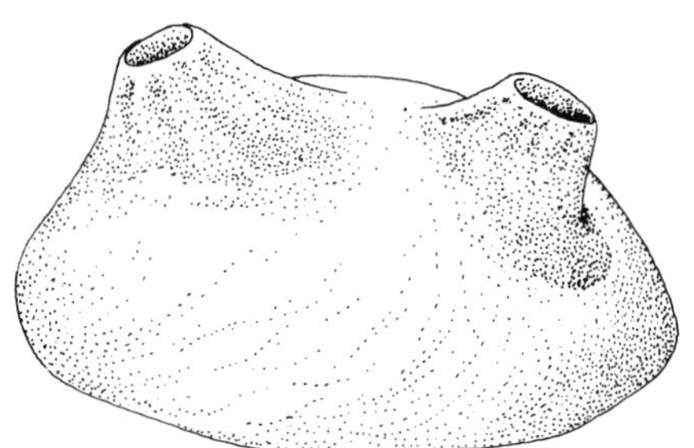

Fig.B. ***DENDRODOA CARNEA*, BLOOD DROP SEA SQUIRT:** Bright red or pink; 6 mm (1/4") tall; attaches to subtidal rocks and shells.

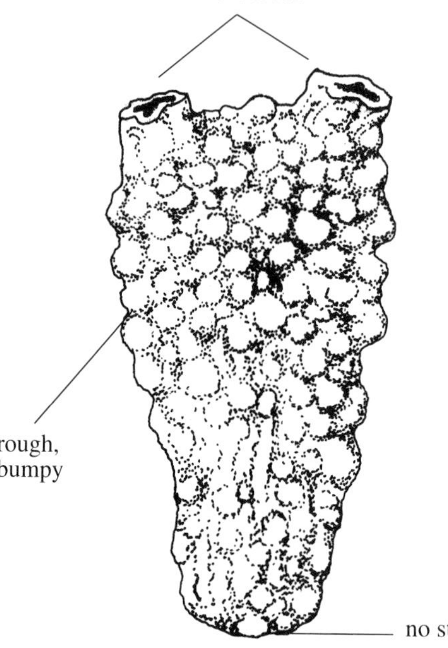

Fig.C. ***STYELA PARTITA*, ATLANTIC ROUGH SEA SQUIRT:** Brownish or yellowish with rough, wrinkled, gristly surface; up to 3 cm (1 1/4") tall; indigenous to this region but much less common than the introduced species, *Styela clava*, the Pacific rough sea squirt (Fig.H)

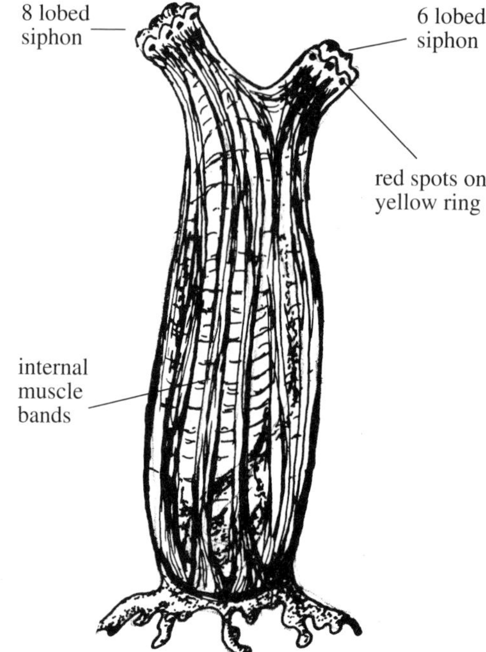

Fig.D. ***CIONA INTESTINALIS*, SEA VASE:** Transparent whitish or yellowish; may have yellow ring and red spots around siphon openings; internal muscle bands often visible through sides; up to 6 cm (2 1/2") tall; less common south of Cape Cod; lives on rocks, pilings, etc. in shallow water. 17.15 E

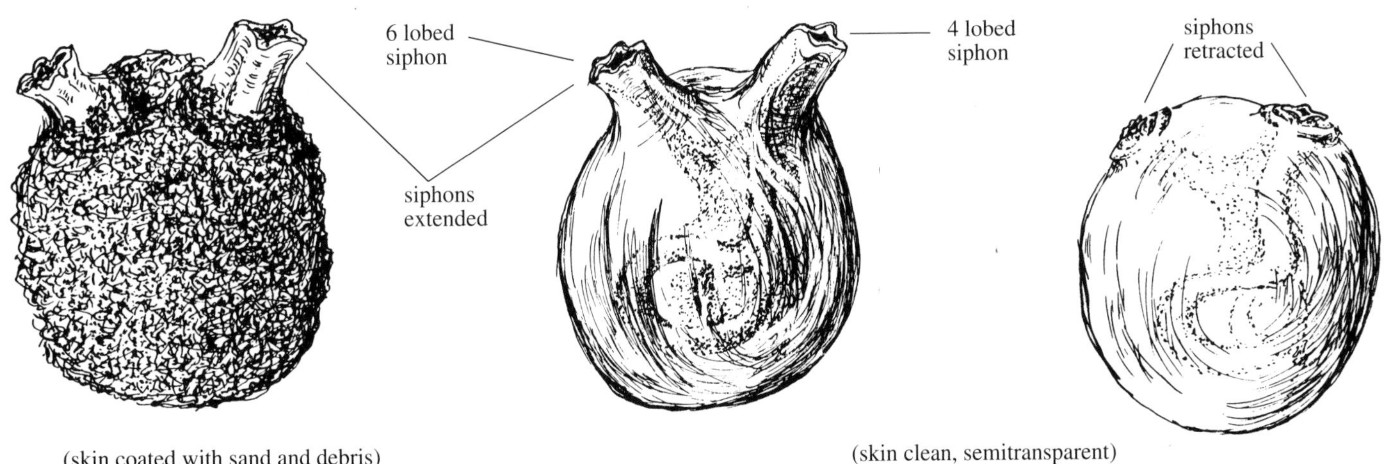

Fig.E. ***MOLGULA* SPP., SEA GRAPES:** The only common species south of Cape Cod, *Molgula manhattensis,* is yellow or orange with darker internal organs often visible inside; surface is smooth but may be encrusted with sand and other debris which can usually be scraped off; up to 3.5 cm (1 1/2") tall; very common on eelgrass, pilings, boats, floats, and many other substrates. A number of other *Molgula* species are common north of Cape Cod. Dissection is required to identify these to species. Refer to R. I. Smith (1964) or Gosner (1971). **17.15 F**

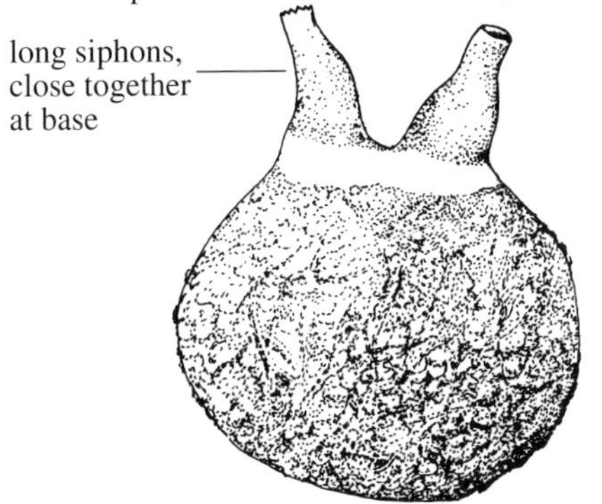

Fig.F. ***BOSTRICHOBRANCHUS PILULARIS:*** Often mud covered, except for an oval area at base of siphons which is free of mud; usually under 12 mm (1/2") in diameter; occurs in subtidal mud and sand.

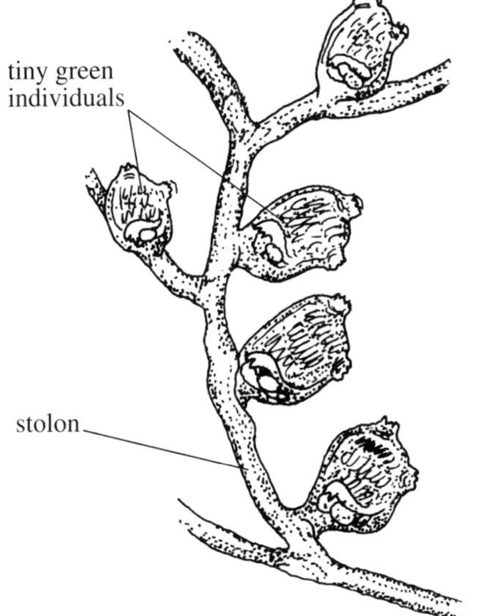

Fig.G. ***PEROPHORA VIRIDIS,* CREEPING TUNICATE:** Translucent greenish; individuals are about 3 mm (1/8") tall; colony may grow over 8 cm (3") long; attaches to rocks, algae, and other solid objects; occurs from Cape Cod south.

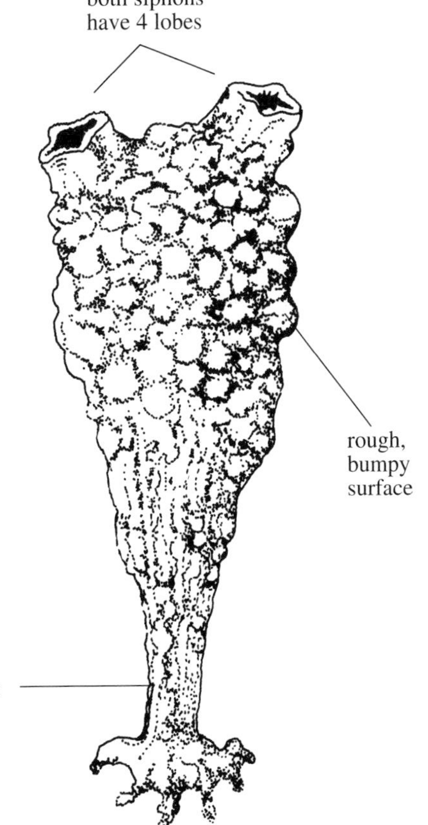

Fig.H. ***STYELA CLAVA,* PACIFIC ROUGH SEA SQUIRT:** Brown or yellow with a very rough, wrinkled, bumpy, gristly surface; up to 15 cm (6") tall; grows in crowded clumps on pilings, lobster pots, fishing nets and other substrates; native to the Philippines and the South Pacific, this species was accidentally brought to California attached to ship bottoms. It appeared in Narragansett Bay in 1976 and spread throughout southern New England by the early 1980's. It has displaced native species and is now a very common fouling organism and a nuisance to fishermen and boaters. **17.15 A**

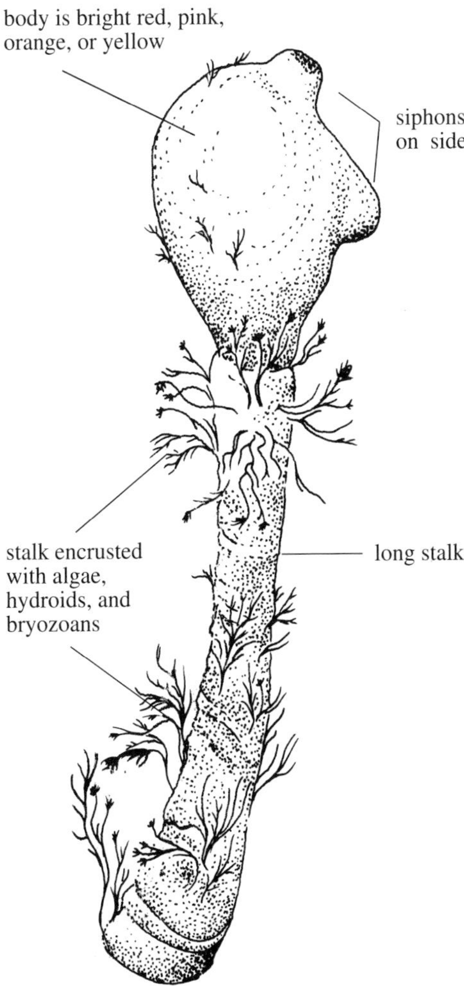

Fig.I. ***BOLTENIA OVIFERA,* STALKED SEA SQUIRT:** Body is bright orange, red, pink, or yellow; stalk is often encrusted with bryozoans, hydroids, and algae; body up to 8 cm (3") tall, stalk may exceed 30 cm (12") in length; common offshore north of Cape Cod; rare south of Cape Cod; sometimes breaks off bottom and washes ashore.

COLONIAL TUNICATES (ASCIDIANS)[1]
PHYLUM CHORDATA, SUBPHYLUM UROCHORDATA, CLASS ASCIDIACEA

Zooids (individual tunicates) form colonies which are embedded in a rubbery, gelatinous, or leathery layer that may be thin and flat or lobed and lumpy; zooids are sometimes arranged in starlike or flowerlike clusters

(Use the key on page 2.06 to determine if you have a colonial tunicate)

#1.Solid color, usually all white; zooids (individuals) in colony cannot be distinguished; with starlike microscopic spicules[2] embedded in tissue; colony forms a thin, flat, leathery coating with numerous pores .... ***Didemnum candidum*, white crust** (Fig.A)

#1.Brown, orange, green, yellow, pink, red or whitish background color; zooids are easily distinguished (especially with a hand lens or dissecting microscope) and may have a contrasting color from the background; zooids in colony are usually arranged in twisting rows or in oval or star shaped clusters (Figs.B-D); no spicules; texture of colony is rubbery or gelatinous .... #2

#2.Dark green, brown or purple background color; with yellowish or whitish zooids (individuals) clustered in numerous distinctive star shaped or oval patterns (Fig.B) like the petals of a flower .... ***Botryllus schlosseri*, golden star tunicate** (Fig.B)

#2.Bright orange, red, pink, yellow or white ground color; zooids may be arranged in twisting rows, star shaped clusters or without any pattern .... #3

#3.Colony forms thin layer with smooth, shiny surface; zooids are arranged in twisting, serpentine rows; overall color is usually bright orange but may be yellow, red or white; very common .... ***Botrylloides diegensis*, Pacific colonial tunicate** (Fig.C)

#3.Thick, hard, rubbery lumps, lobes or slabs; may be smooth and shiny or may be rough with sand grains embedded in the surface; whitish, beige or pink background with brighter red or orange zooids; zooids usually in a circular pattern but may be arranged irregularly .... ***Aplidium* spp., sea pork** (Fig.D)

[1]Refer to Gosner (1971) to identify colonial tunicates found in waters over 30 m (100') deep.

[2]Spicules are microscopic skeletal structures. See page 3.00 for directions on preparing spicules for microscopic examination.

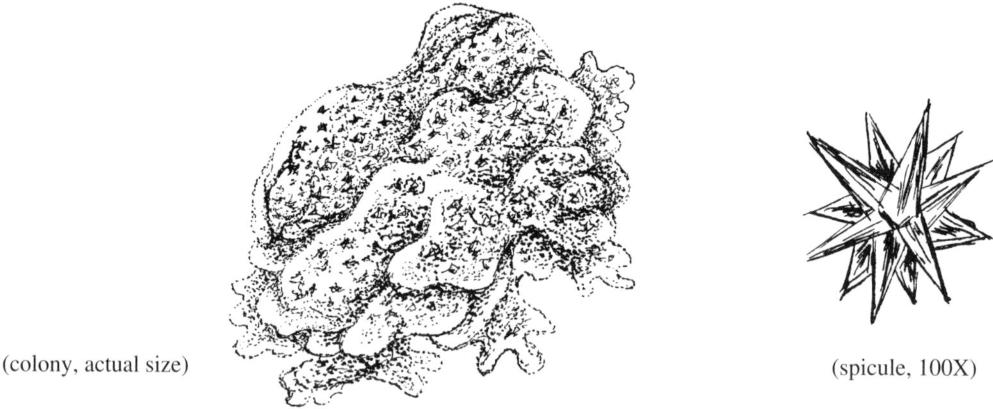

Fig.A. ***DIDEMNUM CANDIDUM*, WHITE CRUST**: Usually white but may be yellowish or reddish; forms a leathery layer about 5 mm (3/16") thick that can extend more than 20 cm (6") in length and width; starlike spicules[2] are less than 20 µm in diameter; grows on boulders below the low tide level. **17.15 B**

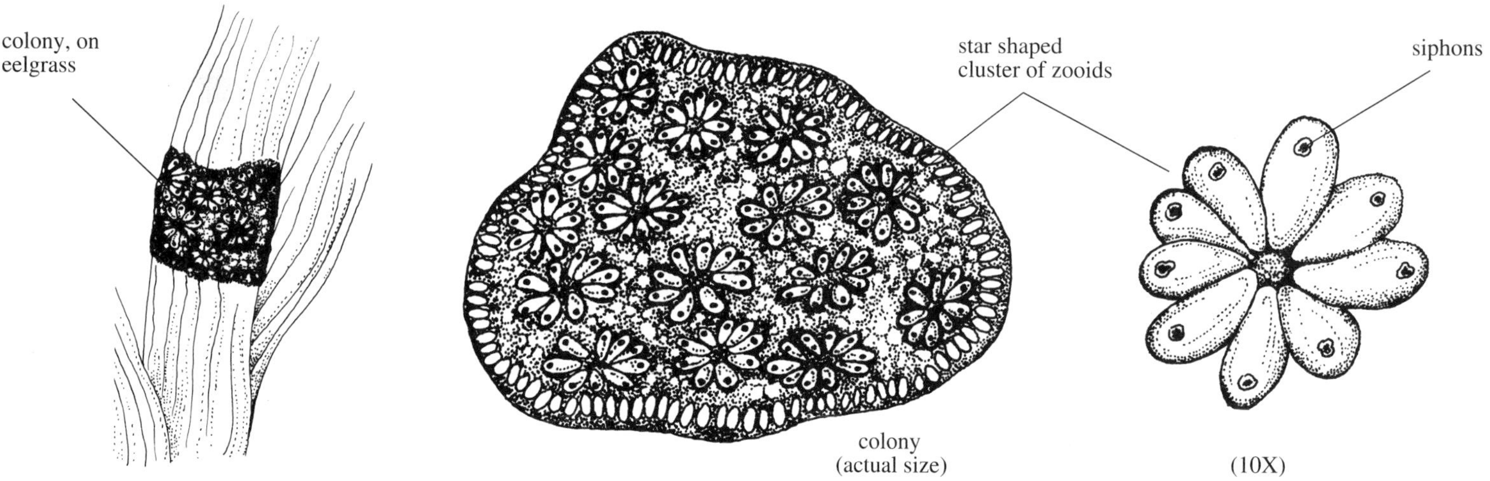

Fig.B. ***BOTRYLLUS SCHLOSSERI*, GOLDEN STAR TUNICATE**: Dark brown, green, or purple background color with yellow or white star shaped clusters of zooids; colony forms thin layer which may be over 7.5 cm (3") in length and width and about 3 mm (1/8") in thickness; individual zooids are tiny, about 2 mm (1/16") long; very common on eelgrass, seaweeds, pilings, and other solid substrates. **17.15 C** **17.15 G**

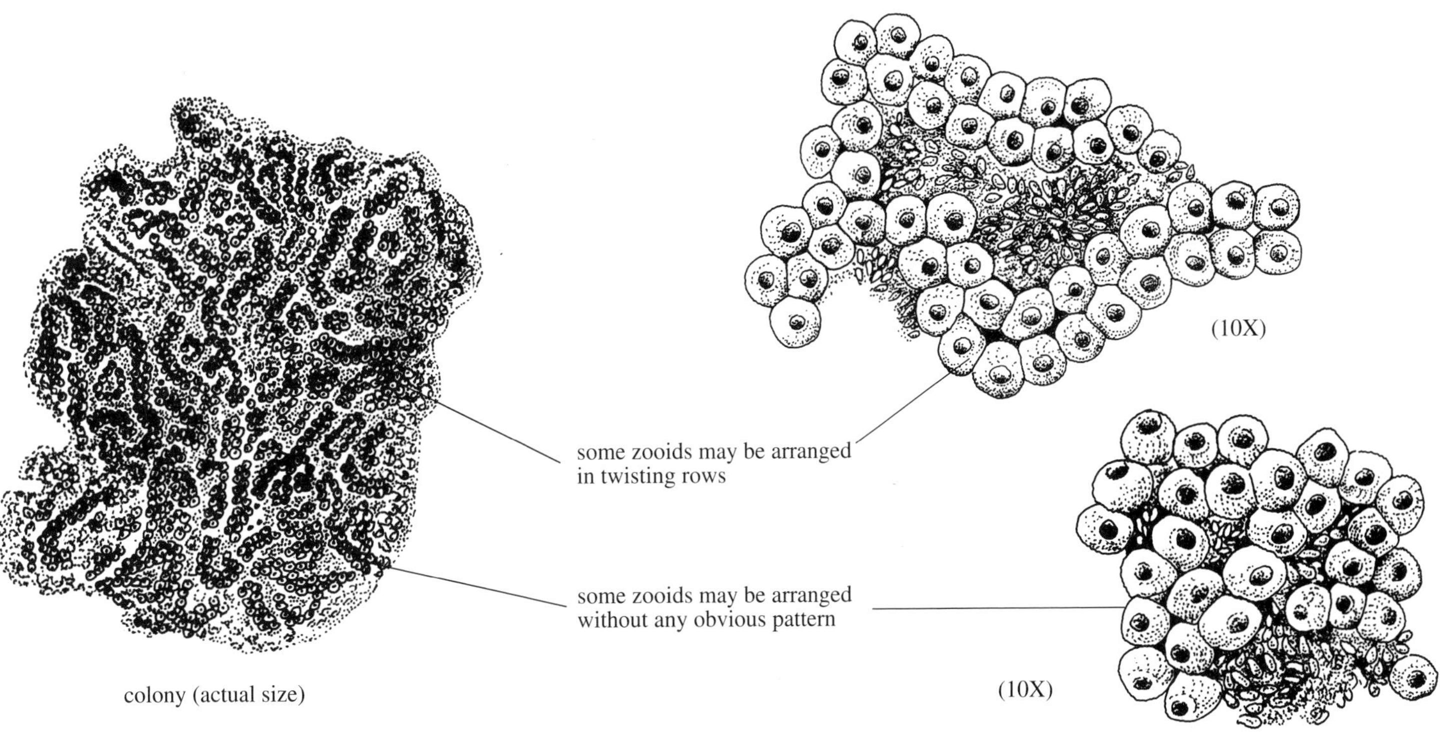

Fig.C. ***BOTRYLLOIDES DIEGENSIS*, PACIFIC COLONIAL TUNICATE**: Usually bright orange but may be yellow, white, or red; colony may be over 10 cm (4") in length and width and about 3 mm (1/8") in thickness; zooids usually arranged in serpentine rows; very common on eelgrass, seaweeds, pilings and other solid substrates in shallow subtidal waters. Native to Japan, this species was accidentally introduced to California. In the late 1970's it was brought to Woods Hole, MA for research and was released into local waters. By the 1980's it became very common in estuaries throughout southern New England. **17.15 D** **17.15 H**

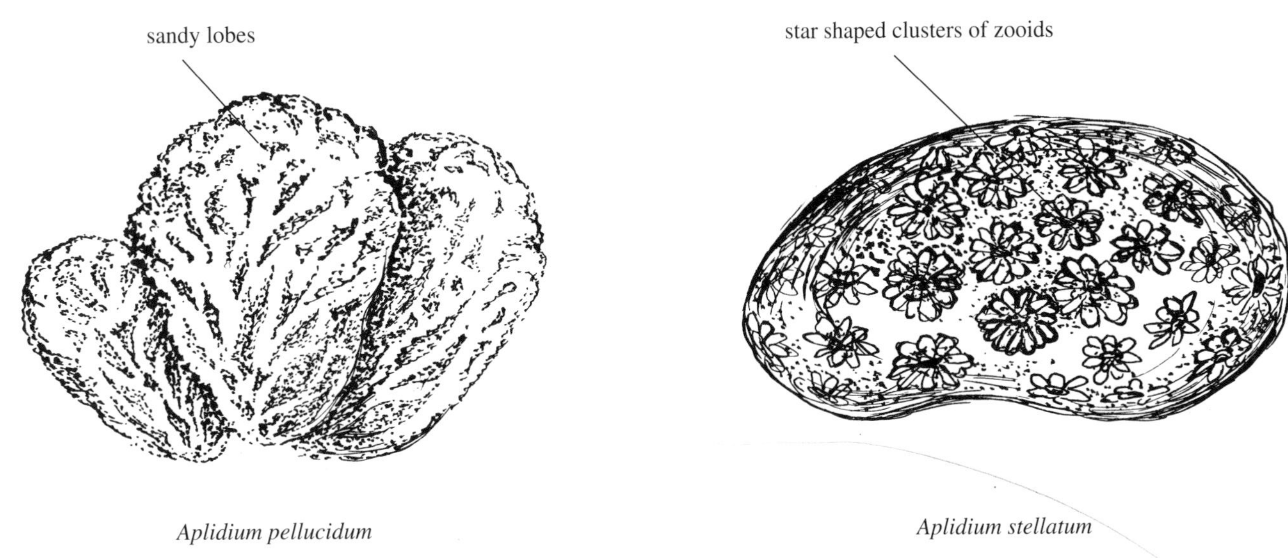

Aplidium pellucidum *Aplidium stellatum*

Fig.D. ***APLIDIUM* SPP. (=*Amaroucium* spp.), SEA PORK**: White, beige, or pink background color with brighter orange or red zooids; colonies may spread over 30 cm (1') or more and may be over 2.5 cm (1") thick; not common. The colonies of one species, *Aplidium pellucidum,* have closely packed, cauliflowerlike lobes with sand embedded in the surface. Colonies of *Aplidium stellatum* form smooth, rubbery lumps or slabs. Colonies of a third species, *Aplidium constellatum*, sometimes form lobes but are not usually embedded with sand. The zooids of this species are usually irregularly arranged. The zooids of the other two species are usually arranged in a circular or starlike pattern. Refer to Gosner (1971) to distinguish between the different *Aplidium* species.

FISHES
PHYLUM CHORDATA, SUBPHYLUM VERTEBRATA, CLASSES CEPHALASPIDOMORPHI (LAMPREYS), ELASMOBRANCHIOMORPHI (CARTILAGINOUS FISHES), AND OSTEICHTHYES (BONY FISHES)

Cold blooded, aquatic vertebrates with fins and gills.

(Use the key on page 2.12 to determine if you have a fish)

#1.With 1 gill opening on each side (Fig.A); gill chamber may be covered by a hard operculum plate (Fig.A) ... **bony fishes (class Osteichthyes)**, #4
#1.With more than 1 gill opening on each side (Figs. B-D); gill chamber not covered by an operculum plate ... #2

#2.With 7 gill openings on each side; mouth does not have jaws (Fig.B) ... ***Petromyzon marinus*, sea lamprey (class Cephalaspidomorphi)** (Fig.B)
#2.With 5 gill openings on each side (Figs.C,D) ... **cartilaginous fishes (class Elasmobranchiomorphi)**, #3

#3.Body is cylindrical, not flat; gill openings are on the sides (Fig.C) ... **sharks (orders Lamniformes and Squaliformes)**, page 13.04
#3.Body is very flat, with broad winglike fins (Fig.D); gill openings are on underside ... **skates and rays (order Rajiformes)**, page 13.06

#4.Fishes that lie flat on one side; both eyes on same side (Fig.E) ... **flatfishes (order Pleuronectiformes)**, page 13.10
#4.Fishes that do not lie flat on one side; with an eye on each side (Fig.A) ... #5

#5.With a tubular snout or bill (Fig.F) ... middle of page 13.07
#5.Without a tubular snout or bill ... #6

#6.With a suction disc on chest (Fig.G) ... middle of page 13.19
#6.Without a suction disc on chest ... **bony fishes (class Osteichthyes) continued**, page 13.02

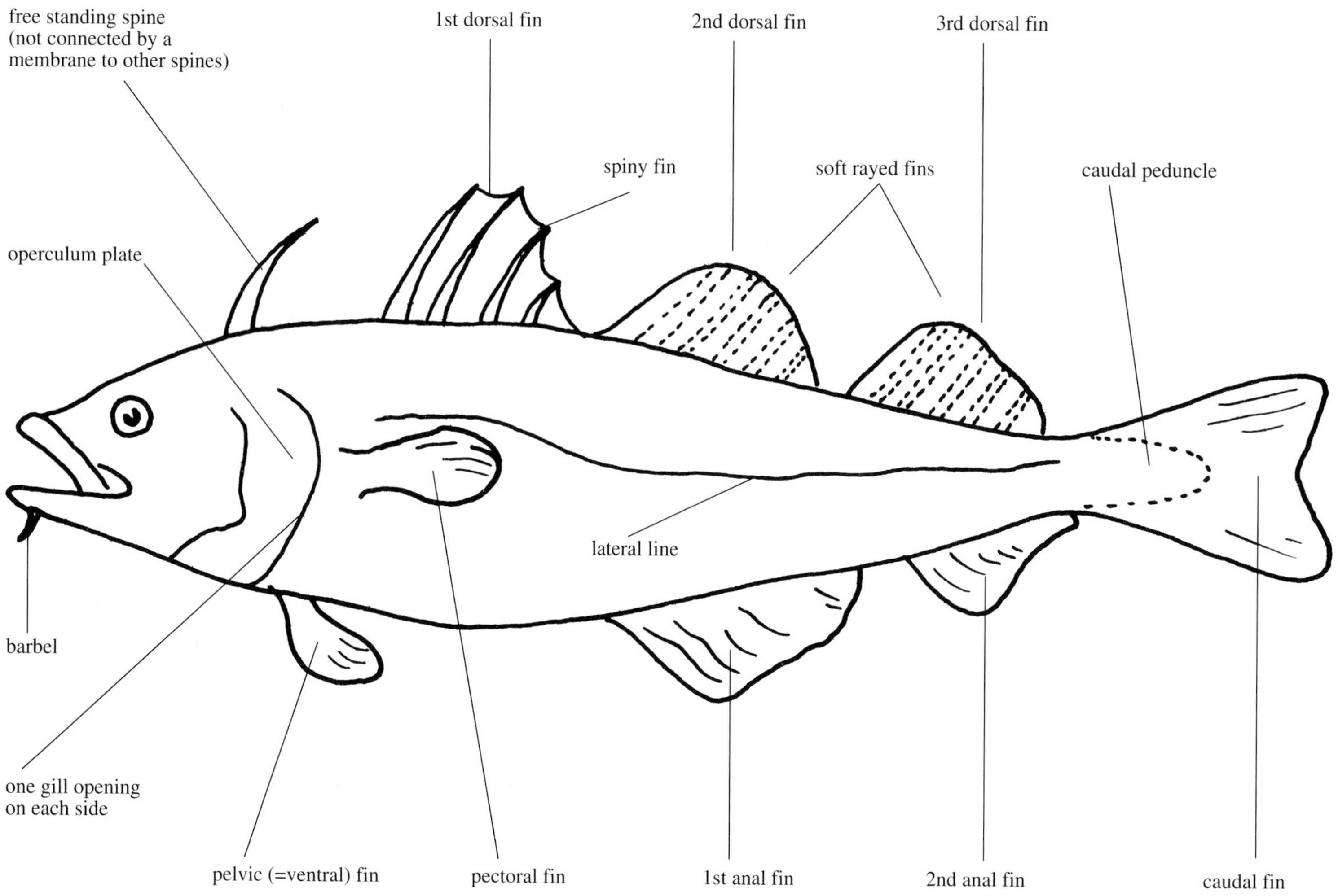

Fig.A. **BONY FISH (COMPOSITE) LABELED WITH TERMS USED IN KEY**

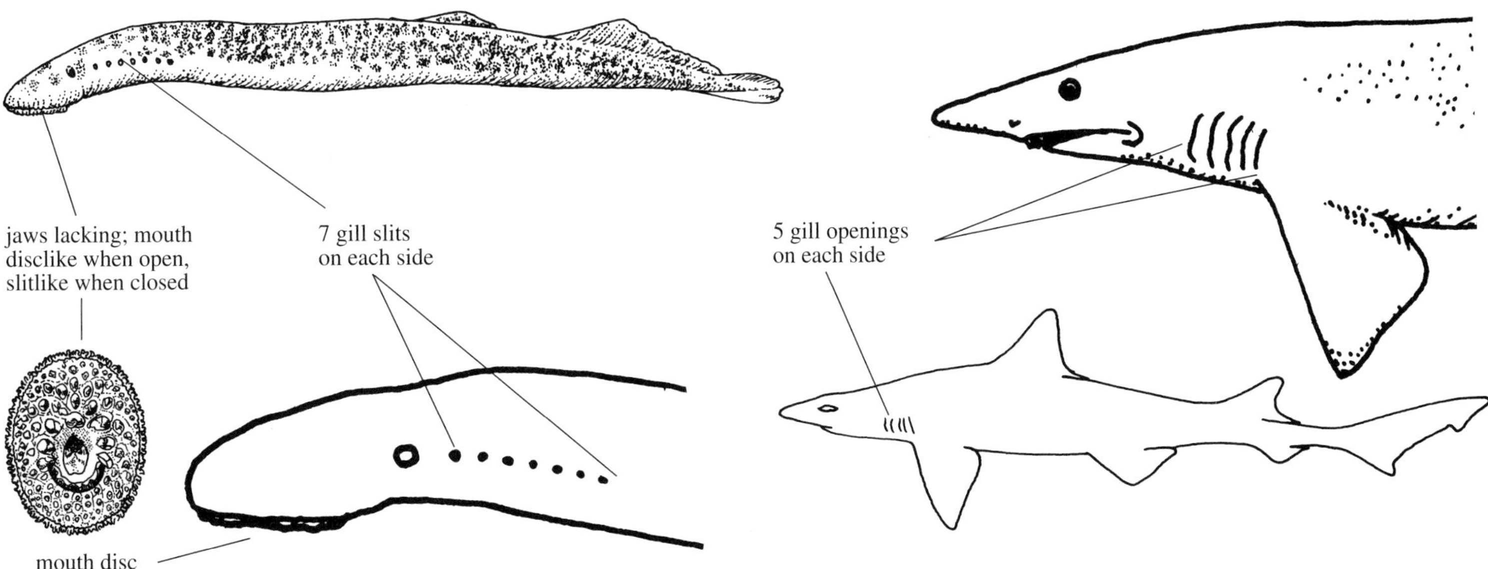

Fig.B. ***PETROMYZON MARINUS*, SEA LAMPREY:** May be brown, green, or red; up to 1 m (3') long; migrates into rivers and streams to spawn. (family Petromyzontidae: lampreys)

Fig.C. **TYPICAL SHARK**

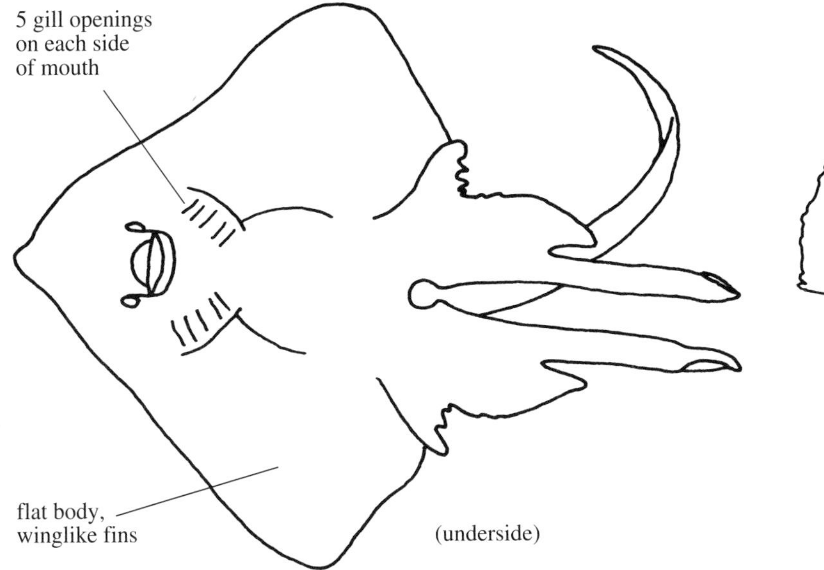

Fig.D. **TYPICAL SKATE OR RAY**

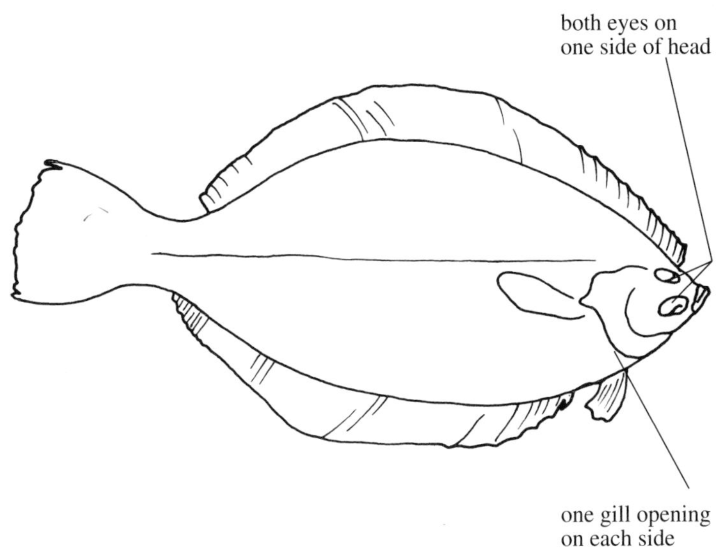

Fig.E. **TYPICAL FLATFISH**

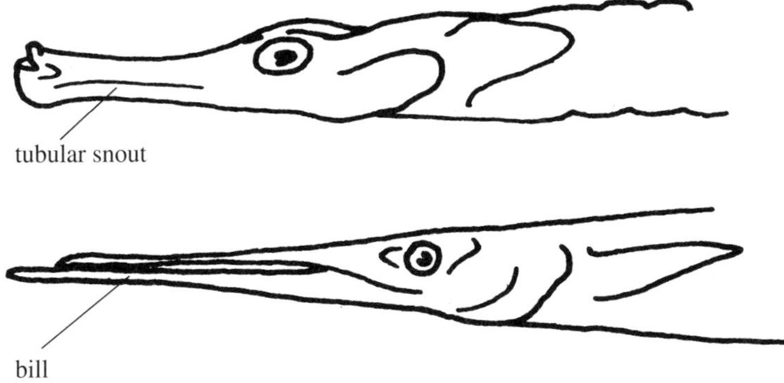

Fig.F. **FISHES WITH TUBULAR SNOUT OR BILL**

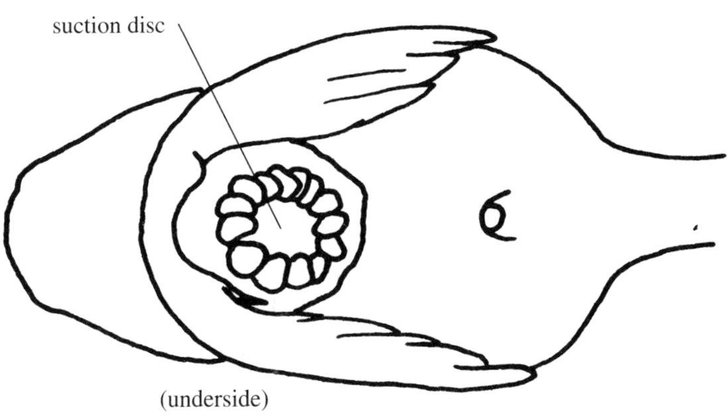

Fig.G. **FISH WITH SUCTION DISC ON CHEST**

BONY FISHES (CONTINUED): PHYLUM CHORDATA, CLASS OSTEICHTHYES

(Fish key begins on page 13.00)

#1.With one dorsal[1] fin (fin on the "back" or "top" of fish); this fin may or may not be preceded by one or more separate, free standing spines[2] (spines that are not connected to others by a membrane) (Figs.A-F) .... #2
#1.With two or more dorsal fins (Figs.G-K) .... #8

#2.With one or more free standing, separate spines[2] or pointed tubercles ("bumps") in front of dorsal fin (Fig.A) .... **sticklebacks, sturgeons, leatherjackets (filefishes), and some fishes in the jack family**, page 13.12
#2.Without any separate spines or tubercles in front of dorsal fin (Figs.B-F) .... #3

#3.Very elongate, slender, eel-like body (Fig.B); dorsal fin is very long, more than 2/3 of the total fish length .... **eels and other elongate fishes**, page 13.08
#3.Body not especially elongate or eel-like (Figs.C-F); dorsal fin about 1/2 or less of the total fish length .... #4

#4.Rear part of dorsal fin is soft rayed[3], front portion is spiny[3] (Fig.C) .... #5
#4.Entire dorsal fin is soft rayed (Figs.D-F) .... #6

#5.Spiny portion of dorsal fin is at least as long as the soft rayed portion .... **wrass family and other families**, page 13.18
#5.Spiny portion of dorsal fin is much shorter than the soft rayed portion .... #11

#6.Tail forked (Fig.D) .... **herrings, anchovies and butterfish families**, page 13.14
#6.Tail rounded or straight, not forked (Figs.E,F) .... #7

#7.With fused beaklike teeth (Fig.E); gill openings are short slits, not covered by operculum plate; no pelvic fin; may or may not be able to inflate like a balloon; may or may not have a caudal (tail) fin .... **ocean sunfish, puffers, and burrfish**, page 13.09
#7.Teeth are pointed or wedge shaped; gill openings are covered by operculum plate; pelvic fin present; not able to inflate; with an obvious caudal (tail) fin (Fig.F) .... **mummichog and killifish family**, page 13.16

#8.Head is broad and armed with bony knobs or sharp spines; pectoral fins are fanlike or winglike (Fig.G)...**searobins, sculpins, and other families**, page 13.20
#8.Head is not particularly broad and not armed with knobs or spines; pectoral fins are not winglike (Figs.H-K) .... #9

#9.Large space between first and second dorsal fins; space at least as long as first dorsal fin (Fig.H) .... page 13.22
#9.Little or no space between first and second dorsal fins (Figs.I-K) .... #10

#10.First dorsal fin spiny[3] (Fig.I) .... #11
#10.First dorsal fin soft rayed[3] (Figs.J,K) .... **family Gadidae: hakes and cods**, #12

#11.Anal fin is long[1], with more than 15 fin rays, or with a row of finlets (tiny fins) behind anal and dorsal fins .... page 13.24
#11.Anal fin is short, with 15 fin rays or less; no finlets behind anal or dorsal fins .... page 13.26

#12.With 2 dorsal fins; second dorsal much longer than first (Fig.J) .... **hakes and allies**, page 13.27
#12.With 3 dorsal fins (Fig.K) .... **cods and allies**, page 13.28

[1]Refer to Fig.A on page 13.00 for terms used in fish key.
[2]Some spines and fins are difficult to see if they are lying flat back against the fish. Scrape your fingernail from back to front along the dorsal surface of the fish to detect and raise up these fins and spines.
[3]Fin spines are rather pointed and stiff whereas soft fin rays are more flexible. Soft fin rays are also segmented giving the appearance of horizontal lines on the fins (see Fig.A on page 13.00).

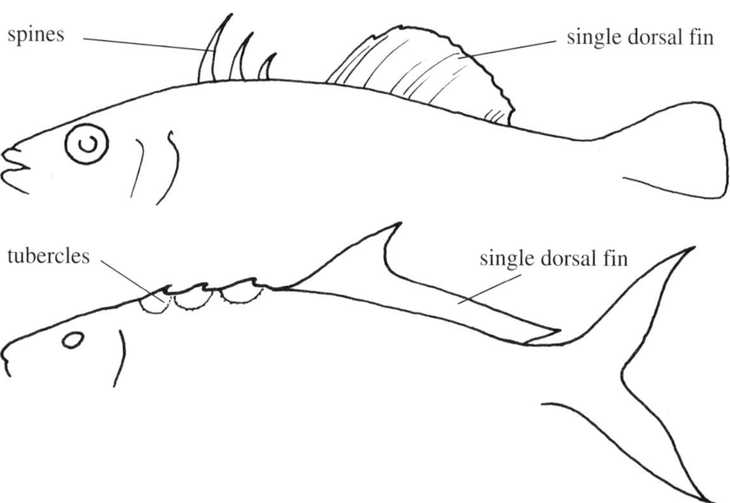

Fig.A. **FISHES WITH SPINES OR TUBERCLES IN FRONT OF SINGLE DORSAL FIN**

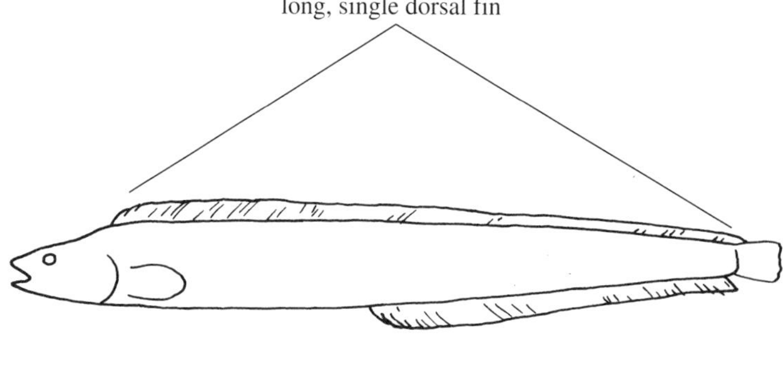

Fig.B. **ELONGATE EEL-LIKE FISH WITH SINGLE DORSAL FIN**

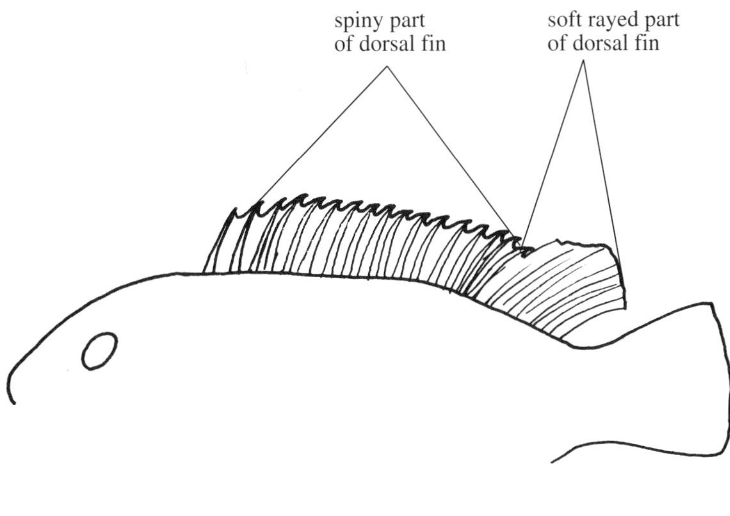

Fig.C. **FISH WITH A SINGLE DORSAL FIN THAT IS PART SPINY AND PART SOFT RAYED**

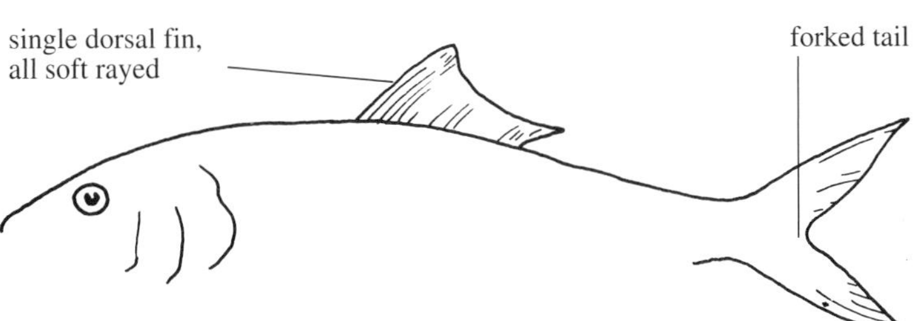

Fig.D. **FISH WITH A FORKED TAIL AND A SINGLE SOFT RAYED DORSAL FIN**

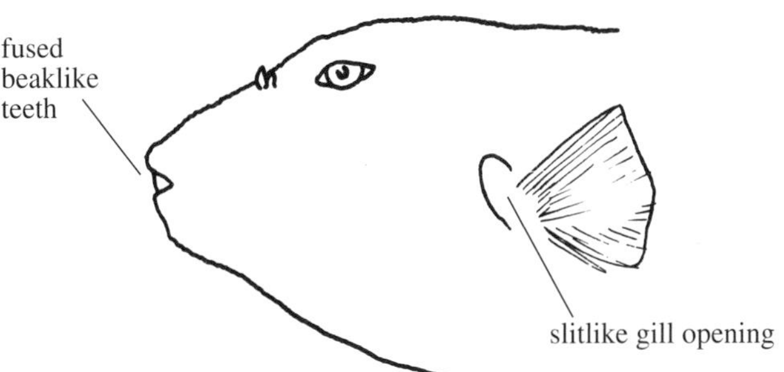

Fig.E. **FISH WITH FUSED BEAKLIKE TEETH, SLITLIKE GILLS, NO PELVIC FIN**

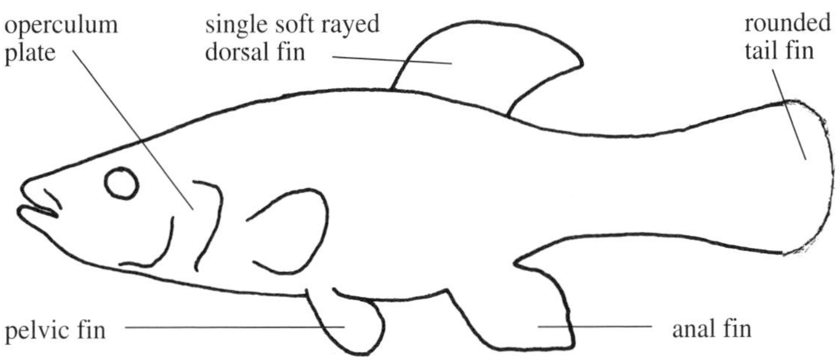

Fig.F. **MUMMICHOG AND KILLIFISH FAMILY**

Fig.G. **SEAROBINS, SCULPINS, AND RELATED FISHES**

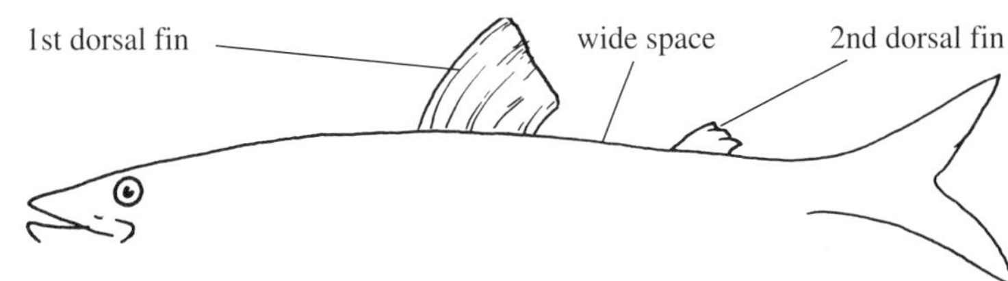

Fig.H. **FISH WITH LARGE SPACE BETWEEN FIRST AND SECOND DORSAL FINS**

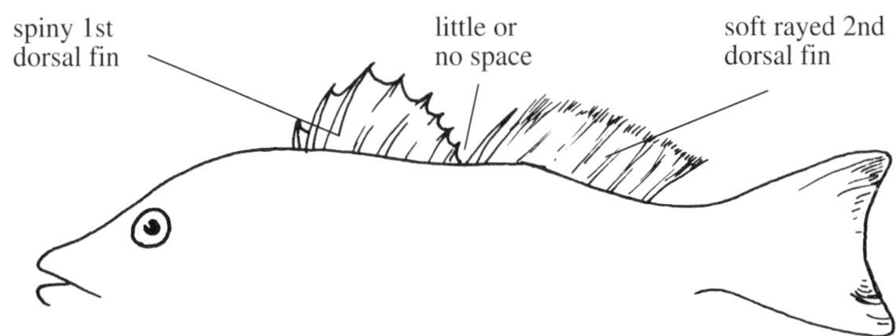

Fig.I. **FISH WITH LITTLE OR NO SPACE BETWEEN TWO DORSAL FINS; FIRST DORSAL FIN IS SPINY AND SECOND IS SOFT RAYED**

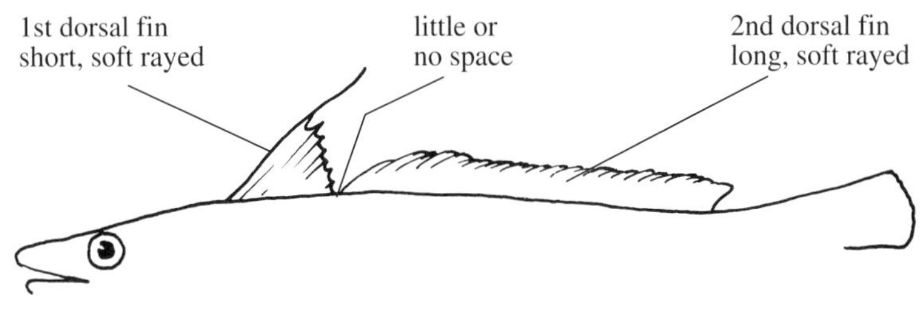

Fig.J. **HAKES AND ALLIES**

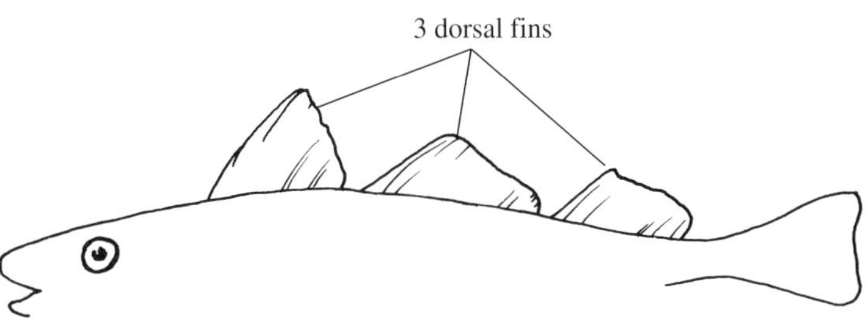

Fig.K. **CODS AND ALLIES**

SHARKS[1]
CLASS ELASMOBRANCHIOMORPHI, ORDERS LAMNIFORMES AND SQUALIFORMES

Cylindrical fishes with 5 gill openings per side.

(Fish key begins on page 13.00)

#1.Second dorsal[2] fin nearly the same size as first dorsal fin (Figs.A-C) .... #2
#1.Second dorsal fin much smaller than the first dorsal fin (Figs.D-G) .... #4

#2.With a spine in front of each of the dorsal fins; with no anal fin, only a pair of pelvic fins .... ***Squalus acanthias*, spiny dogfish** (Fig.A)
#2.Without a spine in front of either of the dorsal fins; with an anal fin and a pair of pelvic fins (Figs.B,C) .... #3

#3.Teeth low and flat; anal fin smaller than first dorsal fin; first dorsal fin begins just behind base of pectoral fins .... ***Mustelus canis*, smooth dogfish** (Fig.B)
#3.Teeth long and sharp; anal fin nearly as large as first dorsal fin; first dorsal fin begins far behind base of pectoral fin .... ***Odontaspis taurus*, sand tiger** (Fig.C)

#4.Head has hammerlike side extensions; eyes are at the ends of the extensions .... ***Sphyrna zygaena*, smooth hammerhead** (Fig.D)
#4.Head does not have side extensions (Figs.E-G) .... #5

#5.Upper portion of caudal (tail) fin very long; nearly as long as head and body combined .... ***Alopias vulpinus*, thresher shark** (Fig.E)
#5.Upper portion of caudal (tail) fin not unusually long; less than half as long as head and body combined (Figs.F,G) .... #6

#6.First dorsal fin begins above the base of the pectoral fins; pectoral fins are relatively broad; less than twice as long as wide .... ***Carcharhinus* spp.[1], sandbar and dusky sharks** (Fig.F)
#6.First dorsal fin begins far behind the base of the pectoral fins; pectoral fins are long and narrow, over twice as long as wide .... ***Prionace glauca*, blue shark** (Fig.G)

[1]This key only includes those sharks that are likely to be found in estuarine waters. Other sharks are common offshore in southern New England which may, on rare occasions, stray into estuarine waters. Refer to Bigelow and Schroeder (1953) or other fish guides to identify any sharks that do not key out here.
[2]Refer to Fig. A on page 13.00 for terms used in fish key.

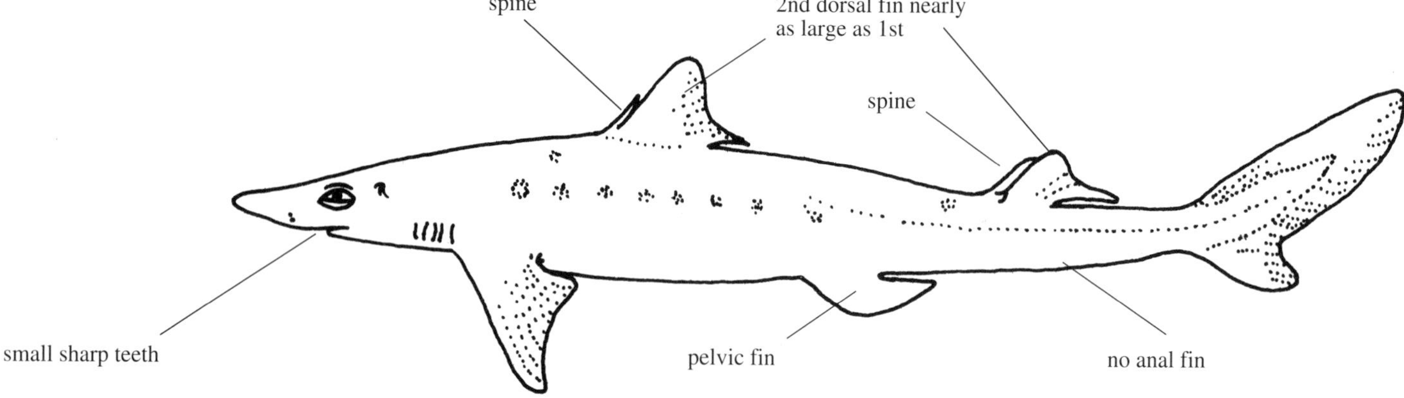

Fig.A. ***SQUALUS ACANTHIAS*, SPINY DOGFISH:** Gray on top, white on bottom, sometimes with white spots on sides; up to about 1.2 m (4') long; very common in bays and sounds. (family Squalidae: dogfish sharks)

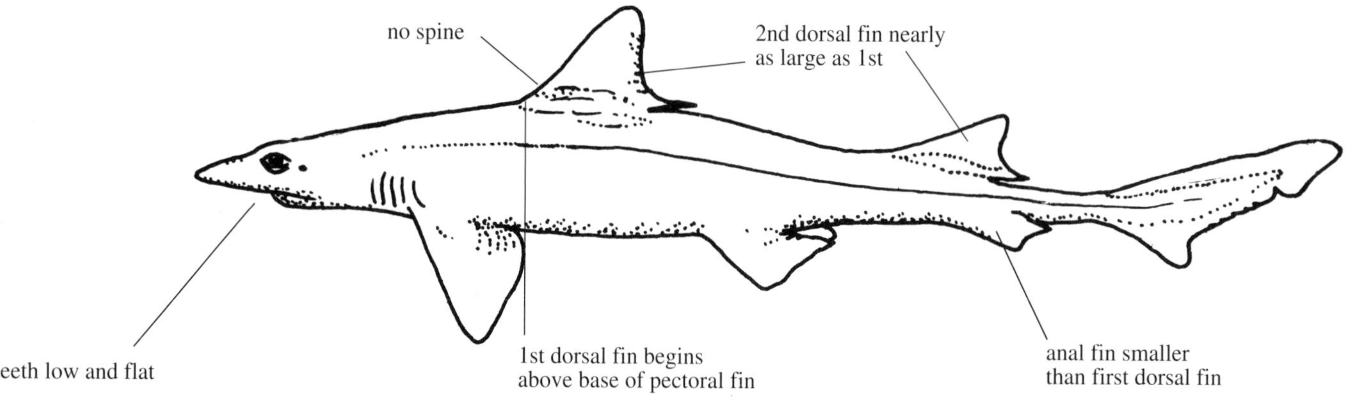

Fig.B. ***MUSTELUS CANIS*, SMOOTH DOGFISH:** Gray on top, whitish on bottom; up to about 1.5 m (5') long; very common in bays and sounds. (family Carcharhinidae: requiem sharks)

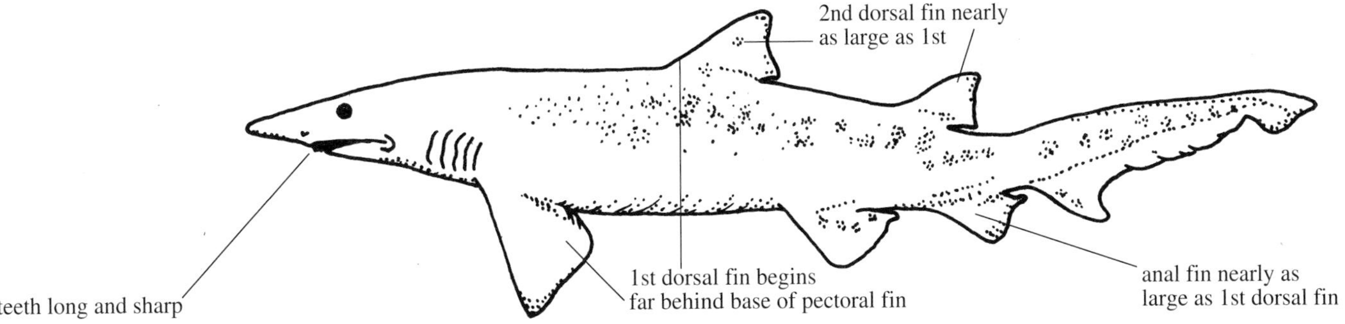

Fig.C. ***ODONTASPIS TAURUS (=Carcharias t.)*, SAND TIGER:** Gray-brown on top, white below, yellowish spots on sides; up to 2.7 m (9') long; common in bays and sounds. (family Odontaspididae: sand tigers)

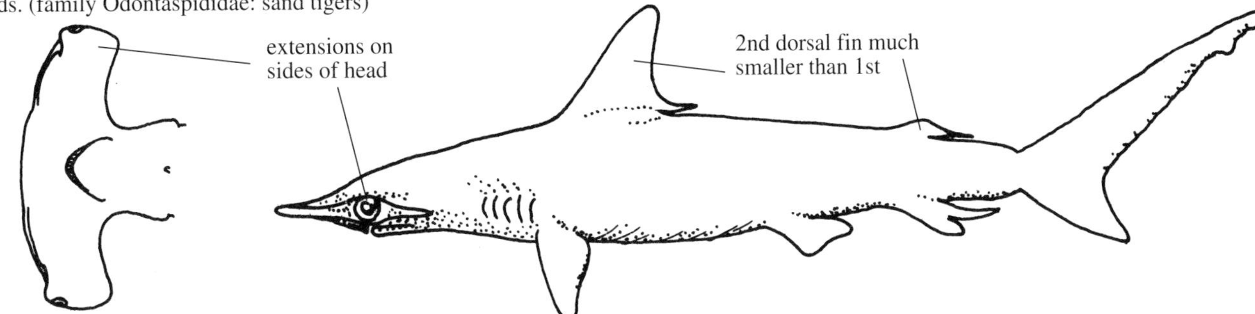

Fig.D. ***SPHYRNA ZYGAENA*, SMOOTH HAMMERHEAD:** Brown or gray on top; grayish-white below; up to 4 m (13') long; not common in estuarine waters. (family Sphyrnidae: hammerhead sharks)

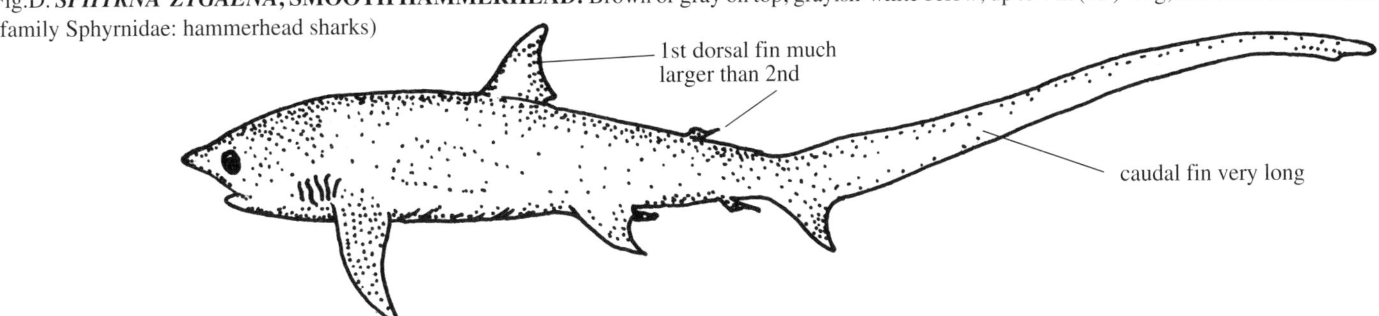

Fig.E. ***ALOPIAS VULPINUS*, THRESHER SHARK:** Gray, blue, or black on top, white below; usually up to about 5 m (16'); not common in estuarine waters. (family Alopiidae: thresher sharks)

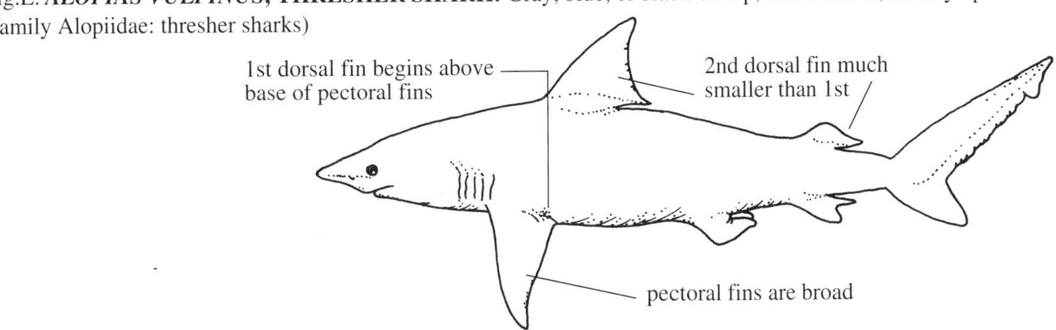

Fig.F. ***CARCHARHINUS* SPP[1]., SANDBAR AND DUSKY SHARKS:** Gray or brown on top, bottom whitish; up to 2.5 m (8') long; not common in estuarine waters. (family Carcharhinidae: requiem sharks)

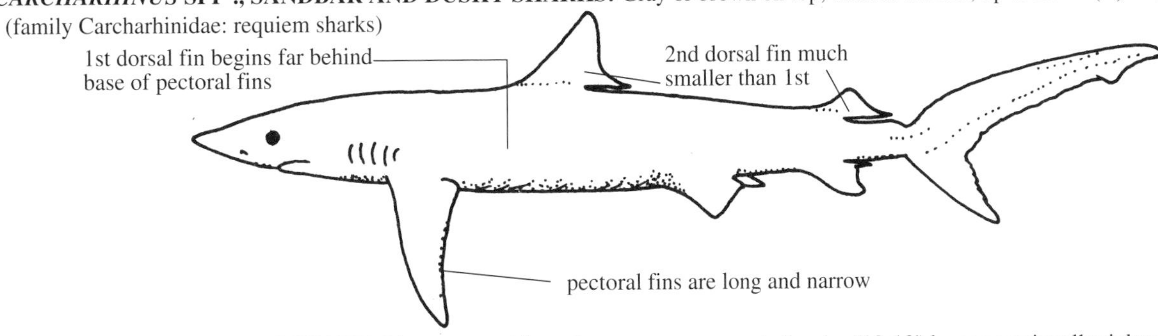

Fig.G. ***PRIONACE GLAUCA*, BLUE SHARK:** Blue on top, white on bottom; averages up to 3 or 4 m (10-13') long; occasionally sighted in bays and sounds. (family Carcharhinidae: requiem sharks)

SKATES AND RAYS
CLASS ELASMOBRANCHIOMORPHI, ORDER RAJIFORMES

Flat cartilaginous fishes with five gill openings per side and with winglike fins.

(Fish key begins on page 13.00)

#1.Without a row of spines on midline of back and tail. (NOTE: a row of spines does occur to each side of the midline) (Fig.A) .... #2
#1.With a row of spines on midline of back and/or tail (Figs.C-E) .... #3

#2.No "eye" spots (see Fig.B) on rear corners of pectoral fins; less than 54 cm (21") long; has maturing or mature external sex characteristics (see Fig.B) at a length of 35 cm (14") or greater; fewer than 64 rows of teeth in upper jaw .... ***Raja erinacea*, little skate** (Figs.A,B)
#2.Often with "eye" spots (see Fig.B) on pectoral fins; may be longer than 54 cm (21"); reaches sexual maturity (see Fig.B) at length of over 54 cm (21"); more than 72 rows of teeth in upper jaw .... ***Raja ocellata*, winter skate** (Figs.A,B)

#3.No fins at end of tail; with large, sharp, saw-edged spine near base of tail .... ***Dasyatis centroura*, roughtail stingray** (Fig.C)
#3.With fins at end of tail; without large spine near base of tail (Figs.D,E) .... #4

#4.Without spines on midline of body; row of spines on midline of tail only; with sharply pointed snout .... ***Raja laevis*, barndoor skate** (Fig.D)
#4.With row of spines on midline of body and tail; with translucent areas on either side of snout .... ***Raja eglanteria*, clearnose skate** (Fig.E)

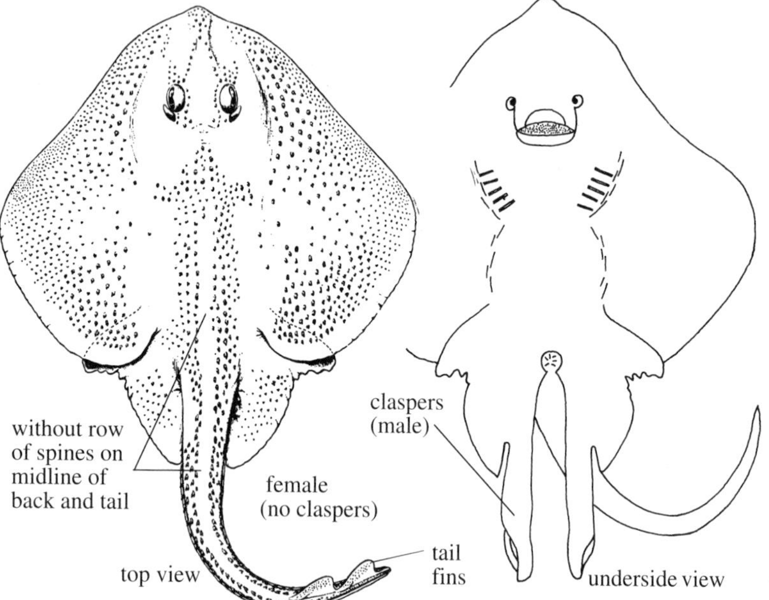

Fig.A. ***RAJA ERINACEA*, LITTLE SKATE:** Brown with dark spots on top, white on bottom; rarely over 54 cm (21") long; very common. **17.16 A**
***RAJA OCELLATA*, WINTER SKATE:** Very similar (see Fig.B) but may have "eye" spots; up to 110 cm (43") long; less common. (family Rajidae: skates)

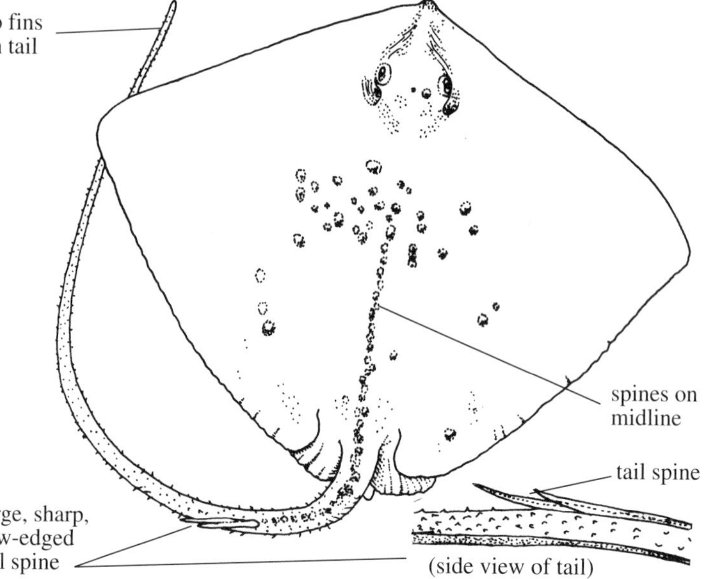

Fig.C. ***DASYATIS CENTROURA*, ROUGHTAIL STINGRAY:** Olive brown or dark brown above, white below; tail black from spine rearward; up to 1.5 m (5') wide and 3 m (10') long; not common in bays or sounds. (family Dasyatidae: stingrays)

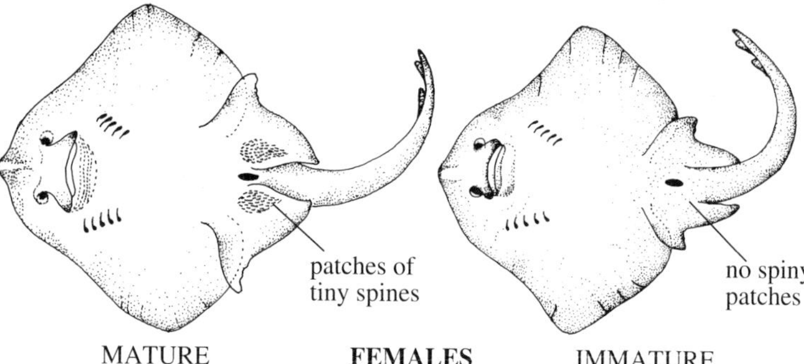

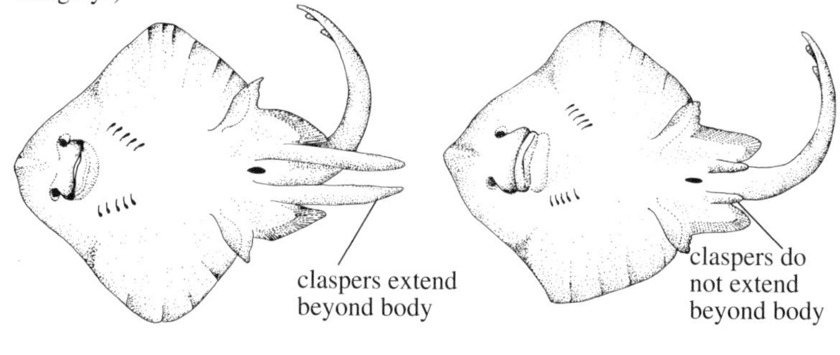

Fig. B. ***RAJA ERINACEA*, LITTLE SKATE**, and ***RAJA OCELLATA*, WINTER SKATE**, are very similar but can be distinguished by size, color, sexual maturity, and teeth (use the key above). If the skate has "eyespots" or if it is longer than 54 cm (21") then it is the winter skate. The eyespots are dark brown spots edged with white. Usually the winter skate has 1-4 of these spots at the rear corner of each pectoral fin. However, the spots may be absent. The little skate has brown spots but not eyespots. If the fish does not have eyespots and is between 35 cm (14") and 54 cm (21") you can use its sexual maturity to determine the species. In this size range little skates are sexually mature or maturing and winter skates are immature. If the skate is less than 35 cm (14") long and doesn't have eyespots you must count the rows of teeth to make a positive identification. Mature females have two patches of spines, one on either side of the vent. Immature females do not have these spines. The spines are hard to see but can be felt if you rub your fingertips in the tail-to-head direction over this area. Mature males have claspers that extend well beyond the rear edge of the body. Immature males have claspers that do not reach the rear edge of the body or barely extend beyond it (Flescher, 1980).

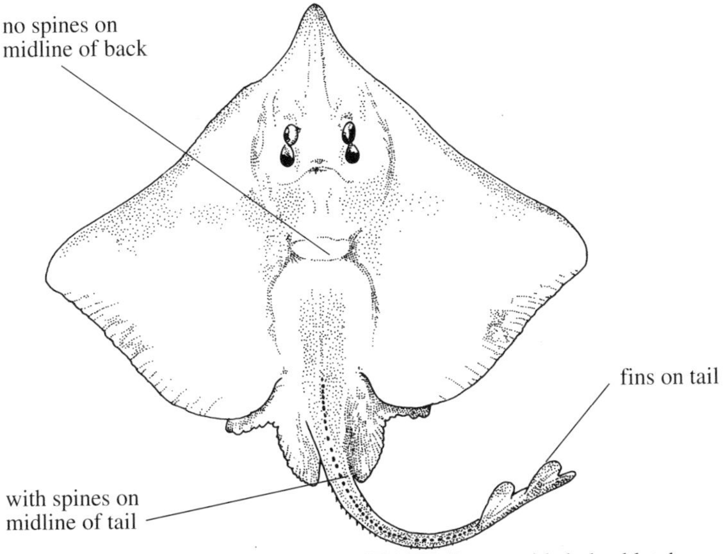

Fig.D. ***RAJA LAEVIS*, BARNDOOR SKATE:** Brown with darker blotches on top, white on bottom; up to 1.8 m (6') long; much less common than the little or winter skates. (family Rajidae: skates)

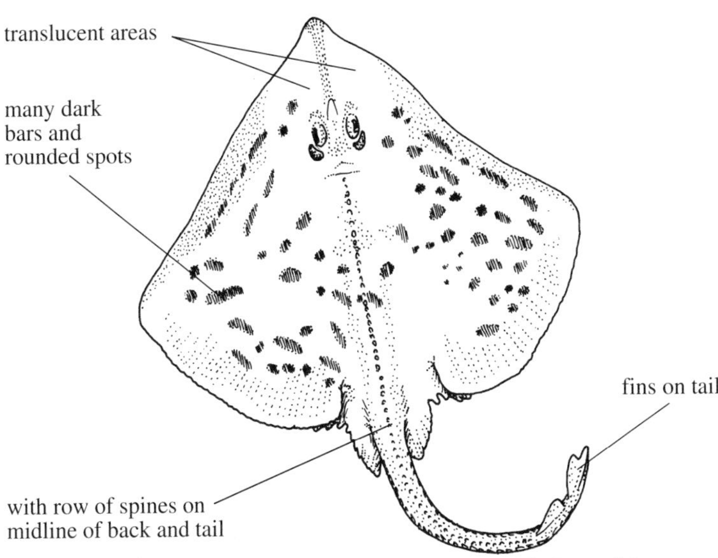

Fig.E. ***RAJA EGLANTERIA*, CLEARNOSE SKATE:** Brownish to gray above with darker bars and round spots, translucent areas on either side of snout, white below; up to 1 m (3') long. (family Rajidae: skates)

BONY FISHES WITH A TUBULAR SNOUT OR BILL: CLASS OSTEICHTHYES

(Fish key begins on page 13.00)

#1.With one or both jaws that are prolonged as a bill (Figs.F,G) .... #2
#1.With jaw bones fused to form a tubular snout, with mouth at its tip (Figs.H,I) .... **family Syngnathidae, pipefishes and seahorses**, #3

#2.Only the lower jaw forms the long bill, upper jaw is short .... ***Hyporhamphus unifasciatus*, silverstripe halfbeak** (Fig.F)
#2.Both jaws form the long bill .... ***Strongylura marina*, Atlantic needlefish** (Fig.G)

#3.Long, thin, eel shaped body, with a caudal ("tail") fin .... ***Syngnathus fuscus*, northern pipefish** (Fig.H)
#3.Head, neck and midbody region is horselike; without a caudal ("tail") fin .... ***Hippocampus erectus*, lined seahorse** (Fig.I)

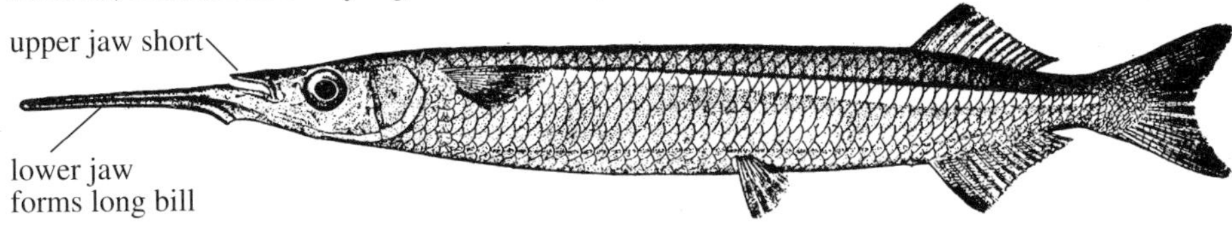

Fig.F. ***HYPORHAMPHUS UNIFASCIATUS*, SILVERSTRIPE HALFBEAK:** Translucent green on top, silvery on sides; less than 25 cm (10") long. (family Exocoetidae: flyingfishes)

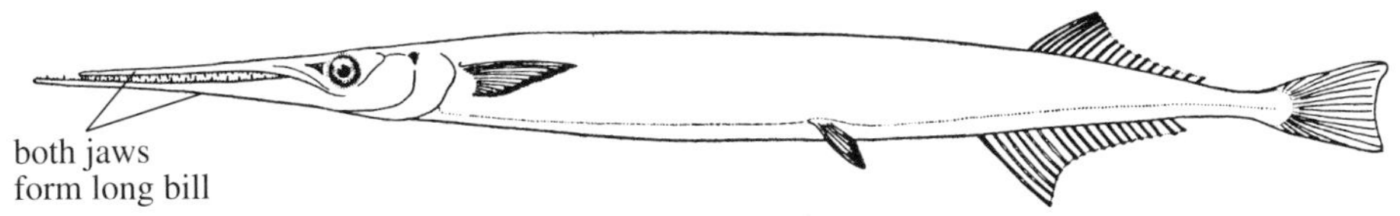

Fig.G. ***STRONGYLURA MARINA*, ATLANTIC NEEDLEFISH:** Greenish on top, silvery on sides; usually 25-50 cm (10-20") long, but may reach 1 m (3'). (family Belonidae: needlefishes)

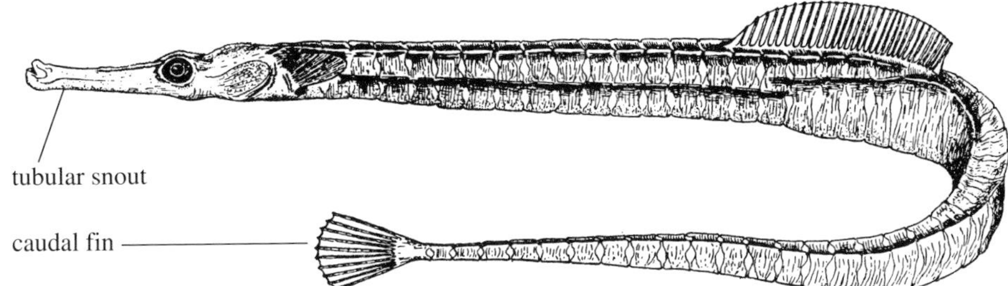

Fig.H. ***SYNGNATHUS FUSCUS*, NORTHERN PIPEFISH:** Green or brown; usually 10-20 cm (4-8") long; very common in estuaries, particularly in eelgrass beds. (family Syngnathidae: pipefishes and seahorses)

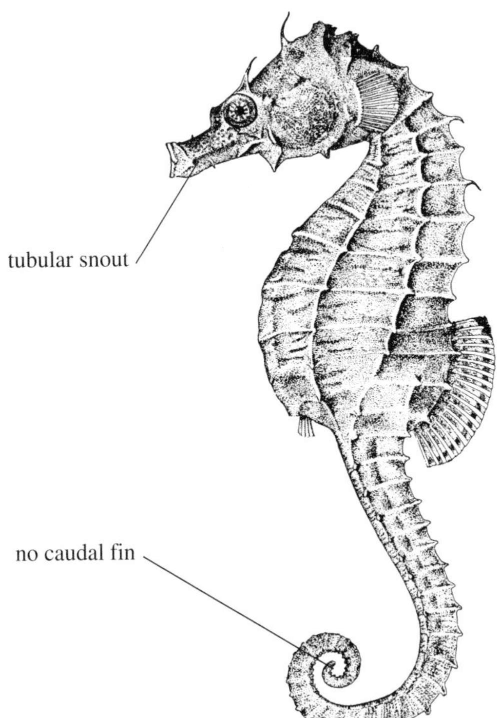

Fig.I. ***HIPPOCAMPUS ERECTUS*, LINED SEAHORSE**: Brown; up to 15 cm (6") long; not common. (family Syngnathidae: pipefishes and seahorses)

EELS AND OTHER ELONGATE BONY FISHES WITH A LONG, SINGLE DORSAL FIN

(Fish key begins on page 13.00)

#1.With an obvious space separating the caudal ("tail") fin from the anal fin[1] (Figs.A-C) .... #2
#1.No obvious space separating the caudal ("tail") fin from the anal fin (Figs.D-G) .... #4

#2.With obvious space separating the caudal fin from dorsal fin (Figs.A-B) .... #3
#2.With no obvious space separating the caudal fin from dorsal fin (Fig.C) .... ***Ulvaria subbifurcata*, radiated shanny** (Fig.C)

#3.Tail is deeply forked; anal fin is less than 1/2 the length of the dorsal fin; no ventral fin .... ***Ammodytes americanus*, American sand lance** (Fig.A)
#3.Tail is rounded or straight; anal fin is more than 2/3 the length of the dorsal fins; ventral fins present, may be long and feelerlike .. **hakes** (Fig.B), page 13.27

#4.With a large space between caudal ("tail") fin and dorsal fin .... ***Macrozoarces americanus*, ocean pout** (Fig.D)
#4.With no space between caudal ("tail") fin and dorsal fin (Figs.E-G) .... #5

#5.Dorsal fin begins above gill opening .... ***Pholis gunnellus*, rock gunnel** (Fig.E)
#5.Dorsal fin begins above or behind tip of pectoral fin .... #6

#6.Dorsal fin begins well behind the pectoral fins; lower jaw projects forward beyond upper jaw .... ***Anguilla rostrata*, American eel** (Fig.F)
#6.Dorsal fin begins above tip of pectoral fins; upper jaw projects forward beyond lower jaw .... ***Conger oceanicus*, conger eel** (Fig.G)

[1] Refer to Fig. A on page 13.00 for terms used in fish key.

Fig.A. ***AMMODYTES AMERICANUS*, AMERICAN SAND LANCE:** Green or brown on top, silvery sides; 10-15 cm (4-6") long. (family Ammodytidae: sand lances)

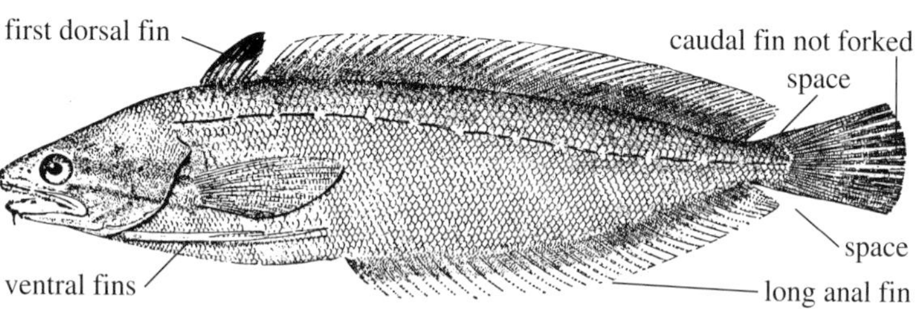

Fig.B. **HAKES** have two dorsal fins. However, sometimes the first dorsal fin is very small and is overlooked. Go to page 13.27.

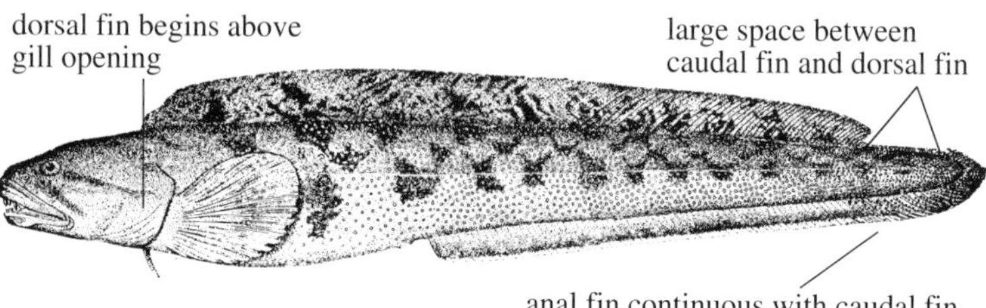

Fig.D. ***MACROZOARCES AMERICANUS*, OCEAN POUT:** Muddy brown or gray with mottled markings; usually 40-75 cm (16-29") long. (family Zoarcidae: eelpouts)

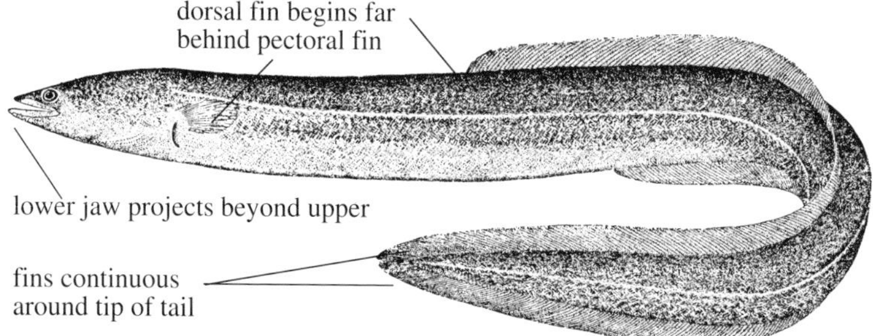

Fig.F. ***ANGUILLA ROSTRATA*, AMERICAN EEL:** Olive green or brown; up to about 1 m (3') long; very common in estuaries. (family Anguillidae: eels)

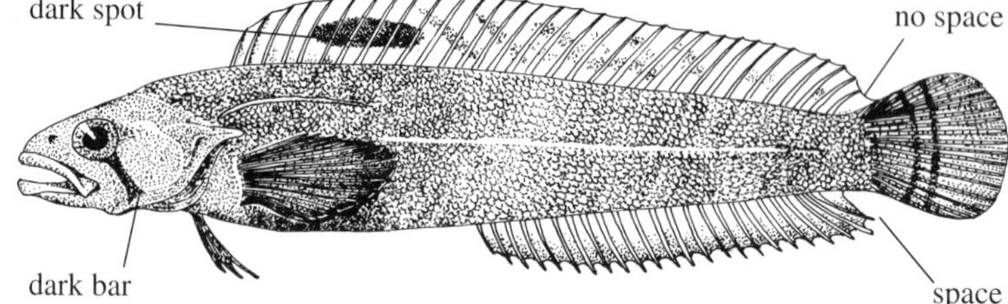

Fig.C. ***ULVARIA SUBBIFURCATA*, RADIATED SHANNY:** Brown with dark blotch on dorsal fin and dark bar under eye; up to 17 cm (7") long; not common. (family Stichaeidae: pricklebacks)

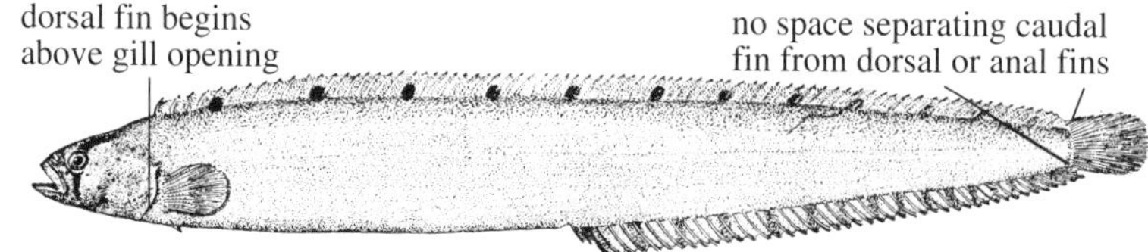

Fig.E. ***PHOLIS GUNNELLUS*, ROCK GUNNEL:** Color variable, yellowish, greenish, brown, or reddish, with black spots along back and dorsal fin; usually less than 20 cm (8") long. (family Pholidae: gunnels)

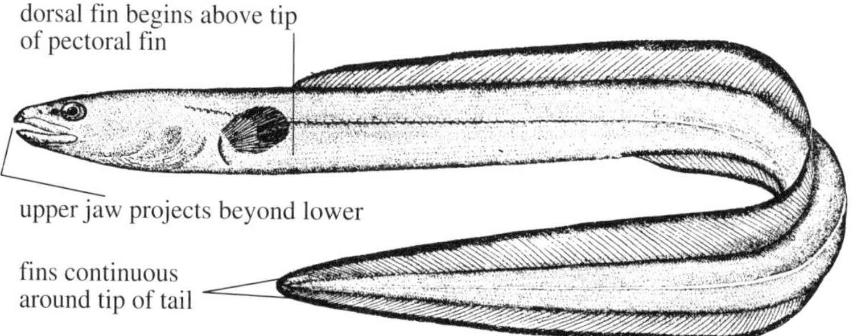

Fig.G. ***CONGER OCEANICUS*, CONGER EEL:** Grayish on back; up to 2 m (7') long. (family Congridae: conger eels)

PUFFERS, BURRFISH, AND OCEAN SUNFISH
CLASS OSTEICHTHYES, ORDER TETRAODONTIFORMES

Fishes with single, all soft rayed dorsal fin; fused beaklike teeth in a tiny mouth; gill openings are short slits; no pelvic fins[1].

(Fish key begins on page 13.00)

#1.With no tail fin; very high dorsal[1] and anal fins; grows very large, over 2 m (6') long .... ***Mola mola*, ocean sunfish** (Fig.A)
#1.With distinct tail fin; rarely over 30 cm (1') long (Figs.B-E) .... #2

#2.Body is hard, rigid, enclosed in a shell-like box of bony plates; body is smooth; belly not able to inflate .... ***Lactophrys trigonus,* trunkfish** (Fig.B)
#2.Body is soft and flexible; may have spiny skin on all or part of the body; belly is able to inflate like a balloon (Figs.C-E) .... #3

#3.Body covered with large bony spines .... ***Chilomycterus schoepfi*, striped burrfish** (Fig.C)
#3.Body smooth or prickly, without large spines .... #4

#4.Skin is smooth except on belly; tail fin is concave (curves inward) .... ***Lagocephalus laevigatus*, smooth puffer** (Fig.D)
#4.Skin is prickly on entire body; tail fin is rounded or straight .... ***Sphoeroides maculatus*, northern puffer** (Fig.E)

[1]Refer to Fig.A on page 13.00 for terms used in fish key.

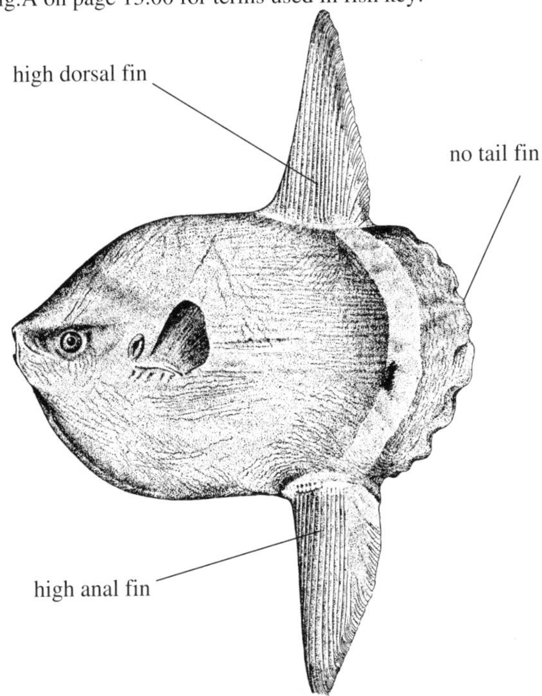

Fig.A. ***MOLA MOLA*, OCEAN SUNFISH:** Dark gray; up to 3 m (10') long, but usually less than 2 m (6 1/2'); frequently sighted at the surface during summer; tall dorsal fin often mistaken for a shark's fin, but it usually flops about and fans the water rather than remaining upright like a shark's dorsal fin. (family Molidae: molas)

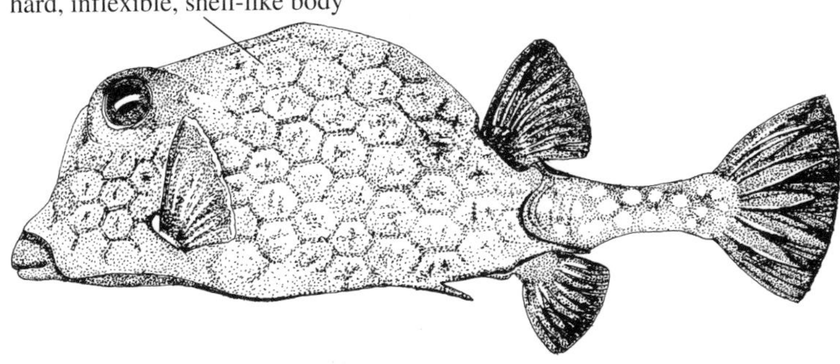

Fig.B. ***LACTOPHRYS TRIGONUS*, TRUNKFISH:** Pale blue-green with black blotches, pentagonal dot pattern; grows up to 45 cm (18") long in tropical waters; small juveniles stray into southern New England on rare occasions. (family Ostraciidae: boxfishes)

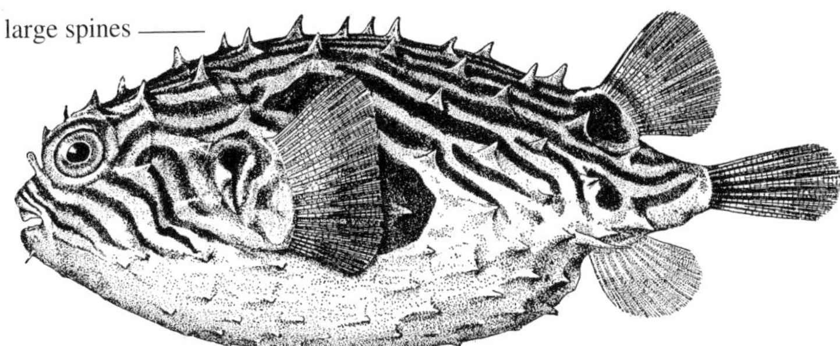

Fig.C. ***CHILOMYCTERUS SCHOEPFI*, STRIPED BURRFISH:** Green, olive, or brown above, belly pale tinted with yellow or orange; up to about 25 cm (10") long. (family Tetraodontidae: puffers)

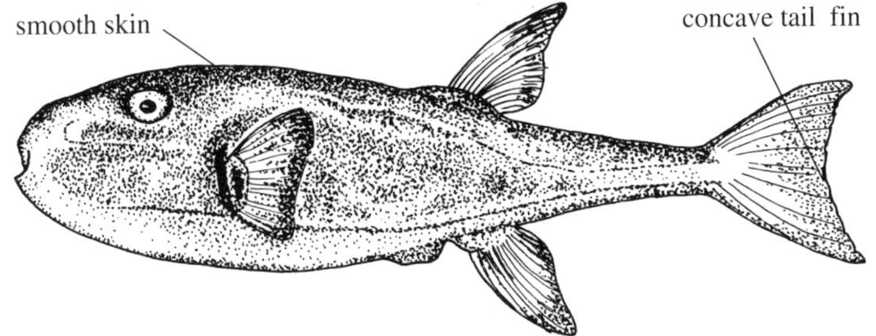

Fig.D. ***LAGOCEPHALUS LAEVIGATUS*, SMOOTH PUFFER:** Dark green above, silvery white below; reported up to 60 cm (2') long but usually much smaller in southern New England. (family Tetraodontidae: puffers)

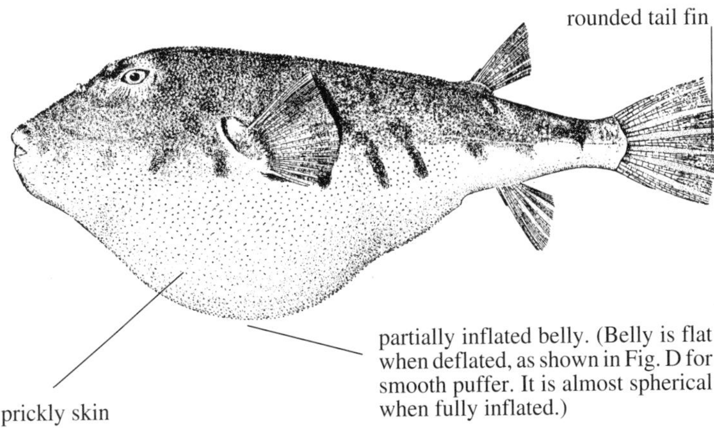

Fig.E. ***SPHOEROIDES MACULATUS*, NORTHERN PUFFER:** Dark olive green or brown above, sides yellow or orange, belly white; up to 25 cm (10") long; the most common puffer in this region. (family Tetraodontidae: puffers)

FLATFISHES : CLASS OSTEICHTHYES, ORDER PLEURONECTIFORMES

Bony fishes that lie flat on one side, both eyes on same side.

(Fish key begins on page 13.00)

#1.Both eyes are on right side (see Fig.D) .... **right-eyed flatfishes** (Figs.A-C), #2
#1.Both eyes are on left side (see Fig.D) .... **left-eyed flatfishes** (Figs.E-H), #4

#2.Upper jaw projects beyond lower jaw; no pectoral[1] fins; no space between ventral and anal fins .... ***Trinectes maculatus*, hogchoker** (Fig.C)
#2.Upper jaw does not project beyond lower jaw; with pectoral fins; with a space between ventral and anal fins (Figs.A,B) .... #3

#3.Lateral line is nearly straight, slightly arched above pectoral fins; 60-76 rays in dorsal fin .... ***Pleuronectes americanus*, winter flounder** (Fig.A)
#3.Lateral line is highly arched above pectoral fins; with 76-85 rays in dorsal fin .... ***Pleuronectes ferrugineus*, yellowtail flounder** (Fig.B)

#4.Teeth very small, not obvious .... #5
#4.With sharply pointed, obvious teeth .... #6

#5.With large mouth; lateral line[1] highly arched; with wide ventral fin; small scales .... ***Scophthalmus aquosus*, windowpane** (Fig.E)
#5.With small mouth; lateral line nearly straight; with narrow ventral fin; large scales .... ***Etropus microstomus*, smallmouth flounder** (Fig.F)

#6.With 4 large, prominent, black "eye" spots; 85-94 rays in dorsal[1] fin .... ***Paralichthys oblongus*, fourspot flounder** (Fig.G)
#6.With or without numerous small dark spots, not "eye" spots; with 72-81 rays in dorsal fin .... ***Paralichthys dentatus*, summer flounder** (Fig.H)

[1]Refer to Fig. A on page 13.00 for terms used in fish key.

RIGHT-EYED FLATFISHES

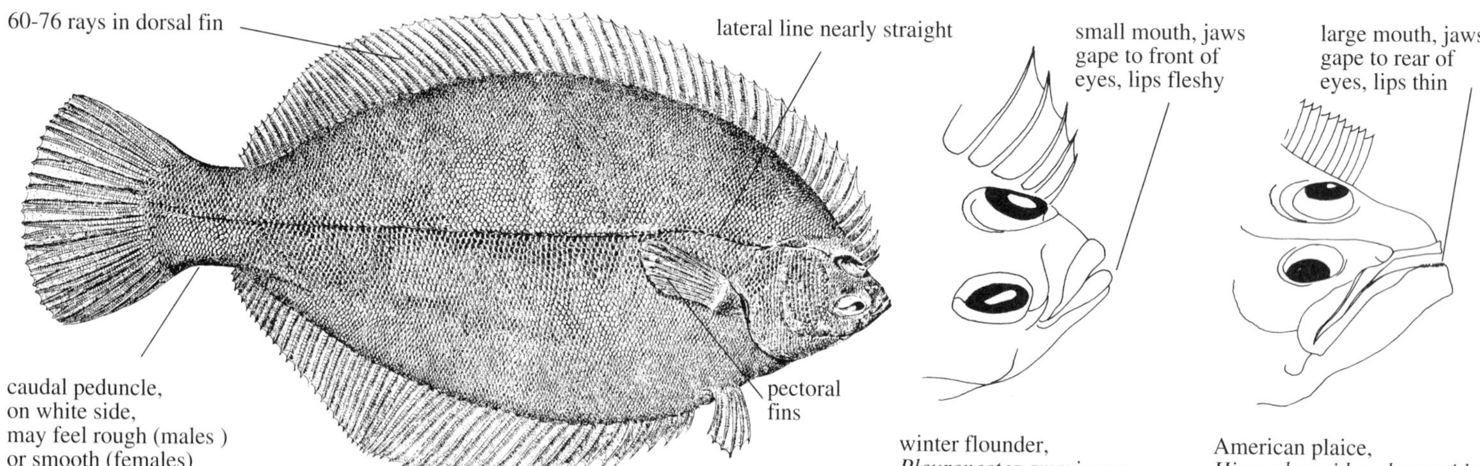

Fig.A. ***PLEURONECTES AMERICANUS (=Pseudopleuronectes a.)*, WINTER FLOUNDER:** Brown on side with eyes, white on other side; usually less than 35 cm (14") long; very common throughout southern New England; the sex of mature winter flounder, about 20 cm (8") or longer, can be determined by rubbing forward on the caudal peduncle on the white side. Males are rough and females are smooth. This difference is most obvious in the spring when they are spawning. American plaice, *Hippoglossoides platessoides*, are common in Gulf of Maine waters over 40 m (125') deep and colder than 13°C (55°F). They rarely stray into shallow estuarine waters. They can be distinguished from winter flounder by the size of the jaw as shown above. (family Pleuronectidae: righteye flounders)

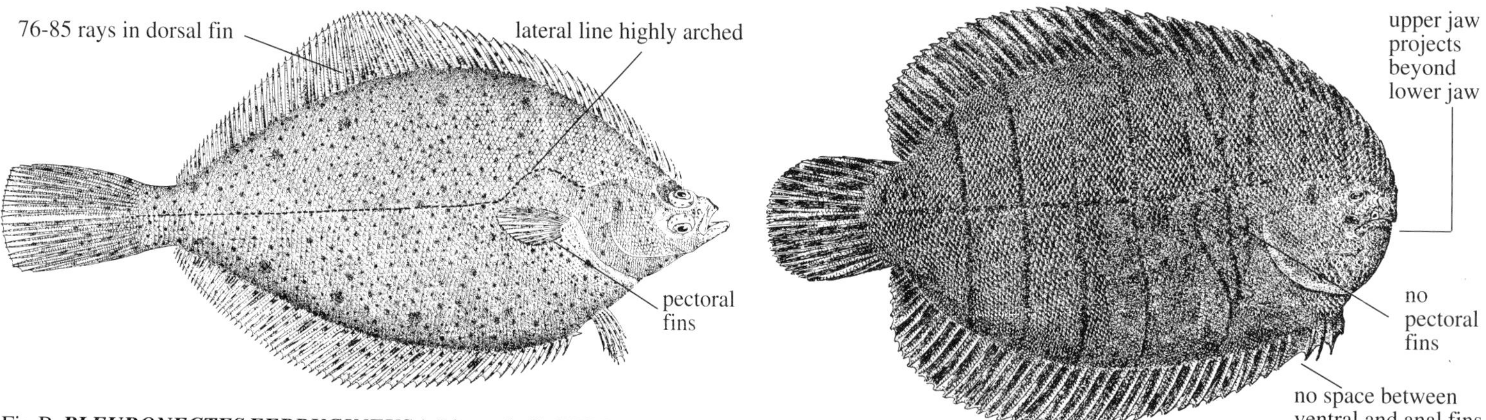

Fig.B. ***PLEURONECTES FERRUGINEUS (=Limanda f.)*, YELLOWTAIL FLOUNDER:** Brown on eyed side, white on other side, tail fin and long fin margins are yellow; usually less than 45 cm (18") long; not common in estuarine waters. (family Pleuronectidae: righteye flounders)

Fig.C. ***TRINECTES MACULATUS*, HOGCHOKER:** Brown on side with eyes, white on other side; up to 20 cm (8") long; occasionally found in bays and sounds, common in some estuaries. (family Soleidae: soles)

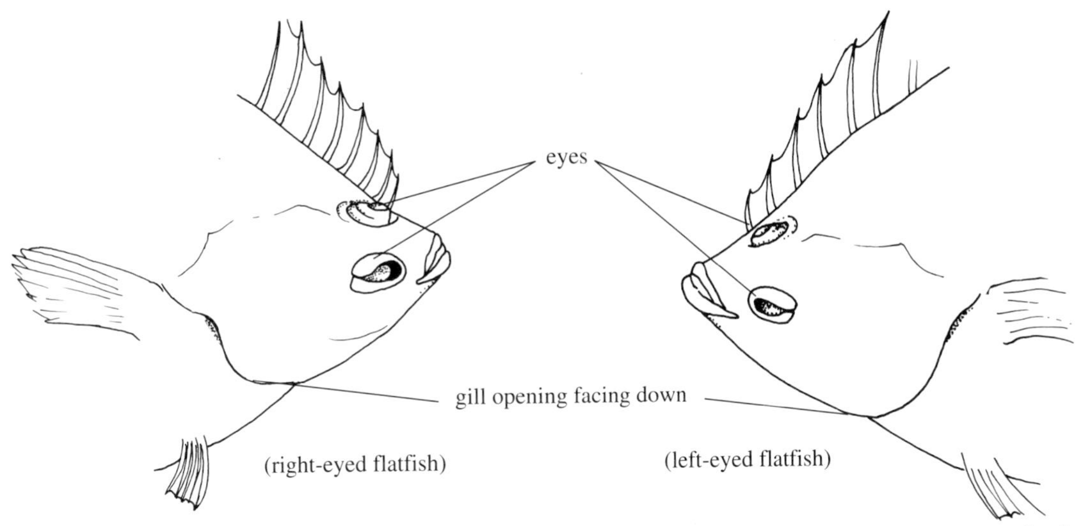

Fig.D. Hold the fish with the gill openings facing down and with the head pointing away from you. Determine if the eyes are on the right or left side of the fish.

LEFT-EYED FLATFISHES

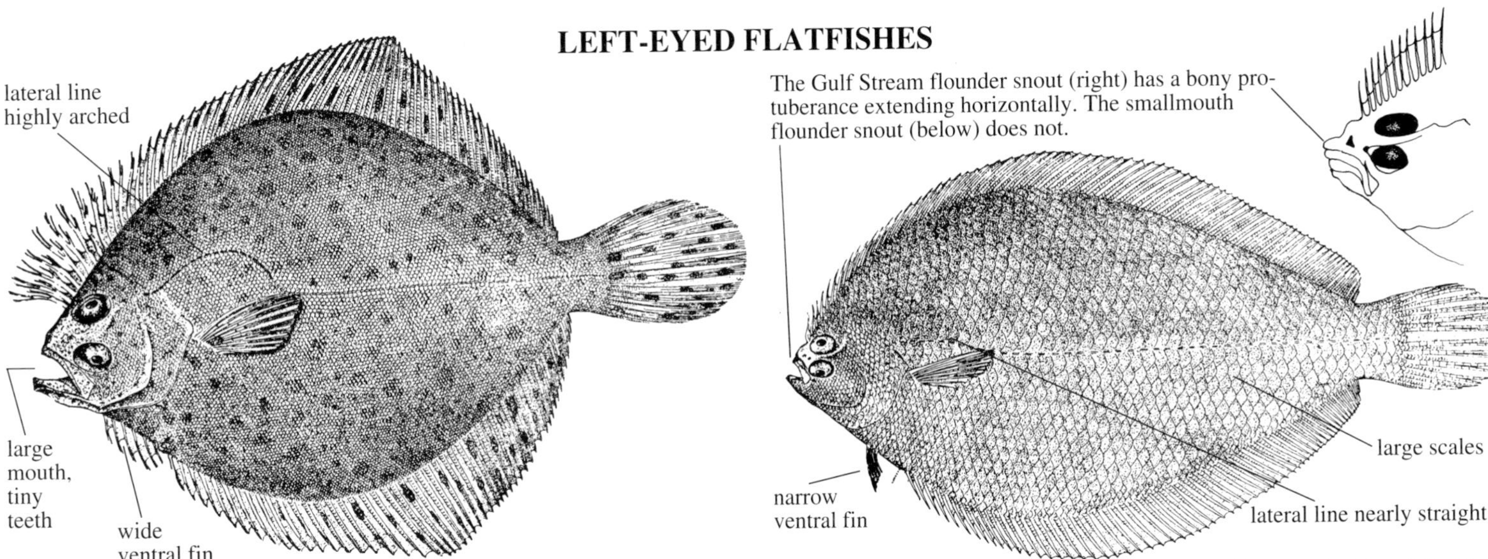

Fig.E. ***SCOPHTHALMUS AQUOSUS*, WINDOWPANE (=sand dab):** Brown with dark and light spots on eyed side, white on other side; up to about 40 cm (16") long; very common throughout southern New England. (family Bothidae: lefteye flounders) **17.16 B**

Fig.F. ***ETROPUS MICROSTOMUS*, SMALLMOUTH FLOUNDER:** Brownish with darker blotches on eyed side; up to 15 cm (6") long; not common. The Gulf Stream flounder, *Citharichthys arctifrons*, is nearly identical to the smallmouth flounder but rarely occurs in waters less than 22 m (72') deep. The two species have different shaped snouts as shown above. (family Bothidae: lefteye flounders)

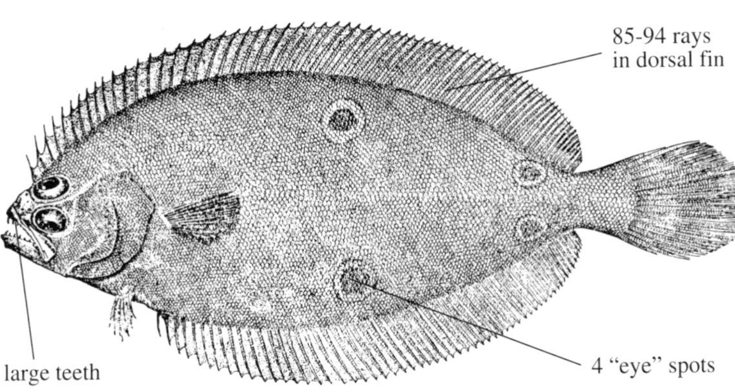

Fig.G. ***PARALICHTHYS OBLONGUS*, FOURSPOT FLOUNDER (=fluke):** Brown on eyed side with four conspicuous black eye spots edged with pink; white on other side; up to 30 cm (12") long; common. (family Bothidae: lefteye flounders)

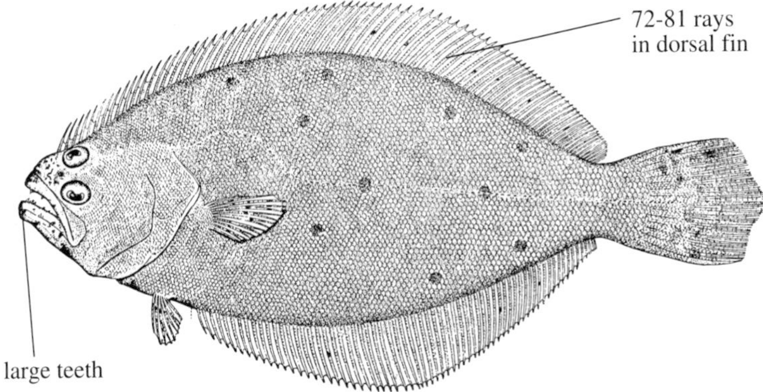

Fig.H. ***PARALICHTHYS DENTATUS*, SUMMER FLOUNDER (=fluke):** Brown on side with eyes, often with darker spots, white on other side; up to 1 m (39") long; common from mid-spring through mid-fall. (family Bothidae: lefteye flounders)

FISHES WITH A SINGLE SOFT RAYED DORSAL[1] FIN PRECEDED BY FREE STANDING SPINES, TUBERCLES, OR A VERY SMALL SPINY FIN

(Fish key begins on page 13.00)

#1.Elongate fish, not particularly deep and thin (Figs.A-E); head region in front of eyes ("forehead") is straight and flat .... #2
#1.Very deep, thin fish, with body flattened from side to side (Figs.F-K); head region in front of eyes ("forehead") is high and arched .... #6

#2.With rows of pointed tubercles ("bumps") along back and sides; with a sharklike tail fin, the upper lobe much longer than the lower; pelvic fins are not spiny .... ***Acipenser* spp., sturgeons** (Fig.E)
#2.With free standing spines in front of dorsal fin; tail fin is not sharklike; pelvic fins have a single, large stout spine (Figs.A-D) .... **sticklebacks**, #3

#3.With 7 or more dorsal spines .... ***Pungitius pungitius*, ninespine stickleback** (Fig.A)
#3.With 5 or fewer dorsal spines (Figs.B-D) .... #4

#4.No plates on sides; 3-4 free standing spines (another spine is attached to the front of the soft dorsal fin) ...***Apeltes quadracus*, fourspine stickleback** (Fig.B)
#4.With many scalelike plates on sides (these plates are nearly transparent, so examine fish very carefully); usually with 3 free standing spines (rarely 2 or 4 spines); the rear spine is just in front of the soft dorsal fin, but not attached to it (Figs.C,D) .... ***Gasterosteus* spp.**, #5

#5.Pelvic fins have one soft ray and a spine; the pelvic fin spine has 1 pointed tooth at base (fig.C); caudal peduncle has a keel (flat ridge) on each side; color of living fish is green, blue, or silvery, without round black spots .... ***Gasterosteus aculeatus*, threespine stickleback** (Fig.C)
#5.Pelvic fins have two soft rays and a spine; the pelvic fin spine has 2 pointed teeth at base (fig.D); caudal peduncle does not have a keel (flat ridge) on each side; color of living fish is lemon yellow with round black spots on sides .... ***Gasterosteus wheatlandi*, blackspotted stickleback** (Fig.D)

#6.With a single dorsal spine, located over the eyes (Figs.F,G) and well in front of dorsal fins .... **leatherjackets (filefishes and triggerfishes)**, #7
#6.With four or more dorsal spines, located just in front of dorsal fin (Figs.H-K) [Spines may be very tiny. Scrape fingernail forward to detect spines.] .... #8

#7.With ventral spine (spine on belly) .... ***Monacanthus hispidus*, planehead filefish** (Fig.F)
#7.Without ventral spine .... ***Aluterus schoepfi*, orange filefish** (Fig.G)

#8.Head region in front of eyes ("forehead") is concave (curves inward) (Figs.H,I) .... #9
#8.Head region in front of eyes ("forehead") is convex (curves outward) (Figs.J,K) .... #10

#9.With long extensions at front of dorsal and anal fins .... ***Selene vomer*, lookdown** (Fig.H)
#9.Without long extensions of dorsal and anal fins .... ***Selene setapinnis*, Atlantic moonfish** (Fig.I)

#10.With long threadlike extensions of numerous dorsal and anal fin rays .... ***Alectis ciliaris*, African pompano** (Fig.J)
#10.Without threadlike extensions .... ***Trachinotus* spp.** (Fig.K)

[1]Refer to Fig.A. on page 13.00 for terms used in fish key.

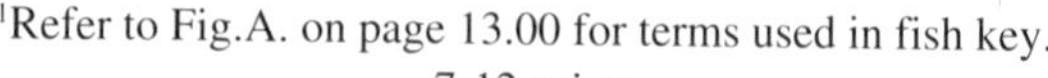

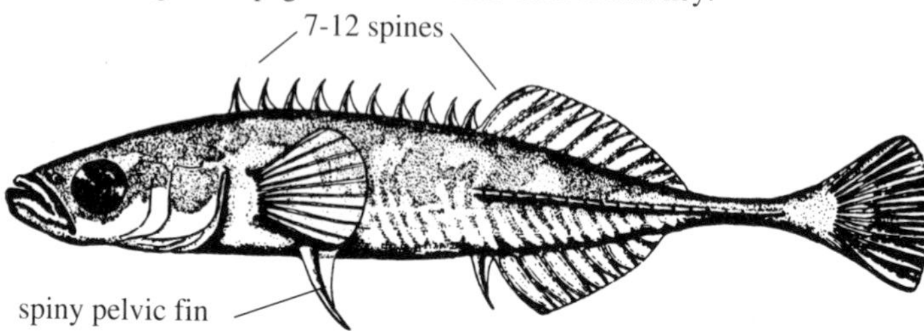

Fig.A. ***PUNGITIUS PUNGITIUS*, NINESPINE STICKLEBACK:** Olive green on top, sides blotchy, belly silvery; average about 5 cm (2") long; common nearshore in eelgrass beds and marshes. (family Gasterosteidae: sticklebacks)

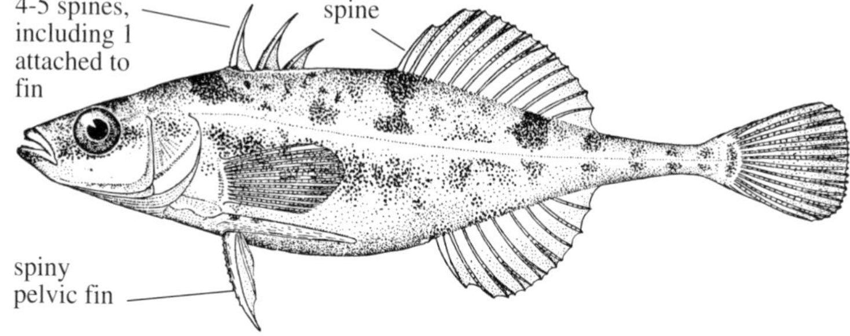

Fig.B. ***APELTES QUADRACUS*, FOURSPINE STICKLEBACK:** Olive green on top, sides mottled, belly silvery; 3-6 cm (1 1/4 - 2 1/2") long; very common in eelgrass beds and marshes. (family Gasterosteidae: sticklebacks)

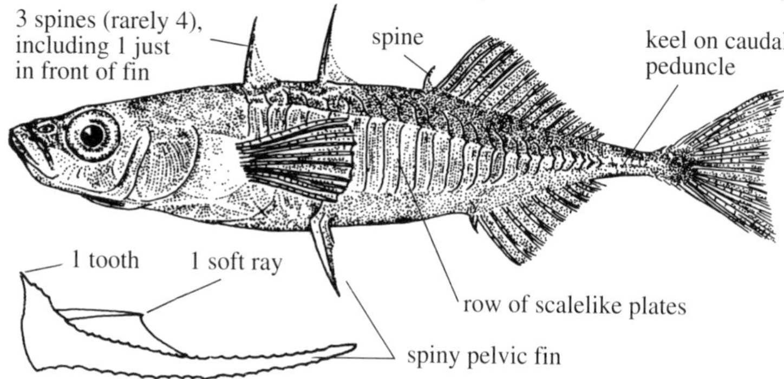

Fig.C. ***GASTEROSTEUS ACULEATUS*, THREESPINE STICKLEBACK:** Grayish or olive green on top, silvery on sides; rarely over 8 cm (3") long; very common nearshore in estuaries. (family Gasterosteidae: sticklebacks)

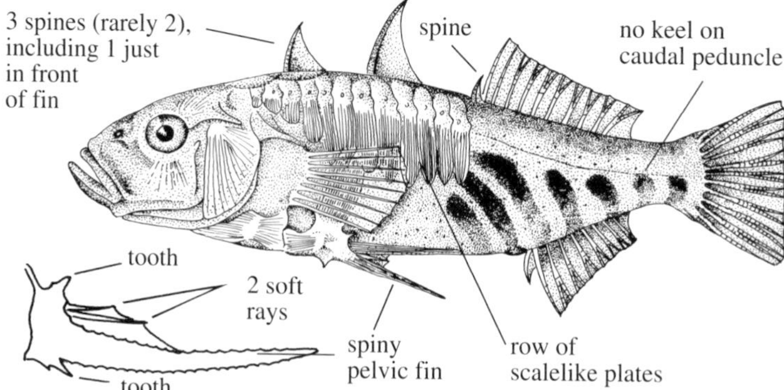

Fig.D. ***GASTEROSTEUS WHEATLANDI*, BLACKSPOTTED STICKLEBACK:** Yellow-green above with black spots on sides, silvery below; up to 8 cm (3") long; occurs nearshore. (family Gasterosteidae: sticklebacks)

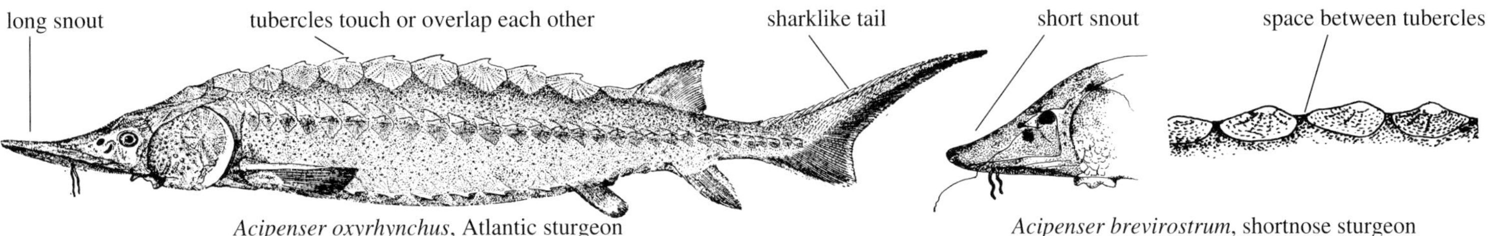

Fig.E. ***ACIPENSER* SPP., STURGEONS:** The Atlantic sturgeon, *A. oxyrhynchus*, is green, gray, or brown on top, pale below; up to 4 m (13') long, usually less than 2 m (6 1/2'). The shortnose sturgeon, *A. brevirostrum*, is similar to the Atlantic sturgeon but is smaller, with a maximum length of 90 cm (35"), has a much shorter snout, and has spaces between the tubercles on its back. It is a rare and endangered species. (family Acipenseridae: sturgeons)

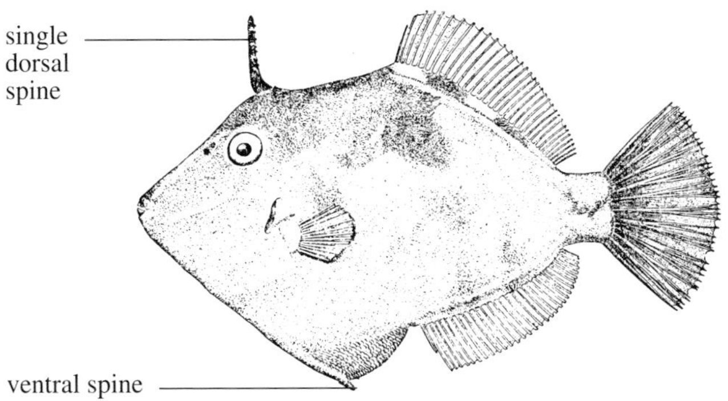

Fig.F. ***MONACANTHUS HISPIDUS*, PLANEHEAD FILEFISH:** Greenish; usually under 10 cm (4") long, up to 25 cm (10"). (family Balistidae: leatherjackets)

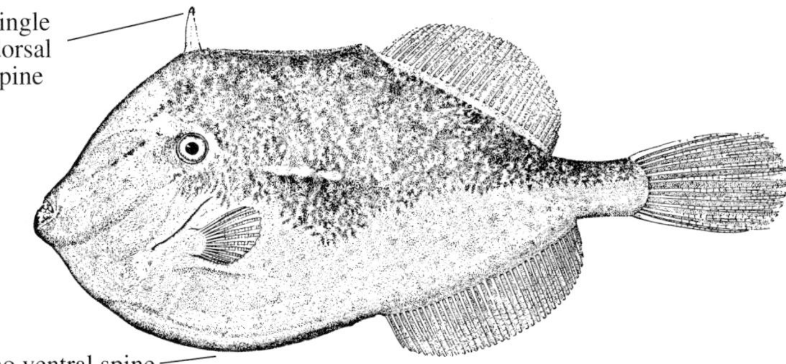

Fig.G. ***ALUTERUS SCHOEPFI*, ORANGE FILEFISH:** Orange or grayish; usually under 25 cm (10") long in our region. (family Balistidae: leatherjackets)

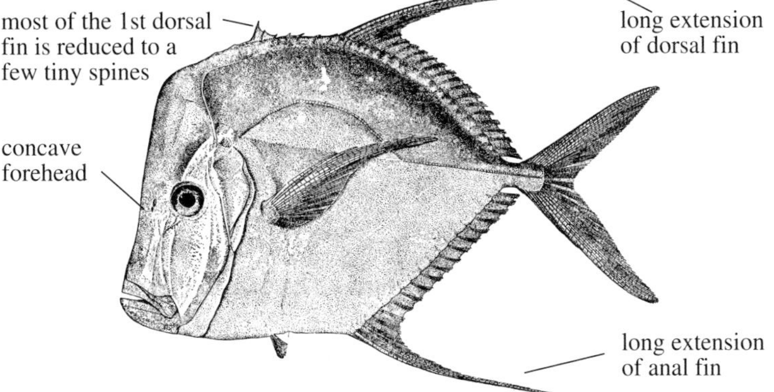

Fig.H. ***SELENE VOMER*, LOOKDOWN:** Very thin, silvery body; usually less than 5 cm (2") long in southern New England, but up to 30 cm (1') elsewhere. (family Carangidae: jacks)

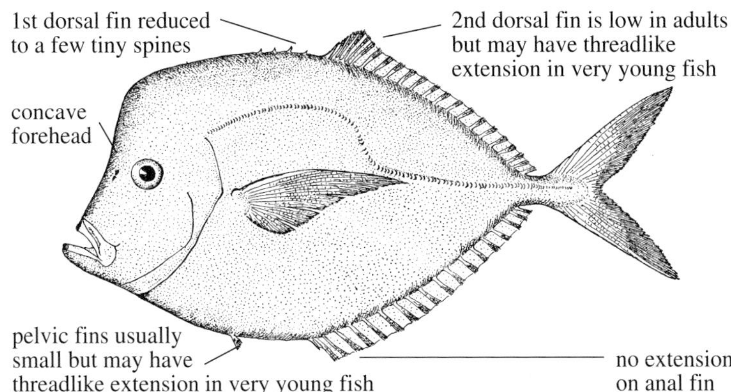

Fig.I. ***SELENE SETAPINNIS*, ATLANTIC MOONFISH:** Very thin, silvery body; usually less than 5 cm (2") long locally but up to 25 cm (10") elsewhere. (family Carangidae: jacks)

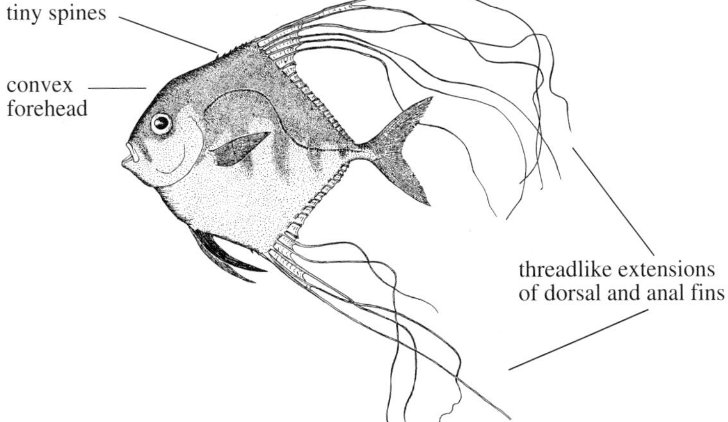

Fig.J. ***ALECTIS CILIARIS (=A. crinitis)*, AFRICAN POMPANO:** Very thin with silver sides; rarely over 10 cm (4") long; occasionally found near shore in late summer and early fall. (family Carangidae: jacks)

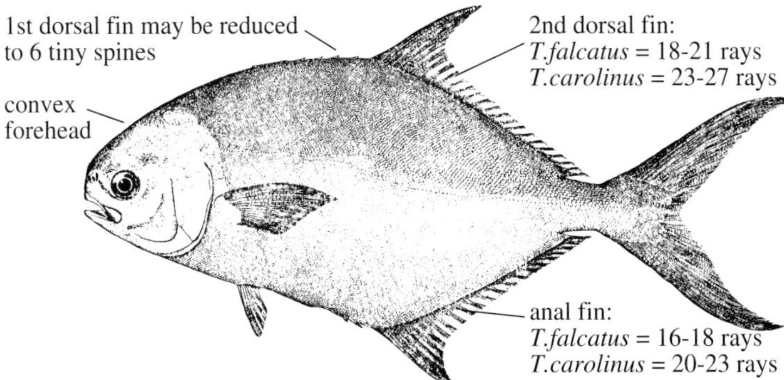

Fig.K. ***TRACHINOTUS* SPP.:** The Florida pompano, *T. carolinus*, is blue or green on back, silvery on sides, yellowish below, fins yellowish; grows to 43 cm (17") long. The permit, *T. falcatus*, is silvery on sides, fins are reddish when young; grows to 80 cm (31") long (see p.13.24, Fig.B). Adults of both species are rare in this region but young permit are occasionally caught in seines near shore. Count fin rays to determine the species. (family Carangidae: jacks)

HERRINGS, ANCHOVIES, AND BUTTERFISHES

Fishes with a single, all soft rayed dorsal[1] fin, and a forked caudal ("tail") fin

(Fish key begins on page 13.00)

#1.Last dorsal fin ray much longer than other rays .... ***Dorosoma cepedianum*, gizzard shad** (Fig.B)
#1.Last dorsal fin ray is not longer than the other rays (Figs. C-L) .... #2

#2.The entire anal fin is behind the dorsal fin (Figs.C-H) .... **family Clupeidae, herrings**, #3
#2.All or the front part of the anal fin is below the dorsal fin (Figs.J-L) .... #8

#3.Large head (from tip of snout to back edge of gill cover) is nearly 1/3 total body length (from tip of snout to rear end of caudal peduncle, see Fig.C); pelvic fins with 7 rays; rear margins of scales are straight and edged with comblike teeth .... ***Brevoortia tyrannus*, Atlantic menhaden** (Fig.C)
#3.Head is 1/4 or less total body length (Figs.D-H); pelvic fins with 8 or 9 rays; rear margins of scales are rounded and smooth .... #4

#4.Dorsal fin begins about midway between head (tip of snout) and start of tail (rear end of caudal peduncle); edge of belly is only slightly saw toothed .... ***Clupea harengus*, Atlantic herring** (Fig.D)
#4.Dorsal fin begins nearer head than tail; edge of belly is very saw toothed (Figs.E-H) .... #5

#5.Tip of lower jaw projects noticeably beyond the upper jaw when mouth is closed; with 18-23 gill rakers (see Fig.A) on lower limb of first gill arch .... ***Alosa mediocris*, hickory shad** (Fig.E)
#5.Tip of lower jaw does not project much beyond the upper jaw when mouth is closed (Figs.F-H); more than 25 gill rakers on lower limb of first gill arch ... #6

#6.Upper edge of lower jaw rises at a slight angle and is nearly straight (Fig.I); tongue is visible in profile when mouth is open (Fig.I); cheek bone (Fig.I) is higher than long .... ***Alosa sapidissima*, American shad** (Fig.F)
#6.Upper edge of lower jaw rises in a steep concave curve (Fig.I); tongue not visible in profile when mouth is open; cheek bone length nearly equals height .. #7

#7.Snout (distance from front edge of eye to tip of upper jaw) is shorter than diameter of eye; lining of belly cavity (slit belly open with knife and look inside) is usually pale grayish or pinkish white; with 38-44 gill rakers on lower limb of first gill arch .... ***Alosa pseudoharengus*, alewife** (Fig.G)
#7.Snout length equals eye diameter; lining of belly cavity is usually blackish; with 41-52 gill rakers on lower limb of first gill arch in adult .... ***Alosa aestivalis*, blueback herring** (Fig.H)

#8.Deep, thin body; jaws do not extend back beyond eyes; dorsal fin about same size as anal fin (Fig.J) .... #9
#8.Elongate body; jaws extend well behind eyes; dorsal fin shorter than anal fin (Figs.K,L) .... **family Engraulidae, anchovies**, #10

#9.Without pelvic fins; single dorsal fin is entirely soft rayed; no spines in front of dorsal fin .... ***Peprilus triacanthus*, butterfish** (Fig.J)
#9.With pelvic fins; with a small spiny rayed dorsal fin or tiny separated spines in front of soft rayed dorsal fin (scrape your fingernail forward along the fish's back in front of the soft rayed dorsal fin to feel if there are any spines) .... **pompanos and other members of the jack family,** page 13.12

#10.Anal fin begins under front of dorsal fin; with indistinct silvery horizontal stripe; 24-27 rays in anal fin .... ***Anchoa mitchilli*, bay anchovy** (Fig.K)
#10.Anal fin begins under rear of dorsal fin; with distinct silvery horizontal stripe; 20-21 rays in anal fin .... ***Anchoa hepsetus*, striped anchovy** (Fig.L)

[1]Refer to Fig. A on page 13.00 for terms used in fish key.

gill cover, lifted and folded forward
upper limb
lower limb
gill rakers
gill filaments
gill arch

Fig.A. **GILL RAKERS:** Gill rakers are rodlike or knoblike bony projections of the gill arch, directed toward the snout on the inner edge of the arch.

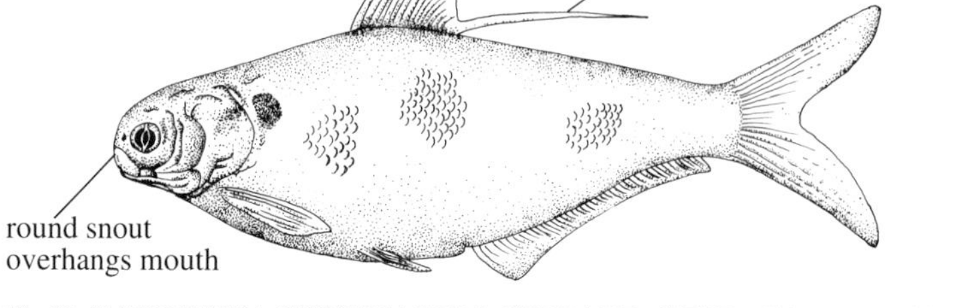

Fig.B. ***DOROSOMA CEPEDIANUM*, GIZZARD SHAD:** Silvery on sides, white underneath, young have round dark spot behind operculum; up to 41 cm (16") long; strays into estuaries from freshwater. (family Clupeidae: herrings)

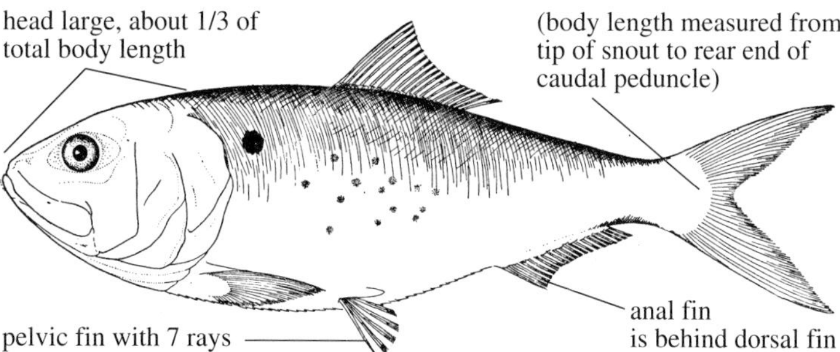

Fig.C. ***BREVOORTIA TYRANNUS*, ATLANTIC MENHADEN (=bunker =pogy):** Silvery sides, darker back; up to about 40 cm (16") long; very common in large schools often near surface. (family Clupeidae: herrings)

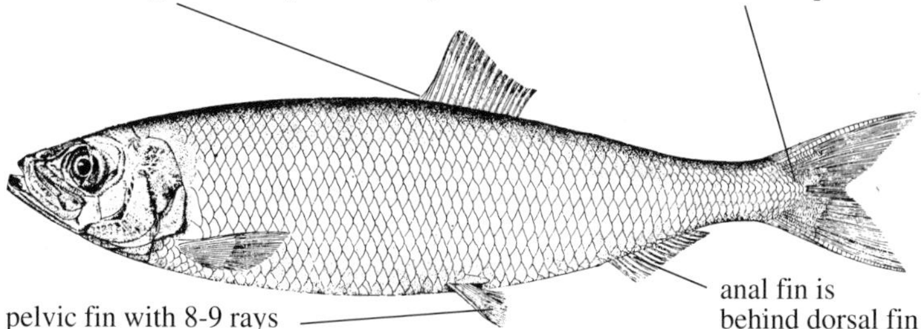

Fig.D. ***CLUPEA HARENGUS*, ATLANTIC HERRING:** Green or blue on top, silvery on sides; up to 46 cm (18") long. (family Clupeidae: herrings)

dorsal fin begins nearer tip of snout than rear end of caudal peduncle
lower jaw projects well beyond upper jaw when mouth is closed
edge of belly is saw toothed
pelvic fin with 8-9 rays
anal fin is behind dorsal fin

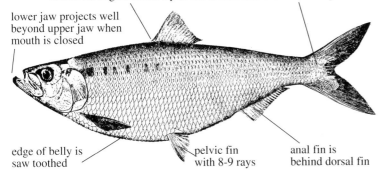

Fig.E. ***ALOSA MEDIOCRIS*, HICKORY SHAD:** Grayish-green above, silvery below; usually 25-45 cm (10-18") long. (family Clupeidae: herrings)

dorsal fin begins nearer tip of snout than rear end of caudal peduncle
snout is shorter than eye diameter
lower jaw projects only slightly beyond upper jaw when mouth is closed
pelvic fin with 8-9 rays
anal fin is behind dorsal fin

Fig.G. ***ALOSA PSEUDOHARENGUS*, ALEWIFE:** Grayish-green on back, silvery sides; up to 40 cm (16") long. (family Clupeidae: herrings)

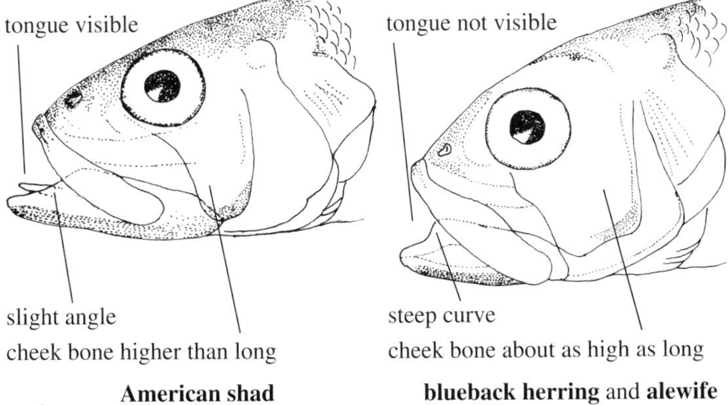

Fig.I. ***ALOSA* SPP.:** The American shad *(A. sapidissima)* can be distinguished from the alewife *(A. pseudoharengus)* and the blueback herring *(A. aestivalis)* using the characteristics shown above.

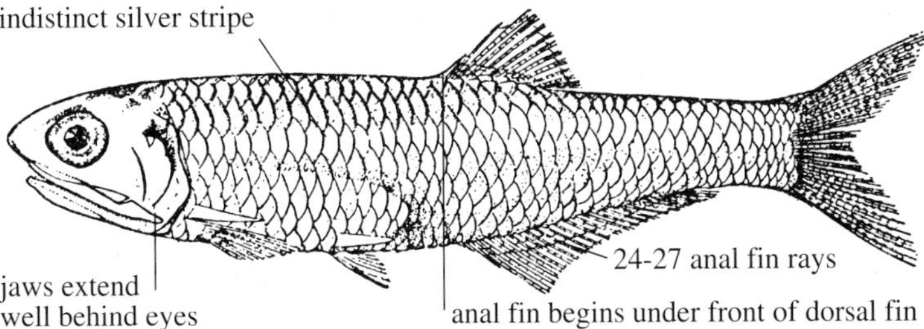

Fig.K. ***ANCHOA MITCHILLI*, BAY ANCHOVY:** Silvery with indistinct silvery horizontal stripe; up to about 9 cm (3 1/2") long. (family Engraulidae: anchovies)

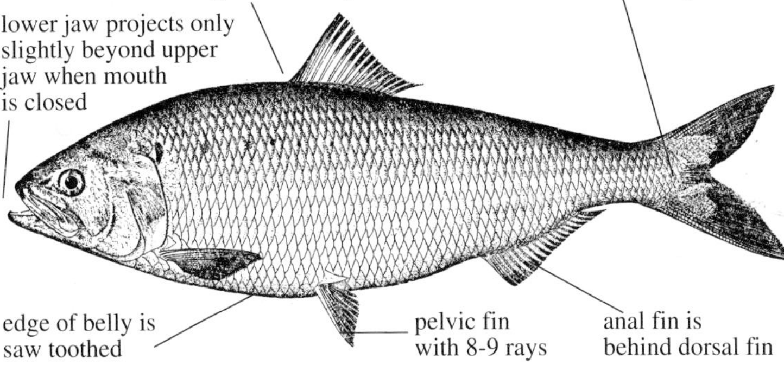

Fig.F. ***ALOSA SAPIDISSIMA*, AMERICAN SHAD:** Green or blue above, silvery on sides; less than 75 cm (30") long. (family Clupeidae: herrings)

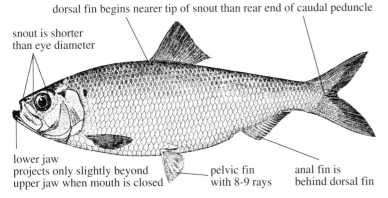

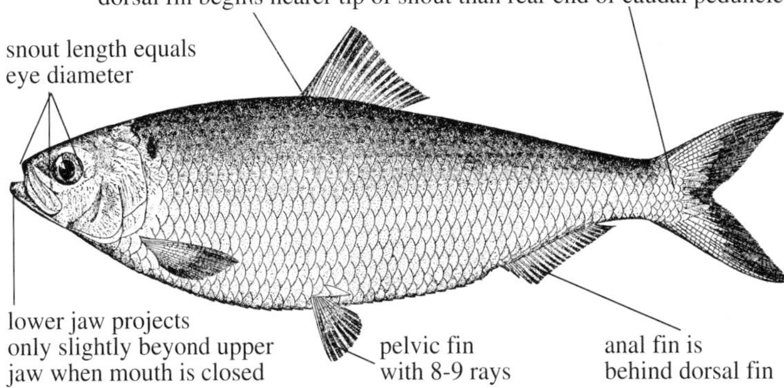

Fig.H. ***ALOSA AESTIVALIS*, BLUEBACK HERRING:** Bluish above, silvery on sides; usually less than 30 cm (12") long. (family Clupeidae: herrings)

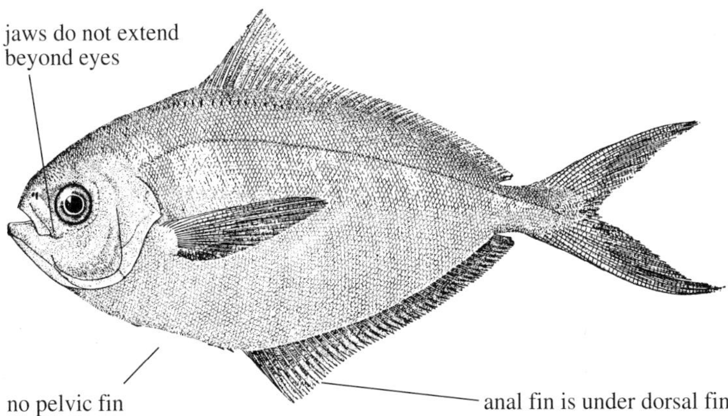

Fig.J. ***PEPRILUS TRIACANTHUS*, BUTTERFISH:** Grayish above, silvery on sides; usually less than 25 cm (10") long. (family Stromateidae: butterfishes)

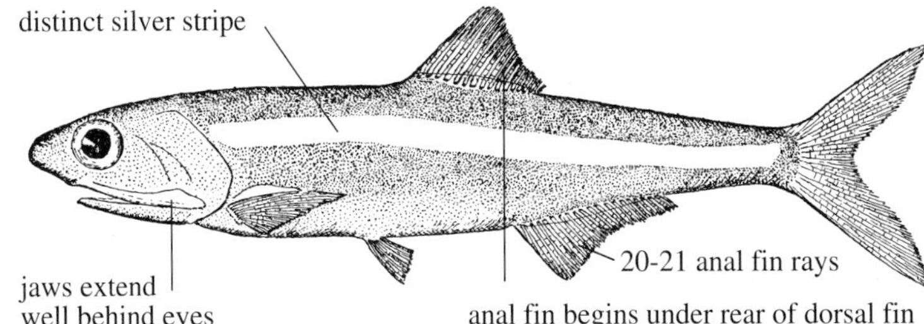

Fig.L. ***ANCHOA HEPSETUS*, STRIPED ANCHOVY:** Silvery with bright, silvery horizontal stripe; up to about 15 cm (6") long. (family Engraulidae: anchovies)

KILLIFISH FAMILY
CLASS OSTEICHTHYES, FAMILY CYPRINODONTIDAE

Fishes with a single, all soft rayed dorsal[1] fin; with pelvic fins; tail not forked.

(Fish key begins on page 13.00)

#1.Dorsal fin begins above or in front of rear tip of pectoral fins (Figs.A,B) .... #2
#1.Dorsal fin begins well behind rear end of pectoral fins (Figs.C-F) .... #3

#2.Deep bodied fish; tail fin is straight; large, wedge shaped teeth with 3 cutting edges (tricuspid) .... ***Cyprinodon variegatus*, sheepshead minnow** (Fig.A)
#2.Not particularly deep bodied; tail fin is rounded; teeth are small and pointed .... ***Lucania parva*, rainwater killifish** (Fig.B)

#3.Dorsal fin taller than long; 8 dorsal fin rays; base of dorsal fin shorter than base of anal fin .... ***Fundulus luciae*, spotfin killifish** (Fig.C)
#3.Dorsal fin as long or longer than tall; 10 or more dorsal fin rays; base of dorsal fin equal to or longer than base of anal fin (Figs.D-F) .... #4

#4.Snout is blunt, distance from eye to tip of snout is equal to eye diameter or less; with 10-12 rays in dorsal fin; without distinct black bands or stripes except when very young, may have indistinct silvery vertical bands .... ***Fundulus heteroclitus*, mummichog** (Fig.D)
#4.Snout is somewhat pointed, distance from eye to tip of snout is longer than eye diameter; with 13-15 rays in dorsal fin; with distinct black vertical or horizontal bands (Figs.E,F) .... #5

#5.Only found in fresh or slightly salty water; mature and immature fish of both sexes have vertical stripes only; base of dorsal fin is same length or shorter than distance from tip of snout to rear edge of eye .... ***Fundulus diaphanus*, banded killifish** (Fig.E)
#5.Very common in estuaries and bays where water is relatively salty or brackish; mature females have horizontal black stripes whereas males and immature females have vertical black stripes; base of dorsal fin is longer than distance from tip of snout to rear of eye .... ***Fundulus majalis*, striped killifish** (Fig.F)

[1]Refer to Fig.A on page 13.00 for terms used in fish key.

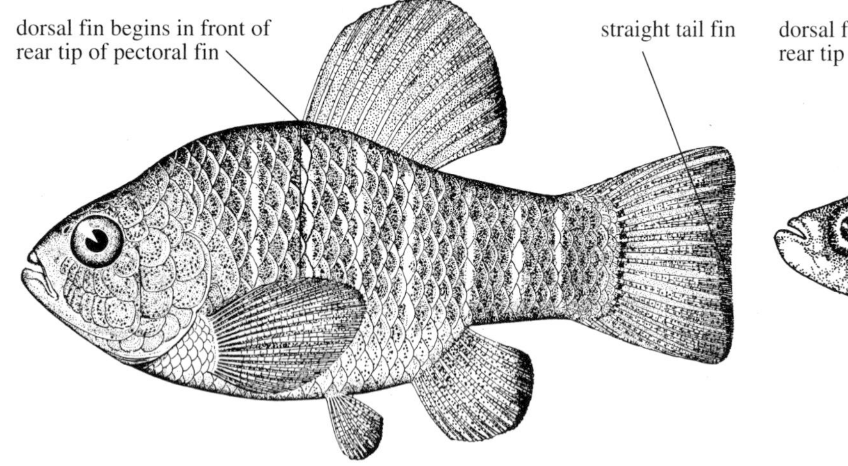

Fig.A. ***CYPRINODON VARIEGATUS*, SHEEPSHEAD MINNOW:** Greenish or brownish above, white below; up to 8 cm (3") long, usually less than 5 cm (2") long.

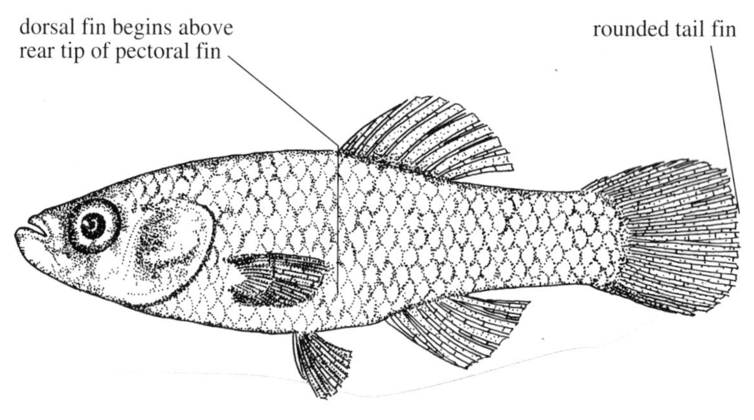

Fig.B. ***LUCANIA PARVA*, RAINWATER KILLIFISH:** Greenish on top, silvery below; up to 6 cm (2 1/2") long.

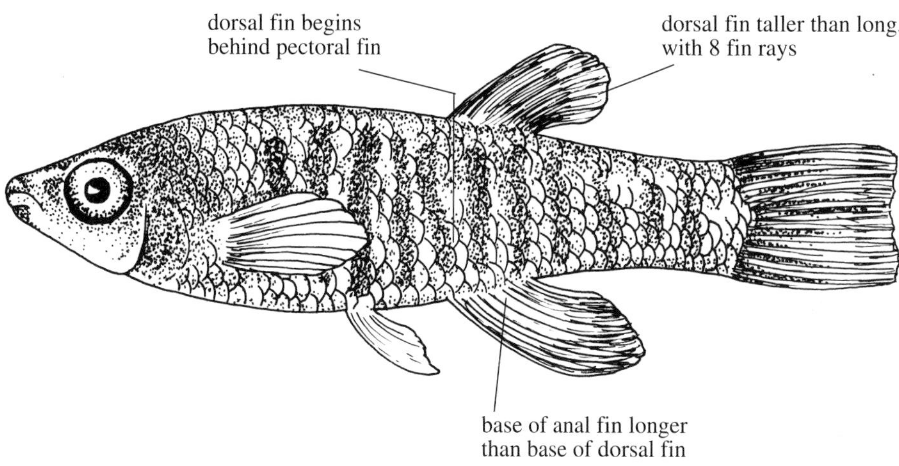

Fig.C. ***FUNDULUS LUCIAE*, SPOTFIN KILLIFISH:** Greenish above, pale below, fins are brownish; up to 5 cm (2") long.

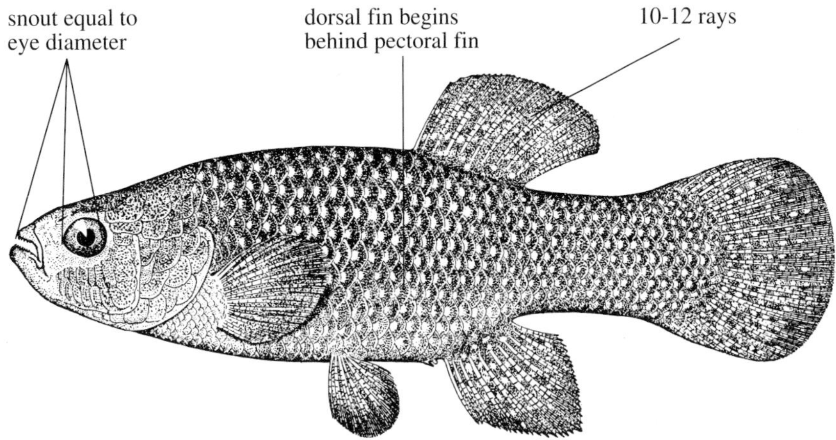

Fig.D. ***FUNDULUS HETEROCLITUS*, MUMMICHOG:** Brown or green, sometimes with lighter or darker indistinct vertical bands; usually 3-6 cm (1 -2 1/2") long, rarely over 10 cm (4") long; very common in estuaries, particularly near tidal marshes.

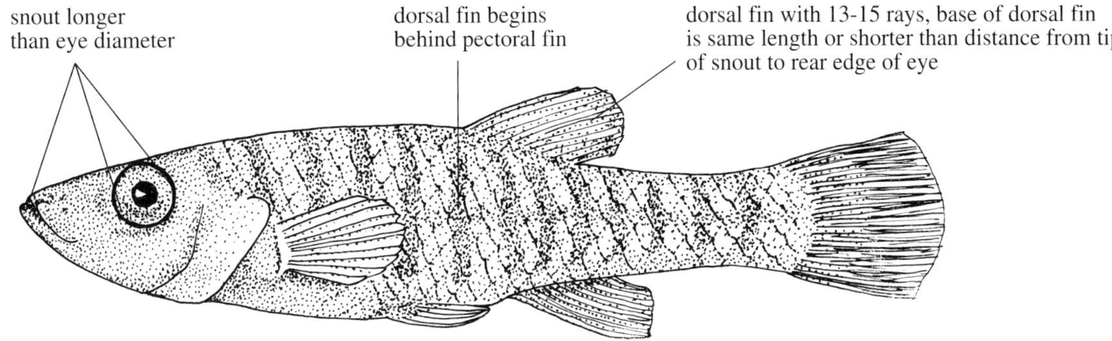

Fig.E. ***FUNDULUS DIAPHANUS*, BANDED KILLIFISH:** Olive green above, lighter below, with vertical bars on sides; up to 10 cm (4") long; only found in fresh or slightly brackish water

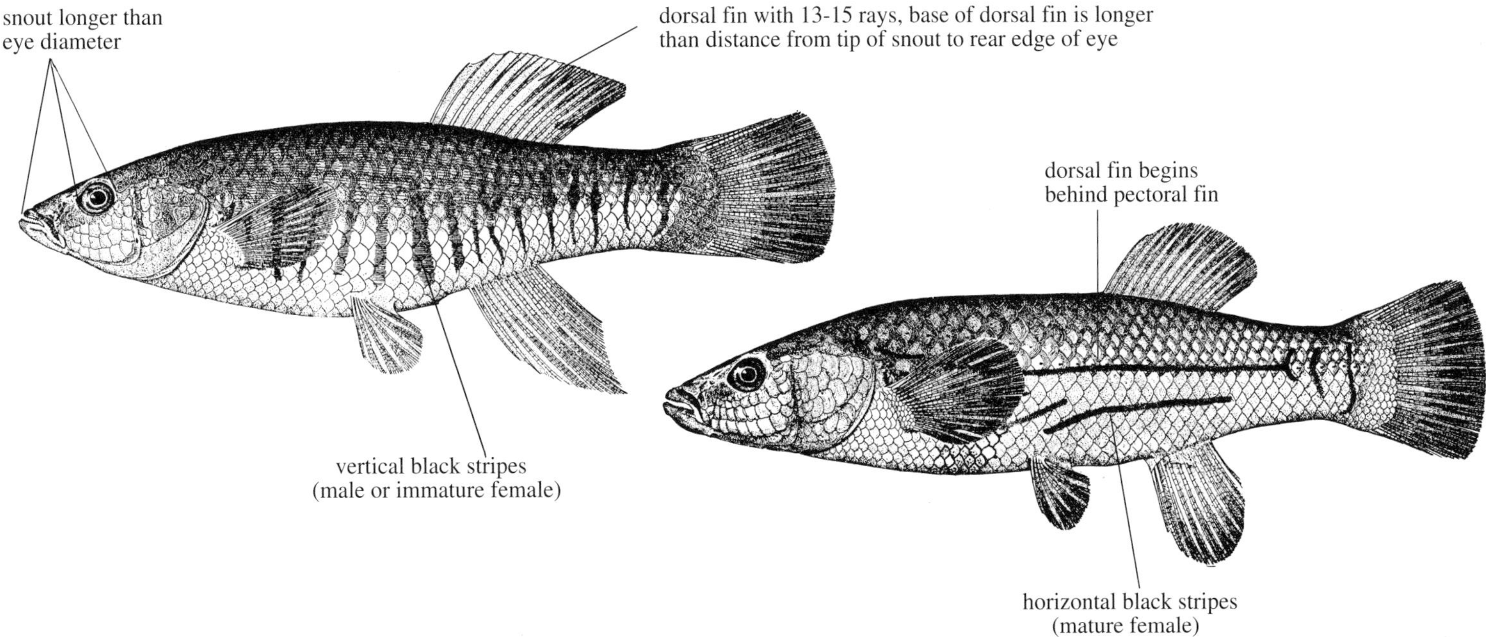

Fig.F. ***FUNDULUS MAJALIS*, STRIPED KILLIFISH:** Silvery sides with black horizontal or vertical stripes; usually 3-6 cm (1 - 2 1/2") long, rarely over 10 cm (4"); very common in estuaries, particularly near tidal marshes.

FISHES WITH A SINGLE DORSAL[1] FIN, PART SPINY AND PART SOFT RAYED

(Fish key begins on page 13.00)

#1.Caudal ("tail") fin is forked (curves deeply inward); pectoral fins are sharply pointed .... ***Stenotomus chrysops*, scup** (Fig.A)
#1.Caudal ("tail") fin is straight or rounded; pectoral fins are rounded (Figs.B-F) .... #2

#2.Bright red body; large eyes (Fig.B) with golden irises; pelvic fins are larger than the pectoral fins .... **family Priacanthidae, bigeyes,** #3
#2.Eyes are not golden or particularly large; pelvic fins are the same size or smaller than the pectoral fins (Figs.C-F) .... #4

#3.Depth of body about 1/2 length[2]; no obvious spine at rear lower corner of preopercle (cheekbone); 17-21 gill rakers[2].... ***Pristigenys alta*, short bigeye** (Fig.B)
#3.Depth of body about 2/5 length; with obvious spine (Fig.B) at corner of preopercle; 15-18 gill rakers .... ***Priacanthus cruentatus*, glasseye snapper** (Fig.B)
#3.Depth of body about 1/3 length; no obvious spine at rear lower corner of preopercle; 23-24 gill rakers .... ***Priacanthus arenatus*, bigeye** (Fig.B)

#4.Head region in front of eyes ("forehead") is concave (curves inward); with a black bar on head through eye and a large black spot on base of dorsal fin .... ***Chaetodon ocellatus*, spotfin butterflyfish** (Fig.C)
#4.Head region in front of eyes ("forehead") is flat or convex (curves outward); no black bar through eye; no spot on dorsal fin (Figs. D-F) .... #5

#5.Dorsal fin about half spiny rayed and half soft rayed; the anal fin is higher than long .... ***Centropristis striata,* black sea bass** (Fig.D)
#5.The soft rayed portion of the dorsal fin is much shorter than the spiny rayed portion; the anal fin is longer than high (Figs.E,F) .... #6

#6.With scales on gill covers; snout somewhat pointed; forehead (above eyes) rather flat; grows up to about 25 cm (10") long .... ***Tautogolabrus adspersus*, cunner** (Fig.E)
#6.Without scales on gill covers; snout blunt; forehead (above eyes) highly arched; grows up to about 90 cm (3') long .... ***Tautoga onitis*, tautog** (Fig.F)

[1]Refer to Fig. A on page 13.00 for terms used in fish key.
[2]Measure body length from tip of snout to rear end of caudal peduncle[1]. Count the gill rakers on the lower limb of first gill arch (see Fig.A on page 13.14).

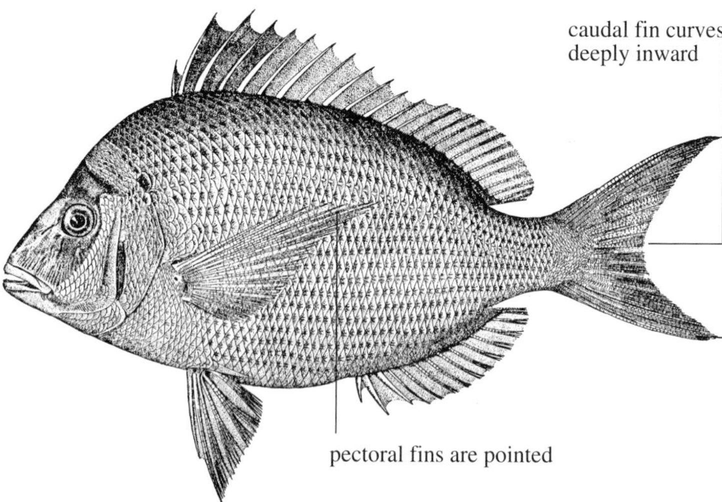

Fig.A. ***STENOTOMUS CHRYSOPS*, SCUP (=porgy):** Silvery, iridescent; usually less than 30 cm (12") long; very common in bays and sounds. (family Sparidae: porgies) **17.16 C**

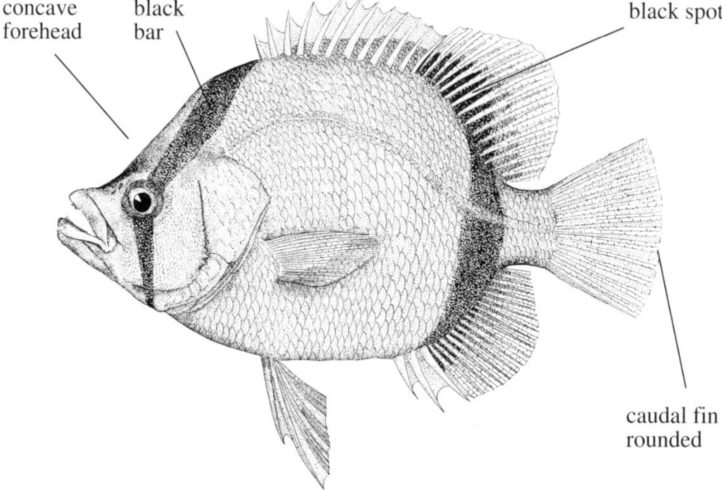

Fig.C. ***CHAETODON OCELLATUS*, SPOTFIN BUTTERFLYFISH:** White, with yellow fins, with a black band through eyes, with a dark spot on base of dorsal fin; up to 15 cm (6") long. (family Chaetodontidae: butterflyfishes)

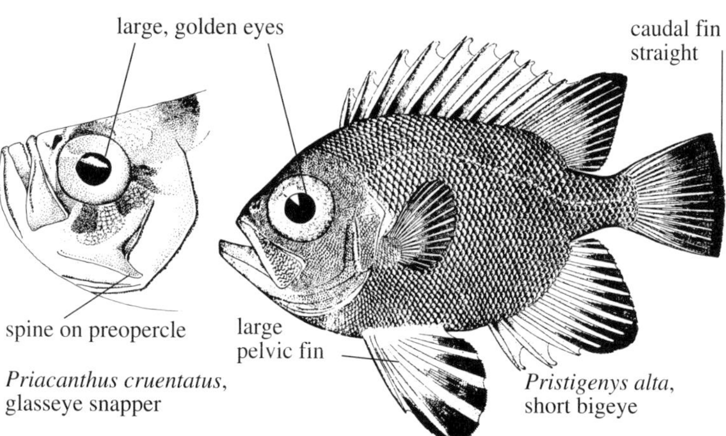

Fig.B. **FAMILY PRIACANTHIDAE, BIGEYES:** Bright red body, golden eyes; usually less than 8 cm (3") long, but may reach 30 cm (1'); refer to couplet #3 in the above key to identify the species.

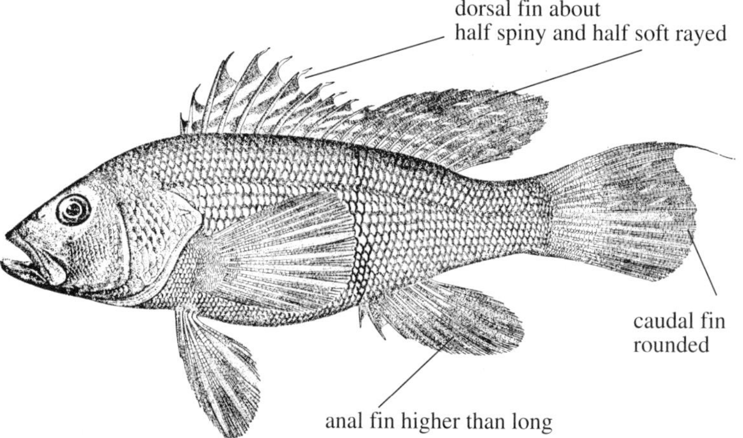

Fig.D. ***CENTROPRISTIS STRIATA*, BLACK SEA BASS:** Gray, brown, or blue-black; up to 50 cm (20") long. (family Serranidae: sea basses)

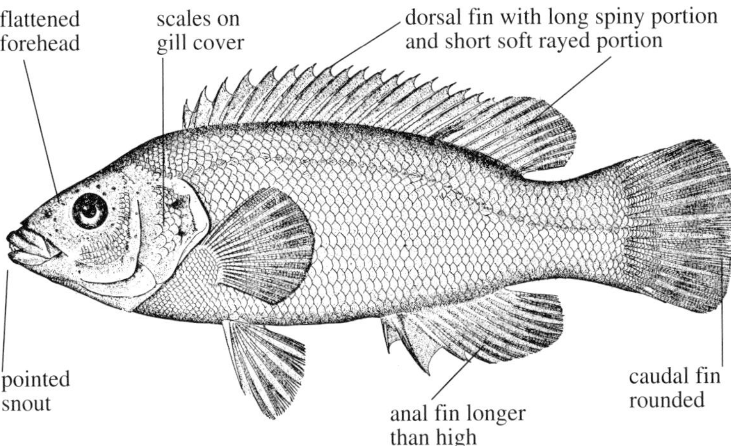

Fig.E. ***TAUTOGOLABRUS ADSPERSUS*, CUNNER (=bergall):** Color variable, often iridescent on a reddish-brown background, sometimes greenish when young; up to 25 cm (10") long; very common throughout southern New England. (family Labridae: wrasses)

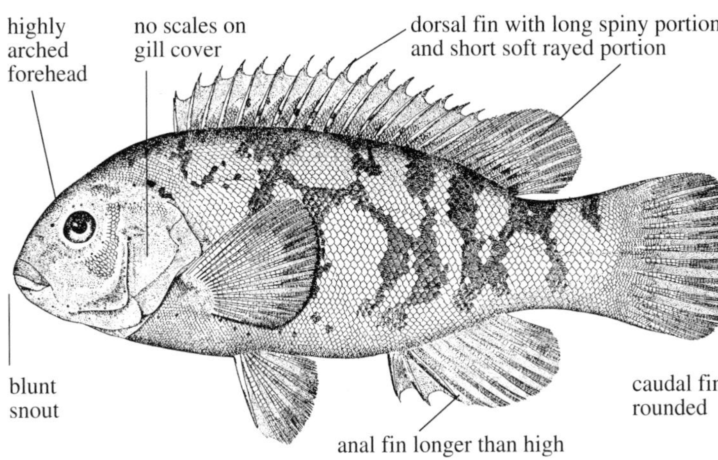

Fig.F. ***TAUTOGA ONITIS*, TAUTOG (=blackfish):** Black or gray, sometimes brown when young; up to about 90 cm (3') long; very common in bays and sounds, especially near rocks and boulders. (family Labridae: wrasses)

FISHES WITH A SUCTION DISC ON CHEST

(Fish key begins on page 13.00)

#1.With rows of pointed tubercles ("bumps") along back and sides .... ***Cyclopterus lumpus*, lumpfish** (Fig.A)
#1.Without rows of tubercles (Figs.B, C) .... #2

#2.Long anal fin, with more than 20 rays; tadpole shaped, body much broader than tail .... ***Liparis* spp., snailfishes** (Fig.B)
#2.Short anal fin, with about 11 rays; not tadpole shaped .... ***Gobiosoma* spp., gobies** (Fig.C)

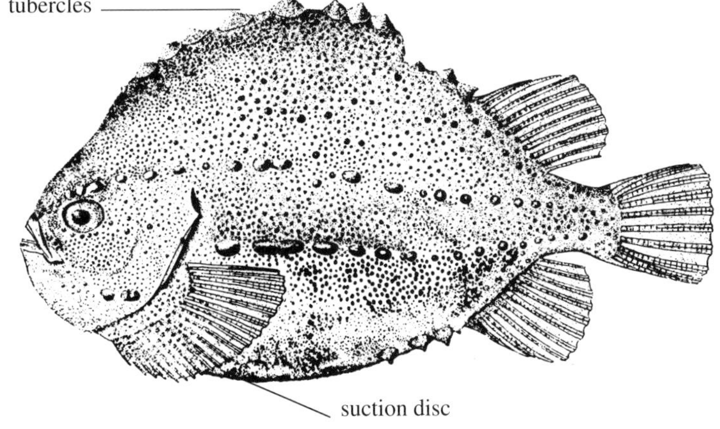

Fig.A. ***CYCLOPTERUS LUMPUS*, LUMPFISH:** Gray, brown, or green; rarely over 10 cm (4") long, but reported to reach up to 58 cm (23"). (family Cyclopteridae: snailfishes)

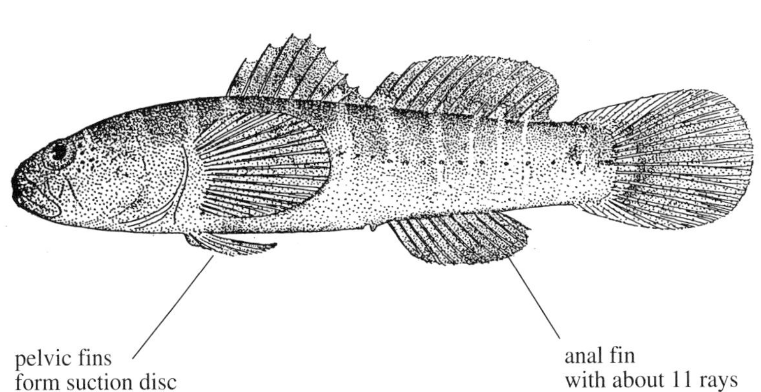

Fig.C. ***GOBIOSOMA* SPP., GOBIES:** Up to 8 cm (3") long. The naked goby *(G. bosc)* is greenish with pale crossbars. The seaboard goby *(G. ginsburgi)* is brown with indistinct crossbars and a row of dark dashes along lateral line. Refer to Thomson et al. (1978) to distinguish these species. (family Gobiidae: gobies)

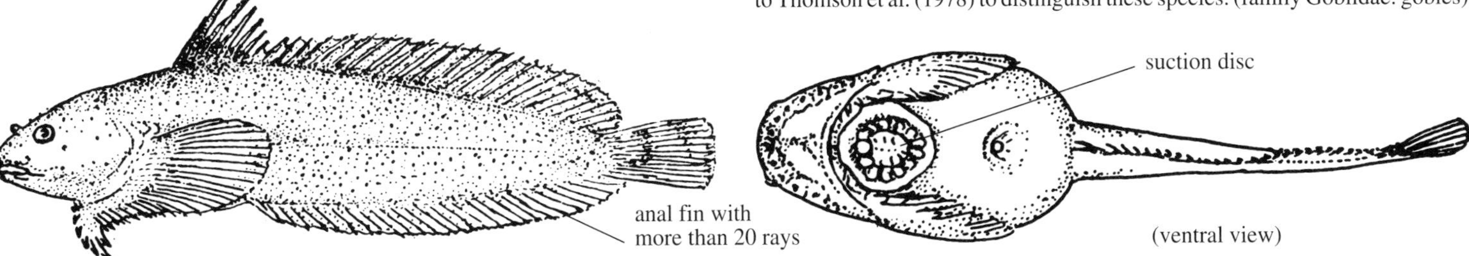

Fig.B. ***LIPARIS* SPP., SNAILFISHES:** The most common species, *Liparis atlanticus*, the Atlantic snailfish, is olive to reddish-brown, with lighter and darker markings, dorsal and anal fins often with cross bars; up to about 13 cm (5") long; occurs in shallow inshore waters, including tidepools. A similar but much less common species, *Liparis inquilinus*, the inquiline snailfish, is highly variable in color, often light to reddish brown with some individuals having spots, stripes, blotches, or bars; up to about 7.5 cm (3") long; dwells inside living sea scallops (*Placopecten magellanicus*) during the daytime, coming out of the scallop at night to feed. *L. atlanticus* has 27-31 pectoral fin rays, 25-29 anal fin rays, and 31-35 dorsal fin rays. *L. inquilinus* has 30-35 pectoral fin rays, 28-31 anal fin rays, and 33-38 dorsal fin rays. (family Cyclopteridae: snailfishes)

SEARHOBINS, SCULPINS, AND SIMILAR FISHES

Fishes with two dorsal[1] fins, a broad head armed with spines, and winglike pectoral fins

(Fish key begins on page 13.00)

#1. Without a fringe of fleshy tabs hanging from lower jaw (Fig.A-F) .... #2
#1. With a fringe of fleshy tabs hanging from lower jaw (Fig.G-I) .... #7

#2. With 3 separate feelers beneath each of the winglike pectoral fins; with a flattened, shovel-like snout (Figs.A,B) .... **family Triglidae, searobins**, #3
#2. No feelers; snout is rounded (Figs.C-F) .... #4

#3. With 1 or 2 obvious horizontal narrow stripes on each side of body; with one dark blotch on pectoral fins; tail fin is straight; pectoral fins reach back to ninth or tenth ray of second dorsal fin .... ***Prionotus evolans*, striped searobin** (Fig.A)
#3. No horizontal stripes (but may have about 5 indistinct, broad vertical bands); with two dark blotches on pectoral fins; tail fin is concave (curves inward); pectoral fins reach back only to fifth or sixth ray of second dorsal fin .... ***Prionotus carolinus*, northern searobin** (Fig.B)

#4. Winglike pectoral fins are very long, reaching nearly to tail; first two spines of first dorsal fin are separate, not connected by a membrane .... ***Dactylopterus volitans*, flying gurnard** (Fig.C)
#4. Winglike pectoral fins are short, reaching back only to the beginning of the second dorsal fin; first two spines of first dorsal fin are not separate from the rest of the dorsal fin (Figs.D-F) .... **family Cottidae, sculpins**, #5

#5. The largest (uppermost) cheek spine is four times as long as the one below it, and extends back to the edge of the gill cover .... ***Myoxocephalus octodecemspinosus*, longhorn sculpin** (Fig.D)
#5. The uppermost cheek spine is no more than twice as long as the one below it, and does not reach more than half way back to gill opening (Figs.E,F) .... #6

#6. Anal fin with 13 or 14 rays; with a tiny pore or slit on each side of throat behind the last gill arch; may grow longer than 20 cm (8") .... ***Myoxocephalus scorpius*, shorthorn sculpin** (Fig.E)
#6. Anal fin with 10 or 11 rays; no pore or slit on sides of throat; never grows longer than 20 cm (8") .... ***Myoxocephalus aenaeus*, grubby** (Fig.F)

#7. Body very broad and flat; with long, separate dorsal spines on tip of snout, the first of which has a flap of skin on its tip used as a fishing lure to attract other fish to eat; very large, often growing over 1 m (3') long .... ***Lophius americanus*, goosefish** (Fig.G)
#7. Body not especially flat; first dorsal fin spines are connected by a membrane; rarely grows over 50 cm (20") long (Figs.H,I) .... #8

#8. First dorsal fin has very ragged outline and is decorated with fleshy tabs; first dorsal fin is longer than second dorsal fin; often bright red or reddish purple .... ***Hemitripterus americanus*, sea raven** (Fig.H)
#8. First dorsal fin is not ragged or decorated; first dorsal fin is shorter than second dorsal fin; olive green or brown .... ***Opsanus tau*, oyster toadfish** (Fig.I)

[1]Refer to Fig.A on page 13.00 for terms used in fish key.

flattened snout
dark horizontal stripes on sides
straight tail fin
3 separate feelers
winglike pectoral fins reach back to 9th or 10th ray of second dorsal fin

Fig.A. ***PRIONOTUS EVOLANS*, STRIPED SEAROBIN:** Reddish brown sides marked with 1 or 2 dark horizontal stripes, pectoral fins are orange to brown with one dark blotch; up to 45 cm (18") long; common south of Cape Cod, rare to the north. (family Triglidae: searobins) **17.16 F**

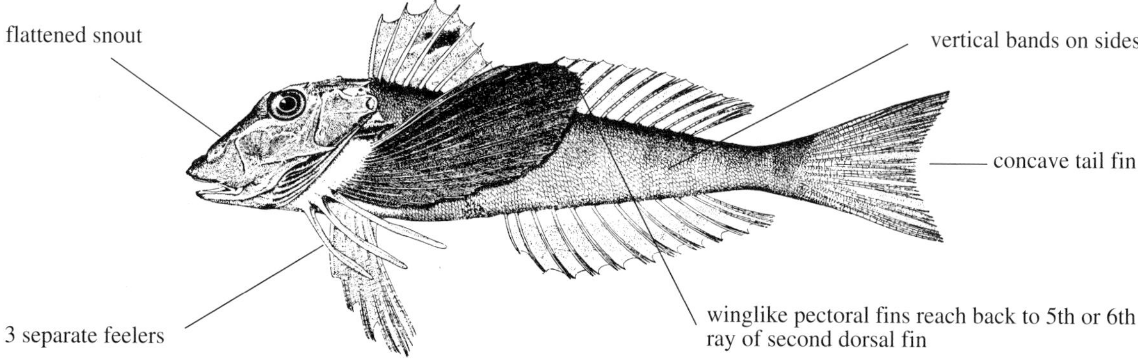

Fig.B. ***PRIONOTUS CAROLINUS*, NORTHERN SEAROBIN:** Brownish or grayish above with about 5 darker vertical bands, pectoral fins yellow or orange marked with two darker bars; usually less than 25 cm (10") long; very common south of Cape Cod, rare to the north. (family Triglidae: searobins)

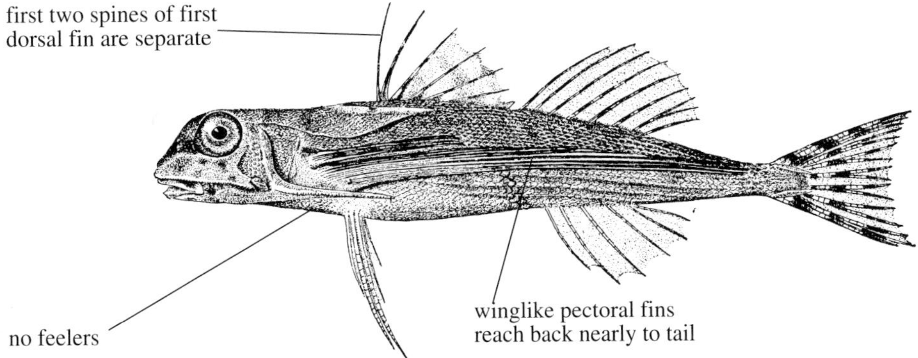

Fig.C. ***DACTYLOPTERUS VOLITANS*, FLYING GURNARD:** Brownish to olive green above, sides with irregular salmon colored markings, winglike pectoral fins with blue markings, reddish cross bars on tail fin; up to about 25 cm (10") long; not common. (family Dactylopteridae: flying gurnards)

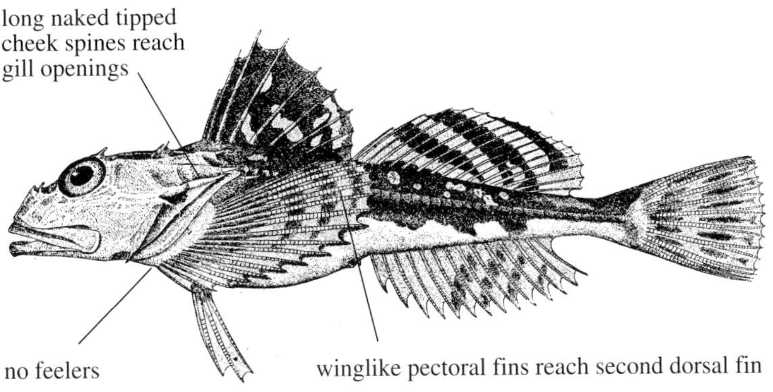

Fig.D. ***MYOXOCEPHALUS OCTODECEMSPINOSUS*, LONGHORN SCULPIN:** Green, yellow, or brown with darker blotches and spots, usually less than 25 cm (10") long. (family Cottidae: sculpins)

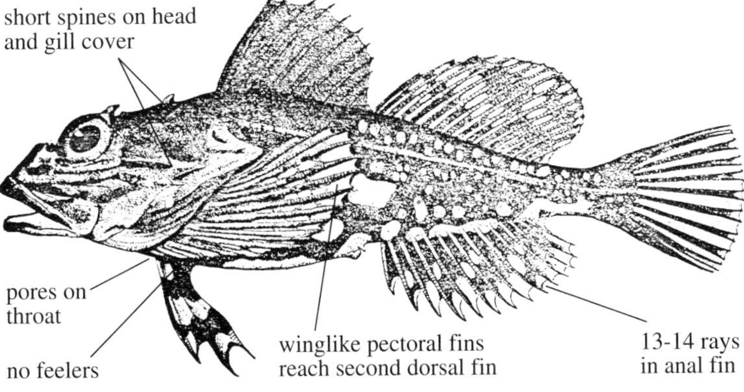

Fig.E. ***MYOXOCEPHALUS SCORPIUS*, SHORTHORN SCULPIN**: Red or brown on top with blotches on sides; rarely over 50 cm (20") long. (family Cottidae: sculpins)

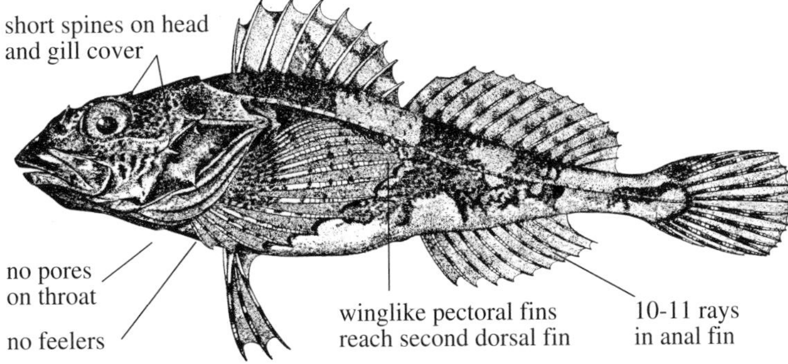

Fig.F. ***MYOXOCEPHALUS AENAEUS*, GRUBBY:** Light or dark gray with darker shading; up to 15 cm (6") long. (family Cottidae: sculpins)

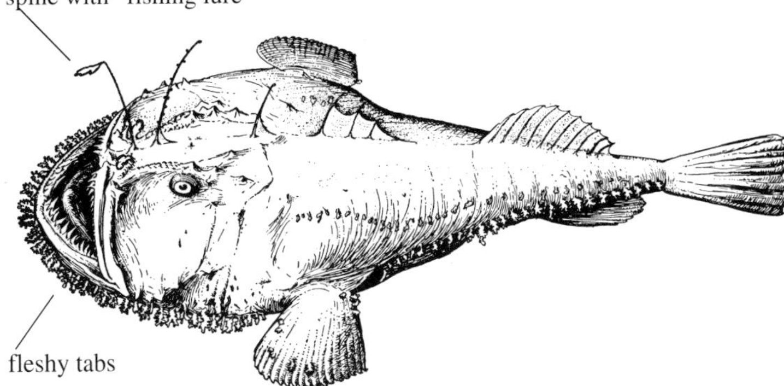

Fig.G. ***LOPHIUS AMERICANUS*, GOOSEFISH (=anglerfish):** Dark brown on top; can grow over 1 m (39") long. (family Lophiidae: goosefishes)

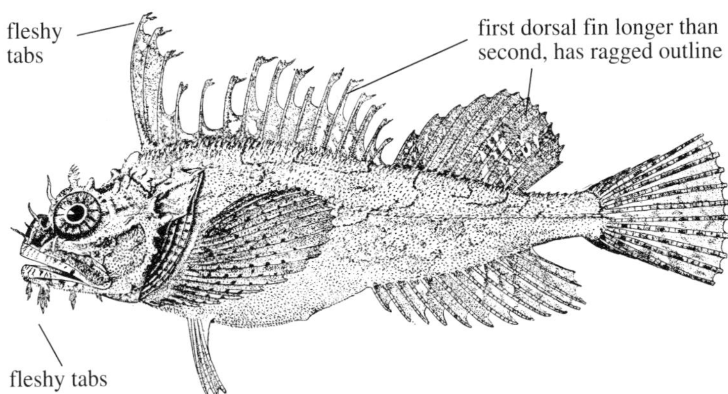

Fig.H. ***HEMITRIPTERUS AMERICANUS*, SEA RAVEN**: Reddish on top, yellow belly; up to 50 cm (20") long. (family Cottidae: sculpins) **17.16 E**

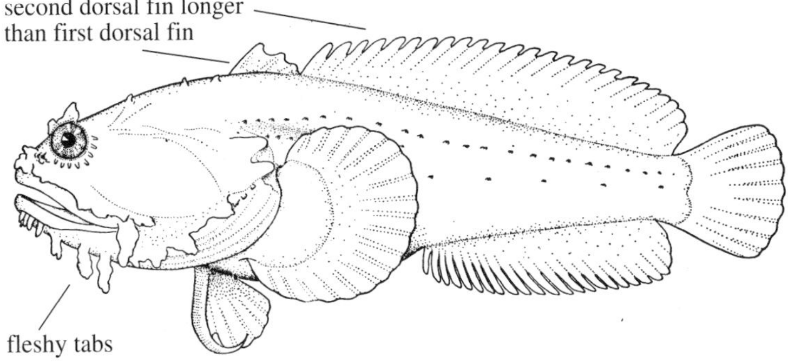

Fig.I. ***OPSANUS TAU*, OYSTER TOADFISH:** Olive green or brown; usually less than 25 cm (10") long. (family Batrachoididae: toadfishes) **17.16 D**

FISHES WITH A LARGE GAP BETWEEN FIRST AND SECOND DORSAL FINS

(Fish key begins on page 13.00)

#1.With a row of finlets (tiny finlike tabs) behind second dorsal[1] and anal fins (Fig.A) ... ***Scomber* spp., mackerels**, #2
#1.No finlets behind second dorsal or anal fins (Figs.B-I) ... #3

#2.Space between dorsal fins longer than first dorsal fin; 11-12 spines in first dorsal fin; no swim bladder ... ***Scomber scombrus,* Atlantic mackerel** (Fig.A)
#2.Space between dorsal fins about same size as first dorsal fin; 9-10 spines in first dorsal fin; with swim bladder ... ***Scomber japonicus,* chub mackerel** (Fig.A)

#3.Second dorsal fin is fleshy, smaller than first dorsal fin, and does not have any fin rays (Figs.B-D) ... #4
#3.Second dorsal fin is as large or larger than first dorsal fin and has soft rays (Figs.E-I) ... #7

#4.Tail fin is straight or slightly concave (curves inward, see Fig.B); up to 11 anal fin rays; often longer than 30 cm (12") ... ***Salmo* spp., salmon and trout**, #5
#4.Tail fin is sharply forked (Figs.C,D); with 12 or more anal fin rays; rarely exceeds 30 cm (12") in length ... #6

#5.Jaws extend to beneath eye; no spots on adipose fin; spots on back extend down sides only to midline ... ***Salmo salar,* Atlantic salmon** (Fig.B)
#5.Jaws extend behind eye; may have spots on adipose fin; spots on back extend down sides below midline ... ***Salmo trutta,* brown trout** (Fig.B)

#6.Jaws do not extend beyond rear edge of eyes; with 15-17 rays in anal fin; body not especially elongate; with small but obvious teeth on jaws and 1 or 2 fangs at tip of tongue ... ***Osmerus mordax*, rainbow smelt** (Fig.C)
#6.Jaws extend well behind eyes; with 12 anal fin rays; body very elongate; with teeth on jaws but not on tongue ... ***Synodus foetens*, inshore lizardfish** (Fig.D)

#7.With large, strong teeth; long, pointed snout ... ***Sphyraena borealis*, northern sennet** (Fig.E)
#7.No teeth; snout is blunt or rounded (Figs.F-I) ... #8

#8.With 11-12 rays in anal fin; anal fin begins directly underneath second dorsal fin; lower jaw is rounded and does not angle sharply upward toward snout (Figs.F,G); rarely found in southern New England ... #9
#8.With at least 15 rays in anal fin; anal fin begins in front of second dorsal fin; lower jaw is flat and angles sharply upward toward snout (Figs.H,I); very common in southern New England ... ***Menidia* spp., silversides**, #11

#9.With a pair of long barbels (threadlike feelers) attached beneath the lower jaw; body is bright red and yellow ... ***Mullus auratus*, red goatfish** (Fig.F)
#9.No barbels (Fig.G); body is greenish above, silvery below ... ***Mugil* spp., mullets**,#10

#10.With a total of 11 spines and rays in anal fin; with only a few scales on second dorsal fin ... ***Mugil cephalus*, striped mullet** (Fig.G)
#10.With a total of 12 spines and rays in anal fin; with many scales on dorsal fin ... ***Mugil curema*, white mullet** (Fig.G)

#11.More than 19 rays in anal fin ... ***Menidia menidia*, Atlantic silverside** (Fig.H)
#11.Fewer than 19 rays in anal fin ... ***Menidia beryllina*, inland silverside** (Fig.I)

[1]Refer to Fig.A on page 13.00 for terms used in fish key.

first dorsal fin has 11-12 spines in *S. scombrus* and 9-10 spines in *S. japonicus.*

dorsal finlets

space between dorsal fins is longer than first dorsal fin in *S. scombrus*. It is about the same size as the first dorsal fin in *S. japonicus.*

anal finlets

Fig.A. ***SCOMBER* SPP., MACKERELS:** The Atlantic mackerel (*S. scombrus*), shown here, is greenish-blue on upper surface with dark vertical bands that do not extend below the midline of the sides; velvety skin with small scales; sides and belly are silvery; up to 50 cm (20") long; very common. The chub mackerel (*S. japonicus*) is similar in overall color to the Atlantic mackerel but has dark spots or blotches that extend beneath the midline of the sides; up to 35 cm (14") long; much less common than *S. scombrus*. (family Scombridae: mackerels and tunas)

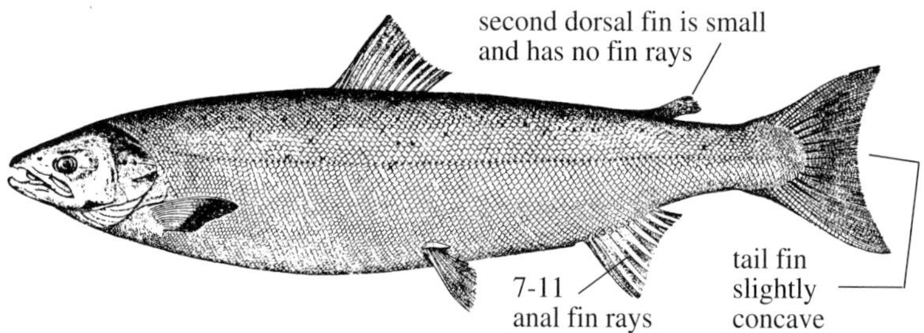

Fig.B. ***SALMO* SPP.:** The Atlantic salmon (*S. salar*), shown here, has a blue-green back, silvery sides, white belly, scattered black spots on sides and head; average length 60-100 cm (2-3'); once common, now rare; restoration programs are underway. The brown trout (*S.trutta*) has black and usually red spots on head, body, and fins; up to 1 m (39") long. Both species spawn in freshwater and may go out to sea to mature. Use key to distinguish. (family Salmonidae: trouts)

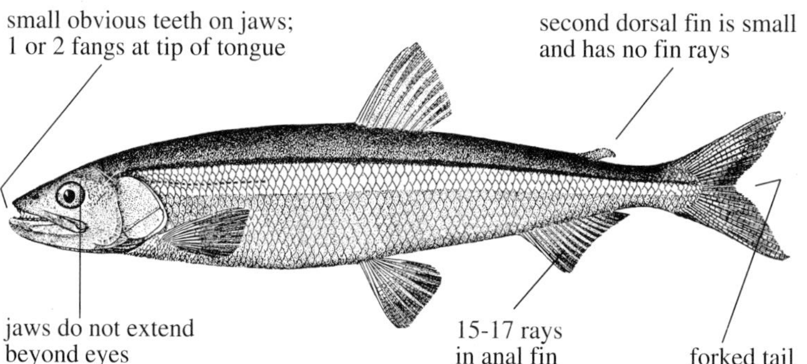

Fig.C. ***OSMERUS MORDAX*, RAINBOW SMELT:** Light green on top, silvery on sides and belly; usually less than 15 cm (6") long; common. (family Osmeridae: smelts)

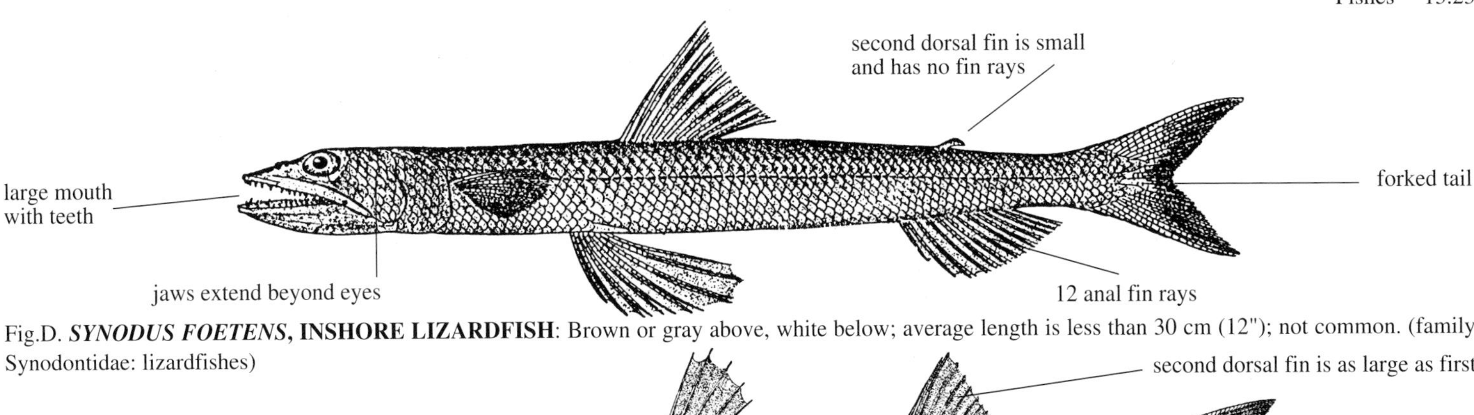

Fig.D. ***SYNODUS FOETENS*, INSHORE LIZARDFISH**: Brown or gray above, white below; average length is less than 30 cm (12"); not common. (family Synodontidae: lizardfishes)

second dorsal fin is as large as first

long jaws,
teeth large and strong

Fig.E. ***SPHYRAENA BOREALIS*, NORTHERN SENNET:** Olive above, silvery below; up to about 30 cm (12") long; occasionally occurs in southern New England. (family Sphyraenidae: barracudas)

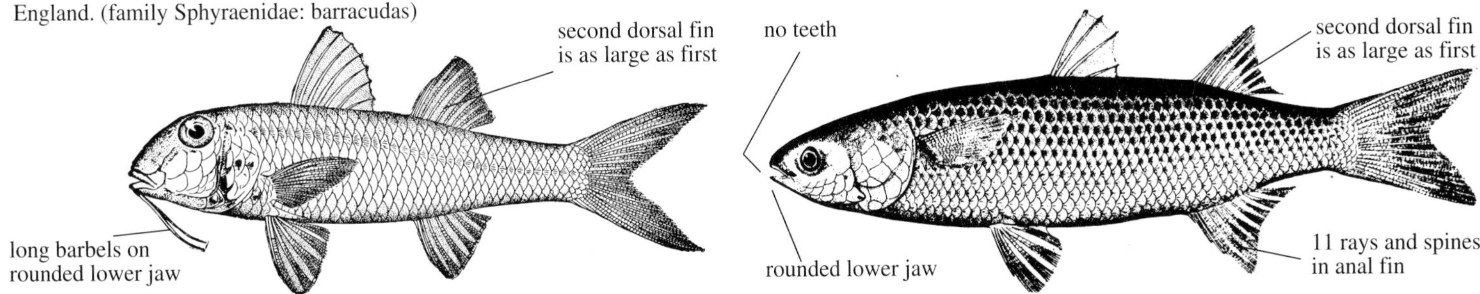

Fig.F. ***MULLUS AURATUS*, RED GOATFISH:** Red on head, back, and sides with red stripe on midline of sides and two yellow stripes below, silver on underside; up to 20 cm (8") long but only smaller juveniles usually occur in southern New England. (family Mullidae: goatfishes)

Fig.G. ***MUGIL CEPHALUS*, STRIPED MULLET** (shown here) and ***MUGIL CUREMA*, WHITE MULLET** (not shown): Both species are dark greenish above, silvery below; usually less than 15 cm (6") long; not common. Use key to distinguish between these two species. (family Mugilidae: mullets)

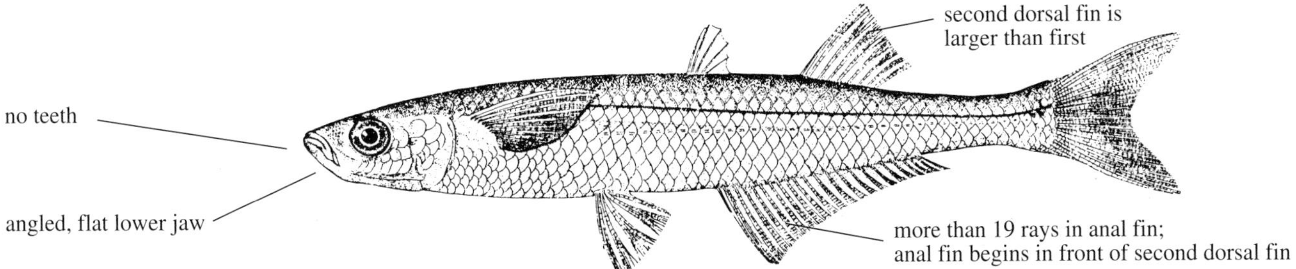

Fig.H. ***MENIDIA MENIDIA*, ATLANTIC SILVERSIDE:** Translucent green on top, sides with silvery horizontal band; up to 12 cm (5") long; very common near shore. (family Atherinidae: silversides)

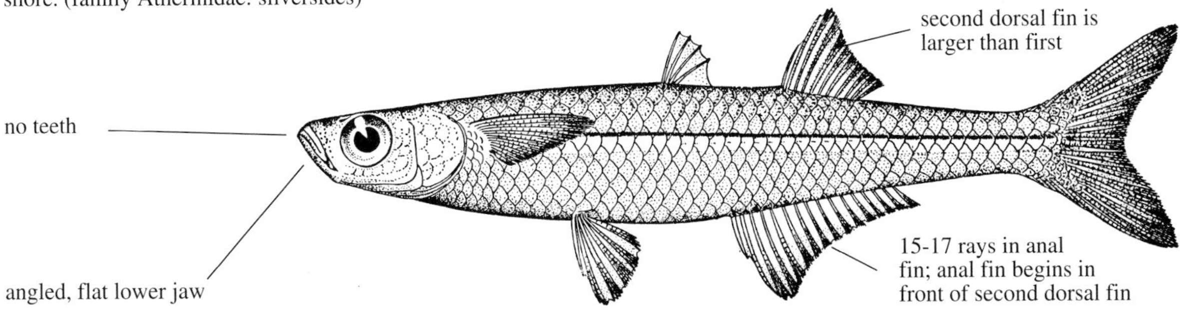

Fig.I. ***MENIDIA BERYLLINA*, INLAND SILVERSIDE:** Translucent green on top, sides with silvery horizontal band; up to 8 cm (3") long; common near shore. (family Atherinidae: silversides)

JACKS AND OTHER FISHES WITH TWO CLOSELY SPACED DORSAL FINS, THE FIRST SPINY AND THE SECOND SOFT RAYED; AND WITH A LONG ANAL[1] FIN OR A ROW OF FINLETS BEHIND ANAL AND DORSAL FINS

(Fish key begins on page 13.00)

#1.With 3 spines in first dorsal fin, the first spine is much stouter than the others and can be locked in an upright position; with a tiny mouth at the tip of its pointed head; no pelvic fins .... ***Balistes capriscus*, gray triggerfish** (Fig.A)
#1.More than 3 spines in first dorsal fin, the first spine is not especially stout and cannot be locked upright; mouth not tiny; with pelvic fins (Figs.B-J) .... #2

#2.First dorsal fin is much lower than the second dorsal fin (Figs.B-D) .... #3
#2.First dorsal fin is as high as or higher than second dorsal fin (Figs.E-J) .... #5

#3.Anal fin is nearly as long as second dorsal fin; without dark vertical bands (Figs.B,C) .... #4
#3.Anal fin is about 1/2 as long as second dorsal fin; young fish have distinct dark vertical bands, older fish do not... ***Seriola zonata*, banded rudderfish** (Fig.D)

#4.With spines in front of anal fin; small jaws extend to front half of eyes; without large teeth; oval shaped, deep body ..... ***Trachinotus falcatus*, permit** (Fig.B)
#4.No spines in front of anal fin; large jaws extend behind eyes; with large teeth .... ***Pomatomus saltatrix*, bluefish** (Fig.C)

#5.With a row of 3 or more finlets behind dorsal and anal fins .... **family Scombridae, tunas[2]** (Fig.E)
#5.With one or no finlets behind dorsal and anal fins (Figs.F-J) .... #6

#6.Without any spines in front of anal fin (page 13.27, Fig.B); anal fin with over 35 rays; without any bony plates along lateral line near posterior end of fish; tail fin not forked .... ***Merluccius bilinearis*, silver hake[3]**, page 13.27
#6.With two spines in front of anal fin; anal fin with fewer than 30 rays; with a row of bony plates along the lateral line near posterior end of fish; tail fin forked (Figs.F-J); caudal peduncle very slender .... #7

#7.With a small detached finlet behind the dorsal fin and another behind the anal fin .... ***Decapterus* spp., scads** (Fig.F)
#7.No finlets behind dorsal or anal fins (Figs.G-J) .... #8

#8.Lateral line is only slightly arched; with noticeably large eyes .... ***Selar crumenophthalmus*, bigeye scad** (Fig.G)
#8.Lateral line is strongly arched; eyes not especially large (Figs.H-J) .... #9

#9.With about 75 bony plates along entire length of lateral line; body slender, more than three times as long as deep .... ***Trachurus lathami*, rough scad** (Fig.H)
#9.With 30 or fewer bony plates along lateral line, plates on rear half of lateral line only; deeper bodied fish, body (from tip of head to base of tail) is less than three times as long as deep (Figs.I,J) .... #10

#10.Most of breast does not have scales; with two pairs of small but plainly visible canine teeth in lower jaw .... ***Caranx hippos*, crevalle jack** (Fig.I)
#10.Entire breast is covered with scales; no teeth in lower jaw .... ***Caranx crysos*, blue runner** (Fig.J)

[1]Refer to Fig. A on page 13.00 for terms used in fish key.
[2]A number of species in the tuna family are common in the open ocean off the coast of southern New England. Some of these species stray near shore on occasion. Refer to a book such as Bigelow and Schroeder (1953) to identify these tunas. Mackerels are also in this family but have widely spaced dorsal fins. See page 13.22.
[3]The first dorsal fin of the silver hake is actually soft rayed but the rays are stiff and may feel somewhat spiny. Thus, the fish is included in this key although it belongs on page 13.27 with the hakes (family Gadidae: cods and hakes).

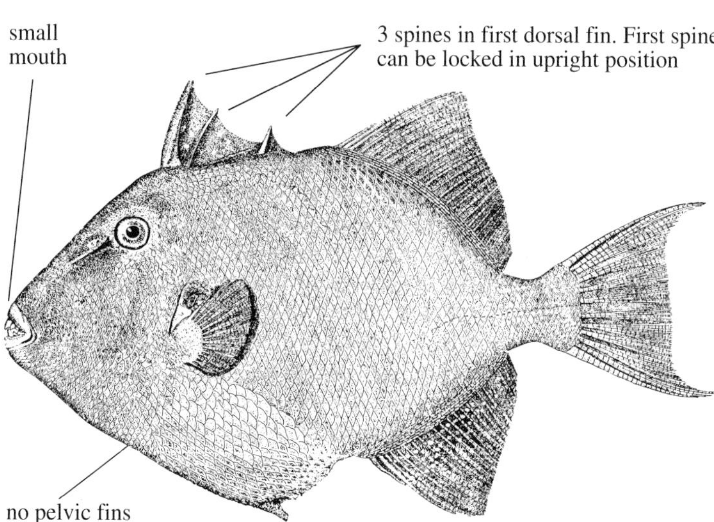

Fig.A. ***BALISTES CAPRISCUS*, GRAY TRIGGERFISH:** May be yellowish or brownish-gray with small violet spots on upper back; up to 50 cm (20") long. (Family Balistidae: leatherjackets)

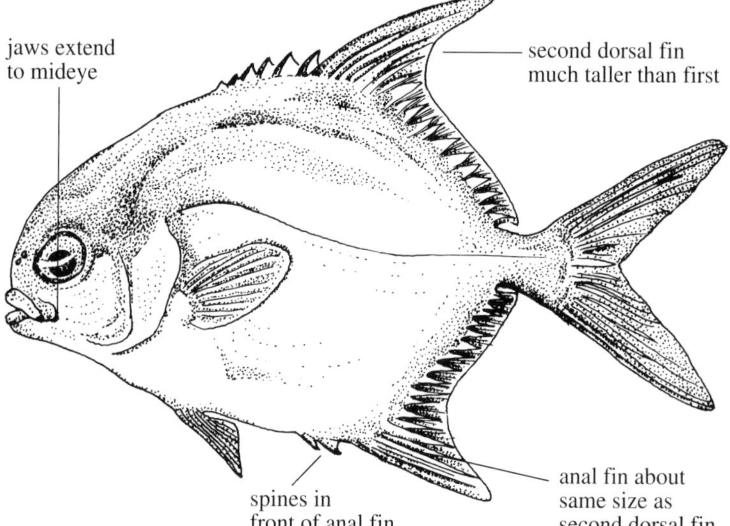

Fig.B. ***TRACHINOTUS FALCATUS*, PERMIT:** Sides usually silvery but sometimes almost black; up to 79 cm (31") long; adults rare in this region, but young sometimes caught in seines near shore. (family Carangidae: jacks)

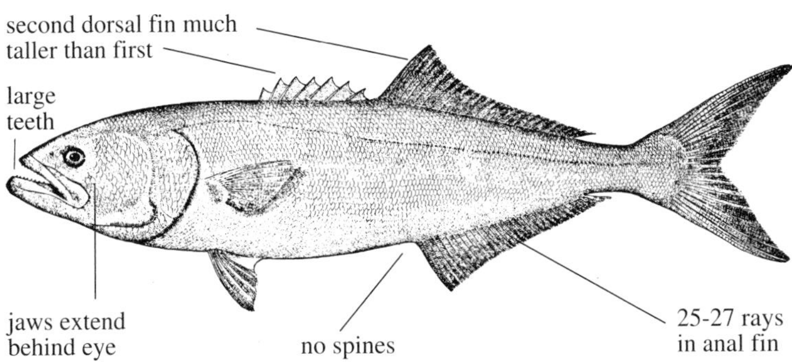

Fig.C. ***POMATOMUS SALTATRIX*, BLUEFISH:** Greenish above, silvery below; rarely over 1 m (39") long; young "snapper" bluefish very common near shore and in estuaries, larger bluefish common offshore. (family Pomatomidae: bluefishes)

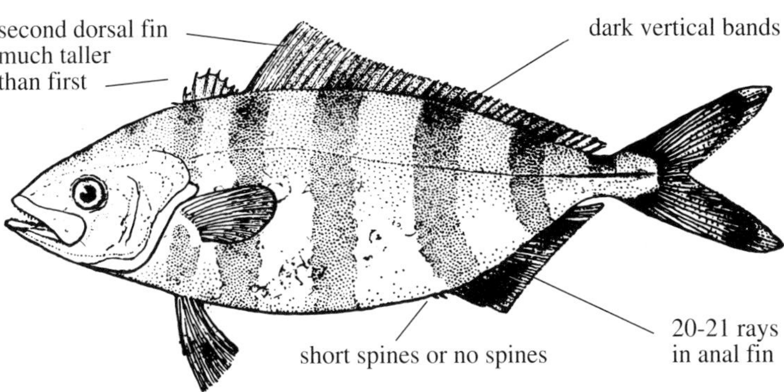

Fig.D. ***SERIOLA ZONATA*, BANDED RUDDERFISH:** Bluish or silvery brown above, paler on sides with dark vertical bands; rarely over 25 cm (10") long. (family Carangidae: jacks)

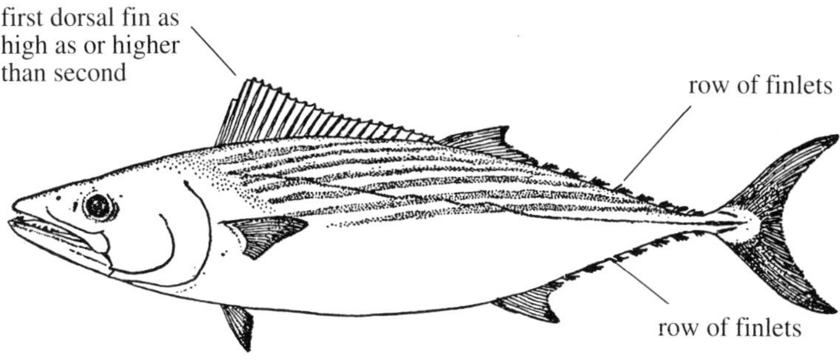

Fig.E. **FAMILY SCOMBRIDAE, TUNAS[2]:** Occasionally the Atlantic bonito (*Sarda sarda*), shown here, or other tuna species will stray into shallow estuarine bays and sounds. They are common offshore. Some tunas reach over 3 m (10') in length but most species that come near shore are under 1 m (39").

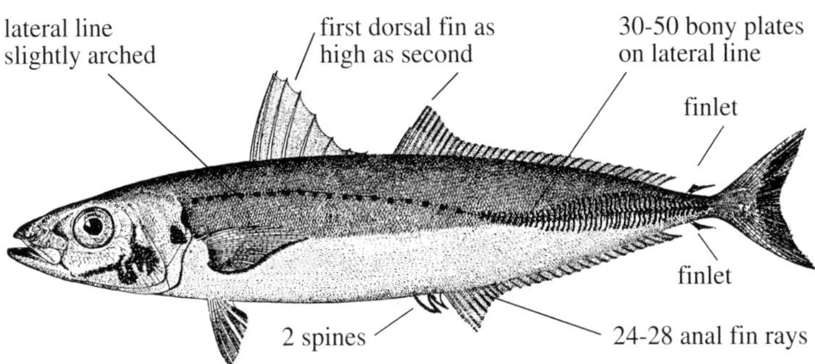

Fig.F. ***DECAPTERUS* SPP., SCADS:** Bluish above, silvery below, dark spot on gill cover; up to about 30 cm (12") long. The mackerel scad (*D. macarellus*) has about 30 bony plates on lateral line and no teeth. The round scad (*D. punctatus*) has 40 or more plates and has teeth. (family Carangidae: jacks)

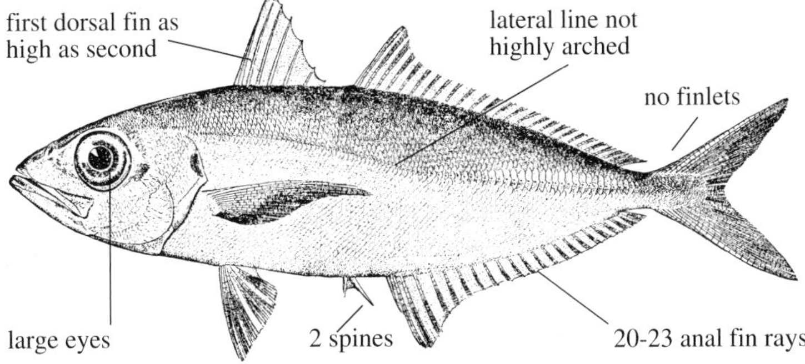

Fig.G. ***SELAR CRUMENOPHTHALMUS*, BIGEYE SCAD:** Bluish above, silvery below; usually less than 25 cm (10") long but grows up to 60 cm (2'). (family Carangidae: jacks)

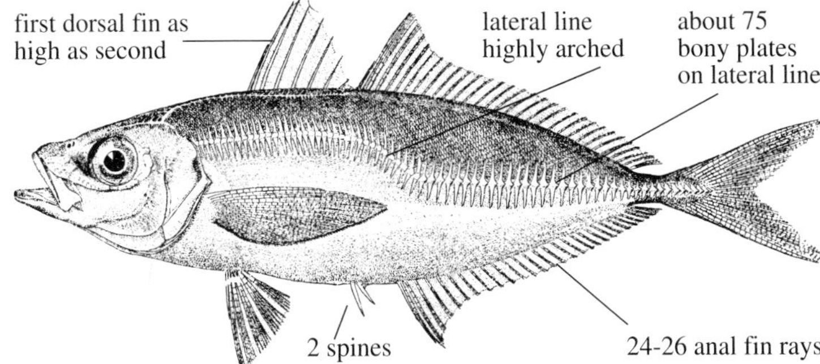

Fig.H. ***TRACHURUS LATHAMI*, ROUGH SCAD:** Bluish-green above, silvery below; up to about 30 cm (12") long. (family Carangidae: jacks)

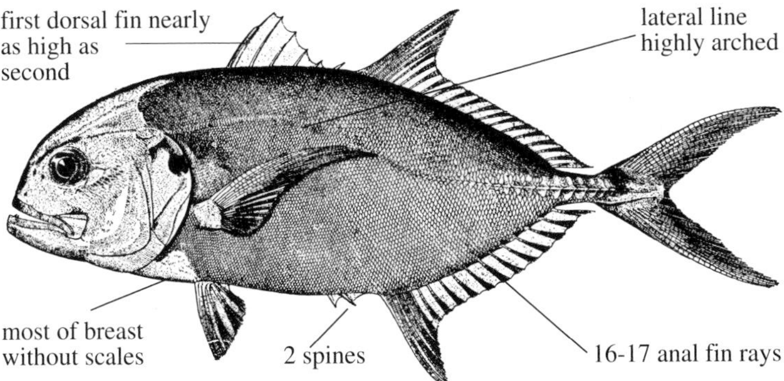

Fig.I. ***CARANX HIPPOS*, CREVALLE JACK:** Green above, bronze or silvery below; reportedly reaches a length of 80 cm (30"). (family Carangidae: jacks)

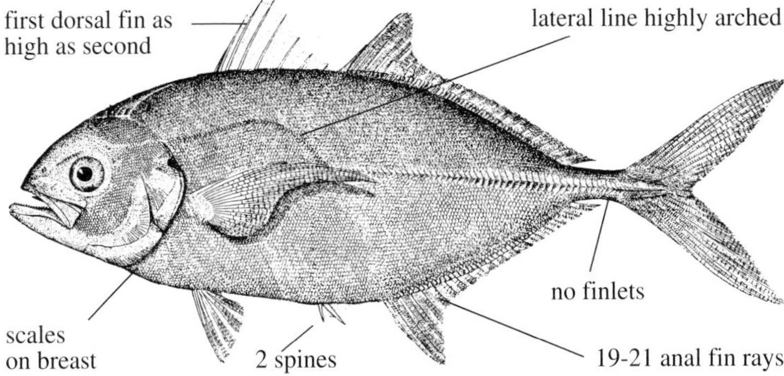

Fig.J. ***CARANX CRYSOS*, BLUE RUNNER:** Greenish bronze above, golden or silvery below; usually up to about 30 cm (12") long, but may reach 60 cm (24"). (family Carangidae: jacks)

FISHES WITH TWO CLOSELY SPACED DORSAL FINS, THE FIRST SPINY AND THE SECOND SOFT RAYED; AND WITH A SHORT ANAL[1] FIN

(Fish key begins on page 13.00)

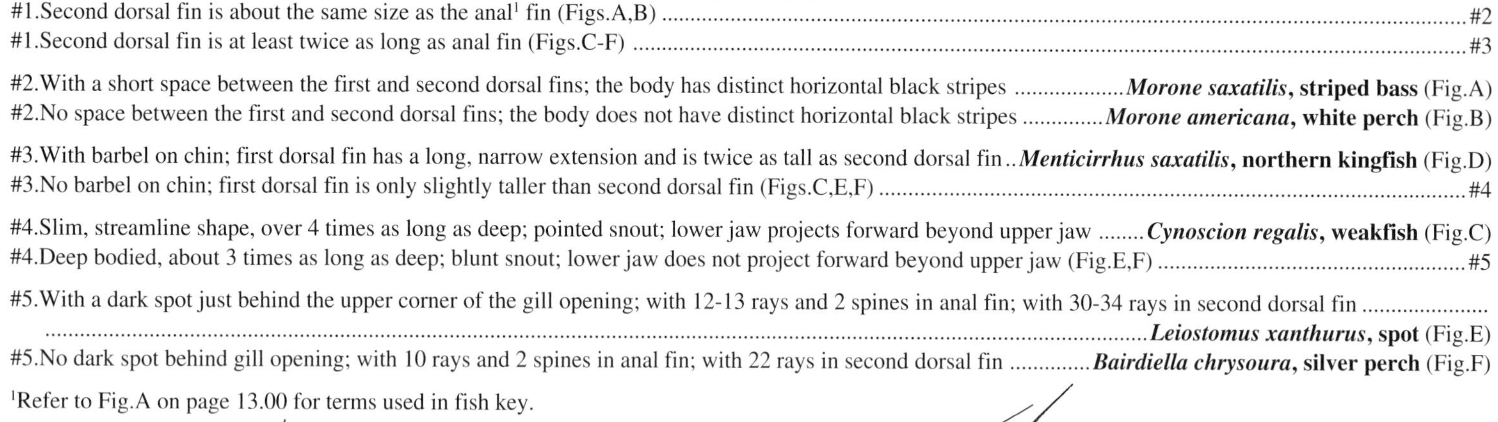

#1.Second dorsal fin is about the same size as the anal[1] fin (Figs.A,B) .... #2
#1.Second dorsal fin is at least twice as long as anal fin (Figs.C-F) .... #3

#2.With a short space between the first and second dorsal fins; the body has distinct horizontal black stripes .... ***Morone saxatilis*, striped bass** (Fig.A)
#2.No space between the first and second dorsal fins; the body does not have distinct horizontal black stripes .... ***Morone americana*, white perch** (Fig.B)

#3.With barbel on chin; first dorsal fin has a long, narrow extension and is twice as tall as second dorsal fin .. ***Menticirrhus saxatilis*, northern kingfish** (Fig.D)
#3.No barbel on chin; first dorsal fin is only slightly taller than second dorsal fin (Figs.C,E,F) .... #4

#4.Slim, streamline shape, over 4 times as long as deep; pointed snout; lower jaw projects forward beyond upper jaw .... ***Cynoscion regalis*, weakfish** (Fig.C)
#4.Deep bodied, about 3 times as long as deep; blunt snout; lower jaw does not project forward beyond upper jaw (Fig.E,F) .... #5

#5.With a dark spot just behind the upper corner of the gill opening; with 12-13 rays and 2 spines in anal fin; with 30-34 rays in second dorsal fin .... ***Leiostomus xanthurus*, spot** (Fig.E)
#5.No dark spot behind gill opening; with 10 rays and 2 spines in anal fin; with 22 rays in second dorsal fin .... ***Bairdiella chrysoura*, silver perch** (Fig.F)

[1]Refer to Fig.A on page 13.00 for terms used in fish key.

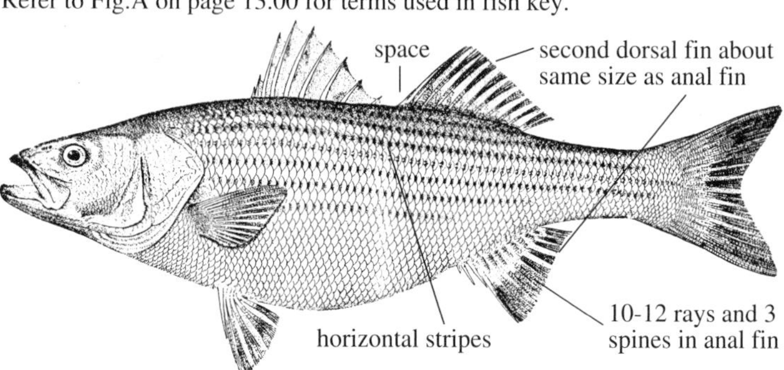

Fig.A. ***MORONE SAXATILIS*, STRIPED BASS:** Grayish-green above, silvery on sides with 7 or 8 distinct black horizontal stripes; up to 1.8 m (6') long, but usually less than 1.5 m (5'). (family Percichthyidae: temperate basses)

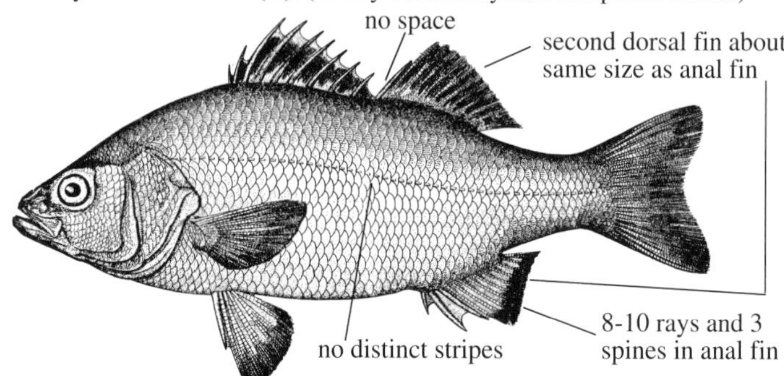

Fig.B. ***MORONE AMERICANA*, WHITE PERCH:** Dark gray-green on upper surface, paler olive or silvery green on sides, white on belly; usually less than 25 cm (10") long. (family Percichthyidae: temperate basses)

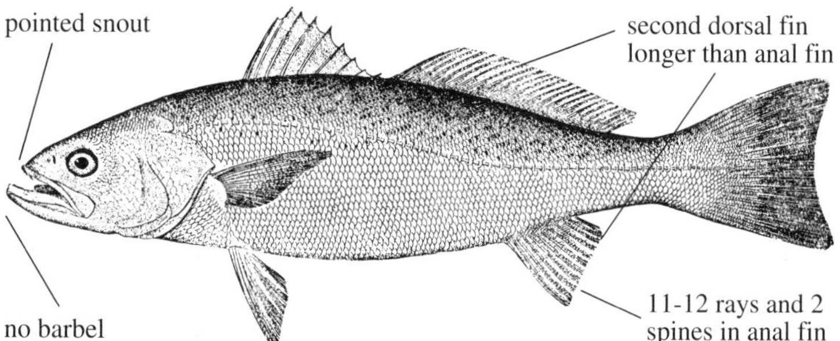

Fig.C. ***CYNOSCION REGALIS*, WEAKFISH:** Light green on back, sides variously colored with large number of small dark spots, lower surface white; up to 90 cm (3') long. (family Sciaenidae: drums)

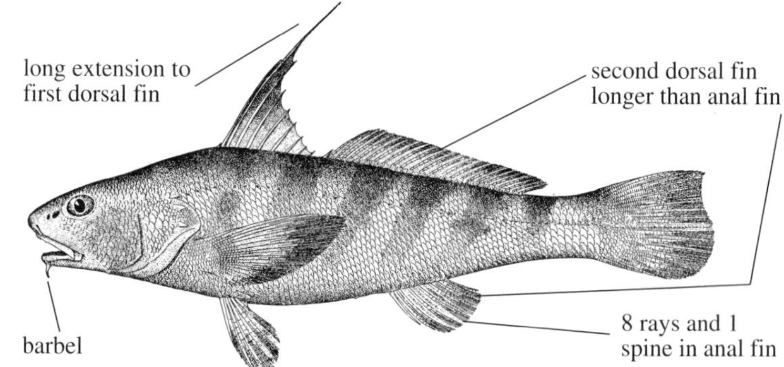

Fig.D. ***MENTICIRRHUS SAXATILIS*, NORTHERN KINGFISH:** Dark gray above, whitish below, sides marked with dark bands; usually less than 25 cm (10") long. (family Sciaenidae: drums)

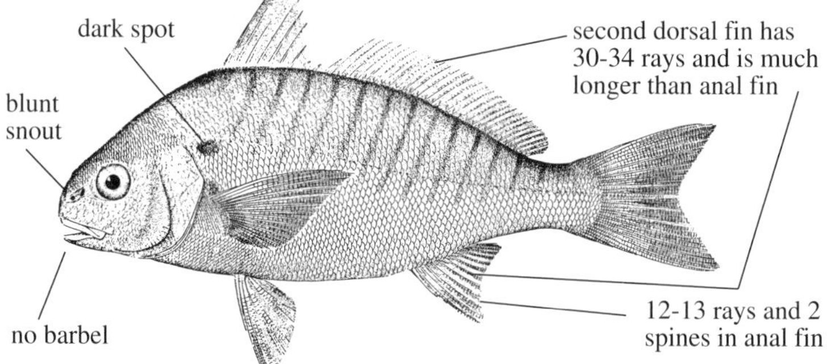

Fig.E. ***LEIOSTOMUS XANTHURUS*, SPOT:** Bluish-gray above, silvery below, dark spot behind gill openings; up to about 25 cm (10") long. (family Sciaenidae: drums)

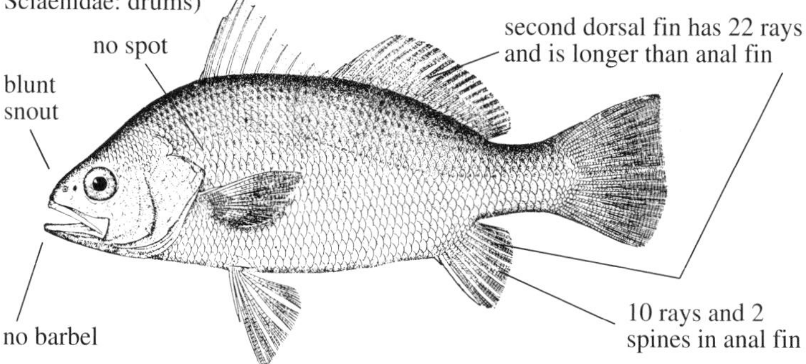

Fig.F. ***BAIRDIELLA CHRYSOURA*, SILVER PERCH:** Greenish above, silvery below, yellowish fins; up to about 20 cm (8") long. (family Sciaenidae: drums)

HAKES: CLASS OSTEICHTHYES, FAMILY GADIDAE (in part)

Fishes with two dorsal[1] fins, both soft rayed, second much longer than first

(Fish key begins on page 13.00)

#1.The first dorsal fin[1] consists of one long ray plus about 50 very short rays, only one dorsal fin is obvious (the second); with three barbels on top of the nose.. .... ***Enchelyopus cimbrius*, fourbeard rockling** (Fig.A)

#1.With two well developed dorsal fins, the first shorter but usually higher than the second; no barbels on top of the nose (Figs.B-E) .... #2

#2.Ventral fins are not long, narrow, and feelerlike; no barbel under chin; first dorsal fin rays may feel rather stiff and spiny .... ***Merluccius bilinearis*, silver hake** (Fig.B)

#2.Ventral fins are long, narrow, and feelerlike; with small barbel under chin; first dorsal fin rays are soft (Figs.C-E) .... #3

#3.First rays of first dorsal fin are not long and threadlike, first dorsal fin is not taller than second; dark brown lateral line broken by a series of whitish dashes .. .. ***Urophycis regia*, spotted hake** (Fig.C)

#3.First rays of first dorsal fin are long and threadlike, first dorsal fin is taller than second; lateral line is pale color and solid, not dashed line (Figs.D,E) .... #4

#4.Two gill rakers on upper arm of first gill arch[2]; 119-148 scales on lateral line from gill opening to caudal (tail) fin .... ***Urophycis tenuis*, white hake** (Fig.D)

#4.Three gill rakers on upper arm of first gill arch; 95-117 rows of scales along the lateral line .... ***Urophycis chuss*, red hake** (Fig.E)

[1]Refer to Fig.A on page 13.00 for terms used in fish key.
[2]Refer to Fig.A on page 13.14 to find gill rakers and gill arches.

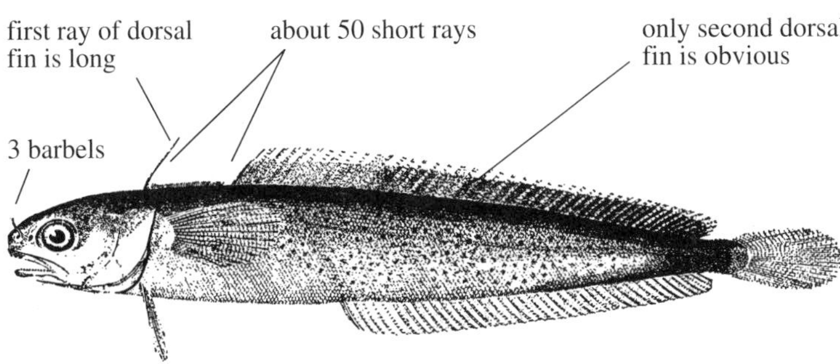

Fig.A. ***ENCHELYOPUS CIMBRIUS*, FOURBEARD ROCKLING:** Dark yellowish olive or brown on back, belly white dotted with brown; up to about 25 cm (10") long; not common.

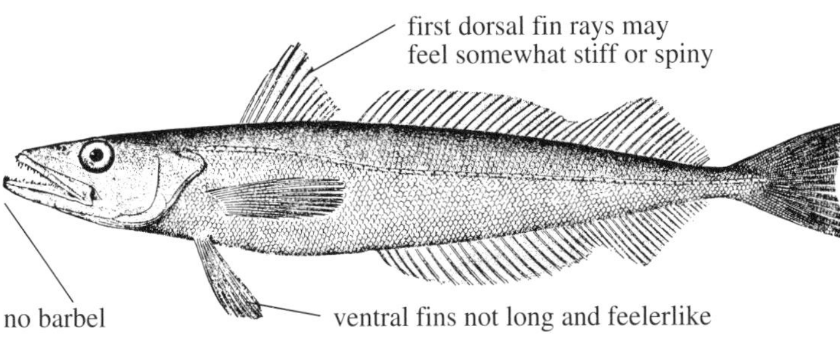

Fig.B. ***MERLUCCIUS BILINEARIS*, SILVER HAKE (=whiting):** Gray on top, silvery on sides and belly; usually less than 50 cm (20") long.

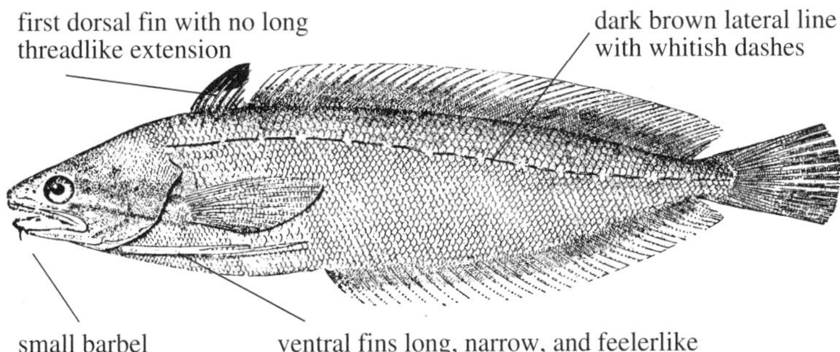

Fig.C. ***UROPHYCIS REGIA,* SPOTTED HAKE:** Dull brown, feelers are whitish, lateral line is brown with white dashes; usually less than 25 cm (10") long.

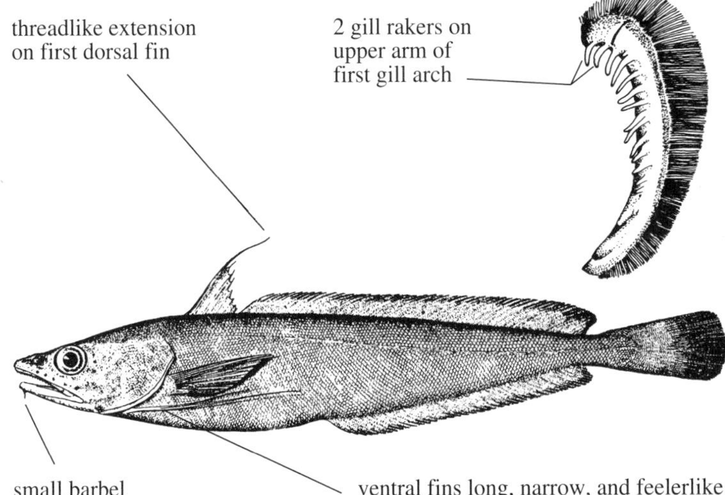

Fig.D. ***UROPHYCIS TENUIS*, WHITE HAKE:** Grayish or purplish; maximum length about 120 cm (4') but average length is under 75 cm (30").

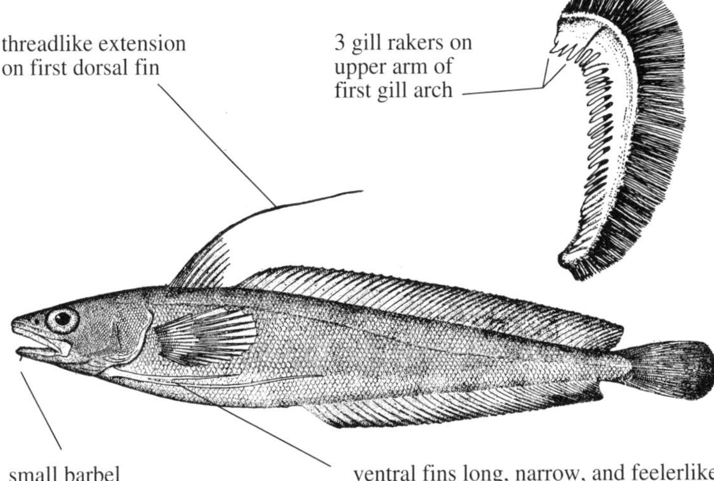

Fig.E. ***UROPHYCIS CHUSS*, RED HAKE (=squirrel hake):** Reddish-brown on top, belly yellowish-white, feeler tinged with yellow; usually less than 40 cm (16") long, with a maximum length of 50 cm (20").

COD FAMILY: CLASS OSTEICHTHYES, FAMILY GADIDAE (in part)

Fishes with three dorsal[1] fins

(Fish key begins on page 13.00)

#1.The lateral line is black; there is a black blotch above the pectoral fin; first dorsal fin is sharply pointed and much taller than the other dorsal fins .... ***Melanogrammus aeglefinus*, haddock** (Fig.A)

#1.The lateral line is pale; there is no black blotch above the pectoral fins (Figs.B-D); first dorsal fin is not sharply pointed and is about the same height as the other dorsal fins .... #2

#2.The lower jaw projects beyond the upper jaw; the chin barbel is very small or absent .... ***Pollachius virens*, pollock** (Fig.B)

#2.The upper jaw projects beyond the lower, the chin barbel is obvious (Figs.C,D) .... #3

#3.The pelvic fins are long and narrow, almost feelerlike, with a long threadlike extension; tail fin is rounded; usually shorter than 25 cm (10") long and maximum length is about 40 cm (16") .... ***Microgadus tomcod*, Atlantic tomcod** (Fig.C)

#3.Pelvic fins are broad with only a short threadlike extension; tail fin is straight or concave (curves inward); often larger than 25 cm (10") and maximum length exceeds 1.5 m (5') .... ***Gadus morhua*, Atantic cod** (Fig.D)

[1]Refer to Fig.A on page 13.00 for terms used in fish key.

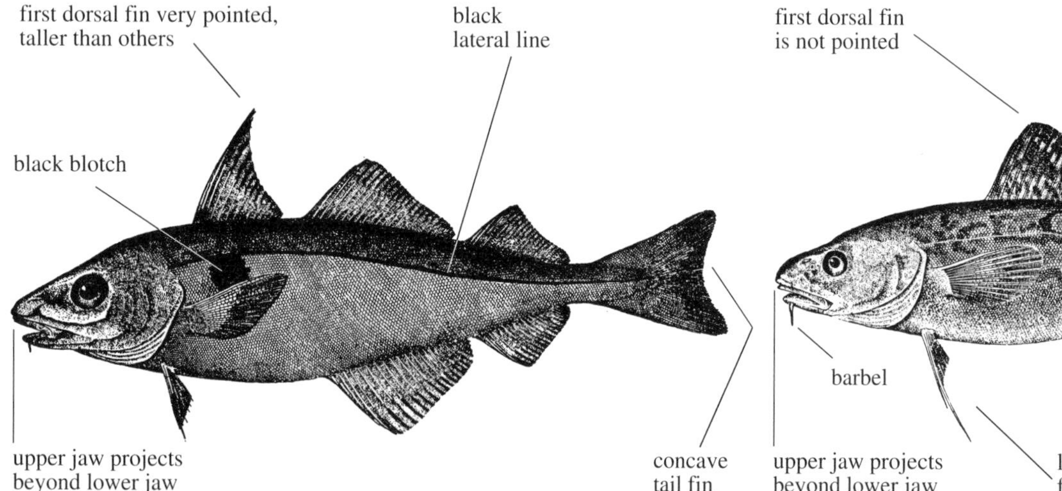

Fig.A. ***MELANOGRAMMUS AEGLEFINUS*, HADDOCK**: Dark purplish gray on back, silvery gray below lateral line; with back lateral line and shoulder patch; rarely grows over 50 cm (20") long but can reach up to 90 cm (3').

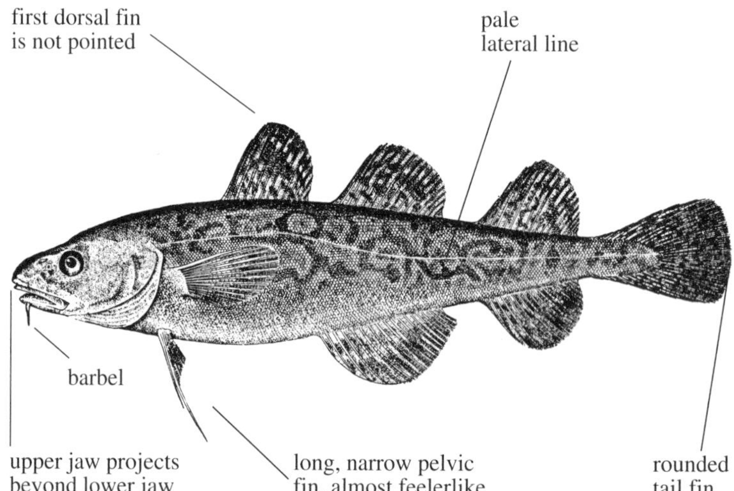

Fig.C. ***MICROGADUS TOMCOD*, ATLANTIC TOMCOD:** Olive green above, dark blotches on sides, lateral line pale, whitish on belly; usually less than 20 cm (8") long; the most common member of the cod family in estuarine waters.

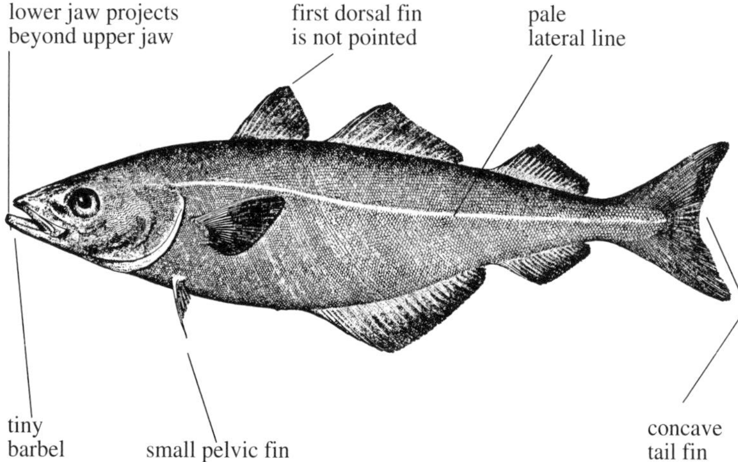

Fig.B. ***POLLACHIUS VIRENS*, POLLOCK:** Green above, gray on sides, silvery gray on belly; rarely over 30 cm (1') long in bays and sounds, but may reach up to 1 m (39") elsewhere.

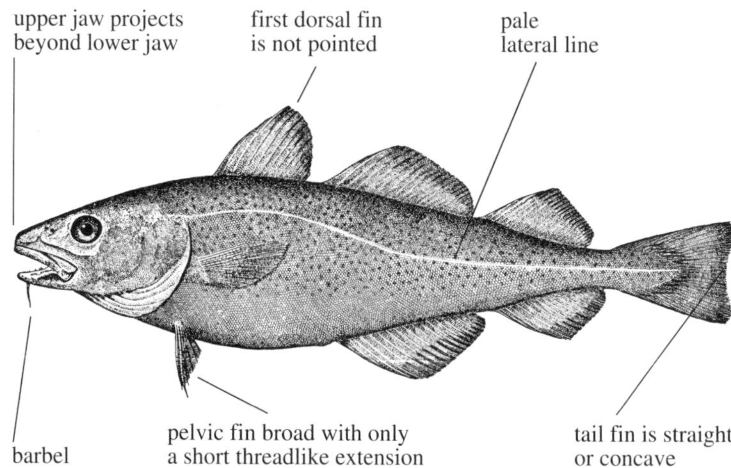

Fig.D. ***GADUS MORHUA*, ATLANTIC COD:** Color variable, gray-green or reddish, spotted, lateral line pale, belly whitish; usually less than 50 cm (20") long, but may reach over 1.5 m (5'); common only in winter and spring in shallow waters under 12 m (40') deep; common year round in deeper water.

FROGS AND TOADS: CLASS AMPHIBIA, ORDER ANURA

Amphibians with hind legs much longer and stronger than front legs; young pass through a larval stage (tadpoles). Most species are unable to tolerate high salinities or very dry environments. No amphibians live in marine waters of New England and only a few species regularly occur along the seashore.

(Use key on page 2.14 to determine if you have a frog or toad)

#1.Large wartlike parotoid glands (Figs.A,B) behind each eye; skin dry and warty .... **toads**, #2

#1.No distinct parotoid glands (Figs.C,D); skin moist and smooth .... **frogs and spadefoots**, #3

#2.Parotoid glands (Fig.A) separated from postorbital ridges (ridges behind eyes) or touch ridge spurs only; usually 1 or 2 warts per dark spot; breast often mottled or spotted .... ***Bufo a. americanus*, eastern American toad** (Fig.A)

#2.Parotoid glands touch postorbital ridges; usually more than 1 or 2 warts per dark spot (Fig.B); breast unmarked or with a large central spot .... ***Bufo woodhousii fowleri*, Fowler's toad** (Fig.B)

#3.Back marked with a dark 'X'; ends of fingers and toes with discs (toe pads); horizontal pupils .... ***Pseudacris c. crucifer*, northern spring peeper** (Fig.C)

#3.Yellowish lines down back; with a black sharp edged spade on hind feet, no toe pads; vertical pupils ... ***Scaphiopus h. holbrookii*, eastern spadefoot** (Fig.D)

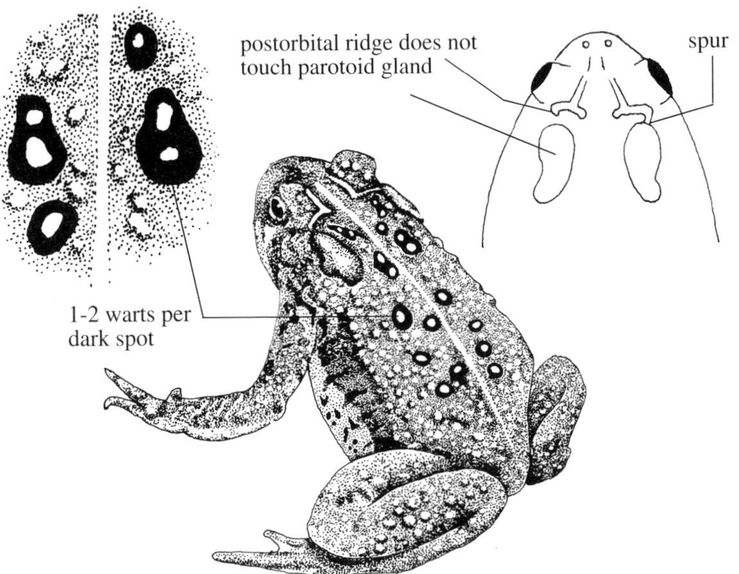

Fig.A. ***BUFO A. AMERICANUS*, EASTERN AMERICAN TOAD:** Brown, gray, or olive; body length up to 11 cm (4 1/2"); reported to occur in tidal marshes but usually found in many terrestrial habitats during most of the year; occurs in fresh or mildly brackish water during breeding season; male call is a long musical trill.

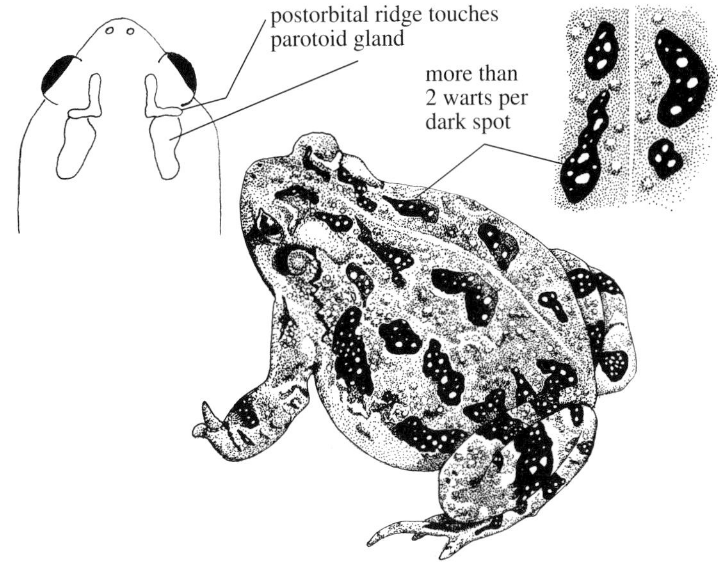

Fig.B. ***BUFO WOODHOUSII FOWLERI*, FOWLER'S TOAD:** Greenish gray; body length up to 7.5 cm (3"); occurs in sandy areas including beaches and dunes; occurs in tidal marshes; male call is a short musical bleat; hybridizes with the American toad and the hybrids are hard to tell apart.

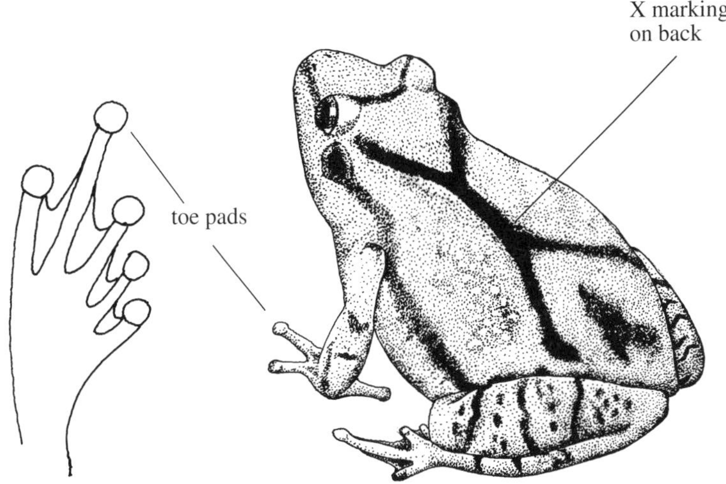

Fig.C. ***PSEUDACRIS C. CRUCIFER*, NORTHERN SPRING PEEPER:** Brown, gray, or olive with an 'X' on back; up to 3 cm (1 1/4") long; rarely seen except in spring breeding season when males call from vegetation near water; occurs in tidal marshes; breeds in mildly brackish water; call is high 'peep.'

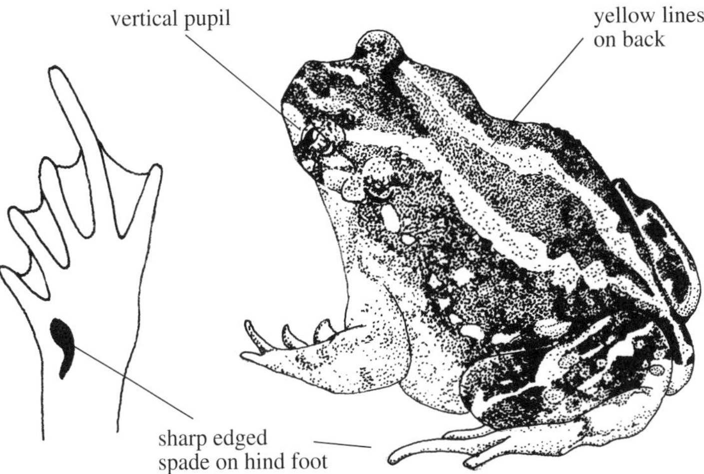

Fig.D. ***SCAPHIOPUS H. HOLBROOKII*, EASTERN SPADEFOOT:** Brown background color with yellow lines running down back from each eye; up to 6 cm (2 1/2") long; occurs in sandy environments such as on Cape Cod and eastern Long Island.

SALAMANDERS: CLASS AMPHIBIA, ORDER CAUDATA

Amphibians with a narrow body and elongate tail; legs approximately equal in size and much shorter than body

(Use key on page 2.14 to determine if you have a salamander)

#1.Back is solid dark gray or black, may or may not have a red or orange stripe on midline .... ***Plethodon cinereus*, redback salamander** (Fig.A)
#1.With yellow or orange round spots on back .... ***Ambystoma maculatum*, spotted salamander** (Fig.B)

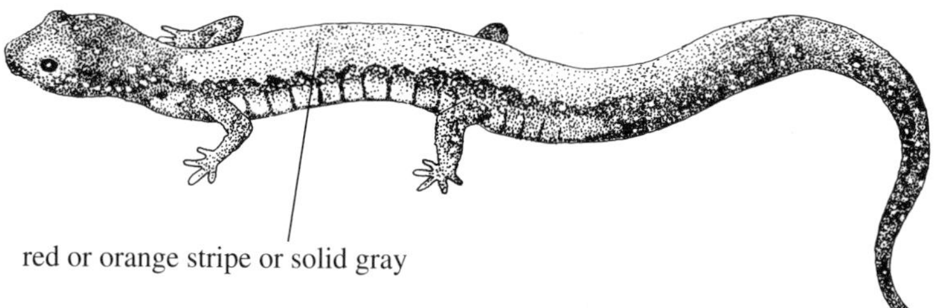

Fig.A. ***PLETHODON CINEREUS*, REDBACK SALAMANDER**: Red or orange stripe on back and tail (except for a leadback variety which is entirely dark); up to 9 cm (3 1/2") long; reported to occur in woods bordering tidal marshes under logs, boards, stones or other cover during the day; not likely to be found in water; salt intolerant.

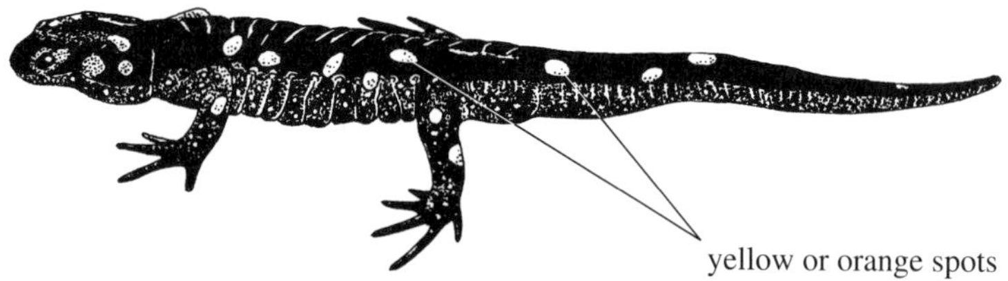

Fig.B. ***AMBYSTOMA MACULATUM*, SPOTTED SALAMANDER**: Back is black or dark gray with an irregular row of yellow or orange spots along each side of back; up to 20 cm (8") long; lives in woods bordering tidal marshes under rotten logs and in rodent tunnels; salt intolerant.

TURTLES[1]: CLASS REPTILIA, ORDER TESTUDINES

Four legged reptiles with a shell

(Use the key on page 2.14 to determine if you have a turtle)

#1.Flipperlike legs; without distinct toes .... **sea turtles[1]**, page 14.04
#1.Legs with distinct toes and claws (Figs.E-I) .... #2

#2.Plastron (shell on underside) small, leaving base of tail and legs well exposed; plastron cross shaped or nearly cross shaped (Fig.C); long tail, more than half the length of the carapace (upper shell); tail saw-toothed .... ***Chelydra s. serpentina*, common snapping turtle[1]** (Fig.E)
#2.Plastron nearly the same length and width as carapace; plastron oval shaped (Fig.D); short tail; tail not saw-toothed .... #3

#3.Carapace is high and dome shaped; plastron not in one piece but hinged near middle .... ***Terrapene c. carolina*, eastern box turtle** (Fig.F)
#3.Carapace not high and dome shaped; plastron in one piece (Figs.G-I) .... #4

#4.Distinct concentric rings or ridges on each scute (plate) of carapace .... ***Malaclemys t. terrapin*, northern diamondback terrapin** (Fig.G)
#4.Faint or no concentric rings or ridges on each scute (Fig.H,I) .... #5

#5.Carapace and head marked with scattered orange or yellow spots .... ***Clemmys guttata*, spotted turtle** (Fig.H)
#5.Carapace without spots; head and neck marked with light lines .... ***Chrysemys p. picta*, eastern painted turtle** (Fig.I)

[1]**WARNING:** Turtles are basically timid animals, but some can inflict a bad bite when picked up or harassed. Avoid getting within reach of snapping jaws, particularly when near a snapping turtle or sea turtle.

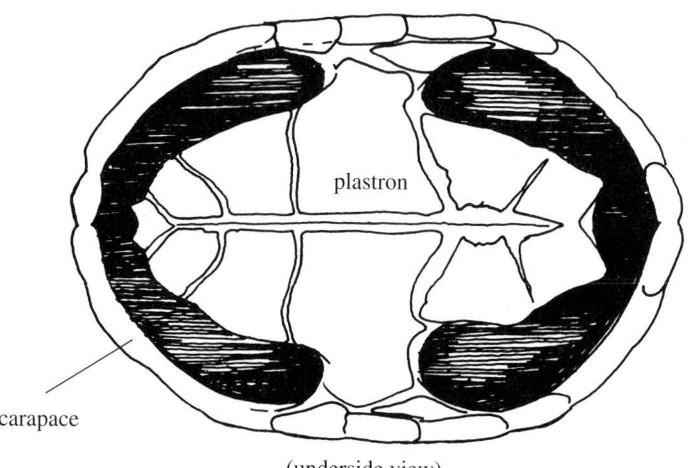

(underside view)

Fig.C. **CROSS SHAPED PLASTRON**

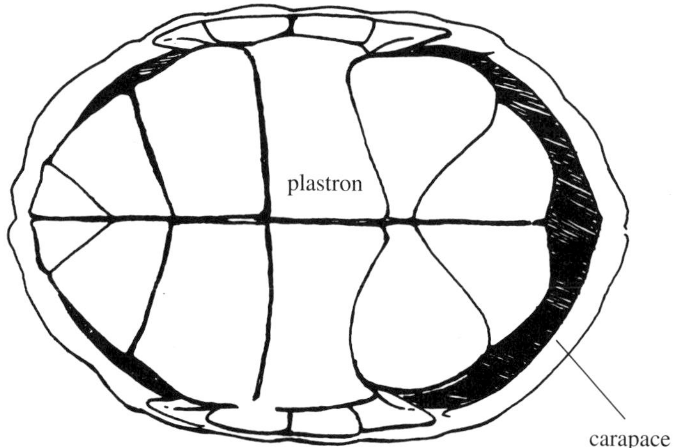

(underside view)

Fig.D. **OVAL PLASTRON**

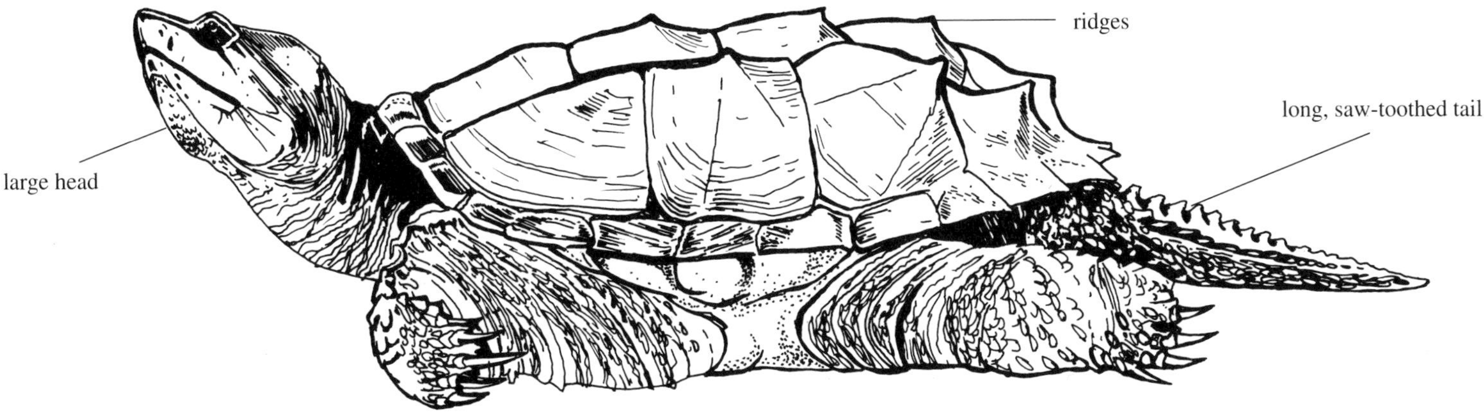

Fig.E. ***CHELYDRA S. SERPENTINA*, COMMON SNAPPING TURTLE**: Black or dark brown carapace; up to about 36 cm (14") long; common in any permanent body of fresh water; enters brackish water and tidal marshes; rather passive in the water, but on land will often strike repeatedly and deliver a nasty bite.

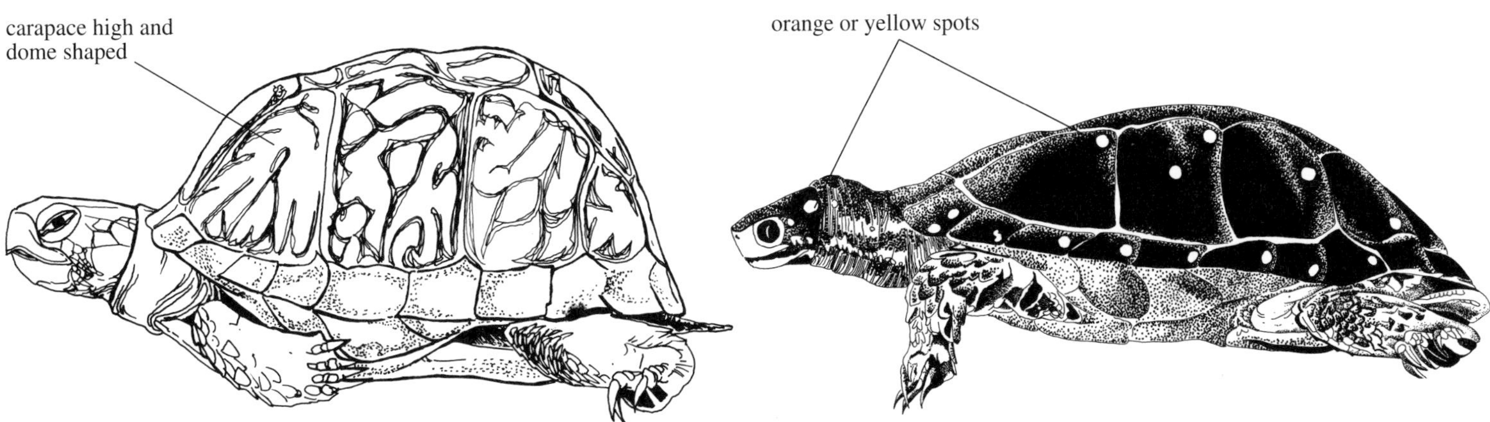

Fig.F. ***TERRAPENE C. CAROLINA*, EASTERN BOX TURTLE:** Carapace is black or brown with yellow, orange, or olive pattern (either light or dark colors can predominate); head and legs with yellow or orange markings; up to 15 cm (6") long; a terrestrial turtle that occurs on the edges of tidal marshes.

Fig.H. ***CLEMMYS GUTTATA*, SPOTTED TURTLE**: Distinct yellow or orange spots on black or brown carapace and on head and neck; up to 12 cm (5") long; reported to occur in tidal marshes, usually found in shallow bodies of fresh water.

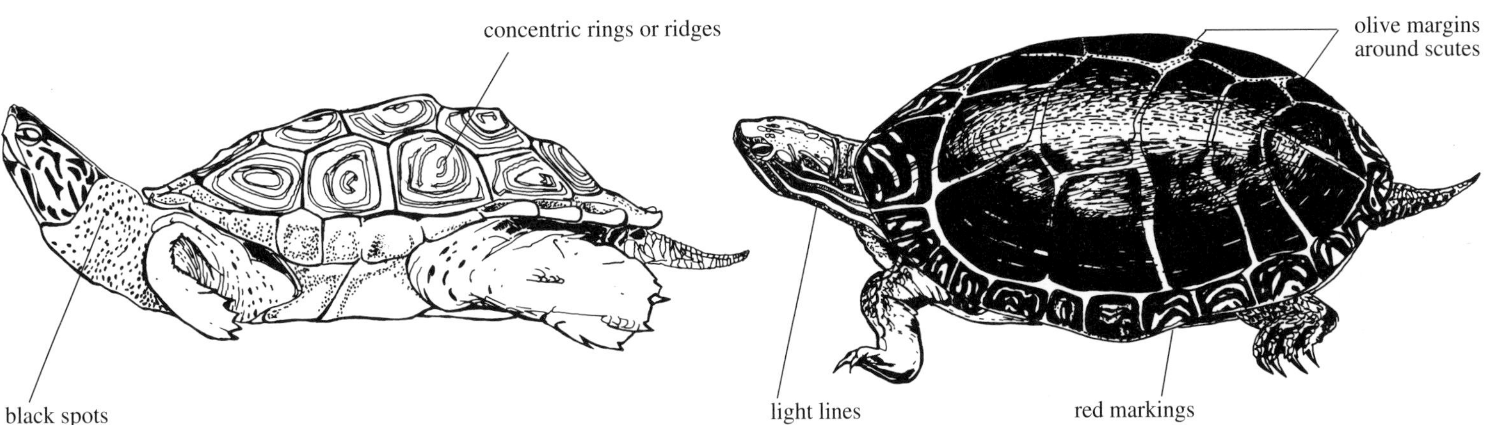

Fig.G. ***MALACLEMYS T. TERRAPIN*, NORTHERN DIAMONDBACK TERRAPIN**: Light brown, gray, or black carapace; each scute (plate) with concentric grooves and ridges or dark and light rings; plastron (lower shell) orange, golden, or greenish; spotted head and legs; up to 23 cm (9 ") long; found only in salt or brackish water; not uncommon in tidal marshes.

Fig.I. ***CHRYSEMYS P. PICTA*, EASTERN PAINTED TURTLE**: Olive to dark brown carapace with olive border around each large scute (plate); marginal scutes with red markings; plastron yellow, sometimes with dark markings; black skin of head with red and yellow lines; up to 15 cm (6") long; occasionally found in tidal marshes, common in fresh water, may be seen basking on logs.

SEA TURTLES[1]: CLASS REPTILIA, ORDER TESTUDINES

Turtles with flipperlike legs; without distinct toes

(Turtle key begins on page 14.02)

#1.Carapace (upper shell) smooth, not composed of scutes (large plates or scales); with several prominent ridges along back .... ***Dermochelys coriacea*, leatherback** (Fig.A)

#1.Carapace composed of numerous scutes; no prominent ridges along back (Figs.B-E) .... #2

#2.Five or more pairs of costal scutes (plates to either side of midline plates), first costal scute touches nuchal scute (plate just behind neck) (Figs.B,C).......... #3

#2.Four pairs of costal scutes; first costal scute does not touch nuchal scute (Figs.D,E) .... #4

#3.Shell is reddish brown; three (rarely four) bridge scutes (plates on underside connecting plastron to carapace, see Fig. B); bridge scutes do not have pores; no interanal scute (small plate at rear end of plastron) .... ***Caretta caretta*, loggerhead** (Fig.B)

#3.Shell is gray or olive green above, yellow on underside; four (rarely five) bridge scutes; bridge scutes have pores; with an interanal scute .... ***Lepidochelys kempii,* Atlantic ridley** (Fig.C)

#4.One pair of scales between eyes; carapace scutes do not overlap (except in very young).. ***Chelonia mydas*, green turtle** (Fig.D)

#4.Two pairs of scales between eyes; carapace scutes overlap (except in very old) .... ***Eretmochelys i. imbricata*, Atlantic hawksbill** (Fig.E)

[1]See warning on page 14.02.

ridges

smooth carapace

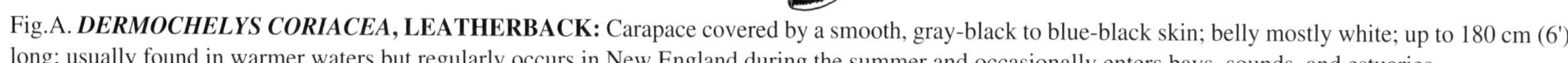

Fig.A. ***DERMOCHELYS CORIACEA*, LEATHERBACK:** Carapace covered by a smooth, gray-black to blue-black skin; belly mostly white; up to 180 cm (6') long; usually found in warmer waters but regularly occurs in New England during the summer and occasionally enters bays, sounds, and estuaries.

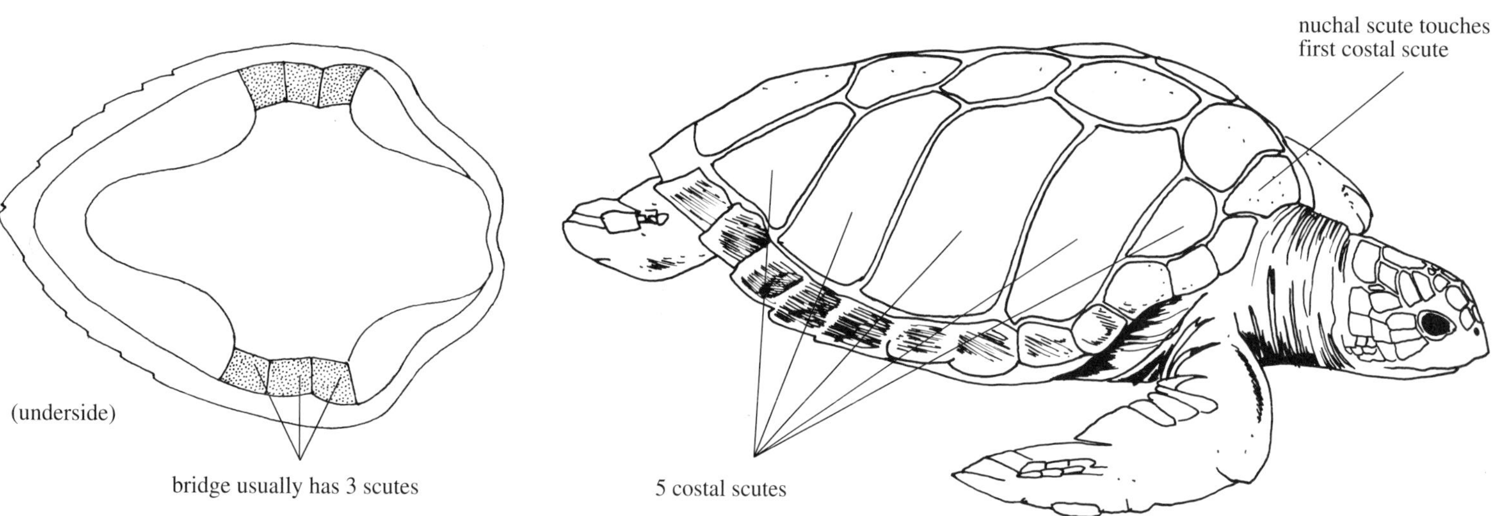

Fig.B. ***CARETTA CARETTA*, LOGGERHEAD:** Reddish brown; up to 120 cm (4') long; usually found in warm Atlantic waters but occasionally seen in southern New England bays and sounds in summer.

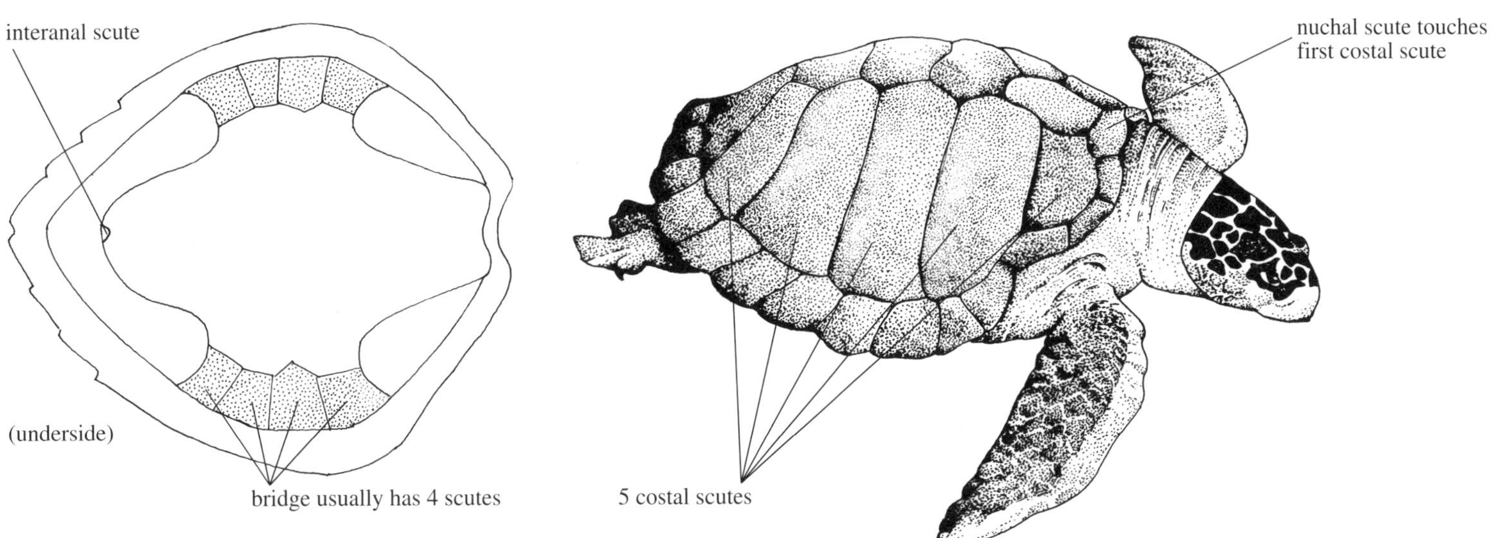

Fig.C. ***LEPIDOCHELYS KEMPII,* ATLANTIC RIDLEY:** Carapace is olive green in older turtles, gray in younger; underside is yellow; up to 70 cm (28") long; usually lives in Gulf of Mexico but immature turtles occur in southern New England in the summer and fall.

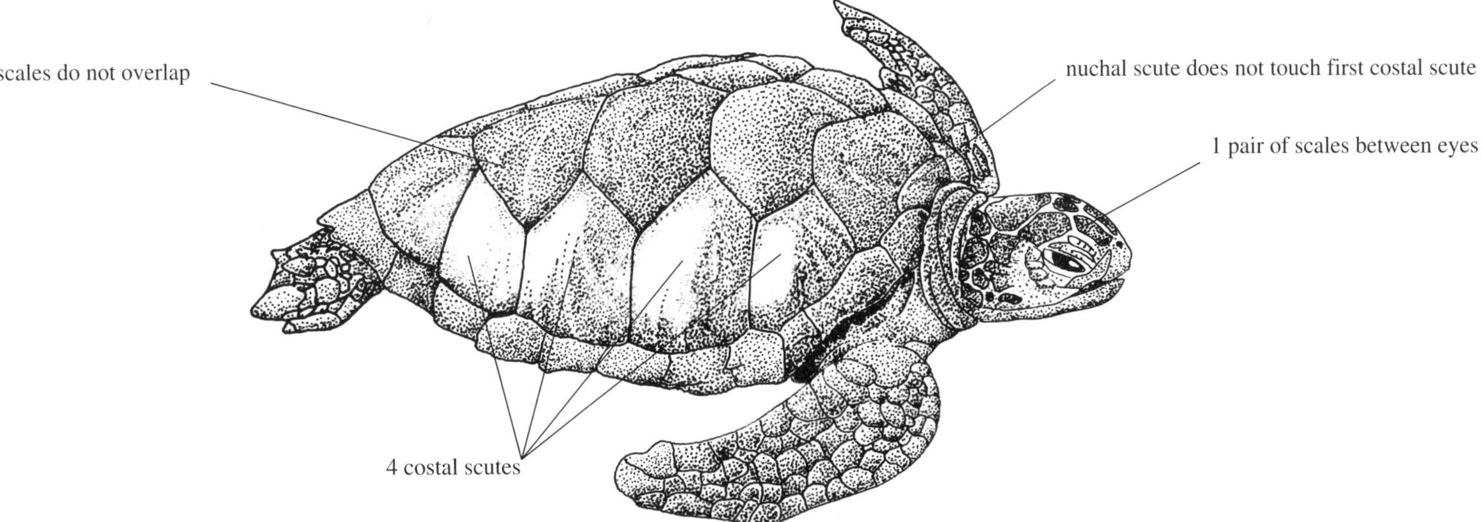

Fig.D. ***CHELONIA MYDAS,* GREEN TURTLE:** Brown or faded olive, often with radiating mottled or wavy dark marks or blotches; up to 120 cm (4') long; usually found in warmer Atlantic waters; rare in estuarine waters, immature turtles occur in southern New England in summer and fall.

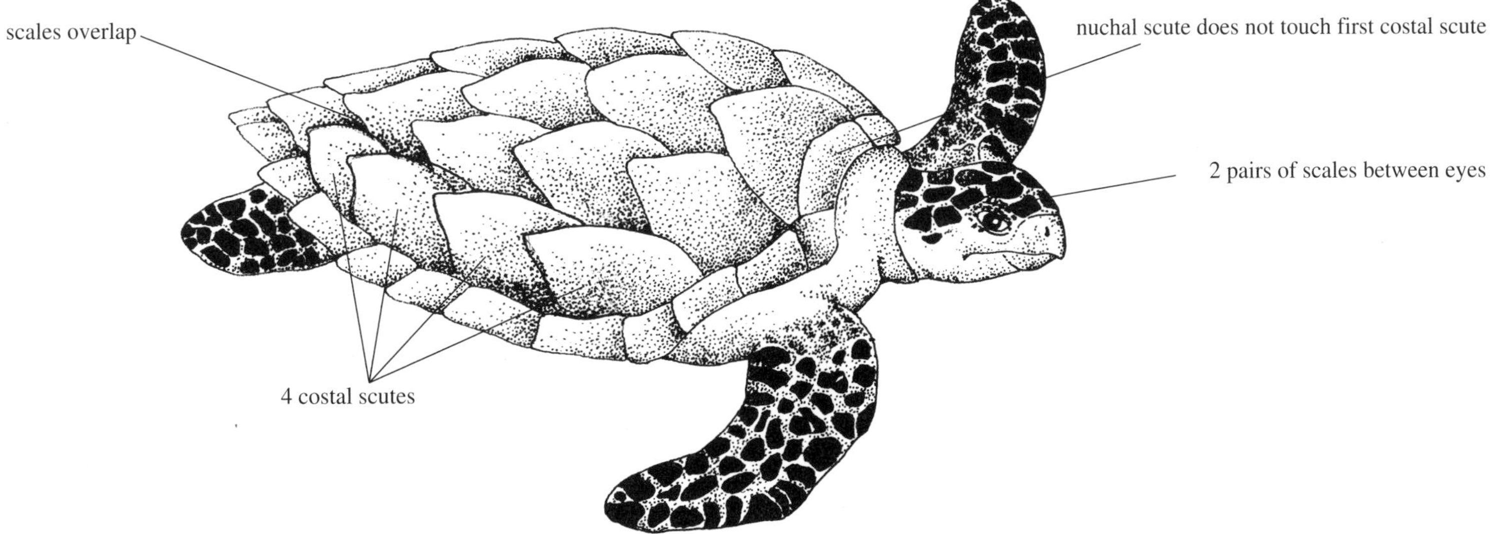

Fig.E. ***ERETMOCHELYS I. IMBRICATA,* ATLANTIC HAWKSBILL:** Brown or tortoiseshell pattern; up to 90 cm (35") long; usually lives in subtropical and tropical waters; rare visitor to southern New England where it occasionally is found far offshore.

SNAKES[1]: CLASS REPTILIA, ORDER SERPENTES

Reptiles without legs, external ears, or moveable eyelids; with forked tongue.

(Use the key on page 2.16 to determine if you have a snake)

#1.Snout upturned; when approached, snake may flatten head and neck and hiss loudly, and/or roll onto back and "play dead" .... ***Heterodon platirhinos*, eastern hognose snake** (Fig.C)

#1.Snout rounded, not upturned (Figs.D-I); does not play dead or behave as described above .... #2

#2.Upper surface of body one solid color[2] (Figs.D,E); scales are smooth (without a raised central ridge, Fig.A) or weakly keeled; anal plate divided (Fig.F) .. #3

#2.Upper surface of body marked with dark spots or blotches (Figs.F,G); scales are keeled (with a raised central ridge, Fig.B); anal plate divided (Fig.F) .... #5

#2.Upper surface of body with three stripes and/or rows of spots (Figs.H,I); stripes or spots are usually yellow but may be brown, green, blue or orange; scales are keeled; anal plate undivided (Fig.I) .... #6

#3.Upper surface of body a bright parrot green .... ***Opheodrys vernalis*, smooth green snake** (Fig.D)

#3.Upper surface of body is black .... #4

#4.Underside (belly) is much lighter than back; belly is very flat; middorsal scales are weakly keeled .... ***Elaphe o. obsoleta*, black rat snake** (Fig.E)

#4.Underside (belly) is black; belly is rounded; scales are smooth .... ***Coluber c. constrictor*, northern black racer** (Fig.E)

#5.Dark crossbands on neck and anterior body, rest of body has dark blotches alternating on back and sides... ***Nerodia s. sipedon*, northern water snake** (Fig.F)

#5.With two parallel rows of blackish spots along back; with a dark downward streak on each side of head... ***Storeria d. dekayi*, northern brown snake** (Fig.G)

#6.Lateral stripes are on scale rows 3 and 4 (3rd and 4th rows of scales up from the large belly scales); tail (from anal plate to tip) is very long and slender (about 1/3 total length of snake); with a brown stripe on outer edge of belly and first two rows of scales ...... ***Thamnophis s. sauritus*, eastern ribbon snake** (Fig.H)

#6.Lateral stripes are on scale rows 2 and 3; tail is about 1/4 of total length; 2 rows of spots on belly .... ***Thamnophis s. sirtalis*, eastern garter snake** (Fig.I)

[1]**WARNING:** Most snakes are inoffensive creatures but many react aggressively when threatened. Handle all snakes with care as many will bite. Do not pick up any snakes you cannot identify.

[2]NOTE: Young snakes have different color patterns than adults. Use Conant and Collins (1991) or Klemens (1993) to identify small snakes that do not key out here.

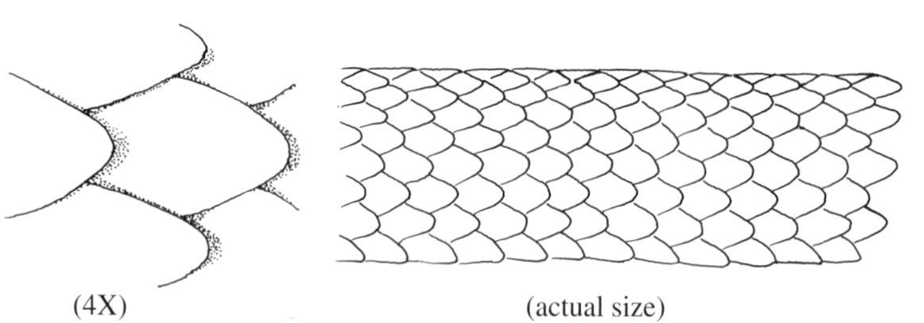

Fig.A. **SMOOTH SCALES:** Scales without a raised central ridge.

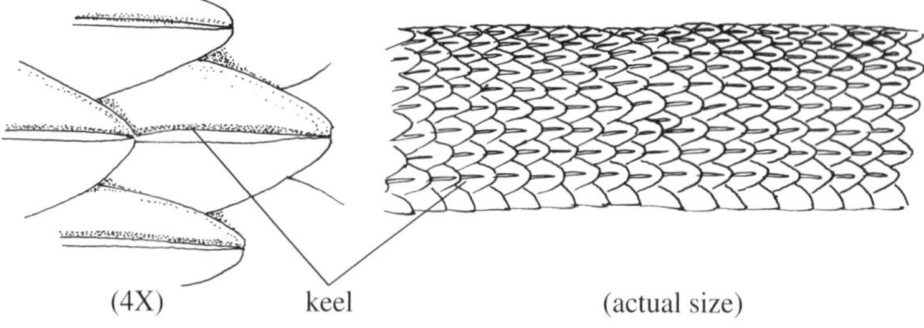

Fig.B. **KEELED SCALES**: Scales with a raised central ridge.

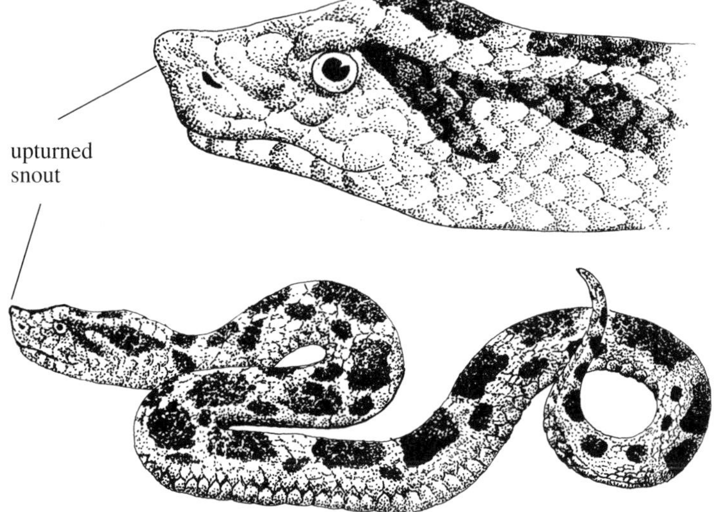

Fig.C. ***HETERODON PLATIRHINOS*, EASTERN HOGNOSE SNAKE:** Normally a spotted snake but may be uniform yellow, brown, gray, red, or black; underside of tail lighter than mottled gray belly; usually up to about 84 cm (33") long; prefers fine sandy habitats and may be locally common on sand dunes.

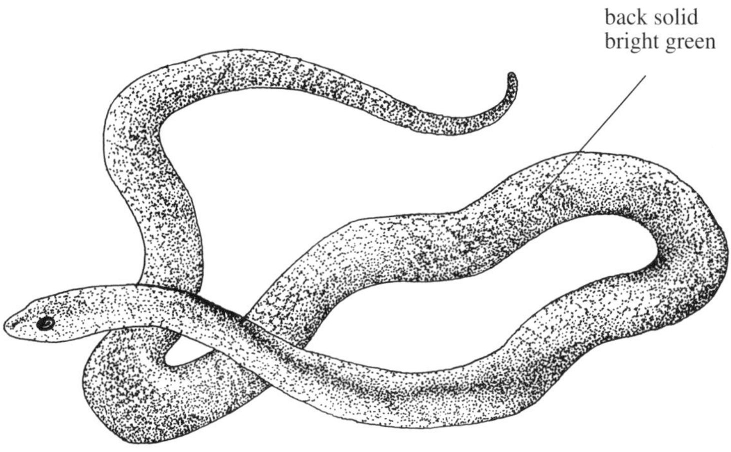

Fig.D. ***OPHEODRYS VERNALIS*, SMOOTH GREEN SNAKE:** Bright green on back, belly cream colored or yellow; usually up to about 51 cm (20") long; found in tidal marshes and other coastal habitats, including islands.

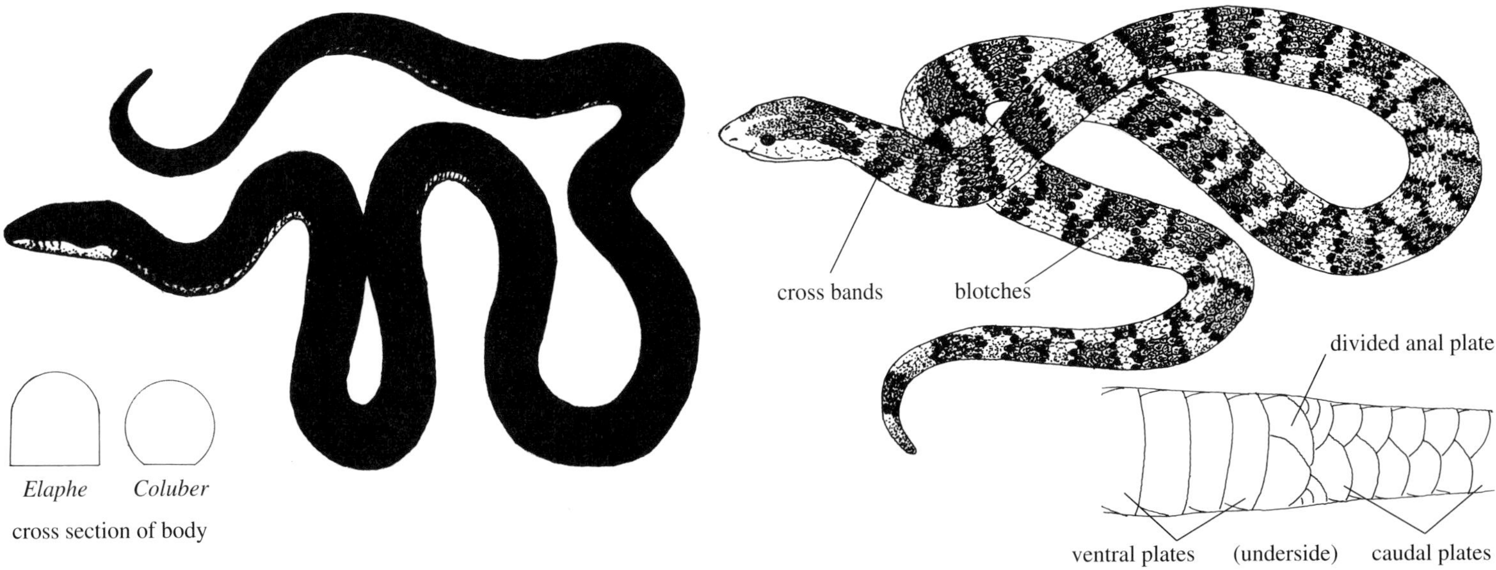

Fig.E. ***ELAPHE O. OBSOLETA,*** **BLACK RAT SNAKE:** Topside is usually all shiny black, but skin between scales may be lighter; belly is yellowish or white; up to about 185 cm (73") long. ***COLUBER C. CONSTRICTOR,*** **NORTHERN BLACK RACER:** All black above and below except for some white on chin and throat; up to 152 cm (60") long. Both species occur in saltmarshes where they feed on small rodents such as the meadow vole, *Microtus*.

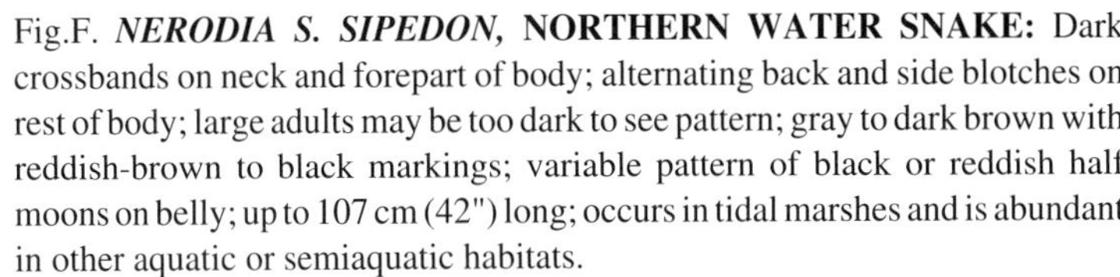

Fig.F. ***NERODIA S. SIPEDON,*** **NORTHERN WATER SNAKE:** Dark crossbands on neck and forepart of body; alternating back and side blotches on rest of body; large adults may be too dark to see pattern; gray to dark brown with reddish-brown to black markings; variable pattern of black or reddish half moons on belly; up to 107 cm (42") long; occurs in tidal marshes and is abundant in other aquatic or semiaquatic habitats.

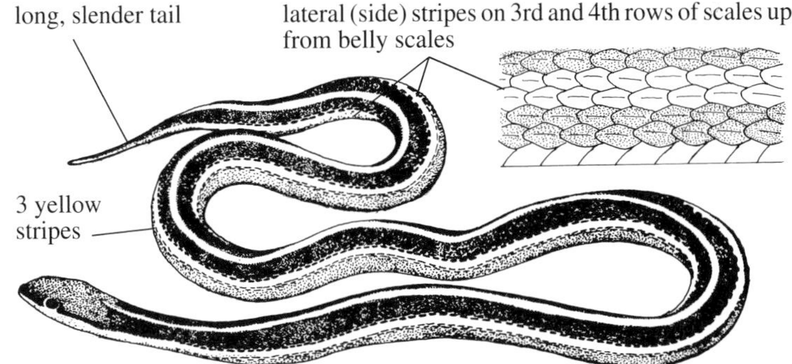

Fig.G. ***STORERIA D. DEKAYI,*** **NORTHERN BROWN SNAKE:** Overall color is light or dark brown with parallel rows of blackish spots along back; up to about 33 cm (13") long; occurs in coastal areas including islands; sometimes found underneath stranded debris just above high tide level.

Fig.H. ***THAMNOPHIS S. SAURITUS,*** **EASTERN RIBBON SNAKE:** Dark background with three bright stripes which are usually yellow but middorsal stripe may be orangish or greenish; with brown stripe on outer edge of belly and first two rows of scales; up to about 66 cm (26") long; occurs in saltmarshes.

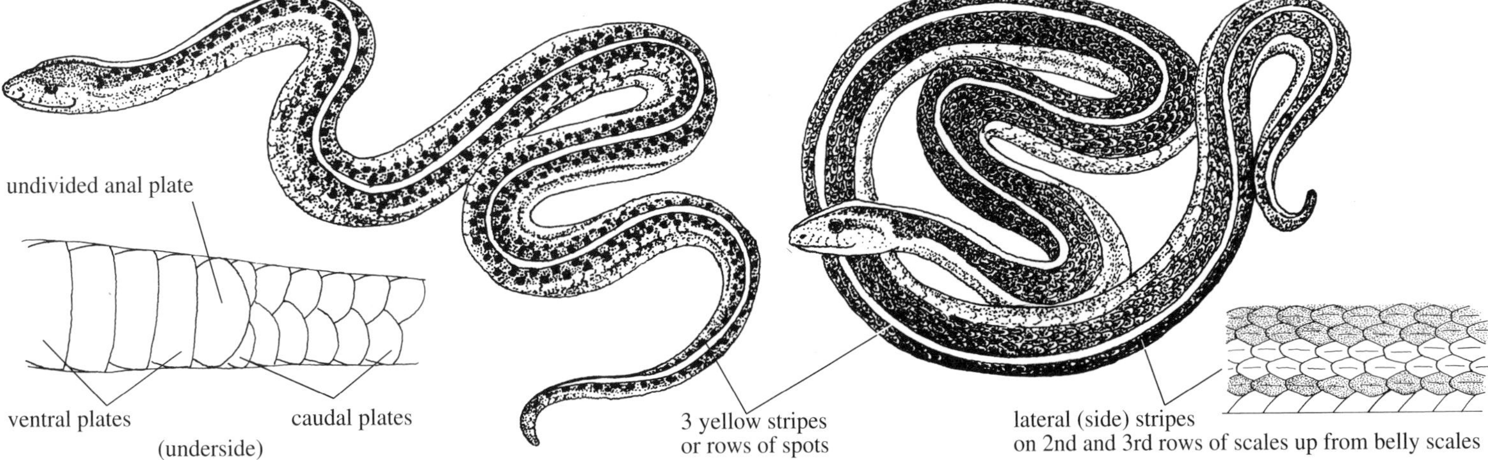

Fig.I. ***THAMNOPHIS S. SIRTALIS,*** **EASTERN GARTER SNAKE:** Variable in color and pattern; usually a dark background color with 3 yellowish stripes, including a stripe down the center of the back; may have a double row of alternating black squares between stripes; either stripes or squares may predominate, or snake may be stripeless; belly yellow or greenish; up to 66 cm (26") long; found in tidal marshes as well as many other coastal habitats, including islands.

BIRDS
PHYLUM CHORDATA, CLASS AVES
Vertebrates with wings and feathers[1]

(Use the key on page 2.14 to determine if you have a bird)

#1. Ducklike (Fig.A); with a relatively long neck, short legs and tail, and webbed feet or lobed toes; often observed swimming (paddling on surface of water or swimming beneath water) ... **waterfowl (ducks, geese, swans, etc.)**, page 15.02

#1. Not ducklike (Figs.B-I); may rest or float on the water but does not swim underwater or paddle for significant distances on water ... #2

#2. Gull-like or ternlike (Figs.B,C); with pointed wings; short legs and fully webbed feet; color is typically gray and white, or black and white, but may be mottled brown when immature; graceful acrobatic flight; often flies over water; may swoop down to rest on land or water and may plunge into water to feed ... **gulls, terns, and seabirds**, page 15.15

#2. Not gull or ternlike (Figs. D-I); with rounded wings and/or is not primarily gray and white or black and white in color ... #3

#3. Waders (Fig.D); shorebirds that walk or run in shallow water or along water's edge on mudflats, beaches and marshes; feed on organisms in water, mud or sand; most species have long legs and/or long, sharply pointed bills ... **wading birds (herons, egrets, and sandpipers)**, page 15.20

#3. Nonwaders (Figs. F-I); do not swim, wade or rest on the water; most species have relatively short legs and short bill ... #4

#4. Fishing birds (Figs. F,G), that dive into water for fish; often seen soaring or hovering with rapidly beating wings just before folding wings and plunging down into water; after fishing, these birds return to perches in trees or on top of poles; they do not paddle, float or wade in water ... **fishing birds**, #5

#4. Land birds (Figs.G-I); birds that rarely or never come into contact with the water; usually seen perching in marsh or upland vegetation, flying or soaring over land or water, hiding in tall grass, or nesting in bluffs, under docks, in trees ... #6

#5. Head is large with shaggy crest (Fig.F); bill is heavy, daggerlike; legs are short; wings are rounded; plunges head first into water; wings and back are blue-gray, belly and neck are white separated by a gray breast band (females also have a reddish brown breastband) ... ***Ceryle alcyon*, belted kingfisher** (Fig.F)

#5. Hawklike (Fig.G), with hooked bill, talons (claws) on feet, long wings; plunges feet first into water; head and underside of wings with black and white pattern ... **osprey and eagles**, page 15.30

#5. Ternlike or gull-like (Fig.B); dives head first; gray and white or black and white ... **terns and seabirds**, page 15.15

#6. Hawklike or owl-like (Fig.G); short-necked bird with talons (strong claws on toes), heavy, hook tipped bill, relatively large, "fierce" eyes, rounded or pointed wings; often seen soaring, circling or hovering ... **birds of prey (falcons, hawks, vultures, owls)**, page 15.29

#6. Not hawklike or owl-like (Figs.H,I); bill is straight or pointed, not hook tipped; claws are not particularly large ... #7

#7. Henlike (Fig.I) with narrow body and rounded wings, stout legs and long toes; secretive and well camouflaged, hiding in marsh grass, usually heard rather than seen; if flushed, will fly short distances with dangling legs; some species have long bills that curve down slightly ... **family Rallidae (in part), rails** (Fig.I)

#7. Not henlike (Fig.H); not particularly secretive, will fly or perch in the open; when at rest may perch in trees and other vegetation, or on telephone wires or walk on ground ... **perching birds and other land birds**, page 15.32

[1]NOTE: Bird lengths given in these keys are measured from tip of bill to end of tail with bird lying on back (see Fig.E). Length data are from R. T. Peterson (1980).

lobed toes

webbed foot

Fig.A. **WATERFOWL**

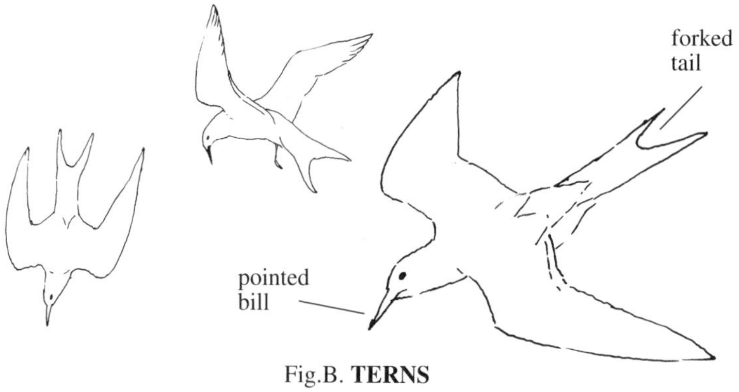

forked tail

pointed bill

Fig.B. **TERNS**

thick bill

rounded or square tail

wide wings

Fig.C. **GULLS**

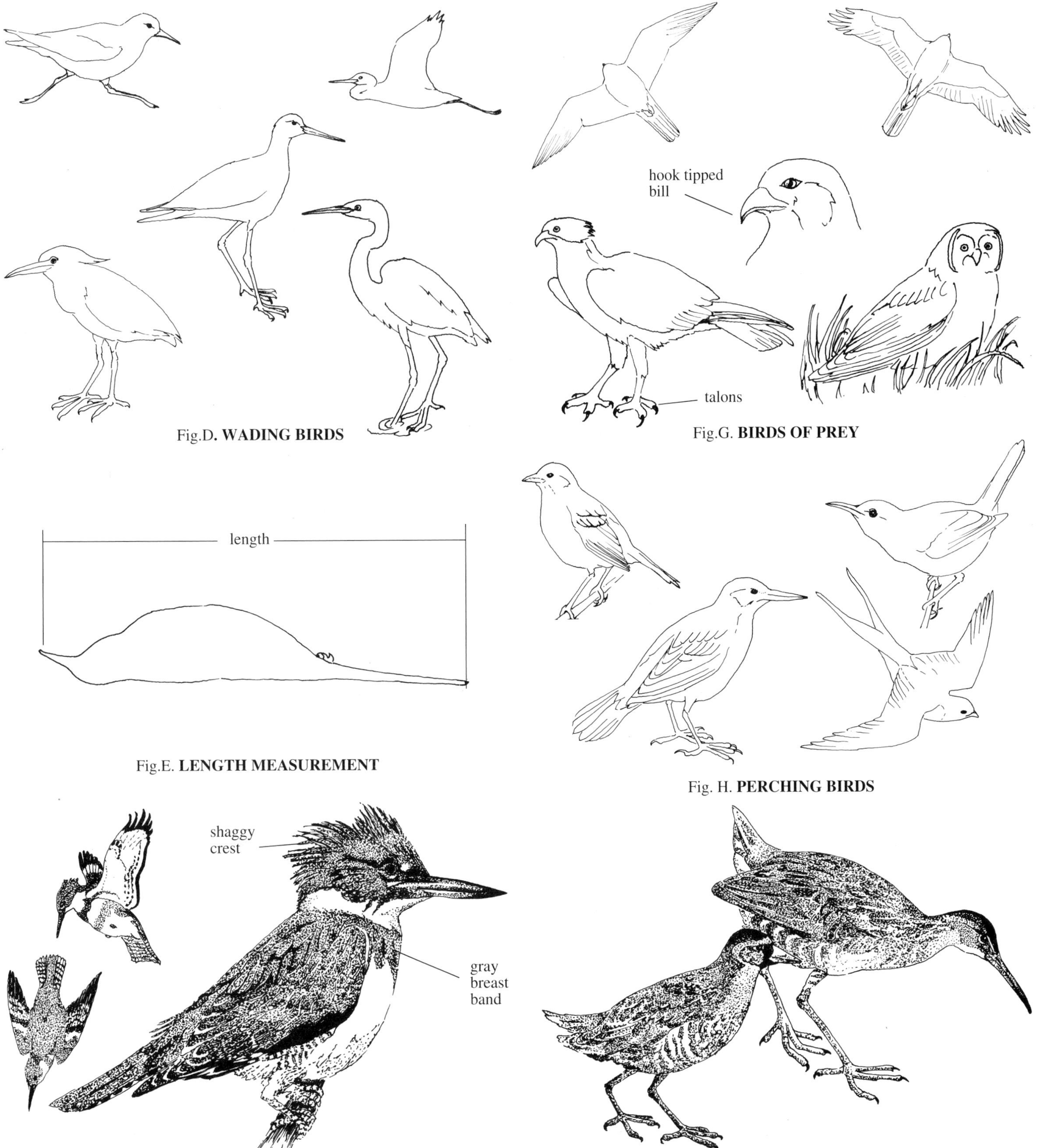

Fig.D. **WADING BIRDS**

Fig.G. **BIRDS OF PREY**

Fig.E. **LENGTH MEASUREMENT**

Fig. H. **PERCHING BIRDS**

Fig.F. ***CERYLE ALCYON* (=*Megaceryle a.*), BELTED KINGFISHER:** Blue-gray above, white belly and throat; up to 33 cm (13") long; hovers over water with rapid wing beat, then dives in head first. (family Alcedinidae: kingfishers)

Fig.I. **FAMILY RALLIDAE (in part), RAILS:** Most species are brownish with white and black stripes and splotches; some rails are up to 48 cm (19") long; common in saltmarshes but rarely seen because they are secretive and well camouflaged.

WATERFOWL (DUCKS, GEESE, SWANS, DIVERS)

Birds with relatively long necks, short legs and tails; with webbed feet or lobed toes; often swim on surface of water and dive beneath water

(Bird key begins on page 15.00)

#1.Bill is ducklike, flattened top to bottom with rounded, spoon shaped tip (Fig. A); toes are webbed (Fig.A) .... #6

#1.Bill is daggerlike, spikelike, or chickenlike, with pointed or hooked tip; bill is not flattened from top to bottom (Figs.B-F); toes may be separate (Figs.C,F) or may be webbed. NOTE: If in doubt, make this choice .... #2

#2.Bill is hook tipped (Fig.B), slender; most of bird is black with orange or yellow chin pouch (Fig.B); often stands on rocks, sometimes with wings outstretched; swims low in water with bill tilted up at an angle; stays underwater for a long time when diving; feet are webbed .... **cormorants** (Fig. B), page 15.04

#2.Tip of bill is pointed (Figs.C-F); no orange or yellow chin pouch; does not often stand on rocks .... #3

#3.Pumps head back and forth when swimming; chickenlike bill extends up onto forehead between eyes (Fig.C); toes are separate, not webbed .... **coots and moorhens** (Fig.C), bottom of page 15.06

#3.Does not pump head back and forth when swimming; bill does not extend onto forehead (Figs.D-F); toes may be webbed (Fig.A) or separate (Fig.F) .... #4

#4.Bill is slender, spikelike, with sawtoothed mandibles (Fig. D); with shaggy or fan shaped crest (Fig.D) on head of all females and some males; flies with head and body at same level; toes are webbed .... **mergansers** (Fig.D), page 15.07

#4.Bill has knob near base (Fig.K); all or most of bird is black .... **scoters** (Fig.K), page 15.11

#4.Bill is daggerlike or chickenlike (Figs.E,F); mandibles are not sawtoothed; head without shaggy or fan shaped crest, but some species have ear tufts (Fig.F) giving head a flat topped appearance; flies with head sagging below body (Fig.E); toes may or may not be webbed .... #5

#5.Bill is heavy, daggerlike (Fig.E); toes are webbed; large bird, often longer than 50 cm (20"); no ear tufts on head; with obvious tail; dark plumage with white chest and/or throat; swims low in water; remains underwater for long period of time when diving .... **loons** (Fig.E), page 15.05

#5.Bill is straight and thin, or daggerlike or chickenlike; toes are separate, not webbed; smaller bird, less than 45 cm (18") in length; some species appear to have no tail; some species have ear tufts giving head a flat topped appearance (Fig.F) .... **grebes** (Fig.F), page 15.06

#5.Bill is flattened from top to bottom and rounded in front (Fig.A); toes are webbed .... #7

#6.Gooselike (Fig.G) or swanlike (Fig.H); neck is very long, making up one-third to one-half of total body length; most species are over 60 cm (2') in length and some exceed 150 cm (5') .... **swans and geese**, page 15.14

#6.Ducklike (Figs.I,J); neck is less than one-third of total body length; most species are under 60 cm (2') in length .... **ducks**, #7

#7.Diving duck; feeds by diving beneath the surface of the water; usually found in deep, open water; often rafts (forms groups floating close together) on water in large numbers; runs and patters on water when taking off (Fig.I); wing is solid color or has white patch .... **diving ducks**, page 15.12

#7.Dabbling duck; feeds by "tipping up" (Fig.J) with head down in water and tail up in air; usually found in relatively shallow, protected water such as estuaries, bays, river mouths; often leaps directly upward from water when taking off; wing patch (speculum) is colorful (blue, green, brown) or white .... **dabbling ducks**, page 15.08

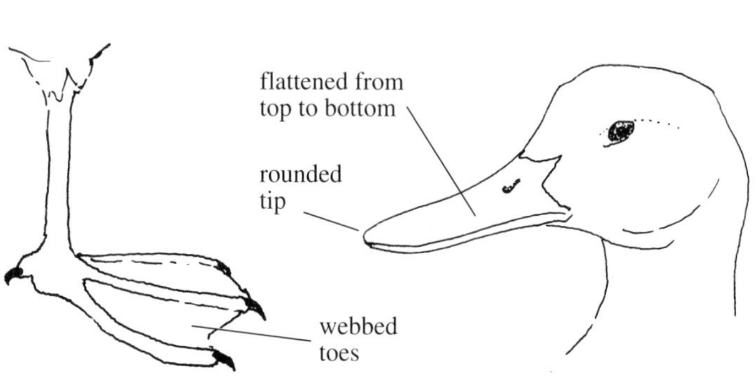

flattened from top to bottom
rounded tip
webbed toes

Fig.A. **DUCKLIKE BILL AND FOOT**

chickenlike bill extends onto forehead
toes not webbed

Fig.C. **COOTS AND MOORHENS**

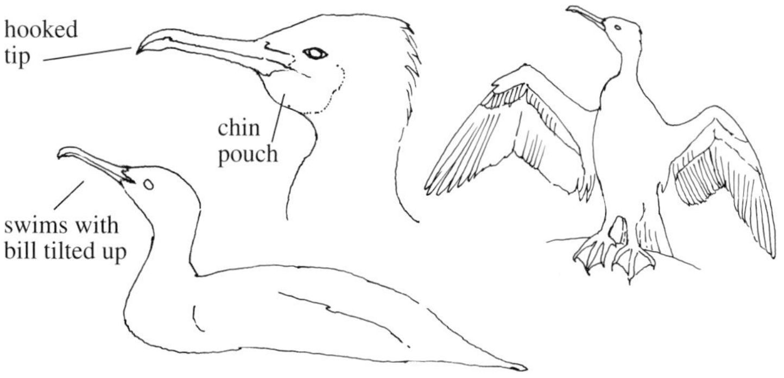

hooked tip
chin pouch
swims with bill tilted up

Fig.B. **CORMORANTS**

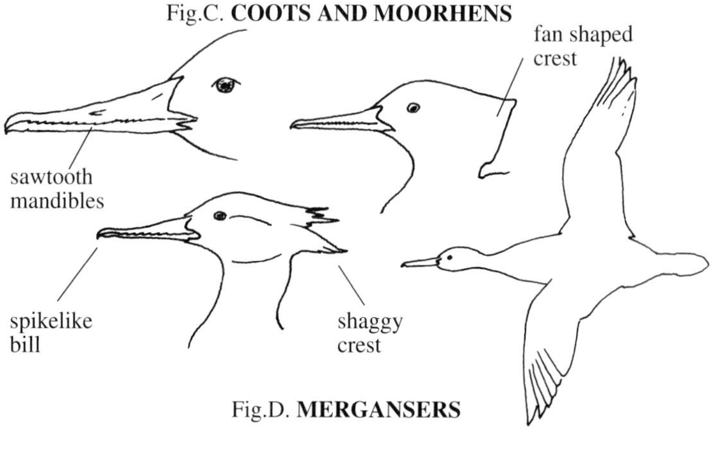

fan shaped crest
sawtooth mandibles
spikelike bill
shaggy crest

Fig.D. **MERGANSERS**

Fig.E. **LOONS**

Fig.H. **SWANS**

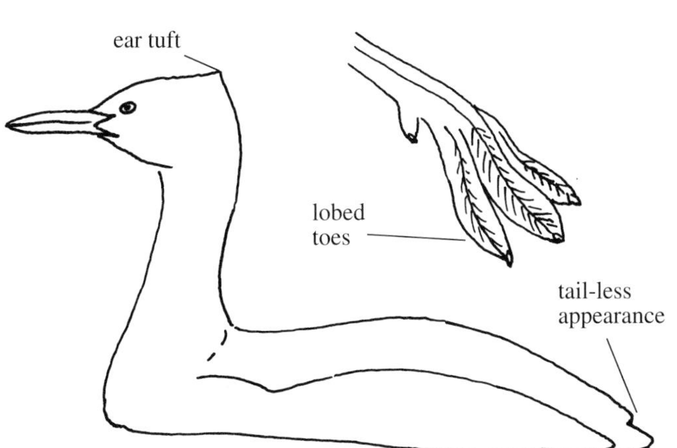

Fig.F. **GREBES**

Fig.I. **DIVING DUCKS**

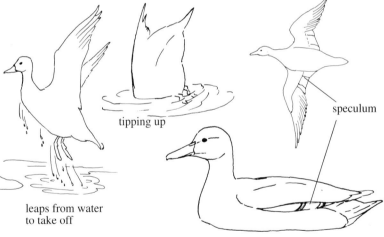

tipping up

speculum

leaps from water
to take off

Fig. J. **DABBLING DUCKS**

Fig. G. **GEESE**

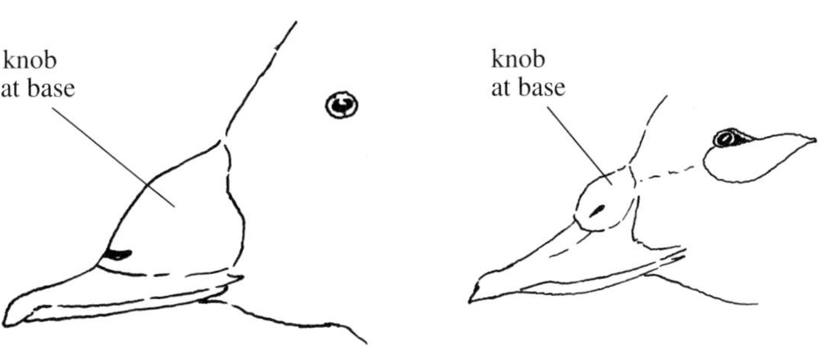

Fig.K. **SCOTER BILLS**

CORMORANTS: FAMILY PHALACROCORACIDAE

Ducklike diving birds with slender, hook tipped bills and an orange or yellow chin pouch

(Use the key on page 15.02 to determine if you have a cormorant)

#1.Belly, breast, and neck are completely black .... adult cormorants, #2
#1.Belly, breast, or neck is white or gray .... immature cormorants, #3

#2.Chin pouch (Fig.A) is orange and is not bordered by a white chin strap; a small crest may or may not be visible on back of the head; this is the only cormorant usually found in this region during the breeding season, approximately April to July .... ***Phalacrocorax auritus*, double-crested cormorant** (Fig.A)
#2.Chin pouch is yellow and is bordered by a white "chin strap" (Fig.B); this is the only cormorant usually found in southern New England during the winter months, December through February .... ***Phalacrocorax carbo*, great cormorant** (Fig.B)

#3.Belly is darker than breast and neck; the most common cormorant in warmer months .... ***Phalacrocorax auritus*, double-crested cormorant** (Fig.A)
#3.Belly is lighter than breast and neck; the only cormorant in winter months .... ***Phalacrocorax carbo*, great cormorant** (Fig.B)

Fig.A. ***PHALACROCORAX AURITUS*, DOUBLE-CRESTED CORMORANT:** Mostly black with orangish chin pouch; up to 83 cm (33") long; excellent diver and underwater swimmer; remains submerged for long time and emerges far from dive site; swims low in water with bill tilted up; often perches on rocks, sometimes with wings outstretched to dry (see Fig.B); migrates south of New England during winter and extends to Newfoundland in summer.

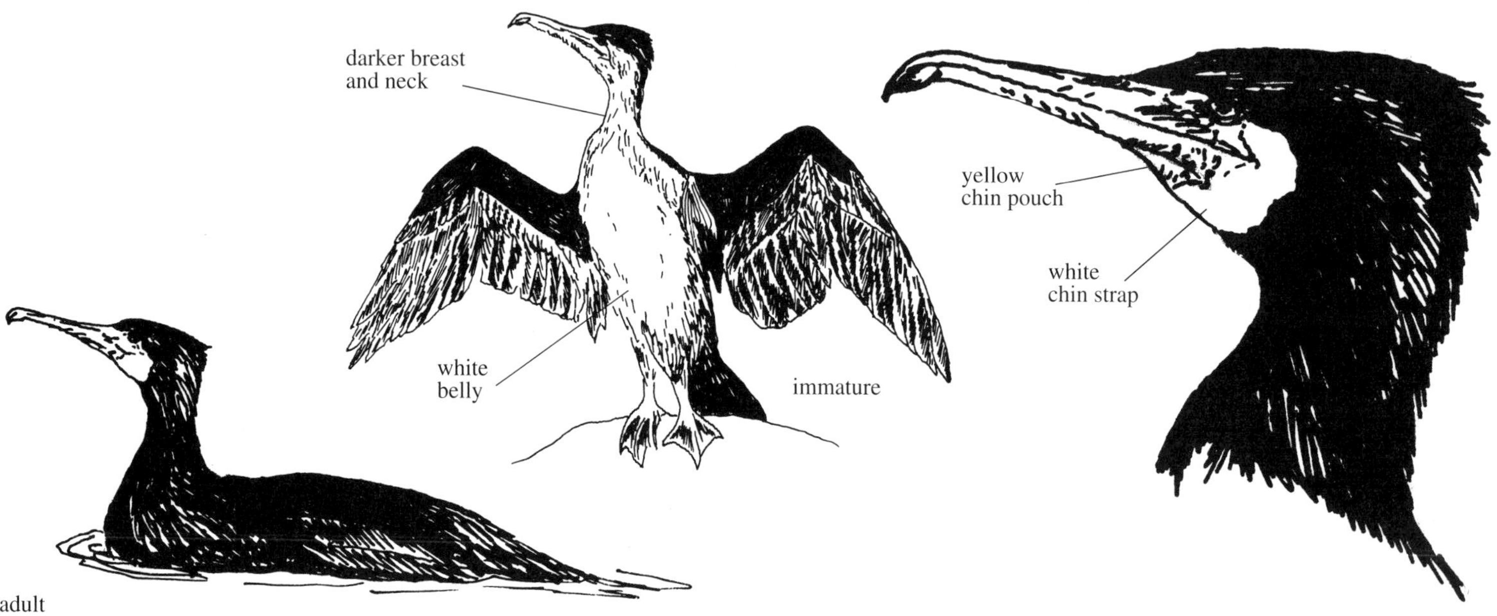

Fig.B. ***PHALACROCORAX CARBO*, GREAT CORMORANT:** Mostly black with yellow chin pouch and white chin strap; up to 93 cm (37") long; breeds in maritime provinces of Canada during summer and migrates south during winter months into southern New England and mid-Atlantic states; behavior similar to double-crested cormorant.

LOONS: FAMILY GAVIIDAE

Ducklike diving birds with daggerlike bills

(Use the key on page 15.02 to determine if you have a loon)

#1.Bill is stout and straight (Fig.A) .... ***Gavia immer*, common loon** (Fig.A)
#1.Bill is thin and upturned (Fig.B) .... ***Gavia stellata*, red-throated loon** (Fig.B)

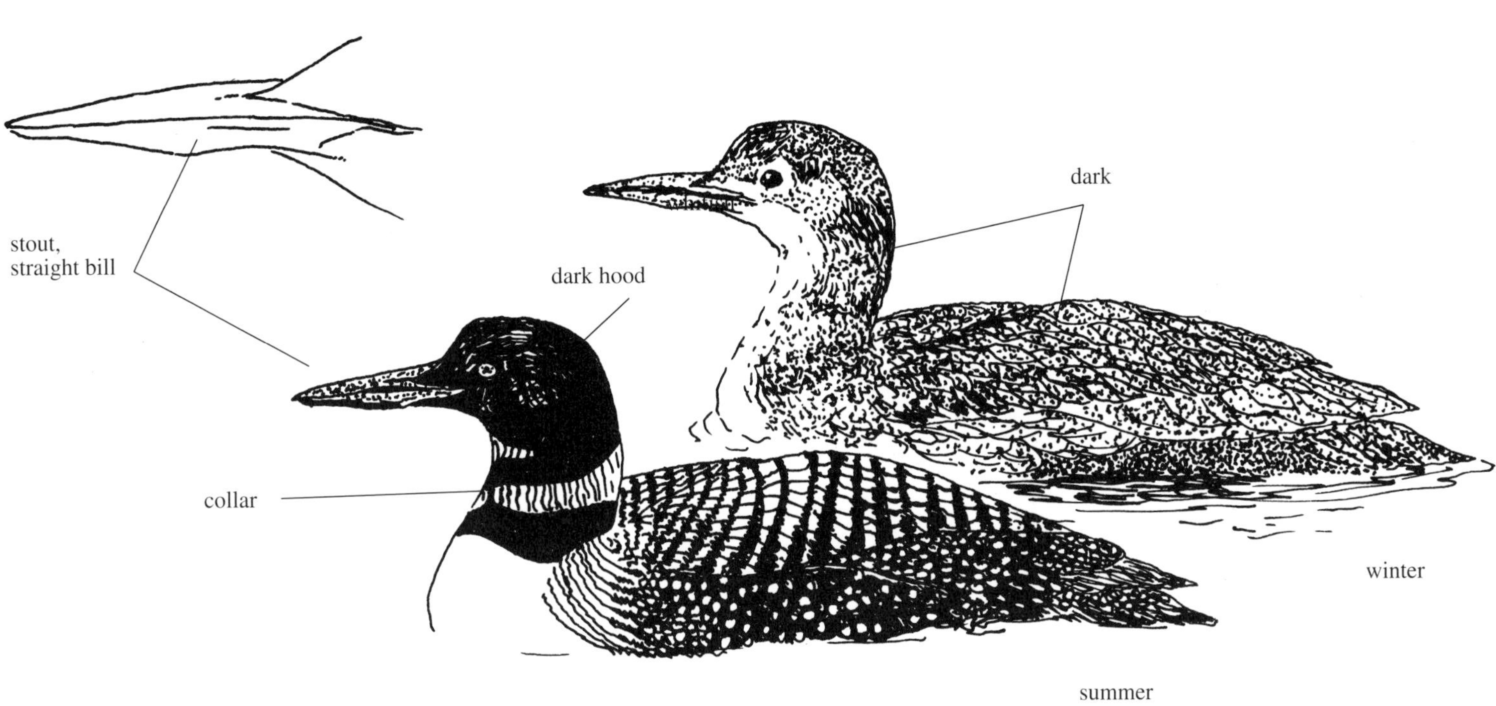

Fig.A. ***GAVIA IMMER*, COMMON LOON:** In summer breeding plummage, the head has a dark hood extending onto throat, a broken white collar and the back is checkered with dark and light cross bands; in winter, the top of the head and back is dark and the underside is whitish; up to 90 cm (36") long; usually observed only during colder months and spring migration.

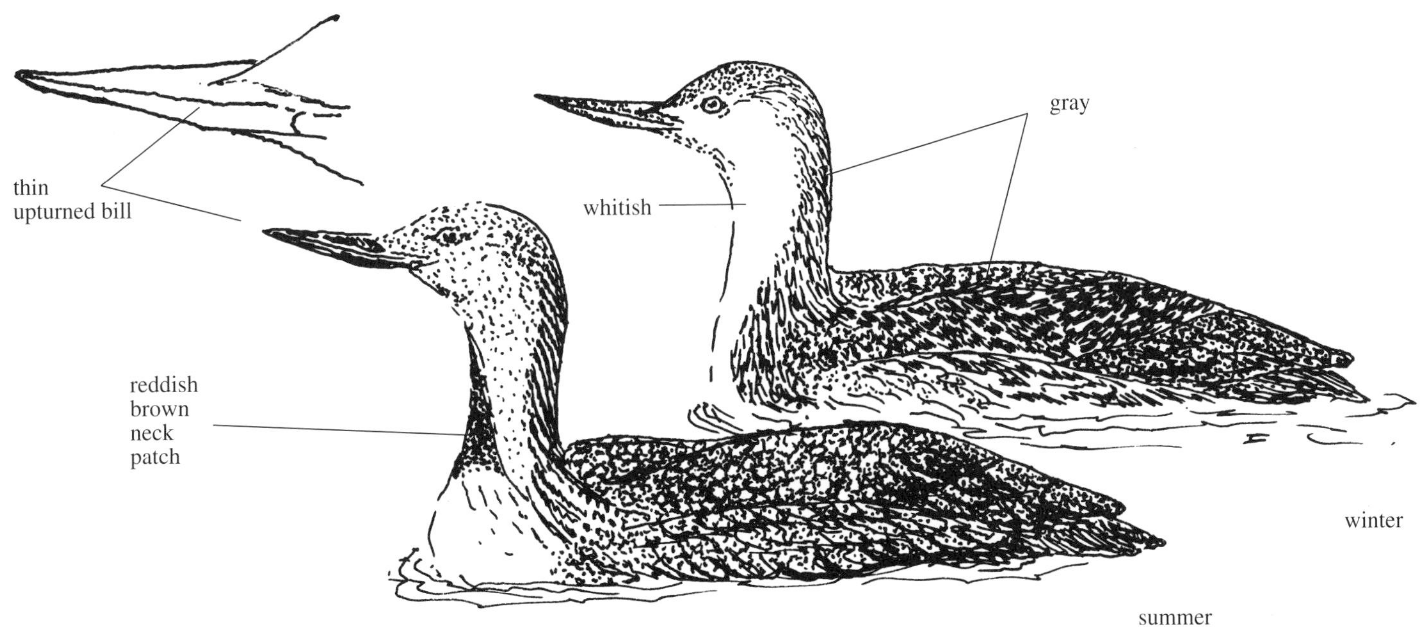

Fig.B. ***GAVIA STELLATA*, RED-THROATED LOON:** In summer breeding plummage, the throat has a reddish-brown throat patch and the head is gray; in winter plummage, the top of the head and back is gray and the underside is whitish; up to 63 cm (25") long; rarely observed along the coast except during colder months.

GREBES: FAMILY PODICIPEDIDAE

Small ducklike diving birds with short bills, lobed toes, and very short tails

(Use the key on page 15.02 to determine if you have a grebe)

#1.Bill is thick and chickenlike (Fig.A); back of head is round without any ear tufts .... ***Podilymbus podiceps*, pied-billed grebe** (Fig.A)
#1.Bill is thin, straight and pointed (Fig.B); head with black "cap" and short ear tufts (Fig.B); found on salt water in colder months only .... #2

#2.Neck and breast are white; face below eyes is white; eyes are red .... ***Podiceps auritus*, horned grebe** (Fig.B)
#2.Neck and breast are gray; face below eyes is gray; adults have a white "chinstrap"; eyes are black .... ***Podiceps grisegena,* red-necked grebe** (Fig.B)

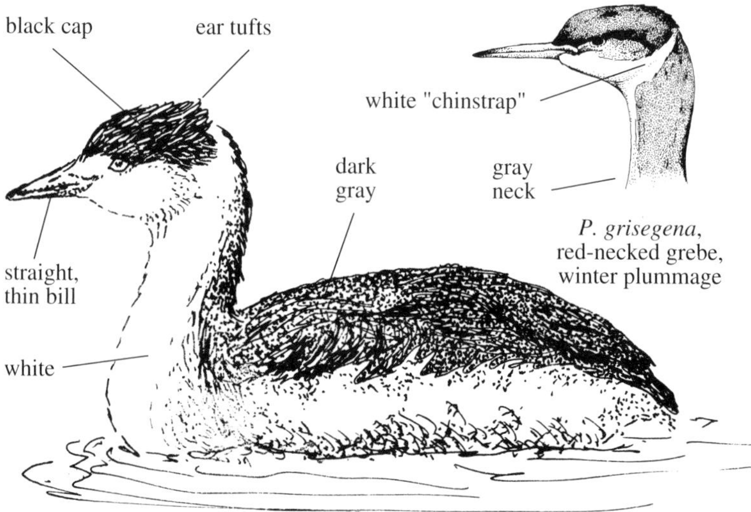

Fig.A. ***PODILYMBUS PODICEPS*, PIED-BILLED GREBE:** Drab brown overall, with white rear end; during breeding season, whitish bill is encircled by a black ring and throat is black; up to 33 cm (13") long; generally solitary; when disturbed, will sink out of sight into water rather than fly away; found on brackish and estuarine waters; seldom on open salt water.

Fig.B. ***PODICEPS* SPP.:** In winter, dark gray above with black cap; occurs on salt water only during colder months; often seen in flocks. *Podiceps auritus*, horned grebe, has a whitish neck and breast, red eyes; up to 38 cm (15") long. *Podiceps grisegena*, red-necked grebe, has a gray neck and breast, adults have a white "chin strap"; black eyes; up to 56 cm (22") long.

COOT AND MOORHEN: FAMILY RALLIDAE (in part)

Waterfowl that pump head back and forth when swimming; with chickenlike bills that extend up onto forehead; toes are not webbed

(Use the key on page 15.02 to determine if you have a coot or moorhen)

#1.Bill is white .... ***Fulica americana*, American coot** (Fig.C)
#1.Bill is red with yellow tip .... ***Gallinula chloropus*, common moorhen** (Fig.D)

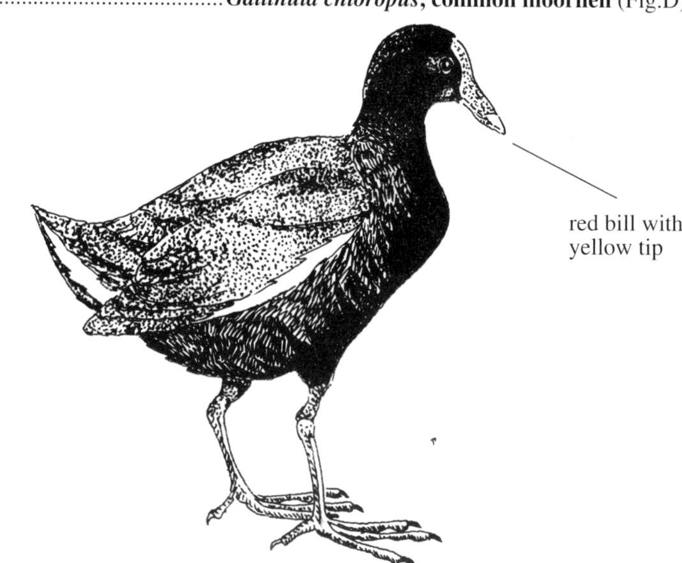

Fig.C. ***FULICA AMERICANA*, AMERICAN COOT:** Gray-black overall with white bill and white spots under tail; up to 40 cm (16") long; runs on water to take off; flies with big feet trailing behind small tail.

Fig.D.***GALLINULA CHLOROPUS*, COMMON MOORHEN:** Brown above, gray below; bill mostly red with yellow tip; up to 33 cm (13") long.

MERGANSERS: FAMILY ANATIDAE (in part)

Waterfowl with slender pointed bills having sawtoothed mandibles; with a crest on the head

(Use the key on page 15.02 to determine if you have a merganser)

#1.Bill is black or dark; crest (Fig.A) on head is wedge or fan shaped and can be raised or lowered .... ***Lophodytes cucullatus*, hooded merganser** (Fig.A)
#1.Bill is red; head is reddish-brown; crest is shaggy, tufted (Fig.B,C) .... **female *Mergus* spp.,** #2
#1.Bill is red; head is green-black; no crest (Fig.C), or if crest is present, is shaggy, tufted (Fig.B) .... **male *Mergus* spp.,** #3

#2.Red of head blends gradually on neck into white of chest (Fig.B) .... **female *Mergus serrator*, red-breasted merganser** (Fig.B)
#2.Red of head ends at a distinct line on neck where white on chest begins (Fig.C) .... **female *Mergus merganser*, common merganser** (Fig.C)

#3.Crest is tufted, shaggy; breast has reddish-brown band, separated from green-black head by white collar (Fig.B) .... **male *Mergus serrator*, red-breasted merganser** (Fig.B)
#3 No crest on head (Fig. C); breast is white, no breast band, no collar .... **male *Mergus merganser*, common merganser** (Fig.C)

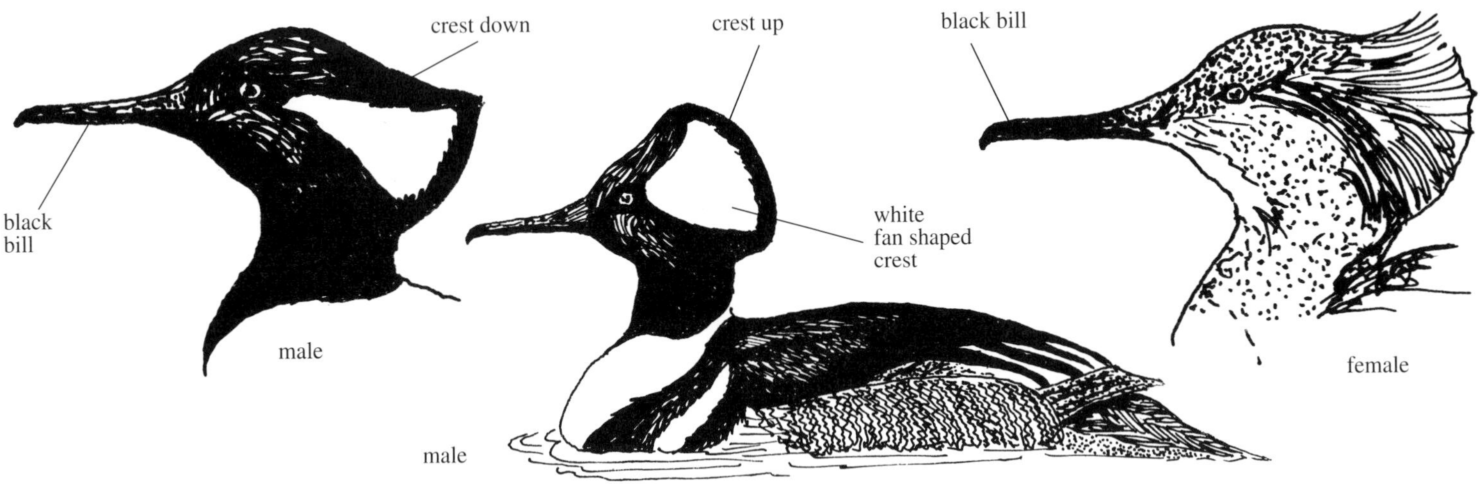

Fig.A. ***LOPHODYTES CUCULLATUS*, HOODED MERGANSER:** Male has distinctive white fan shaped crest which is bordered with black; male has brown sides, black face and back, with white stripes and patches; female is brown overall with white markings; up to 48 cm (19") long.

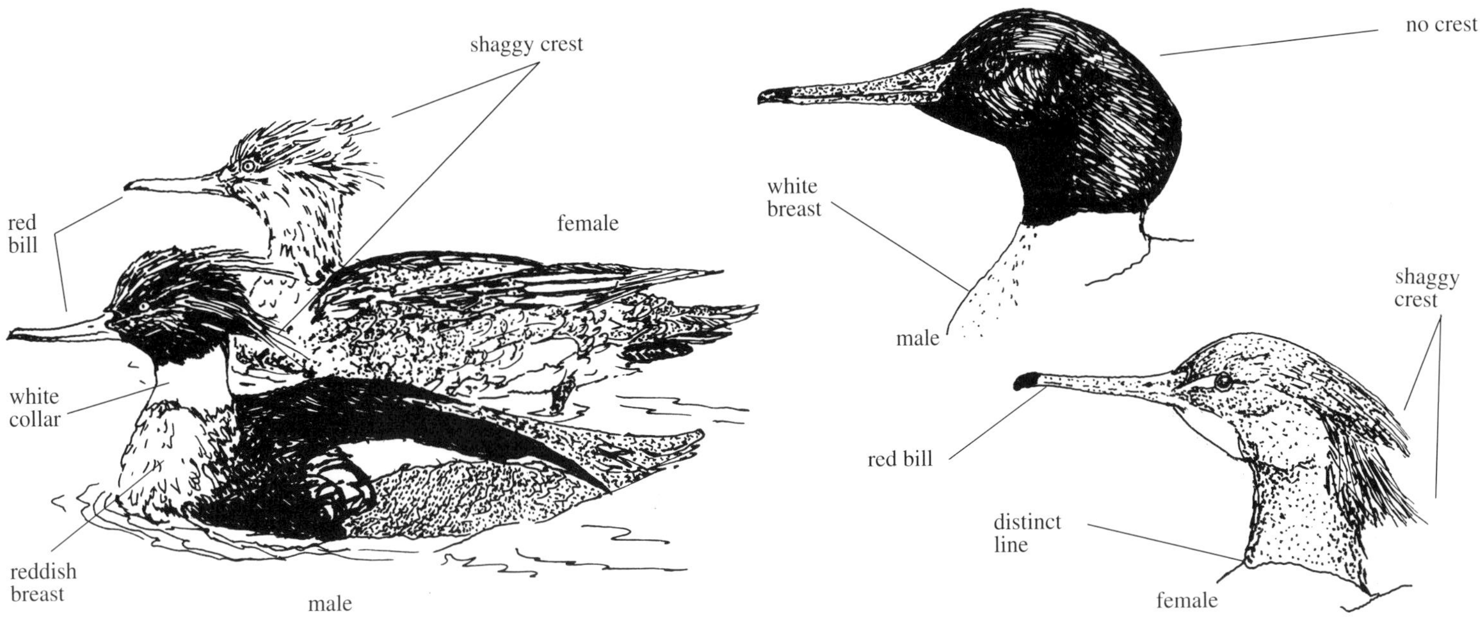

Fig.B. ***MERGUS SERRATOR*, RED-BREASTED MERGANSER:** Male has solid black head with green sheen, wide white collar around neck; rust color breast; female has rust color head and gray back; up to 65 cm (26") long; occurs year-round, common in the winter.

Fig.C. ***MERGUS MERGANSER*, COMMON MERGANSER:** Male has green-black head, white body and breast; female is gray with reddish head; up to 68 cm (27") long; occurs infrequently on salt water in this region, more often seen on tidal fresh water, such as portions of the Connecticut River.

DABBLING DUCKS (SURFACE-FEEDING MARSH DUCKS)
FAMILY ANATIDAE, SUBFAMILY ANATINAE (in part)

Shallow water ducks that feed by upending and usually take off nearly vertically from the water

(Use the key on page 15.02 to determine if you have a dabbling duck)

#1.Entire head is green (Figs.A,B) .... #2
#1.Head is not entirely green (Figs.C-G); may or may not have green markings on head .... #3

#2.Breast is brown; bill is yellowish and not especially long; sides are grayish; violet-blue patch (speculum[2]) on rear edge of wings; may have white neck ring (some hybridized mallards do not have white neck ring) .... ***Anas platyrhynchos*** **(male), mallard** (Fig.A)
#2.Breast is white; bill is bluish and is long and spoon shaped; sides are brown; pale blue patch on front edge of wing .... ***Anas clypeata*** **(male), northern shoveler** (Fig.B)

#3.With narrow green stripe across sides of head through eyes (Figs.C-D) .... #4
#3.Without a narrow green stripe across sides of head through eyes (Figs.E-G) .... #5

#4.Forehead/crown is bright white; with a horizontal white line along the side of the body when the bird is at rest on the water; topside of forewing with a large white patch visible when the bird is in flight .... ***Anas americana*** **(male), American wigeon** (Fig.C)
#4.Forehead/crown is brown; with a vertical white line in front of wing when the bird is at rest on the water; no white patch on topside of forewing .... ***Anas crecca*** **(male), green-winged teal** (Fig.D)

#5.With white markings or patches on head or neck (Figs.E-G) .... #6
#5.Head and neck are entirely brown or mottled[1] brown; no white on head or neck .... page 15.10

#6.With a long flowing crest extending behind head; male has an iridescent green crest with two white stripes, a white collar, and white "chin strap"; female has a grayish-brown head and crest and has a white teardrop shaped eye patch .... ***Aix sponsa*****, wood duck** (Fig.E)
#6.Without any crest (Figs.F,G) .... #7

#7.With a white crescent shaped mark on face between bill and eye; breast and neck are mottled brown; with a pale blue patch on the topside of forewing that may appear as a light horizontal line along the side of the body when the bird is at rest on the water .... ***Anas discors*** **(male), blue-winged teal** (Fig.F)
#7.No white mark in front of eye; breast and most of neck are white; white area of neck extends up the sides of the dark brown head forming a conspicuous point behind eye; with long needlelike tail; slender neck .... ***Anas acuta*** **(male), northern pintail** (Fig.G)

[1]Mottled brown is a mixture of light and dark brown spots and blotches ranging from nearly white to nearly black. The overall color appears brown.
[2]The speculum is a rectangular patch of color on the rear edge of the topside of the wing (see Fig.A on page 15.10).

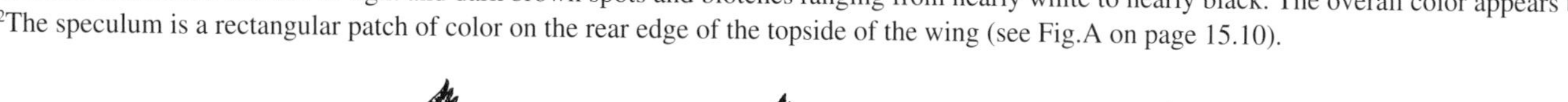

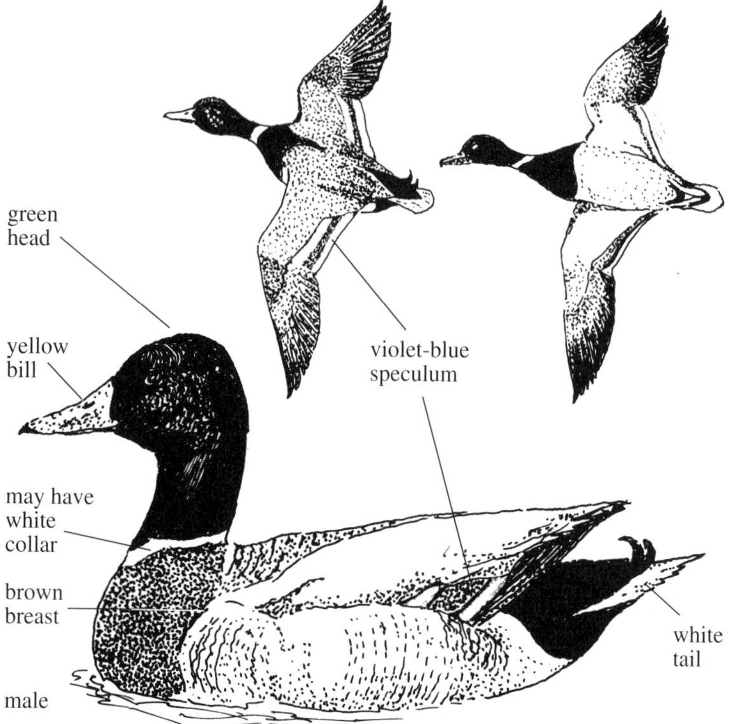

Fig.A. ***ANAS PLATYRHYNCHOS*****, MALLARD:** Male has shiny green head, brown breast, and may have white neck ring; female is mottled[1] brown overall; both sexes have violet-blue speculum[2], yellow bill and whitish tail; up to 70 cm (28") long; one of the most common year-round dabbling ducks in this region.

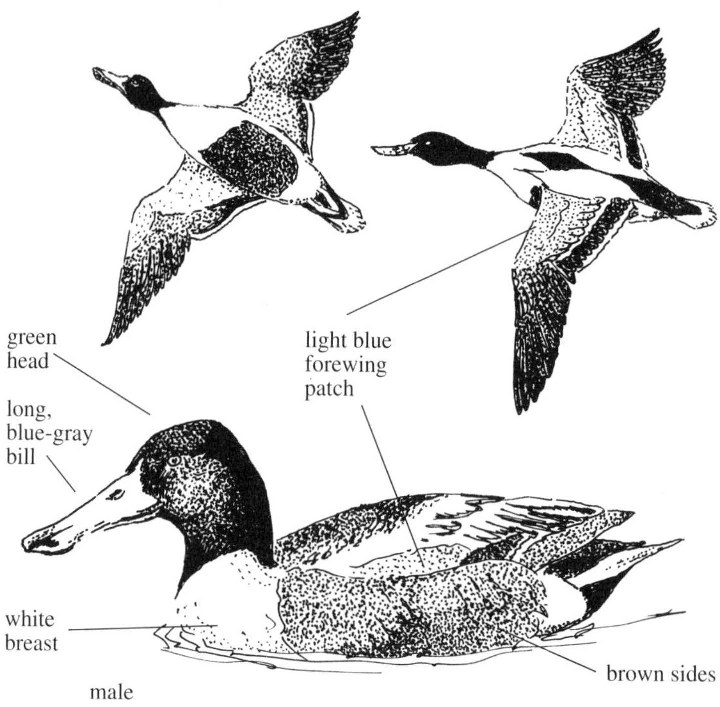

Fig.B. ***ANAS CLYPEATA*****, NORTHERN SHOVELER:** Male has shiny green head, white breast, brown sides, and blue-gray bill; female is mottled[1] brown overall with brown bill; both sexes have a light blue patch on forewing; up to 50 cm (20") long.

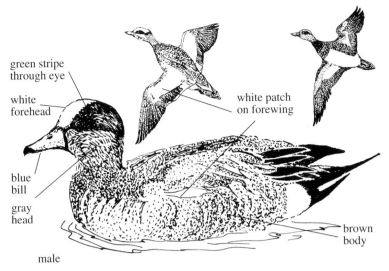

green stripe through eye
white forehead
blue bill
gray head
white patch on forewing
brown body
male

Fig.C. ***ANAS AMERICANA*, AMERICAN WIGEON:** Male has white forehead, green stripe across sides of head through eyes, remainder of head is gray and upper body is brown; female has brown body and gray head; both sexes have a large white patch on forewing, bluish bill, white belly; up to 58 cm (23") long.

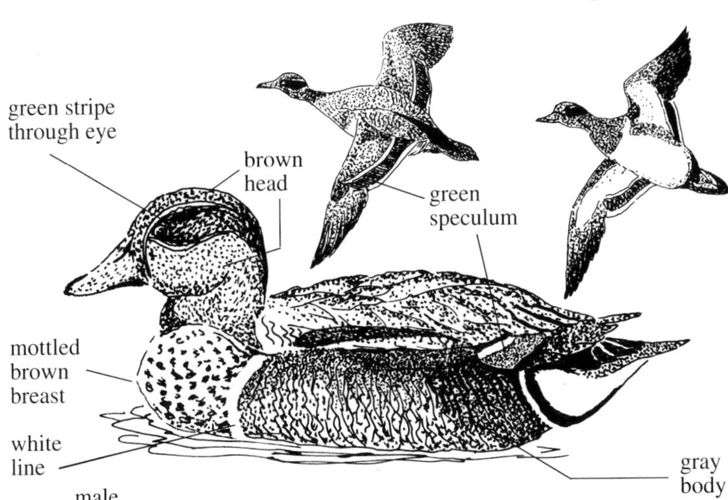

Fig.D. ***ANAS CRECCA*, GREEN-WINGED TEAL:** Male has a brown head with a narrow dark green stripe through eye, mottled[1] brown breast, gray body and, when swimming, with a vertical white line in front of wings; female is mottled brown; both sexes have a green speculum[2]; up to 35 cm (14").

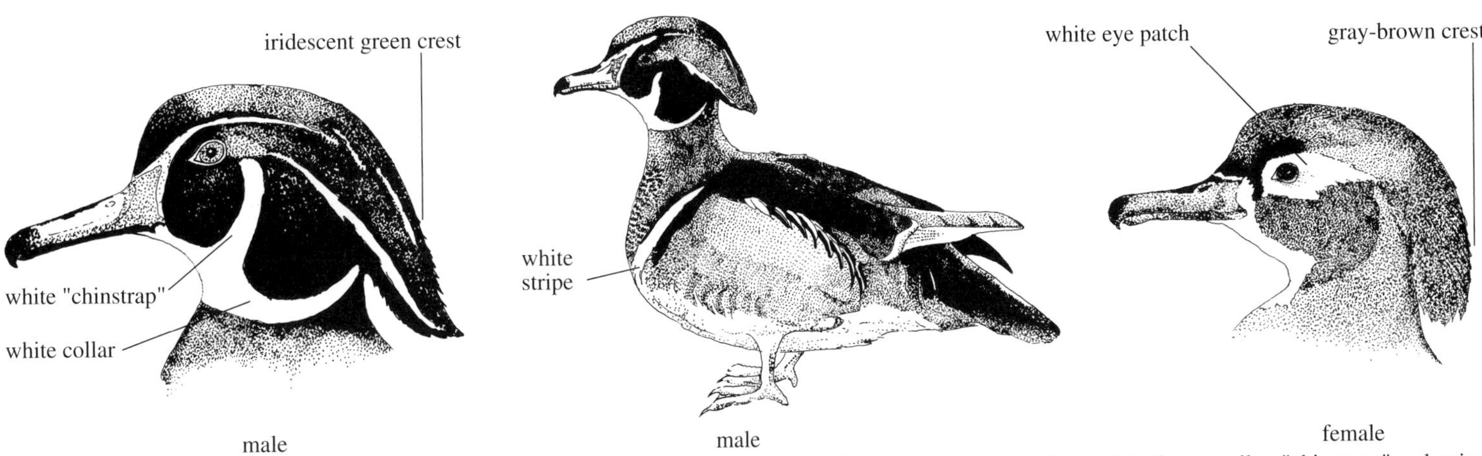

Fig. E. ***AIX SPONSA*, WOOD DUCK:** Male is very colorful with two white stripes on iridescent green crest, with a white throat, collar, "chinstrap," and stripe on breast separating the brown neck from the tan sides, bill and eyes are mostly red, back is dark brown with blue sheen; female is mostly mottled brown with a distinctive white teardrop shaped eye patch; up to 51 cm (20") long; very common in freshwater environments but also occurs in brackish tidal marshes.

Fig.F. ***ANAS DISCORS*, BLUE-WINGED TEAL:** Both sexes are mottled[1] brown overall with light blue patch on forewing; male has a white crescent shaped mark on face between eyes and bill; up to 40 cm (16") long.

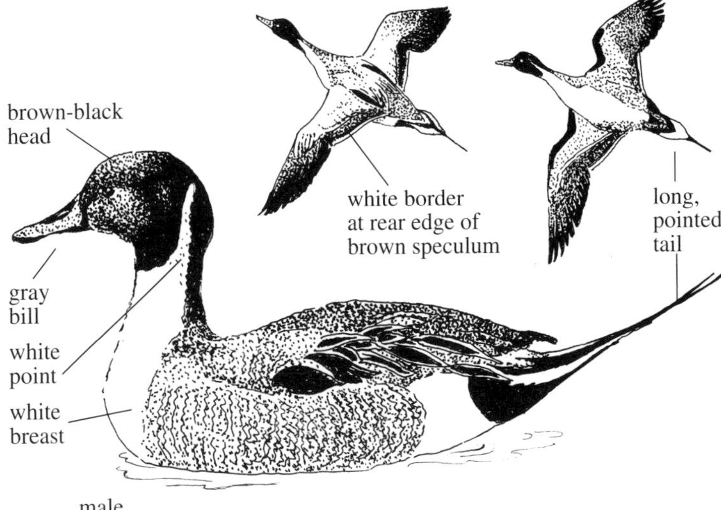

Fig.G. ***ANAS ACUTA*, NORTHERN PINTAIL:** Male has brown-black head, white breast, gray body and wings; female is mottled[1] brown overall; both sexes have a gray bill and a brown speculum[2] bordered by a white line on trailing edge; up to 75 cm (30") long.

DABBLING DUCKS WITH AN ENTIRELY BROWN HEAD AND NECK: FAMILY ANATIDAE, SUBFAMILY ANATINAE (in part)

(The key to the dabbling ducks begins on page 15.08)

#1.With a white teardrop shaped eye patch .... ***Aix sponsa*** **(female[1]), wood duck** (Fig.E, page 15.09)
#1.Without a white eyepatch .... #2

#2.With a violet blue speculum. (The speculum is a rectangular patch of color on the rear edge of the topside of the wing. See Fig.A, this page) .... #3
#2.Speculum is green, brown, or white .... #4

#3.With wide white border along front and back edges of speculum; whitish tail, orange feet; body and head are mottled brown .... ***Anas platyrhynchos*** **(female[1]), mallard** (Fig. A, page 15.08)
#3.With only a thin white border, or no white border visible along edges of speculum; underside of wing with white wing linings (Fig.B, this page) visible when bird is in flight; tail is dark; feet are red or brown; body is very dark brown or black; head is distinctly paler than body .... ***Anas rubripes*** **(male and female), American black duck** (Fig.E, page 15.11)

#4.Speculum is green; topside of forewing may or may not have light wing patch. (Entire wing patch is visible only when bird is flying. A part of the wing patch usually can be seen as a light horizontal line along the side of the body when the bird is at rest on the water. See Fig.C, this page.) .... #5
#4.Speculum is brown or white; no light patch on topside of forewing .... #7

#5.Topside of forewing is dark, no light wing patch .... ***Anas crecca*** **(female[1]), green-winged teal** (Fig.D, page 15.09)
#5.Topside of forewing with a light wing patch (see Fig.C, this page) .... #6

#6.With white patch on topside of forewing; with white belly visible when flying .... ***Anas americana*** **(female[1]), American wigeon** (Fig.C, page 15.09)
#6.With light blue patch on topside of forewing; with dark belly visible when flying .... ***Anas discors*** **(female[1]), blue-winged teal** (Fig.F, page 15.09)

#7.Speculum is white; bill is partially yellow .... ***Anas strepera*** **(male and female), gadwall** (Fig.D, page 15.11)
#7.Speculum is brown with a white border at rear edge; bill is entirely gray .... ***Anas acuta*** **(female[1]), northern pintail** (Fig.G, page 15.09)

[1]NOTE: Most female and immature ducks are difficult to distinguish because they do not have the distinctive color patterns of the males. You can often identify the females and immature birds by their association with males. Descriptions and illustrations of individual species are included with the key to the male dabbling ducks on pages 15.08 and 15.09.

Fig.A. **SPECULUM**

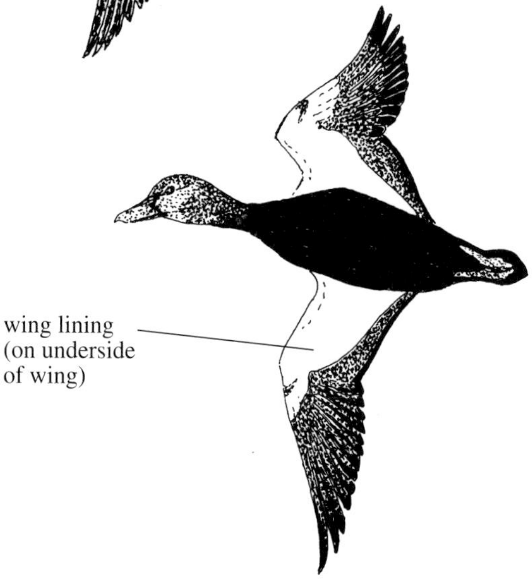

Fig.B. **WING LININGS**

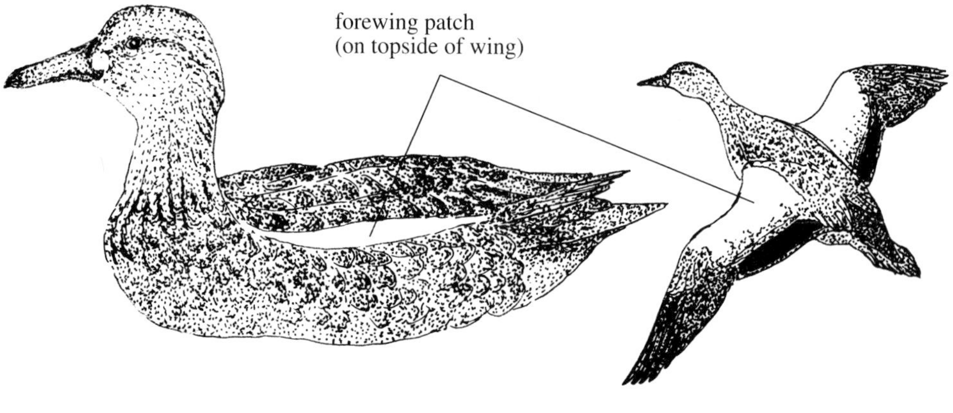

Fig.C. **FOREWING PATCH**

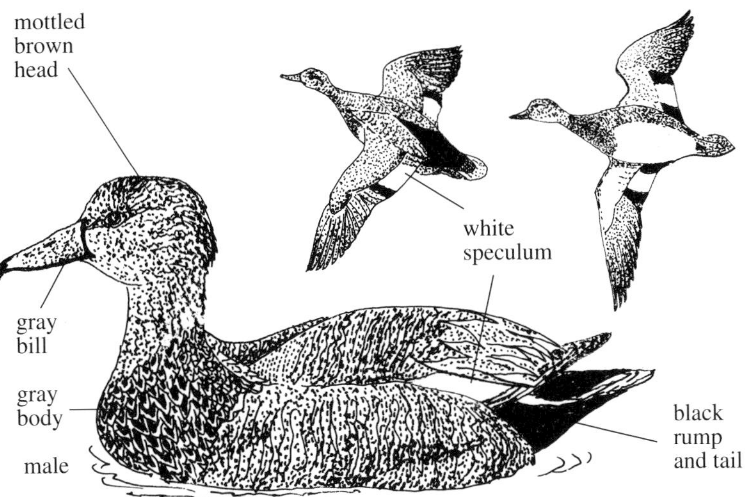

Fig.D. ***ANAS STREPERA*, GADWALL:** Male has brown head and neck, gray wings and body, black rump and tail; female is mottled brown overall; both sexes have a white speculum; up to 58 cm (23") long.

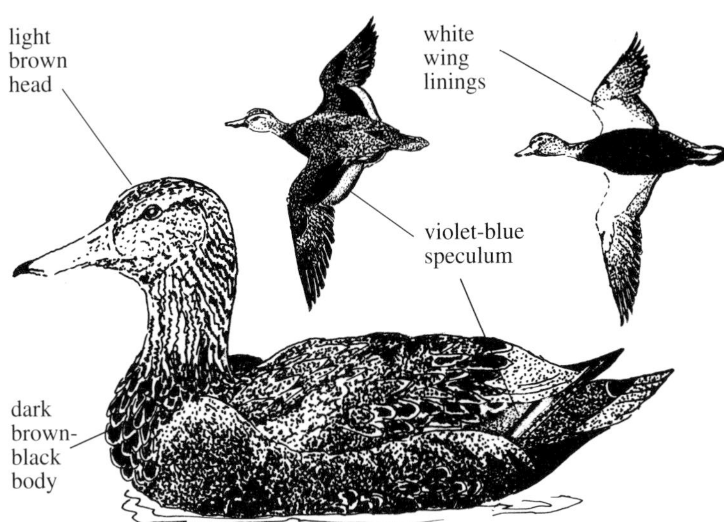

Fig.E. ***ANAS RUBRIPES*, AMERICAN BLACK DUCK:** Both sexes have a dark black-brown body, lighter mottled brown head; wings are dark black-brown above with violet-blue speculum and are mostly white on underside; up to 63 cm (25") long; very common year-round in southern New England.

SCOTERS: FAMILY ANATIDAE, SUBFAMILY ANATINAE [1] (in part)

Diving ducks with all black bodies and colorful bills with knob at base; often observed in large rafts (flocks) in deeper, open water

(Diving duck key begins on page 15.12)

#1.No white markings on head or wings; bill has bright orange-yellow knob at base (Fig.A) .... ***Melanitta nigra*, black scoter** (Fig.A)

#1.With white markings on head or wings .... #2

#2.With small white spot just below eye (Fig.B); with large white wing patch (visible when bird is flying but difficult to see when duck is swimming); bill is orange with black knob at base .... ***Melanitta fusca*, white-winged scoter** (Fig.B)

#2.No white wing patch; with white areas on forehead and back of head (Fig.C); bill brightly patterned with black, orange and white .... ***Melanitta perspicillata*, surf scoter** (Fig.C)

[1]This key is for mature males only. Female and immature scoters are difficult to distinguish. You can identify the female and immature birds by their association with males or by referring to R. T. Peterson (1980), Farrand (1988), or Farrand (1983).

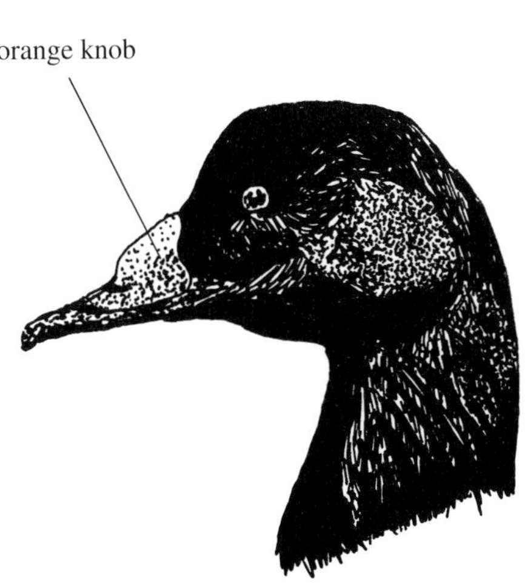

Fig.A. ***MELANITTA NIGRA*, BLACK SCOTER:** Male is black overall with orange-yellow knob on bill; female is dark brown overall with lighter cheeks; up to 48 cm (19") long; the least common scoter species in large mixed flocks which raft together in winter and spring.

Fig.B. ***MELANITTA FUSCA (=M. deglandi)*, WHITE-WINGED SCOTER:** Male is black overall with white patches on wings and small white spot beneath eye; female is dark brown with white wing patches; up to 53 cm (21") long; the most common scoter species in large mixed flocks which raft together in winter and spring.

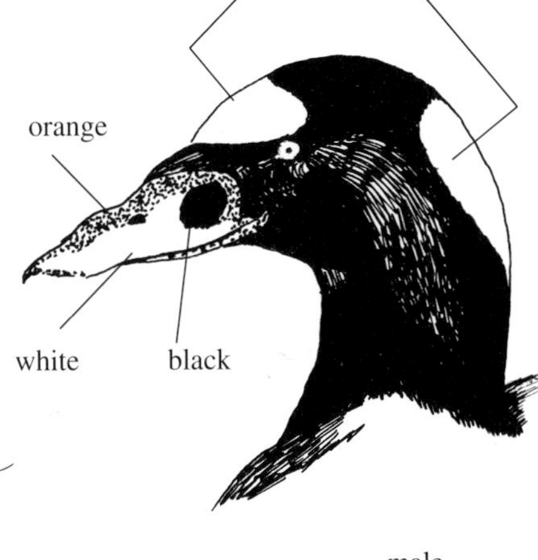

Fig.C. ***MELANITTA PERSPICILLATA*, SURF SCOTER:** Male has 1 or 2 white patches on head, bill is orange, black, and white, body and wings are entirely black; female is dark brown overall and may have lighter spots on cheeks; up to 48 cm (19") long; flocks with other scoters.

DIVING DUCKS (SEA DUCKS AND BAY DUCKS)[1]
FAMILY ANATIDAE, SUBFAMILY ANATINAE (in part)

Ducks which feed by diving beneath the surface and are often observed in large rafts (flocks) in deeper, open water

(Use the key on page 15.02 to determine if you have a diving duck)

#1.Body is completely black or dark; head and/or wings are completely black or with small white markings ... **scoters**, page 15.11
#1.Body has large white or light gray areas (Figs. A-H) ... #2

#2.When floating, duck looks dark on the ends and light in the middle (Figs.A,B); head, chest and tail are dark while wings, sides and belly are light ... #3
#2.Floating duck does not look dark on the ends and light in the middle (Figs. C-H); back may be dark and/or head, neck and chest may have light areas ... #4

#3.Head is reddish-brown; bill is black and long (longer than distance from eye to back of head); middle section is solid white and light gray (without fine gray and white lines across back or sides) ... ***Aythya valisineria*, canvasback** or ***Aythya americana*, redhead** (Fig.A)
#3.Head is black (some green or purple gloss may show at close range); bill is pale blue and moderate length (not longer than distance from eye to back of head); back is patterned with fine gray lines but looks white from a distance ... ***Aythya marila*, greater scaup** or ***Aythya affinis*, lesser scaup** (Fig.B)

#4.Head has large, white, wedge shaped patch which begins behind eye and extends to back of head (Fig.C) ... #5
#4.Head does not have white wedge shaped patch behind and above eye (Figs.D-H) ... #6

#5.Head has a crest that can be raised or lowered (see Fig.A on page 15.07); bill is thin and pointed; sides of body are black and brown; body is slender ... ***Lophodytes cucullatus*, hooded merganser**, page 15.07
#5.Head is puffy, without a crest; bill is flat and spoon shaped; sides of body are white; body is compact ... ***Bucephala albeola*, bufflehead** (Fig. C)

#6.Top of head is white; rest of head is mostly white, with dark cheek patch; tail is long and needlelike ... ***Clangula hyemalis*, oldsquaw** (Fig.D)
#6.Top of head is dark (Figs. E-H); rest of head may be mostly black, white, or may have white patches; tail is not especially long or needlelike ... #7

#7.Breast and neck are dark (black, brown or gray) (Figs.E,F)) ... #8
#7.Breast and neck are white (Figs.G,H) ... #9

#8.Entire head is dark, no white on cheek; with vertical white line in front of each wing; with white ring around bill...***Aythya collaris*, ring-necked duck** (Fig.E)
#8.With white cheek patch; no vertical white line in front of each wing; no ring around bill; often points tail up ... ***Oxyura jamaicensis*, ruddy duck** (Fig.F)

#9.Head is mostly dark (Fig.H); may or may not have a small white spot in front of eye ... #10
#9.Face is white beneath eye; with dark "cap" covering top of head and eyes; with a long sloping forehead ... ***Somateria mollissima*, common eider** (Fig.G)

#10.With a large white spot in front of eye; gray bill is flattened, ducklike; head with no shaggy crest ... ***Bucephala clangula*, common goldeneye** (Fig.H)
#10.With no white spot in front of eye; reddish bill is thin and pointed; females and most males have a shaggy crest (see Figs.B,C on page 15.07) ... ***Mergus* spp., mergansers**, page 15.07

[1]This key is for mature males only. Many female and immature ducks are completely brown, gray or dark overall and are difficult to distinguish because they do not have the distinctive color patterns of the males. Identify female and immature birds by their association with males or refer to Peterson (1980), Farrand (1988), or Farrand (1983).

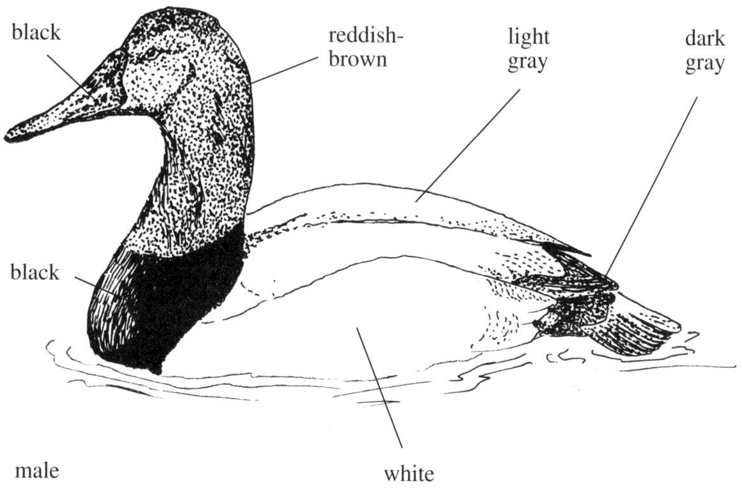

Fig.A. ***AYTHYA VALISINERIA*, CANVASBACK:** Male has reddish-brown head and neck, black chest, light gray back and white sides, black bill; female is gray overall with some rust color in the head and neck; up to 60 cm (24") long. A less common duck, ***Aythya americana*, redhead**, is similar to the canvasback but has gray rather than white sides and the bill is bluish with a black tip.

Fig.B. ***AYTHYA MARILA*, GREATER SCAUP:** Male has dark green head, black chest and tail, gray back and white sides; in flight, trailing edges of wings have broad white stripes; female is dark brown with white band at base of bill; up to 50 cm (20") long. ***Aythya affinis*, lesser scaup**, is very similar to the greater scaup but is much less common. The lesser scaup has a dark purple head that is more pointed on top than the rounded head of the greater scaup.

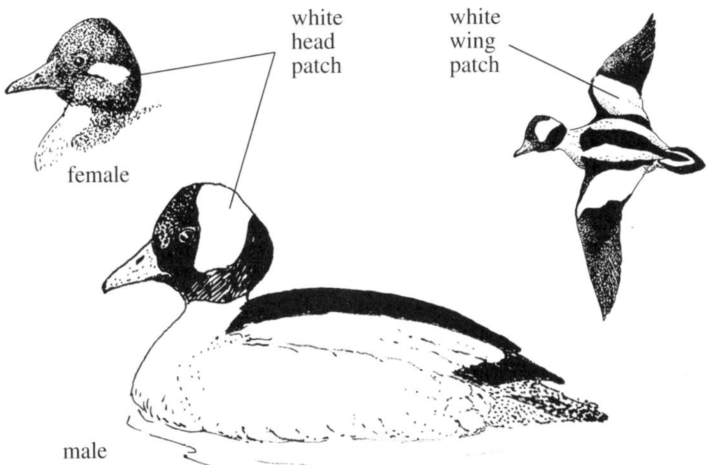

Fig.C. ***BUCEPHALA ALBEOLA*, BUFFLEHEAD:** Male is mostly white with dark green head and large white patch from eye to top of head; female is mostly dark gray with small white patch behind eye; small duck, up to 38 cm (15") long; common in colder months.

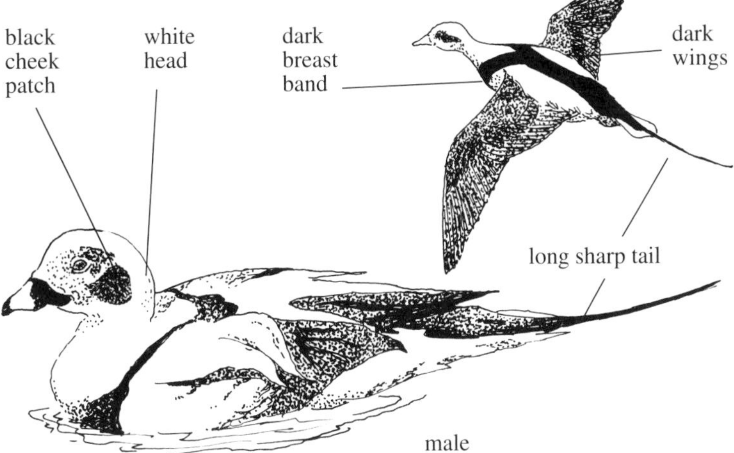

Fig.D. ***CLANGULA HYEMALIS*, OLDSQUAW:** Male in winter has a mostly white body with dark gray band across breast and onto back; head and neck are white with black cheek patch, wings are dark gray; female has dark cheek patch, dark wings, darker back; up to 53 cm (21") long; often observed in winter.

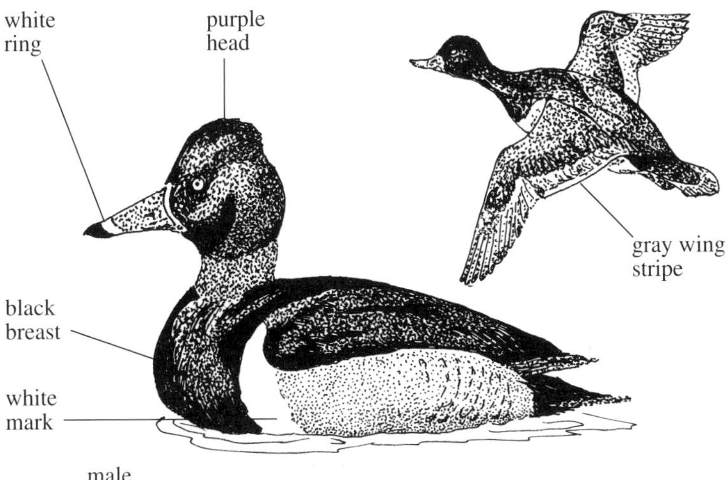

Fig.E. ***AYTHYA COLLARIS*, RING-NECKED DUCK:** Male has dark purple head, black breast, neck, and back, gray sides; female is brown; both sexes have a white ring around bill and gray wing stripe; up to 45 cm (18") long.

Fig.F. ***OXYURA JAMAICENSIS*, RUDDY DUCK:** Male in winter and female year-round have dark gray back, lighter gray sides; male in summer is mostly reddish brown over entire body and wings; both sexes have light cheek patch and dark cap year-round; up to 40 cm (16") long.

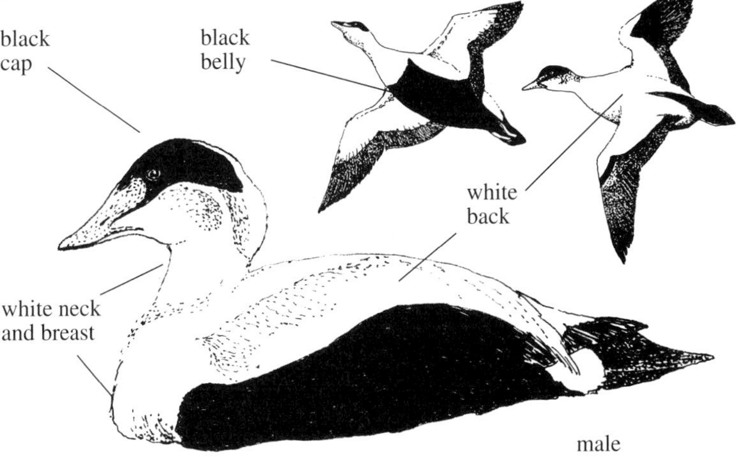

Fig.G. ***SOMATERIA MOLLISSIMA*, COMMON EIDER:** Male has black belly, white back, white neck, breast, and head with black "cap"; female is brown overall; up to 68 cm (27") long.

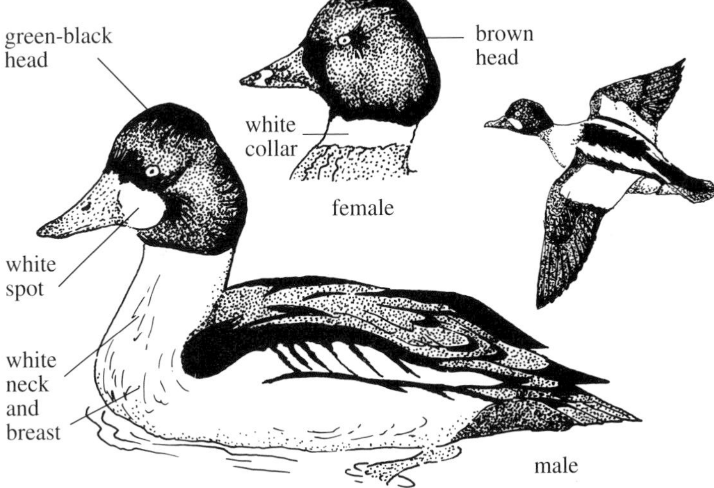

Fig.H. ***BUCEPHALA CLANGULA*, COMMON GOLDENEYE:** Male has mostly white sides, black back, and a green head with white spot on face; female is mostly gray with a brown head and white collar; common in the winter; up to 50 cm (20") long.

SWANS AND GEESE: FAMILY ANATIDAE, SUBFAMILY ANSERINAE

Large waterfowl with very long necks

(Use the key on page 15.02 to determine if you have a swan or goose)

#1.Body, neck, and wings are without any black markings and are completely white (adult) or tinged with brown (immature); very large bird, may reach up to 150 cm (60") in length; neck is longer than the rest of body .... ***Cygnus olor*, mute swan**[1] (Fig.A)

#1.Neck (Figs.C,D) and/or wing tips (Fig.B) are black; not as large as a swan, up to 108 cm (43") in length; neck is not as long as the rest of body ..... **geese**[2], #2

#2.Body and neck are all white (adult) or pale gray (immature); wing tips (Fig.B) are black; bill and feet are pink (adult) or gray (immature) .... ***Chen caerulescens*, snow goose** (Fig.B)

#2.Mostly brown or dark gray body; with black head and neck (Figs. C,D); black legs and feet .... #3

#3.With a broad white "chinstrap" (Fig.C) that extends up over the cheek; black color of neck does not extend over the pale breast region .... ***Branta canadensis*, Canada goose** (Fig.C)

#3.With a small white mark on throat (Fig.D) but without a white "chinstrap"; black color of neck extends onto breast .... ***Branta bernicla*, brant** (Fig.D)

[1]The tundra (=whistling) swan, *Cygnus columbianus (=Olor c.)*, is the only swan native to the Atlantic coast. It is rarely observed except during its fall migration to winter feeding grounds south of Delaware Bay. The bill of the tundra swan is mostly black. The bill of the mute swan is orange with a black base.

[2]Escaped domestic or exotic geese are often found among wild geese; refer to R. I. Peterson (1980) or Farrand (1983) to identify geese that cannot be keyed out here.

Fig.A. ***CYGNUS OLOR*, MUTE SWAN:** Adult is all white, bill is orange with black base, legs and feet are black; up to 150 cm (60") long; wing beats make a high pitched sound; often feeds by "tipping up" (completely submerging head and neck). Immature swans are brownish overall with a pinkish bill. Mute swans were brought to Long Island, NY from Europe in 1912 and are now extremely common throughout southern New England[1].

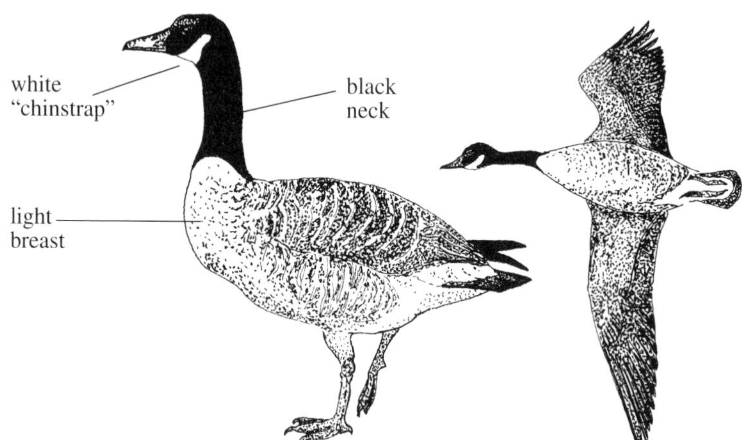

Fig.C. ***BRANTA CANADENSIS*, CANADA GOOSE:** Light brown breast and body, darker brown wings, black neck and head with white "chinstrap," black bill and legs; up to 108 cm (43") long; common year-round; very vocal, noisy honking of flock can be heard from afar, particularly when flying in familiar V-formation; common on open grassy areas such as saltmarshes.

Fig.B. ***CHEN CAERULESCENS*, SNOW GOOSE:** White overall with black wing tips on underside, bill and feet are pink; up to 95 cm (38") long; occasionally observed during fall and winter.

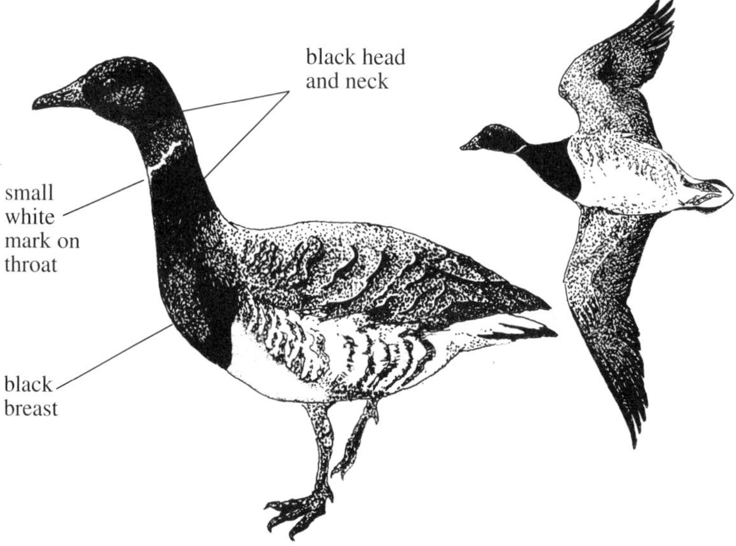

Fig.D. ***BRANTA BERNICLA*, BRANT:** Head, neck, and breast are black with small white mark on neck, belly whitish, wings dark gray; up to 65 cm (26") long; not as common as the Canada goose.

GULLS, TERNS, AND SEABIRDS[1]

Birds with pointed wings, short legs and webbed feet; often observed floating on water or soaring over water; usually gray, black and white

(Bird key begins on page 15.00)

#1.Entire bird, including underside, is blackish except for a white band across rump (front upperside of tail) .... **family Hydrobatidae, storm-petrels**[1] (Fig.A)
#1.Bird is not black overall (belly and underside are usually white) or, if it is black, does not have a white band across rump .... #2

#2.Tail forked (see figures on pages 15.16-15.17); slim body; narrow wings; sharply pointed bill; top of head usually with a dark cap; generally smaller and with shorter legs than gulls; often hovers high over the water and plunges in head first; usually does not float or swim .... **terns and skimmers**, page 15.16
#2.Rounded, square or pointed tail (Figs.B-D); stocky body; wide wings; rather thick bill; usually gull size but may be smaller or larger .... #3

#3.Tail is all white on topside .... #4
#3.Tail is dark on topside, but may or may not have white band across rump (front upperside of tail) .... #5

#4.Tail is pointed; wing tips are black and rest of bird is mostly white, including mantle (topside of wings and across back between wings); bill is long and pointed; dives for fish by making spectacular headfirst plunges into water .... ***Morus bassanus*, northern gannet**[1] (Fig.B)
#4.Tail is rounded or square (see figures on pages 15.18-15.19); wing tips may or may not be black; mantle is gray, black, or brown; does not dive headfirst into water; graceful flier, soars on updrafts; often floats and swims on the surface of the water; perches on dock pilings and gathers in great flocks at garbage dumps; omnivorous (will eat almost anything) .... **gulls**, page 15.18

#5.Tail ends with one or two points because of two long feathers which extend behind tail .... ***Stercorarius* spp., jaegers**[1] (Fig.C)
#5.Tail is rounded or square .... #6

#6.Nostrils are tubular, forming a knoblike bump near base of bill; rarely observed in flocks with adult gulls .... **family Procellariidae, shearwaters**[1] (Fig.D)
#6.Without a knoblike bump near base of bill; usually observed in flocks with adult gulls .... **immature gulls,** page 15.18

[1]Seabirds rarely come within sighting distance of the mainland. Gulls, terns, and skimmers are very common near shore as well as offshore. You are very unlikely to observe seabirds, such as gannets, shearwaters, storm-petrels, or jaegers, unless you are on a boat in open water or on a remote island.

Fig.A. **FAMILY HYDROBATIDAE, STORM-PETRELS[1]:** Black or dark brown overall with a white band across rump; up to 20 cm (8") long; one species skims like a swallow and hovers with feet touching water; often follows ships.

Fig.B. ***MORUS BASSANUS (=Sulla b.)*, NORTHERN GANNET[1]:** White overall, with black wing tips and a tinge of yellow on head; up to 95 cm (38") long; flies rapidly and dives headfirst into water. (family Sulidae)

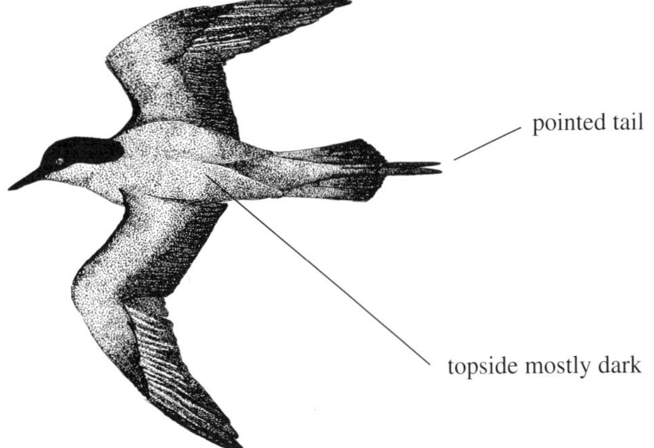

Fig.C. ***STERCORARIUS* SPP., JAEGERS[1]:** Mostly black but may be white on belly and near wing tips; up to 55 cm (22") long; the parasitic jaeger (*Stercorarius parasiticus*) steals food from gulls and terns. (family Laridae)

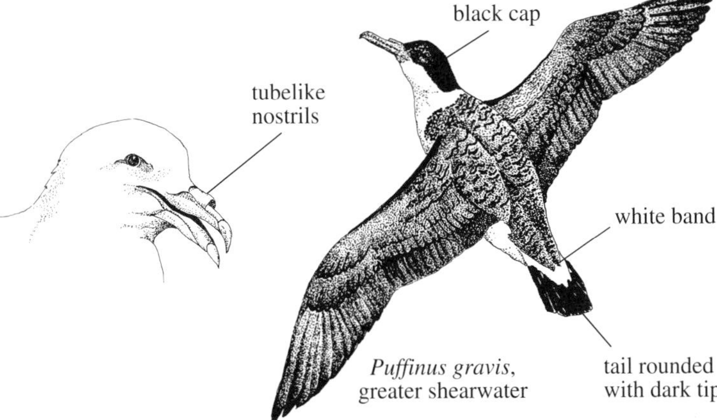

Fig.D. **FAMILY PROCELLARIIDAE, SHEARWATERS[1]**: Black, mottled brown or gray above, usually white on belly but may be dark; one species has a black cap and white stripe across rump; 43-53 cm (17-21") long.

TERNS AND SKIMMER: FAMILY LARIDAE (in part)

Mostly gray, black, and white birds with pointed wings, short legs, and webbed feet; often observed soaring over water or diving into water

(Use the key on page 15.15 to determine if you have a tern)

#1. Entire head, neck, belly, and underside of body is black .... ***Chlidonias niger*, black tern** (Fig.A)
#1. Underside of head, neck, belly, and body is white (Figs.B-G) .... #2

#2. Topside of head, body, and wings are black, undersides are white; bill with lower mandible (jaw, half of beak) longer than the upper (Fig.G); bill is black-tipped, bright orange, flattened laterally (side to side); skims low across water, dipping lower jaw in the water; call sounds like a dog barking, particularly at a distance .... ***Rynchops niger*, black skimmer** (Fig.G)
#2. Topside with some gray or white or mottled brown areas, not entirely black; upper and lower mandibles are about the same length (Figs.B-F) .... #3

#3. Forehead is white, black "cap" on head does not extend to bill and may be reduced to smudging around back of the head (Figs.B,C) .... #4
#3. Forehead and top of head is black, forming a complete black "cap" from base of bill to back of head (Figs.D-F) .... #5
#3. Head is all black or all white, no black cap; tail is rounded or squared off .... **gulls**, page 15.18

#4. Bill is black or dark; "cap" is generally limited to the back of the head and may have "smudgy" edges; looks like the hairline of a partially bald man, with high white forehead; back and neck may be very dark or mottled (spotted or blotchy) .... **winter or immature terns**[1] (Fig.B)
#4. Bill is yellow with black tip; distinct black "cap" on top of head with a clean white forehead; a very small tern, nearly the size of a robin .... ***Sterna antillarum*, least tern** (Fig.C)

#5. Bill is black; legs are dark; mantle is very pale gray; tail is very long with tail feathers that extend well beyond the wing tips when bird is at rest .... ***Sterna dougallii*, roseate tern** (Fig.D)
#5. Bill is orange-red with black tip; legs are orange-red; mantle is gray; tail is not particularly long (Figs.E,F); tail feathers do not extend beyond wing tips when bird is at rest .... #6

#6. Wing tips on topside (upper primaries from "wrist" out) are lighter than rest of wing; top of tail is mostly gray .... ***Sterna forsteri*, Forster's tern** (Fig.E)
#6. Wing tips on topside are darker than rest of wing; top of tail is mostly white .... ***Sterna hirundo*, common tern** (Fig.F)

[1]Immature terns and terns in winter plummage are difficult to identify to species. Identify them with a field guide such as R. T. Peterson (1980) or Farrand (1988).

Fig.A. ***CHLIDONIAS NIGER*, BLACK TERN:** Black head and body, gray wings, back and tail; up to 25 cm (10") long; found on marshes and estuaries.

Fig.B. **WINTER OR IMMATURE TERNS[1]:** In winter, adult terns have a broad white forehead. Rest of plummage similar to summer. Immature terns are darker overall and have a mottled appearance on the mantle.

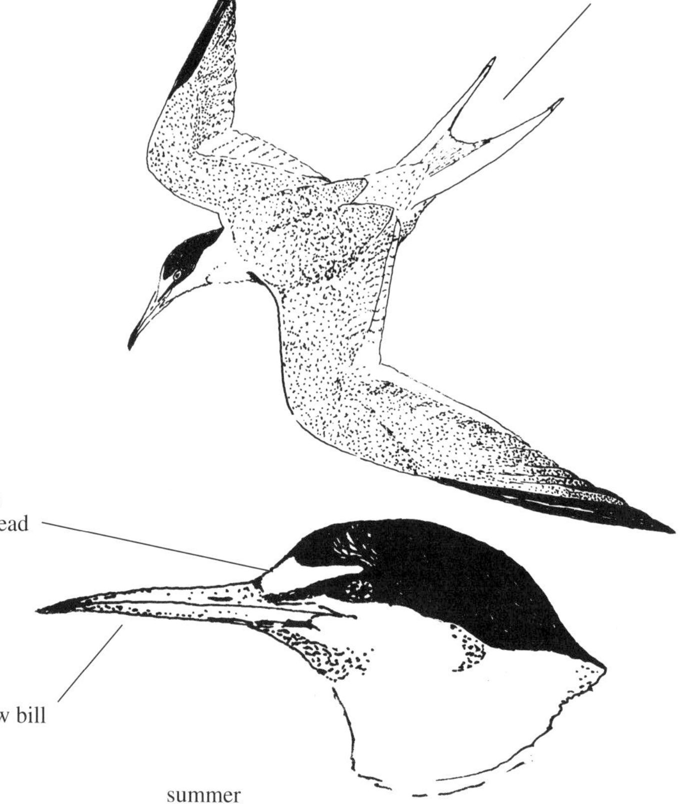

Fig.C. ***STERNA ANTILLARUM* (=*S. albifrons*), LEAST TERN (=little tern):** Pale gray mantle, white body, head with black cap and white forehead, yellow feet and bill; very small tern, up to 23 cm (9").

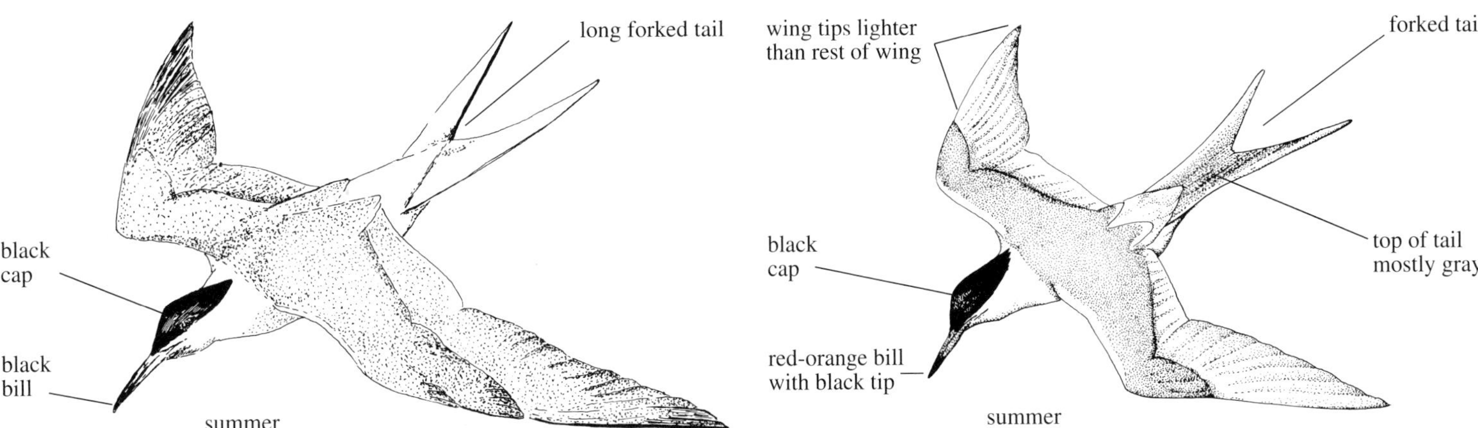

Fig.D. ***STERNA DOUGALLII*, ROSEATE TERN:** Pale gray mantle, white body and tail, black bill, orange-red feet, head with black cap in summer, black cap incomplete in winter; up to 43 cm (17") long; an endangered species that is occasionally observed in the summer or during migrations in spring and fall.

Fig.E. ***STERNA FORSTERI*, FORSTER'S TERN:** Pale gray mantle with whitish wing tips, white body, tail mostly gray on upper side, head with black cap, orange bill with dark tip, legs orange; up to 38 cm (15") long; found on saltmarshes.

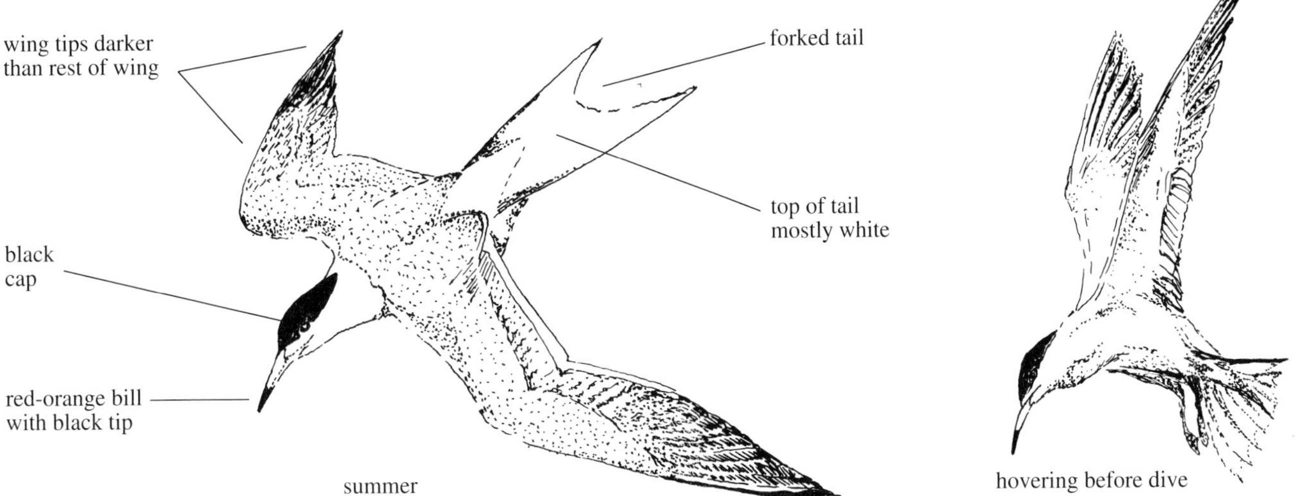

Fig.F. ***STERNA HIRUNDO*, COMMON TERN:** Light gray mantle, white body and tail, orange-red feet, head with black cap and red-orange bill with black tip in summer; in winter, bill is blackish and black cap is incomplete; up to 40 cm (16") long; migrates into southern New England in early May and leaves in mid-September; frequently observed in flocks hovering over schools of small fish that have been driven to the surface by bluefish and plunging head first into the water to feed; establishes very active nesting colonies on remote islands and beaches, defending nests by swooping down in "dive-bomb" flights; the most common tern, but populations are diminishing because of competition with gulls and people.

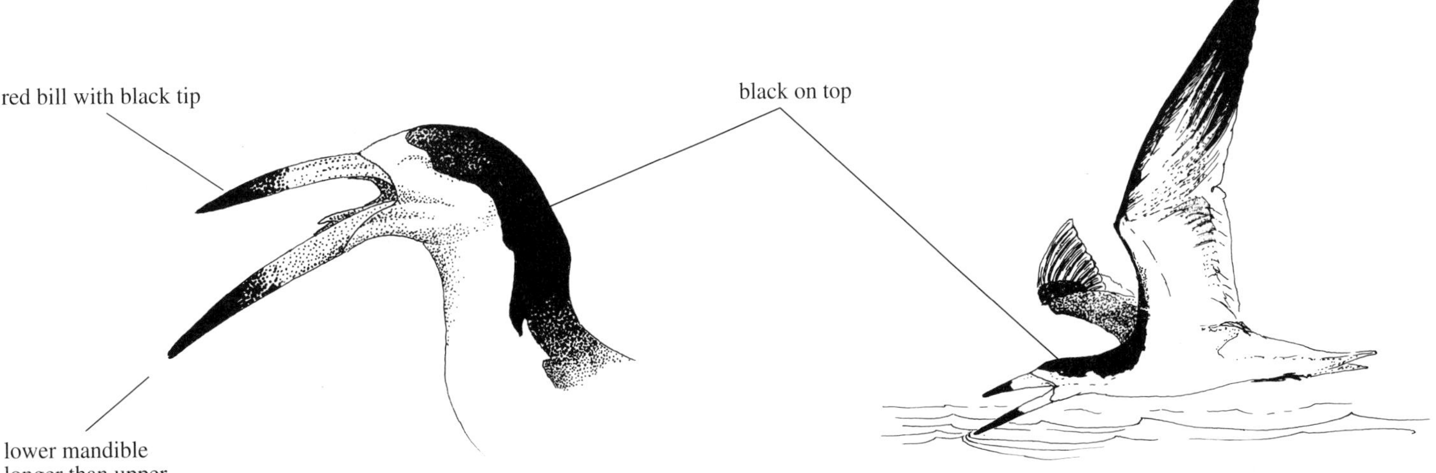

Fig.G. ***RYNCHOPS NIGER*, BLACK SKIMMER:** Black above, white below, bill red with black tip; up to 50 cm (20") long; often flies close to water with lower jaw skimming just beneath surface to catch small fish.

GULLS: FAMILY LARIDAE (in part)

Mostly gray, black, and white birds with pointed wings, short legs, and webbed feet; often observed floating on water or soaring over water

(Key to gulls, terns and seabirds begins on page 15.15)

#1.Mottled brown all over .... **immature gull** (Fig.G)
#1.Underside of body is white, with a black or gray mantle (topside of wings and across back, see Figs.A-F) .... #2

#2.Head is entirely white (Figs.A-C); bill is mostly yellow .... #3
#2.Head is black or has black cap (Figs.D-F) in summer or may be white with a black spot or dark smudge behind eye in winter; bill is black or dark red .... #5

#3.Mantle (topside of wings and across back) is black (Fig.A) .... ***Larus marinus*, great black-backed gull** (Fig.A)
#3.Mantle is gray (Figs.B,C) .... #4

#4.Bill often with a red spot near tip (Fig.B); tan-pink legs; very common "seagull" of most beaches and shores .... ***Larus argentatus*, herring gull** (Fig.B)
#4.Bill is "ringed" (circled) with a dark band near the tip (Fig.C), yellow or greenish legs .... ***Larus delawarensis,* ring-billed gull** (Fig.C)

#5.Tail is rounded or square (Figs.D,E); not usually with black cap; often observed in winter .... #6
#5.Tail is forked (Fig.F); usually with black cap which may or may not be complete; rarely observed in winter .... **terns**, page 15.16

#6.Mantle is light gray and wing tips are white or light gray; with black spot behind eye (Fig.D) on mostly white head in winter (when usually seen), head entirely black in summer; bright red legs .... ***Larus philadelphia*, Bonaparte's gull** (Fig.D)
#6.Mantle is dark gray and wing tips are black; with dark smudge at back of white head (Fig.E) in winter, head entirely black in summer; dark red legs .... ***Larus atricilla*, laughing gull** (Fig.E)

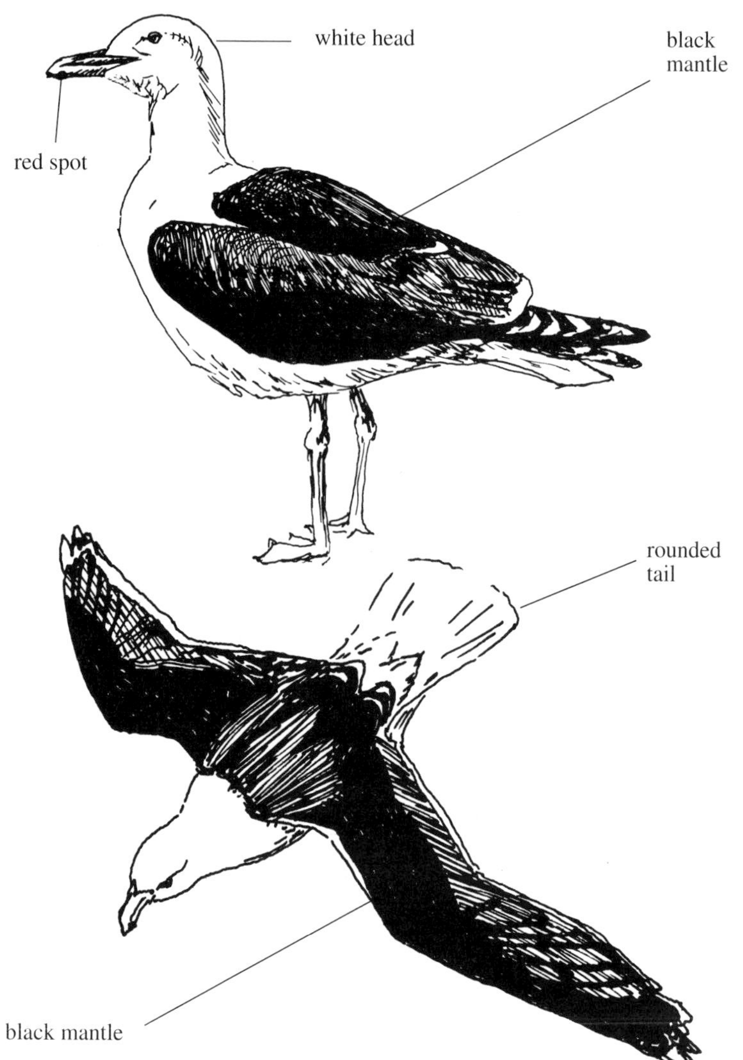

Fig.A. ***LARUS MARINUS*, GREAT BLACK-BACKED GULL:** Black mantle, white head, body, and tail, pinkish-beige legs, yellow bill with red spot; up to 78 cm (31") long; very common year round; a large, aggressive gull which may be displacing the more common herring gull in some places.

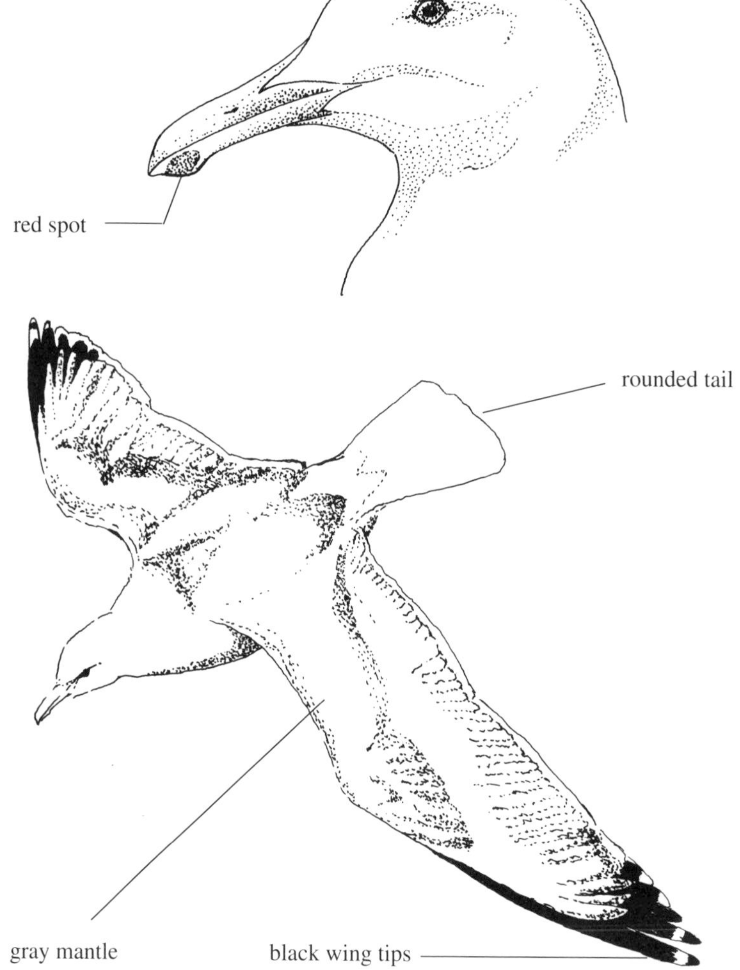

Fig.B. ***LARUS ARGENTATUS*, HERRING GULL:** Gray mantle with black wing tips, white head, body, and tail, pinkish-beige legs, yellow bill with red spot; up to 65 cm (26") long; very common year round; nests in large colonies on islands from early May through July; feeds at dumps in large numbers.

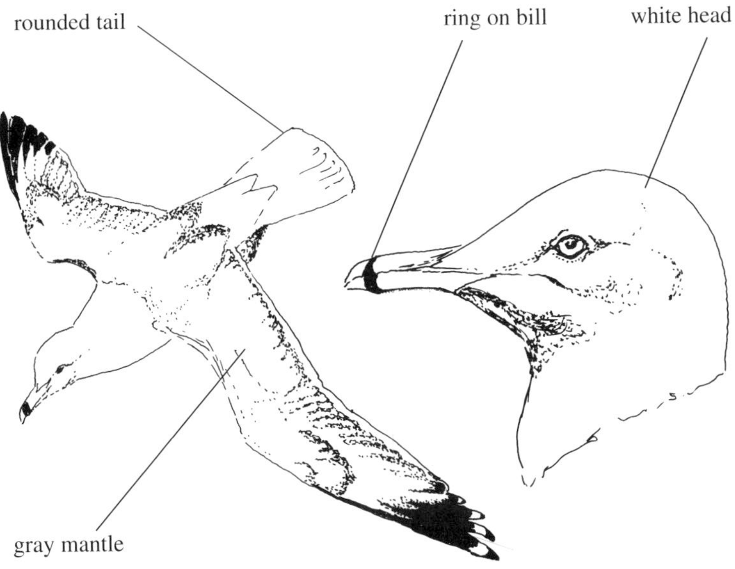

Fig.C. ***LARUS DELAWARENSIS*, RING-BILLED GULL:** Gray mantle with black wing tips, white body and tail, yellow-green legs, yellow bill with black ring; up to 48 cm (19") long; uncommon except in winter.

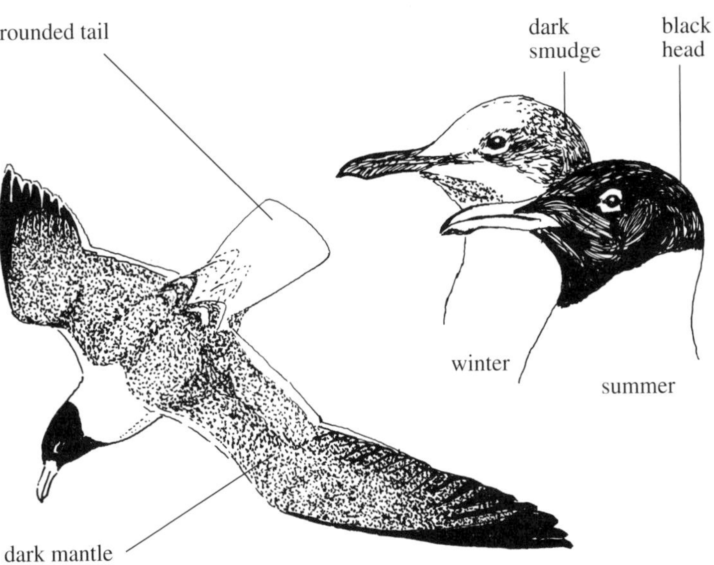

Fig.E. ***LARUS ATRICILLA*, LAUGHING GULL:** Dark gray mantle, black wing tips, white body and tail, dark red legs, head is all black in summer, white with dark smudge in winter; up to 43 cm (17") long; voice is a "ha-ha-ha" laughing sound; not common in southern New England.

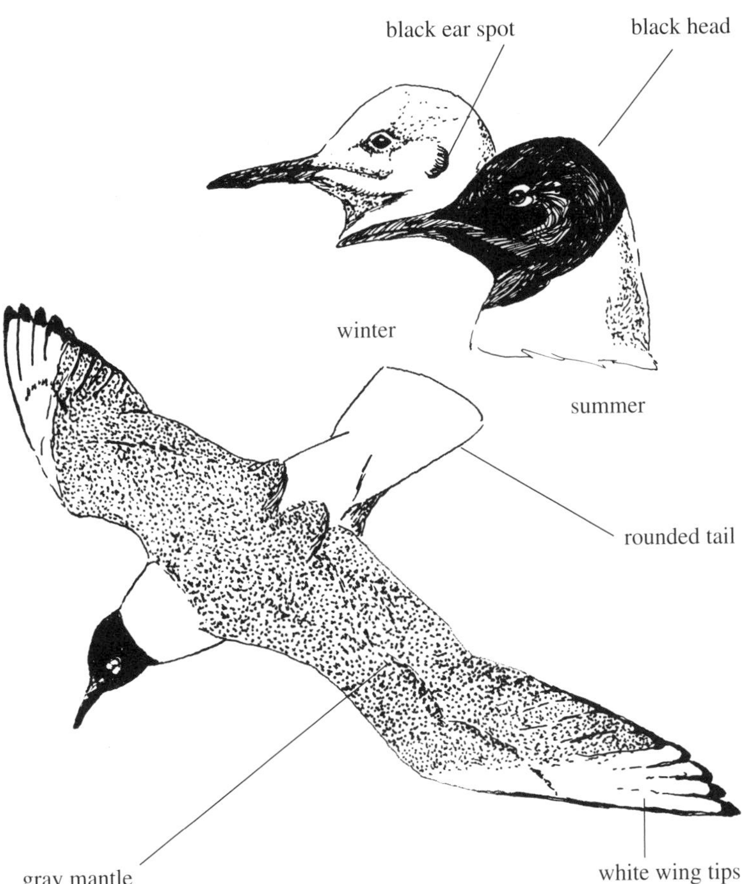

Fig.D. ***LARUS PHILADELPHIA*, BONAPARTE'S GULL:** Light gray mantle, white wing tips, white body and tail, head is all black in summer, white with a black spot behind eye in winter, bright red legs, black bill; up to 33 cm (13") long; not uncommon in winter and during migration periods. Two similar but much rarer species also occur during the winter and migration periods. *Larus ridibundus*, the common black-headed gull, has a dark red bill year round. *Larus minutus*, the little gull, has a black cap in the winter and a dark ear spot.

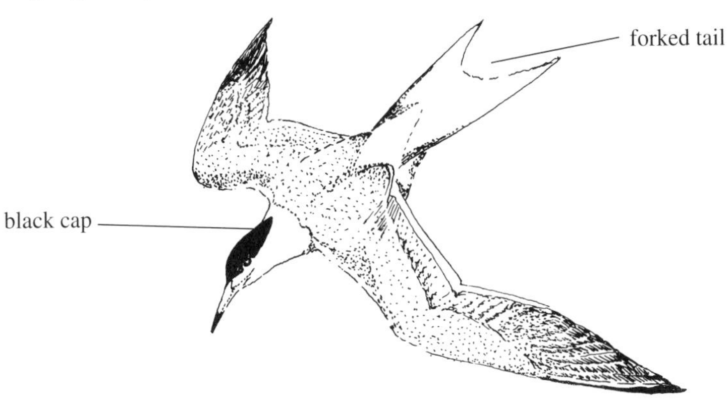

Fig.F. **TERNS:** Gull-like birds with forked tails and black caps. See page 15.16.

Fig.G. **IMMATURE GULLS**: Gulls go through a succession of increasingly lighter mottled brown plumages until they acquire adult plumage at three or four years of age. Immature gulls are difficult to identify to species. Refer to a field guide such as R. I. Peterson (1980) or Farrand (1988) to identify immature gulls.

WADERS: HERONS, EGRETS, SANDPIPERS, PLOVERS, ETC.

Long-legged birds that wade in shallow water or feed along shore at water's edge

(Bird key begins on page 15.00)

#1.Neck is long and thin (Fig.A-C); some species are able to bend the neck in an S-curve or pull the neck in so that the head appears to rest on the shoulders. (If in doubt, make this choice) .... #2

#1.Neck is short or moderate in length (Figs.D-H) .... #6

#2.Flies with head drawn back, neck bent in an S-curve (Fig.A), and legs trailing behind; straight, dagger shaped bill (Fig.A) ..... **herons and egrets**, page 15.22

#2.Flies with neck stretched straight out (Figs.B-E); the legs may (Figs.B,C) or may not (Figs.D,E) trail out behind when flying; bill curves downward (Fig.B) or, if straight, is very slender (Figs.C-E) .... #3

#3.Bill curves downward (Fig.B) .... #4

#3.Bill is straight (Figs.C-E) .... **sandpipers**, #5

#4.Shiny purple-bronze-brown (appears black from a distance) with iridescent green on wings; reaches over 50 cm (20") from tip of bill to end of tail; neck is long and S-shaped; overall appearance is heronlike .... ***Plegadis falcinellus*****, glossy ibis** (Fig.B)

#4.Mottled gray-brown above with distinct stripes on top of head; often with a lighter colored belly; less than 50 cm (20") from tip of bill to end of tail; neck is moderate in length and not usually S-shaped; overall appearance is sandpiperlike (see Fig.B on page 15.25) .... ***Numenius phaeopus*****, whimbrel,** page 15.25

#5.Legs are long, extending beyond tail when in flight (Fig.C); bill is long, at least 4 times as long as distance between front of eyes and base of bill (Fig.C); body may grow to be longer than robin size, longer than 28 cm (11") from tip of bill to end of tail .... page 15.25

#5.Legs are short or moderate in length, do not extend beyond tail when in flight (Figs.D,E); bill is short or moderate in length, no more than 3 times as long as distance between front of eyes and base of bill (Figs.D,E); body is robin size or smaller, no longer than 28 cm (11") from tip of bill to end of tail ...... page 15.26

#6.Neck is short and thick (Figs.E-G); bird often appears to have no neck and a hunched back .... #7

#6.Neck is not particularly short and thick (Figs.D,H); bird has an obvious neck .... #8

#7.A relatively large bird, about the size of a herring gull (common "seagull") or larger, with a total length of 50 cm (20") or more from tip of bill to tip of tail; bill is daggerlike (Fig.G) .... **short neck herons**, couplet #6, page 15.22

#7.Medium to small bird, smaller than a herring gull, less than 50 cm (20") from tip of bill to tip of tail; bill is slender .... #9

#8.Bill is bright orange-red and is flattened laterally (side to side); black head, dark back, white belly; white wing patches are visible when the bird is in flight; often repeatedly makes a sharp and distinctive whistling "cleep" sound .... ***Haematopus palliatus*****, American oystercatcher** (Fig.H)

#8.Bill is dark or black tipped .... #9

#9.Bill is short, rather pigeonlike (Fig.F), often with a slight swelling near tip; neck is short and thick; runs along the shore in "fits and starts" (running, then stopping abruptly); most species have striking black and white patterns on face and neck during summer .... **plovers**, page 15.28

#9.Bill is long and thin (Fig.D) or is daggerlike (Fig.A); no swelling near tip of bill; most species are mottled gray or brown on face and neck during summer; neck is moderate in length and width .... #2 (top of this page)

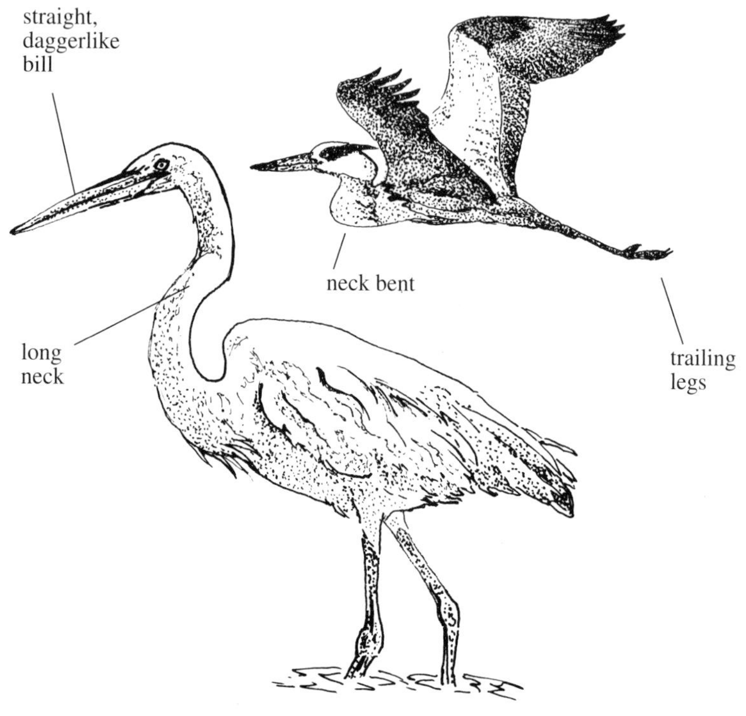

Fig.A. **HERONLIKE WADERS WITH LONG NECKS**

Fig.B. ***PLEGADIS FALCINELLUS*****, GLOSSY IBIS:** Shiny purple-bronze-brown with iridescent green on wings; up to 63 cm (25") long; occasionally seen wading at the edges of tidal marshes. (family Threskiornithidae: ibises)

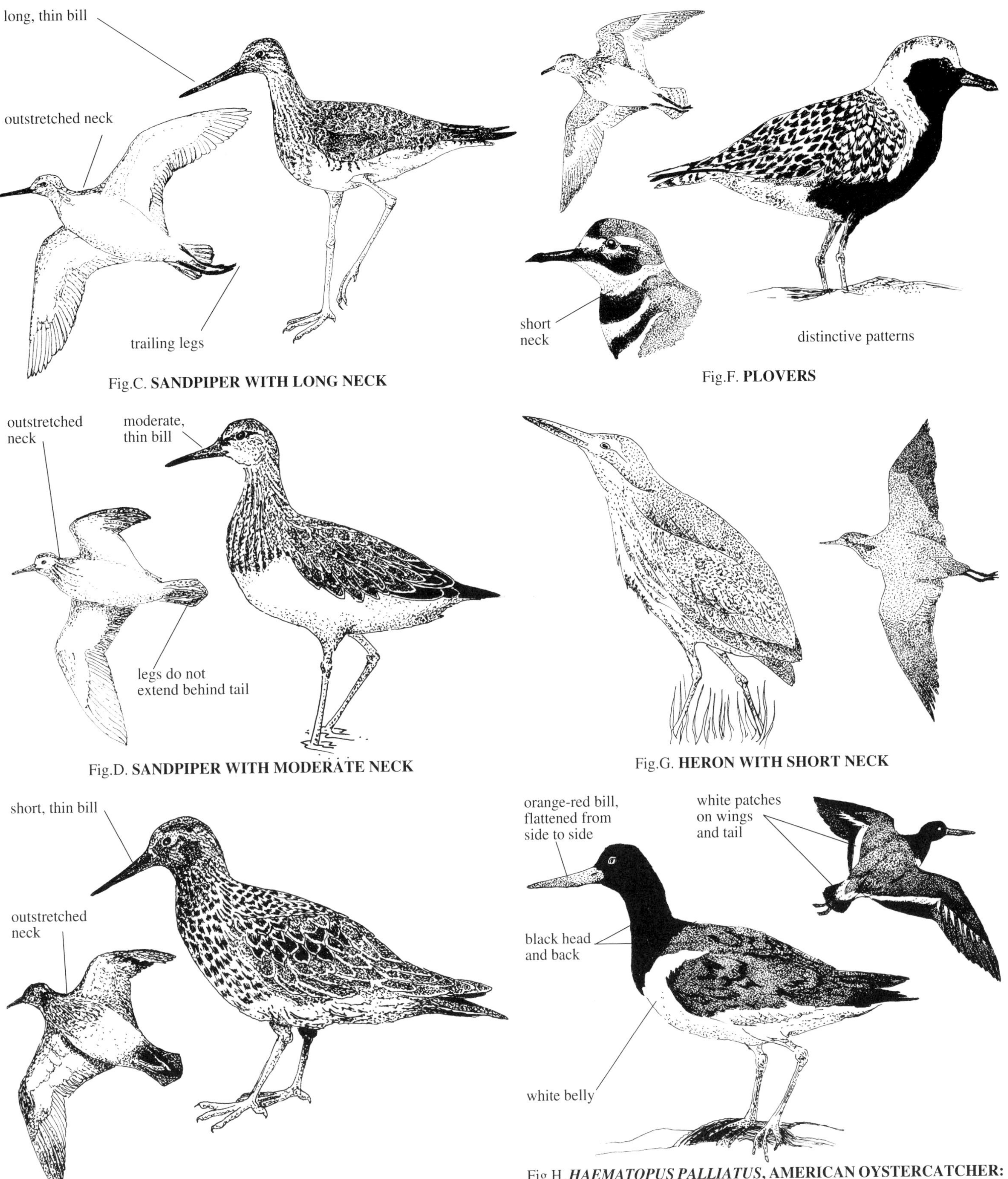

Fig.C. **SANDPIPER WITH LONG NECK**

Fig.F. **PLOVERS**

Fig.D. **SANDPIPER WITH MODERATE NECK**

Fig.G. **HERON WITH SHORT NECK**

Fig.E. **SANDPIPER WITH SHORT NECK**

Fig.H. ***HAEMATOPUS PALLIATUS*, AMERICAN OYSTERCATCHER:** Black head and back, white belly, red-orange bill; up to 53 cm (21") long; occurs on sand beaches and mudflats. (family Haematopodidae: oystercatchers)

HERONS, EGRETS, AND BITTERNS: FAMILY ARDEIDAE (in part)

(Use the key on page 15.20 to determine if you have a heron, egret or bittern)

#1.Neck is long and thin (Figs. A-D) .... #2
#1.Neck is short and thick; bird often appears to have no neck and a hunched back (Figs.F-H); often seen roosting in trees .... #6

#2.Body and wings are mostly white; overall appearance is white but may have small patches of gray or golden brown .... **egrets, white herons,** page 15.24
#2.Body and wings are mostly blue-gray, brown, green or other dark color; overall appearance of bird is not white but may have white areas on head, neck, breast or belly .... #3

#3.Body and wings are mostly blue-gray or steel-gray (Figs.A-C); neck, breast, head or belly may or may not be other colors .... #4
#3.Body and wings are mostly green, dark blue, brown or mottled brown (Figs.D-F); neck, breast, head or belly may or may not be other colors .... #7

#4.Head and cheeks are mostly white with black head plumes or black head cap; bill is yellow; belly and underparts are dark; very large bird, up to 120 cm (4') tall and up to 130 cm (52") from point of bill to end of tail .... ***Ardea herodias*, great blue heron** (Fig.A)
#4.Head and cheeks are bluish or brownish, not white; bill is pale blue; belly and underparts may or may not be white; moderate size bird, up to 65 cm (26") from point of bill to end of tail (Figs.B,C) .... #5

#5.Belly and underparts are dark; at close range, some deep maroon may be seen in the head and neck .... ***Egretta caerulea*, little blue heron** (Fig.B)
#5.Belly and underparts are white; white rump is visible when bird is in flight .... ***Egretta tricolor*, tricolored heron** (Fig.C)

#6.Mostly a combination of gray, white, and black (Figs.G,H); may look gull-like in size and color .... **night herons**, #9
#6.Mostly brown or green (Figs.D-F) .... #7

#7.Wings are dark green or dark blue; head and neck are dark chestnut-brown; back has a bluish or green-blue tint... ***Butorides striatus*, green-backed heron** (Fig.D)
#7.Wings, head and neck are mottled brown (Figs.E,F) .... #8

#8.With black stripe on sides of neck (Fig.E); bill and eyes are yellowish; with black wing tips which are visible when bird is in flight; seldom roosts in trees .... ***Botaurus lentiginosus*, American bittern** (Fig.E)
#8.Without a black stripe on sides of neck; bill is dark; eyes are red; wing tips are brown; often seen roosting in trees .... **immature night heron** (Fig.F)

#9.Top of head is black; back is black; breast, belly, and undersides are white; neck is white .... ***Nycticorax nycticorax*, black-crowned night heron** (Fig.G)
#9.Top of head is white; back is gray; breast, belly, and underside of body are gray; face is black with white patch on cheek .... ***Nyctanassa violacea*, yellow-crowned night heron** (Fig.H)

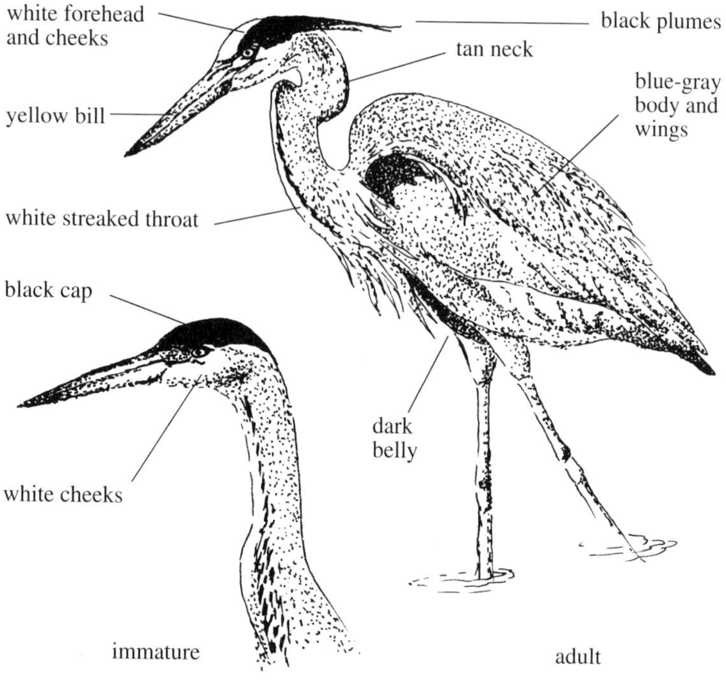

Fig.A. ***ARDEA HERODIAS*, GREAT BLUE HERON:** Body and wings are blue-gray or steel-gray, neck is tan, throat is white edged or streaked with black, head is white with black cap (immature) or black plume (adult), bill is yellow; one of our largest birds, up to 130 cm (52") long; common in warmer months, many great blue herons migrate south but some remain throughout the winter; stands motionless with intense concentration or wades with utmost deliberation in shallow water, poised to strike its daggerlike bill at an unsuspecting fish passing nearby; alarm call is a series of 3-4 loud, hoarse croaks.

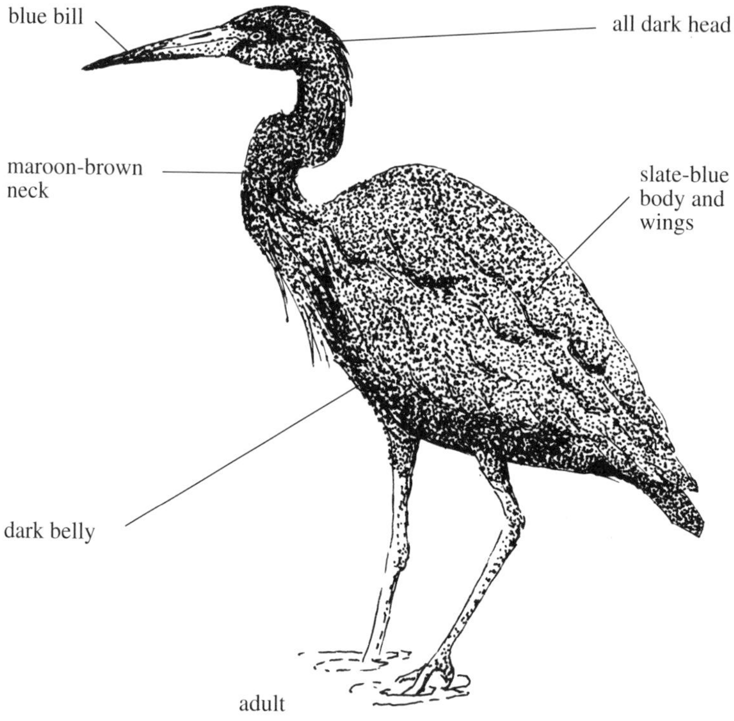

Fig.B. ***EGRETTA CAERULEA (=Florida c.)*, LITTLE BLUE HERON:** Adults are slate-blue overall with a dark maroon-brown neck, immatures are white overall. As they approach breeding age, the white feathers are slowly replaced by blue feathers, resulting in a splotchy dark and light transitional phase (see Fig.B on page 15.24); bill is light-blue, tipped with black; up to 60 cm (2') long; common in summer.

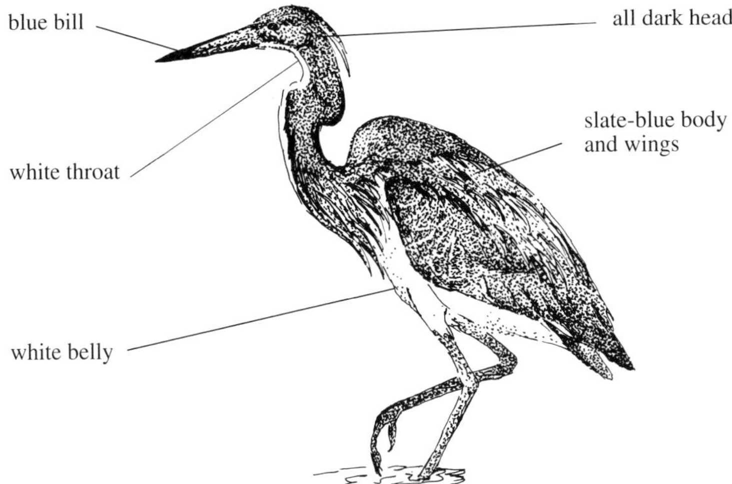

Fig.C. ***EGRETTA TRICOLOR (=Hydranassa t.)*****, TRICOLORED HERON (=Louisiana heron):** Blue-gray head, neck, body, and wings, white belly, throat and rump; up to 65 cm (26") long; not as common as other blue-gray herons.

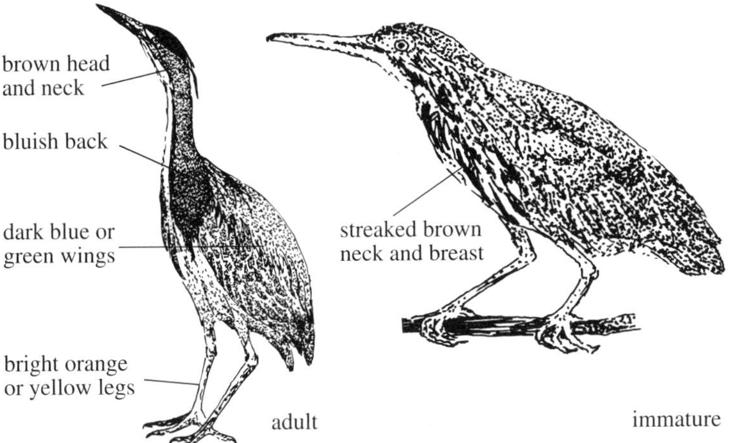

Fig.D. ***BUTORIDES STRIATUS*****, GREEN-BACKED HERON:** Body and wings bluish-green, head and neck brown with white throat, legs greenish-yellow or orange; immature has streaked brown neck and breast; up to 55 cm (22") long; common in warmer months; solitary and secretive; stalks in tall marsh grasses at edges of tidal creeks; when alarmed, jerks tail up and down and stretches neck, often flying away after giving a nasal "skeow" alarm call.

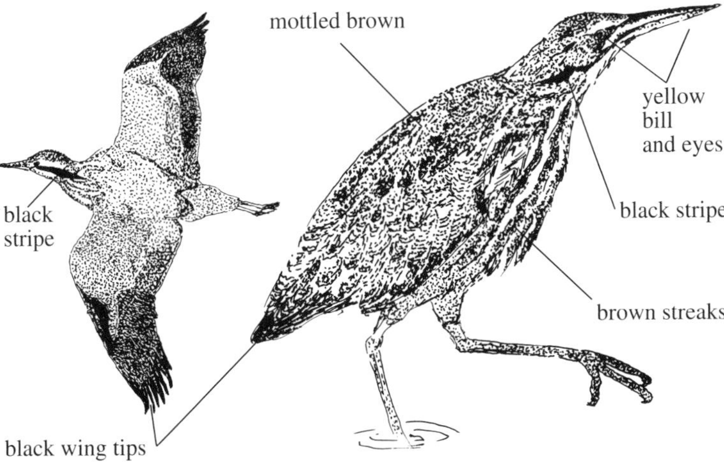

Fig.E. ***BOTAURUS LENTIGINOSUS*****, AMERICAN BITTERN:** Mottled brown head, wings, and body, brown streaks on breast and throat, black stripes on sides of neck, black wing tips, yellow bill and eyes; up to 58 cm (23") long; solitary, secretive; occurs in marsh grass; if disturbed, freezes and points bill up.

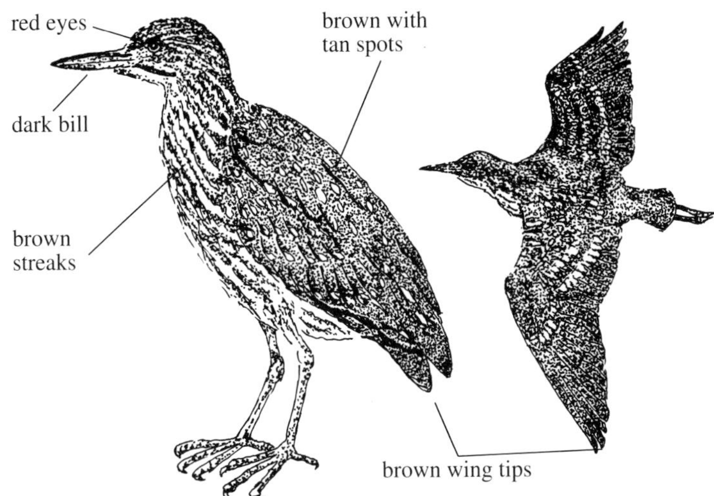

Fig.F. **IMMATURE NIGHT-HERON:** Streaked with brown on breast and head, brown with tan spots on back and wings.

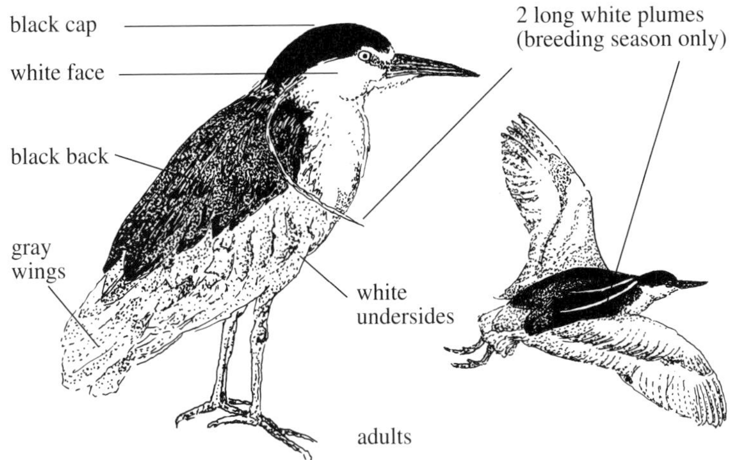

Fig.G. ***NYCTICORAX NYCTICORAX*****, BLACK-CROWNED NIGHT HERON:** Top of head and back is black, breast and undersides are white, wings are gray, eyes are red, bill is black, legs are yellowish; up to 70 cm (28") long; occurs year round, common in warmer months; roosts in trees during day and actively fishes mostly at night; call is a loud single "squawk" often heard at dusk, especially during spring and fall migrations; see Fig.F for immature.

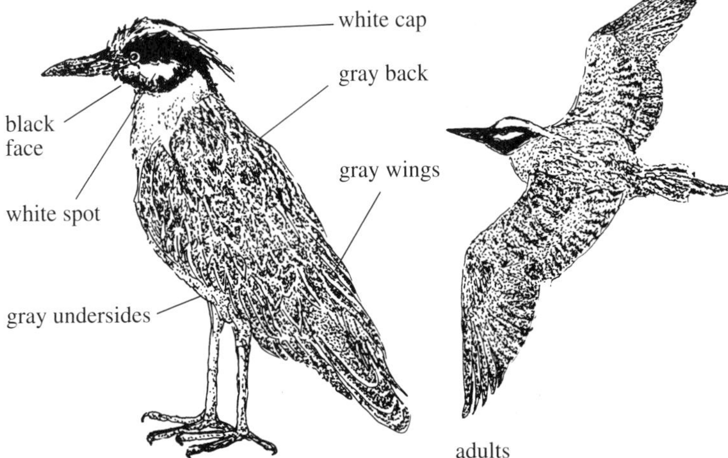

Fig.H.***NYCTANASSA VIOLACEA (=Nycticorax v.)*****, YELLOW-CROWNED NIGHT-HERON:** Top of head is white, back is gray, breast and undersides are gray, face is black with white spot on cheek; up to 70 cm (28") long; occurs in summer, not as common as black-crowned night-heron.

WHITE HERONS AND EGRETS: FAMILY ARDEIDAE (in part)

(Heron and egret key begins on page 15.20)

#1.All plumage (feathers) are completely white .... #2
#1.With patches of brown-gold or blue-gray color .... #5

#2.Bill is yellow or orange .... #3
#2.Bill is black, blue, or dark; not yellow or orange .... #4

#3.Legs and feet are black; large and slender bird, much longer than a common seagull, up to 95 cm (38") from tip of bill to end of tail; back plumes are straight and extend beyond the tail during the breeding season .... ***Casmerodius albus*, great egret** (Fig.A)
#3.Legs and feet are pink, yellow, green, or dusky; a smaller somewhat stocky bird, about the same length as a common seagull, up to 50 cm (20") from tip of bill to end of tail .... ***Bubulcus ibis*, immature cattle egret** (Fig.D)

#4.Bill is bluish with black tip; legs and feet are olive green .... ***Egretta caerulea*, immature little blue heron** (Fig.B)
#4.Bill is black, legs are black with bright yellow feet; with recurved back plumes during breeding season .... ***Egretta thula*, snowy egret** (Fig.C)

#5.With irregular dark patches on white plumage .... ***Egretta caerulea*, little blue heron, in transition from immature to adult plumage** (Fig.B)
#5.With buff (gold-brown) patches on head, back and breast; bill is yellow or orange-pink; legs are pink, yellow, or greenish .... ***Bubulcus ibis*, cattle egret, during breeding season** (Fig.D)

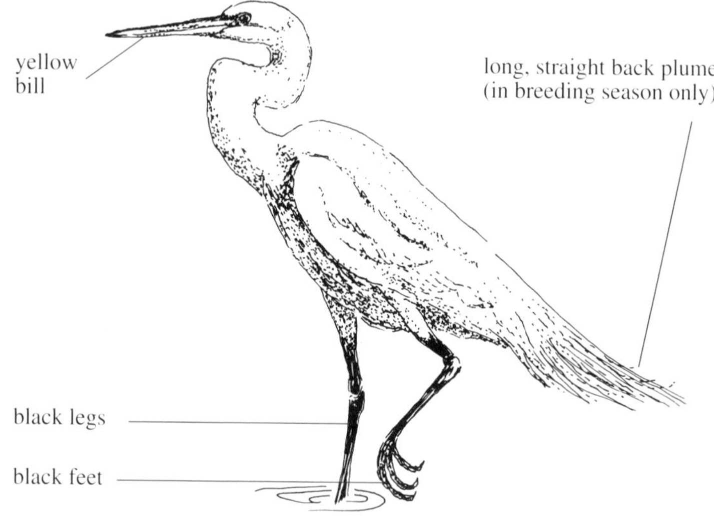

Fig.A. ***CASMERODIUS ALBUS*, GREAT EGRET:** White with a yellow bill, black legs and feet; up to 95 cm (38") long; not as common as the snowy egret.

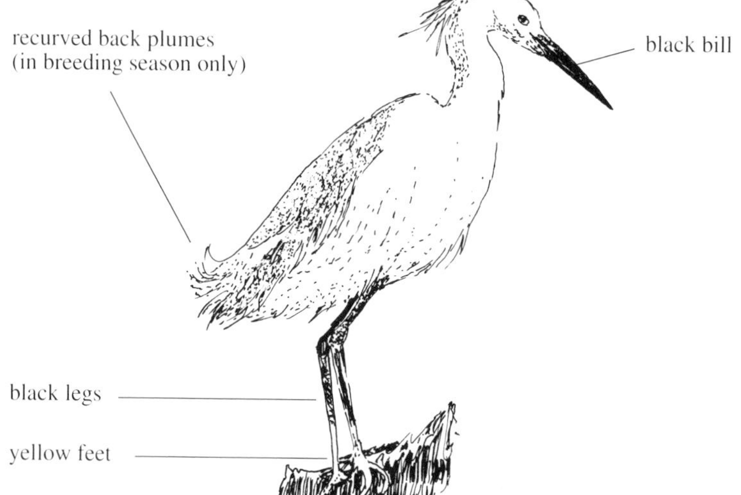

Fig.C. ***EGRETTA THULA*, SNOWY EGRET:** White with a black bill and legs, yellow feet; up to 68 cm (27") long; the most common white heron in this region, especially in summer.

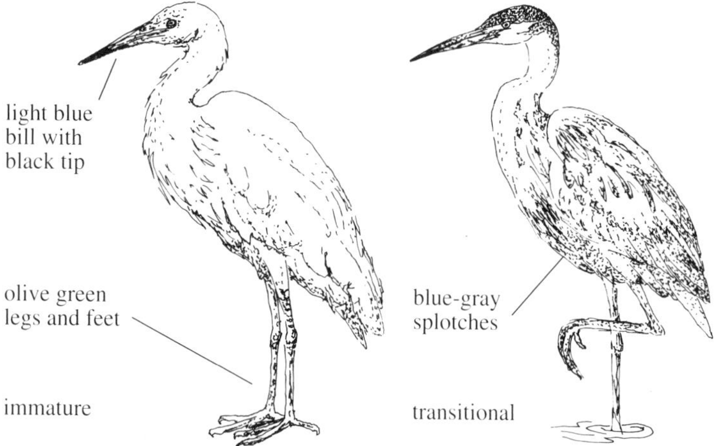

Fig.B. ***EGRETTA CAERULEA (=Florida c.)*, LITTLE BLUE HERON:** White overall when immature, slate-blue overall when adult (see Fig. B on page 15.22). As the heron approaches breeding age, the white feathers are slowly replaced by blue-gray feathers resulting in a splotchy dark and light transitional phase. Bill is light blue, tipped with black, legs and feet are olive green; up to 60 cm (2') long; common in summer.

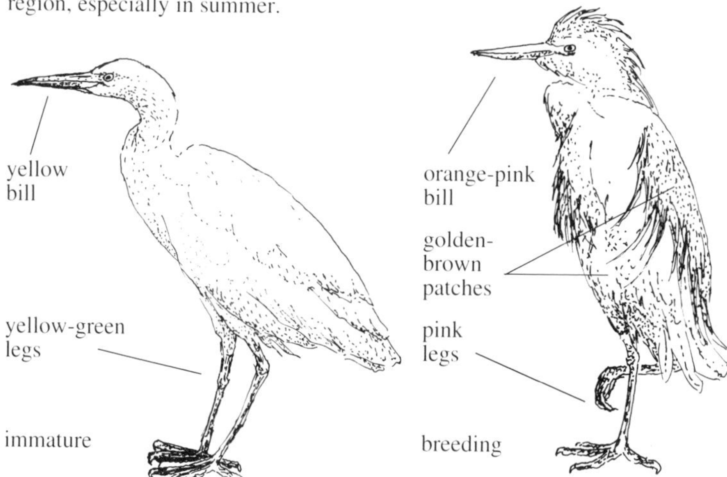

Fig.D. ***BUBULCUS IBIS*, CATTLE EGRET:** In nonbreeding season, entirely white with yellow bill and yellow or greenish legs. In breeding season, with patches of golden-brown on head, back and breast, orange-pink bill, pink legs. Up to 50 cm (20") long; an immigrant from Africa, first found nesting in Florida in 1941, then spread northward along the coast; although not common in southern New England, it is occasionally observed in the summer.

LARGER SANDPIPERS WITH LONG NECKS, LONG BILLS, AND LONG LEGS
FAMILY SCOLOPACIDAE (in part)

Sandpipers that grow larger than robin size; with legs that extend beyond tail when in flight; with a bill that is at least 4 times as long as the distance between the eyes and the base of the bill

(Use the key on page 15.20 to determine if you have a sandpiper)

#1.Legs are bright yellow .... ***Tringa* spp., yellowlegs** (Fig.A)
#1.Legs are gray, green or bluish, not bright yellow .... #2

#2.Bill curves downward (Fig.B) .... ***Numenius phaeopus*, whimbrel** (Fig.B)
#2.Bill is straight (Figs. C,E) .... #3
#2.Bill curves slightly upward (Fig.D) .... ***Limosa* spp., godwits** (Fig.D)

#3.When in flight, shows a white wedge up back (Fig.C) .... ***Limnodromus* spp., dowitchers** (Fig.C)
#3.When in flight, does not show a white wedge up back (Figs.D,E) .... #4

#4.When in flight, white and black bands can be seen on wings (Figs. D,E) .... #5
#4.When in flight, wings do not show white and black bands .... **smaller sandpipers**, page 15.26

#5.Tail with broad black and white bands .... ***Limosa haemastica*, Hudsonian godwit** (Fig.D)
#5.Tail is gray and white .... ***Catoptrophorus semipalmatus*, willet** (Fig.E)

gray back and wings
bright yellow legs

Fig.A. ***TRINGA* SPP., YELLOWLEGS:** Back and wings are dark gray with black and white markings, legs are bright yellow. The greater yellowlegs, *Tringa melanoleuca*, reaches 35 cm (14") in length, has a slightly upturned bill, and a clear three note whistle. The lesser yellowlegs, *Tringa flavipes*, grows up to 28 cm (11") long, has a straight bill, and a weaker one or two note whistle. Both species are common migrants.

brown and tan stripes
down curved bill

Fig.B. ***NUMENIUS PHAEOPUS*, WHIMBREL:** Wings and back are brown, underside tan, head with brown and tan stripes; up to 48 cm (19") long.

straight bill
dark greenish legs
white wedge

Fig.C. ***LIMNODROMUS* SPP., DOWITCHERS:** Back and wings are dark gray with white wedge up back, breast is reddish brown in summer and gray in winter; up to 31 cm (12") long. The short-billed dowitcher, *Limnodromus griseus*, is a common migrant which feeds by pecking in a sewing machine motion on saltmarshes and mudflats.

Fig.D. ***LIMOSA HAEMASTICA*, HUDSONIAN GODWIT:** Wings dark gray with white band, tail with broad black and white bands; gray legs; up to 40 cm (16") long; not uncommon during migration periods. The marbled godwit, *Limosa fedoa*, is tan-brown overall and also occurs during migrations. Both species have a long bill which may be straight or slightly upcurved.

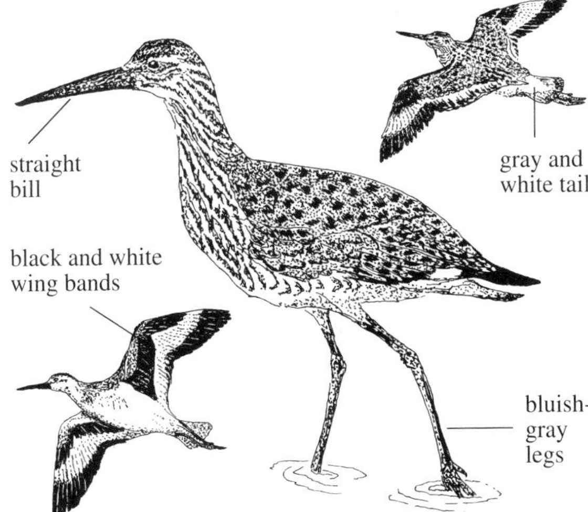

Fig.E. ***CATOPTROPHORUS SEMIPALMATUS*, WILLET:** Gray with black and white bands on wings that can be seen when flying, legs bluish-gray; up to 43 cm (17") long; not common.

SMALLER SANDPIPERS WITH SHORT TO MODERATE SIZE NECKS, BILLS, AND LEGS FAMILY SCOLOPACIDAE (in part)

(Use the key on page 15.20 to determine if you have a sandpiper)

#1. Belly with noticeable black patch (Fig.A); long stout bill droops slightly downward near tip .... ***Calidris alpina*, dunlin** (Fig.A)
#1. No black belly patch (Figs. B-I) .... #2

#2. Breast and belly with round dark spots; when standing, has distinctive teetering behavior, like a see-saw, with tail continuously bobbing up and down; flies stiff winged, taking shallow wingbeats and looking a bit as if it is vibrating through the air rather than flying .... ***Actitis macularia*, spotted sandpiper** (Fig.B)
#2. Breast is streaked, mottled, pale or reddish; belly not spotted (Figs.C-I); behavior while standing or flying not as described above .... #3

#3. With numerous white speckles on back and on top of wings; tail has white sides, a dark center and cross bars .... ***Tringa solitaria*, solitary sandpiper** (Fig.C)
#3. Back and top of wings are not speckled (light streaks may be present at edges of feathers); tail not as described above .... #4

#4. Streaked pattern on breast ends suddenly above pale belly so that bird looks as if it is wearing a bib .... ***Calidris melanotos*, pectoral sandpiper** (Fig.D)
#4. Coloration on breast blends gradually with the coloration on belly (Figs. E-I); bird does not look as if it is wearing a bib .... #5

#5. Breast is mottled brown, gray, or white; not reddish .... #6
#5. Breast is reddish or rusty color .... #11

#6. Legs are yellow or yellow-green .... #7
#6. Legs are black or gray-green, not yellow .... #9

#7. Neck, legs, and bill are long (see Fig.A on page 15.25) .... ***Tringa* spp., yellowlegs**, page 15.25
#7. Neck, legs, and bill are short .... #8

#8. Common in winter on rocky shores, jetties, and breakwaters; dark slate-gray wings and back with white belly; white eye ring and yellowish base of bill are visible at close range .... ***Calidris maritima*, purple sandpiper** (Fig.E)
#8. Common in saltmarshes and muddy shores; wings, back, and breast are streaked brown; bill is entirely black .... ***Calidris minutilla*, least sandpiper** (Fig.F)

#9. Breast is clean white; back is pale gray; shoulders have dark patch; broad white wing stripe visible in flight; common on sandy open beaches where it constantly chases waves up and down the beach .... ***Calidris alba*, sanderling** (Fig.H)
#9. Breast is grayish or brownish, not white; back is brown or gray-brown, not light gray; without dark shoulder patch; without broad white wing stripe visible in flight; does not chase waves up and down beach .... #10

#10. Tip of bill has slight downward droop (Fig.A); breast and back are not mottled or patterned with black markings; robin size, up to 23 cm (9") long .... ***Calidris alpina*, dunlin** (Fig.A)
#10. Tip of bill does not droop downward; back and breast are strongly mottled and patterned with black and dark brown streaks, checks, spots; generally undistinguished, neckless looking, small sparrow size, shorter than 18 cm (7"); the "little brown jobs" of the sandpipers .... ***Calidris* spp., peeps** (Fig.G)

#11. Common on sandy, open beaches where it constantly chases waves up and down the beach; broad white wing stripe and dark rump (Fig.H) visible in flight; does not grow much larger than sparrow size, up to 20 cm (8)" from tip of beak to end of tail; legs and feet are black ...... ***Calidris alba*, sanderling** (Fig.H)
#11. Common on mudflats; does not chase waves as described above; when in flight, shows pale rump (Fig.I) and narrow or no wing stripe; often grows to robin size or larger, over 23 cm (9") long; legs and feet are greenish .... #12

#12. Bill is not especially long; when in flight, does not show white wedge on back; often seen in very large flocks, particularly in the fall, poking around in the mud at low tide .... ***Calidris canutus*, red knot** (Fig.I)
#12. Bill is very long; when in flight, shows a long white wedge up back (see Fig.C on page 15.25); pokes bill into mud with a sewing machinelike motion .... ***Limnodromus* spp., dowitchers**, page 15.25

winter

downward droop at tip of bill

black patch

summer

dark gray legs

Fig.A. ***CALIDRIS ALPINA*, DUNLIN:** With reddish-brown back and black patch on belly during summer, with unpatterned gray-brown back and light gray breast during winter; legs are dark gray; up to 23 cm (9") long; common during winter and migration periods.

winter

dark spots

summer

beige-tan legs

Fig.B. ***ACTITIS MACULARIA*, SPOTTED SANDPIPER:** Brown-gray above, with dark round spots on breast in summer, no breast spots in winter and fall, legs are tan; up to 19 cm (7.5") long; common during summer and migration periods; see description in key of distinctive behavior patterns.

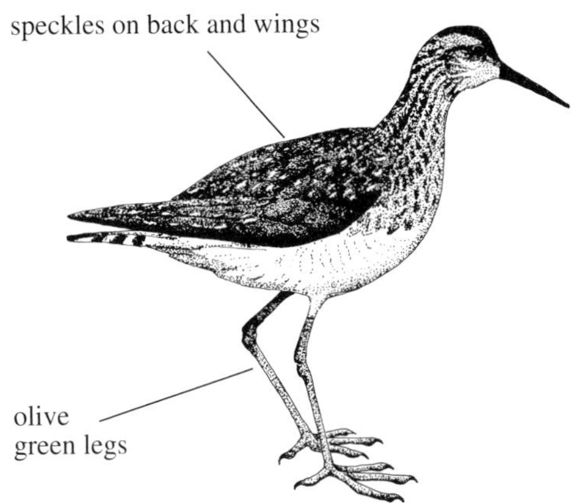

Fig.C.***TRINGA SOLITARIA*, SOLITARY SANDPIPER:** Back dark brown or gray with white specks, tail with white edges and dark cross bands, white eye ring, olive green legs; up to 23 cm (9") long; not common.

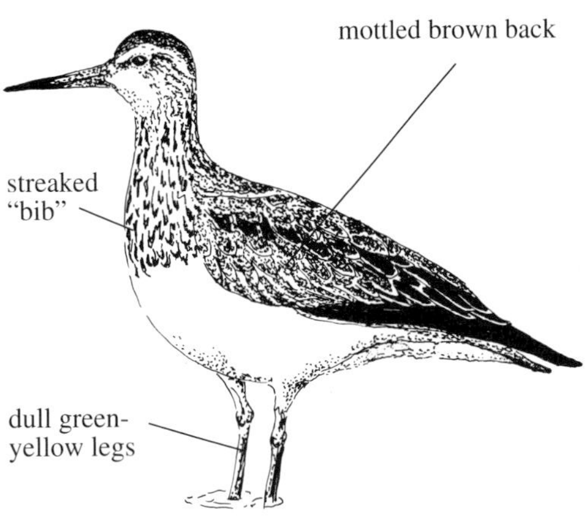

Fig.D.***CALIDRIS MELANOTOS*, PECTORAL SANDPIPER:** Back and breast streaked with brown and black, legs are dull yellow-green; up to 23 cm (9") long; not common.

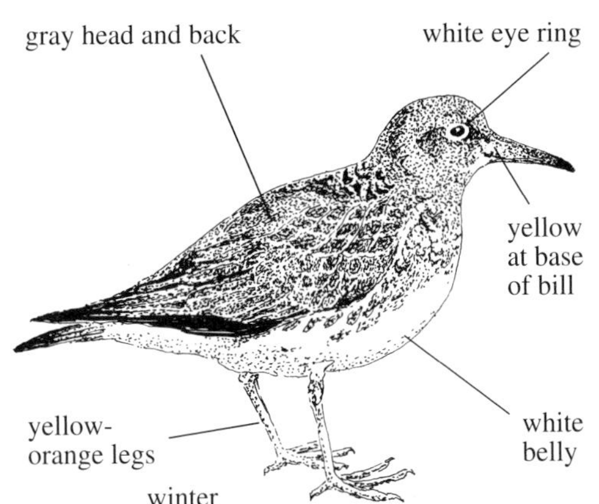

Fig.E.***CALIDRIS MARITIMA*, PURPLE SANDPIPER:** In winter, with gray head, back, and breast, white belly; in summer, back and breast browner and with streaks; yellow legs; yellow at base of bill; white eye ring; up to 23 cm (9") long; common in winter on rocky shores, jetties, and breakwaters.

Fig.F. ***CALIDRIS MINUTILLA*, LEAST SANDPIPER:** Streaked and mottled brown back, head and breast, white belly, yellow-green legs; up to 16 cm (6.5") long; common in saltmarshes and muddy shores during summer and migration periods.

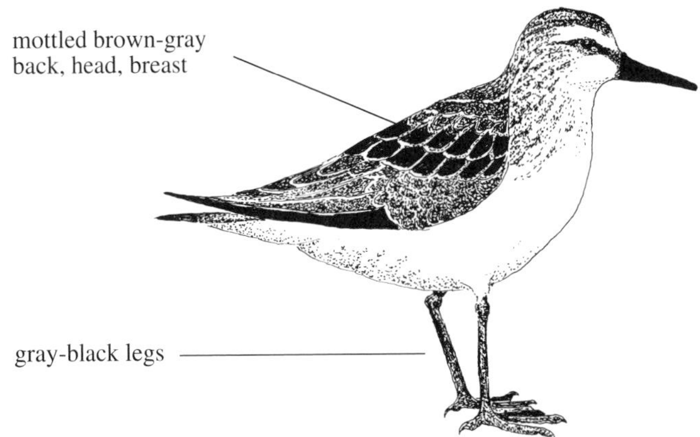

Fig.G.***CALIDRIS* SPP., PEEPS:** Peeps are small, sparrow size sandpipers with a streaked and mottled brown back, head, and breast, white belly, dark gray or black legs; up to 19 cm (7.5") long. The semipalmated sandpiper, *Calidris pusilla*, is the most common of the peeps during the summer and migration periods. Refer to a field guide such as R. T. Peterson (1980) to distinguish between these very similar birds.

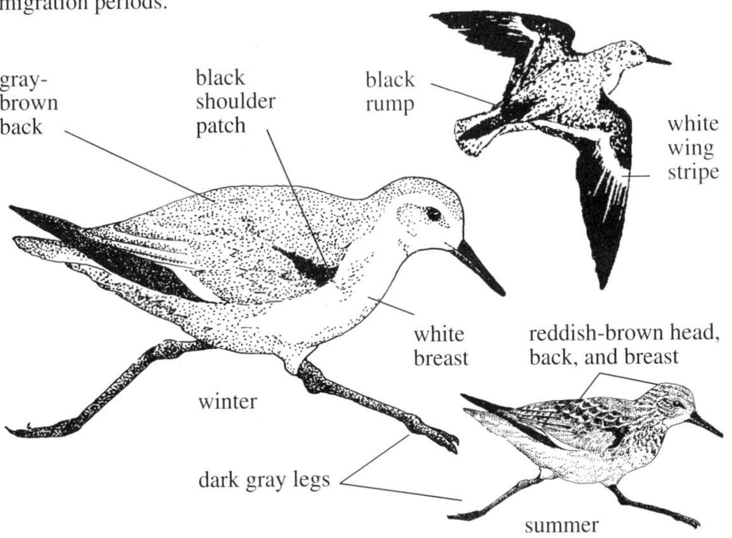

Fig.H.***CALIDRIS ALBA*, SANDERLING:** With reddish-brown head, back, and breast during summer, with pale gray back, white undersides, black shoulder patches in winter; legs are dark gray; up to 20 cm (8") long; common during migration periods and winter; behavior pattern distinctive, see key.

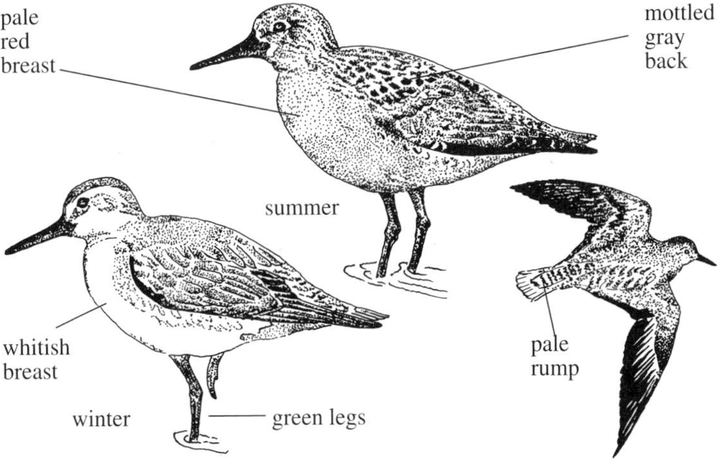

Fig.I. ***CALIDRIS CANUTUS*, RED KNOT:** In summer, with reddish breast and mottled gray back; in winter, with pale breast and gray back; legs are greenish; up to 28 cm (11") long; large flocks seen during migration periods.

PLOVERS: FAMILY CHARADRIIDAE and TURNSTONES: FAMILY SCOLOPACIDAE, in part

Short necked birds with striking black and white markings on face and neck; they run along the shore with quick starts and stops

(Use the key on page 15.20 to determine if you have a plover)

#1.Face and neck with distinct black and white markings (Figs.A-F) .... #2
#1.Face and neck are pale, speckled or mottled; without distinct black and white markings .... **immature plovers or plovers in winter plummage**

#2.Belly, breast and cheeks are black (Figs.A,B); legs are black .... #3
#2.Belly is white (Figs.C-F); neck and cheeks are white and black; legs are yellow or orange .... #4

#3.Axillars ("wingpits") are black; topside of tail and rump is mostly white .... ***Pluvialis squatarola*, black-bellied plover** (Fig.A)
#3.Axillars ("wingpits") are not black; topside of tail and rump is mostly dark .... ***Pluvialis dominica*, lesser golden-plover** (Fig. B)

#4.Face and throat with black and white "harlequin" pattern (Fig.C); wings and back with bright reddish-brown and white patches crossed with black bands (in winter, this basic pattern is not as strikingly colored); bill is sharply pointed and slightly upturned .... ***Arenaria interpres*, ruddy turnstone** (Fig.C)
#4.With one or more broad black and/or white bands (rings) encircling the neck (Figs.D-F); without bright reddish-brown and white patches on wings or back; bill has a slight swelling near tip .... **"belted" or "ring-necked" plovers**, #5

#5.With two black neck rings .... ***Charadrius vociferus*, killdeer** (Fig.D)
#5.With single black and/or white neck ring (Figs.E,F) .... #6

#6.Back and wings are pale sand color; with single black stripe across forehead between eyes; black neck ring may or may not extend completely around throat .... ***Charadrius melodus*, piping plover** (Fig.E)
#6.Back and wings are brown; with white forehead bordered by black stripes above and below, black neck ring extends completely around throat .... ***Charadrius semipalmatus*, semipalmated plover** (Fig.F)

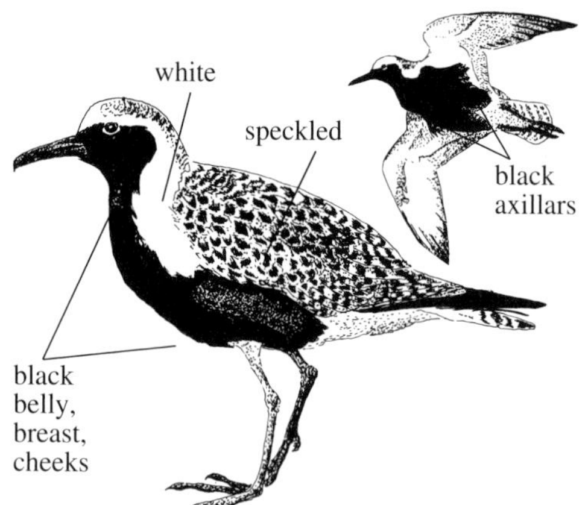

Fig.A. ***PLUVIALIS SQUATAROLA*, BLACK-BELLIED PLOVER:** Top of head and back are speckled black and white, belly, breast, and cheeks are black, axillars ("wingpits") are black (visible only when bird is flying); rump is white; up to 34 cm (13.5") long; common during migratory periods.

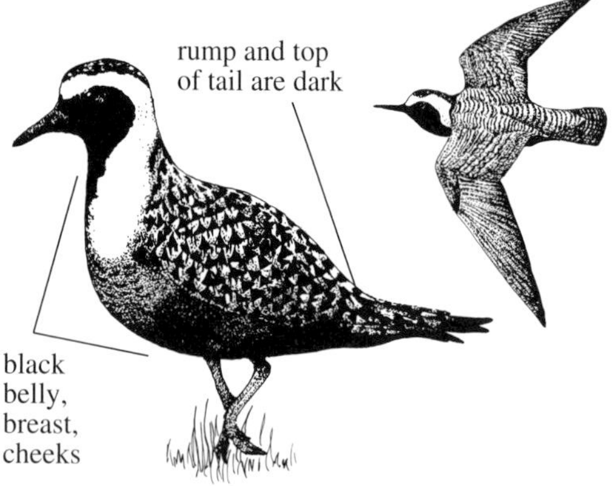

Fig.B. ***PLUVIALIS DOMINICA*, LESSER GOLDEN-PLOVER:** Top of head and back are dark brown with golden speckles; belly, breast, and cheeks are black; rump is dark; up to 28 cm (11") long; not common.

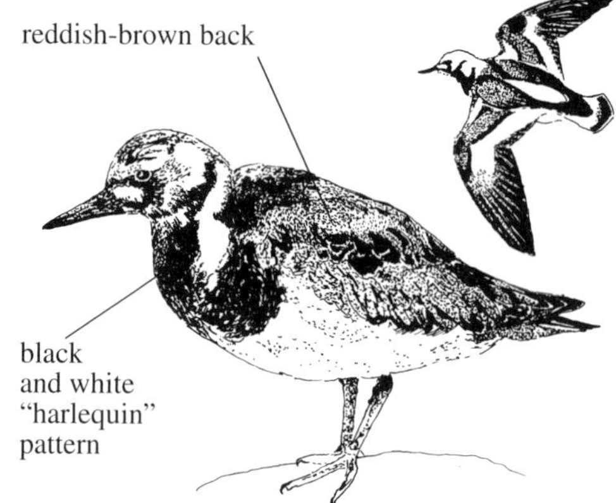

Fig.C. ***ARENARIA INTERPRES*, RUDDY TURNSTONE:** Unique black and white "harlequin" pattern on face and back and breast, reddish-brown on wings and back, orange legs; up to 25 cm (10") long; common during migratory periods.

Fig.D. ***CHARADRIUS VOCIFERUS*, KILLDEER:** Top of head, wings, and back are dark brown, rump is tan; undersides are white, with two black neck rings; up to 28 cm (11") long; common in summer and during migratory periods; voice is a noisy and loud "kill-deeah."

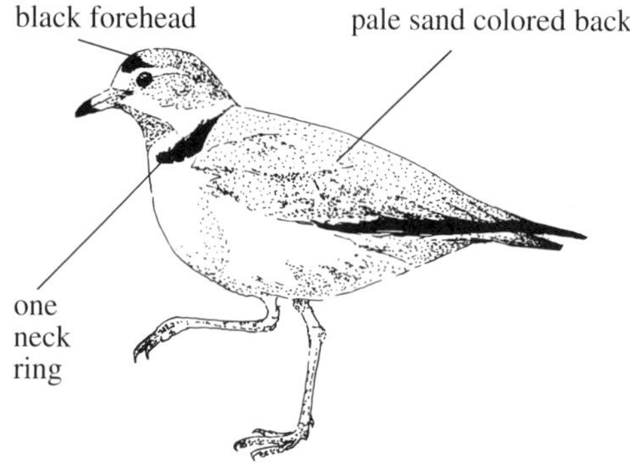

Fig.E. ***CHARADRIUS MELODUS*, PIPING PLOVER:** Back and wings are pale sand color, single black stripe across forehead, black neck ring may or may not completely encircle throat, bill yellow with black tip; up to 19 cm (7.5") long; lives and nests on sandy beaches and dunes; not common.

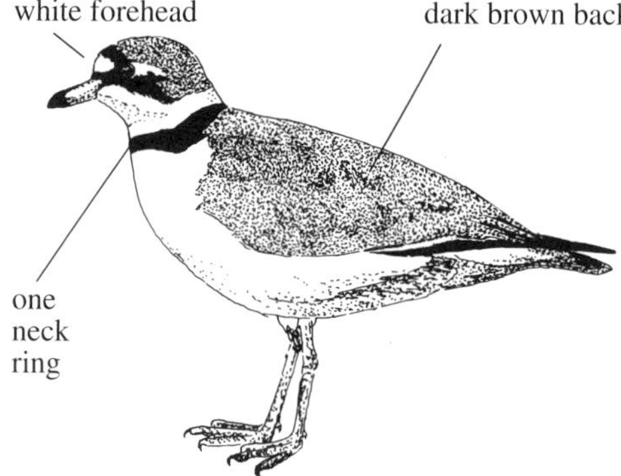

Fig.F. ***CHARADRIUS SEMIPALMATUS*, SEMIPALMATED PLOVER:** Top of head and back are dark brown, forehead white with black stripes above and below, with one black neck band, bill is yellow with black tip; up to 19 cm (7.5") long; common during migratory periods.

BIRDS OF PREY (OWLS, FALCONS, HAWKS, ETC.)

Birds with talons (large claws), hooked bills, large "fierce" looking eyes

(Bird key begins on page 15.00)

#1.Head is large and very round with flattened face formed into a facial disc (Figs. A,B); looks rather neckless; eyes are large and forward facing; legs and toes are feathered; normally solitary, found living alone .... **owls[1], family Strigidae**, #2

#1.Head is small to normal size (Figs. C-F); eyes are somewhat "hooded" and positioned more or less on the sides of the head; legs may be feathered but toes are not; often seen flying during the day; may be found in great numbers, particularly in the fall, during migration .... #3

#2.Brown or fawn color with dark facial disc; small "ear" tufts (Fig.A) may be visible at close range; may be seen flying low over marshes and dunes with a long-winged, mothlike flight .... ***Asio flammeus*, short-eared owl** (Fig.A)

#2.White, with dark flecks or bars; no ear tufts; often perches on a post or sits on a sand dune or hummock .... ***Nyctea scandiaca*, snowy owl** (Fig. B)

#3.Wing tips are rounded or squarish (Fig.C); often observed gliding or soaring .... **hawks, eagles, osprey**, page 15.30

#3.Wing tips are pointed (Figs.D-F); flies with rapid wing beats; rarely observed gliding or soaring .... **falcons, family Falconidae**, #4

#4.Back and tail are reddish brown (wings on male are blue-gray); with TWO sets of black facial markings ("mustaches" AND "sideburns"), one beneath eyes and the other near ears (Fig.D) .... ***Falco sparverius*, American kestrel** (Fig.D)

#4.Back and tail are dark brown (female) or dark blue-gray (male); with ONE set of black facial markings ("mustaches"), beneath eyes only (Figs.E,F) .... #5

#5."Mustaches" are thick, nearly as wide as eyes; larger, crow size, up[2] to 50 cm (20") long .... ***Falco peregrinus*, peregrine falcon** (Fig.E)

#5."Mustaches" are thin, not as wide as eyes; smaller, blue jay size, less than 34 cm (14") long .... ***Falco columbarius*, merlin** (Fig.F)

[1]The two owls included here actively fly and feed during the day. There are also several owl species that occur along the shore and are nocturnal, only active at night. They are rarely observed and are not included in this key. Refer to a field guide such as R. T. Peterson (1980) to identify these owls.

[2]Length is measured from the tip of bill to end of tail. See Fig.E on page 15.01.

Fig.A. ***ASIO FLAMMEUS*, SHORT-EARED OWL:** Streaked brown or tan, dark facial disc, yellow eyes; up to 43 cm (17") long.

no ear tufts
white face disc

Fig.B. ***NYCTEA SCANDIACA*, SNOWY OWL:** White with dark flecks, yellow eyes; up to 68 cm (27") long; occasionally observed during winter.

Fig.C. **BIRDS OF PREY WITH ROUNDED OR SQUARISH WING TIPS**

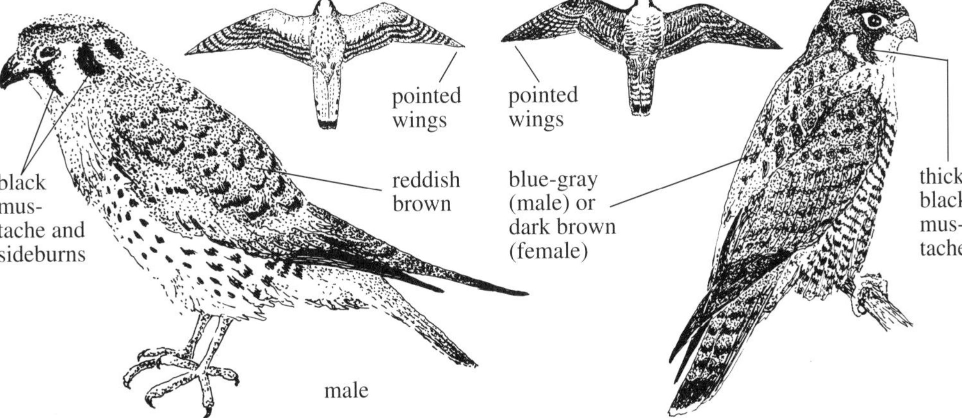

Fig.D. ***FALCO SPARVERIUS*, AMERICAN KESTREL (=sparrow hawk):** Back and tail are reddish-brown, wings of male are blue-gray, with black and white facial markings; up to 30 cm (12") long; common year-round; hovers with rapidly beating wings over open fields or grassy areas; often perches on telephone wires.

Fig.E. ***FALCO PEREGRINUS*, PEREGRINE FALCON:** Back, wings and top of head are blue-gray, undersides are tan with brown spots and streaks, face with thick black sideburns; up to 50 cm (20") long; an endangered species due to the effects of pesticides, occasionally observed during migrations along the coast.

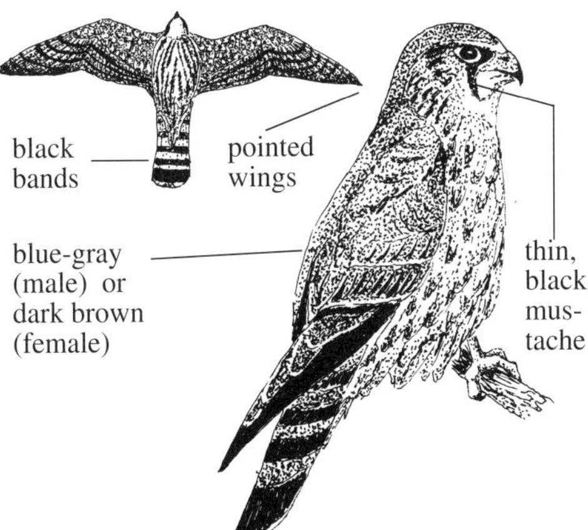

Fig.F. ***FALCO COLUMBARIUS*, MERLIN (=pigeon hawk):** Males are blue-gray above, females and immature birds are dark brown above; both sexes have black bands across tail, narrow black "mustaches," and tan undersides with dark brown streaks; up to 34 cm (14") long; frequently observed during migration periods.

BIRDS OF PREY WITH ROUNDED OR SQUARISH WING TIPS
FAMILIES ACCIPITRIDAE (OSPREY, HAWKS, EAGLES) AND CATHARTIDAE (VULTURES)

(Key to birds of prey begins on page 15.29)

#1.Undersides of wings, breast, and belly are lighter in color than upper sides of wings and back; undersides are whitish or pale brown (Figs. A-E) often with darker bands across tail .... #2

#1.Undersides of wings and body and are mostly or completely black (Figs.F-H); tail and head may or may not be white .... #6

#2.In flight, undersides of wings show a dark "wrist" patch (Fig.A) and may look somewhat checkered; head is mostly white with a dark band running through eyes and across the cheeks to the back of the head; occasionally will hover over water and then plunge into water feet first after fish; flies with wings held in an arched position and with a conspicuous bend in wings .... ***Pandion haliaetus*, osprey** (Fig.A)

#2.Underside of wings without a dark wrist patch visible in flight (Figs. B-E); head is mostly dark; does not plunge into water; glides with wings held out straight or at a slightly upward angle .... #3

#3.With a white rump which is strikingly visible when bird turns in flight (Fig.B); glides low over marsh grasses tilting from side to side with wings held slightly above body level (broad V-shaped dihedral wing position like a turkey vulture); hovers quickly and then drops into grass after prey; with dark owl-like facial disc .... ***Circus cyaneus*, northern harrier** (Fig.B)

#3.Rump is not white; does not glide as described above; without dark facial disc .... #4

#4.Tail is long (Fig.C); when at rest, tip of tail appears square ended or notched; body is slim; wings are short; flies with a pattern of several wingbeats and then a glide .... ***Accipiter* spp., accipiters (bird hawks)** (Fig.C)

#4.Tail is wide, rather fan shaped (Figs.D,E); body is heavy set; wings are broad; often seen sitting in trees quite close to highways; soars and glides in wide circles; during the fall large numbers may be seen soaring in a funnel shaped formation in the sky .... ***Buteo* spp., buteos (buzzard hawks)**, #5

#5.Tail with broad black and white bands; without any dark streaks across belly .... ***Buteo* spp., other buteos** (Fig.D)

#5.Tail with little or no banding; upper (dorsal) side of tail is reddish which can be seen most clearly when bird turns in flight (in strong light, some red may also show through pale underside of tail); with dark streaks across belly .... ***Buteo jamaicensis*, red-tailed hawk** (Fig.E)

#6.Head and tail are completely white (Fig.F); with large yellow bill .... ***Haliaeetus leucocephalus*, bald eagle** (Fig.F)

#6.Head and tail are dark (Figs.F,G), may be black or red .... #7

#7.In flight, some white is visible on underside of wing linings and sometimes on breast; soars with wings stretched flat out .... ***Haliaeetus leucocephalus*, immature bald eagle** (Fig.F)

#7.No white visible .... #8

#8.In flight, underside shows a two-toned black pattern (black and blacker); soars with wings held in a broad V-shape above body (dihedral) and rocks unsteadily from side to side; head is naked (no feathers) and is red in adult and black in immature .... ***Cathartes aura*, turkey vulture** (Fig.G)

#8.In flight, underside is single toned black overall (Fig.H); usually flaps wings steadily, seldom gliding or soaring for more than 2 or 3 seconds except in strong updrafts or when descending; head has feathers .... **crows**, page 15.36 (Fig.H)

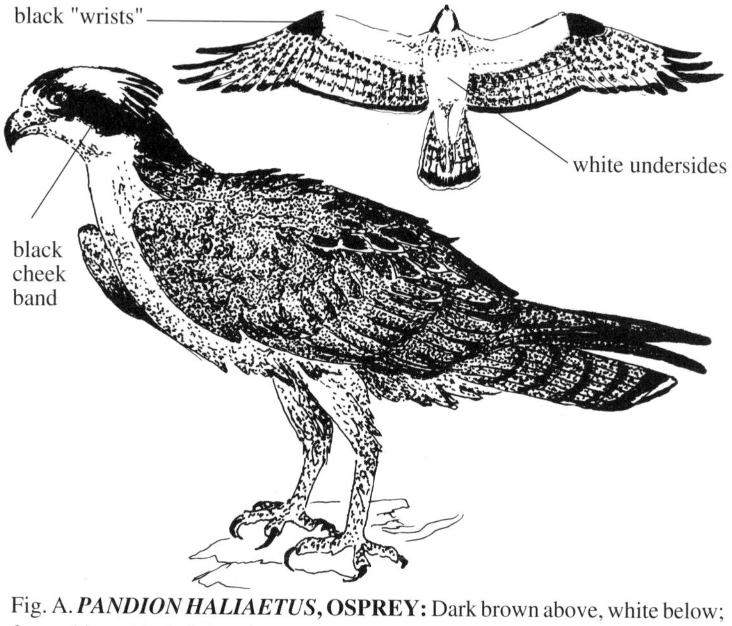

black "wrists"

white undersides

black cheek band

Fig. A. ***PANDION HALIAETUS*, OSPREY:** Dark brown above, white below; face white with dark band across cheek; underside of wings white, with dark "wrist" patch; up to 61 cm (25") long; nest is a large, messy looking conglomeration of sticks atop a dead tree or tall pole; dives feet first into water grabbing fish with talons; population greatly reduced from 1950 to 1970 by effects of pesticides but has increased since DDT was banned in early 1970's.

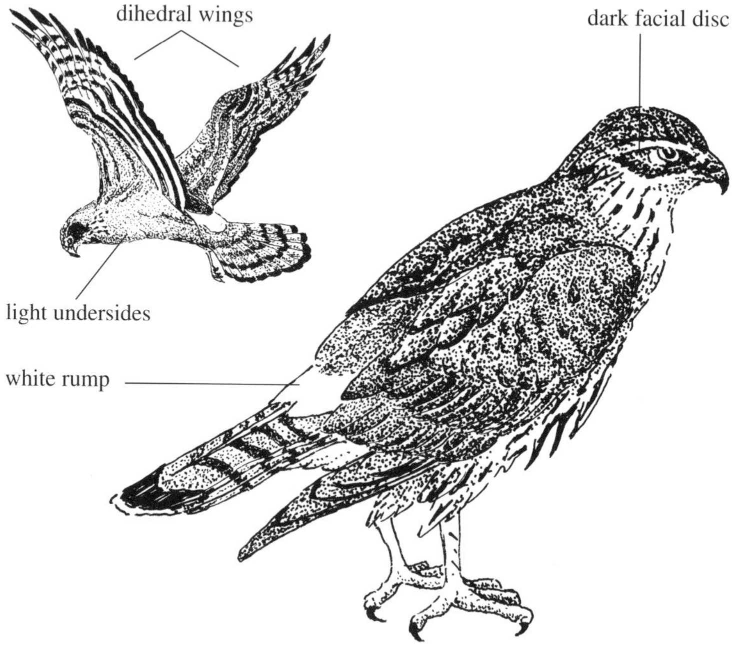

dihedral wings

dark facial disc

light undersides

white rump

Fig.B. ***CIRCUS CYANEUS*, NORTHERN HARRIER (=marsh hawk):** Males are light gray above with dark wing tips, females are dark brown, both sexes have white rump and dark facial discs; up to 60 cm (24") long; occurs year-round.

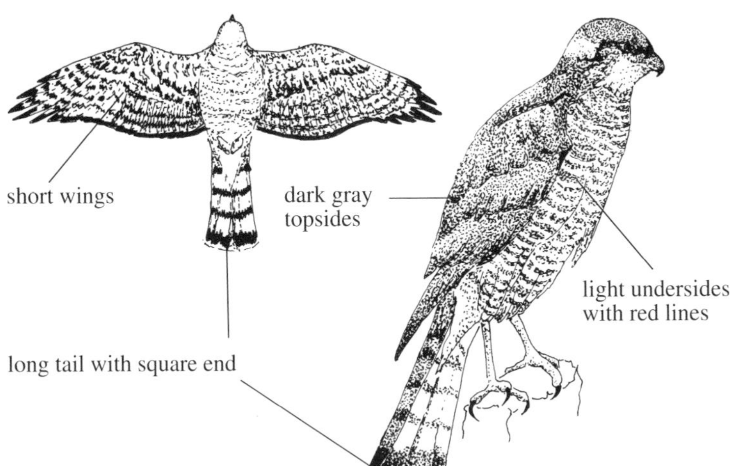

Fig.C. ***ACCIPITER* SPP., ACCIPITERS (bird hawks):** Back is dark gray, breast is light with reddish lines; up to 50 cm (20") long; the sharp-shinned hawk (*A. striatus*), shown above, occurs year-round and is common during migration periods; Cooper's hawk (*A. cooperii*) is less common and has a rounder tail. Refer to a field guide such as R. T. Peterson (1980) to distinguish these species.

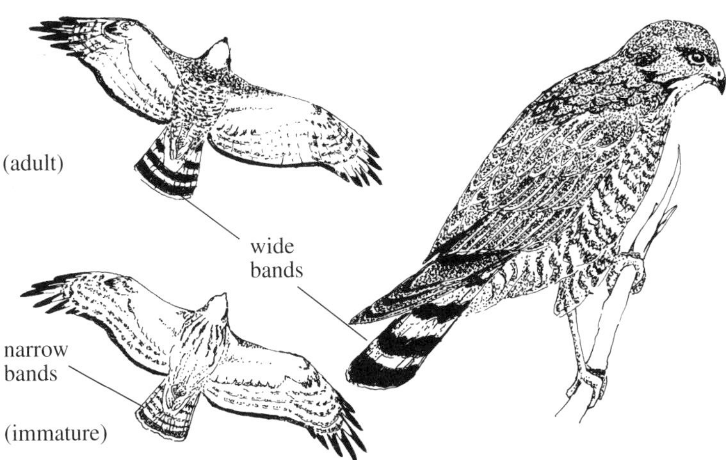

Fig.D. ***BUTEO* SPP., BUTEOS (buzzard hawks):** The broad-winged hawk (*B. platypterus*), red-shouldered hawk (*B. lineatus*), and immature red-tailed hawk (*B. jamaicensis*) all have black bands across tail. They are dark brown above, undersides are whitish or pale red; up to 60 cm (24") long. Refer to a field guide such as R. T. Peterson (1980) to distinguish these species.

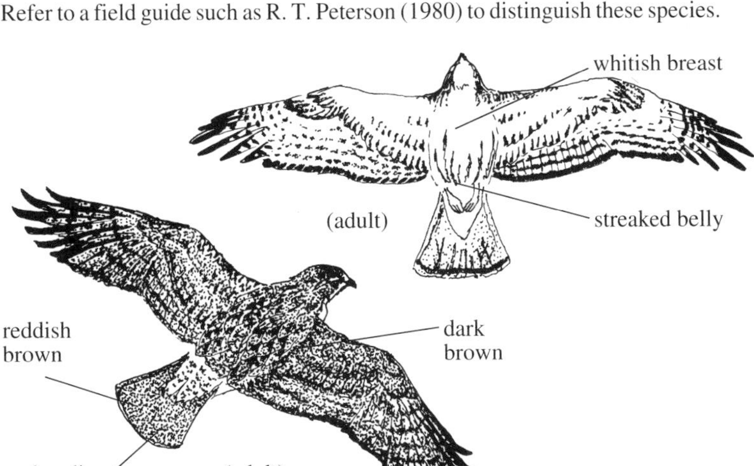

Fig.E. ***BUTEO JAMAICENSIS*, RED-TAILED HAWK:** Adults are dark brown above, with reddish-brown on upperside of tail; underparts are whitish with broad streaks across belly; tail of immature is gray, not red, and may or may not be banded; up to 63 cm (25") long; occurs year-round.

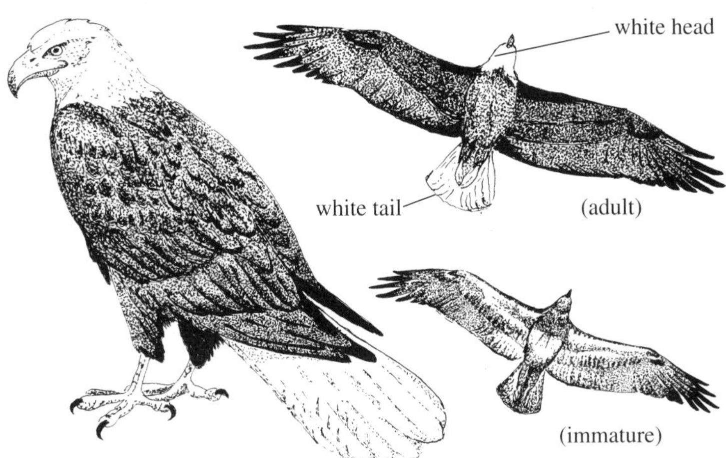

Fig.F. ***HALIAEETUS LEUCOCEPHALUS*, BALD EAGLE:** Adult is black with white head and tail and yellow bill; immature is black with some white in wing linings and breast; up to 108 cm (43") long; occasionally observed in estuaries such as the Connecticut River.

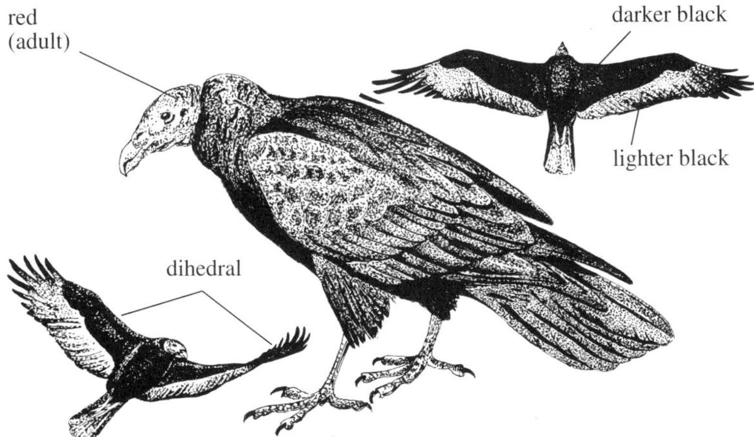

Fig.G. ***CATHARTES AURA*, TURKEY VULTURE:** Black overall with flight feathers somewhat paler than underwing linings, giving wings a two-toned appearance; head is red in adult, dark gray in immature; up to 80 cm (32") long; soars with wings in a dihedral (angled upward).

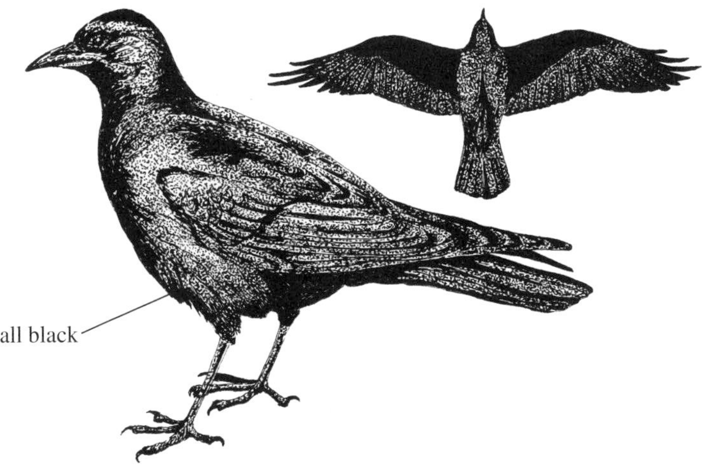

Fig.H. **CROW:** Refer to page 15.36

PERCHING BIRDS[1] (ORDER PASSERIFORMES) AND OTHER LAND BIRDS

(Bird key begins on page 15.00)

#1. All or mostly black, INCLUDING breast and belly (may have an iridescent blue-black sheen, speckles, or a small patch of color on shoulders, but overall appearance is black) .... page 15.36
#1. Not black overall; belly and breast may be lighter than upper sides of body and wings .... #2

#2. Creeps up or down trunks of trees (Figs.E,F); clings to the underside of large branches and hammers or pecks at bark of tree .... #3
#2. Does not creep up or down vertical surfaces of trees (Figs.A-D) .... #4

#3. Creeps UP the tree trunk, tail braced beneath for support .... **family Picidae, woodpeckers** (Fig.E)
#3. Creeps DOWN the tree trunk, head first; with slate-gray back, pale underparts, black or gray cap .... ***Sitta* spp., nuthatches** (Fig.F)

#4. Larger than robin size, longer than 27 cm (11") from tip of bill to end of tail; head is small; body is plump; plumage is tan, blue-gray or mottled; flight is fast, noisy; wing tips are pointed; often seen feeding on the ground in flocks or roosting under bridges, docks, and in abandoned buildings; has low cooing or moaning voice .... **family Columbidae, pigeons and doves** (Fig.A)
#4. Robin size or smaller, less than 27 cm (11") from tip of bill to end of tail; head is not small in proportion to body size (Figs. B-D) .... #5

#5. Head, face and/or breast is entirely black or with distinct black markings such as a black "cap," "mask," "sideburns," stripe across breast, etc .... page 15.34
#5. Without distinct black markings on face or breast .... #6

#6. Tail with one or more distinct white bands, spots, or patches .... page 15.34
#6. Without distinct white markings on tail .... #7

#7. All or part of bird is red, orange, yellow, green, or blue .... page 15.37
#7. Without any red, orange, yellow, green, or blue on body or wings; coloring limited to brown and/or black and/or gray and/or white .... #8

#8. Occurs in large flocks; with many birds flying, landing, perching, and nesting together .... #9
#8. Mostly solitary; usually observed alone or in small numbers .... #11

#9. Underside (breast and belly) is dark brown or black or with numerous gray speckles on dark background .... page 15.36
#9. Underside is light (white, tan) or may have darker spots on lighter background .... #10

#10. Wings are long and pointed; slender with glossy plumage; tiny legs and feet; tiny bills with very wide gaping mouths; flight is fast and erratic, often swooping low to skim just over ground or surface of water; nests in holes in bluffs and banks, under docks and structures built over water; tail is deeply forked or slightly notched in most species .... **family Hirundinidae, swallows** (Fig.B)
#10. Not as described above (Figs. C-D) .... #11

#11. Bill is stout and conical (cone shaped); most species are brownish, streaked, mottled, brown with reddish tinge; round bellied, often feeds on ground .... **family Emberizidae (in part), sparrows and family Fringillidae, finches** (Fig.C)
#11. Bill is not stout and conical .... #12

#12. Bill is slender with slight downward curve; often seen in thickets or marshes clinging to grass and reed stems, with tail cocked high over back; voice may be a scolding buzz or a chanting "tweedle"; brown with white belly, may have white stripes on back or face .... **family Troglodytidae, wrens** (Fig.D)
#12. Not as described above .... refer to a bird identification book[1]

[1]This key includes only the most common species and families of perching birds which are found in coastal habitats. Over 100 species of perching birds occur along the shore. Many of these birds are temporary visitors from upland sites and do not have any special relationship with the marine environment. Furthermore, many are small and difficult to observe closely or to identify. Therefore, a detailed key to species for the perching birds is beyond the scope of this book. Refer to a field guide such as R. T. Peterson (1980), Farrand (1983), or Farrand (1988) if you wish to identify these birds to species.

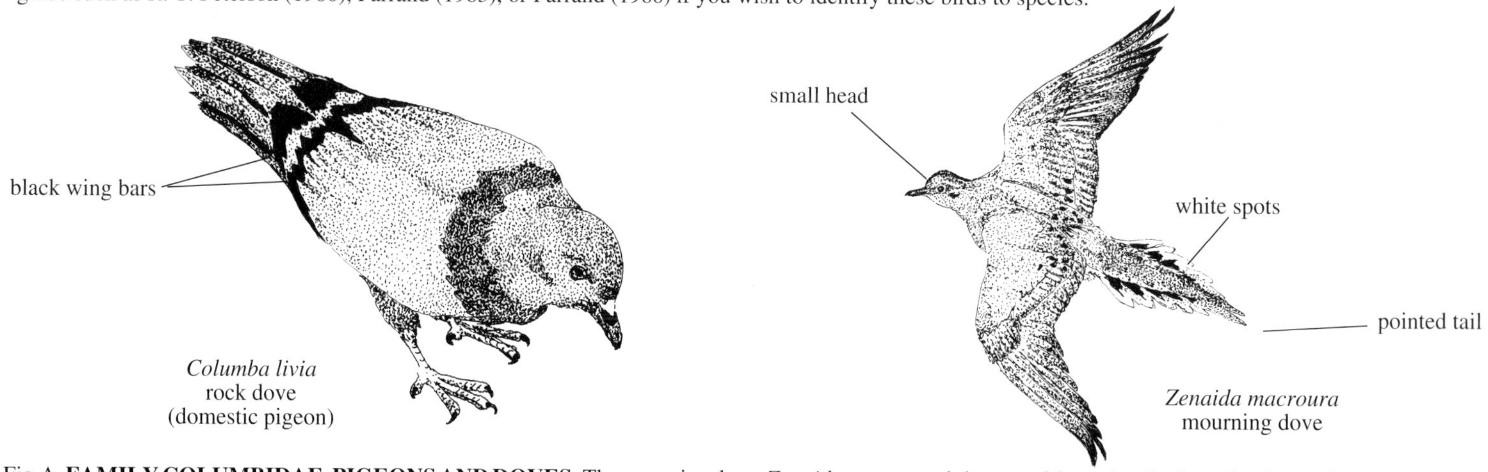

black wing bars

Columba livia
rock dove
(domestic pigeon)

small head

white spots

pointed tail

Zenaida macroura
mourning dove

Fig.A. **FAMILY COLUMBIDAE, PIGEONS AND DOVES:** The mourning dove, *Zenaida macroura*, is brown with a pointed tail that has large white spots. Voice is a mournful "cooo-cooo-cooo" sound. *Columba livia*, the rock dove (common domestic pigeon), has many variations in color, including dark or light gray, white, brown, or blue. Rump is usually white, and wings often have two black bands. Both species reach up to 33 cm (13") in length.

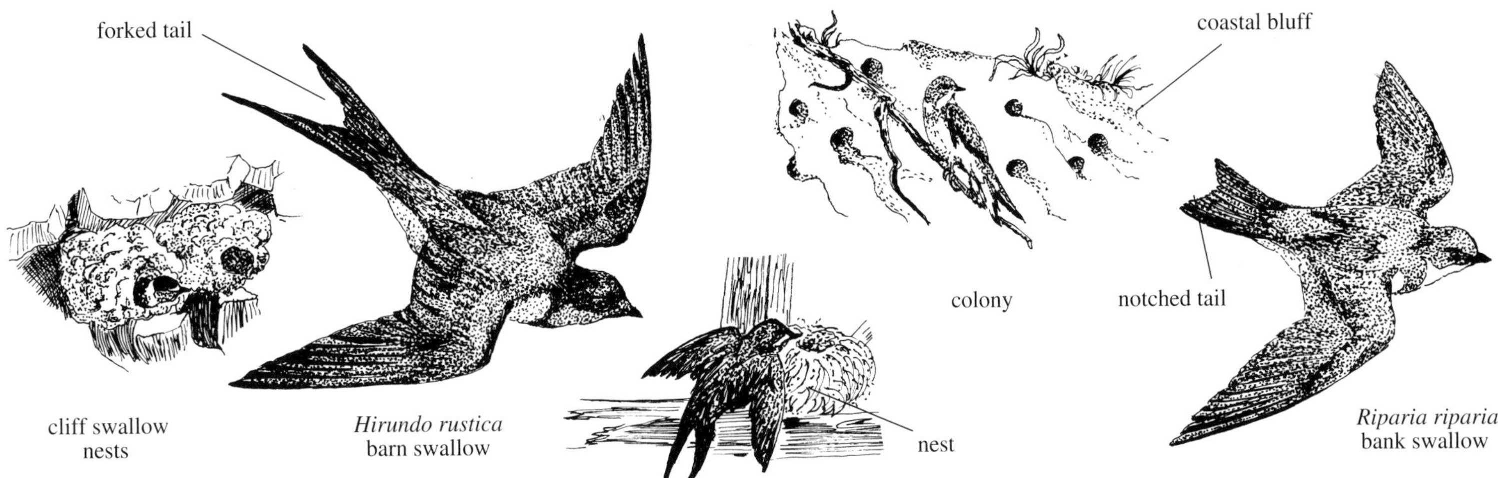

Fig.B. **FAMILY HIRUNDINIDAE, SWALLOWS:** Black, brown, or blue-green above with a white or tan underside; size range is 12-19 cm (5"-7.5"). *Riparia riparia*, the bank swallow, lives in colonies, burrowing numerous holes into the steep sandy sides of many coastal bluffs. The barn swallow, *Hirundo rustica*, has a deeply forked tail, whereas the other swallows have a much smaller notch in their tails. Both the barn swallow and the cliff swallow, *Hirundo pyrrhonota (=Petrochelidon p.)*, build mud nests under waterfront buildings, piers, bridges, cliffs, etc. but the nests of the cliff swallow are juglike or bulb shaped whereas barn swallow nests are more open, bowl shaped. The tree swallow, *Tachycineta bicolor (=Iridoprocne b.)*, has a blue-green back and nests in holes in dead trees or in bird houses placed near the water. Thousands of tree swallows flock along the coast during the fall.

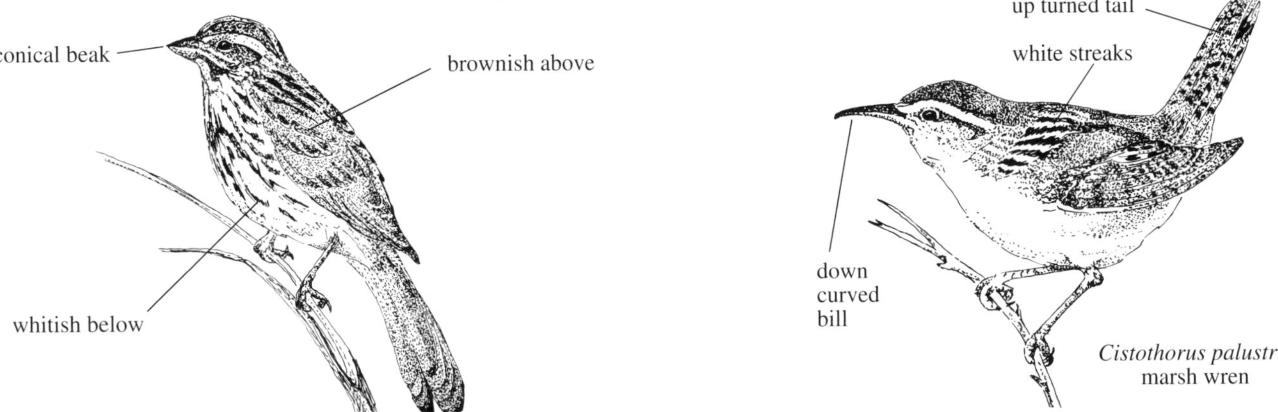

Fig.C. **FAMILY EMBERIZIDAE (in part), SPARROWS AND FAMILY FRINGILLIDAE, FINCHES:** Brownish above, whitish beneath, sometimes with darker streaks, spots, and splotches; 13-18 cm (5"-7") long. Refer to a field guide to distinguish between the numerous species of sparrows and finches that occur in this region. For example, *Melospiza melodia*, the song sparrow, is very common year-round along our coast.

Fig.D. **FAMILY TROGLODYTIDAE, WRENS:** Brown back with white streaks, underside is white or tan; up to 13 cm (5") long; common in saltmarshes and thickets.

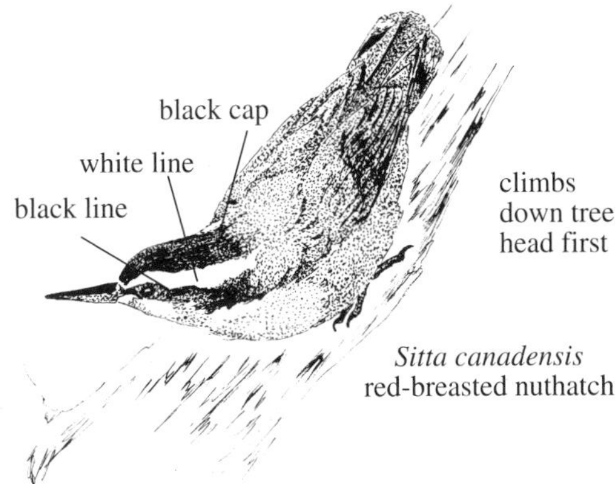

Fig.E. **FAMILY PICIDAE, WOODPECKERS:** The most common woodpecker along the shore, *Colaptes auratus*, the northern flicker, has a dark brown back, white belly and rump, and black speckles on back and belly. Underside of wings and tail is yellow. With a black band across chest and red patch on back of neck. Male has a black "mustache." Up to 35 cm (14") long. Often observed on ground feeding on ants. The downy woodpecker, *Picoides pubescens*, and the hairy woodpecker, *Picoides villosus*, are also found along the shore. They have dark gray wings with white spots. Belly and backs are white. Males have a red spot on back of head. The hairy reaches 24 cm (9.5") in length and the downy 16 cm (6.5").

Fig.F. ***SITTA* SPP., NUTHATCHES:** Gray above, with a black or gray "cap"; small birds, 11-15 cm (4.5"-6") long. *Sitta canadensis*, the red-breasted nuthatch, is reddish on underside, with a black line through eye and a white line above eye. *Sitta carolinensis*, the white-breasted nuthatch, is white on underside with a white face. (family Sittidae)

PERCHING BIRDS WITH BLACK MARKINGS ON HEAD OR WITH WHITE TAIL PATCHES

(Perching bird key begins on page 15.32)

#1.With white band across end of tail (Fig.A); often observed chasing crows and hawks .... ***Tyrannus tyrannus*, eastern kingbird** (Fig.A)
#1.Without a white band across end of tail (Figs. B-K) .... #2

#2.With a bright yellow breast or with bright yellow spots on rump and in front of wings .... #3
#2.Breast or rump is not bright yellow .... #6

#3.With a black V-shaped band across bright yellow breast; with white patches on either side of tail .... ***Sturnella magna*, eastern meadowlark** (Fig.B)
#3.Without a black V on breast .... #4

#4.With a black "mask" or cheek patch covering eyes .... **family Emberizidae, subfamily Parulinae (in part), wood warblers** (Fig.C)
#4.Without a black "mask" or cheek patch .... #5

#5.With a black cap and black wings .... ***Carduelis tristis*, American goldfinch** (Fig.D)
#5.Without a black cap .... #6

#6.Part of head and breast covered with black markings ("cap," "sideburns," "bib," "stripes," etc.) (Figs. E-G); breast is not orange or red; no orange spots on wings and tail .... #7
#6.Top of head with yellow or red spot (spot may or may not be bordered with black) .... ***Regulus* spp., kinglets** (Fig.H)
#6.Entire head and back are dark (black, brown or gray) (Figs. I-K); with orange or red breast or with orange spots on wings and tail .... #8
#6.Not as described above .... page 15.32, couplet #7

#7.With black "sideburns," black breast band, and black "halo"; two small black "horns" sometimes visible .... ***Eremophila alpestris*, horned lark** (Fig.E)
#7.With black cap, black "bib" and white cheeks .... ***Parus atricapillus*, black-capped chickadee** (Fig. F)
#7.With a black face and bib; back of neck is reddish-brown .... ***Calcarius lapponicus*, Lapland longspur** (Fig.G)
#7.None of the above .... page 15.32, couplet #7

#8.Breast is orange; wings with white band .... ***Icterus galbula*, northern oriole** (Fig. I)
#8.Breast is black with white belly; orange patches on wings and tail .... ***Setophaga ruticilla*, American redstart** (Fig. J)
#8.Breast is brick-red; head, wings and tail are black or gray .... ***Turdus migratorius*, American robin** (Fig.K)
#8.None of the above .... page 15.32, couplet #7

kingbird chasing crow

white band at end of tail

Fig.A. ***TYRANNUS TYRANNUS*, EASTERN KINGBIRD:** Black above, white below, with white band across end of tail; up to 20 cm (8") long; sometimes chases crows and hawks. (family Tyrannidae: tyrant flycatchers)

Fig.B. ***STURNELLA MAGNA*, EASTERN MEADOWLARK:** Brown above, breast yellow with black V, white on each side of tail; up to 23 cm (9") long. (family Emberizidae, subfamily Icterinae: blackbirds and allies)

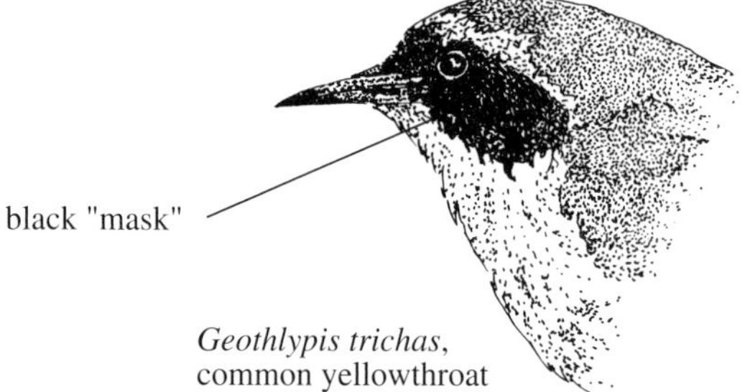

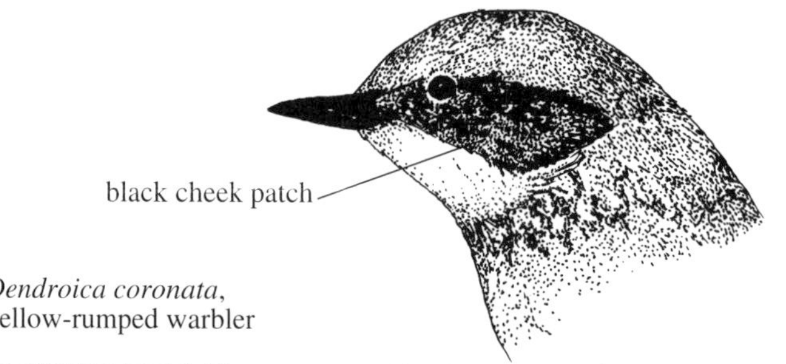

Fig.C. **FAMILY EMBERIZIDAE, SUBFAMILY PARULINAE (in part), WOOD WARBLERS:** The common yellowthroat, *Geothlypis trichas*, has a bright yellow throat and breast, and an olive brown back. The yellow-rumped warbler, *Dendroica coronata*, is mottled with black, gray, and white, with bright yellow patches on rump, in front of each wing, and on top of head. Males of both species have a distinct black cheek patch or a "mask" across face. These warblers reach 15 cm (6") in length. There are many other warbler species without a cheek patch or "mask" that occur along the coast. See footnote on page 15.32.

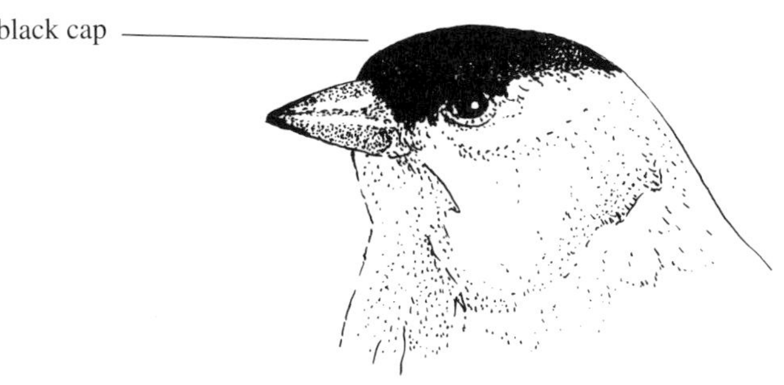

Fig.D. ***CARDUELIS TRISTIS*, AMERICAN GOLDFINCH:** In summer, male is bright yellow with black wings, tail, and "cap" on head; up to 13 cm (5") long. (family Fringillidae: finches)

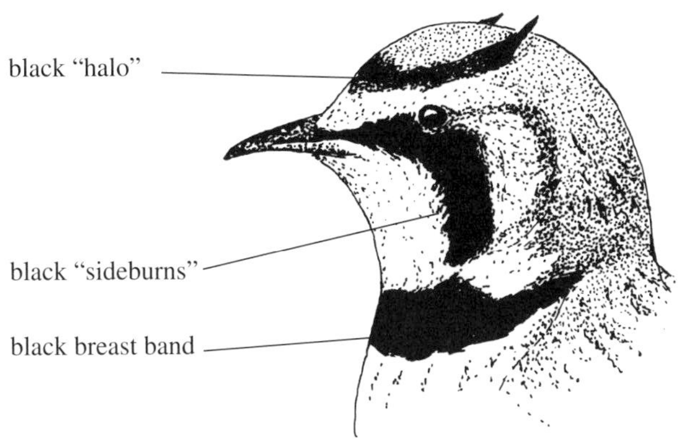

Fig.E. ***EREMOPHILA ALPESTRIS*, HORNED LARK:** Mottled brown overall, with black "sideburns," breast band, and "halo"; up to 20 cm (8") long. (family Alaudidae: larks)

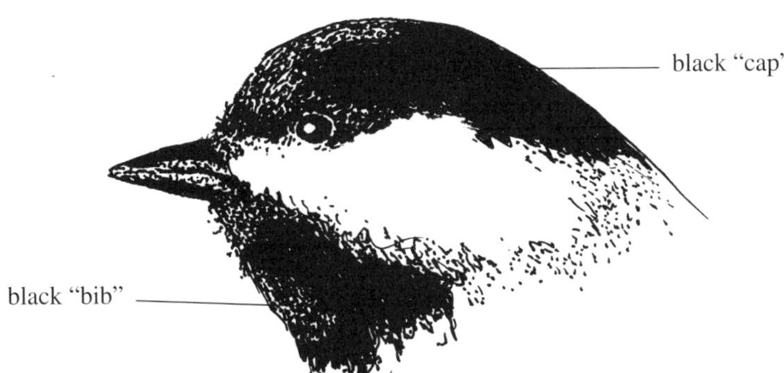

Fig.F. ***PARUS ATRICAPILLUS*, BLACK-CAPPED CHICKADEE:** Gray and tan overall, with black "cap," black "bib," and white cheeks; up to 14 cm (5.5") long. (family Paridae: chickadees and titmice)

Fig.G. ***CALCARIUS LAPPONICUS*, LAPLAND LONGSPUR:** Back and wings are brown, streaked with black and white, belly is white, back of head is brownish, face and throat of male in summer are black outlined with white; up to 16 cm (6.5") long. (family Emberizidae, subfamily Emberizinae: sparrows)

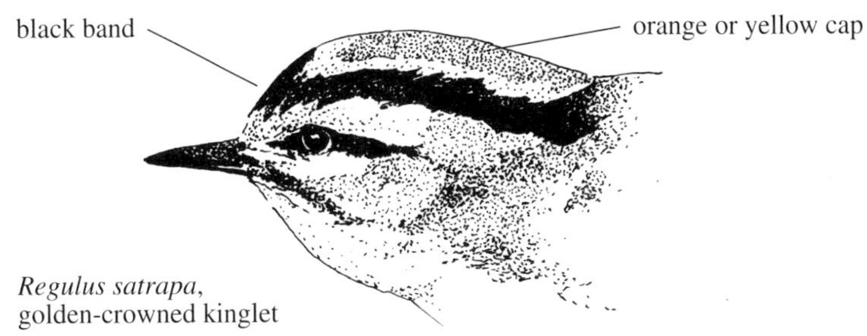

Fig.H. ***REGULUS* SPP., KINGLETS:** Olive gray overall with black and white wing bars; up to 10 cm (4") long. The golden-crowned kinglet, *R. satrapa*, has an orange (male) or yellow (female) cap bordered by a black band. The ruby-crowned kinglet, *R. calendula*, has a red cap (male only) without a black border. (family Muscicapidae: thrushes, kinglets, and allies)

Fig.I. ***ICTERUS GALBULA*, NORTHERN (=Baltimore) ORIOLE:** Male has a bright orange breast and black back, head is solid black; up to 20 cm (8") long. (family Emberizidae, subfamily Icterinae: blackbirds and allies)

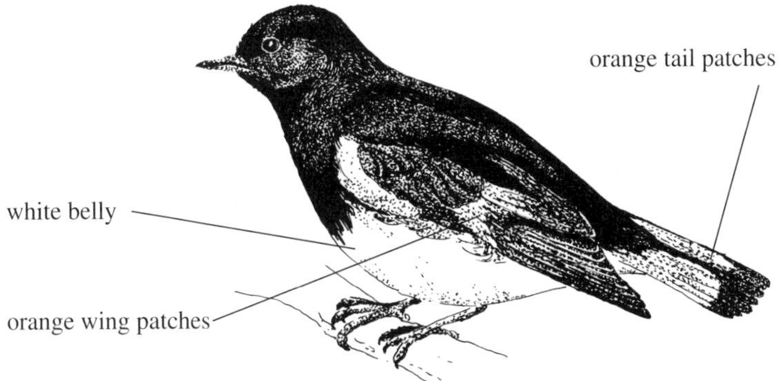

Fig.J. ***SETOPHAGA RUTICILLA*, AMERICAN REDSTART:** Male is black overall with a white belly and with bright orange spots on wings and tail; up to 13 cm (5") long. (family Emberizidae, subfamily Parulinae: wood warblers)

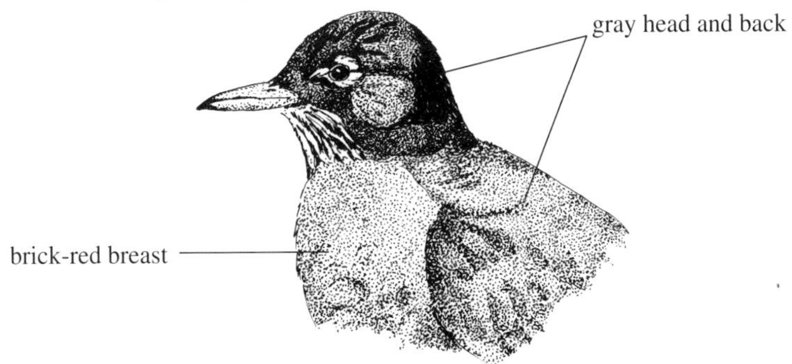

Fig.K. ***TURDUS MIGRATORIUS*, AMERICAN ROBIN:** Dark gray back and head; brick-red breast; up to 28 cm (11") long. (family Muscicapidae: thrushes and allies)

BLACK PERCHING BIRDS

(Perching bird key begins on page 15.32)

#1.Tail is long, extending well beyond the end of the wing tips when the wings are folded back (Figs.A,B) .... **subfamily Icterinae, blackbirds**, #2
#1.Tail is not especially long, most of tail is covered by wings when wings are folded back (Figs. C-F) .... #4

#2.With red and yellow shoulder patches .... ***Agelaius phoeniceus*, red-winged blackbird** (Fig.A)
#2.Shoulders are all black .... #3

#3.Larger than a robin, longer than 28 cm (11"); tail is keel or wedge shaped, broader at the end .... ***Quiscalus quiscula*, common grackle** (Fig.B)
#3.Robin size or smaller, less than 23 cm (9") in length; tail is not wedge shaped (Fig.A) .... **subfamily Icterinae, other blackbirds**[1]

#4.Larger than a robin, more than 28 cm (11") from tip of bill to end of tail; bill is strong and nostrils are covered by forward pointing bristles; voice is a loud and distinctive nasal and rasping "caw" or "car" sound .... ***Corvus* spp., crows** (Fig.C)
#4.Robin size or smaller, less than 28 cm (11") long; bill may be long and sharply pointed or may be very short .... #5

#5.Wings are short and body is plump; looks triangular when flying (Fig.D); bill is black in the winter and yellow in the warmer months; bill, legs, and feet are not especially small; body is heavily speckled in the winter and slightly speckled in the summer .... ***Sturnus vulgaris*, European starling** (Fig. D)
#5.Wings are long, pointed and curved (Figs.E,F); body is slim and streamlined; bill, legs, and feet are tiny; body is solid dark color, not speckled .... #6

#6.Tail is forked and is not especially short; soars in circles and glides between wing flaps .... ***Progne subis*, purple martin** (Fig.E)
#6.Tail is very short and blunt; flight is batlike, twinkling, with short glides between wing flaps .... ***Chaetura pelagica*, chimney swift** (Fig.F)

[1]Several species of smaller blackbirds, less than 23 cm (9") long, are found along the coast, including the rusty blackbird and the brown-headed cowbird. Different species of blackbirds will sometimes flock together. Refer to a bird guide book to identify these species.

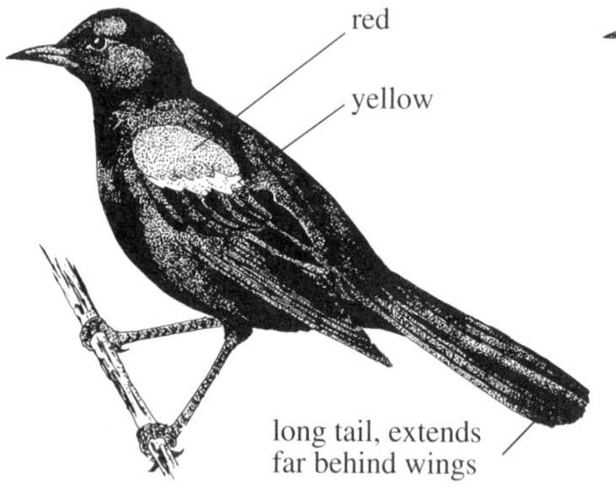

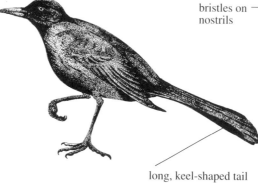

Fig.A. ***AGELAIUS PHOENICEUS*, RED-WINGED BLACKBIRD:** Black, with red shoulder patch ending in yellow margin (if the red is covered only the yellow may be visible); up to 24 cm (9.5") long; often found in large flocks. (family Emberizidae, subfamily Icterinae: blackbirds)

long, keel-shaped tail

Fig.B. ***QUISCALUS QUISCULA*, COMMON GRACKLE:** Iridescent purple-black on head, bronze-black on back; up to 34 cm (13.5") long. (family Emberizidae, subfamily Icterinae: blackbirds)

bristles on
nostrils

tail does not extend
far behind wings

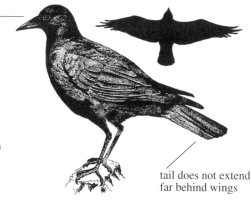

Fig.C. ***CORVUS* SPP., CROWS:** All black, up to 53 cm (21") long. The American crow, *Corvus brachyrhynchos*, makes a distinctive rasping "caw" sound whereas the fish crow, *Corvus ossifragus*, makes a short nasal "car" or "ca" and sometimes a "ca-ha" sound with two syllables. (family Corvidae: crows and jays)

Fig.D. ***STURNUS VULGARIS*, EUROPEAN STARLING:** In colder months, heavily speckled with gray spots on black background, bill dark. In spring and summer, iridescent black with fewer speckles, bill yellow. Up to 21 cm (8.5") long. Often observed in huge, noisy flocks, especially in fall and winter. Starlings were introduced to U.S. in 1890. (family Sturnidae: starlings)

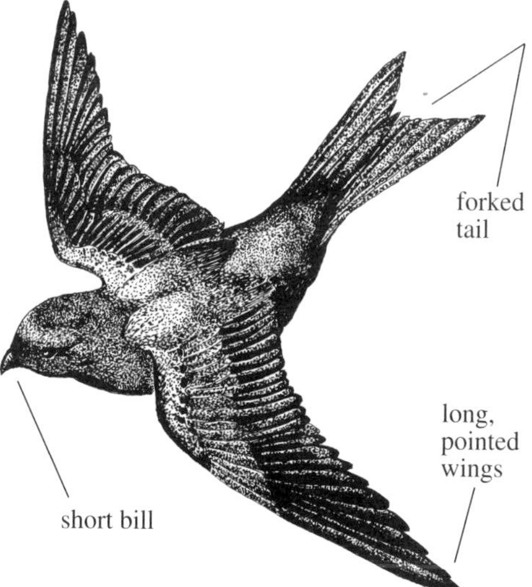

Fig.E. ***PROGNE SUBIS*, PURPLE MARTIN:** Male is blue-black overall; up to 21 cm (8.5") long. (family Hirundinidae: swallows)

Fig.F. ***CHAETURA PELAGICA*, CHIMNEY SWIFT:** Black or dusky overall; up to 14 cm (5.5") long; wings appear to beat alternately rather than together when flying, wings are held stiffly bowed downward when gliding. (family Apodidae: swifts)

HUMMINGBIRDS AND COLORFUL PERCHING BIRDS

(Perching bird key begins on page 15.32)

#1.With a crest on top of the head (Figs. A,B); dominant color is bright red or light blue .... #2
#1.With rounded head, no crest (Figs. C-D); overall color is not bright red or light blue .... #3

#2.Bright red with conical red bill; black facial patches at base of bill .... ***Cardinalis cardinalis*, northern cardinal** (Fig.A)
#2.Blue above and white below, with black "necklace" .... ***Cyanocitta cristata*, blue jay** (Fig.B)

#3.Iridescent green on head, wings and body; wing beat is extremely rapid (blurred) while bird hovers in front of flowers to sip necter using needlelike bill; male has bright red throat; tiny birds, less than 9 cm (3.5") in length .... ***Archilochus colubris*, ruby-throated hummingbird** (Fig. C)
#3.Color is not iridescent green; does not hover in front of flowers .... #4

#4.All or part of bird is yellow or green .... #5
#4.All or part of bird is red or orange .... page 15.34

#5.With black V on breast or with black head or with black face "mask" or with black "cap" .... page 15.34
#5.Without black markings as described above .... #6

#6.With tiny yellow spot on face between eyes or yellow stripes through eyes; overall color of bird is mottled brown with black and white streaks; bill is stout and cone shaped .... **family Emberizidae, subfamily Emberizinae, sparrows** (Fig.D)
#6.Overall color of bird is yellowish or greenish .... **warblers, vireos, flycatchers** (refer to a bird identification book)

crest
black patch

crest
black "necklace"

Fig.A. ***CARDINALIS CARDINALIS*, NORTHERN CARDINAL:** Male is all red, female is brownish with some red on wings and tail, both have black patch at base of bill; up to 23 cm (9") long; not common in coastal habitats. (family Emberizidae, subfamily Cardinalinae: cardinals)

Fig.B. ***CYANOCITTA CRISTATA*, BLUE JAY:** Blue above with white spots on wings and tail, underside is white, with black "necklace"; up to 31 cm (12.5") long; very bold, active, and noisy when disturbed. (family Corvidae: crows and jays)

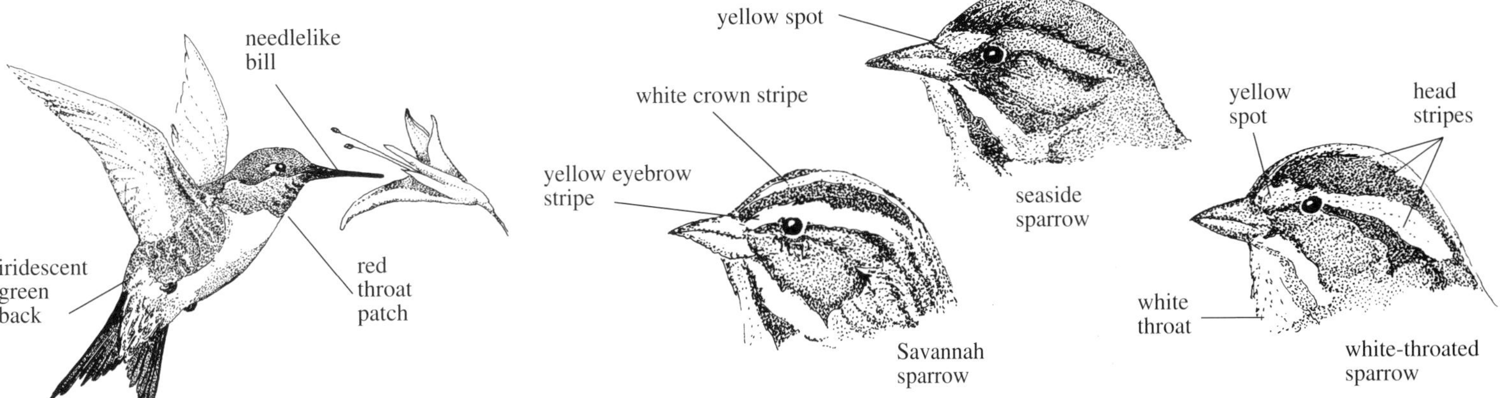

Fig.D. **FAMILY EMBERIZIDAE, SUBFAMILY EMBERIZINAE, SPARROWS:** Several species of sparrows with yellow markings on their face are common in tidal marshes and other coastal habitats. They are all small birds, under 18 cm (7") long and are mottled brown overall with black or white speckles or streaks. The seaside sparrow, *Ammodramus maritimus (=Ammospiza m.)*, has a small bright yellow spot in front of each eye. The white-throated sparrow, *Zonotrichia albicollis*, also has bright yellow spots in front of eyes but has a white throat patch and light and dark stripes over top of head. The Savannah sparrow, *Passerculus sandwichensis*, and the sharp-tailed sparrow, *Ammodramus caudacutus (=Ammospiza c.)*, have yellow "eyebrow" stripes over each eye. Use a bird identification book to distinguish these sparrows.

Fig.C. ***ARCHILOCHUS COLUBRIS*, RUBY-THROATED HUMMINGBIRD:** Iridescent green back, male with red throat; very small, up to 9 cm (3.5") long. (family Trochilidae: hummingbirds)

MARINE MAMMALS: SEALS, PORPOISES, DOLPHINS, AND WHALES PHYLUM CHORDATA, CLASS MAMMALIA, ORDERS CETACEA (WHALES, DOLPHINS, PORPOISES) AND PINNIPEDIA (SEALS)

Mammals with fins or flippers; primarily aquatic, spend all or most of their lives in the water

(Use the key on page 2.12 to determine if you have a marine mammal)

#1. Rear limbs are a pair of flippers, which can be directed backwards and used for swimming or can be positioned under the body and used for walking on the shore; with pair of nostrils at tip of nose, no blowhole on top of head; with whiskers; no dorsal fin (Figs. A-B) .... **seals (order Pinnipedia),** #2

#1. With tail fins or flukes; with 1 or 2 blowholes on top of head; no whiskers; may or may not have a dorsal fin (Figs.C-F) .... **cetaceans (order Cetacea)**, #3

#2. Snout is short, somewhat concave on top, like a cocker spaniel (Fig.A); closed nostril slits form a broad V, almost meeting at the bottom; eyes are about midway between ear holes and tip of nose; color is variable, may be light gray, tan, brown, or black; with irregular small dark spots; maximum length is 170 cm (5.5'); colonies and individuals usually live in coastal waters, such as estuaries, bays, sounds, harbors, and rivers .... ***Phoca vitulina*, harbor seal** (Fig.A)

#2. Not as described above (Fig.B) .... **other seals** (Fig.B)

#3. With dorsal fin (Figs.C-E); tail flukes may or may not rise up out of water when diving .... #4

#3. No dorsal fin (Fig.F) but may have a bumpy ridge along back; tail flukes usually rise up out of water on longer dives .... **some whales** (Fig.F)

#4. Head is rounded with gently sloping forehead; usually less than 3 m (10') long (Figs.C,E); tail flukes may or may not rise up out of water when diving...... #5

#4. Head is flat and V-shaped when viewed from above or is bulbous and squarish; often larger than 3 m (10') long (Figs.D,F); tail flukes usually do not rise up out of water when diving .... #6

#5. Beak is small and indistinct; dorsal fin is short and triangular; usually does not approach moving boats or ride bow waves; the most common cetacean sighted near shore in bays, estuaries, and inlets; maximum length is 1.5 m (5') .... ***Phocoena phocoena*, harbor porpoise** (Fig.C)

#5. Beak is distinct; dorsal fin is tall, pointed, and often curves backwards; may ride boat bow waves; may exceed 1.5 m (5') in length .... **other dolphins** (Fig.E)

#6. Head is bulbous, somewhat squarish when seen from above; with a single blowhole; dorsal fin is broad, located near center of body; no grooves under jaw and belly; no baleen plates; grows up to 6.7 m (22') long; flippers are long and sickle shaped .... ***Globicephala malaena*, pilot whale** (Fig.D)

#6. Head is not bulbous; may have two blowholes; dorsal fin is small, located near rear; may have grooves under lower jaw and belly; mouth may have bony baleen plates, no teeth; grows up to 24 m (78') long; flippers are short .... **other whales** (Fig.F)

[1]Marine mammals are sometimes found stranded, beached, or washed up on shore and may be sick, injured, or dead. Treat them humanely and with care. Immediately contact the Mystic Marinelife Aquarium, the New England Aquarium, or the Okeanos Research Foundation which are members of the Northeast Marine Mammal Stranding Network. They will respond appropriately to the animal's condition and will collect valuable scientific data (Early and McKenzie, 1991).

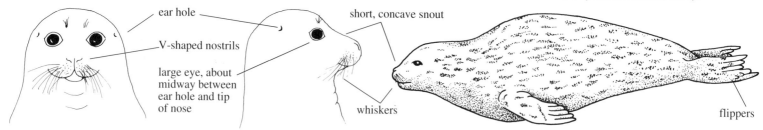

ear hole
short, concave snout
V-shaped nostrils
large eye, about midway between ear hole and tip of nose
whiskers
flippers

Fig.A. ***PHOCA VITULINA*, HARBOR SEAL:** Color is variable, may be light gray, tan, brown, or black; with irregular small dark spots; adults average about 150 cm (5') long with a maximum length of 170 cm (5.5'); lives in coastal waters, such as estuaries, bays, sounds, harbors, and rivers; colonies occur on rocks or ice floes; migrates from the north into southern New England during the winter when it is the most common marine mammal observed near shore.

Halichoerus grypus, gray seal · *Pagophilus groenlandicus*, harp seal · *Cystophora cristata,* hooded seal

Fig.B. **OTHER SEALS** are rarely sighted near the mainland of southern New England, normally living on remote islands and/or in colder waters. Occasionally they wash up on shore, dead or injured (Early and McKenzie, 1991)[1]. Their populations have significantly increased in northern New England and Canada since the passage of marine mammal protection laws. They are likely to become more common winter visitors in southern New England as their populations expand. The gray seal (*Halichoerus grypus*) is large, reaching 2.5 m (8') in length, and has larger spots than the harbor seal. It has a long, straight, donkeylike snout with nostrils that are W-shaped when closed. Its eyes are closer to the ear holes than to the tip of the nose. The hooded seal (*Cystophora cristata*) is also large, reaching 275 cm (9') in length. The male has a distinctive inflatable hoodlike crest overhanging its snout. The harp seal (*Pagophilus groenlandicus*) has a brown saddleshaped marking on its back and sides. It reaches 180 cm (6') in length. Refer to Godin (1977) or Katona et al. (1983) for more information about these seals.

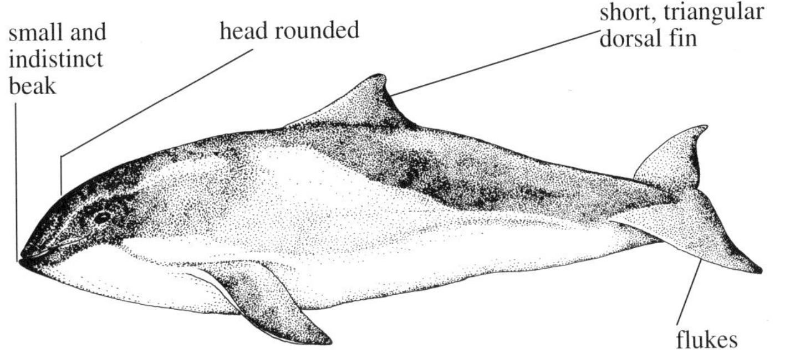

Fig.C. ***PHOCOENA PHOCOENA*, HARBOR PORPOISE:** Dark brown above and white below, sides often speckled or streaked; up to about 1.5 m (5') long; the most common cetacean in the estuaries of southern New England during the warmer months; found near shore in bays, estuaries, and inlets; usually does not approach boats or ride bow waves.

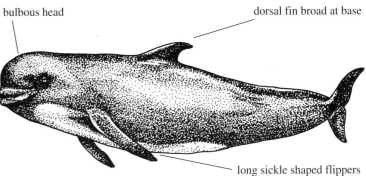

bulbous head
dorsal fin broad at base
long sickle shaped flippers

Fig.D. ***GLOBICEPHALA MALAENA*, PILOT WHALE:** Black with light gray anchor shaped area on chest; up to about 7 m (23') long; occasionally reported in bays and sounds; sometimes an entire school of these whales will become stranded on shore[1].

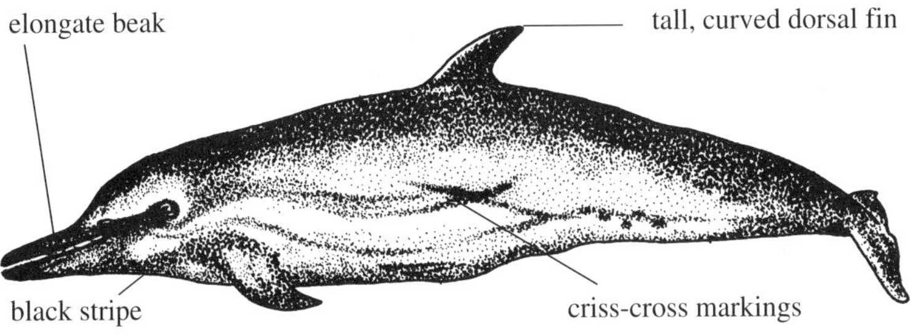

Delphinus delphis, common (=saddleback) dolphin

short beak
tall, curved
dorsal fin
white
patch
yellow-
tan patch

Lagenorhynchus acutus, white-sided dolphin

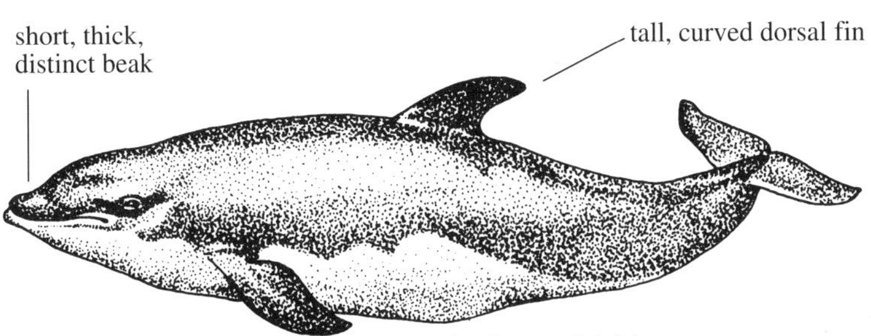

Tursiops truncatus, bottlenose dolphin

Stenella coeruleoalba, striped dolphin

Fig.E. **OTHER DOLPHINS** are infrequent visitors to the estuarine waters of southern New England. They are most often seen offshore or when they become stranded or washed up on shore[1]. Their maximum size is 2-4 m (6-13'). The four species shown above are among the most likely to occur in this region. Several of these species will ride the bow waves of a boat. Refer to Leatherwood et al. (1976), Katona et al. (1983), or Godin (1977) to identify these dolphins.

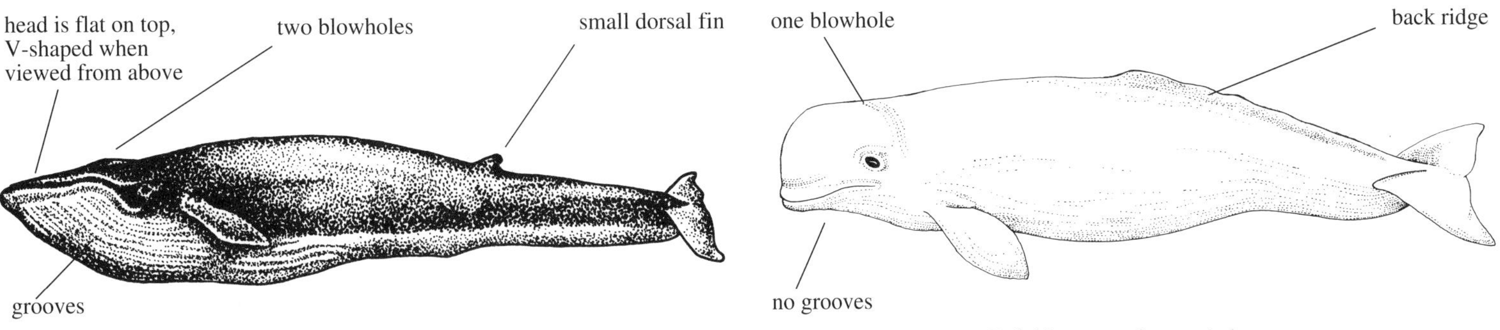

Balaenoptera physalus, finback whale

Delphinapterus leucas, beluga

Fig.F. **OTHER WHALES** rarely stray into shallow estuarine waters in southern New England and when they do, are usually sick, injured, or behaving abnormally. For example, a beluga (*Delphinapterus leucas*), an all white whale that normally resides in Canada, lived for over a year in Long Island Sound during 1985-86 (Overstrom et al., 1991). Whales that are common offshore in this region, such as the minke whale (*Balaenoptera acutorostrata*), the finback whale (*Balaenoptera physalus*), the pygmy sperm whale (*Kogia breviceps*), the humpback whale (*Megaptera novaeangliae*), and other species sometimes become stranded on beaches (Early and McKenzie, 1991)[1]. Refer to Leatherwood et al. (1976), Katona et al. (1983), or Godin (1977) to identify these whales.

TERRESTRIAL MAMMALS: PHYLUM CHORDATA, CLASS MAMMALIA

Mammals with legs, not flippers or fins; primarily land dwelling

(Use the key on page 2.14 to determine if you have a terrestrial mammal)

#1.Mammals larger than mouse size, total length including tail more than 20 cm (8") .... #2
#1.Tiny mammals, mouse size or smaller, total length including tail less than 20 cm (8") .... page 16.04

#2.No tail; usually stands upright on hind legs .... ***Homo sapiens*, human** (Fig.F)
#2.With tail; usually stands on all four legs (Figs.A-E) .... #3

#3.Naked, ratlike tail with no hair (Figs.A,B) .... #4
#3.Tail is hairy, bushy, or cottonlike (Figs.C-E) .... #6

#4.General color of body hair is whitish gray; most of tail is dull pink color .... ***Didelphis virginiana*, opossum** (Fig.A)
#4.Dark brown body and tail .... #5

#5.Tail is flattened from side to side .... ***Ondatra zibethicus*, muskrat** (Fig.B)
#5.Tail is round, not flattened from side to side .... page 16.04

#6.Tail is short, less than 1/3 the length of the head and body (Figs.C-E) .... #7
#6.Tail is long, about 1/2 or more of the length of the head and body .... page 16.06

#7.With hooves; may grow over 1 m (3') tall and 1.8 m (6') long; white underside of tail looks like a flag wagging back and forth as animal darts away .... ***Odocoileus virginianus*, white-tailed deer** (Fig.E)
#7.With padded feet and toes, no hooves; less than 50 cm (20") tall or 1 m (40") long (Figs.C,D) .... #8

#8.Long ears; white and cottony tail; long hind legs .... ***Sylvilagus* spp., cottontail rabbits** (Fig.C)
#8.Short ears; tail is brown or gray; short hind legs .... ***Marmota monax*, woodchuck** (Fig.D)

hairless, pink, round tail

Fig.A. ***DIDELPHIS VIRGINIANA*, OPOSSUM:** General color of hair is whitish gray, tail is dull pinkish and is darker at the base; total length up to about 80 cm (30"), tail up to about 33 cm (13") long; common along shore. (order Marsupialia: pouched mammals)

S. floridanus has a white or brown spot, *S. transitionalis* has a black spot

long ears

tail is short, white, cottonlike

Fig.C. ***SYLVILAGUS* SPP., COTTONTAIL RABBITS:** Body brownish, reddish, or grayish, white cottony tail; average adult length 43 cm (17"). The eastern cottontail (*S. floridanus*) is common on marshes, dunes, and other coastal areas. It has a white or light brown spot on forehead. The New England cottontail (*S. transitionalis*) also occurs on saltmarshes but is much less common. It usually has a black spot on its forehead. (order Lagomorpha: rabbits)

Fig.B. ***ONDATRA ZIBETHICUS*, MUSKRAT:** Brown with black tail; up to about 63 cm (25") total length, tail up to about 27 cm (11") long; not common along seacoast. (order Rodentia: rodents)

Fig.D. ***MARMOTA MONAX*, WOODCHUCK (=groundhog):** Brown with reddish brown undertones, body hairs have somewhat frosted appearance; up to 66 cm (26") total length, tail length up to about 15 cm (6"); common on grassy shorelands. (order Rodentia: rodents)

Fig.E. ***ODOCOILEUS VIRGINIANUS*, WHITE-TAILED DEER:** Reddish brown in summer and grayish or grayish brown in winter; underside of tail is white and is often noticed when deer runs away; up to about 1.8 m (6') long; common on tree covered islands and shoreline areas; often can be seen on tidal wetlands during dusk or dawn; excellent swimmers and have been observed swimming several miles from shore. (order Artiodactyla: hoofed mammals)

Fig.F. ***HOMO SAPIENS*, HUMAN:** Skin color variable, ranging from pink or beige to dark brown; up to about 2.2 m (7') tall; very common along shore, coastal population growing rapidly, displacing many other species of plants and animals; uses marine resources for food, housing, recreation, industry, waste disposal, and many other purposes; impact of humans on marine environment is greater than that of any other species. (order Primates: primates)

BATS: PHYLUM CHORDATA, CLASS MAMMALIA, ORDER CHIROPTERA

Fig.G. **ORDER CHIROPTERA, BATS:** Several species of bats are common along the shores of this region. Refer to Godin (1977) or consult with an expert to identify these species. The two most common brown species are *Myotis lucifugus*, the little brown bat, which reaches a total length of 9 cm (3 1/2") and *Eptesicus fuscus*, the big brown bat, with an average total length of 12 cm (5"). Other species with silver hair and with red hair have also been sighted. A few cases of rabies have been reported in bats and care should be taken in handling living bats.

MICE, VOLES, SHREWS, AND MOLES: PHYLUM CHORDATA, CLASS MAMMALIA

Tiny mammals, mouse size or smaller[1]

(Terrestrial mammal key begins on page 16.02)

#1.With prominent eyes; external ears well developed but may be small and partially hidden by fur; four toes on front feet (Figs.A-F) .... **mice, rats, and voles (order Rodentia: rodents)**, #2

#1.Eyes and ears very tiny and may be hidden by fur (Figs.G-J); five toes on front feet .... **shrews and moles (order Insectivora: insectivores)**, #7

#2.Ears are very small and may be nearly concealed by fur; tail no more than about twice the length of the hind feet (Figs.A,B) .... **voles**, #3

#2.Large, prominent ears; tail more than half the length of the head and body, more than twice the length of the hind feet (Figs.C-F) .... **mice and rats**, #4

#3.Tail about twice as long as hind feet; back is dark brown or gray-black with gray or silver underparts; very common on marshes and beaches .... ***Microtus pennsylvanicus*, meadow vole** (Fig.A)

#3.Tail about same length as hind feet; bright chestnut brown on back and undersides .... ***Microtus pinetorum*, woodland vole** (Fig.B)

#4.Tail hairless, scaly (Figs.C,D); tail same length as or shorter than head and body .... #5

#4.Tail with hair, hair may be thick or sparse (Figs. E,F); tail same length as or longer than head and body .... #6

#5.Tail about same length as head and body; total length, including tail, no more than 19 cm (7 1/2") .... ***Mus musculus*, house mouse** (Fig.C)

#5.Tail shorter than head and body; total length, including tail, may reach up to 39 cm (15") .... ***Rattus norvegicus*, Norway rat** (Fig.D)

#6.Tail about same length as head and body; tail well covered with hair; rear legs and feet somewhat larger than forelegs; white underside; common on dunes and beaches .... ***Peromyscus leucopus*, white-footed mouse** (Fig.E)

#6.Tail longer than head and body; tail sparsely covered with hair; hind feet and legs much larger than forelegs .... ***Zapus hudsonius*, meadow jumping mouse** (Fig.F)

#7.Front feet much broader than hind feet (Figs.G,H); no external ears; hairless nose .... **family Talpidae, moles**, #8

#7.Front feet no broader than hind feet (Figs.I,J); with tiny ears usually concealed by fur; with hair ("whiskers") on nose .... **family Soricidae, shrews**, #9

#8.Nose flattened in front and ringed with fleshy projections; tail covered with short black hair .... ***Condylura cristata*, star-nosed mole** (Fig.G)

#8.Nose pointed; hairless tail .... ***Scalopus aquaticus*, eastern mole** (Fig.H)

#9.Tail nearly as long as body .... ***Sorex cinereus*, masked shrew** (Fig.I)

#9.Tail much less than body length (Fig.J) .... #10

#10.Black to gray black; may be longer than 8.5 cm (3 1/2") total length .... ***Blarina brevicauda*, short-tailed shrew** (Fig.J)

#10.Brownish; up to about 8.5 cm (3 1/2") total length .... ***Cryptotis parva*, least shrew** (Fig.J)

[1]Tiny mammals that do not key out on this page may be juveniles of larger mammals. Go to couplet #2 on page 16.02.

Fig.A. ***MICROTUS PENNSYLVANICUS*, MEADOW VOLE:** Dark brown or gray-black with gray or silvery underparts; total length up to about 18 cm (7") including tail, which is about 4.3 cm (1 3/4") long; one of the most common mammals on marshes and beaches; constructs runway tunnels beneath grass and other ground cover. (order Rodentia: rodents)

Fig.B. ***MICROTUS PINETORUM*, WOODLAND (=pine) VOLE:** Bright brown; up to 13 cm (5") total length including 2 cm (3/4") tail. (order Rodentia: rodents)

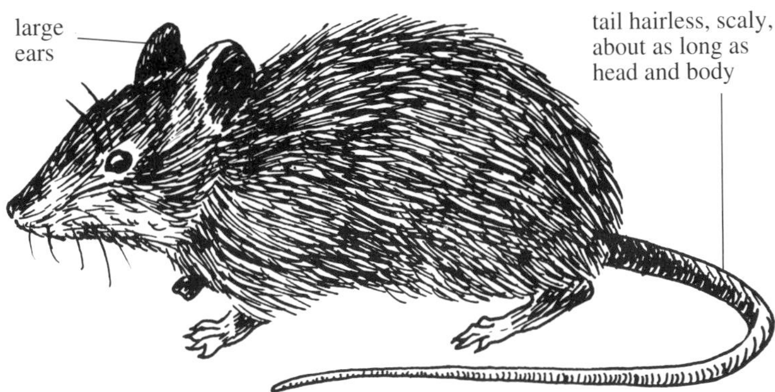

Fig.C. ***MUS MUSCULUS*, HOUSE MOUSE:** Brown or grayish brown on top, gray or light brown underneath; up to 19 cm (7 1/2") total length, tail length up to about 9 cm (3 1/2"). (order Rodentia: rodents)

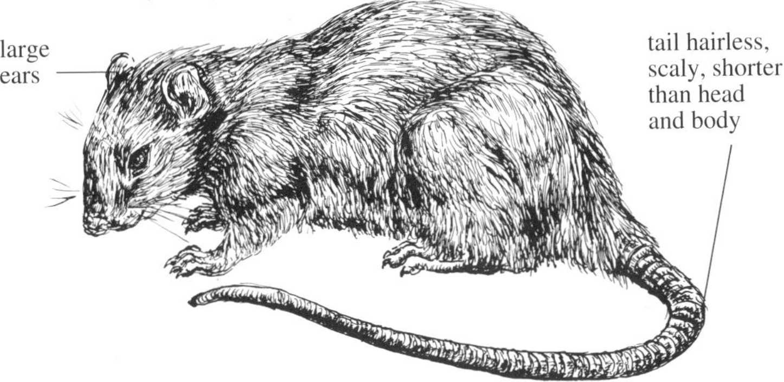

Fig.D. ***RATTUS NORVEGICUS*, NORWAY RAT:** Brown above, yellowish silver below; total length up to about 39 cm (15"), tail length up to about 18 cm (7"); very common in most coastal environments. (order Rodentia: rodents)

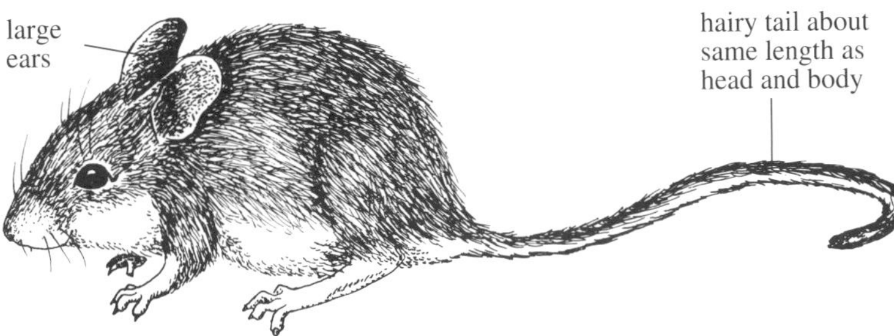

Fig.E. ***PEROMYSCUS LEUCOPUS*, WHITE-FOOTED MOUSE**: Adults are reddish brown on top with white undersides, juveniles are gray; total length up to about 18 cm (7"), tail length up to about 9 cm (3 1/2"); common on dunes and beaches. (order Rodentia: rodents)

Fig.F. ***ZAPUS HUDSONIUS*, MEADOW JUMPING MOUSE:** Back is dark yellow brown, sides are paler, tail gray; up to about 23 cm (9") total length including 14 cm (5 1/2") tail; lives in marshes, dunes and other grassy areas. (order Rodentia: rodents)

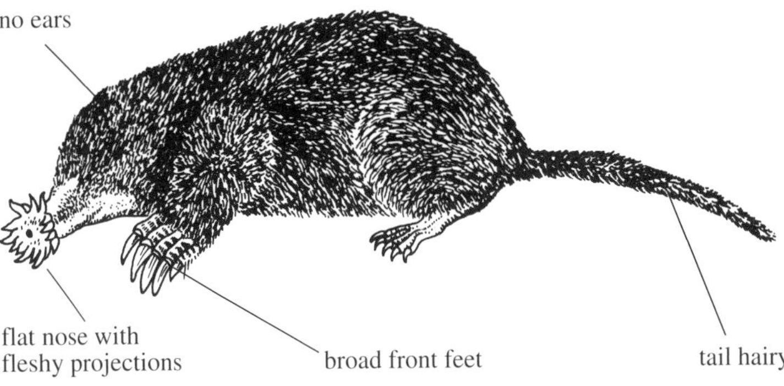

Fig.G. ***CONDYLURA CRISTATA*, STAR-NOSED MOLE:** Glossy black or dark brown; up to about 20 cm (8") total length, tail up to about 9 cm (3 1/2"); found in marshes. (order Insectivora: insectivores)

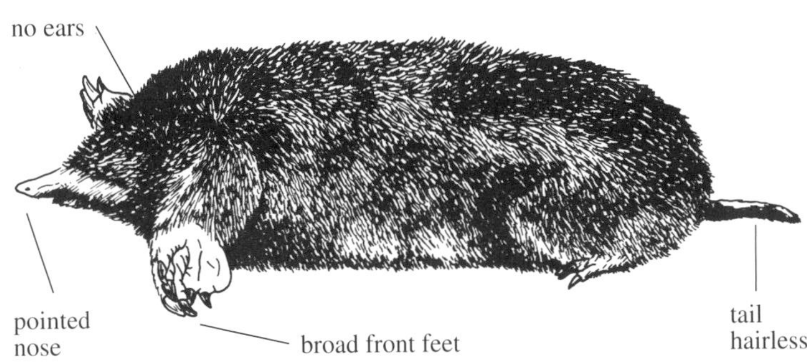

Fig.H. ***SCALOPUS AQUATICUS*, EASTERN MOLE:** Silvery or dark gray, tail and nose are pinkish; up to about 17 cm (6 1/2") total length, tail about 2.9 cm (1 1/8") long; found in marshes and dunes. (order Insectivora: insectivores)

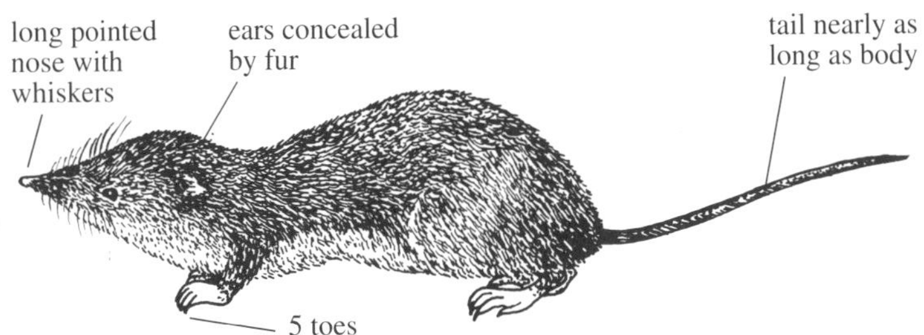

Fig.I. ***SOREX CINEREUS*, MASKED SHREW:** Overall color brownish; up to about 9 cm (3 1/2") total length, tail length up to about 4 cm (1 1/2"); one of the most common mammals on dunes, beaches and marshes. (order Insectivora: insectivores)

Fig.J. ***BLARINA BREVICAUDA*, SHORT-TAILED SHREW:** Black to gray-black; up to about 14 cm (5 1/4") total length, tail length up to about 2.5 cm (1"); common in wooded areas near shore, occasionally found in marshes, beaches or other open shoreline habitats. A similar species, *Cryptotis parva*, the least shrew, is brown; up to about 8.5 cm (3 1/4") total length; not common. (order Insectivora: insectivores)

LARGER MAMMALS WITH LONG, HAIRY TAILS
PHYLUM CHORDATA, CLASS MAMMALIA

(Terrestrial mammal key begins on page 16.02)

#1.Black body with white Y-shaped stripe on back .... ***Mephitis mephitis*, striped skunk** (Fig.A)
#1.No white Y-shaped stripe on back (Figs.B-G) .... #2

#2.Dark brown or black "mask" on face and rings on tail .... ***Procyon lotor,* raccoon** (Fig.B)
#2.No mask on face or rings on tail (Figs.C-G) .... #3

#3.Doglike in appearance; usually greater than 50 cm (20") total length .... **family Canidae, foxes, dogs, and allies** (Fig.C.)
#3.Not doglike; usually less than 50 cm (20") total length (Figs.D-G) .... #4

#4.With long neck; body is very long and slender; tail is long, not especially bushy .... **family Mustelidae, weasels, otters, and allies** (Fig.D)
#4.With short neck; body is not especially long and slender; tail is bushy (Figs.E-G) .... **family Sciuridae, squirrels**, #5

#5.Layer of body skin extends from wrists on forelegs to rear legs and is used as a "sail" to glide from tree to tree .... ***Glaucomys volans*, southern flying squirrel** (Fig.G)
#5.Without a sail-like membrane between fore and hind legs (Figs.E,F) .... #6

#6.Gray to silver gray above with whitish underbody .... ***Sciurus carolinensis*, gray squirrel** (Fig.E)
#6.Reddish with a black line along sides .... ***Tamiasciurus hudsonicus*, red squirrel** (Fig.F)

Fig.A. ***MEPHITIS MEPHITIS*, STRIPED SKUNK:** Black with Y-shaped white stripe on back; up to 70 cm (28") total length, tail length up to 25 cm (10"); common along the shore, especially near human habitation where garbage is available. (order Carnivora: carnivores, family Mustelidae: weasels)

Fig.B. ***PROCYON LOTOR*, RACCOON:** Brownish gray with dark brown or black rings on tail and mask on face; up to 95 cm (37") total length, tail length up to 25 cm (10"); common all along the coast, particularly near shoreline homes where garbage pails provide food; often observed on marshes and beaches. (order Carnivora: carnivores, family Procyonidae: raccoons)

Fig.C. **FAMILY CANIDAE, FOXES, DOGS, AND ALLIES:** The domestic dog (*Canis familiaris*) is the most common member of this family found along the shore. The red fox (*Vulpes vulpes*), shown above, can be sighted on saltmarshes. It is yellowish red overall, tip of tail and underparts are white, feet and back of ears are black; up to about 1 m (39") long. The gray fox (*Urocyon cinereoargenteus*) and even the coyote (*Canis latrans*) may stray onto the coast on rare occasions. Refer to Godin (1977) to identify these animals. (order Carnivora: carnivores)

Fig.D. **FAMILY MUSTELIDAE, WEASELS, OTTERS, MINK, AND ALLIES:** A number of species in this family, including the two shown above, may be seen on rare occasions along the banks of tidal creeks, saltmarshes, and other coastal environments of southern New England. They usually live in freshwater habitats and are exellent swimmers. Most species are mainly nocturnal. Refer to Godin (1977) to identify these animals. (order Carnivora: carnivores)

Fig.E. ***SCIURUS CAROLINENSIS*, GRAY SQUIRREL:** Gray to silver gray above with whitish underbody; up to about 50 cm (20") total length; most common squirrel observed along the coast, particularly near wooded areas. (order Rodentia: rodents, family Sciuridae: squirrels)

Fig.F. ***TAMIASCIURUS HUDSONICUS*, RED SQUIRREL:** Back and tail bright to dull red, underparts are white, with a black line along the sides which is distinct in the summer and may be faint or absent in the winter; smaller and less common than gray squirrel, up to about 38 cm (15") total length. (order Rodentia: rodents, family Sciuridae: squirrels)

Fig.G. ***GLAUCOMYS VOLANS*, SOUTHERN FLYING SQUIRREL:** Grayish brown above, white below; up to 25 cm (10") long; common in maritime forests; active at night, inactive and not usually seen during day. (order Rodentia: rodents, family Sciuridae: squirrels)

COLOR PLATES

Fig. A. ***HALICLONA LOOSANOFFI,* SPONGE**: 5 cm (2") wide. p. 3.04.

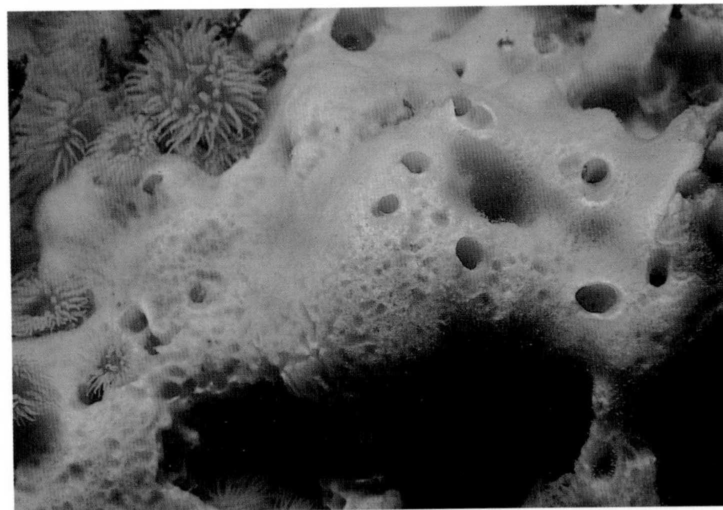

Fig. B. ***HALICHONDRIA BOWERBANKI,* BREAD-CRUMB SPONGE:** 13 cm (5") wide; encrusting form. p. 3.04.

Fig. C. ***MICROCIONA PROLIFERA,* RED BEARD SPONGE**: 7 cm (3") tall; encrusting and erect forms. p. 3.05.

Fig. D. ***CLIONA CELATA,* BORING SPONGE:** 13 cm (5") wide; shown underwater, pores open. p. 3.02.

Fig. E. ***MICROCIONA PROLIFERA,* RED BEARD SPONGE:** 10 cm (4") tall; branching form. p. 3.05.

Fig. F. ***HALICHONDRIA BOWERBANKI,* BREAD-CRUMB SPONGE:** 13 cm (5") wide; erect form. p. 3.04.

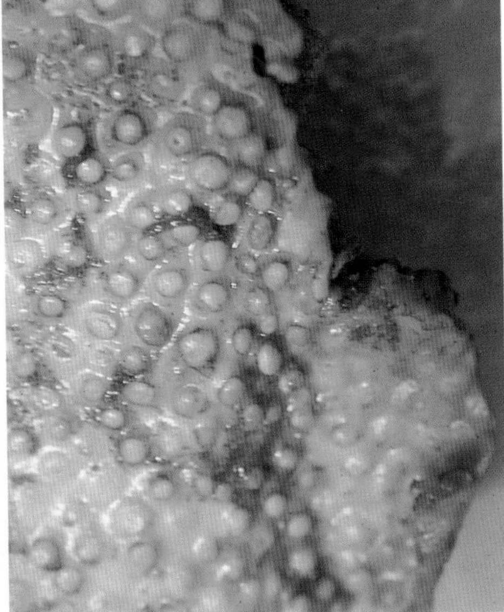

Fig. G. ***CLIONA CELATA,* BORING SPONGE:** 10 cm (4") wide; shown out of water, pores closed. p. 3.02.

Fig. A. ***CHRYSAORA QUINQUECIRRHA*, SEA NETTLE:** 7.5 cm (3") in diameter; umbrella and tentacles contracted. p. 4.01.

Fig. B. ***AURELIA AURITA*, MOON JELLY:** 10 cm (4") in diameter; top view. p. 4.01.

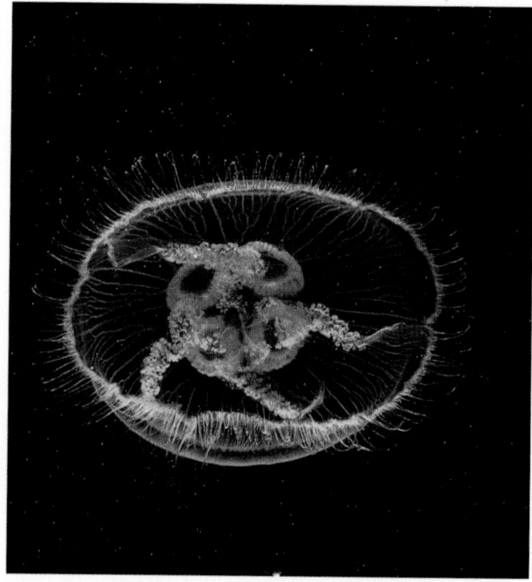

Fig. C. ***AURELIA AURITA*, MOON JELLY:** 10 cm (4") in diameter; underside view. p. 4.01.

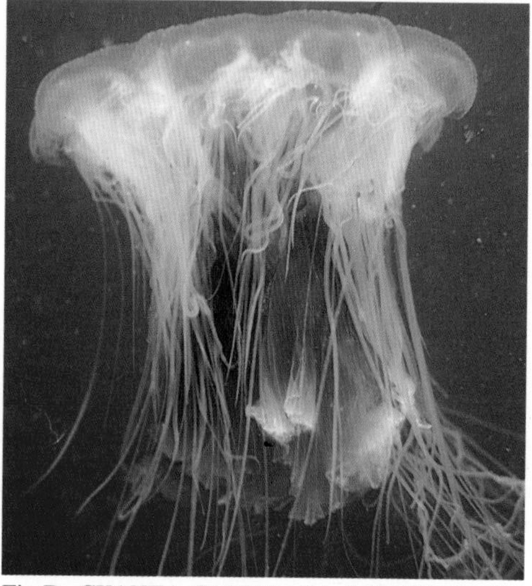

Fig.D. ***CYANEA CAPILLATA*, LION'S MANE JELLYFISH:** 16 cm (6") in diameter; side view. p. 4.01.

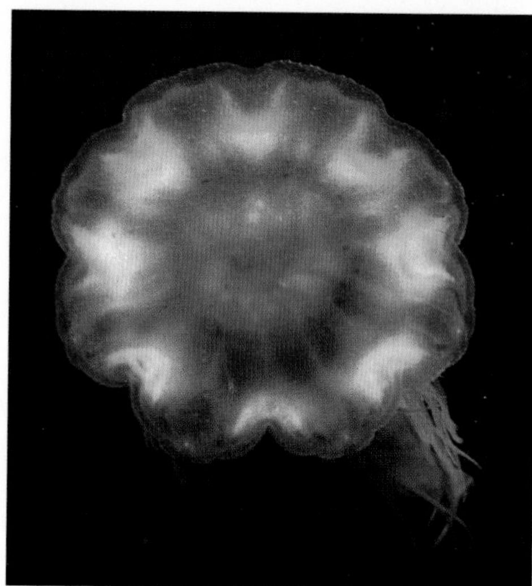

Fig.E. ***CYANEA CAPILLATA*, LION'S MANE JELLYFISH:** 16 cm (6") in diameter; top view. p. 4.01.

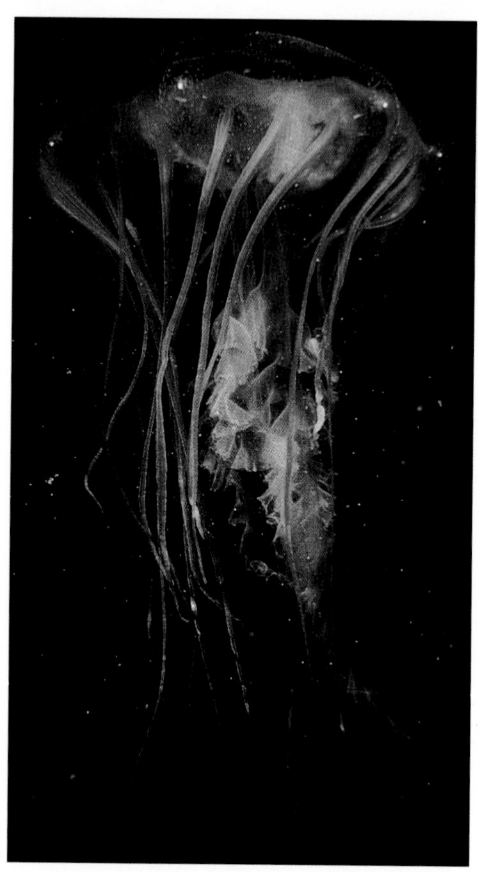

Fig. F. ***CHRYSAORA QUINQUECIRRHA*, SEA NETTLE:** 7.5 cm (3") in diameter; umbrella and tentacles extended. p. 4.01.

Fig. G. ***ASTRANGIA POCULATA*, NORTHERN STAR CORAL**: polyps 12 mm (1/2") tall. p. 4.16.

Fig. H. ***PODOCORYNA CARNEA*, SMOOTH-SPINED SNAILFUR:** growing on longwrist hermit crab; crab shell 2 cm (3/4") long. p. 4.06.

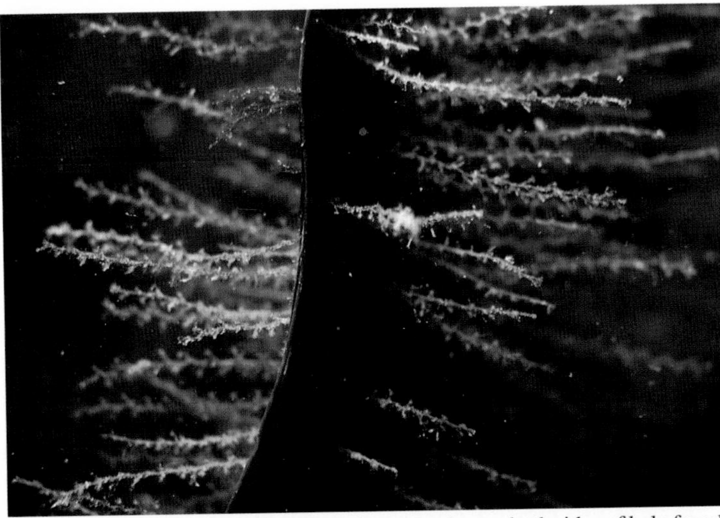

Fig. A. ***OBELIA* SP., HYDROID:** colony growing on both sides of kelp frond; each strand 2.5 cm (1") long. p. 4.09.

Fig. B. ***CAMPANULARIA* SP., HYDROID:** colony growing on blade of eelgrass; colony 2.5 cm (1") long. p. 4.09.

Fig. C. ***DIADUMENE LINEATA,* ORANGESTRIPED GREEN ANEMONE:** 6 mm (1/4") in diameter. p. 4.13.

Fig. D. ***FAGESIA LINEATA,* LINED ANEMONE:** 12 mm (1/2") tall. p. 4.13.

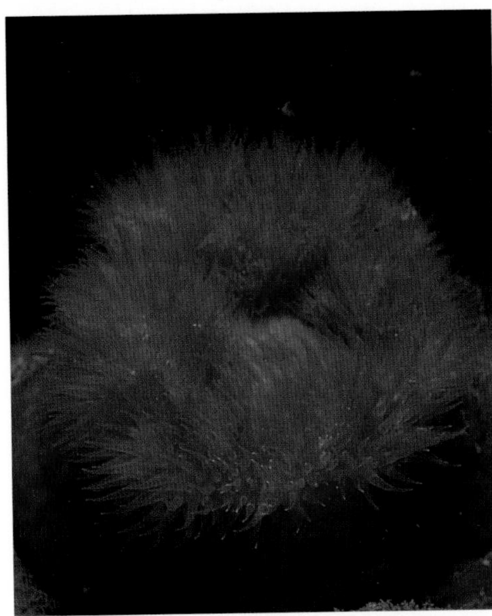

Fig. E. ***METRIDIUM SENILE,* CLONAL PLUMOSE ANEMONE:** 5 cm (2") in diameter; extended form. p. 4.12.

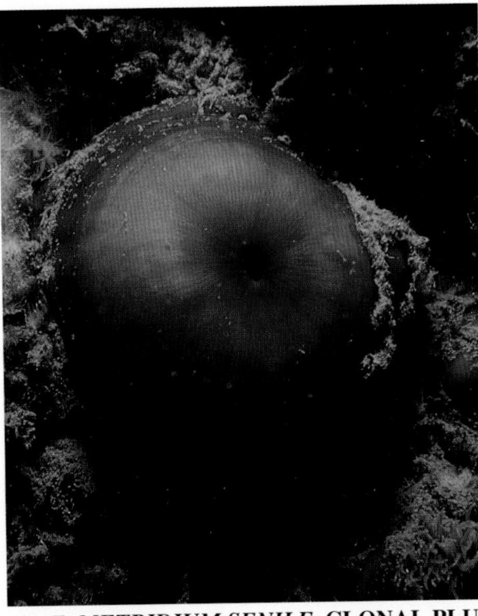

Fig. F. ***METRIDIUM SENILE,* CLONAL PLUMOSE ANEMONE:** 5 cm (2") in diameter; closed form. p. 4.12.

Fig. G. ***DIADUMENE LEUCOLENA,* WHITE ANEMONE:** 2.5 cm (1") long. p. 4.13.

Fig.A. ***CEREBRATULUS LACTEUS,* RIBBON WORM:** 45 cm (18") long. p. 5.07.

Fig.B. ***CEREBRATULUS LACTEUS,* RIBBON WORM:** 12 mm (1/2") wide. p. 5.07.

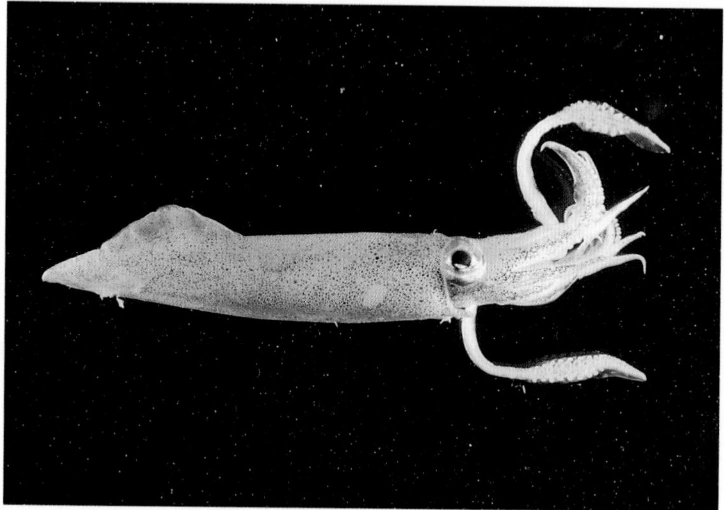

Fig.C. ***LOLIGO PEALEII,* LONGFIN SQUID:** 15 cm (6") long. p. 7.00.

Fig.D. ***TONICELLA MARMOREA,* MOTTLED RED CHITON:** 15 mm (5/8") long. p. 7.00.

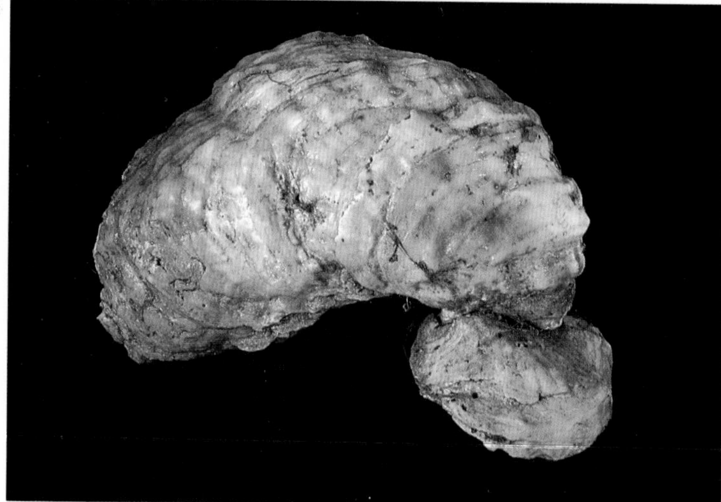

Fig.E. ***CRASSOSTREA VIRGINICA,* EASTERN OYSTER:** 13 cm (5") long. p. 7.15.

Fig.F. ***ENSIS DIRECTUS,* ATLANTIC JACKKNIFE:** 15 cm (6") long; foot extended. p. 7.23.

Fig.A. ***MERCENARIA MERCENARIA,*** **NORTHERN QUAHOG:** 7.5 cm (3") wide. p. 7.18.

Fig.B. ***NUCULA PROXIMA,*** **ATLANTIC NUTCLAM:** 6 mm (1/4") long; inside (left) and outside (right) of shell. p. 7.20.

Fig.C. ***YOLDIA LIMATULA,*** **FILE YOLDIA:** 2.5 cm (1") long; foot extended. p. 7.23.

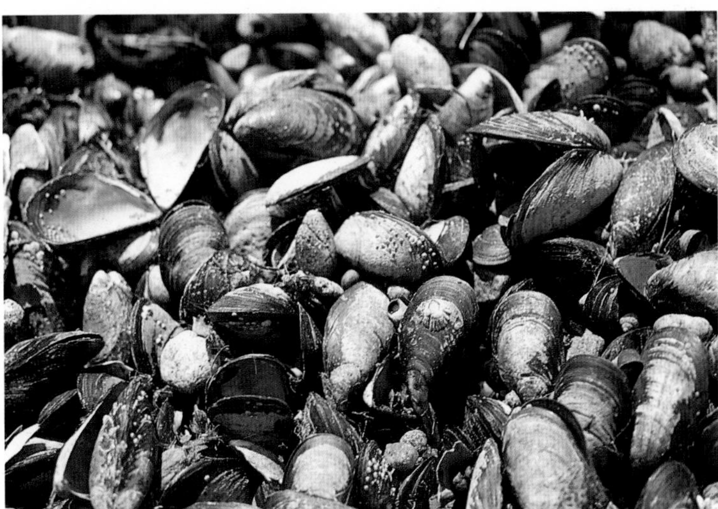

Fig.D. ***MYTILUS EDULIS,*** **BLUE MUSSEL:** 40 cm (16") across field of view. p. 7.19.

Fig.E. ***ASTARTE UNDATA,*** **WAVY ASTARTE:** 2.5 cm (1") wide. p. 7.19.

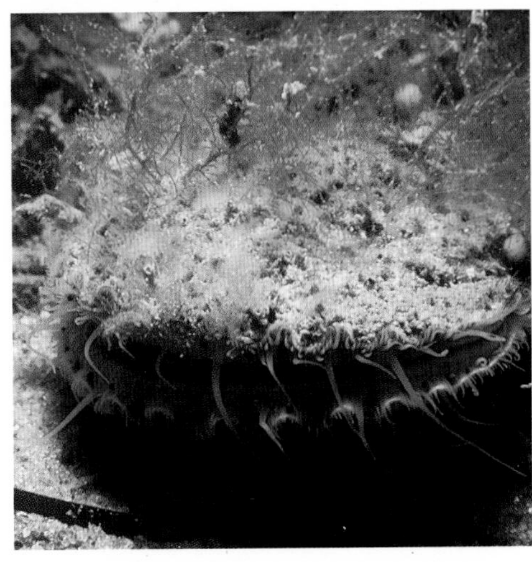

Fig.F. ***ARGOPECTEN IRRADIANS,*** **BAY SCALLOP:** 7.5 cm (3") wide. p. 7.17.

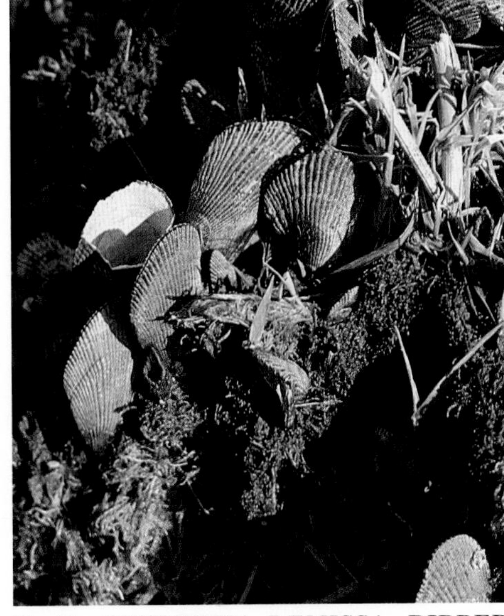

Fig.G. ***GEUKENSIA DEMISSA,*** **RIBBED MUSSEL:** mussels are 7.5 cm (3") long; embedded in saltmarsh peat. p. 7.19.

Fig. A. ***CORYPHELLA VERRUCOSA RUFIBRANCHIALIS,* RED-FINGER AEOLIS:** 2.5 cm (1") long. p. 7.13.

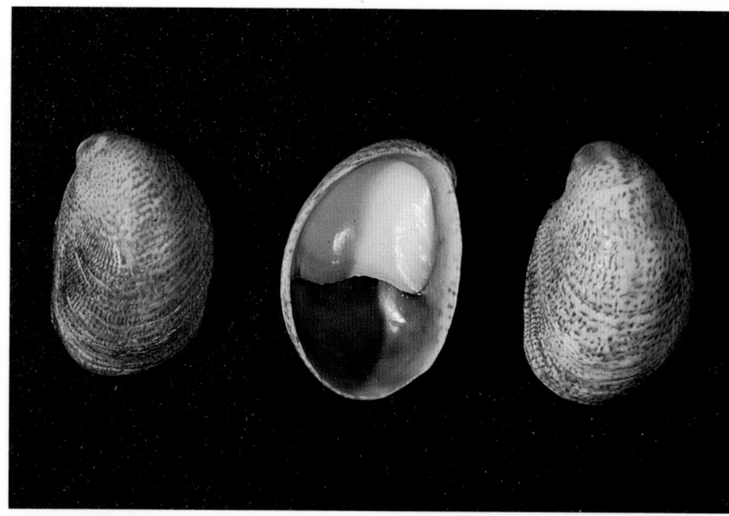

Fig.B. ***CREPIDULA FORNICATA,* COMMON ATLANTIC SLIPPERSNAIL:** 4 cm (1.5") long. p. 7.01.

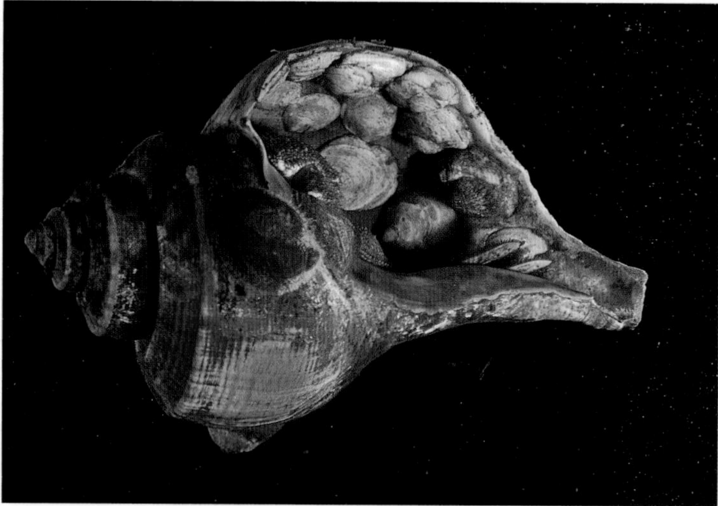

Fig.C. ***BUSYCOTYPUS CANALICULATUS,* CHANNELED WHELK** shell with a number of ***CREPIDULA PLANA,* EASTERN WHITE SLIPPERSNAILS** attached to inside of whelk opening: whelk is 13 cm (5") long. p. 7.10 (whelk) and p. 7.01 (slippersnail).

Fig.D. ***BUSYCOTYPUS CANALICULATUS,* CHANNELED WHELK** producing egg case: egg case is 20 cm (8") long. p. 7.10 (whelk) and p. 2.23 (egg case).

Fig.E. ***UROSALPINX CINEREA,* ATLANTIC OYSTER DRILL:** 2.5 cm (1") long; rock covered with drill egg cases. p. 7.08 (snail) and p. 2.24 (egg case).

Fig.F. ***ANACHIS AVARA,* GREEDY DOVESNAIL:** 15 mm (5/8") long. p. 7.09.

Fig.A. ***LITTORINA OBTUSATA*, YELLOW PERIWINKLE:** 1 cm (3/8") wide; on seaweed. p. 7.05.

Fig.B. ***LITTORINA LITTOREA*, COMMON PERIWINKLE:** 2.5 cm (1") wide; older snail on rock. p. 7.05.

Fig.C. ***LITTORINA LITTOREA*, COMMON PERIWINKLE:** 2 cm (3/4") wide; younger snails on saltmarsh. p. 7.05.

Fig.D. ***LITTORINA SAXATILIS*, ROUGH PERIWINKLE:** 13 mm (1/2") wide. p. 7.05.

Fig.E. ***LACUNA VINCTA*, NORTHERN LACUNA:** 3 mm (1/8") wide; on eelgrass. p. 7.05.

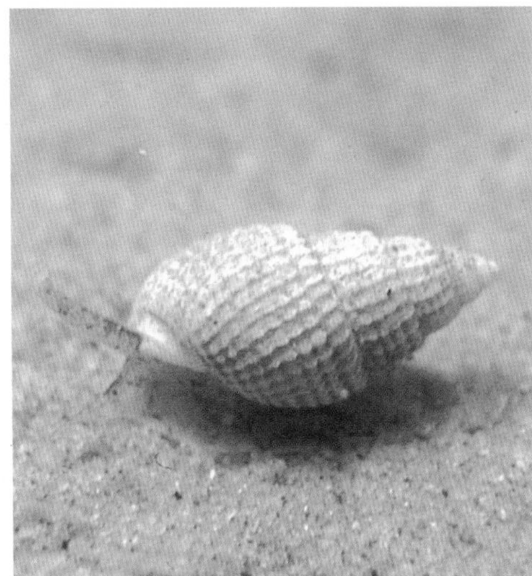

Fig.F. ***ILYANASSA TRIVITTATA*, THREELINE MUDSNAIL:** 15 mm (5/8") long. p. 7.08.

Fig.G. ***ILYANASSA OBSOLETA*, EASTERN MUDSNAIL:** 2 cm (3/4") long. p. 7.09.

Fig.H. ***BUCCINUM UNDATUM*, WAVED WHELK egg case:** 10 cm (4") long. p. 2.23 (egg case) and p. 7.09 (snail).

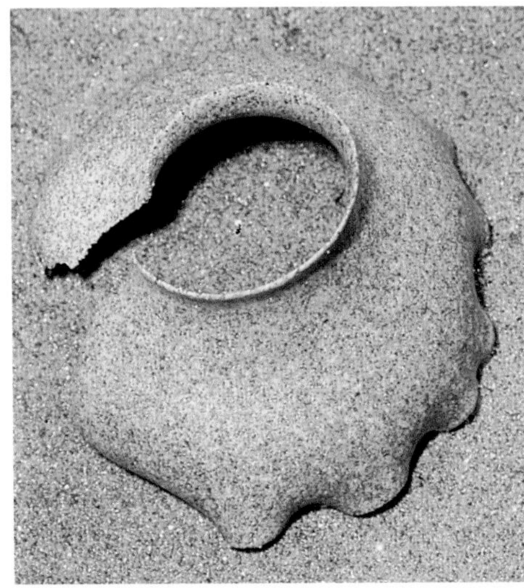

Fig.I. ***EUSPIRA HEROS*, NORTHERN MOONSNAIL egg case:** 15 cm (6") in diameter. p. 2.23 and p. 2.27 (egg case) and p. 7.04 (snail).

Fig.A. ***PECTINARIA GOULDII,* CONE WORM**: 4 cm (1.5") long. p. 8.04.

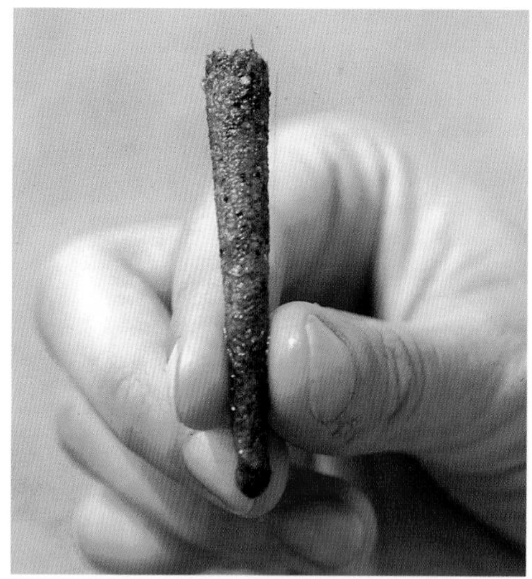

Fig.B. **TUBE OF *PECTINARIA GOULDII,* CONE WORM:** 6 cm (2.5") long. p. 8.04.

Fig.C. ***SPIRORBIS SPIRILLUM,* COILED WORM:** 2 mm (1/16") diameter; also see 17.09E. p. 8.05.

Fig.D. ***HYDROIDES DIANTHUS,* CARNATION WORM:** tubes attached to clam shell; clam shell is 7.5 cm (3") wide. p. 8.05.

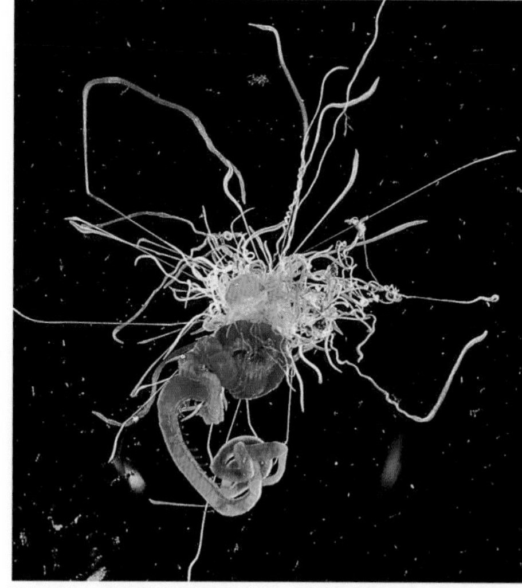

Fig.E. ***POLYCIRRUS EXIMIUS,* BLOOD DROPLET WORM:** 2.5 cm (1") long; with tentacles extended; also see 17.09C. p. 8.07.

Fig.F. ***PHERUSA AFFINIS,* COMMON BROOM WORM:** 6 cm (2.5") long. p. 8.11.

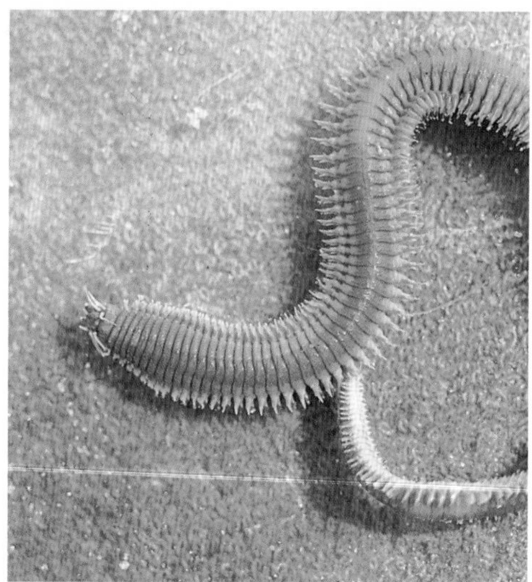

Fig.G. ***NEREIS VIRENS,* COMMON CLAM WORM:** 13 cm (5") long. p. 8.14.

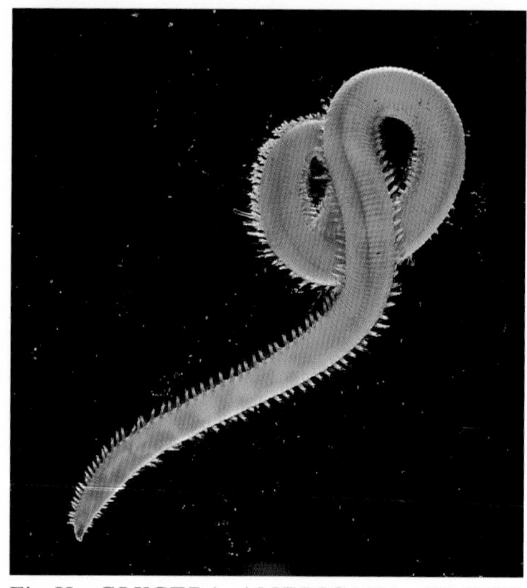

Fig.H. ***GLYCERA AMERICANA,* BLOOD WORM:** 13 cm (5") long. p. 8.18.

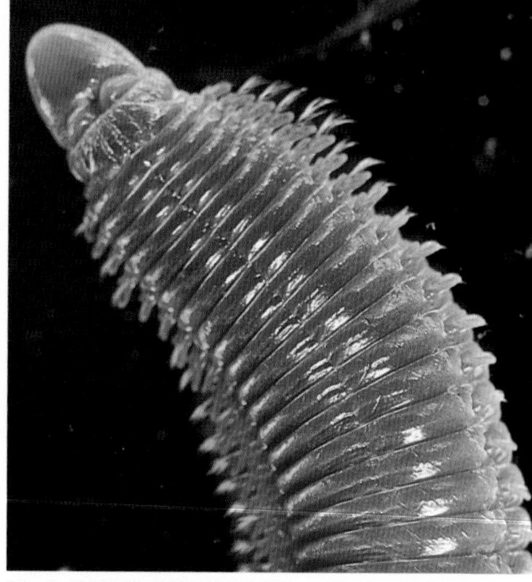

Fig.I. ***LUMBRINERIS* SP., OPAL WORM:** 12 mm (1/2") of underside of head end shown. p. 8.21.

Fig.A. **WORM CASTINGS:** mound 4 cm (1.5") tall; on mudflat. p. 2.27.

Fig.B. ***CHAETOPTERUS VARIOPEDATUS,* PARCHMENT WORM:** 15 cm (6") long. p. 8.10.

Fig.C. ***POLYCIRRUS EXIMIUS,* BLOOD DROPLET WORM:** 2.5 cm (1") long; as found in mud; also see 17.08E. p. 8.07.

Fig.D. ***LEPIDONOTUS SQUAMATUS,* TWELVE-SCALED WORM:** 5 cm (2") long. p. 8.09.

Fig.E. ***SPIRORBIS SPIRILLUM,* COILED WORM:** coiled tubes are 2 mm (1/16") diameter; attached to eelgrass; also see 17.08C. p. 8.05.

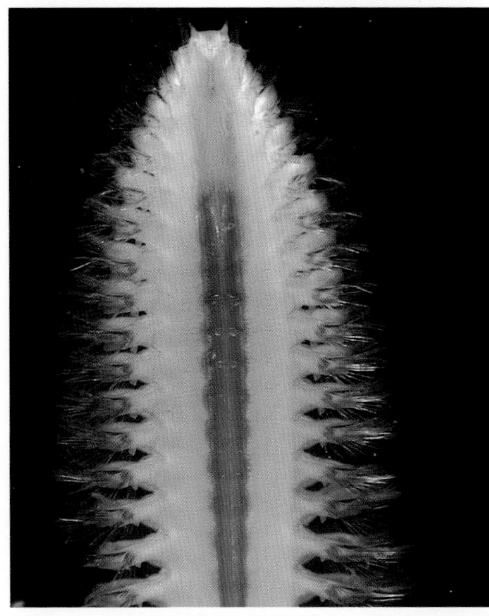

Fig.F. ***NEPHTYS INCISA,* COMMON PAINTED WORM:** 12 mm (1/2") of head end shown. p. 8.17.

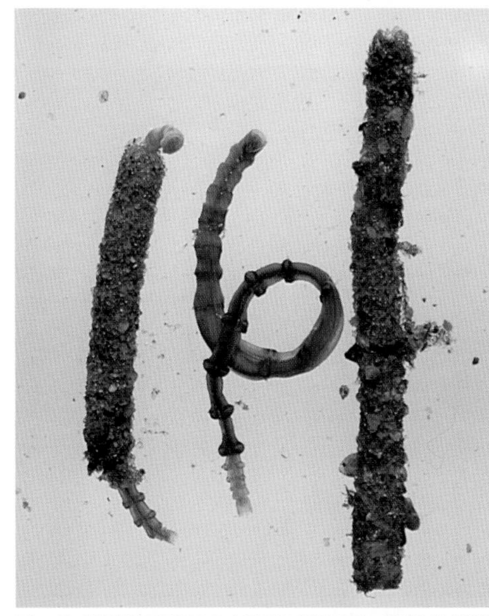

Fig.G. ***CLYMENELLA TORQUATA,* COMMON BAMBOO WORM:** 10 cm (4") long; shown in and out of tube. p. 8.22.

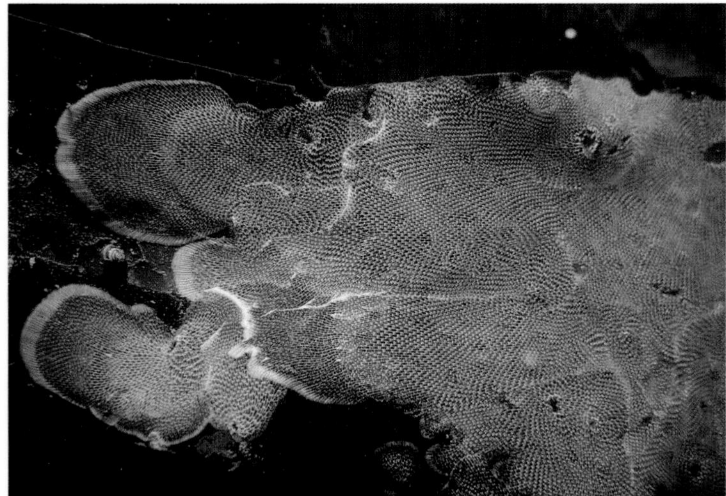

Fig.A. ***MEMBRANIPORA MEMBRANACEA,* LACY BRYOZOAN:** 13 cm (5") across field of view; encrusting on kelp; also see 17.10C. p. 6.05.

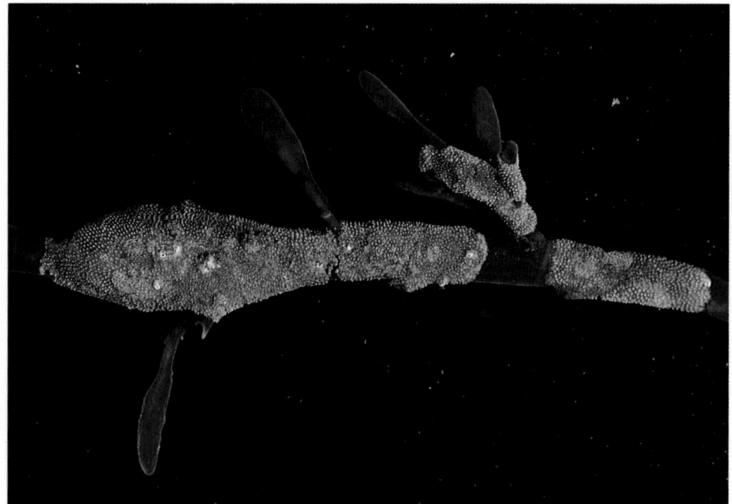

Fig. B. ***SCHIZOPORELLA UNICORNIS,* ENCRUSTING BRYOZOAN:** 10 cm (4") across field of view; encrusting on seaweed; also see 17.10D and E. p. 6.03.

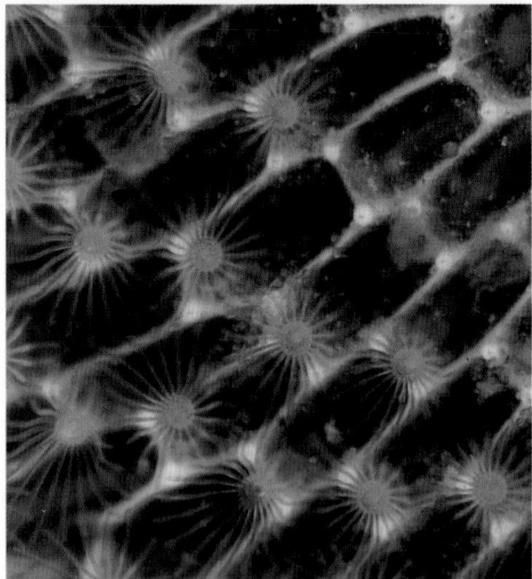

Fig.C. ***MEMBRANIPORA MEMBRANACEA,* LACY BRYOZOAN:** 3 mm (1/8") across field of view; note zooids with tentacles extended. p. 6.05.

Fig. D. ***SCHIZOPORELLA UNICORNIS,* ENCRUSTING BRYOZOAN:** 15 cm (6") across view; encrusting on rock and worm tubes. p. 6.03.

Fig. E. ***SCHIZOPORELLA UNICORNIS,* ENCRUSTING BRYOZOAN:** 6 cm (2 1/2") across field of view; encrusting on mussel shells. p. 6.03.

Fig.F. ***ELECTRA PILOSA,* LACY BRYOZOAN:** 7.5 cm (3") across field of view; encrusting on kelp; also see 17.10G. p. 6.05.

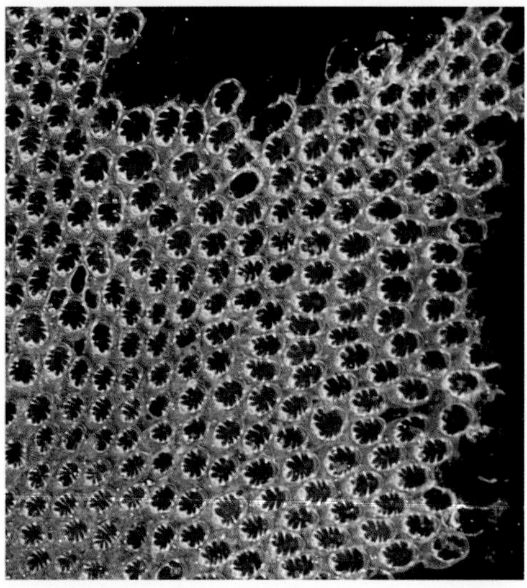

Fig.G. ***ELECTRA PILOSA,* LACY BRYOZOAN:** 1 cm (3/8") across field of view; encrusting on kelp; also see 17.10F. p. 6.05.

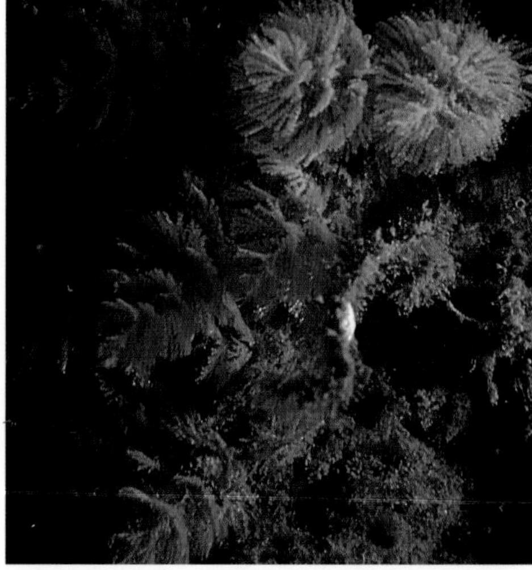

Fig. H. ***BUGULA TURRITA,* SPIRAL-TUFTED BUSHY BRYOZOAN:** 13 cm (5") across field of view. p. 6.00.

Fig.A. ***DANAUS PLEXIPPUS*, MONARCH BUTTERFLY:** 7.5 cm (3") wing span. p. 9.12.

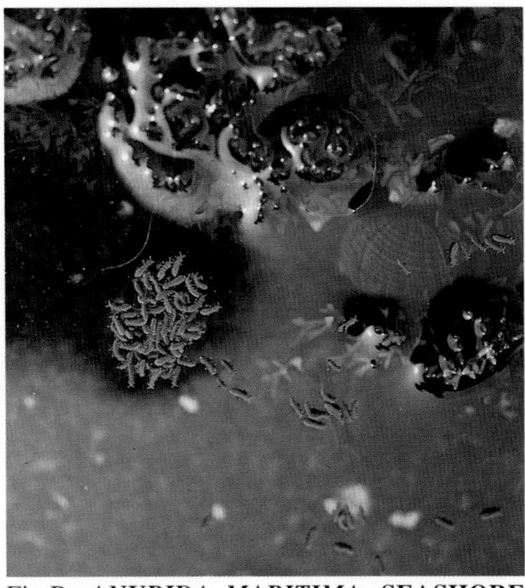

Fig.B. ***ANURIDA MARITIMA*, SEASHORE SPRINGTAIL:** 3 mm (1/8") long; walking on surface of water in tide pool. p. 9.14.

Fig.C. ***ANOPLODACTYLUS LENTUS*, SEA SPIDER:** 2.5 cm (1") leg span; male bearing yellow egg mass. p. 9.03.

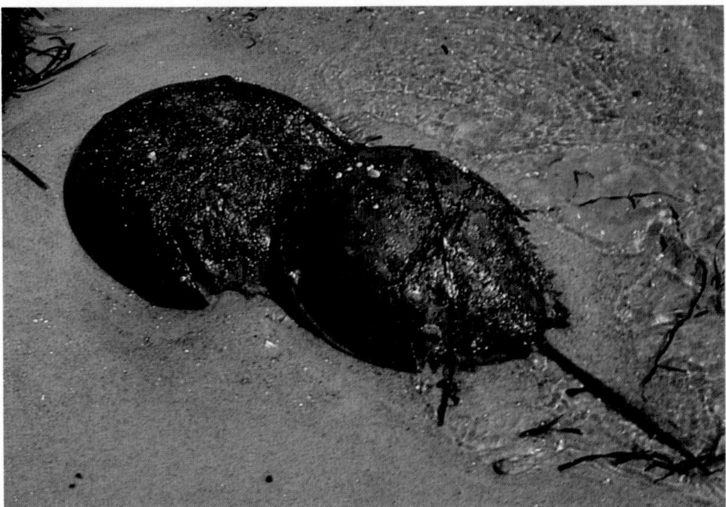

Fig.D. ***LIMULUS POLYPHEMUS*, HORSESHOE CRAB:** 25 cm (10") shell width; female (left) and male (right) spawning on beach above water level. p. 9.01.

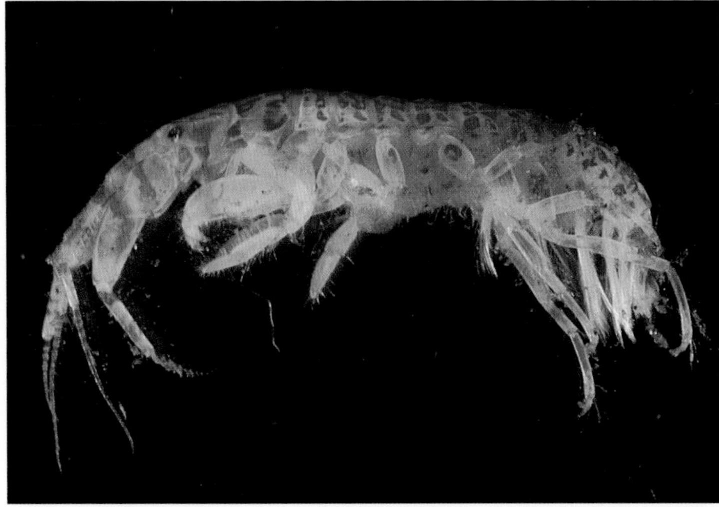

Fig.E. ***UNCIOLA IRRORATA*, AMPHIPOD:** 6 mm (1/4") long. p. 10.05.

Fig.F. ***LEPTOCHEIRUS PINGUIS*, AMPHIPOD:** 12 mm (1/2") long. p. 10.07.

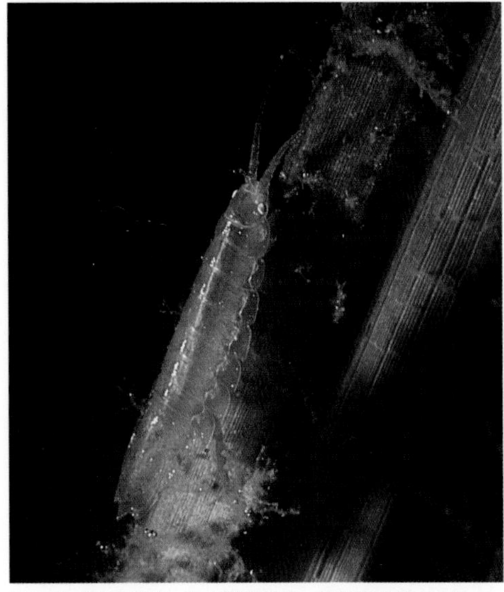

Fig.G. ***IDOTEA BALTHICA*, ISOPOD:** 2.5 cm (1") long; clinging to eelgrass. p. 10.11.

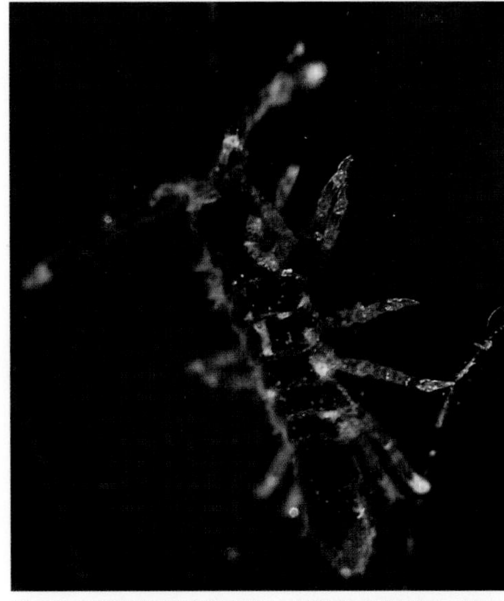

Fig.H. ***ERICHSONELLA FILIFORMIS*, ISOPOD:** 6 mm (1/4") long; on seaweed. p. 10.11.

Fig.A. ***SQUILLA EMPUSA,* MANTIS SHRIMP:** 15 cm (6") long. p. 10.16.

Fig.B. ***CRANGON SEPTEMSPINOSA,* SEVENSPINE BAY SHRIMP:** 5 cm

Fig.C. ***HOMARUS AMERICANUS,* AMERICAN LOBSTER:** 15 cm (6") across field of view. p. 10.18.

Fig.D. ***UCA PUGNAX,* ATLANTIC MARSH FIDDLER CRAB:** 2 cm (3/4") carapace width. p. 10.21.

Fig.E. ***PAGURUS LONGICARPUS,* LONG-WRIST HERMIT CRAB:** 2.5 cm (1") leg span. p. 10.19.

Fig.F. ***PAGURUS POLLICARIS,* FLATCLAW HERMIT CRAB** in shell of *Euspira heros*, northern moonsnail: 7.5 cm (3") leg span. p. 10.19.

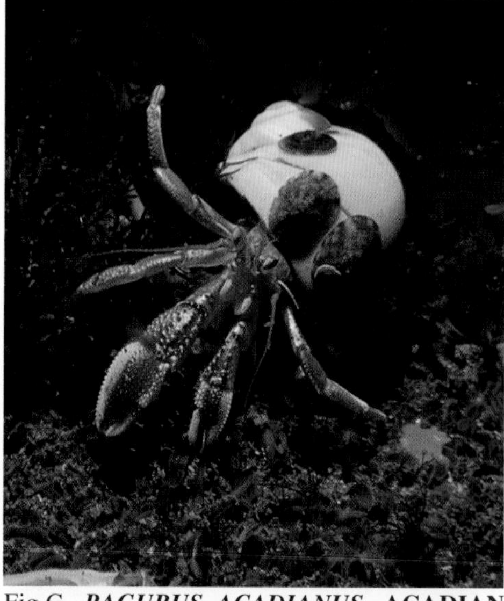

Fig.G. ***PAGURUS ACADIANUS,* ACADIAN HERMIT CRAB** in shell of northern moonsnail; 3 plant limpets, *Notoacmea testudinalis*, are attached to shell; 7.5 cm (3") leg span. p. 10.19.

Fig.A. ***LIBINIA EMARGINATA,* PORTLY SPIDER CRAB:** 10 cm (4") carapace length. p. 10.22.

Fig.B. ***CALLINECTES SAPIDUS,* BLUE CRAB:** 15 cm (6") carapace width; female with red claw tips. p. 10.23.

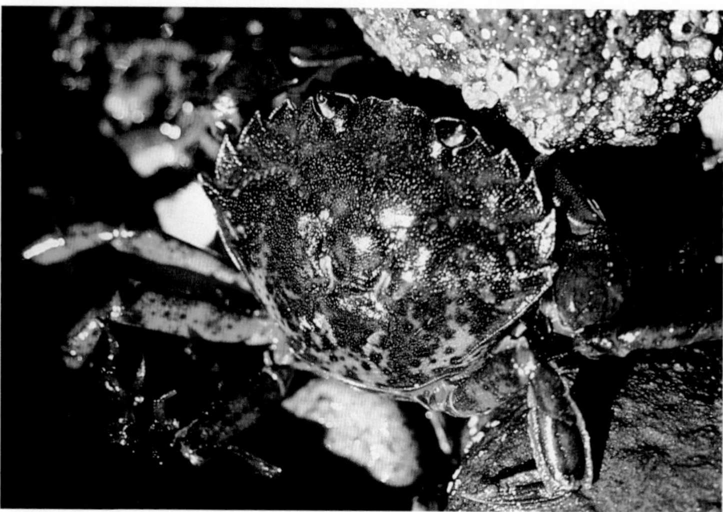

Fig.C. ***CARCINUS MAENAS,* GREEN CRAB**: 7.5 cm (3") carapace width. p. 10.24.

Fig.D. ***CARCINUS MAENAS,* GREEN CRAB:** 5 cm (2") carapace width; female bearing eggs. p. 10.24.

Fig.E. ***CARCINUS MAENAS,* GREEN CRAB:** 7.5 cm (3") carapace width; feeding on *Mya arenaria*, steamer clam. p. 10.24.

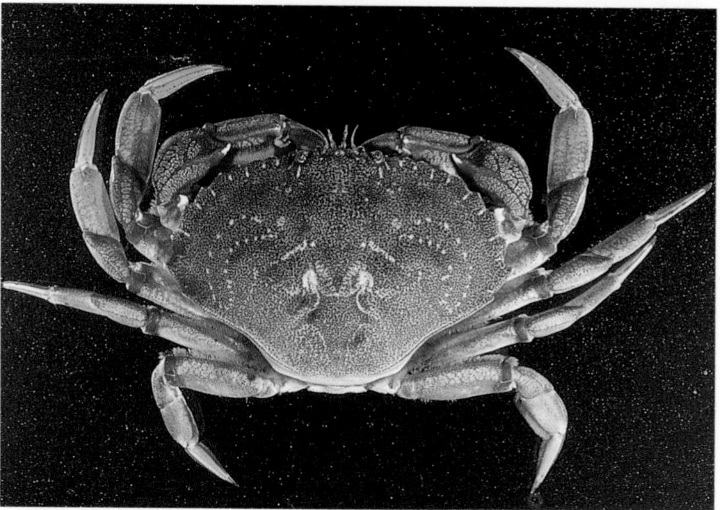

Fig.F. ***CANCER IRRORATUS,* ATLANTIC ROCK CRAB:** 10 cm (4") carapace width. p. 10.24.

Fig.A. ***ASTERIAS VULGARIS,* NORTHERN SEA STAR:** 15 cm (6") in diameter. p. 11.03.

Fig.B. ***ASTERIAS FORBESI,* COMMON SEA STAR:** 15 cm (6") in diameter. p. 11.03.

Fig.C. ***ARBACIA PUNCTULATA,* PURPLE SEA URCHIN:** 5 cm (2") in diameter. p. 11.01.

Fig.D. ***STRONGYLOCENTROTUS DROEBACHIENSIS,* GREEN SEA URCHIN:** 7.5 cm (3") in diameter; note extended tube feet. p. 11.01.

Fig.E. ***HENRICIA SANGUINOLENTA,* BLOOD STAR:** 7.5 cm (3") in diameter. p. 11.03.

Fig.F. ***ECHINARACHNIUS PARMA,* SAND DOLLAR:** 7.5 cm (3") in diameter. p. 11.01.

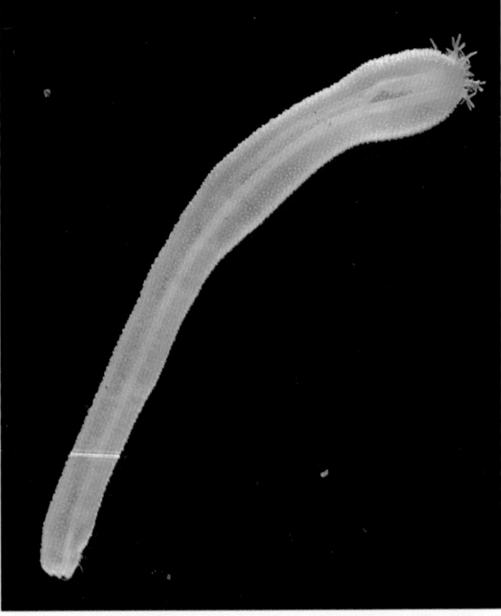

Fig.G. ***LEPTOSYNAPTA TENUIS,* WHITE SYNAPTA:** 10 cm (4") long. p. 11.07.

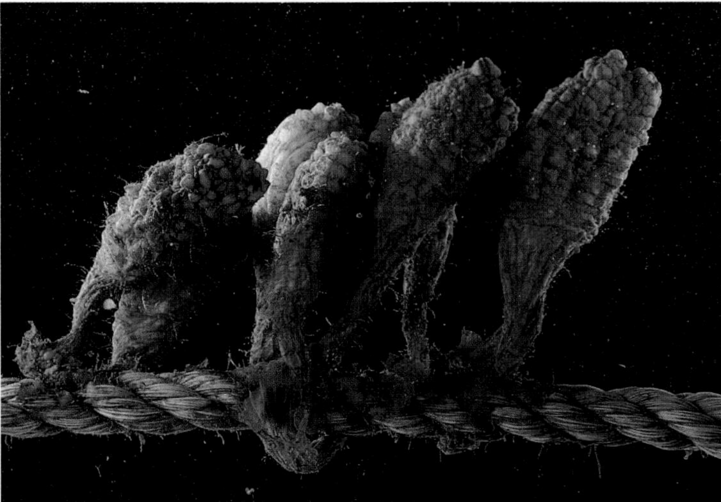
Fig.A. ***STYELA CLAVA*, PACIFIC ROUGH SEA SQUIRT:** 7.5 cm (3") tall. p. 12.01.

Fig.B. ***DIDEMNUM CANDIDUM*, WHITE CRUST:** 13 cm (5") across field of view. p. 12.02.

Fig.C. ***BOTRYLLUS SCHLOSSERI*, GOLDEN STAR TUNICATE:** 6 mm (1/4") diameter of each circular cluster of zooids. p. 12.02.

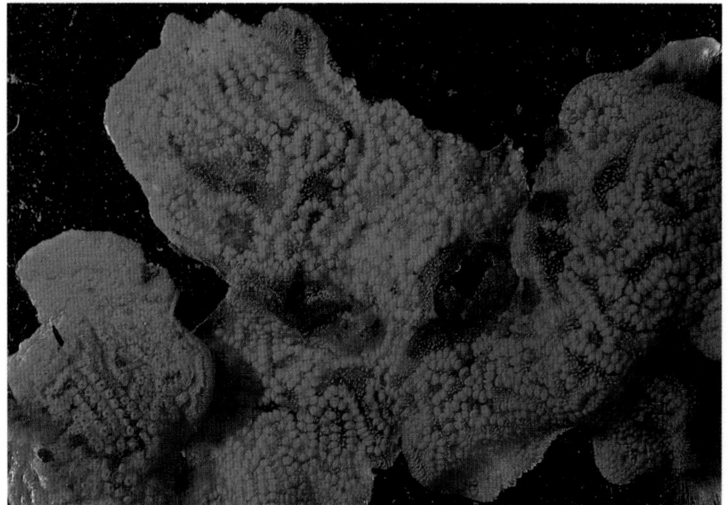
Fig.D. ***BOTRYLLOIDES DIEGENSIS*, PACIFIC COLONIAL TUNICATE**: 7.5 cm (3") across field of view. p. 12.03.

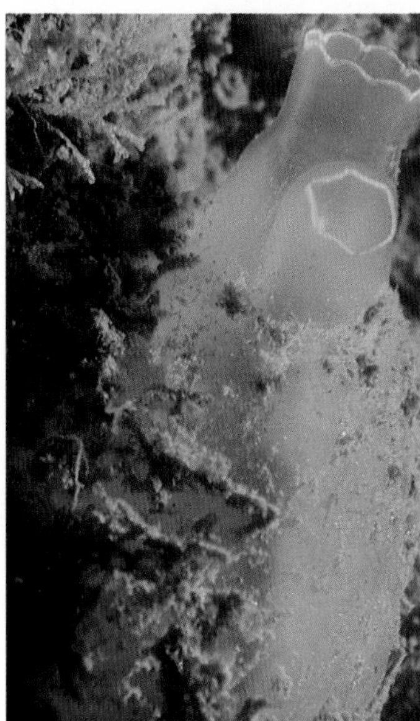
Fig.E. ***CIONA INTESTINALIS*, SEA VASE:** 4 cm (1.5") long. p. 12.00.

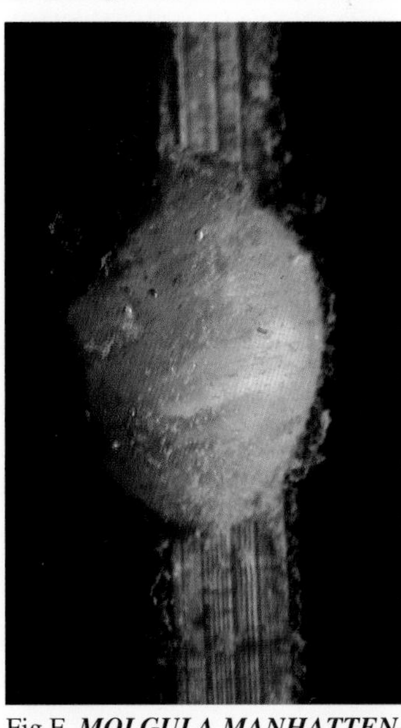
Fig.F. ***MOLGULA MANHATTENSIS*, SEA GRAPE:** 2 cm (3/4") tall; on eelgrass. p. 12.01.

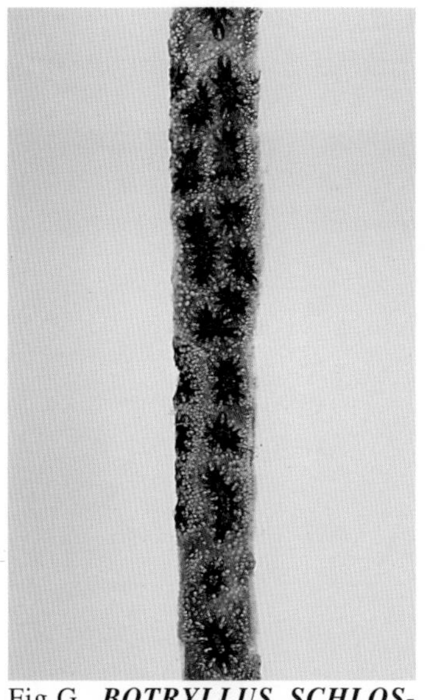
Fig.G. ***BOTRYLLUS SCHLOSSERI*, GOLDEN STAR TUNICATE** on eelgrass: 12 mm (1/2") wide. p. 12.02.

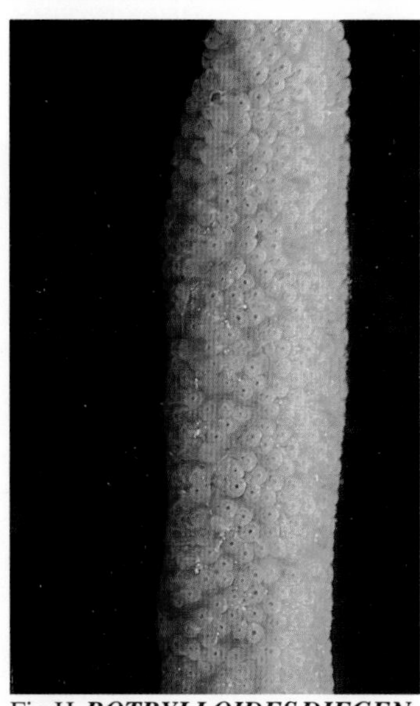
Fig.H. ***BOTRYLLOIDES DIEGENSIS*, PACIFIC COLONIAL TUNICATE** on eelgrass: 12 mm (1/2") wide. p. 12.03.

Fig.A. ***RAJA ERINACEA,* LITTLE SKATE:** 40 cm (16") long. p. 13.06.

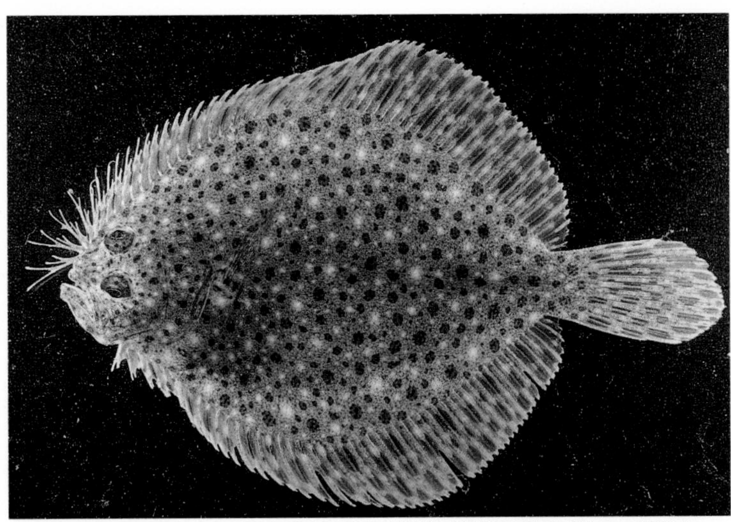

Fig.B. ***SCOPHTHALMUS AQUOSUS,* WINDOWPANE:** 25 cm (10") long. p. 13.11.

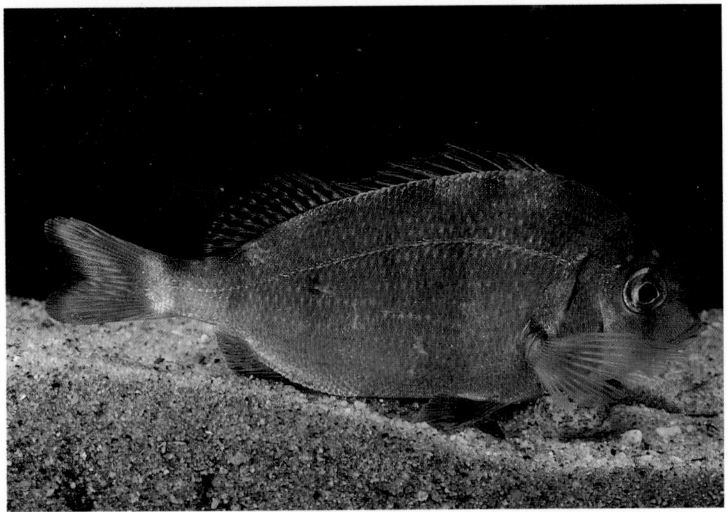

Fig. C. ***STENOTOMUS CHRYSOPS,* SCUP:** 15 cm (6") long. p. 13.18.

Fig. D. ***OPSANUS TAU,* OYSTER TOADFISH:** 15 cm (6") long. p. 13.21.

Fig. E. ***HEMITRIPTERUS AMERICANUS,* SEA RAVEN:** 25 cm (10") long. p. 13.21.

Fig. F. ***PRIONOTUS EVOLANS,* STRIPED SEAROBIN:** 13 cm (5") long. p. 13.20.

LITERATURE CITED

Abbott, R.T. 1954. American seashells. D. Van Nostrand Co., Inc., N.Y.

Agassiz, L. 1862. Contribution to the natural history of the United States of America. Second monograph, Vol. III and Vol. IV. Little Brown and Co., Boston.

Alder, J. and A. Hancock. 1845-55. Monograph of the British nudibranchiate mollusca. Ray Society, London.

American Ornithologists' Union. 1983. Check-list of North American birds, 6th ed. American Ornithologists' Union.

American Ornithologists' Union. 1989. Thirty-seventh supplement to the American Ornithologists' Union check-list of North American birds. Auk 106 (3): 532-538.

Anderson, J.F. and L.A. Magnarelli. 1980. Vertebrate host relationships and distribution of ixodid ticks (Acari: Ixodidae) in Connecticut, USA. J. Med. Entomol. 17(4): 314-323.

Army Corps of Engineers. 1977. Wetland plants of the eastern United States. NADP 200-1-1. Army Corps of Engineers, North Atlantic Division, 90 Church St., N.Y.

Arnett, R.H. Jr. 1968. The beetles of the United States (a manual for identification). The Amer. Entomol. Inst., Ann Arbor, MI.

Arnett, R.H. Jr. 1985. American insects: a handbook of the insects of America north of Mexico. Van Nostrand Reinhold, N.Y.

Arnett, R.H. Jr., N.M. Downie and H.E. Jacques. 1980. How to know the beetles, 2nd ed. William C. Brown Co., Dubuque, IA.

Arnold, A.F. 1901. The sea-beach at ebb tide. Century Company. (Reprinted in 1968 by Dover Publications, Inc., N.Y.)

Babbitt, L.H. 1937. The Amphibia of Connecticut. Conn. State Geol. Nat. Hist. Surv., Bull. 57.

Baker, E.W. et al. 1956. A manual of parasitic mites. Nat'l Pest Control Assoc.

Baker, E.W. and G.W. Wharton. 1952. An introduction to acarology. Macmillan, N.Y.

Barnes, R.D. 1968. Invertebrate zoology. W.B. Saunders Co., Phildelphia, PA.

Bigelow, H.B. and W.C. Schroeder. 1953. Fishes of the Gulf of Maine. U.S. Fish and Wildlife Serv. Bull. 53(74): 1-577. (Reprinted by Harvard University Museum of Comparative Zoology)

Böhlke, J.E. and C.C.G. Chaplin. 1968. Fishes of the Bahamas and adjacent tropical waters. The Academy of Natural Sciences of Philadelphia. Philadelphia, PA.

Borror, D.J. and D.M. Delong. 1971. An introduction to the study of insects. 3rd ed. Holt, Rinehart and Winston, N.Y.

Borror, D.J. and R.E. White. 1970. A field guide to the insects. Houghton Mifflin Co., Boston.

Bousfield, E.L. 1973. Shallow-water Gammaridean Amphipoda of New England. Cornell University Press, Ithaca, N.Y.

Bowman, T.E. and L.G. Abele. 1982. Classification of the recent Crustacea. *In* The biology of Crustacea, Vol. 1, systematics, the fossil record, and biogeography. (D.E. Bliss and L.G. Abele, eds.). Academic Press, N.Y. pp. 1-27.

Britton, W.E. et al. 1923. The Hemiptera or sucking insects of Connecticut. Part IV. Guide to the insects of Connecticut. Conn. State Geol. Nat. Hist. Surv., Bull. 34.

Britton, W.E. and B.H. Walden. 1911. Guide to the insects of Connecticut. Part I: General introduction. Part II: The Euplexoptera and Orthoptera of Connecticut. Conn. State Geol. Nat. Hist. Surv., Bull. 16.

Burgdorfer, W., A.G. Barbour, S.F. Hayes, J.L. Benach, E. Grunwaldt and J. P. Davis. 1982. Lyme disease - a tick-borne spirochetosis? Science 216: 1317-19.

Burt, W.H. and R.P. Grossenheider. 1964. A field guide to the mammals, 2nd ed. Houghton Mifflin Co., Boston.

Bush, L. 1964. Phylum Platyhelminthes. *In* Keys to the marine invertebrates of the Woods Hole region. (R.I. Smith, ed.). Contribution No. 11, Marine Biological Laboratory, Woods Hole, MA, pp. 30-39.

Bush, L.F. 1981. Marine flora and fauna of the northeastern United States. Turbellaria: Acoela and Nemertodermatida. NOAA Tech. Rep. NMFS Circ. 440.

Cable, R.M. 1977. An illustrated laboratory manual of parasitology. Burgess Pub. Co., Minneapolis, MN.

Cairns, S.D. 1981. Marine flora and fauna of the northeastern United States. Scleractinia. NOAA Tech. Rep. NMFS Circ. 438.

Cairns, S.D., D.R. Calder, A. Brinckmann-Voss, C.B. Castro, P.R. Pugh, C.E. Cutress, W.C. Jaap, D.G. Fautin, R.J. Larson, G.R. Harbison, M.N. Arai, and D.M. Opresko. 1991. Common and scientific names of aquatic invertebrates from the United States and Canada: Cnidaria and Ctenophora. Amer. Fish. Soc. Special Publication 22.

Calman, W.T. 1912. The Crustacea of the order Cumacea in the collection of the United States National Museum. Proc. U.S. Nat. Mus. 41: 603-676.

Cheng, T.C. 1967. Marine molluscs as hosts for symbioses: with a review of known parasites of commercially important species. Advan. Mar. Biol. 5: 1-424.

Cheng, T.C. 1973. General parasitology. Academic Press, N.Y.

Chu, H.F. 1949. How to know the immature insects. Wm. C. Brown Co., Dubuque, IA.

Clark, K.B. 1971. Life cycles of southern New England nudibranch molluscs. Ph.D. thesis, Univ. Conn., Storrs, CT.

Coe, W.R. 1912. Echinoderms of Connecticut. Conn. State Geol. Nat. Hist. Surv., Bull. 19. (Reprinted under the title Starfishes, serpent stars, sea urchins and sea cucumbers of the northeast, by Dover Publications, N.Y. 1972)

Coe, W.R. 1936. Sexual phases in *Crepidula*. J. Exper. Zool., 72 (3): 455-477.

Coe, W.R. 1943. Biology of the nemerteans of the Atlantic coast of North America. Trans. Conn. Acad. Arts Sci. 35: 129-328.

Collins, J.T. 1990. Standard common and current scientific names for North American amphibians and reptiles. 3rd ed. Soc. for the Study of Amphibians and Reptiles, Herpetological Circ. 19: 1-41.

Comstock, J.H. (revised by W. J. Gertsch). 1940a. The spider book. Doubleday, Doran and Co., Inc., N.Y.

Comstock, J.H. 1940b. An introduction to entomology. Comstock Publishing Co., Inc., Ithaca, N.Y.

Conant, R. 1975. A field guide to reptiles and amphibians of eastern and central North America. 2nd ed. Houghton Mifflin Co., Boston.

Conant, R. and J.T. Collins. 1991. A field guide to reptiles and amphibians of eastern and central North America. 3rd ed. Houghton Mifflin Co., Boston.

Conn. D.E.P. Wildlife Bureau. 1988. Connecticut's wildlife. A checklist of birds, mammals, reptiles and amphibians. Conn. Dept. Environ. Protect., Wildlife Bur. Pub. NHW-3.

Cook, G.C. and R.O. Brinkurst. 1973. Marine flora and fauna of the northeastern United States. Annelida: Oligochaeta. NOAA Tech. Rep. NMFS Circ. 374.

Covell, C.V. Jr. 1984. A field guide to the moths of eastern North America. Houghton Mifflin Co., Boston.

Crampton, G.C. et al. 1942. The Diptera or true flies of Connecticut, first fascicle. Part VI, Guide to the insects of Connecticut. Conn. State Geol. Nat. Hist. Surv., Bull. 64.

Crane, J.M. 1973. Introduction to marine biology. A laboratory text. Charles E. Merrill Publishing Co., Columbus, OH.

Cressy, R.F. 1978. Marine flora and fauna of the northeastern United States. Crustacea: Branchiura. NOAA Tech. Rep. NMFS Circ. 409.

Crowell, S. 1946. A new sea anemone from Woods Hole, Massachusetts. J. Wash. Acad. Sci. 36: 57-60.

Crosby, C.R. and S.C. Bishop. 1925. Studies in New York spiders, genera:

Ceratinella and *Ceraticelus*. N.Y. State Mus. Bull. 264: 5-71.

Crowder, W. 1931. Between the tides. Dodd, Mead & Co., N.Y.

Cutler, E.B. 1977. Marine flora and fauna of the northeastern United States. Sipuncula. NOAA Tech. Rep. NMFS Circ. 403.

Dall, W.H. 1899. A preliminary catalogue of the shell-bearing marine mollusks and brachiopods of the southeastern coast of the United States. U.S. Nat. Mus. Bull., 37.

Daniels, B.A. and R.T. Sawyer. 1975. The biology of the leech *Myzobdella lugubris* infesting blue crabs and catfish. Biol. Bull. 148: 193-195.

Dawes, B. 1946. The trematoda, with special reference to British and other European forms. Cambridge Univ. Press, Cambridge.

DeGraaf, R.M. and D.D. Rudis. 1983. Amphibians and reptiles of New England. Habitats and natural history. Univ. Mass. Press, Amherst, MA.

DeLong, D.M. 1926. A monographic study of the North American species of the genus *Deltocephalus*. Univ. Studies, The Ohio State Univ., Columbus, OH. Contrib. in Zoology and Entomology, 2(3).

Dillon, E.S. and L.S. Dillon. 1961. A manual of common beetles of eastern North America. Row, Peterson and Co., Evanston, IL.

Dudley, P.L. and P.L. Illg. 1991. Marine flora and fauna of the eastern United States. Copepoda, Cyclopoida: Archinotodelphyidae, Notodelphyidae and Ascidicolidae. NOAA Tech. Rep. NMFS 96.

Duncan, W.H. and M.B. Duncan. 1987. Seaside plants of the Gulf and Atlantic coasts. Smithsonian Inst. Press, Washington, D.C.

Early, G.S. and T.P. McKenzie. 1991. The northeast regional marine mammal stranding network. *In* Marine mammal strandings in the United States: Proceedings of the second marine mammal stranding workshop; 3-5 December, 1987, Miami, FL (J.E. Reynolds and D.K. Odell, eds.). NOAA Tech. Rep. NMFS 98. p. 63-68.

Ehrlich, P.P. and A.H. Ehrlich. 1961. How to know the butterflies. W. C. Brown Co., Dubuque, IA.

Emerton, J.H. 1902. The common spiders of the United States. Ginn and Co. Publishers, Boston.

Fairchild, G.B. 1950. The Diptera or true flies of Connecticut, fourth fascicle, family Tabanidae. Part VI, Guide to the insects of Connecticut. Conn. State Geol. Nat. Hist. Surv., Bull. 75.

Farrand, J. Jr. (ed.). 1983. The Audubon Society master guide to birding. Vol. 1. Loons to sandpipers. Vol. 2. Gulls to dippers. Alfred A. Knopf, N.Y.

Farrand, J. Jr. 1988. Eastern birds. McGraw Hill, N.Y.

Fauchald, K. 1977. The polychaete worms. Definitions and keys to the orders, families and genera. Nat. Hist. Mus. of Los Angeles County, Sci. Series 28.

Fauvel, P. 1923. Polychaetes errantes. Faune de France. Paris. 5:1-488.

Fell, F.J. 1982. Echinodermata. *In* Synopsis and classification of living organisms. (S.P. Parker, ed.). McGraw Hill Book Co., N.Y. pp. 785-818.

Fell, P.E. 1974. Diapause in the gemmules of the marine sponge, *Haliclona loosanoffi*, with a note on the gemmules of *Haliclona oculata*. Biol. Bull. 147: 333-351.

Flescher, D.D. 1980. Guide to some trawl-caught marine fishes from Maine to Cape Hatteras, North Carolina. NOAA Tech. Rep. NMFS Circ. 431.

Fraser, C.M. 1944. Hydroids of the Atlantic coast of North America. Univ. of Toronto Press.

Freeman, J.V. 1987. Immature stages of *Tabanus conterminus* and keys to larvae and pupae of common Tabanidae from United States east coast salt marshes. Ann. Entomol. Soc. Am. 80: 613-623.

Galtsoff, P.S. 1964. The American oyster, *Crassostrea virginica* (Gmelin). Fish. Bull. U.S. Fish and Wildlife Service. 64: 1-480.

George, J.D. and J.J. George. 1979. Marine life. John Wiley and Sons, N.Y.

Godin, A.J. 1977. Wild mammals of New England. The Johns Hopkins Univ. Press, Baltimore, MD.

Goode, H.B. 1884. Natural history of useful aquatic animals. Pt. 3. The foodfishes of the U.S. *In* The fisheries and fishing industries of the United States, Section 1, pp. 169-549, 610-612, 629-681.

Goodwin, G.G. 1935. The mammals of Connecticut. Conn. State Geol. Nat. Hist. Surv., Bull. 53.

Gosner, K.L. 1971. Guide to the identification of marine and estuarine invertebrates. John Wiley and Sons, Inc., N.Y.

Gosner, K.L. 1979. A field guide to the Atlantic seashore. Houghton Mifflin Co., Boston.

Gould, A.A. and W.G. Binney. 1870. Report on the invertebrata of Massachusetts, 2nd. ed. Comprising the Mollusca. Boston, Wright and Potter, State Printers.

Green, J. 1968. Biology of estuarine animals. Univ. of Washington Press, Seattle, WA.

Grimm, F.W. 1975. A review of *Succinnea wilsoni,* a coastal marsh snail of eastern North America. Nautilus 89(2): 39-43.

Hall, E.R. and K.R. Kelson. 1959. The mammals of North America. Ronald Press Co., N.Y.

Hand, C. 1964. Phylum Cnidaria, class Anthozoa. *In* Keys to the marine invertebrates of the Woods Hole region. (R.I. Smith, ed.). Contribution No. 11, Marine Biological Laboratory, Woods Hole, MA, pp. 25-28.

Hargitt, C.W. 1914. The Anthozoa of the Woods Hole region. Bull. U.S. Bur. Fish. 32 (for 1912): 223-254.

Hartman, O. 1944. New England Annelida, Part 2, including the unpublished plates by Verrill with reconstructed captions. Bull. Am. Mus. Nat. Hist. 82(7): 327-344.

Hartman, O. 1945. The marine annelids of North Carolina. Duke Univ. Press, Durham, N.C.

Hartman, O. 1957. Orbiniidae, Apistobranchidae, Paraonidae and Longosomidae. Allan Hancock Pacific Exped. 15(3): 211-392.

Hartman, O. 1966. Polychaeta Myzostomidae and Sedentaria of Antartica. American Geophysical Union Publication No. 1414.

Hartman, W.D. 1958. Natural history of the marine sponges of southern New England. Peabody Museum of Natural History, Yale Univ. Bull., 12.

Hartman, W.D. 1964. Phylum Porifera. *In* Keys to the marine invertebrates of the Woods Hole region. (R.I. Smith, ed.). Contribution No. 11, Marine Biological Laboratory, Woods Hole, MA, pp. 1-7.

Headlee, T. 1945. The mosquitoes of New Jersey and their control. Rutgers Univ. Press, New Brunswick, N. J.

Hedgpeth, J.W. 1948. The pycnogonida of the western north Atlantic and the Caribbean. Proc. U.S. Natn. Mus. 97: 157-342.

Hickman, C.P. 1967. Biology of the invertebrates. C.V. Mosby, Co., St.Louis.

Hincks, T. 1868. A history of the British hydroid zoophytes. John Van Voorst, London.

Ho, J.S. 1977. Marine flora and fauna of the northeastern United States. Copepoda: Lernaeopodidae and Sphyriidae. NOAA Tech. Rep. NMFS Circ. 406.

Ho, J.S. 1978. Marine flora and fauna of the northeastern United States. Copepoda: cyclopoids parasitic on fishes. NOAA Tech. Rep. NMFS Circ. 409.

Holland, W.J. 1968. The moth book. Dover Publications, Inc., N.Y.

Howard, L.O. 1916. The insect book. Doubleday, Page Co., Garden City, N.Y.

Hunter, W.R. and S.C. Brown. 1964. Phylum Mollusca. *In* Keys to the marine invertebrates of the Woods Hole region. (R.I. Smith, ed.). Contribution No. 11, Marine Biological Laboratory, Woods Hole, MA, pp. 129-152.

Hylander, C.J. 1928. The algae of Connecticut. Conn. Geol. Nat. Hist. Surv. Bull., No. 42.

Hyman, L.H. 1939. Some polyclads of the New England coast, especially of the Woods Hole region. Biol. Bull. 76: 127-152.

Hyman, L.H. 1940a. The invertebrates, Vol.I: Protozoa through Ctenophora. McGraw Hill, N.Y.

Hyman, L.H. 1940b. The polyclad flatworms of the Atlantic coast of the United States and Canada. Proc. U.S. Nat. Mus. 89: 449-495.

Hyman, L.H. 1951. The invertebrates, Vol. III: Acanthocephala, Aschelminthes, and Entoprocta, the pseudocoelomate bilateria. McGraw Hill, N.Y.

Jacobson, M.K. and W.K. Emerson. 1971. Shells from Cape Cod to Cape May. Dover Publications, Inc., N.Y. (former title: Shells of the New York City area. Argonaut Books, Inc., Larchmont, N.Y., 1961).

Jamnback, H. and W. Wall. 1959. The common salt marsh Tabanidae of Long Island, New York. N.Y. State Mus. Sci. Serv., Bull. 375.

Jaques, H.E. 1947. How to know the insects. Wm. C. Brown Co., Dubuque, IA.

Jaques, H.E. 1951. How to know the beetles. Wm. C. Brown Co., Dubuque, IA.

Jordan, D.S. and B.W. Evermann. 1896-1900. The fishes of North and Middle America. Bull. U.S. Nat. Mus., 47(1-4).

Joyeux, C. and J.G. Baer. 1936. Cestodes. Faune de France. Paris. Vol. 30.

Kabata, Z. 1979. Parasitic copepoda of British fishes. The Ray Society, London.

Kaston, B.J. 1981. Spiders of Connecticut. Conn. State Geol. Nat. Hist. Surv. Bull. 70 (contains an addendum to the 1948 edition with updated information and corrections).

Katona, S.K., V. Rough and D.T. Richardson. 1983. A field guide to the whales, porpoises and seals of the Gulf of Maine and eastern Canada: Cape Cod to Newfoundland. Charles Scribner's Sons, N.Y.

Keith, A.R. 1969. The mammals of Martha's Vineyard. Dukes County Historical Soc., Inc., Edgartown, MA.

Keppner, E.J. and A.C. Tarjan. 1989. Illustrated key to the genera of free-living marine nematodes of the order Enoplida. NOAA Tech. Rep. NMFS 77.

King, F.W. 1979. The Audubon Society field guide to North American reptiles and amphibians. Alfred A. Knopf, N.Y.

Klemens, M.W. 1993. The amphibians and reptiles of Connecticut and adjacent regions. Conn. Geol. and Nat. Hist. Surv., Bull. 112.

Klots, A.B. 1951. A field guide to the butterflies. Houghton Mifflin Co., Boston.

Kunkel, B.W. 1918. The arthrostraca of Connecticut. Conn. Geol. and Nat. Hist. Surv., Bull. 26.

Lamson, G.H. 1935. The reptiles of Connecticut. Conn. Geol. and Nat. Hist. Surv., Bull. 54.

Larson, R.J. 1976. Marine flora and fauna of the northeastern United States. Cnidaria: Scyphozoa. NOAA Tech. Rep. NMFS Circ. 397.

Lazell, J.D. 1976. This broken archipelago. Cape Cod and the islands, amphibians and reptiles. Demeter Press, Quadrangle/The New York Times Book Co., N.Y.

Leatherwood, S., D. Caldwell and H. Winn. 1976. Whales, dolphins and porpoises of the western North Atlantic, a guide to their identification. NOAA Technical Report NMFS Circ. 396.

Leim, A.H. and W.B. Scott. 1966. Fishes of the Atlantic coast of Canada. Bull. Fish. Res. Bd. Canada, 155.

Levi, H.W. and L.R. Levi. 1968. A guide to spiders and their kin. Golden Press, N.Y.

Light, S.F., et al. 1954. Intertidal invertebrates of the central California coast. Univ. of Calif. Press, Berkeley, CA.

Logier, E.B.S. 1958. The snakes of Ontario. Univ. Toronto Press, Toronto.

Long Island Shell Club. 1988. Seashells of Long Island, New York. Long Island Shell Club, Inc.

Magnarelli, L.A., J.F. Anderson, W. Burgdorfer, and W.A. Chappell. 1984. Parasitism by *Ixodes dammini* (Acari:Ixodidae) and antibodies to spirochaetes in mammals at Lyme disease foci in Connecticut, USA. J. Med. Entomol. 21: 52-57.

Manning, R.B. 1974. Marine flora and fauna of the northeastern United States. Crustacea: Stomatopoda. NOAA Tech. Rep. NMFS Circ. 387.

Manning, R.B. and D.L. Felder. 1991. *Gilvossius*, a new genus of callianassid shrimp from the eastern United States (Crustacea: Decapoda: Thalassinidea). Bull. Mar. Sci. 49: 558-561.

Marcus, E. 1958. Western Atlantic opisthobranchiate gastropods. Amer. Mus. Novitates, No. 1906.

Marcus, E.D.B. 1972. Notes on some opisthobranch gastropods from the Chesapeake Bay. Chesapeake Sci., 13: 300-317.

Matheson, R. 1945. The Diptera or true flies of Connecticut, second fascicle, family Culicidae, the mosquitoes. Part VI, Guide to the insects of Connecticut. Conn. State Geol. Nat. Hist. Surv., Bull. 68.

Mayer, A.G. 1912. Ctenophores of the Atlantic coast of North America. Carnegie Inst. Wash. Publ. 162.

McAlpine, J.F. et al. 1981. Manual of Neartic Diptera. Agriculture Research Branch, Canada.

McCloskey, L.R. 1973. Marine flora and fauna of the northeastern United States. Pycnogonida. NOAA Tech. Rep. NMFS Circ. 386.

Meglitsch, P.A. 1967. Invertebrate zoology. Oxford Univ. Press, N.Y.

Meinkoth, N. 1981. The Audubon Society field guide to North American seashore creatures. Alfred A. Knopf, N.Y.

Menzies, R.J. and D. Frankenberg. 1966. Handbook on the common marine isopod Crustacea of Georgia. Univ. of Georgia Press, Atlanta, GA.

Meyer, M.C. and O.W. Olsen. 1980. Essentials of parasitology (lab manual). Wm. C. Brown Co., Dubuque, IA.

Miner, R.W. 1950. Field book of seashore life. G.P. Putnam's Sons, N.Y.

Moore, G.M. 1964. Phylum Mollusca, shell-less opisthobranchia. *In* Keys to marine invertebrates of the Woods Hole region. (R.I. Smith, ed.). Contrib. No. 11. Marine Biological Laboratory, Woods Hole, MA.

Morris, P.A. 1975. A field guide to the shells of our Atlantic and Gulf coasts. Houghton Mifflin Co., Boston.

Moul, E.T. 1973. Marine flora and fauna of the northeastern United States. Higher plants of the marine fringe. NOAA Technical Report NMFS Circ. 384.

Murie, O.J. 1954. A field guide to animal tracks. Houghton Mifflin, Co., Boston.

Naumov, D.V. 1960. Hydroids and hydromedusae of the U.S.S.R. Zool. Inst. of the Acad. Sci. of the U.S.S.R. No. 70.

Newell, I.M. 1947. A systematic and ecological study of the Halacaridae of eastern North America. Bull. Bingham oceanogr. Coll. 10(3): 1-266.

Nichols, D. and J.A. Cooke. 1971. The Oxford book of invertebrates. Oxford Univ. Press, London.

Niemeyer, V.B. and D.A. Martin. 1967. A guide to the identification of the marine plants and invertebrate animals of tidewater, Virginia. Virginia Instit. of Mar. Sci., Ed. Series #13, Gloucester Pt., VA.

Noble, E.R. and G.A. Noble. 1982. Parasitology: the biology of animal parasites. Lea and Febiger, Philadelphia, PA.

Nutting, C.C. 1899. The hydroids of the Woods Hole region. Bull. U.S. Bur. Fish. 19: 325-386.

Olmstead, N.C. and P.E. Fell. 1974. Tidal marsh invertebrates of Connecticut. Connecticut Arboretum Bull., No. 20. New London, CT.

Osburn, R.C. 1912. The Bryozoa of the Woods Hole region. Bull. Bur. Fish. Wash. (1910) 30: 205-266.

Overstom, N.A., S. Spotte, J.L. Dunn, A.D. Goren, and H.W. Kaufman. 1991. A resident beluhka whale (*Delphinopterus leucas*) in Long Island Sound. *In* Marine mammal strandings in the United States: proceedings of the second marine mammal stranding workshop; 3-5 December, 1987, Miami, FL (J.E. Reynolds and D.K. Odell, eds.). NOAA Tech. Rep. NMFS 98. p. 63-68.

Palmer, E.L. 1957. Palmer's fieldbook of mammals. E.P. Dutton, Co., N.Y.

Paulmier, F.C. 1905. Higher Crustacea of New York City. Bull. N.Y. State Mus. 91: 117-189.

Pawson, D.L. 1977. Marine flora and flora of the northeastern United States. Echinodermata: Holothuroidea. NOAA Tech. Rep. NMFS Circ. 405.

Pechuman, L.L. 1972. The horse and deer flies of New York (Diptera: Tabanidae). Search (Ithaca) 2: 1-72.

Pennak, R.W. 1953. Fresh-water invertebrates of the United States. Ronald Press, N.Y.

Peterson, A. 1939. Keys to the orders of immature stages exclusive of eggs and

pronymphs of N. American insects. Ann. Ent. Soc. Amer. 32: 267-278.
Peterson, R.L. 1966. The mammals of eastern Canada. Oxford Univ. Press, Toronto.
Peterson, R.T. 1980. A field guide to the birds east of the Rockies. Houghton Mifflin Company, Boston.
Petry, L.C. 1968. A beachcomber's botany. The Chatham Conservation Foundation, Inc., Chatham, MA.
Pettibone, M.H. 1963. Marine polychaete worms of the New England region. Part 1. Families Aphroditidae through Throchochaetidae. Bull. U.S. Nat. Mus. 227(1): 1-356.
Pilsbry, H.A. 1916. The sessile barnacles (Cirripedia) contained in the collections of the U.S. National Museum, including a monograph of the American species. Bull. U.S. Nat. Mus. 93: 1-366.
Pritchard, M.H. and G.O.W. Kruse. 1982. The collection and preservation of animal parasites. Univ. of Nebraska Press, Lincoln, NE.
Rathbun, R. 1884. Crustaceans. *In* The fisheries and fishery industries of the United States, section 1, part 5, Natural history of useful aquatic animals. (G.B. Goode, ed.). U.S. Commission of Fish and Fisheries, Washington D.C. pp. 759-830.
Richardson, H. 1905. A monograph on the isopods of North America. Bull. U.S. Nat. Mus. 54: 1-717.
Robbins, C.S., B. Bruun and H.S. Zim. 1966. Birds of North America. Golden Press, N.Y.
Robins, C.R., R.M. Bailey, C.E. Bond, J.R. Brooker, E.A. Lachner, R.N. Lea and W.B. Scott. 1991. Common and scientific names of fishes from the United States and Canada, fifth edition. Amer. Fish. Soc. Special Publication 20.
Rogick, M.D. 1964a. Phylum Entoprocta. *In* Keys to marine invertebrates of the Woods Hole region. (R.I. Smith, ed.). Contrib. No. 11. Marine Biol. Lab., Woods Hole, MA, pp. 165-166.
Rogick, M.D. 1964b. Phylum Ectoprocta. *In* Keys to marine invertebrates of the Woods Hole region. (R.I. Smith, ed.). Contrib. No. 11. Marine Biol. Lab., Woods Hole, MA, pp. 167-187.
Rogick, M.D. and H. Croasdale. 1949. Studies on marine Bryozoa, III. Woods Hole region Bryozoa associated with algae. Biol. Bull. 96: 32-69.
Ryland, J.S. and P.J. Hayward. 1991. Marine flora and fauna of the northeastern United States. Erect Bryozoa. NOAA Tech. Rep. NMFS Circ. 99.
Sawyer, R.T., A.D. Lawler and R.M. Overstreet. 1975. Marine leeches of the eastern United States and the Gulf of Mexico with a key to the species. J. Nat. Hist. 9: 633-667.
Schell, S.C. 1970. How to know the trematodes. Wm. C. Brown Co., Dubuque, IA.
Schmidt, G.D. 1970. How to know the tapeworms. Wm. C. Brown Co., Dubuque, IA.
Schmidt, G.D. and L.S. Roberts. 1981. Foundations of parasitology, 2nd edition. C.V. Mosby, St. Louis, MO.
Schultz, G.A. 1969. How to know the marine isopod crustaceans. Wm. C. Brown Co., Dubuque, IA.
Scott, W.B. and M.G. Scott. 1988. Atlantic fishes of Canada. Can. Bull. Fish. Aquat. Sci. 219.
Serafy, D.K. and F.J. Fell. 1985. Marine flora and fauna of the northeastern United States. Echinodermata: Echinoidea. NOAA Tech. Rep. NMFS Circ. 33.
Sigerfoos, C.P. 1899. A new hydroid from Long Island Sound (*Stylactis hooperi*). Amer. Cat. 33(394): 801-807.
Silberhorn, G.M. 1982. Common plants of the Mid-Atlantic coast. The Johns Hopkins Univ. Press, Baltimore, MD.
Simon, H. 1979. Easy identification guide to North American snakes. Dodd Mead Co., N.Y.
Slater, J.A. and R.M. Baranowski. 1978. How to know the true bugs. Wm. C. Brown Co., Dubuque, IA.
Smith, C.L. 1985. The inland fishes of New York State. N.Y. State Dept. Environ. Conservation.
Smith, R.I. (ed.). 1964. Keys to marine invertebrates of the Woods Hole region. Contrib. No. 11. Marine Biol. Lab., Woods Hole, MA.
Smith, R.I. and J.T. Carlton (ed). 1975. Light's manual: intertidal invertebrates of the central California coast. Univ. of Calif. Press.
Smith, S.I. 1882. Reports on the results of dredging by the U.S. Coast Steamer Blake. XVII, Report on the Crustacea, Part 1. Decapoda. Bull. Mus. Comp. Zool. Harvard. 10: 1-108.
Snodgrass, R.E. 1952. A textbook of arthropod anatomy. Comstock Publishing Associates, Cornell Univ. Press, Ithaca, N.Y.
Stephenson, T.A. 1928, 1935. The British sea anemones. Vol. 1 and Vol. 2. Ray Society, London.
Taylor, S. and M. Villalard. 1979. Seaweeds of the Connecticut shore. 2nd ed. Conn. Arboretum Bull., No. 18. Connecticut College, New London, CT.
Taylor, W.R. 1957. Marine algae of the northeastern coast of North America. 2nd ed. Univ. Michigan Press, Ann Arbor, MI.
Tesky, H.J. 1969. Larvae and pupae of some eastern North American Tabanidae (Diptera). Mem. Ent. Soc. Can. 63: 1-147.
Thomson, K.S., W.H. Weed III, A.G. Taruski and D.E. Simanek. 1978. Saltwater fishes of Connecticut. Conn. Geol. Nat. Hist. Surv., Bull. No. 105.
Tietjen, J.H. 1977. Population distribution and structure of the free living nematodes of Long Island Sound. Mar. Biol. 43: 123-136.
Turgeon, D.D., A.E. Bogan, E.V. Coan, W.K. Emerson, W.G. Lyons, W.L. Pratt, C.F.E. Roper, A. Scheltema, F.G. Thompson, and J.D. Williams. 1988. Common and scientific names of aquatic invertebrates from the United States and Canada: mollusks. Amer. Fish. Soc. Special Publication 16.
Urquhart, F.A. 1949. Introducing the insect. Henry Holt and Company, N.Y.
Ushakov, P.V. 1955. Polychaeta of the far eastern seas of the U.S.S.R. Zoological Institute of the Academy of Sciences of the U.S.S.R., No. 56. (Translated from the Russian by Israel Program for Scientific Translations, Jerusalem, 1965: Available from Office of Technical Services, U.S. Dept. of Commerce, Wash. D.C.)
Uzmann, J.R. 1967. *Histriobdella homari* (Annelida: Polychaeta) in the American lobster, *Homarus americanus*. J. Parasitol. 53: 210-211.
Verrill, A.E. 1880-81. The cephalopods of the northeastern coast of America. Part II. The smaller cephalopods, including the squids and the octopi with other allied forms. Trans. Conn. Acad. Arts Sci. 5: 259-446.
Verrill, A.E. 1881. New England Annelida. Part 1. Historical sketch with annotated lists of the species hitherto recorded. Trans. Conn. Acad. Arts Sci. 4(2): 285-324.
Verrill, A.E. 1892a. The marine nemerteans of New England and adjacent waters. Trans. Conn. Acad. Arts Sci. 8: 328-456.
Verrill, A.E. 1892b. Marine planarians of New England. Trans. Conn. Acad. Arts Sci. 8: 459-520.
Verrill, A.E. 1922. Report of the Canadian Arctic Expedition 1913-18, Vol. VIII, Part G. King's Printer, Ottawa, Canada.
Verrill, A.E. and S.I. Smith. 1873. Report upon the invertebrate animals of Vineyard Sound and the adjacent waters. Rept. U.S. Fish Comm. 1871-1872. Part 1: 298-778.
Viereck, H.L. et al. 1916. The Hymenoptera, or wasp-like insects. Part II. Guide to the insects of Connecticut. Conn. State Geol. Nat. Hist. Surv., Bull. 22.
Watling, L. 1979. Marine flora and fauna of the northeastern United States. Crustacea: Cumacea. NOAA Tech. Rep. NMFS Circ. 423.
Weiss, H.M. 1970. Diet and feeding behavior of the lobster, *Homarus americanus*, in Long Island Sound. Ph.D. thesis, Univ. Conn., Storrs, CT.
Weiss, H.M., D. Glemboski, K. Philips, P. Roper, A. Rosso, T. Sweeney, A. Vittarelli, L. Wahle and J. Weiss. 1995. Plants and animals of Long Island Sound: a documented checklist, bibliography, and computer data base. Project Oceanology, Groton, CT.
Weiss, H.M. and M.W. Dorsey. 1979. Investigating the marine environment:

a sourcebook. Vols. 1-3. Project Oceanology, Groton, CT.

Wells, H.W., M.J. Wells and I.E. Gray. 1960. Marine sponges of North Carolina. Jour. of the Elisha Mitchell Scientific Society 76(2): 200-245.

Wetzel, R.M. 1979. Terrestrial mammals of Connecticut. Univ. Conn., Storrs, CT.

White, R.E. 1983. A field guide to the beetles of North America. Houghton Mifflin Co., Boston.

Wigley, R.L. 1964a. Order Mysidacea. *In* Keys to marine invertebrates of the Woods Hole region. (R.I. Smith, ed.). Contrib. No. 11. Marine Biol. Lab., Woods Hole, MA, pp. 93-95.

Wigley, R. L. 1964b. Order Cumacea. *In* Keys to marine invertebrates of the Woods Hole region. (R.I. Smith, ed.). Contrib. No. 11. Marine Biol. Lab., Woods Hole, MA, pp. 98-102.

Williams, A.B. 1965. Marine decapod crustaceans of the Carolinas. Fishery Bull. U.S. Fish Wildl. Serv. 65(1): 1-298.

Williams, A.B. 1984. Shrimps, lobsters, and crabs of the Atlantic coast of the eastern United States, Maine to Florida. Smithsonian Institution Press, Washington, D.C.

Williams, A.B., L.G. Abele, D.L. Felder, H.H. Hobbs, Jr., R.B. Manning, P.A. McLaughlin, and I. Perez Farfante. 1989. Common and scientific names of aquatic invertebrates from the United States and Canada: decapod crustaceans. Amer. Fish. Soc. Special Publication 17.

Wilson, E.B. 1878. Synopsis of the Pycnogonida of New England. Trans. Conn. Acad. Arts and Sci. 5: 1-26.

Zim, H.S. and H.M. Smith. 1953. Reptiles and amphibians. Simon and Schuster, N.Y.

Zimmer, C. 1980. Cumaceans of the American Atlantic boreal coast region (Crustacea: Peracarida). Smithsonian Contr. Zool. 302.

Zullo, V.A. 1964. Subclass Cirripedia. *In* Keys to marine invertebrates of the Woods Hole region. (R.I. Smith, ed.). Contrib. No. 11. Marine Biol. Lab., Woods Hole, MA, pp. 89-92.

Zullo, V.A. 1979. Marine flora and fauna of the northeastern United States. Arthropoda: Cirripedia. NOAA Tech. Rep. NMFS Circ. 425.

Copyright Acknowledgements

A number of figures have been redrawn or copied from copyright sources. Permissions have been received from the copyright holders for these books and articles. The source location is listed, followed by its location in this book. The style and format are different from the text to reflect the publisher's need for a specialized treatment of acknowledgements required by copyright holders.

Abbott, R.T. 1954 *American Seashells* Van Nostrand, Reinhold, NY.

SOURCE	VIEW/SCIENTIFIC/COMMON NAMES	PAGE FIG
Pg 26 Fig 8	*Nucella (=Thais) lapillus*/Atlantic dogwinkle egg case	2.24 B
Pg 26 Fig 8	*Urosalpinx cinerea*/oyster drill egg case	2.24 C
Pg 26 Fig 8	*Epitonium*/wentletrap egg case	2.23 E
Pg 27 Fig 9	*Nassarius vibex*/bruised nassa egg case	2.24 E
Pg 26 Fig 8	*Busycon carica*/knobbed whelk egg case	2.23 F
Pg 26 Fig 8	*Busycotypus (=Busycon) canaliculatus*/channeled whelk egg case	2.23 G
Pg 26 Fig 8	*Buccinum undatum*/waved whelk egg case	2.23 H
Pg 27 Fig 9	*Bittium alternatum*/alternate bittium egg mass	2.23 K
Pg 27 Fig 9	*Littorina obtusata*/yellow periwinkle egg mass	2.23 M

Alder, J. and A. Hancock. 1845-55. *Monograph of the British Nudibranchiate Mollusca*. The Ray Society, London.

VIEW/SCIENTIFIC/COMMON NAMES	PAGE FIG
Dendronotus frondosus/frond-aeolis	7.12 A
Tenellia (=Embletonia) fuscata	7.12 B
Ancula gibbosa/Atlantic ancula	7.11 C
Alderia modesta (=harvardiensis)/modest alderia	7.13 N
Placida (=Hermaea) dendritica	7.13 O

Arnett, R.H., Jr. 1968. *The Beetles of the United States*. The Catholic University of America Press, Washington, DC. Present copyright by Ross H. Arnett, Jr., The Sandhill Crane Press, Inc., Gainesville, FL.

SOURCE	VIEW/SCIENTIFIC/COMMON NAME	PAGE FIG
Pg 51	family Cicindelidae/tiger beetles	9.19 C
Pg 53	family Carabidae/ground beetles	9.19 D
Pg 191	family Dytiscidae/predaceous diving beetles	9.19 E
Pg 645	family Tenebrionidae/darkling beetles	9.21 E
Pg 535	family Cantharidae/soldier beetles	9.21 F
Pg 465	family Heteroceridae/variegated mud-loving beetles	9.21 G

Barnes, R.D. 1968. *Invertebrate Zoology*. W.B. Saunders Co., Philadelphia, PA. Figures from *Invertebrate Zoology,* Second Edition by Robert Barnes, copyright 1968 by Saunders College Publishing, a division of Holt, Rinehart and Winston, Inc., reprinted by permission of the publisher.

SOURCE	VIEW/SCIENTIFIC/COMMON NAME	PAGE FIG
Pg 207 Fig 10-3A	body segment cross section	8.00 A
Pg 214 Fig 10-10A,B	head and proboscis/*Glycera* spp.	8.18 A
Pg 380 Fig 13-1	dorsal view/*Limulus polyphemus*	9.01 A
Pg 420 Fig 13-38A	*Dermacentor variabilis*/American dog tick	9.09 A
Pg 455 Fig 14-19	fish with fish lice	10.02 A
Pg 194 Fig 9-28	cysts in muscle	2.18 B
Pg 226 Fig 10-23B	tube/*Chaetopterus variopedatus*	8.10 B
Pg 688 Fig 20-11B	*Botryllus schlosseri*/zooids	12.02 B
Pg 215 Fig 10-11A	head/*Diopatra cuprea*	8.13 D
Pg 219 Fig 10-15A	*Hydroides (=Eupomatus) dianthus*/carnation worm	8.05 D
Pg 458 Fig 14-21B	ventral view/*Argulus* sp.	10.03 E
Pg 194 Fig 9-28	free living nematode	5.08 B

Bohlke, J.E. and C.C.G. Chaplin. 1968. *Fishes of the Bahamas and Adjacent Tropical Waters*. The Academy of Natural Sciences of Philadelphia, Philadelphia, PA.

SOURCE	VIEW/SCIENTIFIC/COMMON NAME	PAGE FIG
Pg 683	*Lactophrys trigonus*/trunkfish	13.09B
Pg 308	*Priacanthus cruentatus*/glasseye snapper	13.18B
Pg 308	*Trachinotus falcatus*/permit	13.24B

Borror, D.J. and D.M. Delong. 1971. *An Introduction to the Study of Insects.* Houghton Mifflin Co., Boston, MA. Figures from *An Introduction to the Study of Insects,* Third Edition by D.J. Borror and D. Delong, copyright 1978 by Saunders College Publishing, a division of Holt, Rinehart and Winston, Inc., reprinted by permission of the publisher.

SOURCE	VIEW/SCIENTIFIC/COMMON NAME	PAGE FIG
Pg 162	*Anisolabris maritima*/seaside earwig	9.14 A
Pg 696 Fig A	family Cephidae/stem sawflies	9.28 A
Pg 87	*Machilis maritima*/seashore bristletail	9.14 E

Borror, D.J. and R.E. White. 1970. *A Field Guide to the Insects*. Houghton Mifflin Co., Boston. Acknowledgement is given to the Peterson Field Guide series published by Houghton Mifflin Co. as source material.

SOURCE	VIEW/SCIENTIFIC/COMMON NAME	PAGE FIG
Pg 30	insect body regions	9.10 A
Pg 30	mandibles - grasshopper head	9.10 D
Pg 32	moth head	9.12 A
Pg 72	order Odonata/dragonflies and damselflies	9.13 F
Pg 83	family Tettigoniidae/long-horned grasshoppers	9.15 B
Pg 113	hemiptera beak	9.11 G
Pg 127	family Scutelleridae/shield-backed Bugs	9.16 B
Pg 131	homoptera head side view	9.11 H
Pg 131	planthopper beak side view	9.13 D
Pg 131	delphacid head side view	9.18 C
Pg 133	family Delphacidae/planthoppers	9.18 C
Pg 135	homoptera with wings extended	9.13 D
Pg 135	homoptera side view	9.13 D
Pg 153	family Haliplidae/crawling water beetles	9.19 B
Pg 157	family Hydrophilidae/water scavenger beetles	9.21 C
Pg 211	order Trichoptera/caddisflies, water moths	9.13 C
Pg 263	family Tipulidae/crane flies	9.25 B
Pg 265	family Psychodidae/moth or sand flies	9.25 D
Pg 267	mosquito faces	9.24 A
Pg 269	family Chironomidae/midges	9.25 C
Pg 269	family Simuliidae/black flies	9.25 F

SOURCE	VIEW/SCIENTIFIC/COMMON NAME	PAGE FIG
Pg 269	family Ceratopogonidae/no-see-ums, punkies	9.25 G
Pg 271	mycetophilidae head and eyes	9.25 E
Pg 275	family Rhagionidae/snipe flies	9.22 D
Pg 275	snipe fly antenna	9.22 D
Pg 275	deer fly	9.23 F
Pg 275	tabanid wing	9.23 F
Pg 279	family Dolichopodidae/long-legged flies	9.23 I
Pg 279	family Empididae/dance flies	9.23 J
Pg 281	family Pipunculidae/big-headed flies	9.22 E
Pg 281	family Phoridae/humpbacked flies	9.23 H
Pg 283	antenna with arista	9.22 A
Pg 283	antenna of muscoid flies	9.26 B
Pg 287	muscoidea thorax	9.27 E
Pg 289, 297	wings of muscoid flies	9.26 A
Pg 299	frit fly head	9.27 J
Pg 301	family Ephydridae/shore flies	9.27 I
Pg 319	ovipositors	9.29 J
Pg 323	side view of ichneumon	9.13 E
Pg 323	family Ichneumonidae/ichneumonidid	9.29 C
Pg 329	Chalcidoidea/chalcids	9.29 F
Pg 333	family Cynipidae/gall wasps	9.29 I
Pg 337	family Diapriidae/diapriids	9.29 G
Pg 339	Proctotrupoidea/platygasterids	9.29 H
Pg 345	side view/Myrmicinae/fire ant	9.28 B
Pg 361	Apoidea/bees	9.29 E
Plate 8 Fig 6	family Chrysomelidae/leaf beetles	9.21 H
Plate 14	fly head	9.22 A
Plate 14	Muscoidea/house flies	9.27 E
Plate 14	Sciomyzoidea/marsh flies	9.27 F
Plate 14	family Otitidae/picture-winged flies	9.27 G
Plate 16	Vespoidea/yellowjackets, hornets	9.29 D

Bousfield, E.L. 1973. *Shallow-water Gammaridean Amphipoda of New England*. Cornell Univ. Press, Ithaca and London.

SOURCE	VIEW/SCIENTIFIC/COMMON NAME	PAGE FIG
Pg 280	amphipod tail appendages	10.09 F
Pg 249 Fig 2	family Ampeliscidae/four-eyed amphipods	10.08 A
Pg 226 Fig 1	*Calliopius laeviusculus*/uropod and antenna	10.09 E
Pg 226 Fig 2	family Pleustidae/uropod and antenna	10.09 G
Pg 224 Fig 2	*Listriella* spp.	10.07 E
Pg 225, 251	split telson	10.09 F

Burt, W.H. and R.P. Grossenheider. 1964. *A Field Guide to the Mammals, 2nd edition.* Houghton Mifflin Co., Boston. Acknowledgement is given to the Peterson Field Guide series published by Houghton Mifflin Co. as source material.

SOURCE	VIEW/SCIENTIFIC/COMMON NAME	PAGE FIG
Pg 148	*Zapus hudsonius*/meadow jumping mouse	16.05 F
Pg 117	*Glaucomys volans*/flying squirrel	16.07 G

Chu, H.F. 1949. *How to Know the Immature Insects*. Wm. C. Brown Publishers, Dubuque, IA.

SOURCE	VIEW/SCIENTIFIC/COMMON NAME	PAGE FIG
Pg 76 Fig 175	Carabidae/ground beetle, larvae	9.32 A
Pg 89 Fig 216	Heteroceridae/mud-loving beetle, larvae	9.32 A
Pg 109 Fig A	Coccinelidae/ladybird beetle, larvae	9.32 A
Pg 127 Fig 350	Curculionidae/snout beetles, larvae	9.33 D
Pg 197 Fig 552	Dolichopidae/long-legged fly, larvae	9.34 E
Pg 207 Fig 572	Tabanidae/horse fly, pupae	9.31 E
Pg 200 Fig 559	Cecidomyidae pupae	9.31 F
Pg 202 Fig 561	Mycetophilidae pupae	9.31 F
Pg 206 Fig 570	Tipulidae pupae	9.31 F
Pg 209 Fig 579	Asilidae/flies, pupae	9.31 F
Pg 210 Fig 580	Empidae pupae	9.31 F

Comstock, J.H. 1940. *The Spider Book*. Doubleday, Doran and Co., Inc. NY. Adapted from John Henry Comstock: *The Spider Book*. Revised and edited by W.J. Gertsch. Copyright 1912, 1940 by Doubleday, Doran and Co., Inc. Copyright assigned 1948 to Comstock Publishing Company, Inc. Used by permission of the publisher, Cornell Univ. Press.

SOURCE	VIEW/SCIENTIFIC/COMMON NAME	PAGE FIG
Pg 496	*Neoscona arabesca*	9.06 C
Pg 650	face/family Lycosidae	9.04 C
Pg 135	spinnerets	9.05 G
	cribellum	9.07 E
Pg 343 Fig 339	face/family Theridiidae	9.07 I
Pg 384 Fig 396	*Neriene (=Linyphia) clathrata*	9.07 K

Conant, R. and Collins, J.T. 1991. *A Field Guide to Reptiles and Amphibians of Eastern and Central North America, 3rd ed.* Houghton Mifflin Co., Boston. Acknowledgement is given to the Peterson Field Guide series published by Houghton Mifflin Co. as source material.

SOURCE	VIEW/SCIENTIFIC/COMMON NAME	PAGE FIG
	Scaphiopus holbrookii	14.01 D
	Ambystoma maculatum/spotted salamander	14.02 B
Pl.9	bridge/*Caretta caretta*	14.04 B
Pl.9	*Lepidochelys kempii*/Atlantic ridley	14.05 C
	bridge/*Lepidochelys kempii*	14.05 C
P1.9	*Chelonia mydas*/green turtle	14.05 D
P1.9	*Eretmochelys imbricata*/Atlantic hawksbill	14.05 E
P1.28	*Elaphe obsoleta*/black rat snake	14.07 E
P1.28	cross sections/*Elaphe obsoleta*	14.07 E
P1.22	*Storeria dekayi*/northern brown snake	14.07 G
P1.23	*Thamnophis sauritus*/eastern ribbon snake	14.07 H
P1.24 Fig 58	scale rows/*Thamnophis sauritus*	14.07 H
P1.24 Fig 58	scale rows/*Thamnophis sirtalis sirtalis*	14.07 I

Conant, R. 1975. *A Field Guide to Reptiles and Amphibians of Eastern and Central North America, 2nd ed.* Houghton Mifflin Co., Boston. Acknowledgement is given to the Peterson Field Guide series published by Houghton Mifflin Co. as source material.

SOURCE	VIEW/SCIENTIFIC/COMMON NAME	PAGE FIG
Pg 308	head diagram/*Bufo americanus*	14.01 A
Pg 308	head diagram/*Bufo woodhousii fowleri*	14.01 B

SOURCE	VIEW/SCIENTIFIC/COMMON NAME	PAGE FIG
Pg 318	foot/*Pseudacris* (*Hyla*) *crucifer*	14.01 C
Plate 23	*Thamnophis sirtalis sirtalis*/eastern garter snake	14.07 I
Plate 40	*Plethodon cinereus*/red-backed salamander	14.02 A
Plate 44	*Bufo americanus*/American toad	14.01 A
Plate 47	*Pseudacris* (*Hyla*) *crucifer*/spring peeper	14.01 C
Plate 44	*Bufo woodhousii fowleri*/fowlers toad	14.01 B

Crane, J.M. 1973. *Introduction to Marine Biology.* A Laboratory Text. Charles E. Merrill Publishing Co., Columbus, OH. Illustrations adapted with permission of Merrill, an imprint of Macmillan Publishing Co., from *Introduction to Marine Biology* by J. M. Crane. Copyright 1972 by Merrill Publishing Co.

SOURCE	VIEW/SCIENTIFIC/COMMON NAME	PAGE FIG
	head & proboscis/*Nereis* (=*Neanthes*) *virens*	8.14 A

Daniels, B.A. and R.T. Sawyer. 1975. *The biology of the leech Myzobdella lugubris infesting blue crabs and catfish.* Biological Bulletin 148: 193-195.

SOURCE	SCIENTIFIC/COMMON NAME	PAGE FIG
Pg 195 Fig 1A&B	*Myzobdella lugubris*/leech cocoons	2.19 E
	Myzobdella lugubris/crab leech	8.23 D

Fraser, C.M. 1944. *Hydroids of the Atlantic Coast of North America*. Univ. of Toronto Press. Toronto.

SOURCE	VIEW/SCIENTIFIC/COMMON NAME	PAGE FIG
	closeup/*Podocoryne carnea*	4.06 C
	polyps/*Hydrallmania falcata*	4.07 A
	polyps/*Dynamena* (=*Sertularia*) *pumila*	4.07 B
	polyps/*Sertularella* spp.	4.07 C
	polyps/*Thuiaria* spp.	4.07 D
	reproductive structure/*Halecium* spp.	4.08 B
	polyps/*Obelia geniculata*	4.09 E
	polyps/*Campanularia* (=*Obelia*) *gelatinosa*	4.09 F
	polyps/*Bougainvillea carolinensis*	4.11 C
	colony/*Cordylophora lacustris*	4.11 H

Gosner, K.L. 1971. *Guide to Identification of Marine and Estuarine Invertebrates.* John Wiley and Sons, Inc., NY. Reprinted by permission of John Wiley & Sons, Inc.

SOURCE	VIEW/SCIENTIFIC/COMMON NAME	PAGE FIG
Pg 59 Fig 4.2	spicules, silicious	3.01 K
Pg 60 Fig 4.4A,B	spicules, calcareous	3.01 J
Pg 75 Fig 5.2	hydromedusae	4.00 B
Pg 97 Fig 5.9	hydroid reproductive structures	4.08 A
Pg 234 Fig B	*Lichenopora*/disk-like bryozoan	2.06 C
Pg 239 Fig 13.7B	*Electra pilosa*/lacy bryozoan	6.05 H
Pg 239 Fig 13.7C	*Conopeum triutti*/lacy bryozoan	6.04 A
Pg 239 Fig 13.7E	*Electra crustulenta*/lacy bryozoan	6.04 F
Pg 289 Fig 16.13B	*Elysia chlorotica*/emerald elysia	7.11 F
Pg 347 Fig 17.7M	scale/*Lepidonotus sublevis*/hermit crab scale worm	8.09 A
Pg 347 Fig 17.7N	scale/*Lepidonotus squamatus*/twelve-scaled worm	8.09 A
Pg 374 Fig 17.20C	*Flabelligera affinis*/papillae	8.11 G
Pg 378 Fig 17.23C	tentacles/*Ampharete arctica*	8.07 E
Pg 378 Fig 17.23C	tentacles/*Asabellides oculata*	8.06 D
Pg 482 Fig 21.24C	*Politolana* (=*Cirolana*) *concharum*/telson	10.10 B
Pg 483 Fig 21.21E	*Idotea phosphorea*/telson	10.11 H
Pg 542 Fig 21.55	ventral views/*Callinectes sapidus*	10.23 B
Pg 116 Fig 5.20C	*Stomotoca pterophylla*	4.02 A
Pg 75 Fig 5.2B	*Tamoya haplonema*/sea wasp	4.02 B
Pg 123 Fig 5.24A	*Liriope tetraphylla*	4.02 C
P1.30	*Tima formosa*	4.03 E
Pg 5, 2 Fig 5.2H	*Catablema variscarium*/constricted jellyfish	4.03 F
Pg 119 Fig 5.23B	*Laodicea undulata*	4.03 I
P1.30	*Aequorea* spp.	4.03 L
Pg 94 Fig C	polyp/*Opercularella* spp.	4.05 I
	head/*Cerebratulus lacteus*	5.07 H
	head/*Micrura* spp.	5.07 I
Pg 237 Fig D	*Cribrilina punctata*/encrusting bryozoan	6.03 H
Pg 230 Fig 6	*Triticella* spp.	6.07 H
Pg 279 Fig A, B	teeth/family Pyramidellidae (*Odostomia* sp.)	7.06 A
Pg 289 Fig 16.13G	*Doto coronata*/cerrata	7.12 C
Pg 328 Fig E	*Polygordius* spp./archianellid	8.11 F

Gosner, K.L. 1979. *A Field Guide to the Atlantic Seashore*. Houghton Mifflin Co., Boston. Acknowledgement is given to the Peterson Field Guide series published by Houghton Mifflin Co. as source material.

SOURCE	VIEW/SCIENTIFIC/COMMON NAME	PAGE FIG
Pg 115 Fig 26	*Lichenopora verrucaria*/encrusting bryozoan	6.02 A
Pg 177 Fig 4	*Nereis acuminata* (=*arenaceodentata*) white clam worm	8.14 E
Pg 177 Fig 51-6	*Nereis grayi*/parapodium	8.14 C
Plate 1	sea lettuce	2.02 B
Plate 1	codium	2.03 E
Plate 3	kelp	2.02 B
Plate 4	cord weed	2.03 D
Plate 5	sea potato	2.09 O
Plate 7	Irish moss	2.02 B
Plate 10	spicule/*Didemnum candidum*	12.02 A
Plate 10	*Amaroucium pellucidum*	12.03 D
Plate 10	*Amaroucium stellatum*	12.03 D
Plate 13	*Barentsia* sp.	6.07 B
Plate 15 #6	colony/*Flustrellidra hispida*	6.05 A
Plate 16 #13	*Parasmittina nitida*/encrusting bryozoan	6.03 I
Plate 16 #2	*Schizoporella unicornis*/encrusting bryozoan	6.03 E
Plate 16 #20	*Tegella unicornis*/lacy bryozoan	6.04 D
Plate 16 #21	*Callopora craticula*/lacy bryozoan	6.04 E
Plate 17	*Boltenia ovifera*/stalked sea squirt	12.01 I
Plate 17	*Dendrodoa carnea*/blood-drop sea squirt	12.00 B
Plate 17	*Ciona intestinalis*/sea vase sea squirt	12.00 D
Plate 19	side view/*Crepidula plana*	7.01 D
Plate 20	order Cephalaspidea (*Haminoea solitaria*)/ bubble snails	7.07 F

SOURCE	VIEW/SCIENTIFIC/COMMON NAME	PAGE FIG
Plate 21	*Turbonilla* sp./top whorl	7.06 C
Plate 23	top view/*Pandora gouldiana*	7.21 A
Plate 25	inside view/*Cumingia tellinoides*	7.22 D
Plate 25	*Astarte castanea*/chestnut astarte	7.19 E
Plate 26	inside and top views/*Anadara (=Arca) transversa*	7.16 A
Plate 26	inside and top views/*Anadara (=Arca) ovalis*	7.16 B
Plate 28	inside view/*Mercenaria (=Venus) mercenaria*	7.18 A
Plate 32	*Pleurobrachia pileus*/sea gooseberry	4.17 A
Plate 32	*Beroe* sp./Beroe's comb jelly	4.17 B
Plate 32	*Mnemiopsis leidyi*/common southern comb jelly	4.17 C
Plate 41	capitellid	8.19 C
Plate 42	*Chaetopterus variopedatus*/parchment-tube worm	8.10 C
Plate 42	*Spiochaetopterus oculatus*/glassy-tube worm	8.10 B
Plate 43	*Lepidonotus* spp./cirri	8.09 A
Plate 44	dorid nudibranchs	7.11 A
Plate 44	*Polycera* spp.	7.11 B
Plate 49	*Lernaeenicus* sp./ribbon fish lice	10.02 A
Plate 49	*Aega psora*/isopod, parasitic	10.03 H
Plate 49	bopyrid isopod in shrimp	10.03 H
Plate 50	valviferan isopods	10.11 C
Plate 50	*Erichsonella attenuata*	10.11 J
Plate 55	*Emerita talpoida*/top view	10.19 E
Plate 57	*Upogebia affinis*/coastal mud shrimp	10.18 B
Plate 58	shell/*Uca minax*	10.21 D
Plate 59	*Eurypanopeus depressus*/maxilliped	10.25 C
Plate 62 Fig 47	hole pattern/*Arbacia punctulata*	11.01 B
Plate 62 Fig 47	hole pattern/*Strongylocentrotus droebachiensis*	11.01 C
Plate 10	*Alcyonium digitatum*/soft coral, spicule	4.16 A
Plate 32	*Bolinopsis infundibulum*/common northern comb jelly	4.17 D
	head/*Tetrastemma* spp.	5.07 F
	tentacles/*Phascolopsis gouldii*	5.09 C
P1.16 #5	*Schizomavella auriculata*	6.03 D
Plate 21	*Cerithiopsis greeni*/Green's miniature cerith	7.09 I
Plate 21	*Triphora nigrocincta*/black-line triphora	7.10 D
Plate 26	*Crenella* spp./crenellas	7.17 G
Plate 27	*Barnea truncata*/Atlantic mudpiddock	7.17 H
Plate 27	*Cyrtopleura costata*/angelwing	7.17 H
Plate 24	*Siliqua costata*/Atlantic razor	7.23 C
Plate 24	*Tagellus* spp.	7.23 E
P1.38	anterior end/family Hesionidae	8.16 A
P1.38	family Pilargiidae, *Sigambra tentaculata*	8.16 B
Plate 40	ring of papillae/*Goniada maculata*	8.19 B
Plate 41	*Owenia fusiformis*	8.22 C
P1.64	arm segments/*Ophiopholis aculeata*	11.05 E
P1.64	disc/*Axiognathus squamatus*	11.05 G

Green, J. 1968. *Biology of Estuarine Animals*. Univ. of Washington Press, Seattle.

SOURCE	VIEW/SCIENTIFIC/COMMON NAME	PAGE FIG
Pg 258	*Anurida maritima*/seashore springtail	9.14 D

Grimm, F.W. 1975. *A review of Succinnea wilsoni, a coastal marsh snail of eastern North America*. Nautilus vol. 89(2):40.

VIEW/SCIENTIFIC/COMMON NAME	PAGE FIG
Succinea wilsoni/golden ambersnail	7.07 B

Hall, E.R. and K.R. Kelson. 1959. *The Mammals of North America*. Ronald Press Co., NY. Reprinted by permission of John Wiley and Sons, Inc.

SOURCE	VIEW/SCIENTIFIC/COMMON NAME	PAGE FIG
Pg 52	*Blarina brevicauda*/short-tailed shrew	16.05 J
Pg 72	*Scalopus aquaticus*/eastern mole	16.05 H
Pg 75	*Condylura cristata*/star-nosed mole	16.05 G
Pg 321	*Marmota monax*/woodchuck	16.02 D
Pg 628	*Peromyscus leucopus*/white-footed mouse	16.05 E
Pg 769	*Rattus norvegicus*/Norway rat	16.05 D
Pg 770	*Mus musculus*/house mouse	16.05 C
Pg 855	*Vulpes vulpes*/red fox	16.06 C
Pg 934	*Mephitis mephitis*/skunk	16.06 A
Pg 980	*Phoca vitulina*/harbor seal	16.00 A
Pg 980	*Odocoileus virginianus*/white-tailed deer	16.03 E

Hartman, O. 1944. *New England Annelida, Part 2*, including the unpublished plates by Verrill with reconstructed captions. Bull. Am. Mus. Nat. Hist. vol. 82, article (7):327-344.

VIEW/SCIENTIFIC/COMMON NAME	PAGE FIG
side view/*Spirorbis* sp./coiled worm	8.05 C
top view/*Spirorbis* sp./coiled worm	8.05 C
Paranaitis speciosa	8.15 F

Hartman, O. 1957. *Orbiniidae, Apistobranchidae, Paraonidae and Longosomidae*. Allan Hancock Pacific Exped. 15(3): 211-392.

VIEW/SCIENTIFIC/COMMON NAME	PAGE FIG
top view/*Paraonis gracilis*	8.20 A

Hartman, O. 1966. *Polychaeta Myzostomidae and Sedentaria of Antarctica*. American Geophysical Union Publication No. 1414.

VIEW/SCIENTIFIC/COMMON NAME	PAGE FIG
side view/*Paraonis gracilis*	8.20 A

Hartman, Willard D. 1958. *Natural History of the Marine Sponges of Southern New England*. Bulletin of the Peabody Museum of Natural History, Yale Univ. Bull. 12.

SOURCE	VIEW/SCIENTIFIC/COMMON NAME	PAGE FIG
Fig 10	spicules/*Microciona*	3.03 B
Fig 10	spicules/*Microciona*	3.05 B
Fig 23	spicules/*Haliclona*	3.04 B
Fig 11	spicules/*Lissodendoryx*	3.05 C
Fig 6	spicules/*Halichondria*	3.04 A
Fig 4	spicules/*Cliona* sp. Type I	3.02 D

Headlee, Thomas J. 1945. *The Mosquitoes of New Jersey and their Control.* Trustees of Rutgers College, NJ. Copyright 1945 by Trustees of Rutgers College. Reprinted with permission of Rutgers Univ. Press.

SOURCE	VIEW/SCIENTIFIC/COMMON NAME	PAGE FIG
Pg 35 Fig 12	*Aedes cantator*/brown saltmarsh mosquito	9.24 A
Pg 42 Fig 14	*Aedes sollicitans*/banded saltmarsh mosquito	9.24 A
Pg 39 Fig 1	larvae/*Culicidae*/mosquito	9.33 E

Hickman, C.P. 1967. *Biology of the Invertebrates.* C.V. Mosby, Co., St. Louis.

SOURCE	VIEW/SCIENTIFIC/COMMON NAME	PAGE FIG
Pg 160	comb rows	4.17 C

Jacobson, M.K. and W.K. Emerson. 1971. *Shells from Cape Cod to Cape May.* Dover Publications, Inc., N.Y. (former title: Shells of the New York City Area. Argonaut Books, Inc., Larchmont, NY.

SOURCE	VIEW/SCIENTIFIC/COMMON NAME	PAGE FIG
Pg 45	*Epitonium* sp./wentletrap	7.06 B
Pg 47	*Euspira (=Lunatia) triseriata*/spotted moonsnail	7.04 C
Pg 51	*Crepidula fornicata*/common Atlantic slippersnail	7.01 B
Pg 51	*Crepidula convexa*/convex slippersnail	7.01 C
Pg 53	*Littorina obtusata (=palliata)*/yellow periwinkle	7.05 A
Pg 53	*Littorina saxatilis (=rudis)*/rough periwinkle	7.05 C
Pg 55	*Lacuna vincta*/northern lacuna (=lesser periwinkle or chink shell)	7.05 D
Pg 57	*Mitrella (=Astyris=Columbella) lunata*/ lunar dovesnail	7.09 J
Pg 57	*Anachis (=Columbella) avara*/greedy dovesnail	7.09 K
Pg 59	*Ilyanassa (=Nassarius=) obsoleta*/eastern mud snail (juvenile)	7.09 E
Pg 59	*Ilyanassa (=Nassarius) trivittata*/threeline mudsnail	7.08 C
Pg 59	*Nassarius vibex*/bruised nassa	7.09 F
Pg 65	*Melampus bidentatus*/eastern melampus	7.07 C
Pg 67	*Bittium alternatum (=nigrum)*/alternate bittium	7.06 E
Pg 67	family Pyramidellidae (*Odostomia* sp.)/ rice snail	7.06 A
Pg 68	*Hydrobia totteni (=minuta)*/minute hydrobia	7.06 D
Pg 68	*Kurtziella (=Mangelia) cerina*/wax-colored mangelia	7.09 H
Pg 69	*Acteocina (=Retusa) canaliculata*/channeled barrel-bubble	7.07 E
Pg 73	inner shell edge/*Yoldia limatula*	7.23 B
Pg 73	*Nucula proxima*/nut clam	7.20 D
Pg 73	*Solemya velum*/awning clam	7.17 K
Pg 77	inside view/*Crassostrea (=Ostrea) virginica*	7.15 D
Pg 79	*Anomia simplex*/common jingle	7.20 B
Pg 83	*Pandora gouldiana*/Gould's pandora	7.21 A
Pg 85	*Lyonsia hyalina*/glassy lyonsia	7.17 J
Pg 97	*Mulinia (=Mactra) lateralis*/dwarf surfclam	7.19 F
Pg 97	*Mulinia (=Mactra) lateralis*/dwarf surfclam	7.21 C
Pg 98	*Corbula contracta*/contracted corbula	7.21 B
Pg 99	inner edge/*Mya arenaria*/softshell	7.22 A
Pg 101	*Petricola pholadiformis*/false angelwing	7.17 I
Pg 142	*Macoma tenta*/elongate macoma	7.21 D
P1.61	*Buccinum undatum*/waved whelk	7.09 G

Jaques, H.E. 1947. *How to Know the Insects.* W. C. Brown Publishers, Dubuque, IA.

SOURCE	VIEW/SCIENTIFIC/COMMON NAME	PAGE FIG
Pg 44 Fig 42	insect leg regions	9.10 B
Pg 49 Fig 49A	beetle with wings extended	9.11 E
Pg 49 Fig 49B	bug with wings extended	9.11 G
Pg 49 Fig 49C	grasshopper with wings extended	9.11 F
Pg 102 Fig 197	order Thysanoptera/thrips	9.13 B
Pg 108 Fig 213A	gerrid tarsus	9.17 E
Pg 109 Fig 217	mirid beak	9.17 F
Pg 117 Fig 239	front view/delphacid head	9.18 C
Pg 118 Fig 241	head views/leafhoppers	9.18 A

Kabata, Z. 1979. *Parasitic Copepoda of British Fishes.* The Ray Society, London.

	VIEW/SCIENTIFIC/COMMON NAME	PAGE FIG
	Ergasilus sp.	10.02 C
	order Siphonostomatoida/caligiform fish lice	10.03 D

Katona, S.K., V. Rough, and D.T. Richardson. 1983. *A Field Guide to the Whales, Porpoises and Seals of the Gulf of Maine and Eastern Canada.* Charles Scribner's Sons. Reprinted with the permission of Charles Scribner's Sons, an imprint of Macmillan Publishing Co., NY. from *A Field Guide to the Whales, Porpoises, and Seals of the Gulf of Maine and Eastern Canada* by Steven K. Katona, Valerie Rough, David T. Richardson. Illustrations by John R. Quinn, D.D. Tyler, and Sarah Landry. Illustrations copyright 1983. Sarah Landry, D.D. Tyler, and John R. Quinn.

SOURCE	VIEW/SCIENTIFIC/COMMON NAME	PAGE FIG
Pg 180	side and front view of head/*Phoca vitulina*	16.00 A
Pg 197	head/*Cristophora cristata*/hooded seal	16.00 B
Pg 188	views of head/*Halichoerus grypus*/gray seal	16.00 B
Pg 191	*Pagophilus groenlandicus*/harp seal	16.00 B
Pg 85	*Lagenorhynchus acutus*/white-sided dolphin	16.01 E
Pg 97	*Stenella coeruleoalba*/striped dolphin	16.01 E

Keith, A.R. 1969. *The Mammals of Martha's Vineyard.* Dukes County Historical Soc., Inc. Edgartown, MA.

SOURCE	VIEW/SCIENTIFIC/COMMON NAME	PAGE FIG
	Microtus pennsylvanicus/meadow vole	16.04 A

Leim, A.H. and W.B. Scott. 1966. *Fishes of the Atlantic Coast of Canada.* Bull. Fish. Res. Bd. Canada, 155.

SOURCE	VIEW/SCIENTIFIC/COMMON NAME	PAGE FIG
Pg 266	*Chaetodon ocellatus*/spotfin butterflyfish	13.18 C
Pg 172	*Fundulus diaphanus*/banded killifish	13.17 E
Pg 183	*Gasterosteus wheatlandi*/blackspotted stickleback	13.12 D

Levi, H.W. and L.R. Levi. 1968. *A Guide to Spiders and Their Kin*. Golden Press, NY. From *Spiders and Their Kin* Illustrated by Nicholas Strekalovsky copyright 1968 by Western Publishing Co., Inc. Used by permission.

SOURCE	VIEW/SCIENTIFIC/COMMON NAME	PAGE FIG
Pg 13	tip of leg	9.05 E
Pg 13	tip of leg	9.05 F
Pg 70	face view/family Tetragnathidae	9.06 D
Pg 70, 110, 86	spider eye patterns	9.04 B
Pg 75	face/family Hahniidae	9.05 J
Pg 82, 98	spider eye patterns	9.04 A
Pg 88	face/family Clubionidae	9.05 I
Pg 88	face/family Micryphantidae	9.07 J
Pg 98	face/family Salticidae	9.05 D
Pg 110	face/family Dictynidae	9.07 H
Pg 135	suborder Trombidiformes/mites	9.09 C

Logier, E.B.S. 1958. *The Snakes of Ontario*. Univ. of Toronto Press, Toronto.

SOURCE	VIEW/SCIENTIFIC/COMMON NAME	PAGE FIG
Pg 71 Fig 2G	smooth scales/*Eretmochelys imbricata*	14.06 A
Pg 71 Fig 2E	keeled scales/*Eretmochelys imbricata*	14.06 B
Pg 71 Fig 2H	divided anal plate/*Nerodia (=Natrix) sipedon sipedon*	14.07 F
Pg 71 Fig 2F	undivided anal plate/*Thamnophis sirtalis sirtalis*	14.07 I

Marcus, E.D.B. 1972. *Notes on some opisthobranch gastropods from the Chesapeake Bay*. Chesapeake Sci., Estuaries, Univ. of South Carolina, Columbus, SC., 13: 300-317.

VIEW/SCIENTIFIC/COMMON NAME	PAGE FIG
Elysia catula	7.11 G

McAlpine, J.F. et al. 1981. *Manual of Neartic Diptera*. Agriculture Canada. Agriculture Research Branch, Canada. Illustrations reproduced with the permission of the Minister of Supply & Services, Canada, 1991.

SOURCE	VIEW/SCIENTIFIC/COMMON NAME	PAGE FIG
Pg 113 Fig 144	family Coelopidae/seaweed flies	9.26 D
Pg 113 Fig 143	Milichioidea	9.27 H
Pg 629 Fig 16	dolichopid antenna	9.23 I
Pg 619 Fig 50	empidid antenna	9.23 J

Meglitsch, Paul A. 1967. *Invertebrate Zoology*. Oxford Univ. Press, NY.

SOURCE	VIEW/SCIENTIFIC/COMMON NAME	PAGE FIG
Pg 328 Fig 11-19(A)	*Bothriocephalus* sp./procercoid, coracidium, pleurocercoid	5.05 E

Menzies, R.J. and D. Frankenberg. 1966. *Handbook on the Common Marine Isopod Crustacea of Georgia.* Univ. of Georgia Press, Atlanta, GA.

VIEW/SCIENTIFIC/COMMON NAME	PAGE FIG
top view/*Politolana (=Cirolana) polita*	10.10 B

Miner, Roy Waldo 1950. *Field Book of Seashore Life*. G.P. Putnam's Sons, NY.

SOURCE	VIEW/SCIENTIFIC/COMMON NAME	PAGE FIG
Pg 57	*Polymastia robusta*	3.05 A
Pg 57	spicules, *Polymastia*	3.05 A
Pg 63	*Haliclona (=Chalina) oculata*/deadman's finger sponge	3.03 C
Pg 73	*Isodictya deichmannae*	3.03 A
Pg 113	colony/*Bougainvillea carolinensis*	4.11 C
Pg 119	single polyp/*Obelia geniculata*	4.09 E
Pg 123	polyps/*Halecium* spp.	4.08 B
Pg 125	single polyp/*Campanularia (=Obelia) gelatinosa*	4.09 F
Pg 193	*Astrangia poculata (=danae)*/northern coral	4.16 B
Pg 195	*Ceriantheopsis (=Cerianthus) americanus*	4.14 A
Pg 197	*Edwardsia leidyi*/combjelly parasite anemone	4.15 G
Pg 197	closeup/*Edwardsia elegans*	4.14 B
Pg 197	close up/*Fagesia (=Edwardsia) lineata*	4.13 F
Pg 201	*Haloclava (=Eloactis) producta*/bumpy burrowing anemone	4.15 C
Pg 205 P1.71	oral view/*Tealia (=Urticina) felina (=crassicornis)*	4.13 C
Pg 207	*Paranthus (=Ammophilactis) rapiformus*/ grooved burrowing anemone	4.15 E
Pg 295	whole worm/*Syllis* spp.	8.16 C
Pg 300	body and tail/*Exogene* sp.	8.13 G
Pg 301	whole worm/*Odontosyllis fulgurans*	8.16 C
Pg 309	head/*Harmothoe imbricata*/fifteen-scaled worm	8.09 B
Pg 313	*Pholoe minuta*/slender many-scaled worm	8.09 D
Pg 333	whole worm/*Scoloplos* spp.	8.19 G
Pg 337	spionid tubes	8.11 E
Pg 337	*Polydora ciliata* tube/fine sand tube	2.27 F
Pg 355	*Melinna cristata*	8.06 A
Pg 355	entire worm/*Ampharete acutifrons*	8.06 B
Pg 355	tail/*Ampharete acutifrons*	8.06 B
Pg 355	head region/*Asabellides oculata*	8.06 D
Pg 355	head region/*Ampharete arctica*	8.07 E
Pg 355	*Pista palmata*	8.07 G
Pg 365	*Nicomache lumbricalis*/round-headed bamboo worm	8.22 B
Pg 371	*Scalibregma inflatum*	8.17 A
Pg 371	*Arenicola brasiliensis*/lug worm	8.19 F
Pg 372	*Flabelligera affinis*/mantled broom worm	8.11 G
Pg 372	*Pherusa affinis*/broom worm	8.11 H
Pg 377	crown of tentacles/*Potamilla* sp.	8.05 F
Pg 377	*Sabella microphthalma*/fan or feather duster worm	8.05 G
Pg 417	*Penella* sp.	10.02 A
Pg 417	dorsal view/*Argulus* sp.	10.03 E
Pg 453	family Bopyridae/bopyrid isopod	10.03 H
Pg 537	*Halacarus* sp./water mite	9.09 B
Pg 805	*Tubuliporidae*/panpipe bryozoan	6.01 H
Plate VIII8	head region/spionid	
Pg 133 P1.45	*Eutima mira*	4.03 D
Pg 135 P1.46	*Aglantha digitalis*/pink helmet	4.03 G
Pg 234 P1.46	*Gonionemus vertens*/clinging jellyfish	4.03 H

SOURCE	VIEW/SCIENTIFIC/COMMON NAME	PAGE FIG
Pg 133 P1.45	*Staurophora mertensi*/white-cross jellyfish	4.03 J
Pg 129 P1.43	*Tiaropsis multicirrata*	4.03 K
Pg 131 P1.44	colony/*Calycella syringa*/creeping bell hydroid	4.05 H
Pg 130 P1.44	polyp/*Cuspidella costata*	4.05 H
Pg 130 P1.44	*Lovenella* spp.	4.05 I
Pg 130 P1.44	colony/*Opercularella* spp.	4.05 I
Pg 145 P1.49	*Schizotricha tenella*	4.07 E
Pg 122 P1.41	colony/*Gonothyraea loveni*	4.09 D
Pg 130 P1.44	polyps/*Gonothyraea loveni*	4.09 D
Pg 94 P1.32	*Hybocodon prolifer*	4.10 B
Pg 95 P1.32	colony/*Pennaria tiarella*	4.11 E
Pg 95 P1.32	polyp/*Pennaria tiarella*	4.11 E
Pg 104 P1.35	*Zanclea costata*	4.11 F
Pg 101 P1.33	*Sarsia tubulosa*	4.11 G
Pg 194 P1.67	oral/*Cerianthus borealis*	4.14 A
Pg 210 P1.73	*Actinothoe (=Sagartia) modesta*	4.15 F
Pg 228	*Polychoerus caudatus*	5.01 C
Pg 229	*Childia groenlandica*	5.01 D
Pg 627 Fig 19	family Rissoidae (*Onoba aculeus*)	7.06 F
Color P1.XVII #9	*Doto coronata*/crown doto	7.12 C
Pg 344	*Cirratulus cirratus*/eyed fringed worm	8.08 A
Pg 289	head & tail/*Polygordius* spp.	8.11 F
Pg 701 P1.199& 201	*Pontaster tenuispinus*	11.03 E
Pg 751	disc/*Ophiura sarsi*	11.04 C
Pg 751	disc/*Ophiura robusta*	11.04 D
Pg 742	disc/*Ophiopholis aculeata*	11.05 E
Pg 793	*Caudina arenata*/rat-tailed sea cucumber	11.06 A
Color P1.21	*Chiridota laevis*/silky cucumber	11.07 F

Morris, P.A. 1975. *A Field Guide to the Shells of our Atlantic and Gulf Coasts.* Houghton Mifflin Co., Boston. Acknowledgement is given to the Peterson Field Guide series published by Houghton Mifflin Co. as source material.

SOURCE	VIEW/SCIENTIFIC/COMMON NAME	PAGE FIG
Plate 29 Fig 3*	*Macoma balthica*/Baltic macoma	7.20 A
Plate 23 Fig 10*	*Laevicardium mortoni*/Morton eggcockle	7.20 C
Plate 29 Fig 10*	*Cumingia tellinoides*/Tellin semele	7.22 D
Plate 33 Fig 14*	*Periploma papyratium*/paper spoonclam	7.22 E
P1.18 Fig 7	*Anomia squamula*/prickly jingle shell surface	7.20 B
P1.20 Fig 15	*Mysella planulata*/plate mysella	7.21 F

* = Photo

Murie, O.J. 1954. *A Field Guide to Animal Tracks.* Houghton Mifflin, Co., Boston. Acknowledgement is given to the Peterson Field Guide series published by Houghton Mifflin Co. as source material.

SOURCE	VIEW/SCIENTIFIC/COMMON NAME	PAGE FIG
Pg 11	*Didelphis virginiana*/opossum	16.02 A
Pg 37	*Procyon lotor*/raccoon	16.06 B
Pg 49	*Mustela frenata*/long-tailed weasel	16.07 D
Pg 156	*Sciurus carolinensis*/gray squirrel	16.07 E
Pg 149	*Tamiasciurus hudsonicus*/red squirrel	16.07 F
Pg 175	*Ondatra zibethicus*/muskrat	16.02 B

Nichols, D. and J.A. Cooke. 1971. *The Oxford Book of Invertebrates.* Oxford Univ. Press, London. By permission of Oxford University Press.

SOURCE	VIEW/SCIENTIFIC/COMMON NAME	PAGE FIG
Pg 17 Fig 6	*Peachia*/burrowing anemone	2.00 F
Pg 55 Fig 3	*Helix*/snail	2.00 E
Pg 77 Fig 6	*Spisula*/burrowing clam	2.00 F
Pg 103 Fig 2	*Amphitrite*/burrowing fringed worm	2.00 F
Pg 103 Fig 7	*Arenicola*/burrowing lug worm	2.00 F
Pg 105 Fig 6	*Pectinaria*/burrowing cone worm	2.00 F
Pg 119 Fig 2	*Branchellion* spp./skate leech	8.23 C
	adult tapeworm	5.04 A
	adult/*Bothriocephalus* sp.	5.05 E

Niemeyer, V.B. and D.A. Martin. 1967. *A Guide to the Identification of the Marine Plants and Invertebrate Animals of Tidewater Virginia.* Virginia Institute of Marine Sciences, Ed. Series #13, Gloucester Pt., VA.

VIEW/SCIENTIFIC/COMMON NAME	PAGE FIG
Diopatra cuprea/plumed worm or junk worm	8.13 D

Olmstead, N.C. and P.E. Fell. 1974. *Tidal Marsh Invertebrates of Connecticut.* Connecticut Arboretum Bull., No. 20. New London, CT.

SOURCE	VIEW/SCIENTIFIC/COMMON NAME	PAGE FIG
Pg 25	*Naemia serriata*/ladybird beetle	9.21 D
Pg 29	*Rhytidolomia saucia*/stink bug	9.17 C
Pg 29	*Trigonotylus* sp./plant bug	9.17 F
Pg 31	top/myrmicine ant	9.28 B

Palmer, L.E. 1957. *Palmer's Fieldbook of Mammals.* E.P. Dutton, Co., NY. From *Palmer's Fieldbook of Mammals* by Laurence E. Palmer. Copyright 1957 by E.P. Dutton, renewed 1985 by Katherine Van Winkle Palmer. Reprinted by permission of the publisher, Dutton, an imprint of New American Library, a division of Penguin Books, USA Inc.

VIEW/SCIENTIFIC/COMMON NAME	PAGE FIG
Microtus (=Pitymus) pinetorum/pine vole	16.04 B

Pennak, R.W. 1953. *Fresh-Water Invertebrates of the United States.* Ronald Press, NY. Reprinted by permission of John Wiley and Sons, Inc.

SOURCE	VIEW/SCIENTIFIC/COMMON NAME	PAGE FIG
Pg 610 Fig C	larvae/Hydrophilidae/water scavenger beetle	9.32 A
Pg 622 Fig A	larvae/Chrysomelidae/leaf beetle	9.32 A
Pg 568 Fig B	larvae, side view/*Trichoptera*/caddisfly	9.32 B
Pg 574 Fig A	larvae, dorsal view/*Trichoptera*	9.32 B
Pg 574 Fig B	larvae, hooked claws/*Trichoptera*	9.32 B
Pg 577 Fig F	larvae, sand grain case/*Trichoptera*	9.32 B
Pg 658 Fig A, B	larvae/Tabanidae	9.34 B
Pg 641 Fig A	larvae/Psychodidae/sand fly	9.33 F

SOURCE	VIEW/SCIENTIFIC/COMMON NAME	PAGE FIG
Pg 653 Fig H	larvae/Chironomidae/midge	9.33 G
Pg 582 Fig 362M	pupae, side view/caddisfly	9.31 H
Pg 656 Fig G	larvae/Ceratopogonidae/punky	9.33 H

Peterson, R.L. 1966. *The Mammals of Eastern Canada.* Oxford Univ. Press, Toronto. Illustrations adapted from *The Mammals of Eastern Canada* by R.L. Peterson (Toronto: Oxford University Press Canada, 1966); used by permission of the publisher.

SOURCE	VIEW/SCIENTIFIC/COMMON NAME	PAGE FIG
Fig 53	*Silvilagus floridanus*/cottontail rabbit	16.02 C
	Sorex cinereus/masked shrew	16.05 I

Peterson, R.T. 1980. *A Field Guide to the Birds East of the Rockies.* Houghton Mifflin Co., Boston. Acknowledgement is given to the Peterson Field Guide series published by Houghton Mifflin Co. as source material.

SOURCE	VIEW/SCIENTIFIC/COMMON NAME	PAGE FIG
Pg 33	flying/loon	15.03 E
Pg 35	*Podilymbus podiceps*/pied-billed grebe	15.06 A
Pg 35	foot/grebe	15.03 F
Pg 41	*Phalacrocorax auritus*/double-crested cormorant	15.04 A
Pg 41	*Phalacrocorax carbo*/great cormorant	15.04 B
Pg 43	*Cygnus olor*/mute swan	15.14 A
Pg 43	*Chen caerulescens*/snow goose	15.14 B
Pg 45	*Branta canadensis*/Canada goose	15.14 C
Pg 45	*Branta bernicla*/brant	15.14 D
Pg 46	flying formation/geese	15.03 G
Pg 49	typical female ducks	15.10 A
Pg 49	*Anas clypeata*/northern shoveler	15.08 B
Pg 49	*Anas strepera*/gadwall	15.11 D
Pg 49	*Anas rubripes*/American black duck	15.11 E
Pg 49	taking off/dabbling duck	15.03 J
Pg 51	*Anas americana*/American widgeon	15.09 C
Pg 51	*Anas acuta*/northern pintail	15.09 G
Pg 53	*Anas platyrhynchos*/mallard	15.08 A
Pg 53	forewing patch	15.10 C
Pg 53	*Anas crecca*/green-winged teal	15.09 D
Pg 53	*Anas discors*/blue-winged teal	15.09 F
Pg 55	*Melanitta nigra*/black scoter	15.11 A
Pg 55	*Melanitta fusca (=deglandi)*/white-winged scoter	15.11 B
Pg 55	*Melanitta perspicillata*/surf scoter	15.11 C
Pg 55	taking off/diving ducks	15.03 I
Pg 57	*Somateria mollissima*/common eider	15.13 G
Pg 59	*Aythya valisineria*/canvasback	15.12 A
Pg 59	*Aythya affinis*/lesser scaup	15.12 B
Pg 59	*Aythya marila*/greater scaup	15.12 B
Pg 59	*Aythya collaris*/ring-necked duck	15.13 E
Pg 61	*Bucephala albeola*/bufflehead	15.13 C
Pg 63	*Lophodytes cucullatus*/hooded merganser	15.07 A
Pg 65	coot foot	15.02 C
Pg 65	*Fulica americana*/American coot	15.06 C
Pg 65	*Gallinula chloropus*/common moorhen	15.06 D
Pg 66	speculum	15.10 A

SOURCE	VIEW/SCIENTIFIC/COMMON NAME	PAGE FIG
Pg 69	wing lining	15.10 B
Pg 87	*Larus marinus*/great black-backed gull	15.18 A
Pg 87	*Larus argentatus*/herring gull	15.18 B
Pg 87	*Larus delawarensis*/ring-billed gull	15.19 C
Pg 89	*Larus philadelphia*/Bonaparte's gull	15.19 D
Pg 89	*Larus atricilla*/laughing gull	15.19 E
Pg 97	*Sterna dougallii*/roseate tern	15.17 D
Pg 97	*Sterna antillarum (=albifrons)*/least tern	15.16 C
Pg 97	*Sterna hirundo*/common tern	15.17 F
Pg 97	winter/immature tern	15.16 B
Pg 99	skimmer head	15.17 G
Pg 101	heron flying	15.20 A
Pg 101	*Ardea herodias*/great blue heron	15.22 A
Pg 101	*Egretta (=Florida) caerulea*/little blue heron	15.22 B
Pg 101	*Egretta (=Hydranassa) tricolor*/tricolored or Louisiana heron	15.23 C
Pg 103	great egret wading	15.20 A
Pg 105	*Butorides striatus (=virescens)*/green-backed heron	15.23 D
Pg 105	*Botaurus lentiginosus*/American bittern	15.23 E
Pg 105	immature night heron	15.23 F
Pg 105	herons w/short neck	15.21 G
Pg 109	*Plegadis falcinellus*/glossy ibis	15.20 B
Pg 113, 115	family Rallidae/rails	15.01 I
Pg 119	*Pluvialis squatarola*/black-bellied plover	15.28 A
Pg 119	typical plovers	15.21 F
Pg 121	*Charadrius vociferus*/killdeer	15.28 D
Pg 121	*Charadrius melodus*/piping plover	15.28 E
Pg 121	*Charadrius semipalmatus*/semipalmated plover	15.28 F
Pg 125	*Limnodromus griseus*/short-billed dowitcher	15.25 C
Pg 127	*Limosa haemastica*/Hudsonia godwit	15.25 D
Pg 129	*Tringa melanoleuca*/greater yellowlegs	15.25 A
Pg 131	*Calidris melanotos*/pectoral sandpiper	15.27 D
Pg 131	sandpiper w/moderate neck	15.21 D
Pg 131	*Calidris alba*/sanderling	15.27 H
Pg 133	*Calidris alpina*/dunlin	15.26 A
Pg 133	*Actitis macularia*/spotted sandpiper	15.26 B
Pg 133	sandpiper w/short neck	15.21 E
Pg 133	*Calidris maritima*/purple sandpiper	15.27 E
Pg 135	*Calidris minutilla*/least sandpiper	15.27 F
Pg 135	*Calidris pusilla*/semipalmated sandpiper	15.27 G
Pg 153	*Circus cyaneus*/northern harrier or marsh hawk	15.30 B
Pg 153	*Accipiter striatus*/sharp-shinned hawk	15.31 C
Pg 155	*Buteo jamaicensis*/red-tailed hawk	15.31 E
Pg 159	*Pandion haliaetus*/osprey	15.30 A
Pg 159	*Haliaeetus leucocephalus*/bald eagle	15.31 F
Pg 161	*Cathartes aura*/turkey vulture	15.31 G
Pg 163	*Falco sparverius*/sparrow hawk or American kestrel	15.29 D
Pg 163	*Falco peregrinus*/peregrine falcon	15.29 E
Pg 163	*Falco columbarius*/merlin or pigeon hawk	15.29 F
Pg 164-6	bird of prey wings	15.29 C
Pg 181	*Zenaida macroura*/mourning dove	15.32 A
Pg 187	*Archilochus colubris*/ruby-throated hummingbird	15.37 C

SOURCE	VIEW/SCIENTIFIC/COMMON NAME	PAGE FIG
Pg 187	*Ceryle (=Megaceryle) alcyon*/belted kingfisher	15.01 F
Pg 191	*Colaptes auratus*/northern flicker	15.33 E
Pg 201	*Eremophila alpestris*/horned lark	15.35 E
Pg 203	*Hirundo rustica*/barn swallow	15.33 B
Pg 203	*Progne subis*/purple martin	15.36 E
Pg 205	*Riparia riparia*/bank swallow	15.33 B
Pg 205	*Chaetura pelagica*/chimney swift	15.36 F
Pg 207	*Corvus ossifragus*/fish crow	15.36 C
Pg 209	*Cyanocitta cristata*/blue jay	15.37 B
Pg 213	*Sitta canadensis*/red-breasted nuthatch	15.33 F
Pg 215	*Cistothorus* spp./marsh wren	15.33 D
Pg 217	*Regulus satrapa*/golden-crowned kinglet	15.35 H
Pg 237	*Setophaga ruticilla*/American redstart	15.35 J
Pg 247	*Geothlypis trichas*/common yellowthroat	15.34 C
Pg 253	*Agelaius phoeniceus*/red-winged black-bird	15.36 A
Pg 255	*Quiscalus quiscula*/common grackle	15.36 B
Pg 257	*Sturnella magna*/eastern meadowlark or meadowlark	15.34 B
Pg 257	*Sturnus vulgaris*/starling	15.36 D
Pg 269	*Cardinalis cardinalis*/cardinal	15.37 A
Pg 279	*Zonotrichia albicollis*/white-throated sparrow	15.37 D
Pg 285	typical sparrow	15.33 C
Pg 287	*Passerculus sandwichensis*/savannah sparrow	15.37 D
Pg 289	*Ammodramus (=Ammospiza) maritimus*/ seaside sparrow	15.37 D
Pg 97	*Sterna forsteri*/Forster's tern	15.17 E
Pg 99	*Childonias niger*/black tern	15.16 A
Pg 77	tubelike nostrils	15.15 D
Pg 83	*Stercorarius*/jaegers	15.15 C
Pg 81	*Morus bassanus*/northern gannet	15.15 B
Pg 77	storm petrel hovering	15.15 A
Pg 77	flying/family Hydrobatidae/storm petrel	15.15 A
Pg 35	*Podiceps grisegna*/red-necked grebe	15.06 B

Robbins, C.S., B. Bruun and H.S. Zim. 1966. *Birds of North America*. Golden Press, NY. From *Birds of North America,* Illustrated by Arthur Singer copyright 1983, copyright 1966 Western Publishing Company, Inc. Used by permission.

SOURCE	VIEW/SCIENTIFIC/COMMON NAME	PAGE FIG
Pg 17	length measurement	15.01 E
Pg 35	immature standing/*Phalacrocorax auritus*	15.04 A
Pg 73	*Buteo platypterus*/broad-winged hawk	15.31 D
Pg 95	immature/*Butorides striatus (=virescens)*	15.23 D
Pg 119	sandpiper with long neck	15.21 C
Pg 187	*Picoides villosus*/hairy woodpecker	15.33 E
Pg 193	kingbird chasing crow	15.34 A

Rogick, M.D. and H. Croasdale. 1949. *Studies on Marine Bryozoa, III. Woods Hole Region Bryozoa Associated with Algae*, Biological Bulletin (96:32-69).

SOURCE	VIEW/SCIENTIFIC/COMMON NAME	PAGE FIG
Fig 4	*Aeverrillia (=Buskia) arnata*/stolonate bryozoan	6.07 G
	Alcyonidium polyoum (=mytili)/rubbery bryozoan	6.05 B
Fig 8	*Bowerbankia gracilis*/stolonate bryozoan	6.06 D
Fig 9	*Bowerbankia imbricata*/stolonate bryozoan	6.06 E
Fig 15	*Bugula simplex (=flabellata)*/fan-tufted bushy bryozoan	6.00 B
Fig 16	10X/*Bugula simplex (=flabellata)*	6.00 B
Fig 17	*Bugula turrita*/spiral-tufted bushy bryozoan	6.00 A
Fig 18	10X/*Bugula turrita*	6.00 A
Fig 19	*Callopora aurita*/lacy bryozoan	6.04 C
Fig 26	colony/*Crisia eburnea*	6.01 G
Fig 33	*Flustrellidra hispida*/bristly bryozoan	6.05 A
Fig 42	*Hippothoa hyalina*/encrusting bryozoan	6.03 C
Fig 47	*Microporella ciliata*/encrusting bryozoan	6.03 K
Fig 50	*Pedicellina cernua*/zooid	6.07 A
	Lichenopora sp./encrusting bryozoan	6.02 A
	Electra monostachys (=hastingsae)/lacy bryozoan	6.05 I
	Stephanosella spp.	6.03 F
	Cryptosula (=Lepralia) pallasiana/encrusting bryozoan	6.03 J
	Nolella spp.	6.06 C
	Aetea spp.	6.07 F

Scott, W.B. and M. G. Scott, 1988. *Atlantic Fishes of Canada*. Can. Bull. Fish. Aquat. Sci. 219.

SOURCE	VIEW/SCIENTIFIC/COMMON NAME	PAGE FIG
Pg 613	ventral fin/*Gasterosteus aculeatus*	13.12 C
Pg 613	ventral fin/*Gasterosteus wheatlandi*	13.12 D

Smith, C. Lavett 1985. *The Inland Fishes of New York State.* N.Y. State Dept. Environ. Conservation.

SOURCE	VIEW/SCIENTIFIC/COMMON NAME	PAGE FIG
Pg 71	*Dorosoma cepedianum*/gizzard shad	13.14 B

Smith, R.I. (ed.). 1964. *Keys to Marine Invertebrates of the Woods Hole Region.* Contrib. No. 11. Marine Biol. Lab., Woods Hole, MA.

SOURCE	VIEW/SCIENTIFIC/COMMON NAME	PAGE FIG
Pg 53 Fig 12	*Nereis (=Neanthes) succinea*/parapodium	8.14 B
Pg 53 Fig 13	*Nereis pelagica*/parapodium	8.14 D
Pg 53 Fig 14	*Nereis (=Neanthes) virens*/parapodium	8.14 A
Pg 53 Fig 21	*Schistomeringos (=Stauronereis) rudolphi*	8.12 B
Pg 53 Fig 6	*Polydora* spp.	8.11 D
Pg 55 Fig 23	head/*Syllis* spp.	8.16 C
Pg 55 Fig 28	head/*Odontosyllis fulgurans*	8.16 C
Pg 55 Fig 35	head/*Exogene* sp.	8.13 G
Pg 55 Fig 35	worms with 3-5 tentacles	8.02 B
Pg 55 Fig 37	head/*Autolytus* spp.	8.16 C
Pg 55 Fig 38	gills/*Amphitrite* sp.	8.07 H
Pg 55 Fig 44	*Enoplobranchus sanguineus*/bloody thread worm	8.07 J
Pg 55 Fig 45	*Dodecaceria corallii*/coral worm	8.08 C
Pg 55 Fig 47	head region/*Tharyx acutus*	8.08 D
Pg 55 Fig 53	*Brania* spp.	8.13 F
Pg 57 Fig 50	*Fabricia sabella*/little fan worm	8.05 E
Pg 57 Fig 52	*Sabella crassicornis*/fan or feather duster worm	8.05 H

SOURCE	VIEW/SCIENTIFIC/COMMON NAME	PAGE FIG
Pg 57 Fig 53	collar & eyespots/*Sabella microphthalma*	8.05 G
Pg 57 fig 55	collar & eyespots/*Potamilla* sp.	8.05 F
Pg 57 Fig 63	*Spirorbis spirillum*/counter-clockwise coiled worm	8.05 C
Pg 57 Fig 65	*Spirorbis borealis*/clockwise coiled worm	8.05 C
Pg 57 Fig 73	*Asychis (=Maldanopsis) elongata*/spoon-tailed bamboo worm	8.22 D
Pg 57 Fig 74	*Maldane sarsi*/oval-tailed bamboo worm	8.22 E
Pg 57 Fig 75	*Nephtys incisa (=ingens)*/common painted worm	8.17 C
Pg 57 Fig 80, Pg 59 Fig 81	worms with 1-2 tentacles	8.02 A
Pg 59 Fig 108	*Pectinaria (=Cystenides) gouldii*/cone worm	8.04 A
Pg 59 Fig 109	cone worm tube	8.04 A
Pg 59 Fig 110	*Sabellaria vulgaris*/cement-tube worm	8.04 B
Pg 109 Fig 7	*Limnoria lignorum*/gribble	10.11 E
Pg 123 Fig 6	shell teeth/*Cancer irroratus*	10.24 B
Pg 123 Fig 7	shell teeth/*Cancer borealis*	10.24 C
Pg 125 Fig 39	leg/*Hippolyte zostericola*	10.17 D
Pg 125 Fig 40	leg/*Palaemonetes* spp.	10.17 E
Pg 191 Fig 5	spines on arm/*Axiognathus squamatus*	11.05 G
Pg 191 Fig 6	spines on arm/*Ophiopholis aculeata*	11.05 E
Pg 197 Fig 1	*Saccoglossus kowalewskii*/acorn worm	11.07 G
Pg 13 Fig 14	polyp/*Calycella syringa*	4.05 H
Pg 13 Fig 16	on snail shell/*Podocoryne carnea*	4.06 C
Pg 45 Fig 9	*Zygonmertes virescens*	5.06 C
	head/*Lineus* sp.	5.07 D
Pg 45 Fig 14	*Phascolion strombi*	5.09 B
Pg 55 Fig 46	head/*Cirratulus cirratus*	8.08 A
Pg 57 Fig 59	*Eulalia* spp.	8.15 C
Pg 57 Fig 79	head region/*Podarke*	8.16 A
Pg 59 Fig 88	*Goniada maculata*	8.19 B
Pg 110 Fig 27	Sphaeromatidae	10.11 D
Pg 190 Fig 3	spines on arm/*Ophoderma brevispinium*	11.04 B
Pg 197 Fig 13	*Bostricobranchus pilularis*	12.01 F

Smith, R.I. and J.T. Carlton (ed.). c.1975. *Light's Manual: Intertidal Invertebrates of the Central California Coast. Third Ed.* The Regents of the University of California.

SOURCE	VIEW/SCIENTIFIC/COMMON NAME	PAGE FIG
	open view/*Diadumene (=Haliplanella) luciae*	4.13 D

Snodgrass, R.E. 1952. *A Textbook of Arthropod Anatomy*. Comstock Publishing Associates, Cornell Univ. Press, Ithaca, N.Y. Adapted from R.E. Snodgrass: *A Textbook of Arthropod Anatomy*. Copyright 1952 by Cornell University. Used by permission of the publisher, Cornell University Press.

SOURCE	VIEW/SCIENTIFIC/COMMON NAME	PAGE FIG
	ventral view/*Limulus polyphemus*	9.01 A

Stephenson, T.A. 1928, 1935. *The British Sea Anemones.* Ray Society, London. Vol. 1 and Vol. 2.

VIEW/SCIENTIFIC/COMMON NAME	PAGE FIG
full extension/*Metridium senile*	4.12 B

Taylor, W.R. 1957. *Marine Algae of the Northeastern Coast of North America. 2nd Edition.* Univ. of Michigan Press, Ann Arbor, MI.

SOURCE	VIEW/SCIENTIFIC/COMMON NAME	PAGE FIG
Pg 439	*Corallina officianalis*/calcareous algae	2.03 G
	filamentous algae	2.03 I

Uzmann, J.R. 1967. *Histriobdella homari (Annelida: Polychaeta) in the American Lobster, Homarus americanus.* School of Biological Sciences, University of Nebraska-Lincoln. Journal of Parasitology 53:210-211.

VIEW/SCIENTIFIC/COMMON NAME	PAGE FIG
Histriobdella homari/lobster gill worm	8.23 A

Wells, H.W., M.J. Wells and I.E. Gray. 1960. *Marine sponges of North Carolina.* Journal of the Elisha Mitchell Scientific Society 76(2): 200-245.

SOURCE	VIEW/SCIENTIFIC/COMMON NAME	PAGE FIG
Fig 7	on eelgrass/*Haliclona* sp.	3.04 C
Fig 46	*Suberites ficus*/fig sponge	3.05 D

Williams, A.B. 1984. *Shrimps, Lobsters, and Crabs of the Atlantic Coast of the Eastern United States, Maine to Florida.* c Smithsonian Institution Press, Washington, D.C. Adapted by permission of the Smithsonian Institution Press from *Shrimps, Lobsters, and Crabs of the Atlantic Coast of the Eastern United States, Maine to Florida*, by Austin B. Williams. c Smithsonian Institution, Washington, DC 1984.

SOURCE	VIEW/SCIENTIFIC/COMMON NAME	PAGE FIG
Pg 210 Fig 147b	*Pagurus acadianus*/Acadian hermit crab	10.19 D
Pg 187 Fig A	*Axius serratus*	10.18 B
Pg 187 Fig A	*Gilvossius setimanus (=Callianassa atlantica)*/ ghost shrimp	10.18 B
Pg 309	*Hyas araneus*	10.22 B
Pg 310	*Hyas coarctatus*	10.22 B
Pg 377	anterior teeth/*Callinectes sapidus*	10.23 B
Pg 384	anterior teeth/*Callinectes similis*	10.23 C

Zim, Herbert S. and H.M. Smith. 1953. *Reptiles and Amphibians.* Simon and Schuster, N.Y. Illustrations by James Gordon Irving. Adapted from *REPTILES AND AMPHIBIANS* c. 1953, 1956 Western Publishing Co., Inc. Copyright renewed 1981, 1984. Used by permission.

SOURCE	VIEW/SCIENTIFIC/COMMON NAME	PAGE FIG
Pg 77	keeled scales magnified/*Eretmochelys imbricata*	14.06 B
Pg 102	*Nerodia (=Natrix) sipedon sipedon*/water snake	14.07 F

INDEX

INDEX